# Professional C# 2005

# Professional C# 2005

Christian Nagel
Bill Evjen
Jay Glynn
Karli Watson
Morgan Skinner
Allen Jones

Wiley Publishing, Inc.

# Professional C# 2005

Published by
**Wiley Publishing, Inc.**
10475 Crosspoint Boulevard
Indianapolis, IN 46256
www.wiley.com

Copyright © 2006 by Wiley Publishing, Inc., Indianapolis, Indiana

Published simultaneously in Canada

Library of Congress Card Number: 2005048978

ISBN-13: 978-0-7645-7534-1
ISBN-10: 0-7645-7534-1

Printed in the United States of America

10 9 8 7 6 5 4 3 2

1B/SQ/RQ/QV/IN

No part of this publication may be reproduced, stored in a retrieval system, or transmitted in any form or by any means, electronic, mechanical, photocopying, recording, scanning, or otherwise, except as permitted under Section 107 or 108 of the 1976 United States Copyright Act, without either the prior written permission of the Publisher, or authorization through payment of the appropriate per-copy fee to the Copyright Clearance Center, Inc., 222 Rosewood Drive, Danvers, MA 01923, (978) 750-8400, fax (978) 646-8600. Requests to the Publisher for permission should be addressed to the Legal Department, Wiley Publishing, Inc., 10475 Crosspoint Blvd., Indianapolis, IN 46256, (317) 572-3447, fax (317) 572-4355 or online at http://www.wiley.com/go/permissions.

> **LIMIT OF LIABILITY/DISCLAIMER OF WARRANTY:** THE PUBLISHER AND THE AUTHOR MAKE NO REPRESENTATIONS OR WARRANTIES WITH RESPECT TO THE ACCURACY OR COMPLETENESS OF THE CONTENTS OF THIS WORK AND SPECIFICALLY DISCLAIM ALL WARRANTIES, INCLUDING WITHOUT LIMITATION WARRANTIES OF FITNESS FOR A PARTICULAR PURPOSE. NO WARRANTY MAY BE CREATED OR EXTENDED BY SALES OR PROMOTIONAL MATERIALS. THE ADVICE AND STRATEGIES CONTAINED HEREIN MAY NOT BE SUITABLE FOR EVERY SITUATION. THIS WORK IS SOLD WITH THE UNDERSTANDING THAT THE PUBLISHER IS NOT ENGAGED IN RENDERING LEGAL, ACCOUNTING, OR OTHER PROFESSIONAL SERVICES. IF PROFESSIONAL ASSISTANCE IS REQUIRED, THE SERVICES OF A COMPETENT PROFESSIONAL PERSON SHOULD BE SOUGHT. NEITHER THE PUBLISHER NOT THE AUTHOR SHALL BE LIABLE FOR DAMAGES ARISING HEREFROM. THE FACT THAT AN ORGANIZATION OR WEBSITE IS REFERRED TO IN THIS WORK AS A CITATION AND/OR A POTENTIAL SOURCE OF FURTHER INFORMATION DOES NOT MEAN THAT THE AUTHOR OR THE PUBLISHER ENDORSES THE INFORMATION THE ORGANIZATION OR WEBSITE MAY PROVIDE OR RECOMMENDATIONS IT MAY MAKE. FURTHER, READERS SHOULD BE AWARE THAT INTERNET WEBSITES LISTED IN THIS WORK MAY HAVE CHANGED OR DISAPPEARED BETWEEN WHEN THIS WORK WAS WRITTEN AND WHEN IT IS READ.

For general information on our other products and services please contact our Customer Care Department within the United States at (800) 762-2974, outside the United States at (317) 572-3993 or fax (317) 572-4002.

**Trademarks:** Wiley, the Wiley Publishing logo, Wrox, the Wrox logo, and Programmer to Programmer are trademarks or registered trademarks of John Wiley & Sons, Inc. and/or its affiliates. All other trademarks are the property of their respective owners. Wiley Publishing, Inc., is not associated with any product or vendor mentioned in this book.

Wiley also publishes its books in a variety of electronic formats. Some content that appears in print may not be available in electronic books.

# About the Authors

## Christian Nagel

Christian Nagel is software architect and developer, associate of Thinktecture, who offers training and consulting on how to design and develop Microsoft .NET solutions. He looks back to more than 15 years' experience as a developer and software architect. Christian started his computing career with PDP 11 and VAX/VMS platforms, covering a variety of languages and platforms. Since the year 2000 — when .NET was just a technology preview — he has been working with various .NET technologies to build distributed solutions. With his profound knowledge of Microsoft technologies, he has also written numerous .NET books; is certified as Microsoft Certified Trainer (MCT), Solution Developer (MCSD), and Systems Engineer (MCSE); and is Microsoft Regional Director and MVP for Visual C#. Christian is a speaker at international conferences (TechED, DevDays, VCDC) and is the regional manager of INETA Europe (International .NET User Group Association) supporting .NET user groups. You can contact Christian via his Web site, http://www.christiannagel.com and http://www.thinktecture.com.

## Bill Evjen

Bill Evjen is an active proponent of the .NET technologies and community-based learning initiatives for .NET. He has been actively involved with .NET since the first bits were released in 2000 and has since become president of the St. Louis .NET User Group (http://www.stlusergroups.org). Bill is also the founder and executive director of the International .NET Association (http://www.ineta.org), which represents more than 125,000 members worldwide. Based in St. Louis, Missouri, USA, Bill is an acclaimed author and speaker on ASP.NET and XML Web services. He has written *XML Web Services for ASP.NET*, *Web Services Enhancements: Understanding the WSE for Enterprise Applications*, *Visual Basic .NET Bible*, and *ASP.NET Professional Secrets* (all published by Wiley). Bill is a Technical Director for Reuters, the international news and financial services company. He graduated from Western Washington University in Bellingham, Washington, with a Russian language degree. You can reach Bill at evjen@yahoo.com.

## Jay Glynn

Jay Glynn started writing software nearly 20 years ago, writing applications for the PICK operating system using PICK basic. Since then, he has created software using Paradox PAL and Object PAL, Delphi, VBA, Visual Basic, C, C++, Java, and of course C#. He is currently a Project Coordinator and Architect for a large financial services company in Nashville, Tennessee, working on software for the TabletPC platform. He can be contacted at jlsglynn@hotmail.com.

## Karli Watson

Karli Watson is a freelance author and the technical director of 3form Ltd (http://www.3form.net). Despite starting out by studying nanoscale physics, the lure of cold, hard cash proved too much and dragged Karli into the world of computing. He has since written numerous books on .NET and related technologies, SQL, mobile computing, and a novel that has yet to see the light of day (but that doesn't have any computers in it). Karli is also known for his multicolored clothing, is a snowboarding enthusiast, and still wishes he had a cat.

# About the Authors

## Morgan Skinner

Morgan Skinner began his computing career at a tender age on a Sinclair ZX80 at school, where he was underwhelmed by some code a teacher had written and so began programming in assembly language. After getting hooked on Z80 (which he believes is far better than those paltry 3 registers on the 6502), he graduated through the school's ZX81s to his own ZX Spectrum.

Since then he's used all sorts of languages and platforms, including VAX Macro Assembler, Pascal, Modula2, Smalltalk, X86 assembly language, PowerBuilder, C/C++, VB, and currently C#. He's been programming in .NET since the PDC release in 2000, and liked it so much he joined Microsoft in 2001. He now works in Premier Support for Developers and spends most of his time assisting customers with C#.

You can reach Morgan at http://www.morganskinner.com.

## Allen Jones

Allen Jones has a career spanning 15 years that covers a broad range of IT disciplines, including enterprise management, solution and enterprise architecture, and project management. But software development has always been Allen's passion. Allen has architected and developed Microsoft Windows-based solutions since 1990, including a variety of e-commerce, trading, and security systems.

Allen has co-authored four popular .NET books including the *C# Programmer's Cookbook* (Microsoft Press) and *Programming .NET Security* (O'Reilly), and he is actively involved in the development of courseware for Microsoft Learning covering emerging .NET technologies.

# Credits

**Vice President and Executive Group Publisher**
Richard Swadley

**Vice President and Executive Publisher**
Joseph B. Wikert

**Acquisitions Editor**
Katie Mohr

**Editorial Manager**
Mary Beth Wakefield

**Production Manager**
Tim Tate

**Development Editor**
Sharon Nash

**Production Editor**
Angela Smith

**Technical Editor**
Brian Patterson

**Project Coordinator**
Michael Kruzil

**Graphics and Production Specialists**
Andrea Dahl
Carrie Foster
Lauren Goddard
Denny Hager
Joyce Haughey
Alicia B. South
Julie Trippetti

**Quality Control Technicians**
Leeann Harney
Carl William Pierce
Brian H. Walls

**Proofreading and Indexing**
TECHBOOKS Production Services

To Kalle — Welcome to the family! — *Bill Evjen*

First, I want to thank everyone at Wrox and Microsoft that helped in getting this done. Also, I'd like to thank the other authors for their hard work. Finally, I would like to dedicate this to my wife and my son for putting up with me and the late nights. Without their support and love, none of this really matters. — *Jay Glynn*

To Donna — *Karli Watson*

For my brother, Michael — *Allen Jones*

# Contents

| | |
|---|---|
| Introduction | xxxiii |
| **Part I: The C# Language** | **1** |
| **Chapter 1: .NET Architecture** | **3** |
| The Relationship of C# to .NET | 4 |
| The Common Language Runtime | 4 |
| Advantages of Managed Code | 4 |
| A Closer Look at Intermediate Language | 7 |
| Support for Object Orientation and Interfaces | 8 |
| Distinct Value and Reference Types | 9 |
| Strong Data Typing | 9 |
| Error Handling with Exceptions | 16 |
| Use of Attributes | 17 |
| Assemblies | 17 |
| Private Assemblies | 18 |
| Shared Assemblies | 19 |
| Reflection | 19 |
| .NET Framework Classes | 19 |
| Namespaces | 21 |
| Creating .NET Applications Using C# | 21 |
| Creating ASP.NET Applications | 21 |
| Creating Windows Forms | 24 |
| Windows Controls | 24 |
| Windows Services | 24 |
| The Role of C# in the .NET Enterprise Architecture | 24 |
| Summary | 26 |
| **Chapter 2: C# Basics** | **29** |
| Before We Start | 30 |
| Your First C# Program | 30 |
| The Code | 30 |
| Compiling and Running the Program | 31 |
| A Closer Look | 31 |

# Contents

| | |
|---|---|
| **Variables** | **33** |
| Initialization of Variables | 34 |
| Variable Scope | 35 |
| Constants | 38 |
| **Predefined Data Types** | **39** |
| Value Types and Reference Types | 39 |
| CTS Types | 40 |
| Predefined Value Types | 41 |
| Predefined Reference Types | 44 |
| **Flow Control** | **47** |
| Conditional Statements | 47 |
| Loops | 51 |
| Jump Statements | 54 |
| **Enumerations** | **55** |
| **Arrays** | **57** |
| **Namespaces** | **58** |
| The using Statement | 59 |
| Namespace Aliases | 60 |
| **The Main() Method** | **61** |
| Multiple Main() Methods | 61 |
| Passing Arguments to Main() | 63 |
| **More on Compiling C# Files** | **63** |
| **Console I/O** | **65** |
| **Using Comments** | **67** |
| Internal Comments Within the Source Files | 67 |
| XML Documentation | 68 |
| **The C# Preprocessor Directives** | **70** |
| #define and #undef | 70 |
| #if, #elif, #else, and #endif | 71 |
| #warning and #error | 72 |
| #region and #endregion | 72 |
| #line | 73 |
| #pragma | 73 |
| **C# Programming Guidelines** | **73** |
| Rules for Identifiers | 73 |
| Usage Conventions | 75 |
| **Summary** | **81** |
| **Chapter 3: Objects and Types** | **83** |
| **Classes and Structs** | **84** |
| **Class Members** | **85** |
| Data Members | 85 |

| | |
|---|---:|
| Function Members | 85 |
| readonly Fields | 99 |
| **Structs** | **101** |
| Structs Are Value Types | 102 |
| Structs and Inheritance | 103 |
| Constructors for Structs | 104 |
| **Partial Classes** | **104** |
| **Static Classes** | **106** |
| **The Object Class** | **106** |
| System.Object Methods | 106 |
| The ToString() Method | 108 |
| **Summary** | **110** |

## Chapter 4: Inheritance 111

| | |
|---|---:|
| **Types of Inheritance** | **111** |
| Implementation Versus Interface Inheritance | 111 |
| Multiple Inheritance | 112 |
| Structs and Classes | 112 |
| **Implementation Inheritance** | **113** |
| Virtual Methods | 114 |
| Hiding Methods | 115 |
| Calling Base Versions of Functions | 116 |
| Abstract Classes and Functions | 117 |
| Sealed Classes and Methods | 117 |
| Constructors of Derived Classes | 118 |
| **Modifiers** | **124** |
| Visibility Modifiers | 124 |
| Other Modifiers | 125 |
| **Interfaces** | **126** |
| Defining and Implementing Interfaces | 127 |
| Derived Interfaces | 131 |
| **Summary** | **132** |

## Chapter 5: Operators and Casts 133

| | |
|---|---:|
| **Operators** | **133** |
| Operator Shortcuts | 135 |
| The Ternary Operator | 136 |
| The checked and unchecked Operators | 137 |
| The is Operator | 138 |
| The as Operator | 138 |
| The sizeof Operator | 138 |

xiii

## Contents

| | |
|---|---|
| The typeof Operator | 139 |
| Nullable Types and Operators | 139 |
| The Null Coalescing Operator | 139 |
| Operator Precedence | 140 |
| **Type Safety** | **140** |
| Type Conversions | 141 |
| Boxing and Unboxing | 145 |
| **Comparing Objects for Equality** | **146** |
| Comparing Reference Types for Equality | 146 |
| Comparing Value Types for Equality | 147 |
| **Operator Overloading** | **148** |
| How Operators Work | 149 |
| Operator Overloading Example: The Vector Struct | 150 |
| Which Operators Can You Overload? | 157 |
| **User-Defined Casts** | **157** |
| Implementing User-Defined Casts | 159 |
| Multiple Casting | 165 |
| **Summary** | **169** |

## Chapter 6: Delegates and Events                           171

| | |
|---|---|
| **Delegates** | **171** |
| Declaring Delegates in C# | 173 |
| Using Delegates in C# | 174 |
| **Anonymous Methods** | **176** |
| SimpleDelegate Example | 177 |
| BubbleSorter Example | 180 |
| Multicast Delegates | 183 |
| **Events** | **185** |
| The Receiver's View of Events | 185 |
| Generating Events | 188 |
| **Summary** | **192** |

## Chapter 7: Memory Management and Pointers                 193

| | |
|---|---|
| **Memory Management under the Hood** | **193** |
| Value Data Types | 194 |
| Reference Data Types | 196 |
| Garbage Collection | 198 |
| **Freeing Unmanaged Resources** | **199** |
| Destructors | 199 |
| The IDisposable Interface | 201 |
| Implementing IDisposable and a Destructor | 202 |

## Unsafe Code — 204
- Pointers — 204
- Pointer Example: PointerPlayaround — 214
- Using Pointers to Optimize Performance — 219

**Summary** — 222

# Chapter 8: Strings and Regular Expressions — 223

## System.String — 224
- Building Strings — 225
- StringBuilder Members — 228
- Format Strings — 229

## Regular Expressions — 235
- Introduction to Regular Expressions — 236
- The RegularExpressionsPlayaround Example — 237
- Displaying Results — 240
- Matches, Groups, and Captures — 241

**Summary** — 244

# Chapter 9: Collections — 245

## Examining Groups of Objects — 245
- Collections — 246
- Array Lists — 250
- The Stack Class — 253
- The Queue Class — 256
- The SortedList Class — 257
- Dictionaries and Hashtables — 259
- Generics — 269

**Summary** — 270

# Chapter 10: Generics — 271

## Overview — 272
- Performance — 272
- Type Safety — 273
- Binary Code Reuse — 273
- Code Bloat — 274
- Naming Guidelines — 274

## Generic Collection Classes — 275
- Generic Collections Overview — 275
- Using the List<T> Class — 278

## Contents

| | |
|---|---|
| Using the Queue<T> Class | 283 |
| Using the LinkedList<T> | 287 |
| **Creating Custom Generic Classes** | **293** |
| Default Values | 294 |
| Constraints | 294 |
| **Generic Methods** | **297** |
| **Generic Delegates** | **299** |
| **Other Generic Framework Types** | **301** |
| Nullable<T> | 301 |
| EventHandler<TEventArgs> | 302 |
| ArraySegment<T> | 303 |
| **Summary** | **304** |

## Chapter 11: Reflection                                                      305

| | |
|---|---|
| **Custom Attributes** | **306** |
| Writing Custom Attributes | 306 |
| Custom Attribute Example: WhatsNewAttributes | 310 |
| **Reflection** | **314** |
| The System.Type Class | 314 |
| The TypeView Example | 316 |
| The Assembly Class | 319 |
| Completing the WhatsNewAttributes Example | 321 |
| **Summary** | **325** |

## Chapter 12: Errors and Exceptions                                           327

| | |
|---|---|
| **Looking into Errors and Exception Handling** | **327** |
| Exception Classes | 328 |
| Catching Exceptions | 330 |
| User-Defined Exception Classes | 340 |
| **Summary** | **348** |

## Chapter 13: Threading                                                      349

| | |
|---|---|
| **Threading** | **349** |
| **Applications with Multiple Threads** | **351** |
| **Manipulating Threads** | **351** |
| The ThreadPlayaround Sample | 355 |
| Thread Priorities | 358 |
| Synchronization | 359 |
| **Creating Threads Using ThreadPool** | **364** |
| **Summary** | **368** |

# Contents

## Part II: The .NET Environment — 369

### Chapter 14: Visual Studio 2005 — 371

**Working with Visual Studio 2005** — **371**
   Creating a Project — 377
   Solutions and Projects — 383
   Windows Application Code — 387
   Reading in Visual Studio 6 Projects — 387
   Exploring and Coding a Project — 388
   Building a Project — 399
   Debugging — 404
**Refactoring** — **408**
**Summary** — **410**

### Chapter 15: Assemblies — 411

**What Are Assemblies?** — **411**
   The Answer to DLL Hell — 412
   Features of Assemblies — 413
   Application Domains and Assemblies — 413
**Assembly Structure** — **417**
   Assembly Manifests — 418
   Namespaces, Assemblies, and Components — 419
   Private and Shared Assemblies — 419
   Viewing Assemblies — 420
   Building Assemblies — 421
**Cross-Language Support** — **425**
   The CTS and the CLS — 425
   Language Independence in Action — 427
   CLS Requirements — 436
**Global Assembly Cache** — **438**
   Native Image Generator — 438
   Global Assembly Cache Viewer — 439
   Global Assembly Cache Utility (gacutil.exe) — 441
**Creating Shared Assemblies** — **441**
   Shared Assembly Names — 441
   Creating a Shared Assembly — 444
**Configuration** — **449**
   Configuration Categories — 450
   Versioning — 451
   Configuring Directories — 460
**Summary** — **462**

# Contents

## Chapter 16: .NET Security — 463

### Code Access Security — 464
- Code Groups — 465
- Code Access Permissions and Permissions Sets — 471
- Policy Levels: Machine, User, and Enterprise — 476

### Support for Security in the Framework — 478
- Demanding Permissions — 479
- Requesting Permissions — 480
- Implicit Permission — 484
- Denying Permissions — 485
- Asserting Permissions — 486
- Creating Code Access Permissions — 487
- Declarative Security — 488

### Managing Security Policies — 489
- The Security Configuration File — 489
- Managing Code Groups and Permissions — 492
- Turning Security On and Off — 493
- Resetting Security Policy — 493
- Creating a Code Group — 493
- Deleting a Code Group — 494
- Changing a Code Group's Permissions — 494
- Creating and Applying Permissions Sets — 495
- Distributing Code Using a Strong Name — 497
- Distributing Code Using Certificates — 499
- Managing Zones — 504

### Role-Based Security — 506
- The Principal — 507
- Windows Principal — 508
- Roles — 509
- Declarative Role-Based Security — 509

### Summary — 510

## Chapter 17: Localization — 513

### Namespace System.Globalization — 514
- Unicode Issues — 514
- Cultures and Regions — 515
- Cultures in Action — 520
- Sorting — 524

### Resources — 526
- Creating Resource Files — 526
- Resource File Generator — 527

|  |  |
|---|---|
| ResourceWriter | 527 |
| Using Resource Files | 528 |
| The System.Resources Namespace | 533 |
| **Localization Example Using Visual Studio** | **534** |
| Changing the Culture Programmatically | 539 |
| Using Custom Resource Messages | 541 |
| Automatic Fallback for Resources | 542 |
| Outsourcing Translations | 543 |
| **Localization with ASP.NET** | **544** |
| **A Custom Resource Reader** | **545** |
| Creating a DatabaseResourceReader | 546 |
| Creating a DatabaseResourceSet | 547 |
| Creating a DatabaseResourceManager | 548 |
| Client Application for DatabaseResourceReader | 549 |
| **Creating Custom Cultures** | **549** |
| **Summary** | **550** |

## Chapter 18: Deployment — 551

|  |  |
|---|---|
| **Designing for Deployment** | **551** |
| **Deployment Options** | **552** |
| Xcopy | 552 |
| Copy Web Tool | 552 |
| Publishing Web Sites | 552 |
| Deployment Projects | 552 |
| ClickOnce | 553 |
| **Deployment Requirements** | **553** |
| **Simple Deployment** | **554** |
| Xcopy | 554 |
| Xcopy and Web Applications | 555 |
| Copy Web Tool | 555 |
| Publishing a Web Site | 555 |
| **Installer Projects** | **556** |
| What Is Windows Installer? | 556 |
| Creating Installers | 557 |
| **ClickOnce** | **567** |
| ClickOnce Operation | 567 |
| Publishing an Application | 568 |
| ClickOnce Settings | 568 |
| Application Cache | 569 |
| Security | 569 |
| Advanced Options | 570 |
| **Summary** | **576** |

# Contents

## Part III: Data — 577

### Chapter 19: Data Access with .NET — 579

**ADO.NET Overview** — 580
- Namespaces — 580
- Shared Classes — 581
- Database-Specific Classes — 581

**Using Database Connections** — 582
- Managing Connection Strings — 584
- Using Connections Efficiently — 585
- Transactions — 588

**Commands** — 589
- Executing Commands — 590
- Calling Stored Procedures — 594

**Fast Data Access: The Data Reader** — 597

**Managing Data and Relationships: The DataSet Class** — 600
- Data Tables — 601
- Data Columns — 602
- Data Relationships — 608
- Data Constraints — 609

**XML Schemas** — 612
- Generating Code with XSD — 613

**Populating a DataSet** — 619
- Populating a DataSet Class with a Data Adapter — 619
- Populating a DataSet from XML — 620

**Persisting DataSet Changes** — 620
- Updating with Data Adapters — 621
- Writing XML Output — 623

**Working with ADO.NET** — 625
- Tiered Development — 625
- Key Generation with SQL Server — 627
- Naming Conventions — 629

**Summary** — 630

### Chapter 20: .NET Programming with SQL Server 2005 — 633

**.NET Runtime Host** — 634
**Microsoft.SqlServer.Server** — 635
**User-Defined Types** — 636
- Creating UDTs — 636
- Using UDTs — 642
- Using UDTs from Client-Side Code — 642

xx

## Contents

| | |
|---|---:|
| **User-Defined Aggregates** | **643** |
| Creating User-Defined Aggregates | 644 |
| Using User-Defined Aggregates | 645 |
| **Stored Procedures** | **645** |
| Creating Stored Procedures | 645 |
| Using Stored Procedures | 646 |
| **User-Defined Functions** | **647** |
| Creating User-Defined Functions | 647 |
| Using User-Defined Functions | 648 |
| **Triggers** | **648** |
| Creating Triggers | 649 |
| Using Triggers | 650 |
| **XML Data Type** | **650** |
| Tables with XML Data | 651 |
| Query of Data | 653 |
| XML Data Modification Language (XML DML) | 654 |
| XML Indexes | 655 |
| Strongly Typed XML | 656 |
| **Summary** | **657** |

## Chapter 21: Manipulating XML                                    659

| | |
|---|---:|
| **XML Standards Support in .NET** | **660** |
| **Introducing the System.Xml Namespace** | **660** |
| **Using MSXML in .NET** | **661** |
| **Using System.Xml Classes** | **663** |
| **Reading and Writing Streamed XML** | **664** |
| Using the XmlReader Class | 664 |
| Validating with XmlReader | 668 |
| Using the XmlWriter Class | 670 |
| **Using the DOM in .NET** | **672** |
| Using the XmlDocument Class | 673 |
| **Using XPathNavigators** | **678** |
| The System.Xml.XPath Namespace | 678 |
| The System.Xml.Xsl Namespace | 684 |
| **XML and ADO.NET** | **689** |
| Converting ADO.NET Data to XML | 689 |
| Converting XML to ADO.NET Data | 696 |
| Reading and Writing a DiffGram | 699 |
| **Serializing Objects in XML** | **701** |
| Serialization without Source Code Access | 708 |
| **Summary** | **711** |

## Contents

### Chapter 22: Working with Active Directory — 713

- **The Architecture of Active Directory** — 714
  - Features — 714
  - Active Directory Concepts — 715
  - Characteristics of Active Directory Data — 719
  - Schema — 719
- **Administration Tools for Active Directory** — 721
  - Active Directory Users and Computers — 721
  - ADSI Edit — 722
- **Programming Active Directory** — 723
  - Classes in System.DirectoryServices — 725
  - Binding — 725
  - Getting Directory Entries — 730
  - Object Collections — 731
  - Cache — 732
  - Creating New Objects — 733
  - Updating Directory Entries — 734
  - Accessing Native ADSI Objects — 735
  - Searching in Active Directory — 736
- **Searching for User Objects** — 740
  - User Interface — 740
  - Get the Schema Naming Context — 741
  - Get the Property Names of the User Class — 742
  - Search for User Objects — 743
- **DSML** — 745
  - Classes in System.DirectoryServices.Protocols — 746
  - Searching for Active Directory Objects with DSML — 746
- **Summary** — 748

## Part IV: Windows Applications — 749

### Chapter 23: Windows Forms — 751

- **Creating a Windows Form Application** — 752
  - Class Hierarchy — 757
- **Control Class** — 759
  - Size and Location — 759
  - Appearance — 760
  - User Interaction — 760
  - Windows Functionality — 761
  - Miscellaneous Functionality — 762

| Standard Controls and Components | **762** |
|---|---|
| Button | 762 |
| CheckBox | 764 |
| RadioButton | 764 |
| ComboBox, ListBox, and CheckedListBox | 765 |
| DateTimePicker | 767 |
| ErrorProvider | 767 |
| HelpProvider | 769 |
| ImageList | 769 |
| Label | 769 |
| ListView | 770 |
| PictureBox | 772 |
| ProgressBar | 772 |
| TextBox, RichTextBox and MaskedTextBox | 773 |
| Panel | 774 |
| FlowLayoutPanel and TableLayoutPanel | 774 |
| SplitContainer | 775 |
| TabControl and TabPages | 776 |
| ToolStrip | 776 |
| MenuStrip | 779 |
| ContextMenuStrip | 779 |
| ToolStripMenuItem | 779 |
| ToolStripManager | 780 |
| ToolStripContainer | 780 |
| **Forms** | **780** |
| Form Class | 781 |
| Multiple Document Interface (MDI) | 786 |
| Custom Controls | 787 |
| **Summary** | **799** |

## Chapter 24: Viewing .NET Data — 801

| **The DataGridView Control** | **801** |
|---|---|
| Displaying Tabular Data | 802 |
| Data Sources | 803 |
| **DataGridView Class Hierarchy** | **813** |
| **Data Binding** | **816** |
| Simple Binding | 816 |
| Data-Binding Objects | 817 |
| **Visual Studio .NET and Data Access** | **822** |
| Creating a Connection | 822 |
| Selecting Data | 825 |

xxiii

# Contents

| | |
|---|---|
| Updating the Data Source | 826 |
| Building a Schema | 827 |
| Other Common Requirements | 832 |
| **Summary** | **840** |

## Chapter 25: Graphics with GDI+ — 841

| | |
|---|---|
| **Understanding Drawing Principles** | **842** |
| GDI and GDI+ | 842 |
| Drawing Shapes | 844 |
| Painting Shapes Using OnPaint() | 847 |
| Using the Clipping Region | 848 |
| **Measuring Coordinates and Areas** | **850** |
| Point and PointF | 851 |
| Size and SizeF | 852 |
| Rectangle and RectangleF | 853 |
| Region | 854 |
| **A Note about Debugging** | **855** |
| **Drawing Scrollable Windows** | **856** |
| **World, Page, and Device Coordinates** | **863** |
| **Colors** | **863** |
| Red-Green-Blue (RGB) Values | 863 |
| The Named Colors | 864 |
| Graphics Display Modes and the Safety Palette | 865 |
| The Safety Palette | 866 |
| **Pens and Brushes** | **866** |
| Brushes | 866 |
| Pens | 867 |
| **Drawing Shapes and Lines** | **868** |
| **Displaying Images** | **870** |
| **Issues When Manipulating Images** | **873** |
| **Drawing Text** | **874** |
| **Simple Text Example** | **874** |
| **Fonts and Font Families** | **876** |
| **Example: Enumerating Font Families** | **878** |
| **Editing a Text Document: The CapsEditor Sample** | **880** |
| The Invalidate() Method | 885 |
| Calculating Item Sizes and Document Size | 886 |
| OnPaint() | 887 |
| Coordinate Transforms | 889 |
| Responding to User Input | 890 |

# Contents

| Printing | 893 |
|---|---|
| Implementing Print and Print Preview | 895 |
| **Summary** | **899** |

## Part V: Web Applications — 901

### Chapter 26: ASP.NET Pages — 903

| **ASP.NET Introduction** | **904** |
|---|---|
| State Management in ASP.NET | 905 |
| **ASP.NET Web Forms** | **905** |
| The ASP.NET Code Model | 909 |
| ASP.NET Server Controls | 910 |
| **ADO.NET and Data Binding** | **926** |
| Updating the Event-Booking Application | 926 |
| More on Data Binding | 933 |
| **Application Configuration** | **939** |
| **Summary** | **941** |

### Chapter 27: ASP.NET Development — 943

| **Custom Controls** | **944** |
|---|---|
| User Controls | 944 |
| User Controls in PCSDemoSite | 950 |
| Custom Controls | 952 |
| **Master Pages** | **956** |
| Master Pages in PCSDemoSite | 958 |
| **Site Navigation** | **960** |
| Navigation in PCSDemoSite | 962 |
| **Security** | **963** |
| Adding Forms Authentication using the Security Wizard | 964 |
| Implementing a Login System | 969 |
| Login Web Server Controls | 970 |
| Securing Directories | 971 |
| Security in PCSDemoSite | 972 |
| **Themes** | **974** |
| Applying Themes to Pages | 974 |
| Defining Themes | 975 |
| Themes in PCSDemoSite | 975 |
| **Summary** | **979** |

xxv

# Contents

## Part VI: Communication — 981

### Chapter 28: Web Services — 983

**SOAP** — 984
**WSDL** — 985
**Web Services** — 987
    Exposing Web Services — 987
    Consuming Web Services — 990
**Extending the Event-Booking Example** — 993
    The Event-Booking Web Service — 993
    The Event-Booking Client — 997
**Exchanging Data Using SOAP Headers** — 1001
**Summary** — 1007

### Chapter 29: .NET Remoting — 1009

**What Is .NET Remoting?** — 1010
    Application Types and Protocols — 1010
    CLR Object Remoting — 1011
**.NET Remoting Overview** — 1011
**Contexts** — 1014
    Activation — 1015
    Attributes and Properties — 1015
    Communication between Contexts — 1016
**Remote Objects, Clients, and Servers** — 1016
    Remote Objects — 1017
    A Simple Server — 1018
    A Simple Client — 1019
**.NET Remoting Architecture** — 1020
    Channels — 1020
    Formatters — 1025
    ChannelServices and RemotingConfiguration — 1025
    Object Activation — 1027
    Message Sinks — 1030
    Passing Objects in Remote Methods — 1031
    Lifetime Management — 1036
**Miscellaneous .NET Remoting Features** — 1039
    Configuration Files — 1039
    Hosting Servers in ASP.NET — 1050
    Classes, Interfaces, and Soapsuds — 1051

|   |   |
|---|---|
| Asynchronous Remoting | 1053 |
| Security with .NET Remoting | 1054 |
| Remoting and Events | 1056 |
| Call Contexts | 1062 |
| **Summary** | **1064** |

## Chapter 30: Enterprise Services — 1065

### Overview — 1065

|   |   |
|---|---|
| History | 1066 |
| Where to Use Enterprise Services | 1067 |
| Contexts | 1067 |
| Automatic Transactions | 1068 |
| Distributed Transactions | 1068 |
| Object Pooling | 1068 |
| Role-based Security | 1068 |
| Queued Components | 1069 |
| Loosely Coupled Events | 1069 |
| Services without Components | 1069 |

### Creating a Simple COM+ Application — 1070

|   |   |
|---|---|
| Class ServicedComponent | 1070 |
| Sign the Assembly | 1070 |
| Assembly Attributes | 1071 |
| Creating the Component | 1072 |

### Deployment — 1073

|   |   |
|---|---|
| Automatic Deployment | 1073 |
| Manual Deployment | 1073 |
| Creating an Installer Package | 1074 |

### Component Services Explorer — 1075
### Client Application — 1077
### Transactions — 1078

|   |   |
|---|---|
| ACID Properties | 1078 |
| Transaction Attributes | 1079 |
| Transaction Results | 1079 |

### Sample Application — 1080

|   |   |
|---|---|
| Entity Classes | 1081 |
| The OrderControl Component | 1084 |
| The OrderData Component | 1085 |
| The OrderLineData Component | 1088 |
| Client Application | 1089 |

### Services without Components — 1090
### Summary — 1093

# Contents

## Chapter 31: Message Queuing — 1095

### Overview — 1095
- When to Use Message Queuing — 1096
- Message Queuing Features — 1098

### Message Queuing Products — 1098

### Message Queuing Architecture — 1099
- Messages — 1099
- Message Queue — 1100

### Message Queuing Administrative Tools — 1101
- Creating Message Queues — 1101
- Message Queue Properties — 1101

### Programming Message Queuing — 1103
- Creating a Message Queue — 1103
- Finding a Queue — 1103
- Opening Known Queues — 1104
- Sending a Message — 1106
- Receiving Messages — 1109

### Course Order Application — 1111
- Course Order Class Library — 1111
- Course Order Message Sender — 1114
- Sending Priority and Recoverable Messages — 1115
- Course Order Message Receiver — 1116

### Receiving Results — 1120
- Acknowledgement Queues — 1120
- Response Queues — 1120

### Transactional Queues — 1121
### Message Queue Installation — 1122
### Summary — 1123

## Chapter 32: Future of Distributed Programming — 1125

### Problems Today — 1126
### Web Services — 1126
- Security — 1128
- Reliability — 1129
- Transactions — 1131
- Performance — 1133

### WCF Overview — 1134
### Programming with WCF — 1137
- Contracts — 1137
- Service Implementation — 1139
- Binding — 1141

## Contents

| | |
|---|---|
| Hosting | 1143 |
| Clients | 1144 |
| **Preparing for WCF** | **1145** |
| .NET Remoting | 1145 |
| ASP.NET Web Services | 1146 |
| Enterprise Services | 1146 |
| Message Queuing | 1147 |
| **Summary** | **1148** |

# Part VII: Interop     1149

## Chapter 33: COM Interoperability     1151

| | |
|---|---|
| **.NET and COM** | **1152** |
| Metadata | 1152 |
| Freeing Memory | 1153 |
| Interfaces | 1153 |
| Method Binding | 1155 |
| Data Types | 1155 |
| Registration | 1155 |
| Threading | 1156 |
| Error Handling | 1158 |
| Event Handling | 1158 |
| **Marshaling** | **1159** |
| **Using a COM Component from a .NET Client** | **1159** |
| Creating a COM Component | 1159 |
| Creating a Runtime Callable Wrapper | 1163 |
| Threading Issues | 1166 |
| Adding Connection Points | 1166 |
| Using ActiveX Controls in Windows Forms | 1168 |
| Using COM Objects from within ASP.NET | 1171 |
| **Using a .NET Component from a COM Client** | **1171** |
| COM Callable Wrapper | 1172 |
| Creating a .NET Component | 1172 |
| Creating a Type Library | 1173 |
| COM Interop Attributes | 1175 |
| COM Registration | 1178 |
| Creating a COM Client | 1179 |
| Adding Connection Points | 1181 |
| Creating a Client with a Sink Object | 1182 |
| Running Windows Forms Controls in Internet Explorer | 1183 |
| **Summary** | **1184** |

# Contents

## Part VIII: Windows Base Services — 1185

### Chapter 34: Manipulating Files and the Registry — 1187

**Managing the File System** — **1188**
- .NET Classes That Represent Files and Folders — 1189
- The Path Class — 1191
- Example: A File Browser — 1192

**Moving, Copying, and Deleting Files** — **1197**
- Example: FilePropertiesAndMovement — 1197
- Looking at the Code for FilePropertiesAndMovement — 1198

**Reading and Writing to Files** — **1201**
- Reading a File — 1202
- Writing to a File — 1204
- Streams — 1205
- Buffered Streams — 1207
- Reading and Writing to Binary Files Using FileStream — 1208
- Reading and Writing to Text Files — 1213

**Reading Drive Information** — **1220**

**File Security** — **1222**
- Reading ACLs from a File — 1222
- Reading ACLs from a Directory — 1224
- Adding and Removing ACLs from a File — 1225

**Reading and Writing to the Registry** — **1226**
- The Registry — 1227
- The .NET Registry Classes — 1229
- Example: SelfPlacingWindow — 1232

**Summary** — **1238**

### Chapter 35: Accessing the Internet — 1239

**The WebClient Class** — **1240**
- Downloading Files — 1240
- Basic Web Client Example — 1240
- Uploading Files — 1242

**WebRequest and WebResponse Classes** — **1242**
- Other WebRequest and WebResponse Features — 1243

**Displaying Output as an HTML Page** — **1245**
- Allowing Simple Web Browsing from Your Applications — 1246
- Launching Internet Explorer Instances — 1248

# Contents

| | |
|---|---|
| Giving Your Application More IE Type Features | 1248 |
| Showing Documents Using the WebBrowser Control | 1254 |
| Printing Using the WebBrowser Control | 1255 |
| Displaying the Code of a Requested Page | 1256 |
| The WebRequest and WebResponse Hierarchy | 1257 |
| **Utility Classes** | **1258** |
| URIs | 1258 |
| IP Addresses and DNS Names | 1259 |
| **Lower-Level Protocols** | **1262** |
| Lower-Level Classes | 1263 |
| **Summary** | **1268** |

## Chapter 36: Windows Services — 1271

| | |
|---|---|
| **What Is a Windows Service?** | **1271** |
| **Windows Services Architecture** | **1272** |
| Service Program | 1273 |
| Service Control Program | 1275 |
| Service Configuration Program | 1275 |
| **System.ServiceProcess Namespace** | **1275** |
| **Creating a Windows Service** | **1275** |
| A Class Library Using Sockets | 1276 |
| TcpClient Example | 1279 |
| Windows Service Project | 1281 |
| Threading and Services | 1287 |
| Service Installation | 1287 |
| Installation Program | 1287 |
| **Monitoring and Controlling the Service** | **1292** |
| MMC Computer Management | 1293 |
| net.exe | 1293 |
| sc.exe | 1294 |
| Visual Studio Server Explorer | 1295 |
| ServiceController Class | 1295 |
| **Troubleshooting** | **1301** |
| Interactive Services | 1302 |
| Event Logging | 1302 |
| Performance Monitoring | 1309 |
| **Power Events** | **1314** |
| **Summary** | **1314** |

xxxi

## Part IX: Appendices (Web Site Only)

| | |
|---|---|
| Appendix A: Principles of Object-Oriented Programming | 1319 |
| Appendix B: C# for Visual Basic 6 Developers | 1357 |
| Appendix C: C# for Java Developers | 1405 |
| Appendix D: C# for C++ Developers | 1433 |
| Index | 1487 |

# Introduction

If we were to describe the C# language and its associated environment, the .NET Framework, as the most important new technology for developers for many years, we would not be exaggerating. .NET is designed to provide a new environment within which you can develop almost any application to run on Windows, while C# is a new programming language that has been designed specifically to work with .NET. Using C# you can, for example, write a dynamic Web page, an XML Web service, a component of a distributed application, a database access component, a classic Windows desktop application, or even a new smart client application that allows for online/offline capabilities. This book covers the .NET Framework 2.0, the third release of the framework. If you are coding using version 1.0 or 1.1, there may be sections of the book that will not work for you. We try to notify you of items that are new to the .NET Framework 2.0 specifically.

Don't be fooled by the .NET label. The NET bit in the name is there to emphasize Microsoft's belief that distributed applications, in which the processing is distributed between client and server, are the way forward, but C# is not just a language for writing Internet or network-aware applications. It provides a means for you to code up almost any type of software or component that you might need to write for the Windows platform. Between them, C# and .NET are set both to revolutionize the way that you write programs, and to make programming on Windows much easier than it has ever been.

That's quite a substantial claim, and it needs to be justified. After all, we all know how quickly computer technology changes. Every year Microsoft brings out new software, programming tools, or versions of Windows, with the claim that these will be hugely beneficial to developers. So what's different about .NET and C#?

## The Significance of .NET and C#

In order to understand the significance of .NET, it is useful to remind ourselves of the nature of many of the Windows technologies that have appeared in the past ten years or so. Although they may look quite different on the surface, all of the Windows operating systems from Windows 3.1 (introduced in 1992) through Windows Server 2003 have the same familiar Windows API at their core. As we've progressed through new versions of Windows, huge numbers of new functions have been added to the API, but this has been a process of evolving and extending the API rather than replacing it.

The same can be said for many of the technologies and frameworks that we've used to develop software for Windows. For example, **COM (Component Object Model)** originated as **OLE (Object Linking and Embedding)**. At the time, it was, to a large extent, simply a means by which different types of Office documents could be linked, so that, for example, you could place a small Excel spreadsheet in your Word document. From that it evolved into COM, **DCOM (Distributed COM)**, and eventually COM+ — a sophisticated technology that formed the basis of the way almost all components communicated, as well as implementing transactions, messaging services, and object pooling.

Microsoft chose this evolutionary approach to software for the obvious reason that it is concerned about backward compatibility. Over the years a huge base of third-party software has been written for

# Introduction

Windows, and Windows wouldn't have enjoyed the success it has had if every time Microsoft introduced a new technology it broke the existing code base!

While backward compatibility has been a crucial feature of Windows technologies and one of the strengths of the Windows platform, it does have a big disadvantage. Every time some technology evolves and adds new features, it ends up a bit more complicated than it was before.

It was clear that something had to change. Microsoft couldn't go on forever extending the same development tools and languages, always making them more and more complex in order to satisfy the conflicting demands of keeping up with the newest hardware and maintaining backward compatibility with what was around when Windows first became popular in the early 1990s. There comes a point where you have to start with a clean slate if you want a simple yet sophisticated set of languages, environments, and developer tools, which makes it easy for developers to write state-of-the-art software.

This fresh start is what C# and .NET are all about. Roughly speaking, .NET is a framework—an API—for programming on the Windows platform. Along with the .NET Framework, C# is a language that has been designed from scratch to work with .NET, as well as to take advantage of all the progress in developer environments and in our understanding of object-oriented programming principles that have taken place over the past 20 years.

Before we continue, we should make it clear that backward compatibility has not been lost in the process. Existing programs will continue to work, and .NET was designed with the ability to work with existing software. Presently, communication between software components on Windows almost entirely takes place using COM. Taking account of this, .NET does have the ability to provide wrappers around existing COM components so that .NET components can talk to them.

It is true that you don't need to learn C# in order to write code for .NET. Microsoft has extended C++, provided another new language called J#, and made substantial changes to Visual Basic to turn it into the more powerful language Visual Basic .NET, in order to allow code written in either of these languages to target the .NET environment. These other languages, however, are hampered by the legacy of having evolved over the years rather than having been written from the start with today's technology in mind.

This book will equip you to program in C#, while at the same time provide the necessary background in how the .NET architecture works. We will not only cover the fundamentals of the C# language but also go on to give examples of applications that use a variety of related technologies, including database access, dynamic Web pages, advanced graphics, and directory access. The only requirement is that you be familiar with at least one other high-level language used on Windows — either C++, Visual Basic, or J++.

## *Advantages of .NET*

We've talked in general terms about how great .NET is, but we haven't said much about how it helps to make your life as a developer easier. In this section, we'll discuss some of the improved features of .NET in brief.

- ❑   **Object-Oriented Programming** — both the .NET Framework and C# are entirely based on object-oriented principles right from the start.
- ❑   **Good Design** — a base class library, which is designed from the ground up in a highly intuitive way.

- **Language Independence** — with .NET, all of the languages Visual Basic .NET, C#, J#, and managed C++ compile to a common **Intermediate Language**. This means that languages are interoperable in a way that has not been seen before.

- **Better Support for Dynamic Web Pages** — while ASP offered a lot of flexibility, it was also inefficient because of its use of interpreted scripting languages, and the lack of object-oriented design often resulted in messy ASP code. .NET offers an integrated support for Web pages, using a new technology — ASP.NET. With ASP.NET, code in your pages is compiled, and may be written in a .NET-aware high-level language such as C#, J#, or Visual Basic 2005.

- **Efficient Data Access** — a set of .NET components, collectively known as ADO.NET, provides efficient access to relational databases and a variety of data sources. Components are also available to allow access to the file system, and to directories. In particular, XML support is built into .NET, allowing you to manipulate data, which may be imported from or exported to non-Windows platforms.

- **Code Sharing** — .NET has completely revamped the way that code is shared between applications, introducing the concept of the **assembly**, which replaces the traditional DLL. Assemblies have formal facilities for versioning, and different versions of assemblies can exist side by side.

- **Improved Security** — each assembly can also contain built-in security information that can indicate precisely who or what category of user or process is allowed to call which methods on which classes. This gives you a very fine degree of control over how the assemblies that you deploy can be used.

- **Zero Impact Installation** — there are two types of assembly: shared and private. Shared assemblies are common libraries available to all software, while private assemblies are intended only for use with particular software. A private assembly is entirely self-contained, so the process of installing it is simple. There are no registry entries; the appropriate files are simply placed in the appropriate folder in the file system.

- **Support for Web Services** — .NET has fully integrated support for developing Web services as easily as you'd develop any other type of application.

- **Visual Studio 2005** — .NET comes with a developer environment, Visual Studio 2005, which can cope equally well with C++, C#, J#, and Visual Basic 2005, as well as with ASP.NET code. Visual Studio 2005 integrates all the best features of the respective language-specific environments of Visual Studio .NET 2002/2003 and Visual Studio 6.

- **C#** — C# is a new object-oriented language intended for use with .NET.

We will be looking more closely at the benefits of the .NET architecture in Chapter 1.

# What's New in the .NET Framework 2.0

The first version of the .NET Framework (1.0) was released in 2002 to much enthusiasm. The latest version, the .NET Framework 2.0, was introduced in 2005 and is considered a major release of the framework.

With each release of the framework, Microsoft has always tried to ensure that there were minimal breaking changes to code developed. Thus far, they have been very successful at this goal.

# Introduction

> Make sure that you create a staging server to completely test the upgrade of your applications to the .NET Framework 2.0 as opposed to just upgrading a live application.

The following details some of the changes that are new to the .NET Framework 2.0 as well as new additions to Visual Studio 2005 — the development environment for the .NET Framework 2.0.

## *SQL Server integration*

After a long wait, the latest version of SQL Server has finally been released. This version, SQL Server 2005, is quite special in so many ways. Most importantly for the .NET developer is that SQL Server 2005 is now hosting the CLR. Microsoft has developed their .NET offering for developers so that the .NET Framework 2.0, Visual Studio 2005 and SQL Server 2005 are all now tied together — meaning that these three products are now released in unison. This is quite important as it is rather well known that most applications built use all three of these pieces and that they all need to be upgraded together in such a way that they work with each other in a seamless manner.

Due to the fact that SQL Server 2005 now hosts the CLR, this means that you can now avoid building database aspects of your application using the T-SQL programming language. Instead, you can now build items such as your stored procedures, triggers and even data types in any of the .NET-compliant languages, such as C#.

SQL Server Express is the 2005 version of SQL Server that replaces MSDE. This version doesn't have the strict limitations MSDE had.

## *64-Bit support*

Most programming today is done on 32-bit machines. It was a monumental leap forward in application development when computers went from 16-bit to 32-bit. More and more enterprises are moving to the latest and greatest 64-bit servers from companies such as Intel (Itanium chips) and AMD (x64 chips) and the .NET Framework 2.0 has now been 64-bit enabled for this great migration.

Microsoft has been working hard to make sure that everything you build in the 32-bit world of .NET will run in the 64-bit world. This means that everything you do with SQL Server 2005 or ASP.NET will not be affected by moving to 64-bit. Microsoft themselves made a lot of changes to the CLR in order to get a 64-bit version of .NET to work. Changes where made to things such as garbage collection (to handle larger amounts of data), the JIT compilation process, exception handling, and more.

Moving to 64-bit gives you some powerful additions. The most important (and most obvious reason) is that 64-bit servers give you a larger address space. Going to 64-bit also allows for things like larger primitive types. For instance, an integer value of $2^{32}$ will give you 4,294,967,296 — while an integer value of $2^{64}$ will give you 18,446,744,073,709,551,616. This comes in quite handy for those applications that need to calculate things such as the U.S. debt or other high numbers.

Companies such as Microsoft and IBM are pushing their customers to take a look at 64-bit. One of the main areas of focus are on database and virtual storage capabilities as this is seen as an area in which it makes a lot of sense to move to 64-bit for.

# Introduction

Visual Studio 2005 can install and run on a 64-bit computer. This IDE has both 32-bit and 64-bit compilers on it. One final caveat is that the 64-bit .NET Framework is meant only for Windows Server 2003 SP1 or better as well as other 64-bit Microsoft operating systems that might come our way.

When you build your applications in Visual Studio 2005, you can change the build properties of your application so that it compiles specifically for 64-bit computers. To find this setting, you will need to pull up your application's properties and click on the Build tab from within the Properties page. On the Build page, click on the Advanced button and this will pull up the Advanced Compiler Setting dialog. From this dialog, you can change the target CPU from the bottom of the dialog. From here, you can establish your application to be built for either an Intel 64-bit computer or an AMD 64-bit computer. This is shown here in Figure I-1.

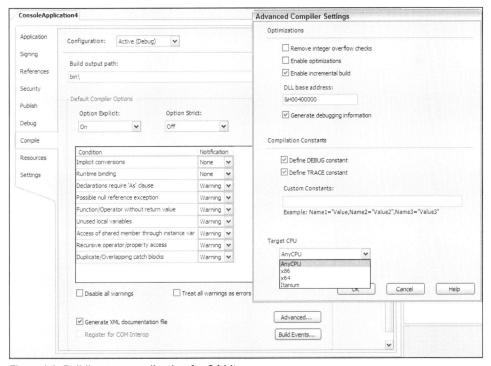

Figure I-1: Building your application for 64-bit

## *Generics*

In order to make collections a more powerful feature and also increase their efficiency and usability, generics were introduced to the .NET Framework 2.0. This introduction to the underlying framework means that languages such as C# and Visual Basic 2005 can now build applications that use generic types. The idea of generics is nothing new. They look similar to C++ templates but are a bit different. You can also find generics in other languages, such as Java. Their introduction into the .NET Framework 2.0 languages is a huge benefit for the user.

# Introduction

Generics enable you to make a generic collection that is still strongly typed — providing fewer chances for errors (because they occur at runtime), increasing performance, and giving you Intellisense features when you are working with the collections.

To utilize generics in your code, you will need to make reference to the `System.Collections.Generic` namespace. This will give you access to generic versions of the `Stack`, `Dictionary`, `SortedDictionary`, `List` and `Queue` classes. The following demonstrates the use of a generic version of the `Stack` class:

```
void Page_Load(object sender, EventArgs e)
{
    System.Collections.Generic.Stack<string> myStack =
        New System.Collections.Generic.Stack<string>();
    myStack.Push("St. Louis Rams");
    myStack.Push("Indianapolis Colts");
    myStack.Push("Minnesota Vikings");

    Array myArray;
    myArray = myStack.ToArray();

    foreach(string item in myArray)
    {
        Label1.Text += item + "<br />";
    }
}
```

In the above example, the `Stack` class is explicitly cast to be of type `string`. Here, you specify the collection type with the use of brackets. This example, casts the `Stack` class to type `string` using `Stack<string>`. If you wanted to cast it to something other than a `Stack` class of type `string` (for instance, `int`), then you would specify `Stack<int>`.

Because the collection of items in the `Stack` class is cast to a specific type immediately as the `Stack` class is created, the `Stack` class no longer casts everything to type `object` and then later (in the `foreach` loop) to type `string`. This process is called boxing, and it is expensive. Because this code is specifying the types up front, the performance is increased for working with the collection.

In addition to just working with various collection types, you can also use generics with classes, delegates, methods and more. Chapter 10 of this book covers generics in detail.

## *Anonymous methods*

Anonymous methods enable you to put programming steps within a delegate that you can then later execute instead of creating an entirely new method. For instance, if you were not using anonymous methods, you would use delegates in a manner similar to the following:

```
public partial class Default_aspx
{
    void Page_Load(object sender, EventArgs e)
    {
        this.Button1.Click += ButtonWork;
    }
```

# Introduction

```
    void ButtonWork(object sender, EventArgs e)
    {
        Label1.Text = "You clicked the button!";
    }
}
```

But using anonymous methods, you can now put these actions directly in the delegate as shown here in the following example:

```
public partial class Default_aspx
{
    void Page_Load(object sender, EventArgs e)
    {
        this.Button1.Click += delegate(object myDelSender, EventArgs myDelEventArgs)
        {
            Label1.Text = "You clicked the button!";
        };
    }
}
```

When using anonymous methods, there is no need to create a separate method. Instead you place the necessary code directly after the delegate declaration. The statements and steps to be executed by the delegate are placed between curly braces and closed with a semicolon.

## Nullable types

Due to the fact that generics has been introduced into the underlying .NET Framework 2.0, it is now possible to create nullable value types — using `System.Nullable<T>`. This is ideal for situations such as creating sets of nullable items of type `int`. Before this, it was always difficult to create an `int` with a null value from the get-go or to later assign null values to an `int`.

To create a nullable type of type `int`, you would use the following syntax:

```
System.Nullable<int> x = new System.Nullable<int>;
```

There is a new type modifier that you can also use to create a type as nullable. This is shown in the following example:

```
int? salary = 800000
```

This ability to create nullable types is not a C#-only item as this ability was built into .NET Framework itself and, as stated, is there due to the existence of the new generics feature in .NET. For this reason, you will also find nullable types in Visual Basic 2005 as well.

## Iterators

Iterators enable you to use `foreach` loops on your own custom types. To accomplish this, you need to have your class implement the `IEnumerable` interface as shown here:

# Introduction

```
using System;
using Systm.Collections;

public class myList
{
    internal object[] elements;
    internal int count;

    public IEnumerator GetEnumerator()
    {
        yield return "St. Louis Rams";
        yield return "Indianapolis Colts";
        yield return "Minnesota Vikiings";
    }
}
```

In order to use the `IEnumerator` interface, you will need to make a reference to the `System.Collections` namespace. With this all in place, you can then iterate through the custom class as shown here:

```
void Page_Load(object sender, EventArgs e)
{
    myList IteratorList = new myList();

    foreach(string item in IteratorList)
    {
        Response.Write(item.ToString() + "<br />");
    }
}
```

## *Partial Classes*

Partial classes are a new feature to the .NET Framework 2.0 and again C# takes advantage of this addition. Partial classes allow you to divide up a single class into multiple class files, which are later combined into a single class when compiled.

To create a partial class, you simply need to use the `partial` keyword for any classes that are to be joined together with a different class. The `partial` keyword precedes the `class` keyword for the classes that are to be combined with the original class. For instance, you might have a simple class called `Calculator` as shown here:

```
public class Calculator
{
    public int Add(int a, int b)
    {
        return a + b;
    }
}
```

From here, you can create a second class that attaches itself to this first class as shown here in the following example:

```
    public partial class Calculator
    {
        public int Subtract(int a, int b)
        {
            return a - b;
        }
    }
```

When compiled, these classes will be brought together into a single `Calculator` class instance as if they were built together to begin with.

# Where C# Fits In

In one sense, C# can be seen as being the same thing to programming languages as .NET is to the Windows environment. Just as Microsoft has been adding more and more features to Windows and the Windows API over the past decade, Visual Basic 2005 and C++ have undergone expansion. Although Visual Basic and C++ have ended up as hugely powerful languages as a result of this, both languages also suffer from problems due to the legacies of how they have evolved.

In the case of Visual Basic 6 and earlier versions, the main strength of the language was the fact that it was simple to understand and didn't make many programming tasks easy, largely hiding the details of the Windows API and the COM component infrastructure from the developer. The downside to this was that Visual Basic was never truly object-oriented, so that large applications quickly became disorganized and hard to maintain. As well, because Visual Basic's syntax was inherited from early versions of BASIC (which, in turn, was designed to be intuitively simple for beginning programmers to understand, rather than to write large commercial applications), it didn't really lend itself to well-structured or object-oriented programs.

C++, on the other hand, has its roots in the ANSI C++ language definition. It isn't completely ANSI-compliant for the simple reason that Microsoft first wrote its C++ compiler before the ANSI definition had become official, but it comes close. Unfortunately, this has led to two problems. First, ANSI C++ has its roots in a decade-old state of technology, and this shows up in a lack of support for modern concepts (such as Unicode strings and generating XML documentation), and for some archaic syntax structures designed for the compilers of yesteryear (such as the separation of declaration from definition of member functions). Second, Microsoft has been simultaneously trying to evolve C++ into a language that is designed for high-performance tasks on Windows, and in order to achieve that they've been forced to add a huge number of Microsoft-specific keywords as well as various libraries to the language. The result is that on Windows, the language has become a complete mess. Just ask C++ developers how many definitions for a string they can think of: `char*`, `LPTSTR`, `string`, `CString` (MFC version), `CString` (WTL version), `wchar_t*`, `OLECHAR*`, and so on.

Now enter .NET — a completely new environment that is going to involve new extensions to both languages. Microsoft has gotten around this by adding yet more Microsoft-specific keywords to C++, and by completely revamping Visual Basic into Visual Basic .NET into Visual Basic 2005, a language that retains some of the basic VB syntax but that is so different in design that we can consider it to be, for all practical purposes, a new language.

# Introduction

It's in this context that Microsoft has decided to give developers an alternative — a language designed specifically for .NET, and designed with a clean slate. Visual C# 2005 is the result. Officially, Microsoft describes C# as a "simple, modern, object-oriented, and type-safe programming language derived from C and C++." Most independent observers would probably change that to "derived from C, C++, and Java." Such descriptions are technically accurate but do little to convey the beauty or elegance of the language. Syntactically, C# is very similar to both C++ and Java, to such an extent that many keywords are the same, and C# also shares the same block structure with braces ({}) to mark blocks of code, and semicolons to separate statements. The first impression of a piece of C# code is that it looks quite like C++ or Java code. Beyond that initial similarity, however, C# is a lot easier to learn than C++, and of comparable difficulty to Java. Its design is more in tune with modern developer tools than both of those other languages, and it has been designed to give us, simultaneously, the ease of use of Visual Basic, and the high-performance, low-level memory access of C++ if required. Some of the features of C# are:

- Full support for classes and object-oriented programming, including both interface and implementation inheritance, virtual functions, and operator overloading.
- A consistent and well-defined set of basic types.
- Built-in support for automatic generation of XML documentation.
- Automatic cleanup of dynamically allocated memory.
- The facility to mark classes or methods with user-defined attributes. This can be useful for documentation and can have some effects on compilation (for example, marking methods to be compiled only in debug builds).
- Full access to the .NET base class library, as well as easy access to the Windows API (if you really need it, which won't be all that often).
- Pointers and direct memory access are available if required, but the language has been designed in such a way that you can work without them in almost all cases.
- Support for properties and events in the style of Visual Basic.
- Just by changing the compiler options, you can compile either to an executable or to a library of .NET components that can be called up by other code in the same way as ActiveX controls (COM components).
- C# can be used to write ASP.NET dynamic Web pages and XML Web services.

Most of the above statements, it should be pointed out, do also apply to Visual Basic 2005 and Managed C++. The fact that C# is designed from the start to work with .NET, however, means that its support for the features of .NET is both more complete, and offered within the context of a more suitable syntax than for those other languages. While the C# language itself is very similar to Java, there are some improvements, in particular, Java is not designed to work with the .NET environment.

Before we leave the subject, we should point out a couple of limitations of C#. The one area the language is not designed for is time-critical or extremely high performance code — the kind where you really are worried about whether a loop takes 1,000 or 1,050 machine cycles to run through, and you need to clean up your resources the millisecond they are no longer needed. C++ is likely to continue to reign supreme among low-level languages in this area. C# lacks certain key facilities needed for extremely high performance apps, including the ability to specify inline functions and destructors that are guaranteed to run at particular points in the code. However, the proportions of applications that fall into this category are very low.

# Introduction

## What You Need to Write and Run C# Code

The .NET Framework will run on Windows 98, 2000, XP, and 2003. In order to write code using .NET, you will need to install the .NET SDK unless you are using Windows Server 2003, which comes with the .NET Framework 1.0 and 1.1 already installed. If you are going to work through the examples in this book though, you are going to want to install the .NET Framework 2.0 — even if you are running Windows Server 2003 as the .NET Framework 2.0 is not included on this server as a default.

Also, unless you are intending to write your C# code using a text editor or some other third party developer environment, you will almost certainly also want Visual Studio 2005. The full SDK isn't needed to run managed code, but the .NET runtime is needed. You may find you need to distribute the .NET runtime with your code for the benefit of those clients who do not have it already installed.

## What This Book Covers

In this book, we start by reviewing the overall architecture of .NET in the next chapter in order to give us the background we need to be able to write managed code. After that the book is divided into a number of sections that cover both the C# language and its application in a variety of areas.

### Part I: The C# Language

This section gives us a good grounding in the C# language itself. This section doesn't presume knowledge of any particular language, although it does assume you are an experienced programmer. We start by looking at C#'s basic syntax and data types, and then discuss the object-oriented features of C# before moving on to look at more advanced C# programming topics.

### Part II: The .NET Environment

In this section, we look at the principles of programming in the .NET environment. In particular, we look at Visual Studio .NET, security, threading deployment of .NET applications, and how to generate your own libraries as assemblies.

### Part III: Data

Here we look at accessing databases with ADO.NET, and at interacting with directories and Active Directory. We also extensively cover support in .NET for XML and on the Windows operating system side, and the .NET features of SQL Server 2005.

### Part IV: Windows Applications

This section focuses on building classic Windows applications, which are called Windows Forms in .NET. Windows Forms are the thick-client version of applications, and using .NET to build these types of applications is a quick and easy way of accomplishing this task. In addition to looking at Windows Forms, we will take a look at GDI+, which is the technology we will use for building applications that include advanced graphics.

# Introduction

## *Part V: Web Applications*

In this section, we cover writing components that will run on Web sites, serving up Web pages. This covers the tremendous amount of new features that ASP.NET 2.0 provides.

## *Part VI: Communication*

This section is all about communication. Here we cover Web services for platform-independent communication, .NET Remoting for communication between .NET clients and servers, Enterprise Services for the services in the background and DCOM communication. With message queuing asynchronous, disconnected communication is shown. The chapter "Future of Distributed Programming" prepares you for the future so you can make the correct communication choices for your current solutions.

## *Part VII: Interop*

Backward compatibility with COM is an important part of .NET. Too many COM components and applications have been developed. This section shows how to use existing COM components with .NET applications, and the other way around, how to use .NET components within COM applications.

## *Part VIII: Windows Base Services*

This section, the concluding part of the main body of the book, covers accessing the file and registry, accessing the Internet through your applications, and working with Windows Services.

## *Part IX: Appendices (Web Site Only)*

This section includes several appendices detailing the principles of object-oriented programming as well as programming language-specific information about C#. These appendices are available as PDFs on the Web site accompanying this book (`http://www.wrox.com`).

# Conventions

We have used a number of different styles of text and layout in the book to help differentiate between the different kinds of information. Here are examples of the styles we use and an explanation of what they mean:

Bullets appear indented, with each new bullet marked as follows:

- **Important Words** are in a bold type font.
- Keys that you press on the keyboard, like *Ctrl* and *Enter*, are in italics.

Code appears in a number of different ways. If it's a word that we're talking about in the text — for example, when discussing the `if...else` loop — it's in `this font`. If it's a block of code that you can type in as a program and run, then it's also in a gray box:

```
    public static void Main()
    {
        AFunc(1,2,"abc");
    }
```

Sometimes you'll see code in a mixture of styles, like this:

```
// If we haven't reached the end, return true, otherwise
// set the position to invalid, and return false.
pos++;
if (pos < 4)
    return true;
else {
    pos = -1;
    return false;
}
```

The code with a white background is code we've already looked at and that we don't wish to examine further.

*Advice, hints, and background information come in an italicized, indented font like this.*

> **Important pieces of information come in boxes like this.**

We demonstrate the syntactical usage of methods, properties (and so on) using the following format:

```
Regsvcs BookDistributor.dll [COM+AppName] [TypeLibrary.tbl]
```

Here, italicized parts indicate object references, variables, or parameter values to be inserted; the square braces indicate optional parameters.

# Source Code

As you work through the examples in this book, you may choose either to type in all the code manually or to use the source code files that accompany the book. All of the source code used in this book is available for download at http://www.wrox.com. Once at the site, simply locate the book's title (either by using the Search box or by using one of the title lists) and click the Download Code link on the book's detail page to obtain all the source code for the book.

*Because many books have similar titles, you may find it easiest to search by ISBN; this book's ISBN is 0-7645-7534-1.*

Once you download the code, just decompress it with your favorite compression tool. Alternately, you can go to the main Wrox code download page at http://www.wrox.com/dynamic/books/download.aspx to see the code available for this book and all other Wrox books.

# Introduction

## Errata

We make every effort to ensure that there are no errors in the text or in the code. However, no one is perfect, and mistakes do occur. If you find an error in one of our books, like a spelling mistake or faulty piece of code, we would be very grateful for your feedback. By sending in errata you may save another reader hours of frustration, and at the same time you will be helping us provide even higher quality information.

To find the errata page for this book, go to `http://www.wrox.com` and locate the title using the Search box or one of the title lists. Then, on the book details page, click the Book Errata link. On this page you can view all errata that have been submitted for this book and posted by Wrox editors. A complete book list including links to each book's errata is also available at `http://www.wrox.com/misc-pages/booklist.shtml`.

If you don't spot "your" error already on the Book Errata page, go to `http://www.wrox.com/contact/techsupport.shtml` and complete the form there to send us the error you have found. We'll check the information and, if appropriate, post a message to the book's errata page and fix the problem in subsequent editions of the book.

## p2p.wrox.com

For author and peer discussion, join the P2P forums at `p2p.wrox.com`. The forums are a Web-based system for you to post messages relating to Wrox books and related technologies and interact with other readers and technology users. The forums offer a subscription feature to e-mail you topics of interest of your choosing when new posts are made to the forums. Wrox authors, editors, other industry experts, and your fellow readers are present on these forums.

At `http://p2p.wrox.com` you will find a number of different forums that will help you not only as you read this book, but also as you develop your own applications. To join the forums, just follow these steps:

1. Go to `p2p.wrox.com` and click the Register link.
2. Read the terms of use and click Agree.
3. Supply the required information to join as well as any optional information you wish to provide and click Submit.

You will receive an e-mail with information describing how to verify your account and complete the joining process.

> *You can read messages in the forums without joining P2P, but you must join in order to post your own messages.*

Once you join, you can post new messages and respond to other users' posts. You can read messages at any time on the Web. If you would like to have new messages from a particular forum e-mailed to you, click the Subscribe to this Forum icon by the forum name in the forum listing.

For more information about how to use the Wrox P2P, be sure to read the P2P FAQs for answers to questions about how the forum software works as well as many common questions specific to P2P and Wrox books. To read the FAQs, click the FAQ link on any P2P page.

# Part I
# The C# Language

Chapter 1: .NET Architecture

Chapter 2: C# Basics

Chapter 3: Objects and Types

Chapter 4: Inheritance

Chapter 5: Operators and Casts

Chapter 6: Delegates and Events

Chapter 7: Memory Management and Pointers

Chapter 8: Strings and Regular Expressions

Chapter 9: Collections

Chapter 10: Generics

Chapter 11: Reflection

Chapter 12: Errors and Exceptions

Chapter 13: Threading

# .NET Architecture

Throughout this book, we emphasize that the C# language cannot be viewed in isolation, but must be considered in parallel with the .NET Framework. The C# compiler specifically targets .NET, which means that all code written in C# will always run within the .NET Framework. This has two important consequences for the C# language:

- The architecture and methodologies of C# reflect the underlying methodologies of .NET.
- In many cases, specific language features of C# actually depend upon features of .NET, or of the .NET base classes.

Because of this dependence, it is important to gain some understanding of the architecture and methodology of .NET before you begin C# programming. That is the purpose of this chapter.

This chapter begins by going over what happens when all code (including C#) that targets .NET is compiled and run. Once you have this broad overview, you take a more detailed look at the *Microsoft Intermediate Language* (MSIL or simply IL), the assembly language that all compiled code ends up in on .NET. In particular, you see how IL, in partnership with the *Common Type System* (CTS) and *Common Language Specification* (CLS), works to give you interoperability between languages that target .NET. This chapter also discusses where common languages (including Visual Basic and C++) fit into .NET.

Next, you move on to examine some of the other features of .NET, including assemblies, namespaces, and the .NET base classes. The chapter finishes with a brief look at the kinds of applications you can create as a C# developer.

Chapter 1

# The Relationship of C# to .NET

C# is a relatively new programming language and is significant in two respects:

- ❑ It is specifically designed and targeted for use with Microsoft's .NET Framework (a feature-rich platform for the development, deployment, and execution of distributed applications).
- ❑ It is a language based on the modern object-oriented design methodology, and when designing it Microsoft learned from the experience of all the other similar languages that have been around since object-oriented principles came to prominence some 20 years ago.

One important thing to make clear is that C# is a language in its own right. Although it is designed to generate code that targets the .NET environment, it is not itself part of .NET. Some features are supported by .NET but not by C#, and you might be surprised to learn that some features of the C# language are not supported by .NET (for example, some instances of operator overloading)!

However, because the C# language is intended for use with .NET, it is important for you to have an understanding of this Framework if you want to develop applications in C# effectively. So, this chapter takes some time to peek underneath the surface of .NET. Let's get started.

# The Common Language Runtime

Central to the .NET Framework is its runtime execution environment, known as the *Common Language Runtime* (CLR) or the *.NET runtime*. Code running under the control of the CLR is often termed *managed code*.

However, before it can be executed by the CLR, any source code that you develop (in C# or some other language) needs to be compiled. Compilation occurs in two steps in .NET:

1. Compilation of source code to IL
2. Compilation of IL to platform-specific code by the CLR

This two-stage compilation process is very important, because the existence of the IL (managed code) is the key to providing many of the benefits of .NET.

## *Advantages of Managed Code*

Microsoft intermediate language shares with Java byte code the idea that it is a low-level language with a simple syntax (based on numeric codes rather than text), which can be very quickly translated into native machine code. Having this well-defined universal syntax for code has significant advantages.

### *Platform independence*

First, it means that the same file containing byte code instructions can be placed on any platform; at runtime the final stage of compilation can then be easily accomplished so that the code will run on that particular platform. In other words, by compiling to IL you obtain platform independence for .NET, in much the same way as compiling to Java byte code gives Java platform independence.

# .NET Architecture

You should note that the platform independence of .NET is only theoretical at present because, at the time of writing, a complete implementation of .NET is only available for Windows. However, a partial implementation is available (see, for example, the Mono project, an effort to create an open source implementation of .NET, at www.go-mono.com/).

## *Performance improvement*

Although we previously made comparisons with Java, IL is actually a bit more ambitious than Java byte code. IL is always *Just-In-Time* compiled (known as JIT compilation), whereas Java byte code was often interpreted. One of the disadvantages of Java was that, on execution, the process of translating from Java byte code to native executable resulted in a loss of performance (with the exception of more recent cases, where Java is JIT compiled on certain platforms).

Instead of compiling the entire application in one go (which could lead to a slow start-up time), the JIT compiler simply compiles each portion of code as it is called (just-in-time). When code has been compiled once, the resultant native executable is stored until the application exits, so that it does not need to be recompiled the next time that portion of code is run. Microsoft argues that this process is more efficient than compiling the entire application code at the start, because of the likelihood that large portions of any application code will not actually be executed in any given run. Using the JIT compiler, such code will never be compiled.

This explains why we can expect that execution of managed IL code will be almost as fast as executing native machine code. What it doesn't explain is why Microsoft expects that we will get a performance *improvement*. The reason given for this is that, because the final stage of compilation takes place at runtime, the JIT compiler will know exactly what processor type the program will run on. This means that it can optimize the final executable code to take advantage of any features or particular machine code instructions offered by that particular processor.

Traditional compilers will optimize the code, but they can only perform optimizations that are independent of the particular processor that the code will run on. This is because traditional compilers compile to native executable before the software is shipped. This means that the compiler doesn't know what type of processor the code will run on beyond basic generalities, such as that it will be an x86-compatible processor or an Alpha processor. Visual Studio 6, for example, optimizes for a generic Pentium machine, so the code that it generates cannot take advantage of hardware features of Pentium III processors. On the other hand, the JIT compiler can do all the optimizations that Visual Studio 6 can, and in addition it will optimize for the particular processor the code is running on.

## *Language interoperability*

The use of IL not only enables platform independence; it also facilitates *language interoperability*. Simply put, you can compile to IL from one language, and this compiled code should then be interoperable with code that has been compiled to IL from another language.

You're probably now wondering which languages aside from C# are interoperable with .NET, so the following sections briefly discuss how some of the other common languages fit into .NET.

### Visual Basic 2005

Visual Basic .NET 2002 had undergone a complete revamp from Visual Basic 6 to bring it up-to-date with the first version of the .NET Framework. The Visual Basic language itself had dramatically evolved from

VB6 and this meant that VB6 was not a suitable language for running .NET programs. For example, VB6 is heavily integrated into COM and works by exposing only event handlers as source code to the developer — most of the background code is not available as source code. Not only that, it does not support implementation inheritance, and the standard data types Visual Basic 6 uses are incompatible with .NET.

Visual Basic 6 was upgraded to Visual Basic .NET in 2002, and the changes that were made to the language are so extensive you might as well regard Visual Basic as a new language. Existing Visual Basic 6 code does not compile to the present Visual Basic 2005 code (or to Visual Basic .NET 2002 and 2003 for that matter). Converting a Visual Basic 6 program to Visual Basic 2005 requires extensive changes to the code. However, Visual Studio 2005 (the upgrade of Visual Studio for use with .NET) can do most of the changes for you. If you attempt to read a Visual Basic 6 project into Visual Studio 2005, it will upgrade the project for you, which means that it will rewrite the Visual Basic 6 source code into Visual Basic 2005 source code. Although this means that the work involved for you is heavily cut down, you will need to check through the new Visual Basic 2005 code to make sure that the project still works as intended because the conversion might not be perfect.

One side effect of this language upgrade is that it is no longer possible to compile Visual Basic 2005 to native executable code. Visual Basic 2005 compiles only to IL, just as C# does. If you need to continue coding in Visual Basic 6, you can do so, but the executable code produced will completely ignore the .NET Framework, and you'll need to keep Visual Studio 6 installed if you want to continue to work in this developer environment.

## Visual C++ 2005

Visual C++ 6 already had a large number of Microsoft-specific extensions on Windows. With Visual C++ .NET, extensions have been added to support the .NET Framework. This means that existing C++ source code will continue to compile to native executable code without modification. It also means, however, that it will run independently of the .NET runtime. If you want your C++ code to run within the .NET Framework, you can simply add the following line to the beginning of your code:

```
#using <mscorlib.dll>
```

You can also pass the flag /clr to the compiler, which then assumes that you want to compile to managed code, and will hence emit IL instead of native machine code. The interesting thing about C++ is that when you compile to managed code, the compiler can emit IL that contains an embedded native executable. This means that you can mix managed types and unmanaged types in your C++ code. Thus the managed C++ code

```
class MyClass
{
```

defines a plain C++ class, whereas the code

```
__gc class MyClass
{
```

will give you a managed class, just as if you'd written the class in C# or Visual Basic 2005. The advantage of using managed C++ over C# code is that you can call unmanaged C++ classes from managed C++ code without having to resort to COM interop.

# .NET Architecture

The compiler raises an error if you attempt to use features that are not supported by .NET on managed types (for example, templates or multiple inheritance of classes). You will also find that you will need to use nonstandard C++ features (such as the __gc keyword shown in the previous code) when using managed classes.

Because of the freedom that C++ allows in terms of low-level pointer manipulation and so on, the C++ compiler is not able to generate code that will pass the CLR's memory type safety tests. If it's important that your code is recognized by the CLR as memory type safe, you'll need to write your source code in some other language (such as C# or Visual Basic 2005).

### Visual J# 2005

The latest language to be added to the mix is Visual J# 2005. Prior to .NET Framework 1.1, users were able to use J# only after making a separate download. Now the J# language is built into the .NET Framework. Because of this, J# users are able to take advantage of all the usual features of Visual Studio 2005. Microsoft expects that most J++ users will find it easiest to use J# if they want to work with .NET. Instead of being targeted at the Java runtime libraries, J# uses the same base class libraries that the rest of the .NET-compliant languages use. This means that you can use J# for building ASP.NET Web applications, Windows Forms, XML Web services, and everything else that is possible—just as C# and Visual Basic 2005 can.

### Scripting languages

Scripting languages are still around, although in general, their importance is likely to decline with the advent of .NET. JScript, on the other hand, has been upgraded to JScript .NET. You can now write ASP.NET pages in JScript .NET, run JScript .NET as a compiled rather than an interpreted language, and write strongly typed JScript .NET code. With ASP.NET there is no reason to use scripting languages in server-side Web pages. VBA is, however, still used as a language for Microsoft Office and Visual Studio macros.

### COM and COM+

Technically speaking, COM and COM+ aren't technologies targeted at .NET, because components based on them cannot be compiled into IL (although it's possible to do so to some degree using managed C++, if the original COM component was written in C++). However, COM+ remains an important tool, because its features are not duplicated in .NET. Also, COM components will still work—and .NET incorporates COM interoperability features that make it possible for managed code to call up COM components and vice versa (this is discussed in Chapter 33, "COM Interoperability"). In general, however, you will probably find it more convenient for most purposes to code new components as .NET components, so that you can take advantage of the .NET base classes as well as the other benefits of running as managed code.

## A Closer Look at Intermediate Language

From what you learned in the previous section, Microsoft intermediate language obviously plays a fundamental role in the .NET Framework. As C# developers, we now understand that our C# code will be compiled into IL before it is executed (indeed, the C# compiler *only* compiles to managed code). It makes sense, then, to now take a closer look at the main characteristics of IL, because any language that targets .NET would logically need to support the main characteristics of IL, too.

# Chapter 1

Here are the important features of IL:

- ❏ Object orientation and use of interfaces
- ❏ Strong distinction between value and reference types
- ❏ Strong data typing
- ❏ Error handling through the use of exceptions
- ❏ Use of attributes

The following sections take a closer look at each of these characteristics.

## Support for Object Orientation and Interfaces

The language independence of .NET does have some practical limitations. IL is inevitably going to implement some particular programming methodology, which means that languages targeting it are going to have to be compatible with that methodology. The particular route that Microsoft has chosen to follow for IL is that of classic object-oriented programming, with single implementation inheritance of classes.

*If you are unfamiliar with the concepts of object orientation, refer to Appendix A for more information. Appendix A is posted at* www.wrox.com.

In addition to classic object-oriented programming, IL also brings in the idea of interfaces, which saw their first implementation under Windows with COM. .NET interfaces are not the same as COM interfaces; they do not need to support any of the COM infrastructure (for example, they are not derived from IUnknown, and they do not have associated GUIDs). However, they do share with COM interfaces the idea that they provide a contract, and classes that implement a given interface must provide implementations of the methods and properties specified by that interface.

You have now seen that working with .NET means compiling to IL, and that in turn means that you will need to use traditional object-oriented methodologies. However, that alone is not sufficient to give you language interoperability. After all, C++ and Java both use the same object-oriented paradigms, but they are still not regarded as interoperable. We need to look a little more closely at the concept of language interoperability.

To start with, we need to consider exactly what we mean by language interoperability. After all, COM allowed components written in different languages to work together in the sense of calling each other's methods. What was inadequate about that? COM, by virtue of being a binary standard, did allow components to instantiate other components and call methods or properties against them, without worrying about the language the respective components were written in. In order to achieve this, however, each object had to be instantiated through the COM runtime, and accessed through an interface. Depending on the threading models of the relative components, there may have been large performance losses associated with marshaling data between apartments or running components or both on different threads. In the extreme case of components hosted as an executable rather than DLL files, separate processes would need to be created in order to run them. The emphasis was very much that components could talk to each other but only via the COM runtime. In no way with COM did components written in different languages directly communicate with each other, or instantiate instances of each other — it was always done with COM as an intermediary. Not only that, but the COM architecture did not permit implementation inheritance, which meant that it lost many of the advantages of object-oriented programming.

An associated problem was that, when debugging, you would still have to debug components written in different languages independently. It was not possible to step between languages in the debugger. So what we *really* mean by language interoperability is that classes written in one language should be able to talk directly to classes written in another language. In particular:

- A class written in one language can inherit from a class written in another language.
- The class can contain an instance of another class, no matter what the languages of the two classes are.
- An object can directly call methods against another object written in another language.
- Objects (or references to objects) can be passed around between methods.
- When calling methods between languages you can step between the method calls in the debugger, even when this means stepping between source code written in different languages.

This is all quite an ambitious aim, but amazingly, .NET and IL have achieved it. In the case of stepping between methods in the debugger, this facility is really offered by the Visual Studio .NET IDE rather than by the CLR itself.

## *Distinct Value and Reference Types*

As with any programming language, IL provides a number of predefined primitive data types. One characteristic of IL, however, is that it makes a strong distinction between value and reference types. *Value types* are those for which a variable directly stores its data, whereas *reference types* are those for which a variable simply stores the address at which the corresponding data can be found.

In C++ terms, reference types can be considered to be similar to accessing a variable through a pointer, whereas for Visual Basic, the best analogy for reference types are objects, which in Visual Basic 6 are always accessed through references. IL also lays down specifications about data storage: instances of reference types are always stored in an area of memory known as the *managed heap*, whereas value types are normally stored on the *stack* (although if value types are declared as fields within reference types, they will be stored inline on the heap). Chapter 2, "C# Basics," discusses the stack and the heap and how they work.

## *Strong Data Typing*

One very important aspect of IL is that it is based on exceptionally *strong data typing*. That means that all variables are clearly marked as being of a particular, specific data type (there is no room in IL, for example, for the `Variant` data type recognized by Visual Basic and scripting languages). In particular, IL does not normally permit any operations that result in ambiguous data types.

For instance, Visual Basic 6 developers are used to being able to pass variables around without worrying too much about their types, because Visual Basic 6 automatically performs type conversion. C++ developers are used to routinely casting pointers between different types. Being able to perform this kind of operation can be great for performance, but it breaks type safety. Hence, it is permitted only under certain circumstances in some of the languages that compile to managed code. Indeed, pointers (as opposed to references) are permitted only in marked blocks of code in C#, and not at all in Visual Basic (although they are allowed in managed C++). Using pointers in your code causes it to fail the memory type safety checks performed by the CLR.

You should note that some languages compatible with .NET, such as Visual Basic 2005, still allow some laxity in typing, but that is only possible because the compilers behind the scenes ensure the type safety is enforced in the emitted IL.

Although enforcing type safety might initially appear to hurt performance, in many cases the benefits gained from the services provided by .NET that rely on type safety far outweigh this performance loss. Such services include:

- Language interoperability
- Garbage collection
- Security
- Application domains

The following sections take a closer look at why strong data typing is particularly important for these features of .NET.

## *The importance of strong data typing for language interoperability*

If a class is to derive from or contains instances of other classes, it needs to know about all the data types used by the other classes. This is why strong data typing is so important. Indeed, it is the absence of any agreed system for specifying this information in the past that has always been the real barrier to inheritance and interoperability across languages. This kind of information is simply not present in a standard executable file or DLL.

Suppose that one of the methods of a Visual Basic 2005 class is defined to return an `Integer` — one of the standard data types available in Visual Basic 2005. C# simply does not have any data type of that name. Clearly, you will only be able to derive from the class, use this method, and use the return type from C# code, if the compiler knows how to map Visual Basic 2005's `Integer` type to some known type that is defined in C#. So how is this problem circumvented in .NET?

### Common Type System

This data type problem is solved in .NET through the use of the *Common Type System* (CTS). The CTS defines the predefined data types that are available in IL, so that all languages that target the .NET Framework will produce compiled code that is ultimately based on these types.

For the previous example, Visual Basic 2005's `Integer` is actually a 32-bit signed integer, which maps exactly to the IL type known as `Int32`. This will therefore be the data type specified in the IL code. Because the C# compiler is aware of this type, there is no problem. At source code level, C# refers to `Int32` with the keyword `int`, so the compiler will simply treat the Visual Basic 2005 method as if it returned an `int`.

# .NET Architecture

The CTS doesn't merely specify primitive data types but a rich hierarchy of types, which includes well-defined points in the hierarchy at which code is permitted to define its own types. The hierarchical structure of the Common Type System reflects the single-inheritance object-oriented methodology of IL, and resembles Figure 1-1.

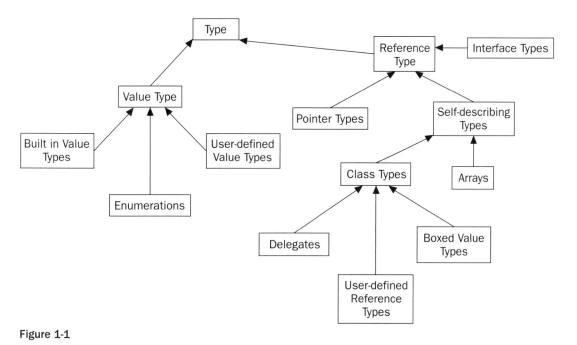

**Figure 1-1**

The following table explains the types shown in Figure 1-1.

| Type | Meaning |
| --- | --- |
| Type | Base class that represents any type. |
| Value Type | Base class that represents any value type. |
| Reference Types | Any data types that are accessed through a reference and stored on the heap. |
| Built-in Value Types | Includes most of the standard primitive types, which represent numbers, Boolean values, or characters. |
| Enumerations | Sets of enumerated values. |
| User-defined Value Types | Types that have been defined in source code and are stored as value types. In C# terms, this means any struct. |
| Interface Types | Interfaces. |
| Pointer Types | Pointers. |

*Table continued on following page*

| Type | Meaning |
| --- | --- |
| `Self-describing Types` | Data types that provide information about themselves for the benefit of the garbage collector (see the next section). |
| `Arrays` | Any type that contains an array of objects. |
| `Class Types` | Types that are self-describing but are not arrays. |
| `Delegates` | Types that are designed to hold references to methods. |
| `User-defined Reference Types` | Types that have been defined in source code and are stored as reference types. In C# terms, this means any class. |
| `Boxed Value Types` | A value type that is temporarily wrapped in a reference so that it can be stored on the heap. |

We won't list all of the built-in value types here, because they are covered in detail in Chapter 3, "Objects and Types." In C#, each predefined type recognized by the compiler maps onto one of the IL built-in types. The same is true in Visual Basic 2005.

## Common Language Specification

The Common Language Specification (CLS) works with the CTS to ensure language interoperability. The CLS is a set of minimum standards that all compilers targeting .NET must support. Because IL is a very rich language, writers of most compilers will prefer to restrict the capabilities of a given compiler to only support a subset of the facilities offered by IL and the CTS. That is fine, as long as the compiler supports everything that is defined in the CLS.

> It is perfectly acceptable to write non–CLS-compliant code. However, if you do, the compiled IL code isn't guaranteed to be fully language interoperable.

For example, take case sensitivity. IL is case sensitive. Developers who work with case-sensitive languages regularly take advantage of the flexibility this case sensitivity gives them when selecting variable names. Visual Basic 2005, however, is not case sensitive. The CLS works around this by indicating that CLS-compliant code should not expose any two names that differ only in their case. Therefore, Visual Basic 2005 code can work with CLS-compliant code.

This example shows that the CLS works in two ways. First, it means that individual compilers do not have to be powerful enough to support the full features of .NET — this should encourage the development of compilers for other programming languages that target .NET. Second, it provides a guarantee that, if you restrict your classes to exposing only CLS-compliant features, code written in any other compliant language can use your classes.

The beauty of this idea is that the restriction to using CLS-compliant features applies only to public and protected members of classes and public classes. Within the private implementations of your classes, you can write whatever non-CLS code you want, because code in other assemblies (units of managed code, see later in this chapter) cannot access this part of your code anyway.

# .NET Architecture

We won't go into the details of the CLS specifications here. In general, the CLS won't affect your C# code very much, because there are very few non–CLS-compliant features of C# anyway.

## *Garbage collection*

The *garbage collector* is .NET's answer to memory management, and in particular to the question of what to do about reclaiming memory that running applications ask for. Up until now two techniques have been used on the Windows platform for deallocating memory that processes have dynamically requested from the system:

- ❑ Make the application code do it all manually.
- ❑ Make objects maintain reference counts.

Having the application code responsible for deallocating memory is the technique used by lower-level, high-performance languages such as C++. It is efficient, and it has the advantage that (in general) resources are never occupied for longer than necessary. The big disadvantage, however, is the frequency of bugs. Code that requests memory also should explicitly inform the system when it no longer requires that memory. However, it is easy to overlook this, resulting in memory leaks.

Although modern developer environments do provide tools to assist in detecting memory leaks, they remain difficult bugs to track down, because they have no effect until so much memory has been leaked that Windows refuses to grant any more to the process. By this point, the entire computer may have appreciably slowed down due to the memory demands being made on it.

Maintaining reference counts is favored in COM. The idea is that each COM component maintains a count of how many clients are currently maintaining references to it. When this count falls to zero, the component can destroy itself and free up associated memory and resources. The problem with this is that it still relies on the good behavior of clients to notify the component that they have finished with it. It only takes one client not to do so, and the object sits in memory. In some ways, this is a potentially more serious problem than a simple C++-style memory leak, because the COM object may exist in its own process, which means that it will never be removed by the system (at least with C++ memory leaks, the system can reclaim all memory when the process terminates).

The .NET runtime relies on the garbage collector instead. This is a program whose purpose is to clean up memory. The idea is that all dynamically requested memory is allocated on the heap (that is true for all languages, although in the case of .NET, the CLR maintains its own managed heap for .NET applications to use). Every so often, when .NET detects that the managed heap for a given process is becoming full and therefore needs tidying up, it calls the garbage collector. The garbage collector runs through variables currently in scope in your code, examining references to objects stored on the heap to identify which ones are accessible from your code — that is to say which objects have references that refer to them. Any objects that are not referred to are deemed to be no longer accessible from your code and can therefore be removed. Java uses a system of garbage collection similar to this.

Garbage collection works in .NET because IL has been designed to facilitate the process. The principle requires that you cannot get references to existing objects other than by copying existing references and that IL is type safe. In this context, what we mean is that if any reference to an object exists, then there is sufficient information in the reference to exactly determine the type of the object.

It would not be possible to use the garbage collection mechanism with a language such as unmanaged C++, for example, because C++ allows pointers to be freely cast between types.

# Chapter 1

One important aspect of garbage collection is that it is not deterministic. In other words, you cannot guarantee when the garbage collector will be called; it will be called when the CLR decides that it is needed (unless you explicitly call the collector), though it is also possible to override this process and call up the garbage collector in your code.

## Security

.NET can really excel in terms of complementing the security mechanisms provided by Windows because it can offer code-based security, whereas Windows only really offers role-based security.

*Role-based security* is based on the identity of the account under which the process is running (that is, who owns and is running the process). Code-based security on the other hand is based on what the code actually does and on how much the code is trusted. Thanks to the strong type safety of IL, the CLR is able to inspect code before running it in order to determine required security permissions. .NET also offers a mechanism by which code can indicate in advance what security permissions it will require to run.

The importance of *code-based security* is that it reduces the risks associated with running code of dubious origin (such as code that you've downloaded from the Internet). For example, even if code is running under the administrator account, it is possible to use code-based security to indicate that that code should still not be permitted to perform certain types of operation that the administrator account would normally be allowed to do, such as read or write to environment variables, read or write to the registry, or access the .NET reflection features.

Security issues are covered in more depth in Chapter 16, ".NET Security."

## Application domains

Application domains are an important innovation in .NET and are designed to ease the overhead involved when running applications that need to be isolated from each other, but that also need to be able to communicate with each other. The classic example of this is a Web server application, which may be simultaneously responding to a number of browser requests. It will, therefore, probably have a number of instances of the component responsible for servicing those requests running simultaneously.

In pre-.NET days, the choice would be between allowing those instances to share a process, with the resultant risk of a problem in one running instance bringing the whole Web site down, or isolating those instances in separate processes, with the associated performance overhead.

Up until now, the only means of isolating code has been through processes. When you start a new application, it runs within the context of a process. Windows isolates processes from each other through address spaces. The idea is that each process has available 4GB of virtual memory in which to store its data and executable code (4GB is for 32-bit systems; 64-bit systems use more memory). Windows imposes an extra level of indirection by which this virtual memory maps into a particular area of actual physical memory or disk space. Each process gets a different mapping, with no overlap between the actual physical memories that the blocks of virtual address space map to (see Figure 1-2).

# .NET Architecture

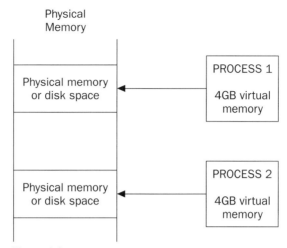

Figure 1-2

In general, any process is able to access memory only by specifying an address in virtual memory — processes do not have direct access to physical memory. Hence it is simply impossible for one process to access the memory allocated to another process. This provides an excellent guarantee that any badly behaved code will not be able to damage anything outside its own address space. (Note that on Windows 95/98, these safeguards are not quite as thorough as they are on Windows NT/2000/XP/2003, so the theoretical possibility exists of applications crashing Windows by writing to inappropriate memory.)

Processes don't just serve as a way to isolate instances of running code from each other. On Windows NT/2000/XP/2003 systems, they also form the unit to which security privileges and permissions are assigned. Each process has its own security token, which indicates to Windows precisely what operations that process is permitted to do.

Although processes are great for security reasons, their big disadvantage is in the area of performance. Often, a number of processes will actually be working together, and therefore need to communicate with each other. The obvious example of this is where a process calls up a COM component, which is an executable, and therefore is required to run in its own process. The same thing happens in COM when surrogates are used. Because processes cannot share any memory, a complex marshaling process has to be used to copy data between the processes. This results in a very significant performance hit. If you need components to work together and don't want that performance hit, then you have to use DLL-based components and have everything running in the same address space — with the associated risk that a badly behaved component will bring everything else down.

*Application domains* are designed as a way of separating components without resulting in the performance problems associated with passing data between processes. The idea is that any one process is divided into a number of application domains. Each application domain roughly corresponds to a single application, and each thread of execution will be running in a particular application domain (see Figure 1-3).

15

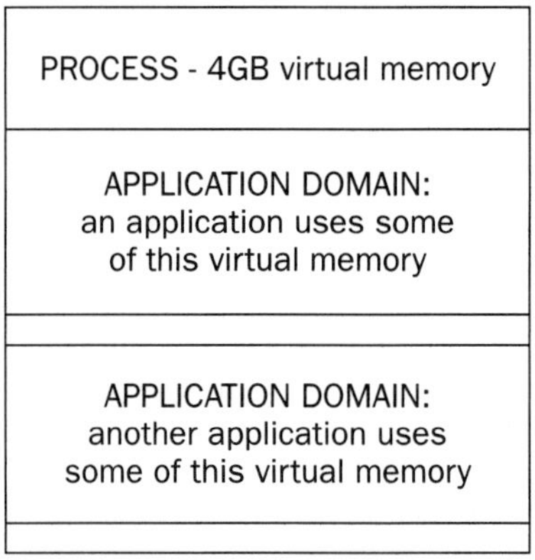

```
┌─────────────────────────────────┐
│  PROCESS - 4GB virtual memory   │
├─────────────────────────────────┤
│      APPLICATION DOMAIN:        │
│      an application uses some   │
│       of this virtual memory    │
├─────────────────────────────────┤
│                                 │
│      APPLICATION DOMAIN:        │
│     another application uses    │
│     some of this virtual memory │
│                                 │
└─────────────────────────────────┘
```

**Figure 1-3**

If different executables are running in the same process space, they are clearly able to easily share data, because theoretically they can directly see each other's data. However, although this is possible in principle, the CLR makes sure that this does not happen in practice by inspecting the code for each running application, to ensure that the code cannot stray outside its own data areas. This sounds at first sight like an almost impossible trick to pull off—after all, how can you tell what the program is going to do without actually running it?

In fact, it is usually possible to do this because of the strong type safety of the IL. In most cases, unless code is using unsafe features such as pointers, the data types it is using will ensure that memory is not accessed inappropriately. For example, .NET array types perform bounds checking to ensure that no out-of-bounds array operations are permitted. If a running application does need to communicate or share data with other applications running in different application domains, it must do so by calling on .NET's remoting services.

Code that has been verified to check that it cannot access data outside its application domain (other than through the explicit remoting mechanism) is said to be *memory type-safe*. Such code can safely be run alongside other type-safe code in different application domains within the same process.

## *Error Handling with Exceptions*

The .NET Framework is designed to facilitate handling of error conditions using the same mechanism, based on exceptions, that is employed by Java and C++. C++ developers should note that because of IL's stronger typing system, there is no performance penalty associated with the use of exceptions with IL in the way that there is in C++. Also, the `finally` block, which has long been on many C++ developers' wish list, is supported by .NET and by C#.

Exceptions are covered in detail in Chapter 12, "Errors and Exceptions." Briefly, the idea is that certain areas of code are designated as exception handler routines, with each one able to deal with a particular error condition (for example, a file not being found, or being denied permission to perform some operation). These conditions can be defined as narrowly or as widely as you want. The exception architecture ensures that when an error condition occurs, execution can immediately jump to the exception handler routine that is most specifically geared to handle the exception condition in question.

# .NET Architecture

The architecture of exception handling also provides a convenient means to pass an object containing precise details of the exception condition to an exception handling routine. This object might include an appropriate message for the user and details of exactly where in the code the exception was detected.

Most exception handling architecture, including the control of program flow when an exception occurs, is handled by the high-level languages (C#, Visual Basic 2005, C++), and is not supported by any special IL commands. C#, for example, handles exceptions using `try{}`, `catch{}`, and `finally{}` blocks of code. (For more details, see Chapter 12.)

What .NET does do, however, is provide the infrastructure to allow compilers that target .NET to support exception handling. In particular, it provides a set of .NET classes that can represent the exceptions, and the language interoperability to allow the thrown exception objects to be interpreted by the exception handling code, irrespective of what language the exception handling code is written in. This language independence is absent from both the C++ and Java implementations of exception handling, although it is present to a limited extent in the COM mechanism for handling errors, which involves returning error codes from methods and passing error objects around. The fact that exceptions are handled consistently in different languages is a crucial aspect of facilitating multi-language development.

## Use of Attributes

*Attributes* are a feature that is familiar to developers who use C++ to write COM components (through their use in Microsoft's COM Interface Definition Language [IDL]). The initial idea of an attribute was that it provided extra information concerning some item in the program that could be used by the compiler.

Attributes are supported in .NET — and hence now by C++, C#, and Visual Basic 2005. What is, however, particularly innovative about attributes in .NET is that a mechanism exists whereby you can define your own custom attributes in your source code. These user-defined attributes will be placed with the metadata for the corresponding data types or methods. This can be useful for documentation purposes, where they can be used in conjunction with reflection technology in order to perform programming tasks based on attributes. Also, in common with the .NET philosophy of language independence, attributes can be defined in source code in one language, and read by code that is written in another language.

Attributes are covered in Chapter 11, "Reflection."

## Assemblies

An *assembly* is the logical unit that contains compiled code targeted at the .NET Framework. Assemblies are not covered in great detail in this chapter because they are covered in detail in Chapter 15, "Assemblies," but we summarize the main points here.

An assembly is completely self-describing, and is a logical rather than a physical unit, which means that it can be stored across more than one file (indeed dynamic assemblies are stored in memory, not on file at all). If an assembly is stored in more than one file, there will be one main file that contains the entry point and describes the other files in the assembly.

Note that the same assembly structure is used for both executable code and library code. The only real difference is that an executable assembly contains a main program entry point, whereas a library assembly doesn't.

17

# Chapter 1

An important characteristic of assemblies is that they contain metadata that describes the types and methods defined in the corresponding code. An assembly, however, also contains assembly metadata that describes the assembly itself. This assembly metadata, contained in an area known as the *manifest*, allows checks to be made on the version of the assembly, and on its integrity.

> *ildasm, a Windows-based utility, can be used to inspect the contents of an assembly, including the manifest and metadata. ildasm is discussed in Chapter 15.*

The fact that an assembly contains program metadata means that applications or other assemblies that call up code in a given assembly do not need to refer to the registry, or to any other data source, in order to find out how to use that assembly. This is a significant break from the old COM way of doing things, in which the GUIDs of the components and interfaces had to be obtained from the registry, and in some cases, the details of the methods and properties exposed would need to be read from a type library.

Having data spread out in up to three different locations meant there was the obvious risk of something getting out of synchronization, which would prevent other software from being able to use the component successfully. With assemblies, there is no risk of this happening, because all the metadata is stored with the program executable instructions. Note that even though assemblies are stored across several files, there are still no problems with data going out of synchronization. This is because the file that contains the assembly entry point also stores details of, and a hash of, the contents of the other files, which means that if one of the files gets replaced, or in any way tampered with, this will almost certainly be detected and the assembly will refuse to load.

Assemblies come in two types: *shared* and *private* assemblies.

## Private Assemblies

Private assemblies are the simplest type. They normally ship with software and are intended to be used only with that software. The usual scenario in which you will ship private assemblies is when you are supplying an application in the form of an executable and a number of libraries, where the libraries contain code that should only be used with that application.

The system guarantees that private assemblies will not be used by other software, because an application may only load private assemblies that are located in the same folder that the main executable is loaded in, or in a subfolder of it.

Because you would normally expect that commercial software would always be installed in its own directory, this means that there is no risk of one software package overwriting, modifying, or accidentally loading private assemblies intended for another package. Because private assemblies can be used only by the software package that they are intended for, this means that you have much more control over what software uses them. There is, therefore, less need to take security precautions because there is no risk, for example, of some other commercial software overwriting one of your assemblies with some new version of it (apart from the case where software is designed specifically to perform malicious damage). There are also no problems with name collisions. If classes in your private assembly happen to have the same name as classes in someone else's private assembly, that doesn't matter, because any given application will only be able to see the one set of private assemblies.

Because a private assembly is entirely self-contained, the process of deploying it is simple. You simply place the appropriate file(s) in the appropriate folder in the file system (no registry entries need to be made). This process is known as *zero impact (xcopy) installation*.

# .NET Architecture

## Shared Assemblies

Shared assemblies are intended to be common libraries that any other application can use. Because any other software can access a shared assembly, more precautions need to be taken against the following risks:

- Name collisions, where another company's shared assembly implements types that have the same names as those in your shared assembly. Because client code can theoretically have access to both assemblies simultaneously, this could be a serious problem.

- The risk of an assembly being overwritten by a different version of the same assembly — the new version being incompatible with some existing client code.

The solution to these problems involves placing shared assemblies in a special directory subtree in the file system, known as the *global assembly cache* (GAC). Unlike with private assemblies, this cannot be done by simply copying the assembly into the appropriate folder — it needs to be specifically installed into the cache. This process can be performed by a number of .NET utilities and involves carrying out certain checks on the assembly, as well as setting up a small folder hierarchy within the assembly cache that is used to ensure assembly integrity.

To avoid the risk of name collisions, shared assemblies are given a name based on private key cryptography (private assemblies are simply given the same name as their main file name). This name is known as a *strong name*, is guaranteed to be unique, and must be quoted by applications that reference a shared assembly.

Problems associated with the risk of overwriting an assembly are addressed by specifying version information in the assembly manifest and by allowing side-by-side installations.

## Reflection

Because assemblies store metadata, including details of all the types and members of these types that are defined in the assembly, it is possible to access this metadata programmatically. Full details of this are given in Chapter 11, "Reflection." This technique, known as *reflection*, raises interesting possibilities, because it means that managed code can actually examine other managed code, or can even examine itself, to determine information about that code. This is most commonly used to obtain the details of attributes, although you can also use reflection, among other purposes, as an indirect way of instantiating classes or calling methods, given the names of those classes on methods as strings. In this way, you could select classes to instantiate methods to call at runtime, rather than compile time, based on user input (dynamic binding).

# .NET Framework Classes

Perhaps one of the biggest benefits of writing managed code, at least from a developer's point of view, is that you get to use the .NET *base class library*.

The .NET base classes are a massive collection of managed code classes that allow you to do almost any of the tasks that were previously available through the Windows API. These classes follow the same object model IL uses, based on single inheritance. This means that you can either instantiate objects of whichever .NET base class is appropriate, or you can derive your own classes from them.

# Chapter 1

The great thing about the .NET base classes is that they have been designed to be very intuitive and easy to use. For example, to start a thread, you call the `Start()` method of the `Thread` class. To disable a `TextBox`, you set the `Enabled` property of a `TextBox` object to `false`. This approach — while familiar to Visual Basic and Java developers, whose respective libraries are just as easy to use — will be a welcome relief to C++ developers, who for years have had to cope with such API functions as `GetDIBits()`, `RegisterWndClassEx()`, and `IsEqualIID()`, as well as a whole plethora of functions that required Windows handles to be passed around.

On the other hand, C++ developers always had easy access to the entire Windows API, whereas Visual Basic 6 and Java developers were more restricted in terms of the basic operating system functionality that they have access to from their respective languages. What is new about the .NET base classes is that they combine the ease of use that was typical of the Visual Basic and Java libraries with the relatively comprehensive coverage of the Windows API functions. Many features of Windows still are not available through the base classes, and for those you will need to call into the API functions, but in general, these are now confined to the more exotic features. For everyday use, you will probably find the base classes adequate. And if you do need to call into an API function, .NET offers a so-called *platform-invoke* that ensures data types are correctly converted, so the task is no harder than calling the function directly from C++ code would have been — regardless of whether you are coding in C#, C++, or Visual Basic 2005.

> *WinCV, a Windows-based utility, can be used to browse the classes, structs, interfaces, and enums in the base class library. WinCV is discussed in Chapter 14, "Visual Studio 2005."*

Although Chapter 3 is nominally dedicated to the subject of base classes, in reality, once we have completed our coverage of the syntax of the C# language, most of the rest of this book shows you how to use various classes within the .NET base class library. That is how comprehensive base classes are. As a rough guide, the areas covered by the .NET base classes include:

- Core features provided by IL (including the primitive data types in the CTS discussed in Chapter 3, "Objects and Types")
- Windows GUI support and controls (see Chapter 23, "Windows Forms")
- Web Forms (ASP.NET, discussed in Chapters 26, "ASP.NET Pages" and 27, "ASP.NET Development")
- Data Access (ADO.NET; see Chapters 19, "Data Access with .NET," 20, ".NET Programming with SQL Server 2005," and 21, "Manipulating XML")
- Directory Access (see Chapter 22, "Working with Active Directory")
- File system and registry access (see Chapter 34, "Manipulating Files and the Registry")
- Networking and Web browsing (see Chapter 35, "Accessing the Internet")
- .NET attributes and reflection (see Chapter 11, "Reflection")
- Access to aspects of the Windows OS (environment variables and so on; see Chapter 16, ".NET Security")
- COM interoperability (see Chapters 30, "Enterprise Services" and 33, "COM Interoperability")

Incidentally, according to Microsoft sources, a large proportion of the .NET base classes have actually been written in C#!

## Namespaces

*Namespaces* are the way that .NET avoids name clashes between classes. They are designed to avoid the situation in which you define a class to represent a customer, name your class `Customer`, and then someone else does the same thing (a likely scenario — the proportion of businesses that have customers seems to be quite high).

A namespace is no more than a grouping of data types, but it has the effect that the names of all data types within a namespace automatically get prefixed with the name of the namespace. It is also possible to nest namespaces within each other. For example, most of the general-purpose .NET base classes are in a namespace called `System`. The base class `Array` is in this namespace, so its full name is `System.Array`.

.NET requires all types to be defined in a namespace; for example, you could place your `Customer` class in a namespace called `YourCompanyName`. This class would have the full name `YourCompanyName.Customer`.

> *If a namespace is not explicitly supplied, the type will be added to a nameless global namespace.*

Microsoft recommends that for most purposes you supply at least two nested namespace names: the first one refers to the name of your company, and the second one refers to the name of the technology or software package that the class is a member of, such as `YourCompanyName.SalesServices.Customer`. This protects, in most situations, the classes in your application from possible name clashes with classes written by other organizations.

Chapter 2, "C# Basics," looks more closely at namespaces.

# Creating .NET Applications Using C#

C# can also be used to create console applications: text-only applications that run in a DOS window. You'll probably use console applications when unit testing class libraries, and for creating Unix or Linux daemon processes. However, more often you'll use C# to create applications that use many of the technologies associated with .NET. This section gives you an overview of the different types of applications that you can write in C#.

## Creating ASP.NET Applications

Active Server Pages (ASP) is a Microsoft technology for creating Web pages with dynamic content. An ASP page is basically an HTML file with embedded chunks of server-side VBScript or JavaScript. When a client browser requests an ASP page, the Web server delivers the HTML portions of the page, processing the server-side scripts as it comes to them. Often these scripts query a database for data, and mark up that data in HTML. ASP is an easy way for clients to build browser-based applications.

However, ASP is not without its shortcomings. First, ASP pages sometimes render slowly because the server-side code is interpreted instead of compiled. Second, ASP files can be difficult to maintain because they were unstructured; the server-side ASP code and plain HTML are all jumbled up together. Third, ASP sometimes makes development difficult because there is little support for error handling and type-checking. Specifically, if you are using VBScript and want to implement error handling in your pages, you have to use the `On Error Resume Next` statement, and follow every component call with a check to `Err.Number` to make sure that the call had gone well.

ASP.NET is a complete revision of ASP that fixes many of its problems. It does not replace ASP; rather, ASP.NET pages can live side by side on the same server with legacy ASP applications. Of course, you can also program ASP.NET with C#!

The following section explores the key features of ASP.NET. For more details, refer to Chapters 26, "ASP.NET Pages" and 27, "ASP.NET Development."

## *Features of ASP.NET*

First, and perhaps most important, ASP.NET pages are *structured*. That is, each page is effectively a class that inherits from the .NET `System.Web.UI.Page` *class*, and can override a set of methods that are evoked during the `Page` object's lifetime. (You can think of these events as page-specific cousins of the `OnApplication_Start` and `OnSession_Start` events that went in the `global.asa` files of plain old ASP.) Because you can factor a page's functionality into event handlers with explicit meanings, ASP.NET pages are easier to understand.

Another nice thing about ASP.NET pages is that you can create them in Visual Studio 2005, the same environment in which you create the business logic and data access components that those ASP.NET pages use. A Visual Studio 2005 project, or *solution*, contains all of the files associated with an application. Moreover, you can debug your classic ASP pages in the editor as well; in the old days of Visual InterDev, it was often a vexing challenge to configure InterDev and the project's Web server to turn debugging on.

For maximum clarity, the ASP.NET `code-behind` feature lets you take the structured approach even further. ASP.NET allows you to isolate the server-side functionality of a page to a class, compile that class into a DLL, and place that DLL into a directory below the HTML portion. A `code-behind` directive at the top of the page associates the file with its DLL. When a browser requests the page, the Web server fires the events in the class in the page's `code-behind` DLL.

Last but not least, ASP.NET is remarkable for its increased performance. Whereas classic ASP pages are interpreted with each page request, the Web server caches ASP.NET pages after compilation. This means that subsequent requests of an ASP.NET page execute more quickly than the first.

ASP.NET also makes it easy to write pages that cause forms to be displayed by the browser, which you might use in an intranet environment. The traditional wisdom is that form-based applications offer a richer user interface, but are harder to maintain because they run on so many different machines. For this reason, people have relied on form-based applications when rich user interfaces were a necessity and extensive support could be provided to the users.

With the advent of Internet Explorer 5 and the lackluster performance of Navigator 6, however, the advantages of form-based applications are clouded. IE 5's consistent and robust support for DHTML allows the programmer to create Web-based applications that are every bit as pretty as their fat client equivalents. Of course, such applications necessitate standardizing on IE and not supporting Navigator. In many industrial situations, this standardization is now common.

# .NET Architecture

## *Web Forms*

To make Web page construction even easier, Visual Studio 2005 supplies *Web Forms*. They allow you to build ASP.NET pages graphically in the same way that Visual Basic 6 or C++ Builder windows are created; in other words, by dragging controls from a toolbox onto a form, then flipping over to the code aspect of that form, and writing event handlers for the controls. When you use C# to create a Web Form, you are creating a C# class that inherits from the `Page` base class, and an ASP.NET page that designates that class as its code-behind. Of course, you don't have to use C# to create a Web Form; you can use Visual Basic 2005 or another .NET-compliant language just as well.

In the past, the difficulty of Web development discouraged some teams from attempting it. To succeed in Web development, you had to know so many different technologies, such as VBScript, ASP, DHTML, JavaScript, and so on. By applying the Form concepts to Web pages, Web Forms have made Web development considerably easier.

## Web server controls

The controls used to populate a Web Form are not controls in the same sense as ActiveX controls. Rather, they are XML tags in the ASP.NET namespace that the Web browser dynamically transforms into HTML and client-side script when a page is requested. Amazingly, the Web server is able to render the same server-side control in different ways, producing a transformation appropriate to the requestor's particular Web browser. This means that it is now easy to write fairly sophisticated user interfaces for Web pages, without having to worry about how to ensure that your page will run on any of the available browsers — because Web Forms will take care of that for you.

You can use C# or Visual Basic 2005 to expand the Web Form toolbox. Creating a new server-side control is simply a matter of implementing .NET's `System.Web.UI.WebControls.WebControl` class.

## *XML Web services*

Today, HTML pages account for most of the traffic on the World Wide Web. With XML, however, computers have a device-independent format to use for communicating with each other on the Web. In the future, computers may use the Web and XML to communicate information rather than dedicated lines and proprietary formats such as *Electronic Data Interchange* (EDI). XML Web services are designed for a service-oriented Web, in which remote computers provide each other with dynamic information that can be analyzed and reformatted, before final presentation to a user. An XML Web service is an easy way for a computer to expose information to other computers on the Web in the form of XML.

In technical terms, an XML Web service on .NET is an ASP.NET page that returns XML instead of HTML to requesting clients. Such pages have a `code-behind` DLL containing a class that derives from the `WebService` class. The Visual Studio 2005 IDE provides an engine that facilitates Web service development.

An organization might choose to use XML Web services for two main reasons. The first reason is that they rely on HTTP; XML Web services can use existing networks (HTTP) as a medium for conveying information. The other is that because XML Web services use XML, the data format is self-describing, non-proprietary, and platform-independent.

# Chapter 1

## *Creating Windows Forms*

Although C# and .NET are particularly suited to Web development, they still offer splendid support for so-called *fat-client* or *thick-client* apps, applications that have to be installed on the end user's machine where most of the processing takes place. This support is from *Windows Forms*.

A Windows Form is the .NET answer to a Visual Basic 6 Form. To design a graphical window interface, you just drag controls from a toolbox onto a Windows Form. To determine the window's behavior, you write event-handling routines for the form's controls. A Windows Form project compiles to an executable that must be installed alongside the .NET runtime on the end user's computer. Like other .NET project types, Windows Form projects are supported by both Visual Basic 2005 and C#. Chapter 23, "Windows Forms," examines Windows Forms more closely.

## *Windows Controls*

Although Web Forms and Windows Forms are developed in much the same way, you use different kinds of controls to populate them. Web Forms use Web server controls, and Windows Forms use *Windows Controls*.

A Windows Control is a lot like an ActiveX control. After a Windows Control is implemented, it compiles to a DLL that must be installed on the client's machine. In fact, the .NET SDK provides a utility that creates a wrapper for ActiveX controls, so that they can be placed on Windows Forms. As is the case with Web Controls, Windows Control creation involves deriving from a particular class, `System.Windows.Forms.Control`.

## *Windows Services*

A Windows Service (originally called an NT Service) is a program designed to run in the background in Windows NT/2000/XP/2003 (but not Windows 9x). Services are useful where you want a program to be running continuously and ready to respond to events without having been explicitly started by the user. A good example would be the World Wide Web Service on Web servers, which listens out for Web requests from clients.

It is very easy to write services in C#. .NET Framework base classes are available in the `System.Service Process` namespace that handle many of the boilerplate tasks associated with services, and in addition, Visual Studio .NET allows you to create a C# Windows Service project, which uses C# source code for a basic Windows service. Chapter 36, "Windows Services," explores how to write C# Windows Services.

# The Role of C# in the .NET Enterprise Architecture

C# requires the presence of the .NET runtime, and it will probably be a few years before most clients — particularly most home computers — have .NET installed. In the meantime, installing a C# application is likely to mean also installing the .NET redistributable components. Because of that, it is likely that we will see many C# applications first in the enterprise environment. Indeed, C# arguably presents an outstanding opportunity for organizations that are interested in building robust, n-tiered client-server applications.

When combined with ADO.NET, C# has the ability to access quickly and generically data stores such as SQL Server and Oracle databases. The returned datasets can easily be manipulated using the ADO.NET object model, and automatically render as XML for transport across an office intranet.

Once a database schema has been established for a new project, C# presents an excellent medium for implementing a layer of data access objects, each of which could provide insertion, updates, and deletion access to a different database table.

Because it's the first component-based C language, C# is a great language for implementing a business object tier, too. It encapsulates the messy plumbing for inter-component communication, leaving developers free to focus on gluing their data access objects together in methods that accurately enforce their organizations' business rules. Moreover, with attributes, C# business objects can be outfitted for method-level security checks, object pooling, and JIT activation supplied by COM+ Services. Furthermore, .NET ships with utility programs that allow your new .NET business objects to interface with legacy COM components.

To create an enterprise application with C#, you create a Class Library project for the data access objects and another for the business objects. While developing, you can use Console projects to test the methods on your classes. Fans of extreme programming can build Console projects that can be executed automatically from batch files to unit test that working code has not been broken.

On a related note, C# and .NET will probably influence the way you physically package your reusable classes. In the past, many developers crammed a multitude of classes into a single physical component because this arrangement made deployment a lot easier; if there was a versioning problem, you knew just where to look. Because deploying .NET enterprise components involves simply copying files into directories, developers can now package their classes into more logical, discrete components without encountering "DLL Hell."

Last but not least, ASP.NET pages coded in C# constitute an excellent medium for user interfaces. Because ASP.NET pages compile, they execute quickly. Because they can be debugged in the Visual Studio 2005 IDE, they are robust. Because they support full-scale language features like early binding, inheritance, and modularization, ASP.NET pages coded in C# are tidy and easily maintained.

Seasoned developers acquire a healthy skepticism about strongly hyped new technologies and languages and are reluctant to utilize new platforms simply because they are urged to. If you're an enterprise developer in an IT department, though, or if you provide application services across the World Wide Web, let us assure you that C# and .NET offer at least four solid benefits, even if some of the more exotic features like XML Web services and server-side controls don't pan out:

- ❑ Component conflicts will become infrequent and deployment is easier, because different versions of the same component can run side by side on the same machine without conflicting.
- ❑ Your ASP.NET code won't look like spaghetti code.
- ❑ You can leverage a lot of the functionality in the .NET base classes.
- ❑ For applications requiring a Windows Forms user interface, C# makes it very easy to write this kind of application.

Windows Forms have to some extent been downplayed in the past year due to the advent of Web Forms and Internet-based applications. However, if you or your colleagues lack expertise in JavaScript, ASP, or related technologies, Windows Forms are still a viable option for creating a user interface with speed and ease. Just remember to factor your code so that the user interface logic is separate from the business logic and the data access code. Doing so will allow you to migrate your application to the browser at some point in the future if you need to do so. Also, it is likely that Windows Forms will remain the dominant user interface for applications for use in homes and small businesses for a long time to come. In addition to this, the new smart client features of Windows Forms (the ability to easily work in an online/offline mode) will bring a new round of exciting applications.

## Summary

This chapter has covered a lot of ground, briefly reviewing important aspects of the .NET Framework and C#'s relationship to it. It started by discussing how all languages that target .NET are compiled into Microsoft intermediate language (IL) before this is compiled and executed by the Common Language Runtime (CLR). This chapter also discussed the roles of the following features of .NET in the compilation and execution process:

- Assemblies and .NET base classes
- COM components
- JIT compilation
- Application domains
- Garbage Collection

Figure 1-4 provides an overview of how these features come into play during compilation and execution.

You learned about the characteristics of IL, particularly its strong data typing and object-orientation, and how these characteristics influence the languages that target .NET, including C#. You also learned how the strongly typed nature of IL enables language interoperability, as well as CLR services such as garbage collection and security.

Finally, you learned how C# can be used as the basis for applications that are built upon several .NET technologies, including ASP.NET.

Chapter 2 discusses how to write code in C#.

# .NET Architecture

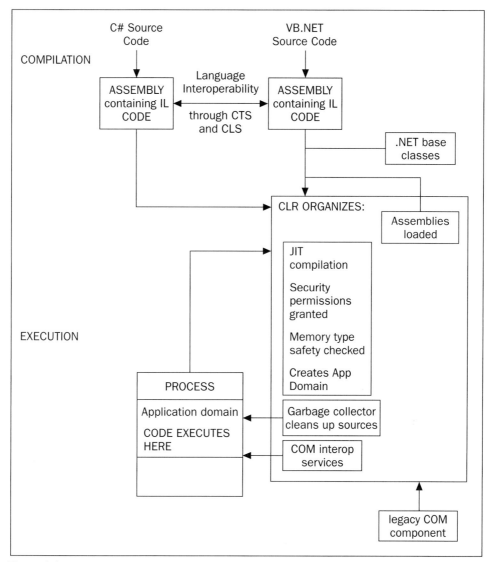

Figure 1-4

# C# Basics

Now that you understand a little more about what C# can do, you will want to learn how to use it. This chapter on the basics of C# gives you a good start in that direction by providing you with a basic knowledge of the fundamentals of C# programming, which we build on in subsequent chapters. The main topics we cover are:

- Declaring variables
- Initialization and scope of variables
- Predefined C# data types
- Dictating the flow of execution within a C# program using loops and conditional statements
- Enumerations
- Namespaces
- The `Main()` method
- Basic command-line C# compiler options
- Using `System.Console` to perform console I/O
- Using documentation features in C# and Visual Studio .NET
- C# identifiers and keywords
- Recommended guidelines and conventions for good programming in C#

By the end of this chapter, you will know enough C# to write simple programs, though without using inheritance or other object-oriented features, which are covered in the following chapters.

# Chapter 2

# Before We Start

As already mentioned, C# is an object-oriented language. As we get you up to speed in the fundamentals of the C# language, we will be assuming that you have a good grasp of the concepts behind object-oriented (OO) programming. In other words, we will expect you to understand what we mean by *classes*, *objects*, *interfaces*, and *inheritance*. If you have programmed in C++ or Java before, you should have a pretty good grounding in object-oriented programming (OOP). However, if you do not have a background in OOP, plenty of good sources of information are available on this subject. You can start with Appendix A, which presents a detailed introduction to OOP concepts and is posted at www.wrox.com.

If you are an experienced developer in Visual Basic 6, C++, or Java, you should note that we make many comparisons between C#, C++, Java, and Visual Basic 6 as we walk you through the basics of C#. However, you might prefer to learn C# initially by reading a comparison between C# and your selected language. If so, we have also made available separate documents for download on the Wrox Press Web site (www.wrox.com) that give introductions to C# from the point of view of each of those languages.

# Your First C# Program

Let's start in the traditional way by compiling and running the simplest possible C# program — a simple class consisting of a console application that writes a message to the screen.

## The Code

Type the following into a text editor (such as Notepad), and save it with a .cs extension (for example, First.cs):

```csharp
using System;

namespace Wrox.ProCSharp.Basics
{
    class MyFirstCSharpClass
    {
        static void Main()
        {
            Console.WriteLine("This isn't at all like Java!");
            Console.ReadLine();
            return;
        }
    }
}
```

*The following chapters present a number of code samples. The most common technique for writing C# programs is to use Visual Studio 2005 to generate a basic project and add your own code to it. However, because the aim of these early chapters is to teach the C# language, we are going to keep things simple and avoid relying on Visual Studio 2005 until Chapter 14, "Visual Studio 2005." Instead, we will present the code as simple files that you can type in using any text editor and compile from the command line.*

# C# Basics

## Compiling and Running the Program

You can compile this program by simply running the C# command-line compiler (`csc.exe`) against the source file, like this:

**csc First.cs**

If you want to compile code from the command line using the `csc` command, you should be aware that the .NET command-line tools, including `csc`, are only available if certain environment variables have been set up. Depending on how you installed .NET (and Visual Studio 2005), this may or may not be the case on your machine.

> *If you do not have the environment variables set up, you have the following two options. The first is to run the batch file* `%Microsoft Visual Studio 2005%\Common7\Tools\vcvars32.bat` *from the command prompt before running* `csc`, *where* `%Microsoft Visual Studio 2005` *is the folder to which Visual Studio 2005 has been installed. The second (easier) way is to use the Visual Studio 2005 command prompt instead of the usual command prompt window. You will find the Visual Studio .NET command prompt in the Start Menu, under Programs, Microsoft Visual Studio2005, Microsoft Visual Studio Tools. It is simply a command prompt window that automatically runs* `vcvars32.bat` *when it opens.*

Compiling the code produces an executable file named `First.exe`, which you can run from the command line or from Windows Explorer like any other executable. Give it a try:

**csc First.cs**

```
Microsoft (R) Visual C# .NET Compiler version 8.00.40607.16
for Microsoft (R) Windows (R) .NET Framework version 2.0.40607
Copyright (C) Microsoft Corporation 2001-2003. All rights reserved.
```

**First.exe**

```
This isn't at all like Java!
```

Well, maybe that message isn't quite true! This program has some fairly fundamental similarities to Java, although there are one or two points (such as the capitalized `Main()` function) to catch out the unwary Java or C++ developer. Let's look a little more closely at what's going on in the code.

## A Closer Look

First, a few general comments about C# syntax. In C#, as in other C-style languages, most statements end in a semicolon (`;`) and can continue over multiple lines without needing a continuation character (such as the underscore in Visual Basic). Statements can be joined into blocks using curly braces (`{}`). Single-line comments begin with two forward slash characters (`//`), and multi-line comments begin with a slash and an asterisk (`/*`) and end with the same combination reversed (`*/`). In these aspects, C# is identical to C++ and Java, but different from Visual Basic. It is the semicolons and curly braces that give C# code such a different visual appearance to Visual Basic code. If your background is predominantly Visual Basic, take extra care to remember the semicolon at the end of every statement. Omitting this is usually the biggest single cause of compilation errors among developers new to C-style languages.

31

The first couple of lines in the previous code example have to do with *namespaces* (mentioned later in this chapter), which are a way to group together associated classes. This concept will be familiar to Java and C++ developers but may be new to Visual Basic 6 developers. C# namespaces are basically the same as C++ namespaces or, equivalently, Java packages, but there is no comparable concept in Visual Basic 6. The namespace keyword declares the namespace your class should be associated with. All code within the following braces is regarded as being within that namespace. The using statement specifies a namespace that the compiler should look at to find any classes that are referenced in your code but that aren't defined in the current namespace. This serves the same purpose as the import statement in Java and the using namespace statement in C++.

```
using System;

namespace Wrox.ProCSharp.Basics
{
```

The reason for the presence of the using statement in the First.cs file is that you are going to use a library class, System.Console. The using System statement allows you to refer to this class simply as Console (and similarly for any other classes in the System namespace). The standard System namespace is where the most commonly used .NET types reside. It is important to realize that everything you do in C# depends on the .NET base classes; in this case, you are using the Console class within the System namespace in order to write to the console window.

> *Because almost every C# program uses classes in the System namespace, we will assume that a* using System; *statement is present in the file for all code snippets in this chapter.*

Note that C# has no built-in keywords of its own for input or output; it is completely reliant on the .NET classes.

Next, you declare a class ostensibly called MyFirstClass. However, because it has been placed in a namespace called Wrox.ProCSharp.Basics, the fully qualified name of this class is Wrox.ProCSharp.Basics.MyFirstCSharpClass:

```
    class MyFirstCSharpClass
    {
```

As in Java, all C# code must be contained within a class. Classes in C# are similar to classes in Java and C++, and very roughly comparable to class modules in Visual Basic 6. The class declaration consists of the class keyword, followed by the class name and a pair of curly braces. All code associated with the class should be placed between these braces.

Next you declare a method called Main(). Every C# executable (such as console applications, Windows applications, and Windows services) must have an entry point—the Main() method (note the capital M):

```
        static void Main()
        {
```

The method is called when the program is started, like the main() function in C++ or Java, or Sub Main() in a Visual Basic 6 module. This method must return either nothing (void) or an integer (int). A C# method corresponds to a method in C++ and Java (sometimes referred to in C++ as a member function). It also corresponds to either a Visual Basic Function or a Visual Basic Sub, depending on whether the method returns anything (unlike Visual Basic, C# makes no conceptual distinction between functions and subroutines).

Note the format of method definitions in C#:

```
[modifiers] return_type MethodName([parameters])
{
   // Method body. NB. This code block is pseudo-code
}
```

Here, the first square brackets represent certain optional keywords. Modifiers are used to specify certain features of the method you are defining, such as where the method can be called from. In this case, you have two modifiers: `public` and `static`. The `public` modifier means that the method can be accessed from anywhere, so it can be called from outside your class. This is the same meaning as `public` in C++ and Java, and `Public` in Visual Basic. The `static` modifier indicates that the method does not operate on a specific instance of your class and therefore is called without first instantiating the class. This is important because you are creating an executable rather than a class library. Once again, this has the same meaning as the `static` keyword in C++ and Java, though in this case there is no Visual Basic equivalent (the `Static` keyword in Visual Basic has a different meaning). You set the return type to `void`, and in the example, you don't include any parameters.

Finally, we come to the code statements themselves:

```
Console.WriteLine("This isn't at all like Java!");
Console.ReadLine();
return;
```

In this case, you simply call the `WriteLine()` method of the `System.Console` class to write a line of text to the console window. `WriteLine()` is a `static` method, so you don't need to instantiate a `Console` object before calling it.

`Console.ReadLine()` reads user input. Adding this line forces the application to wait for the carriage return key to be hit before the application exits, and, in the case of Visual Studio 2005, the console window disappears.

You then call `return` to exit from the method (and, because this is the `Main()` method, the program). You specified `void` in your method header, so you don't return any parameters. The `return` statement is equivalent to `return` in C++ and Java, and `Exit Sub` or `Exit Function` in Visual Basic.

Now that you have had a taste of basic C# syntax, you are ready to go into more detail with the various aspects of C#. Because it is virtually impossible to write any non-trivial program without *variables*, we will start by looking at variables in C#.

# Variables

You declare variables in C# using the following syntax:

```
datatype identifier;
```

## Chapter 2

For example:

```
int i;
```

This statement declares an `int` named `i`. The compiler won't actually let you use this variable until you have initialized it with a value, but the declaration allocates four bytes on the stack to hold the value.

Once it has been declared, you can assign a value to the variable using the assignment operator, =:

```
i = 10;
```

You can also declare the variable and initialize its value at the same time:

```
int i = 10;
```

This syntax is identical to C++ and Java syntax but very different from Visual Basic syntax for declaring variables. If you are coming from Visual Basic 6, you should also be aware that C# doesn't distinguish between objects and simple types, so there is no need for anything like the `Set` keyword, even if you want your variable to refer to an object. The C# syntax for declaring variables is the same no matter what the data type of the variable.

If you declare and initialize more than one variable in a single statement, all of the variables will be of the same data type:

```
int x = 10, y =20;     // x and y are both ints
```

To declare variables of different types, you need to use separate statements. Don't assign different data types within a multiple variable declaration:

```
int x = 10;
bool y = true;            // Creates a variable that stores true or false
int x = 10, bool y = true;   // This won't compile!
```

Notice the // and the text after in the preceding examples. These are comments. The // character sequence tells the compiler to ignore the text that follows. Comments in code are further explained later in this chapter.

## *Initialization of Variables*

Variable initialization demonstrates another example of C#'s emphasis on safety. Briefly, the C# compiler requires that any variable be initialized with some starting value before you refer to that variable in an operation. Most modern compilers will flag violations of this as a warning, but the ever-vigilant C# compiler treats such violations as errors. This prevents you from unintentionally retrieving junk values from memory that is left over from other programs.

C# has two methods for ensuring that variables are initialized before use:

❑ Variables that are fields in a class or struct, if not initialized explicitly, are by default zeroed out when they are created.

# C# Basics

❑ Variables that are local to a method must be explicitly initialized in your code prior to any statements in which their values are used. In this case, the initialization doesn't have to happen when the variable is declared, but the compiler will check all possible paths through the method and will flag an error if it detects any possibility of the value of a local variable being used before it is initialized.

C#'s approach contrasts with that of C++, in which the compiler leaves it up to the programmer to make sure that variables are initialized before use, and that of Visual Basic, in which all variables are zeroed out automatically.

For example, you can't do the following in C#:

```csharp
public static int Main()
{
   int d;
   Console.WriteLine(d);   // Can't do this! Need to initialize d before use
   return 0;
}
```

Notice that this code snippet demonstrates defining `Main()` so it returns an `int` instead of `void`.

When you attempt to compile these lines, you will receive this kind of error message:

```
Use of unassigned local variable 'd'
```

The same rules apply to reference types as well. Consider the following statement:

```csharp
Something objSomething;
```

In C++, this line would create an instance of the `Something` class on the stack. In C#, this same line of code would only create a *reference* for a `Something` object, but this reference does not yet actually refer to any object. Any attempt to call a method or property against this variable would result in an error.

Instantiating a reference object in C# requires use of the `new` keyword. You create a reference as shown in the previous example and then point the reference at an object allocated on the heap using the `new` keyword:

```csharp
objSomething = new Something();   // This creates a Something on the heap
```

## *Variable Scope*

The *scope* of a variable is the region of code from which the variable can be accessed. In general, the scope is determined by the following rules:

❑ A *field* (also known as a member variable) of a class is in scope for as long as its containing class is in scope (this is the same as for C++, Java, and VB).

❑ A *local variable* is in scope until a closing brace indicates the end of the block statement or method in which it was declared.

# Chapter 2

❑ A local variable that is declared in a `for`, `while`, or similar statement is in scope in the body of that loop. (C++ developers will note that this is the same behavior as the ANSI standard for C++. Early versions of the Microsoft C++ compiler did not comply with this standard, but scoped such variables to remain in scope after the loop terminated.)

## Scope clashes for local variables

It's common in a large program to use the same variable name for different variables in different parts of the program. This is fine as long as the variables are scoped to completely different parts of the program so there is no possibility for ambiguity. However, bear in mind that local variables with the same name can't be declared twice in the same scope, so you can't do this:

```
int x = 20;
// some more code
int x = 30;
```

Consider the following code sample:

```
using System;

namespace Wrox.ProCSharp.Basics
{
   public class ScopeTest
   {
      public static int Main()
      {
         for (int i = 0; i < 10; i++)
         {
            Console.WriteLine(i);
         }   // i goes out of scope here

         // We can declare a variable named i again, because
         // there's no other variable with that name in scope
         for (int i = 9; i >= 0; i--)
         {
            Console.WriteLine(i);
         }   // i goes out of scope here
         return 0;
      }
   }
}
```

This code simply prints out the numbers from 0 to 9, and then back again from 9 to 0, using a `for` loop. The important thing to note is that you declare the variable `i` twice in this code, within the same method. You can do this because `i` is declared in two separate loops, so each `i` variable is local to its own loop.

Here's another example:

```
       public static int Main()
       {
          int j = 20;
          for (int i = 0; i < 10; i++)
          {
```

```
            int j = 30;    // Can't do this - j is still in scope
            Console.WriteLine(j + i);
        }
        return 0;
    }
```

If you try to compile this, you'll get an error:

```
ScopeTest.cs(12,14): error CS0136: A local variable named 'j' cannot be declared in
this scope because it would give a different meaning to 'j', which is already used
in a 'parent or current' scope to denote something else
```

This is because the variable j, which is defined before the start of the for loop, is still in scope within the for loop, and won't go out of scope until the Main() method has finished executing. Although the second j (the illegal one) is in the loop's scope, that scope is nested within the Main() method's scope. The compiler has no way to distinguish between these two variables, so it won't allow the second one to be declared. This is again different from C++ where variable hiding is permitted.

## *Scope clashes for fields and local variables*

In certain circumstances, however, you can distinguish between two identifiers with the same name (although not the same fully qualified name) and the same scope, and in this case the compiler will allow you to declare the second variable. The reason is that C# makes a fundamental distinction between variables that are declared at the type level (fields) and variables declared within methods (local variables).

Consider the following code snippet:

```
using System;

namespace Wrox.ProCSharp.Basics
{
    class ScopeTest2
    {
        static int j = 20;

        public static void Main()
        {
            int j = 30;
            Console.WriteLine(j);
            return;
        }
    }
}
```

This code will compile, even though you have two variables named j in scope within the Main() method: the j that was defined at the class level, and doesn't go out of scope until the class is destroyed (when the Main() method terminates, and the program ends); and the j defined in Main(). In this case, the new variable named j that you declare in the Main() method *hides* the class-level variable with the same name, so when you run this code, the number 30 will be displayed.

However, what if you want to refer to the class-level variable? You can actually refer to fields of a class or struct from outside the object, using the syntax object.fieldname. In the previous example, you are accessing a static field (we look at what this means in the next section) from a static method, so you can't use an instance of the class; you just use the name of the class itself:

```
...
public static void Main()
{
    int j = 30;
    Console.WriteLine(ScopeTest2.j);
}
...
```

If you were accessing an instance field (a field that belongs to a specific instance of the class), you would need to use the `this` keyword instead. This keyword performs the same role as `this` in C++ and Java, and `Me` in Visual Basic.

## Constants

Prefixing a variable with the `const` keyword when it is declared and initialized designates that variable as a constant. As the name implies, a constant is a variable whose value cannot be changed throughout its lifetime:

```
const int a = 100;    // This value cannot be changed
```

Constants will be familiar to Visual Basic and C++ developers. C++ developers should, however, note that C# does not permit all the subtleties of C++ constants. In C++, not only could variables be declared as constant, but depending on the declaration, you could have constant pointers, variable pointers to constants, constant methods (that don't change the contents of the containing object), constant parameters to methods, and so on. These subtleties have been discarded in C#, and all you can do is declare local variables and fields to be constant.

Constants have the following characteristics:

- ❏ They must be initialized when they are declared, and once a value has been assigned, it can never be overwritten.
- ❏ The value of a constant must be computable at compile time. Therefore, you can't initialize a constant with a value taken from a variable. If you need to do this, you will need to use a read-only field (this is explained in Chapter 3, "Objects and Types").
- ❏ Constants are always implicitly static. However, notice that you don't have to (and, in fact, are not permitted to) include the `static` modifier in the constant declaration.

At least three advantages exist to using constants in your programs:

- ❏ Constants make your programs easier to read by replacing magic numbers and strings with readable names whose values are easy to understand.
- ❏ Constants make your programs easier to modify. For example, assume that you have a `SalesTax` constant in one of your C# programs, and that constant is assigned a value of 6 percent. If the sales tax rate changes at a later point in time, you can modify the behavior of all tax calculations simply by assigning a new value to the constant; you don't have to hunt throughout your code for the value .06 and change each one, hoping that you've found all of them.

# C# Basics

❑ Constants make it easier to avoid mistakes in your programs. If you attempt to assign another value to a constant somewhere in your program other than at the point where the constant is declared, the compiler will flag the error.

## Predefined Data Types

Now that you have seen how to declare variables and constants, this section takes a closer look at the data types available in C#. As you will see, C# is a lot fussier about the types available and their definitions than some other languages are.

### *Value Types and Reference Types*

Before examining the data types in C#, it is important to understand that C# distinguishes between two categories of data type:

❑ Value types

❑ Reference types

The next few sections look in detail at the syntax for value and reference types. Conceptually, the difference is that a *value type* stores its value directly, whereas a *reference type* stores a reference to the value. Compared to other languages, value types in C# are basically the same thing as simple types (integer, float, but not pointers or references) in Visual Basic or C++. Reference types are the same as reference types in Visual Basic, or are similar to types accessed through pointers in C++.

These types are stored in different places in memory; value types are stored in an area known as the *stack*, and reference types are stored in an area known as the *managed heap*. It is important to be aware of whether a type is a value type or a reference type because of the different effect that assignment has. For example, int is a value type, which means that the following statement will result in two locations in memory storing the value 20:

```
// i and j are both of type int
i = 20;
j = i;
```

However, consider the following code. For this code, assume you have defined a class called Vector. Assume that Vector is a reference type and has an int member variable called Value:

```
Vector x, y;
x = new Vector();
x.Value = 30;    // Value is a field defined in Vector class
y = x;
Console.WriteLine(y.Value);
y.Value = 50;
Console.WriteLine(x.Value);
```

The crucial point to understand is that after executing this code, there is only one Vector object around. x and y both point to the memory location that contains this object. Because x and y are variables of a reference type, declaring each variable simply reserves a reference—it doesn't instantiate an object of the given type. This is the same as declaring a pointer in C++ or an object reference in Visual Basic. In neither case does an object actually get created. In order to create an object you have to use the `new` keyword, as shown. Because x and y refer to the same object, changes made to x will affect y and vice versa. Hence the code will display 30 then 50.

> *C++ developers should note that this syntax is like a reference, not a pointer. We use the . notation, not ->, to access object members. Syntactically, C# references look more like C++ reference variables. However, behind the superficial syntax, the real similarity is with C++ pointers.*

If a variable is a reference, it is possible to indicate that it does not refer to any object by setting its value to `null`:

```
y = null;
```

This is just the same as setting a reference to `null` in Java, a pointer to `NULL` in C++, or an object reference in Visual Basic to `Nothing`. If a reference is set to `null`, then clearly it is not possible to call any non-static member functions or fields against it; doing so would cause an exception to be thrown at runtime.

In languages like C++, the developer could choose whether a given value was to be accessed directly or via a pointer. Visual Basic was more restrictive, taking the view that COM objects were reference types and simple types were always value types. C# is similar to Visual Basic in this regard: whether a variable is a value or reference is determined solely by its data type, so `int`, for example, is always a value type. It is not possible to declare an `int` variable as a reference (although in Chapter 5, "Operators and Casts" which covers *boxing*, you see it is possible to wrap value types in references of type `object`).

In C#, basic data types like `bool` and `long` are value types. This means that if you declare a `bool` variable and assign it the value of another `bool` variable, you will have two separate `bool` values in memory. Later, if you change the value of the original `bool` variable, the value of the second `bool` variable does not change. These types are copied by value.

In contrast, most of the more complex C# data types, including classes that you yourself declare, are reference types. They are allocated upon the heap, have lifetimes that can span multiple function calls, and can be accessed through one or several aliases. The Common Language Runtime (CLR) implements an elaborate algorithm to track which reference variables are still reachable, and which have been orphaned. Periodically, the CLR will destroy orphaned objects and return the memory that they once occupied back to the operating system. This is done by the garbage collector.

C# has been designed this way because high performance is best served by keeping primitive types (like `int` and `bool`) as value types, while having larger types that contain many fields (as is usually the case with classes) as reference types. If you want to define your own type as a value type, you should declare it as a struct.

## CTS Types

As mentioned in Chapter 1, ".NET Architecture," the basic predefined types recognized by C# are not intrinsic to the language but are part of the .NET Framework. For example, when you declare an `int` in C#, what you are actually declaring is an instance of a .NET struct, `System.Int32`. This may sound like an esoteric point, but it has a profound significance: it means that you are able to treat all the primitive data types syntactically as if they were classes that supported certain methods. For example, to convert an `int` i to a `string`, you can write:

# C# Basics

```
string s = i.ToString();
```

It should be emphasized that, behind this syntactical convenience, the types really are stored as primitive types, so there is absolutely no performance cost associated with the idea that the primitive types are notionally represented by .NET structs.

The following sections review the types that are recognized as built-in types in C#. Each type is listed, along with its definition and the name of the corresponding .NET type (CTS type). C# has 15 predefined types, 13 value types, and 2 (`string` and `object`) reference types.

## Predefined Value Types

The built-in value types represent primitives, such as integer and floating-point numbers, character, and Boolean types.

### Integer types

C# supports eight predefined integer types:

| Name   | CTS Type      | Description            | Range (min:max)                                                        |
|--------|---------------|------------------------|------------------------------------------------------------------------|
| sbyte  | System.SByte  | 8-bit signed integer   | -128:127 ($-2^7:2^7-1$)                                                |
| short  | System.Int16  | 16-bit signed integer  | -32,768:32,767 ($-2^{15}:2^{15}-1$)                                    |
| int    | System.Int32  | 32-bit signed integer  | -2,147,483,648:2,147,483,647 ($-2^{31}:2^{31}-1$)                      |
| long   | System.Int64  | 64-bit signed integer  | -9,223,372,036,854,775,808: 9,223,372,036,854,775,807 ($-2^{63}:2^{63}-1$) |
| byte   | System.Byte   | 8-bit unsigned integer | 0:255 ($0:2^8-1$)                                                      |
| ushort | System.UInt16 | 16-bit unsigned integer| 0:65,535 ($0:2^{16}-1$)                                                |
| uint   | System.UInt32 | 32-bit unsigned integer| 0:4,294,967,295 ($0:2^{32}-1$)                                         |
| ulong  | System.UInt64 | 64-bit unsigned integer| 0:18,446,744,073,709,551,615 ($0:2^{64}-1$)                            |

Future versions of Windows will target 64-bit processors, which can move bits into and out of memory in larger chunks to achieve faster processing times. Consequently, C# supports a rich palette of signed and unsigned integer types ranging in size from 8 to 64 bits.

Many of these type names will be new to Visual Basic. C++ and Java developers should be careful; some of the names of C# types are the same as C++ and Java types, but the types have different definitions. For example, in C#, an `int` is always a 32-bit signed integer. In C++ an `int` is a signed integer, but the number of bits is platform-dependent (32 bits on Windows). In C#, all data types have been defined in a platform-independent manner to allow for the possible future porting of C# and .NET to other platforms.

A `byte` is the standard 8-bit type for values in the range 0 to 255 inclusive. Be aware that, in keeping with its emphasis on type safety, C# regards the `byte` type and the `char` type as completely distinct, and any programmatic conversions between the two must be explicitly requested. Also be aware that unlike the other types in the integer family, a `byte` type is by default unsigned. Its signed version bears the special name `sbyte`.

With .NET, a `short` is no longer quite so short; it is now 16 bits long. The `int` type is 32 bits long. The `long` type reserves 64 bits for values. All integer-type variables can be assigned values in decimal or in hex notation. The latter require the `0x` prefix:

```
long x = 0x12ab;
```

If there is any ambiguity about whether an integer is `int`, `uint`, `long`, or `ulong`, it will default to an `int`. To specify which of the other integer types the value should take, you can append one of the following characters to the number:

```
uint ui = 1234U;
long l = 1234L;
ulong ul = 1234UL;
```

You can also use lowercase `u` and `l`, although the latter could be confused with the integer 1 (one).

## *Floating-point types*

Although C# provides a plethora of integer data types, it supports floating-point types as well. They will be familiar to C and C++ programmers:

| Name | CTS Type | Description | Significant Figures | Range (approximate) |
|---|---|---|---|---|
| `float` | `System.Single` | 32-bit single-precision floating point | 7 | $\pm 1.5 \times 10^{-45}$ to $\pm 3.4 \times 10^{38}$ |
| `double` | `System.Double` | 64-bit double-precision floating point | 15/16 | $\pm 5.0 \times 10^{-324}$ to $\pm 1.7 \times 10^{308}$ |

The `float` data type is for smaller floating-point values, for which less precision is required. The `double` data type is bulkier than the `float` data type, but offers twice the precision (15 digits).

If you hard-code in a non-integer number (such as 12.3) in your code, the compiler will normally assume you want the number interpreted as a double. If you want to specify that the value is a `float`, you append the character F (or f) to it:

```
float f = 12.3F;
```

## *The decimal type*

In addition, there is a `decimal` type representing higher precision floating-point numbers:

| Name | CTS Type | Description | Significant Figures | Range (approximate) |
|---|---|---|---|---|
| decimal | System.Decimal | 128-bit high precision decimal notation | 28 | $\pm 1.0 \times 10^{-28}$ to $\pm 7.9 \times 10^{28}$ |

One of the great things about the CTS and C# is the provision of a dedicated decimal type for financial calculations. How you use the 28 digits that the decimal type provides is up to you. In other words, you can track smaller dollar amounts with greater accuracy for cents, or larger dollar amounts with more rounding in the fractional area. You should bear in mind, however, that decimal is not implemented under the hood as a primitive type, so using decimal will have a performance impact on your calculations.

To specify that your number is of a decimal type rather than a double, float, or an integer, you can append the M (or m) character to the value as shown in the following example:

```
decimal d = 12.30M;
```

## *The Boolean type*

The C# bool type is used to contain Boolean values of either true or false:

| Name | CTS Type | Values |
|---|---|---|
| bool | System.Boolean | true or false |

You cannot implicitly convert bool values to and from integer values. If a variable (or a function return type) is declared as a bool, you can only use values of true and false. You will get an error if you try to use zero for false and a non-zero value for true.

## *The character type*

For storing the value of a single character, C# supports the char data type:

| Name | CTS Type | Values |
|---|---|---|
| char | System.Char | Represents a single 16-bit (Unicode) character |

Although this data type has a superficial resemblance to the char type provided by C and C++, there is a significant difference. C++ char represents an 8-bit character, whereas a C# char contains 16 bits. This is part of the reason that implicit conversions between the char type and the 8-bit byte type are not permitted.

Although 8 bits may be enough to encode every character in the English language and the digits 0–9, they aren't enough to encode every character in more expansive symbol systems (such as Chinese). In a gesture toward universality, the computer industry is moving away from the 8-bit character set and toward the 16-bit Unicode scheme, of which the ASCII encoding is a subset.

Literals of type char are signified by being enclosed in single quotes, for example 'A'. If you try to enclose a character in double quotes, the compiler will treat this as a string and throw an error.

As well as representing chars as character literals, you can represent them with 4-digit hex Unicode values (for example '\u0041'), as integer values with a cast (for example, (char)65), or as hexadecimal values ('\x0041'). They can also be represented by an escape sequence:

| Escape Sequence | Character |
| --- | --- |
| \' | Single quote |
| \" | Double quote |
| \\ | Backslash |
| \0 | Null |
| \a | Alert |
| \b | Backspace |
| \f | Form feed |
| \n | Newline |
| \r | Carriage return |
| \t | Tab character |
| \v | Vertical tab |

C++ developers should note that because C# has a native string type, you don't need to represent strings as arrays of chars.

## Predefined Reference Types

C# supports two predefined reference types:

| Name | CTS Type | Description |
| --- | --- | --- |
| object | System.Object | The root type, from which all other types in the CTS derive (including value types) |
| string | System.String | Unicode character string |

### The object type

Many programming languages and class hierarchies provide a root type, from which all other objects in the hierarchy derive. C# and .NET are no exception. In C#, the object type is the ultimate parent type from which all other intrinsic and user-defined types derive. This is a key feature of C#, which distinguishes it from both Visual Basic and C++, although its behavior here is very similar to Java. All types

# C# Basics

implicitly derive ultimately from the `System.Object` class. This means that you can use the `object` type for two purposes:

❑ You can use an `object` reference to bind to an object of any particular subtype. For example, in Chapter 5, "Operators and Casts," you see how you can use the `object` type to box a value object on the stack to move it to the heap. `object` references are also useful in reflection, when code must manipulate objects whose specific types are unknown. This is similar to the role played by a void pointer in C++ or by a `Variant` data type in VB.

❑ The `object` type implements a number of basic, general-purpose methods, which include `Equals()`, `GetHashCode()`, `GetType()`, and `ToString()`. Responsible user-defined classes may need to provide replacement implementations of some of these methods using an object-oriented technique known as *overriding*, which is discussed in Chapter 4, "Inheritance." When you override `ToString()`, for example, you equip your class with a method for intelligently providing a string representation of itself. If you don't provide your own implementations for these methods in your classes, the compiler will pick up the implementations in `object`, which may or may not be correct or sensible in the context of your classes.

The `object` type is examined in more detail in subsequent chapters.

## *The string type*

Veterans of C and C++ probably have battle scars from wrestling with C-style strings. A C or C++ string was nothing more than an array of characters, so the client programmer had to do a lot of work just to copy one string to another or to concatenate two strings. In fact, for a generation of C++ programmers, implementing a string class that wrapped up the messy details of these operations was a rite of passage requiring many hours of teeth gnashing and head scratching. Visual Basic programmers had a somewhat easier life, with a string type, while Java people had it even better, with a `String` class that is in many ways very similar to C# string.

C# recognizes the `string` keyword, which under the hood is translated to the .NET class, `System.String`. With it, operations like string concatenation and string copying are a snap:

```
string str1 = "Hello ";
string str2 = "World";
string str3 = str1 + str2;  // string concatenation
```

Despite this style of assignment, `string` is a reference type. Behind the scenes, a `string` object is allocated on the heap, not the stack, and when you assign one string variable to another string, you get two references to the same string in memory. However, with `string` there are some differences from the usual behavior for reference types. For example, should you then make changes to one of these strings, note that this will create an entirely new `string` object, leaving the other string unchanged. Consider the following code:

```
using System;

class StringExample
{
   public static int Main()
   {
      string s1 = "a string";
```

45

```
            string s2 = s1;
            Console.WriteLine("s1 is " + s1);
            Console.WriteLine("s2 is " + s2);
            s1 = "another string";
            Console.WriteLine("s1 is now " + s1);
            Console.WriteLine("s2 is now " + s2);
            return 0;
        }
    }
```

The output from this is:

```
s1 is a string
s2 is a string
s1 is now another string
s2 is now a string
```

Changing the value of s1 had no effect on s2, contrary to what you'd expect with a reference type! What's happening here is that when s1 is initialized with the value a string, a new string object is allocated on the heap. When s2 is initialized, the reference points to this same object, so s2 also has the value a string. However, when you now change the value of s1, instead of replacing the original value, a new object will be allocated on the heap for the new value. The s2 variable will still point to the original object, so its value is unchanged. Under the hood, this happens as a result of operator overloading, a topic that is explored in Chapter 5, "Operators and Casts." In general, the string class has been implemented so that its semantics follow what you would normally intuitively expect for a string.

String literals are enclosed in double quotes ("..."); if you attempt to enclose a string in single quotes, the compiler will take the value as a char, and throw an error. C# strings can contain the same Unicode and hexadecimal escape sequences as chars. Because these escape sequences start with a backslash, you can't use this character unescaped in a string. Instead, you need to escape it with two backslashes (\\):

```
string filepath = "C:\\ProCSharp\\First.cs";
```

Even if you are confident you can remember to do this all the time, it can prove annoying typing all those double backslashes. Fortunately, C# gives you an alternative. You can prefix a string literal with the at character (@) and all the characters in it will be treated at face value; they won't be interpreted as escape sequences:

```
string filepath = @"C:\ProCSharp\First.cs";
```

This even allows you to include line breaks in your string literals:

```
string jabberwocky = @"'Twas brillig and the slithy toves
Did gyre and gimble in the wabe.";
```

Then the value of jabberwocky would be this:

```
'Twas brillig and the slithy toves
Did gyre and gimble in the wabe.
```

# Flow Control

This section looks at the real nuts and bolts of the language: the statements that allow you to control the *flow* of your program rather than executing every line of code in the order it appears in the program.

## *Conditional Statements*

Conditional statements allow you to branch your code depending on whether certain conditions are met or on the value of an expression. C# has two constructs for branching code — the `if` statement, which allows you to test whether a specific condition is met, and the `switch` statement, which allows you to compare an expression with a number of different values.

### *The if statement*

For conditional branching, C# inherits the C and C++ `if...else` construct. The syntax should be fairly intuitive for anyone who has done any programming with a procedural language:

```
if (condition)
    statement(s)
else
    statement(s)
```

If more than one statement is to be executed as part of either condition, these statements will need to be joined together into a block using curly braces (`{ ... }`). (This also applies to other C# constructs where statements can be joined into a block, such as the `for` and `while` loops):

```
bool isZero;
if (i == 0)
{
    isZero = true;
    Console.WriteLine("i is Zero");
}
else
{
    isZero = false;
    Console.WriteLine("i is Non-zero");
}
```

The syntax here is similar to C++ and Java but once again different from Visual Basic. Visual Basic developers should note that C# does not have any statement corresponding to Visual Basic's `EndIf`. Instead, the rule is that each clause of an `if` contains just one statement. If you need more than one statement, as in the preceding example, you should enclose the statements in braces, which will cause the whole group of statements to be treated as a single block statement.

If you want to, you can use an `if` statement without a final `else` statement. You can also combine `else if` clauses to test for multiple conditions:

```
using System;

namespace Wrox.ProCSharp.Basics
{
```

```csharp
class MainEntryPoint
{
   static void Main(string[] args)
   {
      Console.WriteLine("Type in a string");
      string input;
      input = Console.ReadLine();
      if (input == "")
      {
         Console.WriteLine("You typed in an empty string");
      }
      else if (input.Length < 5)
      {
         Console.WriteLine("The string had less than 5 characters");
      }
      else if (input.Length < 10)
      {
         Console.WriteLine("The string had at least 5 but less than 10
            characters");
      }
      Console.WriteLine("The string was " + input);
   }
}
}
```

There is no limit to how many `else if`'s you can add to an `if` clause.

You'll notice that the previous example declares a string variable called `input`, gets the user to enter text at the command line, feeds this into `input`, and then tests the length of this string variable. The code also shows how easy string manipulation can be in C#. To find the length of `input`, for example, use `input.Length`.

One point to note about `if` is that you don't need to use the braces if there's only one statement in the conditional branch:

```csharp
if (i == 0)
    Console.WriteLine("i is Zero");         // This will only execute if i == 0
Console.WriteLine("i can be anything");    // Will execute whatever the
                                           // value of i
```

However, for consistency, many programmers prefer to use curly braces whenever they use an `if` statement.

The `if` statements presented also illustrate some of the C# operators that compare values. Note in particular that, like C++ and Java, C# uses `==` to compare variables for equality. Do not use `=` for this purpose. A single `=` is used to assign values.

In C#, the expression in the `if` clause must evaluate to a Boolean. C++ programmers should be particularly aware of this; unlike C++, it is not possible to test an integer (returned from a function, say) directly. In C#, you have to convert the integer that is returned to a Boolean `true` or `false`, for example by comparing the value with zero or with `null`:

```
if (DoSomething() != 0)
{
    // Non-zero value returned
}
else
{
    // Returned zero
}
```

This restriction is there in order to prevent some common types of runtime bugs that occur in C++. In particular, in C++ it was common to mistype = when == was intended, resulting in unintentional assignments. In C# this will normally result in a compile-time error, because unless you are working with `bool` values, = will not return a `bool`.

## *The switch statement*

The `switch...case` statement is good for selecting one branch of execution from a set of mutually exclusive ones. It will be familiar to C++ and Java programmers and is similar to the `Select Case` statement in Visual Basic.

It takes the form of a `switch` argument followed by a series of `case` clauses. When the expression in the `switch` argument evaluates to one of the values beside a `case` clause, the code immediately following the `case` clause executes. This is one example where you don't need to use curly braces to join statements into blocks; instead, you mark the end of the code for each case using the `break` statement. You can also include a `default` case in the `switch` statement, which will execute if the expression evaluates to none of the other cases. The following `switch` statement tests the value of the `integerA` variable:

```
switch (integerA)
{
    case 1:
        Console.WriteLine("integerA =1");
        break;
    case 2:
        Console.WriteLine("integerA =2");
        break;
    case 3:
        Console.WriteLine("integerA =3");
        break;
    default:
        Console.WriteLine("integerA is not 1,2, or 3");
        break;
}
```

Note that the case values must be constant expressions; variables are not permitted.

Though the `switch...case` statement should be familiar to C and C++ programmers, C#'s `switch...case` is a bit safer than its C++ equivalent. Specifically, it prohibits fall-through conditions in almost all cases. This means that if a `case` clause is fired early on in the block, later clauses cannot be fired unless you use a `goto` statement to mark that you want them fired too. The compiler enforces this restriction by flagging every `case` clause that is not equipped with a `break` statement as an error similar to this:

```
Control cannot fall through from one case label ('case 2:') to another
```

Although it is true that fall-through behavior is desirable in a limited number of situations, in the vast majority of cases it is unintended and results in a logical error that's hard to spot. Isn't it better to code for the norm rather than for the exception?

By getting creative with `goto` statements (which C# does support) however, you can duplicate fall-through functionality in your `switch...cases`. However, if you find yourself really wanting to, you probably should reconsider your approach. The following code illustrates both how to use `goto` to simulate fall-through, and how messy the resultant code can get:

```
// assume country and language are of type string
switch(country)
{
    case "America":
        CallAmericanOnlyMethod();
        goto case "Britain";
    case "France":
        language = "French";
        break;
    case "Britain":
        language = "English";
        break;
}
```

There is one exception to the no–fall-through rule, however, in that you can fall through from one case to the next if that case is empty. This allows you to treat two or more cases in an identical way (without the need for `goto` statements):

```
switch(country)
{
    case "au":
    case "uk":
    case "us":
        language = "English";
        break;
    case "at":
    case "de":
        language = "German";
        break;
}
```

One intriguing point about the `switch` statement in C# is that the order of the cases doesn't matter — you can even put the `default` case first! As a result, no two cases can be the same. This includes different constants that have the same value, so you can't, for example, do this:

```
// assume country is of type string
const string england = "uk";
const string britain = "uk";
switch(country)
{
    case england:
    case britain:    // this will cause a compilation error
        language = "English";
        break;
}
```

# C# Basics

The previous code also shows another way in which the `switch` statement is different in C# from C++: In C#, you are allowed to use a string as the variable being tested.

## Loops

C# provides four different loops (`for`, `while`, `do...while`, and `foreach`) that allow you to execute a block of code repeatedly until a certain condition is met. The `for`, `while`, and `do...while` loops are essentially identical to those encountered in C++.

### The for loop

C# `for` loops provide a mechanism for iterating through a loop where you test whether a particular condition holds before you perform another iteration. The syntax is

```
for (initializer; condition; iterator)
    statement(s)
```

where

- ❑ The initializer is the expression evaluated before the first loop is executed (usually initializing a local variable as a loop counter).
- ❑ The condition is the expression checked before each new iteration of the loop (this must evaluate to `true` for another iteration to be performed).
- ❑ The iterator is an expression evaluated after each iteration (usually incrementing the loop counter). The iterations end when the condition evaluates to `false`.

The `for` loop is a so-called pre-test loop, because the loop condition is evaluated before the loop statements are executed, and so the contents of the loop won't be executed at all if the loop condition is `false`.

The `for` loop is excellent for repeating a statement or a block of statements for a predetermined number of times. The following example is typical of the use of a `for` loop. The following code will write out all the integers from 0 to 99:

```
for (int i = 0; i < 100; i = i+1)    // this is equivalent to
                                      // For i = 0 To 99 in VB.
{
    Console.WriteLine(i);
}
```

Here, you declare an `int` called `i` and initialize it to zero. This will be used as the loop counter. You then immediately test whether it is less than 100. Because this condition evaluates to `true`, you execute the code in the loop, displaying the value 0. You then increment the counter by one, and walk through the process again. Looping ends when `i` reaches 100.

Actually, the way the preceding loop is written isn't quite how you would normally write it. C# has a shorthand for adding 1 to a variable, so instead of `i = i + 1`, you can simply write `i++`:

```
for (int i = 0; i < 100; i++)
{
    // etc.
```

C# `for` loop syntax is far more powerful than the Visual Basic `For...Next` loop, because the iterator can be any statement. In Visual Basic, all you can do is add or subtract some number from the loop control variable. In C# you can do anything; for example, you can multiply the loop control variable by 2.

It's not unusual to nest `for` loops so that an inner loop executes once completely for each iteration of an outer loop. This scheme is typically employed to loop through every element in a rectangular multi-dimensional array. The outermost loop loops through every row, and the inner loop loops through every column in a particular row. The following code displays rows of numbers. It also uses another `Console` method, `Console.Write()`, which does the same as `Console.WriteLine()` but doesn't send a carriage return to the output.

```csharp
using System;

namespace Wrox.ProCSharp.Basics
{
    class MainEntryPoint
    {
        static void Main(string[] args)
        {
            // This loop iterates through rows...
            for (int i = 0; i < 100; i+=10)
            {
                // This loop iterates through columns...
                for (int j = i; j < i + 10; j++)
                {
                    Console.Write(" " + j);
                }
                Console.WriteLine();
            }
        }
    }
}
```

Although `j` is an integer, it will be automatically converted to a string so that the concatenation can take place. C++ developers will note that this is far easier than string handling ever was in C++; for Visual Basic developers this is familiar ground.

C programmers should take note of one particular feature of the preceding example. The counter variable in the innermost loop is effectively re-declared with each successive iteration of the outer loop. This syntax is legal not only in C# but in C++ as well.

The preceding sample results in this output:

**csc NumberTable.cs**

```
Microsoft (R) Visual C# .NET Compiler version 7.10.3052.4
for Microsoft (R) .NET Framework version 1.0.4322
Copyright (C) Microsoft Corporation 2001-2002. All rights reserved.
```

# C# Basics

```
 0  1  2  3  4  5  6  7  8  9
10 11 12 13 14 15 16 17 18 19
20 21 22 23 24 25 26 27 28 29
30 31 32 33 34 35 36 37 38 39
40 41 42 43 44 45 46 47 48 49
50 51 52 53 54 55 56 57 58 59
60 61 62 63 64 65 66 67 68 69
70 71 72 73 74 75 76 77 78 79
80 81 82 83 84 85 86 87 88 89
90 91 92 93 94 95 96 97 98 99
```

Although it is technically possible to evaluate something other than a counter variable in a `for` loop's test condition, it is certainly not typical. It is also possible to omit one (or even all) of the expressions in the `for` loop. In such situations, however, you should consider using the `while` loop.

## *The while loop*

The `while` loop is identical to the `while` loop in C++ and Java, and the `While...Wend` loop in Visual Basic. Like the `for` loop, `while` is a pre-test loop. The syntax is similar, but `while` loops take only one expression:

```
while(condition)
    statement(s);
```

Unlike the `for` loop, the `while` loop is most often used to repeat a statement or a block of statements for a number of times that is not known before the loop begins. Usually, a statement inside the `while` loop's body will set a Boolean flag to `false` on a certain iteration, triggering the end of the loop, as in the following example:

```
bool condition = false;
while (!condition)
{
    // This loop spins until the condition is true
    DoSomeWork();
    condition = CheckCondition();    // assume CheckCondition() returns a bool
}
```

All of C#'s looping mechanisms, including the `while` loop, can forego the curly braces that follow them if they intend to repeat just a single statement and not a block of statements. Again, many programmers consider it good practice to use braces all of the time.

## *The do...while loop*

The `do...while` loop is the post-test version of the `while` loop. It does the same thing with the same syntax as `do...while` in C++ and Java, and the same thing as `Loop...While` in Visual Basic. This means that the loop's test condition is evaluated after the body of the loop has been executed. Consequently, `do...while` loops are useful for situations in which a block of statements must be executed at least one time, as in this example:

```
bool condition;
do
{
    // this loop will at least execute once, even if Condition is false
    MustBeCalledAtLeastOnce();
    condition = CheckCondition();
} while (condition);
```

## The foreach loop

The `foreach` loop is the final C# looping mechanism that we discuss. Whereas the other looping mechanisms were present in the earliest versions of C and C++, the `foreach` statement is a new addition (borrowed from Visual Basic), and a very welcome one at that.

The `foreach` loop allows you to iterate through each item in a collection. For the time being we won't worry about exactly what a collection is — it is explained fully in Chapter 9, "Collections." For now, we will just say that it is an object that contains other objects. Technically, to count as a collection, it must support an interface called `IEnumerable`. Examples of collections include C# arrays, the collection classes in the `System.Collection` namespaces, and user-defined collection classes. You can get an idea of the syntax of `foreach` from the following code, if you assume that `arrayOfInts` is (unsurprisingly) an array if ints:

```
foreach (int temp in arrayOfInts)
{
    Console.WriteLine(temp);
}
```

Here, `foreach` steps through the array one element at a time. With each element, it places the value of the element in the `int` variable called `temp`, and then performs an iteration of the loop.

An important point to note with `foreach` is that you can't change the value of the item in the collection (`temp` in the preceding code), so code such as the following will not compile:

```
foreach (int temp in arrayOfInts)
{
    temp++;
    Console.WriteLine(temp);
}
```

If you need to iterate through the items in a collection and change their values, you will need to use a `for` loop instead.

## Jump Statements

C# provides a number of statements that allow you to jump immediately to another line in the program. The first of these is, of course, the notorious `goto` statement.

# C# Basics

## *The goto statement*

The `goto` statement allows you to jump directly to another specified line in the program, indicated by a *label* (this is just an identifier followed by a colon):

```
goto Label1;
   Console.WriteLine("This won't be executed");
Label1:
   Console.WriteLine("Continuing execution from here");
```

A couple of restrictions are involved with `goto`. You can't jump into a block of code such as a `for` loop, you can't jump out of a class, and you can't exit a `finally` block after `try...catch` blocks (Chapter 12, "Errors and Exceptions," looks at exception handling with `try...catch...finally`).

The reputation of the `goto` statement probably precedes it, and in most circumstances, its use is sternly frowned upon. In general, it certainly doesn't conform to good object-oriented programming practice. However, there is one place where it is quite handy: jumping between cases in a `switch` statement, particularly because C#'s `switch` is so strict on fall-through. You saw the syntax for this earlier in this chapter.

## *The break statement*

You have already met the `break` statement briefly—when you used it to exit from a case in a `switch` statement. In fact, `break` can also be used to exit from `for`, `foreach`, `while`, or `do...while` loops too. Control will switch to the statement immediately after the end of the loop.

If the statement occurs in a nested loop, control will switch to the end of the innermost loop. If the break occurs outside of a `switch` statement or a loop, a compile-time error will occur.

## *The continue statement*

The `continue` statement is similar to `break`, and must also be used within a `for`, `foreach`, `while`, or `do...while` loop. However, it exits only from the current iteration of the loop, meaning execution will restart at the beginning of the next iteration of the loop, rather than outside the loop altogether.

## *The return statement*

The `return` statement is used to exit a method of a class, returning control to the caller of the method. If the method has a return type, `return` must return a value of this type; otherwise if the method returns `void`, you should use `return` without an expression.

# Enumerations

An *enumeration* is a user-defined integer type. When you declare an enumeration, you specify a set of acceptable values that instances of that enumeration can contain. Not only that, but you can give the values user-friendly names. If, somewhere in your code, you attempt to assign a value that is not in the acceptable set of values to an instance of that enumeration, the compiler will flag an error. This concept may be new to Visual Basic programmers. C++ does support enumerations (or enums), but C# enumerations are far more powerful than their C++ counterparts.

Creating an enumeration can end up saving you lots of time and headaches in the long run. At least three benefits exist to using enumerations instead of plain integers:

- ❏ As mentioned, enumerations make your code easier to maintain by helping to ensure that your variables are assigned only legitimate, anticipated values.

- ❏ Enumerations make your code clearer by allowing you to refer to integer values by descriptive names rather than by obscure "magic" numbers.

- ❏ Enumerations make your code easier to type, too. When you go to assign a value to an instance of an enumerated type, the Visual Studio .NET IDE will, through IntelliSense, pop up a list box of acceptable values in order to save you some keystrokes and to remind you of what the possible options are.

You can define an enumeration as follows:

```
public enum TimeOfDay
{
   Morning = 0,
   Afternoon = 1,
   Evening = 2
}
```

In this case, you use an integer value to represent each period of the day in the enumeration. You can now access these values as members of the enumeration. For example, `TimeOfDay.Morning` will return the value 0. You will typically use this enumeration to pass an appropriate value into a method and iterate through the possible values in a `switch` statement:

```
class EnumExample
{
   public static int Main()
   {
      WriteGreeting(TimeOfDay.Morning);
      return 0;
   }

   static void WriteGreeting(TimeOfDay timeOfDay)
   {
      switch(timeOfDay)
      {
         case TimeOfDay.Morning:
            Console.WriteLine("Good morning!");
            break;
         case TimeOfDay.Afternoon:
            Console.WriteLine("Good afternoon!");
            break;
         case TimeOfDay.Evening:
            Console.WriteLine("Good evening!");
            break;
         default:
            Console.WriteLine("Hello!");
            break;
      }
   }
}
```

# C# Basics

The real power of enums in C# is that behind the scenes they are instantiated as structs derived from the base class, `System.Enum`. This means it is possible to call methods against them to perform some useful tasks. Note that because of the way the .NET Framework is implemented there is no performance loss associated with treating the enums syntactically as structs. In practice, once your code is compiled, enums will exist as primitive types, just like `int` and `float`.

You can retrieve the string representation of an enum as in the following example, using the earlier `TimeOfDay` enum:

```
TimeOfDay time = TimeOfDay.Afternoon;
Console.WriteLine(time.ToString());
```

This will return the string `Afternoon`.

Alternatively you can obtain an enum value from a string.

```
TimeOfDay time2 = (TimeOfDay) Enum.Parse(typeof(TimeOfDay), "afternoon", true);
Console.WriteLine((int)time2);
```

This code snippet illustrates both obtaining an enum value from a string and converting to an integer. To convert from a string, you need to use the static `Enum.Parse()` method, which as shown here takes three parameters. The first is the type of enum you want to consider. The syntax is the keyword `typeof` followed by the name of the enum class in brackets. (Chapter 5, "Operators and Casts," explores the `typeof` operator in more detail.) The second parameter is the string to be converted, and the third parameter is a `bool` indicating whether or not you should ignore case when doing the conversion. Finally, note that `Enum.Parse()` actually returns an object reference—you need to explicitly convert this to the required enum type (this is an example of an unboxing operation). For the preceding code, this returns the value 1 as an object, corresponding to the enum value of `TimeOfDay.Afternoon`. On converting explicitly to an `int`, this produces the value 1 again.

Other methods on `System.Enum` do things like return the number of values in an enum definition or list the names of the values. Full details are in the MSDN documentation.

## Arrays

We won't say too much about arrays in this chapter, because arrays and collections are covered in detail in Chapter 9, "Collections." However, we'll give you just enough syntax here that you can code 1-dimensional arrays. Arrays in C# are declared by fixing a set of square brackets to the end of the variable type of the individual elements (note that all the elements in an array must be of the same data type).

> *A note to Visual Basic users: arrays in C# use square brackets, not parentheses. C++ users will be familiar with the square brackets, but should carefully check the code presented here because C# syntax for actually declaring array variables is not the same as C++ syntax.*

For example, whereas `int` represents a single integer, `int[]` represents an array of integers:

```
int[] integers;
```

# Chapter 2

To initialize the array with specific dimensions, you can use the `new` keyword, giving the size in the square brackets after the type name:

```
// Create a new array of 32 ints
int[] integers = new int[32];
```

All arrays are reference types and follow reference semantics. Hence, in this code, even though the individual elements are primitive value types, the `integers` array is a reference type. So if you later write

```
int [] copy = integers;
```

this will simply assign the variable `copy` to refer to the same array — it won't create a new array.

To access an individual element within the array, you use the usual syntax, placing the index of the element in square brackets after the name of the array. All C# arrays use zero-based indexing, so you can reference the first variable with the index zero:

```
integers[0] = 35;
```

Similarly, you reference the 32 element value with an index value of 31:

```
integers[31] = 432;
```

C#'s array syntax is flexible. In fact, C# allows you to declare arrays without initializing them, so that the array can be dynamically sized later in the program. With this technique, you are basically creating a `null` reference, and later pointing that reference at a dynamically allocated stretch of memory locations requested with the `new` keyword:

```
int[] integers;
integers = new int[32];
```

You can find out how many elements are in any array by using this syntax:

```
int numElements = integers.Length;    // integers is any reference to an array.
```

# Namespaces

As you have seen, namespaces provide a way of organizing related classes and other types. Unlike a file or a component, a namespace is a logical rather than a physical grouping. When you define a class in a C# file, you can include it within a namespace definition. Later, when you define another class that performs related work in another file, you can include it within the same namespace, creating a logical grouping that gives an indication to other developers using the classes how they are related and used:

```
namespace CustomerPhoneBookApp
{
    using System;

    public struct Subscriber
    {
```

# C# Basics

```
        // Code for struct here...
    }
}
```

Placing a type in a namespace effectively gives that type a long name, consisting of the type's namespace as a series of names separated with periods (.), terminating with the name of the class. In the preceding example, the full name of the `Subscriber` struct is `CustomerPhoneBookApp.Subscriber`. This allows distinct classes with the same short name to be used within the same program without ambiguity.

You can also nest namespaces within other namespaces, creating a hierarchical structure for your types:

```
namespace Wrox
{
    namespace ProCSharp
    {
        namespace Basics
        {
            class NamespaceExample
            {
                // Code for the class here...
            }
        }
    }
}
```

Each namespace name is composed of the names of the namespaces it resides within, separated with periods, starting with the outermost namespace and ending with its own short name. So the full name for the `ProCSharp` namespace is `Wrox.ProCSharp`, and the full name of `NamespaceExample` class is `Wrox.ProCSharp.Basics.NamespaceExample`.

You can use this syntax to organize the namespaces in your namespace definitions too, so the previous code could also be written as follows:

```
namespace Wrox.ProCSharp.Basics
{
    class NamespaceExample
    {
        // Code for the class here...
    }
}
```

Note that you are not permitted to declare a multipart namespace nested within another namespace.

Namespaces are not related to assemblies. It is perfectly acceptable to have different namespaces in the same assembly or to define types in the same namespace in different assemblies.

## The using Statement

Obviously, namespaces can grow rather long and tiresome to type, and the ability to indicate a particular class with such specificity may not always be necessary. Fortunately, as noted at the beginning of the chapter, C# allows you to abbreviate a class's full name. To do this, you list the class's namespace at the top of the file, prefixed with the `using` keyword. Throughout the rest of the file, you can refer to the types in the namespace simply by their type names.

```
using System;
using Wrox.ProCSharp;
```

As remarked earlier, virtually all C# source code will start with the statement `using System;` simply because so many useful classes supplied by Microsoft are contained in the `System` namespace.

If two namespaces referenced by `using` statements contain a type of the same name, you will have to use the full (or at least, a longer) form of the name to ensure that the compiler knows which type is to be accessed. For example, say classes called `NamespaceExample` exist both in the `Wrox.ProCSharp.Basics` and `Wrox.ProCSharp.OOP` namespaces. If you then create a class called `Test` in the `Wrox.ProCSharp` namespace, and instantiate one of the `NamespaceExample` classes in this class, you need to specify which of these two classes you're talking about:

```
using Wrox.ProCSharp;

class Test
{
   public static int Main()
   {
      Basics.NamespaceExample nSEx = new Basics.NamespaceExample();
      // do something with the nSEx variable
      return 0;
   }
}
```

Because `using` statements occur at the top of C# files, in the same place that C and C++ list `#include` statements, it's easy for programmers moving from C++ to C# to confuse namespaces with C++-style header files. Don't make this mistake. The `using` statement does no physical linking between files, and C# has no equivalent to C++ header files.

Your organization will probably want to spend some time developing a namespace schema so that its developers can quickly locate functionality that they need and so that the names of the organization's homegrown classes won't conflict with those in off-the-shelf class libraries. Guidelines on establishing your own namespace scheme along with other naming recommendations are discussed later in this chapter.

## *Namespace Aliases*

Another use of the `using` keyword is to assign aliases to classes and namespaces. If you have a very long namespace name that you want to refer to several times in your code but don't want to include in a simple `using` statement (for example, to avoid type name conflicts), you can assign an alias to the namespace. The syntax for this is:

```
using alias = NamespaceName;
```

The following example (a modified version of the previous example) assigns the alias `Introduction` to the `Wrox.ProCSharp.Basics` namespace, and uses this to instantiate a `NamespaceExample` object, which is defined in this namespace. Notice the use of the namespace alias qualifier (::). This forces the search to start with the Introduction namespace alias. If a class called Introduction had been introduced in the same scope, a conflict would happen. The :: operator allows the alias to be referenced even if the conflict exists. The NamespaceExample class has one method, GetNamespace(), which uses the GetType() method exposed by every class to access a Type object representing the class's type. You use this object to return a name of the class's namespace:

```
using System;
using Introduction = Wrox.ProCSharp.Basics;

class Test
{
   public static int Main()
   {
      Introduction::NamespaceExample NSEx =
         new Introduction::NamespaceExample();

      Console.WriteLine(NSEx.GetNamespace());

      return 0;
   }
}


namespace Wrox.ProCSharp.Basics
{
   class NamespaceExample
   {
      public string GetNamespace()
      {
         return this.GetType().Namespace;
      }
   }
}
```

# The Main() Method

You saw at the start of this chapter that C# programs start execution at a method named Main(). As you saw earlier, this must be a static method of a class (or struct), and must have a return type of either int or void.

Although it is common to specify the public modifier explicitly, because by definition the method must be called from outside the program, it doesn't actually matter what accessibility level you assign to the entry point method — it will run even if you mark the method as private.

## Multiple Main() Methods

When a C# console or Windows application is compiled, by default the compiler looks for exactly one Main() method in any class matching the signature that was just described and makes that class method the entry point for the program. If there is more than one Main() method, the compiler will return an error message. For example, consider the following code called MainExample.cs:

```csharp
using System;

namespace Wrox.ProCSharp.Basics
{
   class Client
   {
      public static int Main()
      {
         MathExample.Main();
         return 0;
      }
   }

   class MathExample
   {
      static int Add(int x, int y)
      {
         return x + y;
      }

      public static int Main()
      {
         int i = Add(5,10);
         Console.WriteLine(i);
         return 0;
      }
   }
}
```

This contains two classes, both of which have a `Main()` method. If you try to compile this code in the usual way, you will get the following errors:

**csc MainExample.cs**

```
Microsoft (R) Visual C# .NET Compiler version 8.00.40607.16
for Microsoft (R) Windows (R) .NET Framework version 2.0.40607
Copyright (C) Microsoft Corporation 2001-2003. All rights reserved.

MainExample.cs(7,23): error CS0017: Program 'MainExample.exe' has more than
one entry point defined: 'Wrox.ProCSharp.Basics.Client.Main()'
MainExample.cs(21,23): error CS0017: Program 'MainExample.exe' has more than
one entry point defined: 'Wrox.ProCSharp.Basics.MathExample.Main()'
```

However, you can explicitly tell the compiler which of these methods to use as the entry point for the program using the `/main` switch, together with the full name (including namespace) of the class to which the `Main()` method belongs:

**csc MainExample.cs /main:Wrox.ProCSharp.Basics.MathExample**

# C# Basics

## Passing Arguments to Main()

The examples so far have only shown the `Main()` method without any parameters. However, when the program is invoked, you can get the CLR to pass any command-line arguments to the program by including a parameter. This parameter is a string array, traditionally called `args` (although C# will accept any name). The program can use this array to access any options passed through the command line when the program is started.

The following sample, `ArgsExample.cs`, loops through the string array passed in to the `Main()` method and writes the value of each option to the console window:

```csharp
using System;

namespace Wrox.ProCSharp.Basics
{
   class ArgsExample
   {
      public static int Main(string[] args)
      {
         for (int i = 0; i < args.Length; i++)
         {
            Console.WriteLine(args[i]);
         }
         return 0;
      }
   }
}
```

You can compile this as usual using the command line. When you run the compiled executable, you can pass in arguments after the name of the program, for example:

**ArgsExample /a /b /c**

```
/a
/b
/c
```

# More on Compiling C# Files

So far, you have seen how to compile console applications using `csc.exe`, but what about other types of applications? What if you want to reference a class library? The full set of compilation options for the C# compiler is of course detailed in the MSDN documentation, but we list here the most important options.

To answer the first question, you can specify what type of file you want to create using the `/target` switch, often abbreviated to `/t`. This can be one of the following:

# Chapter 2

| Option | Output |
|---|---|
| `/t:exe` | A console application (the default) |
| `/t:library` | A class library with a manifest |
| `/t:module` | A component without a manifest |
| `/t:winexe` | A Windows application (without a console window) |

If you want a non-executable file (such as a DLL) to be loadable by the .NET runtime, you must compile it as a library. If you compile a C# file as a module, no assembly will be created. Although modules cannot be loaded by the runtime, they can be compiled into another manifest using the `/addmodule` switch.

Another option we need to mention is `/out`. This allows you to specify the name of the output file produced by the compiler. If the `/out` option isn't specified, the compiler will base the name of the output file on the name of the input C# file, adding an extension according to the target type (for example, exe for a Windows or console application, or dll for a class library). Note that the `/out` and `/t`, or `/target`, options must precede the name of the file you want to compile.

If you want to reference types in assemblies that aren't referenced by default, you can use the `/reference` or `/r` switch, together with the path and file name of the assembly. The following example demonstrates how you can compile a class library and then reference that library in another assembly. It consists of two files:

- The class library
- A console application, which will call a class in the library

The first file is called `MathLibrary.cs` and contains the code for your DLL. To keep things simple, it contains just one (public) class, `MathLib`, with a single method that adds two `int`s:

```
namespace Wrox.ProCSharp.Basics
{
    public class MathLib
    {
        public int Add(int x, int y)
        {
            return x + y;
        }
    }
}
```

You can compile this C# file into a .NET DLL using the following command:

**csc /t:library MathLibrary.cs**

The console application, `MathClient.cs`, will simply instantiate this object and call its `Add()` method, displaying the result in the console window:

# C# Basics

```
using System;

namespace Wrox.ProCSharp.Basics
{
   class Client
   {
      public static void Main()
      {
         MathLib mathObj = new MathLib();
         Console.WriteLine(mathObj.Add(7,8));
      }
   }
}
```

You can compile this code using the `/r` switch to point at or reference the newly compiled DLL:

**csc MathClient.cs /r:MathLibrary.dll**

You can then run it as normal just by entering `MathClient` at the command prompt. This displays the number 15 — the result of your addition.

## Console I/O

By this point, you should have a basic familiarity with C#'s data types, as well as some knowledge of how the thread-of-control moves through a program that manipulates those data types. In this chapter, you have also used several of the `Console` class's static methods used for reading and writing data. Because these methods are so useful when writing basic C# programs, this section quickly goes over them in a little more detail.

To read a line of text from the console window, you use the `Console.ReadLine()` method. This will read an input stream (terminated when the user presses the `Return` key) from the console window and return the input string. There are also two corresponding methods for writing to the console, which you have already used extensively:

- ❑ `Console.Write()` — Writes the specified value to the console window.
- ❑ `Console.WriteLine()` — This does the same, but adds a new line character at the end of the output.

Various forms (overloads) of these methods exist for all of the predefined types (including `object`), so in most cases you don't have to convert values to strings before you display them.

For example, the following code lets the user input a line of text, and displays that text:

```
string s = Console.ReadLine();
Console.WriteLine(s);
```

`Console.WriteLine()` also allows you to display formatted output in a way comparable to C's `printf()` function. To use `WriteLine()` in this way, you pass in a number of parameters. The first is a string containing markers in curly braces where the subsequent parameters will be inserted into the text. Each marker contains a zero-based index for the number of the parameter in the following list. For example, {0} represents the first parameter in the list. Consider the following code:

```
int i = 10;
int j = 20;
Console.WriteLine("{0} plus {1} equals {2}", i, j, i + j);
```

This code displays:

```
10 plus 20 equals 30
```

You can also specify a width for the value, and justify the text within that width, using positive values for right justification and negative values for left justification. To do this, you use the format {n,w}, where n is the parameter index and w is the width value:

```
int i = 940;
int j = 73;
Console.WriteLine(" {0,4}\n+{1,4}\n ----\n {2,4}", i, j, i + j);
```

The result of this is:

```
  940
+  73
 ----
 1013
```

Finally, you can also add a format string, together with an optional precision value. It is not possible to give a complete list of possible format strings, since, as you see in Chapter 8, "Strings and Regular Expressions," it is possible to define your own format strings. However, the main ones in use for the predefined types are as follows:

| String | Description |
| --- | --- |
| C | Local currency format. |
| D | Decimal format. Converts an integer to base 10, and pads with leading zeros if a precision specifier is given. |
| E | Scientific (exponential) format. The precision specifier sets the number of decimal places (6 by default). The case of the format string (e or E) determines the case of the exponential symbol. |
| F | Fixed-point format; the precision specifier controls the number of decimal places. Zero is acceptable. |
| G | General format. Uses E or F formatting, depending on which is the most compact. |
| N | Number format. Formats the number with commas as thousands separators, for example 32,767.44. |
| P | Percent format. |
| X | Hexadecimal format. The precision specifier can be used to pad with leading zeros. |

# C# Basics

Note that the format strings are normally case-insensitive, except for `e`/`E`.

If you want to use a format string, you should place it immediately after the marker that gives the parameter number and field width, and separated from it by a colon. For example, to format a `decimal` value as currency for the computer's locale, with precision to two decimal places, you would use C2:

```
decimal i = 940.23m;
decimal j = 73.7m;
Console.WriteLine(" {0,9:C2}\n+{1,9:C2}\n ---------\n {2,9:C2}", i, j, i + j);
```

The output of this in the United States is:

```
    $940.23
+    $73.70
 ---------
  $1,013.93
```

As a final trick, you can also use placeholder characters instead of these format strings to map out formatting. For example:

```
double d = 0.234;
Console.WriteLine("{0:#.00}", d);
```

This displays as .23, because the # symbol is ignored if there is no character in that place, and zeros will either be replaced by the character in that position if there is one or else printed as a zero.

# Using Comments

The next topic looks very simple on the surface — adding comments to your code.

## *Internal Comments Within the Source Files*

As noted earlier in this chapter, C# uses the traditional C-type single-line (`// ...`) and multi-line (`/* ... */`) comments:

```
// This is a single-line comment
/* This comment
   spans multiple lines */
```

Everything in a single-line comment, from the `//` to the end of the line, will be ignored by the compiler, and everything from an opening `/*` to the next `*/` in a multi-line comment combination will be ignored. Obviously, you can't include the combination `*/` in any multi-line comments, because this will be treated as the end of the comment.

It is actually possible to put multi-line comments within a line of code:

```
Console.WriteLine(/* Here's a comment! */ "This will compile");
```

Inline comments like this should be used with care because they can make code hard to read. However, they can be useful when debugging if, say, you temporarily want to try running the code with a different value somewhere:

```
DoSomething(Width, /*Height*/ 100);
```

Comment characters included in string literals are, of course, treated like normal characters:

```
string s = "/* This is just a normal string */";
```

## XML Documentation

In addition to the C-type comments, illustrated in the preceding section, C# has a very neat feature that we can't omit from this chapter: the ability to produce documentation in XML format automatically from special comments. These comments are single-line comments, but begin with three slashes (///), instead of the usual two. Within these comments, you can place XML tags containing documentation of the types and type members in your code.

The following tags are recognized by the compiler:

| Tag | Description |
| --- | --- |
| `<c>` | Marks up text within a line as code, for example:<br>`<c>int i = 10;</c>` |
| `<code>` | Marks multiple lines as code. |
| `<example>` | Marks up a code example. |
| `<exception>` | Documents an exception class. (Syntax verified by the compiler.) |
| `<include>` | Includes comments from another documentation file. (Syntax verified by the compiler.) |
| `<list>` | Inserts a list into the documentation. |
| `<param>` | Marks up a method parameter. (Syntax verified by the compiler.) |
| `<paramref>` | Indicates that a word is a method parameter. (Syntax verified by the compiler.) |
| `<permission>` | Documents access to a member. (Syntax verified by the compiler.) |
| `<remarks>` | Adds a description for a member. |
| `<returns>` | Documents the return value for a method. |
| `<see>` | Provides a cross-reference to another parameter. (Syntax verified by the compiler.) |
| `<seealso>` | Provides a "see also" section in a description. (Syntax verified by the compiler.) |
| `<summary>` | Provides a short summary of a type or member. |
| `<value>` | Describes a property. |

# C# Basics

To see how this works, add some XML comments to the `MathLibrary.cs` file from the "More on Compiling C# Files" section, and call it `Math.cs`. You will add a `<summary>` element for the class and for its `Add()` method, and also a `<returns>` element and two `<param>` elements for the `Add()` method:

```csharp
// Math.cs
namespace Wrox.ProCSharp.Basics
{

   ///<summary>
   ///    Wrox.ProCSharp.Basics.Math class.
   ///    Provides a method to add two integers.
   ///</summary>
   public class Math
   {
      ///<summary>
      ///    The Add method allows us to add two integers
      ///</summary>
      ///<returns>Result of the addition (int)</returns>
      ///<param name="x">First number to add</param>
      ///<param name="y">Second number to add</param>
      public int Add(int x, int y)
      {
         return x + y;
      }
   }
}
```

The C# compiler can extract the XML elements from the special comments and use them to generate an XML file. To get the compiler to generate the XML documentation for an assembly, you specify the `/doc` option when you compile, together with the name of the file you want to be created:

**csc /t:library /doc:Math.xml Math.cs**

The compiler will throw an error if the XML comments do not result in a well-formed XML document.

This will generate an XML file named `Math.xml`, which looks like this:

```xml
<?xml version="1.0"?>
<doc>
   <assembly>
      <name>Math</name>
   </assembly>
   <members>
      <member name="T:Wrox.ProCSharp.Basics.Math">
         <summary>
            Wrox.ProCSharp.Basics.Math class.
            Provides a method to add two integers.
         </summary>
      </member>
      <member name=
            "M:Wrox.ProCSharp.Basics.Math.Add(System.Int32,System.Int32)">
         <summary>
```

```
                The Add method allows us to add two integers
            </summary>
            <returns>Result of the addition (int)</returns>
            <param name="x">First number to add</param>
            <param name="y">Second number to add</param>
        </member>
    </members>
</doc>
```

Notice how the compiler has actually done some work for you; it has created an `<assembly>` element and also added a `<member>` element for each type or member of a type in the file. Each `<member>` element has a `name` attribute with the full name of the member as its value, prefixed by a letter that indicates whether this is a type (`T:`), field (`F:`), or member (`M:`).

# The C# Preprocessor Directives

Besides the usual keywords, most of which you have now encountered, C# also includes a number of commands that are known as *preprocessor directives*. These commands never actually get translated to any commands in your executable code, but instead they affect aspects of the compilation process. For example, you can use preprocessor directives to prevent the compiler from compiling certain portions of your code. You might do this if you are planning to release two versions of the code — a basic version and an enterprise version that will have more features. You could use preprocessor directives to prevent the compiler from compiling code related to the additional features when you are compiling the basic version of the software. Another scenario is that you might have written bits of code that are intended to provide you with debugging information. You probably don't want those portions of code compiled when you actually ship the software.

The preprocessor directives are all distinguished by beginning with the # symbol.

> *C++ developers will recognize the preprocessor directives as something that plays an important part in C and C++. However, there aren't as many preprocessor directives in C#, and they are not used as often. C# provides other mechanisms, such as custom attributes, that achieve some of the same effects as C++ directives. Also, note that C# doesn't actually have a separate preprocessor in the way that C++ does. The so-called preprocessor directives are actually handled by the compiler. Nevertheless, C# retains the name preprocessor directive because these commands give the impression of a preprocessor.*

The next sections briefly cover the purposes of the preprocessor directives.

## #define and #undef

`#define` is used like this:

```
#define DEBUG
```

What this does is tell the compiler that a symbol with the given name (in this case `DEBUG`) exists. It is a little bit like declaring a variable, except that this variable doesn't really have a value — it just exists. And this symbol isn't part of your actual code; it exists only for the benefit of the compiler, while the compiler is compiling the code, and has no meaning within the C# code itself.

# C# Basics

`#undef` does the opposite, and removes the definition of a symbol:

```
#undef DEBUG
```

If the symbol doesn't exist in the first place, then `#undef` has no effect. Similarly, `#define` has no effect if a symbol already exists.

You need to place any `#define` and `#undef` directives at the beginning of the C# source file, before any code that declares any objects to be compiled.

`#define` isn't much use on its own, but when combined with other preprocessor directives, especially `#if`, it becomes very powerful.

> *Incidentally, you might notice some changes from the usual C# syntax. Preprocessor directives are not terminated by semicolons, and normally constitute the only command on a line. That's because for the preprocessor directives, C# abandons its usual practice of requiring commands to be separated by semicolons. If it sees a preprocessor directive, it assumes the next command is on the next line.*

## #if, #elif, #else, and #endif

These directives inform the compiler whether or not to compile a block of code. Consider this method:

```
int DoSomeWork(double x)
{
   // do something
   #if DEBUG
      Console.WriteLine("x is " + x);
   #endif
}
```

This code will compile as normal, except for the `Console.WriteLine()` method call that is contained inside the `#if` clause. This line will only be executed if the symbol DEBUG has been defined by a previous `#define` directive. When the compiler finds the `#if` directive, it checks to see if the symbol concerned exists, and only compiles the code inside the `#if` clause if the symbol does exist. Otherwise, the compiler simply ignores all the code until it reaches the matching `#endif` directive. Typical practice is to define the symbol DEBUG while you are debugging, and have various bits of debugging-related code inside `#if` clauses. Then, when you are close to shipping, you simply comment out the `#define` directive, and all the debugging code miraculously disappears, the size of the executable file gets smaller, and your end users don't get confused by being shown debugging information. (Obviously, you would do more testing to make sure your code still works without DEBUG defined). This technique is very common in C and C++ programming and is known as *conditional compilation*.

The `#elif` (=`else if`) and `#else` directives can be used in `#if` blocks and have the intuitively obvious meanings. It is also possible to nest `#if` blocks:

```
#define ENTERPRISE
#define W2K

// further on in the file
```

71

```
#if ENTERPRISE
    // do something
    #if W2K
        // some code that is only relevant to enterprise
        // edition running on W2K
    #endif
#elif PROFESSIONAL
    // do something else
#else
    // code for the leaner version
#endif
```

Note that, unlike the situation in C++, using `#if` is not the only way to compile code conditionally. C# provides an alternative mechanism through the `Conditional` attribute, which is explored in Chapter 11, "Reflection."

`#if` and `#elif` support a limited range of logical operators too, using the operators !, ==, !=, and ||. A symbol is considered to be `true` if it exists and `false` if it doesn't. For example:

```
#if W2K && (ENTERPRISE==false)    // if W2K is defined but ENTERPRISE isn't
```

# #warning and #error

Two other very useful preprocessor directives are `#warning` and `#error`. These will respectively cause a warning or an error to be raised when the compiler encounters them. If the compiler sees a `#warning` directive, it will display whatever text appears after the `#warning` to the user, after which compilation continues. If it encounters a `#error` directive, it will display the subsequent text to the user as if it were a compilation error message and then immediately abandon the compilation, so no IL code will be generated.

You can use these directives as checks that you haven't done anything silly with your `#define` statements; you can also use the `#warning` statements to remind yourself to do something:

```
#if DEBUG && RELEASE
    #error "You've defined DEBUG and RELEASE simultaneously!"
#endif

#warning "Don't forget to remove this line before the boss tests the code!"
    Console.WriteLine("*I hate this job*");
```

# #region and #endregion

The `#region` and `#endregion` directives are used to indicate that a certain block of code is to be treated as a single block with a given name, like this:

```
#region Member Field Declarations
    int x;
    double d;
    Currency balance;
#endregion
```

This doesn't look that useful by itself; it doesn't affect the compilation process in any way. However, the real advantage is that these directives are recognized by some editors, including the Visual Studio .NET editor. These editors can use these directives to lay out your code better on the screen. You see how this works in Chapter 14, "Visual Studio 2005."

## #line

The `#line` directive can be used to alter the file name and line number information that is output by the compiler in warnings and error messages. You probably won't want to use this directive that often. Its main use occurs if you are coding in conjunction with some other package that alters the code you are typing in before sending it to the compiler, since this will mean line numbers, or perhaps the file names reported by the compiler, won't match up to the line numbers in the files or the file names you are editing. The `#line` directive can be used to restore the match. You can also use the syntax `#line default` to restore the line to the default line numbering:

```
#line 164 "Core.cs"    // we happen to know this is line 164 in the file
                       // Core.cs, before the intermediate
                       // package mangles it.

// later on

#line default          // restores default line numbering
```

## #pragma

The `#pragma` directive can either suppress or restore specific compiler warnings. Unlike command-line options, the `#pragma` directive can be implemented on a class or method level, allowing a fine-grain control of what warnings are suppressed and when. The following example disables the field not used warning and then restores it after the `MyClass` class compiles.

```
#pragma warning disable 169
public class MyClass
{
   int neverUsedField;
}
#pragma warning restore 169
```

# C# Programming Guidelines

This final section of this chapter looks at the guidelines you need to bear in mind when writing C# programs.

## Rules for Identifiers

This section examines the rules governing what names you can use for variables, classes, methods, and so on. Note that the rules presented in this section are not merely guidelines: They are enforced by the C# compiler.

# Chapter 2

Identifiers are the names you give to variables, to user-defined types such as classes and structs, and to members of these types. Identifiers are case-sensitive, so for example variables named `interestRate` and `InterestRate` would be recognized as different variables. Following are a couple of rules determining what identifiers you can use in C#:

- ❑ They must begin with a letter or underscore, although they can contain numeric characters.
- ❑ You can't use C# keywords as identifiers.

C# has the following reserved keywords:

| | | | | |
|---|---|---|---|---|
| abstract | do | Implicit | params | switch |
| as | double | In | private | this |
| base | else | Int | protected | throw |
| bool | enum | Interface | public | true |
| break | event | Internal | readonly | try |
| byte | explicit | Is | ref | typeof |
| case | extern | lock | return | uint |
| catch | false | long | sbyte | ulong |
| char | finally | namespace | sealed | unchecked |
| checked | fixed | new | short | unsafe |
| class | float | null | sizeof | ushort |
| const | for | object | stackalloc | using |
| continue | foreach | operator | static | virtual |
| decimal | goto | out | string | volatile |
| default | if | override | struct | void |
| delegate | | | | while |

If you do need to use one of these words as an identifier (for example, if you are accessing a class written in a different language), you can prefix the identifier with the @ symbol to indicate to the compiler that what follows is to be treated as an identifier, not as a C# keyword (so `abstract` is not a valid identifier, but `@abstract` is).

Finally, identifiers can also contain Unicode characters, specified using the syntax \uXXXX, where XXXX is the four-digit hex code for the Unicode character. The following are some examples of valid identifiers:

- ❑ Name
- ❑ überfluß
- ❑ _Identifier
- ❑ \u005fIdentifier

The last two items in this list are identical and interchangeable (because 005f is the Unicode code for the underscore character), so obviously these identifiers couldn't both be declared in the same scope. Note that although syntactically you are allowed to use the underscore character in identifiers, this isn't recommended in most situations, because it doesn't follow the guidelines for naming variables that Microsoft has written to ensure that developers use the same conventions, making it easier to read each other's code.

## Usage Conventions

In any development language, there usually arise certain traditional programming styles. The styles are not part of the language itself but are conventions concerning, for example, how variables are named or how certain classes, methods, or functions are used. If most developers using that language follow the same conventions, it makes it easier for different developers to understand each other's code — which in turn generally helps program maintainability. For example, a common (though not universal) convention in Visual Basic 6 was that variables that represents strings have names beginning with lowercase s or lowercase str, as in the Visual Basic 6 statements Dim sResult As String or Dim strMessage As String. Conventions do, however, depend on the language and the environment. For example, C++ developers programming on the Windows platform have traditionally used the prefixes psz or lpsz to indicate strings — char *pszResult; char *lpszMessage; — but on Unix machines it's more common not to use any such prefixes: char *Result; char *Message;.

You'll notice from the sample code in this book that the convention in C# is to name variables without prefixes: string Result; string Message;.

> *The convention by which variable names are prefixed with letters that represent the data type is known as Hungarian notation. It means that other developers reading the code can immediately tell from the variable name what data type the variable represents. Hungarian notation is widely regarded as redundant in these days of smart editors and IntelliSense.*

Whereas, with many languages, usage conventions simply evolved as the language was used, with C# and the whole of the .NET Framework Microsoft has written very comprehensive usage guidelines, which are detailed in the .NET/C# MSDN documentation. This should mean that, right from the start, .NET programs will have a high degree of interoperability in terms of developers being able to understand code. The guidelines have also been developed with the benefit of some twenty years hindsight in object-oriented programming, and as a result have been carefully thought out and appear to have been well received in the developer community to judge by the relevant newsgroups. Hence the guidelines are well worth following.

It should be noted, however, that the guidelines are not the same as language specifications. You should try to follow the guidelines when you can. Nevertheless, you won't run into problems if you do have a good reason for not doing so — for example, you won't get a compilation error because you don't follow these guidelines. The general rule is that if you don't follow the usage guidelines you must have a convincing reason. Departing from the guidelines should be a positive decision rather than simply not bothering. Also, if you compare the guidelines with the samples in the remainder of this book, you'll notice that in numerous examples in this book, we have chosen not to follow the conventions. That's usually because the conventions are designed for much larger programs than our samples, and although they are great if you are writing a complete software package, they are not really so suitable for small 20-line standalone programs. In many cases, following the conventions would have made our samples harder rather than easier to follow.

# Chapter 2

The full guidelines for good programming style are quite extensive. This section is confined to describing some of the more important guidelines, as well as the ones most likely to surprise you. If you want to make absolutely certain that your code follows the usage guidelines completely, you will need to refer to the MSDN documentation.

## *Naming conventions*

One important aspect to making your programs understandable is how you choose to name your items — and that includes naming variables, methods, classes, enumerations, and namespaces.

It is intuitively obvious that your names should reflect the purpose of the item and should be designed not to clash with other names. The general philosophy in the .NET Framework is also that the name of a variable should reflect the purpose of that variable instance and not the data type. For example, `height` is a good name for a variable, whereas `integerValue` isn't. However, you will probably feel that that principle is an ideal that is hard to achieve. Particularly when you are dealing with controls, in most cases, you'll probably feel happier sticking with variable names like `confirmationDialog` and `chooseEmployeeListBox`, which do indicate the data type in the name.

The following sections look at some of the things you need to think about when choosing names.

### Casing of names

In many cases you should use *Pascal casing* for names. Pascal casing means that the first letter of each word in a name is capitalized: `EmployeeSalary`, `ConfirmationDialog`, `PlainTextEncoding`. You will notice that essentially all of the names of namespaces, classes, and members in the base classes follow Pascal casing. In particular, the convention of joining words using the underscore character is discouraged. So you should try not to use names like `employee_salary`. It has also been common in other languages to use all capitals for names of constants. This is not advised in C#, because such names are harder to read — the convention is to use Pascal casing throughout:

```
const int MaximumLength;
```

The only other casing scheme that you are advised to use is *camel casing*. Camel casing is similar to Pascal casing, except that the first letter of the first word in the name is not capitalized: `employeeSalary`, `confirmationDialog`, `plainTextEncoding`. Following are three situations in which you are advised to use camel casing:

❑   For names of all private member fields in types:

```
public int subscriberID;
```

   Note, however, that often it is conventional to prefix names of member fields with an underscore:

```
public int subscriberID;
```

❑   For names of all parameters passed to methods:

```
public void RecordSale(string salesmanName, int quantity);
```

❑   To distinguish items that would otherwise have the same name. A common example is when a property wraps around a field:

76

```csharp
    private string employeeName;

    public string EmployeeName
    {
       get
       {
          return employeeName;
       }
    }
```

If you are doing this, you should always use camel casing for the private member and Pascal casing for the public or protected member, so that other classes that use your code see only names in Pascal case (except for parameter names).

You should also be wary about case-sensitivity. C# is case-sensitive, so it is syntactically correct for names in C# to differ only by the case, as in the previous examples. However, you should bear in mind that your assemblies might at some point be called from Visual Basic .NET applications—and *Visual Basic .NET is not case-sensitive*. Hence, if you do use names that differ only by case, it is important to do so only in situations in which both names will never be seen outside your assembly. (The previous example qualifies as okay because camel case is used with the name that is attached to a `private` variable.) Otherwise you may prevent other code written in Visual Basic .NET from being able to use your assembly correctly.

## Name styles

You should try to be consistent about your style of names. For example, if one of the methods in a class is called `ShowConfirmationDialog()`, then you should not give another method a name like `ShowDialogWarning()`, or `WarningDialogShow()`. The other method should be called `ShowWarningDialog()`. Get the idea?

## Namespace names

Namespace names are particularly important to design carefully in order to avoid risk of ending up with the same name for one of your namespaces as someone else uses. Remember, namespace names are the *only* way that .NET distinguishes names of objects in shared assemblies. So if you use the same namespace name for your software package as another package, and both packages get installed on the same computer, there are going to be problems. Because of this, it's almost always a good idea to create a top-level namespace with the name of your company, and then nest successive namespaces that narrow down the technology, group, or department you are working in or the name of the package your classes are intended for. Microsoft recommends namespace names that begin with `<CompanyName>.<TechnologyName>` as in these two examples:

```
WeaponsOfDestructionCorp.RayGunControllers
WeaponsOfDestructionCorp.Viruses
```

# Chapter 2

## Names and keywords

It is important that the names do not clash with any keywords. In fact, if you attempt to name an item in your code with a word that happens to be a C# keyword, you'll almost certainly get a syntax error because the compiler will assume the name refers to a statement. However, because of the possibility that your classes will be accessed by code written in other languages, it is important that you also don't use names that are keywords in other .NET languages. Generally speaking, C++ keywords are similar to C# keywords, so confusion with C++ is unlikely, and those commonly encountered keywords that are unique to Visual C++ tend to start with two underscore characters. Like C#, C++ keywords are spelled in lowercase, so if you hold to the convention of naming your public classes and members with Pascal-style names, they will always have at least one uppercase letter in their names, and there will be no risk of clashes with C++ keywords. On the other hand, you are more likely to have problems with Visual Basic .NET, which has many more keywords than C# does, and being non–case-sensitive means you cannot rely on Pascal-style names for your classes and methods.

The following table lists the keywords and standard function calls in Visual Basic .NET, which should if possible be avoided, in whatever case combination, for your public C# classes:

| | | | |
|---|---|---|---|
| Abs | Do | Loc | RGB |
| Add | Double | Local | Right |
| AddHandler | Each | Lock | RmDir |
| AddressOf | Else | LOF | Rnd |
| Alias | ElseIf | Log | RTrim |
| And | Empty | Long | SaveSettings |
| Ansi | End | Loop | Second |
| AppActivate | Enum | LTrim | Seek |
| Append | EOF | Me | Select |
| As | Erase | Mid | SetAttr |
| Asc | Err | Minute | SetException |
| Assembly | Error | MIRR | Shared |
| Atan | Event | MkDir | Shell |
| Auto | Exit | Module | Short |
| Beep | Exp | Month | Sign |
| Binary | Explicit | MustInherit | Sin |
| BitAnd | ExternalSource | MustOverride | Single |
| BitNot | False | MyBase | SLN |
| BitOr | FileAttr | MyClass | Space |
| BitXor | FileCopy | Namespace | Spc |
| Boolean | FileDateTime | New | Split |

# C# Basics

| | | | |
|---|---|---|---|
| ByRef | FileLen | Next | Sqrt |
| Byte | Filter | Not | Static |
| ByVal | Finally | Nothing | Step |
| Call | Fix | NotInheritable | Stop |
| Case | For | NotOverridable | Str |
| Catch | Format | Now | StrComp |
| CBool | FreeFile | NPer | StrConv |
| CByte | Friend | NPV | Strict |
| CDate | Function | Null | String |
| CDbl | FV | Object | Structure |
| CDec | Get | Oct | Sub |
| ChDir | GetAllSettings | Off | Switch |
| ChDrive | GetAttr | On | SYD |
| Choose | GetException | Open | SyncLock |
| Chr | GetObject | Option | Tab |
| CInt | GetSetting | Optional | Tan |
| Class | GetType | Or | Text |
| Clear | GoTo | Overloads | Then |
| CLng | Handles | Overridable | Throw |
| Close | Hex | Overrides | TimeOfDay |
| Collection | Hour | ParamArray | Timer |
| Command | If | Pmt | TimeSerial |
| Compare | Iif | PPmt | TimeValue |
| Const | Implements | Preserve | To |
| Cos | Imports | Print | Today |
| CreateObject | In | Private | Trim |
| CShort | Inherits | Property | Try |
| CSng | Input | Public | TypeName |
| CStr | InStr | Put | TypeOf |
| CurDir | Int | PV | UBound |
| Date | Integer | QBColor | UCase |
| DateAdd | Interface | Raise | Unicode |
| DateDiff | Ipmt | RaiseEvent | Unlock |

79

## Chapter 2

| | | | |
|---|---|---|---|
| DatePart | IRR | Randomize | Until |
| DateSerial | Is | Rate | Val |
| DateValue | IsArray | Read | Weekday |
| Day | IsDate | ReadOnly | While |
| DDB | IsDbNull | ReDim | Width |
| Decimal | IsNumeric | Remove | With |
| Declare | Item | RemoveHandler | WithEvents |
| Default | Kill | Rename | Write |
| Delegate | Lcase | Replace | WriteOnly |
| DeleteSetting | Left | Reset | Xor |
| Dim | Lib | Resume | Year |
| Dir | Line | Return | |

## Use of properties and methods

One area that can cause confusion in a class is whether a particular quantity should be represented by a property or a method. The rules here are not hard and fast, but in general, you ought to use a property if something really should look and feel like a variable. (If you're not sure what a property is, see Chapter 3, "Objects and Types.") This means, among other things, that:

- ❑ Client code should be able to read its value. Write-only properties are not recommended, so for example use a `SetPassword()` method, not a write-only `Password` property.

- ❑ Reading the value should not take too long. The fact that something is a property usually suggests that reading it will be relatively quick.

- ❑ Reading the value should not have any observable and unexpected side effect. Further, setting the value of a property should not have any side effect that is not directly related to the property. Setting the width of a dialog box has the obvious effect of changing the appearance of the dialog box on the screen. That's fine, as that's obviously related to the property in question.

- ❑ It should be possible to set properties in any order. In particular, it is not good practice when setting a property to throw an exception because another related property has not yet been set. For example, if in order to use a class that accesses a database you need to set `ConnectionString`, `UserName`, and `Password`, then the author of the class should make sure the class is implemented so the user really can set them in any order.

- ❑ Successive reads of a property should give the same result. If the value of a property is likely to change unpredictably, you should code it up as a method instead. `Speed`, in a class that monitors the motion of an automobile, is not a good candidate for a property. Use a `GetSpeed()` method here; on the other hand, `Weight` and `EngineSize` are good candidates for properties because they will not change for a given object.

If the item you are coding satisfies all of the preceding criteria, it is probably a good candidate for a property. Otherwise you should use a method.

## C# Basics

### *Use of fields*

The guidelines are pretty simple here. Fields should almost always be private, except that in some cases it may be acceptable for constant or read-only fields to be public. The reason is that if you make a field public, you may hinder your ability to extend or modify the class in the future.

The previous guidelines should give you a rough idea of good practices, and you should also use them in conjunction with good object-oriented programming style.

It's also worth bearing in mind that Microsoft has been fairly careful about being consistent and has followed its own guidelines when writing the .NET base classes. So a very good way to get an intuitive feel for the conventions to follow when writing .NET code is to simply look at the base classes — see how classes, members, and namespaces are named, and how the class hierarchy works. If you try to write your code in the same style as the base classes, you shouldn't go wrong.

# Summary

This chapter examined some of the basic syntax of C#, covering the areas needed to write simple C# programs. It has covered a lot of ground, but much of it will be instantly recognizable to developers who are familiar with any C-style language (or even JavaScript). Some of the topics covered include:

- Variable scope and access levels
- Declaring variables of various data types
- Controlling the flow of execution within a C# program
- Comments and XML documentation
- Preprocessor directives
- Usage guidelines and naming conventions, the guidelines that you should adhere to when writing C# code, so that your code follows normal .NET practice and can be easily understood by others

You have seen that C# syntax is similar to C++ and Java syntax, although there are many minor differences. You have also seen that in many areas this syntax is combined with facilities to write code very quickly, for example high-quality string handling facilities. C# also has a strongly defined type system, based on a distinction between value and reference types. Chapters 3 and 4 cover the C# object-oriented programming features.

# Objects and Types

So far, you've been introduced to some of the main building blocks that make up the C# language, including declaring variables, data types, and program flow statements, and you have seen a couple of very short complete programs containing little more than the Main() method. What you haven't really seen is how you can put all these together to form a longer, complete program. The key to this lies in working with classes — the subject of this chapter. In particular, this chapter covers:

- ❏ The differences between classes and structs
- ❏ Fields, properties, and methods
- ❏ Passing values by value and reference
- ❏ Method overloading
- ❏ Constructors and static constructors
- ❏ Read-only fields
- ❏ The Object class, from which all other types are derived

Inheritance and features related to inheritance are discussed in Chapter 4, "Inheritance."

> This chapter introduces the basic syntax associated with classes. However, we assume that you are already familiar with the underlying principles of using classes — for example, that you know what a constructor or a property is, and this chapter is largely confined to applying those principles in C# code. If you are not familiar with the concept of the class, you might want to take a look at Appendix A, which is available with the code downloads for the book on the Web at www.wrox.com.

# Chapter 3

This chapter introduces and explains those concepts that are not necessarily supported by most object-oriented languages. For example, although object constructors are a widely used concept that you should be familiar with, static constructors are something new to C#, so this chapter explains how static constructors work.

# Classes and Structs

Classes and structs are essentially templates from which you can create objects. Each object contains data and has methods to manipulate and access that data. The class defines what data and functionality each particular object (called an *instance*) of that class can contain. For example, if you have a class that represents a customer, it might define fields such as `CustomerID`, `FirstName`, `LastName`, and `Address`, which you will use to hold information about a particular customer. It might also define functionality that acts upon the data stored in these fields. You can then instantiate an object of this class to represent one specific customer, set the field values for that instance, and use its functionality.

```
class PhoneCustomer
{
   public const string DayOfSendingBill = "Monday";
   public int CustomerID;
   public string FirstName;
   public string LastName;
}
```

Structs differ from classes in the way that they are stored in memory and accessed (classes are reference types stored in the heap, structs are value types stored on the stack), and in some of the features (for example, structs don't support inheritance). You will tend to use structs for smaller data types for performance reasons. In terms of syntax, however, structs look very similar to classes; the main difference is that you use the keyword `struct` instead of `class` to declare them. For example, if you wanted all `PhoneCustomer` instances to be allocated on the stack instead of the managed heap, you could write:

```
struct PhoneCustomerStruct
{
   public const string DayOfSendingBill = "Monday";
   public int CustomerID;
   public string FirstName;
   public string LastName;
}
```

For both classes and structs, you use the keyword `new` to declare an instance: This keyword creates the object and initializes it; in the following example, the default behavior is to zero out its fields:

```
PhoneCustomer myCustomer = new PhoneCustomer();           // works for a class
PhoneCustomerStruct myCustomer2 = new PhoneCustomerStruct();// works for a struct
```

In most cases, you'll find you use classes much more often than structs. For this reason, this chapter discusses classes first, and then points out the differences between classes and structs and the specific reasons why you might choose to use a struct instead of a class. Unless otherwise stated, however, you can assume that code presented for a class will work equally well for a struct.

# Class Members

The data and functions within a class are known as the class's *members*. Microsoft's official terminology distinguishes between data members and function members. As well as these members, classes can also contain nested types (such as other classes). All members of a class can be declared as `public` (in which case they are directly accessible from outside the class) or as `private` (in which case they are only visible to other code within the class), just as in Visual Basic, C++, and Java. C# also has variants on this theme, such as `protected` (which indicates a member is visible only to the class in question and to any derived classes). Chapter 4 provides a comprehensive list of the different accessibilities.

## Data Members

Data members are those members that contain the data for the class—fields, constants, and events. Data members can be either static (associated with the class as a whole) or instance (each instance of the class has its own copy of the data). As usual for object-oriented languages, a class member is always an instance member unless it is explicitly declared as `static`.

*Fields* are any variables associated with the class. You have already seen fields being used in the `PhoneCustomer` class in the previous example.

Once you have instantiated a `PhoneCustomer` object, you can then access these fields using the `Object.FieldName` syntax as shown in this example:

```
PhoneCustomer Customer1 = new PhoneCustomer();
Customer1.FirstName = "Simon";
```

*Constants* can be associated with classes in the same way as variables. You declare a constant using the `const` keyword. Once again, if it is declared as `public`, it will be accessible from outside the class.

```
class PhoneCustomer
{
    public const string DayOfSendingBill = "Monday";
    public int CustomerID;
    public string FirstName;
    public string LastName;
}
```

*Events* are class members that allow an object to notify a caller whenever something noteworthy happens, such as a field or property of the class changing, or some form of user interaction occurring. The client can have code known as an event handler that reacts to the event. Chapter 6, "Delegates and Events," look at events in detail.

## Function Members

Function members are those members that provide some functionality for manipulating the data in the class. They include methods, properties, constructors, finalizers, operators, and indexers.

*Methods* are functions that are associated with a particular class. They can be either instance methods, which work on a particular instance of a class, or static methods, which provide more generic functionality that doesn't require you to instantiate a class (like the `Console.WriteLine()` method). Methods are discussed in the next section.

*Properties* are sets of functions that can be accessed from the client in a similar way to the public fields of the class. C# provides a specific syntax for implementing read and write properties on your classes, so you don't have to jury-rig methods whose names have the words `Get` or `Set` embedded in them. Because there's a dedicated syntax for properties that is distinct from that for normal functions, the illusion of objects as actual things is strengthened for client code.

*Constructors* are special functions that are called automatically when an object is instantiated. They must have the same name as the class to which they belong, and cannot have a return type. Constructors are useful for initializing the values of fields.

*Finalizers* are similar to constructors, but are called when the CLR detects that an object is no longer needed. They have the same name as the class, preceded by a tilde (~). C++ programmers should note that finalizers are used much less frequently than their nearest C++ equivalent, destructors, because the CLR handles garbage collection automatically. Also, it is impossible to predict precisely when a finalizer will be called. Finalizers are discussed in Chapter 7, "Memory Management and Pointers."

*Operators* at their simplest are actions like + or –. When you add two integers, you are, strictly speaking, using the + operator for integers. However, C# also allows you to specify how existing operators will work with your own classes (*operator overloading*). Chapter 5, "Operators and Casts," looks at operators in detail.

*Indexers* allow your objects to be indexed in the same way as an array or collection. This topic is also covered in Chapter 5.

## *Methods*

In Visual Basic, C, and C++, you could define global functions that were not associated with a particular class. This is not the case in C#. As noted earlier, in C# every function must be associated with a class or struct.

Note that official C# terminology does in fact make a distinction between functions and methods. In this terminology, the term "function member" includes not only methods, but also other non-data members of a class or struct. This includes indexers, operators, constructors, destructors, and also — perhaps somewhat surprisingly — properties. These are contrasted with data members: fields, constants, and events. This chapter is confined to looking at methods.

### Declaring methods

The syntax for defining a method in C# is just what you'd expect from a C-style language, and is virtually identical to the syntax in C++ and Java. The main syntactical difference from C++ is that, in C#, each method is separately declared as public or private. It is not possible to use `public:` blocks to group several method definitions. Also, all C# methods are declared and defined in the class definition. There is no facility in C# to separate the method implementation as there is in C++.

# Objects and Types

In C#, the definition of a method consists of any method modifiers (such as the method's accessibility), the type of the return value, followed by the name of the method, followed by a list of input arguments enclosed in parentheses, followed by the body of the method enclosed in curly braces:

```
[modifiers] return_type MethodName([parameters])
{
   // Method body
}
```

Each parameter consists of the name of the type of the parameter, and the name by which it can be referenced in the body of the method. Also, if the method returns a value, a return statement must be used with the return value to indicate the exit point. For example:

```
public bool IsSquare(Rectangle rect)
{
   return (rect.Height == rect.Width);
}
```

This code uses one of the .NET base classes, `System.Drawing.Rectangle`, which represents a rectangle.

If the method doesn't return anything, you specify a return type of void, because you can't omit the return type altogether; and if it takes no arguments, you still need to include an empty set of parentheses after the method name (as with the `Main()` method). In this case, including a return statement is optional — the method returns automatically when the closing curly brace is reached. You should note that a method can contain as many return statements as required:

```
public bool IsPositive(int value)
{
   if (value < 0)
      return false;
   return true;
}
```

## Invoking methods

The syntax for invoking a method is exactly the same in C# as it is in C++ and Java, and the only difference between C# and Visual Basic is that round brackets must always be used when invoking the method in C# — this is actually simpler than the Visual Basic 6 set of rules whereby brackets were sometimes necessary and at other times not allowed.

The following example, `MathTest`, illustrates the syntax for definition of and instantiation of classes, and definition and invocation of methods. Besides the class that contains the `Main()` method, it defines a class named `MathTest`, which contains a couple of methods and a field.

```
using System;

namespace Wrox.ProCSharp.MathTestSample
{
   class MainEntryPoint
   {
      static void Main()
```

87

```csharp
    {
        // Try calling some static functions
        Console.WriteLine("Pi is " + MathTest.GetPi());
        int x = MathTest.GetSquareOf(5);
        Console.WriteLine("Square of 5 is " + x);

        // Instantiate at MathTest object
        MathTest math = new MathTest();   // this is C#'s way of
                                          // instantiating a reference type

        // Call non-static methods
        math.value = 30;
        Console.WriteLine(
            "Value field of math variable contains " + math.value);
        Console.WriteLine("Square of 30 is " + math.GetSquare());
    }
}

// Define a class named MathTest on which we will call a method
class MathTest
{
    public int value;

    public int GetSquare()
    {
        return value*value;
    }

    public static int GetSquareOf(int x)
    {
        return x*x;
    }

    public static double GetPi()
    {
        return 3.14159;
    }
}
```

Running the `MathTest` example produces these results:

**csc MathTest.cs**

```
Microsoft (R) Visual C# .NET Compiler version 8.00.40607.16
for Microsoft (R) Windows (R) .NET Framework version 2.0.40607
Copyright (C) Microsoft Corporation 2001-2003. All rights reserved.

MathTest.exe
Pi is 3.14159
Square of 5 is 25
Value field of math variable contains 30
Square of 30 is 900
```

# Objects and Types

As you can see from the code, the `MathTest` class contains a field that contains a number, as well as a method to find the square of this number. It also contains two static methods, one to return the value of pi and one to find the square of the number passed in as a parameter.

Some features of this class are not really good examples of C# program design. For example, `GetPi()` would usually be implemented as a `const` field, but following good design here would mean using some concepts that we have not yet introduced.

Most of the syntax in the preceding example should be familiar to C++ and Java developers. If your background is in Visual Basic, then just think of the `MathTest` class as being like a Visual Basic class module that implements fields and methods. There are a couple of points to watch out for though, whatever your language.

## Passing parameters to methods

Arguments can in general be passed into methods by reference or by value. When a variable is passed by reference, the called method gets the actual variable—so any changes made to the variable inside the method persist when the method exits. On the other hand, if a variable is passed by value, the called method gets an identical copy of the variable—which means any changes made are lost when the method exits. For complex data types, passing by reference is more efficient because of the large amount of data that must be copied when passing by value.

In C#, all parameters are passed by value unless you specifically say otherwise. This is the same behavior as in C++ but the opposite of Visual Basic. However, you need to be careful in understanding the implications of this for reference types. Because reference type variables only hold a reference to an object, it is this reference that will be copied, not the object itself. Hence, changes made to the underlying object will persist. Value type variables, in contrast, hold the actual data, so a copy of the data itself will be passed into the method. An `int`, for instance, is passed by value to a method, and any changes that the method makes to the value of that `int` do not change the value of the original `int` object. Conversely, if an array or any other reference type, such as a class, is passed into a method, and the method uses the reference to change a value in that array, the new value is reflected in the original array object.

Here is an example, `ParameterTest.cs`, that demonstrates this:

```
using System;

namespace Wrox.ProCSharp.ParameterTestSample
{
    class ParameterTest
    {
        static void SomeFunction(int[] ints, int i)
        {
            ints[0] = 100;
            i = 100;
        }

        public static int Main()
        {
            int i = 0;
            int[] ints = { 0, 1, 2, 4, 8 };
            // Display the original values
```

```
            Console.WriteLine("i = " + i);
            Console.WriteLine("ints[0] = " + ints[0]);
            Console.WriteLine("Calling SomeFunction...");

            // After this method returns, ints will be changed,
            // but i will not
            SomeFunction(ints, i);
            Console.WriteLine("i = " + i);
            Console.WriteLine("ints[0] = " + ints[0]);
            return 0;
        }
    }
}
```

The output of this is:

**csc ParameterTest.cs**

```
Microsoft (R) Visual C# .NET Compiler version 8.00.40607.16
for Microsoft (R) Windows (R) .NET Framework version 2.0.40607
Copyright (C) Microsoft Corporation 2001-2003. All rights reserved.

ParameterTest.exe
i = 0
ints[0] = 0
Calling SomeFunction...
i = 0
ints[0] = 100
```

Notice how the value of i remains unchanged, but the value changed in ints is also changed in the original array.

The behavior of strings is different again. This is because strings are immutable (if you alter a string's value, you create an entirely new string), so strings don't display the typical reference-type behavior. Any changes made to a string within a method call won't affect the original string. This point is discussed in more detail in Chapter 8, "Strings and Regular Expressions."

## ref parameters

Passing variables by value is the default. You can, however, force value parameters to be passed by reference. To do so, you use the ref keyword. If a parameter is passed to a method, and if the input argument for that method is prefixed with the ref keyword, any changes that the method makes to the variable will affect the value of the original object:

```
static void SomeFunction(int[] ints, ref int i)
{
    ints[0] = 100;
    i = 100;    // the change to i will persist after SomeFunction() exits
}
```

# Objects and Types

You will also need to add the `ref` keyword when you invoke the method:

```
SomeFunction(ints, ref i);
```

Adding the `ref` keyword in C# serves the same purpose as using the `&` syntax in C++ to specify passing by reference. However, C# makes the behavior more explicit (thus hopefully preventing bugs) by requiring the use of the `ref` keyword when invoking the method.

Finally, it is also important to understand that C# continues to apply initialization requirements to parameters passed to methods. Any variable must be initialized before it is passed into a method, whether it is passed in by value or reference.

## out parameters

In C-style languages, it is common for functions to be able to output more than one value from a single routine. This is accomplished using output parameters, by assigning the output values to variables that have been passed to the method by reference. Often, the starting values of the variables that are passed by reference are unimportant. Those values will be overwritten by the function, which may never even look at any previous value.

It would be convenient if you could use the same convention in C#. However, C# requires that variables be initialized with a starting value before they are referenced. Although you could initialize your input variables with meaningless values before passing them into a function that will fill them with real, meaningful ones, this practice seems at best needless and at worst confusing. However, there is a way to short-circuit the C# compiler's insistence on initial values for input arguments.

You do this with the `out` keyword. When a method's input argument is prefixed with `out`, that method can be passed a variable that has not been initialized. The variable is passed by reference, so any changes that the method makes to the variable will persist when control returns from the called method. Again, you also need to use the `out` keyword when you call the method, as well as when you define it:

```
static void SomeFunction(out int i)
{
    i = 100;
}

public static int Main()
{
    int i; // note how i is declared but not initialized
    SomeFunction(out i);
    Console.WriteLine(i);
    return 0;
}
```

The `out` keyword is an example of something new in C# that has no analogy in either Visual Basic or C++, and which has been introduced to make C# more secure against bugs. If an `out` parameter isn't assigned a value within the body of the function, the method won't compile.

## Method overloading

C# supports method overloading—several versions of the method that have different signatures (that is, the name, number of parameters, and parameter types). However, C# does not support default parameters in the way that, say, C++ or Visual Basic do. In order to overload methods, you simply declare the methods with the same name but different numbers or types of parameters:

```
class ResultDisplayer
{
   void DisplayResult(string result)
   {
      // implementation
   }

   void DisplayResult(int result)
   {
      // implementation
   }
}
```

Because C# does not support optional parameters, you will need to use method overloading to achieve the same effect:

```
class MyClass
{
   int DoSomething(int x)    // want 2nd parameter with default value 10
   {
      DoSomething(x, 10);
   }

   int DoSomething(int x, int y)
   {
      // implementation
   }
}
```

As in any language, method overloading carries with it the potential for subtle runtime bugs if the wrong overload is called. Chapter 4 discusses how to code defensively against these problems. For now, you should know that C# does place some minimum differences on the parameters of overloaded methods:

- ❑ It is not sufficient for two methods to differ only in their return type.
- ❑ It is not sufficient for two methods to differ only by virtue of a parameter having been declared as `ref` or `out`.

## *Properties*

Properties are unusual in that they represent an idea that C# has taken from Visual Basic, not from C++/Java. The idea of a property is that it is a method or pair of methods that are dressed to look like a field as far as any client code is concerned. A good example of this is the `Height` property of a Windows Form. Suppose you have the following code:

```
// mainForm is of type System.Windows.Forms
mainForm.Height = 400;
```

# Objects and Types

On executing this code, the height of the window will be set to 400 and you will see the window resize on the screen. Syntactically, this code looks like you're setting a field, but in fact you are calling a property accessor that contains code to resize the form.

To define a property in C#, you use the following syntax:

```csharp
public string SomeProperty
{
   get
   {
      return "This is the property value";
   }
   set
   {
      // do whatever needs to be done to set the property
   }
}
```

The `get` accessor takes no parameters and must return the same type as the declared property. You should not specify any explicit parameters for the `set` accessor either, but the compiler assumes it takes one parameter, which is of the same type again, and which is referred to as `value`. As an example, the following code contains a property called `ForeName`, which sets a field called `foreName` and applies a length limit:

```csharp
private string foreName;

public string ForeName
{
   get
   {
      return foreName;
   }
   set
   {
      if (value.Length > 20)
         // code here to take error recovery action
         // (eg. throw an exception)
      else
         foreName = value;
   }
}
```

Note the naming convention used here. You take advantage of C#'s case-sensitivity by using the same name, Pascal-cased for the public property and camel-cased for the equivalent private field if there is one. Some developers prefer to use field names that are prefixed by an underscore: `_foreName`; this provides an extremely convenient way of identifying fields.

Visual Basic 6 programmers should remember that C# does not distinguish between Visual Basic 6 `Set` and Visual Basic 6 `Let`: In C#, the write accessor is always identified with the keyword, `set`.

## Read-only and write-only properties

It is possible to create a read-only property by simply omitting the `set` accessor from the property definition. Thus, to make `ForeName` read-only in the previous example:

```
private string foreName;

public string ForeName
{
   get
   {
      return foreName;
   }
}
```

It is similarly possible to create a write-only property by omitting the `get` accessor. However, this is regarded as poor programming practice because it could be confusing to authors of client code. In general, it is recommended that if you are tempted to do this, you should use a method instead.

## Access modifiers for properties

C# does allow the `set` and `get` accessors to have differing access modifiers. This would allow a property to have a public `get` and a private or protected `set`. This can help control how or when a property can be set. In the following code example, notice that the `set` has a private access modifier and the `get` does not have any. In this case the `get` takes on the access level of the property. One of the accessors must follow the access level of the property. A compile error will be generated if the `get` accessor has the `protected` access level associated with it because that would make both accessors have a different access level than the property.

```
public string Name
{
  get
  {
    return _name;
  }
  private set
  {
    _name = value;
  }
}
```

## A note about inlining

Some developers may worry that the previous sections have presented a number of situations in which standard C# coding practices have led to very small functions — for example, accessing a field via a property instead of directly. Is this going to hurt performance because of the overhead of the extra function call? The answer is that there is no need to worry about performance loss from these kinds of programming methodologies in C#. Recall that C# code is compiled to IL, then JIT compiled at runtime to native executable code. The JIT compiler is designed to generate highly optimized code and will ruthlessly inline code as appropriate (in other words, replace function calls by inline code). A method or property whose implementation simply calls another method or returns a field will almost certainly be inlined. Note, however, that the decision of where to inline is made entirely by the CLR. There is no way

## Objects and Types

for you to control which methods are inlined by using, for example, some keyword similar to the `inline` keyword of C++.

### Constructors

The syntax for declaring basic constructors in C# is the same as in Java and C++. You declare a method that has the same name as the containing class and that does not have any return type:

```
public class MyClass
{
   public MyClass()
   {
   }
   // rest of class definition
```

As in C++ and Java, it's not necessary to provide a constructor for your class. We haven't supplied one for any of the examples so far in the book. In general, if you don't supply any constructor, the compiler will just make up a default one for you behind the scenes. It'll be a very basic constructor that just initializes all the member fields by zeroing them out (null reference for reference types, zero for numeric data types, and false for bools). Often, that will be adequate; if not, you'll need to write your own constructor.

> **For C++ programmers:** Because primitive fields in C# are by default initialized by being zeroed out, whereas primitive fields in C++ are by default uninitialized, you may find you don't need to write constructors in C# as often as you would in C++.

Constructors follow the same rules for overloading as other methods (that is, you can provide as many overloads to the constructor as you want, provided they are clearly different in signature):

```
public MyClass()    // zero-parameter constructor
{
   // construction code
}
public MyClass(int number)    // another overload
{
   // construction code
}
```

Note, however, that if you supply any constructors that take parameters, the compiler will not automatically supply a default one. This is done only if you have not defined any constructors at all. In the following example, because a one-parameter constructor is defined, the compiler assumes that this is the only constructor you want to be available and so will not implicitly supply any others:

```
public class MyNumber
{
   private int number;
   public MyNumber(int number)
   {
      this.number = number;
   }
}
```

This code also illustrates typical use of the `this` keyword to distinguish member fields from parameters of the same name. If you now try instantiating a `MyNumber` object using a no-parameter constructor, you will get a compilation error:

```
MyNumber numb = new MyNumber();    // causes compilation error
```

We should mention that it is possible to define constructors as private or protected, so that they are invisible to code in unrelated classes too:

```
public class MyNumber
{
   private int number;
   private MyNumber(int number)    // another overload
   {
      this.number = number;
   }
}
```

This example hasn't actually defined any public or even any protected constructors for `MyNumber`. This would actually make it impossible for `MyNumber` to be instantiated by outside code using the `new` operator (though you might write a public static property or method in `MyNumber` that can instantiate the class). This is useful in two situations:

❑   If your class serves only as a container for some static members or properties and therefore should never be instantiated

❑   If you want the class to only ever be instantiated by calling some static member function (this is the so-called class factory approach to object instantiation)

## Static constructors

One novel feature of C# is that it is also possible to write a static no-parameter constructor for a class. Such a constructor will be executed only once, as opposed to the constructors written so far, which are instance constructors, and are executed whenever an object of that class is created. There is no equivalent to the static constructor in C++ or Visual Basic 6.

```
class MyClass
{
   static MyClass()
   {
      // initialization code
   }
   // rest of class definition
}
```

One reason for writing a static constructor would be if your class has some static fields or properties that need to be initialized from an external source before the class is first used.

The .NET runtime makes no guarantees about when a static constructor will be executed, so you should not place any code in it that relies on it being executed at a particular time (for example, when an assembly is loaded). Nor is it possible to predict in what order static constructors of different classes will execute.

## Objects and Types

However, what is guaranteed is that the static constructor will run at most once, and that it will be invoked before your code makes any reference to the class. In C#, the static constructor usually seems to be executed immediately before the first call to any member of the class.

Notice that the static constructor does not have any access modifiers. It's never called by any other C# code, but always by the .NET runtime when the class is loaded, so any access modifier like `public` or `private` would be meaningless. For this same reason, the static constructor cannot ever take any parameters, and there can only be one static constructor for a class. It should also be obvious that a static constructor can only access static members, not instance members, of the class.

Note that it is possible to have a static constructor and a zero-parameter instance constructor defined in the same class. Although the parameter lists are identical, there is no conflict because the static constructor is executed when the class is loaded, but the instance constructor is executed whenever an instance is created — so there won't be any confusion about which constructor gets executed when.

Note that if you have more than one class that has a static constructor, the static constructor that will be executed first is undefined. This means that you should not put any code in a static constructor that depends on other static constructors having been or not having been executed. On the other hand, if any static fields have been given default values, these will be allocated before the static constructor is called.

The next example illustrates the use of a static constructor. The example is imaginatively called `StaticConstructor` and is based on the idea of a program that has user preferences (which are presumably stored in some configuration file). To keep things simple, we'll assume just one user preference — a quantity called `BackColor`, which might represent the background color to be used in an application. And because we don't want to get into the details of writing code to read data from an external source here, we'll make the assumption that the preference is to have a background color of red on weekdays and green on weekends. All the program will do is display the preference in a console window — but this is enough to see a static constructor at work.

```csharp
namespace Wrox.ProCSharp.StaticConstructorSample
{
    public class UserPreferences
    {
        public static readonly Color BackColor;

        static UserPreferences()
        {
            DateTime now = DateTime.Now;
            if (now.DayOfWeek == DayOfWeek.Saturday
               || now.DayOfWeek == DayOfWeek.Sunday)
                BackColor = Color.Green;
            else
                BackColor = Color.Red;
        }

        private UserPreferences()
        {
        }
    }
}
```

This code shows how the color preference is stored in a static variable, which is initialized in the static constructor. This field is declared as read-only, which means that its value can only be set in a constructor. You learn about read-only fields in more detail later in this chapter. The code makes use of a couple of useful structs that have been supplied by Microsoft as part of the framework class library, `System.DateTime.` and `System.Drawing.Color. DateTime` implements a static property, `Now`, which returns the current time, and an instance property, `DayOfWeek`, which works out what day of the week a date-time represents. `Color` (which is discussed in Chapter 25, "Graphics with GDI+") is used to store colors. It implements various static properties, such as `Red` and `Green` as used in this example, which return commonly used colors. In order to use `Color`, you need to reference the `System.Drawing.dll` assembly when compiling, and you must add a `using` statement for the `System.Drawing` namespace:

```
using System;
using System.Drawing;
```

You test the static constructor with this code:

```
class MainEntryPoint
{
   static void Main(string[] args)
   {
      Console.WriteLine("User-preferences: BackColor is: " +
                       UserPreferences.BackColor.ToString());
   }
}
```

Compiling and running this code results in this output:

**StaticConstructor.exe**

```
User-preferences: BackColor is: Color [Red]
```

## Calling constructors from other constructors

You may sometimes find yourself in the situation where you have several constructors in a class, perhaps to accommodate some optional parameters, for which the constructors have some code in common. For example, consider this:

```
class Car
{
   private string description;
   private uint nWheels;
   public Car(string model, uint nWheels)
   {
      this.description = description;
      this.nWheels = nWheels;
   }

   public Car(string model)
   {
      this.description = description;
      this.nWheels = 4;
   }
// etc.
```

Both constructors initialize the same fields. It would clearly be neater to place all the code in one place, and C# has a special syntax, known as a constructor initializer, to allow this.

```
class Car
{
   private string description;
   private uint nWheels;

   public Car(string model, uint nWheels)
   {
      this.description = description;
      this.nWheels = nWheels;
   }

   public Car(string model) : this(model, 4)
   {
   }
   // etc
```

In this context, the `this` keyword simply causes the constructor with the nearest matching parameters to be called. Note that any constructor initializer is executed before the body of the constructor. Say the following code is run:

```
Car myCar = new Car("Proton Persona");
```

In this example, the two-parameter constructor executes before any code in the body of the one-parameter constructor (though in this particular case, because there is no code in the body of the one-parameter constructor, it makes no difference).

A C# constructor initializer may contain either one call to another constructor in the same class (using the syntax just presented) or one call to a constructor in the immediate base class (using the same syntax, but using the keyword `base` instead of `this`). It is not possible to put more than one call in the initializer.

The syntax for constructor initializers in C# is similar to that for constructor initialization lists in C++, but C++ developers should beware. Behind the similarity in syntax, C# initializers follow very different rules for what can be placed in them. Whereas you can use a C++ initialization list to indicate initial values of any member variables or to call a base constructor, the only thing you can put in a C# initializer is one call to one other constructor. This forces C# classes to follow a strict sequence for how they get constructed, whereas C++ allows some laxity. This issue is studied more in Chapter 4, where you see that the sequence enforced by C# arguably amounts to no more than good programming practice anyway.

## *readonly Fields*

The concept of a constant as a variable that contains a value that cannot be changed is something that C# shares with most programming languages. However, constants don't necessarily meet all requirements. On occasion, you may have some variable whose value shouldn't be changed, but where the value is not known until runtime. C# provides another type of variable that is useful in this scenario: the `readonly` field.

The `readonly` keyword gives a bit more flexibility than `const`, allowing for the case in which you might want a field to be constant but also need to carry out some calculations to determine its initial value. The rule is that you can assign values to a `readonly` field inside a constructor, but not anywhere else. It's also possible for a `readonly` field to be an instance rather than a static field, having a different value for each instance of a class. This means that, unlike a `const` field, if you want a `readonly` field to be static, you have to declare it as such.

Suppose you have an MDI program that edits documents, but that for licensing reasons you want to restrict the number of documents that can be opened simultaneously. Now assume that you are selling different versions of the software, and it's possible that customers can upgrade their licenses to open more documents simultaneously. Clearly this means you can't hard-code the maximum number in the source code. You'd probably need a field to represent this maximum number. This field will have to be read in — perhaps from a registry key or some other file storage — each time the program is launched. So your code might look something like this:

```
public class DocumentEditor
{
    public static readonly uint MaxDocuments;

    static DocumentEditor()
    {
        MaxDocuments = DoSomethingToFindOutMaxNumber();
    }
}
```

In this case, the field is static, because the maximum number of documents needs to be stored only once per running instance of the program. This is why it is initialized in the static constructor. If you had an instance `readonly` field, you would initialize it in the instance constructor(s). For example, presumably each document you edit has a creation date, which you wouldn't want to allow the user to change (because that would be rewriting the past!). Note that the field is also public — you don't normally need to make `readonly` fields private, because by definition they cannot be modified externally (the same principle also applies to constants).

As noted earlier, date is represented by the class `System.DateTime`. The following code uses a `System.DateTime` constructor that takes three parameters (the year, month, and day of the month — you can find details of this and other `DateTime` constructors in the MSDN documentation):

```
public class Document
{
    public readonly DateTime CreationDate;

    public Document()
    {
        // read in creation date from file. Assume result is 1 Jan 2002
        // but in general this can be different for different instances
        // of the class
        CreationDate = new DateTime(2002, 1, 1);
    }
}
```

`CreationDate` and `MaxDocuments` in the previous code snippet are treated like any other field, except that because they are read-only, they cannot be assigned to outside the constructors.

# Objects and Types

```
void SomeMethod()
{
   MaxDocuments = 10;    // compilation error here. MaxDocuments is readonly
}
```

It's also worth noting that you don't have to assign a value to a `readonly` field in a constructor. If you don't do so, it will be left with the default value for its particular data type or whatever value you initialized it to at its declaration. That applies to both static and instance `readonly` fields.

# Structs

So far, you have seen how classes offer a great way of encapsulating objects in your program. You have also seen how they are stored on the heap in a way that gives you much more flexibility in data lifetime, but with a slight cost in performance. This performance cost is small thanks to the optimizations of managed heaps. However, in some situations all you really need is a small data structure. In this case, a class provides more functionality than you need, and for performance reasons you will probably prefer to use a struct. Look at this example:

```
class Dimensions
{
   public double Length;
   public double Width;
}
```

This code defines a class called `Dimensions`, which simply stores the length and width of some item. Perhaps you're writing a furniture-arranging program to let people experiment with rearranging their furniture on the computer and you want to store the dimensions of each item of furniture. It looks like you're breaking the rules of good program design by making the fields public, but the point is that you don't really need all the facilities of a class for this at all. All you have is two numbers, which you'll find convenient to treat as a pair rather than individually. There is no need for lots of methods, or for you to be able to inherit from the class, and you certainly don't want to have the .NET runtime go to the trouble of bringing in the heap with all the performance implications, just to store two doubles.

As mentioned earlier in this chapter, the only thing you need to change in the code to define a type as a struct instead of a class is to replace the keyword `class` with `struct`:

```
struct Dimensions
{
   public double Length;
   public double Width;
}
```

Defining functions for structs is also exactly the same as defining them for classes. The following code demonstrates a constructor and a property for a struct:

```
struct Dimensions
{
   public double Length;
   public double Width;
```

## Chapter 3

```
        Dimensions(double length, double width)
        { Length=length; Width=width; }

        public int Diagonal
        {
            {
                get
                {
                    return Math.Sqrt(Length*Length + Width*Width);
                }
            }
        }
}
```

In many ways, you can think of structs in C# as being like scaled-down classes. They are basically the same as classes, but designed more for cases where you simply want to group some data together. They differ from classes in the following ways:

- ❑ Structs are value types, not reference types. This means they are stored either in the stack or inline (if they are part of another object that is stored on the heap) and have the same lifetime restrictions as the simple data types.
- ❑ Structs do not support inheritance.
- ❑ There are some differences in the way constructors work for structs. In particular, the compiler always supplies a default no-parameter constructor, which you are not permitted to replace.
- ❑ With a struct, you can specify how the fields are to be laid out in memory (this is examined in Chapter 11, "Reflection," which covers attributes).

Because structs are really intended to group data items together, you'll sometimes find that most or all of their fields are declared as public. This is, strictly speaking, contrary to the guidelines for writing .NET code—according to Microsoft, fields (other than `const` fields) should always be private and wrapped by public properties. However, for simple structs, many developers would nevertheless consider public fields to be acceptable programming practice.

> *C++ developers beware; structs in C# are very different from classes in their implementation. This is very different than the situation in C++, for which classes and structs are virtually the same thing.*

The following sections look at some of these differences in more detail.

## *Structs Are Value Types*

Although structs are value types, you can often treat them syntactically in the same way as classes. For example, with the definition of the `Dimensions` class in the previous section, you could write:

```
        Dimensions point = new Dimensions();
        point.Length = 3;
        point.Width = 6;
```

# Objects and Types

Note that because structs are value types, the `new` operator does not work in the same way as it does for classes and other reference types. Instead of allocating memory on the heap, the `new` operator simply calls the appropriate constructor, according to the parameters passed to it, initializing all fields. Indeed, for structs it is perfectly legal to write:

```
Dimensions point;
point.Length = 3;
point.Width = 6;
```

If `Dimensions` was a class, this would produce a compilation error, because `point` would contain an uninitialized reference — an address that points nowhere, so you could not start setting values to its fields. For a struct, however, the variable declaration actually allocates space on the stack for the entire struct, so it's ready to assign values to. Note, however, that the following code would cause a compilation error, with the compiler complaining that you are using an uninitialized variable:

```
Dimensions point;
Double D = point.Length;
```

Structs follow the same rules as any other data type: everything must be initialized before use. A struct is considered fully initialized either when the `new` operator has been called against it, or when values have been individually assigned to all its fields. And of course, a struct defined as a member field of a class is initialized by being zeroed-out automatically when the containing object is initialized.

The fact that structs are value types will affect performance, though depending on how you use your struct, this can be good or bad. On the positive side, allocating memory for structs is very fast because this takes place inline or on the stack. The same goes for removing structs when they go out of scope. On the other hand, whenever you pass a struct as a parameter or assign a struct to another struct (as in A=B, where A and B are structs), the full contents of the struct are copied, whereas for a class only the reference is copied. This will result in a performance loss that depends on the size of the struct — this should emphasize the fact that structs are really intended for small data structures. Note, however, that when passing a struct as a parameter to a method, you can avoid this performance loss by passing it as a `ref` parameter — in this case only the address in memory of the struct will be passed in, which is just as fast as passing in a class. On the other hand, if you do this, you'll have to be aware that it means the called method can in principle change the value of the struct.

## Structs and Inheritance

Structs are not designed for inheritance. This means that it is not possible to inherit from a struct. The only exception to this is that structs, in common with every other type in C#, derive ultimately from the class `System.Object`. Hence, structs also have access to the methods of `System.Object`, and it is even possible to override them in structs — an obvious example would be overriding the `ToString()` method. The actual inheritance chain for structs is that each struct derives from a class, `System.ValueType`, which in turn derives from `System.Object`. `ValueType` does not add any new members to `Object`, but provides implementations of some of them that are more suitable for structs. Note that you cannot supply a different base class for a struct: Every struct is derived from `ValueType`.

## Constructors for Structs

You can define constructors for structs in exactly the same way that you can for classes, except that you are not permitted to define a constructor that takes no parameters. This may seem nonsensical, and the reason is buried in the implementation of the .NET runtime. Some rare circumstances exist in which the .NET runtime would not be able to call a custom zero-parameter constructor that you have supplied. Microsoft has therefore taken the easy way out and banned zero-parameter constructors for structs in C#.

That said, the default constructor, which initializes all fields to zero values, is always present implicitly, even if you supply other constructors that take parameters. It's also impossible to circumvent the default constructor by supplying initial values for fields. The following code will cause a compile-time error:

```
struct Dimensions
{
   public double Length = 1;      // error. Initial values not allowed
   public double Width = 2;       // error. Initial values not allowed
```

Of course, if `Dimensions` had been declared as a class, this code would have compiled without any problems.

Incidentally, you can supply a `Close()` or `Dispose()` method for a struct in the same way you do for a class.

# Partial Classes

The `partial` keyword allows the class, struct, or interface to span across multiple files. Typically a class will reside entirely in a single file. However, in situations where multiple developers need access to the same class, or more likely in the situation where a code generator of some type is generating part of a class, then having the class in multiple files can be beneficial.

The way that the `partial` keyword is used is to simply place partial before class, struct, or interface. In the following example the class `TheBigClass` resides in two separate source files, `BigClassPart1.cs` and `BigClassPart2.cs`:

```
//BigClassPart1.cs
partial class TheBigClass
{
  public void MethodOne()
   {
   }
}

//BigClassPart2.cs
partial class TheBigClass
{
  public void MethodTwo()
   {
   }
}
```

# Objects and Types

When the project that these two source files are part of is compiled, a single type called `TheBigClass` will be created with two methods, `MethodOne()` and `MethodTwo()`.

If any of the following keywords are used in describing the class, the same must apply to all partials of the same type:

- public
- private
- protected
- internal
- abstract
- sealed
- base class
- new
- generic constraints

Nested partials are allowed as long as the partial keyword precedes the class keyword in the nested type. Attributes, XML comments, interfaces, generic-type parameter attributes, and members will be combined when the partial types are compiled into the type. Given the two source files:

```
//BigClassPart1.cs
[CustomAttribute]
partial class TheBigClass : TheBigBaseClass, IBigClass
{
  public void MethodOne()
  {
  }
}

//BigClassPart2.cs
[AnotherAttribute]
partial class TheBigClass : IOtherBigClass
{
  public void MethodTwo()
  {
  }
}
```

After the compile, the equivalent source file would be:

```
[CustomAttribute]
[AnotherAttribute]
partial class TheBigClass : TheBigBaseClass, IBigClass, IOtherBigClass
{
  public void MethodOne()
  {
  }
```

```
    public void MethodTwo()
    {
    }
}
```

# Static Classes

Earlier, this chapter discussed static constructors and how they allowed the initialization of static member variables. If a class contains nothing but static methods and properties, the class itself can become static. A static class is functionally the same as creating a class with a private static constructor. An instance of the class can never be created. By using the `static` keyword, the compiler can help by checking that instance members are never accidentally added to the class. If they are, a compile error happens. This can help guarantee that an instance is never created. The syntax for a static class looks like this:

```
static class StaticUtilities
{
  public static void HelperMethod()
  {
  }
}
```

An object of type `StaticUtilities` is not needed to call the `HelperMethod()`. The type name is used to make the call:

```
StaticUtilities.HelperMethod();
```

# The Object Class

As indicated earlier, all .NET classes are ultimately derived from `System.Object`. In fact, if you don't specify a base class when you define a class, the compiler will automatically assume that it derives from `Object`. Because inheritance has not been used in this chapter, every class you have seen here is actually derived from `System.Object`. (As noted earlier, for structs this derivation is indirect: A struct is always derived from `System.ValueType`, which in turn derives from `System.Object`.)

The practical significance of this is that, besides the methods and properties and so on that you define, you also have access to a number of public and protected member methods that have been defined for the `Object` class. These methods are available in all other classes that you define.

## System.Object Methods

The methods defined in `Object` are as shown in the following table:

# Objects and Types

| Method | Access Modifiers | Purpose |
|---|---|---|
| `string ToString()` | `public virtual` | Returns a string representation of the object |
| `int GetHashTable()` | `public virtual` | Used if implementing dictionaries (hash tables) |
| `bool Equals(object obj)` | `public virtual` | Compares instances of the object for equality |
| `bool Equals(object objA, object objB)` | `public static` | Compares instances of the object for equality |
| `bool ReferenceEquals (object objA, object objB)` | `public static` | Compares whether two references refer to the same object |
| `Type GetType()` | `Public` | Returns details of the type of the object |
| `object MemberwiseClone()` | `Protected` | Makes a shallow copy of the object |
| `void Finalize()` | `protected virtual` | This is the .NET version of a destructor |

You haven't yet seen enough of the C# language to be able to understand how to use all these methods. For the time being, the following list simply summarizes the purpose of each method, with the exception of `ToString()`, which is examined in more detail.

- `ToString()` — This is intended as a fairly basic, quick-and-easy string representation; use it when you just want a quick idea of the contents of an object, perhaps for debugging purposes. It provides very little choice of how to format the data: For example, dates can in principle be expressed in a huge variety of different formats, but `DateTime.ToString()` does not offer you any choice in this regard. If you need a more sophisticated string representation that, for example, takes account of your formatting preferences or of the culture (the locale), then you should implement the `IFormattable` interface (see Chapter 8, "Strings and Regular Expressions").

- `GetHashCode()` — This is used if objects are placed in a data structure known as a map (also known as a hash table or dictionary). It is used by classes that manipulate these structures in order to determine where to place an object in the structure. If you intend your class to be used as key for a dictionary, you will need to override `GetHashCode()`. Some fairly strict requirements exist for how you implement your overload, and you learn about those when you examine dictionaries in Chapter 9, "Collections."

- `Equals()` (both versions) and `ReferenceEquals()` — As you'll gather by the existence of three different methods aimed at comparing the equality of objects, the .NET Framework has quite a sophisticated scheme for measuring equality. Subtle differences exist between how these three methods, along with the comparison operator, ==, are intended to be used. Not only that, but restrictions also exist on how you should override the virtual, one-parameter version of `Equals()` if you choose to do so, because certain base classes in the `System.Collections` namespace call the method and expect it to behave in certain ways. You explore the use of these methods in Chapter 5, "Operators and Casts," when you examine operators.

- `Finalize()` — This method is covered in Chapter 7, "Memory Management and Pointers." It is intended as the nearest that C# has to C++-style destructors, and is called when a reference object is garbage collected to clean up resources. The `Object` implementation of `Finalize()` actually does nothing and is ignored by the garbage collector. You will normally override `Finalize()` if an object owns references to unmanaged resources that need to be removed when the object is deleted. The garbage collector cannot do this directly because it only knows about managed resources, so it relies on any finalizers that you supply.

- `GetType()` — This method returns an instance of a class derived from `System.Type`. This object can provide an extensive range of information about the class of which your object is a member, including base type, methods, properties, and so on. `System.Type` also provides the entry point into .NET's reflection technology. Chapter 11, "Reflection," examines this topic.

- `MemberwiseClone()` — This is the only member of `System.Object` that isn't examined in detail anywhere in the book. There is no need to, because it is fairly simple in concept. It simply makes a copy of the object and returns a reference (or in the case of a value type, a boxed reference) to the copy. Note that the copy made is a shallow copy — this means that it copies all the value types in the class. If the class contains any embedded references, then only the references will be copied, not the objects referred to. This method is protected and so cannot be called to copy external objects. It is also not virtual, so you cannot override its implementation.

## The ToString() Method

You've already encountered `ToString()` in Chapter 2, "C# Basics." It provides the most convenient way to get a quick string representation of an object.

For example:

```
int i = -50;
string str = i.ToString();   // returns "-50"
```

Here's another example:

```
enum Colors {Red, Orange, Yellow};
// later on in code...
Colors favoriteColor = Colors.Orange;
string str = favoriteColor.ToString();      // returns "Orange"
```

`Object.ToString()` is actually declared as virtual, and all these examples are taking advantage of the fact that its implementation in the C# predefined data types has been overridden for us in order to return correct string representations of those types. You might not think that the `Colors` enum counts as a predefined data type. It actually gets implemented as a struct derived from `System.Enum`, and `System.Enum` has a rather clever override of `ToString()` that deals with all the enums you define.

If you don't override `ToString()` in classes that you define, your classes will simply inherit the `System.Object` implementation — which displays the name of the class. If you want `ToString()` to return a string that contains information about the value of objects of your class, then you will need to override it. To illustrate this, the following example, `Money`, defines a very simple class, also called `Money`, which represent U.S. currency amounts. `Money` simply acts as a wrapper for the decimal class but supplies a `ToString()` method. Note that this method must be declared as `override` because it is replacing

# Objects and Types

(overriding) the `ToString()` method supplied by `Object`. Chapter 4 discusses overriding in more detail. The complete code for this example is as follows. Note that it also illustrates use of properties to wrap fields:

```
using System;

namespace Wrox.ProCSharp.OOCSharp
{
   class MainEntryPoint
   {
      static void Main(string[] args)
      {
         Money cash1 = new Money();
         cash1.Amount = 40M;
         Console.WriteLine("cash1.ToString() returns: " + cash1.ToString());
         Console.ReadLine();
      }
   }
   class Money
   {
      private decimal amount;

      public decimal Amount
      {
         get
         {
            return amount;
         }
         set
         {
            amount = value;
         }
      }
      public override string ToString()
      {
         return "$" + Amount.ToString();
      }
   }
}
```

This example is here just to illustrate syntactical features of C#. C# already has a predefined type to represent currency amounts, `decimal`, so in real life, you wouldn't write a class to duplicate this functionality unless you wanted to add various other methods to it. And in many cases, due to formatting requirements, you'd probably use the `String.Format()` method (which is covered in Chapter 8) rather than `ToString()` to display a currency string.

In the `Main()` method you first instantiate a `Money` object, then a `BetterMoney` object. In both cases you call `ToString()`. For the `Money` object, you'll pick up the `Object` version of this method that displays class information. For the `BetterMoney` object, you'll pick up your own override. Running this code gives the following results:

```
StringRepresentations
cash1.ToString() returns: $40
```

109

Chapter 3

# Summary

This chapter examined C# syntax for declaring and manipulating objects. You have seen how to declare static and instance fields, properties, methods, and constructors. You have also seen that C# adds some new features not present in the OOP model of some other languages: Static constructors provide a means of initializing static fields, whereas structs allow you to define high-performance types, albeit with a more restricted feature set, which do not require the use of the managed heap. You have also seen how all types in C# derive ultimately from the type `System.Object`, which means that all types start with a basic set of useful methods, including `ToString()`.

Chapter 4, "Inheritance," examines implementation and interface inheritance in C#.

# Inheritance

Chapter 3, "Objects and Types," examined how to use individual classes in C#. The focus in that chapter was on how to define methods, constructors, properties, and other members of a single class (or a single struct). Although you did learn that all classes ultimately derive from the class `System.Object`, you did not see how to create a hierarchy of inherited classes. Inheritance is the subject of this chapter. It briefly discusses the scope of C#'s support for inheritance before examining in detail how to code first implementation inheritance and then interface inheritance in C#. Note that this chapter presumes familiarity with the basic concepts of inheritance, including virtual functions and overriding. This chapter concentrates on the syntax used to provide inheritance and inheritance-related topics, such as virtual functions, and on those aspects of the C# inheritance model that are particular to C# and not necessarily shared by other object-oriented languages.

## Types of Inheritance

This chapter starts off by reviewing exactly what C# does and does not support as far as inheritance is concerned.

### Implementation Versus Interface Inheritance

Gurus of object-oriented programming will know that there are two distinct types of inheritance: implementation inheritance and interface inheritance.

- **Implementation inheritance** means that a type derives from a base type, taking all the base type's member fields and functions. With implementation inheritance, a derived type adopts the base type's implementation of each function, unless it is indicated in the definition of the derived type that a function implementation is to be overridden. This type of inheritance is most useful when you need to add functionality to an existing type, or where a number of related types share a significant amount of common functionality. A good example of this comes in the Windows Forms classes, which are discussed in Chapter 23,

"Windows Forms," along with the base class `System.Windows.Forms.Control`, which provides a very sophisticated implementation of a generic Windows control, and numerous other classes such as `System.Windows.Forms.TextBox` and `System.Windows.Forms.ListBox` that derive from `Control` and override functions or provide new functions to implement specific types of control.

- **Interface inheritance** means that a type inherits only the signatures of the functions, but does not inherit any implementations. This type of inheritance is most useful when you want to specify that a type makes certain features available. For example, certain types can indicate that they provide a resource cleanup method called `Dispose()` by deriving from an interface, `System.IDisposable` (see Chapter 7, "Memory Management and Pointers"). Because the way that one type cleans up resources is likely to be very different from the way that another type cleans up resources, there is no point defining any common implementation, so interface inheritance is appropriate here. Interface inheritance is often regarded as providing a contract: By deriving from an interface, a type is guaranteed to provide certain functionality to clients.

Traditionally, languages such as C++ have been very strong on implementation inheritance. Indeed, implementation inheritance has been at the core of the C++ programming model. On the other hand, Visual Basic 6 did not support any implementation inheritance of classes but did support interface inheritance thanks to its underlying COM foundations.

C# has both implementation and interface inheritance. There is arguably no preference, because both types of inheritance are fully built into the language from the ground up. This makes it easy for you to choose the best architecture for your solution.

## *Multiple Inheritance*

Some languages such as C++ support what is known as *multiple inheritance*, in which a class derives from more than one other class. The benefits of using of multiple inheritance are debatable: On the one hand, there is no doubt that it is possible to use multiple inheritance to write extremely sophisticated, yet compact, code, as demonstrated by the C++ ATL library. On the other hand, code that uses multiple implementation inheritance is often difficult to understand and debug (a point that is equally well demonstrated by the C++ ATL library). As mentioned, making it easy to write robust code was one of the crucial design goals behind the development of C#. Accordingly, C# does not support multiple implementation inheritance. It does, however, allow types to derive from multiple interfaces. This means that a C# class can derive from one other class, and any number of interfaces. Indeed, we can be more precise: Thanks to the presence of `System.Object` as a common base type, every C# class (except for `Object`) has exactly one base class, and may additionally have any number of base interfaces.

## *Structs and Classes*

Chapter 3 distinguishes between structs (value types) and classes (reference types). One restriction of using a struct is that structs do not support inheritance, beyond the fact that every struct is automatically derived from `System.ValueType`. In fact we should be more careful. It's true that it is not possible to code a type hierarchy of structs; however, it is possible for structs to implement interfaces. In other words, structs don't really support implementation inheritance, but they do support interface inheritance. Indeed, we can summarize the situation for any types that you define as follows:

# Inheritance

- **Structs** are always derived from `System.ValueType`. They can also derive from any number of interfaces.
- **Classes** are always derived from one other class of your choosing. They can also derive from any number of interfaces.

## Implementation Inheritance

If you want to declare that a class derives from another class, use the following syntax:

```
class MyDerivedClass : MyBaseClass
{
   // functions and data members here
}
```

*This syntax is very similar to C++ and Java syntax. However, C++ programmers, who will be used to the concepts of public and private inheritance, should note that C# does not support private inheritance, hence the absence of a public or private qualifier on the base class name. Supporting private inheritance would have complicated the language for very little gain. In practice, private inheritance is used extremely rarely in C++ anyway.*

If a class (or a struct) also derives from interfaces, the list of base class and interfaces is separated by commas:

```
public class MyDerivedClass : MyBaseClass, IInterface1, IInterface2
{
        // etc.
```

For a struct, the syntax is as follows:

```
public struct MyDerivedStruct : IInterface1, IInterface2
{
        // etc.
```

If you do not specify a base class in a class definition, the C# compiler will assume that `System.Object` is the base class. Hence, the following two pieces of code yield the same result:

```
class MyClass : Object   // derives from System.Object
{
   // etc.
}
```

and

```
class MyClass     // derives from System.Object
{
   // etc.
}
```

For the sake of simplicity, the second form is more common.

Because C# supports the `object` keyword, which serves as a pseudonym for the `System.Object` class, you can also write:

```
class MyClass : object    // derives from System.Object
{
   // etc.
}
```

If you want to reference the `Object` class, use the `object` keyword, which is recognized by intelligent editors such as Visual Studio .NET and thus facilitates editing your code.

## Virtual Methods

By declaring a base class function as `virtual`, you allow the function to be overridden in any derived classes:

```
class MyBaseClass
{
   public virtual string VirtualMethod()
   {
      return "This method is virtual and defined in MyBaseClass";
   }
}
```

It is also permitted to declare a property as `virtual`. For a virtual or overridden property, the syntax is the same as for a non-virtual property, with the exception of the keyword `virtual`, which is added to the definition. The syntax looks like this:

```
public virtual string ForeName
{
   get { return fName; }
   set { fName = value; }
}
private string foreName;
```

For simplicity, the following discussion focuses mainly on methods, but it applies equally well to properties.

The concepts behind virtual functions in C# are identical to standard OOP concepts. You can override a virtual function in a derived class, and when the method is called, the appropriate method for the type of object is invoked. In C#, functions are not virtual by default, but (aside from constructors) can be explicitly declared as `virtual`. This follows the C++ methodology: for performance reasons, functions are not virtual unless indicated. In Java, by contrast, all functions are virtual. C# differs from C++ syntax, however, because it requires you to declare when a derived class's function overrides another function, using the `override` keyword:

# Inheritance

```
class MyDerivedClass : MyBaseClass
{
   public override string VirtualMethod()
   {
      return "This method is an override defined in MyDerivedClass";
   }
}
```

This syntax for method overriding removes potential runtime bugs that can easily occur in C++, when a method signature in a derived class unintentionally differs slightly from the base version, resulting in the method failing to override the base version. In C# this is picked up as a compile-time error, because the compiler would see a function marked as `override` but no base method for it to override.

Neither member fields nor static functions can be declared as virtual. The concept simply wouldn't make sense for any class member other than an instance function member.

## *Hiding Methods*

If a method with the same signature is declared in both base and derived classes, but the methods are not declared as `virtual` and `override`, respectively, then the derived class version is said to *hide* the base class version.

In most cases, you would want to override methods rather than hide them; by hiding them you risk calling the "wrong" method for a given class instance. However, as shown in the following example, C# syntax is designed to ensure that the developer is warned at compile time about this potential problem, thus making it safer to hide methods if that is your intention. This also has versioning benefits for developers of class libraries.

Suppose you have a class called `HisBaseClass`:

```
class HisBaseClass
{
   // various members
}
```

At some point in the future you write a derived class that adds some functionality to `HisBaseClass`. In particular, you add a method called `MyGroovyMethod()`, which is not present in the base class:

```
class MyDerivedClass: HisBaseClass
{
   public int MyGroovyMethod()
   {
      // some groovy implementation
      return 0;
   }
}
```

One year later, you decide to extend the functionality of the base class. By coincidence, you add a method that is also called `MyGroovyMethod()` and has the same name and signature as yours, but probably doesn't do the same thing. When you compile your code using the new version of the base class, you have a potential clash because your program won't know which method to call. It's all perfectly legal C#, but because your `MyGroovyMethod()` is not intended to be related in any way to the base class `MyGroovyMethod()`, the result of running this code does not yield the result you want. Fortunately, C# has been designed in such a way that it copes very well when conflicts of this type arise.

In these situations, C# generates a compilation warning. That reminds you to use the `new` keyword to declare that you intend to hide a method, like this:

```
class MyDerivedClass : HisBaseClass
{
   public new int MyGroovyMethod()
   {
      // some groovy implementation
      return 0;
   }
}
```

However, because your version of `MyGroovyMethod()` is not declared as `new`, the compiler will pick up on the fact that it's hiding a base class method without being instructed to do so and generate a warning (this applies whether or not you declared `MyGroovyMethod()` as `virtual`). If you want, you can rename your version of the method. This is the recommended course of action, because it will eliminate future confusion. However, if you decide not to rename your method for whatever reason (for example, you've published your software as a library for other companies, so you can't change the names of methods), all your existing client code will still run correctly, picking up your version of `MyGroovyMethod()`. That's because any existing code that accesses this method must be doing so through a reference to `MyDerivedClass` (or a further derived class).

Your existing code cannot access this method through a reference to `HisBaseClass`; it would generate a compilation error when compiled against the earlier version of `HisBaseClass`. The problem can only happen in client code you have yet to write. C# arranges things so that you get a warning that a potential problem might occur in future code — and you will need to pay attention to this warning, and take care not to attempt to call your version of `MyGroovyMethod()` through any reference to `HisBaseClass` in any future code you add. However, all your existing code will still work fine. It may be a subtle point, but it's quite an impressive example of how C# is able to cope with different versions of classes.

## *Calling Base Versions of Functions*

C# has a special syntax for calling base versions of a method from a derived class: `base.<MethodName>()`. For example, if you want a method in a derived class to return 90 percent of the value returned by the base class method, you can use the following syntax:

```
class CustomerAccount
{
   public virtual decimal CalculatePrice()
   {
      // implementation
      return 0.0M;
```

```
        }
    }
    class GoldAccount : CustomerAccount
    {
        public override decimal CalculatePrice()
        {
            return base.CalculatePrice() * 0.9M;
        }
    }
```

Java uses a similar syntax, with the exception that Java uses the keyword `super` rather than `base`. C++ has no similar keyword but instead requires specification of the class name (`CustomerAccount::CalculatePrice()`). Any equivalent to `base` in C++ would have been ambiguous because C++ supports multiple inheritance.

Note that you can use the `base.<MethodName>()` syntax to call any method in the base class — you don't have to call it from inside an override of the same method.

## Abstract Classes and Functions

C# allows both classes and functions to be declared as abstract. An abstract class cannot be instantiated, whereas an abstract function does not have an implementation, and must be overridden in any non-abstract derived class. Obviously, an abstract function is automatically virtual (although you don't need to supply the `virtual` keyword; doing so results in a syntax error). If any class contains any abstract functions, that class is also abstract and must be declared as such:

```
abstract class Building
{
    public abstract decimal CalculateHeatingCost();   // abstract method
}
```

C++ developers will notice some syntactical differences in C# here. C# does not support the `=0` syntax to declare abstract functions. In C#, this syntax would be misleading because `=<value>` is allowed in member fields in class declarations to supply initial values:

```
abstract class Building
{
    private bool damaged = false;   // field
    public abstract decimal CalculateHeatingCost();   // abstract method
}
```

*C++ developers should also note the slightly different terminology: In C++, abstract functions are often described as pure virtual; in the C# world, the only correct term to use is abstract.*

## Sealed Classes and Methods

C# allows classes and methods to be declared as `sealed`. In the case of a class, this means that you can't inherit from that class. In the case of a method, this means that you can't override that method.

```csharp
sealed class FinalClass
{
   // etc
}
class DerivedClass : FinalClass        // wrong. Will give compilation error
{
   // etc
}
```

*Java developers will recognize* `sealed` *as the C# equivalent of Java's* `final`.

The most likely situation in which you'll mark a class or method as `sealed` will be if the class or method is internal to the operation of the library, class, or other classes that you are writing, so you are sure that any attempt to override some of its functionality will cause problems. You might also mark a class or method as `sealed` for commercial reasons, in order to prevent a third party from extending your classes in a manner that is contrary to the licensing agreements. In general, however, you should be careful about marking a class or member as `sealed`, because by doing so you are severely restricting how it can be used. Even if you don't think it would be useful to inherit from a class or override a particular member of it, it's still possible that at some point in the future someone will encounter a situation you hadn't anticipated in which it is useful to do so. The .NET base class library frequently uses sealed classes in order to make these classes inaccessible to third-party developers who might want to derive their own classes from them. For example, `string` is a sealed class.

Declaring a method as `sealed` serves a similar purpose as for a class, although you rarely will want to declare a method as `sealed`.

```csharp
class MyClass
{
   public sealed override void FinalMethod()
   {
      // etc.
   }
}
class DerivedClass : MyClass
{
   public override void FinalMethod()      // wrong. Will give compilation error
   {
   }
}
```

It does not make sense to use the `sealed` keyword on a method unless that method is itself an override of another method in some base class. If you are defining a new method and you don't want anyone else to override it, you would not declare it as `virtual` in the first place. If, however, you have overridden a base class method, the `sealed` keyword provides a way of ensuring that the override you supply to a method is a "final" override in the sense that no one else can override it again.

## Constructors of Derived Classes

Chapter 3 discusses how constructors can be applied to individual classes. An interesting question arises as to what happens when you start defining your own constructors for classes that are part of a hierarchy, inherited from other classes that may also have custom constructors.

# Inheritance

Assume you have not defined any explicit constructors for any of your classes. This means that the compiler supplies default zeroing-out constructors for all your classes. There is actually quite a lot going on under the hood when that happens, but the compiler is able to arrange it so that things work out nicely throughout the class hierarchy and every field in every class gets initialized to whatever its default value is. When you add a constructor of your own, however, you are effectively taking control of construction. This has implications right down through the hierarchy of derived classes, and you have to make sure that you don't inadvertently do anything to prevent construction through the hierarchy from taking place smoothly.

You might be wondering why there is any special problem with derived classes. The reason is that when you create an instance of a derived class, there is actually more than one constructor at work. The constructor of the class you instantiate isn't by itself sufficient to initialize the class—the constructors of the base classes must also be called. That's why we've been talking about construction through the hierarchy.

To see why base class constructors must be called, you're going to develop an example based on a cell phone company called MortimerPhones. The example contains an abstract base class, `GenericCustomer`, which represents any customer. There is also a (non-abstract) class, `Nevermore60Customer`, that represents any customer on a particular rate called the `Nevermore60` rate. All customers have a name, represented by a private field. Under the `Nevermore60` rate, the first few minutes of the customer's call time are charged at a higher rate, necessitating the need for the field `highCostMinutesUsed`, which details how many of these higher-cost minutes each customer has used up. The class definitions look like this:

```
abstract class GenericCustomer
{
    private string name;
    // lots of other methods etc.
}
class Nevermore60Customer : GenericCustomer
{
    private uint highCostMinutesUsed;
    // other methods etc.
}
```

We won't worry about what other methods might be implemented in these classes, because we are concentrating solely on the construction process here. And if you download the sample code for this chapter, you'll find that the class definitions include only the constructors.

Take a look at what happens when you use the `new` operator to instantiate a `Nevermore60Customer`:

```
GenericCustomer customer = new Nevermore60Customer();
```

Clearly both of the member fields `name` and `highCostMinutesUsed` must be initialized when `customer` is instantiated. If you don't supply constructors of your own, but rely simply on the default constructors, then you'd expect `name` to be initialized to the `null` reference, and `highCostMinutesUsed` to zero. Let's look in a bit more detail at how this actually happens.

The `highCostMinutesUsed` field presents no problem: the default `Nevermore60Customer` constructor supplied by the compiler will initialize this field to zero.

What about `name`? Looking at the class definitions, it's clear that the `Nevermore60Customer` constructor can't initialize this value. This field is declared as private, which means that derived classes don't have access to it. So the default `Nevermore60Customer` constructor simply won't know that this field exists. The only code items that have that knowledge are other members of `GenericCustomer`. This means that if `name` is going to be initialized, that'll have to be done by some constructor in `GenericCustomer`. No matter how big your class hierarchy is, this same reasoning applies right down to the ultimate base class, `System.Object`.

Now that you have an understanding of the issues involved, you can look at what actually happens whenever a derived class is instantiated. Assuming default constructors are used throughout, the compiler first grabs the constructor of the class it is trying to instantiate, in this case `Nevermore60Customer`. The first thing that the default `Nevermore60Customer` constructor does is attempt to run the default constructor for the immediate base class, `GenericCustomer`. Then the `GenericCustomer` constructor attempts to run the constructor for its immediate base, `System.Object`. `System.Object` doesn't have any base classes, so its constructor just executes and returns control to the `GenericCustomer` constructor. That constructor now executes, initializing `name` to `null`, before returning control to the `Nevermore60Customer` constructor. That constructor in turn executes, initializing `highCostMinutesUsed` to zero, and exits. At this point, the `Nevermore60Customer` instance has been successfully constructed and initialized.

The net result of all this is that the constructors are called in order of `System.Object` first, then progressing down the hierarchy until the compiler reaches the class being instantiated. Notice also that in this process, each constructor handles initialization of the fields in its own class. That's how it should normally work, and when you start adding your own constructors you should try to stick to that principle.

Notice the order in which this happens. It's always the base class constructors that get called first. This means that there are no problems with a constructor for a derived class invoking any base class methods, properties, and any other members that it has access to, because it can be confident that the base class has already been constructed and its fields initialized. It also means that if the derived class doesn't like the way that the base class has been initialized, it can change the initial values of the data, provided it has access to do so. However, good programming practice almost invariably means you'll try to prevent that situation from occurring if you can, and you will trust the base class constructor to deal with its own fields.

Now that you know how the process of construction works, you can start fiddling with it by adding your own constructors.

## *Adding a no-parameter constructor in a hierarchy*

We'll take the simplest case first and see what happens if you simply replace the default constructor somewhere in the hierarchy with another constructor that takes no parameters. Suppose that you decide that you want everyone's name to be initially set to the string `"<no name>"` instead of to the `null` reference. You'd modify the code in `GenericCustomer` like this:

```
public abstract class GenericCustomer
{
   private string name;
   public GenericCustomer()
      : base()   // we could omit this line without affecting the compiled code
   {
      name = "<no name>";
   }
```

Adding this code will work fine. `Nevermore60Customer` still has its default constructor, so the sequence of events described earlier will proceed as before, except that the compiler will use the custom `GenericCustomer` constructor instead of generating a default one, so the `name` field will always be initialized to `"<no name>"` as required.

Notice that in your constructor, you've added a call to the base class constructor before the `GenericCustomer` constructor is executed, using a syntax similar to that used earlier when we discussed how to get different overloads of constructors to call each other. The only difference is that this time you use the `base` keyword instead of `this`, to indicate it's a constructor to the `base` class rather than a constructor to the current class you want to call. There are no parameters in the brackets after the `base` keyword — that's important because it means you are not passing any parameters to the base constructor, so the compiler will have to look for a parameterless constructor to call. The result of all this is that the compiler will inject code to call the `System.Object` constructor, just as would happen by default anyway.

In fact, you can omit that line of code, and write the following (as was done for most of the constructors so far in the chapter):

```
public GenericCustomer()
{
    name = "<no name>";
}
```

If the compiler doesn't see any reference to another constructor before the opening curly brace, it assumes that you intended to call the base class constructor; this fits in with the way default constructors work.

The `base` and `this` keywords are the only keywords allowed in the line that calls another constructor. Anything else causes a compilation error. Also note that only one other constructor can be specified.

So far, this code works fine. One good way to mess up the progression through the hierarchy of constructors, however, is to declare a constructor as `private`:

```
private GenericCustomer()
{
    name = "<no name>";
}
```

If you try this, you'll find you get an interesting compilation error, which could really throw you if you don't understand how construction down a hierarchy works:

```
'Wrox.ProCSharp.GenericCustomer()' is inaccessible due to its protection level
```

The interesting thing is that the error occurs not in the `GenericCustomer` class, but in the derived class, `Nevermore60Customer`. What's happened is that the compiler has tried to generate a default constructor for `Nevermore60Customer`, but has not been able to because the default constructor is supposed to invoke the no-parameter `GenericCustomer` constructor. By declaring that constructor as `private`, you've made it inaccessible to the derived class. A similar error occurs if you supply a constructor to `GenericCustomer`, which takes parameters, but at the same time you fail to supply a no-parameter constructor. In this case the compiler will not generate a default constructor for `GenericCustomer`, so when it tries to generate the default constructors for any derived class, it'll again find that it can't because a no-parameter base class constructor is not available. A workaround would be to add your own constructors to the derived classes, even if you don't actually need to do anything in these constructors, so that the compiler doesn't try to generate any default constructor for them.

Now that you have all the theoretical background you need, you're ready to move on to an example of how you can neatly add constructors to a hierarchy of classes. In the next section, you start adding constructors that take parameters to the MortimerPhones example.

## *Adding constructors with parameters to a hierarchy*

You're going to start with a one-parameter constructor for `GenericCustomer`, which controls that customers can be instantiated only when they supply their names:

```
abstract class GenericCustomer
{
   private string name;
   public GenericCustomer(string name)
   {
      this.name = name;
   }
}
```

So far, so good. However, as mentioned previously, this will cause a compilation error when the compiler tries to create a default constructor for any derived classes, because the default compiler-generated constructors for `Nevermore60Customer` will try to call a no-parameter `GenericCustomer` constructor and `GenericCustomer` does not possess such a constructor. Therefore, you'll need to supply your own constructors to the derived classes to avoid a compilation error:

```
class Nevermore60Customer : GenericCustomer
{
   private uint highCostMinutesUsed;
   public Nevermore60Customer(string name)
      : base(name)
   {
   }
}
```

Now instantiation of `Nevermore60Customer` objects can only take place when a string containing the customer's name is supplied, which is what you want anyway. The interesting thing is what the `Nevermore60Customer` constructor does with this string. Remember that it can't initialize the `name` field itself, because it has no access to private fields in its base class. Instead, it passes the name through to the base class for the `GenericCustomer` constructor to handle. It does this by specifying that the base class constructor to be executed first is the one that takes the name as a parameter. Other than that, it doesn't take any action of its own.

Next, you're going to investigate what happens if you have different overloads of the constructor as well as a class hierarchy to deal with. To this end, assume that Nevermore60 customers may have been referred to MortimerPhones by a friend as part of one of those sign-up-a-friend-and-get-a-discount offers. This means that when you construct a `Nevermore60Customer`, you may need to pass in the referrer's name as well. In real life, the constructor would have to do something complicated with the name, like process the discount, but here you'll just store the referrer's name in another field.

# Inheritance

The `Nevermore60Customer` definition will now look like this:

```
class Nevermore60Customer : GenericCustomer
{
   public Nevermore60Customer(string name, string referrerName)
      : base(name)
   {
      this.referrerName = referrerName;
   }

   private string referrerName;
   private uint highCostMinutesUsed;
```

The constructor takes the name and passes it to the `GenericCustomer` constructor for processing. `referrerName` is the variable that is your responsibility here, so the constructor deals with that parameter in its main body.

However, not all `Nevermore60Customers` will have a referrer, so you still need a constructor that doesn't require this parameter (or a constructor that gives you a default value for it). In fact, you will specify that if there is no referrer, then the `referrerName` field should be set to "`<None>`", using the following one-parameter constructor:

```
public Nevermore60Customer(string name)
   : this(name, "<None>")
{
}
```

You've now got all your constructors set up correctly. It's instructive to examine the chain of events that now occurs when you execute a line like this:

```
GenericCustomer customer = new Nevermore60Customer("Arabel Jones");
```

The compiler sees that it needs a one-parameter constructor that takes one string, so the constructor it will identify is the last one that you've defined:

```
public Nevermore60Customer(string Name)
   : this(Name, "<None>")
```

When you instantiate `customer`, this constructor will be called. It immediately transfers control to the corresponding `Nevermore60Customer` two-parameter constructor, passing it the values "`Arabel Jones`", and "`<None>`". Looking at the code for this constructor, you see that it in turn immediately passes control to the one-parameter `GenericCustomer` constructor, giving it the string "`Arabel Jones`", and in turn that constructor passes control to the `System.Object` default constructor. Only now do the constructors execute. First, the `System.Object` constructor executes. Next comes the `GenericCustomer` constructor, which initializes the `name` field. Then the `Nevermore60Customer` two-parameter constructor gets control back, and sorts out initializing the `referrerName` to "`<None>`". Finally, the `Nevermore60Customer` one-parameter constructor gets to execute; this constructor doesn't do anything else.

# Chapter 4

As you can see, this is a very neat and well-designed process. Each constructor handles initialization of the variables that are obviously its responsibility, and in the process your class has been correctly instantiated and prepared for use. If you follow the same principles when you write your own constructors for your classes, you should find that even the most complex classes get initialized smoothly and without any problems.

## Modifiers

You have already encountered quite a number of so-called modifiers — keywords that can be applied to a type or to a member. Modifiers can indicate the visibility of a method, such as `public` or `private`, or the nature of an item, such as whether a method is `virtual` or `abstract`. C# has a number of modifiers, and at this point it's worth taking a minute to provide the complete list.

### *Visibility Modifiers*

Visibility modifiers indicate which other code items can view an item.

| Modifier | Applies To | Description |
| --- | --- | --- |
| `public` | Any types or members | The item is visible to any other code. |
| `protected` | Any member of a type, also any nested type | The item is visible only to any derived type. |
| `internal` | Any member of a type, also any nested type | The item is visible only within its containing assembly. |
| `private` | Any types or members | The item is visible only inside the type to which it belongs. |
| `protected internal` | Any member of a type, also any nested type | The item is visible to any code within its containing assembly and also to any code inside a derived type. |

Note that type definitions can be public or private, depending on whether you want the type to be visible outside its containing assembly.

```
public class MyClass
{
   // etc.
```

You cannot define types as protected, internal, or protected internal, because these visibility levels would be meaningless for a type contained in a namespace. Hence these visibilities can only be applied to members. However, you can define nested types (that is, types contained within other types) with these visibilities, because in this case the type also has the status of a member. Hence, the following code is correct:

# Inheritance

```
public class OuterClass
{
  protected class InnerClass
  {
        // etc.
  }
  // etc.
}
```

If you have a nested type, the inner type is always able to see all members of the outer type. Therefore with the preceding code, any code inside `InnerClass` always has access to all members of `OuterClass`, even where those members are private.

## Other Modifiers

The modifiers in the following table can be applied to members of types, and have various uses. A few of these modifiers also make sense when applied to types.

| Modifier | Applies To | Description |
| --- | --- | --- |
| `new` | Function members | The member hides an inherited member with the same signature. |
| `static` | All members | The member does not operate on a specific instance of the class. |
| `virtual` | Classes and function members only | The member can be overridden by a derived class. |
| `abstract` | Function members only | A virtual member that defines the signature of the member, but doesn't provide an implementation. |
| `override` | Function members only | The member overrides an inherited virtual or abstract member. |
| `sealed` | Classes | The member overrides an inherited virtual member, but cannot be overridden by any classes that inherit from this class. Must be used in conjunction with `override`. |
| `extern` | static [DllImport] methods only | The member is implemented externally, in a different language. |

Of these, `internal` and `protected internal` are the ones that are new to C# and the .NET Framework. `internal` acts in much the same way as `public`, but access is confined to other code in the same assembly — that is, code that is being compiled at the same time in the same program. You can use `internal` to ensure all the other classes that you are writing have access to a particular member, while at the same time hiding it from other code written by other organizations. `protected internal` combines protected and internal, but in an OR sense, not an AND sense. A protected internal member can be seen by any code in the same assembly. It can also be seen by any derived classes, even those in other assemblies.

# Chapter 4

# Interfaces

As mentioned earlier, by deriving from an interface a class is declaring that it implements certain functions. Because not all object-oriented languages support interfaces, this section examines C#'s implementation of interfaces in detail.

> *Developers familiar with COM should be aware that, although conceptually C# interfaces are similar to COM interfaces, they are not the same thing. The underlying architecture is different. For example, C# interfaces do not derive from IUnknown. A C# interface provides a contract stated in terms of .NET functions. Unlike a COM interface, a C# interface does not represent any kind of binary standard.*

This section illustrates interfaces by presenting the complete definition of one of the interfaces that has been predefined by Microsoft, `System.IDisposable`. `IDisposable` contains one method, `Dispose()`, which is intended to be implemented by classes to clean up code:

```
public interface IDisposable
{
    void Dispose();
}
```

This code shows that declaring an interface works syntactically in pretty much the same way as declaring an abstract class. You should be aware, however, that it is not permitted to supply implementations of any of the members of an interface. In general, an interface can only contain declarations of methods, properties, indexers, and events.

You can never instantiate an interface; it only contains the signatures of its members. An interface has neither constructors (how can you construct something that you can't instantiate?) nor fields (because that would imply some internal implementation). An interface definition is also not allowed to contain operator overloads, though that's not because there is any problem in principle with declaring them — there isn't; it is because interfaces are usually intended to be public contracts, and having operator overloads would cause some incompatibility problems with other .NET languages, such as Visual Basic .NET, which do not support operator overloading.

It is also not permitted to declare modifiers on the members in an interface definition. Interface members are always implicitly `public`, and cannot be declared as `virtual` or `static`. That's up to implementing classes to decide. It is therefore fine for implementing classes to declare access modifiers, as is done in the example in this section.

Take for example `IDisposable`. If a class wants to declare publicly that it implements the `Dispose()` method, it must implement `IDisposable` — which in C# terms means that the class derives from `IDisposable`.

```
class SomeClass : IDisposable
{
    // this class MUST contain an implementation of the
    // IDisposable.Dispose() method, otherwise
    // you get a compilation error
    public void Dispose()
    {
```

# Inheritance

```
            // implementation of Dispose() method
        }
        // rest of class
    }
```

In this example, if `SomeClass` derives from `IDisposable` but doesn't contain a `Dispose()` implementation with the exact same signature as defined in `IDisposable`, you get a compilation error because the class would be breaking its agreed contract to implement `IDisposable`. Of course, there's no problem for the compiler about a class having a `Dispose()` method but not deriving from `IDisposable`. The problem, then, would be that other code would have no way of recognizing that `SomeClass` has agreed to support the `IDisposable` features.

> `IDisposable` *is a relatively simple interface because it defines only one method. Most interfaces will contain more members.*

Another good example of an interface is provided by the `foreach` loop in C#. In principle, the `foreach` loop works internally by querying the object to find out whether it implements an interface called `System.Collections.IEnumerable`. If it does, the C# compiler will inject IL code, which uses the methods on this interface to iterate through the members of the collection. If it doesn't, `foreach` will raise an exception. The `IEnumerable` interface is examined in more detail in Chapter 9, "Collections." It's worth pointing out that both `IEnumerable` and `IDisposable` are somewhat special interfaces to the extent that they are actually recognized by the C# compiler, which takes account of these interfaces in the code that it generates. Obviously, any interfaces that you define yourself won't be so privileged!

## *Defining and Implementing Interfaces*

This section illustrates how to define and use interfaces through developing a short program that follows the interface inheritance paradigm. The example is based on bank accounts. Assume you are writing code that will ultimately allow computerized transfers between bank accounts. And assume for this example that there are many companies that may implement bank accounts, but they have all mutually agreed that any classes that represent bank accounts will implement an interface, `IBankAccount`, which exposes methods to deposit or withdraw money, and a property to return the balance. It is this interface that will allow outside code to recognize the various bank account classes implemented by different bank accounts. Although the aim is to allow the bank accounts to talk to each other to allow transfers of funds between accounts, we won't introduce that feature just yet.

To keep things simple, you will keep all the code for the example in the same source file. Of course, if something like the example were used in real life, you could surmise that the different bank account classes would not only be compiled to different assemblies but would be hosted on different machines owned by the different banks. (How .NET assemblies hosted on different machines can communicate is explored in Chapter 29, ".NET Remoting.") That's all much too complicated for our purposes here. However, to maintain some attempt at realism, you will define different namespaces for the different companies.

To begin, you need to define the `IBank` interface:

```
namespace Wrox.ProCSharp
{
    public interface IBankAccount
    {
```

```
            void PayIn(decimal amount);
            bool Withdraw(decimal amount);
            decimal Balance
            {
                get;
            }
        }
    }
```

Notice the name of the interface, `IBankAccount`. It's a convention that an interface name traditionally starts with the letter I, so that you know that it's an interface.

> Chapter 2, "C# Basics," pointed out that, in most cases, .NET usage guidelines discourage the so-called Hungarian notation in which names are preceded by a letter that indicates the type of object being defined. Interfaces are one of the few exceptions in which Hungarian notation is recommended.

The idea is that you can now write classes that represent bank accounts. These classes don't have to be related to each other in any way; they can be completely different classes. They will, however, all declare that they represent bank accounts by the mere fact that they implement the `IBankAccount` interface.

Let's start off with the first class, a saver account run by the Royal Bank of Venus:

```
namespace Wrox.ProCSharp.VenusBank
{
    public class SaverAccount : IBankAccount
    {
        private decimal balance;
        public void PayIn(decimal amount)
        {
            balance += amount;
        }
        public bool Withdraw(decimal amount)
        {
            if (balance >= amount)
            {
                balance -= amount;
                return true;
            }
            Console.WriteLine("Withdrawal attempt failed.");
            return false;
        }
        public decimal Balance
        {
            get
            {
                return balance;
            }
        }
        public override string ToString()
        {
            return String.Format("Venus Bank Saver: Balance = {0,6:C}", balance);
        }
    }
}
```

# Inheritance

It should be pretty obvious what the implementation of this class does. You maintain a private field, `balance`, and adjust this amount when money is deposited or withdrawn. You display an error message if an attempt to withdraw money fails because there is insufficient money in the account. Notice also that, because we want to keep the code as simple as possible, you are not implementing extra properties, such as the account holder's name! In real life that would be pretty essential information, but for this example it's unnecessarily complicated.

The only really interesting line in this code is the class declaration:

```
public class SaverAccount : IBankAccount
```

You've declared that `SaverAccount` derives from one interface, `IBankAccount`, and you have not explicitly indicated any other base classes (which of course means that `SaverAccount` derives directly from `System.Object`). By the way, derivation from interfaces acts completely independently from derivation from classes.

Being derived from `IBankAccount` means that `SaverAccount` gets all the members of `IBankAccount`. But because an interface doesn't actually implement any of its methods, `SaverAccount` must provide its own implementations of all of them. If any implementations are missing, you can rest assured that the compiler will complain. Recall also that the interface just indicates the presence of its members. It's up to the class to decide if it wants any of them to be `virtual` or `abstract` (though `abstract` functions are of course only allowed if the class itself is `abstract`). For this particular example, you don't have any reason to make any of the interface functions virtual.

To illustrate how different classes can implement the same interface, assume the Planetary Bank of Jupiter also implements a class to represent one of its bank accounts — a Gold Account:

```
namespace Wrox.ProCSharp.JupiterBank
{
   public class GoldAccount : IBankAccount
   {
      // etc
   }
}
```

We won't present details of the `GoldAccount` class here; in the sample code, it's basically identical to the implementation of `SaverAccount`. We stress that `GoldAccount` has no connection with `VenusAccount`, other than that they happen to implement the same interface.

Now that you have your classes, you can test them out. You first need a couple of `using` statements:

```
using System;
using Wrox.ProCSharp;
using Wrox.ProCSharp.VenusBank;
using Wrox.ProCSharp.JupiterBank;
```

Now you need a `Main()` method:

```
namespace Wrox.ProCSharp
{
   class MainEntryPoint
   {
```

```
        static void Main()
        {
            IBankAccount venusAccount = new SaverAccount();
            IBankAccount jupiterAccount = new GoldAccount();
            venusAccount.PayIn(200);
            venusAccount.Withdraw(100);
            Console.WriteLine(venusAccount.ToString());
            jupiterAccount.PayIn(500);
            jupiterAccount.Withdraw(600);
            jupiterAccount.Withdraw(100);
            Console.WriteLine(jupiterAccount.ToString());
        }
    }
}
```

This code (which if you download the sample, you can find in the file `BankAccounts.cs`) produces this output:

```
C:> BankAccounts
Venus Bank Saver: Balance = £100.00
Withdrawal attempt failed.
Jupiter Bank Saver: Balance = £400.00
```

The main point to notice about this code is the way that you have declared both your reference variables as `IBankAccount` references. This means that they can point to any instance of any class that implements this interface. It does, however, mean that you can only call methods that are part of this interface through these references — if you want to call any methods implemented by a class that are not part of the interface, you need to cast the reference to the appropriate type. In the example code, you were able to call `ToString()` (not implemented by `IBankAccount`) without any explicit cast, purely because `ToString()` is a `System.Object` method, so the C# compiler knows that it will be supported by any class (put differently, the cast from any interface to `System.Object` is implicit). Chapter 5, "Operators and Casts," covers the syntax for how to perform casts.

Interface references can in all respects be treated like class references — but the power of an interface reference is that it can refer to any class that implements that interface. For example, this allows you to form arrays of interfaces, where each element of the array is a different class:

```
IBankAccount[] accounts = new IBankAccount[2];
accounts[0] = new SaverAccount();
accounts[1] = new GoldAccount();
Note, however, that we'd get a compiler error if we tried something like this
accounts[1] = new SomeOtherClass();     // SomeOtherClass does NOT implement
                                        // IBankAccount: WRONG!!
```

This causes a compilation error similar to this:

```
Cannot implicitly convert type 'Wrox.ProCSharp.SomeOtherClass' to
'Wrox.ProCSharp.IBankAccount'
```

## Derived Interfaces

It's possible for interfaces to inherit from each other in the same way that classes do. This concept is illustrated by defining a new interface, `ITransferBankAccount`, which has the same features as `IBankAccount` but also defines a method to transfer money directly to a different account:

```
namespace Wrox.ProCSharp
{
   public interface ITransferBankAccount : IBankAccount
   {
      bool TransferTo(IBankAccount destination, decimal amount);
   }
}
```

Because `ITransferBankAccount` derives from `IBankAccount`, it gets all the members of `IBankAccount` as well as its own. That means that any class that implements (derives from) `ITransferBankAccount` must implement all the methods of `IBankAccount`, as well as the new `TransferTo()` method defined in `ITransferBankAccount`. Failure to implement all of these methods will result in a compilation error.

Note that `TransferTo()` method uses an `IBankAccount` interface reference for the destination account. This illustrates the usefulness of interfaces: When implementing and then invoking this method, you don't need to know anything about what type of object you are transferring money to—all you need to know is that this object implements `IBankAccount`.

To illustrate `ITransferBankAccount`, assume that the Planetary Bank of Jupiter also offers a current account. Most of the implementation of the `CurrentAccount` class is identical to the implementations of `SaverAccount` and `GoldAccount` (again, this is just in order to keep this example simple—that won't normally be the case), so in the following code just the differences are highlighted:

```
public class CurrentAccount : ITransferBankAccount
{
   private decimal balance;
   public void PayIn(decimal amount)
   {
      balance += amount;
   }
   public bool Withdraw(decimal amount)
   {
      if (balance >= amount)
      {
         balance -= amount;
         return true;
      }
      Console.WriteLine("Withdrawal attempt failed.");
      return false;
   }
   public decimal Balance
   {
      get
      {
         return balance;
      }
```

```
        }
        public bool TransferTo(IBankAccount destination, decimal amount)
        {
            bool result;
            if ((result = Withdraw(amount)) == true)
                destination.PayIn(amount);
            return result;
        }
        public override string ToString()
        {
            return String.Format("Jupiter Bank Current Account: Balance = {0,6:C}",
                                                                        balance);
        }
    }
}
```

The class can be demonstrated with this code:

```
static void Main()
{
    IBankAccount venusAccount = new SaverAccount();
    ITransferBankAccount jupiterAccount = new CurrentAccount();
    venusAccount.PayIn(200);
    jupiterAccount.PayIn(500);
    jupiterAccount.TransferTo(venusAccount, 100);
    Console.WriteLine(venusAccount.ToString());
    Console.WriteLine(jupiterAccount.ToString());
}
```

This code (`CurrentAccount.cs`) produces the following output, which as you can verify shows the correct amounts have been transferred:

```
C:> CurrentAccount
Venus Bank Saver: Balance = £300.00
Jupiter Bank Current Account: Balance = £400.00
```

# Summary

This chapter examined how to code inheritance in C#. You have seen that C# offers rich support for both multiple interface and single implementation inheritance, as well as provides a number of useful syntactical constructs designed to assist in making code more robust, such as the `override` keyword, which indicates when a function should override a base function; the `new` keyword, which indicates when a function hides a base function; and the rigid rules for constructor initializers that are designed to ensure that constructors are designed to interoperate in a robust manner.

Chapter 5 examines C#'s support for operators, operator overloads, and casting between types.

# Operators and Casts

The preceding chapters have covered most of what you need to start writing useful programs using C#. This chapter completes the discussion of the essential language elements and goes on to discuss powerful aspects of C# that allow you to extend the capabilities of the C# language. Specifically, this chapter discusses the following:

- The operators available in C#
- The idea of equality when dealing with reference and value types
- Data conversion between the primitive data types
- Converting value types to reference types using boxing
- Converting between reference types by casting
- Overloading the standard operators to support operations on the custom types you define
- Adding cast operators to the custom types you define to support seamless data type conversions

## Operators

Although most of C#'s operators should be familiar to C and C++ developers, this section discusses the most important ones for the benefit of new programmers and Visual Basic converts, and to shed light on some of the changes introduced with C#.

# Chapter 5

C# supports the operators listed in the following table, although four (`sizeof`, `*`, `->`, and `&`) are only available in unsafe code (code that bypasses C#'s type safety checking), which is discussed in Chapter 7, "Memory Management and Pointers":

| Category | Operator |
| --- | --- |
| Arithmetic | `+ - * / %` |
| Logical | `& | ^ ~ && || !` |
| String concatenation | `+` |
| Increment and decrement | `++ --` |
| Bit shifting | `<< >>` |
| Comparison | `== != < > <= >=` |
| Assignment | `= += -= *= /= %= &= |= ^= <<= >>=` |
| Member access (for objects and structs) | `.` |
| Indexing (for arrays and indexers) | `[ ]` |
| Cast | `( )` |
| Conditional (the Ternary Operator) | `?:` |
| Delegate concatenation and removal (discussed in Chapter 6, "Delegates and Events") | `+ -` |
| Object Creation | `new` |
| Type information | `sizeof` (unsafe code only) `is typeof as` |
| Overflow exception control | `checked unchecked` |
| Indirection and Address | `* -> &` (unsafe code only) `[ ]` |
| Namespace alias qualifier (discussed in Chapter 2, "C# Basics") | `::` |
| Null coalescing operator | `??` |

One of the biggest pitfalls to watch out for when using C# operators is that, like other C-style languages, C# uses different operators for assignment =, and comparison ==. For instance, the following statement means *let x equal three*:

```
x = 3;
```

If you now want to compare x to a value, you need to use the double equals sign ==:

```
if (x == 3)
```

# Operators and Casts

Fortunately, C#'s strict type safety rules prevent the very common C error where assignment is performed instead of comparison in logical statements. This means that in C# the following statement will generate a compiler error:

```
if (x = 3)
```

Visual Basic programmers who are accustomed to using the ampersand (&) character to concatenate strings will have to make an adjustment. In C#, the plus sign (+) is used instead, whereas & denotes a bit-wise AND between two different integer values. | allows you to perform a bit-wise OR between two integers. Visual Basic programmers also might not recognize the modulus (%) arithmetic operator. This returns the remainder after division, so for example x % 5 returns 2 if x is equal to 7.

You will use few pointers in C#, so you will use few indirection operators. Specifically, the only place you will use them is within blocks of unsafe code, because that's the only place in C# where pointers are allowed. Pointers and unsafe code are discussed in Chapter 7.

## *Operator Shortcuts*

The following table shows the full list of shortcut assignment operators available in C#.

| Shortcut Operator | Equivalent To |
|---|---|
| x++, ++x | x = x + 1 |
| x--, --x | x = x - 1 |
| x += y | x = x + y |
| x -= y | x = x - y |
| x *= y | x = x * y |
| x /= y | x = x / y |
| x %= y | x = x % y |
| x >>= y | x = x >> y |
| x <<= y | x = x << y |
| x &= y | x = x & y |
| x |= y | x = x | y |
| x ^= y | x = x ^ y |

You may be wondering why there are two examples each for the ++ increment and the -- decrement operators. Placing the operator *before* the expression is known as a *prefix*, and placing the operator *after* the expression is known as a *postfix*, and there is a difference in the way they behave.

The increment and decrement operators can act both as whole expressions and within expressions. When used by themselves the effect of both the prefix and postfix versions is identical and corresponds to the statement x = x + 1. When used within larger expressions, the prefix operator will increment the value of x *before* the expression is evaluated; in other words, x is incremented and the new value is used in the expression. In contrast, the postfix operator increments the value of x *after* the expression is evaluated — the expression is evaluated using the original value of x. The following example uses the increment operator (++) as an example to demonstrate the difference between the prefix and postfix behavior:

```
int x = 5;
if (++x == 6)
{
    Console.WriteLine("This will execute");
}
if (x++ == 7)
{
    Console.WriteLine("This won't");
}
```

The first if condition evaluates to true, because x is incremented from 5 to 6 before the expression is evaluated. The condition in the second if statement is false, however, because x is incremented to 7 only after the entire expression has been evaluated (while x = 6).

The prefix and postfix operators --x and x-- behave in the same way, but decrement rather than increment the operand.

The other shortcut operators, such as += and -=, require two operands, and are used to modify the value of the first operand by performing an arithmetic, logical, or bit-wise operation on it. For example, the next two lines are equivalent:

```
x += 5;
x = x + 5;
```

## *The Ternary Operator*

The ternary operator (?:) is a shorthand form of the if...else construction. It gets its name from the fact that it involves three operands. It allows you to evaluate a condition, returning one value if that condition is true, or another value if it is false. The syntax is

```
condition ? true_value : false_value
```

Here, *condition* is the Boolean expression to be evaluated, *true_value* is the value that will be returned if *condition* is true, and *false_value* is the value that will be returned otherwise.

When used sparingly, the ternary operator can add a dash of terseness to your programs. It is especially handy for providing one of a couple of arguments to a function that is being invoked. You can use it to quickly convert a Boolean value to a string value of true or false. It is also handy for displaying the correct singular or plural form of a word, for example:

```
int x = 1;
string s = x.ToString() + " ";
s += (x == 1 ? "man" : "men");
Console.WriteLine(s);
```

# Operators and Casts

This code displays 1 man if x is equal to one but will display the correct plural form for any other number. Note, however, that if your output needs to be localized to different languages, you will have to write more sophisticated routines to take account of the different grammatical rules of different languages.

## The checked and unchecked Operators

Consider the following code:

```
byte b = 255;
b++;
Console.WriteLine(b.ToString());
```

The `byte` data type can only hold values in the range zero to 255, so incrementing the value of b causes an overflow. How the CLR handles this depends on a number of issues, including compiler options, so whenever there's a risk of an unintentional overflow, you need some way of making sure that you get the result you want.

To do this, C# provides the `checked` and `unchecked` operators. If you mark a block of code as `checked`, the CLR will enforce overflow checking, and throw an `OverflowException` if an overflow occurs. Let's change the code to include the `checked` operator:

```
byte b = 255;
checked
{
    b++;
}
Console.WriteLine(b.ToString());
```

When you try to run this code, you will get an error message like this:

```
Unhandled Exception: System.OverflowException: Arithmetic operation resulted in an
overflow.
   at Wrox.ProCSharp.Basics.OverflowTest.Main(String[] args)
```

*You can enforce overflow checking for all unmarked code in your program by specifying the* /checked *compiler option.*

If you want to suppress overflow checking, you can mark the code as `unchecked`:

```
byte b = 255;
unchecked
{
    b++;
}
Console.WriteLine(b.ToString());
```

In this case, no exception will be raised, but you will lose data — because the `byte` type can't hold a value of 256, the overflowing bits will be discarded, and your b variable will hold a value of zero.

Note that `unchecked` is the default behavior. The only time you are likely to need to explicitly use the `unchecked` keyword is if you need a few unchecked lines of code inside a larger block that you have explicitly marked as `checked`.

## The is Operator

The `is` operator allows you to check whether an object is compatible with a specific type. For example, to check whether a variable is compatible with the `object` type:

*The phrase "is compatible" means that an object is either of that type or is derived from that type.*

```
int i = 10;
if (i is object)
{
    Console.WriteLine("i is an object");
}
```

`int`, like all C# data types, inherits from `object`; therefore the expression `i is object` will evaluate to `true`, and the message will be displayed.

## The as Operator

The `as` operator is used to perform explicit type conversions of reference types. If the type being converted is compatible with the specified type, conversion is performed successfully. However, if the types are incompatible, the `as` operator returns the value `null`. As shown in the following code, attempting to convert an `object` reference to a `string` will return null if the `object` reference does not actually refer to a `string` instance:

```
object o1 = "Some String";
object o2 = 5;

string s1 = o1 as string;    // s1 = "Some String"
string s2 = o2 as string;    // s2 = null
```

The `as` operator allows you to perform a safe type conversion in a single step without the need to first test the type using the `is` operator and then perform the conversion.

## The sizeof Operator

You can determine the size (in bytes) required on the stack by a value type using the `sizeof` operator:

```
unsafe
{
    Console.WriteLine(sizeof(int));
}
```

This will display the number 4, because an `int` is four bytes long.

Notice that you can only use the `sizeof` operator in unsafe code. Chapter 7 looks at unsafe code in more detail.

# Operators and Casts

## The typeof Operator

The `typeof` operator returns a `System.Type` object representing a specified type. For example, `typeof(string)` will return a `Type` object representing the `System.String` type. This is useful when you want to use reflection to find out information about an object dynamically. Chapter 11 looks at reflection.

## Nullable Types and Operators

If you use nullable types in your programs, you must always consider the effect a `null` value can have when used in conjunction with the various operators. Usually, when using a unary or binary operator with nullable types, the result will be `null` if one or both of the operands is `null`. For example:

```
int? a = null;

int? b = a + 4;      // b = null
int? c = a * 5;      // c = null
```

However, when comparing nullable types, if only one of the operands is `null`, the comparison will always equate to `false`. This means you cannot assume a condition is `true` just because its opposite is `false`, as often happens in programs using non-nullable types. For example:

```
int? a = null;
int? b = -5;

if (a >= b)
    System.Console.WriteLine("a >= b");
else
    System.Console.WriteLine("a < b");
```

*The possibility of a `null` value means that you cannot freely combine nullable and non-nullable types in an expression. This is discussed in the "Type Conversions" section later in this chapter.*

## The Null Coalescing Operator

The null coalescing operator (`??`) provides a shorthand mechanism to cater to the possibility of `null` values when working with nullable and reference types. The operator is placed between two operands—the first operand must be a nullable type or reference type, and the second operand must be of the same type as the first or of a type that is implicitly convertible to the type of the first operand. The null coalescing operator evaluates as follows: if the first operand is not `null`, then the overall expression has the value of the first operand. However, if the first operand is `null`, the overall expression has the value of the second operand. For example:

```
int? a = null;
int b;

b = a ?? 10;     // b has the value 10
a = 3;
b = a ?? 10;     // b has the value 3
```

If the second operand cannot be implicitly converted to the type of the first operand, a compile-time error is generated.

## *Operator Precedence*

The following table shows the order of precedence of the C# operators. The operators at the top of the table are those with the highest precedence (that is, the ones evaluated first in an expression containing multiple operators).

| Group | Operators |
| --- | --- |
| Primary | `() . [] x++ x-- new typeof sizeof checked unchecked` |
| Unary | `+ - ! ~ ++x --x` and casts |
| Multiplication/Division | `* / %` |
| Addition/Subtraction | `+ -` |
| Bitwise shift operators | `<< >>` |
| Relational | `< > <= >= is as` |
| Comparison | `== !=` |
| Bitwise AND | `&` |
| Bitwise XOR | `^` |
| Bitwise OR | `|` |
| Boolean AND | `&&` |
| Boolean OR | `||` |
| Ternary operator | `?:` |
| Assignment | `= += -= *= /= %= &= |= ^= <<= >>= >>>=` |

*In complex expressions, you should avoid relying on operator precedence to produce the correct result. Using parentheses to specify the order in which you want operators applied clarifies your code and avoids potential confusion.*

# Type Safety

Chapter 1, ".NET Architecture," noted that the Intermediate Language (IL) enforces strong type safety upon its code. Strong typing enables many of the services provided by .NET, including security and language interoperability. As you would expect from a language compiled into IL, C# is also strongly typed. Among other things, this means that data types are not always seamlessly interchangeable. This section looks at conversions between primitive types.

# Operators and Casts

C# also supports conversions between different reference types and allows you to define how data types that you create behave when converted to and from other types. Both these topics are discussed later in this chapter.

Generics, a new feature included in C# 2.0, allow you to avoid some of the most common situations in which you would need to perform type conversions. See Chapter 10, "Generics," for details.

## Type Conversions

Often, you need to convert data from one type to another. Consider the following code:

```
byte value1 = 10;
byte value2 = 23;
byte total;
total = value1 + value2;
Console.WriteLine(total);
```

When you attempt to compile these lines, you get the error message

```
Cannot implicitly convert type 'int' to 'byte'
```

The problem here is that when you add two bytes together, the result will be returned as an `int`, not as another `byte`. This is because a `byte` can only contain eight bits of data, so adding two bytes together could very easily result in a value that can't be stored in a single `byte`. If you do want to store this result in a `byte` variable, you're going to have to convert it back to a `byte`. The following sections discuss two conversion mechanisms supported by C# — *implicit* and *explicit*.

### Implicit conversions

Conversion between types can normally be achieved automatically (implicitly) only if you can guarantee that the value is not changed in any way. This is why the previous code failed; by attempting a conversion from an `int` to a `byte`, you were potentially losing three bytes of data. The compiler isn't going to let you do that unless you explicitly tell it that that's what you want to do. If you store the result in a `long` instead of a `byte`, however, you'll have no problems:

```
byte value1 = 10;
byte value2 = 23;
long total;              // this will compile fine
total = value1 + value2;
Console.WriteLine(total);
```

This is because a `long` holds more bytes of data than a `byte`, so there is no risk of data being lost. In these circumstances, the compiler is happy to make the conversion for you, without you needing to ask for it explicitly.

The following table shows the implicit type conversions supported in C#.

| From | To |
|---|---|
| sbyte | short, int, long, float, double, decimal |
| byte | short, ushort, int, uint, long, ulong, float, double, decimal |
| short | int, long, float, double, decimal |
| ushort | int, uint, long, ulong, float, double, decimal |
| int | long, float, double, decimal |
| uint | long, ulong, float, double, decimal |
| long, ulong | float, double, decimal |
| float | double |
| char | ushort, int, uint, long, ulong, float, double, decimal |

As you would expect, you can only perform implicit conversions from a smaller integer type to a larger one, not from larger to smaller. You can also convert between integers and floating-point values; however, the rules are slightly different here. Though you can convert between types of the same size, such as int/uint to float and long/ulong to double, you can also convert from long/ulong back to float. You might lose four bytes of data doing this, but this only means that the value of the float you receive will be less precise than if you had used a double; this is regarded by the compiler as an acceptable possible error because the magnitude of the value is not affected. You can also assign an unsigned variable to a signed variable so long as the limits of value of the unsigned type fit between the limits of the signed variable.

Nullable types introduce additional considerations when implicitly converting value types:

❏ Nullable types implicitly convert to other nullable types following the conversion rules described for non-nullable types in the previous table; that is, int? implicitly converts to long?, float?, double?, and decimal?.

❏ Non-nullable types implicitly convert to nullable types according to the conversion rules described in the preceding table; that is, int implicitly converts to long?, float?, double?, and decimal?.

❏ Nullable types *do not* implicitly convert to non-nullable types; you must perform an explicit conversion as described in the next section. This is because there is the chance a nullable type will have the value null, which cannot be represented by a non-nullable type.

## *Explicit conversions*

Many conversions cannot be implicitly made between types, and the compiler will give an error if any are attempted. These are some of the conversions that cannot be made implicitly:

❏ int to short — May lose data

❏ int to uint — May lose data

❏ uint to int — May lose data

- `float` to `int` — Will lose everything after the decimal point
- Any numeric type to `char` — Will lose data
- Decimal to any numeric type — Because the decimal type is internally structured differently from both integers and floating-point numbers
- `int?` to `int` — The nullable type may have the value `null`

However, you can explicitly carry out such conversions using *casts*. When you cast one type to another, you deliberately force the compiler to make the conversion. A cast looks like this:

```
long val = 30000;
int i = (int)val;   // A valid cast. The maximum int is 2147483647
```

You indicate the type to which you're casting by placing its name in parentheses before the value to be converted. If you are familiar with C, this is the typical syntax for casts. If you are familiar with the C++ special cast keywords such as `static_cast`, these do not exist in C# and you have to use the older C-type syntax.

Casting can be a dangerous operation to undertake. Even a simple cast from a `long` to an `int` can cause problems if the value of the original `long` is greater than the maximum value of an `int`:

```
long val = 3000000000;
int i = (int)val;      // An invalid cast. The maximum int is 2147483647
```

In this case, you will not get an error, but you also will not get the result you expect. If you run this code and output the value stored in i, this is what you get:

```
-1294967296
```

It is good practice to assume that an explicit cast will not give the results you expect. As you saw earlier, C# provides a `checked` operator that you can use to test whether an operation causes an arithmetic overflow. You can use the `checked` operator to check that a cast is safe and to force the runtime to throw an overflow exception if it isn't:

```
long val = 3000000000;
int i = checked ((int)val);
```

Bearing in mind that all explicit casts are potentially unsafe, you should take care to include code in your application to deal with possible failures of the casts. Chapter 12, "Errors and Exceptions," introduces structured exception handling using the `try` and `catch` statements.

Using casts, you can convert most primitive data types from one type to another; for example, in this code the value 0.5 is added to `price`, and the total is cast to an `int`:

```
double price = 25.30;
int approximatePrice = (int)(price + 0.5);
```

This will give the price rounded to the nearest dollar. However, in this conversion, data is lost — namely everything after the decimal point. Therefore, such a conversion should never be used if you want to go on to do more calculations using this modified price value. However, it is useful if you want to output the approximate value of a completed or partially completed calculation—if you do not want to bother the user with lots of figures after the decimal point.

This example shows what happens if you convert an unsigned integer into a `char`:

```
ushort c = 43;
char symbol = (char)c;
Console.WriteLine(symbol);
```

The output is the character that has an ASCII number of 43, the + sign. You can try out any kind of conversion you want between the numeric types (including `char`), and it will work, such as converting a `decimal` into a `char`, or vice versa.

Converting between value types is not just restricted to isolated variables, as you have seen. You can convert an array element of type `double` to a struct member variable of type `int`:

```
struct ItemDetails
{
    public string Description;
    public int ApproxPrice;
}

//...

double[] Prices = { 25.30, 26.20, 27.40, 30.00 };

ItemDetails id;
id.Description = "Whatever";
id.ApproxPrice = (int)(Prices[0] + 0.5);
```

To convert a nullable type to a non-nullable type or another nullable type where data loss may occur, you must use an explicit cast. Importantly, this is true even when converting between elements with the same basic underlying type, for example, `int?` to `int` or `float?` to `float`. This is because the nullable type may have the value `null`, which cannot be represented by the non-nullable type. As long as an explicit cast between two equivalent non-nullable types is possible, so is the explicit cast between nullable types. However, if casting from a nullable to non-nullable type and the variable has the value `null`, an `InvalidOperationException` is thrown. For example:

```
int? a = null;
int  b = (int)a;    // Will throw exception
```

Using explicit casts and a bit of care and attention, you can convert any instance of a simple value type to almost any other. However there are limitations on what you can do with explicit type conversions— as far as value types are concerned, you can only convert to and from the numeric and `char` types and `enum` types. You can't directly cast Booleans to any other type or vice versa.

If you need to convert between numeric and string, methods are provided in the .NET class library. The `Object` class implements a `ToString()` method, which has been overridden in all the .NET predefined types and which returns a string representation of the object:

# Operators and Casts

```
int i = 10;
string s = i.ToString();
```

Similarly, if you need to parse a string to retrieve a numeric or Boolean value, you can use the `Parse()` method supported by all the predefined value types:

```
string s = "100";
int i = int.Parse(s);
Console.WriteLine(i + 50);   // Add 50 to prove it is really an int
```

Note that `Parse()` will register an error by throwing an exception if it is unable to convert the string (for example, if you try to convert the string `Hello` to an integer). Exceptions are covered in Chapter 12.

## Boxing and Unboxing

In Chapter 2, "C# Basics," you learned that all types, both the simple predefined types such as `int` and `char`, and the complex types such as classes and structs, derive from the `object` type. This means that you can treat even literal values as though they were objects:

```
string s = 10.ToString();
```

However, you also saw that C# data types are divided into value types, which are allocated on the stack, and reference types, which are allocated on the heap. How does this square with the ability to call methods on an `int`, if the `int` is nothing more than a four-byte value on the stack?

The way C# achieves this is through a bit of magic called *boxing*. Boxing and its counterpart, *unboxing*, allow you to convert value types to reference types and then back to value types. This is included in the section on casting because this is essentially what you are doing—you are casting your value to the `object` type. Boxing is the term used to describe the transformation of a value type to a reference type. Basically, the runtime creates a temporary reference-type box for the object on the heap.

This conversion can occur implicitly, as in the preceding example, but you can also perform it manually:

```
int i = 20;
object o = i;
```

Unboxing is the term used to describe the reverse process, where the value of a previously boxed value type is cast back to a value type. We use the term *cast* here, because this has to be done explicitly. The syntax is similar to explicit type conversions already described:

```
int i = 20;
object o = i;        // Box the int
int j = (int)o;      // Unbox it back into an int
```

You can only unbox a variable that has previously been boxed. If you executed the last line when `o` is not a boxed `int`, you will get an exception thrown at runtime.

One word of warning: When unboxing, you have to be careful that the receiving value variable has enough room to store all the bytes in the value being unboxed. C#'s ints, for example, are only 32 bits long, so unboxing a long value (64 bits) into an int as shown here will result in an InvalidCastException:

```
long a = 333333423;
object b = (object)a;
int c = (int)b;
```

# Comparing Objects for Equality

After discussing operators and briefly touching on the equality operator, it is worth considering for a moment what equality means when dealing with instances of classes and structs. Understanding the mechanics of object equality is essential for programming logical expressions and is important when implementing operator overloads and casts, which is the topic of the rest of this chapter.

The mechanisms of object equality are different depending on whether you are comparing reference types (instances of classes), or value types (the primitive data types, instances of structs or enums). The following sections look at the equality of reference and value types independently.

## Comparing Reference Types for Equality

One aspect of System.Object that can look surprising at first sight is the fact that it defines three different methods for comparing objects for equality: ReferenceEquals() and two versions of Equals(). Add to this the comparison operator (==), and you actually have four ways of comparing for equality. Some subtle differences exist between the different methods, which are examined next.

### The ReferenceEquals() method

ReferenceEquals() is a static method that tests whether two references refer to the same instance of a class; specifically whether the two references contain the same address in memory. As a static method, it is not possible to override, so the System.Object implementation is what you always have. ReferenceEquals() will always return true if supplied with two references that refer to the same object instance, and false otherwise. It does, however, consider null to be equal to null:

```
SomeClass x, y;
x = new SomeClass();
y = new SomeClass();
bool B1 = ReferenceEquals(null, null);    // returns true
bool B2 = ReferenceEquals(null,x);        // returns false
bool B3 = ReferenceEquals(x, y);          // returns false because x and y
                                          // point to different objects
```

### The virtual Equals() method

The System.Object implementation of the virtual version of Equals() also works by comparing references. However, because this method is virtual, you can override it in your own classes in order to compare objects by value. In particular, if you intend instances of your class to be used as keys in a dictionary, you will need to override this method to compare values. Otherwise, depending on how you override Object.GetHashCode(), the dictionary class that contains your objects will either not work

# Operators and Casts

at all or will work very inefficiently. One point you should note when overriding `Equals()` is that your override should never throw exceptions. Once again, this is because doing so could cause problems for dictionary classes and possibly certain other .NET base classes that internally call this method.

## The static Equals() method

The `static` version of `Equals()` actually does the same thing as the virtual instance version. The difference is that the static version takes two parameters and compares them for equality. This method is able to cope when either of the objects is `null`, and therefore, provides an extra safeguard against throwing exceptions if there is a risk that an object might be `null`. The `static` overload first checks whether the references it has been passed are `null`. If they are both `null`, it returns `true` (because `null` is considered to be equal to `null`). If just one of them is `null`, it returns `false`. If both references actually refer to something, it calls the virtual instance version of `Equals()`. This means that when you override the instance version of `Equals()`, the effect is as if you were overriding the static version as well.

## Comparison operator (==)

The comparison operator can be best seen as an intermediate option between strict value comparison and strict reference comparison. In most cases, writing

```
bool b = (x == y);    // x, y object references
```

means that you are comparing references. However, it is accepted that there are some classes whose meanings are more intuitive if they are treated as values. In those cases, it is better to override the comparison operator to perform a value comparison. Overriding operators is discussed next, but the obvious example of this is the `System.String` class for which Microsoft has overridden this operator to compare the contents of the strings rather than their references.

# Comparing Value Types for Equality

When comparing value types for equality, the same principles hold as for reference types: `Reference Equals()` is used to compare references, `Equals()` is intended for value comparisons, and the comparison operator is viewed as an intermediate case. However the big difference is that value types need to be boxed in order to convert them to references so that methods can be executed on them. In addition, Microsoft has already overloaded the instance `Equals()` method in the `System.ValueType` class in order to test equality appropriate to value types. If you call `sA.Equals(sB)` where `sA` and `sB` are instances of some struct, the return value will be `true` or `false` according to whether `sA` and `sB` contain the same values in all their fields. On the other hand, no overload of `==` is available by default for your own structs. Writing `(sA == sB)` in any expression will result in a compilation error unless you have provided an overload of `==` in your code for the struct in question.

Another point is that `ReferenceEquals()` always returns `false` when applied to value types, because to call this method, the value types will need to be boxed into objects. Even if you write

```
bool b = ReferenceEquals(v,v);    // v is a variable of some value type
```

you will still get the answer of `false` because `v` will be boxed separately when converting each parameter, which means you get different references. Calling `ReferenceEquals()` to compare value types doesn't really make much sense.

Although the default override of `Equals()` supplied by `System.ValueType` will almost certainly be adequate for the vast majority of structs that you define, you might want to override it again for your own structs in order to improve performance. Also, if a value type contains reference types as fields, you might want to override `Equals()` to provide appropriate semantics for these fields, because the default override of `Equals()` will simply compare their addresses.

# Operator Overloading

This section looks at another type of member that you can define for a class or a struct: the *operator overload*.

Operator overloading is something that will be familiar to C++ developers. However, because the concept will be new to both Java and Visual Basic developers, we explain it here. C++ developers will probably prefer to skip ahead to the main example.

The point of operator overloading is that you don't always just want to call methods or properties on objects. Often you need to do things like adding quantities together, multiplying them, or performing logical operations such as comparing objects. Suppose you had defined a class that represents a mathematical matrix. Now in the world of math, matrices can be added together and multiplied, just like numbers. So it's quite plausible that you'd want to write code like this:

```
Matrix a, b, c;
// assume a, b and c have been initialized
Matrix d = c * (a + b);
```

By overloading the operators, you can tell the compiler what + and * do when used in conjunction with a `Matrix`, allowing you to write code like this. If you were coding in a language that didn't support operator overloading, you would have to define methods to perform those operations. The result would certainly be less intuitive, and would probably look something like this:

```
Matrix d = c.Multiply(a.Add(b));
```

With what you've learned so far, operators like + and * have been strictly for use with the predefined data types, and for good reason: the compiler knows what all the common operators mean for those data types. For example, it knows how to add two `long`s or how to divide one `double` by another `double`, and can generate the appropriate intermediate language code. When you define your own classes or structs, however, you have to tell the compiler everything: what methods are available to call, what fields to store with each instance, and so on. Similarly, if you want to use operators with your own types, you'll have to tell the compiler what the relevant operators mean in the context of that class. The way you do that is by defining overloads for the operators.

The other thing we should stress is that overloading isn't just concerned with arithmetic operators. You also need to consider the comparison operators, ==, <, >, !=, >=, and <=. Take the statement `if (a==b)`. For classes, this statement will, by default, compare the references a and b — it tests to see if the references point to the same location in memory, rather than checking to see if the instances actually contain the same data. For the `string` class, this behavior is overridden so that comparing strings really does compare the contents of each string. You might want to do the same for your own classes. For structs, the == operator doesn't do anything at all by default. Trying to compare two structs to see if they are equal produces a compilation error unless you explicitly overload == to tell the compiler how to perform the comparison.

# Operators and Casts

A large number of situations exist in which being able to overload operators will allow you to generate more readable and intuitive code, including:

- Almost any mathematical object such as coordinates, vectors, matrices, tensors, functions, and so on. If you are writing a program that does some mathematical or physical modeling, you will almost certainly use classes representing these objects.
- Graphics programs that use mathematical or coordinate-related objects when calculating positions on screen.
- A class that represents an amount of money (for example, in a financial program).
- A word processing or text analysis program that uses classes representing sentences, clauses and so on; you might want to use operators to combine sentences (a more sophisticated version of concatenation for strings).

However, there are also many types for which operator overloading would not be relevant. Using operator overloading inappropriately will make code that uses your types far more difficult to understand. For example, multiplying two `DateTime` objects just doesn't make any sense conceptually.

## How Operators Work

To understand how to overload operators, it's quite useful to think about what happens when the compiler encounters an operator. Using the addition operator (+) as an example, suppose the compiler processes the following lines of code:

```
int a = 3;
uint b = 2;
double d = 4.0;
long l = a + b;
double x = d + a;
```

What happens when the compiler encounters the following line?

```
long l = a + b;
```

The compiler identifies that it needs to add two integers and assign the result to a `long`. However, the expression a + b is really just an intuitive and convenient syntax for calling a method that adds two numbers together .The method takes two parameters, a and b, and returns their sum. Therefore, the compiler does the same thing as it does for any method call — it looks for the best matching overload of the addition operator based on the parameter types; in this case, one that takes two integers. As with normal overloaded methods, the desired return type does not influence the compiler's choice as to which version of a method it calls. As it happens, the overload called in the example takes two `int` parameters and returns an `int`; this return value is subsequently converted to a `long`.

The next line causes the compiler to use a different overload of the addition operator:

```
double x = d + a;
```

In this instance, the parameters are a `double` and an `int`, but as it happens there isn't an overload of the addition operator that takes this combination of parameters. Instead, the compiler identifies the best matching overload of the addition operator as being the version that takes two doubles as its parameters, and implicitly casts the `int` to a `double`. Adding two doubles requires a different process than adding two integers. Floating-point numbers are stored as a mantissa and an exponent. Adding them involves bit-shifting the mantissa of one of the `double`s so that the two exponents have the same value, adding the mantissas, then shifting the mantissa of the result and adjusting its exponent to maintain the highest possible accuracy in the answer.

Now, you're in a position to see what happens if the compiler finds something like this:

```
Vector vect1, vect2, vect3;
// initialize vect1 and vect2
vect3 = vect1 + vect2;
vect1 = vect1*2;
```

Here, `Vector` is the struct, which is defined in the following section. The compiler will see that it needs to add two `Vector` instances, `vect1` and `vect2`, together. It'll look for an overload of the addition operator, which takes two `Vector` instances as its parameters.

If the compiler finds an appropriate overload, it'll call up the implementation of that operator. If it can't find one, it'll look to see if there is any other overload for + that it can use as a best match — perhaps something that has two parameters of other data types that can be implicitly converted to `Vector` instances. If the compiler can't find a suitable overload, it'll raise a compilation error, just as it would if it couldn't find an appropriate overload for any other method call.

## *Operator Overloading Example: The Vector Struct*

This section demonstrates operator overloading through developing a struct named `Vector` that represents a 3-dimensional mathematical vector. Don't worry if mathematics is not your strong point — we'll keep the vector example very simple. As far as you are concerned, a 3D-vector is just a set of three numbers (doubles) that tell you how far something is moving. The variables representing the numbers are called x, y, and z: x tells you how far something moves East, y tells you how far it moves North, and z tells you how far it moves upward (in height). Combine the three numbers together and you get the total movement. For example, if x=3.0, y=3.0, and z=1.0 (which you'd normally write as (3.0, 3.0, 1.0), you're moving 3 units East, 3 units North, and rising upward by 1 unit.

You can add or multiply vectors by other vectors or by numbers. Incidentally, in this context we use the term *scalar*, which is math-speak for a simple number — in C# terms that's just a `double`. The significance of addition should be clear. If you move first by the vector (3.0, 3.0, 1.0) then you move by the vector (2.0, -4.0, -4.0), the total amount you have moved can be worked out by adding the two vectors. Adding vectors means adding each component individually, so you get (5.0, -1.0, -3.0). In this context, mathematicians write c=a+b, where a and b are the vectors and c is the resulting vector. You want to be able to use the `Vector` struct the same way.

> *The fact that this example will be developed as a struct rather than a class is not significant. Operator overloading works in the same way for both structs and classes.*

The following is the definition for `Vector` — containing the member fields, constructors, and a `ToString()` override so you can easily view the contents of a `Vector`, and finally that operator overload:

# Operators and Casts

```
namespace Wrox.ProCSharp.OOCSharp
{
    struct Vector
    {
        public double x, y, z;

        public Vector(double x, double y, double z)
        {
            this.x = x;
            this.y = y;
            this.z = z;
        }

        public Vector(Vector rhs)
        {
            x = rhs.x;
            y = rhs.y;
            z = rhs.z;
        }

        public override string ToString()
        {
            return "( " + x + " , " + y + " , " + z + " )";
        }
```

This example has two constructors that require the initial value of the vector to be specified, either by passing in the values of each component or by supplying another Vector whose value can be copied. Constructors like the second one that takes single Vector argument are often termed *copy constructors*, because they effectively allow you to initialize a class or struct instance by copying another instance. Note that to keep things simple, the fields are left as `public`. We could have made them `private` and written corresponding properties to access them, but it wouldn't have made any difference to the example, other than to make the code longer.

Here is the interesting part of the Vector struct — the operator overload that provides support for the addition operator:

```
        public static Vector operator + (Vector lhs, Vector rhs)
        {
            Vector result = new Vector(lhs);
            result.x += rhs.x;
            result.y += rhs.y;
            result.z += rhs.z;
            return result;
        }
    }
}
```

The operator overload is declared in much the same way as a method, except the `operator` keyword tells the compiler it's actually an operator overload you're defining. The `operator` keyword is followed by the actual symbol for the relevant operator, in this case the addition operator (+). The return type is whatever type you get when you use this operator. Adding two vectors results in a vector, so the return type is Vector. For this particular override of the addition operator, the return type is the same as the containing class, but that's not necessarily the case as you see later in this example. The two parameters are the things you're operating on. For binary operators (those that take two parameters), like the addition and subtraction operators, the first parameter is the value on the left of the operator, and the second parameter is the value on the right.

C# requires that all operator overloads are declared as `public` and `static`, which means that they are associated with their class or struct, not with a particular instance. Because of this, the body of the operator overload has no access to non-static class members and has no access to the `this` identifier. This is fine because the parameters provide all the input data the operator needs to know to perform its task.

Now that you understand the syntax for the addition operator declaration, you can look at what happens inside the operator:

```
{
    Vector result = new Vector(lhs);
    result.x += rhs.x;
    result.y += rhs.y;
    result.z += rhs.z;
    return result;
}
```

This part of the code is exactly the same as if you were declaring a method, and you should easily be able to convince yourself that this really will return a vector containing the sum of `lhs` and `rhs` as defined. You simply add the members x, y, and z together individually.

Now all you need to do is write some simple code to test the `Vector` struct. Here it is:

```
static void Main()
{
    Vector vect1, vect2, vect3;
    vect1 = new Vector(3.0, 3.0, 1.0);
    vect2 = new Vector(2.0, -4.0, -4.0);
    vect3 = vect1 + vect2;
    Console.WriteLine("vect1 = " + vect1.ToString());
    Console.WriteLine("vect2 = " + vect2.ToString());
    Console.WriteLine("vect3 = " + vect3.ToString());
}
```

Saving this code as `Vectors.cs`, and compiling and running it returns this result:

**Vectors**

```
vect1 = ( 3 , 3 , 1 )
vect2 = ( 2 , -4 , -4 )
vect3 = ( 5 , -1 , -3 )
```

## Adding more overloads

In addition to adding vectors, you can multiply and subtract them and compare their values. In this section, you develop the Vector example further by adding a few more operator overloads. You won't develop the complete set that you'd probably need for a fully functional `Vector` type, but enough to demonstrate some other aspects of operator overloading. First, you'll overload the multiplication operator to support multiplying vectors by a scalar and multiplying vectors by another vector.

Multiplying a vector by a scalar simply means multiplying each component individually by the scalar: for example, 2 * (1.0, 2.5, 2.0) returns (2.0, 5.0, 4.0). The relevant operator overload looks like this:

```
public static Vector operator * (double lhs, Vector rhs)
{
    return new Vector(lhs * rhs.x, lhs * rhs.y, lhs * rhs.z);
}
```

This by itself, however, is not sufficient. If a and b are declared as type Vector, it will allow you to write code like this:

```
b = 2 * a;
```

The compiler will implicitly convert the integer 2 to a double in order to match the operator overload signature. However, code like the following will not compile:

```
b = a * 2;
```

The thing is that the compiler treats operator overloads exactly like method overloads. It examines all the available overloads of a given operator to find the best match. The preceding statement requires the first parameter to be a Vector and the second parameter to be an integer, or something that an integer can be implicitly converted to. You have not provided such an overload. The compiler can't start swapping the order of parameters so the fact that you've provided an overload that takes a double followed by a Vector is not sufficient. You need to explicitly define an overload that takes a Vector followed by a double as well. There are two possible ways of implementing this. The first way involves breaking down the vector multiplication operation in the same way that you've done for all operators so far:

```
public static Vector operator * (Vector lhs, double rhs)
{
    return new Vector(rhs * lhs.x, rhs * lhs.y, rhs *lhs.z);
}
```

Given that you've already written code to implement essentially the same operation, however, you might prefer to reuse that code by writing:

```
public static Vector operator * (Vector lhs, double rhs)
{
    return rhs * lhs;
}
```

This code works by effectively telling the compiler that if it sees a multiplication of a Vector by a double, it can simply reverse the parameters and call the other operator overload. Which you prefer is to some extent a matter of preference. The sample code for this chapter uses the second version, because it looks neater and illustrates the idea in action. This version also makes for more maintainable code, because it saves duplicating the code to perform the multiplication in two separate overloads.

Next, you need to overload the multiplication operator to support vector multiplication. Mathematics provides a couple of ways of multiplying vectors together, but the one we are interested in here is known as the *dot product* or *inner product*, and it actually gives a scalar as a result. That's the reason for this example, to demonstrate that arithmetic operators don't have to return the same type as the class in which they are defined.

In mathematical terms, if you have two vectors (x, y, z) and (X, Y, Z), then the inner product is defined to be the value of x*X + y*Y + z*Z. That might look like a strange way to multiply two things together, but it's actually very useful, because it can be used to calculate various other quantities. Certainly, if you ever end up writing code that displays complex 3D graphics, for example using Direct3D or DirectDraw, you'll almost certainly find your code needs to work out inner products of vectors quite often as an intermediate step in calculating where to place objects on the screen. What concerns us here is that we want people using your Vector to be able to write double X = a*b to calculate the dot product of two Vector objects (a and b). The relevant overload looks like this:

```
public static double operator * (Vector lhs, Vector rhs)
{
    return lhs.x * rhs.x + lhs.y * rhs.y + lhs.z * rhs.z;
}
```

Now that you understand the arithmetic operators, you can check that they work using a simple test method:

```
static void Main()
{
    // stuff to demonstrate arithmetic operations
    Vector vect1, vect2, vect3;
    vect1 = new Vector(1.0, 1.5, 2.0);
    vect2 = new Vector(0.0, 0.0, -10.0);
    vect3 = vect1 + vect2;
    Console.WriteLine("vect1 = " + vect1);
    Console.WriteLine("vect2 = " + vect2);
    Console.WriteLine("vect3 = vect1 + vect2 = " + vect3);
    Console.WriteLine("2*vect3 = " + 2*vect3);
    vect3 += vect2;
    Console.WriteLine("vect3+=vect2 gives " + vect3);
    vect3 = vect1*2;
    Console.WriteLine("Setting vect3=vect1*2 gives " + vect3);
    double dot = vect1*vect3;
    Console.WriteLine("vect1*vect3 = " + dot);
}
```

Running this code (Vectors2.cs) produces this result:

**Vectors2**

```
vect1 = ( 1 , 1.5 , 2 )
vect2 = ( 0 , 0 , -10 )
vect3 = vect1 + vect2 = ( 1 , 1.5 , -8 )
2*vect3 = ( 2 , 3 , -16 )
vect3+=vect2 gives ( 1 , 1.5 , -18 )
Setting vect3=vect1*2 gives ( 2 , 3 , 4 )
vect1*vect3 = 14.5
```

This shows that the operator overloads have given the correct results, but if you look at the test code closely, you might be surprised to notice that it actually used an operator that hadn't been overloaded — the addition assignment operator, +=:

```
vect3 += vect2;
Console.WriteLine("vect3 += vect2 gives " + vect3);
```

Although += normally counts as a single operator, it can be broken down into two steps: the addition and the assignment. Unlike C++, C# won't actually allow you to overload the = operator, but if you overload +, the compiler will automatically use your overload of + to work out how to carry out a += operation. The same principle works for the all of the assignment operators such as -=, *=, /=, &=, and so on.

## Overloading the comparison operators

C# has six comparison operators, and they come in three pairs:

- == and !=
- \> and <
- \>= and <=

C# requires that you overload these operators in pairs. That is, if you overload ==, you must overload != too; otherwise, you get a compiler error. In addition, the comparison operators must return a `bool`. This is the fundamental difference between these operators and the arithmetic operators. The result of adding or subtracting two quantities, for example, can theoretically be any type depending on the quantities. You've already seen that multiplying two `Vector` objects can be implemented to give a scalar. Another example involves the .NET base class `System.DateTime`. It's possible to subtract two `DateTime` instances, but the result is not a `DateTime`; instead it is a `System.TimeSpan` instance. By contrast, it doesn't really make much sense for a comparison to return anything other than a `bool`.

> *If you overload == and !=, you must also override the* `Equals()` *and* `GetHashCode()` *methods inherited from* `System.Object`, *otherwise you'll get a compiler warning. The reasoning is that the* `Equals()` *method should implement the same kind of equality logic as the == operator.*

Apart from these differences, overloading the comparison operators follows the same principles as overloading the arithmetic operators. However, comparing quantities isn't always as simple as you'd think. For example, if you simply compare two object references, you will compare the memory address where the objects are stored. This is rarely the desired behavior of a comparison operator, and so you must code the operator to compare the value of the objects and return the appropriate Boolean response. The following example overrides the == and != operators for the `Vector` struct. Here's the implementation of ==:

```
public static bool operator == (Vector lhs, Vector rhs)
{
   if (lhs.x == rhs.x && lhs.y == rhs.y && lhs.z == rhs.z)
      return true;
   else
      return false;
}
```

This approach simply compares two Vector objects for equality based on the values of their components. For most structs, that is probably what you will want to do, though in some cases you may need to think carefully about what you mean by equality. For example, if there are embedded classes, should you simply compare whether the references point to the same object (*shallow comparison*) or whether the values of the objects are the same (*deep comparison*)?

> *Don't be tempted to overload the comparison operator by calling the instance version of the* Equals() *method inherited from* System.Object. *If you do and then an attempt is made to evaluate* (objA == objB) *when* objA *happens to be* null, *you will get an exception as the .NET runtime tries to evaluate* null.Equals(objB). *Working the other way around (overriding* Equals() *to call the comparison operator) should be safe.*

You also need to override the != operator. The simple way to do it is like this:

```
public static bool operator != (Vector lhs, Vector rhs)
{
   return ! (lhs == rhs);
}
```

As usual, you should quickly check that your override works with some test code. This time you'll define three Vector objects and compare them:

```
static void Main()
{
    Vector vect1, vect2, vect3;
    vect1 = new Vector(3.0, 3.0, -10.0);
    vect2 = new Vector(3.0, 3.0, -10.0);
    vect3 = new Vector(2.0, 3.0, 6.0);
    Console.WriteLine("vect1==vect2 returns   " + (vect1==vect2));
    Console.WriteLine("vect1==vect3 returns   " + (vect1==vect3));
    Console.WriteLine("vect2==vect3 returns   " + (vect2==vect3));
    Console.WriteLine();
    Console.WriteLine("vect1!=vect2 returns   " + (vect1!=vect2));
    Console.WriteLine("vect1!=vect3 returns   " + (vect1!=vect3));
    Console.WriteLine("vect2!=vect3 returns   " + (vect2!=vect3));
}
```

Compiling this code (the Vectors3.cs sample in the code download) generates this compiler warning because you haven't overridden Equals() for your Vector. For our purposes here, that doesn't matter, so we will ignore it.

**csc Vectors3.cs**

```
Microsoft (R) Visual C# 2005 Compiler version 8.00.50215.33
for Microsoft (R) Windows (R) 2005 Framework version 2.0.50215
Copyright (C) Microsoft Corporation 2001-2005. All rights reserved.


Vectors3.cs(5,11): warning CS0660: 'Wrox.ProCSharp.OOCSharp.Vector' defines
        operator == or operator != but does not override Object.Equals(object o)
Vectors3.cs(5,11): warning CS0661: 'Wrox.ProCSharp.OOCSharp.Vector' defines
        operator == or operator != but does not override Object.GetHashCode()
```

## Operators and Casts

Running the example produces these results at the command line:

**Vectors3**

```
vect1==vect2 returns  True
vect1==vect3 returns  False
vect2==vect3 returns  False

vect1!=vect2 returns  False
vect1!=vect3 returns  True
vect2!=vect3 returns  True
```

### Which Operators Can You Overload?

It is not possible to overload all of the available operators. The operators that you can overload are listed in the following table.

| Category | Operators | Restrictions |
| --- | --- | --- |
| Arithmetic binary | +, *, /, -, % | None. |
| Arithmetic unary | +, -, ++, -- | None. |
| Bitwise binary | &, \|, ^, <<, >> | None. |
| Bitwise unary | !, ~<br>true, false | The `true` and `false` operators must be overloaded as a pair. |
| Comparison | ==, !=<br>>=, <=<br>>, < | Comparison operators must be overloaded in pairs. |
| Assignment | +=, -=, *=, /=, >>=,<br><<=, %=, &=, \|=, ^= | You cannot explicitly overload these operators; they are overridden implicitly when you override the individual operators such as +, -, %, and so on. |
| Index | [] | You cannot overload the index operator directly. The indexer member type, discussed in Chapter 2, "C# Basics," allows you to support the index operator on your classes and structs. |
| Cast | () | You cannot overload the cast operator directly. User-defined casts (discussed next) allow you to define custom cast behavior. |

## User-Defined Casts

Earlier, this chapter examined how you can convert values between predefined data types. You saw that this is done through a process of *casting*. You also saw that C# allows two different types of casts: implicit and explicit.

157

For an explicit cast, you *explicitly* mark the cast in your code by writing the destination data type inside parentheses:

```
int I = 3;
long l = I;              // implicit
short s = (short)I;      // explicit
```

For the predefined data types, explicit casts are required where there is a risk that the cast might fail or some data might be lost. The following are some examples:

- When converting from an `int` to a `short`, because the short might not be large enough to hold the value of the `int`.
- When converting from signed to unsigned data types will return incorrect results if the signed variable holds a negative value.
- When converting from floating-point to integer data types, the fractional part of the number will be lost.
- When converting from a nullable type to a non-nullable type, a value of `null` will cause an exception.

The idea is that by making the cast explicit in your code, C# forces you to affirm that you understand there is a risk of data loss, and therefore presumably you have written your code to take this into account.

Because C# allows you to define your own data types (structs and classes), it follows that you will need the facility to support casts to and from those data types. The mechanism is that you can define a cast as a member operator of one of the relevant classes. Your cast operator must be marked as either `implicit` or `explicit` to indicate how you are intending it to be used. The expectation is that you follow the same guidelines as for the predefined casts: if you know the cast is always safe whatever the value held by the source variable, then you define it as `implicit`. If, on the other hand, you know there is a risk of something going wrong for certain values — perhaps some loss of data or an exception being thrown — then you should define the cast as `explicit`.

> You should define any custom casts you write as explicit if there are any source data values for which the cast will fail or if there is any risk of an exception being thrown.

The syntax for defining a cast is similar to that for overloading operators discussed earlier in this chapter. This is not a coincidence, because a cast is regarded as an operator whose effect is to convert from the source type to the destination type. To illustrate the syntax, the following is taken from an example `struct` named `Currency`, which is introduced later in this section:

```
public static implicit operator float (Currency value)
{
    // processing
}
```

# Operators and Casts

The return type of the operator defines the target type of the cast operation, and the single parameter is the source object for the conversion. The cast defined here allows you to implicitly convert the value of a `Currency` into a `float`. Note that if a conversion has been declared as `implicit`, the compiler will permit its use either implicitly or explicitly. If it has been declared as `explicit`, the compiler will only permit it to be used explicitly. In common with other operator overloads, casts must be declared as both `public` and `static`.

> *C++ developers will notice that this is different from C++, in which casts are instance members of classes.*

## Implementing User-Defined Casts

This section illustrates the use of implicit and explicit user-defined casts in an example called `Simple Currency` (which, as usual, is found in the code download). In this example, you define a struct, `Currency`, which holds a positive USD ($) monetary value. C# provides the `decimal` type for this purpose, but it is possible you might still want to write your own struct or class to represent monetary values if you want to perform sophisticated financial processing and therefore want to implement specific methods on such a class.

> *The syntax for casting is the same for structs and classes. This example happens to be for a struct, but would work just as well if you declared* `Currency` *as a class.*

Initially, the definition of the `Currency` struct is as follows:

```
struct Currency
{
   public uint Dollars;
   public ushort Cents;

   public Currency(uint dollars, ushort cents)
   {
      this.Dollars = dollars;
      this.Cents = cents;
   }

   public override string ToString()
   {
      return string.Format("${0}.{1,-2:00}", Dollars,Cents);
   }
```

The use of unsigned data types for the `Dollar` and `Cents` fields ensures that a `Currency` instance can only hold positive values. It is restricted this way in order to illustrate some points about explicit casts later on. You might want to use a class like this to hold, for example, salary information for employees of a company (people's salaries tend not to be negative!). To keep the class simple, the fields are public, but usually, you would make them `private` and define corresponding properties for the dollars and cents.

Start off by assuming that you want to be able to convert `Currency` instances to `float` values, where the integer part of the `float` represents the dollars. In other words, you would like to be able to write code like this:

```
Currency balance = new Currency(10,50);
float f = balance;   // We want f to be set to 10.5
```

To be able to do this, you need to define a cast. Hence, you add the following to your `Currency` definition:

```
public static implicit operator float (Currency value)
{
    return value.Dollars + (value.Cents/100.0f);
}
```

This cast is implicit. This is a sensible choice in this case, because, as should be clear from the definition of `Currency`, any value that can be stored in the currency can also be stored in a `float`. There's no way that anything should ever go wrong in this cast.

> There is a slight cheat here — in fact, when converting a uint to a float, there can be a loss in precision, but Microsoft has deemed this error sufficiently marginal to count the uint-to-float cast as implicit anyway.

However, if you have a `float` that you would like to be converted to a `Currency`, the conversion is not guaranteed to work: a `float` can store negative values, which `Currency` instances can't; and a `float` can store numbers of a far higher magnitude than can be stored in the (`uint`) `Dollar` field of `Currency`. So if a `float` contains an inappropriate value, converting it to a `Currency` could give unpredictable results. As a result of this risk, the conversion from `float` to `Currency` should be defined as explicit. Here is the first attempt, which won't give quite the correct results, but it is instructive to examine why:

```
public static explicit operator Currency (float value)
{
    uint dollars = (uint)value;
    ushort cents = (ushort)((value-dollars)*100);
    return new Currency(dollars, cents);
}
```

The following code will now successfully compile:

```
float amount = 45.63f;
Currency amount2 = (Currency)amount;
```

However, the following code, if you tried it, would generate a compilation error, because it attempts to use an explicit cast implicitly:

```
float amount = 45.63f;
Currency amount2 = amount;   // wrong
```

By making the cast explicit, you warn the developer to be careful because data loss might occur. However, as you soon see, this isn't how you want your `Currency` struct to behave. Try writing a test harness and running the sample. Here is the `Main()` method, which instantiates a `Currency` struct and attempts a few conversions. At the start of this code, you write out the value of balance in two different ways (because this will be needed to illustrate something later on in the example):

```
static void Main()
{
    try
    {
        Currency balance = new Currency(50,35);
        Console.WriteLine(balance);
```

```
            Console.WriteLine("balance is " + balance);
            Console.WriteLine("balance is (using ToString()) " +
               balance.ToString());
            float balance2= balance;
            Console.WriteLine("After converting to float, = " + balance2);
            balance = (Currency) balance2;
            Console.WriteLine("After converting back to Currency, = " + balance);

            Console.WriteLine("Now attempt to convert out of range value of " +
                        "-$100.00 to a Currency:");
            checked
            {
               balance = (Currency) (-50.5);
               Console.WriteLine("Result is " + balance.ToString());
            }
         }
         catch(Exception e)
         {
            Console.WriteLine("Exception occurred: " + e.Message);
         }
      }
}
```

Notice that the entire code is placed in a `try` block to catch any exceptions that occur during your casts. Also, the lines that test converting an out-of-range value to `Currency` are placed in a `checked` block in an attempt to trap negative values. Running this code gives this output:

**SimpleCurrency**

```
50.35
Balance is $50.35
Balance is (using ToString()) $50.35
After converting to float, = 50.35
After converting back to Currency, = $50.34
Now attempt to convert out of range value of -$100.00 to a Currency:
Result is $4294967246.60486
```

This output shows that the code didn't quite work as expected. First, converting back from `float` to `Currency` gave a wrong result of $50.34 instead of $50.35. Second, no exception was generated when you tried to convert an obviously out-of-range value.

The first problem is caused by rounding errors. If a cast is used to convert from a `float` to a `uint`, the computer will *truncate* the number rather than *rounding* it. The computer stores numbers in binary rather than decimal, and the fraction 0.35 cannot be exactly represented as a binary fraction (just like 1/3 cannot be represented exactly as a decimal fraction; it comes out as 0.3333 recurring). So, the computer ends up storing a value very slightly lower than 0.35, and which can be represented exactly in binary format. Multiply by 100 and you get a number fractionally less than 35, which gets truncated to 34 cents. Clearly in this situation, such errors caused by truncation are serious, and the way to avoid them is to ensure that some intelligent rounding is performed in numerical conversions instead. Luckily, Microsoft has written a class that will do this: `System.Convert`. `System.Convert` contains a large number of static methods to perform various numerical conversions, and the one that we want is `Convert.ToUInt16()`. Note that the extra care taken by the `System.Convert` methods does come at a performance cost, so you should only use them when you need them.

Now let's examine why the expected overflow exception didn't get thrown. The problem here is this: the place where the overflow really occurs isn't actually in the `Main()` routine at all — it is inside the code for the cast operator, which is called from the `Main()` method. And that code wasn't marked as `checked`.

The solution here is to ensure that the cast itself is computed in a `checked` context too. With both of these changes, the revised code for the conversion looks like this:

```
public static explicit operator Currency (float value)
{
    checked
    {
        uint dollars = (uint)value;
        ushort cents = Convert.ToUInt16((value-dollars)*100);
        return new Currency(dollars, cents);
    }
}
```

Note that you use `Convert.ToUInt16()` to calculate the cents, as described earlier, but you do not use it for calculating the dollar part of the amount. `System.Convert` is not needed when working out the dollar amount because truncating the `float` value is what you want there.

> It is worth noting that the `System.Convert` methods also carry out their own overflow checking. Hence, for the particular case we are considering, there is no need to place the call to `Convert.ToUInt16()` inside the checked context. The checked context is still required, however, for the explicit casting of value to dollars.

You won't see a new set of results with this new `checked` cast just yet, because you have some more modifications to make to the `SimpleCurrency` example later in this section.

> If you are defining a cast that will be used very often, and for which performance is at an absolute premium, you may prefer not to do any error checking. That's also a legitimate solution, provided the behavior of your cast and the lack of error checking are very clearly documented.

## Casts between classes

The `Currency` example involves only classes that convert to or from `float` — one of the predefined data types. However, it is not necessary to involve any of the simple data types. It is perfectly legitimate to define casts to convert between instances of different structs or classes that you have defined. You need to be aware of a couple of restrictions, however:

- You cannot define a cast if one of the classes is derived from the other (these types of cast already exist, as you will see).
- The cast must be defined inside the definition of either the source or destination data type.

To illustrate these requirements, suppose you have the class hierarchy shown in Figure 5-1.

# Operators and Casts

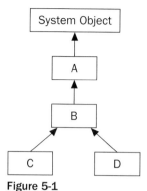

Figure 5-1

In other words, classes C and D are indirectly derived from A. In this case, the only legitimate user-defined cast between A, B, C, or D would be to convert between classes C and D, because these classes are not derived from each other. The code to do so might look like this (assuming you want the casts to be explicit, which is usually the case when defining casts between user-defined casts):

```
public static explicit operator D(C value)
{
    // and so on
}
public static explicit operator C(D value)
{
    // and so on
}
```

For each of these casts, you have a choice of where you place the definitions — inside the class definition of C or inside the class definition of D, but not anywhere else. C# requires you to put the definition of a cast inside either the source class (or struct) or the destination class (or struct). A side effect of this is that you can't define a cast between two classes unless you have access to edit the source code for at least one of them. This is sensible because it prevents third parties from introducing casts into your classes.

Once you have defined a cast inside one of the classes, you can't also define the same cast inside the other class. Obviously, there should be only one cast for each conversion — otherwise the compiler wouldn't know which one to pick.

## Casts between base and derived classes

To see how these casts work, start by considering the case where the source and destination are both reference types, and consider two classes, MyBase and MyDerived, where MyDerived is derived directly or indirectly from MyBase.

First, from MyDerived to MyBase; it is always possible (assuming the constructors are available) to write:

```
MyDerived derivedObject = new MyDerived();
MyBase baseCopy = derivedObject;
```

In this case, you are casting implicitly from `MyDerived` to `MyBase`. This works because of the rule that any reference to a type `MyBase` is allowed to refer to objects of class `MyBase` or to objects of anything derived from `MyBase`. In OO programming, instances of a derived class are, in a real sense, instances of the base class, plus something extra. All the functions and fields defined on the base class are defined in the derived class too.

Alternatively, you can write:

```
MyBase derivedObject = new MyDerived();
MyBase baseObject = new MyBase();
MyDerived derivedCopy1 = (MyDerived) derivedObject;   // OK
MyDerived derivedCopy2 = (MyDerived) baseObject;      // Throws exception
```

This code is perfectly legal C# (in a syntactic sense, that is) and illustrates casting from a base class to a derived class. However, the final statement will throw an exception when executed. What happens when you perform the cast is that the object being referred to is examined. Because a base class reference can in principle refer to a derived class instance, it is possible that this object is actually an instance of the derived class that you are attempting to cast to. If that's the case, the cast succeeds, and the derived reference is set to refer to the object. If, however, the object in question is not an instance of the derived class (or of any class derived from it), the cast fails and an exception is thrown.

Notice the casts that the compiler has supplied, which convert between base and derived class, do not actually do any data conversion on the object in question. All they do is set the new reference to refer to the object if it is legal for that conversion to occur. To that extent, these casts are very different in nature from the ones that you will normally define yourself. For example, in the `SimpleCurrency` example earlier, you defined casts that convert between a `Currency` struct and a `float`. In the `float`-to-`Currency` cast, you actually instantiated a new `Currency` struct and initialized it with the required values. The predefined casts between base and derived classes do not do this. If you actually want to convert a `MyBase` instance into a real `MyDerived` object with values based on the contents of the `MyBase` instance, you would not be able to use the cast syntax to do this. The most sensible option is usually to define a derived class constructor that takes a base class instance as a parameter, and have this constructor perform the relevant initializations:

```
class DerivedClass : BaseClass
{
    public DerivedClass(BaseClass rhs)
    {
        // initialize object from the Base instance
    }
    // etc.
```

## Boxing and unboxing casts

The previous discussion focused on casting between base and derived classes where both participants were reference types. Similar principles apply when casting value types, although in this case it is not possible to simply copy references—some copying of data must take place.

It is not, of course, possible to derive from structs or primitive value types. So, casting between base and derived structs invariably means casting between a primitive type or a struct and `System.Object` (theoretically, it is possible to cast between a struct and `System.ValueType`, though it is hard to see why you would want to do this).

## Operators and Casts

The cast from any struct (or primitive type) to `object` is always available as an implicit cast — because it is a cast from a derived to a base type — and is just the familiar process of boxing. For example, with the `Currency` struct:

```
Currency balance = new Currency(40,0);
object baseCopy = balance;
```

When this implicit cast is executed, the contents of `balance` are copied onto the heap into a boxed object, and the `baseCopy` object reference set to this object. What actually happens behind the scenes is this: When you originally defined the `Currency` struct, the .NET Framework implicitly supplied another (hidden) class, a boxed `Currency` class, which contains all the same fields as the `Currency` struct, but is a reference type, stored on the heap. This happens whenever you define a value type — whether it is a `struct` or `enum`, and similar boxed reference types exist corresponding to all the primitive value types of `int`, `double`, `uint`, and so on. It is not possible, nor necessary, to gain direct programmatic access to any of these boxed classes in source code, but they are the objects that are working behind the scenes whenever a value type is cast to `object`. When you implicitly cast `Currency` to `object`, a boxed `Currency` instance gets instantiated and initialized with all the data from the `Currency` struct. In the preceding code, it is this boxed `Currency` instance that `baseCopy` will refer to. By these means, it is possible for casting from derived to base type to work syntactically in the same way for value types as for reference types.

Casting the other way is known as *unboxing*. Just as for casting between a base reference type and a derived reference type, it is an explicit cast, because an exception will be thrown if the object being cast is not of the correct type:

```
object derivedObject = new Currency(40,0);
object baseObject = new object();
Currency derivedCopy1 = (Currency)derivedObject;   // OK
Currency derivedCopy2 = (Currency)baseObject;      // Exception thrown
```

This code works analogously to the similar code presented earlier for reference types. Casting `derivedObject` to `Currency` works fine because `derivedObject` actually refers to a boxed `Currency` instance — the cast will be performed by copying the fields out of the boxed `Currency` object into a new `Currency` struct. The second cast fails because `baseObject` does not refer to a boxed `Currency` object.

When using boxing and unboxing, it is important to understand both processes actually copy the data into the new boxed or unboxed object. Hence, manipulations on the boxed object, for example, will not affect the contents of the original value type.

## *Multiple Casting*

One thing you will have to watch for when you are defining casts is that if the C# compiler is presented with a situation in which no direct cast is available to perform a requested conversion, it will attempt to find a way of combining casts to do the conversion. For example, with the `Currency` struct, suppose the compiler encounters a couple of lines of code like this:

```
Currency balance = new Currency(10,50);
long amount = (long)balance;
double amountD = balance;
```

165

You first initialize a `Currency` instance, and then you attempt to convert it to a `long`. The trouble is that you haven't defined the cast to do that. However, this code will still compile successfully. What will happen is that the compiler will realize that you have defined an implicit cast to get from `Currency` to `float`, and the compiler already knows how to explicitly cast a `float` to a `long`. Hence, it will compile that line of code into IL code that converts `balance` first to a `float`, and then converts that result to a `long`. The same thing happens in the final line of the code, when you convert `balance` to a `double`. However, because the cast from `Currency` to `float` and the predefined cast from `float` to `double` are both implicit, you can write this conversion in your code as an implicit cast. If you'd preferred, you could have specified the casting route explicitly:

```
Currency balance = new Currency(10,50);
long amount = (long)(float)balance;
double amountD = (double)(float)balance;
```

However, in most cases, this would be seen as needlessly complicating your code. The following code by contrast would produce a compilation error:

```
Currency balance = new Currency(10,50);
long amount = balance;
```

The reason is the best match for the conversion that the compiler can find is still to convert first to `float` then to `long`. The conversion from `float` to `long` needs to be specified explicitly, though.

All this by itself shouldn't give you too much trouble. The rules are, after all, fairly intuitive and designed to prevent any data loss from occurring without the developer knowing about it. However, the problem is that if you are not careful when you define your casts, it is possible for the compiler to figure out a path that leads to unexpected results. For example, suppose it occurs to someone else in the group writing the `Currency` struct that it would be useful to be able to convert a `uint` containing the total number of cents in an amount into a `Currency` (cents not dollars because the idea is not to lose the fractions of a dollar). So, this cast might be written to try to achieve this:

```
public static implicit operator Currency (uint value)
{
    return new Currency(value/100u, (ushort)(value%100));
} // Don't do this!
```

Note the u after the first 100 in this code to ensure that `value/100u` is interpreted as a `uint`. If you'd written `value/100`, the compiler would have interpreted this as an `int`, not a `uint`.

`Don't do this` is clearly commented in this code, and here's why. Look at the following code snippet; all it does is convert a `uint` containing 350 into a `Currency` and back again. What do you think `bal2` will contain after executing this?

```
uint bal = 350;
Currency balance = bal;
uint bal2 = (uint)balance;
```

The answer is not 350 but 3! And it all follows logically. You convert 350 implicitly to a `Currency`, giving the result `balance.Dollars=3, balance.Cents=50`. Then the compiler does its usual figuring out of best path for the conversion back. `Balance` ends up getting implicitly converted to a `float` (value 3.5), and this gets converted explicitly to a `uint` with value 3.

## Operators and Casts

Of course, other instances exist in which converting to another data type and back again causes data loss. For example, converting a `float` containing 5.8 to an `int` and back to a `float` again will lose the fractional part, giving a result of 5, but there is a slight difference in principle between losing the fractional part of a number and dividing an integer by more than 100! `Currency` has suddenly become a rather dangerous class that does strange things to integers!

The problem is that there is a conflict between how your casts interpret integers. The casts between `Currency` and `float` interpret an integer value of 1 as corresponding to one dollar, but the latest `uint`-to-`Currency` cast interprets this value as one cent. This is an example of very poor design. If you want your classes to be easy to use, you should make sure all your casts behave in a way that is mutually compatible, in the sense that they intuitively give the same results. In this case, the solution is obviously to rewrite the `uint`-to-`Currency` cast so that it interprets an integer value of 1 as one dollar:

```
public static implicit operator Currency (uint value)
{
   return new Currency(value, 0);
}
```

Incidentally, you might wonder whether this new cast is necessary at all. The answer is that it could be useful. Without this cast, the only way for the compiler to carry out a `uint`-to-`Currency` conversion would be via a `float`. Converting directly is a lot more efficient in this case, so having this extra cast gives performance benefits, but you need to make sure it gives the same result as you would get going via a `float`, which you have now done. In other situations, you may also find that separately defining casts for different predefined data types allows more conversions to be implicit rather than explicit, though that's not the case here.

A good test of whether your casts are compatible is to ask whether a conversion will give the same results (other than perhaps a loss of accuracy as in `float`-to-`int` conversions), irrespective of which path it takes. The `Currency` class provides a good example of this. Look at this code:

```
Currency balance = new Currency(50, 35);
ulong bal = (ulong) balance;
```

At present, there is only one way that the compiler can achieve this conversion: by converting the `Currency` to a `float` implicitly, then to a `ulong` explicitly. The `float`-to-`ulong` conversion requires an explicit conversion, but that's fine because you have specified one here.

Suppose, however, that you then added another cast, to convert implicitly from a `Currency` to a `uint`. You will actually do this by modifying the `Currency` struct by adding the casts both to and from `uint`. This code is available as the `SimpleCurrency2` example:

```
public static implicit operator Currency (uint value)
{
   return new Currency(value, 0);
}

public static implicit operator uint (Currency value)
{
   return value.Dollars;
}
```

Now the compiler has another possible route to convert from `Currency` to `ulong`: to convert from `Currency` to `uint` implicitly then to `ulong` implicitly. Which of these two routes will it take? C# does have some precise rules (which are not detailed in this book; if you are interested, details are in the MSDN documentation) to say how the compiler decides which is the best route if there are several possibilities. The best answer is that you should design your casts so that all routes give the same answer (other than possible loss of precision), in which case it doesn't really matter which one the compiler picks. (As it happens in this case, the compiler picks the `Currency`-to-`uint`-to-`ulong` route in preference to `Currency`-to-`float`-to-`ulong`.)

To test the `SimpleCurrency2` sample, add this code to the test code for `SimpleCurrency`:

```
try
{
    Currency balance = new Currency(50,35);
    Console.WriteLine(balance);
    Console.WriteLine("balance is " + balance);
    Console.WriteLine("balance is (using ToString()) " + balance.ToString());

    uint balance3 = (uint) balance;
    Console.WriteLine("Converting to uint gives " + balance3);
```

Running the sample now gives these results:

**SimpleCurrency2**

```
50
balance is $50.35
balance is (using ToString()) $50.35
Converting to uint gives 50
After converting to float, = 50.35
After converting back to Currency, = $50.34
Now attempt to convert out of range value of -$100.00 to a Currency:
Exception occurred: Arithmetic operation resulted in an overflow.
```

The output shows that the conversion to `uint` has been successful, though as expected, you have lost the cents part of the `Currency` in making this conversion. Casting a negative `float` to `Currency` has also produced the expected overflow exception now that the `float`-to-`Currency` cast itself defines a checked context.

However, the output also demonstrates one last potential problem that you need to be aware of when working with casts. The very first line of output has not displayed the balance correctly, displaying `50` instead of `$50.35`. Consider these lines:

```
Console.WriteLine(balance);
Console.WriteLine("balance is " + balance);
Console.WriteLine("balance is (using ToString()) " + balance.ToString());
```

Only the last two lines correctly display the `Currency` as a string. So what's going on? The problem here is that when you combine casts with method overloads, you get another source of unpredictability. We will look at these lines in reverse order.

# Operators and Casts

The third `Console.WriteLine()` statement explicitly calls the `Currency.ToString()` method ensuring the `Currency` is displayed as a string. The second does not do so. However, the string literal `"balance is"` passed to `Console.WriteLine()` makes it clear to the compiler that the parameter is to be interpreted as a string. Hence, the `Currency.ToString()` method will be called implicitly.

The very first `Console.WriteLine()` method, however, simply passes a raw `Currency` struct to `Console.WriteLine()`. Now, `Console.WriteLine()` has many overloads, but none of them takes a `Currency` struct. So the compiler will start fishing around to see what it can cast the `Currency` to in order to make it match up with one of the overloads of `Console.WriteLine()`. As it happens, one of the `Console.WriteLine()` overloads is designed to display `uint`s quickly and efficiently, and it takes a `uint` as a parameter, and you have now supplied a cast that converts `Currency` implicitly to `uint`.

In fact, `Console.WriteLine()` has another overload that takes a `double` as a parameter and displays the value of that `double`. If you look closely at the output from the first `SimpleCurrency` example, you will find the very first line of output displayed `Currency` as a `double`, using this overload. In that example, there wasn't a direct cast from `Currency` to `uint`, so the compiler picked `Currency-to-float-to-double` as its preferred way of matching up the available casts to the available `Console.WriteLine()` overloads. However, now that there is a direct cast to `uint` available in `SimpleCurrency2`, the compiler has opted for this route.

The upshot of this is that if you have a method call that takes several overloads, and you attempt to pass it a parameter whose data type doesn't match any of the overloads exactly, then you are forcing the compiler to decide not only what casts to use to perform the data conversion, but which overload, and hence which data conversion, to pick. The compiler always works logically and according to strict rules, but the results may not be what you expected. If there is any doubt, you are better off specifying which cast to use explicitly.

## Summary

This chapter looked at the standard operators provided by C#, described the mechanics of object equality, and examined how the compiler converts the standard data types from one to another. It also demonstrated how you can implement custom operator support on your data types using operator overloads. Finally, the chapter looked at a special type of operator overload, the cast operator, which allows you to specify how instances of your types are converted to other data types.

Chapter 6 focuses on two closely related member types that you can implement in your types to support very clean event-based object models: delegates and events.

# 6

# Delegates and Events

Callback functions are an important part of programming in Windows. If you have a background in C or C++ programming, you have seen callbacks used in many of the Windows APIs. With the addition of the `AddressOf` keyword, Visual Basic developers are now able to take advantage of the API that once was off limits. Callback functions are really pointers to a method call. Also known as function pointers, they are a very powerful programming feature. .NET has implemented the concept of a function pointer in the form of delegates. What makes them special is that unlike the C function pointer, the .NET delegate is type-safe. What this means is that a function pointer in C is nothing but a pointer to a memory location. You have no idea what that pointer is really pointing to. Things like parameters and return types are not known. As you see in this chapter, .NET has made delegates a type-safe operation. Later in the chapter you see how .NET uses delegates as the means of implementing events.

## Delegates

Delegates exist for situations in which you want to pass methods around to other methods. To see what that means, consider this line of code:

```
int i = int.Parse("99");
```

You are so used to passing data to methods as parameters, as in this example, you don't consciously think about it; and for this reason the idea of passing methods around instead of data might sound a little strange. However, there are cases in which you have a method that does something, and rather than operating on data, the method might need to do something that involves invoking another method. To complicate things further, you do not know at compile-time what this second method is. That information is available only at runtime and hence will need to be passed in as a parameter to the first method. That might sound confusing but should be clearer with a couple of examples:

## Chapter 6

- **Starting Threads** — It is possible in C# to tell the computer to start some new sequence of execution in parallel with what it is currently doing. Such a sequence is known as a thread, and starting one up is done using the `Start()` method on an instance of one of the base classes, `System.Threading.Thread`. If you tell the computer to start a new sequence of execution, you have to tell it where to start that sequence. You have to supply it with the details of a method in which execution can start. In other words, the `Thread.Start()` method has to take a parameter that defines the method to be invoked by the thread.

- **Generic Library Classes** — Many libraries contain code to perform various standard tasks. It is usually possible for these libraries to be self-contained, in the sense that you know when you write to the library exactly how the task must be performed. However, sometimes the task contains some subtask, which only the individual client code that uses the library knows how to perform. For example, say you want to write a class that takes an array of objects and sorts them into ascending order. Part of the sorting process involves repeatedly taking two of the objects in the array and comparing them in order to see which one should come first. If you want to make the class capable of sorting arrays of any object, there is no way that it can tell in advance how to do this comparison. The client code that hands your class the array of objects will also have to tell your class how to do this comparison for the particular objects it wants sorted. The client code will have to pass your class details of an appropriate method that can be called and does the comparison.

- **Events** — The general idea here is that often you have code that needs to be informed when some event takes place. GUI programming is full of situations like this. When the event is raised, the runtime will need to know what method should be executed. This is done by passing the method that handles the event as a parameter to a delegate. This is discussed later in the chapter.

So, now that you understand the principle that, sometimes, methods need to take details of other methods as parameters, you need to figure out how you can do that. The simplest way would appear to be to just pass in the name of a method as a parameter. To take the example from threading, suppose you are going to start a new thread, and you have a method called `EntryPoint()`, which is where you want your thread to start running:

```
void EntryPoint()
{
    // do whatever the new thread needs to do
}
```

Alternatively, you can start the new thread off with some code like this:

```
Thread NewThread = new Thread();
Thread.Start(EntryPoint);                       // WRONG
```

In fact, this is the simple way of doing it, and it is what some languages, such as C and C++, do in this kind of situation (in C and C++, the parameter `EntryPoint` is the function pointer).

Unfortunately, this direct approach causes some problems with type safety, and it also neglects the fact that when you are doing object-oriented programming, methods rarely exist in isolation, but usually need to be associated with a class instance before they can be called. As a result of these problems, the .NET Framework does not syntactically permit this direct approach. Instead, if you want to pass methods around, you have to wrap up the details of the method in a new kind of object, a delegate. Delegates quite simply are a special type of object — special in the sense that, whereas all the objects defined up to now contain data, a delegate just contains the details of a method.

## Declaring Delegates in C#

When you want to use a class in C#, you do so in two stages. First, you need to define the class—that is, you need to tell the compiler what fields and methods make up the class. Then (unless you are using only static methods), you instantiate an object of that class. With delegates it is the same thing. You have to start off by defining the delegates you want to use. In the case of delegates, defining them means telling the compiler what kind of method a delegate of that type will represent. Then, you have to create one or more instances of that delegate.

The syntax for defining delegates looks like this:

```
delegate void VoidOperation(uint x);
```

In this case, you have defined a delegate called `VoidOperation`, and you have indicated that each instance of this delegate can hold a reference to a method that takes one `uint` parameter and returns `void`. The crucial point to understand about delegates is that they are very type-safe. When you define the delegate, you have to give full details of the signature of the method that it is going to represent.

> **One good way of understanding delegates is by thinking of a delegate as something that gives a name to a method signature.**

Suppose you wanted to define a delegate called `TwoLongsOp` that will represent a function that takes two `long`s as its parameters and returns a `double`. You could do it like this:

```
delegate double TwoLongsOp(long first, long second);
```

Or, to define a delegate that will represent a method that takes no parameters and returns a `string`, you might write this:

```
delegate string GetAString();
```

The syntax is similar to that for a method definition, except that there is no method body and the definition is prefixed with the keyword `delegate`. Because what you are doing here is basically defining a new class, you can define a delegate in any of the same places that you would define a class—that is to say either inside another class or outside of any class and in a namespace as a top-level object. Depending on how visible you want your definition to be, you can apply any of the normal access modifiers to delegate definitions—`public`, `private`, `protected`, and so on:

```
public delegate string GetAString();
```

*We really mean what we say when we describe defining a delegate as defining a new class. Delegates are implemented as classes derived from the class* `System.MulticastDelegate`, *which is derived from the base class,* `System.Delegate`. *The C# compiler is aware of this class and uses its delegate syntax to shield you from the details of the operation of this class. This is another good example of how C# works in conjunction with the base classes to make programming as easy as possible.*

After you have defined a delegate, you can create an instance of it so that you can use it to store details of a particular method.

## Chapter 6

*There is an unfortunate problem with terminology here. With classes there are two distinct terms—class, which indicates the broader definition, and object, which means an instance of the class. Unfortunately, with delegates there is only the one term. When you create an instance of a delegate, what you have created is also referred to as a delegate. You need to be aware of the context to know which meaning we are using when we talk about delegates.*

## Using Delegates in C#

The following code snippet demonstrates the use of a delegate. It is a rather long-winded way of calling the `ToString()` method on an `int`:

```
private delegate string GetAString();

static void Main(string[] args)
{
   int x = 40;
   GetAString firstStringMethod = new GetAString(x.ToString);
   Console.WriteLine("String is" + firstStringMethod());
   // With firstStringMethod initialized to x.ToString(),
   // the above statement is equivalent to saying
   // Console.WriteLine("String is" + x.ToString());
```

In this code, you instantiate a delegate of type `GetAString`, and you initialize it so that it refers to the `ToString()` method of the integer variable x. Delegates in C# always syntactically take a one-parameter constructor, the parameter being the method to which the delegate will refer. This method must match the signature with which you originally defined the delegate. So in this case, you would get a compilation error if you tried to initialize `firstStringMethod` with any method that did not take parameters and return a string. Notice that because `int.ToString()` is an instance method (as opposed to a static one) you need to specify the instance (x) as well as the name of the method to initialize the delegate properly.

The next line actually uses the delegate to display the string. In any code, supplying the name of a delegate instance, followed by brackets containing any parameters, has exactly the same effect as calling the method wrapped by the delegate. Hence, in the preceding code snippet, the `Console.WriteLine()` statement is completely equivalent to the commented-out line.

One feature of delegates is that they are type-safe to the extent that they ensure the signature of the method being called is correct. However, interestingly, they do not care what type of object the method is being called against or even whether the method is a static method or an instance method.

> **An instance of a given delegate can refer to any instance or static method on any object of any type, provided that the signature of the method matches the signature of the delegate.**

To demonstrate this, the following example expands the previous code snippet so that it uses the `firstStringMethod` delegate to call a couple of other methods on another object—an instance method and a static method. For this, you use the `Currency` struct, which is defined as follows:

# Delegates and Events

```csharp
struct Currency
{
   public uint Dollars;
   public ushort Cents;

   public Currency(uint dollars, ushort cents)
   {
      this.Dollars = dollars;
      this.Cents = cents;
   }

   public override string ToString()
   {
      return string.Format("${0}.{1,-2:00}", Dollars,Cents);
   }

   public static explicit operator Currency (float value)
   {
      checked
      {
         uint dollars = (uint)value;
         ushort cents = (ushort)((value-dollars)*100);
         return new Currency(dollars, cents);
      }
   }

   public static implicit operator float (Currency value)
   {
      return value.Dollars + (value.Cents/100.0f);
   }

   public static implicit operator Currency (uint value)
   {
      return new Currency(value, 0);
   }

   public static implicit operator uint (Currency value)
   {
      return value.Dollars;
   }
}
```

Notice that the `Currency` struct has its own overload of `ToString()`. To demonstrate using delegates with static methods, this code also adds a static method with the same signature to `Currency`:

```csharp
struct Currency
{
   public static string GetCurrencyUnit()
   {
      return "Dollar";
   }
```

Now you can use your `GetAString` instance as follows:

```
private delegate string GetAString();

static void Main(string[] args)
{
   int x = 40;
   GetAString firstStringMethod = new GetAString(x.ToString);
   Console.WriteLine("String is " + firstStringMethod());
   Currency balance = new Currency(34, 50);
   firstStringMethod = new GetAString(balance.ToString);
   Console.WriteLine("String is " + firstStringMethod());
   firstStringMethod = new GetAString(Currency.GetCurrencyUnit);
   Console.WriteLine("String is " + firstStringMethod());
```

This code shows how you can call a method via a delegate and subsequently reassign the delegate to refer to different methods on different instances of classes, even static methods or methods against instances of different types of class, provided that the signature of each method matches the delegate definition.

However, you still haven't seen the process of actually passing a delegate to another method. Nor have you actually achieved anything particularly useful yet. It is possible to call the `ToString()` method of `int` and `Currency` objects in a much more straightforward way than using delegates! Unfortunately, the nature of delegates requires a fairly complex example before you can really appreciate their usefulness. The next section presents two delegate examples. The first one simply uses delegates to call a couple of different operations. It illustrates how to pass delegates to methods and how you can use arrays of delegates — although arguably it still doesn't do much that you couldn't do a lot more simply without delegates. Then, a second, much more complex example of a `BubbleSorter` class is presented, which implements a method to sort out arrays of objects into increasing order. This class would be difficult to write without delegates.

## Anonymous Methods

Up to this point, a method must already exist in order for the delegate to work (that is, the delegate is defined with the same signature as the method(s) it will be used with). However there is another way to use delegates — with anonymous methods. An anonymous method is a block of code that is used as the parameter for the delegate.

The syntax for defining a delegate with an anonymous method doesn't change. It's when the delegate is instantiated that things change. The following is a very simple console app that shows how using an anonymous method can work:

```
namespace ConsoleApplication1
{
  class Program
  {
    delegate string delegateTest(string val);
```

```csharp
      static void Main(string[] args)
      {
        string mid = ", middle part,";

        delegateTest anonDel = delegate(string param)
        {
          param += mid;
          param += " and this was added to the string.";
          return param;
        };

        Console.WriteLine(anonDel("Start of string"));

      }
    }
  }
```

The delegate `delegateTest` is defined as a class-level variable. It takes a single string parameter. Where things become different is in the `Main` method. When `anonDel` is defined, instead of passing in a known method name, a simple block of code is used:

```csharp
{
   param += mid;
   param += " and this was added to the string.";
   return param;
};
```

As you can see, the block of code uses a method-level string variable, `mid`, which is defined outside of the anonymous method and adds it to the parameter that was passed in. The code then returns the string value. When the delegate is called, a string is passed in as the parameter and the returned string is output to the console.

The benefit of anonymous methods is to reduce overhead. A method doesn't have to be defined just to be used by the delegate. This becomes very evident when defining the delegate for an event. (Events are discussed later in this chapter.) This can help reduce the complexity of code, especially where there are several events defined.

A couple of rules must be followed when using anonymous methods. You can't have a jump statement (`break`, `goto`, or `continue`) in an anonymous method that has a target outside of the anonymous method. The reverse is also true — a jump statement outside the anonymous method cannot have a target inside the anonymous method.

Unsafe code cannot be accessed inside an anonymous method. Also, `ref` and `out` parameters that are used outside of the anonymous method cannot be accessed. Other variables defined outside of the anonymous method can be used.

## SimpleDelegate Example

This example defines a `MathsOperations` class that has a couple of static methods to perform two operations on doubles. Then you use delegates to call up these methods. The math class looks like this:

```csharp
class MathsOperations
{
   public static double MultiplyByTwo(double value)
   {
      return value*2;
   }

   public static double Square(double value)
   {
      return value*value;
   }
}
```

You call up these methods like this:

```csharp
using System;

namespace SimpleDelegate
{
    delegate double DoubleOp(double x);

    class MainEntryPoint
    {
       static void Main()
       {
          DoubleOp [] operations =
             {
                new DoubleOp(MathsOperations.MultiplyByTwo),
                new DoubleOp(MathsOperations.Square)
             };

          for (int i=0 ; i<operations.Length ; i++)
          {
             Console.WriteLine("Using operations[{0}]:", i);
             ProcessAndDisplayNumber(operations[i], 2.0);
             ProcessAndDisplayNumber(operations[i], 7.94);
             ProcessAndDisplayNumber(operations[i], 1.414);
             Console.WriteLine();
          }
       }

       static void ProcessAndDisplayNumber(DoubleOp action, double value)
       {
          double result = action(value);
          Console.WriteLine(
             "Value is {0}, result of operation is {1}", value, result);
       }
```

In this code, you instantiate an array of `DoubleOp` delegates (remember that once you have defined a delegate class, you can basically instantiate instances just like you can with normal classes, so putting some into an array is no problem). Each element of the array gets initialized to refer to a different operation implemented by the `MathOperations` class. Then, you loop through the array, applying each operation

# Delegates and Events

to three different values. This illustrates one way of using delegates — that you can group methods together into an array using them, so that you can call several methods in a loop.

The key lines in this code are the ones in which you actually pass each delegate to the `ProcessAndDisplayNumber()` method, for example:

```
ProcessAndDisplayNumber(operations[i], 2.0);
```

Here, you are passing in the name of a delegate but without any parameters. Given that `operations[i]` is a delegate, syntactically:

- ❏     `operations[i]` means *the delegate* (that is, the method represented by the delegate).
- ❏     `operations[i](2.0)` means *actually call this method, passing in the value in parentheses*.

The `ProcessAndDisplayNumber()` method is defined to take a delegate as its first parameter:

```
static void ProcessAndDisplayNumber(DoubleOp action, double value)
```

Then, when in this method, you call:

```
double result = action(value);
```

This actually causes the method that is wrapped up by the `action` delegate instance to be called and its return result stored in `Result`.

Running this example gives the following:

```
SimpleDelegate
Using operations[0]:
Value is 2, result of operation is 4
Value is 7.94, result of operation is 15.88
Value is 1.414, result of operation is 2.828

Using operations[1]:
Value is 2, result of operation is 4
Value is 7.94, result of operation is 63.0436
Value is 1.414, result of operation is 1.999396
```

If anonymous methods were used in this example, the first class, `MathOperations`, could be completely eliminated. The `Main` method would then look like this:

```
static void Main()
{
  DoubleOp multByTwo = delegate(double val) {return val * 2;}
  DoubleOp square = delegate(double val) {return val * val;}

  DoubleOp [] operations = {multByTwo, square};

  for (int i=0 ; i<operations.Length ; i++)
  {
```

```
        Console.WriteLine("Using operations[{0}]:", i);
        ProcessAndDisplayNumber(operations[i], 2.0);
        ProcessAndDisplayNumber(operations[i], 7.94);
        ProcessAndDisplayNumber(operations[i], 1.414);
        Console.WriteLine();
    }
}
```

Running this version will give the same results as the previous example. The advantage is that it eliminated a class.

## *BubbleSorter Example*

You are now ready for an example that will show delegates working in a situation in which they are very useful. You are going to write a class called `BubbleSorter`. This class implements a static method, `Sort()`, which takes as its first parameter an array of objects, and rearranges this array into ascending order. For example, if you were to pass it this array of `int`s: {0, 5, 6, 2, 1}, it would rearrange this array into {0, 1, 2, 5, 6}.

The bubble-sorting algorithm is a well-known and very simple way of sorting numbers. It is best suited to small sets of numbers, because for larger sets of numbers (more than about 10) far more efficient algorithms are available). It works by repeatedly looping through the array, comparing each pair of numbers and, if necessary, swapping them, so that the largest numbers progressively move to the end of the array. For sorting `int`s, a method to do a bubble sort might look like this:

```
        for (int i = 0; i < sortArray.Length; i++)
        {
           for (int j = i + 1; j < sortArray.Length; j++)
           {
              if (sortArray[j] < sortArray[i])   // problem with this test
              {
                 int temp = sortArray[i];   // swap ith and jth entries
                 sortArray[i] = sortArray[j];
                 sortArray[j] = temp;
              }
           }
        }
```

This is all very well for `int`s, but you want your `Sort()` method to be able to sort any object. In other words, if some client code hands you an array of `Currency` structs or any other class or struct that it may have defined, you need to be able to sort the array. This presents a problem with the line `if(sortArray[j] < sortArray[i])` in the preceding code, because that requires you to compare two objects on the array to see which one is greater. You can do that for `int`s, but how are you to do it for some new class that is unknown or undecided until runtime? The answer is the client code that knows about the class will have to pass in a delegate wrapping a method that will do the comparison.

You define the delegate like this:

```
        delegate bool CompareOp(object lhs, object rhs);
```

And you give your Sort method this signature:

```
static public void Sort(object [] sortArray, CompareOp gtMethod)
```

The documentation for this method states that gtMethod must refer to a static method that takes two arguments, and returns true if the value of the second argument is *greater than* (that is, should come later in the array than) the first one.

> *Although you are using delegates here, it is possible to solve this problem alternatively by using interfaces. .NET in fact makes the* IComparer *interface available for that purpose. However, delegates are used here because this is still the kind of problem that lends itself to delegates.*

Now you are all set. Here is the definition for the BubbleSorter class:

```
class BubbleSorter
{
   static public void Sort(object [] sortArray, CompareOp gtMethod)
   {
      for (int i=0 ; i<sortArray.Length ; i++)
      {
         for (int j=i+1 ; j<sortArray.Length ; j++)
         {
            if (gtMethod(sortArray[j], sortArray[i]))
            {
               object temp = sortArray[i];
               sortArray[i] = sortArray[j];
               sortArray[j] = temp;
            }
         }
      }
   }
}
```

To use this class, you need to define some other class, which you can use to set up an array that needs sorting. For this example, assume that the Mortimer Phones mobile phone company has a list of employees and wants them sorted according to salary. The employees are each represented by an instance of a class, Employee, which looks like this:

```
class Employee
{
   private string name;
   private decimal salary;

   public Employee(string name, decimal salary)
   {
      this.name = name;
      this.salary = salary;
   }

   public override string ToString()
   {
      return string.Format(name + ", {0:C}", salary);
   }
```

```
        public static bool RhsIsGreater(object lhs, object rhs)
        {
            Employee empLhs = (Employee) lhs;
            Employee empRhs = (Employee) rhs;
            return (empRhs.salary > empLhs.salary) ? true : false;
        }
    }
```

Notice that in order to match the signature of the `CompareOp` delegate, you had to define `RhsIsGreater` in this class as taking two object references, rather than `Employee` references as parameters. This means that you had to cast the parameters into `Employee` references in order to perform the comparison.

Now you are ready to write some client code to request a sort:

```
using System;

namespace Wrox.ProCSharp.AdvancedCSharp
{
    delegate bool CompareOp(object lhs, object rhs);

    class MainEntryPoint
    {
        static void Main()
        {
            Employee [] employees =
                {
                    new Employee("Bugs Bunny", 20000),
                    new Employee("Elmer Fudd", 10000),
                    new Employee("Daffy Duck", 25000),
                    new Employee("Wiley Coyote", (decimal)1000000.38),
                    new Employee("Foghorn Leghorn", 23000),
                    new Employee("RoadRunner'", 50000)};
            CompareOp employeeCompareOp = new CompareOp(Employee.RhsIsGreater);
            BubbleSorter.Sort(employees, employeeCompareOp);

            for (int i=0 ; i<employees.Length ; i++)
                Console.WriteLine(employees[i].ToString());
        }
    }
}
```

Running this code shows that the `Employees` are correctly sorted according to salary:

**BubbleSorter**
Elmer Fudd, $10,000.00
Bugs Bunny, $20,000.00
Foghorn Leghorn, $23,000.00
Daffy Duck, $25,000.00
RoadRunner, $50,000.00
Wiley Coyote, $1,000,000.38

# Delegates and Events

## Multicast Delegates

So far, each of the delegates you have used wraps just one single method call. Calling the delegate amounts to calling that method. If you want to call more than one method, you need to make an explicit call through a delegate more than once. However, it is possible for a delegate to wrap more than one method. Such a delegate is known as a *multicast delegate*. If a multicast delegate is called, it will successively call each method in order. For this to make sense, the delegate signature must return a void (otherwise, where would all the return values go?), and in fact, if the compiler sees a delegate that returns a void, it automatically assumes you mean a multicast delegate. Consider the following code, which is adapted from the SimpleDelegate example. Although the syntax is the same as before, it is actually a multicast delegate, Operations, that gets instantiated:

```
delegate void DoubleOp(double value);
//   delegate double DoubleOp(double value);   // can't do this now

class MainEntryPoint
{
   static void Main()
   {
      DoubleOp operations = new DoubleOp(MathOperations.MultiplyByTwo);
      operations += new DoubleOp(MathOperations.Square);
```

In the earlier example, you wanted to store references to two methods so you instantiated an array of delegates. Here, you simply add both operations into the same multicast delegate. Multicast delegates recognize the operators + and +=. Alternatively, you can also expand the last two lines of the preceding code as in this snippet:

```
DoubleOp operation1 = new DoubleOp(MathOperations.MultiplyByTwo);
DoubleOp operation2 = new DoubleOp(MathOperations.Square);
DoubleOp operations = operation1 + operation2;
```

Multicast delegates also recognize the operators − and −= to remove method calls from the delegate.

> *In terms of what's going on under the hood, a multicast delegate is a class derived from* System.MulticastDelegate, *which in turn is derived from* System.Delegate. System.Multicast Delegate *has additional members to allow chaining of method calls together into a list.*

To illustrate the use of multicast delegates, the following code recasts the SimpleDelegate example into a new example, MulticastDelegate. Because you now need the delegate to refer to methods that return void, you have to rewrite the methods in the MathOperations class, so they display their results instead of returning them:

```
class MathOperations
{
   public static void MultiplyByTwo(double value)
   {
      double result = value*2;
      Console.WriteLine(
         "Multiplying by 2: {0} gives {1}", value, result);
   }
```

```csharp
        public static void Square(double value)
        {
            double result = value*value;
            Console.WriteLine("Squaring: {0} gives {1}", value, result);
        }
    }
```

To accommodate this change, you also have to rewrite `ProcessAndDisplayNumber`:

```csharp
static void ProcessAndDisplayNumber(DoubleOp action, double valueToProcess)
{
   Console.WriteLine("\nProcessAndDisplayNumber called with value = " +
                     valueToProcess);
   action(valueToProcess);
}
```

Now you can try out your multicast delegate like this:

```csharp
        static void Main()
        {
            DoubleOp operations = new DoubleOp(MathOperations.MultiplyByTwo);
            operations += new DoubleOp(MathOperations.Square);

            ProcessAndDisplayNumber(operations, 2.0);
            ProcessAndDisplayNumber(operations, 7.94);
            ProcessAndDisplayNumber(operations, 1.414);
            Console.WriteLine();
        }
```

Now, each time `ProcessAndDisplayNumber` is called, it will display a message to say that it has been called. Then the following statement will cause each of the method calls in the `action` delegate instance to be called in succession:

```csharp
action(value);
```

Running this code gives this result:

```
MulticastDelegate

ProcessAndDisplayNumber called with value = 2
Multiplying by 2: 2 gives 4
Squaring: 2 gives 4

ProcessAndDisplayNumber called with value = 7.94
Multiplying by 2: 7.94 gives 15.88
Squaring: 7.94 gives 63.0436

ProcessAndDisplayNumber called with value = 1.414
Multiplying by 2: 1.414 gives 2.828
Squaring: 1.414 gives 1.999396
```

# Delegates and Events

If you are using multicast delegates, you should be aware that the order in which methods chained to the same delegate will be called is formally undefined. You should, therefore, avoid writing code that relies on such methods being called in any particular order.

## Events

Windows-based applications are message-based. This means that the application is communicating with Windows and Windows is communicating with the application by using predefined messages. These messages are structures that contain various pieces of information that the application and Windows will use to determine what to do next. Prior to libraries such as MFC or to development environments such as Visual Basic, the developer would have to handle the message that Windows sends to the application. Visual Basic and now .NET wrap some of these incoming messages as something called events. If you need to react to a specific incoming message, you would handle the corresponding event. A common example of this is when the user clicks a button on a form. Windows is sending a `WM_MOUSECLICK` message to the button's message handler (sometimes referred to as the Windows Procedure or WndProc). To the .NET developer this is exposed as the `OnClick` event of the button.

In developing object-based applications, another form of communication between objects is required. When something of interest happens in one of your objects, chances are that other objects will want to be informed. Again, events come to the rescue. Just as the .NET Framework wraps up Windows messages in events, you can also utilize events as the communications medium between your objects.

Delegates are used as the means of wiring up the event when the message is received by the application.

Believe it or not, in the preceding section on delegates, you learned just about everything you need to know to understand how events work. However, one of the great things about how Microsoft has designed C# events is that you don't actually need to understand anything about the underlying delegates in order to use them. So, this section starts off with a short discussion of events from the point of view of the client software. It focuses on what code you need to write in order to receive notifications of events, without worrying too much about what is happening behind the scenes — just so you can see how easy handling events really is. After that, you write an example that generates events, and as you do so, you should see how the relationship between events and delegates work.

The discussion in this section will be of most use to C++ developers because C++ does not have any concept similar to events. C# events, on the other hand, are quite similar in concept to Visual Basic events, although the syntax and the underlying implementation are different in C#.

> *In this context, the term event is used in two different senses. First, as something interesting that happens; and second, as a precisely defined object in the C# language — the object that handles the notification process. When we mean the latter, we will usually refer to it either as a C# event or, when the meaning is obvious from the context, simply as an event.*

### The Receiver's View of Events

The event receiver is any application, object, or component that wants to be notified when something happens. To go along with the receiver there will of course be the event sender. The sender's job will be to raise the event. The sender can be either another object or assembly in your application, or in the case of system events such as mouse clicks or keyboard entry, the sender will be the .NET runtime. It is important to note that the sender of the event will not have any knowledge of who or what the receiver is. This is what makes events so useful.

Now, somewhere inside the event receiver will be a method that is responsible for handling the event. This event handler will be executed each time the event that it is registered to is raised. This is where the delegate comes in. Because the sender has no idea who the receiver(s) will be, there cannot be any type of reference set between the two. So the delegate is used as the intermediary. The sender defines the delegate that will be used by the receiver. The receiver registers the event handler with the event. The process of hooking up the event handler is known as wiring up an event. A simple example of wiring up the `Click` event will help illustrate this process.

First, create a simple Windows Forms application. Drag over a button control from the toolbox and place it on the form. In the properties window rename the button to `btnOne`. In the code editor, add the following line of code in the `Form1` constructor:

```
btnOne.Click += new EventHandler(Button_Click);
```

Now in Visual Studio you should have noticed that after you typed in the += operator all you had to do was press the Tab key a couple of times and the editor will do the rest of the work for you. In most cases this is fine. However, in this example the default handler name is not being used, so you should just enter the text yourself.

What is happening is that you are telling the runtime that when the `Click` event of `btnOne` is raised, that `Button_Click` method should be executed. `EventHandler` is the delegate that the event uses to assign the handler (`Button_Click`) to the event (`Click`). Notice that you used the += operator to add this new method to the delegate list. This is just like the multicast example that you looked at earlier in this chapter. This means that you can add more than one handler for any event. Because this is a multicast delegate, all of the rules about adding multiple methods apply; however, there is no guarantee as to the order that the methods are called. Go ahead and drag another button onto the form and rename it to `btnTwo`. Now connect the `btnTwo` `Click` event to the same `Button_Click` method, as shown here:

```
btnOne.Click += new EventHandler(Button_Click);
btnTwo.Click += new EventHandler(Button_Click);
```

The `EventHandler` delegate is defined for you in the .NET Framework. It is in the `System` namespace and all of the events that are defined in the .NET Framework use it. As discussed earlier, a delegate requires that all of the methods that are added to the delegate list must have the same signature. This obviously holds true for event delegates as well. Here is the `Button_Click` method defined:

```
private void Button_Click(object sender, EventArgs e)
{

}
```

A few things are important about this method. First, it always returns `void`. Event handlers cannot return a value. Next are the parameters. As long as you use the `EventHandler` delegate, your parameters will be `object` and `EventArgs`. The first parameter is the object that raised the event. In this example it is either `btnOne` or `btnTwo`, depending on which button is clicked. By sending a reference to the object that raised the event you can assign the same event handler to more than one object. For example,

# Delegates and Events

you can define one button click handler for several buttons and then determine which button was clicked by asking the sender parameter.

The second parameter, `EventArgs`, is an object that contains other potentially useful information about the event. This parameter could actually be any type as long as it is derived from `EventArgs`. The `MouseDown` event uses the `MouseDownEventArgs`. It contains properties for which button was used, the X and Y coordinates of the pointer, and other info related to the event. Notice the naming pattern of ending the type with `EventArgs`. Later in the chapter you see how to create and use a custom `EventArgs`-based object.

The name of the method should also be mentioned. As a convention, any event handlers follow a naming convention of `object_event`. `object` is the object that is raising the event and `event` is the event being raised. There is a convention and for readability's sake it should be followed.

The last thing to do in this example is to add some code to actually do something in the handler. Now remember that two buttons are using the same handler. So first you have to determine which button raises the event, and then you can call the action that should be performed. In this example, you can just output some text to a label control on the form. Drag a label control from the toolbox onto the form and name it `lblInfo`. Then write the following code on the `Button_Click` method:

```
if(((Button)sender).Name == "btnOne")
   lblInfo.Text = "Button One was pressed";
else
   lblInfo.Text = "Button Two was pressed";
```

Notice that because the sender parameter is sent as object, you will have to cast it to whatever object is raising the event, in this case `Button`. In this example, you use the `Name` property to determine what button raised the event; however, you can also use another property. The `Tag` property is handy to use in this scenario, because it can contain anything that you want to place in it. To see how the multicast capability of the event delegate works, add another method to the `btnTwo Click` event. Use the default method name. The constructor of the form should look something like this now:

```
btnOne.Click += new EventHandler(Button_Click);
btnTwo.Click += new EventHandler(Button_Click);
btnTwo.Click += new EventHandler(btnTwo_Click);
```

If you let Visual Studio create the stub for you, you will have the following method at the end of the source file. However, you have to add the call to the `MessageBox` function.

```
private void btnTwo_Click(object sender, EventArgs e)
{
   MessageBox.Show("This only happens in Button 2 click event");
}
```

If you go back and make use of anonymous methods, the methods `Button_Click` and `btnTwo_Click` would not be needed. The code for the events would like this:

```
btnOne.Click += new EventHandler(lblInfo.Text = "Button One was pressed";);
btnTwo.Click += new EventHandler(lblInfo.Text = "Button Two was pressed";);
btnTwo.Click += new EventHandler(MessageBox.Show
                    ("This only happens in Button 2 click event"););
```

187

# Chapter 6

When you run this example, clicking `btnOne` will change the text in the label. Clicking `btnTwo` will not only change the text but also display the `MessageBox`. Again the important thing to remember is that there is no guarantee that the label text changes before the `MessageBox` appears, so be careful not to write dependent code in the handlers.

You might have had to learn a lot of concepts to get this far, but the amount of coding you need to do in the receiver is fairly trivial. Also bear in mind that you will find yourself writing event receivers a lot more often than you write event senders. At least in the field of the Windows user interface, Microsoft has already written all the event senders you are likely to need (these are in the .NET base classes, in the `Windows.Forms` namespace).

## *Generating Events*

Receiving events and responding to them is only one side of the story. To be really useful you need the ability to generate events and raise them in your code. The example in this section looks at creating, raising, receiving, and optionally canceling an event.

The example has a form raise an event that will be listened to by another class. When the event is raised, the receiving object will determine if the process should execute and then cancel the event if the process cannot continue. The goal in this case is to determine whether the number of seconds of the current time is greater than or less than 30. If the number of seconds is less than 30, a property is set with a string that represents the current time; if the number of seconds is greater than 30, the event is canceled and the time string is set to an empty string.

The form used to generate the event has a button and a label on it. In the example code download the button is named `btnRaise` and the label is `lblInfo`; however, you can use any name you want for your labels. After you have created the form and added the two controls you will be able to create the event and the corresponding delegate. Add the following code in the class declaration section of the form class:

```
public delegate void ActionEventHandler(object sender, ActionCancelEventArgs ev);
public static event ActionEventHandler Action;
```

So what exactly is going on with these two lines of code? First you are declaring a new delegate type of `ActionEventHandler`. The reason that you have to create a new one and not use one of the predefined delegates in the .NET Framework is that there will be a custom `EventArgs` class used. Remember the method signature must match the delegate. So you now have a delegate to use; the next line actually defines the event. In this case the `Action` event is defined, and the syntax for defining the event requires that you specify the delegate that will be associated with the event. You can also use a delegate that is defined in the .NET Framework. Nearly 100 classes are derived from the `EventArgs` class, so you might find one that works for you. Again, because a custom `EventArgs` class is used in this example, a new delegate type has to be created that matches it.

The new `EventArgs`-based class, `ActionCancelEventArgs`, is actually derived from `CancelEventArgs`, which is derived from `EventArgs`. `CancelEventArgs` adds the `Cancel` property. `Cancel` is a Boolean that informs the sender object that the receiver wants to cancel or stop the event processing. In the `ActionCancelEventArgs` class a `Message` property has been added. This is a string property that will contain textual information on the processing state of the event. Here is the code for the `ActionCancelEventArgs` class:

```
public class ActionCancelEventArgs : System.ComponentModel.CancelEventArgs
{

  string _msg = "";

  public ActionCancelEventArgs()    : base()  {}

  public ActionCancelEventArgs(bool cancel) : base(cancel)   {}

  public ActionCancelEventArgs(bool cancel, string message) : base(cancel)
  {
    _msg = message;
  }

  public string Message
  {
    get {return _msg;}
    set {_msg = value;}
  }
}
```

You can see that all an `EventArgs`-based class does is carry information about an event to and from the sender and receiver. Most times the information used from the `EventArgs` class will be used by the receiver object in the event handler. However, sometimes the event handler can add information into the `EventArgs` class and it will be available to the sender. This is how the example uses the `EventArgs` class. Notice that a couple of constructors are available in the `EventArgs` class. This extra flexibility adds to the usability of the class by others.

At this point, an event has been declared, the delegate has been defined, and the `EventArgs` class has been created. The next thing that has to happen is that the event needs to be raised. The only thing that you really need to do is make a call to the event with the proper parameters as shown in this example:

```
ActionCancelEventArgs ev = new CancelEventArgs();
Action(this, ev);
```

Simple enough. Create the new `ActionCancelEventArgs` class and pass it in as one of the parameters to the event. However, there is one small problem. What if the event hasn't been used anywhere yet? What if an event handler has not yet been defined for the event? The `Action` event would actually be null. If you tried to raise the event, you would get a null reference exception. If you wanted to derive a new form class and use the form that has the `Action` event defined as the base, you would have to do something else whenever the `Action` event is raised. Currently you would have to enable another event handler in the derived form in order to get access to it. To make this process a little easier and to catch the null reference error you have to create a method with the name `OnEventName` where `EventName` is the name of the event. The example has a method named `OnAction`. Here is the complete code for the `OnAction` method.

```
protected void OnAction(object sender, ActionCancelEventArgs ev)
{
  if(Action != null)
    Action(sender, ev);
}
```

## Chapter 6

Not much to it but it does accomplish what is needed. By making the method protected, only derived classes have access to it. You can also see that the event is tested against null before it is raised. If you were to derive a new class that contains this method and event, you would have to override the `OnAction` method and then you would be hooked into the event. To do this, you would have to call `base.OnAction()` in the override. Otherwise, the event would not be raised. This naming convention is used throughout the .NET Framework and is documented in the .NET SDK documentation.

Notice the two parameters that are passed into the `OnAction` method. They should look familiar to you because they are the same parameters that will need to be passed to the event. If the event needed to be raised from another object other than the one that the method is defined in, you would need to make the accessor internal or public and not protected. Sometimes it makes sense to have a class that consists of nothing but event declarations and that these events are called from other classes. You would still want to create the `OnEventName` methods. However, in that case they might be static methods.

So now that the event has been raised, something needs to handle it. Create a new class in the project and call it `BusEntity`. Remember that the goal of this project is to check the seconds property of the current time, and if it is less than 30, set a string value to the time, and if it is greater than 30, set the string to `::` and cancel the event. Here is the code:

```csharp
using System;
using System.IO;
using System.ComponentModel;

namespace SimpleEvent
{
  public class BusEntity
  {

    string _time = "";

    public BusEntity()
    {
      Form1.Action += new Form1.ActionEventHandler(Form1_Action);
    }

    private void Form1_Action(object sender, ActionCancelEventArgs ev)
    {
      ev.Cancel = !DoActions();
      if(ev.Cancel)
        ev.Message = "Wasn't the right time.";
    }

    private bool DoActions()
    {
      bool retVal = false;
      DateTime tm = DateTime.Now;

      if(tm.Second < 30)
      {
        _time = "The time is " + DateTime.Now.ToLongTimeString();
        retVal = true;
      }
```

```
        else
            _time = "";

        return retVal;

    }

    public string TimeString
    {
        get {return _time;}
    }

  }
}
```

In the constructor, the handler for the `Form1.Action` event is declared. Notice the syntax is very similar to the `Click` event that you registered earlier. Because you used the same pattern for declaring the event, the usage syntax stays consistent as well. Something else worth mentioning at this point is how you were able to get a reference to the `Action` event without having a reference to `Form1` in the `BusEntity` class. Remember that in the `Form1` class the `Action` event is declared static. This isn't a requirement, but it does make it easier to create the handler. You could have declared the event public, but then an instance of `Form1` would need to be referenced.

When you coded the event in the constructor, you called the method that was added to the delegate list `Form1_Action`, in keeping with the naming standards. In the handler a decision on whether or not to cancel the event needs to be made. The `DoActions` method returns a Boolean value based on the time criteria described earlier. `DoAction` also sets the `_time` string to the proper value.

Next, the `DoActions` return value is set to the `ActionCancelEventArgs Cancel` property. Remember that `EventArg` classes generally do not do anything other than carry values to and from the event senders and receivers. If the event is canceled (`ev.Cancel = true`), the `Message` property is also set with a string value that describes why the event was canceled.

Now if you look at the code in the `btnRaise_Click` event handler again you will be able to see how the `Cancel` property is used

```
    private void btnRaise_Click(object sender, EventArgs e)
    {
      ActionCancelEventArgs cancelEvent = new ActionCancelEventArgs();
      OnAction(this, cancelEvent);
      if(cancelEvent.Cancel)
        lblInfo.Text = cancelEvent.Message;
      else
        lblInfo.Text = _busEntity.TimeString;
    }
```

Note that the `ActionCancelEventArgs` object is created. Next the event `Action` is raised, passing in the newly created `ActionCancelEventArgs` object. When the `OnAction` method is called and the event is raised, the code in the `Action` event handler in the `BusEntity` object is executed. If there were other objects that had registered for the `Action` event, they too would execute. Something to keep in mind is that if there were other objects handling this event, they would all see the same `ActionCancelEventArgs` object. If you needed to keep up with which object canceled the event and whether more than one object canceled the event, you would need some type of list-based data structure in the `ActionCancelEventArgs` class.

After the handlers that have been registered with the event delegate have been executed, you can query the `ActionCancelEventArgs` object to see if it has been canceled. If it has been canceled, `lblInfo` will contain the `Message` property value. If the event has not been canceled, the `lblInfo` will show the current time.

This should give you a basic idea of how you can utilize events and the `EventArgs`-based object in the event to pass information around in your applications.

## Summary

This chapter gave you the basics of delegates and events. You learned how to declare a delegate and add methods to the delegate list. You also learned the process of declaring event handlers to respond to an event, as well as how to create a custom event and use the patterns for raising the event.

As a .NET developer, you will be using delegates and events extensively, especially when developing Windows Forms applications. Events are the means that the .NET developer has to monitor the various Windows messages that occur while the application is executing. Otherwise you would have to monitor the WndProc and catch the `WM_MOUSEDOWN` message instead of getting the mouse `Click` event for a button.

The use of delegates and events in the design of a large application can reduce dependencies and the coupling of layers. This allows you to develop components that have a higher reusability factor.

# Memory Management and Pointers

This chapter looks at various aspects of memory management and memory access. Although the runtime takes much of the responsibility for memory management away from the programmer, it is useful to understand how memory management works and important to know how to work with unmanaged resources efficiently.

If you have a good understanding of memory management and knowledge of the pointer capabilities provided by C#, you are also better positioned to integrate C# code with legacy code and perform efficient memory manipulation in performance-critical systems.

Specifically, this chapter discusses:

- ❑  How the runtime allocates space on the stack and the heap
- ❑  How garbage collection works
- ❑  How to use destructors and the `System.IDisposable` interface to ensure unmanaged resources are released correctly
- ❑  The syntax for using pointers in C#
- ❑  How to use pointers to implement high-performance stack-based arrays

## Memory Management under the Hood

One of the advantages of C# programming is that the programmer doesn't need to worry about detailed memory management; in particular, the garbage collector deals with the problem of memory cleanup on your behalf. The result is that you get something that approximates the efficiency of languages like C++ without the complexity of having to handle memory management yourself as you do in C++. However, although you don't need to manage memory manually, if you need to write efficient code, it still pays to understand what is going on behind the scenes. This section takes a look at what happens in the computer's memory when you allocate variables.

> *The precise details of much of the content of this section are undocumented. You should interpret this section as a simplified guide to the general processes rather than as a statement of exact implementation.*

## Value Data Types

Windows uses a system known as *virtual addressing*, in which the mapping from the memory address seen by your program to the actual location in hardware memory is entirely managed by Windows. The result of this is that each process on a 32-bit processor sees 4GB of available memory, irrespective of how much hardware memory you actually have in your computer (on 64-bit processors this number will be greater). This 4GB of memory contains everything that is part of the program, including the executable code, any DLLs loaded by the code, and the contents of all variables used when the program runs. This 4GB of memory is known as the *virtual address space* or *virtual memory*. For convenience in this chapter it is referred to simply as *memory*.

Each memory location in the available 4GB is numbered starting from zero. To access a value stored at a particular location in memory, you need to supply the number that represents that memory location. In any compiled high-level language, including C#, Visual Basic, C++, and Java, the compiler converts human-readable variable names into memory addresses that the processor understands.

Somewhere inside a process's virtual memory is an area known as the *stack*. The stack stores value data types that are not members of objects. In addition, when you call a method, the stack is used to hold a copy of any parameters passed to the method. To understand how the stack works, you need to understand the importance of variable scope in C#. It is *always* the case that if a variable a goes into scope before variable b, then b will go out of scope first. Look at this code:

```
{
    int a;
    // do something
    {
        int b;
        // do something else
    }
}
```

First, a gets declared. Then, inside the inner code block, b gets declared. Then the inner code block terminates and b goes out of scope; then a goes out of scope. So, the lifetime of b is entirely contained within the lifetime of a. The idea that you always deallocate variables in the reverse order to how you allocate them is crucial to the way the stack works.

You don't know exactly where in the address space the stack is — you don't need to know for C# development. A *stack pointer* (a variable maintained by the operating system) identifies the next free location on the stack. When your program first starts running, the stack pointer will point to just past the end of the block of memory that is reserved for the stack. The stack actually fills downward, from high memory addresses to low addresses. As data is put on the stack, the stack pointer is adjusted accordingly, so it always points to just past the next free location. This is illustrated in Figure 7-1, which shows a stack pointer with a value of 800000 (0xC3500 in hex) and the next free location is the address 799999.

# Memory Management and Pointers

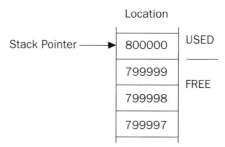

**Figure 7-1**

The following code instructs the compiler that you need space in memory to store an integer and a double, and these memory locations are referred to as `nRacingCars` and `engineSize`. The line that declares each variable indicates the point at which you will start requiring access to this variable, and the closing curly brace of the block in which the variables are declared identifies the point at which both variables go out of scope.

```
{
    int nRacingCars = 10;
    double engineSize = 3000.0;
    // do calculations;
}
```

Assuming you use the stack shown in Figure 7-1, when the variable `nRacingCars` comes into scope and is assigned the value `10`, the value `10` is placed in locations `799996` through `799999`, the four bytes just below the location pointed to by the stack pointer. (Four bytes because that's how much memory is needed to store an `int`.) To accommodate this, 4 is subtracted from the value of the stack pointer, so it now points to the location `799996`, just after the new first free location (`799995`).

The next line of code declares the variable `engineSize` (a `double`) and initializes it to the value `3000.0`. A `double` occupies 8 bytes, so the value `3000.0` will be placed in locations `799988` through `799995` on the stack, and the stack pointer is decremented by 8, so that once again, it points just after the next free location on the stack.

When `engineSize` goes out of scope, the computer knows that it is no longer needed. As a result of the way variable lifetimes are always nested, you can guarantee that, whatever else has happened while `engineSize` was in scope, the stack pointer is now pointing to the location where `engineSize` is stored. To remove `engineSize` from the stack, the stack pointer is incremented by 8, so that it now points to the location immediately after the end of `engineSize`. At this point in the code, you are at the closing curly brace and so `nRacingCars` also goes out of scope. The stack pointer gets incremented by 4. When another variable comes into scope after `engineSize` and `nRacingCars` have been removed from the stack, it would overwrite the memory descending from location `799999`, where `nRacingCars` used to be stored.

If the compiler hits a line like `int i, j`, the order of coming into scope looks indeterminate. Both variables are declared at the same time and go out of scope at the same time. In this situation, it doesn't matter in what order the two variables are removed from memory. The compiler internally always ensures that the one that was put in memory first is removed last, thus preserving the rule about no crossover of variable lifetimes.

# Chapter 7

# *Reference Data Types*

Although the stack gives very high performance, it is not flexible enough to be used for all variables. The requirement that the lifetimes of variables must be nested is too restrictive for many purposes. Often, you will want to use a method to allocate memory to store some data and be able to keep that data available long after that method has exited. This possibility exists whenever storage space is requested with the new operator — as is the case for all reference types. That's where the *managed heap* comes in.

If you have done any C++ coding that required low-level memory management, you will be familiar with the heap. The managed heap is not quite the same as the heap C++ uses; the managed heap works under the control of the garbage collector and provides significant benefits when compared to traditional heaps.

The managed heap (or heap for short) is just another area of memory from the process's available 4GB. The following code demonstrates how the heap works and how memory is allocated for reference data types:

```
void DoWork()
{
    Customer arabel;
    arabel = new Customer();
    Customer mrJones = new Nevermore60Customer();
}
```

This code assumes the existence of two classes, Customer and Nevermore60Customer. These classes are in fact taken from the Mortimer Phones examples in Appendix A (which is posted at www.wrox.com).

First, you declare a Customer reference called arabel. The space for this will be allocated on the stack, but remember that this is only a reference, not an actual Customer object. The arabel reference takes up 4 bytes, enough space to hold the address at which a Customer object will be stored. (You need 4 bytes to represent a memory address as an integer value between 0 and 4GB.)

The next line

```
arabel = new Customer();
```

does several things. First, it allocates memory on the heap to store a Customer object (a real object, not just an address). Then it sets the value of the variable arabel to the address of the memory it has allocated to the new Customer object. (It also calls the appropriate Customer() constructor to initialize the fields in the class instance, but we won't worry about that here.)

The Customer instance is not placed on the stack — it is placed on the heap. In this example, you don't know precisely how many bytes a Customer object occupies, but assume for the sake of argument it is 32. These 32 bytes contain the instance fields of Customer as well as some information that .NET uses to identify and manage its class instances.

To find a storage location on the heap for the new Customer object, the .NET runtime will look through the heap and grab the first contiguous, unused block of 32 bytes. Again for the sake of argument, assume that this happens to be at address 200000, and that the arabel reference occupied locations 799996 through 799999 on the stack. This means that before instantiating the arabel object, the memory contents will look similar to Figure 7-2.

# Memory Management and Pointers

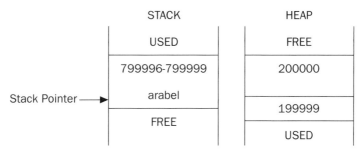

**Figure 7-2**

After allocating the new `Customer` object, the contents of memory will look like Figure 7-3. Note that unlike the stack, memory in the heap is allocated upward, so the free space can be found above the used space.

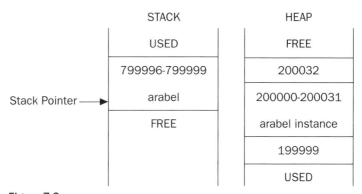

**Figure 7-3**

The next line of code both declares a `Customer` reference and instantiates a `Customer` object. In this instance, space on the stack for the `mrJones` reference is allocated and space for the `mrJones` object is allocated on the heap in a single line of code:

```
Customer mrJones = new Nevermore60Customer();
```

This line allocates 4 bytes on the stack to hold the `mrJones` reference, stored at locations `799992` through `799995`. The `mrJones` object is allocated space on the heap starting at location `200032`.

It is clear from the example that the process of setting up a reference variable is more complex than that for setting up a value variable, and there is a performance overhead. In fact, the process is somewhat oversimplified here, because the .NET runtime needs to maintain information about the state of the heap, and this information needs to be updated whenever new data is added to the heap. Despite these overheads, you now have a mechanism for allocating variables that is not constrained by the limitations of the stack. By assigning the value of one reference variable to another of the same type, you have two variables that reference the same object in memory. When a reference variable goes out of scope, it is

# Chapter 7

removed from the stack as described in the previous section, but the data for a referenced object is still sitting on the heap. The data will remain on the heap until either the program terminates, or the garbage collector removes it, which will only happen when it is no longer referenced by any variables.

That's the power of reference data types, and you will see this feature used extensively in C# code. It means that you have a high degree of control over the lifetime of your data, because it is guaranteed to exist in the heap as long as you are maintaining some reference to it.

## Garbage Collection

The previous discussion and diagrams show the managed heap working very much like the stack, to the extent that successive objects are placed next to each other in memory. This means that you can work out where to place the next object by using a heap pointer that indicates the next free memory location, and which gets adjusted as you add more objects to the heap. However, things are complicated because the lives of the heap-based objects are not coupled to the scope of the individual stack-based variables that reference them.

When the garbage collector runs, it will remove all those objects from the heap that are no longer referenced. Immediately after it has done this, the heap will have objects scattered on it, mixed up with memory that has just been freed (see Figure 7-4).

Figure 7-4

If the managed heap stayed like this, allocating space for new objects would be an awkward process, with the runtime having to search through the heap for a block of memory big enough to store each new object. However, the garbage collector doesn't leave the heap in this state. As soon as the garbage collector has freed up all the objects it can, it compacts the heap by moving all remaining objects to form one contiguous block of memory. This means that the heap can continue working just like the stack as far as locating where to store new objects is concerned. Of course, when the objects are moved about, all the references to those objects need to be updated with the correct new addresses, but the garbage collector handles that too.

This action of compacting by the garbage collector is where the managed heap really works differently from old unmanaged heaps. With the managed heap, it is just a question of reading the value of the heap

# Memory Management and Pointers

pointer, rather than iterating through a linked list of addresses to find somewhere to put the new data. For this reason, instantiating an object under .NET is much faster. Interestingly, accessing objects tends to be faster too, because the objects are compacted toward the same area of memory on the heap, resulting in less page swapping. Microsoft believes that these performance gains more than compensate for the performance penalty that you get whenever the garbage collector needs to do some work to compact the heap and change all those references to objects it has moved.

> *Generally, the garbage collector runs when the .NET runtime determines that a garbage collection is required. You can force the garbage collector to run at a certain point in your code by calling* `System.GC.Collect()`. *The* `System.GC` *class is a .NET class that represents the garbage collector, and the* `Collect()` *method initiates a garbage collection. The GC class is intended for rare situations in which you know that it's a good time to call the garbage collector; for example, if you have just dereferenced a large number of objects in your code. However, the logic of the garbage collector does not guarantee that all unreferenced objects will be removed from the heap in a single garbage collection pass.*

## Freeing Unmanaged Resources

The presence of the garbage collector means that you will usually not worry about objects that you no longer need; you will simply allow all references to those objects to go out of scope and allow the garbage collector to free memory as required. However, the garbage collector does not know how to free unmanaged resources (such as file handles, network connections, and database connections). When managed classes encapsulate direct or indirect references to unmanaged resources, you need to make special provision to ensure that the unmanaged resources are released when an instance of the class is garbage collected.

When defining a class, you can use two mechanisms to automate the freeing of unmanaged resources. These mechanisms are often implemented together because each provides a slightly different approach to the solution of the problem. The mechanisms are as follows:

- ❏ Declaring a destructor (or finalizer) as a member of your class
- ❏ Implementing the `System.IDisposable` interface in your class

The following sections discuss each of these mechanisms in turn, and then look at how to implement them together for best effect.

### *Destructors*

You've seen that constructors allow you to specify actions that must take place whenever an instance of a class is created. Conversely, destructors are called before an object is destroyed by the garbage collector. Given this behavior, a destructor would initially seem like a great place to put code to free unmanaged resources and perform a general cleanup. Unfortunately, things are not so straightforward.

> *Although we talk about destructors in C#, in the underlying .NET architecture these are known as finalizers. When you define a destructor in C#, what is emitted into the assembly by the compiler is actually a method called* `Finalize()`. *That's something that doesn't affect any of your source code, but you'll need to be aware of the fact if you need to examine the contents of an assembly.*

# Chapter 7

The syntax for a destructor will be familiar to C++ developers. It looks like a method, with the same name as the containing class, but prefixed with a tilde (~). It has no return type, and takes no parameters and no access modifiers. Here is an example:

```
class MyClass
{
    ~MyClass()
    {
        // destructor implementation
    }
}
```

When the C# compiler compiles a destructor, it implicitly translates the destructor code to the equivalent of a `Finalize()` method that ensures the `Finalize()` method of the parent class is executed. The following example shows the C# code equivalent to the IL that the compiler would generate for the ~MyClass destructor:

```
protected override void Finalize()
{
    try
    {
        // destructor implementation
    }
    finally
    {
        base.Finalize();
    }
}
```

As shown, the code implemented in the ~MyClass destructor is wrapped in a `try` block contained in the `Finalize()` method. A call to the parent's `Finalize()` method is ensured by placing the call in a `finally` block. `try` and `finally` blocks are discussed in Chapter 12, "Errors and Exceptions."

Experienced C++ developers make extensive use of destructors, sometimes not only to clean up resources but also to provide debugging information or perform other tasks. C# destructors are used far less than their C++ equivalents. The problem with C# destructors when compared with their C++ counterparts is that they are nondeterministic. When a C++ object is destroyed, its destructor runs immediately. However, because of the way the garbage collector works, there is no way to know when an object's destructor will actually execute. Hence, you cannot place any code in the destructor that relies on being run at a certain time, and you shouldn't rely on the destructor being called for different class instances in any particular order. When your object is holding scarce and critical resources that need to be freed as soon as possible, you don't want to wait for garbage collection.

Another problem with C# destructors is that the implementation of a destructor delays the final removal of an object from memory. Objects that do not have a destructor get removed from memory in one pass of the garbage collector, but objects that have destructors require two passes to be destroyed: The first one calls the destructor without removing the object, and the second actually deletes the object. In addition, the runtime uses a single thread to execute the `Finalize()` methods of all objects. If you use destructors frequently, and use them to execute lengthy cleanup tasks, the impact on performance can be noticeable.

# Memory Management and Pointers

## *The IDisposable Interface*

In C#, the recommended alternative to using a destructor is using the `System.IDisposable` interface. The `IDisposable` interface defines a pattern (with language-level support) that provides a deterministic mechanism for freeing unmanaged resources and avoids the garbage collector–related problems inherent with destructors. The `IDisposable` interface declares a single method named `Dispose()`, which takes no parameters and returns `void`. Here is an implementation for `MyClass`:

```
class MyClass : IDisposable
{
   public void Dispose()
   {
      // implementation
   }
}
```

The implementation of `Dispose()` should explicitly free all unmanaged resources used directly by an object and call `Dispose()` on any encapsulated objects that also implement the `IDisposable` interface. In this way, the `Dispose()` method provides precise control over when unmanaged resources are freed.

Suppose you have a class named `ResourceGobbler`, which relies on the use of some external resource and implements `IDisposable`. If you want to instantiate an instance of this class, use it, and then dispose of it, you could do it like this:

```
ResourceGobbler theInstance = new ResourceGobbler();

// do your processing

theInstance.Dispose();
```

Unfortunately, this code fails to free the resources consumed by `theInstance` if an exception occurs during processing, and so you should write the code as follows using a `try` block (which is discussed fully in Chapter 12):

```
ResourceGobbler theInstance = null;

try
{
   theInstance = new ResourceGobbler();

   // do your processing
}
finally
{
   if (theInstance != null) theInstance.Dispose();
}
```

This version ensures that `Dispose()` is always called on `theInstance` and that any resources consumed by it are always freed, even if an exception occurs during processing. However, it would make for confusing code if you always had to repeat such a construct. C# offers a syntax that you can use to guarantee that `Dispose()` will automatically be called against an object that implements `IDisposable` when its reference goes out of scope. The syntax to do this involves the `using` keyword — though now in a very different context, which has nothing to do with namespaces. The following code generates IL code equivalent to the `try` block just shown:

```
using (ResourceGobbler theInstance = new ResourceGobbler())
{
   // do your processing
}
```

The `using` statement, followed in brackets by a reference variable declaration and instantiation, will cause that variable to be scoped to the accompanying statement block. In addition, when that variable goes out of scope, its `Dispose()` method will be called automatically, even if an exception occurs. However, if you are already using `try` blocks to catch other exceptions, it is cleaner and avoids additional code indentation if you avoid the `using` statement and simply call `Dispose()` in the `Finally` clause of the existing `try` block.

> *For some classes, the notion of a* `Close()` *method is more logical than* `Dispose()`; *for example, when dealing with files or database connections. In these cases it is common to implement the* `IDisposable` *interface and then implement a separate* `Close()` *method that simply calls* `Dispose()`. *This approach provides clarity in the use of your classes but also supports the* `using` *statement provided by C#.*

## Implementing IDisposable and a Destructor

The previous sections discussed two alternatives for freeing unmanaged resources used by the classes you create:

- ❑ The execution of a destructor is enforced by the runtime but is nondeterministic and places an unacceptable overhead on the runtime because of the way garbage collection works.

- ❑ The `IDisposable` interface provides a mechanism that allows users of a class to control when resources are freed, but requires discipline to ensure that `Dispose()` is called.

In general, the best approach is to implement both mechanisms in order to gain the benefits of both while overcoming their limitations. You implement `IDisposable` on the assumption that most programmers will call `Dispose()` correctly, but implement a destructor as a safety mechanism in case `Dispose()` is not called. Here is an example of a dual implementation:

```
public class ResourceHolder : IDisposable
{
    private bool isDisposed = false;

    public void Dispose()
    {
       Dispose(true);
       GC.SuppressFinalize(this);
    }

    protected virtual void Dispose(bool disposing)
    {
       if (!isDisposed)
       {
```

```
            if (disposing)
            {
                // Cleanup managed objects by calling their
                // Dispose() methods.
            }
            // Cleanup unmanaged objects
        }
        isDisposed = true;
    }

    ~ResourceHolder()
    {
        Dispose (false);
    }

    public void SomeMethod()
    {
        // Ensure object not already disposed before execution of any method
        if(isDisposed)
        {
            throw new ObjectDisposedException("ResourceHolder");
        }

        // method implementation...
    }
}
```

You can see from this code that there is a second `protected` overload of `Dispose()`, which takes one `bool` parameter—and this is the method that does all cleaning up. `Dispose(bool)` is called by both the destructor and by `IDisposable.Dispose()`. The point of this approach is to ensure that all cleanup code is in one place.

The parameter passed to `Dispose(bool)` indicates whether `Dispose(bool)` has been invoked by the destructor or by `IDisposable.Dispose()`—`Dispose(bool)` should not be invoked from anywhere else in your code. The idea is this:

❑  If a consumer calls `IDisposable.Dispose()`, that consumer is indicating that all managed and unmanaged resources associated with that object should be cleaned up.

❑  If a destructor has been invoked, all resources still need to be cleaned up. However, in this case, you know that the destructor must have been called by the garbage collector and you should not attempt to access other managed objects because you can no longer be certain of their state. In this situation, the best you can do is clean up the known unmanaged resources, and hope that any referenced managed objects also have destructors that will perform their own cleaning up.

The `isDisposed` member variable indicates whether the object has already been disposed and allows you to ensure you do not try to dispose of member variables more than once. It also allows you to test whether an object has been disposed before executing any instance methods, as shown in `SomeMethod()`. This simplistic approach is not thread-safe and depends on the caller ensuring only one thread is calling the method concurrently. Requiring a consumer to enforce synchronization is a reasonable assumption and one that is used repeatedly throughout the .NET class libraries (in the Collection classes for example). Threading and synchronization are discussed in Chapter 13, "Threading."

Finally, `IDisposable.Dispose()` contains a call to the method `System.GC.SuppressFinalize()`. `GC` is the class that represents the garbage collector, and the `SuppressFinalize()` method tells the garbage collector that a class no longer needs to have its destructor called. Because your implementation of `Dispose()` has already done all the cleanup required, there's nothing left for the destructor to do. Calling `SuppressFinalize()` means that the garbage collector will treat that object as if it doesn't have a destructor at all.

# Unsafe Code

As you have just seen, C# is very good at hiding much of the basic memory management from the developer, thanks to the garbage collector and the use of references. However, cases exist in which you will want direct access to memory. For example, you might want to access a function in an external (non-.NET) DLL that requires a pointer to be passed as a parameter (as many Windows API functions do), or possibly for performance reasons. This section examines C#'s facilities that provide direct access to the contents of memory.

## *Pointers*

Although we are introducing *pointers* as if they are a new topic, in reality pointers are not new at all. You have been using references freely in your code, and a reference is simply a type-safe pointer. You have already seen how variables that represent objects and arrays actually store the memory address of where the corresponding data (the *referent*) is stored. A pointer is simply a variable that stores the address of something else in the same way as a reference. The difference is that C# does not allow you direct access to the address contained in a reference variable. With a reference, the variable is treated syntactically as if it stores the actual contents of the referent.

C# references are designed to make the language simpler to use and to prevent you from inadvertently doing something that corrupts the contents of memory. With a pointer, on the other hand, the actual memory address is available to you. This gives you a lot of power to perform new kinds of operations. For example, you can add 4 bytes to the address, so that you can examine or even modify whatever data happens to be stored 4 bytes further on in memory.

The two main reasons for using pointers are as follows:

❑   **Backwards compatibility** — Despite all of the facilities provided by the .NET runtime, it is still possible to call native Windows API functions, and for some operations, this may be the only way to accomplish your task. These API functions are generally written in C and often require pointers as parameters. However, in many cases it is possible to write the `DllImport` declaration in a way that avoids use of pointers; for example, by using the `System.IntPtr` class.

❑   **Performance** — On those occasions where speed is of the utmost importance, pointers can provide a route to optimized performance. Provided you know what you are doing, you can ensure that data is accessed or manipulated in the most efficient way. However, be aware that more often than not, there are other areas of your code where you can make the necessary performance improvements without resorting to using pointers. Try using a code profiler to look for the bottlenecks in your code — one comes with Visual Studio 2005.

# Memory Management and Pointers

Low-level memory access comes at a price. The syntax for using pointers is more complex than that for reference types and pointers are unquestionably more difficult to use correctly. You need good programming skills and an excellent ability to think carefully and logically about what your code is doing in order to use pointers successfully. If you are not careful, it is very easy to introduce subtle, difficult-to-find bugs into your program using pointers. For example, it is easy to overwrite other variables, cause stack overflows, access areas of memory that don't store any variables, or even overwrite information about your code that is needed by the .NET runtime, thereby crashing your program.

In addition, if you use pointers your code must be granted a high level of trust by the runtime's code access security mechanism or it will not be allowed to execute. Under the default code access security policy, this is only possible if your code is running on the local machine. If your code must be run from a remote location, such as the Internet, users must grant your code additional permissions for it to work. Unless the users trust you and your code, they are unlikely to grant these permissions. Code access security is discussed more in Chapter 16, ".NET Security."

Despite these issues, pointers remain a very powerful and flexible tool in the writing of efficient code and are worth learning about.

> *We strongly advise against using pointers unnecessarily because your code will not only be harder to write and debug, but it will also fail the memory type-safety checks imposed by the CLR, which is discussed in Chapter 1, ".NET Architecture."*

## *Writing unsafe code*

As a result of the risks associated with pointers, C# allows the use of pointers only in blocks of code that you have specifically marked for this purpose. The keyword to do this is unsafe. You can mark an individual method as being unsafe like this:

```
unsafe int GetSomeNumber()
{
    // code that can use pointers
}
```

Any method can be marked as unsafe, irrespective of what other modifiers have been applied to it (for example, static methods or virtual methods). In the case of methods, the unsafe modifier applies to the method's parameters, allowing you to use pointers as parameters. You can also mark an entire class or struct as unsafe, which means that all of its members are assumed to be unsafe:

```
unsafe class MyClass
{
    // any method in this class can now use pointers
}
```

Similarly, you can mark a member as unsafe:

```
class MyClass
{
    unsafe int *pX;    // declaration of a pointer field in a class
}
```

Or you can mark a block of code within a method as `unsafe`:

```
void MyMethod()
{
   // code that doesn't use pointers
   unsafe
   {
      // unsafe code that uses pointers here
   }
   // more 'safe' code that doesn't use pointers
}
```

Note, however, that you cannot mark a local variable by itself as `unsafe`:

```
int MyMethod()
{
   unsafe int *pX;    // WRONG
}
```

If you want to use an unsafe local variable, you will need to declare and use it inside a method or block that is unsafe. There is one more step before you can use pointers. The C# compiler rejects unsafe code unless you tell it that your code includes unsafe blocks. The flag to do this is `unsafe`. Hence, to compile a file named `MySource.cs` that contains unsafe blocks (assuming no other compiler options), the command is:

```
csc /unsafe MySource.cs
```

or:

```
csc -unsafe MySource.cs
```

*If you are using Visual Studio 2005, you will find the option to compile unsafe code in the Build tab of the project properties window.*

## Pointer syntax

Once you have marked a block of code as `unsafe`, you can declare a pointer using this syntax:

```
int* pWidth, pHeight;
double* pResult;
byte*[] pFlags;
```

This code declares four variables: `pWidth` and `pHeight` are pointers to integers, `pResult` is a pointer to a `double`, and `pFlags` is an array of pointers to bytes. It is common practice to use the prefix p in front of names of pointer variables to indicate that they are pointers. When used in a variable declaration, the symbol * indicates that you are declaring a pointer (that is, something that stores the address of a variable of the specified type).

# Memory Management and Pointers

*C++ developers should be aware of the syntax difference between C++ and C#. The C# statement* `int* pX, pY;` *corresponds to the C++ statement* `int *pX, *pY;`. *In C#, the* `*` *symbol is associated with the type rather than the variable name.*

Once you have declared variables of pointer types, you can use them in the same way as normal variables, but first you need to learn two more operators:

- `&` means *take the address of*, and converts a value data type to a pointer, for example `int` to `*int`. This operator is known as the *address operator*.
- `*` means *get the contents of this address*, and converts a pointer to a value data type (for example, `*float` to `float`). This operator is known as the *indirection operator* (or sometimes as the *dereference operator*).

You will see from these definitions that `&` and `*` have the opposite effect to one another.

*You might be wondering how it is possible to use the symbols* `&` *and* `*` *in this manner, because these symbols also refer to the operators of bitwise AND (*`&`*) and multiplication (*`*`*). Actually, it is always possible for both you and the compiler to know what is meant in each case, because with the new pointer meanings, these symbols always appear as unary operators — they only act on one variable and appear in front of that variable in your code. On the other hand, bitwise AND and multiplication are binary operators — they require two operands.*

The following code shows examples of how to use these operators:

```
int x = 10;
int* pX, pY;
pX = &x;
pY = pX;
*pY = 20;
```

You start off by declaring an integer, x, with the value 10 followed by two pointers to integers, pX and pY. You then set pX to point to x (that is, you set the contents of pX to be the address of x). Then you assign the value of pX to pY, so that pY also points to x. Finally, in the statement `*pY = 20`, you assign the value 20 as the contents of the location pointed to by pY — in effect changing x to 20 because pY happens to point to x. Note that there is no particular connection between the variables pY and x. It's just that at the present time, pY happens to point to the memory location at which x is held.

To get a better understanding of what is going on, consider that the integer x is stored at memory locations `0x12F8C4` through `0x12F8C7` (1243332 to 1243335 in decimal) on the stack (there are 4 locations because an `int` occupies 4 bytes). Because the stack allocates memory downward, this means that the variables pX will be stored at locations `0x12F8C0` to `0x12F8C3`, and pY will end up at locations `0x12F8BC` to `0x12F8BF`. Note that pX and pY also occupy 4 bytes each. That is not because an `int` occupies 4 bytes. It's because on a 32-bit processor you need 4 bytes to store an address. With these addresses, after executing the previous code, the stack will look like Figure 7-5.

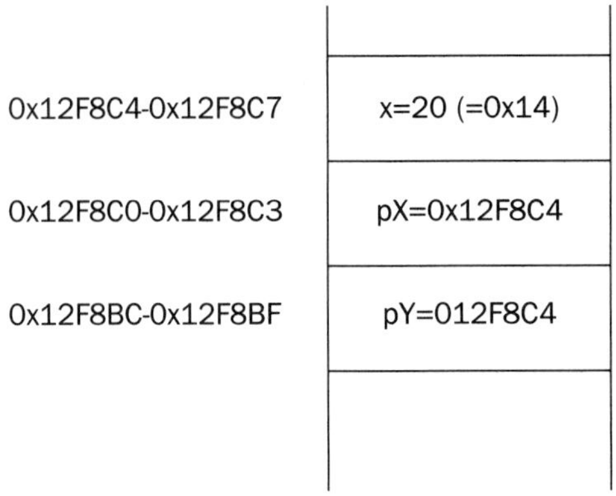

|                      |              |
|----------------------|--------------|
| 0x12F8C4-0x12F8C7    | x=20 (=0x14) |
|                      |              |
| 0x12F8C0-0x12F8C3    | pX=0x12F8C4  |
|                      |              |
| 0x12F8BC-0x12F8BF    | pY=012F8C4   |
|                      |              |

**Figure 7-5**

*Although this process is illustrated with integers, which will be stored consecutively on the stack on a 32-bit processor, this doesn't happen for all data types. The reason is that 32-bit processors work best retrieving data from memory in 4-byte chunks. Memory on such machines tends to be divided into 4-byte blocks, and each block is sometimes known under Windows as a DWORD because this was the name of a 32-bit unsigned int in pre-.NET days. It is most efficient to grab DWORDs from memory—storing data across DWORD boundaries normally gives a hardware performance hit. For this reason, the .NET runtime normally pads out data types so that the memory they occupy is a multiple of 4. For example, a short occupies 2 bytes, but if a short is placed on the stack, the stack pointer will still be decremented by 4, not 2, so that the next variable to go on the stack will still start at a DWORD boundary.*

You can declare a pointer to any value type (that is, any of the predefined types `uint`, `int`, `byte`, and so on, or to a struct). However, it is not possible to declare a pointer to a class or array; this is because doing so could cause problems for the garbage collector. In order to work properly, the garbage collector needs to know exactly what class instances have been created on the heap, and where they are, but if your code started manipulating classes using pointers, you could very easily corrupt the information on the heap concerning classes that the .NET runtime maintains for the garbage collector. In this context, any data type that the garbage collector can access is known as a *managed type*. Pointers can only be declared as *unmanaged types* because the garbage collector cannot deal with them.

## *Casting pointers to integer types*

Because a pointer really stores an integer that represents an address, you won't be surprised to know that the address in any pointer can be converted to or from any integer type. Pointer-to-integer-type conversions must be explicit. Implicit conversions are not available for such conversions. For example, it is perfectly legitimate to write the following:

```
int x = 10;
int* pX, pY;
pX = &x;
pY = pX;
*pY = 20;
uint y = (uint)pX;
int* pD = (int*)y;
```

# Memory Management and Pointers

The address held in the pointer pX is cast to a uint and stored in the variable y. You have then cast y back to an int* and stored it in the new variable pD. Hence, now pD also points to the value of x.

The primary reason for casting a pointer value to an integer type is to display it. The Console.Write() and Console.WriteLine() methods do not have any overloads that can take pointers, but will accept and display pointer values that have been cast to integer types:

```
Console.WriteLine("Address is " + pX);          // wrong -- will give a
                                                // compilation error
Console.WriteLine("Address is " + (uint)pX);    // OK
```

You can cast a pointer to any of the integer types. However, because an address occupies 4 bytes on 32-bit systems, casting a pointer to anything other than a uint, long, or ulong is almost certain to lead to overflow errors. (An int causes problems because its range is from roughly –2 billion to 2 billion, whereas an address runs from zero to about 4 billion.) When C# is released for 64-bit processors, an address will occupy 8 bytes. Hence, on such systems, casting a pointer to anything other than ulong is likely to lead to overflow errors. It is also important to be aware that the checked keyword does not apply to conversions involving pointers. For such conversions, exceptions will not be raised when overflows occur, even in a checked context. The .NET runtime assumes that if you are using pointers you know what you are doing and are not worried about possible overflows.

## Casting between pointer types

You can also explicitly convert between pointers pointing to different types. For example:

```
byte aByte = 8;
byte* pByte= &aByte;
double* pDouble = (double*)pByte;
```

This is perfectly legal code, though again, if you try something like this, be careful. In this example, if you look at the double value pointed to by pDouble, you will actually be looking up some memory that contains a byte (aByte), combined with some other memory, and treating it as if this area of memory contained a double, which won't give a meaningful value. However, you might want to convert between types in order to implement the equivalent of a C union, or you might want to cast pointers to other types into pointers to sbyte in order to examine individual bytes of memory.

## void pointers

If you want to maintain a pointer, but do not want to specify what type of data it points to, you can declare it as a pointer to a void:

```
int* pointerToInt;
void* pointerToVoid;
pointerToVoid = (void*)pointerToInt;
```

The main use of this is if you need to call an API function that requires void* parameters. Within the C# language, there isn't a great deal that you can do using void pointers. In particular, the compiler will flag an error if you attempt to dereference a void pointer using the * operator.

## Chapter 7

### *Pointer arithmetic*

It is possible to add or subtract integers to and from pointers. However, the compiler is quite clever about how it arranges for this to be done. For example, suppose you have a pointer to an `int` and you try to add 1 to its value. The compiler will assume you actually mean you want to look at the memory location following the `int`, and hence will increase the value by 4 bytes — the size of an `int`. If it is a pointer to a `double`, adding 1 will actually increase the value of the pointer by 8 bytes, the size of a `double`. Only if the pointer points to a `byte` or `sbyte` (1 byte each) will adding 1 to the value of the pointer actually change its value by 1.

You can use the operators +, -, +=, -=, ++, and -- with pointers, with the variable on the right-hand side of these operators being a `long` or `ulong`.

> *It is not permitted to carry out arithmetic operations on void pointers.*

For example, assume these definitions:

```
uint u = 3;
byte b = 8;
double d = 10.0;
uint* pUint= &u;        // size of a uint is 4
byte* pByte = &b;       // size of a byte is 1
double* pDouble = &d;   // size of a double is 8
```

Next, assume the addresses to which these pointers point are:

- pUint: 1243332
- pByte: 1243328
- pDouble: 1243320

Then execute this code:

```
++pUint;                // adds (1*4) = 4 bytes to pUint
pByte -= 3;             // subtracts (3*1) = 3 bytes from pByte
double* pDouble2 = pDouble + 4; // pDouble2 = pDouble + 32 bytes (4*8 bytes)
```

The pointers now contain:

- pUint: 1243336
- pByte: 1243325
- pDouble2: 1243352

> The general rule is that adding a number X to a pointer to type T with value P gives the result P + X*(sizeof(T)).

# Memory Management and Pointers

*You need to be aware of the previous rule. If successive values of a given type are stored in successive memory locations, pointer addition works very well to allow you to move pointers between memory locations. If you are dealing with types such as byte or char, though, whose sizes are not multiples of 4, successive values will not by default be stored in successive memory locations.*

You can also subtract one pointer from another pointer, provided both pointers point to the same data type. In this case, the result is a `long` whose value is given by the difference between the pointer values divided by the size of the type that they represent:

```
double* pD1 = (double*)1243324;    // note that it is perfectly valid to
                                   // initialize a pointer like this.
double* pD2 = (double*)1243300;
long L = pD1-pD2;                  // gives the result 3 (=24/sizeof(double))
```

## The sizeof operator

This section has been referring to the sizes of various data types. If you need to use the size of a type in your code, you can use the `sizeof` operator, which takes the name of a data type as a parameter and returns the number of bytes occupied by that type. For example:

```
int x = sizeof(double);
```

This will set x to the value 8.

The advantage of using `sizeof` is that you don't have to hardcode data type sizes in your code, making your code more portable. For the predefined data types, `sizeof` returns the following values:

```
sizeof(sbyte) = 1;          sizeof(byte) = 1;
sizeof(short) = 2;          sizeof(ushort) = 2;
sizeof(int) = 4;            sizeof(uint) = 4;
sizeof(long) = 8;           sizeof(ulong) = 8;
sizeof(char) = 2;           sizeof(float) = 4;
sizeof(double) = 8;         sizeof(bool) = 1;
```

You can also use `sizeof` for structs that you define yourself, though in that case, the result depends on what fields are in the struct. You cannot use `sizeof` for classes, and it can only be used in an `unsafe` code block.

## Pointers to structs: The pointer member access operator

Pointers to structs work in exactly the same way as pointers to the predefined value types. There is, however, one condition — the struct must not contain any reference types. This is due to the restriction mentioned earlier that pointers cannot point to any reference types. To avoid this, the compiler will flag an error if you create a pointer to any struct that contains any reference types.

# Chapter 7

Suppose you had a struct defined like this:

```
struct MyStruct
{
    public long X;
    public float F;
}
```

You could define a pointer to it like this:

```
MyStruct* pStruct;
```

Then you could initialize it like this:

```
MyStruct Struct = new MyStruct();
pStruct = &Struct;
```

It is also possible to access member values of a struct through the pointer:

```
(*pStruct).X = 4;
(*pStruct).F = 3.4f;
```

However, this syntax is a bit complex. For this reason, C# defines another operator that allows you to access members of structs through pointers using a simpler syntax. It is known as the *pointer member access operator*, and the symbol is a dash followed by a greater-than sign, so it looks like an arrow: ->.

> C++ developers will recognize the pointer member access operator, because C++ uses the same symbol for the same purpose.

Using the pointer member access operator, the previous code can be rewritten:

```
pStruct->X = 4;
pStruct->F = 3.4f;
```

You can also directly set up pointers of the appropriate type to point to fields within a struct:

```
long* pL = &(Struct.X);
float* pF = &(Struct.F);
```

or, equivalently:

```
long* pL = &(pStruct->X);
float* pF = &(pStruct->F);
```

## Pointers to class members

As indicated earlier, it is not possible to create pointers to classes. That's because the garbage collector does not maintain any information about pointers, only about references, so creating pointers to classes could cause garbage collection to not work properly.

212

However, most classes do contain value type members, and you might want to create pointers to them. This is possible but requires a special syntax. For example, suppose you rewrite the struct from the previous example as a class:

```
class MyClass
{
    public long X;
    public float F;
}
```

Then you might want to create pointers to its fields, X and F, in the same way as you did earlier. Unfortunately, doing so will produce a compilation error:

```
MyClass myObject = new MyClass();
long* pL = &(myObject.X);    // wrong -- compilation error
float* pF = &(myObject.F);   // wrong -- compilation error
```

Although X and F are unmanaged types, they are embedded in an object, which sits on the heap. During garbage collection, the garbage collector might move MyObject to a new location, which would leave pL and pF pointing to the wrong memory addresses. Because of this the compiler will not let you assign addresses of members of managed types to pointers in this manner.

The solution is to use the `fixed` keyword, which tells the garbage collector that there may be pointers referencing members of certain objects, so those objects must not be moved. The syntax for using `fixed` looks like this if you just want to declare one pointer:

```
MyClass myObject = new MyClass();
fixed (long* pObject = &(myObject.X))
{
    // do something
}
```

You define and initialize the pointer variable in the brackets following the keyword `fixed`. This pointer variable (pObject in the example) is scoped to the `fixed` block identified by the curly braces. In doing this, the garbage collector knows not to move the myObject object while the code inside the `fixed` block is executing.

If you want to declare more than one pointer, you can place multiple `fixed` statements before the same code block:

```
MyClass myObject = new MyClass();
fixed (long* pX = &(myObject.X))
fixed (float* pF = &(myObject.F))
{
    // do something
}
```

You can nest entire `fixed` blocks if you want to fix several pointers for different periods:

```
MyClass myObject = new MyClass();
fixed (long* pX = &(myObject.X))
{
   // do something with pX
   fixed (float* pF = &(myObject.F))
   {
      // do something else with pF
   }
}
```

You can also initialize several variables within the same `fixed` block, provided they are of the same type:

```
MyClass myObject = new MyClass();
MyClass myObject2 = new MyClass();
fixed (long* pX = &(myObject.X), pX2 = &(myObject2.X))
{
   // etc.
```

In all these cases, it is immaterial whether the various pointers you are declaring point to fields in the same or different objects or to static fields not associated with any class instance.

## Pointer Example: PointerPlayaround

This section presents an example that uses pointers. The following code is an example named `PointerPlayaround`. It does some simple pointer manipulation and displays the results, allowing you to see what is happening in memory and where variables are stored:

```
using System;

namespace Wrox.ProCSharp.Chapter07
{
   class MainEntryPoint
   {
      static unsafe void Main()
      {
         int x=10;
         short y = -1;
         byte y2 = 4;
         double z = 1.5;
         int* pX = &x;
         short* pY = &y;
         double* pZ = &z;

         Console.WriteLine(
            "Address of x is 0x{0:X}, size is {1}, value is {2}",
            (uint)&x, sizeof(int), x);
         Console.WriteLine(
            "Address of y is 0x{0:X}, size is {1}, value is {2}",
            (uint)&y, sizeof(short), y);
```

# Memory Management and Pointers

```csharp
            Console.WriteLine(
                "Address of y2 is 0x{0:X}, size is {1}, value is {2}",
                (uint)&y2, sizeof(byte), y2);
            Console.WriteLine(
                "Address of z is 0x{0:X}, size is {1}, value is {2}",
                (uint)&z, sizeof(double), z);
            Console.WriteLine(
                "Address of pX=&x is 0x{0:X}, size is {1}, value is 0x{2:X}",
                (uint)&pX, sizeof(int*), (uint)pX);
            Console.WriteLine(
                "Address of pY=&y is 0x{0:X}, size is {1}, value is 0x{2:X}",
                (uint)&pY, sizeof(short*), (uint)pY);
            Console.WriteLine(
                "Address of pZ=&z is 0x{0:X}, size is {1}, value is 0x{2:X}",
                (uint)&pZ, sizeof(double*), (uint)pZ);

            *pX = 20;
            Console.WriteLine("After setting *pX, x = {0}", x);
            Console.WriteLine("*pX = {0}", *pX);

            pZ = (double*)pX;
            Console.WriteLine("x treated as a double = {0}", *pZ);

            Console.ReadLine();
        }
    }
}
```

This code declares four value variables:

- ❑ An `int x`
- ❑ A `short y`
- ❑ A `byte y2`
- ❑ A `double z`

It also declares pointers to three of these values: `pX`, `pY`, and `pZ`.

Next, you display the values of these variables as well as their sizes and addresses. Note that in taking the address of `pX`, `pY`, and `pZ`, you are effectively looking at a pointer *to* a pointer — an address of an address of a value. Notice that, in accordance with the usual practice when displaying addresses, you have used the `{0:X}` format specifier in the `Console.WriteLine()` commands to ensure that memory addresses are displayed in hexadecimal format.

Finally, you use the pointer `pX` to change the value of `x` to `20` and do some pointer casting to see what happens if you try to treat the content of `x` as if it were a `double`.

Compiling and running this code results in the following output. This screen output demonstrates the effects of attempting to compile both with and without the `/unsafe` flag:

```
csc PointerPlayaround.cs
Microsoft (R) Visual C# 2005 Compiler version 8.00.50215.33
for Microsoft (R) Windows (R) 2005 Framework version 2.0.50215
Copyright (C) Microsoft Corporation 2001-2005. All rights reserved.

PointerPlayaround.cs(7,26): error CS0227: Unsafe code may only appear if
        compiling with /unsafe

csc /unsafe PointerPlayaround.cs
Microsoft (R) Visual C# 2005 Compiler version 8.00.50215.33
for Microsoft (R) Windows (R) 2005 Framework version 2.0.50215
Copyright (C) Microsoft Corporation 2001-2005. All rights reserved.

PointerPlayaround
Address of x is 0x12F4B0, size is 4, value is 10
Address of y is 0x12F4AC, size is 2, value is -1
Address of y2 is 0x12F4A8, size is 1, value is 4
Address of z is 0x12F4A0, size is 8, value is 1.5
Address of pX=&x is 0x12F49C, size is 4, value is 0x12F4B0
Address of pY=&y is 0x12F498, size is 4, value is 0x12F4AC
Address of pZ=&z is 0x12F494, size is 4, value is 0x12F4A0
After setting *pX, x = 20
*pX = 20
x treated as a double = 2.86965129997082E-308
```

Checking through these results confirms the description of how the stack operates that was given in the "Memory Management under the Hood" section earlier in this chapter. It allocates successive variables moving downward in memory. Notice how it also confirms that blocks of memory on the stack are always allocated in multiples of 4 bytes. For example, y is a short (of size 2), and has the (decimal) address 1242284, indicating that the memory locations reserved for it are locations 1242284 through 1242287. If the .NET runtime had been strictly packing up variables next to each other, Y would have occupied just two locations, 1242284 and 1242285.

The next example illustrates pointer arithmetic, as well as pointers to structs and class members. This example is called call PointerPlayaround2. To start off, you define a struct named CurrencyStruct, which represents a currency value as dollars and cents. You also define an equivalent class named CurrencyClass:

```
struct CurrencyStruct
{
   public long Dollars;
   public byte Cents;

   public override string ToString()
   {
      return "$" + Dollars + "." + Cents;
   }
}

class CurrencyClass
{
   public long Dollars;
   public byte Cents;
```

```
        public override string ToString()
        {
            return "$" + Dollars + "." + Cents;
        }
    }
```

Now that you have your struct and class defined, you can apply some pointers to them. Following is the code for the new example. Because the code is fairly long, we will go through it in detail. You start off by displaying the size of `CurrencyStruct`, creating a couple of `CurrencyStruct` instances and creating some `CurrencyStruct` pointers. You use the `pAmount` pointer to initialize the members of the `amount1` `CurrencyStruct` and then display the addresses of your variables:

```
public static unsafe void Main()
{
    Console.WriteLine(
        "Size of CurrencyStruct struct is " + sizeof(CurrencyStruct));
    CurrencyStruct amount1, amount2;
    CurrencyStruct* pAmount = &amount1;
    long* pDollars = &(pAmount->Dollars);
    byte* pCents = &(pAmount->Cents);

    Console.WriteLine("Address of amount1 is 0x{0:X}", (uint)&amount1);
    Console.WriteLine("Address of amount2 is 0x{0:X}", (uint)&amount2);
    Console.WriteLine("Address of pAmount is 0x{0:X}", (uint)&pAmount);
    Console.WriteLine("Address of pDollars is 0x{0:X}", (uint)&pDollars);
    Console.WriteLine("Address of pCents is 0x{0:X}", (uint)&pCents);
    pAmount->Dollars = 20;
    *pCents = 50;
    Console.WriteLine("amount1 contains " + amount1);
```

Now you do some pointer manipulation that relies on your knowledge of how the stack works. Due to the order in which the variables were declared, you know that `amount2` will be stored at an address immediately below `amount1`. The `sizeof(CurrencyStruct)` operator returns 16 (as demonstrated in the screen output coming up), so `CurrencyStruct` occupies a multiple of 4 bytes. Therefore, after you decrement your currency pointer, it will point to `amount2`:

```
    --pAmount;    // this should get it to point to amount2
    Console.WriteLine("amount2 has address 0x{0:X} and contains {1}",
        (uint)pAmount, *pAmount);
```

Notice that when you call `Console.WriteLine()` you display the contents of `amount2` but you haven't yet initialized it. What gets displayed will be random garbage—whatever happened to be stored at that location in memory before execution of the example. There is an important point here: normally, the C# compiler would prevent you from using an uninitialized variable, but when you start using pointers, it is very easy to circumvent many of the usual compilation checks. In this case, you have done so because the compiler has no way of knowing that you are actually displaying the contents of `amount2`. Only you know that, because your knowledge of the stack means you can tell what the effect of decrementing `pAmount` will be. Once you start doing pointer arithmetic, you find you can access all sorts of variables and memory locations that the compiler would usually stop you from accessing, hence the description of pointer arithmetic as unsafe.

Next you do some pointer arithmetic on your `pCents` pointer. `pCents` currently points to `amount1.Cents`, but the aim here is to get it to point to `amount2.Cents`, again using pointer operations instead of directly telling the compiler that's what you want to do. To do this, you need to decrement the address `pCents` contains by `sizeof(Currency)`:

```
// do some clever casting to get pCents to point to cents
// inside amount2
CurrencyStruct* pTempCurrency = (CurrencyStruct*)pCents;
pCents = (byte*) ( --pTempCurrency );
Console.WriteLine("Address of pCents is now 0x{0:X}", (uint)&pCents);
```

Finally, you use the `fixed` keyword to create some pointers that point to the fields in a class instance, and use these pointers to set the value of this instance. Notice that this is also the first time that you have been able to look at the address of an item stored on the heap rather than the stack:

```
Console.WriteLine("\nNow with classes");
// now try it out with classes
CurrencyClass amount3 = new CurrencyClass();

fixed(long* pDollars2 = &(amount3.Dollars))
fixed(byte* pCents2 = &(amount3.Cents))
{
   Console.WriteLine(
      "amount3.Dollars has address 0x{0:X}", (uint)pDollars2);
   Console.WriteLine(
      "amount3.Cents has address 0x{0:X}", (uint) pCents2);
   *pDollars2 = -100;
   Console.WriteLine("amount3 contains " + amount3);
}
```

Compiling and running this code gives output similar to this:

```
csc /unsafe PointerPlayaround2.cs
Microsoft (R) Visual C# 2005 Compiler version 8.00.50215.33
for Microsoft (R) Windows (R) 2005 Framework version 2.0.50215
Copyright (C) Microsoft Corporation 2001-2005. All rights reserved.

PointerPlayaround2
Size of CurrencyStruct struct is 16
Address of amount1 is 0x12F4A4
Address of amount2 is 0x12F494
Address of pAmount is 0x12F490
Address of pDollars is 0x12F48C
Address of pCents is 0x12F488
amount1 contains $20.50
amount2 has address 0x12F494 and contains $0.0
Address of pCents is now 0x12F488

Now with classes
amount3.Dollars has address 0xA64414
amount3.Cents has address 0xA6441C
amount3 contains $-100.0
```

# Memory Management and Pointers

*These results were obtained using the .NET Framework version 2.0 Beta 2. You might find that the actual addresses displayed are different if you run the sample on a different version of .NET.*

Notice in this output the uninitialized value of `amount2` that is displayed and that the size of the `CurrencyStruct` struct is 16 — somewhat larger than you would expect given the sizes of its fields (a `long` and a `byte` should total 9 bytes). This is the effect of word alignment that was discussed earlier.

## Using Pointers to Optimize Performance

Until now, all of the examples have been designed to demonstrate the various things that you can do with pointers. We have played around with memory in a way that is probably interesting only to people who like to know what's happening under the hood, but doesn't really help you to write better code. Here you're going to apply your understanding of pointers and see an example in which judicious use of pointers will have a significant performance benefit.

### Creating stack-based arrays

This section looks at one of the main areas in which pointers can be useful; creating high-performance, low-overhead arrays on the stack. As discussed in Chapter 2, "C# Basics," C# includes rich support for handling arrays. Although C# makes it very easy to use both one-dimensional and rectangular or jagged multidimensional arrays, it suffers from the disadvantage that these arrays are actually objects; they are instances of `System.Array`. This means that the arrays are stored on the heap with all of the overhead that this involves. There may be occasions when you need to create a short-lived high-performance array and don't want the overhead of reference objects. You can do this using pointers, although as you see in this section, this is only easy for one-dimensional arrays.

To create a high-performance array, you need to use a new keyword: `stackalloc`. The `stackalloc` command instructs the .NET runtime to allocate an amount of memory on the stack. When you call `stackalloc`, you need to supply it with two pieces of information:

- ❑ The type of data you want to store
- ❑ How many of these data items you need to store

For example, to allocate enough memory to store 10 `decimal` data items, you can write:

```
decimal* pDecimals = stackalloc decimal[10];
```

This command simply allocates the stack memory; it doesn't attempt to initialize the memory to any default value. This is fine for the purpose of this example because you are creating a high-performance array, and initializing values unnecessarily would hurt performance.

Similarly, to store 20 `double` data items, you write:

```
double* pDoubles = stackalloc double[20];
```

Although this line of code specifies the number of variables to store as a constant, this can equally be a quantity evaluated at runtime. So you can write the previous example like this:

```
int size;
size = 20;    // or some other value calculated at run-time
double* pDoubles = stackalloc double[size];
```

You will see from these code snippets that the syntax of `stackalloc` is slightly unusual. It is followed immediately by the name of the data type you want to store (and this must be a value type), and then by the number of items you need space for in square brackets. The number of bytes allocated will be this number multiplied by `sizeof(data type)`. The use of square brackets in the preceding code sample suggests an array, which isn't too surprising. If you have allocated space for 20 doubles, then what you have is an array of 20 doubles. The simplest type of array that you can have is a block of memory that stores one element after another (see Figure 7-6).

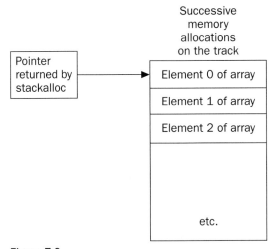

**Figure 7-6**

This diagram also shows the pointer returned by `stackalloc`, which is always a pointer to the allocated data type that points to the top of the newly allocated memory block. To use the memory block you simply dereference the returned pointer. For example, to allocate space for 20 doubles and then set the first element (element 0 of the array) to the value 3.0, write this:

```
double* pDoubles = stackalloc double [20];
*pDoubles = 3.0;
```

To access the next element of the array, you use pointer arithmetic. As described earlier, if you add 1 to a pointer, its value will be increased by the size of whatever data type it points to. In this case, this will be just enough to take you to the next free memory location in the block that you have allocated. So, you can set the second element of the array (element number 1) to the value 8.4 like this:

```
double* pDoubles = stackalloc double [20];
*pDoubles = 3.0;
*(pDoubles+1) = 8.4;
```

By the same reasoning, you can access the element with index X of the array with the expression `*(pDoubles+X)`.

# Memory Management and Pointers

Effectively, you have a means by which you can access elements of your array, but for general-purpose use this syntax is too complex. Fortunately, C# defines an alternative syntax using square brackets. C# gives a very precise meaning to square brackets when they are applied to pointers; if the variable p is any pointer type and X is an integer, then the expression p[X] is always interpreted by the compiler as meaning *(p+X). This is true for all pointers, not only those initialized using stackalloc. With this shorthand notation, you now have a very convenient syntax for accessing your array. In fact, it means that you have exactly the same syntax for accessing one-dimensional stack-based arrays as you do for accessing heap-based arrays that are represented by the System.Array class:

```
double* pDoubles = stackalloc double [20];
pDoubles[0] = 3.0;    // pDoubles[0] is the same as *pDoubles
pDoubles[1] = 8.4;    // pDoubles[1] is the same as *(pDoubles+1)
```

*This idea of applying array syntax to pointers isn't new. It has been a fundamental part of both the C and C++ languages ever since those languages were invented. Indeed, C++ developers will recognize the stack-based arrays they can obtain using* stackalloc *as being essentially identical to classic stack-based C and C++ arrays. It is this syntax and the way it links pointers and arrays that was one of the reasons why the C language became popular in the 1970s, and the main reason why the use of pointers became such a popular programming technique in C and C++.*

Although your high-performance array can be accessed in the same way as a normal C# array, a word of caution is in order. The following code in C# raises an exception:

```
double[] myDoubleArray = new double [20];
myDoubleArray[50] = 3.0;
```

The exception occurs because you are trying to access an array using an index that is out of bounds; the index is 50, whereas the maximum allowed value is 19. However, if you declare the equivalent array using stackalloc, there is no object wrapped around the array that can perform bounds checking. Hence, the following code will *not* raise an exception:

```
double* pDoubles = stackalloc double [20];
pDoubles[50] = 3.0;
```

In this code, you allocate enough memory to hold 20 doubles. Then you set sizeof(double) memory locations starting at the location given by the start of this memory + 50*sizeof(double) to hold the double value 3.0. Unfortunately, that memory location is way outside the area of memory that you have allocated for the doubles. There is no knowing what data might be stored at that address. At best, you may have used some currently unused memory, but it is equally possible that you may have just overwritten some locations in the stack that were being used to store other variables or even the return address from the method currently being executed. Once again, you see that the high performance to be gained from pointers comes at a cost; you need to be certain you know what you are doing, or you will get some very strange runtime bugs.

## *QuickArray example*

The discussion of pointers ends with a stackalloc example called QuickArray. In this example, the program simply asks users how many elements they want to be allocated for an array. The code then uses stackalloc to allocate an array of longs that size. The elements of this array are populated with the squares of the integers starting with 0 and the results displayed on the console:

```csharp
using System;

namespace Wrox.ProCSharp.Chapter07
{
    class MainEntryPoint
    {
        static unsafe void Main()
        {
            Console.Write("How big an array do you want? \n> ");
            string userInput = Console.ReadLine();
            uint size = uint.Parse(userInput);

            long* pArray = stackalloc long [(int)size];
            for (int i=0 ; i<size ; i++)
                pArray[i] = i*i;

            for (int i=0 ; i<size ; i++)
                Console.WriteLine("Element {0} = {1}", i, *(pArray+i));
        }
    }
}
```

Here is the output for the `QuickArray` example:

```
QuickArray
How big an array do you want?
> 15
Element 0 = 0
Element 1 = 1
Element 2 = 4
Element 3 = 9
Element 4 = 16
Element 5 = 25
Element 6 = 36
Element 7 = 49
Element 8 = 64
Element 9 = 81
Element 10 = 100
Element 11 = 121
Element 12 = 144
Element 13 = 169
Element 14 = 196
```

# Summary

Remember, to become a truly proficient C# programmer, you must have a solid understanding of how memory allocation and garbage collection works. This chapter provided a description of how the CLR manages and allocates memory on the heap and the stack. It also discussed how to write classes that free unmanaged resources correctly, and how to use pointers in C#. These are both advanced topics that are poorly understood and often implemented incorrectly by novice programmers.

Chapter 8 discusses strings and a powerful mechanism for string manipulation: regular expressions.

# Strings and Regular Expressions

In the beginning of this book, you have been almost constantly using strings and have taken for granted the stated mapping that the `string` keyword in C# actually refers to the .NET base class `System.String`. `System.String` is a very powerful and versatile class, but it is by no means the only string-related class in the .NET armory. This chapter starts off by reviewing the features of `System.String`, and then looks at some quite nifty things you can do with strings using some of the other .NET classes — in particular those in the `System.Text` and `System.Text.Regular Expressions` namespaces. This chapter covers the following areas:

- **Building strings** — If you're performing repeated modifications on a string, for example in order to build up a lengthy string prior to displaying it or passing it to some other method or application, the `String` class can be very inefficient. For this kind of situation, another class, `System.Text.StringBuilder` is more suitable, because it has been designed exactly for this situation.

- **Formatting expressions** — You also take a closer look at those formatting expressions that have been used in the `Console.WriteLine()` method throughout these last few chapters. These formatting expressions are processed using a couple of useful interfaces, `IFormatProvider` and `IFormattable`, and by implementing these interfaces on your own classes, you can actually define your own formatting sequences so that `Console.WriteLine()` and similar classes will display the values of your classes in whatever way you specify.

- **Regular expressions** — .NET also offers some very sophisticated classes that deal with the situation in which you need to identify or extract substrings that satisfy certain fairly sophisticated criteria; for example, finding all occurrences within a string where a character or set of characters is repeated, finding all words that begin with s and contain at least one n, or strings that adhere to employee ID or Social Security number constructions. Although you can write methods to perform this kind of processing using the `String` class, such methods are cumbersome to write. Instead, you can use some classes from `System.Text.Regular Expressions`, which are designed specifically to perform this kind of processing.

# Chapter 8

# System.String

Before examining the other string classes, this section quickly reviews some of the available methods on the String class.

System.String is a class specifically designed to store a string and allow a large number of operations on the string. Also, because of the importance of this data type, C# has its own keyword and associated syntax to make it particularly easy to manipulate strings using this class.

You can concatenate strings using operator overloads:

```
string message1 = "Hello";         // returns "Hello"
message1 += ", There";             // returns "Hello, There"
string message2 = message1 + "!";  // returns "Hello, There!"
```

C# also allows extraction of a particular character using an indexer-like syntax:

```
char char4 = message[4];    // returns 'a'. Note the char is zero-indexed
```

This enables you to perform such common tasks as replacing characters, removing whitespace, and capitalization. The following table introduces the key methods.

| Method | Purpose |
| --- | --- |
| Compare | Compares the contents of strings, taking into account the culture (locale) in assessing equivalence between certain characters |
| CompareOrdinal | Same as Compare but doesn't take culture into account |
| Concat | Combines separate string instances into a single instance |
| CopyTo | Copies a specific number of characters from the selected index to a entirely new instance of an array |
| Format | Formats a string containing various values and specifiers for how each value should be formatted |
| IndexOf | Locates the first occurrence of a given substring or character in the string |
| IndexOfAny | Locates the first occurrence of any one of a set of characters in the string |
| Insert | Inserts a string instance into another string instance at a specified index |
| Join | Builds a new string by combining an array of strings |
| LastIndexOf | Same as IndexOf, but finds the last occurrence |
| LastIndexOfAny | Same as IndexOfAny, but finds the last occurrence |
| PadLeft | Pads out the string by adding a specified repeated character to the left side of the string |
| PadRight | Pads out the string by adding a specified repeated character to the right side of the string |

# Strings and Regular Expressions

| Method | Purpose |
| --- | --- |
| `Replace` | Replaces occurrences of a given character or substring in the string with another character or substring |
| `Split` | Splits the string into an array of substrings, the breaks occurring wherever a given character occurs |
| `Substring` | Retrieves the substring starting at a specified position in the string |
| `ToLower` | Converts string to lowercase |
| `ToUpper` | Converts string to uppercase |
| `Trim` | Removes leading and trailing whitespace |

*Please note that this table is not comprehensive but is intended to give you an idea of the features offered by strings.*

## Building Strings

As you have seen, `String` is an extremely powerful class that implements a large number of very useful methods. However, the `String` class has a shortcoming that makes it very inefficient for making repeated modifications to a given string — it is actually an *immutable* data type, which means that once you initialize a string object, that string object can never change. The methods and operators that appear to modify the contents of a string actually create new strings, copying across the contents of the old string if necessary. For example, look at the following code:

```
string greetingText = "Hello from all the guys at Wrox Press. ";
greetingText += "We do hope you enjoy this book as much as we enjoyed writing it.";
```

What happens when this code executes is this: first, an object of type `System.String` is created and initialized to hold the text `Hello from all the guys at Wrox Press.` Note the space *after* the full stop. When this happens, the .NET runtime allocates just enough memory in the string to hold this text (39 chars), and the variable `greetingText` is set to refer to this string instance.

In the next line, syntactically it looks like some more text is being added onto the string — though it is not. Instead, what happens is that a new string instance is created with just enough memory allocated to store the combined text — that's 103 characters in total. The original text, `Hello from all the people at Wrox Press.`, is copied into this new string instance along with the extra text, `We do hope you enjoy this book as much as we enjoyed writing it`. Then, the address stored in the variable `greetingText` is updated, so the variable correctly points to the new `String` object. The old `String` object is now unreferenced — there are no variables that refer to it — and so will be removed the next time the garbage collector comes along to clean out any unused objects in your application.

By itself, that doesn't look too bad, but suppose you wanted to encode that string by replacing each letter (not the punctuation) with the character that has an ASCII code further on in the alphabet, as part of some extremely simple encryption scheme. This would change the string to `Ifmmp gspn bmm uif hvst bu Xspy Qsftt. Xf ep ipqf zpv fokpz uijt cppl bt nvdi bt xf fokpzfe xsjujoh ju`. Several ways of doing this exist, but the simplest and (if you are restricting yourself to using the `String` class) almost

225

certainly the most efficient way is to use the `String.Replace()` method, which replaces all occurrences of a given substring in a string with another substring. Using `Replace()`, the code to encode the text looks like this:

```
string greetingText = "Hello from all the guys at Wrox Press. ";
greetingText += "We do hope you enjoy this book as much as we enjoyed writing it.";

for(int i = (int)'z'; i>=(int)'a' ; i--)
{
    char old1 = (char)i;
    char new1 = (char)(i+1);
    greetingText = greetingText.Replace(old1, new1);
}

for(int i = (int)'Z'; i>=(int)'A' ; i--)
{
    char old1 = (char)i;
    char new1 = (char)(i+1);
    greetingText = greetingText.Replace(old1, new1);
}

Console.WriteLine("Encoded:\n" + greetingText);
```

*For simplicity, this code doesn't wrap Z to A or z to a. These letters get encoded to [ and {, respectively.*

Here, the `Replace` method works in a fairly intelligent way, to the extent that it won't actually create a new string unless it actually makes some changes to the old string. The original string contained 23 different lowercase characters and 3 different uppercase ones. The `Replace` method will therefore have allocated a new string 26 times in total, each new string storing 103 characters. That means that as a result of the encryption process there will be string objects capable of storing a combined total of 2,678 characters now sitting on the heap waiting to be garbage-collected! Clearly, if you use strings to do text processing extensively, your applications will run into severe performance problems.

To address this kind of issue, Microsoft has supplied the `System.Text.StringBuilder` class. `StringBuilder` isn't as powerful as `String` in terms of the number of methods it supports. The processing you can do on a `StringBuilder` is limited to substitutions and appending or removing text from strings. However, it works in a much more efficient way.

When you construct a string using the `String` class, just enough memory gets allocated to hold the string. The `StringBuilder`, however, does better than this and normally allocates more memory than is actually needed. You, as a developer, have the option to indicate how much memory the `StringBuilder` should allocate, but if you don't, the amount will default to some value that depends on the size of the string that the `StringBuilder` instance is initialized with. The `StringBuilder` class has two main properties:

❑ `Length`, which indicates the length of the string that it actually contains

❑ `Capacity`, which indicates the maximum length of the string in the memory allocation

Any modifications to the string take place within the block of memory assigned to the `StringBuilder` instance, which makes appending substrings and replacing individual characters within strings very efficient. Removing or inserting substrings is inevitably still inefficient, because it means that the following part of the string has to be moved. Only if you perform some operation that exceeds the capacity of the string is it necessary to allocate new memory and possibly move the entire contained string. In adding extra capacity, based on our experiments the `StringBuilder` appears to double its capacity if it detects the capacity has been exceeded and no new value for the capacity has been set.

For example, if you use a `StringBuilder` object to construct the original greeting string, you might write this code:

```
StringBuilder greetingBuilder =
   new StringBuilder("Hello from all the guys at Wrox Press. ", 150);
greetingBuilder.Append("We do hope you enjoy this book as much as we enjoyed
                        writing it");
```

*In order to use the* `StringBuilder` *class, you will need a* `System.Text` *reference in your code.*

This code sets an initial capacity of 150 for the `StringBuilder`. It is always a good idea to set some capacity that covers the likely maximum length of a string, to ensure the `StringBuilder` doesn't need to relocate because its capacity was exceeded. Theoretically, you can set as large a number as you can pass in an `int`, although the system will probably complain that it doesn't have enough memory if you actually try to allocate the maximum of 2 billion characters (this is the theoretical maximum that a `StringBuilder` instance is in principle allowed to contain).

When the preceding code is executed, it first creates a `StringBuilder` object that looks like Figure 8-1.

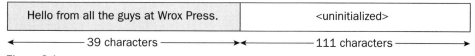

Figure 8-1

Then, on calling the `Append()` method, the remaining text is placed in the empty space, without the need for more memory allocation. However, the real efficiency gain from using a `StringBuilder` comes when you are making repeated text substitutions. For example, if you try to encrypt the text in the same way as before, you can perform the entire encryption without allocating any more memory whatsoever:

```
StringBuilder greetingBuilder =
   new StringBuilder("Hello from all the guys at Wrox Press. ", 150);
greetingBuilder.Append("We do hope you enjoy this book as much as we enjoyed
                        writing it");

for(int i = (int)'z'; i>=(int)'a' ; i--)
{
   char old1 = (char)i;
   char new1 = (char)(i+1);
   greetingBuilder = greetingBuilder.Replace(old1, new1);
}

for(int i = (int)'Z'; i>=(int)'A' ; i--)
{
   char old1 = (char)i;
```

```
        char new1 = (char)(i+1);
        greetingBuilder = greetingBuilder.Replace(old1, new1);
    }

    Console.WriteLine("Encoded:\n" + greetingBuilder.ToString());
```

This code uses the `StringBuilder.Replace()` method, which does the same thing as `String.Replace()`, but without copying the string in the process. The total memory allocated to hold strings in the preceding code is 150 for the `StringBuilder` instance, as well as the memory allocated during the string operations performed internally in the final `Console.WriteLine()` statement.

Normally, you will want to use `StringBuilder` to perform any manipulation of strings and `String` to store or display the final result.

## StringBuilder Members

You have seen a demonstration of one constructor of `StringBuilder`, which takes an initial string and capacity as its parameters. There are others. For example, you can supply only a string:

```
StringBuilder sb = new StringBuilder("Hello");
```

Or you can create an empty `StringBuilder` with a given capacity:

```
StringBuilder sb = new StringBuilder(20);
```

Apart from the `Length` and `Capacity` properties, there is a read-only `MaxCapacity` property that indicates the limit to which a given `StringBuilder` instance is allowed to grow. By default, this is given by `int.MaxValue` (roughly 2 billion, as noted earlier), but you can set this value to something lower when you construct the `StringBuilder` object:

```
// This will both set initial capacity to 100, but the max will be 500.
// Hence, these StringBuilder can never grow to more than 500 characters,
// otherwise it will raise exception if you try to do that.
StringBuilder sb = new StringBuilder(100, 500);
```

You can also explicitly set the capacity at any time, though an exception will be raised if you set it to a value less than the current length of the string or a value that exceeds the maximum capacity:

```
StringBuilder sb = new StringBuilder("Hello");
sb.Capacity = 100;
```

The following table lists the main `StringBuilder` methods.

| Method | Purpose |
| --- | --- |
| `Append()` | Appends a string to the current string |
| `AppendFormat()` | Appends a string that has been worked out from a format specifier |
| `Insert()` | Inserts a substring into the current string |

# Strings and Regular Expressions

| Method | Purpose |
|---|---|
| `Remove()` | Removes characters from the current string |
| `Replace()` | Replaces all occurrences of a character by another character or a substring with another substring in the current string |
| `ToString()` | Returns the current string cast to a `System.String` object (overridden from `System.Object`) |

Several overloads of many of these methods exist.

> `AppendFormat()` *is actually the method that is ultimately called when you call* `Console.WriteLine()`, *which has responsibility for working out what all the format expressions like* `{0:D}` *should be replaced with. This method is examined in the next section.*

There is no cast (either implicit or explicit) from `StringBuilder` to `String`. If you want to output the contents of a `StringBuilder` as a `String`, you must use the `ToString()` method.

Now that you have been introduced to the `StringBuilder` class and shown some of the ways in which you can use it to increase performance, you should be aware that this class will not always give you the increased performance that you are looking for. Basically, the `StringBuilder` class should be used when you are manipulating multiple strings. However, if you are just doing something as simple as concatenating two strings, you will find that `System.String` will be better performing.

## *Format Strings*

So far, a large number of classes and structs have been written for the code samples presented in this book, and they have normally implemented a `ToString()` method in order to be able to display the contents of a given variable. However, quite often users might want the contents of a variable to be displayed in different, often culture- and locale-dependent, ways. The .NET base class, `System.DateTime`, provides the most obvious example of this. For example, you might want to display the same date as 10 June 2006, 10 Jun 2006, 6/10/06 (USA), 10/6/06 (UK), or 10.06.2006 (Germany).

Similarly, the `Vector` struct in Chapter 3, "Objects and Types," implements the `Vector.ToString()` method to display the vector in the format `(4, 56, 8)`. There is, however, another very common way of writing vectors, in which this vector would appear as `4i + 56j + 8k`. If you want the classes that you write to be user-friendly, they need to support the facility to display their string representations in any of the formats that users are likely to want to use. The .NET runtime defines a standard way that this should be done: the `IFormattable` interface. Showing how to add this important feature to your classes and structs is the subject of this section.

As you probably know, you need to specify the format in which you want a variable displayed when you call `Console.WriteLine()`. Therefore, this section uses this method as an example, although most of the discussion applies to any situation in which you want to format a string. For example, if you want to display the value of a variable in a list box or text box, you will normally use the `String.Format()` method to obtain the appropriate string representation of the variable. However, the actual format specifiers you use to request a particular format are identical to those passed to `Console.WriteLine()`. Hence, you will focus on `Console.WriteLine()` as an example. You start by examining what actually happens when you supply a format string to a primitive type, and from this you will see how you can plug in format specifiers for your own classes and structs into the process.

Chapter 2, "C# Basics," uses format strings in `Console.Write()` and `Console.WriteLine()` like this:

```
double d = 13.45;
int i = 45;
Console.WriteLine("The double is {0,10:E} and the int contains {1}", d, i);
```

The format string itself consists mostly of the text to be displayed, but wherever there is a variable to be formatted, its index in the parameter list appears in braces. You might also include other information inside the brackets concerning the format of that item. For example, you can include

❑ The number of characters to be occupied by the representation of the item, prefixed by a comma. A negative number indicates that the item should be left-justified, whereas a positive number indicates that it should be right-justified. If the item actually occupies more characters than have been requested, it will still appear in full.

❑ A format specifier, preceded by a colon. This indicates how you want the item to be formatted. For example, you can indicate whether you want a number to be formatted as a currency or displayed in scientific notation.

The following table lists the common format specifiers for the numeric types, which were briefly discussed in Chapter 2.

| Specifier | Applies To | Meaning | Example |
|---|---|---|---|
| C | Numeric types | Locale-specific monetary value | $4834.50 (USA)<br>£4834.50 (UK) |
| D | Integer types only | General integer | 4834 |
| E | Numeric types | Scientific notation | 4.834E+003 |
| F | Numeric types | Fixed-point decimal | 4384.50 |
| G | Numeric types | General number | 4384.5 |
| N | Numeric types | Common locale-specific format for numbers | 4,384.50 (UK/USA)<br>4 384,50 (continental Europe) |
| P | Numeric types | Percentage notation | 432,000.00% |
| X | Integer types only | Hexadecimal format | 1120 (If you want to display 0x1120, you will have to write out the 0x separately) |

If you want an integer to be padded with zeros, you can use the format specifier 0 (zero) repeated as many times as the number length is required. For example, the format specifier `0000` will cause 3 to be displayed as `0003`, and `99` to be displayed as `0099`, and so on.

It is not possible to give a complete list, because other data types can add their own specifiers. Showing how to define your own specifiers for your own classes is the aim of this section.

## *How the string is formatted*

As an example of how strings are formatted, if you execute the following statement:

```
Console.WriteLine("The double is {0,10:E} and the int contains {1}", d, i);
```

`Console.WriteLine()` just passes the entire set of parameters to the static method, `String.Format()`. This is the same method that you would call if you wanted to format these values for use in a string to be displayed in a text box, for example. The implementation of the three-parameter overload of `WriteLine()` basically does this:

```
// Likely implementation of Console.WriteLine()

public void WriteLine(string format, object arg0, object arg1)
{
    Console.WriteLine(string.Format(format, arg0, arg1));
}
```

The one-parameter overload of this method, which is in turn getting called in the preceding code sample, simply writes out the contents of the string it has been passed, without doing any further formatting on it.

`String.Format()` now needs to construct the final string by replacing each format specifier with a suitable string representation of the corresponding object. However, as you saw earlier, for this process of building up a string you need a `StringBuilder` instance rather than a `string` instance. In this example, a `StringBuilder` instance is created and initialized with the first known portion of the string, the text "The double is ". Next, the `StringBuilder.AppendFormat()` method is called, passing in the first format specifier, `{0,10:E}`, as well as the associated object, `double`, in order to add the string representation of this object to the string object being constructed. This process continues with `StringBuilder.Append()` and `StringBuilder.AppendFormat()` being called repeatedly until the entire formatted string has been obtained.

Now comes the interesting part; `StringBuilder.AppendFormat()` has to figure out how to format the object. First, it probes the object to find out whether it implements an interface in the `System` namespace called `IFormattable`. You can find this out quite simply by trying to cast an object to this interface and seeing whether the cast succeeds, or by using the C# `is` keyword. If this test fails, `AppendFormat()` calls the object's `ToString()` method, which all objects either inherit from `System.Object` or override. This is exactly what happens here, because none of the classes written so far have implemented this interface. That is why the overrides of `Object.ToString()` have been sufficient to allow the structs and classes from earlier chapters such as `Vector` to get displayed in `Console.WriteLine()` statements.

However, all of the predefined primitive numeric types do implement this interface, which means that for those types, and in particular for `double` and `int` in the example, the basic `ToString()` method inherited from `System.Object` will not be called. To understand what happens instead, you need to examine the `IFormattable` interface.

`IFormattable` defines just one method, which is also called `ToString()`. However, this method takes two parameters as opposed to the `System.Object` version, which doesn't take any parameters. The following code shows the definition of `IFormattable`:

```
interface IFormattable
{
    string ToString(string format, IFormatProvider formatProvider);
}
```

The first parameter that this overload of `ToString()` expects is a string that specifies the requested format. In other words, it is the specifier portion of the string that appears inside the braces (`{}`) in the string originally passed to `Console.WriteLine()` or `String.Format()`. For example, in the example the original statement was:

```
Console.WriteLine("The double is {0,10:E} and the int contains {1}", d, i);
```

Hence, when evaluating the first specifier, `{0,10:E}`, this overload will be called against the `double` variable, d, and the first parameter passed to it will be E. `StringBuilder.AppendFormat()` will pass in here the text that appears after the colon in the appropriate format specifier from the original string.

We won't worry about the second `ToString()` parameter in this book. It is a reference to an object that implements the `IFormatProvider` interface. This interface gives further information that `ToString()` might need to consider when formatting the object such as culture-specific details (a .NET culture is similar to a Windows locale; if you are formatting currencies or dates, you need this information). If you are calling this `ToString()` overload directly from your source code, you might want to supply such an object. However, `StringBuilder.AppendFormat()` passes in null for this parameter. If `formatProvider` is null, then `ToString()` is expected to use the culture specified in the system settings.

Getting back to the example, the first item you want to format is a `double`, for which you are requesting exponential notation, with the format specifier E. The `StringBuilder.AppendFormat()` method establishes that the `double` does implement `IFormattable`, and will therefore call the two-parameter `ToString()` overload, passing it the string E for the first parameter and null for the second parameter. It is now up to the double's implementation of this method to return the string representation of the double in the appropriate format, taking into account the requested format and the current culture. `StringBuilder.AppendFormat()` will then sort out padding the returned string with spaces, if necessary, to fill the 10 characters the format string specified.

The next object to be formatted is an `int`, for which you are not requesting any particular format (the format specifier was simply `{1}`). With no format requested, `StringBuilder.AppendFormat()` passes in a null reference for the format string. The two-parameter overload of `int.ToString()` is expected to respond appropriately. No format has been specifically requested, therefore it will call the no-parameter `ToString()` method.

This entire string formatting process is summarized in Figure 8-2.

# Strings and Regular Expressions

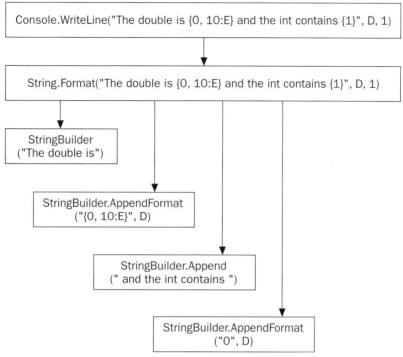

Figure 8-2

## *The FormattableVector example*

Now that you know how format strings are constructed, in this section you extend the Vector example from earlier in the book, so that you can format vectors in a variety of ways. You can download the code for this example from www.wrox.com. Now that you understand the principles involved, you will discover the actual coding is quite simple. All you need to do is implement IFormattable and supply an implementation of the ToString() overload defined by that interface.

The format specifiers you are going to support are as follows:

❑ N — Should be interpreted as a request to supply a quantity known as the Norm of the Vector. This is just the sum of squares of its components, which for mathematics buffs happens to be equal to the square of the length of the Vector, and is usually displayed between double vertical bars, like this: ||34.5||.

❑ VE — Should be interpreted as a request to display each component in scientific format, just as the specifier E applied to a double indicates (2.3E+01, 4.5E+02, 1.0E+00).

❑ IJK — Should be interpreted as a request to display the vector in the form 23i + 450j + 1k.

❑ Anything else should simply return the default representation of the Vector (23, 450, 1.0).

## Chapter 8

To keep things simple, you are not going to implement any option to display the vector in combined IJK and scientific format. You will, however, make sure you test the specifier in a case-insensitive way, so that you allow ijk instead of IJK. Note that it is entirely up to you which strings you use to indicate the format specifiers.

To achieve this, you first modify the declaration of Vector so it implements IFormattable:

```
struct Vector : IFormattable
{
    public double x, y, z;

    // Beginning part of Vector
```

Now you add your implementation of the two-parameter ToString() overload:

```
public string ToString(string format, IFormatProvider formatProvider)
{
    if (format == null)
        return ToString();
    string formatUpper = format.ToUpper();
    switch (formatUpper)
    {
        case "N":
            return "|| " + Norm().ToString() + " ||";
        case "VE":
            return String.Format("( {0:E}, {1:E}, {2:E} )", x, y, z);
        case "IJK":
            StringBuilder sb = new StringBuilder(x.ToString(), 30);
            sb.Append(" i + ");
            sb.Append(y.ToString());
            sb.Append(" j + ");
            sb.Append(z.ToString());
            sb.Append(" k");
            return sb.ToString();
        default:
            return ToString();
    }
}
```

That is all you have to do! Notice how you take the precaution of checking whether format is null before you call any methods against this parameter — you want this method to be as robust as reasonably possible. The format specifiers for all the primitive types are case-insensitive, so that's the behavior that other developers are going to expect from your class too. For the format specifier VE, you need each component to be formatted in scientific notation, so you just use String.Format() again to achieve this. The fields x, y, and z are all doubles. For the case of the IJK format specifier, there are quite a few substrings to be added to the string, so you use a StringBuilder object to improve performance.

For completeness, you also reproduce the no-parameter ToString() overload developed earlier:

```
public override string ToString()
{
    return "( " + x + ", " + y + ", " + z + " )";
}
```

Finally, you need to add a `Norm()` method that computes the square (norm) of the vector, because we didn't actually supply this method when we developed the `Vector` struct:

```
public double Norm()
{
   return x*x + y*y + z*z;
}
```

Now you can try out your formattable vector with some suitable test code:

```
static void Main()
{
   Vector v1 = new Vector(1,32,5);
   Vector v2 = new Vector(845.4, 54.3, -7.8);
   Console.WriteLine("\nIn IJK format,\nv1 is {0,30:IJK}\nv2 is {1,30:IJK}",
                     v1, v2);
   Console.WriteLine("\nIn default format,\nv1 is {0,30}\nv2 is {1,30}", v1, v2);
   Console.WriteLine("\nIn VE format\nv1 is {0,30:VE}\nv2 is {1,30:VE}", v1, v2);
   Console.WriteLine("\nNorms are:\nv1 is {0,20:N}\nv2 is {1,20:N}", v1, v2);
}
```

The result of running this sample is this:

```
FormattableVector
In IJK format,
v1 is              1 i + 32 j + 5 k
v2 is        845.4 i + 54.3 j + -7.8 k

In default format,
v1 is                    ( 1 , 32 , 5 )
v2 is             ( 845.4 , 54.3 , -7.8 )

In VE format
v1 is ( 1.000000E+000, 3.200000E+001, 5.000000E+000 )
v2 is ( 8.454000E+002, 5.430000E+001, -7.800000E+000 )

Norms are:
v1 is               || 1050 ||
v2 is          || 717710.49 ||
```

This shows that your custom specifiers are being picked up correctly.

# Regular Expressions

*Regular expressions* are part of those small technology areas that are incredibly useful in a wide range of programs, yet rarely used among developers. You can think of regular expressions as a mini-programming language with one specific purpose: to locate substrings within a large string expression. It is not a new technology; it originated in the UNIX environment and is commonly used with the Perl programming language. Microsoft ported it onto Windows, where up until now it has been used mostly with scripting languages. Regular expressions are today, however, supported by a number of .NET classes in the namespace `System.Text.RegularExpressions`. You can also find the use of regular expressions in various parts of the .NET Framework. For instance, you will find that they are used within the ASP.NET Validation server controls.

If you are not familiar with the regular expressions language, this section gives a very basic introduction to both regular expressions and their related .NET classes. If you are already familiar with regular expressions, you'll probably want to just skim through this section to pick out the references to the .NET base classes. You might like to know that the .NET regular expression engine is designed to be mostly compatible with Perl 5 regular expressions, although it has a few extra features.

## Introduction to Regular Expressions

The regular expressions language is designed specifically for string processing. It contains two features:

- A set of *escape codes* for identifying specific types of characters. You will be familiar with the use of the * character to represent any substring in DOS expressions. (For example, the DOS command `Dir Re*` lists the files with names beginning with `Re`.) Regular expressions use many sequences like this to represent items such as *any one character, a word break, one optional character,* and so on.
- A system for grouping parts of substrings and intermediate results during a search operation.

With regular expressions, you can perform quite sophisticated and high-level operations on strings. For example, you can

- Identify (and perhaps either flag or remove) all repeated words in a string (for example, "The computer books books" to "The computer books")
- Convert all words to title case (for example, "this is a Title" to "This Is A Title")
- Convert all words longer than three characters to title case (for example, "this is a Title" to "This is a Title")
- Ensure that sentences are properly capitalized
- Separate the various elements of a URI (for example, given `http://www.wrox.com`, extract the protocol, computer name, file name, and so on)

Of course, all of these tasks can be performed in C# using the various methods on `System.String` and `System.Text.StringBuilder`. However, in some cases, this would involve writing a fair amount of C# code. If you use regular expressions, this code can normally be compressed to just a couple of lines. Essentially, you instantiate a `System.Text.RegularExpressions.RegEx` object (or, even simpler, invoke a static `RegEx()` method), pass it the string to be processed, and pass in a regular expression (a string containing the instructions in the regular expressions language), and you're done.

A regular expression string looks at first sight rather like a regular string, but interspersed with escape sequences and other characters that have a special meaning. For example, the sequence \b indicates the beginning or end of a word (a word boundary), so if you wanted to indicate you were looking for the characters th at the beginning of a word, you would search for the regular expression, \bth. (that is, the sequence word boundary -t-h). If you wanted to search for all occurrences of th at the end of a word, you would write th\b (the sequence t-h-word boundary). However, regular expressions are much more

# Strings and Regular Expressions

sophisticated than that and include, for example, facilities to store portions of text that are found in a search operation. This section merely scratches the surface of the power of regular expressions.

Suppose your application needed to convert U.S. phone numbers to an international format. In the United States, the phone numbers have this format: 314-123-1234, which is often written as (314) 123-1234. When converting this national format to an international format you have to include +1 (the country code of the United States) and add brackets around the area code: +1 (314) 123-1234. As find-and-replace operations go, that's not too complicated, but would still require some coding effort if you were going to use the `String` class for this purpose (which would mean that you would have to write your code using the methods available on `System.String`).The regular expressions language allows you to construct a short string that achieves the same result.

This section is intended only as a very simple example, so it concentrates on searching strings to identify certain substrings, not on modifying them.

## *The RegularExpressionsPlayaround Example*

For the rest of this section, you develop a short example that illustrates some of the features of regular expressions and how to use the .NET regular expressions engine in C# by performing and displaying the results of some searches. The text you are going to use as your sample document is an introduction to a Wrox Press book on ASP.NET (Professional ASP.NET 2.0, ISBN 0-7645-7610-0):

```
string Text =
@"This comprehensive compendium provides a broad and thorough investigation of all
aspects of programming with ASP.NET. Entirely revised and updated for the 2.0
Release of .NET, this book will give you the information you need to master ASP.NET
and build a dynamic, successful, enterprise Web application.";
```

*This code is valid C# code, despite all the line breaks. It nicely illustrates the utility of verbatim strings that are prefixed by the @ symbol.*

This text is referred to as the *input string*. To get your bearings and get used to the regular expressions .NET classes, you start with a basic plain text search that doesn't feature any escape sequences or regular expression commands. Suppose that you want to find all occurrences of the string `ion`. This search string is referred to as the *pattern*. Using regular expressions and the `Text` variable declared previously, you can write this:

```
string Pattern = "ion";
MatchCollection Matches = Regex.Matches(Text, Pattern,
                                  RegexOptions.IgnoreCase |
                                  RegexOptions.ExplicitCapture);
foreach (Match NextMatch in Matches)
{
   Console.WriteLine(NextMatch.Index);
}
```

This code uses the static method `Matches()` of the `Regex` class in the `System.Text.RegularExpressions` namespace. This method takes as parameters some input text, a pattern, and a set of optional flags taken from the `RegexOptions` enumeration. In this case, you have specified that all searching should be case-insensitive. The other flag, `ExplicitCapture`, modifies the way that the match is collected in a way that, for your purposes, makes the search a bit more efficient—you see why this is later (although it does have other uses that we won't explore here). `Matches()` returns a reference to a `MatchCollection` object. A *match* is the technical term for the results of finding an instance of the pattern in the expression. It is represented by the class `System.Text.RegularExpressions.Match`. Therefore, you return a `Match Collection` that contains all the matches, each represented by a `Match` object. In the preceding code, you simply iterate over the collection, and use the `Index` property of the `Match` class, which returns the index in the input text of where the match was found. Running this code results in three matches. The following table details some of the `RegexOptions` enumerations.

| Member Name | Description |
| --- | --- |
| `CultureInvariant` | Specifies that the culture of the string is ignored |
| `ExplicitCapture` | Modifies the way the match is collected by making sure that valid captures are the ones that are explicitly named |
| `IgnoreCase` | Ignores the case of the string that is input |
| `IgnorePatternWhitespace` | Removes unescaped whitespace from the string and enables comments that are specified with the pound or hash sign |
| `Multiline` | Changes the characters ^ and $ so that they are applied to the beginning and end of each line and not to just to the beginning and end of the entire string |
| `RightToLeft` | Causes the inputted string to be read from right to left instead of the default left to right (ideal for some Asian and other languages that are read in this direction) |
| `Singleline` | Specifies a single-line mode were the meaning of the dot (.) is changed to match every character |

So far, nothing is really new from the preceding example apart from some .NET base classes. However, the power of regular collections really comes from that pattern string. The reason is that the pattern string doesn't have to only contain plain text. As hinted at earlier, it can also contain what are known as *meta-characters*, which are special characters that give commands, as well as escape sequences, which work in much the same way as C# escape sequences. They are characters preceded by a backslash (\) and have special meanings.

For example, suppose you wanted to find words beginning with n. You could use the escape sequence \b, which indicates a word boundary (a word boundary is just a point where an alphanumeric character precedes or follows a whitespace character or punctuation symbol). You would write this:

```
string Pattern = @"\bn";
MatchCollection Matches = Regex.Matches(Text, Pattern,
                                RegexOptions.IgnoreCase |
                                RegexOptions.ExplicitCapture);
```

Notice the @ character in front of the string. You want the \b to be passed to the .NET regular expressions engine at runtime—you don't want the backslash intercepted by a well-meaning C# compiler that thinks it's an escape sequence intended for itself! If you want to find words ending with the sequence ion, you write this:

# Strings and Regular Expressions

```
string Pattern = @"ion\b";
```

If you want to find all words beginning with the letter `a` and ending with the sequence `ion` (which has as its only match the word *application* in the example), you will have to put a bit more thought into your code. You clearly need a pattern that begins with `\ba` and ends with `ion\b`, but what goes in the middle? You need to somehow tell the application that between the `n` and the `ion` there can be any number of characters as long as none of them are whitespace. In fact, the correct pattern looks like this:

```
string Pattern = @"\ba\S*ion\b";
```

Eventually you will get used to seeing weird sequences of characters like this when working with regular expressions. It actually works quite logically. The escape sequence `\S` indicates any character that is not a whitespace character. The `*` is called a *quantifier*. It means that the preceding character can be repeated any number of times, including zero times. The sequence `\S*` means *any number of characters as long as they are not whitespace characters*. The preceding pattern will, therefore, match any single word that begins with `a` and ends with `ion`.

The following table lists some of the main special characters or escape sequences that you can use. It is not comprehensive, but a fuller list is available in the MSDN documentation.

| Symbol | Meaning | Example | Matches |
|---|---|---|---|
| ^ | Beginning of input text | ^B | B, but only if first character in text |
| $ | End of input text | X$ | X, but only if last character in text |
| . | Any single character except the newline character (\n) | i.ation | isation, ization |
| * | Preceding character may be repeated 0 or more times | ra*t | rt, rat, raat, raaat, and so on |
| + | Preceding character may be repeated 1 or more times | ra+t | rat, raat, raaat and so on, (but not rt) |
| ? | Preceding character may be repeated 0 or 1 times | ra?t | rt and rat only |
| \s | Any whitespace character | \sa | [space]a, \ta, \na (\t and \n have the same meanings as in C#) |
| \S | Any character that isn't a whitespace | \SF | aF, rF, cF, but not \tf |
| \b | Word boundary | ion\b | Any word ending in ion |
| \B | Any position that isn't a word boundary | \BX\B | Any X in the middle of a word |

If you want to search for one of the meta-characters, you can do so by escaping the corresponding character with a backslash. For example, . (a single period) means any single character other than the newline character, whereas \. means a dot.

You can request a match that contains alternative characters by enclosing them in square brackets. For example, [1|c] means one character that can be either 1 or c. If you wanted to search for any occurrence of the words map or man, you would use the sequence ma[n|p]. Within the square brackets, you can also indicate a range, for example [a-z] to indicate any single lowercase letter, [A-E] to indicate any uppercase letter between A and E, or [0-9] to represent a single digit. If you want to search for an integer (that is, a sequence that contains only the characters 0 through 9), you could write [0-9]+ (note the use of the + character to indicate there must be at least one such digit, but there may be more than one — so this would match 9, 83, 854, and so on).

## *Displaying Results*

In this section, you code the RegularExpressionsPlayaround example, so you can get a feel for how the regular expressions work.

The core of the example is a method called WriteMatches(), which writes out all the matches from a MatchCollection in a more detailed format. For each match, it displays the index of where the match was found in the input string, the string of the match, and a slightly longer string, which consists of the match plus up to ten surrounding characters from the input text — up to 5 characters before the match and up to 5 afterward (it is fewer than 5 characters if the match occurred within 5 characters of the beginning or end of the input text). In other words, a match on the word messaging that occurs near the end of the input text quoted earlier would display and messaging of d (five characters before and after the match), but a match on the final word data would display g of data. (only one character after the match), because after that you get to the end of the string. This longer string lets you see more clearly where the regular expression locates the match:

```
static void WriteMatches(string text, MatchCollection matches)
{
    Console.WriteLine("Original text was: \n\n" + text + "\n");
    Console.WriteLine("No. of matches: " + matches.Count);
    foreach (Match nextMatch in matches)
    {
        int Index = nextMatch.Index;
        string result = nextMatch.ToString();
        int charsBefore = (Index < 5) ? Index : 5;
        int fromEnd = text.Length - Index - result.Length;
        int charsAfter = (fromEnd < 5) ? fromEnd : 5;
        int charsToDisplay = charsBefore + charsAfter + result.Length;

        Console.WriteLine("Index: {0}, \tString: {1}, \t{2}",
            Index, result,
            text.Substring(Index - charsBefore, charsToDisplay));
    }
}
```

The bulk of the processing in this method is devoted to the logic of figuring out how many characters in the longer substring it can display without overrunning the beginning or end of the input text. Note that you use another property on the Match object, Value, which contains the string identified for the match.

# Strings and Regular Expressions

Other than that, `RegularExpressionsPlayaround` simply contains a number of methods with names like `Find1`, `Find2`, and so on, which perform some of the searches based on the examples in this section. For example, `Find2` looks for any string that contains a at the beginning of a word:

```
static void Find2()
{
   string text = @"This comprehensive compendium provides a broad and thorough
      investigation of all aspects of programming with ASP.NET. Entirely revised and
      updated for the 2.0 Release of .NET, this book will give you the information
      you need to master ASP.NET and build a dynamic, successful, enterprise Web
      application.";
   string pattern = @"\ba";
   MatchCollection matches = Regex.Matches(text, pattern,
      RegexOptions.IgnoreCase);
   WriteMatches(text, matches);
}
```

Along with this comes a simple `Main()` method that you can edit to select one of the `Find<n>()` methods:

```
static void Main()
{
   Find1();
   Console.ReadLine();
}
```

The code also needs to make use of the `RegularExpressions` namespace:

```
using System;
using System.Text.RegularExpressions;
```

Running the example with the `Find1()` method shown previously gives these results:

```
RegularExpressionsPlayaround
Original text was:

This comprehensive compendium provides a broad and thorough investigation of all
aspects of programming with ASP.NET. Entirely revised and updated for the 2.0
Release of .NET, this book will give you the information you need to master ASP.NET
and build a dynamic, successful, enterprise Web application.

No. of matches: 1
Index: 291,     String: application,     Web application.
```

## Matches, Groups, and Captures

One nice feature of regular expressions is that you can group characters. It works the same way as compound statements in C#. In C# you can group any number of statements by putting them in braces, and the result is treated as one compound statement. In regular expression patterns, you can group any characters (including meta-characters and escape sequences), and the result is treated as a single character. The only difference is that you use parentheses instead of braces. The resultant sequence is known as a *group*.

For example, the pattern (an) + locates any recurrences of the sequence an. The + quantifier applies only to the previous character, but because you have grouped the characters together, it now applies to repeats of an treated as a unit. This means that if you apply (an)+ to the input text, bananas came to Europe late in the annals of history, the anan from bananas is identified. On the other hand, if you write an+, the program selects the ann from annals, as well as two separate sequences of an from bananas. The expression (an)+ identifies occurrences of an, anan, ananan, and so on, whereas the expression an+ identifies occurrences of an, ann, annn, and so on.

> You might wonder why with the preceding example (an)+ picks out anan *from the word banana but doesn't identify either of the two occurrences of* an *from the same word. The rule is that matches must not overlap. If there are a couple of possibilities that would overlap, then by default the longest possible sequence will be matched.*

However, groups are actually more powerful than that. By default, when you form part of the pattern into a group, you are also asking the regular expression engine to remember any matches against just that group, as well as any matches against the entire pattern. In other words, you are treating that group as a pattern to be matched and returned in its own right. This can actually be extremely useful if you want to break up strings into component parts.

For example, URIs have the format: *<protocol>*://*<address>*:*<port>*, where the port is optional. An example of this is http://www.wrox.com:4355. Suppose you want to extract the protocol, the address, and the port from a URI, where you know that there may or may not be whitespace (but no punctuation) immediately following the URI. You could do so using this expression:

```
\b(\S+)://(\S+)(?::(\S+))?\b
```

Here is how this expression works: First, the leading and trailing \b sequences ensure that you only consider portions of text that are entire words. Within that, the first group, (\S+)://, identifies one or more characters that don't count as whitespace, and which are followed by ://—the http:// at the start of an HTTP URI. The brackets cause the http to be stored as a group. The subsequent (\S+) identifies the string www.wrox.com in the URI. This group will end either when it encounters the end of the word (the closing \b) or a colon (:) as marked by the next group.

The next group identifies the port (:4355). The following ? indicates that this group is optional in the match—if there is no :xxxx, this won't prevent a match from being marked. This very important, because the port number is not always specified in a URI—in fact it is absent most of the time. However, things are a bit more complicated than that. You want to indicate that the colon might or might not appear too, but you don't want to store this colon in the group. You've achieved this by having two nested groups. The inner (\S+) identifies anything that follows the colon (for example, 4355). The outer group contains the inner group preceded by the colon, and this group in turn is preceded by the sequence ?:. This sequence indicates that the group in question should not be saved (you only want to save 4355; you don't need :4355 as well!). Don't get confused by the two colons following each other—the first colon is part of the ?: sequence that says "don't save this group," and the second is text to be searched for.

If you run this pattern on the following string, you'll get one match: http://www.wrox.com.

```
Hey I've just found this amazing URI at http:// what was it -- oh yes
http://www.wrox.com
```

# Strings and Regular Expressions

Within this match, you will find the three groups just mentioned as well as a fourth group, which represents the match itself. Theoretically, it is possible that each group itself might return no, one, or more than one match. Each of these individual matches is known as a *capture*. So, the first group, (\S+), has one capture, http. The second group also has one capture (www.wrox.com). The third group, however, has no captures, because there is no port number on this URI.

Notice that the string contains a second http://. Although this does match up to the first group, it will not be captured by the search because the entire search expression does not match this part of the text.

There isn't space to show any examples of C# code that uses groups and captures, but you should know that the .NET RegularExpressions classes support groups and captures, through classes known as Group and Capture. Also, the GroupCollection and CaptureCollection classes represent collections of groups and captures. The Match class exposes the Groups() method, which returns the corresponding GroupCollection object. The Group class correspondingly implements the Captures() method, which returns a CaptureCollection. The relationship between the objects is shown in Figure 8-3.

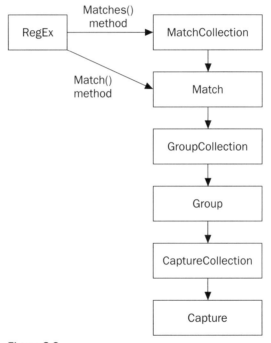

Figure 8-3

You might not want to return a Group object every time you just want to group some characters. A fair amount of overhead is involved in instantiating the object, which is not necessary if all you want is to group some characters as part of your search pattern. You can disable this by starting the group with the character sequence ?: for an individual group, as was done for the URI example, or for all groups by specifying the RegExOptions.ExplicitCaptures flag on the RegEx.Matches() method, as was done in the earlier examples.

Chapter 8

# Summary

You have quite a number of available data types at your disposal when working with the .NET Framework. One of the most used types in your applications (especially apps that focus on the submission and retrieval of data) is the `String` data type. The `string`, being as important as it is, is the reason that this book has a complete chapter focused on how to use the `string` data type and manipulate it in your applications.

When working with strings in the past, it was quite common just to slice and dice the strings as needed using concatenation. With the .NET Framework, you can use the `StringBuilder` class to accomplish a lot of this task with better performance than before.

Last, but hardly least, advanced string manipulation using regular expressions is an excellent tool to search through and validate your strings.

# 9

# Collections

In some situations it is necessary to hold more than a single item in your data collection. You might want to hold a group or collection of data that is related in some fashion in a larger construct. The C# language and the .NET Framework provide you with a number of opportunities for performing this type of value sorting in your code.

This chapter shows you how to work with groups of objects. It takes a close look at array lists, dictionaries, and collections as well as how to use them properly in your C# code for the best possible performance.

## Examining Groups of Objects

This section looks at how the .NET base classes support data structures that consist of a group of similar objects. Chapter 3, "Objects and Types," introduced the ordinary array, the simplest data structure of this kind. The ordinary array is an instance of the class `System.Array` namespace, but C# wraps its own syntax around this class. `System.Array` has two advantages: it is relatively efficient for accessing an individual element given its index, and it has its own C# syntax, which obviously makes using it more intuitive. However, it also has a huge disadvantage: you must specify its size when you instantiate it. There is no facility for adding, inserting, or removing elements later on. You also have to have a numeric index in order to be able to access an element. This is not particularly useful if, for example, you are dealing with a set of employee records and need to look up a given record from the name of the employee.

.NET has quite extensive support for a number of other data structures that are useful in different circumstances. Not only that, but there are also a number of interfaces that classes can implement in order to declare that they support all the functionality of a particular type of data structure. This chapter surveys many of these structures:

- ❑ Collections
- ❑ Array lists

- ❑ Stacks
- ❑ Queues
- ❑ SortedLists
- ❑ Dictionaries (also sometimes known as maps)

With the exception of the basic `System.Array`, all the data structure classes are located in the `System.Collections` namespace.

> *The name* `System.Collections` *reflects another of those terminology ambiguities that plague computing. Collection is often used informally to denote any data structure. However, it also has the more specific meaning of a class that implements* `IEnumerable` *or* `ICollection` — *a particular type of data structure that you investigate later in this chapter. This chapter always uses the term collection to refer to the more specific meaning, except where .NET base class names force us to use it in the general sense.*

## Collections

The idea of a *collection* is that it represents a set of objects that you can access by stepping through each element in turn. In particular, you access the set of objects by using a `foreach` loop. For example, when you write something like the following code, you are assuming that the variable messageSet is a collection:

```
foreach (string nextMessage in messageSet)
{
    DoSomething(nextMessage);
}
```

The ability to use a `foreach` loop is the main purpose of collections. They offer little in the way of additional features.

Over the next couple of pages, you look in more detail at what a collection is, and you implement your own collection by converting the Vector example from Chapter 3. The broad concepts behind collections are actually not new to the .NET Framework. Collections have been a part of COM for years and have also been used in Visual Basic 6 with the convenient `For...Each` syntax. Java also has a `foreach` loop, and in both cases the underlying architecture is very similar to that for .NET collections.

### What is a collection?

Internally, an object is a collection if it is able to supply a reference to a related object, known as an *enumerator*, which is able to step through the items in the collection. More specifically, a collection must implement the interface `System.Collections.IEnumerable`. `IEnumerable` defines just one method and looks like this:

```
interface IEnumerable
{
    IEnumerator GetEnumerator();
}
```

# Collections

The purpose of `GetEnumerator()` is to return the enumerator object. As you can gather from the preceding code, the enumerator object is expected to implement an interface, `System.Collections.IEnumerator`.

> *An additional collections interface, `ICollection`, is derived from `IEnumerable`. More sophisticated collections will implement this interface as well. Besides `GetEnumerator()`, it implements a property that returns the number of elements in the collection. It also features support for copying the collection to an array and can supply information indicating if it is thread-safe. However, this example only considers the simpler collection interface, `IEnumerable`.*

`IEnumerator` looks like this:

```
interface IEnumerator
{
    object Current { get; }
    bool MoveNext();
    void Reset();
}
```

`IEnumerator` is intended to work like this — the object that implements it should be associated with one particular collection. When this object is first initialized, it does not yet refer to any elements in the collection, and you must call `MoveNext()`, which moves the enumerator so that it refers to the first element in the collection. You can then retrieve this element with the `Current` property. `Current` returns an object reference, so you will have to cast it to the type of object you are expecting to find in the collection. You can do whatever you want with that object, then move to the next item in the collection by calling `MoveNext()` again. You repeat this process until there are no more items in the collection — you will know this has happened when the `Current` property returns `null`.

You can return to the start of the collection by calling the `Reset()` method at any time. Note that `Reset()` actually returns to just before the start of the collection so if you call this method, you must call `MoveNext()` again to get to the first element.

You can see from this example that the point of the collection is simply to provide a way of stepping through all the elements when you don't want to supply an index, and you are happy to rely on the collection itself to choose the order in which the elements are returned to you. This usually means that you are not bothered about the order in which the elements are retrieved, as long as you get to see all of them, although in some cases a particular collection might be instructed to return the elements in a certain order.

In one sense, a collection is a very basic type of group of objects, because it does not allow you to add or remove items from the group. All you can do is retrieve the items in an order determined by the collection and examine them. It is not even possible to replace or modify items in the collection, because the `Current` property is read-only. The most frequent use of the collection is to give you the syntactical convenience of the `foreach` loop.

Arrays are considered collections, as should be obvious because the `foreach` command works successfully with arrays. For the particular case of arrays, the enumerator supplied by the `System.Array` class steps through the elements in increasing order of index from zero upward.

# Chapter 9

In fact, the previous `foreach` loop in C# is just a syntactical shortcut for writing the following code:

```
{
    IEnumerator enumerator = MessageSet.GetEnumerator();
    string nextMessage;
    enumerator.MoveNext();
    while ( (nextMessage = enumerator.Current) != null)
    {
        DoSomething(nextMessage);    // We only have read access
                                     // to NextMessage
        enumerator.MoveNext();
    }
}
```

Note the enclosing curly braces framing the previous code snippet. They are supplied to ensure that this code has exactly the same effect as the earlier `foreach` loop. If they weren't included, this code would have differed to the extent that the `nextMessage` and `enumerator` variables would have remained in scope after the loop had finished being executed.

One important aspect of collections is that the enumerator is returned as a separate object. It should not be the same object as the collection itself. The reason is to allow for the possibility that more than one enumerator might be applied simultaneously to the same collection.

## *Adding collection support to the Vector struct*

The `Vector` struct started in Chapter 3 is about to get another extension with collection support.

So far, the `Vector` struct contains a `Vector` instance with three components, x, y, and z, and because an indexer was defined in Chapter 3, it is possible to treat a `Vector` instance as an array, so that you can access the x-component by writing `SomeVector[0]`, the y-component by writing `SomeVector[1]`, and the z-component by writing `SomeVector[2]`.

You now extend the `Vector` struct into a new code sample, the `VectorAsCollection` project, in which it is also possible to iterate through the components of a `Vector` by writing code like this:

```
foreach (double component in someVector)
   Console.WriteLine("Component is " + component);
```

Your first task is to mark `Vector` as a collection by having it implement the `IEnumerable` interface. You start by modifying the declaration of the `Vector` struct:

```
struct Vector : IFormattable, IEnumerable
{
    public double x, y, z;
```

Note that the `IFormattable` interface is present because you added support for string format specifiers earlier. Now you need to implement the `IEnumerable` interface:

```
        public IEnumerator GetEnumerator()
        {
            return new VectorEnumerator(this);
        }
```

# Collections

The implementation of `GetEnumerator()` could hardly be simpler, but it depends on the existence of a new class, `VectorEnumerator`, which you need to define. Because `VectorEnumerator` is not a class that any outside code has to see directly, you declare it as a private class inside the `Vector` struct. Its definition looks like this:

```
private class VectorEnumerator : IEnumerator
{
   Vector theVector;        // Vector object that this enumerator refers to
   int location;            // which element of theVector the enumerator is
                            // currently referring to

   public VectorEnumerator(Vector theVector)
   {
      this.theVector = theVector;
      location = -1;
   }

   public bool MoveNext()
   {
      ++location;
      return (location > 2) ? false : true;
   }

   public object Current
   {
      get
      {
         if (location < 0 || location > 2)
            throw new InvalidOperationException(
               "The enumerator is either before the first element or " +
               "after the last element of the Vector");
         return theVector[(uint)location];
      }
   }

   public void Reset()
   {
      location = -1;
   }
}
```

As required for an enumerator, `VectorEnumerator` implements the `IEnumerator` interface. It also contains two member fields, `theVector`, which is a reference to the `Vector` (the collection) that this enumerator is to be associated with, and `location`, an `int` that indicates the enumerator's reference point in the collection — put differently, whether the `Current` property should retrieve the x, y, or z component of the vector.

The way, you will work in this case is by treating `location` as an index and internally implementing the `enumerator` to access `Vector` as an array. When accessing `Vector` as an array, the valid indices are 0, 1, and 2 — you will extend this by using -1 as the value that indicates where the enumerator is before the start of the collection, and 3 to indicate that it is beyond the end of the collection. Hence, the initialization of this field to -1 in the `VectorEnumerator` constructor:

```
public VectorEnumerator(Vector theVector)
{
    this.theVector = theVector;
    location = -1;
}
```

Notice the constructor also takes a reference to the `Vector` instance that you are to enumerate—this was supplied in the `Vector.GetEnumerator()` method:

```
public IEnumerator GetEnumerator()
{
    return new VectorEnumerator(this);
}
```

## Array Lists

An *array list* is very similar to an array, except that it has the ability to grow. It is represented by the class `System.Collections.ArrayList`.

The `ArrayList` class also has some similarities with the `StringBuilder` class. Just as a `StringBuilder` allocates enough space in memory to store a certain number of characters and allows you to manipulate characters within the space, the `ArrayList` allocates enough memory to store a certain number of object references. You can then efficiently manipulate these object references. If you try to add more objects to the `ArrayList` than permitted, it will automatically increase its capacity by allocating a new area of memory big enough to hold twice as many elements as the current capacity and relocate the objects to this new location.

The simplest form of instantiation of an `ArrayList` is illustrated here:

```
ArrayList baseballTeams = new ArrayList();
```

With this type of instantiation, the `ArrayList` object is created with a capacity of 16—meaning that there are 16 items in the array. In order to get at the `ArrayList` class, you need to make a reference to the `System.Collections` namespace in your project. You can also instantiate an `ArrayList` by indicating the initial capacity you want. For example:

```
ArrayList baseballTeams = new ArrayList(20);
```

It is also possible to set the capacity of the `ArrayList` directly after a generic instantiation with the use of the `Capacity` property as shown in the following example:

```
ArrayList baseballTeams = new ArrayList();
baseballTeams.Capacity = 20;
```

Note, however, that changing the capacity causes the entire `ArrayList` to be reallocated to a new block of memory with the required capacity. Some other important notes to understand about the capacity of the `ArrayList` are in the area of capacity growth. Initially, as stated, the default capacity of an `ArrayList` object is set to 16 items. The idea of an `ArrayList` is that it can dynamically grow as needed. However, when you add the 17th element to the default `ArrayList`, what happens is that a new `ArrayList` object is created—but double the size (an `ArrayList` with 32 elements). Once the new `ArrayList` is created, the contents of the original `ArrayList` are copied over to the new `ArrayList` instance. Once copied over, the original `ArrayList` is then marked for garbage collection. This growth behavior is the same if you set the capacity of the `ArrayList` yourself. For instance, if you use the following construction:

```
ArrayList baseballTeams = new ArrayList(20);
```

an `ArrayList` is created with 20 items. On adding the 21st item to the `ArrayList`, a new `ArrayList` is created — but this time, the new `ArrayList` created contains 40 items in the collection. Just remember that when the `ArrayList` is forced to dynamically grow, it simply doubles itself.

The number of elements in the `ArrayList` can be obtained with the `Count` property:

```
int nBaseballTeams = baseballTeams.Count;
```

Once the `ArrayList` is instantiated, you can then add elements using the `Add()` method. This console application example uses the `Add()` method and then displays each of the items that were added:

```
ArrayList baseballTeams = new ArrayList();
baseballTeams.Add("St. Louis Cardinals");
baseballTeams.Add("Seattle Mariners");
baseballTeams.Add("Florida Marlins");

foreach (string item in baseballTeams)
{
    Console.Write(item + "\n");
}

Console.Readline();
```

One thing to note about adding items to the `ArrayList` is that the `ArrayList` treats all its elements as `object` references. That means you can store whatever objects you like in an `ArrayList`, but when accessing the objects, you will need to cast them back to the appropriate data type, as shown here:

```
string element1 = (string)baseballTeams[1];
```

In addition to casting this item from the `ArrayList` to a `string`, the preceding example is specifying a specific item in the collection based upon an indexer. In this example, `element1` is assigned a value of `Seattle Mariners`. When adding items to the `ArrayList`, you can also specify the location of the item being added using the `Insert()` method. This is illustrated in the following example:

```
baseballTeams.Insert(1, "San Francisco Giants");   // inserts at position 1
```

There is also a useful override of `Insert` that allows you to insert all the elements of a collection into an `ArrayList`, given an `ICollection` interface reference.

You can remove elements at a specific point in the collection with the use of the `RemoveAt()` method. This is done using the following construction:

```
baseballTeams.RemoveAt(1);    // removes object at position 1
```

You can also supply an object reference to another method, `Remove()`. However, it is important to note that this takes longer because it will cause the `ArrayList` to make a linear search through the array to find the object.

Note that adding or removing an element causes all subsequent elements to have to be correspondingly shifted in memory, even if no reallocation of the entire `ArrayList` is needed.

So far, you've seen the basics of adding and removing items from the `ArrayList` collection. Another way of adding items to the `ArrayList` is through the use of the `AddRange()` method. The `AddRange()` method allows you to add an entire collection of items at a time. Going back to the previous baseball teams example, add some additional items. This time though, add a collection of items that are represented in a string array. This is illustrated in the following example:

```
ArrayList baseballTeams = new ArrayList();
baseballTeams.Add("St. Louis Cardinals");
baseballTeams.Add("Seattle Mariners");
baseballTeams.Add("Florida Marlins");

string[] myStringArray = new string[2];
myStringArray[0] = "San Francisco Giants";
myStringArray[1] = "Los Angeles Dodgers";

baseballTeams.AddRange(myStringArray);

foreach (string item in baseballTeams)
{
    Console.Write(item + "\n");
}

Console.Readline();
```

This example creates a string array, adds two items to the array, and then uses the `AddRange()` method of the `ArrayList` object to add the entire string array in one line. Once added to the `ArrayList`, there are then five items in the collection, which are then displayed to the console.

The `RemoveRange()` method allows you to specify a range of items that are to be removed from a collection of items in the `ArrayList`. The `RemoveRange()` method takes two parameters — the first being the location to start from and the second being the number of items to remove from that point.

For instance, add this one line of code to the example and see what happens to the items in the `ArrayList`:

```
ArrayList baseballTeams = new ArrayList();
baseballTeams.Add("St. Louis Cardinals");
baseballTeams.Add("Seattle Mariners");
baseballTeams.Add("Florida Marlins");

string[] myStringArray = new string[2];
myStringArray[0] = "San Francisco Giants";
myStringArray[1] = "Los Angeles Dodgers";

baseballTeams.AddRange(myStringArray);
```

# Collections

```
    baseballTeams.RemoveRange(2, 2);

    foreach (string item in baseballTeams)
    {
       Console.Write(item + "\n");
    }

    Console.Readline();
```

This use of the `RemoveRange()` method states that the items to be removed should start from the index position of 2 (`"Florida Marlins"`) and that two items should be removed. This means that `Florida Marlins` and `San Francisco Giants` will be removed from the `ArrayList` collection of items.

Another interesting method of the `ArrayList` object is the `GetRange()` method. This is used if you want to copy over a specific range of items to a new `ArrayList`. For example, suppose that you have an `ArrayList` as shown earlier that contains five baseball teams. If you need a new `ArrayList` object that will contain only a subset of these five baseball teams, you would accomplish this task as shown here:

```
    ArrayList secondArray = new ArrayList(baseballTeams.GetRange(2, 2));
```

The `GetRange()` method works similarly to the `AddRange()` method. It takes two parameters — the first is the place in the index to start and the second is the number of items to copy. In this example, a new `ArrayList` object is created that copies two items from the previous `ArrayList`. The two items copied are at the index positions of 2 and 3, whose values are `Florida Marlins` and `San Francisco Giants`. In addition to the `GetRange()` method, you will also find the `SetRange()` and `InsertRange()` methods that are there for placing items in an `ArrayList`.

An array list can be really useful if you need to build up an array of objects but you do not know in advance how big the array is going to be. In that case, you can construct the array in an `ArrayList`, and then copy the `ArrayList` back to a plain old array when you have finished, provided that you actually need the data as an array (this would be the case, for example, if the array is to be passed to a method that expects an array as a parameter). The relationship between `ArrayList` and `Array` is in many ways similar to that between `StringBuilder` and `String`.

Unfortunately, unlike the `StringBuilder` class, there is no single method to do this conversion from an `ArrayList` to an `Array`. You have to use a loop to manually copy back references. Note, however, that you are only copying the references, not the objects, so this should not result in much of a performance hit:

```
    // strings is an ArrayList instance being used to store string instances
    string[] myStringArray = new string[baseballTeams.Count];
    for (int i=0 ; i< baseballTeams.Count ; i++)
       myStringArray[i] = (string)baseballTeams[i];
```

## *The Stack Class*

A `Stack` is another collection type that is ideal for working with data items that are considered temporary and are disposable after their use by your application. The `Stack` class creates collections in a structure called *Last In First Out* (LIFO). This means that the items that are pulled from the collection are in the reverse order in which they are input into the collection. This is illustrated in Figure 9-1.

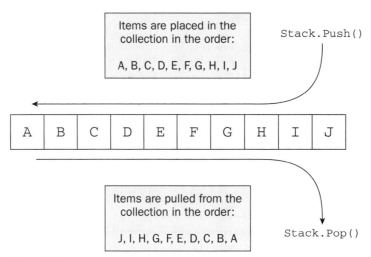

Figure 9-1

Items are placed into a Stack using the Push() method, while items are pulled from the collection using the Pop() method. This section starts by looking at populating a Stack object and reading back the values. This is illustrated in the following console application example:

```
Stack alphabet = new Stack();
alphabet.Push("A");
alphabet.Push("B");
alphabet.Push("C");

foreach (string item in alphabet)
{
   Console.Write(item);
}

Console.ReadLine();
```

To code this example, you have to first make a reference to the System.Collections namespace in order to get at the Stack class. In this case, a Stack object is instantiated and using the Stack object's Push() method, the letters A, B, and C are added to the collection (in that order). Then the items of the Stack collection are iterated through and written to the console screen. This produces the following results:

CBA

In this example, items are read in the order of CBA because items are read from a Stack collection in the reverse order in which they were set into the collection.

It is also possible to use the Pop() method to pull items from a Stack object. However, the big difference in pulling them off the collection using the Pop() method and just iterating through them as shown in the preceding example is that when you use the Pop() method, the item is pulled from the collection permanently. For instance, take a look at the following code example, which utilizes the Pop() method:

# Collections

```
Stack alphabet = new Stack();
alphabet.Push("A");
alphabet.Push("B");
alphabet.Push("C");

Console.Write("First Iteration: ");

foreach (string item in alphabet)
{
   Console.Write(item);
}

Console.WriteLine("\nItem pulled from collection: " + alphabet.Pop().ToString());
Console.Write("Second iteration: ");

foreach (string item in alphabet)
{
   Console.Write(item);
}

Console.ReadLine();
```

In this case, the items A, B, and C are placed in the collection and written to the console screen. From here, one of the items is popped from the collection using:

```
alphabet.Pop()
```

The value of the item popped from the collection is then written to the screen. Then the alphabet collection is iterated through again, but this time you will notice that the letter C is missing from the collection. The reason is that this item was popped off the collection permanently. Running this application produces the following results to the console screen:

```
First iteration: CBA
Item pulled from collection: C
Second iteration: BA
```

In regards to the `Pop()` method, if you are interested in keeping the items as part of the collection, you can always use the `Peek()` method, which allows you to pull the latest item from the collection without removing it from the overall collection as the `Pop()` method would do.

The following table details some of the methods of the `Stack` class.

| Method | Description |
| --- | --- |
| Clear | Removes all the items from the collection |
| Clone | Creates a shadow copy of the collection |
| CopyTo | Copies the collection to an existing one-dimensional array |
| GetEnumerator | Returns an enumerator for the collection |

*Table continued on following page*

255

| Method | Description |
| --- | --- |
| Peek | Returns the top-most object from the Stack without removing it from the entire collection |
| Pop | Returns the top-most object from the Stack and removes it from the collection |
| Push | Places items in the Stack |
| ToArray | Copies the Stack to a new array |

## *The Queue Class*

You will find that working with the Queue class and the collection it creates is similar to working with the Stack class. The big difference is that the Queue class creates collections in a structure referred to as *First In First Out* (FIFO). This means that items that are placed in the collection are pulled from the collection in the same order in which they were placed. This is illustrated in Figure 9-2.

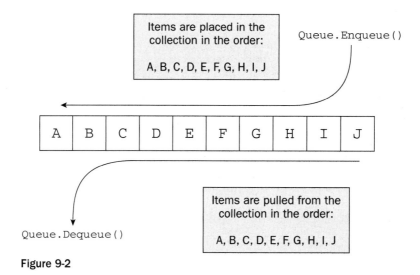

Figure 9-2

Items are placed into the collection using the Enqueue() method, and they are pulled from the collection using the Dequeue() method. If you take the example from the Stack object and modify it so that it uses the Queue object instead, it will produce different results. The code for this example is shown here:

```
Queue alphabet = new Queue();
alphabet.Enqueue("A");
alphabet.Enqueue("B");
alphabet.Enqueue("C");

Console.Write("First Iteration: ");

foreach (string item in alphabet)
```

```
    {
        Console.Write(item);
    }

    Console.WriteLine("\nItem pulled from collection: " +
        alphabet.Dequeue().ToString());
    Console.Write("Second iteration: ");

    foreach (string item in alphabet)
    {
        Console.Write(item);
    }

    Console.ReadLine();
```

In this example, the `Queue` class is used to store the values A, B, and C. Once stored, the items are iterated through and written to the console screen. From here, one of the items is removed from the collection. Much like the `Stack` class's `Pop()` method, the `Queue` class uses the `Dequeue()` method and also permanently removes the item from the collection. This is illustrated in the second iteration through the collection. The result of running this application is shown here:

```
First iteration: ABC
Item pulled from collection: A
Second iteration: BC
```

The following table details some of the methods of the `Queue` class.

| Method | Description |
| --- | --- |
| `Clear` | Removes all the items from the collection |
| `Clone` | Creates a shadow copy of the collection |
| `Contains` | Determines whether an element is in the collection |
| `CopyTo` | Copies the collection to an existing one-dimensional array |
| `Dequeue` | Returns the first-place object in the `Queue` and removes it from the collection |
| `Enqueue` | Places items in the `Queue` |
| `GetEnumerator` | Returns an enumerator for the collection |
| `Peek` | Returns the top-most object from the `Queue` without removing it from the entire collection |
| `ToArray` | Copies the `Queue` to a new array |

## *The SortedList Class*

The `SortedList` class creates collections that are meant to be worked with in a different manner than when working with FIFO/LIFO collections. In working with the items in a `SortedList` collection, each item placed in the collection is assigned an identifying key that is later used in reference to the item.

Like the `ArrayList` class, when you instantiate the `SortedList` object, it is initially given a default capacity of 16. You place items in the collection using the `Add()` method:

```
SortedList footballTeams = new SortedList();
footballTeams.Add(1, "St. Louis Rams");
footballTeams.Add(2, "Kansas City Chiefs");
footballTeams.Add(3, "Indianapolis Colts");

for (int i = 0; i < footballTeams.Count; i++)
{
    Console.WriteLine("KEY: " + footballTeams.GetKey(i) +
        "   VALUE: " + footballTeams.GetByIndex(i));
}

Console.ReadLine();
```

In this example, three items are added to the `SortedList` collection. Each string is assigned an associated key for the item placed. In this case, the keys are of type `int`: 1, 2, and 3. However, you could just have easily used a `string` value for the key, as shown here:

```
footballTeams.Add("Winner", "St. Louis Rams");
```

It is possible to iterate through values and keys of a `SortedList` collection by using either the `GetKeyList()` or `GetValueList()` methods. For instance, you can iterate through the values of the `footballTeams` collection as illustrated here:

```
foreach (string item in footballTeams.GetValueList())
{
    Console.WriteLine(item);
}
```

Here is an iteration through the keys of a `SortedList` collection:

```
foreach (int item in footballTeams.GetKeyList())
{
    Console.WriteLine(item);
}
```

Notice in this example that you cast the keys coming from the `SortedList` as of type `int` because this is the value you used. If you used `string` values for the keys, then, of course, you would have to cast item to `string` as well.

The following table details the methods of the `SortedList` class.

| Method | Description |
|---|---|
| Add | Places an item in the collection |
| Clear | Removes all the items from the collection |
| Clone | Creates a shallow copy of the collection |

# Collections

| Method | Description |
| --- | --- |
| `ContainsKey` | Determines whether an item is in the collection based upon a key value |
| `ContainsValue` | Determines whether an item is in the collection based upon an item value |
| `CopyTo` | Copies the collection to an existing one-dimensional array |
| `GetByIndex` | Returns the value of an item at a specified index |
| `GetEnumerator` | Returns an enumerator for the collection |
| `GetKey` | Returns the value of an item at a specified key |
| `GetKeyList` | Returns a collection of keys from the `SortedList` |
| `GetValueList` | Returns a collection of values from the `SortedList` |
| `Remove` | Removes an item from the collection based upon the item's key value |
| `RemoveAt` | Removes an item from the collection based upon the index value of the item |
| `SetByIndex` | Replaces the value at a specified index in the collection |

## Dictionaries and Hashtables

*Dictionaries* represent a very sophisticated data structure that allows you to access an element based on some key, which can be of any data type you want. They are also known as *maps* or *hash tables*. Dictionaries are great if you want to store objects as if they were an array, but where you want to use some other data type rather than a numeric type to index into the structure. They also allow you to add and remove items freely, a bit like an `ArrayList`, but without the performance overhead of having to shift subsequent items in memory.

The kinds of situations in which dictionaries can be useful are illustrated using the `MortimerPhones Employees` example, which you develop later in this section. This example assumes that Mortimer Phones (the mobile phone company that was first introduced in Chapter 3) has some software that processes details of its employees. To that end, you need a data structure — something like an array — that contains data for employees. You assume that each Mortimer Phones employee is identified by an employee ID, which is a set of characters such as B342 or W435, and is stored as an `EmployeeID` object. Each employee's details are stored as an `EmployeeData` object; for the example, this just contains the employee's ID, name, and salary.

Suppose you have this `EmployeeID`

```
EmployeeID id = new EmployeeID("W435");
```

and a variable called `employees`, which you can treat syntactically as an array of `EmployeeData` objects. In actuality, this is not an array; it is a dictionary, and because it is a dictionary, you can get the details of an employee with the previously declared ID like this:

```
EmployeeData theEmployee = employees[id];
    // Note that id is NOT a numeric type - it is an EmployeeID instance
```

259

That's the power of dictionaries. They look like arrays (but are more powerful than that; they are more like `ArrayLists` because you can dynamically set their capacity, and add and remove elements), but you don't have to use an integer to index into them; you can use any data type you want. For a dictionary, this is called a *key* rather than an index. Roughly speaking, what happens is that the dictionary takes the key supplied when you access an element (in the preceding example this is the ID object) and it does some processing on the value of this key. This processing returns an integer that depends on the value of the key, and is used to work out where in the array the entry should be stored or retrieved from. Here is a short list of other examples where you might want to use a dictionary to store objects:

- If you want to store details of employees or other people, indexed by their Social Security numbers. Although the Social Security number is basically an integer, you cannot use an array with Social Security numbers as the index because a U.S. Social Security number theoretically can go up to the value of 999999999. On a 32-bit system you'd never fit an array that big in a program's address space! Most of the array would be empty anyway. Using a dictionary, you can have a Social Security number to index an employee, but still keep the dictionary size small.
- If you want to store addresses, indexed by zip code. In the United States, zip codes are just numbers, but in Canada and the United Kingdom they use letters and numbers together.
- If you want to store any data for objects or people, indexed by the name of the object or person.

Although the effect of a dictionary is that it looks to client code much like a dynamic array with a very flexible means of indexing into it, a lot of work goes on behind the scenes to bring this about. In principle you can use an object of any class as an index key for dictionaries. However, you must implement certain features on a class before it can be used as a key. This also pertains to the `GetHashCode()` method that all classes and structs inherit from `System.Object`. This section takes a closer look under the hood at what a dictionary is, how it works, and how `GetHashCode()` is involved. Then, you move on to the `MortimerPhonesEmployees` example, which demonstrates how to use a dictionary and how to set up a class so that it can be used as a key.

## Dictionaries in real life

The term *dictionary* is used because the structure is very similar to a real-life dictionary. In a real dictionary you will normally want to look up the meaning of a word (or in the case of a foreign dictionary, the details of how to translate a word). The couple of lines of text that give the meaning (or the translation) are the data you are really interested in. The fact that a large dictionary has tens of thousands of data items in it is no problem when you want to look up a meaning, because you just look for the word in alphabetical order. In a sense, the word you are looking up is equivalent to the key that you use to get at the data you are really interested in. It is not really the word itself you are interested in so much as the data associated with it. The word just provides the means to locate the entry in the dictionary. So, you need three things to build a dictionary:

- The data you want to look up
- The key
- The algorithm that allows you to find where the data is in the dictionary

The algorithm is a crucial part of the dictionary. Just knowing the key is not sufficient — you also need a way that you can use the key to find out the location of the item in the data structure. In real-life dictionaries, this algorithm is provided by arranging words in alphabetical order.

# Collections

## Dictionaries in .NET

In .NET, the basic dictionary is represented by the class `Hashtable`, which works on the same principles as a real-life dictionary, except that it assumes that the key and item are both of type `Object`. This means that a `Hashtable` can store whatever data structure you want. By contrast, a real-life dictionary uses strings as the keys.

Although `Hashtable` represents the generic will-store-anything dictionary, it is permissible to define your own more specialized dictionary classes. Microsoft has provided an abstract base class, `DictionaryBase`, which provides basic dictionary functionality, and from which you can derive your classes. There is also a ready-made .NET base class, `System.Collections.Specialized.StringDictionary`, which you should use in place of `Hashtable` if your keys are strings.

When you create a `Hashtable` object, you can indicate its initial capacity, just as you would for `StringBuilder` and `ArrayList`:

```
Hashtable employees = new Hashtable(53);
```

As usual, there are many other constructors, but this is the one you will probably use most often. Notice the unusual size of the initial capacity: 53. There is a good reason for this. Due to the internal algorithms used in dictionaries, they work most efficiently if their capacity is a prime number.

Adding an object to the `Hashtable` is done with the `Add()` method, but `Hashtable.Add()` takes two parameters, both of which are object references. The first is a reference to the key; the second is a reference to the data. Carrying on with the `EmployeeID` and `EmployeeData` classes from the example, you would instantiate the various objects as such:

```
EmployeeID id;
EmployeeData data;

// initialize id and data to refer to some employee
// assume employees is a Hashtable instance
//that contains EmployeeData references

employees.Add(id, data);
```

To retrieve the data for an item, you need to supply the key. `Hashtable` implements an indexer so that you can retrieve data — this is how you get the array syntax discussed earlier:

```
EmployeeData data = employees[id];
```

You can also remove items from the dictionary by supplying the key of the object to be removed:

```
employees.Remove(id);
```

You can find out how many items are in the hash table using the `Count` property:

```
int nEmployees = employees.Count;
```

Notice, however, that there is no `Insert()` method. You have not yet seen how a dictionary works internally, but there is no difference between adding and inserting data. Unlike an array or an `ArrayList`, you don't find one big block of data at the beginning of the structure and an empty block at the end. Instead, the situation looks more like the diagram in Figure 9-3, in which any unmarked parts of the dictionary are empty.

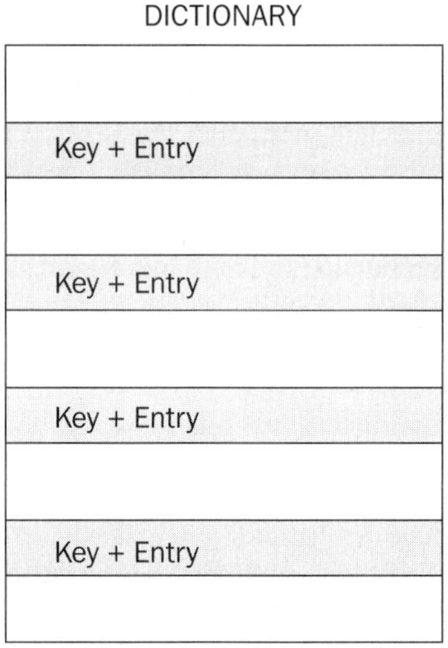

DICTIONARY

| |
|---|
| Key + Entry |
| |
| Key + Entry |
| |
| Key + Entry |
| |
| Key + Entry |
| |

**Figure 9-3**

When you add an entry, it will actually be placed at some location that could be anywhere in the dictionary. How the location is worked out from the key is something that you don't need to know about when you are using the dictionary. The important point is that the algorithm used to work out the location of an item is reliable. As long as you remember what the key is, you can just hand it to the `Hashtable` object, and it will be able to use the key to quickly work out where the item is and retrieve it for you. You see how the algorithm works later in this section. (Hint: It relies on the key's `GetHashCode()` method.)

Note that the diagram in Figure 9-3 is simplified. Each key/entry pair is not actually stored inside the dictionary structure—as is common for reference types, what is stored are the object references that indicate where on the heap the objects themselves are located.

## How the dictionary works

So far, you've seen that dictionaries (hash tables) are extremely convenient to use, but there is a snag: `Hashtable` (and indeed any other dictionary class) uses some sort of algorithm to work out where to place each object based on the key, and that algorithm isn't entirely provided by the `Hashtable` class. It has two stages, and the code for one of these stages must be provided by the `key` class. If you are using a class that Microsoft has written, and which can be used as a key (such as `String`), there's no problem (Microsoft will have written all the code already). However, if the `key` class is one that you have written, you will have to write this part of the algorithm yourself.

In computer parlance, the part of the algorithm implemented by the `key` class is known as a *hash* (hence the term *hash table*), and the `Hashtable` class looks in a very particular place for the hash algorithm. It

# Collections

looks in your object's `GetHashCode()` method, which it inherits from `System.Object`. Whenever a dictionary class needs to work out where an item should be located, it simply calls the key object's `GetHashCode()` method. This is why it was emphasized when discussing `System.Object()` that if you override `GetHashCode()`, there are fairly stringent requirements on how you do it, because your implementation needs to behave in certain ways for dictionary classes to work correctly. (If you don't intend your class to ever be used as a key in a dictionary, there's no need to override `GetHashCode()`.)

The way it works is that `GetHashCode()` returns an `int`, and it somehow uses the value of the key to generate this `int`. `Hashtable` will take this `int` and do some other processing on it that involves some sophisticated mathematical calculations, and which returns the index of where in the dictionary an item with the given hash should be stored. We won't go into this part of the algorithm — that part has already been coded by Microsoft, so you don't need to know about it. What you should know is that it involves prime numbers and is the reason why the hash table capacity should be a prime number.

For this to work properly, you need to adhere to some fairly strict requirements for the `GetHashCode()` override, as mentioned earlier. These requirements are going to sound quite abstract and daunting, but don't worry too much. As the `MortimerPhonesEmployees` example demonstrates, it is not at all difficult to code a key class that satisfies these requirements:

- ❏ It should be fast (because placing or retrieving entries in a dictionary is supposed to be fast).
- ❏ It must be consistent; if you regard two keys as representing the same value, they must give the same value for the hash.
- ❏ It should ideally give values that are likely to be evenly distributed across the entire range of numbers that an `int` can store.

The reason for this last condition is because of a potential problem; what happens if you get two entries in the dictionary whose hashes both give the same index?

If this happens, the dictionary class will have to start fiddling about looking for the nearest available free location to store the second item — and will have to do some searching in order to retrieve this item later on. This is obviously going to hurt performance, and clearly, if lots of your keys are tending to give the same indexes for where they should be stored, this kind of clash becomes more likely. However, because of the way Microsoft's part of the algorithm works, this risk is minimized when the calculated hash values are evenly distributed between `int.MinValue` and `int.MaxValue`.

The risk of clashes between keys also increases as the dictionary gets fuller, so it's normally a good idea to make sure the capacity of the dictionary is substantially greater than the number of elements actually in it. For this reason, `Hashtable` will automatically relocate to increase its capacity well before it actually becomes full. The proportion of the table that is full is termed the *load*, and you can set the maximum value that you want the load to reach before `Hashtable` relocates in another of the `Hashtable` constructors:

```
// capacity =50, Max Load = 0.5
Hashtable employees = new Hashtable(50, 0.5);
```

The smaller the maximum load, the more efficiently your hash table works and the more memory it occupies. Incidentally, when a hash table relocates in order to increase its capacity, it always chooses a prime number as its new capacity.

Another important point mentioned earlier is that the hashing algorithm must be consistent. If two objects contain what you regard as the same data, they must give the same hash value, and this is where the important restrictions on how you override the `Equals()` and `GetHashCode()` methods of `System.Object` come in. You see, the way that the `Hashtable` determines whether two keys A and B are equal is that it calls `A.Equals(B)`. This means you must ensure that the following is always true:

> If `A.Equals(B)` **is true, then** `A.GetHashCode()` **and** `B.GetHashCode()` **must always return the same hash code.**

This probably seems a fairly subtle point, but it is crucial. If you contrived some way of overriding these methods so that the preceding statement is not always true, a hash table that uses instances of this class as its keys will simply not work properly. Instead, you'll find funny things happening. For example, you might place an object in the hash table and then discover that you can never retrieve it, or you might try to retrieve an entry and get the wrong entry returned.

*For this reason, the C# compiler will display a compilation warning if you supply an override for* `Equals()` *but don't supply an override for* `GetHashCode()`.

For `System.Object` this condition is true, because `Equals()` simply compares references, and `GetHashCode()` actually returns a hash that is based solely on the address of the object. This means that hash tables based on a key that doesn't override these methods will work correctly. However, the problem with this way of doing things is that keys are regarded as equal only if they are the same object. That means that when you place an object in the dictionary, you then have to hang on to the reference to the key. You can't simply instantiate another key object later that has the same value, because the same value is defined as meaning the very same instance. This means that if you don't override the `Object` versions of `Equals()` and `GetHashCode()`, your class won't be very convenient to use in a hash table. It makes more sense to implement `GetHashCode()` to generate a hash based on the value of the key rather than its address in memory. This is why you will invariably need to override `GetHashCode()` and `Equals()` for any class that you want to be used as a key.

Incidentally, `System.String` has had these methods overloaded appropriately. `Equals()` has been overloaded to provide value comparison, and `GetHashCode()` has also been correspondingly overloaded to return a hash based on the value of the string. For this reason, it is convenient to use strings as keys in a dictionary.

## *The MortimerPhonesEmployees example*

The `MortimerPhonesEmployees` example is a program that sets up a dictionary of employees. As mentioned earlier, the dictionary is indexed using `EmployeeID` objects, and each item stored in the dictionary is an `EmployeeData` object that stores details of an employee. The program simply instantiates a dictionary, adds a couple of employees to it, and then invites the user to type in employee IDs. For each ID the user types in, the program attempts to use the ID to index a dictionary and retrieve the employee's details. The process iterates until the user types in X. The example, when run, looks like this:

```
MortimerPhonesEmployees
Enter employee ID (format:A999, X to exit)> B001
Employee: B001: Mortimer           $100,000.00
```

```
Enter employee ID (format:A999, X to exit)> W234
Employee: W234: Arabel Jones          $10,000.00

Enter employee ID (format:A999, X to exit)> X
```

This example contains a number of classes. In particular, you need the `EmployeeID` class, which is the key used to identify employees, and the `EmployeeData` class that stores employee data. We will examine the `EmployeeID` class first, because this is the one where all the action happens in terms of preparing it to be used as a dictionary key. The definition of this class is as follows:

```
class EmployeeID
{
    private readonly char prefix;
    private readonly int number;


    public EmployeeID(string id)
    {
        prefix = (id.ToUpper())[0];
        number = int.Parse(id.Substring(1,3));
    }

    public override string ToString()
    {
        return prefix.ToString() + string.Format("{0,3:000}", number);
    }

    public override int GetHashCode()
    {
        return ToString().GetHashCode();
    }

    public override bool Equals(object obj)
    {
        EmployeeID rhs = obj as EmployeeID;
        if (rhs == null)
            return false;
        if (prefix == rhs.prefix && number == rhs.number)
            return true;
        return false;
    }
}
```

The first part of the class definition simply stores the actual ID. Remember that the ID takes a format such as `B001` or `W234`. It consists of a single letter prefix, followed by three numeric characters. You store this as a `char` for the prefix and an `int` for the remainder of the code.

The constructor simply takes a string and breaks it up to form these fields. Note that to keep the example simple, no error checking is performed. Just assume the string passed into the constructor is in the correct format. The `ToString()` method simply returns the ID as a string:

```
return prefix.ToString() + string.Format("{0,3:000}", number);
```

Note the format specifier (3:000) that ensures the int containing the number is padded with zeros, so you get, for example, B001, and not B1.

Now you come to the two method overrides that you need for the dictionary. First, you have overridden Equals() so that it compares the values of EmployeeID instances:

```
public override bool Equals(object obj)
{
    EmployeeID rhs = obj as EmployeeID;
    if (rhs == null)
        return false;
    if (prefix == rhs.prefix && number == rhs.number)
        return true;
    return false;
}
```

This is the first time you have seen an example of an override of Equals(). Notice that your first task is to check whether the object passed as a parameter is actually an EmployeeID instance. If it isn't, then it obviously isn't going to equal this object, so you return false. You test the type by attempting to cast it to EmployeeID using C#'s as keyword. Once you have established that you have an EmployeeID object, you just compare the values of the fields to see if they contain the same values as this object.

The implementation of GetHashCode() is shorter, though at first sight it is perhaps harder to understand what's going on:

```
public override int GetHashCode()
{
    string str = this.ToString();
    return str.GetHashCode();
}
```

Earlier, you learned some strict requirements that the calculated hash code has to satisfy. Of course, all sorts of ways exist to devise simple and efficient hashing algorithms. Generally, taking the fields, multiplying them by large prime numbers, and adding the results together is a good way to do this. However, for convenience, Microsoft has already implemented a sophisticated, yet efficient hashing algorithm for the String class, so you may as well take advantage of that. String.GetHashCode() produces well-distributed numbers based on the contents of the string. It satisfies all the requirements of a hash code.

The only disadvantage of leveraging this method is that some performance loss is associated with converting your EmployeeID class to a string in the first place. If you are concerned about that and need the last ounce of performance in your hashing algorithms, you will need to design your own hash. Designing hashing algorithms is a complex topic that we cannot discuss in depth in this book. However, we will suggest one simple approach to the problem, which is to multiply numbers based on the component fields of the class by different prime numbers (for mathematical reasons, multiplying by different prime numbers helps to prevent different combinations of values of the fields from giving the same hash code). The following snippet shows a suitable implementation of GetHashCode():

```
public override int GetHashCode()   // alternative implementation
{
    return (int)prefix*13 + (int)number*53;
}
```

This particular example works more quickly than the `ToString()`-based algorithm used in the example but has the disadvantage that the hash codes generated by different `EmployeeID`s are less likely to be evenly spread across the range of `int`. Incidentally, the primitive numeric types do have `GetHashCode()` methods defined, but these methods simply return the value of the variable, and are hence not particularly useful. The primitive types aren't really intended to be used as keys.

Notice that the `GetHashCode()` and `Equals()` implementations do between them satisfy the requirements for equality mentioned earlier. With the override of `Equals()`, two `EmployeeID` objects will be considered equal if, and only if, they have the same values of `prefix` and `number`. However, in that case `ToString()` provides the same value for both of them, and so they will give the same hash code. That's the crucial test that must be satisfied.

Next is the class that contains the employee data. The definition of this class is fairly basic and intuitive:

```csharp
class EmployeeData
{
   private string name;
   private decimal salary;
   private EmployeeID id;

   public EmployeeData(EmployeeID id, string name, decimal salary)
   {
      this.id = id;
      this.name = name;
      this.salary = salary;
   }

   public override string ToString()
   {
      StringBuilder sb = new StringBuilder(id.ToString(), 100);
      sb.Append(": ");
      sb.Append(string.Format("{0,-20}", name));
      sb.Append(" ");
      sb.Append(string.Format("{0:C}", salary));
      return sb.ToString();
   }
}
```

Notice how once again for performance reasons, you use a `StringBuilder` object to generate the string representation of an `EmployeeData` object. Finally, you create the test harness. This is defined in the `TestHarness` class:

```csharp
class TestHarness
{

   Hashtable employees = new Hashtable(31);

   public void Run()
   {
      EmployeeID idMortimer = new EmployeeID("B001");
      EmployeeData mortimer = new EmployeeData(idMortimer, "Mortimer",
                                               100000.00M);
      EmployeeID idArabel = new EmployeeID("W234");
```

```csharp
        EmployeeData arabel= new EmployeeData(idArabel, "Arabel Jones",
                                        10000.00M);

        employees.Add(idMortimer, mortimer);
        employees.Add(idArabel, arabel);

        while (true)
        {
            try
            {
                Console.Write("Enter employee ID (format:A999, X to exit)> ");
                string userInput = Console.ReadLine();
                userInput = userInput.ToUpper();
                if (userInput == "X")
                    return;
                EmployeeID id = new EmployeeID(userInput);
                DisplayData(id);
            }
            catch (Exception e)
            {
                Console.WriteLine("Exception occurred. Did you use the correct
                                format for the employee ID?");
                Console.WriteLine(e.Message);
                Console.WriteLine();
            }

            Console.WriteLine();
        }
    }

    private void DisplayData(EmployeeID id)
    {
        object empobj = employees[id];
        if (empobj != null)
        {
            EmployeeData employee = (EmployeeData)empobj;
            Console.WriteLine("Employee: " + employee.ToString());
        }
        else
            Console.WriteLine("Employee not found: ID = " + id);
    }
}
```

`TestHarness` contains the member field, which actually is the dictionary.

As usual for a dictionary, you set the initial capacity to a prime number; in this case, 31. The guts of the test harness are in the `Run()` method. This method first sets up details for two employees—`mortimer` and `arabel`—and adds their details to the dictionary:

```csharp
        employees.Add(idMortimer, mortimer);

        employees.Add(idArabel, arabel);
```

# Collections

Next, you enter the `while` loop that repeatedly asks the user to input an `employeeID`. There is a `try` block inside the `while` loop, which is just there to trap any problems caused by the user typing in something that's not the correct format for an `EmployeeID`, which would cause the `EmployeeID` constructor to throw an exception when it tries to construct an ID from the string:

```
string userInput = Console.ReadLine();
userInput = userInput.ToUpper();
if (userInput == "X")
    return;
EmployeeID id = new EmployeeID(userInput);
```

If the `EmployeeID` is constructed correctly, you display the associated employee by calling a method, `DisplayData()`. This is the method in which you finally get to access the dictionary with array syntax. Indeed, retrieving the employee data for the employee with this ID is the first thing you do in this method:

```
private void DisplayData(EmployeeID id)
{
    object empobj = employees[id];
```

If there is no employee with that ID in the dictionary, `employees[id]` will return `null`, which is why you check for a `null` reference and display an appropriate error message if you find one. Otherwise, you simply cast your returned `empobj` reference to an `EmployeeData`. (Remember that `Hashtable` is a very generic dictionary class; it is storing objects, so retrieving an element from it will return an object reference, which you need to cast back to the type that you originally placed in the dictionary.) Once you have your `EmployeeID` reference, you can simply display the employee data using the `EmployeeData.ToString()` method:

```
        EmployeeData employee = (EmployeeData)empobj;
        Console.WriteLine("Employee: " + employee.ToString());
```

The final part of the code — the `Main()` method — kicks off the whole example. This simply instantiates a `TestHarness` object and runs it:

```
static void Main()
{
    TestHarness harness = new TestHarness();
    harness.Run();
}
```

## *Generics*

To make collections, a more powerful feature and also increase their efficiency and usability, generics were introduced to C# with the release of the .NET Framework 2.0. The idea of generics is nothing new. They are a tad similar to C++ templates. You can also find generics in other languages, such as Java. Their introduction into the .NET Framework 2.0 languages is a huge benefit for the developer.

Generics enable you to make a generic collection that is still strongly typed — providing fewer chances for errors (because they occur at design time), increasing performance, and giving you IntelliSense features when you are working with the collections.

## Chapter 9

The `System.Collections.Generic` namespace gives you access to generic versions of the `Stack`, `Dictionary`, `SortedDictionary`, `List`, and `Queue` classes.

Generics are covered in detail in Chapter 10.

# Summary

This chapter took a look at working with different sorts of collections in your code. It discussed array lists, dictionaries, and collections. In addition to these types of collections, if you look in the SDK documentation of all the collections that implement the `ICollection` or `IEnumerable` interfaces, you will actually find a long list of available classes at your disposal. Included in this list of classes, you will find a collection that should satisfy your needs. When implementing a collection in your code, think through the size, type, and performance that your collection requires and consider all your options. The .NET Framework provides a tremendous number of possibilities for this type of work.

# 10
# Generics

One of the biggest changes of the C# language and the CLR is the introduction of generics. With .NET 1.0, creating a flexible class or method that should use classes that are not known at compile time must be based on the `Object` class. With the `Object` class, there's no type safety during compile time. Casting is necessary. Also, using the `Object` class for value types has a performance impact.

.NET 2.0 supports generics. With generics the `Object` class is no longer necessary in such scenarios. Generic classes make use of generic types that are replaced with specific types as needed. This allows for type safety: the compiler complains if a specific type is not supported with the generic class.

Generics are a great feature, especially with collection classes. Most of the .NET 1.0 collection classes are based on the `Object` type. .NET 2.0 offers new collection classes that are implemented as generics.

Generics are not limited to classes; in this chapter, you also see generics with delegates, interfaces, and methods.

This chapter discusses the following:

- ❑ Generics overview
- ❑ Generic collection classes
- ❑ Creating custom generic classes
- ❑ Generic methods
- ❑ Generic delegates
- ❑ Other generic framework types

# Chapter 10

# Overview

Generics are not a completely new construct; similar concepts exist with other languages. For example, C++ templates can be compared to generics. However, there's a big difference between C++ templates and .NET generics. With C++ templates the source code of the template is required when a template is instantiated with a specific type. Contrary to C++ templates, generics are not only a construct of the C# language; generics are defined with the CLR. This makes it possible to instantiate generics with a specific type in Visual Basic even though the generic class was defined with C#.

The following sections look into the advantages and disadvantages of generics.

## Performance

One of the big advantages of generics is performance. In Chapter 9, collection classes from the namespace `System.Collections` were used to work with multiple objects. Adding a value type to such a collection results in boxing and unboxing when the value type is converted to a reference type and vice versa.

> *Boxing and unboxing is discussed in Chapter 5, "Operators and Casts." Here is just a short refresher about these terms.*
>
> *Value types are stored on the stack. Reference types are stored on the heap. C# classes are reference type; structs are value types. .NET makes it easy to convert value types to reference types, and so you can use a value type everywhere an object (which is a reference type) is needed. For example, an int can be assigned to an object. The conversion from a value type to a reference type is known as boxing. Boxing happens automatically if a method requires an object as a parameter, and a value type is passed. On the other side, a boxed value type can be converted to a value type using unboxing. With unboxing the cast operator is required.*

The following example shows the `ArrayList` class from the namespace `System.Collections`. `ArrayList` stores objects, the `Add()` method is defined to require an object as a parameter, and so an integer type is boxed. When the values from an `ArrayList` are read, unboxing occurs when the object is converted to an integer type. This may be obvious with the cast operator that is used to assign the first element of the `ArrayList` collection to the variable `i1`, but also happens inside the `foreach` statement where the variable `i2` of type `int` is accessed:

```
ArrayList list = new ArrayList();
list.Add(44);    // boxing - convert a value type to a reference type

int i1 = (int)list[0];   // unboxing - convert a reference type to a value type

foreach (int i2 in list)
{
   Console.WriteLine(i2);   // unboxing
}
```

Boxing and unboxing is easy to use, but it has a big performance impact, especially when iterating through many items.

Instead of using objects, the `List<T>` class from the namespace `System.Collections.Generic` allows you to define the type when it is used. In the example here, the generic type of the `List<T>` class is

# Generics

defined as `int`, and so the `int` type is used inside the class that is generated dynamically from the JIT compiler. Boxing and unboxing no longer happens:

```
List<int> list = new List<int>();
list.Add(44);   // no boxing - value types are stored in the List<int>

int i1 = list[0];   // no unboxing, no cast needed

foreach (int i2 in list)
{
    Console.WriteLine(i2);
}
```

## Type Safety

Another feature of generics is type safety. As with the `ArrayList` class, if objects are used, any type can be added to this collection. This example shows adding an integer, a string, and an object of type `MyClass` to the collection of type `ArrayList`:

```
ArrayList list = new ArrayList();
list.Add(44);
list.Add("mystring");
list.Add(new MyClass());
```

Now if this collection is iterated using the following `foreach` statement which iterates using integer elements, the compiler accepts this code. However, because not all elements in the collection can be cast to an `int`, a runtime exception will occur:

```
foreach (int i in list)
{
    Console.WriteLine(i);
}
```

Errors should be detected as early as possible. With the generic class `List<T>`, the generic type `T` defines what types are allowed. With a definition of `List<int>`, only integer types can be added to the collection. The compiler doesn't compile this code because the `Add()` method has invalid arguments:

```
List<int> list = new List<int>();
list.Add(44);
list.Add("mystring");       // compile time error
list.Add(new MyClass());    // compile time error
```

## Binary Code Reuse

Generics allow better binary code reuse. A generic class can be defined once and can be instantiated with many different types. You needn't access the source code as is necessary with C++ templates.

As an example, here the `List<T>` class from the namespace `System.Collections.Generic` in the assembly mscorlib is instantiated with an `int`, a string, and a `MyClass` type:

```
List<int> list = new List<int>();
list.Add(44);

List<string> stringList = new List<string>();
stringList.Add("mystring");

List<MyClass> myclassList = new List<MyClass>();
myClassList.Add(new MyClass());
```

Generic types can be defined in one language and used from any other .NET language.

## Code Bloat

How much code is created with generics when instantiating them with different specific types?

Because a generic class definition goes into the assembly, instantiating generic classes with specific types doesn't duplicate these classes in the IL code. However, when the generic classes are compiled by the JIT compiler to native code, a new class for every specific value type is created. Reference types share all the same implementation of the same native class. This is because with reference types only a 4-byte memory address (with 32-bit systems) is needed within the generic instantiated class to reference a reference type. Value types are contained within the memory of the generic instantiated class, and because every value type can have different memory requirements, a new class for every value type is instantiated.

## Naming Guidelines

If generics are used in the program, it helps when generic types can be distinguished from non-generic types. Here are naming guidelines for generic types:

- ❑ Generic type names should be prefixed with the letter T.
- ❑ If the generic type can be replaced by any class because there's no special requirement, and only one generic type is used, the character T is good as a generic type name:

```
public class List<T> { }

public class LinkedList<T> { }
```

- ❑ If there's a special requirement for a generic type (for example, it must implement an interface or derive from a base class), or if two or more generic types are used, descriptive names should be used for the type names:

```
public delegate void EventHandler<TEventArgs>(object sender, TEventArgs e);

public delegate TOutput Converter<TInput, TOutput>(TInput from);

public class SortedList<TKey, TValue> { }
```

# Generics

## Generic Collection Classes

Many generic interfaces and collection classes are defined in the namespace `System.Collections.Generic`. These classes can be used instead of the collection classes that were discussed in Chapter 9, "Collections." Many of the classes dealt with in the previous chapter have a similar generic class, so this section does not differentiate between a list and a dictionary but focuses on generic features instead.

## *Generic Collections Overview*

Before taking a closer look at how to use the collection classes, this section gives you an overview of which generic collection classes and interfaces are available.

The major interfaces and their functionality are defined in the following table.

| Interface | Methods and Properties | Description |
| --- | --- | --- |
| ICollection<T> | Add(), Clear(), Contains(), CopyTo(), Remove() Count, IsReadOnly | The interface ICollection<T> is implemented by collection classes. Methods of this interface can be used to add and remove elements from the collection. The generic interface ICollection<T> inherits from the non-generic interface IEnumerable. With this it is possible to pass objects implementing ICollection<T> to methods that require IEnumerable objects as parameters. |
| IList<T> | Insert(), RemoveAt(), IndexOf() Item | The interface IList<T> allows you to access a collection using an indexer. It is also possible to insert or remove elements at any position of the collection. Similar to ICollection<T>, the interface IList<T> inherits from IEnumerable. |
| IEnumerable<T> | GetEnumerator() | The interface IEnumerable<T> is required if a foreach statement is used with the collection. This interface defines the method GetEnumerator() that returns an enumerator implementing IEnumerator<T>. The generic interface IEnumerable<T> inherits from the non-generic interface IEnumerable. |

*Table continued on following page*

275

| Interface | Methods and Properties | Description |
|---|---|---|
| `IEnumerator<T>` | `Current` | The `foreach` statement uses an enumerator implementing `IEnumerator<T>` for accessing all elements in a collection. The interface `IEnumerator<T>` inherits from the non-generic interfaces `IEnumerator` and `IDisposable`. The interface `IEnumerator` defines the methods `MoveNext()` and `Reset()`, `IEnumerator<T>` defines the type-safe version of the property `Current`. |
| `IDictionary<TKey, TValue>` | `Add()`, `ContainsKey()`, `Remove()`, `TryGetValue()`, `Item`, `Keys`, `Values` | The interface `IDictionary<K, V>` is implemented by collections whose elements have a key and a value. |
| `IComparer<T>` | `Compare()` | The interface `IComparer<T>` is used to sort elements inside a collection with the `Compare()` method. |
| `IEqualityComparer<T>` | `Equals()`, `GetHashCode()` | `IEqualityComparer<T>` is the second interface to compare objects. With this interface the objects can be compared for equality. The method `GetHashCode()` should return a unique value for every object. The method `Equals()` returns `true` if the objects are equal, `false` otherwise. |

The generic collection classes and their functionality are shown in the following table.

| Class | Implemented Interfaces | Description |
|---|---|---|
| `List<T>` | `IList<T>` `ICollection<T>` `IEnumerable<T>` | The `List<T>` class is the generic replacement for the `ArrayList` class. Similarly to the `ArrayList` class, the `List<T>` class can grow and shrink dynamically. Besides the implementation of the three implemented interfaces, this class also supports additional functionality like sorting and reversing the elements in the collection. |
| `Dictionary<TKey, TValue>` | `IDictionary<TKey, TValue>` `ICollection<KeyValuePair<TKey, TValue>>` `IEnumerable <KeyValuePair<TKey, TValue>>` `ISerializable` `IDeserializationCallback` | `Dictionary<TKey, TValue>` is a collection class that stores key and value pairs. |

# Generics

| Class | Implemented Interfaces | Description |
|---|---|---|
| SortedList<TKey, TValue> | IDictionary<TKey, TValue><br>ICollection<KeyValuePair<TKey, TValue>><br>IEnumerable<KeyValuePair<TKey, TValue>> | SortedList<TKey, TValue> is similar to Dictionary<TKey, TValue> with the difference that this collection is sorted by the key. |
| LinkedList<T> | ICollection<T><br>IEnumerable<T><br>ISerializable<br>IDeserializationCallback | LinkedList<T> is a double-linked list. With a double-linked list one element references the next and the previous. |
| Queue<T> | ICollection<T><br>IEnumerable<T> | Queue<T> is a collection with first-in, first-out behavior. The element that was added first will be read first from the queue. This is similar to a print-queue where the oldest print jobs are processed first.<br>The method Enque() adds an object to the end of the queue; the method Deque() returns and removes an object from the beginning of the queue. With the method Peek() it is possible to read the first object from the queue without removing it. |
| Stack<T> | ICollection<T><br>IEnumerable<T> | Stack<T> is a collection with first-in, last-out behavior. The element that was added last will be read first from the stack. The Stack<T> offers the methods Push() and Pop(). With Push() an object is added to the end of the stack, while Pop() reads and removes the object from the end of the stack. The method Peek() reads the last object from the stack without removing it. |

The .NET Framework offers some generic collection base classes that can be used to create a custom generic collection class. The classes in the following table are found in the namespace System.Collections.ObjectModel.

277

| Class | Implemented Interfaces | Description |
|---|---|---|
| `Collection<T>` | `IList<T>`<br>`ICollection<T>`<br>`IEnumerable<T>` | The class `Collection<T>` can be used as a base class for a custom generic collection class. It implements the interfaces `IList<T>`, `ICollection<T>`, and `IEnumerable<T>`. Behind the scenes, this class makes use of the `List<T>` class. However, it doesn't offer all the methods that `List<T>` does. So with a custom generic collection class you can offer the methods that are appropriate for the use case.<br>With a custom collection class you can access the underlying `List<T>` object with the protected property `Items`. |
| `ReadOnly Collection<T>` | `IList<T>`<br>`ICollection<T>`<br>`IEnumerable<T>` | `ReadOnlyCollection<T>` is a read-only version of the class `Collection<T>`. All the methods from the interfaces that allow adding and removing elements are explicitly implemented and throw a `NotSupportedException`.<br>An object of this class can be created by passing any collection that implements the `IList<T>` interface to the constructor. |
| `KeyedCollection <TKey, TItem>` | `IList<TItem>`<br>`ICollection<TItem>`<br>`IEnumerable<TItem>` | `KeyedCollection<TKey, TItem>` is an abstract base class that can be used for custom collection classes that have a key and a value. This class inherits from `Collection<TItem>`. |

## Using the List<T> Class

The class `List<T>` in the namespace `System.Collections.Generic` is a very similar in its usage to the `ArrayList` class from the namespace `System.Collections`. This class implements the `IList`, `ICollection`, and `IEnumerable` interfaces. Because Chapter 9 already discussed the methods of these interfaces, this section looks at how to use the `List<T>` class.

The following example uses the class `Racer` as elements to be added to the collection to represent a Formula-1 racer. This class has two fields, a name and a car, that can be accessed with properties. With the constructor of the class the name of the racer and the car can be passed to set the members. The method `ToString()` is overridden to return the name of the racer and the car:

```
public class Racer
{
    private string name;
    public string Name
    {
```

```
            get
            {
                return name;
            }
        }

        private string car;
        public string Car
        {
            get
            {
                return car;
            }
        }

        public Racer(string name, string car)
        {
            this.name = name;
            this.car = car;
        }

        public override string ToString()
        {
            return name + ", " + car;
        }
    }
```

The variable `racers` is defined to be of type `List<Racer>`. With the `new` operator a new object of the same type is created. Here the default constructor of the `List<T>` class is used. This class also has a constructor to reserve memory for a specific number of items, and a constructor to copy elements from another collection of type `List<T>`.

Because the class `List<T>` was instantiated with the concrete class `Racer`, now only `Racer` objects can be added with the `Add()` method. With the class `List<T>`, the `Add()` method is defined as `void Add(T item)`. In the following sample code five Formula-1 racers are created and added to the collection. Then, using the `foreach` statement, every team in the collection is iterated to be displayed on the console:

```
        List<Racer> racers = new List<Racer>();
        racers.Add(new Racer("Michael Schumacher", "Ferrari"));
        racers.Add(new Racer("Juan Pablo Montoya", "McLaren-Mercedes"));
        racers.Add(new Racer("Kimi Raikkonen", "McLaren-Mercedes"));
        racers.Add(new Racer("Mark Webber", "Williams-BMW"));
        racers.Add(new Racer("Rubens Barichello", "Ferrari"));

        foreach (Racer r in racers)
        {
            Console.WriteLine(r);
        }
```

With the `List<T>` class, not only can you add items and access them by using an enumerator; this class also has methods to insert and remove elements, clear the collection, and copy the elements to an array. Even more powerful functionality is discussed next. `List<T>` offers methods to search and to convert elements, reverse the order, and so on.

## Chapter 10

### *Finding elements*

In this section, you search for all racers in the collection that drive a Ferrari.

The `List<T>` class offers `Find()` and `FindAll()` methods with these declarations:

```
public T Find(Predicate<T> match);
public List<T> FindAll(Predicate<T> match);
```

Both methods require a `Predicate<T>` as an argument. `Predicate<T>` is a delegate that references a predicate method. A predicate is a method that returns a Boolean value. If the predicate returns `true`, there's a match and the element is found. If it returns `false`, the element is not added to the result of the search. With the definition of `Predicate<T>`, the predicate must have a single argument of type `T`. The `Find()` method returns the first element with a predicate match, and the `FindAll()` method returns all elements with a predicate match in a list collection.

So you have to define a predicate. You use the predicate method `DrivingCarPredicate()` for finding a racer with a specific car. This method is defined in the class `FindRacer`, which can be initialized with the car to search. `DrivingCarPredicate()` receives a `Racer` object and compares the car of the `Racer` object with the car that is set in the constructor to return `true` or `false` accordingly:

```
public class FindRacer
{
    private string car;
    public FindRacer(string car)
    {
        this.car = car;
    }

    public bool DrivingCarPredicate(Racer racer)
    {
        return racer.Car == car;
    }
}
```

To find the specific racers, the `FindRacer` class is initiated and initialized with a Ferrari, because you want to find all Ferrari racers. With the `FindAll()` method of the `List<T>` class, a new predicate delegate is instantiated, and this predicate delegate receives the `finder.DrivingCarPredicate` method. `FindAll()` returns a list of type `List<Racer>` that is used with the `foreach` to iterate all returned racers to display them on the console:

```
FindRacer finder = new FindRacer("Ferrari");

foreach (Racer racer in
        racers.FindAll(new Predicate<Racer>(finder.DrivingCarPredicate)))
{
    Console.WriteLine(racer);
}
```

As a result, Michael Schumacher and Rubens Barichello are displayed on the console.

# Generics

## Performing some action

Template delegates are not only used with the `Find()`/`FindAll()` methods; they are also used to perform some action with every element. The `List<T>` class offers a `ForEach()` method that uses an `Action<T>` delegate to perform some action with every element in the collection. The delegate `Action<T>` has a void return type.

In the example, the `ForEach()` method is used to display every racer to the console. Because here you just iterate through all racer objects and other initialization data is not needed with the iteration (such as the car with the `FindAll()` method), an anonymous method that has a `Racer` parameter is defined. The implementation of the anonymous method writes the racer to the console:

```
racers.ForEach(delegate(Racer r) { Console.WriteLine(r); });
```

*Anonymous methods are discussed in Chapter 6, "Delegates and Events."*

If only the racers where the previously used predicate applies should be written to the console, the methods `ForEach()` and `FindAll()` can be combined. With the list returned from `FindAll()`, the `ForEach()` method is invoked:

```
// display all Ferrari drivers on the console
FindRacer finder = new FindRacer("Ferrari");
racers.FindAll(new Predicate<Racer>(finder.DrivingCarPredicate)).
      ForEach(delegate(Racer r) { Console.WriteLine(r); });
```

This way, the complete `foreach` code block can be reduced to a single line of code. Of course it takes some time to get used to this coding style. If the implementation of anonymous methods are needed more than once, don't use anonymous methods. A helper method can do the task and help with reuse.

## Sorting

The `List<T>` class allows sorting its elements. The `Sort()` method has several overloads defined. The arguments that can be passed are a generic delegate `Comparison<T>`, the generic interface `IComparer<T>`, and a range together with the generic interface `IComparer<T>`:

```
public void List<T>.Sort();
public void List<T>.Sort(Comparison<T>);
public void List<T>.Sort(IComparer<T>);
public void List<T>.Sort(Int32, Int32, IComparer<T>);
```

The `Sort()` method without arguments is possible only if the elements in the collection implement the interface `IComparable`.

`Comparison<T>` is a delegate to a method that has two parameters of type `T` and a return type `int`. If the parameter values are equal, the method must return 0. If the first parameter is less than the second, a value less than zero must be returned; otherwise a value greater than zero is returned.

With a simple implementation for the comparison method, an anonymous method can be used. The two parameters are of type `Racer`, and in the implementation the `Name` properties are compared by using the string method `CompareTo()`:

281

```
racers.Sort(delegate(Racer r1, Racer r2) {
    return r1.Name.CompareTo(r2.Name); });
```

After the method has been invoked, the complete racer list is sorted based on the name of the racer.

Instead of using a delegate, the interface `IComparer<T>` also can be used to sort the collection. The class `RacerComparer` implements the interface `IComparer<T>` for `Racer` types. This class allows you to sort either by the name of the racer or by the car. Whether the sort should happen by the name or by the car is defined with the inner enumeration type `CompareType`. The `CompareType` is set with the constructor of the class `RacerComparer`. The interface `IComparer<Racer>` defines the method `Compare` that is required for sorting. In the implementation of this method, the `CompareTo()` method of the `String` class is used — either on the car or on the name:

```
public class RacerComparer : IComparer<Racer>
{
    public enum CompareType
    {
        Name,
        Car
    }

    private CompareType compareType;
    public RacerComparer(CompareType compareType)
    {
        this.compareType = compareType;
    }

    public int Compare(Racer x, Racer y)
    {
        int result = 0;
        switch (compareType)
        {
            case CompareType.Name:
                result = x.Name.CompareTo(y.Name);
                break;
            case CompareType.Car:
                result = x.Car.CompareTo(y.Car);
                break;
        }
        return result;
    }
}
```

When the racers collection is sorted, a new instance of the `RacerComparer` class is passed, and here the sort is done by the car:

```
racers.Sort(new RacerComparer(RacerComparer.CompareType.Car));
```

## Type conversion

With the `List<T>` method `ConvertAll()`, all types of a collection can be converted to a different type. The `ConvertAll()` method uses a `Converter` delegate that is defined like this:

# Generics

```
public sealed delegate TOutput Converter<TInput, TOutput>(TInput from);
```

The generic types `TInput` and `TOutput` are used with the conversion. `TInput` is the argument of the delegate method and `TOutput` is the return type.

In this example all `Racer` types should be converted to `Person` types. Whereas the `Racer` type contains a name and a car, the `Person` type contains a `firstname` and a `lastname`. For the conversion, the car of the racer can be ignored but the name must be converted to a `firstname` and `lastname`:

```
public class Person
{
    private string firstname;
    private string lastname;

    public Person(string firstname, string lastname)
    {
        this.firstname = firstname;
        this.lastname = lastname;
    }

    public override string ToString()
    {
        return firstname + " " + lastname;
    }
}
```

The conversion happens by invoking the `racers.ConvertAll<Person>()` method. The argument of this method is defined as an anonymous method with an argument of type `Racer` and a `Person` type that is returned. In the implementation of the anonymous method a new `Person` object is created and returned. For the `Person` object, the `Name` of the `Racer` is converted to `firstname` and `lastname`:

```
List<Person> persons = racers.ConvertAll<Person>(delegate(Racer r) {
    int ixSeparator = r.Name.LastIndexOf(' ') + 1;
    string lastname = r.Name.Substring(ixSeparator,
        r.Name.Length - ixSeparator);
    string firstname = r.Name.Substring(0, ixSeparator - 1);
    return new Person(firstname, lastname);
});
```

The result of the conversion is a list containing the converted `Person` objects: `persons` of type `List<Person>`.

## Using the Queue<T> Class

The class `Queue<T>` has the same functionality as the `Queue` class discussed in Chapter 9; that is, it is just a generic version of a queue. Elements are processed *First-In, First-Out* (FIFO).

The sample application for the `Queue<T>` class is a document management application. One thread is used to add documents to the queue, and another thread reads documents from the queue and processes them.

The elements stored in the queue are of type `Document`. The `Document` class defines a title and content:

```
public class Document
{
   private string title;
   public string Title
   {
      get
      {
         return title;
      }
   }

   private string content;
   public string Content
   {
      get
      {
         return content;
      }
   }

   public Document(string title, string content)
   {
      this.title = title;
      this.content = content;
   }
}
```

The `DocumentManager` class is a thin layer around the `Queue<T>` class. The class `DocumentManager` defines how to handle documents: adding documents to the queue with the `AddDocument()` method, and getting documents from the queue with the `GetDocument()` method.

Inside the `AddDocument()` method, the document is added to the end of the queue using the `Enqueue()` method. The first document from the queue is read with the `Dequeue()` method inside `GetDocument()`. Because multiple threads can access the `DocumentManager` concurrently, the access of the queue is locked with the `lock` statement.

*Threading and the lock statement are discussed in Chapter 13, "Threading."*

`IsDocumentAvailable` is a read-only Boolean property that returns `true` if there are documents in the queue and `false` if not:

```
public class DocumentManager
{
   private readonly Queue<Document> documentQueue = new Queue<Document>();

   public void AddDocument(Document doc)
   {
      lock (this)
      {
         documentQueue.Enqueue(doc);
      }
   }
```

```csharp
        public Document GetDocument()
        {
            Document doc = null;
            lock (this)
            {
                doc = documentQueue.Dequeue();
            }
            return doc;
        }

        public bool IsDocumentAvailable
        {
            get
            {
                return documentQueue.Count > 0;
            }
        }
    }
```

The class `ProcessDocuments` processes documents from the queue in a separate thread. The only method that can be accessed from the outside is `Start()`. In the `Start()` method a new thread is instantiated. A `ProcessDocuments` object is created for starting the thread, and the `Run()` method is defined as the start method of the thread. `ThreadStart` is a delegate that references the method to be started by the thread. After creating the `Thread` object, the thread is started by calling the method `Thread.Start()`.

With the `Run()` method of the `ProcessDocuments` class an endless loop is defined. Within this loop, the property `IsDocumentAvailable` is used to see if there is a document in the queue. If there is a document in the queue, the document is taken from the `DocumentManager` and processed. Processing here is only writing information to the console. In a real application, the document could be written to a file, to the database, or sent across the network.

```csharp
    public class ProcessDocuments
    {
        public static void Start(DocumentManager dm)
        {
            new Thread(new ProcessDocuments(dm).Run).Start();
        }

        protected ProcessDocuments(DocumentManager dm)
        {
            documentManager = dm;
        }

        private DocumentManager documentManager;

        protected void Run()
        {
            while (true)
            {
                if (documentManager.IsDocumentAvailable)
                {
                    Document doc = documentManager.GetDocument();
```

# Chapter 10

```
            Console.WriteLine("Processing document {0}", doc.Title);
         }
         Thread.Sleep(new Random().Next(20));
      }
   }
}
```

In the `Main()` method of the application a `DocumentManager` object is instantiated, and the document processing thread is started. Then 1000 documents are created and added to the `DocumentManager`. With a real application, documents can be received from a Web service.

```
class Program
{
   static void Main(string[] args)
   {
      DocumentManager dm = new DocumentManager();

      ProcessDocuments.Start(dm);

      // Create documents and add them to the DocumentManager
      for (int i = 0; i < 1000; i++)
      {
         Document doc = new Document("Doc " + i.ToString(), "content");
         dm.AddDocument(doc);
         Console.WriteLine("added document {0}", doc.Title);
         Thread.Sleep(new Random().Next(20));
      }
   }
}
```

When you start the application, the documents are added and removed from the queue as shown in Figure 10-1.

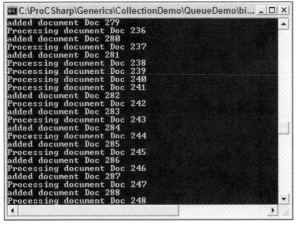

Figure 10-1

# Generics

## Using the LinkedList<T>

A collection class that has no similar version with a non-generic collection is LinkedList<T>. LinkedList<T> is a doubly linked list where one element references the next and the previous one as shown in Figure 10-2.

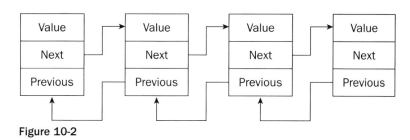

Figure 10-2

The advantage of a linked list is that if elements should be inserted in the middle of a list, the linked list is very fast. When an element is inserted only the Next reference of the previous element and the Previous reference of the next element must be changed to reference the inserted element. With a collection class, when an element is inserted all following elements must be moved.

Of course, there's also a disadvantage with linked lists. Linked lists can only be accessed one after the other. It takes a long time to find an element that's somewhere in the middle or at the end of the list.

The sample application uses a linked list LinkedList<T> together with a list List<T>. The linked list contains documents as in the previous example, but the documents have an additional priority associated with them. The documents will be sorted inside the linked list depending on the priority. If multiple documents have the same priority, the elements are sorted depending on the time the document was inserted.

Figure 10-3 describes the collections of the sample application. LinkedList<Document> is the linked list containing all the Document objects. The figure shows the title and the priority of the documents. The title indicates when the document was added to the list: The first document added has the title One, the second document Two, and so on. You can see that the documents One and Four have the same priority, 8, but because One was added before Four, it is earlier in the list.

When new documents are added to the linked list, they should be added after the last document that has the same priority. A LinkedList<Document> collection contains elements of type LinkedListNode<Document>. The class LinkedListNode<T> adds Next and Previous properties to walk from one node to the next. For referencing such elements, the List<T> is defined as List<LinkedListNode<Document>>. For fast access to the last document of every priority, the collection List<LinkedListNode> contains up to 10 elements, each referencing the last document of every priority. In the upcoming discussion the references to the last documents of every priority is called *priority node*.

# Chapter 10

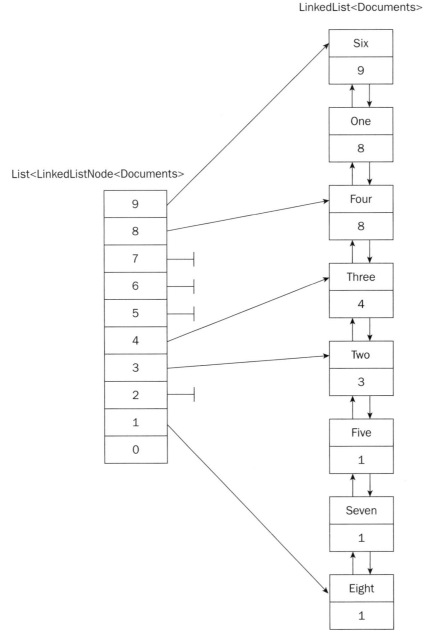

**Figure 10-3**

From the previous example, the Document class is extended to contain the priority. The priority is set with the constructor of the class:

```csharp
public class Document
{
   private string title;
   public string Title
   {
      get
      {
         return title;
      }
   }

   private string content;
   public string Content
   {
      get
      {
         return content;
      }
   }

   private byte priority;
   public byte Priority
   {
      get
      {
         return priority;
      }
   }

   public Document(string title, string content, byte priority)
   {
      this.title = title;
      this.content = content;
      this.priority = priority;
   }
}
```

The heart of the solution is the `PriorityDocumentManager` class. This class is very easy to use. With the public interface of this class new `Document` elements can be added to the linked list, the first document can be retrieved, and for testing purposes it also has a method to display all elements of the collection as they are linked in the list.

The class `PriorityDocumentManager` contains two collections. The collection of type `LinkedList<Document>` contains all documents. The collection of type `List<LinkedListNode<Document>>` contains references of up to 10 elements that are entry points to add new documents with a specific priority. Both collection variables are initialized with the constructor of the class `PriorityDocumentManager`. The list collection is also initialized with `null`:

```csharp
public class PriorityDocumentManager
{
   private readonly LinkedList<Document> documentList;

   // priorities 0..9
```

# Chapter 10

```
            private readonly List<LinkedListNode<Document>> priorityNodes;

            public PriorityDocumentManager()
            {
                documentList = new LinkedList<Document>();

                priorityNodes = new List<LinkedListNode<Document>>(10);
                for (int i = 0; i < 10; i++)
                {
                    priorityNodes.Add(new LinkedListNode<Document>(null));
                }
            }
```

Part of the public interface of the class is the method `AddDocument()`. `AddDocument()` does nothing more than call the private method `AddDocumentToPriorityNode()`. The reason for having the implementation inside a different method is that `AddDocumentToPriorityNode()` may be called recursively, as you see soon:

```
            public void AddDocument(Document d)
            {
                AddDocumentToPriorityNode(d, d.Priority);
            }
```

The first action that is done in the implementation of `AddDocumentToPriorityNode()` is a check if the priority fits in the allowed priority range. Here the allowed range is between 0 and 9. If a wrong value is passed, an exception of type `ArgumentException` is thrown.

Next you check if there's already a priority node with the same priority as the priority that was passed. If there's no such priority node in the list collection, `AddDocumentToPriorityNode()` is invoked recursively with the priority value decremented to check for a priority node with the next lower priority.

If there's no priority node with the same priority or any priority with a lower value, the document can be safely added to the end of the linked list by calling the method `AddLast()`. Also, the linked list node is referenced by the priority node that's responsible for the priority of the document.

If there's an existing priority node, you can get the position inside the linked list where the document should be inserted. Here you must differentiate if a priority node already exists with the correct priority, or if there's just a priority node that references a document with a lower priority. In the first case you can just insert the new document after the position that's referenced by the priority node. Because the priority node always must reference the last document with a specific priority, the reference of the priority node must be set. It gets more complex if just a priority node referencing a document with a lower priority exists. Here the document must be inserted before all documents with the same priority as the priority node. To get the first document of the same priority, a `while` loop iterates through all linked list nodes using the `Previous` property until a linked list node is reached that has a different priority. This way, you know the position where the document must be inserted, and the priority node can be set:

```
            private void AddDocumentToPriorityNode(Document doc, int priority)
            {
                if (priority > 9 || priority < 0)
                    throw new ArgumentException("Priority must be between 0 and 9");
```

# Generics

```
            if (priorityNodes[priority].Value == null)
            {
               priority--;
               if (priority >= 0)
               {
                  // check for the next lower priority
                  AddDocumentToPriorityNode(doc, priority);
               }
               else // now no priority node exists with the same priority or lower
                    // add the new document to the end
               {
                  documentList.AddLast(doc);
                  priorityNodes[doc.Priority] = documentList.Last;
               }
               return;
            }
            else // a priority node exists
            {
               LinkedListNode<Document> priorityNode = priorityNodes[priority];
               if (priority == doc.Priority)      // priority node with the same
                                                  // priority exists
               {
                  documentList.AddAfter(priorityNode, doc);

                  // set the priority node to the last document with the same priority
                  priorityNodes[doc.Priority] = priorityNode.Next;
               }
               else // only priority node with a lower priority exists
               {
                  // get the first node of the lower priority
                  LinkedListNode<Document> firstPriorityNode = priorityNode;
                  while (firstPriorityNode.Previous != null &&
                         firstPriorityNode.Previous.Value.Priority ==
                             priorityNode.Value.Priority)
                  {
                     firstPriorityNode = priorityNode.Previous;
                  }

                  documentList.AddBefore(firstPriorityNode, doc);

                  // set the priority node to the new value
                  priorityNodes[doc.Priority] = firstPriorityNode.Previous;
               }
            }
         }
      }
```

Now only simple methods are left for discussion. `DisplayAllNodes()` just does a `foreach` loop to display the priority and the title of every document to the console.

The method `GetDocument()` returns the first document (the document with the highest priority) from the linked list and removes it from the list:

```csharp
    public void DisplayAllNodes()
    {
        foreach (Document doc in documentList)
        {
            Console.WriteLine("priority: {0}, title {1}", doc.Priority, doc.Title);
        }
    }

    // returns the document with the highest priority (that's first
    // in the linked list)
    public Document GetDocument()
    {
        Document doc = documentList.First.Value;
        documentList.RemoveFirst();
        return doc;
    }
}
```

In the `Main()` method the `PriorityDocumentManager` is used to demonstrate its functionality. Eight new documents with different priorities are added to the linked list, and then the complete list is displayed:

```csharp
static void Main(string[] args)
{
    PriorityDocumentManager pdm = new PriorityDocumentManager();
    pdm.AddDocument(new Document("one", "Sample", 8));
    pdm.AddDocument(new Document("two", "Sample", 3));
    pdm.AddDocument(new Document("three", "Sample", 4));
    pdm.AddDocument(new Document("four", "Sample", 8));
    pdm.AddDocument(new Document("five", "Sample", 1));
    pdm.AddDocument(new Document("six", "Sample", 9));
    pdm.AddDocument(new Document("seven", "Sample", 1));
    pdm.AddDocument(new Document("eight", "Sample", 1));

    pdm.DisplayAllNodes();

    Console.ReadLine();
}
```

Figure 10-4 shows the result of the running program. You can see that the documents are sorted first by the priority and second by when the document was added.

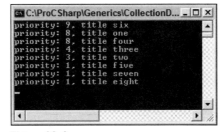

**Figure 10-4**

# Generics

# Creating Custom Generic Classes

Now that you've seen how to use many of the generic classes offered by the .NET Framework, you can step into creating custom generic classes.

A generic class is defined similarly to a normal class with the generic type declaration. The generic type can then be used within the class as a field member, or with parameter types of methods:

```csharp
public class MyGeneric<T>
{
   private T member;

   public void Method(T obj)
   {
   }
}
```

Every class that deals with the object type is a possible candidate for a generic implementation. Also, if classes make use of hierarchies, generics can be very helpful in making casting unnecessary.

Here you rework the `DocumentManager` class that was defined earlier. You can build this class with enough flexibility to not only support the `Document` type. The new version of this class is listed here:

```csharp
public class DocumentManager<T>
{
   private readonly Queue<T> documentQueue = new Queue<T>();

   public void AddDocument(T doc)
   {
      lock (this)
      {
         documentQueue.Enqueue(doc);
      }
   }

   public T GetDocument()
   {
      T doc = default(T);
      lock (this)
      {
         doc = documentQueue.Dequeue();
      }
      return doc;
   }

   public bool IsDocumentAvailable
   {
      get
      {
         return (documentQueue.Count > 0) ? true : false;
      }
   }
}
```

The `Document` class has previously been used by the `DocumentManager`. Now the class is defined as a generic class that makes use of type `T`. The `DocumentManager` is flexible and can use any type for `T`. This type can be used with variables inside the class. As shown here, the generic type can also be used when using a generic type as `Queue<T>`. The same type that is used to instantiate the `DocumentManager<T>` class is used to instantiate the `Queue<T>` class:

```
public class DocumentManager<T>
{
    private readonly Queue<T> documentQueue = new Queue<T>();
```

The methods `AddDocument()` and `GetDocument()` have defined `T` as the parameter and return type:

```
    public void AddDocument(T doc)
    {
        //...
    }

    public T GetDocument()
    {
        //...
    }
}
```

## *Default Values*

It is not possible to assign `null` with generic types. The reason is that a generic type can also be instantiated as a value type, and `null` is allowed only with reference types. To circumvent this problem, you can use the `default` keyword. With the `default` keyword `null` is assigned to reference types and `0` is assigned to value types.

```
        T doc = default(T);
```

## *Constraints*

You have to do more to make the class `ProcessDocuments` generic. Because the class `ProcessDocuments` invokes methods of the `Document` class, a `where` clause must be defined to specify the methods and properties that must be available with the generic type. The `where` clause can require a generic type to implement an interface or to derive from a specific base class.

The new version of the class `ProcessDocuments` is made independent of the `Document` class and also independent of the `DocumentManager`. This is done by defining the interfaces `IDocument` and `IDocumentManager<T>`. These interfaces define the methods and properties that are used by `ProcessDocuments<T, U>`.

The interface `IDocument` defines the read-only properties `Title` and `Content`:

```
public interface IDocument
{
    string Title
    {
        get;
    }
```

# Generics

```
        string Content
        {
            get;
        }
    }
```

The previously created class `Document` now implements the interface `IDocument`:

```
    public class Document : IDocument
    {
        //...
```

`IDocumentManager<T>` is a generic interface. Type `T` for the methods of this interface can be instantiated on a case-by-case basis:

```
    public interface IDocumentManager<T>
    {
        void AddDocument(T doc);
        T GetDocument();
        bool IsDocumentAvailable
        {
            get;
        }
    }
```

The class `DocumentManager<T>` now implements the interface `IDocumentManager<T>`. The generic type for the interface is defined by the class `DocumentManager<T>`:

```
    public class DocumentManager<T>
        : IDocumentManager<T>
    {
```

The class `ProcessDocuments` now is changed to use two generic types: `TDocument` and `TDocumentManager`. The first `where` clause defines that the type `TDocument` must implement the interface `IDocument`. One type that can be used for `TDocument` is `Document`, because this class implements the interface `IDocument`. However, any other type that implements the interface `IDocument` can be used for `TDocument`. The `where` clause for the type `TDocumentManager` defines that this type must implement the interface `IDocumentManager<TDocument>`. So in case `Document` is used for `TDocument`, `TDocumentManager` must be a class that implements `IDocumentManager<Document>`.

The generic types `TDocument` and `TDocumentManager` are now used in the implementation:

```
    public class ProcessDocuments<TDocument, TDocumentManager>
        where TDocument : IDocument
        where TDocumentManager : IDocumentManager<TDocument>
    {
        public static void Start(TDocumentManager dm)
        {
            new Thread(
                new ProcessDocuments<TDocument, TDocumentManager>(dm).Run).Start();
```

```
    }

        protected ProcessDocuments(TDocumentManager dm)
        {
            documentManager = dm;
        }

        private TDocumentManager documentManager;

        protected void Run()
        {
           while (true)
           {
              if (documentManager.IsDocumentAvailable)
              {
                 T doc = documentManager.GetDocument();
                 Console.WriteLine("Processing document {0}", doc.Title);
              }
              Thread.Sleep(new Random().Next(20));
           }
        }
    }
```

In the `Main()` method the `DocumentManager` now is initiated by using the `Document` class. The static method `Start()` of the class `ProcessDocuments` is invoked by defining the `Document` class as a parameter for `TDocument`, and `DocumentManager<Document>` as the parameter for `TDocumentManager`:

```
    static void Main(string[] args)
    {
        DocumentManager<Document> dm = new DocumentManager<Document>();

        ProcessDocuments<Document, DocumentManager<Document>>.Start(dm);

        for (int i = 0; i < 1000; i++)
        {
            Document doc = new Document("Doc " + i.ToString(), "content");
            dm.AddDocument(doc);
            Console.WriteLine("added document {0}", doc.Title);
            Thread.Sleep(new Random().Next(20));
        }
    }
```

In case new objects of a generic type must be instantiated in a generic class, the `where` clause can be extended with the *constructor constraint* `new()`. This constructor constraint defines that a default constructor must be available with the generic type:

```
public class MyClass<T>
   where T : IFoo, new()
{
   //...
```

*With .NET 2.0 only constructor constraints for the default constructor can be defined. It is not possible to define a constructor constraint for other constructors.*

# Generic Methods

In addition to defining generic classes, it is also possible to define generic methods. With a generic method the generic type is defined with the method declaration.

The method Swap<T> defines T as a generic type that is used for two arguments and a variable temp:

```
void Swap<T>(ref T x, ref T y)
{
   T temp;
   temp = x;
   x = y;
   y = temp;
}
```

A generic method can be invoked by assigning the generic type with the method call:

```
int i = 4;
int j = 5;
Swap<int>(ref i, ref j);
```

However, because the C# compiler can get the type of the parameters by calling the Swap method, it is not required to assign the generic type with the method call. The generic method can be invoked as simply as non-generic methods:

```
int i = 4;
int j = 5;
Swap(ref i, ref j);
```

Here's an example where a generic method is used to accumulate all elements of a collection. For showing the features of generic methods, the following Account class that contains a name and a balance is used.

```
public class Account
{
   private string name;
   public string Name
   {
      get
      {
         return name;
      }
   }

   private decimal balance;
   public decimal Balance
   {
      get
      {
         return balance;
      }
   }
```

```csharp
    public Account(string name, Decimal balance)
    {
        this.name = name;
        this.balance = balance;
    }
}
```

All the accounts where the balance should be accumulated are added to an accounts list of type `List<Account>`:

```csharp
List<Account> accounts = new List<Account>();
accounts.Add(new Account("Christian", 1500));
accounts.Add(new Account("Sharon", 2200));
accounts.Add(new Account("Katie", 1800));
```

A traditional way to accumulate all `Account` objects is by looping through all `Account` objects with a `foreach` statement as shown here. Because the `foreach` statement is using the `IEnumerable` interface to iterate the elements of a collection, the argument of the `AccumulateSimple()` method is of type `IEnumerable`. This way, the `AccumulateSimple()` method can be used with all collection classes that implement the interface `IEnumerable`. In the implementation of this method the property `Balance` of the `Account` object is directly accessed:

```csharp
public static class Algorithm
{
    public static decimal AccumulateSimple(IEnumerable e)
    {
        decimal sum = 0;
        foreach (Account a in e)
        {
            sum += a.Balance;
        }
        return sum;
    }
}
```

The `Accumulate` method is invoked this way:

```csharp
decimal amount = Algorithm.AccumulateSimple(accounts);
```

The problem with the first implementation is that it works only with `Account` objects. This can be avoided by using a generic method.

The second version of the `Accumulate()` method accepts any type that implements the interface `IAccount`. As you've seen earlier with generic classes, generic types can be restricted with the `where` clause. The same clause that is used with generic classes can be used with generic methods. The parameter of the `Accumulate()` method is changed to `IEnumerable<T>`. `IEnumerable<T>` is a generic version of the interface `IEnumerable` that is implemented by the generic collection classes:

```csharp
public static decimal Accumulate<TAccount>(IEnumerable<TAccount> coll)
        where TAccount : IAccount
    {
```

# Generics

```
       decimal sum = 0;

       foreach (TAccount a in coll)
       {
           sum += a.Balance;
       }
       return sum;
}
```

> One important restriction of the where clause with C# 2.0 is that it's not possible to define operators that must be implemented by the generic type. Operators cannot be defined in interfaces. With the where clause it is only possible to define base classes, interfaces, and the default constructor.

The new `Accumulate()` method can be invoked by using the template parameter:

```
       decimal amount = Algorithm.Accumulate<Account>(accounts);
```

Because the template parameter can be automatically inferred by the compiler from the parameter type of the method, it is valid to invoke the `Accumulate()` method this way:

```
       decimal amount = Algorithm.Accumulate(accounts);
```

The requirement for the generic types to implement the interface `IAccount` may be too restrictive. This requirement can be changed by using generic delegates. In the next section, the `Accumulate()` method will be changed to be independent of any interface.

## Generic Delegates

As discussed in Chapter 6, "Events and Delegates," delegates are type-safe references to methods. With generic delegates, the parameters of the delegate can be defined later.

The method `Accumulate()` is changed to have two generic types. `TInput` is the type of the objects that are accumulated and `TSummary` is the returned type. The first parameter of `Accumulate` is the interface `IEnumerable<T>`, as it was before. The second parameter requires the `Action` delegate to reference a method that is invoked to accumulate all balances.

With the implementation, the method referenced by the `Action` delegate is now invoked for every element, and then the sum of the calculation is returned:

```
       public delegate TSummary Action<TInput, TSummary>(TInput t, TSummary u);

       public static TSummary Accumulate<TInput, TOutput>(IEnumerable<T> coll,
           Action<TInput, TSummary> action)
       {
           TSummary sum = default(TSummary);
```

```
        foreach (TInput input in coll)
        {
            sum = action(input, sum);
        }
        return sum;
    }
```

The method `Accumulate` can be invoked using an anonymous method that defines that the balance of the account should be added to the second parameter:

```
decimal amount = Accumulate<Account, decimal>(
        accounts, delegate(Account a, decimal d) { return a.Balance + d; });
```

If the addition of `Account` balances is needed more than once, it is useful to move the functionality into a separate method, `AccountAdder()`:

```
static decimal AccountAdder(Account a, decimal d)
{
    return a.Balance + d;
}
```

And use the `AccountAdder` method with the `Accumulate` method:

```
decimal amount = Accumulate<Account, decimal>(
        accounts, AccountAdder);
```

The method referenced by the `Action` delegate can implement any logic; for example, a multiplication could be done instead of a summation.

The `Accumulate()` method is made more flexible with the `AccumulateIf()` method. With `AccumulateIf()`, an additional parameter of type `Predicate<T>` is used. The delegate `Predicate<T>` references the method that will be invoked to check whether the account should be part of the accumulation. In the `foreach` statement, the `action` method will be invoked only if the predicate `match` returns `true`:

```
        public static TSummary AccumulateIf<TInput, TSummary>(
            IEnumerable<TInput> coll,
            Action<TInput, TSummary> action,
            Predicate<TInput> match)
    {
        TSummary sum = default(TSummary);

        foreach (TInput a in coll)
        {
            if (match(a))
            {
                sum = action(a, sum);
            }
        }

        return sum;
    }
```

# Generics

Calling the method `AccumulateIf()` can have an implementation for the accumulation and an implementation for the predicate. Here, only the accounts with a balance higher than 2000 are accumulated:

```
decimal amount = Algorithm.AccumulateIf<Account, decimal>(
   accounts,
   delegate(Account a, decimal d) { return a.Balance + d; },
   delegate(Account a) {return a.Balance > 2000 ? true : false; });
```

## Other Generic Framework Types

In addition to the `System.Collections.Generic` namespace, the .NET Framework has other uses for generic types. The structs and delegates discussed here are all in the `System` namespace and serve different purposes.

This section discusses the following:

- ❑ The struct `Nullable<T>`
- ❑ The delegate `EventHandler<TEventArgs>`
- ❑ The struct `ArraySegment<T>`

### Nullable<T>

A number in the database and a number in a programming language have an important different characteristic insofar as the number of the database can be null. A number in C# cannot be null. Int32 is a struct, and because structs are implemented as value types, it cannot be null.

The problem doesn't exist only with databases but also with mapping XML data to .NET types.

This difference often causes headaches and lot of additional work to map the data. One solution could be to map numbers from databases and XML files to reference types, because reference types can have a null value. However, this also means additional overhead during runtime.

With the structure `Nullable<T>` this can be easily solved. In the example, `Nullable<T>` is instantiated with `Nullable<int>`. The variable x can now be used like an `int`, assigning values and using operators to do some calculation. This behavior is made possible by casting operators of the `Nullable<T>` type. However, x can also be `null`. The `Nullable<T>` properties `HasValue` and `Value` can check if there is a value, and the value can be accessed:

```
Nullable<int> x;
x = 4;
x += 3;
if (x.HasValue)
{
   int y = x.Value;
}
x = null;
```

Because nullable types are used very often, C# has a special syntax for defining variables of this type. Instead of using the syntax with the generic structure, the ? operator can be used. In the following example, the variables x1 and x2 both are instances of a nullable int type:

```
Nullable<int> x1;
int? x2;
```

A nullable type can be compared with null and numbers as shown. Here the value of x is compared with null, and if it is not null, it is compared with a value smaller than 0:

```
int? x = GetNullableType();
if (x == null)
    Console.WriteLine("x is null");
else if (x < 0)
    Console.WriteLine("x is smaller than 0");
```

Nullable types can also be used with arithmetic operators. The variable x3 is the sum of the variables x1 and x2. If any of the nullable types has a null value, the result is null:

```
int? x1 = GetNullableType();
int? x2 = GetNullableType();
int? x3 = x1 + x2;
```

Non-nullable types can be converted to nullable types. With the conversion from a non-nullable type to a nullable type, an implicit conversion is possible where casting is not required. This conversion always succeeds:

```
int y1 = 4;
int? x1 = y1;
```

The other way around, the conversion from a nullable type to a non-nullable type, can fail. If the nullable type has a null value and the null value is assigned to a non-nullable type, an exception of type InvalidOperationException is thrown. That's the reason the cast operator is required to do an explicit conversion:

```
int? x1 = GetNullableType();
int y1 = (int)x1;
```

Instead of doing an explicit cast, it is also possible to convert a nullable type to a non-nullable type with the coalescing operator. The coalescing operator has the syntax ?? to define a default value for the conversion in case the nullable type has a value of null. Here, y1 gets the value 0 if x1 is null:

```
int? x1 = GetNullableType();
int y1 = x1 ?? 0;
```

## *EventHandler<TEventArgs>*

With Windows Forms and Web applications, delegates for many different event handlers are defined. Some of the event handlers are listed here:

# Generics

```
public sealed delegate void EventHandler(object sender, EventArgs e);
public sealed delegate void PaintEventHandler(object sender, PaintEventArgs e);
public sealed delegate void MouseEventHandler(object sender, MouseEventArgs e);
```

These delegates have in common that the first argument is always the sender, who was the origin of the event, and the second argument is of a type to contain information specific to the event.

With the new `EventHandler<TEventArgs>`, it is not necessary to define a new delegate for every event handler. As you can see, the first parameter is defined the same way as before, but the second parameter is a generic type TEventArgs. The `where` clause defines that the type for TEventArgs must derive from the base class EventArgs:

```
public sealed delegate void EventHandler<TEventArgs>(object sender, TEventArgs e)
    where TEventArgs : EventArgs
```

## ArraySegment<T>

The struct `ArraySegment<T>` represents a segment of an array. If parts of an array are needed, a segment can be used. With the struct `ArraySegment<T>`, the information about the segment (the offset and count) is contained within this structure.

In the example the variable `arr` is defined as an `int` array with 8 elements. The variable `segment` of type `ArraySegment<int>` is used to represent a segment of the integer array. The segment is initialized with the constructor where the array is passed together with an offset and an item count. Here the offset is set to 2, so you start with the third element, and the count is set to 3, so 6 is the last element of the segment.

The array behind the array segment can be accessed with the `Array` property. `ArraySegment<T>` also has the properties `Offset` and `Count` that indicate the initialized values to define the segment. The `for` loop is used to iterate through the array segment. The first expression of the `for` loop is initialized to the offset where the iteration should begin. With the second expression the count of the element numbers in the segment is used to check if the iteration should stop. Within the `for` loop the elements contained by the segment are accessed with the `Array` property:

```
int[] arr = {1, 2, 3, 4, 5, 6, 7, 8};
ArraySegment<int> segment = new ArraySegment<int>(arr, 2, 3);

for (int i = segment.Offset; i < segment.Offset + segment.Count; i++)
{
    Console.WriteLine(segment.Array[i]);
}
```

With the example so far, you might question the usefulness of the `ArraySegment<T>` structure. However, the `ArraySegment<T>` can also be passed as an argument to methods. This way, just a single argument is needed instead of three that define the offset and count in addition to the array.

The method `WorkWithSegment()` gets an `ArraySegment<string>` as a parameter. In the implementation of this method, the properties `Offset`, `Count`, and `Array` are used as before:

# Chapter 10

```
void WorkWithSegment(ArraySegment<string> segment)
{
    for (int i = segment.Offset; i < segment.Offset + segment.Count; i++)
    {
        Console.WriteLine(segment.Array[i]);
    }
}
```

> It's important to note that array segments don't copy the elements of the originating array. Instead, the originating array can be accessed through ArraySegment<T>. If elements of the array segment are changed, the changes can be seen in the original array.

# Summary

This chapter introduced a very important new feature of .NET 2.0: generics. With generic classes you can create type-independent classes, and generic methods allow type-independent methods. Interfaces, structs, and delegates can be created in a generic way as well. Generics make new programming style possible. You've seen how algorithms, particularly actions and predicates, can be implemented to be used with different classes — and all type-safe. Generic delegates make it possible to decouple algorithms from collections.

A major use of generics is with collection classes. The framework has been extended with the namespace System.Collections.Generic that includes generic versions of the collection classes from the System.Collections namespace. You looked at using several generic collection classes such as List<T>, Queue<T>, and LinkedList<T>.

Other .NET Framework types include are Nullable<T>, EventHandler<TEventArgs>, and ArraySegment<T>.

# 11
# Reflection

*Reflection* is a generic term that describes the ability to inspect and manipulate program elements at runtime. For example, reflection allows you to:

- ❏ Enumerate the members of a type
- ❏ Instantiate a new object
- ❏ Execute the members of an object
- ❏ Find out information about a type
- ❏ Find out information about an assembly
- ❏ Inspect the custom attributes applied to a type
- ❏ Create and compile a new assembly

This list represents a great deal of functionality and encompasses some of the most powerful and complex capabilities provided by the .NET Framework class library. Unfortunately, this chapter does not have the space to cover all the capabilities of reflection and so it focuses on those elements you are likely to use frequently.

The discussion begins with custom attributes, a mechanism that allows you to associate custom metadata with program elements. This metadata is created at compile time and embedded in an assembly. You can then inspect the metadata at runtime using some of the capabilities of reflection.

After looking at custom attributes, the chapter looks at some of the fundamental classes that enable reflection, including the `System.Type` and `System.Reflection.Assembly` classes, which provide the access points for much of what you can do with reflection.

To demonstrate custom attributes and reflection, you develop an example based on a company that regularly ships upgrades to its software, and wants to have details of these upgrades documented automatically. In the example, you define custom attributes that indicate the date when program elements where last modified, and what changes were made. You then use reflection to develop an application that looks for these attributes in an assembly, and can automatically display all the details about what upgrades have been made to the software since a given date.

Another example in this chapter considers an application that reads from or writes to a database and uses custom attributes as a way of marking which classes and properties correspond to which database tables and columns. By reading these attributes from the assembly at runtime, the program is able to automatically retrieve or write data to the appropriate location in the database, without requiring specific logic for each table or column.

## Custom Attributes

You've seen how you can define attributes on various items within your program. These attributes have been defined by Microsoft as part of the .NET Framework class library, many of which receive special support by the C# compiler. This means that for those particular attributes, the compiler could customize the compilation process in specific ways; for example, laying out a struct in memory according to the details in the `StructLayout` attributes.

The .Net Framework also allows you to define your own attributes. Clearly, these attributes will not have any effect on the compilation process, because the compiler has no intrinsic awareness of them. However, these attributes will be emitted as metadata in the compiled assembly when they are applied to program elements.

By itself, this metadata might be useful for documentation purposes, but what makes attributes really powerful is that using reflection, your code can read this metadata and use it to make decisions at runtime. This means that the custom attributes that you define can have a direct effect on how your code runs. For example, custom attributes can be used to enable declarative code access security checks for custom permission classes, associate information with program elements that can then be used by testing tools, or when developing extensible frameworks that allow the loading of plugins or modules.

### *Writing Custom Attributes*

To understand how to write custom attributes, it is useful to know what the compiler does when it encounters an element in your code that has a custom attribute applied to it. To take the database example, suppose you have a C# property declaration that looks like this:

```
[FieldName("SocialSecurityNumber")]
public string SocialSecurityNumber
{
    get {
        // etc.
```

When the C# compiler recognizes that this property has an attribute applied to it (`FieldName`), it will start by appending the string `Attribute` to this name, forming the combined name `FieldNameAttribute`. The compiler will then search all the namespaces in its search path (those namespaces that have been mentioned in a `using` statement) for a class with the specified name. Note that if you mark an item with an attribute whose name already ends in the string `Attribute`, the compiler won't add the string to the name a second time, leaving the attribute name unchanged. Therefore, the preceding code is equivalent to this:

```csharp
[FieldNameAttribute("SocialSecurityNumber")]
public string SocialSecurityNumber
{
   get {
   // etc.
```

The compiler expects to find a class with this name, and it expects this class to be derived directly or indirectly from System.Attribute. The compiler also expects that this class contains information that governs the use of the attribute. In particular, the attribute class needs to specify the following:

- ❏ The types of program elements to which the attribute can be applied (classes, structs, properties, methods, and so on).
- ❏ Whether it is legal for the attribute to be applied more than once to the same program element.
- ❏ Whether the attribute, when applied to a class or interface, is inherited by derived classes and interfaces.
- ❏ The mandatory and optional parameters the attribute takes.

If the compiler cannot find a corresponding attribute class, or it finds one but the way that you have used that attribute doesn't match the information in the attribute class, the compiler will raise a compilation error. For example, if the attribute class indicates that the attribute can only be applied to classes, but you have applied it to a struct definition, a compilation error will occur.

To continue with the example, assume you have defined the FieldName attribute like this:

```csharp
[AttributeUsage(AttributeTargets.Property,
   AllowMultiple=false,
   Inherited=false)]
public class FieldNameAttribute : Attribute
{
   private string name;
   public FieldNameAttribute(string name)
   {
      this.name = name;
   }
}
```

The following sections discuss each element of this definition.

## *AttributeUsage attribute*

The first thing to note is that the attribute class itself is marked with an attribute — the System.AttributeUsage attribute. This is an attribute defined by Microsoft for which the C# compiler provides special support. (You could argue that AttributeUsage isn't an attribute at all; it is more like a meta-attribute, because it applies only to other attributes, not simply to any class.) The primary purpose of AttributeUsage is to identify the types of program elements to which your custom attribute can be applied. This information is given by the first parameter of the AttributeUsage attribute — this parameter is mandatory, and is of an enumerated type, AttributeTargets. In the previous example, you have indicated that the FieldName attribute can be applied only to properties, which is fine, because that is exactly what you have applied it to in the earlier code fragment. The members of the `AttributeTargets` enumeration are

- All
- Assembly
- Class
- Constructor
- Delegate
- Enum
- Event
- Field
- GenericParameter (.NET 2.0 only)
- Interface
- Method
- Module
- Parameter
- Property
- ReturnValue
- Struct

This list identifies all of the program elements to which you can apply attributes. Note that when applying the attribute to a program element, you place the attribute in square brackets immediately before the element. However, two values in the preceding list do not correspond to any program element: `Assembly` and `Module`. An attribute can be applied to an assembly or module as a whole instead of to an element in your code; in this case the attribute can be placed anywhere in your source code, but needs to be prefixed with the `Assembly` or `Module` keyword:

```
[assembly:SomeAssemblyAttribute(Parameters)]
[module:SomeAssemblyAttribute(Parameters)]
```

When indicating the valid target elements of a custom attribute, you can combine these values using the bitwise OR operator. For example, if you wanted to indicate that your `FieldName` attribute can be applied to both properties and fields, you would write:

```
    [AttributeUsage(AttributeTargets.Property | AttributeTargets.Field,
        AllowMultiple=false,
        Inherited=false)]
    public class FieldNameAttribute : Attribute
```

You can also use `AttributeTargets.All` to indicate that your attribute can be applied to all types of program elements. The `AttributeUsage` attribute also contains two other parameters, `AllowMultiple` and `Inherited`. These are specified using the syntax of `<ParameterName>=<ParameterValue>`,

# Reflection

instead of simply giving the values for these parameters. These parameters are optional—you can omit them if you want.

The `AllowMultiple` parameter indicates whether an attribute can be applied more than once to the same item. The fact that it is set to `false` here indicates that the compiler should raise an error if it sees something like this:

```
[FieldName("SocialSecurityNumber")]
[FieldName("NationalInsuranceNumber")]
public string SocialSecurityNumber
{
    // etc.
```

If the `Inherited` parameter is set to `true`, an attribute applied to a class or interface will also automatically be applied to all derived classes or interfaces. If the attribute is applied to a method or property, it will automatically apply to any overrides of that method or property and so on.

## Specifying attribute parameters

This section examines how you can specify the parameters that your custom attribute takes. The way it works is that when the compiler encounters a statement such as

```
[FieldName("SocialSecurityNumber")]
public string SocialSecurityNumber
{
    // etc.
```

it examines the parameters passed into the attribute—in this case a string—and looks for a constructor for the attribute that takes exactly those parameters. If the compiler finds an appropriate constructor, the compiler will emit the specified metadata to the assembly. If the compiler doesn't find an appropriate constructor, a compilation error occurs. As discussed later in this chapter, reflection involves reading metadata (attributes) from assemblies and instantiating the attribute classes they represent. Because of this, the compiler must ensure an appropriate constructor exists that will allow the runtime instantiation of the specified attribute.

In the example, you have supplied just one constructor for `FieldNameAttribute`, and this constructor takes one string parameter. Therefore, when applying the `FieldName` attribute to a property, you must supply one string as a parameter, as you have done in the preceding sample code.

If you want to allow a choice of what types of parameters should be supplied with an attribute, you can provide different constructor overloads, although normal practice is to supply just one constructor, and use properties to define any other optional parameters, as explained next.

## Specifying optional attribute parameters

As demonstrated with reference to the `AttributeUsage` attribute, an alternative syntax exists by which optional parameters can be added to an attribute. This syntax involves specifying the names and values of the optional parameters. It works through `public` properties or fields in the attribute class. For example, suppose you modified the definition of the `SocialSecurityNumber` property as follows:

```
[FieldName("SocialSecurityNumber", Comment="This is the primary key field")]
public string SocialSecurityNumber
{

    // etc.
```

In this case, the compiler recognizes the `<ParameterName>= <ParameterValue>` syntax of the second parameter and does not attempt to match this parameter to a `FieldNameAttribute` constructor. Instead, it looks for a `public` property or field (although public fields are not considered good programming practice, so normally you will work with properties) of that name that it can use to set the value of this parameter. If you want the previous code to work, you have to add some code to `FieldNameAttribute`:

```
[AttributeUsage(AttributeTargets.Property,
    AllowMultiple=false,
    Inherited=false)]
public class FieldNameAttribute : Attribute
{
    private string comment;
    public string Comment
    {
        get
        {
            return comment;
        }
        set
        {
            comment = value;
        }
    }

    // etc.
```

## Custom Attribute Example: WhatsNewAttributes

In this section, you start developing the `WhatsNewAttributes` example described earlier, which provides for an attribute that indicates when a program element was last modified. This is a rather more ambitious code sample than many of the others in that it consists of three separate assemblies:

- The `WhatsNewAttributes` assembly, which contains the definitions of the attributes
- The `VectorClass` assembly, which contains the code to which the attributes have been applied
- The `LookUpWhatsNew` assembly, which contains the project that displays details of items that have changed

Of these, only `LookUpWhatsNew` is a console application of the type that you have used up until now. The remaining two assemblies are libraries — they each contain class definitions, but no program entry point. For the `VectorClass` assembly, this means that the entry point and test harness class have been removed from the `VectorAsCollection` sample, leaving only the `Vector` class.

# Reflection

Managing three related assemblies by compiling at the command line is tricky; and although the commands for compiling all these source files are provided separately, you might prefer to edit the code sample (which you can download from the Wrox Web site at www.wrox.com) as a combined Visual Studio .NET solution as discussed in Chapter 14, "Visual Studio 2005." The download includes the required Visual Studio 2005 solution files.

## *The WhatsNewAttributes library assembly*

This section starts off with the core `WhatsNewAttributes` assembly. The source code is contained in the file `WhatsNewAttributes.cs`, which is in the WhatsNewAttributes project of the WhatsNewAttributes solution in the example code for this chapter. The syntax for doing this is quite simple. At the command line you supply the flag `target:library` to the compiler. To compile `WhatsNewAttributes`, type:

```
csc /target:library WhatsNewAttributes.cs
```

The `WhatsNewAttributes.cs` file defines two attribute classes, `LastModifiedAttribute` and `SupportsWhatsNewAttribute`. `LastModifiedAttribute` is the attribute that you can use to mark when an item was last modified. It takes two mandatory parameters (parameters that are passed to the constructor): the date of the modification and a string containing a description of the changes. There is also one optional parameter named `issues` (for which a `public` property exists), which can be used to describe any outstanding issues for the item.

In real life you would probably want this attribute to apply to anything. To keep the code simple, its usage is limited here to classes and methods. You will allow it to be applied more than once to the same item (`AllowMultiple=true`) because an item might be modified more than once, and each modification will have to be marked with a separate attribute instance.

`SupportsWhatsNew` is a smaller class representing an attribute that doesn't take any parameters. The idea of this attribute is that it's an assembly attribute that is used to mark an assembly for which you are maintaining documentation via the `LastModifiedAttribute`. This way, the program that will examine this assembly later on knows that the assembly it is reading is one on which you are actually using your automated documentation process. Here is the complete source code for this part of the example:

```
using System;

namespace Wrox.ProCSharp.WhatsNewAttributes
{
   [AttributeUsage(
      AttributeTargets.Class | AttributeTargets.Method,
      AllowMultiple=true, Inherited=false)]
   public class LastModifiedAttribute : Attribute
   {
      private DateTime dateModified;
      private string changes;
      private string issues;

      public LastModifiedAttribute(string dateModified, string changes)
      {
         this.dateModified = DateTime.Parse(dateModified);
         this.changes = changes;
      }
```

```
        public DateTime DateModified
        {
           get
           {
              return dateModified;
           }
        }

        public string Changes
        {
           get
           {
              return changes;
           }
        }

        public string Issues
        {
           get
           {
              return issues;
           }
           set
           {
              issues = value;
           }
        }
     }

     [AttributeUsage(AttributeTargets.Assembly)]
     public class SupportsWhatsNewAttribute : Attribute
     {
     }
}
```

This code should be clear with reference to previous descriptions. Notice, however, that we have not bothered to supply `set` accessors to the `Changes` and `DateModified` properties. There is no need for these accessors, because you are requiring these parameters to be set in the constructor as mandatory parameters. You need the `get` accessors so that you can read the values of these attributes.

## The VectorClass assembly

Next, you need to use these attributes. To this end, you use a modified version of the earlier `VectorAs Collection` sample. Note that you need to reference the `WhatsNewAttributes` library that you have just created. You also need to indicate the corresponding namespace with a `using` statement so the compiler can recognize the attributes:

```
using System;
using Wrox.ProCSharp.WhatsNewAttributes;
using System.Collections;
using System.Text;
[assembly: SupportsWhatsNew]
```

In this code, you have also added the line that will mark the assembly itself with the `SupportsWhatsNew` attribute.

Now for the code for the `Vector` class. You are not making any major changes to this class; you only add a couple of `LastModified` attributes to mark out the work that you have done on this class in this chapter, and `Vector` is defined as a class instead of a struct to simplify the code (of the next iteration of the sample) that displays the attributes. (In the `VectorAsCollection` sample, `Vector` is a struct, but its enumerator is a class. This means the next iteration of the sample would have had to pick out both classes and structs when looking at the assembly, which would have made the example less straightforward.)

```
namespace Wrox.ProCSharp.VectorClass
{
    [LastModified("14 Feb 2002", "IEnumerable interface implemented " +
        "So Vector can now be treated as a collection")]
    [LastModified("10 Feb 2002", "IFormattable interface implemented " +
        "So Vector now responds to format specifiers N and VE")]
    class Vector : IFormattable, IEnumerable
    {
        public double x, y, z;

        public Vector(double x, double y, double z)
        {
            this.x = x;
            this.y = y;
            this.z = z;
        }

        [LastModified("10 Feb 2002",
                    "Method added in order to provide formatting support")]
        public string ToString(string format, IFormatProvider formatProvider)
        {
            if (format == null)
                return ToString();
```

You also mark the contained `VectorEnumerator` class as new:

```
        [LastModified("14 Feb 2002",
                    "Class created as part of collection support for Vector")]
        private class VectorEnumerator : IEnumerator
        {
```

To compile this code from the command line, type the following:

```
csc /target:library /reference:WhatsNewAttributes.dll VectorClass.cs
```

That's as far as you can get with this example for now. You can't run anything yet, because all you have are two libraries. You develop the final part of the example, in which you look up and display these attributes, as soon as you've had a look at how reflection works.

# Chapter 11

# Reflection

This section takes a closer look at the `System.Type` class, which lets you access information concerning the definition of any data type. It then discusses the `System.Reflection.Assembly` class, which you can use to access information about an assembly, or to load that assembly into your program. Finally, you combine the code in this section with the code of the previous section to complete the `WhatsNewAttributes` sample.

## The System.Type Class

So far you have used the `Type` class only to hold the reference to a type as follows:

```
Type t = typeof(double);
```

Although previously referred to as a class, `Type` is an abstract base class. Whenever you instantiate a `Type` object, you are actually instantiating a class derived from `Type`. `Type` has one derived class corresponding to each actual data type, though in general the derived classes simply provide different overloads of the various `Type` methods and properties that return the correct data for the corresponding data type. They do not generally add new methods or properties. In general, three common ways exist of obtaining a `Type` reference that refers to any given type:

- ❑ You can use the C# `typeof` operator as in the preceding code. This operator takes the name of the type (not in quote marks, however) as a parameter.
- ❑ You can use the `GetType()` method, which all classes inherit from `System.Object`:

```
double d = 10;
Type t = d.GetType();
```

`GetType()` is called against a variable, rather than taking the name of a type. Note, however, that the `Type` object returned is still associated with only that data type. It does not contain any information that relates to that instance of the type. The `GetType()` method can be useful if you have a reference to an object, but are not sure what class that object is actually an instance of.

- ❑ You can call the `static` method of the `Type` class, `GetType()`:

```
Type t = Type.GetType("System.Double");
```

`Type` is really the gateway to much of the reflection functionality. It implements a huge number of methods and properties — far too many to provide a comprehensive list here. However, the following subsections should give you some idea of the kinds of things you can do with the `Type` class. Note that the available properties are all read-only; you use `Type` to find out about the data type — you can't use it to make any modifications to the type!

### Type properties

You can split the properties implemented by `Type` into three categories:

- ❑ A number of properties retrieve the strings containing various names associated with the class:

# Reflection

| Property | Returns |
|---|---|
| `Name` | The name of the data type |
| `FullName` | The fully qualified name of the data type (including the namespace name) |
| `Namespace` | The name of the namespace in which the data type is defined |

❏ It is also possible to retrieve references to further type objects that represent related classes:

| Property | Returns Type Reference Corresponding To |
|---|---|
| `BaseType` | Immediate base type of this type |
| `UnderlyingSystemType` | The type that this type maps to in the .NET runtime (recall that certain .NET base types actually map to specific predefined types recognized by IL) |

❏ A number of Boolean properties indicate whether or not this type is, for example, a class, an enum, and so on. These properties include `IsAbstract`, `IsArray`, `IsClass`, `IsEnum`, `IsInterface`, `IsPointer`, `IsPrimitive` (one of the predefined primitive data types), `IsPublic`, `IsSealed`, and `IsValueType`.

For example, using a primitive data type:

```
Type intType = typeof(int);
Console.WriteLine(intType.IsAbstract);     // writes false
Console.WriteLine(intType.IsClass);        // writes false
Console.WriteLine(intType.IsEnum);         // writes false
Console.WriteLine(intType.IsPrimitive);    // writes true
Console.WriteLine(intType.IsValueType);    // writes true
```

Or using the `Vector` class:

```
Type vecType = typeof(Vector);
Console.WriteLine(vecType.IsAbstract);     // writes false
Console.WriteLine(vecType.IsClass);        // writes true
Console.WriteLine(vecType.IsEnum);         // writes false
Console.WriteLine(vecType.IsPrimitive);    // writes false
Console.WriteLine(vecType.IsValueType);    // writes false
```

You can also retrieve a reference to the assembly that the type is defined in. This is returned as a reference to an instance of the `System.Reflection.Assembly` class, which is examined shortly:

```
Type t = typeof (Vector);
Assembly containingAssembly = new Assembly(t);
```

## Methods

Most of the methods of `System.Type` are used to obtain details of the members of the corresponding data type — the constructors, properties, methods, events, and so on. Quite a large number of methods exist, but they all follow the same pattern. For example, two methods retrieve details of the methods of the data type: `GetMethod()` and `GetMethods()`. `GetMethod()` returns a reference to a `System.Reflection.MethodInfo` object, which contains details of a method. `GetMethods()` returns an array of such references. The difference is that `GetMethods()` returns details of all the methods, whereas `GetMethod()` returns details of just one method with a specified parameter list. Both methods have overloads that take an extra parameter, a `BindingFlags` enumerated value that indicates which members should be returned — for example, whether to return public members, instance members, static members, and so on.

So, for example, the simplest overload of `GetMethods()` takes no parameters and returns details of all the public methods of the data type:

```
Type t = typeof(double);
MethodInfo[] methods = t.GetMethods();
foreach (MethodInfo nextMethod in methods)
{
    // etc.
```

The following member methods of `Type` follow the same pattern:

| Type of Object Returned | Methods (The Method with the Plural Name Returns an Array) |
|---|---|
| `ConstructorInfo` | `GetConstructor()`, `GetConstructors()` |
| `EventInfo` | `GetEvent()`, `GetEvents()` |
| `FieldInfo` | `GetField()`, `GetFields()` |
| `InterfaceInfo` | `GetInterface()`, `GetInterfaces()` |
| `MemberInfo` | `GetMember()`, `GetMembers()` |
| `MethodInfo` | `GetMethod()`, `GetMethods()` |
| `PropertyInfo` | `GetProperty()`, `GetProperties()` |

The `GetMember()` and `GetMembers()` methods return details of any or all members of the data type, irrespective of whether these members are constructors, properties, methods, and so on. Finally, note that it is possible to invoke members either by calling the `InvokeMember()` method of `Type` or by calling the `Invoke()` method of the `MethodInfo`, `PropertyInfo`, and the other classes.

## *The TypeView Example*

This section demonstrates some of the features of the `Type` class with a short example, `TypeView`, which you can use to list the members of a data type. The example demonstrates how to use `TypeView` for a `double`; however, you can swap this type with any other data type just by changing one line of the code for the sample. `TypeView` displays far more information than can be displayed in a console window, so we're going to take a break from our normal practice and display the output in a message box. Running `TypeView` for a `double` produces the results shown in Figure 11-1.

# Reflection

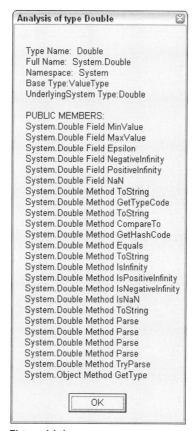

Figure 11-1

The message box displays the name, full name, and namespace of the data type as well as the name of the underlying type and the base type. Next, it simply iterates through all the public instance members of the data type, displaying for each member the declaring type, the type of member (method, field, and so on) and the name of the member. The *declaring type* is the name of the class that actually declares the type member (for example, `System.Double` if it is defined or overridden in `System.Double`, or the name of the relevant base type if the member is simply inherited from some base class).

`TypeView` does not display signatures of methods, because you are retrieving details of all public instance members through `MemberInfo` objects, and information about parameters is not available through a `MemberInfo` object. In order to retrieve that information, you would need references to `MethodInfo` and other more specific objects, which means you would need to obtain details of each type of member separately.

`TypeView` does display details of all public instance members, but it happens that for doubles, the only ones defined are fields and methods. You will compile `TypeView` as a console application — there is no problem with displaying a message box from a console application. However, the fact that you are using a message box means that you need to reference the base class assembly `System.Windows.Forms.dll`, which contains the classes in the `System.Windows.Forms` namespace in which the `MessageBox` class that you will need is defined. The code for `TypeView` is as follows. To begin, you need to add a couple of `using` statements:

```
using System;
using System.Text;
using System.Windows.Forms;
using System.Reflection;
```

You need `System.Text` because you will be using a `StringBuilder` object to build up the text to be displayed in the message box, and `System.Windows.Forms` for the message box itself. The entire code is in one class, `MainClass`, which has a couple of `static` methods and one `static` field, a `StringBuilder` instance called `OutputText`, which will be used to build up the text to be displayed in the message box. The main method and class declaration look like this:

```
class MainClass
{
    static void Main()
    {
        // modify this line to retrieve details of any
        // other data type
        Type t = typeof(double);

        AnalyzeType(t);
        MessageBox.Show(OutputText.ToString(), "Analysis of type "
                                               + t.Name);
        Console.ReadLine();
    }
```

The `Main()` method implementation starts by declaring a `Type` object to represent your chosen data type. You then call a method, `AnalyzeType()`, which extracts the information from the `Type` object and uses it to build up the output text. Finally, you show the output in a message box. Using the `MessageBox` class is fairly intuitive. You just call its `static Show()` method, passing it two strings, which will, respectively, be the text in the box and the caption. `AnalyzeType()` is where the bulk of the work is done:

```
        static void AnalyzeType(Type t)
        {
            AddToOutput("Type Name:   " + t.Name);
            AddToOutput("Full Name:   " + t.FullName);
            AddToOutput("Namespace:   " + t.Namespace);
            Type tBase = t.BaseType;
            if (tBase != null)
                AddToOutput("Base Type:" + tBase.Name);
            Type tUnderlyingSystem = t.UnderlyingSystemType;
            if (tUnderlyingSystem != null)
                AddToOutput("UnderlyingSystem Type:" + tUnderlyingSystem.Name);

            AddToOutput("\nPUBLIC MEMBERS:");
            MemberInfo [] Members = t.GetMembers();
            foreach (MemberInfo NextMember in Members)
            {
```

# Reflection

```
            AddToOutput(NextMember.DeclaringType + " " +
            NextMember.MemberType + " " + NextMember.Name);
      }
   }
```

You implement the `AnalyzeType()` method by calling various properties of the `Type` object to get the information you need concerning the type names, then call the `GetMembers()` method to get an array of `MemberInfo` objects that you can use to display the details of each member. Note that you use a helper method, `AddToOutput()`, to build up the text to be displayed in the message box:

```
static void AddToOutput(string Text)
{
    OutputText.Append("\n" + Text);
}
```

Compile the `TypeView` assembly using this command:

```
csc /reference:System.Windows.Forms.dll TypeView.cs
```

## The Assembly Class

The `Assembly` class is defined in the `System.Reflection` namespace, and provides access to the metadata for a given assembly. It also contains methods to allow you to load and even execute an assembly—assuming the assembly is an executable. Like the `Type` class, `Assembly` contains a large number of methods and properties—too many to cover here. Instead, this section is confined to covering those methods and properties that you need to get started, and which you will use to complete the `WhatsNewAttributes` example.

Before you can do anything with an `Assembly` instance, you need to load the corresponding assembly into the running process. You can do this with either the static members `Assembly.Load()` or `Assembly.LoadFrom()`. The difference between these methods is that `Load()` takes the name of the assembly, and the runtime searches in a variety of locations in an attempt to locate the assembly. These locations include the local directory and the global assembly cache. `LoadFrom()` takes the full path name of an assembly and does not attempt to find the assembly in any other location:

```
Assembly assembly1 = Assembly.Load("SomeAssembly");
Assembly assembly2 = Assembly.LoadFrom
   (@"C:\My Projects\Software\SomeOtherAssembly");
```

A number of other overloads of both methods exist, which supply additional security information. Once you have loaded an assembly, you can use various properties on it to find out, for example, its full name:

```
string name = assembly1.FullName;
```

### Finding out about types defined in an assembly

One nice feature of the `Assembly` class is that it allows you to obtain details of all the types that are defined in the corresponding assembly. You simply call the `Assembly.GetTypes()` method, which returns an array of `System.Type` references containing details of all the types. You can then manipulate these `Type` references as explained in the previous section:

```
Type[] types = theAssembly.GetTypes();
foreach(Type definedType in types)
{
    DoSomethingWith(definedType);
}
```

## *Finding out about custom attributes*

The methods you use to find out which custom attributes are defined on an assembly or type depend on what type of object the attribute is attached to. If you want to find out what custom attributes are attached to an assembly as a whole, you need to call a `static` method of the `Attribute` class, `GetCustomAttributes()`, passing in a reference to the assembly:

```
Attribute[] definedAttributes =
        Attribute.GetCustomAttributes(assembly1);
        // assembly1 is an Assembly object
```

*This is actually quite significant. You may have wondered why, when we defined custom attributes, we had to go to all the trouble of actually writing classes for them, and why Microsoft hadn't come up with some simpler syntax. Well, the answer is here. The custom attributes do genuinely exist as objects, and when an assembly is loaded you can read in these attribute objects, examine their properties, and call their methods.*

`GetCustomAttributes()`, used to get assembly attributes, has a couple of overloads. If you call it without specifying any parameters other than an assembly reference, it will simply return all the custom attributes defined for that assembly. You can also call `GetCustomAttributes()` specifying a second parameter, which is a `Type` object that indicates the attribute class in which you are interested. In this case `GetCustomAttributes()` returns an array consisting of all the attributes present that are of the specified type.

Note that all attributes are retrieved as plain `Attribute` references. If you want to call any of the methods or properties you defined for your custom attributes, you will need to cast these references explicitly to the relevant custom attribute classes. You can obtain details of custom attributes that are attached to a given data type by calling another overload of `Assembly.GetCustomAttributes()`, this time passing a `Type` reference that describes the type for which you want to retrieve any attached attributes. On the other hand, if you want to obtain attributes that are attached to methods, constructors, fields, and so on, you will need to call a `GetCustomAttributes()` method that is a member of one of the classes `MethodInfo`, `ConstructorInfo`, `FieldInfo`, and so on.

If you only expect a single attribute of a given type, you can call the `GetCustomAttribute()` method instead, which returns a single `Attribute` object. You will use `GetCustomAttribute()` in the `WhatsNewAttributes` example to find out whether the `SupportsWhatsNew` attribute is present in the assembly. To do this, you call `GetCustomAttribute()`, passing in a reference to the `WhatsNewAttributes` assembly, and the type of the `SupportWhatsNewAttribute` attribute. If this attribute is present, you get an `Attribute` instance. If no instances of it are defined in the assembly, you get `null`. And if two or more instances are found, `GetCustomAttribute()` throws a `System.Reflection.AmbiguousMatchException`:

```
Attribute supportsAttribute =
        Attribute.GetCustomAttributes(assembly1,
            typeof(SupportsWhatsNewAttribute));
```

# Reflection

## Completing the WhatsNewAttributes Example

You now have enough information to complete the `WhatsNewAttributes` example by writing the source code for the final assembly in the sample, the `LookUpWhatsNew` assembly. This part of the application is a console application. However, it needs to reference the other assemblies of `WhatsNewAttributes` and `VectorClass`. Although this is going to be a command-line application, you will follow the previous `TypeView` sample in actually displaying your results in a message box, because there is a lot of text output — too much to show in a console window screenshot.

The file is called `LookUpWhatsNew.cs`, and the command to compile it is

```
csc /reference:WhatsNewAttributes.dll /reference:VectorClass.dll LookUpWhatsNew.cs
```

In the source code of this file, you first indicate the namespaces you want to infer. `System.Text` is there because you need to use a `StringBuilder` object again:

```
using System;
using System.Reflection;
using System.Windows.Forms;
using System.Text;
using Wrox.ProCSharp.VectorClass;
using Wrox.ProCSharp.WhatsNewAttributes;

namespace Wrox.ProCSharp.LookUpWhatsNew
{
```

The class that contains the main program entry point as well as the other methods is `WhatsNewChecker`. All the methods you define are in this class, which also has two static fields: `outputText`, which contains the text as you build it up in preparation for writing it to the message box, and `backDateTo`, which stores the date you have selected. All modifications made since this date will be displayed. Normally, you would display a dialog box inviting the user to pick this date, but we don't want to get sidetracked into that kind of code. For this reason, `backDateTo` is hard-coded to a value of 1 Feb 2002. You can easily change this date if you want when you download the code:

```
    class WhatsNewChecker
    {
        static StringBuilder outputText = new StringBuilder(1000);
        static DateTime backDateTo = new DateTime(2002, 2, 1);

        static void Main()
        {
            Assembly theAssembly = Assembly.Load("VectorClass");
            Attribute supportsAttribute =
                Attribute.GetCustomAttribute(
                    theAssembly, typeof(SupportsWhatsNewAttribute));
            string Name = theAssembly.FullName;

            AddToMessage("Assembly: " + Name);
            if (supportsAttribute == null)
            {
                AddToMessage(
                    "This assembly does not support WhatsNew attributes");
                return;
```

```
            }
        else
            AddToMessage("Defined Types:");

        Type[] types = theAssembly.GetTypes();
        foreach(Type definedType in types)
            DisplayTypeInfo(theAssembly, definedType);

        MessageBox.Show(outputText.ToString(),
            "What\'s New since " + backDateTo.ToLongDateString());
        Console.ReadLine();
    }
```

The `Main()` method first loads the `VectorClass` assembly, and verifies that it is marked with the `SupportsWhatsNew` attribute. You know `VectorClass` has the `SupportsWhatsNew` attribute applied to it because you have only recently compiled it, but this is a check that would be worth making if the user was given a choice of what assembly they wanted to check.

Assuming all is well, you use the `Assembly.GetTypes()` method to get an array of all the types defined in this assembly, and then loop through them. For each one, you call a method, `DisplayTypeInfo()`, which will add the relevant text, including details of any instances of `LastModifiedAttribute`, to the `outputText` field. Finally, you show the message box with the complete text. The `DisplayTypeInfo()` method looks like this:

```
        static void DisplayTypeInfo(Assembly theAssembly, Type type)
        {
            // make sure we only pick out classes
            if (!(type.IsClass))
                return;
            AddToMessage("\nclass " + type.Name);

            Attribute [] attribs = Attribute.GetCustomAttributes(type);
            if (attribs.Length == 0)
                AddToMessage("No changes to this class\n");
            else
                foreach (Attribute attrib in attribs)
                    WriteAttributeInfo(attrib);

            MethodInfo [] methods = type.GetMethods();
            AddToMessage("CHANGES TO METHODS OF THIS CLASS:");
            foreach (MethodInfo nextMethod in methods)
            {
                object [] attribs2 =
                    nextMethod.GetCustomAttributes(
                        typeof(LastModifiedAttribute), false);
                if (attribs2 != null)
                {
                    AddToMessage(
                        nextMethod.ReturnType + " " + nextMethod.Name + "()");
                    foreach (Attribute nextAttrib in attribs2)
                        WriteAttributeInfo(nextAttrib);
                }
            }
        }
```

Notice that the first thing you do in this method is check whether the `Type` reference you have been passed actually represents a class. Because, in order to keep things simple, you have specified that the `LastModified` attribute can only be applied to classes or member methods, you would be wasting your time doing any processing if the item is not a class (it could be a class, delegate, or enum).

Next, you use the `Attribute.GetCustomAttributes()` method to find out if this class does have any `LastModifiedAttribute` instances attached to it. If it does, you add their details to the output text, using a helper method, `WriteAttributeInfo()`.

Finally, you use the `Type.GetMethods()` method to iterate through all the member methods of this data type, and then do the same with each method as you did for the class—check if it has any `LastModifiedAttribute` instances attached to it and, if so, display them using `WriteAttributeInfo()`.

The next bit of code shows the `WriteAttributeInfo()` method, which is responsible for working out what text to display for a given `LastModifiedAttribute` instance. Note that this method is passed an `Attribute` reference, so it needs to cast this to a `LastModifiedAttribute` reference first. After it has done that, it uses the properties that you originally defined for this attribute to retrieve its parameters. It checks that the date of the attribute is sufficiently recent before actually adding it to the text for display:

```
static void WriteAttributeInfo(Attribute attrib)
{

    LastModifiedAttribute lastModifiedAttrib =
        attrib as LastModifiedAttribute;
    if (lastModifiedAttrib == null)
        return;

    // check that date is in range
    DateTime modifiedDate = lastModifiedAttrib.DateModified;
    if (modifiedDate < backDateTo)
        return;

    AddToMessage("   MODIFIED: " +
        modifiedDate.ToLongDateString() + ":");
    AddToMessage("     " + lastModifiedAttrib.Changes);
    if (lastModifiedAttrib.Issues != null)
        AddToMessage("     Outstanding issues:" +
            lastModifiedAttrib.Issues);
}
```

Finally, here is the helper `AddToMessage()` method:

```
        static void AddToMessage(string message)
        {
           outputText.Append("\n" + message);
        }
    }
}
```

Running this code produces the results shown in Figure 11-2.

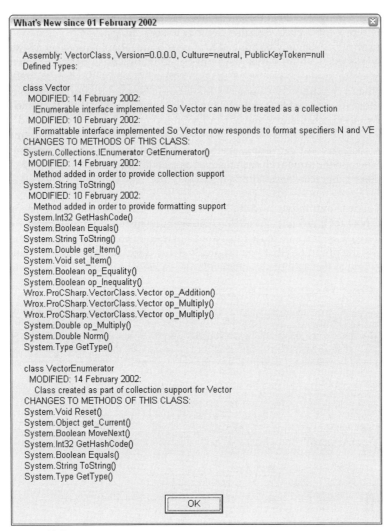

Figure 11-2

Notice that when you list the types defined in the `VectorClass` assembly, you actually pick up two classes: `Vector` and the embedded `VectorEnumerator` class. Also notice that because the `backDateTo` date of 1 Feb is hard-coded in this example, you actually pick up the attributes that are dated 14 Feb (when you added the collection support) but not those dated 14 Jan (when you added the `IFormattable` interface).

## Summary

This chapter did not attempt to cover the entire topic of reflection. Reflection is an extensive subject worthy of a book of its own. Instead, it looked at the `Type` and `Assembly` classes, which are the primary entry points through which you can access the extensive capabilities provided by reflection.

In addition, this chapter demonstrated a specific aspect of reflection that you are likely to use more often than any other — the inspection of custom attributes. You learned how to define and apply your own custom attributes, and how to retrieve information about custom attributes at runtime.

Chapter 12 looks at exceptions and structured exception handing.

# 12
# Errors and Exceptions

Errors happen, and it isn't always because of the person who coded the application. Sometimes your application will generate an error because of an action that was initiated by the end user of your application. In any case, you should anticipate errors occurring in your applications and code accordingly.

The .NET Framework has enhanced the ways in which you deal with errors. C#'s mechanism for handling error conditions allows you to provide custom handling for each type of error condition as well as to separate code that identifies errors from the code that handles them.

The main topics covered in this chapter include:

- ❑ Looking at the exception classes
- ❑ Using `try – catch – finally` to capture exceptions
- ❑ Creating user-defined exceptions

By the end of the chapter, you will have a good handle on advanced exception handling in your C# applications.

## Looking into Errors and Exception Handling

No matter how good your coding is, your programs should be able to handle any possible errors that may occur. For example, in the middle of some complex processing your code may discover that it doesn't have permission to read a file, or while it is sending network requests the network may go down. In such exceptional situations, it is not enough for a method to simply return an appropriate error code — there might be 15 or 20 nested method calls, so what you really want the program to do is jump back up through all those 15 or 20 calls in order to exit the task completely and take the appropriate counteractions. The C# language has very good facilities to handle this kind of situation, through the mechanism known as *exception handling*.

> *Error-handling facilities in Visual Basic 6 are very restricted and essentially limited to the* On Error GoTo *statement. If you are coming from a Visual Basic 6 background, you will find C# exceptions open up a whole new world of error handling in your programs. On the other hand, Java and C++ developers will be familiar with the principle of exceptions because these languages also handle errors in a similar way to C#. Developers using C++ are sometimes wary of exceptions because of possible C++ performance implications, but this is not the case in C#. Using exceptions in C# code in general does not adversely affect performance. Visual Basic 2005 developers will find that working with exceptions in C# is very similar using exceptions in Visual Basic (except for the syntax differences).*

# Exception Classes

In C#, an exception is an object created (or *thrown*) when a particular exceptional error condition occurs. This object contains information that should help track down the problem. Although you can create your own exception classes (and you will be doing so later), .NET provides you with many predefined exception classes.

## Base class exception classes

This section provides a quick survey of some of the exceptions available in the .NET Base Class Library. Microsoft has provided a large number of exception classes in .NET — too many to provide a comprehensive list here. This class hierarchy diagram in Figure 12-1 shows but a few of these classes, to give you a sense of the general pattern.

All the classes in Figure 12-1 are part of the System namespace, with the exception of IOException and the classes derived from IOException, which are part of the namespace System.IO. The System.IO namespace deals with reading and writing data to files. In general, there is no specific namespace for exceptions; exception classes should be placed in whatever namespace is appropriate to the classes that can generate them — hence IO-related exceptions are in the System.IO namespace, and you will find exception classes in quite a few of the base class namespaces.

The generic exception class, System.Exception, is derived from System.Object, as you would expect for a .NET class. In general, you should not throw generic System.Exception objects in your code, because they provide no specifics of the error condition.

Two important classes in the hierarchy are derived from System.Exception:

❑ System.SystemException — This class is for exceptions that are usually thrown by the .NET runtime or that are considered to be of a generic nature and might be thrown by almost any application. For example, StackOverflowException will be thrown by the .NET runtime if it detects the stack is full. On the other hand, you might choose to throw ArgumentException or its subclasses in your own code, if you detect that a method has been called with inappropriate arguments. Subclasses of System.SystemException include classes that represent both fatal and non-fatal errors.

❑ System.ApplicationException — This class is important, because it is the intended base for any class of exception defined by third parties. Hence, if you define any exceptions covering error conditions unique to your application, you should derive these directly or indirectly from System.ApplicationException.

# Errors and Exceptions

Other exception classes that might come in handy include the following:

- `StackOverflowException`—This exception is thrown when the area of memory allocated to the stack is full. A stack overflow can occur if a method continuously calls itself recursively. This is generally a fatal error, because it prevents your application from doing anything apart from terminating (in which case it is unlikely that even the `finally` block will execute). Trying to handle errors like this yourself is usually pointless.

- `EndOfStreamException`—The usual cause of an `EndOfStreamException` is an attempt to read past the end of a file. A *stream* represents a flow of data between data sources. Streams are covered in detail in Chapter 35, "Accessing the Internet."

- `OverflowException`—An `OverflowException` is what happens if you attempt to cast an `int` containing a value of -40 to a `uint` in a `checked` context.

The other exception classes shown in Figure 12-1 are not discussed here; you should be able to guess their purposes by looking at their names.

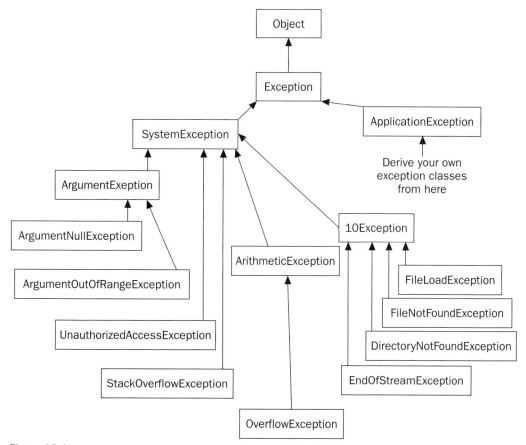

**Figure 12-1**

# Chapter 12

The class hierarchy for exceptions is somewhat unusual in that most of these classes do not add any functionality to their respective base classes. However, in the case of exception handling, the common reason for adding inherited classes is to indicate more specific error conditions, and there is often no need to override methods or add any new ones (although it is not uncommon to add extra properties that carry extra information about the error condition). For example, you might have a base `ArgumentException` class intended for method calls where inappropriate values are passed in, and an `ArgumentNullException` class derived from it, which is intended to handle a `null` argument if passed.

## Catching Exceptions

Given that the .NET Framework includes a spade of predefined base class exception objects, how do you use them in your code to trap error conditions? In order to deal with possible error conditions in C# code, you will normally divide the relevant part of your program into blocks of three different types:

- `try` blocks encapsulate the code that forms part of the normal operation of your program, but which might encounter some serious error conditions.
- `catch` blocks encapsulate the code that deals with the various error conditions that your code might have encountered by working through any of the code in the accompanying `try` block.
- `finally` blocks encapsulate the code that cleans up any resources or takes any other action that you will normally want done at the end of a `try` or `catch` block. It is important to understand that the `finally` block is executed whether or not an exception is thrown. Because the aim is that the `finally` block contains cleanup code that should always be executed, the compiler will flag an error if you place a `return` statement inside a `finally` block. For an example of using the `finally` block, you might close any connections that were opened in the `try` block. It is also important to understand that the `finally` block is completely optional. If you don't have a requirement for any cleanup code, there is no need for this block.

So how do these blocks fit together to trap error conditions? Here's how:

1. The execution flow first enters the `try` block.
2. If no errors occur in the `try` block, execution proceeds normally through the block, and when the end of the `try` block is reached, the flow of execution jumps to the `finally` block if one is present (Step 5). However, if an error does occur within the `try` block, execution jumps to a `catch` block (next step).
3. The error condition is handled in the `catch` block.
4. At the end of the `catch` block, execution automatically transfers to the `finally` block if one is present.
5. The `finally` block is executed.

The C# syntax used to bring all this about looks roughly like this:

```
try
{
    // code for normal execution
}
```

```
catch
{
    // error handling
}
finally
{
    // clean up
}
```

Actually, a few variations on this theme exist:

- You can omit the `finally` block because it is optional.
- You can also supply as many `catch` blocks as you want to handle specific types of errors.
- You can omit the `catch` blocks altogether, in which case the syntax serves not to identify exceptions, but as a way of guaranteeing that code in the `finally` block will be executed when execution leaves the `try` block. This is useful if the `try` block contains several exit points.

So far so good, but the question that has yet to be answered is this: If the code is running in the `try` block, how does it know when to switch to the `catch` block if an error has occurred? If an error is detected, the code does something known as *throwing an exception*. In other words, it instantiates an exception object class and throws it:

```
throw new OverflowException();
```

Here you have instantiated an exception object of the `OverflowException` class. As soon as the computer encounters a `throw` statement inside a `try` block, it immediately looks for the `catch` block associated with that `try` block. If there is more than one `catch` block associated with the `try` block, it identifies the correct `catch` block by checking which exception class the `catch` block is associated with. For example, when the `OverflowException` object is thrown, execution jumps to the following `catch` block:

```
catch (OverflowException ex)
{
    // exception handling here
}
```

In other words, the computer looks for the `catch` block that indicates a matching exception class instance of the same class (or of a base class).

With this extra information, you can expand the `try` block just demonstrated. Assume, for the sake of argument, that there are two possible serious errors that can occur in the `try` block: an overflow and an array out of bounds. Assume that your code contains two Boolean variables, `Overflow` and `OutOfBounds`, which indicate whether these conditions exist. You have already seen that a predefined exception class exists to indicate overflow (`OverflowException`); similarly, an `IndexOutOfRangeException` class exists to handle an array out-of-bounds.

Now your `try` block looks like this:

```
try
{
    // code for normal execution

    if (Overflow == true)
        throw new OverflowException();

    // more processing

    if (OutOfBounds == true)
        throw new IndexOutOfRangeException();

    // otherwise continue normal execution
}
catch (OverflowException ex)
{
    // error handling for the overflow error condition
}
catch (IndexOutOfRangeException ex)
{
    // error handling for the index out of range error condition
}
finally
{
    // clean up
}
```

So far, this might not look that much different from what you could have done with the Visual Basic 6 On Error GoTo statement (with the exception perhaps that the different parts in the code are separated). C#, however, provides a far more powerful and flexible mechanism for error handling.

This is because you can have `throw` statements that are nested in several method calls inside the `try` block, but the same `try` block continues to apply even as execution flow enters these other methods. If the computer encounters a `throw` statement, it immediately goes back up through all the method calls on the stack, looking for the end of the containing `try` block and the start of the appropriate `catch` block. During this process, all the local variables in the intermediate method calls will correctly go out of scope. This makes the `try...catch` architecture well suited to the situation described at the beginning of this section, where the error occurs inside a method call that is nested inside 15 or 20 method calls, and processing has to stop immediately.

As you can probably gather from this discussion, `try` blocks can play a very significant part in controlling the flow of execution of your code. However, it is important to understand that exceptions are intended for exceptional conditions, hence their name. You wouldn't want to use them as a way of controlling when to exit a `do...while` loop.

## Implementing multiple catch blocks

The easiest way to see how `try...catch...finally` blocks work in practice is with a couple of examples. The first example is called `SimpleExceptions`. It repeatedly asks the user to type in a number and then displays it. However, for the sake of this example, imagine that the number has to be between 0

# Errors and Exceptions

and 5, otherwise the program won't be able to process the number properly. Therefore you will throw an exception if the user types in anything outside of this range.

The program then continues to ask for more numbers for processing until the user simply presses the Enter key without entering anything.

> *You should note that this code does not provide a good example of when to use exception handling. As already indicated, the idea of exceptions is that they are provided for exceptional circumstances. Users are always typing in silly things, so this situation doesn't really count. Normally, your program will handle incorrect user input by performing an instant check and asking the user to retype the input if there is a problem. However, generating exceptional situations is difficult in a small example that you can read through in a few minutes! So, we will tolerate this bad practice for now in order to demonstrate how exceptions work. The examples that follow present more realistic situations.*

The code for `SimpleExceptions` looks like this:

```csharp
using System;

namespace Wrox.ProCSharp.AdvancedCSharp
{
   public class MainEntryPoint
   {
      public static void Main()
      {
         string userInput;
         while (true)
         {
            try
            {
               Console.Write("Input a number between 0 and 5 " +
                  "(or just hit return to exit)> ");
               userInput = Console.ReadLine();
               if (userInput == "")
                  break;
               int index = Convert.ToInt32(userInput);
               if (index < 0 || index > 5)
                  throw new IndexOutOfRangeException(
                     "You typed in " + userInput);
               Console.WriteLine("Your number was " + index);
            }
            catch (IndexOutOfRangeException ex)
            {
               Console.WriteLine("Exception: " +
                  "Number should be between 0 and 5. " + ex.Message);
            }
            catch (Exception ex)
            {
               Console.WriteLine(
                  "An exception was thrown. Message was: " + ex.Message);
            }
            catch
            {
               Console.WriteLine("Some other exception has occurred");
```

```
            }
            finally
            {
                Console.WriteLine("Thank you");
            }
        }
      }
    }
}
```

The core of this code is a `while` loop, which continually uses `Console.ReadLine()` to ask for user input. `ReadLine()` returns a string, so your first task is to convert it to an `int` using the `System.Convert.ToInt32()` method. The `System.Convert` class contains various useful methods to perform data conversions and provides an alternative to the `int.Parse()` method. In general, `System.Convert` contains methods to perform various type conversions. Recall that the C# compiler resolves `int` to instances of the `System.Int32` base class.

> It is also worth pointing out that the parameter passed to the catch block is scoped to that catch block — which is why you are able to use the same parameter name, ex, in successive catch blocks in the preceding code.

In the preceding example, you also check for an empty string, because this is your condition for exiting the `while` loop. Notice how the `break` statement actually breaks right out of the enclosing `try` block as well as the `while` loop because this is valid behavior. Of course, once execution breaks out of the `try` block, the `Console.WriteLine()` statement in the `finally` block is then executed. Although you just display a greeting here, more commonly, you will be doing tasks like closing file handles and calling the `Dispose()` method of various objects in order to perform any cleaning up. Once the computer leaves the `finally` block, it simply carries on executing unto the next statement that it would have executed, had the `finally` block not been present. In the case of this example though, you iterate back to the start of the `while` loop, and enter the `try` block once again (unless the `finally` block was entered as a result of executing the `break` statement in the `while` loop, in which case you simply exit the `while` loop).

Next, you check for your exception condition:

```
if (index < 0 || index > 5)
    throw new IndexOutOfRangeException("You typed in " + userInput);
```

When throwing an exception, you need to choose what type of exception to throw. Although the class `System.Exception` is available, it is only intended as a base class; it is considered bad programming practice to throw an instance of this class as an exception, because it conveys no information about the nature of the error condition. Instead, the .NET Framework contains many other exception classes that are derived from `System.Exception`. Each of these matches a particular type of exception condition, and you are free to define your own ones as well. The idea is that you give as much information as possible about the particular exception condition by throwing an instance of a class that matches the particular error condition. In the preceding example, `System.IndexOutOfRangeException` is the best choice in the circumstances. `IndexOutOfRangeException` has several constructor overloads. The one chosen in the example takes a string, which describes the error. Alternatively, you might choose to derive your own custom `Exception` object that describes the error condition in the context of your application.

## Errors and Exceptions

Suppose the user then types a number that is not between 0 and 5. This will be picked up by the `if` statement and an `IndexOutOfRangeException` object will be instantiated and thrown. At this point the computer will immediately exit the `try` block and hunt for a `catch` block that handles `IndexOutOfRangeException`. The first `catch` block it encounters is this:

```
catch (IndexOutOfRangeException ex)
{
   Console.WriteLine(
      "Exception: Number should be between 0 and 5." + ex.Message);
}
```

Because this `catch` block takes a parameter of the appropriate class, the `catch` block will be passed the exception instance and executed. In this case, you display an error message and the `Exception.Message` property (which corresponds to the string you passed to the `IndexOutOfRange`'s constructor). After executing this `catch` block, control then switches to the `finally` block, just as if no exception had occurred.

Notice that in the example, you have also provided another `catch` block:

```
catch (Exception ex)
{
   Console.WriteLine("An exception was thrown. Message was: " + ex.Message);
}
```

This `catch` block would also be capable of handling an `IndexOutOfRangeException` if it weren't for the fact that such exceptions will already have been caught by the previous `catch` block — a reference to a base class can also refer to any instances of classes derived from it, and all exceptions are derived from `System.Exception`. So why doesn't this `catch` block get executed? The answer is that the computer executes only the first suitable `catch` block it finds from the list of available `catch` blocks. So why is this second `catch` block even here? Well, it is not only your code that is covered by the `try` block; inside the block, you actually make three separate calls to methods in the `System` namespace (`Console.ReadLine()`, `Console.Write()`, and `Convert.ToInt32()`), and any of these methods might throw an exception.

If you type in something that's not a number — say a or hello — the `Convert.ToInt32()` method will throw an exception of the class `System.FormatException` to indicate that the string passed into `ToInt32()` is not in a format that can be converted to an `int`. When this happens, the computer will trace back through the method calls, looking for a handler that can handle this exception. Your first `catch` block (the one that takes an `IndexOutOfRangeException`) won't do. The computer then looks at the second `catch` block. This one will do because `FormatException` is derived from `Exception`, so a `FormatException` instance can be passed in as a parameter here.

The structure of the example is actually fairly typical of a situation with multiple `catch` blocks. You start off with `catch` blocks that are designed to trap very specific error conditions. Then, you finish with more general blocks that will cover any errors for which you have not written specific error handlers. Indeed, the order of the `catch` blocks is important. If you had written the previous two blocks in the opposite order, the code would not have compiled, because the second `catch` block is unreachable (the `Exception catch` block would catch all exceptions). Therefore, the uppermost `catch` blocks should be the most granular options available and ending with the most general options.

However, in the previous example, you have a third `catch` block listed in the code:

```
catch
{
    Console.WriteLine("Some other exception has occurred");
}
```

This is the most general `catch` block of all—it doesn't take any parameter. The reason this `catch` block is here is to catch exceptions thrown by other code that isn't written in C# or isn't even managed code at all. You see, it is a requirement of the C# language that only instances of classes derived from `System.Exception` can be thrown as exceptions, but other languages might not have this restriction—C++, for example, allows any variable whatsoever to be thrown as an exception. If your code calls into libraries or assemblies that have been written in other languages, it might find an exception has been thrown that is not derived from `System.Exception`, although in many cases, the .NET `PInvoke` mechanism will trap these exceptions and convert them into .NET `Exception` objects. However, there is not that much that this `catch` block can do, because you have no idea what class the exception might represent.

> *For this particular example, there is no point in adding this catch-all catch handler. Doing this is useful if you are calling into some other libraries that are not .NET-aware and which might throw exceptions. However, it is included it in the example to illustrate the principle.*

Now that you have analyzed the code for the example, you can run it. The following output illustrates what happens with different inputs and demonstrates both the `IndexOutOfRangeException` and the `FormatException` being thrown:

```
SimpleExceptions
Input a number between 0 and 5 (or just hit return to exit)> 4
Your number was 4
Thank you
Input a number between 0 and 5 (or just hit return to exit)> 0
Your number was 0
Thank you
Input a number between 0 and 5 (or just hit return to exit)> 10
Exception: Number should be between 0 and 5. You typed in 10
Thank you
Input a number between 0 and 5 (or just hit return to exit)> hello
An exception was thrown. Message was: Input string was not in a correct format.
Thank you
Input a number between 0 and 5 (or just hit return to exit)>
Thank you
```

## Catching exceptions from other code

The previous example demonstrated the handling of two exceptions. One of them, `IndexOutOfRangeException`, was thrown by your own code. The other, `FormatException`, was thrown from inside one of the base classes. It is very common for code in a library to throw an exception if it detects that some problem has occurred, or if one of the methods has been called inappropriately by being passed the wrong parameters. However, library code rarely attempts to catch exceptions; this is regarded as the responsibility of the client code.

Often, you will find that exceptions get thrown from the base class libraries while you are debugging. The process of debugging to some extent involves determining why exceptions have been thrown and

# Errors and Exceptions

removing the causes. Your aim should be to ensure that by the time the code is actually shipped, exceptions do occur only in very exceptional circumstances, and if at all possible, are handled in some appropriate way in your code.

## *System.Exception properties*

The example has only illustrated the use of the `Message` property of the exception object. However, a number of other properties are available in `System.Exception`, as shown in the following table.

| Property | Description |
| --- | --- |
| Data | This provides you with the ability to add key/value statements to the exception that can be used to supply extra information about the exception. This is a new property in the .NET Framework 2.0. |
| HelpLink | This is a link to a help file that provides more information about the exception. |
| InnerException | If this exception was thrown inside a `catch` block, then `InnerException` contains the exception object that sent the code into that `catch` block. |
| Message | This is text that describes the error condition. |
| Source | This is the name of the application or object that caused the exception. |
| StackTrace | This provides details of the method calls on the stack (to help track down the method that threw the exception). |
| TargetSite | This is a .NET reflection object that describes the method that threw the exception. |

Of these properties, `StackTrace` and `TargetSite` are supplied automatically by the .NET runtime if a stack trace is available. `Source` will always be filled in by the .NET runtime as the name of the assembly in which the exception was raised (though you might want to modify the property in your code to give more specific information), whereas `Data`, `Message`, `HelpLink`, and `InnerException` must be filled in by the code that threw the exception, by setting these properties immediately before throwing the exception. For example, the code to throw an exception might look something like this:

```
if (ErrorCondition == true)
{
   Exception myException = new ClassmyException("Help!!!!");
   myException.Source = "My Application Name";
   myException.HelpLink = "MyHelpFile.txt";
   myException.Data["ErrorDate"] = DateTime.Now;
   myException.Data.Add("AdditionalInfo", "Contact Bill from the Blue Team");
   throw myException;
}
```

Here, `ClassMyException` is the name of the particular exception class you are throwing. Note that it is common practice for the names of all exception classes to end with `Exception`. Also note that the `Data` property is assigned in two possible ways.

## What happens if an exception isn't handled?

Sometimes an exception might be thrown, but there might not be a `catch` block in your code that is able to handle that kind of exception. The `SimpleExceptions` example can serve to illustrate this. Suppose, for example, you omitted the `FormatException` and catch-all `catch` blocks, and only supplied the block that traps an `IndexOutOfRangeException`. In that circumstance, what would happen if a `FormatException` got thrown?

The answer is that the .NET runtime would catch it. Later in this section, you learn how you can nest `try` blocks, and in fact, there is already a nested `try` block behind the scenes in the example. The .NET runtime has effectively placed the entire program inside another huge `try` block—it does this for every .NET program. This `try` block has a `catch` handler that can catch any type of exception. If an exception occurs that your code doesn't handle, the execution flow will simply pass right out of your program and get trapped by this `catch` block in the .NET runtime. However, the results of this probably won't be what you want. What happens is that the execution of your code will be terminated promptly and the user will see a dialog box that complains that your code hasn't handled the exception, as well as any details about the exception the .NET runtime was able to retrieve. At least the exception will have been caught though! This is what actually happened earlier in Chapter 2, "C# Basics," in the `Vector` example when the program threw an exception.

In general, if you are writing an executable, you should try to catch as many exceptions as you reasonably can, and handle them in a sensible way. If you are writing a library, it is normally best not to handle exceptions (unless a particular exception represents something wrong in your code that you can handle), but instead, assume that the calling code will handle any errors it encounters. However, you may nevertheless want to catch any Microsoft-defined exceptions, so that you can throw your own exception objects that give more specific information to the client code.

## Nested try blocks

One nice feature of exceptions is that you can nest `try` blocks inside each other, like this:

```
try
{
    // Point A
    try
    {
        // Point B
    }
    catch
    {
        // Point C
    }
    finally
    {
        // clean up
    }
    // Point D
}
catch
{
    // error handling
}
```

```
finally
{
    // clean up
}
```

Although each `try` block is only accompanied by one `catch` block in this example, you could string several `catch` blocks together too. This section takes a closer look at how nested `try` blocks work.

If an exception is thrown inside the outer `try` block but outside the inner `try` block (points A and D), the situation is no different from any of the scenarios you have seen before: either the exception is caught by the outer `catch` block and the outer `finally` block is executed, or the `finally` block is executed and the .NET runtime handles the exception.

If an exception is thrown in the inner `try` block (point B), and there is a suitable inner `catch` block to handle the exception, then again you are in familiar territory: the exception is handled there, and the inner `finally` block is executed before execution resumes inside the outer try block (at point D).

Now suppose an exception occurs in the inner `try` block but there *isn't* a suitable inner `catch` block to handle it. This time, the inner `finally` block is executed as usual, but then the .NET runtime will have no choice but to leave the entire inner `try` block in order to search for a suitable exception handler. The next obvious place to look is in the outer `catch` block. If the system finds one here, that handler will be executed and then the outer `finally` block. If there is no suitable handler here, the search for one will go on. In this case it means the outer `finally` block will be executed, and then, because there are no more `catch` blocks, control will transfer to the .NET runtime. Note that at no point is the code beyond point D in the outer `try` block executed.

An even more interesting thing happens if an exception is thrown at point C. If the program is at point C it must be already processing an exception that was thrown at point B. It is in fact quite legitimate to throw another exception from inside a `catch` block. In this case, the exception is treated as if it had been thrown by the outer `try` block, so flow of execution will immediately leave the inner `catch` block, and execute the inner `finally` block, before the system searches the outer `catch` block for a handler. Similarly, if an exception is thrown in the inner `finally` block, control will immediately transfer to the best appropriate handler, with the search starting at the outer `catch` block.

> **It is perfectly legitimate to throw exceptions from `catch` and `finally` blocks.**

Although the situation has been shown with just two `try` blocks, the same principles hold no matter how many `try` blocks you nest inside each other. At each stage, the .NET runtime will smoothly transfer control up through the `try` blocks, looking for an appropriate handler. At each stage, as control leaves a `catch` block, any cleanup code in the corresponding `finally` block (if present) will be executed, but no code outside any `finally` block will be run until the correct `catch` handler has been found and run.

You have now seen how having nested `try` blocks can work. The obvious next question is why would you want to do that? There are two reasons:

- ❑ To modify the type of exception thrown
- ❑ To enable different types of exception to be handled in different places in your code

## Modifying the type of exception

Modifying the type of the exception can be useful when the original exception thrown does not adequately describe the problem. What typically happens is that something—possibly the .NET runtime—throws a fairly low-level exception that says something like an overflow occurred (`OverflowException`) or an argument passed to a method was incorrect (a class derived from `ArgumentException`). However, because of the context in which the exception occurred, you will know that this reveals some other underlying problem (for example, an overflow can only have happened at that point in your code because a file you have just read contained incorrect data). In that case, the most appropriate thing that your handler for the first exception can do is throw another exception that more accurately describes the problem, so that another `catch` block further along can deal with it more appropriately. In this case, it can also forward the original exception through a property implemented by `System.Exception` called `InnerException`. `InnerException` simply contains a reference to any other related exception that was thrown—in case the ultimate handler routine will need this extra information.

Of course, the situation also exists where an exception occurs inside a `catch` block. For example, you might normally read in some configuration file that contains detailed instructions for handling the error, and it might turn out that this file is not there.

## Handling different exceptions in different places

The second reason for having nested `try` blocks is so that different types of exceptions can be handled at different locations in your code. A good example of this is if you have a loop where various exception conditions can occur. Some of these might be serious enough that you need to abandon the entire loop, while others might be less serious and simply require that you abandon that iteration and move on to the next iteration around the loop. You could achieve this by having one `try` block inside the loop, which handles the less serious error conditions, and an outer `try` block outside the loop, which handles the more serious error conditions. You see how this works in the next exceptions example.

# User-Defined Exception Classes

You are now ready to look at a second example that illustrates exceptions. This example, called `MortimerColdCall`, contains two nested `try` blocks and also illustrates the practice of defining your own custom exception classes, and throwing another exception from inside a `try` block.

This example returns to the Mortimer Phones mobile phone company used in Chapter 4, "Inheritance." The example assumes that Mortimer Phones wants to have additional customers. Its sales team is going to ring up a list of people in order to invite them to become customers, a practice known in sales jargon as cold-calling people. To this end, you have a text file available that contains the names of the people to be cold-called. The file should be in a well-defined format in which the first line contains the number of people in the file and each subsequent line contains the name of the next person. In other words, a correctly formatted file of names might look like this:

```
4
George Washington
Zbigniew Harlequin
John Adams
Thomas Jefferson
```

# Errors and Exceptions

Because this is only an example, you are not really going to cold-call these people! This version of cold-calling is designed to display the name of the person on the screen (perhaps for the sales guy to read). That's why you only put names, and not phone numbers in the file.

Your program will ask the user for the name of the file and will then simply read it in and display the names of people.

That sounds like a simple task, but even so, a couple of things can go wrong and require you to abandon the entire procedure:

- ❑ The user might type the name of a file that doesn't exist. This will be caught as a `FileNotFound` exception.

- ❑ The file might not be in the correct format. There are two possible problems here. First, the first line of the file might not be an integer. Second, there might not be as many names in the file as the first line of the file indicates. In both cases, you want to trap this oddity as a custom exception that has been written specially for this purpose, `ColdCallFileFormatException`.

There is also something else that could go wrong that won't cause you to abandon the entire process but will mean you need to abandon that person and move on to the next person in the file (and hence this will need to be trapped by an inner `try` block). Some people are spies working for rival land-line telephone companies, and obviously, you wouldn't want to let these people know what you are up to by accidentally phoning one of them. Your research has indicated that you can identify who the land-line spies are because their names begin with Z. Such people should have been screened out when the data file was first prepared, but just in case any have slipped through, you will need to check each name in the file and throw a `LandLineSpyFoundException` if you detect a land-line spy. This, of course, is another custom exception object.

Finally, you will implement this example by coding a class, `ColdCallFileReader`, which maintains the connection to the cold-call file and retrieves data from it. You will code this class in a very safe way, which means its methods will all throw exceptions if they are called inappropriately; for example, if a method that will read a file is called before the file has even been opened. For this purpose, you will write another exception class, `UnexpectedException`.

## Catching the user-defined exceptions

Let's start with the `Main()` method of the `MortimerColdCall` sample, which catches your user-defined exceptions. Note that you will need to call up file-handling classes in the `System.IO` namespace as well as the `System` namespace.

```
using System;
using System.IO;

namespace Wrox.ProCSharp.AdvancedCSharp
{
   class MainEntryPoint
   {
      static void Main()
      {
         string fileName;
         Console.Write("Please type in the name of the file " +
```

```csharp
            "containing the names of the people to be cold-called > ");
        fileName = Console.ReadLine();
        ColdCallFileReader peopleToRing = new ColdCallFileReader();

        try
        {
            peopleToRing.Open(fileName);
            for (int i=0 ; i<peopleToRing.NPeopleToRing; i++)
            {
                peopleToRing.ProcessNextPerson();
            }
            Console.WriteLine("All callers processed correctly");
        }
        catch(FileNotFoundException ex)
        {
            Console.WriteLine("The file {0} does not exist", fileName);
        }
        catch(ColdCallFileFormatException ex)
        {
            Console.WriteLine(
           "The file {0} appears to have been corrupted", fileName);
            Console.WriteLine("Details of problem are: {0}", ex.Message);
            if (ex.InnerException != null)
                Console.WriteLine(
                    "Inner exception was: {0}", ex.InnerException.Message);
        }
        catch(Exception ex)
        {
            Console.WriteLine("Exception occurred:\n" + ex.Message);
        }
        finally
        {
            peopleToRing.Dispose();
        }
        Console.ReadLine();
    }
}
```

This code is little more than a loop to process people from the file. You start off by asking the user for the name of the file. Then you instantiate an object of a class called `ColdCallFileReader`, which is defined shortly. The `ColdCallFileReader` class is the class that handles the file reading. Notice that you do this outside the initial `try` block—that's because the variables that you instantiate here need to be available in the subsequent `catch` and `finally` blocks, and if you declared them inside the `try` block they'd go out of scope at the closing curly brace of the `try` block, which would not be a good thing.

In the `try` block, you open the file (using the `ColdCallFileReader.Open()` method) and loop over all the people in it. The `ColdCallFileReader.ProcessNextPerson()` method reads in and displays the name of the next person in the file, while the `ColdCallFileReader.NPeopleToRing` property tells you how many people should be in the file (obtained by reading the first line of the file).

There are three `catch` blocks, one for `FileNotFoundException`, one for `ColdCallFileFormat Exception`, and one to trap any other .NET exceptions.

# Errors and Exceptions

In the case of a `FileNotFoundException`, you display a message to that effect. Notice that in this `catch` block, the exception instance is not actually used at all. This `catch` block is used to illustrate the user-friendliness of the application. Exception objects generally contain technical information that is useful for developers, but not the sort of stuff you want to show to your end users. So in this case, you create a simpler message of your own.

For the `ColdCallFileFormatException` handler, you have done the opposite, and illustrated how to give fuller technical information, including details of the inner exception, if one is present.

Finally, if you catch any other generic exceptions, you display a user-friendly message, instead of letting any such exceptions fall through to the .NET runtime. Note that you have chosen not to handle any other exceptions not derived from `System.Exception`, because you are not calling directly into non-.NET code.

The `finally` block is there to clean up resources. In this case, this means closing any open file — performed by the `ColdCallFileReader.Dispose()` method.

## Throwing the user-defined exceptions

Now take a look at the definition of the class that handles the file reading and (potentially) throws your user-defined exceptions: `ColdCallFileReader`. Because this class maintains an external file connection, you will need to make sure it gets disposed of correctly in accordance with the principles laid down for the disposing of objects in Chapter 4. Hence, you derive this class from `IDisposable`.

First, you declare some variables:

```
class ColdCallFileReader :IDisposable
{
    FileStream fs;
    StreamReader sr;
    uint nPeopleToRing;
    bool isDisposed = false;
    bool isOpen = false;
```

`FileStream` and `StreamReader`, both in the `System.IO` namespace, are the base classes that you will use to read the file. `FileStream` allows you to connect to the file in the first place, whereas `StreamReader` is specially geared up to reading text files, and implements a method, `StreamReader()`, which reads a line of text from a file. You look at `StreamReader` more closely in Chapter 35, which discusses file handling in depth.

The `isDisposed` field indicates whether the `Dispose()` method has been called. `ColdCallFileReader` is implemented so that once `Dispose()` has been called, it is not permitted to reopen connections and reuse the object. `isOpen` is also used for error checking — in this case, checking whether the `StreamReader` actually connects to an open file.

The process of opening the file and reading in that first line — the one that tells you how many people are in the file — is handled by the `Open()` method:

```
public void Open(string fileName)
{
    if (isDisposed)
        throw new ObjectDisposedException("peopleToRing");
```

```
            fs = new FileStream(fileName, FileMode.Open);
            sr = new StreamReader(fs);
            try
            {
                string firstLine = sr.ReadLine();
                nPeopleToRing = uint.Parse(firstLine);
                isOpen = true;
            }
            catch (FormatException ex)
            {
                throw new ColdCallFileFormatException(
                    "First line isn\'t an integer", ex);
            }
        }
```

The first thing you do in this method (as with all other `ColdCallFileReader` methods) is check whether the client code has inappropriately called it after the object has been disposed of, and throw a predefined `ObjectDisposedException` object if that has occurred. The `Open()` method checks the `isDisposed` field to see whether `Dispose()` has already been called. Because calling `Dispose()` implies the caller has now finished with this object, you regard it as an error to attempt to open a new file connection if `Dispose()` has been called.

Next, the method contains the first of two inner `try` blocks. The purpose of this one is to catch any errors resulting from the first line of the file not containing an integer. If that problem arises, the .NET runtime will throw a `FormatException`, which you trap and convert to a more meaningful exception that indicates there is actually a problem with the format of the cold-call file. Note that `System.FormatException` is there to indicate format problems with basic data types, not with files, and so is not a particularly useful exception to pass back to the calling routine in this case. The new exception thrown will be trapped by the outermost `try` block. Because no cleanup is needed here, there is no need for a `finally` block.

If everything is fine, you set the `isOpen` field to `true` to indicate that there is now a valid file connection from which data can be read.

The `ProcessNextPerson()` method also contains an inner `try` block:

```
        public void ProcessNextPerson()
        {
            if (isDisposed)
                throw new ObjectDisposedException("peopleToRing");
            if (!isOpen)
                throw new UnexpectedException(
                    "Attempted to access cold call file that is not open");
            try
            {
                string name;
                name = sr.ReadLine();
                if (name == null)
                    throw new ColdCallFileFormatException("Not enough names");
                if (name[0] == 'Z')
                {
                    throw new LandLineSpyFoundException(name);
                }
```

# Errors and Exceptions

```
            Console.WriteLine(name);
        }
        catch(LandLineSpyFoundException ex)
        {
            Console.WriteLine(ex.Message);
        }

        finally
        {
        }
    }
```

Two possible problems exist with the file here (assuming there actually is an open file connection; the `ProcessNextPerson()` method checks this first). First, you might read in the next name and discover that it is a land-line spy. If that condition occurs, the exception is trapped by the first of the `catch` blocks in this method. Because that exception has been caught here, inside the loop, it means that execution can subsequently continue in the `Main()` method of the program, and the subsequent names in the file will continue to be processed.

A problem might also occur if you try to read the next name and discover that you have already reached the end of the file. The way that the `StreamReader` object's `ReadLine()` method works is if it has gone past the end of the file, it doesn't throw an exception, but simply returns `null`. So if you find a null string, you know that the format of the file was incorrect because the number in the first line of the file indicated a larger number of names than were actually present in the file. If that happens, you throw a `ColdCallFileFormatException`, which will be caught by the outer exception handler (which will cause execution to terminate).

Once again, you don't need a `finally` block here because there is no cleanup to do; however, this time an empty one is there, just to show that you can do so, if you want.

The example is nearly finished. You have just two more members of `ColdCallFileReader` to look at: the `NPeopleToRing` property, which returns the number of people supposed to be in the file, and the `Dispose()` method, which closes an open file. Notice that the `Dispose()` method just returns if it has already been called — this is the recommended way of implementing it. It also checks that there actually is a file stream to close before closing it. This example is here to illustrate defensive coding techniques, so that's what you are doing!

```
        public uint NPeopleToRing
        {
            get
            {
                if (isDisposed)
                    throw new ObjectDisposedException("peopleToRing");
                if (!isOpen)
                    throw new UnexpectedException(
                        "Attempted to access cold call file that is not open");
                return nPeopleToRing;
            }
        }

        public void Dispose()
```

```
    {
        if (isDisposed)
            return;

        isDisposed = true;
        isOpen = false;
        if (fs != null)
        {
            fs.Close();
            fs = null;
        }
    }
}
```

## *Defining the exception classes*

Finally, you need to define your own three exception classes. Defining your own exception is quite easy, because there are rarely any extra methods to add. It is just a case of implementing a constructor to ensure that the base class constructor is called correctly. Here is the full implementation of `LandLineSpyFoundException`:

```
class LandLineSpyFoundException : ApplicationException
{
    public LandLineSpyFoundException(string spyName)
        :   base("LandLine spy found, with name " + spyName)
    {
    }

    public LandLineSpyFoundException(
        string spyName, Exception innerException)
        :   base(
            "LandLine spy found with name " + spyName, innerException)
    {
    }
}
```

Notice that it is derived from `ApplicationException`, as you would expect for a custom exception. In fact, if you'd been going about this even more formally, you would probably have put in an intermediate class, something like `ColdCallFileException`, derived from `ApplicationException`, and derived both of your exception classes from this class, just to make sure that the handling code has that extra fine degree of control over which exception handler handles which exception. However, to keep the example simple, you won't do that.

You have done one bit of processing in `LandLineSpyFoundException`. You have assumed the message passed into its constructor is just the name of the spy found, and so you turn this string into a more meaningful error message. You have also provided two constructors, one that simply takes a message, and one that also takes an inner exception as a parameter. When defining your own exception classes, it is best to include, as a minimum, at least these two constructors (although you won't actually be using the second `LandLineSpyFoundException` constructor in this example).

Now for the `ColdCallFileFormatException`. This follows the same principles as the previous exception, except that you don't do any processing on the message:

```csharp
    class ColdCallFileFormatException : ApplicationException
    {
        public ColdCallFileFormatException(string message)
            : base(message)
        {
        }

        public ColdCallFileFormatException(
            string message, Exception innerException)
            : base(message, innerException)
        {
        }
    }
```

And finally, `UnexpectedException`, which looks much the same as `ColdCallFileFormatException`:

```csharp
    class UnexpectedException : ApplicationException
    {
        public UnexpectedException(string message)
            : base(message)
        {
        }

        public UnexpectedException(string message, Exception innerException)
            : base(message, innerException)
        {
        }
    }
```

Now you are ready to test the program. First, try the `people.txt` file whose contents you displayed earlier. This has four names (which match the number given in the first line of the file) including one spy. Then try the following `people2.txt` file, which has an obvious formatting error:

```
49
George Washington
Zbigniew Harlequin
John Adams
Thomas Jefferson
```

Finally, try the example but specify the name of a file that does not exist, `people3.txt`, say. Running the program three times for the three file names gives these results:

**MortimerColdCall**
```
Please type in the name of the file containing the names of the people to be cold-
called > people.txt
George Washington
LandLine spy found, with name Zbigniew Harlequin
John Adams
Thomas Jefferson
All callers processed correctly
```

347

## Chapter 12

```
MortimerColdCall
Please type in the name of the file containing the names of the people to be cold-
called > people2.txt
George Washington
LandLine spy found, with name Zbigniew Harlequin
John Adams
Thomas Jefferson
The file people2.txt appears to have been corrupted
Details of the problem are: Not enough names


MortimerColdCall
Please type in the name of the file containing the names of the people to be cold-
called > people3.txt
The file people3.txt does not exist
```

In the end, this little application shows you a number of different ways in which you can handle the errors and exceptions that you might find in your own applications.

## Summary

This chapter took a close look at the rich mechanism C# has for dealing with error conditions through exceptions. You are not limited to the generic error codes that could be output from your code, but you have the ability to go in and uniquely handle the most granular of error conditions. Sometimes these error conditions are provided to you through the .NET Framework itself, but at other times, you might want to go in and code your own error conditions as was shown in this chapter. In either case, you have a lot of ways of protecting the workflow of your applications from unnecessary and dangerous faults.

# 13
# Threading

This chapter looks at the support that C# and the .NET base classes offer for developing applications that employ the use of multiple threads. It briefly examines the `Thread` and the `ThreadPool` classes, through which much of the threading support takes place, and you develop a couple of examples that illustrate threading principles. Then you examine some of the issues that arise with thread synchronization. Due to the complexity of the subject, the emphasis of this chapter is solely on understanding some of the basic principles involved through some simple sample applications. This chapter focuses on

- ❑ How to start a thread
- ❑ Providing thread priorities
- ❑ Controlling access to objects through synchronization

By the end of the chapter, you will feel quite comfortable working with threads in your code. The following section starts by running through the basics of threading.

## Threading

A *thread* is an independent stream of instructions in a program. All your C# programs up to this point have one entry point — the `Main()` method. Execution starts with the first statement in the `Main()` method and continues until that method returns.

This program structure is all very well for programs in which there is one identifiable sequence of tasks, but often a program actually needs to be doing more than one thing at the same time; for example, when you start up Internet Explorer and get increasingly frustrated with the time it takes a page to load. Eventually, you get so fed up (if you're like me, after about 2 seconds!) that you click the Back button or type in some other URL. For this to work, Internet Explorer must be doing at least three things:

# Chapter 13

- Grabbing the data for the page as it is returned from the Internet, along with any accompanying files
- Rendering the page
- Watching for any user input that might indicate the user wants Internet Explorer to do something else instead (for example, watching for button clicks)

The same situation applies to any case where a program is performing some task while at the same time displaying a dialog box that gives you the chance to cancel the task at any time.

Let's look at the Internet Explorer example in more detail. We will simplify the problem by ignoring the task of storing the data as it arrives from the Internet and assume that Internet Explorer is simply faced with two tasks:

- Displaying the page
- Watching for user input

Assume that this is a Web page that takes a long time to display; it might have some processor-intensive JavaScript in it, or it might contain a marquee element in it that needs to be updated continually. One way that you can approach this situation is to write a method that does a little bit of work in rendering the page. After a short time, say, a twentieth of a second, the method checks to see if there has been any user input. If so, the input is processed (which may mean canceling the rendering task). Otherwise, the method carries on rendering the page for another twentieth of the second.

This approach works, but it is going to be a very complicated method to implement. Also, it totally ignores the event-based architecture of Windows. Recall from the coverage of events earlier in the book that if any user input arrives, the system will want to notify the application by raising an event. To modify your method to allow Windows to use events, you would do the following:

- Write an event handler that responds to user input. The response may include setting some flag to indicate that rendering should stop.
- Write a method that handles the rendering. This method is designed to be executed whenever you are not doing anything else.

This solution is better, because it works with the Windows event architecture. However, look at what it has to do. For starters, it will have to time itself carefully. While this method is running, the computer cannot respond to any user input. That means this method will have to make a note of the time that it gets called, continue monitoring the time as it works, and return as soon as a fairly suitable period of time has elapsed (the absolute maximum to retain user responsiveness would be a bit less than a tenth of a second). Furthermore, before this method returns, it will need to store the exact state it was at when it was interrupted, so that the next time it is called it can carry on. It is certainly possible to write a method that would do that, and in the days of Windows 3.1, that's exactly what you would have had to do to handle this sort of situation. Luckily, NT 3.1 and then Windows 95 brought multithreaded processes, which provide a far more convenient solution to this type of problem.

# Applications with Multiple Threads

The preceding example illustrates the situation in which an application needs to do more than one thing, so the obvious solution is to give the application more than one thread of execution. As mentioned, a thread represents the sequence of instructions that the computer executes. There is no reason why an application should only have one such sequence. In fact, it can have as many as you want. All that is required is that each time you create a new thread of execution, you indicate a method at which execution should start. The first thread in an application always starts at the `Main()` method because the first thread is started by the .NET runtime, and `Main()` is the method that the .NET runtime selects. Subsequent threads will be started internally by your application, which means that your application chooses where those threads start.

So far, we have spoken rather loosely about threads happening at the same time. In fact, one processor can do only one thing at a time. If you have a multiprocessor system, it is theoretically possible for more than one instruction to be executed simultaneously — one on each processor. However, for the majority of us who work on single-processor computers, things just don't happen simultaneously. What actually happens is that the Windows operating system gives the appearance of many processes taking place at the same time by a procedure known as *pre-emptive multitasking*.

Pre-emptive multitasking means that Windows picks a thread in some process and allows that thread to run for a short period of time. Microsoft has not documented the duration of this period, because it is one of those internal operating system parameters that it wants to be free to tweak as Windows evolves in order to maintain optimum performance. In any case, it is not the kind of information you need to know to run the Windows applications. In human terms, this time is very short — certainly no more than milliseconds. It is known as the thread's *time slice*. When the time slice is finished, Windows takes control back and selects another thread, which will then be allocated a time slice. These time slices are so short that we get the illusion of lots of things happening simultaneously.

Even when your application only has one thread, this process of pre-emptive multitasking is going on because many other processes are running on the system, and each process needs to be given time slices for each of its threads. That's how, when you have lots of windows on your screen, each one representing a different process, you can still click on any of them and have it appear to respond straight away. The response isn't instantaneous — it happens the next time the thread in the relevant process that is responsible for handling user input from that window gets a time slice. However, unless the system is very busy, the wait before that happens is so short that you don't notice it.

# Manipulating Threads

Threads are manipulated using the class `Thread`, which can be found in the `System.Threading` namespace. An instance of `Thread` represents one thread, or one sequence of execution. You can create another thread by simply instantiating another instance of the `Thread` object. Let's next look at starting a thread.

To make the following code snippets more concrete, suppose you are writing a graphics image editor, and the user requests to change the color depth of the image. For a large image this can take a while. It's the type of situation where you'd probably create a separate thread to do the processing so that you don't tie up the user interface while the color depth change is happening. To start up a thread, you first need to instantiate a thread object:

```
// entryPoint has been declared previously as a delegate
// of type ThreadStart
Thread depthChangeThread = new Thread(entryPoint);
```

Here you have given the variable the name `depthChangeThread`.

> *Additional threads that are created within an application in order to perform some task are often known as worker threads.*

The preceding code shows that the `Thread` constructor requires one parameter, which is used to indicate the entry point of the thread — that is, the method at which the thread starts executing. Because you are passing in the details of a method, this is a situation that calls for the use of delegates. In fact, a delegate has already been defined in the `System.Threading` class. It is called `ThreadStart`, and its signature looks like this:

```
public delegate void ThreadStart();
```

The parameter you pass to the constructor must be a delegate of this type (another way using anonymous methods is shown shortly).

After doing this, however, the new thread isn't actually doing anything yet. It is simply sitting there waiting to be started. You start a thread by calling the `Thread.Start()` method.

Suppose you have a method, `ChangeColorDepth()`, which does this processing:

```
void ChangeColorDepth()
{
    // processing to change color depth of image
}
```

You would arrange for this processing to be performed with this code:

```
ThreadStart entryPoint = new ThreadStart(ChangeColorDepth);
Thread depthChangeThread = new Thread(entryPoint);
depthChangeThread.Name = "DepthChange Thread";
depthChangeThread.Start();
```

After this point, two threads are running simultaneously.

In this code, you have also assigned a user-friendly name to the thread using the `Thread.Name` property (see Figure 13-1). It's not necessary to do this, but it can be useful.

Note that because the thread entry point (`ChangeColorDepth()` in this example) cannot take any parameters, you will have to find some other means of passing in any information that the method needs. The most obvious way would be to use member fields of the class this method is a member of. In addition to not being able to take any parameters in, the method also cannot return anything. (Where would any return value be returned to? As soon as this method returns a value, the thread that is running it will terminate, so there is nothing around to receive any return value and you can hardly return it to the thread that invoked this thread, because that thread will presumably be busy doing something else.)

# Threading

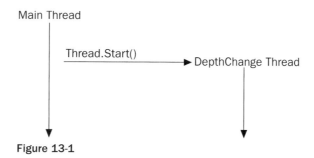

Figure 13-1

The .NET Framework 2.0 introduces some new features that also change the way in which you can start threads. This latest iteration of the .NET Framework introduces anonymous methods that now enable you to avoid creating a separate method and allow you to place the code block of the method directly in the delegate declaration instead. This new addition considerably changes the way in which you can start up your threads (as was earlier shown with the ChangeColorDepth() method).

If you want to use anonymous methods (this option is only available in C# and is not available in Visual Basic), you would alter the ChangeColorDepth() method to the following:

```
void ChangeColorDepth()
{
    Thread depthChangeThread = new Thread(delegate()
    {
        // processing to change color depth of image
    });

    depthChangeThread.Name = "DepthChange Thread";
    depthChangeThread.Start();

}
```

As you can see from this example, using anonymous threads provides a cleaner block of code that is also easier to follow. Using anonymous methods also means that there is no need to then employ the ThreadStart delegate.

Once you have started a thread, you can also suspend, resume, or abort it. Suspending a thread means pausing the thread or putting it to sleep — the thread will simply not run for a specific period of time, which also means it will not take up any processor time while it waits. It then can later be resumed, which means it will simply carry on from the point at which it was most recently suspended. If a thread is aborted, it will stop running altogether. Windows will permanently destroy all data that it maintains relating to that thread, so the thread subsequently cannot be restarted after it is aborted.

Continuing with the image editor example, assume that for some reason the user interface thread displays a dialog giving the user a chance to suspend temporarily the conversion process (it is not usual for a user to want to do this, but it is only an example; a more realistic example might be the user pausing the playing of a sound or video file). You code the response like this in the main thread:

```
depthChangeThread.Suspend();
```

If the user subsequently asks for the processing to resume, use this method:

```
depthChangeThread.Resume();
```

Finally, if the user (more realistically) decides against the conversion after all and chooses to cancel it, you then use the `Abort()` method:

```
depthChangeThread.Abort();
```

It is important to note that the `Suspend()` and `Abort()` methods do not necessarily work instantly. In the case of `Suspend()`, .NET might allow the thread being suspended to execute a few more instructions in order to reach a point at which .NET regards the thread as safely suspendable. This is for technical reasons — really to ensure the correct operation of the garbage collector (for details see the MSDN documentation). In the case of aborting a thread, the `Abort()` method actually works by throwing a `ThreadAbortException` in the affected thread. `ThreadAbortException` is a special exception class that is never handled. This ensures that any associated `finally` blocks are executed before the thread that is currently executing code inside `try` blocks is killed. Furthermore, this ensures that any appropriate cleaning up of resources can be done and also gives the thread a chance to make sure that any data it was manipulating (for example, fields of a class instance that will remain around after the thread has been killed) is left in a valid state.

> *Prior to .NET, aborting a thread in this way was not recommended except in extreme cases because the affected thread simply was killed immediately, which meant that any data it was manipulating could be left in an invalid state, and any resources the thread was using would be left open. The exception mechanism used by .NET in this situation means that aborting threads is safer.*

Although this exception mechanism makes aborting a thread safe, it does mean that aborting a thread might actually take some time, because theoretically there is no limit on how long code in a `finally` block could take to execute. Due to this, after aborting a thread, you might want to wait until the thread has actually been killed before continuing any processing. You would really only wait if any of your subsequent processing relies on the other thread having been killed. You can wait for a thread to terminate by calling the `Join()` method:

```
depthChangeThread.Abort();
depthChangeThread.Join();
```

`Join()` also has other overloads that allow you to specify a time limit on how long you are prepared to wait. If the time limit is reached, execution will continue anyway. If no time limit is specified, the thread that is waiting will wait for as long as it has to.

The previous code snippets will result in one thread performing actions on another thread (or at least in the case of `Join()`, waiting for another thread). However, what happens if the main thread wants to perform some actions on itself? In order to do this it needs a reference to a thread object that represents its own thread. It can get such a reference using a static property, `CurrentThread`, of the `Thread` class:

```
Thread myOwnThread = Thread.CurrentThread;
```

# Threading

`Thread` is actually a slightly unusual class to manipulate because there is always one thread present even before you instantiate any others—the thread that you are currently executing. This means that you can manipulate the class in two ways:

- ❏ You can instantiate a thread object, which will then represent a running thread and whose instance members apply to that running thread.
- ❏ You can call any of a number of static methods. These generally apply to the thread you are actually calling the method from.

One static method you might want to call is `Sleep()`. This method puts the running thread to sleep for a set period of time, after which it will continue.

## The ThreadPlayaround Sample

To illustrate how to use threads, in this section you build a small sample program called `Thread Playaround`. The aim of this example is to give you a feel for how manipulating threads works, so it is not intended to illustrate any realistic programming situations.

The core of the `ThreadPlayaround` sample is a short method, `DisplayNumbers()`, that counts up to a large number, displaying every so often its current count. `DisplayNumbers()` starts by displaying the name and culture of the thread that it is being run on:

```
static void DisplayNumbers()
{
    Thread thisThread = Thread.CurrentThread;
    string name = thisThread.Name;
    Console.WriteLine("Starting thread: " + name);
    Console.WriteLine(name + ": Current Culture = " +
                     thisThread.CurrentCulture);

    for (int i=1 ; i<= 8*interval ; i++)
    {
        if (i%interval == 0)
            Console.WriteLine(name + ": count has reached " + i);
    }
}
```

The limit of the count depends on `interval`, a field whose value is typed by the user. If the user types `100`, you will count up to `800`, displaying the values `100`, `200`, `300`, `400`, `500`, `600`, `700`, and `800`. If the user types `1000`, you will count up to `8000`, displaying the values `1000`, `2000`, `3000`, `4000`, `5000`, `6000`, `7000`, and `8000` along the way, and so on. This might all seem like a pointless exercise, but the purpose of it is to tie up the processor for a period while allowing you to see how far the processor is progressing with its task.

`ThreadPlayaround` starts a second worker thread, which will run `DisplayNumbers()`, but immediately after starting the worker thread, the main thread begins executing the same method. This means that you should see both counts happening at the same time.

## Chapter 13

The `Main()` method for `ThreadPlayaround` and its containing class looks like this:

```
class EntryPoint
{
    static int interval;

    static void Main()
    {
        Console.Write("Interval to display results at?> ");
        interval = int.Parse(Console.ReadLine());

        Thread thisThread = Thread.CurrentThread;
        thisThread.Name = "Main Thread";

        ThreadStart workerStart = new ThreadStart(StartMethod);
        Thread workerThread = new Thread(workerStart);
        workerThread.Name = "Worker";
        workerThread.Start();

        DisplayNumbers();
        Console.WriteLine("Main Thread Finished");

        Console.ReadLine();
    }
}
```

The start of the class declaration is shown here so that you can see that `interval` is a static field of this class. In the `Main()` method, you first ask the user for the interval. Then you retrieve a reference to the thread object that represents the main thread — this is done so that you can give this thread a name and see what's going on in the output.

Next, you create the worker thread, set its name, and start it off by passing it a delegate that indicates that the method it must start in is a method called `workerStart`. Finally, you call the `DisplayNumbers()` method to start counting. The entry point for the worker thread is this:

```
static void StartMethod()
{
    DisplayNumbers();
    Console.WriteLine("Worker Thread Finished");
}
```

Note that all these methods are static methods in the same class, `EntryPoint`. Note also that the two counts take place entirely separately, because the variable `i` in the `DisplayNumbers()` method that is used to do the counting is a local variable. Local variables are not only scoped to the method they are defined in but are also visible only to the thread that is executing that method. If another thread starts executing the same method, that thread will get its own copy of the local variables. You start by running the code and selecting a relatively small value of 100 for the interval:

**ThreadPlayaround**
```
Interval to display results at?> 100
Starting thread: Main Thread
Main Thread: Current Culture = en-US
```

# Threading

```
Main Thread: count has reached 100
Main Thread: count has reached 200
Main Thread: count has reached 300
Main Thread: count has reached 400
Main Thread: count has reached 500
Main Thread: count has reached 600
Main Thread: count has reached 700
Main Thread: count has reached 800
Main Thread Finished
Starting thread: Worker
Worker: Current Culture = en-US
Worker: count has reached 100
Worker: count has reached 200
Worker: count has reached 300
Worker: count has reached 400
Worker: count has reached 500
Worker: count has reached 600
Worker: count has reached 700
Worker: count has reached 800
Worker Thread Finished
```

As far as threads working in parallel are concerned, this doesn't immediately look like it's working too well! You see that the main thread starts, counts up to 800, and then claims to finish. The worker thread then starts and runs through separately.

The problem here is actually that starting a thread is a major process. After instantiating the new thread, the main thread comes across this line of code:

```
    workerThread.Start();
```

This call to `Thread.Start()` informs Windows that the new thread is to be started, then immediately returns. While you are counting up to 800, Windows is busily making the arrangements for the thread to be started. This internally means, among other things, allocating various resources for the thread, and performing various security checks. By the time the new thread is actually starting up, the main thread has already finished its work!

You can solve this problem by choosing a larger interval, so that both threads spend longer in the `DisplayNumbers()` method. Try `1000000` this time:

**ThreadPlayaround**
```
Interval to display results at?> 1000000
Starting thread: Main Thread
Main Thread: Current Culture = en-US
Main Thread: count has reached 1000000
Starting thread: Worker
Worker: Current Culture = en-US
Main Thread: count has reached 2000000
Worker: count has reached 1000000
Main Thread: count has reached 3000000
Worker: count has reached 2000000
Main Thread: count has reached 4000000
Worker: count has reached 3000000
```

```
Main Thread: count has reached 5000000
Main Thread: count has reached 6000000
Worker: count has reached 4000000
Main Thread: count has reached 7000000
Worker: count has reached 5000000
Main Thread: count has reached 8000000
Main Thread Finished
Worker: count has reached 6000000
Worker: count has reached 7000000
Worker: count has reached 8000000
Worker Thread Finished
```

Now you can see the threads really working in parallel. The main thread starts and counts up to one million. At some point, while the main thread is counting the next million numbers, the worker thread starts off, and from then on, the two threads progress at the same rate until they both finish.

It is important to understand that unless you are running a multiprocessor computer, using two threads in a CPU-intensive task will not have saved any time. On a single-processor machine, having both threads count up to 8 million will have taken just as long as having one thread count up to 16 million. Arguably, it will take slightly longer, because with the extra thread around, the operating system has to do a little bit more thread switching, but this difference will be negligible. The advantage of using more than one thread is twofold. First, you gain responsiveness, in that one of the threads could be dealing with user input while the other thread does some work behind the scenes. Second, you will save time if at least one thread is doing something that doesn't involve CPU time, such as waiting for data to be retrieved from the Internet, because the other threads can carry out their processing while the inactive thread(s) are waiting.

## *Thread Priorities*

What happens if you are going to have multiple threads running in your application, but some threads are more important than others? For this, it is possible to assign different priorities to different threads within a process. In general, a thread will not be allocated any time slices if there are any higher-priority threads working. The advantage of this is that you can guarantee user responsiveness by assigning a slightly higher priority to a thread that handles receiving user input. For most of the time, such a thread will have nothing to do, and the other threads can carry on their work. However, if the user does anything, this thread will immediately take priority over other threads in your application for the short time that it spends handling the event.

High-priority threads can completely block threads of lower priority, so you should be careful when changing thread priorities. You should also be aware that thread priorities are treated differently on different operating systems. The thread priorities are defined as values of the `ThreadPriority` enumeration. The possible values are `Highest`, `AboveNormal`, `Normal`, `BelowNormal`, and `Lowest`.

You should note that each process has a base priority, and that these values are relative to the priority of your process. Giving a thread a higher priority might ensure that it gets priority over other threads in that process, but there might still be other processes running on the system whose threads get an even higher priority. Windows tends to give a higher priority to its own operating system threads.

# Threading

You can see the effect of changing a thread priority by making the following change to the `Main()` method in the `ThreadPlayaround` sample:

```
ThreadStart workerStart = new ThreadStart(StartMethod);
Thread workerThread = new Thread(workerStart);
workerThread.Name = "Worker";

workerThread.Priority = ThreadPriority.AboveNormal;

workerThread.Start();
```

This indicates that the worker thread should have a slightly higher priority than the main thread. The result is dramatic:

```
ThreadPlayaroundWithPriorities
Interval to display results at?> 1000000
Starting thread: Main Thread
Main Thread: Current Culture = en-US
Starting thread: Worker
Worker: Current Culture = en-US
Main Thread: count has reached 1000000
Worker: count has reached 1000000
Worker: count has reached 2000000
Worker: count has reached 3000000
Worker: count has reached 4000000
Worker: count has reached 5000000
Worker: count has reached 6000000
Worker: count has reached 7000000
Worker: count has reached 8000000
Worker Thread Finished
Main Thread: count has reached 2000000
Main Thread: count has reached 3000000
Main Thread: count has reached 4000000
Main Thread: count has reached 5000000
Main Thread: count has reached 6000000
Main Thread: count has reached 7000000
Main Thread: count has reached 8000000
Main Thread Finished
```

This shows that when the worker thread has an `AboveNormal` priority, the main thread scarcely gets a look-in once the worker thread has started.

## Synchronization

One crucial aspect of working with threads is the *synchronization* of access to any variables that more than one thread has access to. Synchronization means that only one thread should be able to access the variable at any one time. If you do not ensure that access to variables is synchronized, subtle bugs can result. This section briefly reviews some of the main issues involved.

# Chapter 13

## *What is synchronization?*

The issue of synchronization arises because what looks like a single statement in your C# source code in most cases will translate into many statements in the final compiled assembly language machine code. Take, for example, the following statement:

```
message += ", there";    // message variable is a string that contains "Hello"
```

This statement looks syntactically in C# like one statement, but it actually involves a large number of operations when the code is being executed. Memory will need to be allocated to store the new longer string; the variable `message` will need to be set to refer to the new memory; the actual text will need to be copied, and so on.

Obviously, the case is exaggerated here by selecting a string — one of the more complex data types — as an example, but even when performing arithmetic operations on primitive numeric types, there is quite often more going on behind the scenes than you would imagine from looking at the C# code. In particular, many operations cannot be carried out directly on variables stored in memory locations, and their values have to be separately copied into special locations in the processor known as *registers*.

In a situation where a single C# statement translates into more than one native machine code command, it is quite possible that the thread's time slice might end in the middle of executing that statement process. If this happens, another thread in the same process might be given a time slice, and, if access to variables involved with that statement (here: `message`) is not synchronized, this other thread might attempt to read or write to the same variables. In the example, was the other thread intended to see the new value of message or the old value?

The problems can get even worse than this. The statement used in the example is relatively simple, but in a more complicated statement, some variable might have an undefined value for a brief period, while the statement is being executed. If another thread attempts to read that value in that instant, it might simply read garbage. More seriously, if two threads simultaneously try to write data to the same variable, it is almost certain that that variable will contain an incorrect value afterward.

Synchronization is not an issue that affects the `ThreadPlayaround` sample, because both threads use mostly local variables. The only variable that both threads have access to is the `interval` field, but this field is initialized by the main thread before any other thread starts, and subsequently only reads from either thread, so there is still not a problem. Synchronization issues only arise if at least one thread is writing to a variable while other threads are either reading or writing to it.

Fortunately, C# provides an extremely easy way of synchronizing access to variables, and the C# language keyword that does it is `lock`. You use `lock` like this:

```
lock (x)
{
   DoSomething();
}
```

What the `lock` statement does is wrap an object known as a *mutual exclusion lock*, or *mutex*, around the variable in the round brackets. The mutex will remain in place while the compound statement attached to the `lock` keyword is executed. While the mutex is wrapped around a variable, no other thread is permitted access to that variable. You can see this with the preceding code; the compound statement will execute, and

# Threading

eventually this thread will lose its time slice. If the next thread to gain the time slice attempts to access the variable x, access to the variable will be denied. Instead, Windows will simply put the thread to sleep until the mutex has been released.

The `Mutex` object does allow you to lock an object from another thread (thereby blocking the thread) regardless of where that thread originates. The `Mutex` object allows for locking of objects whether the second thread is contained within the same process or is originating in an entirely different process. Therefore, the `Mutex` object is a *system-wide* solution to thread synchronization.

The mutex is the simplest of a number of mechanisms that can be used to control access to variables. We don't have the space to go into the others here, but they are all controlled through the .NET base class `System.Threading.Monitor`. In fact, the C# `lock` statement is simply a C# syntax wrapper around a couple of method calls to this class.

In general, you should synchronize variables wherever there is a risk that any thread might try writing to a variable at the same time as other threads are trying to read from or write to the same variable. There is not space here to cover the details of thread synchronization; it is a fairly big topic in its own right. The following sections are confined to pointing out a couple of the potential pitfalls.

## Synchronization issues

Synchronizing threads is vital in multithreaded applications. However, it's an area in which it is important to proceed carefully because a number of subtle and hard-to-detect bugs can easily arise, in particular *deadlocks* and *race conditions*.

### Don't overuse synchronization

Although thread synchronization is important, it is important to use it only where it is necessary because it can impact performance for two reasons. First, there is some overhead associated with actually putting a lock on an object and taking it off, though this is admittedly minimal. Second, and more importantly, the more thread synchronization you have, the more threads can get held up waiting for objects to be released. Remember that if one thread holds a lock on any object, any other thread that needs to access that object will simply halt execution until the lock is released. It is important, therefore, that you place as little code inside `lock` blocks as you can without causing thread synchronization bugs. In this sense, you can think of `lock` statements as temporarily disabling the multithreading ability of an application, and therefore temporarily removing all the benefits of multithreading.

However, the dangers of using synchronization too often (performance and responsiveness go down) are not as great as the dangers associated with not using synchronization when you need it (subtle runtime bugs that are very hard to track down).

### Deadlocks

A *deadlock* (or a deadly embrace) is a bug that can occur when two threads have to access resources that are locked by the other. Suppose one thread is running the following code, where a and b are two object references that both threads have access to:

```
lock (a)
{
   // do something
```

```
        lock (b)
        {
            // do something
        }
    }
}
```

At the same time, another thread is running this code:

```
lock (b)
{
    // do something

    lock (a)
    {
        // do something
    }
}
```

Depending on the times that the threads come across the various statements, the following scenario is quite possible: the first thread acquires a lock on a, while at about the same time the second thread acquires a lock on b. A short time later, the first thread comes across the `lock(b)` statement, and immediately goes to sleep, waiting for the lock on b to be released. Soon afterward, the second thread comes across its `lock(a)` statement and also puts itself to sleep, ready for Windows to wake it up the instant the lock on a gets released. Unfortunately, the lock on a is never going to be released because the first thread, which owns this lock, is sleeping and won't wake up until the lock on b gets released, which won't happen until the second thread wakes up. The result is deadlock. Both threads just permanently sit there doing nothing, each waiting for the other thread to release its lock. This kind of problem can cause an entire application to just hang, so that you have no choice but to use the Task Manager to terminate the entire process.

> *In this situation, it is not possible for another thread to release the locks; a mutual exclusion lock can only be released by the thread that claims the lock in the first place.*

Deadlocks can usually be avoided by having both threads claim locks on objects in the same order. In the preceding example, if the second thread claimed the locks in the same order as the first thread, a first, then b, whichever thread has the lock on a first would completely finish its task and then the other thread would start. This way, no deadlock can occur.

You might think that it is easy to avoid coding deadlocks — after all, in the example, it looks fairly obvious that a deadlock could occur so you probably wouldn't write that code in the first place. However, remember that different locks can occur in different method calls. With this example, the first thread might actually be executing this code:

```
lock (a)
{
    // do bits of processing

    CallSomeMethod()
}
```

# Threading

Here, `CallSomeMethod()` might call other methods, and so on, and buried in there somewhere is a `lock(b)` statement. In this situation, it might not be nearly so obvious when you write your code that you are allowing a possible deadlock.

## Race conditions

A *race condition* is somewhat subtler than a deadlock. It rarely halts execution of a process, but it can lead to data corruption. It is hard to give a precise definition of a race, but it generally occurs when several threads attempt to access the same data, and do not adequately take account of what the other threads are doing. Race conditions are best understood using an example.

Suppose you have an array of objects, where each element in the array needs to be processed somehow, and you have a number of threads that are between them doing this processing. You might have an object, for example, `ArrayController`, which contains the array of objects as well as an `int` that indicates how many of them have been processed, and therefore, which one should be processed next. `ArrayController` might implement this method:

```
public int GetObject(int index)
{

    // returns the object at the given index.

}
```

It also implements this read/write property:

```
public int ObjectsProcessed
{

    // indicates how many of the objects have been processed.

}
```

Now, each thread that is helping to process the objects might execute some code that looks like this:

```
lock(ArrayController)
{
   int nextIndex = ArrayController.ObjectsProcessed;
   Console.WriteLine("Object to be processed next is " + nextIndex);
   ++ArrayController.ObjectsProcessed;
   object next = ArrayController.GetObject(nextIndex);
}
ProcessObject(next);
```

This by itself should work, but suppose that in an attempt to avoid tying up resources for longer than necessary, you decide not to hold the lock on `ArrayController` while you're displaying the user message. Therefore, you rewrite the preceding code like this:

```
lock(ArrayController)
{
   int nextIndex = ArrayController.ObjectsProcessed;
}
```

```
    Console.WriteLine("Object to be processed next is " + nextIndex);

    lock(ArrayController)
    {
       ++ArrayController.ObjectsProcessed;
       object next = ArrayController.GetObject(nextIndex);
    }

    ProcessObject(next);
```

Here, you have a possible problem. What could happen is that one thread gets an object (say, the 11th object in the array), and displays the message saying that it is about to process this object. Meanwhile, a second thread also starts executing the same code, calls `ObjectsProcessed`, and determines that the next object to be processed is the 11th object, because the first thread hasn't yet updated `ArrayController.ObjectsProcessed`. While the second thread is happily writing to the console that it will now process the 11th object, the first thread acquires another lock on the `ArrayController` and inside this lock increments `ObjectsProcessed`. Unfortunately, it is too late. Both threads are now committed to processing the same object — a textbook example of a race condition.

For both deadlocks and race conditions, it is not often obvious when the condition can occur; and when it does, it is hard to identify the bug. In general, this is an area where you largely learn from experience. However, it is important to consider very carefully all the parts of the code where you need synchronization when you are writing multithreaded applications to check whether there is any possibility of deadlocks or race conditions arising. Keep in mind that you cannot predict the exact times that different threads will encounter different instructions.

# Creating Threads Using ThreadPool

So far, you have looked at creating and destroying threads by working with a single thread at a time using the `Thread` class. It is important to note that it is expensive (CPU intensive) to build up and destroy threads in this manner. For this reason, the CLR contains a built-in thread pool for you to use for your applications. This thread pool can be accessed via the `ThreadPool` class.

The `ThreadPool` class will work to reuse existing threads from a managed pool of threads and when it is done using the thread, the thread will simply be returned to the thread pool for reuse. `ThreadPool` contains the ability to access 25 available threads (per processor).

Using the `ThreadPool` class is far easier than creating threads using the `Thread` class as was shown earlier in this chapter. However, when deciding whether to create threads using the `ThreadPool` class or the `Thread` class, you should take some of the following points into consideration.

You should use the `ThreadPool` class when you are interested in achieving the following:

- ❑ When you are interested in creating and destroying threads in the easiest manner possible
- ❑ When the performance of how your application uses threads is of high priority

# Threading

You should instead use the `Thread` class when you are interested in achieving the following:

- When you are interested in controlling the priority of the threads created
- When you want the thread you are working with to maintain its identity, which is associated with the thread over various operations and time intervals
- When you are working with threads that might be long-lived threads

The following example looks at how to create a thread using the `ThreadPool` class. First, create a console application. The code for this application is as follows:

```
using System;
using System.Collections.Generic;
using System.Text;
using System.Threading;

namespace ConsoleApplication1
{
    class Program
    {
        static int interval;

        static void Main(string[] args)
        {
            Console.Write("Interval to display results at?> ");
            interval = int.Parse(Console.ReadLine());

            ThreadPool.QueueUserWorkItem(new WaitCallback(StartMethod));
            Thread.Sleep(100);
            ThreadPool.QueueUserWorkItem(new WaitCallback(StartMethod));
            Console.ReadLine();

        }

        static void StartMethod(Object stateInfo)
        {
            DisplayNumbers("Thread " + DateTime.Now.Millisecond.ToString());
            Console.WriteLine("Thread Finished");
        }

        static void DisplayNumbers(string GivenThreadName)
        {
            Console.WriteLine("Starting thread: " + GivenThreadName);

            for (int i = 1; i <= 8 * interval; i++)
            {
                if (i % interval == 0)
                {
                    Console.WriteLine("Count has reached " + i);
                    Thread.Sleep(1000);
                }
            }
        }
    }
}
```

The first thing to pay attention to is that the `System.Threading` namespace is imported into the page in order to gain access to the `ThreadPool` class. This example is similar to an earlier example used in this chapter. Instead of creating an instance of the `Thread` class (as was done earlier), you simply need to call the `ThreadPool.QueueUserWorkItem()` method. You can go about calling this method in a couple of ways. Shown above is one variation on making this call. Below is another method to use:

```
ThreadPool.QueueUserWorkItem(new WaitCallback(StartMethod));
```

It would have also been possible to simply using the following construct:

```
ThreadPool.QueueUserWorkItem(StartMethod);
```

After the first invocation of the `QueueUserWorkItem` method, the main thread is put to sleep for 100 milliseconds before a second thread in the managed thread pool is used. You do this by simply using another instance of the `QueueUserWorkItem` method invocation.

When run, you will see results similar to the following in the console:

```
Interval to display results at?> 100
Starting thread: Thread 265
Count has reached 100
Starting thread: Thread 359
Count has reached 100
Count has reached 200
Count has reached 200
Count has reached 300
Count has reached 300
Count has reached 400
Count has reached 400
Count has reached 500
Count has reached 500
Count has reached 600
Count has reached 600
Count has reached 700
Count has reached 700
Count has reached 800
Count has reached 800
Thread Finished
Thread Finished
```

When using the `WaitCallBack` delegate, you also have the ability to pass in a parameter as well. This is illustrated in this partial code example:

```
ThreadPool.QueueUserWorkItem(new WaitCallback(StartMethod), "First Thread");
Thread.Sleep(100);
ThreadPool.QueueUserWorkItem(new WaitCallback(StartMethod), "Second Thread");
Console.ReadLine();
```

As you can see, a string is also passed in with the `WaitCallBack` delegate. This is then used in the `StartMethod` method as illustrated here:

# Threading

```
static void StartMethod(Object stateInfo)
{
    DisplayNumbers("Thread " + stateInfo.ToString());
    Console.WriteLine("Thread Finished");
}
```

These changes produce the following results:

```
Interval to display results at?> 100
Starting thread: Thread First Thread
Count has reached 100
Starting thread: Thread Second Thread
Count has reached 100
Count has reached 200
Count has reached 200
Count has reached 300
Count has reached 300
Count has reached 400
Count has reached 400
Count has reached 500
Count has reached 500
Count has reached 600
Count has reached 600
Count has reached 700
Count has reached 700
Count has reached 800
Count has reached 800
Thread Finished
Thread Finished
```

It is also possible to get a series of properties about the thread you are working with using the `Thread` object. To pull some of the information on the thread being executed, change the `DisplayNumbers` method as follows:

```
static void DisplayNumbers(string GivenThreadName)
{
    Console.WriteLine("Starting thread: " + GivenThreadName);

    for (int i = 1; i <= 8 * interval; i++)
    {
        if (i % interval == 0)
        {
            Console.WriteLine("Count has reached " + i);
            Console.WriteLine("CurrentCulture: " +
               Thread.CurrentThread.CurrentCulture.ToString());
            Console.WriteLine("IsThreadPoolThread: " +
               Thread.CurrentThread.IsThreadPoolThread.ToString());
            Console.WriteLine("ManagedThreadId: " +
               Thread.CurrentThread.ManagedThreadId.ToString());
            Console.WriteLine("Priority: " +
               Thread.CurrentThread.Priority.ToString());
            Console.WriteLine("ThreadState: " +
               Thread.CurrentThread.ThreadState.ToString());
```

```
            Thread.Sleep(1000);
        }
    }
}
```

In this example, you use the `Thread.CurrentThread` property to get at the information available for the particular thread that is currently being executed. This will produce the following results (a partial sample of the output):

```
Count has reached 100
CurrentCulture: en-US
IsThreadPoolThread: True
ManagedThreadId: 10
Priority: Normal
ThreadState: Background
```

Remember, in the end, you can create threads using the `Thread` or the `ThreadPool` class. Each one has some pros and cons, but you will find that it is pretty simple to work with .NET threading in any case.

# Summary

This chapter took a quick look at how to code applications that utilize multiple threads using the `System.Threading` namespace. Using multithreading in your applications takes careful planning. Too many threads can cause resource issues and not enough threads can cause your applications to seem sluggish and to perform rather poorly.

The `System.Threading` namespace in the .NET Framework does allow you to manipulate threads; however, this does not mean that the .NET Framework handles all the difficult tasks of multithreading for you. You have to consider thread priority and synchronization issues. This chapter discussed these issues and how to code for them in your C# applications. It also looked at the problems associated with deadlocks and race conditions.

Just remember that if you are going to use multithreading in your C# applications, careful planning should be a big part of your efforts.

# Part II
# The .NET Environment

Chapter 14: Visual Studio 2005

Chapter 15: Assemblies

Chapter 16: .NET Security

Chapter 17: Localization

Chapter 18: Deployment

# 14

# Visual Studio 2005

At this point you should be familiar with the C# language and almost ready to move on to the applied sections of the book, which look at how to use C# to program a variety of applications. Before doing that, however, you need to examine how you can use Visual Studio and some of the features provided by the .NET environment to get the best from your programs.

This chapter looks at what programming in the .NET environment means in practice. It covers Visual Studio, the main development environment in which you will write, compile, debug, and optimize your C# programs, and provides guidelines for writing good applications. Visual Studio is the main IDE used for everything from writing Web Forms, Windows Forms, XML Web services, and more. For more details on Windows Forms and how to write user interface code, see Chapter 23, "Windows Forms."

## Working with Visual Studio 2005

Visual Studio 2005 is a fully integrated development environment. It is designed to make the process of writing your code, debugging it, and compiling it to an assembly to be shipped as easy as possible. What this means in practice is that Visual Studio gives you a very sophisticated multiple-document-interface application in which you can do just about everything related to developing your code. It offers these features:

- ❑ **Text editor.** Using this editor, you can write your C# (as well as Visual Basic 2005, J#, and C++) code. This text editor is quite sophisticated. For example, as you type, it automatically lays out your code by indenting lines, matching start and end brackets of code blocks, and color-coding keywords. It also performs some syntax checks as you type and underlines code that causes compilation errors, also known as design-time debugging. In addition it features IntelliSense, which automatically displays the names of classes, fields, or methods as you begin to type them. As you start typing parameters to methods, it will also show you the parameter lists for the available overloads. Figure 14-1 shows the IntelliSense feature in action with one of the .NET base classes, `ListBox`.

# Chapter 14

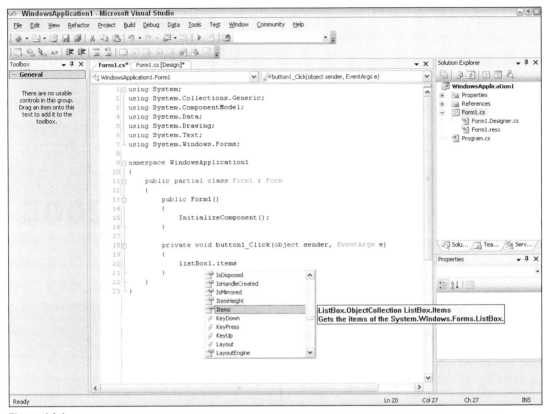

Figure 14-1

> A useful shortcut to remember is that by pressing CTRL+SPACE, you can bring back the IntelliSense list box if you need it and if for any reason it's not visible.

- ❑ **Design view editor.** This editor enables you to place user-interface and data-access controls in your project; Visual Studio automatically adds the necessary C# code to your source files to instantiate these controls in your project. (This is possible because all .NET controls are instances of particular base classes.)

- ❑ **Supporting windows.** These windows allow you to view and modify aspects of your project, such as the classes in your source code as well as the available properties (and their startup values) for Windows Forms and Web Forms classes. You can also use these windows to specify compilation options, such as which assemblies your code needs to reference.

- ❑ **The ability to compile from within the environment.** Instead of having to run the C# compiler from the command line, you can simply select a menu option to compile the project and Visual Studio will call the compiler for you and pass all the relevant command-line parameters to the compiler, detailing such things as which assemblies to reference and what type of assembly you want to be emitted (executable or library .dll, for example). If you want, it can also run the compiled executable for you so you can see whether it runs satisfactorily. You can even choose between different build configurations (for example, a release or debug build).

# Visual Studio 2005

- **Integrated debugger.** It's in the nature of programming that your code won't run correctly the first time you try it. Or the second time. Or the third time. Visual Studio seamlessly links up to a debugger for you, allowing you to set breakpoints and watches on variables from within the environment.

- **Integrated MSDN help.** Visual Studio enables you to access the MSDN documentation from within the IDE. For example, if you're not sure of the meaning of a keyword while using the text editor, simply select the keyword and press the F1 key, and Visual Studio accesses MSDN to show you related topics. Similarly, if you're not sure what a certain compilation error means, you can bring up the documentation for that error by selecting the error message and pressing F1.

- **Access to other programs.** Visual Studio can also access a number of other utilities that allow you to examine and modify aspects of your computer or network, without you having to leave the developer environment. Among the tools available, you can check running services and database connections, look directly into your SQL Server tables, and even browse the Web using an Internet Explorer window.

If you've developed previously using C++ or Visual Basic, you will already be familiar with the relevant Visual Studio 6 version of the IDE, and many of the features in the preceding list will not be new to you. What is new in Visual Studio is that it combines all the features that were previously available across all Visual Studio 6 development environments. This means that whatever language you used in Visual Studio 6, you'll find some new features in Visual Studio. For example, in the older Visual Basic environment, you could not compile separate debug and release builds. On the other hand, if you are coming to C# from a background of C++, much of the support for data access and the ability to drop controls into your application with a click of the mouse, which has long been part of the Visual Basic developer's experience, will be new to you. In the C++ development environment drag-and-drop support is limited to the most common user-interface controls.

> *C++ developers will miss two Visual Studio 6 features in Visual Studio 2005: edit-and-continue debugging and an integrated profiler. Visual Studio 2005 also does not include a full profiler application. Instead, you will find a number of .NET classes that assist with profiling in the* `System.Diagnostics` *namespace. The perfmon profiling tool is available from the command line (just type perfmon) and has a number of new .NET-related performance monitors.*

Whatever your background, you will find the overall look of the Visual Studio 2005 developer environment has changed since days of Visual Studio 6 to accommodate the new features, the single cross-language IDE, and the integration with .NET. There are new menu and toolbar options, and many of the existing ones from Visual Studio 6 have been renamed. So you'll have to spend some time familiarizing yourself with the layout and commands available in Visual Studio 2005.

The differences between Visual Studio 2002/2003 and Visual Studio 2005 are a few nice additions that facilitate working in Visual Studio 2005. The biggest changes in Visual Studio 2005 include the ability to refactor code, which allows you to extract methods, globally rename variables, and perform other quick actions upon an entire project of code.

One of the biggest items to notice with your installation of Visual Studio 2005 is that this new IDE works with the .NET Framework 2.0. In fact, when you install Visual Studio 2005, you will also be installing the .NET Framework 2.0 if it isn't already installed. Visual Studio 2005 is not built to work with version 1.0 or 1.1 of the .NET Framework, which means that if you still want to develop 1.0 or 1.1 applications, you will want to keep Visual Studio 2002 or 2003, respectively, installed on your machine. Installing Visual Studio 2005 installs a complete and new copy of Visual Studio and does not upgrade the previous Visual Studio 2002 or 2003 IDEs. The three copies of Visual Studio will then run side-by-side.

# Chapter 14

Note that if you attempt to open your Visual Studio 2002 or 2003 projects using Visual Studio 2005, the IDE will warn you that your solution will be upgraded to Visual Studio 2005 if you continue by popping up the Visual Studio Conversion Wizard (see Figure 14-2).

**Figure 14-2**

The upgrade wizard has been dramatically improved from Visual Studio 2003 to this newer one provided by Visual Studio 2005. This new wizard can make backup copies of the solutions that are being backed up (see Figure 14-3) and it can also back up solutions that are contained within source control.

It is also possible to have Visual Studio generate a conversion report for you in the conversion process's final step. The report will then be viewable directly in the document window of Visual Studio. This report is illustrated (done with a simple conversion) in Figure 14-4.

# Visual Studio 2005

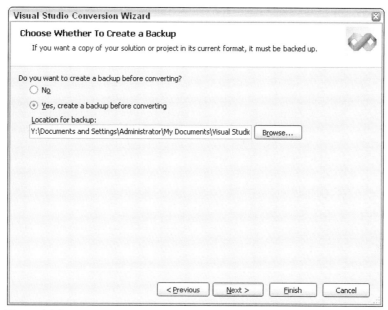

Figure 14-3

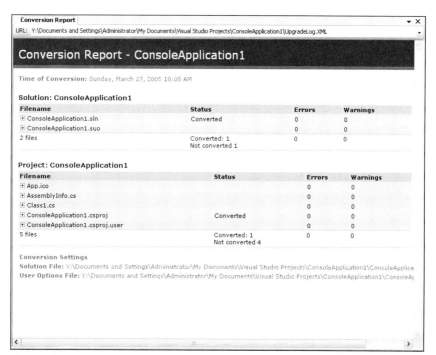

Figure 14-4

# Chapter 14

Remember that you shouldn't upgrade production solutions without testing your programs first in a staging environment to ensure your application will not be affected by the changes between versions 1.0/1.1 and 2.0 of the .NET Framework.

Because this is a professional-level book, it doesn't look in detail at every feature or menu option available in Visual Studio 2005. Surely you will be able to find your way around the IDE. The real aim of the Visual Studio coverage is to ensure that you are sufficiently familiar with the concepts involved when building and debugging a C# application, so you can make the most of working with Visual Studio 2005. Figure 14-5 shows what your screen might look like when working in Visual Studio 2005. (Note that because the appearance of Visual Studio is highly customizable, the windows might not be in the same locations or different windows might be visible when you launch this development environment.)

The following sections take you through the process of creating, coding, and debugging a project, showing what Visual Studio can do to help you at each stage.

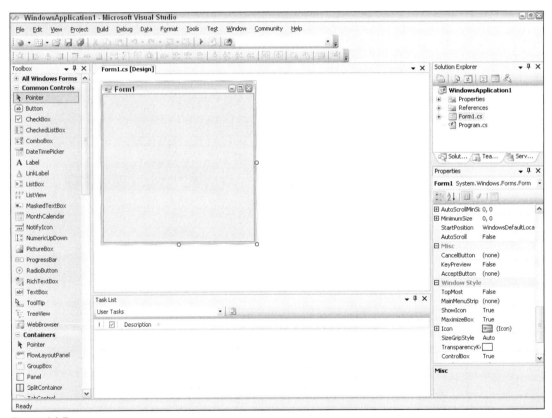

Figure 14-5

# Visual Studio 2005

## Creating a Project

Once you have installed Visual Studio 2005, you will want to start your first project. With Visual Studio, you rarely start with a blank file and then add C# code, in the way that you've been doing in the previous chapters in this book. (Of course, the option of asking for an empty application project is there if you really do want to start writing your code from scratch or if you are going to create a solution that will contain a number of projects.) Instead, the idea is that you tell Visual Studio roughly what type of project you want to create, and it will generate the files and C# code that provides a framework for that type of project. You then work by adding your code to this outline. For example, if you want to build a Windows GUI-interface-based application (or, in .NET terminology, a Windows Form), Visual Studio will start you off with a file containing C# source code that creates a basic form. This form is capable of talking to Windows and receiving events. It can be maximized, minimized, or resized; all you have to do is add the controls and functionality you want. If your application is intended to be a command-line utility (a console application), Visual Studio will give you a basic namespace, class, and a `Main()` method to start you off.

Last, but hardly least, when you create your project, Visual Studio also sets up the compilation options that you are likely to supply to the C# compiler — whether it is to compile to a command-line application, a library, or a Windows application. It will also tell the compiler which base class libraries you will need to reference (a Windows GUI application will need to reference many of the `Windows.Forms`-related libraries; a console application probably won't). You can of course modify all these settings as you are editing, if you need to.

The first time you start Visual Studio, you will be presented with a blank IDE (see Figure 14-6). The Start Page is an HTML page that contains various links to useful Web sites, and enables you to open existing projects or start a new project altogether.

Figure 14-6 shows the type of Start Page you get after you've used Visual Studio 2005; it includes a list of the most recently edited projects. You can just click one of these projects to open it again.

### Selecting a project type

You can create a new project by selecting File ➪ New Project from the Visual Studio menu. From here you will get the New Project dialog box (see Figure 14-7) — and your first inkling of the variety of different projects you can create.

# Chapter 14

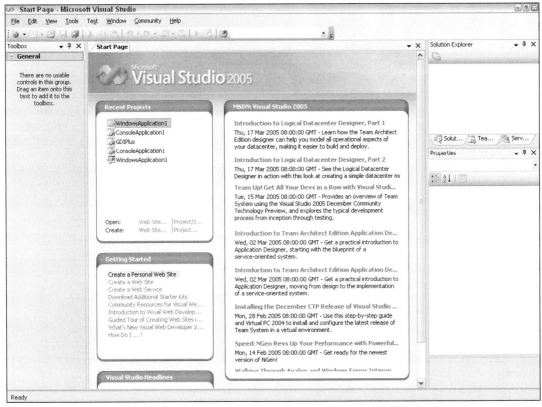

Figure 14-6

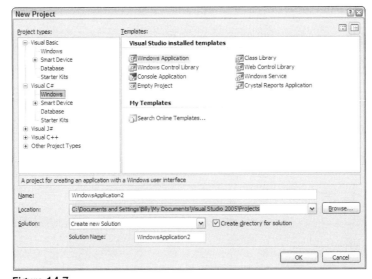

Figure 14-7

# Visual Studio 2005

Using this dialog box, you effectively select the initial framework files and code you want Visual Studio to generate for you, the type of compilation options you want, and the compiler you want to compile your code with—either the Visual C#, Visual Basic 2005, Visual J#, or Visual C++ compiler. You can immediately see the language integration that Microsoft has promised for .NET at work here! This particular example uses a C# console application.

> *We don't have space to cover all the various options for different types of projects here. On the C++ side, all the old C++ project types are there—MFC application, ATL project, and so on. On the Visual Basic 2005 side, the options have changed somewhat. For example, you can create a Visual Basic 2005 command-line application (Console Application), a .NET component (Class Library), a .NET control (Windows Control Library), and more. However, you cannot create an old-style COM-based control (the .NET control is intended to replace such ActiveX controls).*

The following table lists all the options that are available to you under Visual C# Projects. Note that some other more specialized C# template projects are available under the Other Projects option.

| If you choose... | You get the C# code and compilation options to generate... |
|---|---|
| Windows Application | A basic empty form that responds to events. |
| Class Library | A .NET class that can be called up by other code. |
| Windows Control Library | A .NET class that can be called up by other code and that has a user interface. (Like an old-style ActiveX control.) |
| ASP.NET Web Application | An ASP.NET-based Web site: ASP.NET pages and C# classes that generate the HTML response sent to browsers from those pages. |
| ASP.NET Web Service | A C# class that acts as a fully operational Web service. |
| ASP.NET Mobile Web Application | An application type that allows you to build ASP.NET pages that target mobile devices. |
| Web Control Library | A control that can be called up by ASP.NET pages, to generate the HTML code that gives the appearance of a control when displayed on a browser. |
| Console Application | An application that runs at the command-line prompt, or in a console window. |
| Windows Service | A service that runs in the background on Windows NT and Windows 2000. |
| Crystal Reports Windows Application | A project for creating a C# application with a Windows user interface and a sample Crystal Report. |
| SQL Server Project | A project for creating classes to use in SQL Server. |
| Pocket PC 2003 Application | A project for creating a .NET Compact Framework 2.0 forms application for Pocket PC 2003 and later. |
| Pocket PC 2003 Class Library | A project for creating a .NET Compact Framework 2.0 class library (.dll) for Pocket PC 2003 and later. |

*Table continued on following page*

| If you choose... | You get the C# code and compilation options to generate... |
|---|---|
| Pocket PC 2003 Control Library | A project for creating .NET Compact Framework 2.0 controls for Pocket PC 2003 and later. |
| Pocket PC 2003 Console Application | A project for creating a .NET Compact Framework 2.0 non-graphical application for Pocket PC 2003 and later. |
| Pocket PC 2003 Empty Project | An empty project for creating a .NET Compact Framework 2.0 application for Pocket PC 2003 and later. |
| Smartphone 2003 Application | A project for creating a .NET Compact Framework 1.0 forms application for Smartphone 2003 and later. |
| Smartphone 2003 Class Library | A project for creating .NET Compact Framework 1.0 class library (.dll) for Smartphone 2003 and later. |
| Smartphone 2003 Console Application | A project for creating a .NET Compact Framework 1.0 non-graphical application for Smartphone 2003 and later. |
| Smartphone 2003 Empty Project | An empty project for creating a .NET Compact Framework 1.0 application for Smartphone 2003 and later. |
| Windows CE 5.0 Application | A project for creating a .NET Compact Framework 2.0 forms application for Windows CE 5.0 and later. |
| Windows CE 5.0 Class Library | A project for creating a .NET Compact Framework 2.0 class library (.dll) for Windows CE 5.0 and later. |
| Windows CE 5.0 Control Library | A project for creating .NET Compact Framework 2.0 controls for Windows CE 5.0 and later. |
| Windows CE 5,0 Console Application | A project for creating a .NET Compact Framework 2.0 command-line application for Windows CE 5.0 and later. |
| Windows CE 5,0 Empty Project | An empty project for creating a .NET Compact Framework 2.0 application for Windows CE 5.0 and later. |
| Excel Workbook | A project for creating managed code extensions behind a new or existing Excel 2003 workbook. |
| Word Document | A project for creating managed code extensions behind a new or existing Word 2003 document. |
| Excel Template | A project for creating managed code extensions behind a new or existing Excel 2003 template. |
| Word Template | A project for creating managed code extensions behind a new or existing Word 2003 template. |
| Empty Project | Installs nothing. You have to write all your code from scratch; but you still get the benefit of all the Visual Studio facilities when you are writing. |

# Visual Studio 2005

| If you choose... | You get the C# code and compilation options to generate... |
|---|---|
| Empty Web Project | The same as Empty Project, but the compilation settings are set to instruct the compiler to generate code for ASP.NET pages. |
| New Project In Existing Folder | New project files for an empty project. Use this option if you have some straight C# source code (for example, typed in a text editor) and want to turn it into a Visual Studio project. |

This isn't a full list. Various types of starter kits, such as a screen saver starter kit and a movie collection starter kit, are also available. Also, a test application is available that allows you to create a project that contains tests.

## *The newly created console project*

When you click OK after selecting the Console Application option, Visual Studio gives you a couple of files, including a source code file, `Program.cs`, which contains the initial framework code. Figure 14-8 shows what code Visual Studio has written for you.

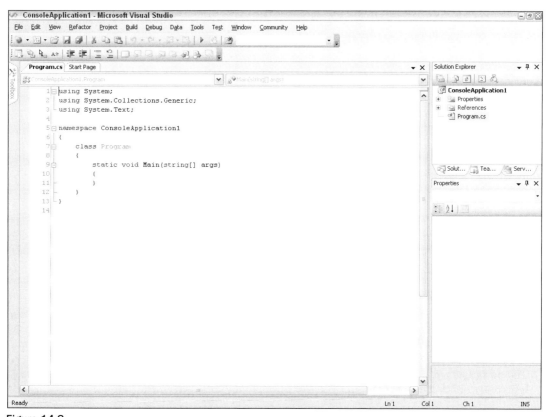

Figure 14-8

## Chapter 14

As you can see, you have a C# program that doesn't do anything yet but contains the basic items required in any C# executable program: a namespace and a class that contains the `Main()` method, which is the program's entry point. (Strictly speaking, the namespace isn't necessary, but it would be very bad programming practice not to declare one.) This code is all ready to compile and run, which you can do immediately by pressing the F5 key or by selecting the Debug menu and choosing Start. However, before you do that, add the following line of code — to make your application actually do something!

```
static void Main(string[] args)
{
    Console.WriteLine("Hello from all the folks at Wrox Press");
}
```

If you compile and run the project, you'll see a console window that stays barely long enough onscreen so you have time to read the message. The reason this happens is that Visual Studio, remembering the settings you specified when you created the project, arranged for it to be compiled and run as a console application. Windows then realizes that it has to run a console application but doesn't have a console window to run it from. So Windows creates a console window and runs the program. As soon as the program exits, Windows recognizes that it doesn't need the console window anymore and promptly removes it. That's all very logical but doesn't help you very much if you actually want to look at the output from your project!

A good way to avoid this problem is to insert the following line just before the `Main()` method returns in your code.

```
static void Main(string[] args)
{
    Console.WriteLine("Hello from all the folks at Wrox Press");
    Console.ReadLine();
}
```

That way, your code will run, display its output, and come across the `Console.ReadLine()` statement, at which point it will wait for you to press the Return (or Enter) key before the program exits. This means that the console window will hang around until you press Return.

Note that all this is only an issue for console applications that you test-run from Visual Studio — if you are writing a Windows application, the window displayed by the application will automatically remain onscreen until you exit it. Similarly, if you run a console application from the command-line prompt, you won't have any problems about the window disappearing.

### Other files created

The `Program.cs` source code file isn't the only file that Visual Studio has created for you. If you take a look in the folder in which you asked Visual Studio to create your project, you will see not just the C# file, but a complete directory structure that looks like what is shown in Figure 14-9.

The two folders, `bin` and `obj`, store compiled and intermediate files. Subfolders of `obj` hold various temporary or intermediate files; subfolders of `bin` hold the compiled assemblies.

# Visual Studio 2005

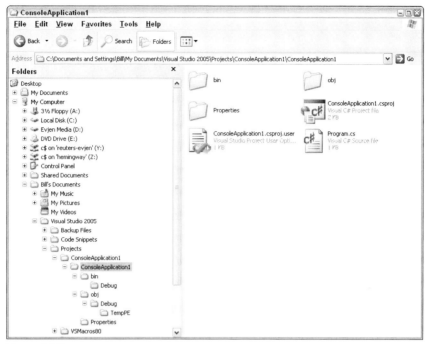

**Figure 14-9**

*Traditionally, Visual Basic developers would simply write the code and then run it. Before shipping, the code would then have to be compiled into an executable; Visual Basic tended to hide the process of compilation when debugging. In C#, it's more explicit: to run the code, you have to compile (or build) it first, which means an assembly must be created somewhere.*

The remaining files in the project's main folder, `ConsoleApplication1`, are there for Visual Studio's benefit. They contain information about the project (for example, the files it contains) so that Visual Studio knows how to have the project compiled and how to read it in the next time you open the project.

## Solutions and Projects

One important distinction you must understand is that between a project and a solution:

- ❏ A *project* is a set of all the source code files and resources that will compile into a single assembly (or in some cases, a single module). For example, a project might be a class library or a Windows GUI application.

- ❏ A *solution* is the set of all the projects that make up a particular software package (application).

To understand this distinction, look at what happens when you ship a project—the project consists of more than one assembly. For example, you might have a user interface, custom controls, and other components that ship as libraries of the parts of the application. You might even have a different user interface

383

for administrators. Each of these parts of the application might be contained in a separate assembly, and hence, they are regarded by Visual Studio as a separate project. However, it is quite likely that you will be coding these projects in parallel and in conjunction with each other. Thus, it is quite useful to be able to edit them all as one single unit in Visual Studio. Visual Studio allows this by regarding all the projects as forming one solution, and treats the solution as the unit that it reads in and allows you to work on.

Up until now we have been loosely talking about creating a console project. In fact, in the example you are working on, Visual Studio has actually created a solution for you — though this particular solution contains just one project. You can see the situation in a window in Visual Studio known as the Solution Explorer (see Figure 14-10), which contains a tree structure that defines your solution.

**Figure 14-10**

Figure 14-10 shows that the project contains your source file, `Program.cs`, as well as another C# source file, `AssemblyInfo.cs` (found in the Properties folder), which allows you to provide information that describes the assembly as well as the ability to specify versioning information. (You look at this file in detail in Chapter 15, "Assemblies.") The Solution Explorer also indicates the assemblies that your project references according to namespace. You can see this by expanding the References folder in the Solution Explorer.

If you haven't changed any of the default settings in Visual Studio, you will probably find the Solution Explorer in the top-right corner of your screen. If you can't see it, just go to the View menu and select Solution Explorer.

The solution is described by a file with the extension `.sln` — in this example, it's `Console Application1.sln`. The project is described by various other files in the project's main folder. If you attempt to edit these files using Notepad, you'll find that they are mostly plain text files; and, in accordance with the principle that .NET and .NET tools rely on open standards wherever possible, they are mostly in XML format.

> *C++ developers will recognize that a Visual Studio solution corresponds to an old Visual C++ project workspace (stored in a `.dsw` file) and a Visual Studio project corresponds to an old C++ project (`.dsp` file). By contrast, Visual Basic developers will recognize that a solution corresponds to an old Visual Basic project group (`.vbg` file), and the .NET project corresponds to an old Visual Basic project (`.vbp` file). Visual Studio differs from the old Visual Basic IDE in that it always creates a solution for you automatically. In Visual Studio 6, Visual Basic developers would get a project; however, they would have to request a project group from the IDE separately.*

# Visual Studio 2005

## Adding another project to the solution

As you work through the following sections you will see how Visual Studio works with Windows applications as well as console ones. To that end, you will create a Windows project called BasicForm that you will add to your current solution, BasicConsoleApp.

*This means you'll end up with a solution containing a Windows application and a console application. That's not a very common scenario — you're more likely to have one application and a number of libraries — but it allows you to see more code! You might, however, create a solution like this if, for example, you are writing a utility that you want to run either as a Windows application or as a command-line utility.*

You can create the new project in two ways. You can select New Project from the File menu (as you've done already) or you can select Add ⇨ New Project from the File menu. If you select New Project from the File menu, this will bring up the familiar New Project dialog box; this time, however, you'll notice a drop-down list near the bottom of the dialog box (see Figure 14-11). This selection allows you to specify whether you want to create a new solution for this project or add it to the existing solution.

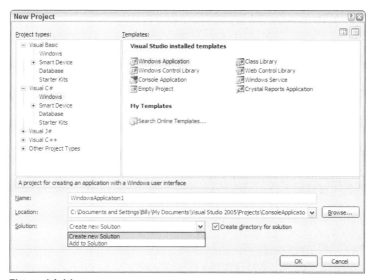

Figure 14-11

If you select Add to Solution, you will get a new project so that the ConsoleApplication1 solution now contains a console application and a Windows application.

*In accordance with the language-independence of Visual Studio, the new project doesn't have to be a C# project. It's perfectly acceptable to put a C# project, a Visual Basic 2005 project, and a C++ project in the same solution. But we'll stick with C# here since this is a C# book!*

Of course, this means that ConsoleApplication1 isn't really an appropriate name for the solution anymore! To change the name, you can right-click on the name of the solution and select Rename from the context menu. Call the new solution DemoSolution. The Solution Explorer window now looks like Figure 14-12.

385

Chapter 14

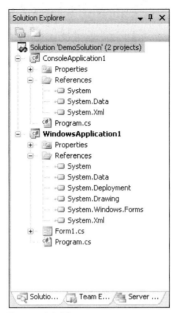

**Figure 14-12**

You can see from this that Visual Studio has made your newly added Windows project automatically reference some of the extra base classes that are important for Windows Forms functionality.

You'll notice if you look in Windows Explorer that the name of the solution file has changed to DemoSolution.sln. In general, if you want to rename any files, the Solution Explorer window is the best place to do so, because Visual Studio will then automatically update any references to that file in the other project files. If you just rename files using Windows Explorer, you might find you break the solution because Visual Studio won't be able to locate all the files it needs to read in. You will then have to manually edit the project and solution files to update the file references.

## Setting the startup project

One thing you'll need to bear in mind if you have multiple projects in a solution is that only one of them can be run at a time! When you compile the solution, all the projects in it will be compiled. However, you have to specify which one is the one you want Visual Studio to start running when you press F5 or select Start. If you have one executable and several libraries that it calls, then this will clearly be the executable. In this case, where you have two independent executables in the project, you'd simply have to debug each in turn.

You can tell Visual Studio which project to run by right-clicking that project in the Solution Explorer window and selecting Set as Startup Project from the context menu. You can tell which one is the current startup project — it is the one that appears in bold in the Solution Explorer window (WindowsApplication1 in Figure 14-12).

## Windows Application Code

A Windows application contains a lot more code right from the start than a console application when Visual Studio first creates it. That's because creating a window is an intrinsically more complex process. Chapter 23 discusses the code for a Windows application in detail; for now, take a look at the code in the `Form1` class in the WindowsApplication1 project to see for yourself how much is auto-generated.

## Reading in Visual Studio 6 Projects

If you are coding in C#, you won't need to read in any old Visual Studio 6 projects because C# doesn't exist in Visual Studio 6. However, language interoperability is a key part of the .NET Framework, so you might want your C# code to work alongside code written in Visual Basic or in C++. In that situation, you might have to edit projects that were created with Visual Studio 6.

Visual Studio has no problems reading in and upgrading Visual Studio 6 projects and workspaces. The situation is different for C++, Visual Basic, and J++ projects:

❑ In Visual C++, no change to the source code is needed. All your old Visual C++ code still works fine with the new C++ compiler. Obviously it is not managed code, but it will still compile to code that runs outside the .NET runtime; if you want your code to integrate with the .NET Framework, you will need to edit it. If you get Visual Studio to read in an old Visual C++ project, it will simply add a new solution file and updated project files. It will leave the old `.dsw` and `.dsp` files unchanged so that the project can still be edited by Visual Studio 6, if necessary.

❑ In the case of Visual Basic, things are a bit more complicated. As mentioned in Chapter 1, ".NET Architecture," although Visual Basic 2005 has been designed very much around Visual Basic 6.0 and shares much of the same syntax, it is in many ways a new language. In Visual Basic 6.0, the source code largely consisted of the event handlers for the controls. In Visual Basic 2005, the code that actually instantiates the main window and many of its controls is not part of Visual Basic but is instead hidden behind the scenes as part of the configuration of your project. In contrast, Visual Basic 2005 works in the same way as C#, by putting the entire program out in the open as source code, so all the code that displays the main window and all the controls on it needs to be in the source file. Also, like C#, Visual Basic 2005 requires everything to be object-oriented and part of a class, whereas VB didn't even recognize the concept of classes in the .NET sense. If you try to read a Visual Basic project with Visual Studio, it will have to upgrade the entire source code to Visual Basic 2005 before it can handle it—and this involves making a lot of changes to the Visual Basic code. Visual Studio can, to a large extent, make these changes automatically and will then create a new Visual Basic 2005 solution for you. You will find that the source code it gives you looks very different from the corresponding Visual Basic code, and you will still need to check carefully through the generated code to make sure the project still works correctly. You might even find areas of code where Visual Studio has left comments to the effect that it can't figure out exactly what you wanted the code to do, and you might have to edit the code manually.

❑ As far as Microsoft is concerned, J++ is now an obsolete language and is not directly supported in .NET. However, in order that existing J++ code can continue to operate, separate tools are available to allow J++ code to work with .NET. Visual Studio 2005 includes the J# development environment and will work with J++ code. There is also a utility that can convert legacy J++ code to C# code—similar to the Visual Basic 6 to Visual Basic 2005 upgrade facility. These tools are grouped under the name JUMP (Java User Migration Path) and at the time of writing are neither bundled with .NET nor Visual Studio; you can download them instead at http://msdn.microsoft.com/vjsharp/jump/default.aspx.

# Chapter 14

## Exploring and Coding a Project

This section looks at the features that Visual Studio provides to help you add code to your project.

### The folding editor

One really exciting feature of Visual Studio is its use of a folding editor as its default code editor (see Figure 14-13).

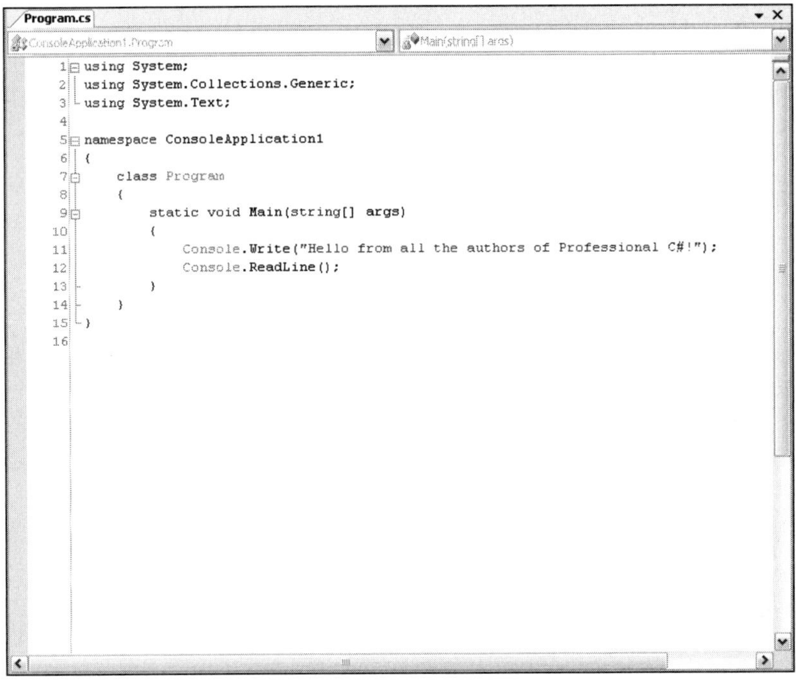

**Figure 14-13**

Figure 14-13 shows the code for the console application that you generated earlier. Notice those little minus signs on the left-hand side of the window. These signs mark the points where the editor assumes a new block of code (or documentation comment) begins. You can click these icons to close up the view of the corresponding block of code just as you would close a node in a tree control (see Figure 14-14).

This means that while you are editing you can focus on just the areas of code you want to look at, and you can hide the bits of code you're not interested in. If you don't like the way the editor has chosen to block off your code, you can indicate your own blocks of collapsing code with the C# preprocessor directives, #region and #endregion, which were examined earlier in the book. For example, if you wanted to collapse the code inside the Main() method, you would add the code shown in Figure 14-15.

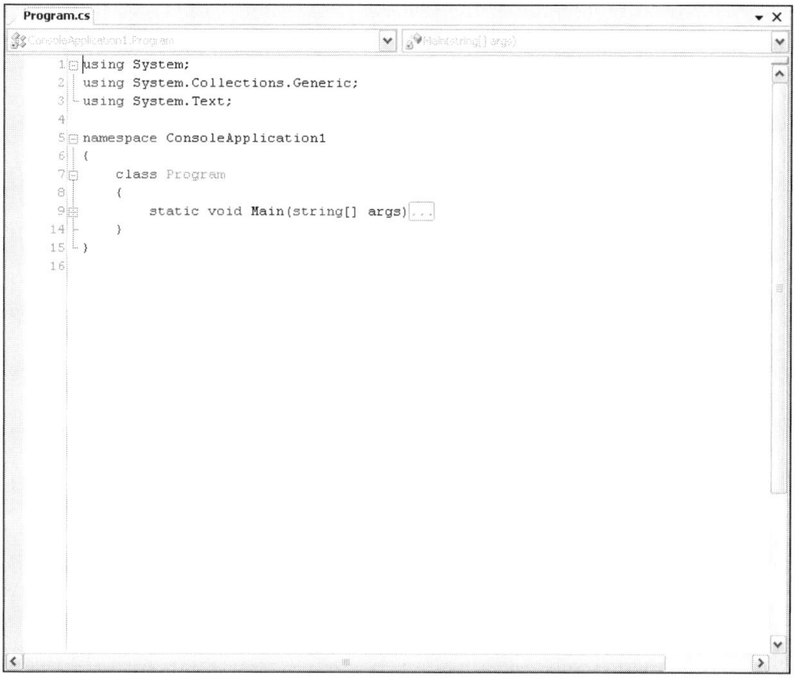

# Visual Studio 2005

Figure 14-14

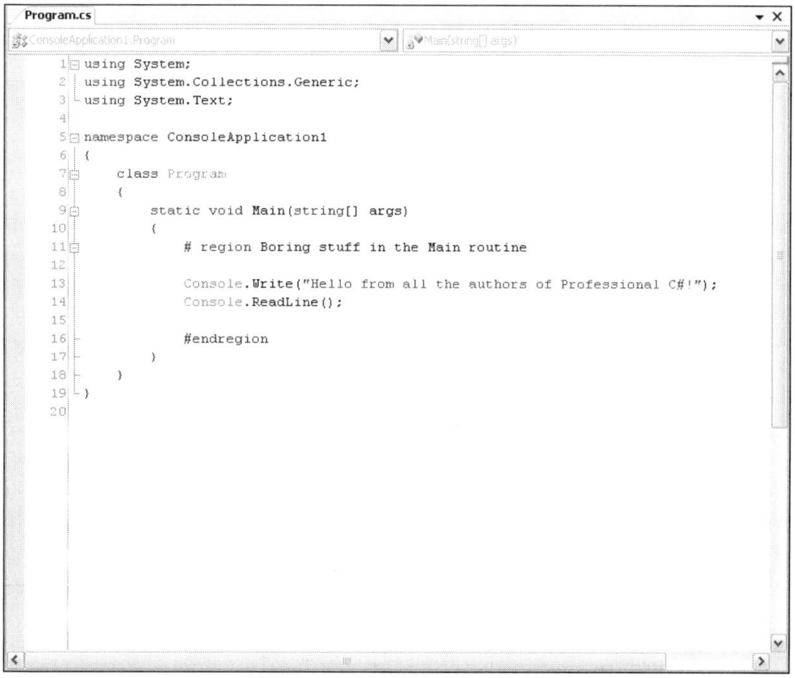

Figure 14-15

## Chapter 14

The code editor will automatically detect the `#region` block and place a new minus sign by the `#region` directive as shown in Figure 14-15, allowing you to close the region. Enclosing this code in a region means that you can get the editor to close the block of code (see Figure 14-16), marking the area with the comment you specified in the `#region` directive. The compiler, however, ignores the directives and compiles the `Main()` method as normal.

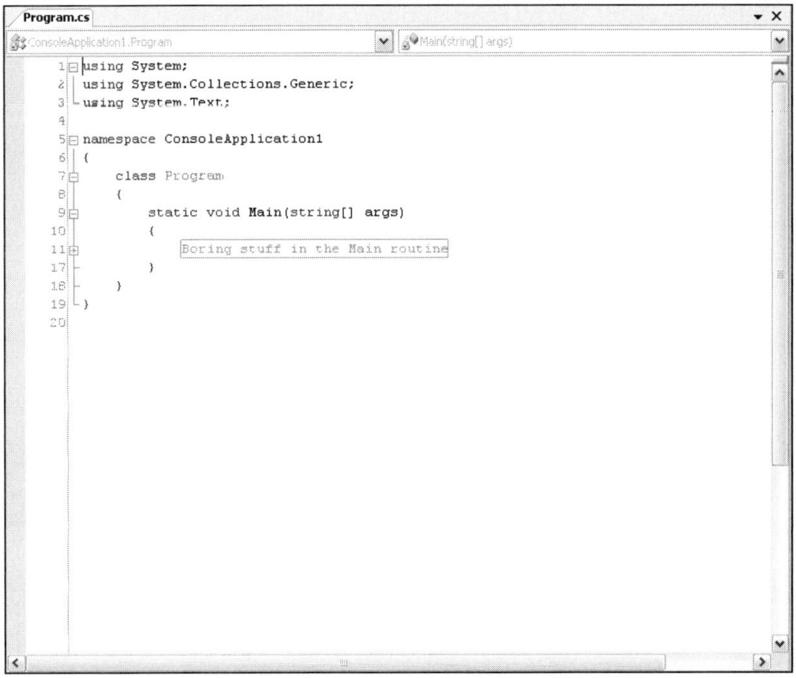

**Figure 14-16**

In addition to the folding editor feature, Visual Studio's code editor brings across all the familiar functionality from Visual Studio 6. In particular it features IntelliSense, which not only saves you typing, but also ensures that you use the correct parameters. C++ developers will notice that the Visual Studio IntelliSense feature is a bit more robust than the Visual Studio 6 version and also works more quickly. You will also notice that IntelliSense has been improved in Visual Studio 2005. It is now smarter in that it remembers your preferred choices and starts off with this choice instead of starting directly at the beginning of the sometimes rather lengthy lists that IntelliSense can now provide.

The code editor also performs some syntax checking on your code and underlines most syntax errors with a short wavy line, even before you compile the code. Hovering the mouse pointer over the underlined text brings up a small box telling you what the error is. Visual Basic developers have been familiar with this feature, known as *design-time debugging*, for years; now C# and C++ developers can benefit from it as well.

## Visual Studio 2005

### Other windows

In addition to the code editor, Visual Studio provides a number of other windows that allow you to view your project from different points of view.

*The rest of this section describes a number of other windows. If one of these windows is not visible on your screen, you can select it from the View menu. To show the Design View and Code Editor, right-click the file name in the Solution Explorer and select View Designer or View Code from the context menu, or select the item from the toolbar at the top of the Solution Explorer. The Design View and Code Editor both share the same tabbed window.*

### The Design View window

If you are designing a user interface application, such as a Windows application, Windows control library, or an ASP.NET application, you will use the Design View window. This window presents a visual overview of what your form will look like. You normally use the Design View window in conjunction with a window known as the Toolbox. The Toolbox contains a large number of .NET components that you can drag onto your program (see Figure 14-17).

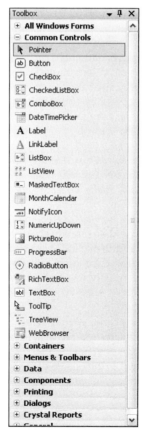

Figure 14-17

391

# Chapter 14

The principle of the Toolbox was applied in all development environments in Visual Studio 6, but with .NET the number of components available from the Toolbox has vastly increased. The categories of components available through the Toolbox depend, to some extent, on the type of project you are editing — for example, you'll get a far wider range when you are editing the WindowsApplication1 project in the DemoSolution solution than you do when you are editing the ConsoleApplication1 project. The most important ranges of items available include the following:

- ❑ **Data.** Classes that allow you to connect to data sources and manage the data they contain. Here you will find components for working with Microsoft SQL Server, Oracle, and any OleDb data source.

- ❑ **Windows Forms Controls (labeled as Common Controls).** Classes that represent visual controls such as text boxes, list boxes, or tree views for working with thick-client applications.

- ❑ **Web Forms Controls (labeled as Standard).** Classes that basically do the same thing as Windows controls, but that work in the context of Web browsers, and that work by sending HTML output to simulate the controls to the browser.

- ❑ **Components.** Miscellaneous .NET classes that perform various useful tasks on your machine, such as connecting to directory services or to the event log.

You can also add your own custom categories to the Toolbox by right-clicking on any category and selecting Add Tab from the context menu. You can also place other tools in the Toolbox by selecting Choose Items from the same context menu — this is particularly useful for adding your favorite COM components and ActiveX controls, which are not present in the Toolbox by default. If you add a COM control, you can still click to place it in your project just as you would with a .NET control. Visual Studio automatically adds all the required COM interoperability code to allow your project to call up the control. In this case, what is actually added to your project is a .NET control that Visual Studio creates behind the scenes and that acts as a wrapper for your COM control.

> *C++ developers will recognize the Toolbox as Visual Studio's (much enhanced) version of the resource editor. Visual Basic developers might not be that impressed at first; after all, Visual Studio 6 also has a Toolbox. However, the Toolbox in Visual Studio has a dramatically different effect on your source code than its precursor.*

To see how the Toolbox works, place a text box in your basic form project. You simply click the TextBox control contained within the Toolbox and then click again to place it in the form in the design view (or if you prefer, you can simply drag and drop the control directly onto the design surface). Now the design view looks like Figure 14-18, showing roughly what WindowsApplication1 will look like if you compile and run it.

If you look at the code view of your form, you see that Visual Studio 2005 doesn't add the code that instantiates a `TextBox` object to go on the form directly here as it did in previous versions of the IDE. Instead, you will need to expand the plus sign next to `Form1.cs` in the Visual Studio Solution Explorer. Here you will find a file that is dedicated to the design of the form and the controls that are placed on the form — `Form1.Designer.cs`. In this class file, you will find a new member variable in the `Form1` class:

```
partial class Form1
{
    private System.Windows.Forms.TextBox textBox1;
```

# Visual Studio 2005

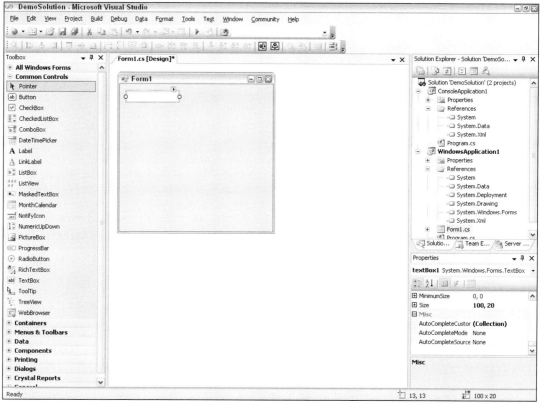

Figure 14-18

There is also some code to initialize it in the method, `InitializeComponent()`, which is called from the `Form1` constructor:

```
/// <summary>
/// Required method for Designer support - do not modify
/// the contents of this method with the code editor.
/// </summary>
private void InitializeComponent()
{
   this.textBox1 = new System.Windows.Forms.TextBox();
   this.SuspendLayout();
   //
   // textBox1
   //
   this.textBox1.Location = new System.Drawing.Point(13, 13);
   this.textBox1.Name = "textBox1";
   this.textBox1.Size = new System.Drawing.Size(100, 20);
   this.textBox1.TabIndex = 0;
   //
   // Form1
   //
```

```csharp
            this.AutoScaleDimensions = new System.Drawing.SizeF(6F, 13F);
            this.AutoScaleMode = System.Windows.Forms.AutoScaleMode.Font;
            this.ClientSize = new System.Drawing.Size(292, 273);
            this.Controls.Add(this.textBox1);
            this.Name = "Form1";
            this.Text = "Form1";
            this.ResumeLayout(false);
            this.PerformLayout();

        }
```

In one sense, there is no difference between the code editor and the design view; they simply present different views of the same code. What actually happened when you clicked to add the `TextBox` into the design view is that the editor placed the preceding extra code in your C# source file for you. The design view simply reflects this change because Visual Studio is able to read your source code and determine from it what controls should be around when the application starts up. This is a fundamental shift from the old Visual Basic way of looking at things, in which everything was based around the visual design. Now, your C# source code is what fundamentally controls your application, and the design view is just a different way of viewing the source code. Incidentally, if you do write any Visual Basic 2005 code with Visual Studio, you'll find the same principles at work.

If you'd wanted to, you could have worked the other way around; if you manually added the same code to your C# source files, Visual Studio would have automatically detected from the code that your application contained a `TextBox` control, and would have shown it in the design view at the designated position. It is best to add these controls visually, and let Visual Studio handle the initial code generation — it's a lot quicker and less error-prone to click the mouse button a couple of times than to type a few lines of code!

Another reason for adding these controls visually is that, to recognize that they are there, Visual Studio does need the relevant code to conform to certain criteria — and code that you write by hand might not do so. In particular, you'll notice that the `InitializeComponent()` method that contains the code to initialize the `TextBox` is commented to warn you against modifying it. That's because this is the method that Visual Studio looks at in order to determine what controls are around when your application starts up. If you create and define a control somewhere else in your code, Visual Studio won't be aware of it, and you won't be able to edit it in the design view or certain other useful windows.

In fact, despite the warnings, you can modify the code in `InitializeComponent()`, provided you are careful. There's generally no harm in changing the values of some of the properties, for example, so that a control displays different text or so that it is a different size. In practice, the developer studio is pretty robust when it comes to working around any other code you place in this method. Just be aware that if you make too many changes to `InitializeComponent()`, you do run the risk that Visual Studio won't recognize some of your controls. We should stress that this won't affect your application whatsoever when it is compiled, but it might disable some of the editing features of Visual Studio for those controls. Hence, if you want to add any other substantial initialization, it's probably better to do so in the `Form1` constructor or in some other method.

## The Properties window

This is another window that has its origins in the old Visual Basic IDE. You know from the first part of the book that .NET classes can implement properties. In fact, as you'll discover when building Windows Forms (see Chapter 23), the .NET base classes that represent forms and controls have a lot of properties that define their action or appearance—properties such as Width, Height, Enabled (whether the user can type input to the control), and Text (the text displayed by the control)—and Visual Studio knows about many of these properties. The Properties window, shown in Figure 14-19, displays and allows you to edit the initial values of most of these properties for the controls that Visual Studio has been able to detect by reading your source code.

**Figure 14-19**

> The Properties window can also show events. You can view events for what you are focused on in the IDE or selected in the drop-down list box directly in the Properties window by clicking the icon that looks like a lightning flash at the top of the window.

At the top of the Properties window is a list box that allows you to select which control you want to view. In the example in this chapter, you've selected Form1, the main form class for your WindowsApplication1 project, and have edited the text to "Basic Form—Hello!" If you now check the source code you can see that what you have actually done is edit the source code—using a friendlier user interface:

```
this.AutoScaleDimensions = new System.Drawing.SizeF(6F, 13F);
this.AutoScaleMode = System.Windows.Forms.AutoScaleMode.Font;
this.ClientSize = new System.Drawing.Size(292, 273);
this.Controls.Add(this.textBox1);
this.Name = "Form1";
this.Text = "Basic Form - Hello";
this.ResumeLayout(false);
this.PerformLayout();
```

# Chapter 14

Not all the properties shown in the Properties window are explicitly mentioned in your source code. For those that aren't, Visual Studio will display the default values that were set when the form was created and that are set when the form is actually initialized. Obviously, if you change a value for one of these properties in the Properties window, a statement explicitly setting that property will magically appear in your source code — and vice versa. It is interesting to note that if a property is changed from its original value, this property will then appear in bold type within the list box of the Properties window. Sometimes double-clicking the property in the Properties window returns the value back to its original value.

The Properties window provides a convenient way to get a broad overview of the appearance and properties of a particular control or window.

> *It is interesting to note that the Properties window is implemented as a* `System.Windows.Forms.PropertyGrid` *instance, which will internally use the reflection technology described in Chapter 11, "Reflection," to identify the properties and property values to display.*

## The Class View window

Unlike the Properties window, the Class View window, shown in Figure 14-20, owes its origins to the C++ (and J++) developer environments. This window will be new to Visual Basic developers because Visual Basic 6 did not even support the concept of the class, other than in the sense of a COM component. The Class View is not actually treated by Visual Studio as a window in its own right — rather it is an additional tab to the Solution Explorer window. By default, the Class View will not even appear in the Visual Studio Solution Explorer. To invoke the Class View, select View ➪ Other Windows ➪ Class View. The Class View (see Figure 14-20) shows the hierarchy of the namespaces and classes in your code. It gives you a tree view that you can expand to see what namespaces contain what classes and what classes contain what members.

Figure 14-20

A nice feature of the Class View is that if you right-click the name of any item for which you have access to the source code, the context menu features the Go To Definition option, which takes you to the definition of the item in the code editor. Alternatively, you can do this by double-clicking the item in Class View (or, indeed, by right-clicking the item you want in the source code editor and choosing the same option from the resulting context menu). The context menu also gives you the option to add a field, method, property, or indexer to a class. This means that you specify the details of the relevant member in a dialog box, and the code gets added for you. This might not be that useful in the case of fields or methods, which can be quickly added to your code; however, you might find this feature helpful in the case of properties and indexers, where it can save you quite a bit of typing.

### The Object Browser window

One important aspect of programming in the .NET environment is being able to find out what methods and other code items are available in the base classes and any other libraries that you are referencing from your assembly. This feature is available through a window called the Object Browser. You can access this window by selecting Object Browser from the View menu in Visual Studio 2005.

The Object Browser window is quite similar to the Class View window in that it displays a tree view that gives the class structure of your application, allowing you to inspect the members of each class. The user interface is slightly different in that it displays class members in a separate pane rather than in the tree view itself. The real difference is that it lets you look at not just the namespaces and classes in your project but also the ones in all the assemblies referenced by the project. Figure 14-21 shows the Object Browser viewing the `SystemException` class from the .NET base classes.

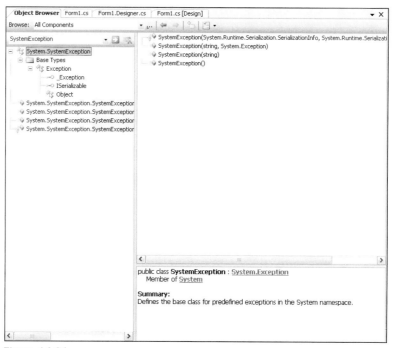

Figure 14-21

## Chapter 14

The only point you have to watch with the Object Browser is that it groups classes by the assembly in which they are located first and by namespace second. Unfortunately, because namespaces for the base classes are often spread across several assemblies, this means you might have trouble locating a particular class unless you know what assembly it is in.

The Object Browser is there to view .NET objects. If for any reason you want to investigate installed COM objects, you'll find that the OLEView tool previously used in the C++ IDE is still available — it's located in the folder C:\Program Files\Microsoft Visual Studio 8\Common7\Tools\Bin along with several other similar utilities.

> *Visual Basic developers should not confuse the .NET Object Browser with the Object Browser of the Visual Basic 6 IDE. The .NET Object Browser is there to view .NET classes, whereas the tool of that name in Visual Basic 6 is used to view COM components. If you want the functionality of the old Object Browser, you should now use the OLEView tool.*

### The Server Explorer window

You can use the Server Explorer window, shown in Figure 14-22, to find out about aspects of the computers in your network while coding.

**Figure 14-22**

As you can see from the screenshot, among the things you can access through the Server Explorer are database connections, information about services, event logs, and more.

The Server Explorer is linked to the Properties window so that if you open the Services node, for example, and click a particular service, the properties of that service will be displayed in the Properties window.

### Pin buttons

While exploring Visual Studio, you might have noticed that many of the windows have some interesting functionality more reminiscent of toolbars. In particular, apart from the code editor, they can all be docked. Another, very new, feature of them is that when they are docked, they have an extra icon that looks like a pin next to the minimize button in the top-right corner of each window. This icon really does act like a pin — it can be used to pin the windows open. When they are pinned (the pin is displayed vertically), they behave just like the regular windows that you are used to. When they are unpinned, however (the pin is displayed horizontally), they only remain open as long as they have the focus. As soon as they lose the focus (because you clicked or moved your mouse somewhere else) they smoothly retreat into the main border around the entire Visual Studio application. (You can also feel the speed of your computer by how fast or slow they open and close).

Pinning and unpinning windows provides another way of making the best use of the limited space on your screen. It's not really been seen a great deal in Windows before, though a few third-party applications such as PaintShop Pro have used similar concepts. Pinned windows have, however, been around on many Unix-based systems for quite a while.

## Building a Project

This section examines the options that Visual Studio gives you for building your project.

### Building, compiling, and making

Before examining the various build options, it's important to clarify some terminology. You'll often see three different terms used in connection with the process of getting from your source code to some sort of executable code: compiling, building, and making. The origin of these various terms comes from the fact that until recently, the process of getting from source code to executable code involved more than one step (and this is still the case in C++). This was due in large part to the number of source files in a program. In C++, for example, each source file needs to be compiled individually. This leads to what are known as object files, each containing something like executable code, but where each object file relates to only one source file. In order to generate an executable, these object files need to be linked together, a process that is officially known as linking. The combined process was usually referred to — at least on the Windows platform — as building your code. However, in C# terms the compiler is more sophisticated and is able to read in and treat all your source files as one block. Hence, there isn't really a separate linking stage, so in the context of C# the terms *compile* and *build* are used interchangeably.

In addition to this, the term *make* basically means the same as *build*, though it's not really used in the context of C#. The term originated on old mainframe systems on which, when a project was composed of many source files, a separate file would be written that contained instructions to the compiler on how to build a project — which files to include and what libraries to link to and so on. This file was generally known as a make file and is still quite standard on Unix systems. Make files are not normally needed on Windows, though you can still write them (or get Visual Studio to generate them) if you need to.

### Debug and release builds

The idea of having separate builds is very familiar to C++ developers and less so to those with a Visual Basic background. The point here is that when you are debugging you typically want your executable to behave differently than it does when you are ready to ship the software. When you are ready to ship your software, you want the size of the executable to be as small as possible and the executable itself to be as fast as possible. Unfortunately, these requirements aren't really compatible with your needs when you are debugging code, as explained in the following sections.

#### Optimization

High performance is achieved partly by the compiler doing a lot of optimizations on the code. This means that the compiler actively looks at your source code as it's compiling in order to identify places where it can modify the precise details of what you're doing in a way that doesn't change the overall effect, but that makes things more efficient. For example, if the compiler encountered the following source code:

```
double InchesToCm(double Ins)
{
    return Ins*2.54;
}

// later on in the code

Y = InchesToCm(X);
```

it might replace it with this:

```
Y = X * 2.54;
```

Or it might replace this code

```
{
    string Message = "Hi";
    Console.WriteLine(Message);
}
```

with this:

```
Console.WriteLine("Hi");
```

By doing so, it bypasses having to declare an unnecessary object reference in the process.

It's not possible to exactly pin down what optimizations the C# compiler does — nor whether the two previous examples actually would occur with any particular example, because those kinds of details are not documented (chances are that for managed languages such as C#, the previous optimizations would occur at JIT compilation time, not when the C# compiler compiles source code to assembly). For obvious commercial reasons, companies that write compilers are usually quite reluctant to give too many details about the tricks that their compilers use. We should stress that optimizations do not affect your source code — they affect only the contents of the executable code. However, the previous examples should give you a good idea of what to expect from optimizations.

The problem is that although optimizations like the previous ones help a great deal in making your code run faster, they aren't that helpful for debugging. Suppose with the first example that you want to set a breakpoint inside the `InchesToCm()` method to see what's going on in there. How can you possibly do that if the executable code doesn't actually have an `InchesToCm()` method because the compiler has removed it? And how can you set a watch on the `Message` variable when that doesn't exist in the compiled code either?

## Debugger symbols

When you're debugging, you often have to look at values of variables, and you will specify them by their source code names. The trouble is that executable code generally doesn't contain those names — the compiler replaces the names with memory addresses. .NET has modified this situation somewhat, to the

# Visual Studio 2005

extent that certain items in assemblies are stored with their names, but this is only true of a small minority of items — such as public classes and methods — and those names will still be removed when the assembly is JIT-compiled. Asking the debugger to tell you what the value is in the variable called `HeightInInches` isn't going to get you very far if, when the debugger examines the executable code, it sees only addresses and no reference to the name `HeightInInches` anywhere. So, to debug properly, you need to have extra debugging information made available in the executable. This information includes, among other things, names of variables and line information that allows the debugger to match up which executable machine assembly language instructions correspond to those of your original source code instructions. You won't, however, want that information in a release build, both for commercial reasons (debugging information makes it a lot easier for other people to disassemble your code) and because it increases the size of the executable.

### Extra source code debugging commands

A related issue is that quite often while you are debugging there will be extra lines in your code to display crucial debugging-related information. Obviously you want the relevant commands removed entirely from the executable before you ship the software. You could do this manually, but wouldn't it be so much easier if you could simply mark those statements in some way so that the compiler ignores them when it is compiling your code to be shipped? You've already seen in the first part of the book how this can be done in C# by defining a suitable processor symbol, and possibly using this in conjunction with the `Conditional` attribute, giving you what is known as *conditional compilation*.

What all these factors add up to is that you need to compile almost all commercial software in a slightly different way when debugging, compared to the final product that is shipped. Visual Studio is able to take this into account because, as you have already seen, it stores details of all the options that it is supposed to pass to the compiler when it has your code compiled. All that Visual Studio has to do in order to support different types of builds is to store more than one set of such details. The different sets of build information are referred to as configurations. When you create a project, Visual Studio automatically gives you two configurations, called Debug and Release:

- ❑ The Debug configuration commonly specifies that no optimizations are to take place, extra debugging information is to be present in the executable, and the compiler is to assume that the debug preprocessor symbol `Debug` is present unless it is explicitly `#undefined` in the source code.

- ❑ The Release configuration specifies that the compiler should optimize, that there should be no extra debugging information in the executable, and that the compiler should not assume that any particular preprocessor symbol is present.

You can define your own configurations as well. You might want to do this, for example, if you want to set up professional-level builds and enterprise-level builds so you can ship two versions of the software. In the past, because of issues concerning the Unicode character encodings being supported on Windows NT but not on Windows 95, it was common for C++ projects to feature a Unicode configuration and an MBCS (multibyte character set) configuration.

### *Selecting a configuration*

One obvious question is that, because Visual Studio stores details of more than one configuration, how does it determine which one to use when arranging for a project to be built? The answer is that there is always an active configuration, which is the configuration that will be used when you ask Visual Studio to build a project. (Note that configurations are set for each project rather than for each solution.)

## Chapter 14

By default, when you create a project, the debug configuration is the active configuration. You can change which configuration is the active one by clicking the Build menu option and selecting the Configuration Manager item. It is also available through a drop-down menu in the main Visual Studio toolbar.

### *Editing configurations*

In addition to choosing the active configuration, you can also examine and edit the configurations. To do this, you select the relevant project in the Solution Explorer and then select the Properties from the Project menu. This brings up a very sophisticated dialog box. (Alternatively, you can access the same dialog box by right-clicking the name of the project in the Solution Explorer and then selecting Properties from the context menu.)

This dialog contains a tree view, which allows you to select quite a lot of different general areas to examine or edit. We don't have space to show all of these areas but we will show a couple of the most important ones.

Figure 14-23 shows a tabbed view of the available properties for a particular application. This screenshot shows the general application settings for the ConsoleApplication1 project that you created earlier in the chapter.

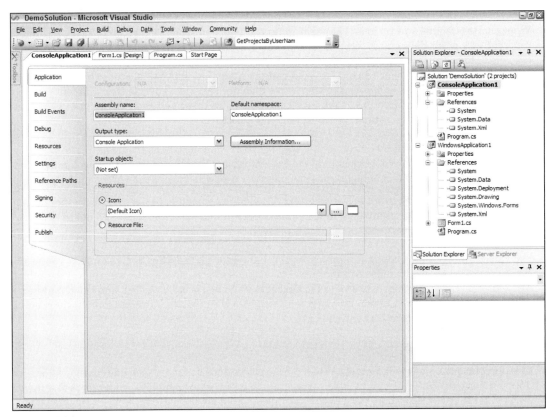

Figure 14-23

# Visual Studio 2005

Among the points to note are that you can select the name of the assembly as well as the type of assembly to be generated. The options here are Console Application, Windows Application, and Class Library. You can, of course, change the assembly type if you want. (Though arguably, if you want, you might wonder why you didn't pick the correct project type at the time that you asked Visual Studio to generate the project for you in the first place!)

Figure 14-24 shows the build configuration properties. You'll notice that a dropdown list near the top of the dialog box allows you to specify which configuration you want to look at. In this case you can see — in the case of the Debug configuration — that the compiler assumes that the DEBUG and TRACE preprocess or symbols have been defined. Also, the code is not optimized and extra debugging information is generated.

In general, it's not that often that you'll have to adjust the configuration settings. However, if you ever do need to use them, you now know the difference between the available configuration properties.

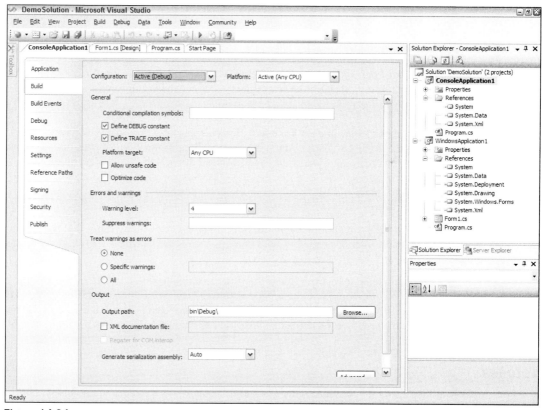

Figure 14-24

403

# Chapter 14

## Debugging

After the long discussion about building and build configurations, you might be surprised to learn that this chapter is not going to spend a great deal of time discussing debugging itself. The reason for that is that the principles and the process of debugging—setting breakpoints and examining the values of variables—isn't really significantly different in Visual Studio from in any of the various Visual Studio 6 IDEs. Instead, this section briefly reviews the features offered by Visual Studio, focusing on those areas that might be new to some developers. It also discusses how to deal with exceptions, because these can cause problems during debugging.

In C#, as in pre-.NET languages, the main technique involved in debugging is simply setting breakpoints and using them to examine what is going on in your code at a certain point in its execution.

### Breakpoints

You can set breakpoints from Visual Studio on any line of your code that is actually executed. The simplest way is to click the line in the code editor, within the shaded area toward the far left of the document window (or press the F9 key when the appropriate line is selected). This sets up a breakpoint on that particular line, which causes execution to break and control to be transferred to the debugger as soon as that line is reached in the execution process. As in previous versions of Visual Studio, a breakpoint is indicated by a large circle to the left of the line in the code editor. Visual Studio also highlights the line by displaying the text and background in a different color. Clicking the circle again removes the breakpoint.

If breaking every time at a particular line isn't adequate for your particular problem, you can also set conditional breakpoints. To do this, select Debug ⇨ Windows ⇨ Breakpoints. This brings up a dialog box asking you for details of the breakpoint you want to set. Among the options available, you can:

- ❏ Specify that execution should break only after the breakpoint has been passed a certain number of times.

- ❏ Specify that the breakpoint should come into effect only every so-many times that the line is reached, for example every twentieth time that a line is executed. (This is useful when debugging large loops.)

- ❏ Set the breakpoints relative to a variable rather than to an instruction. In this case, the value of the variable will be monitored and the breakpoints will be triggered whenever the value of this variable changes. You might find, however, that using this option slows down your code considerably. Checking whether the value of a variable has changed after every instruction adds a lot of processor time.

### Watches

After a breakpoint has been hit you will usually want to investigate the values of variables. The simplest way to do this is to hover the mouse cursor over the name of the variable in the code editor. This causes a little box that shows the value of that variable to pop up, which can also be expanded to greater detail. This is shown in Figure 14-25.

# Visual Studio 2005

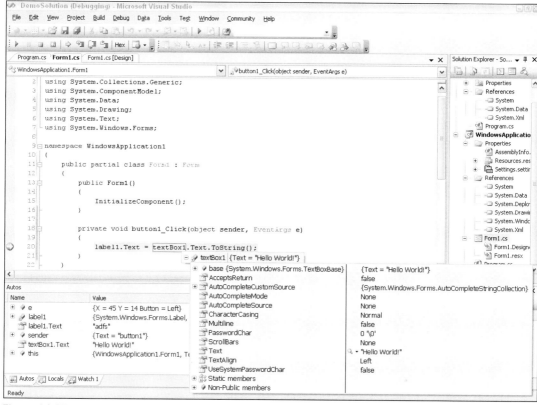

Figure 14-25

However, you might also prefer to use the Watch window to examine the contents of variables. The Watch window (shown in Figure 14-26) is a tabbed window that appears only when the program is running under the debugger.

Variables that are classes or structs are shown with a + icon next to them, which you can click to expand the variable and see the values of its fields.

The three tabs to this window are each designed to monitor different variables:

- **Autos** monitors the last few variables that have been accessed as the program was executing.
- **Locals** monitors variables that are accessible in the method currently being executed.
- **Watch** monitors any variables that you have explicitly specified by typing their names into the Watch window.

405

# Chapter 14

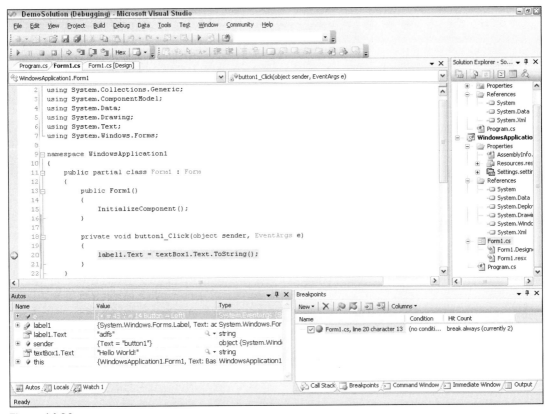

Figure 14-26

## Exceptions

Exceptions are great when you ship your application and in making sure that error conditions are handled in an appropriate way within your application. Used well, they can ensure that your application copes with difficulties well and the user never gets presented with a technical dialog box. Unfortunately, exceptions are not so great when you're trying to debug your application. The problem is twofold:

- ❏ If an exception occurs when you're debugging, you often don't want it to be handled automatically — especially if automatically handling it means retiring gracefully and terminating execution! Rather, you want the debugger to help you find out why the exception has occurred. Of course the trouble is that if you have written good, robust, defensive code, your program will automatically handle almost anything — including the bugs that you want to detect!

- ❏ If an exception occurs that you haven't written a handler for, the .NET runtime will still go off looking for a handler. But by the time it discovers that there isn't one, it will have terminated your program. There won't be a call stack left and you won't be able to look at the values of any of your variables, because they will all have gone out of scope.

Of course, you can set breakpoints in your catch blocks, but that often doesn't help very much because when the `catch` block is reached, flow of execution will, by definition, have exited the corresponding `try` block. That means that the variables you probably wanted to examine the values of in order to find out what's gone wrong will have gone out of scope. You won't even be able to look at the stack trace to find out what method was being executed when the `throw` statement occurred — because control will have left that method. Setting the breakpoints at the `throw` statement will of course solve this, except that if you are coding defensively there will be a lot of `throw` statements in your code. How can you tell which one is the one that threw the exception?

In fact, Visual Studio provides a very neat answer to all of this. If you look into the main Debug menu, you'll find a menu item called Exceptions. This item opens the Exceptions dialog box (see Figure 14-27), which allows you to specify what happens when an exception is thrown. You can choose to continue execution or to stop and start debugging — in which case execution stops and the debugger steps in at the `throw` statement itself.

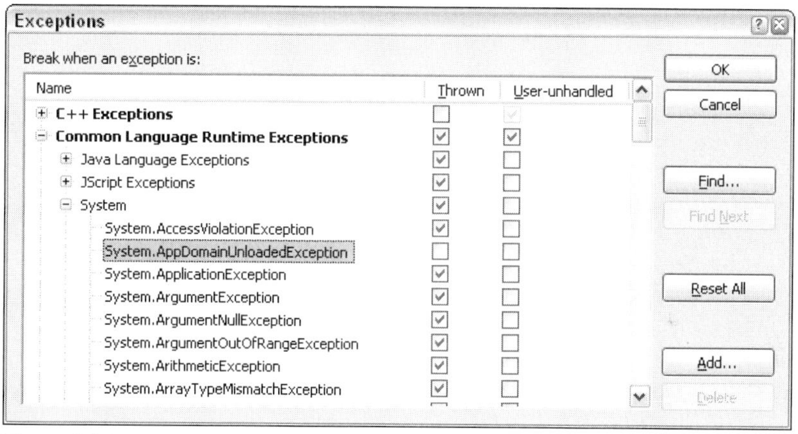

Figure 14-27

What makes this a really powerful tool is that you can customize the behavior according to which class of exception is thrown. For example, in Figure 14-24, we've told Visual Studio to break into the debugger whenever it encounters any exception thrown by a .NET base class, but not to break into the debugger if the exception is an `AppDomainUnloadedException`.

Visual Studio knows about all the exception classes available in the .NET base classes, and also about quite a few exceptions that can be thrown outside the .NET environment. Visual Studio isn't automatically aware of your own custom exception classes that you write, but you can manually add your exception classes to the list and thereby specify which of your exceptions should cause execution to stop immediately. To do this, just click the Add button (which is enabled when you have selected a top-level node from the tree) and type in the name of your exception class.

# Chapter 14

# Refactoring

Many developers develop their applications first for functionality and then, once the functionality is in place, they *re-work* their applications to make them more manageable and more readable. This process is referred to as *refactoring*. Refactoring is the process of reworking code for readability, performance, providing type safety, and lining applications up to better adhere to standard OO (object-oriented) programming practices.

For this reason, the C# environment of Visual Studio 2005 now includes a set of refactoring tools. You can find these tools under the Refactoring option in the Visual Studio menu. To show this in action, create a new class called Car in Visual Studio:

```
using System;
using System.Collections.Generic;
using System.Text;

namespace ConsoleApplication1
{
    public class Car
    {
        public string _color;
        public string _doors;

        public int Go()
        {
            int speedMph = 100;
            return speedMph;
        }
    }
}
```

Now from here, suppose that in the idea of refactoring, you want to change the code a bit so that the _color and the _door variables are encapsulated into public .NET properties. The refactoring capabilities of Visual Studio 2005 allow you to simply right-click either of these properties in the document window and select Refactor ➪ Encapsulate Field. This will pull up the Encapsulate Field dialog shown in Figure 14-28.

From this dialog, you can provide the name of the property and click the OK button. This will turn the selected public field into a private field while also encapsulating the field into a public .NET property. After clicking OK, the code will have been reworked to the following (after redoing both fields):

```
using System;
using System.Collections.Generic;
using System.Text;

namespace ConsoleApplication1
{
    public class Car
    {
```

```
        private string _color;

        public string Color
        {
            get { return _color; }
            set { _color = value; }
        }
        private string _doors;

        public string Doors
        {
            get { return _doors; }
            set { _doors = value; }
        }

        public int Go()
        {
            int speedMph = 100;
            return speedMph;
        }
    }
}
```

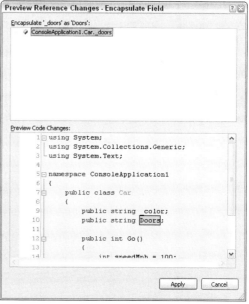

Figure 14-28

As you can see, these wizards make it quite simple to refactor your code not just on one page but for an entire application. Also included are abilities to do the following:

- Rename method names, local variables, fields, and more
- Extract methods from a selection of code
- Extract interfaces based upon a set of existing type members
- Promote local variables to parameters
- Rename or reorder parameters

You will find the new refactoring abilities provided by Visual Studio 2005 a great way to get you the cleaner, more readable, better structured code that you are looking for.

## Summary

This chapter looked at one of the most important programming tools in the .NET environment — Visual Studio 2005. The bulk of the chapter examined how this tool facilitates writing code in C# (and C++ and Visual Basic 2005).

Visual Studio 2005 is one of the easiest development environments to work with in the programming world. You will find that Visual Studio makes RAD development easy to achieve, but at the same time, you can dig deep in the mechanics of how your applications are created. This chapter took a close look at using Visual Studio for everything from refactoring, to reading in Visual Studio 6 projects, to debugging, plus many of the windows available to Visual Studio.

Chapter 15 looks at assemblies in detail.

# 15
# Assemblies

An *assembly* is the .NET term for a deployment and configuration unit. This chapter discusses exactly what assemblies are, how they can be applied, and why they are such a useful feature. In particular, this chapter covers the following topics:

- The innovations offered by assemblies over previous technologies
- How to create and view assemblies
- What the Common Language Specification means, and how cross-language support is made possible
- How to share assemblies

The chapter begins with an overview of assemblies.

## What Are Assemblies?

Before the .NET platform was introduced, you had to deal with the predecessors of assemblies: normal DLLs exporting global functions and COM DLLs exporting COM classes. Microsoft itself introduced the phrase "DLL Hell" to describe traditional problems with DLLs — problems known all too well.

Often applications break because a newly installed application overwrites a DLL that has also been used by another application. Sometimes the installation replaces a new DLL with an old one, because the installation program does not correctly check the versions or the versions are not correctly set. More often, an old DLL is replaced by a new version. Normally, this shouldn't be a problem — the new DLL should be backward-compatible with the old version; however, often that is not the case.

# Chapter 15

Windows 2000 introduced the *side-by-side* feature, which allows the installation of DLLs in the application's directory. With side-by-side, you can install a different version of an already installed, shared DLL to the directory of the application. The `LoadLibrary()` Win32 API call was rewritten so that it first checks for a `.local` file in the application directory. If it is found, the API first checks if a DLL was in the same directory of the application, before the other mechanisms are used to find a shared DLL. This also modifies the fixed path that is in the registry for COM DLLs. Side-by-side is an afterthought and doesn't solve all the issues, and even introduces some new problems with COM DLLs. Another feature of Windows 2000 or later Windows operating systems that deals with DLL Hell is file protection: system DLLs are protected from being overwritten by unauthorized parties. All of these features deal with the symptoms, not with the causes themselves.

The versioning problems of DLLs exist because it's not clear which version of a specific DLL is needed by each application. Dependencies are not tracked or enforced with the traditional DLL architecture. COM DLLs seem to solve a lot of the DLL problems because of a better separation of the implementation and the interface. The interface is a contract between the client and the component, which, according to COM rules, should never be changed and thus cannot break. However, even with COM, changes of implementations can break existing applications.

Side-by-side also supports COM DLLs. If you have ever tried side-by-side with COM DLLs, you have seen that it's just a hack. New problems arise when using side-by-side COM DLLs. If you're installing the same DLL over the old one (without uninstalling the old DLL), what happens when two versions of the same component use different threading configurations? The configuration information is taken from the last installed version. This problem exists because the configuration of a COM component is not stored in the component DLL itself but in the registry.

## *The Answer to DLL Hell*

The .NET platform's answer to DLL Hell and to all of its problems is *assemblies*. Assemblies are self-describing installation units, consisting of one or more files. One assembly could be a single DLL or EXE that includes metadata, or it can be made of different files, for example, resource files, metadata, DLLs, and an EXE. Installation of an assembly can be as simple as copying all of its files. An *xcopy* installation can be done. Another big feature of assemblies is that they can be *private* or *shared*. With COM this differentiation doesn't exist, because practically all COM components are shared. If you search for a COM component in the registry or use OleView, you have to walk through hundreds and hundreds of components. Only a small number of these components were ever meant to be used from more than one application; however, every component must have a global unique identifier (GUID).

There's a big difference between private and shared assemblies. Many developers will be happy with just private assemblies. No special management, registration, versioning, and so on is needed with private assemblies. The only application that could have version problems with private assemblies is your own application. The private components you use within your application are installed at the same time as the application itself. Local application directories are used for the assemblies of the components, so you shouldn't have any versioning problems. No other application will ever overwrite your private assemblies. Of course it is still a good idea to use version numbers for private assemblies too. This helps a lot with code changes, but it's not a requirement of .NET.

With private assemblies you can still have versioning problems during development time. For example, if a component you use in your application references version 1 of assembly X, and you use version 2 of assembly X in your application, which version of the assembly is copied to your application directory?

# Assemblies

The answer depends on what assembly you have referenced first—this versioning problem must be solved during development time. On the installed system, a hot fix can be easily applied to an application by simply replacing a private assembly with a new version. The only application that could have problems with the new version is the one where this fix is applied, because no other applications can be influenced.

When using shared assemblies, several applications can use this assembly and have a dependency on it. With shared assemblies, many rules must be fulfilled—a shared assembly must have a special version number, a unique name, and usually it's installed in the *global assembly cache*.

## Features of Assemblies

The features of assemblies can be summarized as follows:

- Assemblies are *self-describing*. It's no longer necessary to pay attention to registry keys for apartments, to get the type library from some other place, and so on. Assemblies include metadata that describes the assembly. The metadata includes the types exported from the assembly and a manifest; the next section describes the function of a manifest.

- *Version dependencies* are recorded inside an assembly manifest. By storing the version of any referenced assemblies in the manifest of the assembly, you are able to know exactly the version number of the referenced assembly that was used during development. The version of the referenced assembly that will be used can be configured by the developer and the system administrator. Later in this chapter, you learn which version policies are available and how they work.

- Assemblies can be loaded *side-by-side*. With Windows 2000 you already have a side-by-side feature where different versions of the same DLL can be used on a system. .NET extends this functionality of Windows 2000, allowing different versions of the same assembly to be used inside a single process! How is this useful? If assembly A references version 1 of the shared assembly Shared, and assembly B uses version 2 of the shared assembly Shared, and you are using both assembly A and B, you need both versions of the shared assembly Shared in your application—and with .NET both versions are loaded and used.

- Application isolation is ensured using *application domains*. With application domains a number of applications can run independently inside a single process. Faults in one application cannot directly affect other applications inside the same process.

- Installation can be as easy as copying the files that belong to an assembly. An xcopy can be enough. This feature is named *no-touch deployment*. However, there are cases in which no-touch deployment cannot be applied, and a normal Windows installation is required. Deployment of applications is discussed in Chapter 18, "Deployment."

## Application Domains and Assemblies

Before .NET, processes were used as isolation boundaries, with every process having its private virtual memory; an application running in one process could not write to the memory of another application and thereby crash the other application. The process was used as an isolation and security boundary between applications. With the .NET architecture you have a new boundary for applications: *application domains*. With managed IL code the runtime can ensure that access to the memory of another application inside a single process can't happen. Multiple applications can run in a single process within multiple application domains (see Figure 15-1).

413

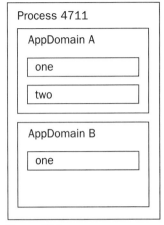
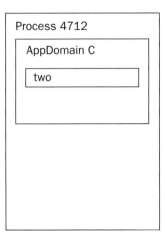

Figure 15-1

An assembly is loaded into an application domain. In Figure 15-1 you can see process 4711 with two application domains. In application domain A, the objects one and two are instantiated, one in assembly One, and two in assembly Two. The second application domain in process 4711 has an instance one. To minimize memory consumption, the code of assemblies is only loaded once into an application domain. Instance and static members are not shared between application domains. It's not possible to directly access objects within another application domain; a proxy is needed instead. So in Figure 15-1, the object one in application domain B cannot directly access the objects one or two in application domain A without a proxy.

*Chapter 29, ".NET Remoting" offers more about proxies and communication across application domains.*

The `AppDomain` class is used to create and terminate application domains, load and unload assemblies and types, and to enumerate assemblies and threads in a domain. In this section, you program a small example to see application domains in action.

First, create a C# Console Application called `AssemblyA`. In the `Main()` method add a `Console.WriteLine()` so that you can see when this method gets called. In addition, add the class `Demo` with a constructor with two `int` values as arguments, which will be used to create instances with the `AppDomain` class. The `AssemblyA.exe` assembly will be loaded from the second application that will be created:

```
using System;

namespace Wrox.ProCSharp.Assemblies.AppDomains
{
    public class Demo
    {
        public Demo(int val1, int val2)
        {
            Console.WriteLine("Constructor with the values {0}, {1}" +
                " in domain {2} called", val1, val2,
                AppDomain.CurrentDomain.FriendlyName);
        }
    }
}
```

```csharp
class Program
{
    static void Main(string[] args)
    {
        Console.WriteLine("Main in domain {0} called",
            AppDomain.CurrentDomain.FriendlyName);
    }
}
```

Running the application produces the output shown in Figure 15-2.

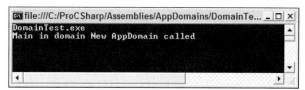

**Figure 15-2**

The second project you create is again a C# Console Application: DomainTest. First, display the name of the current domain using the property FriendlyName of the AppDomain class. With the Create Domain() method, a new application domain with the friendly name New AppDomain is created. Then load the assembly AssemblyA into the new domain and call the Main() method by calling ExecuteAssembly():

```csharp
using System;
namespace Wrox.ProCSharp.Assemblies.AppDomains
{
    class Program
    {
        static void Main(string[] args)
        {
            AppDomain currentDomain = AppDomain.CurrentDomain;
            Console.WriteLine(currentDomain.FriendlyName);
            AppDomain secondDomain =
                AppDomain.CreateDomain("New AppDomain");
            secondDomain.ExecuteAssembly("AssemblyA.exe");
        }
    }
}
```

Before starting the program DomainTest.exe, reference the assembly AssemblyA.exe with the DomainTest project. Referencing the assembly with Visual Studio 2005 copies the assembly to the project directory, so that the assembly can be found. If the assembly cannot be found, a System.IO.FileNotFoundException exception is thrown.

When DomainTest.exe is run, you get the console output shown in Figure 15-3. DomainTest.exe is the friendly name of the first application domain. The second line is the output of the newly loaded assembly in the New AppDomain. With a process viewer, you will not see the process AssemblyA.exe executing because there's no new process created. AssemblyA is loaded into the process DomainTest.exe.

**Figure 15-3**

Instead of calling the `Main()` method in the newly loaded assembly, you can also create a new instance. In the following example, replace the `ExecuteAssembly()` method with a `CreateInstance()`. The first argument is the name of the assembly, `AssemblyA`. The second argument defines the type that should be instantiated: `Wrox.ProCSharp.Assemblies.AppDomains.Demo`. The third argument, `true`, means that case is ignored. `System.Reflection.BindingFlags.CreateInstance` is a binding flag enumeration value to specify that the constructor should be called:

```
AppDomain secondDomain =
    AppDomain.CreateDomain("New AppDomain");
// secondDomain.ExecuteAssembly("AssemblyA.exe");
secondDomain.CreateInstance("AssemblyA",
    "Wrox.ProCSharp.Assemblies.AppDomains.Demo", true,
    System.Reflection.BindingFlags.CreateInstance,
    null, new object[] {7, 3}, null, null, null);
```

Figure 15-4 shows the result of a successful run of the application.

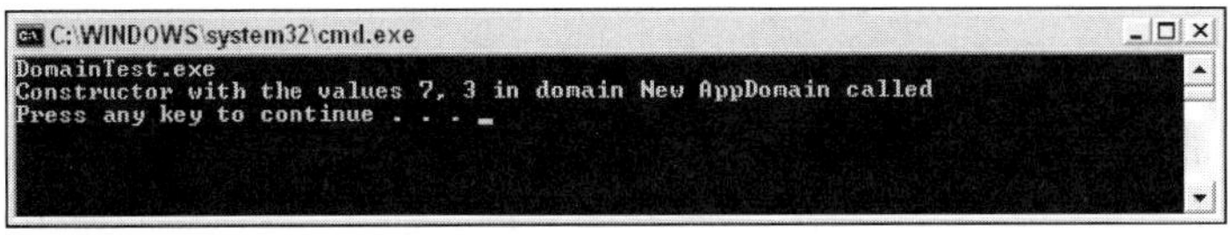

**Figure 15-4**

Now you have seen how to create and call application domains. In runtime hosts, application domains are created automatically. ASP.NET creates an application domain for each Web application that runs on a Web server. Internet Explorer creates application domains in which managed controls will run. For applications, it can be useful to create application domains if you want to unload an assembly. You can unload assemblies only by terminating an application domain.

> Application domains are an extremely useful construct if assemblies are loaded dynamically, and the requirement exists to unload assemblies after use. Within the primary application domain it is not possible to get rid of loaded assemblies. However, it is possible to end application domains where all assemblies loaded just within the application domain are cleaned from the memory.

# Assembly Structure

An assembly consists of assembly metadata describing the complete assembly, type metadata describing the exported types and methods, MSIL code, and resources. All these parts can be inside of one file or spread across several files.

In this example (see Figure 15-5), the assembly metadata, type metadata, MSIL code, and resources are all in one file — Component.dll. The assembly consists of a single file.

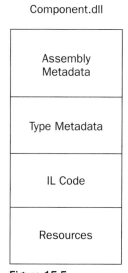

Figure 15-5

The second example shows a single assembly spread across three files (see Figure 15-6). Component.dll has assembly metadata, type metadata, and MSIL code, but no resources. The assembly uses a picture from picture.jpeg that is not embedded inside Component.dll, but is referenced from within the assembly metadata. The assembly metadata also references a module called util.netmodule, which itself includes only type metadata and MSIL code for a class. A module has no assembly metadata, thus the module itself has no version information; it also cannot be installed separately. All three files in this example make up a single assembly; the assembly is the installation unit. It would also be possible to put the manifest in a different file.

# Chapter 15

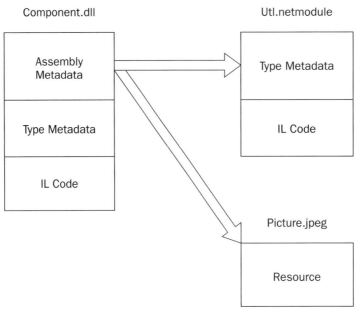

**Figure 15-6**

## Assembly Manifests

An important part of an assembly is a *manifest*, which is part of the metadata. It describes the assembly with all the information that's needed to reference it and lists all its dependencies. The parts of the manifest are as follows:

- ❑ **Identity.** (name, version, culture, and public key)
- ❑ **A list of files.** Files belonging to this assembly. A single assembly must have at least one file, but may contain a number of files.
- ❑ **A list of referenced assemblies.** All assemblies used from the assembly are documented inside the manifest. This reference information includes the version number and the public key, which is used to uniquely identify assemblies. The public key is discussed later in this chapter.
- ❑ **A set of permission requests.** These are the permissions needed to run this assembly. You can find more information about permissions in Chapter 16, ".NET Security."
- ❑ **Exported types.** These are included if they are defined within a module and the module is referenced from the assembly; otherwise they are not part of the manifest. A module is a unit of reuse. The type description is stored as metadata inside the assembly. You can get the structures and classes with the properties and methods from the metadata. This replaces the type library that was used with COM to describe the types. For the use of COM clients it's easy to generate a type library out of the manifest. The reflection mechanism uses the information about the exported types for late binding to classes. See Chapter 11, "Reflection," for more information about reflection.

# Assemblies

## Namespaces, Assemblies, and Components

You might be a little bit confused by the meanings of namespaces, types, assemblies, and components. How does a namespace fit into the assembly concept? The namespace is completely independent of an assembly. You can have different namespaces in a single assembly, but the same namespace can be spread across assemblies. The namespace is just an extension of the type name — it belongs to the name of the type. Thus, the real name of the class Demo you used before is Wrox.ProCSharp.Assemblies.AppDomains.Demo.

The diagram in Figure 15-7 should help to make this concept clearer. It shows three assemblies, which you build later in this chapter — an assembly written with C++/CLI, one with Visual Basic, and one with C#. All these assemblies have classes in the same namespace: Wrox.ProCSharp.Assemblies.CrossLanguage. The assembly HelloCSharp, in addition, has a Math class that's in the namespace Wrox.Utils.

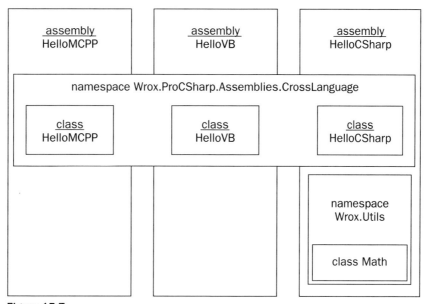

Figure 15-7

## Private and Shared Assemblies

Assemblies can be shared or private. A *private assembly* is found either in the same directory as the application, or within one of its subdirectories. With a private assembly, it's not necessary to think about naming conflicts with other classes or versioning problems. The assemblies that are referenced during the build process are copied to the application directory. Private assemblies are the normal way to build assemblies, especially when applications and components are built within the same company.

When using *shared assemblies*, you have to be aware of some rules. The assembly must be unique and therefore must also have a unique name called a *strong name*. Part of the strong name is a mandatory version number. Shared assemblies will mostly be used when a vendor, different from that of the application, builds the component, or when a large application is split into subprojects.

# Chapter 15

## Viewing Assemblies

Assemblies can be viewed using the command-line utility ildasm, the MSIL disassembler. You can open an assembly by starting ildasm from the command line with the assembly as an argument or by selecting the File ⇨ Open menu.

Figure 15-8 shows ildasm opening the example that you build a little later in the chapter, HelloCSharp.exe. ildasm shows the manifest and the HelloCSharp type in the Wrox.ProCSharp.Assemblies.CrossLanguage namespace. When you open the manifest, you can see the version number and the assembly attributes, as well as the referenced assemblies and their versions. You can see the MSIL code by opening the methods of the class.

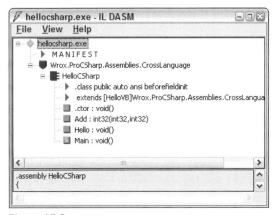

**Figure 15-8**

## ildasm symbols

The following table lists the symbols used with ildasm.

| Symbol | Description |
| --- | --- |
| | Represents a namespace. |
| | Represents a reference type, a class. Similar symbols are used by value types (structs) that have a light color, delegates that are real classes with the MSIL code, interfaces that have an "I" in the graphic, and enumerations with an "E." |
| | Represents a method and get and set accessors of a property; an "S" in the graphic means that this method is static. |
| | Represents a field. |
| | Represents an event. |

# Assemblies

| Symbol | Description |
|---|---|
| ▲ | Represents a property. |
| ▶ | This means that more information is available (for example, manifest information or information about a class declaration). |

> In addition to using ildasm, the .NET Reflector is another great tool to use to analyze assemblies. The .NET Reflector allows type and member search, call and callee graphs, and decompiles IL code to C#, C++, or Visual Basic. You can download this tool from http://www.aisto.com/roeder/dotnet.

## Building Assemblies

Now that you know what assemblies are, it is time to build some. Of course, you have already built assemblies in previous chapters, because a .NET executable counts as an assembly. This section looks at special options for assemblies.

### Creating modules and assemblies

All C# project types in Visual Studio create an assembly. Whether you choose a DLL or EXE project type, an assembly is always created. With the command-line C# compiler *csc*, it's also possible to create modules. A module is a DLL without assembly attributes (so it's not an assembly, but it can be added to assemblies at a later time). The command

```
csc /target:module hello.cs
```

creates a module `hello.netmodule`. You can view this module using ildasm.

A module also has a manifest, but there is no `.assembly` entry inside the manifest (except for the external assemblies that are referenced) because a module has no assembly attributes. It's not possible to configure versions or permissions with modules; that can only be done at the assembly scope. You can find references to assemblies in the manifest of the module. With the `/addmodule` option of csc, it's possible to add modules to existing assemblies.

To compare modules to assemblies, create a simple class A and compile it by using the following command:

```
csc /target:module A.cs
```

The compiler generates the file `A.netmodule`, which doesn't include assembly information (as you can see using ildasm looking at the manifest information). The manifest of the module shows the referenced assembly mscorlib and the `.module` entry in Figure 15-9.

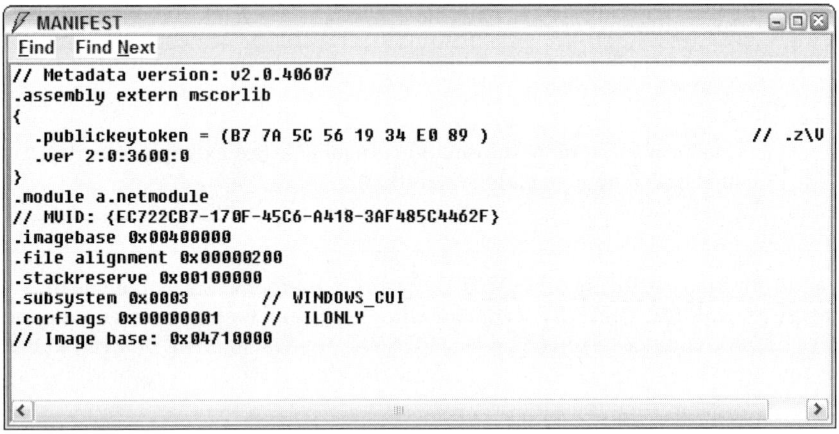

```
MANIFEST
Find  Find Next
// Metadata version: v2.0.40607
.assembly extern mscorlib
{
  .publickeytoken = (B7 7A 5C 56 19 34 E0 89 )                // .z\U
  .ver 2:0:3600:0
}
.module a.netmodule
// MVID: {EC722CB7-170F-45C6-A418-3AF485C4462F}
.imagebase 0x00400000
.file alignment 0x00000200
.stackreserve 0x00100000
.subsystem 0x0003       // WINDOWS_CUI
.corflags 0x00000001    // ILONLY
// Image base: 0x04710000
```

Figure 15-9

Next, create an assembly B that includes the module A.netmodule. It's not necessary to have a source file to generate this assembly. The command to build the assembly is:

```
csc /target:library /addmodule:A.netmodule /out:B.dll
```

Looking at the assembly using ildasm, you can only find a manifest. In the manifest, the assembly mscorlib is referenced. Next, you see the assembly section with a hash algorithm and the version. The number of the algorithm defines the type of the algorithm that was used to create the hash code of the assembly. When creating an assembly programmatically it is possible to select the algorithm. Part of the manifest is a list of all modules belonging to the assembly. In Figure 15-10 you see .module A. netmodule, which belongs to the assembly. Classes exported from modules are part of the assembly manifest; classes exported from the assembly itself are not.

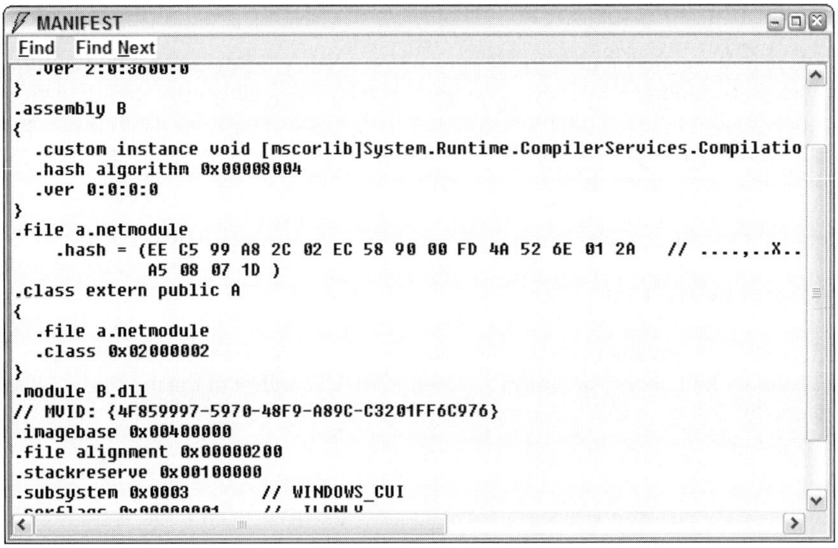

```
MANIFEST
Find  Find Next
  .ver 2:0:3600:0
}
.assembly B
{
  .custom instance void [mscorlib]System.Runtime.CompilerServices.Compilatio
  .hash algorithm 0x00008004
  .ver 0:0:0:0
}
.file a.netmodule
      .hash = (EE C5 99 A8 2C 02 EC 58 90 00 FD 4A 52 6E 01 2A  // ....,..X..
               A5 08 07 1D )
.class extern public A
{
  .file a.netmodule
  .class 0x02000002
}
.module B.dll
// MVID: {4F859997-5970-48F9-A89C-C3201FF6C976}
.imagebase 0x00400000
.file alignment 0x00000200
.stackreserve 0x00100000
.subsystem 0x0003       // WINDOWS_CUI
 corflags 0x00000001    // ILONLY
```

Figure 15-10

# Assemblies

What's the purpose of modules? Modules can be used for faster startup of assemblies because not all types are inside a single file. The modules are loaded only when needed. Another reason to use modules is if you want to create an assembly with more than one programming language; one module could be written using Visual Basic, another module could be written using C#, and these two modules could be included in a single assembly.

## Creating assemblies using Visual Studio

As already mentioned, all project types in Visual Studio create assemblies. With Visual Studio 2005 there's no support for creating modules directly.

When creating a Visual Studio project, the source file `AssemblyInfo.cs` is generated automatically. You can use the normal source code editor to configure the assembly attributes in this file. This is the file generated from the wizard:

```
using System.Reflection;
using System.Runtime.CompilerServices;
//
// General Information about an assembly is controlled through the
// following set of attributes. Change these attribute values to modify
// the information associated with an assembly.
//
[assembly: AssemblyTitle("DomainTest")]
[assembly: AssemblyDescription("")]
[assembly: AssemblyConfiguration("")]
[assembly: AssemblyCompany("")]
[assembly: AssemblyProduct("DomainTest")]
[assembly: AssemblyCopyright("Copyright @ Wrox Press 2005")]
[assembly: AssemblyTrademark("")]
[assembly: AssemblyCulture("")]
//
// Version information for an assembly consists of the following four
// values:
//
//      Major Version
//      Minor Version
//      Build Number
//      Revision
//
// You can specify all the values or you can default the Revision and
// Build Numbers by using the '*' as shown below:
[assembly: AssemblyVersion("1.0.*")]
```

This file is used for configuration of the assembly manifest. The compiler reads the assembly attributes to inject the specific information into the manifest.

`[assembly]` and `[module]` are assembly-level attributes. Assembly-level attributes are, in contrast to the other attributes, not attached to a specific language element. The arguments that can be used for the assembly attribute are classes of the namespaces `System.Reflection`, `System.Runtime.CompilerServices`, and `System.Runtime.InteropServices`.

*You can read more about attributes and how to create and use custom attributes in Chapter 11, "Reflection."*

423

The following table contains a list of assembly attributes defined within the `System.Reflection` namespace.

| Assembly Attribute | Description |
| --- | --- |
| `AssemblyCompany` | Specifies the company name. |
| `AssemblyConfiguration` | Specifies build information such as retail or debugging information. |
| `AssemblyCopyright` and `AssemblyTrademark` | Hold the copyright and trademark information. |
| `AssemblyDefaultAlias` | Can be used if the assembly name is not easily readable (such as a GUID when the assembly name is created dynamically). With this attribute an alias name can be specified. |
| `AssemblyDescription` | Describes the assembly or the product. Looking at the properties of the executable file this value shows up as Comments. |
| `AssemblyProduct` | Specifies the name of the product where the assembly belongs. |
| `AssemblyInformationalVersion` | This attribute isn't used for version checking when assemblies are referenced, it is for information only. It is very useful to specify the version of an application that uses multiple assemblies. Opening the properties of the executable you can see this value as the Product Version. |
| `AssemblyTitle` | Used to give the assembly a friendly name. The friendly name can include spaces. With the file properties you can see this value as Description. |

Here's an example of how these attributes might be configured:

```
[assembly: AssemblyTitle("Professional C#")]
[assembly: AssemblyDescription("")]
[assembly: AssemblyConfiguration("Retail version")]
[assembly: AssemblyCompany("Wrox Press")]
[assembly: AssemblyProduct("Wrox Professional Series")]
[assembly: AssemblyCopyright("Copyright (C) Wrox Press 2005")]
[assembly: AssemblyTrademark("Wrox is a registered trademark of " +
    "John Wiley & Sons, Inc.")]
[assembly: AssemblyCulture("en-US")]
```

The following attributes correspond to classes in the `System.Runtime.CompilerServices` namespace:

- `AssemblyCulture` tells about the culture of the assembly. Cultures are discussed in Chapter 17, "Localization."

- `AssemblyVersion` specifies the version number of the assembly. Versioning plays an important part for shared assemblies.

# Assemblies

*Additional COM interoperability attributes within the* `System.Runtime.InteropServices` *namespace can be used to make .NET types visible to COM, to specify application IDs, for example. COM interoperability is the subject of Chapter 33.*

## Cross-Language Support

One of the best features of COM is its support for multiple languages. It's possible to create a COM component with Visual Basic and to make use of it from within a scripting client such as JScript. On the other hand, it's also possible to create a COM component using C++ that a Visual Basic program cannot make use of. A scripting client has different requirements than a Visual Basic client, and a C++ client is able to use many more COM features than any other client language.

When you write COM components, it's always necessary to have the client programming language in mind. The server must be developed for a specific client language or for a group of client languages. If you are designing a COM component for a scripting client, this component can also be used from within C++, but then the C++ client has some disadvantages. Many rules must be followed when different clients should be supported, and the compiler can't help with COM; the COM developer has to know the requirements of the client language and has to create the interfaces accordingly.

How does this compare with the .NET platform? With the *Common Type System* (CTS), .NET defines how value types and reference types can be defined from a .NET language and the memory layout of such types. But the CTS does not guarantee that a type which is defined from any language can be used from any other language. This is the role of the *Common Language Specification* (CLS). The CLS defines the minimum requirement of types that must be supported by a .NET language.

The CTS and CLS were briefly mentioned in Chapter 1, ".NET Architecture." This section goes deeper and explores the following:

- ❑ Both CTS and CLS.
- ❑ Language independence in action by creating a C++, Visual Basic, and a C# class that derive from each other. You look at the MSIL code that's generated from these compilers.
- ❑ The requirements of the CLS.

### The CTS and the CLS

All types are declared with the guidance of the CTS. The CTS defines a set of rules that language compilers must follow to define, reference, use, and store reference and value types. Therefore, by following the CTS, objects written in different languages can interact with each other.

However, not all types are available to all programming languages. To build components accessible from all .NET languages, use the CLS. With the CLS the compiler can check for valid code according to the CLS specification.

Any language that supports .NET isn't just restricted to the common subset of features that is defined with the CLS; even with .NET it's still possible to create components that cannot be used from different languages. Supporting all languages is much easier with .NET than it was with COM. If you do restrict yourself to the CLS, it's *guaranteed* that this component can be used from all languages. It is most likely that libraries written by third parties will restrict themselves to the CLS to make the library available to all languages.

The .NET Framework was designed from the ground up to support multiple languages. During the design phase of .NET, Microsoft invited many compiler vendors to build their own .NET languages. Microsoft itself delivers Visual Basic, C++/CLI, C#, J#, and JScript .NET. In addition, more than 50 languages from different vendors, such as COBOL, Smalltalk, Perl, and Eiffel, are available. Each of these languages has its specific advantages and many different features. The compilers of all these languages have been extended to support .NET.

> **The CLS is the minimum specification of requirements that a language must support. This means that if you restrict your public methods to the CLS, all languages supporting .NET can use your classes!**

Most, but not all, of the classes in the .NET Framework are CLS-compliant. The non-compliant classes and methods are specially marked as not compliant in the MSDN documentation. One example is the `UInt32` structure in the `System` namespace. `UInt32` represents a 32-bit unsigned integer. Not all languages (including Visual Basic and J#) support unsigned data types; such data types are not CLS-compliant.

Figure 15-11 shows the relation of the CLS to the CTS and how types of programming languages relate.

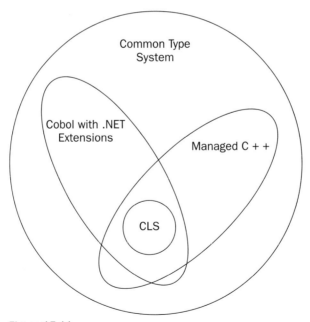

Figure 15-11

# Assemblies

## Language Independence in Action

This section shows CLS in action. The first assembly created includes a base class with Visual C++. The second assembly has a Visual Basic class that inherits from the C++ class. The third assembly is a C# Console Application with a class deriving from the Visual Basic code, and a `Main` function that's using the C# class. The implementation should just show how the languages make use of .NET classes, and how they handle numbers, so all these classes have a simple `Hello()` method where the `System.Console` class is used, and an `Add()` method where two numbers are added. Figure 15-12 shows the UML class diagram with these classes and methods.

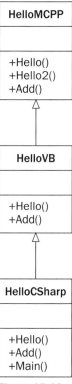

Figure 15-12

## Writing the C++/CLI class

The first project type you create for this example is a .NET Class Library, which is created from the Visual C++ Projects project type of Visual Studio, and named `HelloCPP` (see Figure 15-13). Name the solution `LanguageIndependence`.

# Chapter 15

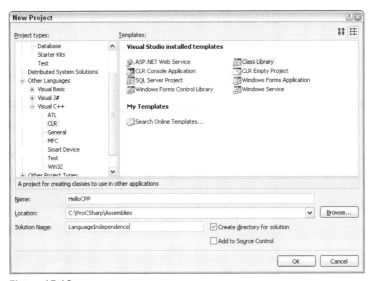

Figure 15-13

The application wizard generates a class `Class1` marked with `ref` to make the class a managed type. Without a special attribute, the class would be a normal unmanaged C++ class generating native code. This class is in the file `HelloCPP.h`:

```
// HelloCPP.h
#pragma once
using namespace System;

namespace HelloCPP
{
    public ref class Class1
    {
        // TODO: Add your methods for this class here.
    };
}
```

For demonstration purposes, change the namespace and class name, and add three methods to the class. The virtual method `Hello2()` uses a C runtime function, `printf()`, that demonstrates the use of native code within a managed class. To make this method available the header file `stdio.h` must be included. Within the `Hello()` method you are using the `Console` managed class from the `System` namespace. The C++ `using namespace` statement is similar to the C# `using` statement. `using namespace System` opens the `System` namespace, so you don't have to write `System::Console::WriteLine()`. Mark the method `Hello()` with the `virtual` keyword, so that it can be overridden. `Hello()` will be overridden in the Visual Basic and C# classes. Similar to C#, C++ member functions are not `virtual` by default. Add a third method, `Add()`, which returns the sum of two `int` arguments, to the class so that you can compare the generated MSIL to the different languages to see how they handle numbers. All three examples use the same namespace: `Wrox.ProCSharp.Assemblies.CrossLanguage`.

428

## Assemblies

```cpp
// HelloMCPP.h
#pragma once

#include <stdio.h>
using namespace System;
namespace Wrox
{
   namespace ProCSharp
   {
      namespace Assemblies
      {
         namespace CrossLanguage
         {
            public ref class HelloCPP
            {
            public:
               virtual void Hello()
               {
                  Console::WriteLine("Hello, C++/CLI");
               }
               virtual void Hello2()
               {
                  printf("Hello, calling native code\n");
               }
               int Add(int val1, int val2)
               {
                  return val1 + val2;
               }
            };
         }
      }
   }
}
```

To allow all .NET languages to use the class HelloCPP, the assembly should be marked CLS compliant. Add the assembly attribute [CLSCompliant] to the file AssemblyInfo.cpp. Because the class CLSCompliantAttribute is in the namespace System, the namespace must be imported.

```cpp
//...
using namespace System;

//...
[assembly:ComVisible(false)];
[assembly:CLSCompliant(true)];
```

To compare the programs with running code, this example uses the release build instead of the debug configuration. With debug configurations you can see some non-optimized IL code. Looking at the generated DLL using ildasm (see Figure 15-14), in addition to the class HelloCPP with its members you will also find the static method printf(). This method calls a native unmanaged function using pinvoke.

hellocpp.dll - IL DASM
File View Help
hellocpp.dll
MANIFEST
<CppImplementationDetails>
<CrtImplementationDetails>
Wrox.ProCSharp.Assemblies.CrossLanguage
Wrox.ProCSharp.Assemblies.CrossLanguage.HelloCF
.class public auto ansi beforefieldinit
.ctor : void()
Add : int32(int32,int32)
Hello : void()
Hello2 : void()
_CrtImplementationDetails
HINSTANCE__
IMAGE_AUX_SYMBOL_TYPE
IMPORT_OBJECT_NAME_TYPE
IMPORT_OBJECT_TYPE
.assembly HelloCPP

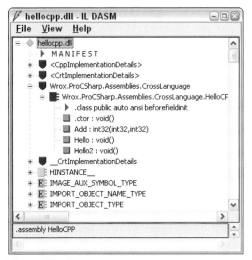

Figure 15-14

The `Hello2()` method (see Figure 15-15) pushes the address of the field `$ArrayType$$$BY0BM@$$CBD`, which keeps the string on the stack. In line `IL_0005` a call to the static `printf()` method can be seen where a pointer to the string "`Hello, calling native code`" is passed.

Wrox.ProCSharp.Assemblies.CrossLanguage.HelloCPP::Hello2 : void()
Find Find Next
.method public hidebysig newslot virtual
instance void Hello2() cil managed
{
// Code size 12 (0xc)
.maxstack 1
IL_0000: ldsflda valuetype '<CppImplementationDetails>'.$ArrayType$$$BY0
IL_0005: call vararg int32 modopt([mscorlib]System.Runtime.CompilerSe
IL_000a: pop
IL_000b: ret
} // end of method HelloCPP::Hello2

Figure 15-15

`printf()` itself is called via the *platform invoke* mechanism (see Figure 15-16). With the platform invoke, you can call all native functions like the C runtime and Win32 API calls.

The `Hello()` method (see Figure 15-17) is completely made up of MSIL code; there's no native code. Also the string "`Hello, C++/CLI`" is a managed string written into the assembly and put onto the stack with `ldstr`. In line `IL_0005` you are calling the `WriteLine()` method of the `System.Console` class using the string from the stack.

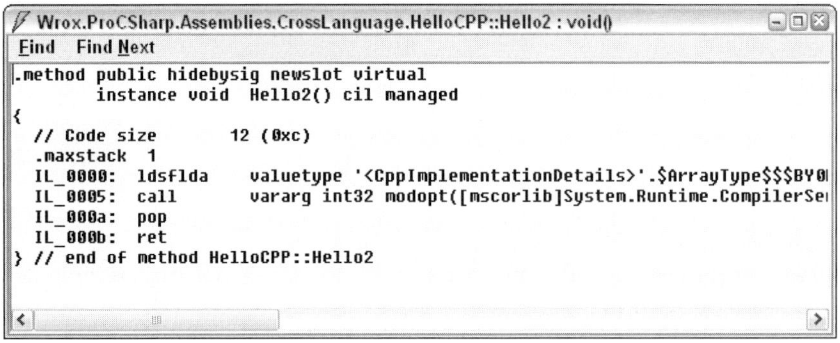

# Assemblies

To demonstrate how numbers are used within C++/CLI, take a look at the MSIL code of the `Add()` method (see Figure 15-18). The passed arguments are put on the stack with `ldarg.1` and `ldarg.2`, add adds the stack values and puts the result on the stack, and in line `IL_0003` the result is returned.

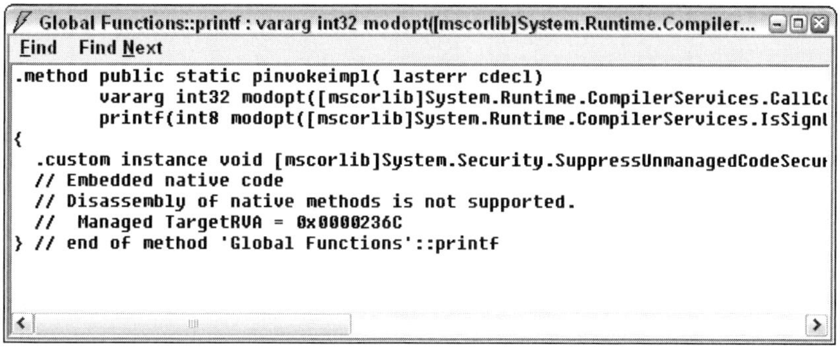

```
.method public static pinvokeimpl( lasterr cdecl)
        vararg int32 modopt([mscorlib]System.Runtime.CompilerServices.CallC(
        printf(int8 modopt([mscorlib]System.Runtime.CompilerServices.IsSign
{
  .custom instance void [mscorlib]System.Security.SuppressUnmanagedCodeSecur
  // Embedded native code
  // Disassembly of native methods is not supported.
  //   Managed TargetRVA = 0x0000236C
} // end of method 'Global Functions'::printf
```

Figure 15-16

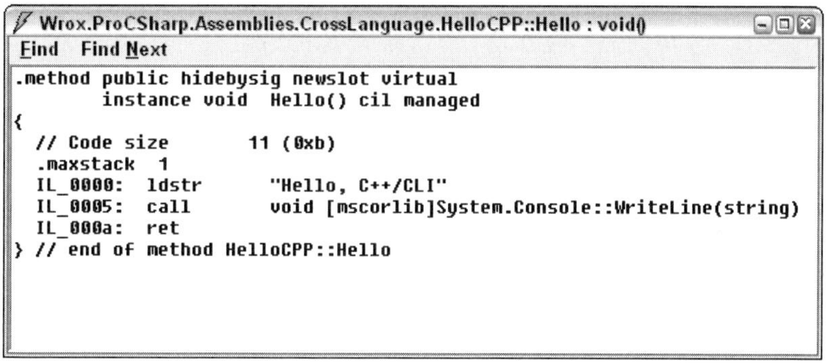

```
.method public hidebysig newslot virtual
        instance void  Hello() cil managed
{
  // Code size       11 (0xb)
  .maxstack  1
  IL_0000:  ldstr      "Hello, C++/CLI"
  IL_0005:  call       void [mscorlib]System.Console::WriteLine(string)
  IL_000a:  ret
} // end of method HelloCPP::Hello
```

Figure 15-17

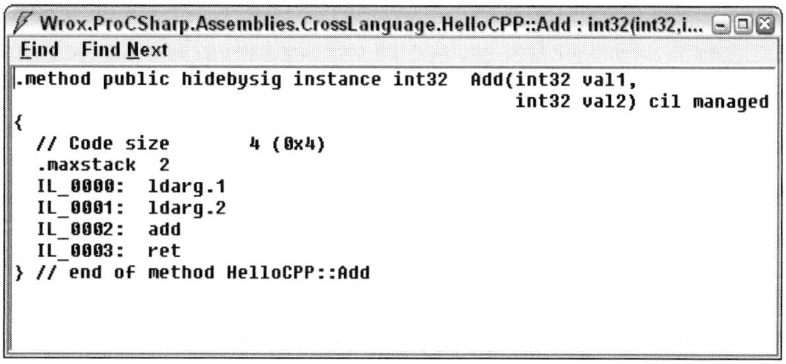

```
.method public hidebysig instance int32  Add(int32 val1,
                                              int32 val2) cil managed
{
  // Code size       4 (0x4)
  .maxstack  2
  IL_0000:  ldarg.1
  IL_0001:  ldarg.2
  IL_0002:  add
  IL_0003:  ret
} // end of method HelloCPP::Add
```

Figure 15-18

# Chapter 15

> What's the advantage of using C++/CLI compared to C# and other languages of the .NET Framework? C++/CLI makes it easier to make traditional C++ code available to .NET. MSIL code and native code can be mixed easily.

## Writing the Visual Basic class

In this section, you use Visual Basic to create a class. Again, use the Class Library wizard, and name the project `HelloVB` (see Figure 15-19).

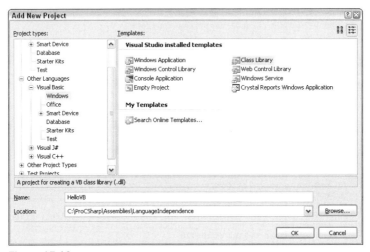

Figure 15-19

Change the namespace of the class to `Wrox.ProCSharp.Assemblies.CrossLanguage`. In a Visual Basic project, you can do this by changing the root namespace of the project in the project properties, as demonstrated in Figure 15-20.

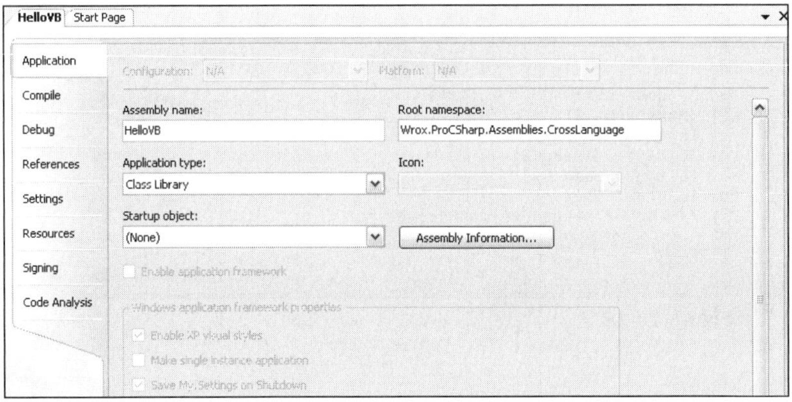

Figure 15-20

## Assemblies

To make it possible to derive the class from `HelloCPP`, a reference to `HelloCPP.dll` is needed. Add the reference to the C++ project by selecting Project ➪ Add Reference. After building the assembly the reference can be seen inside the manifest: `.assembly extern HelloCPP` (see Figure 15-21). Adding the reference to the project copies the referenced assembly to the output directory of the Visual Basic project, so that you are independent of later changes made to the original referenced assembly.

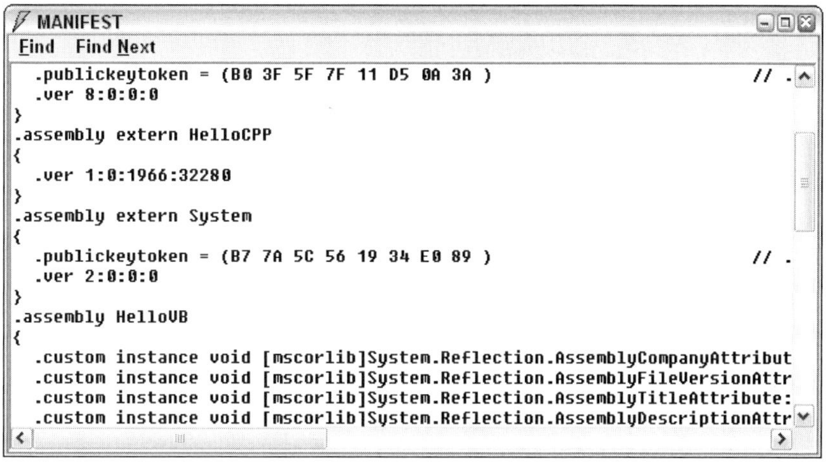

```
MANIFEST
Find  Find Next
    .publickeytoken = (B0 3F 5F 7F 11 D5 0A 3A )         // .
    .ver 8:0:0:0
}
.assembly extern HelloCPP
{
    .ver 1:0:1966:32280
}
.assembly extern System
{
    .publickeytoken = (B7 7A 5C 56 19 34 E0 89 )         // .
    .ver 2:0:0:0
}
.assembly HelloVB
{
    .custom instance void [mscorlib]System.Reflection.AssemblyCompanyAttribut
    .custom instance void [mscorlib]System.Reflection.AssemblyFileVersionAttr
    .custom instance void [mscorlib]System.Reflection.AssemblyTitleAttribute:
    .custom instance void [mscorlib]System.Reflection.AssemblyDescriptionAttr
```

Figure 15-21

Create the class `HelloVB` using the following code. The class `HelloVB` inherits from `HelloMCPP`. Visual Basic uses the keyword `Inherits` to derive from a base class. `Inherits` must be in the line after the `Class` statement. Override the `Hello()` method in the base class. The Visual Basic `Overrides` keyword does the same thing as the C# `override` keyword. In the implementation of the `Hello()` method, the `Hello()` method of the base class is called using the Visual Basic keyword `MyBase`. The `MyBase` keyword is the same as `base` in C#. The method `Add()` is implemented so that you can examine the generated MSIL code to see how Visual Basic works with numbers. The `Add()` method from the base class is not virtual, so it can't be overridden. Visual Basic uses the keyword `Shadows` to hide a method of a base class. `Shadows` is similar to C#'s `new` modifier. The C# `new` modifier was introduced in Chapter 4, "Inheritance."

```vb
Public Class HelloVB
    Inherits HelloCPP

    Public Overrides Sub Hello()
       MyBase.Hello()
       Console.WriteLine("Hello, Visual Basic")
    End Sub

    Public Shadows Function Add(ByVal val1 As Integer, _
                                ByVal val2 As Integer) As Integer
        Return val1 + val2
    End Function
End Class
```

Now look at the MSIL code generated from the Visual Basic compiler.

The `HelloVB.Hello()` method (see Figure 15-22) first calls the `Hello()` method of the base class `HelloMCPP`. In line `IL_0006`, a string stored in the metadata is pushed on the stack using `ldstr`.

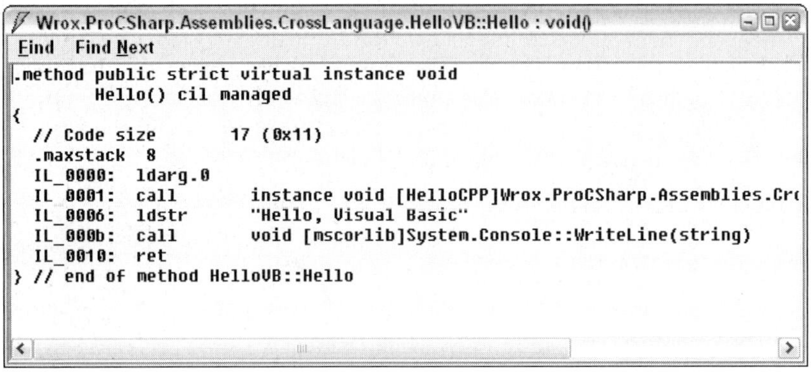
Wrox.ProCSharp.Assemblies.CrossLanguage.HelloVB::Hello : void()
Find   Find Next
.method public strict virtual instance void
        Hello() cil managed
{
  // Code size       17 (0x11)
  .maxstack  8
  IL_0000:  ldarg.0
  IL_0001:  call       instance void [HelloCPP]Wrox.ProCSharp.Assemblies.Cr
  IL_0006:  ldstr      "Hello, Visual Basic"
  IL_000b:  call       void [mscorlib]System.Console::WriteLine(string)
  IL_0010:  ret
} // end of method HelloVB::Hello
Figure 15-22

The other method (see Figure 15-23) you are looking at is `Add()`. Visual Basic uses `add.ovf` instead of the `add` method that was used in the C++/CLI-generated MSIL code. This is just a single MSIL statement that's different between C++ and Visual Basic, but the statement `add.ovf` generates more lines of native code because `add.ovf` performs overflow checking. If the result of the addition of the two arguments is too large to be represented in the target type, `add.ovf` generates an exception of type `OverflowException`. In contrast, `add` just performs an addition of the two values, whether or not the target fits. In the case where the target is not big enough, the true value of the summation is lost, which results in a wrong number. So, `add` is faster, but `add.ovf` is safer.

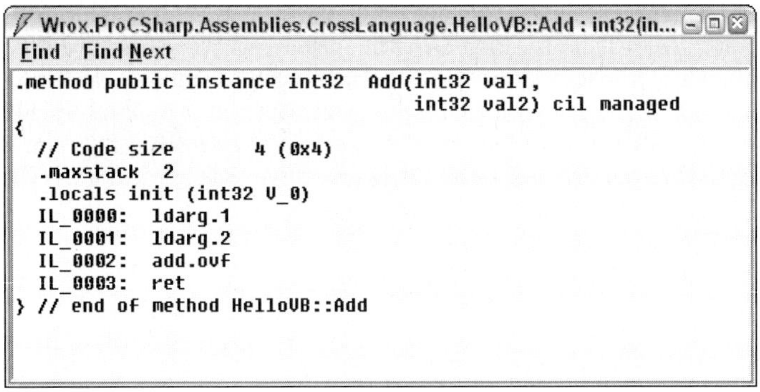
Wrox.ProCSharp.Assemblies.CrossLanguage.HelloVB::Add : int32(in...
Find   Find Next
.method public instance int32  Add(int32 val1,
                                   int32 val2) cil managed
{
  // Code size       4 (0x4)
  .maxstack  2
  .locals init (int32 V_0)
  IL_0000:  ldarg.1
  IL_0001:  ldarg.2
  IL_0002:  add.ovf
  IL_0003:  ret
} // end of method HelloVB::Add
Figure 15-23

## Writing the C# class

The third class is created using C#, which is the language this book is written about. For this project, create a C# Console Application called `HelloCSharp`. Add a reference to the `HelloVB` and the `HelloCPP` assembly, because the C# class will derive from the Visual Basic class.

# Assemblies

Use the following code to create the class `HelloCSharp`. The methods implemented in the C# class are similar to the C++/CLI and the Visual Basic classes. `Hello()` is an overridden method of the base class; `Add()` is a new method:

```
using System;

namespace Wrox.ProCSharp.Assemblies.CrossLanguage
{
    public class HelloCSharp : HelloVB
    {
        public HelloCSharp()
        {
        }
        public override void Hello()
        {
            base.Hello();
            Console.WriteLine("Hello, C#");
        }
        public new int Add(int val1, int val2)
        {
            return val1 + val2;
        }
    }

    class Program
    {
        static void Main()
        {
            HelloCSharp hello = new HelloCSharp();
            hello.Hello();
        }
    }
}
```

As you can see in Figure 15-24, the generated MSIL code for the `Hello()` method is the same as the MSIL code from the Visual Basic compiler.

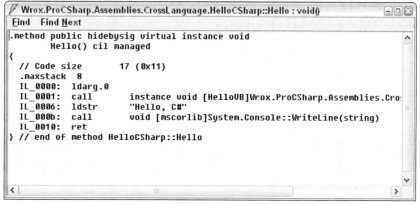

Figure 15-24

The `Add()` method (see Figure 15-25) differs, and yet is similar to the C++/CLI code. Doing calculations, the C# compiler doesn't use the methods with overflow checking if the default compiler settings are configured in the Visual Studio project. The faster MSIL method `add` is used instead of `add.ovf`; but it's possible to change this option by using the configuration properties of C# and Visual Basic projects. Setting "Check for overflow underflow" to `true` in a C# project, the MSIL code that the C# compiler generates for this example will be the same as that generated by the Visual Basic compiler. Unlike Visual Basic, with C# it's also possible to choose this option on an expression-by-expression basis with the `checked` and `unchecked` operators. The `checked` and `unchecked` operators are discussed in Chapter 5, "Operators and Casts."

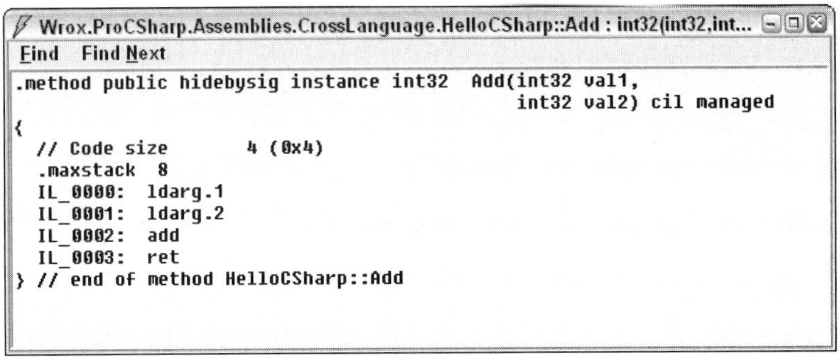
Wrox.ProCSharp.Assemblies.CrossLanguage.HelloCSharp::Add : int32(int32,int...
Find Find Next
.method public hidebysig instance int32 Add(int32 val1,
int32 val2) cil managed
{
// Code size 4 (0x4)
.maxstack 8
IL_0000: ldarg.1
IL_0001: ldarg.2
IL_0002: add
IL_0003: ret
} // end of method HelloCSharp::Add

Figure 15-25

Finally, in Figure 15-26 you can see the console application output.

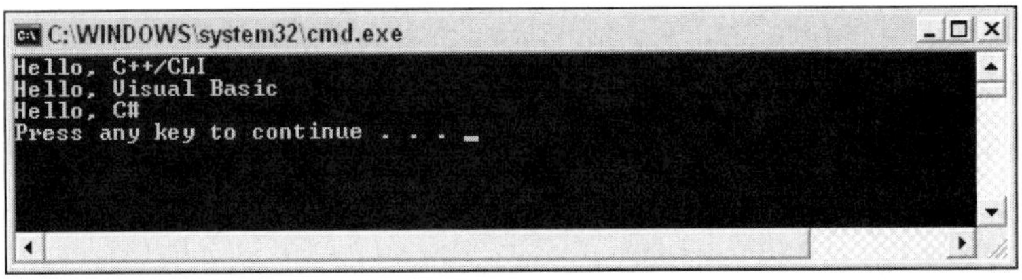
C:\WINDOWS\system32\cmd.exe
Hello, C++/CLI
Hello, Visual Basic
Hello, C#
Press any key to continue . . .

Figure 15-26

*Because all the .NET languages generate MSIL code and all the languages make use of the classes in the .NET Framework, it's often said that there is no difference regarding performance. As you can see, however, small differences are still there. First, depending on the language, some languages support different data types from others. Second, the generated MSIL code can still be different. One example that you've seen is that the number calculations are implemented differently: whereas the default configuration of Visual Basic is for safety, the default for C# is for speed. C# is also more flexible.*

## CLS Requirements

You saw the CLS in action when you looked at cross-language inheritance between C++/CLI, Visual Basic, and C#. Until now you didn't pay any attention to the CLS requirements when building your project. You were lucky — the methods defined in the base classes were callable from the derived classes.

# Assemblies

If a method had the `System.UInt32` data type as one of its arguments, you wouldn't be able to use it from Visual Basic. Unsigned data types are not CLS-compliant; for a .NET language, it's not necessary to support this data type.

The CLS exactly defines the requirements to make a component CLS-compliant, which enables it to be used with different .NET languages. With COM you had to pay attention to language-specific requirements when designing a component. JScript had different requirements from Visual Basic 6, and the requirements of Visual J++ were different again. This is no longer the case with .NET. To design a component that should be used from other languages, you just have to make it CLS-compliant; it's guaranteed that this component can be used from all .NET languages. If you mark a class as CLS-compliant, the compiler can warn you about non-compliant methods.

All .NET languages must support the CLS. When talking about .NET languages it's important to differentiate between *.NET consumer* and *.NET extender* tools.

A .NET consumer language just uses classes from the .NET Framework—it can't create .NET classes that can be used from other languages. A consumer tool can use any CLS-compliant class. A .NET extender tool has the requirements of a consumer and in addition can inherit any CLS-compliant .NET class and define new CLS-compliant classes that can be used by consumers. C++, Visual Basic, and C# all are extender tools. With these languages, it's possible to create CLS-compliant classes.

## *The CLSCompliant attribute*

With the `CLSCompliant` attribute, you can mark your assembly to be CLS-compliant. Doing this guarantees that the classes in this assembly can be used from all .NET consumer tools. The compiler issues warnings when you are using non-CLS-compliant data types in public and protected methods. The data types you use in the private implementation don't matter—when using other languages outside of the class, you don't have direct access to private methods anyway.

To get compiler warnings when a data type is not compliant in public and protected methods, you set the attribute `CLSCompliant` in the assembly by adding this attribute to the file `AssemblyInfo.cs`. To make a class CLS-compliant it is also necessary that the base classes are CLS compliant, so you must apply this attribute not only to the C# class but also to the Visual Basic and C++ base classes.

```
[assembly: System.CLSCompliant(true)]
```

This way, all the defined types and public methods inside the assembly must be compliant. Using a non-compliant `uint` type as argument type, you get this error from the compiler:

```
error CS3001: Argument type uint is not CLS-compliant
```

When you mark an assembly as compliant, it's still possible to define methods that are not compliant. This can be useful if you want to override some method to make it available with both compliant and non-compliant argument data types. The methods that are not compliant must be marked, within the class, by the `CLSCompliant` attribute with a value of `false`. The `CLSCompliant` attribute can be applied to types, methods, properties, fields, and events:

```
[CLSCompliant(false)]
void Method(uint i)
{
   //...
```

437

## Chapter 15

### *CLS rules*

The requirements for an assembly to be CLS-compliant are as follows:

- All types appearing in a method prototype must be CLS-compliant.
- Array elements must have a CLS-compliant element type. Arrays must also be 0-indexed.
- A CLS-compliant class must inherit from a CLS-compliant class. System.Object is CLS-compliant.
- Although method names in CLS-compliant classes are not case-sensitive, method names may not only be different in their case.
- Enumerations must be of type Int16, Int32, or Int64. Enumerations of other types are not compliant.

All the listed requirements only apply to public and protected members. The private implementation itself doesn't matter — non-compliant types can be used there, and the assembly is still compliant.

In addition to these naming guidelines to support multiple languages, it's necessary to pay attention to method names where the type is part of the name. Data type names are language-specific, for example, the C# int, long, and float types are equivalent to the Visual Basic Integer, Long, and Single types. When a data type name is used in a name of a method, the universal type names — Int32, Int64, and Single — and not the language-specific type names should be used:

```
int ReadInt32();
long ReadInt64();
float ReadSingle();
```

Complying with the CLS specs and guidelines, it's easy to create components that can be used from multiple languages. It's not necessary to test the component by using all .NET consumer languages.

## Global Assembly Cache

The *global assembly cache* is, as the name implies, a cache for globally available assemblies. Most shared assemblies are installed inside this cache, but some private assemblies can also be found there. If a private assembly is compiled to native code using the native image generator, the compiled native code goes into this cache, too!

This section explores creating native images at installation time and viewing shared assemblies with the Global Assembly Cache Viewer and the Global Assembly Cache Utility.

### *Native Image Generator*

With the native image generator Ngen.exe, you can compile the IL code to native code at installation time. This way the program can start faster because the compilation during runtime is no longer necessary. The ngen utility installs the native image in the native image cache. The physical directory of the native image cache is <windows>\assembly\NativeImages<RuntimeVersion>.

# Assemblies

With `ngen install myassembly`, you can compile the MSIL code to native code and install it into the native image cache. This should be done from an installation program if you would like to put the assembly in the native image cache.

With ngen you can also display all assemblies from the native image cache with the option `display`. If you add an assembly name to the `display` option you get the information about all installed versions of this assembly and the assemblies that are dependent on the native assembly, as shown in Figure 15-27.

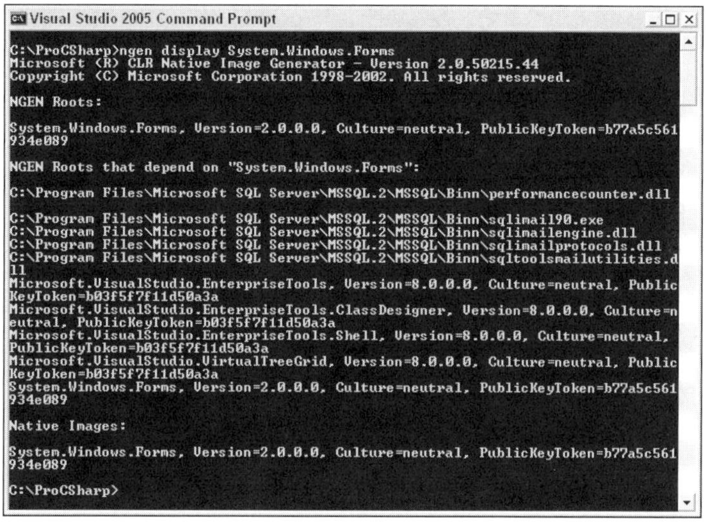

**Figure 15-27**

If the security of the system changes, it's not sure if the native image has the security requirements it needs for running the application. This is why the native images become invalid with a system configuration change. With the command `ngen update` all native images are rebuilt to include the new configurations.

## Global Assembly Cache Viewer

The global assembly cache can be displayed using shfusion.dll, which is a Windows shell extension to view and manipulate the contents of the cache. A Windows shell extension is a COM DLL that integrates with the Windows explorer. You just have to start the explorer and go to the `<windir>/assembly` directory.

Figure 15-28 shows the Assembly Cache Viewer.

With the Assembly Cache Viewer, you can see the Global Assembly Name, Type, Version, Culture, and the Public Key Token. With the Type you can see if the assembly was installed using the native image generator. When you select an assembly using the context menu, it's possible to delete an assembly and to view the properties (see Figure 15-29).

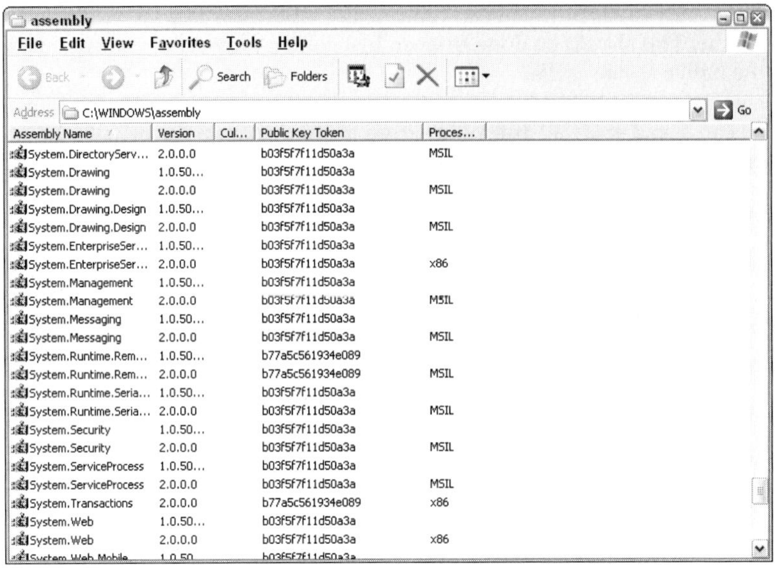

# Chapter 15

Figure 15-28

Figure 15-29

You can see the real files and directories behind the assembly cache by checking the directory from the command line. Inside the `<windir>\assembly` directory there's a GAC and NativeImages_<runtime version> directory. GAC is the directory for shared assemblies, and in NativeImages_<runtime version> you can find the assemblies compiled to native code. If you go deeper in the directory structure you will find directory names that are similar to the assembly names, and below that a version directory and the assemblies themselves. This allows an installation of different versions of the same assembly.

# Assemblies

## Global Assembly Cache Utility (gacutil.exe)

The assembly viewer can be used to view and delete assemblies with the Windows explorer, but it's not possible to use it from scripting code that can be used from installation programs. `gacutil.exe` is a utility to install, uninstall, and list assemblies using the command line.

The following list explains some of the gacutil options:

- **gacutil /l** lists all assemblies from the assembly cache
- **gacutil /i mydll** installs the shared assembly mydll into the assembly cache
- **gacutil /u mydll** uninstalls the assembly mydll

# Creating Shared Assemblies

Assemblies can be isolated for use by a single application—not sharing an assembly is the default. When using private assemblies, it's not necessary to pay attention to any requirements that are necessary for sharing.

This section explores the following:

- Strong names as a requirement for shared assemblies
- Creating shared assemblies
- Installing shared assemblies in the global assembly cache
- Delayed signing of shared assemblies

## Shared Assembly Names

The goal of a shared assembly name is that it must be globally unique, and it must be possible to protect the name. At no time can any other person create an assembly using the same name.

COM solved the first problem by using a globally unique identifier (GUID). The second problem, however, still existed because anyone could steal the GUID and create a different object with the same identifier. Both problems are solved with *strong names* of .NET assemblies.

A strong name is made of these items:

- The *name* of the assembly itself.
- A *version number*. This allows it to use different versions of the same assembly at the same time. Different versions can also work side-by-side and can be loaded concurrently inside the same process.
- A *public key* guarantees that the strong name is unique. It also guarantees that a referenced assembly cannot be replaced from a different source.
- A *culture*. Cultures are discussed in Chapter 17, "Localization."

# Chapter 15

> **A shared assembly must have a strong name to uniquely identify the assembly.**

A strong (shared) name is a simple text name accompanied by a version number, a public key, and a culture. You wouldn't create a new public key with every assembly, but you'd have one in your company, so the key uniquely identifies your company's assemblies.

However, this key cannot be used as a trust key. Assemblies can carry Authenticode signatures to build up a trust. The key for the Authenticode signature can be a different one from the key used for the strong name.

> *For development purposes a different public key can be used and later be exchanged easily with the real key. This feature is discussed later in the section "Delayed signing of assemblies."*

To uniquely identify the assemblies in your companies, a useful namespace hierarchy should be used to name your classes. Here is a simple example showing how to organize namespaces: Wrox Press can use the major namespace `Wrox` for its classes and namespaces. In the hierarchy below the namespace, the namespaces must be organized so that all classes are unique. Every chapter of this book uses a different namespace of the form `Wrox.ProCSharp.<Chapter>`; this chapter uses `Wrox.ProCSharp.Assemblies`. So if there is a class `Hello` in two different chapters there's no conflict because of different namespaces. Utility classes that are used across different books can go into the namespace `Wrox.Utilities`.

A company name commonly used as the first part of the namespace is not necessarily unique, so something more must be used to build a strong name. For this the public key is used. Because of the public/private key principle in strong names, no one without access to your private key can destructively create an assembly that could be unintentionally called by the client.

## *Public key cryptography*

If you already know about public key cryptography, you can skip this section. This is just a simple introduction to keys. For encryption you have to differentiate between *symmetric* encryption and *public/private key* encryption.

With a symmetric key, the same key can be used for encryption and decryption, but this is not the case with a public/private key pair. If something is encrypted using a public key, it can be decrypted with the corresponding private key, but it is not possible with the public key. This also works the other way around: if something is encrypted using a private key, it can be decrypted by using the corresponding public key but not the private key.

Public and private keys are always created as a pair. The public key can be made available to everybody, and it can even be put on a Web site, but the private key must be safely locked away. Following are some examples where these public and private keys are used.

If Sarah sends a mail to Julian, and Sarah wants to make sure that no one else but Julian can read the mail, she uses Julian's public key. The message is encrypted using Julian's public key. Julian opens the mail and can decrypt it using his secretly stored private key. This guarantees that no one else except Julian can read Sarah's mail.

# Assemblies

There's one problem left: Julian can't be sure that the mail comes from Sarah. Anyone could use Julian's public key to encrypt mails sent to Julian. We can extend this principle. Let's start again with Sarah sending a mail to Julian. Before Sarah encrypts the mail using Julian's public key, she adds her signature and encrypts the signature using her own private key. Then she encrypts the mail using Julian's public key. Therefore, it is guaranteed that no one else but Julian can read the mail. When Julian decrypts the mail, he detects an encrypted signature. The signature can be decrypted using Sarah's public key. For Julian it's not a problem to access Sarah's public key, because this key is public. After decrypting the signature, Julian can be sure that Sarah has sent the mail.

The next section looks at how this public/private key principle is used with assemblies.

## Integrity using strong names

A public/private key pair must be used to create a shared component. The compiler writes the public key to the manifest, creates a hash of all files that belong to the assembly, and signs the hash with the private key, which is not stored within the assembly. It is then guaranteed that no one can change your assembly. The signature can be verified with the public key.

During development, the client assembly must reference the shared assembly. The compiler writes the public key of the referenced assembly to the manifest of the client assembly. To reduce storage, it is not the public key that is written to the manifest of the client assembly, but a public key token. The public key token consists of the last eight bytes of a hash of the public key, and that is unique.

At runtime, during loading of the shared assembly (or at install-time if the client is installed using the native image generator), the hash of the shared component assembly can be verified by using the public key stored inside the client assembly. Only the owner of the private key can change the shared component assembly. There is no way a component `Math` that was created by vendor A and referenced from a client can be replaced by a component from a hacker. Only the owner of the private key can replace the shared component with a new version. Integrity is guaranteed in so far as the shared assembly comes from the expected publisher.

Figure 15-30 shows a shared component with a public key referenced by a client assembly that has a public key token of the shared assembly inside the manifest.

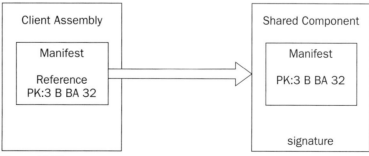

**Figure 15-30**

# Chapter 15

## Creating a Shared Assembly

In the next example, you create a shared assembly and a client that uses it.

Creating shared assemblies is not much different than creating private assemblies. Create a simple Visual C# Class Library project with the name `SharedDemo`. Change the namespace to `Wrox.ProCSharp.Assemblies.Sharing`, and the class name to `SharedDemo`. Enter the following code. In the constructor of the class all lines of a file are read into a `StringCollection`. The name of the file is passed as an argument to the constructor. The method `GetQuoteOfTheDay()` just returns a random string of the collection.

```
using System;
using System.Collections.Generic;
using System.IO;

namespace Wrox.ProCSharp.Assemblies.Sharing
{
    public class SharedDemo
    {
        private List<string> quotes;
        private Random random;

        public SharedDemo(string filename)
        {
            quotes = new List<string>();
            Stream stream = File.OpenRead(filename);
            StreamReader streamReader = new StreamReader(stream);
            string quote;
            while ((quote = streamReader.ReadLine()) != null)
            {
                quotes.Add(quote);
            }
            streamReader.Close();
            stream.Close();
            random = new Random();
        }

        public string GetQuoteOfTheDay()
        {
            int index = random.Next(1, quotes.Count);
            return quotes[index];
        }
    }
}
```

### Create a strong name

A strong name is needed to share this assembly. You can create such a name with the *strong name tool* (sn):

```
sn -k mykey.snk
```

The strong name utility generates and writes a public/private key pair, and writes this pair to a file; here the file is `mykey.snk`.

# Assemblies

With Visual Studio 2005 you can sign the assembly with the project properties by selecting the Signing tab as shown in Figure 15-31. You can also create keys with this tool. However, you don't need to create a key file for every project. Just a few keys for the complete company can be used instead. It is useful to create different keys depending on security requirements (see Chapter 16, ".NET Security").

Setting the signing option with Visual Studio adds the /keyfile option to the compiler setting. Visual Studio also allows you to create a keyfile that is secured with a password. Such a file has the file extension pfx (see Figure 15-31).

After rebuilding, the public key can be found inside the manifest. You can verify this using ildasm as shown in Figure 15-32.

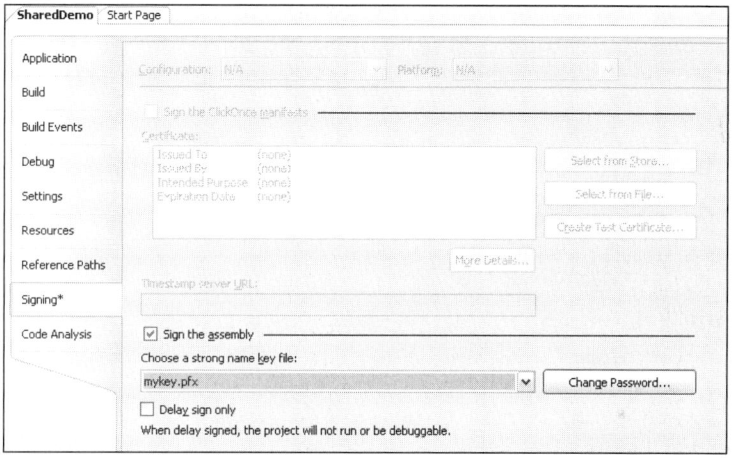

Figure 15-31

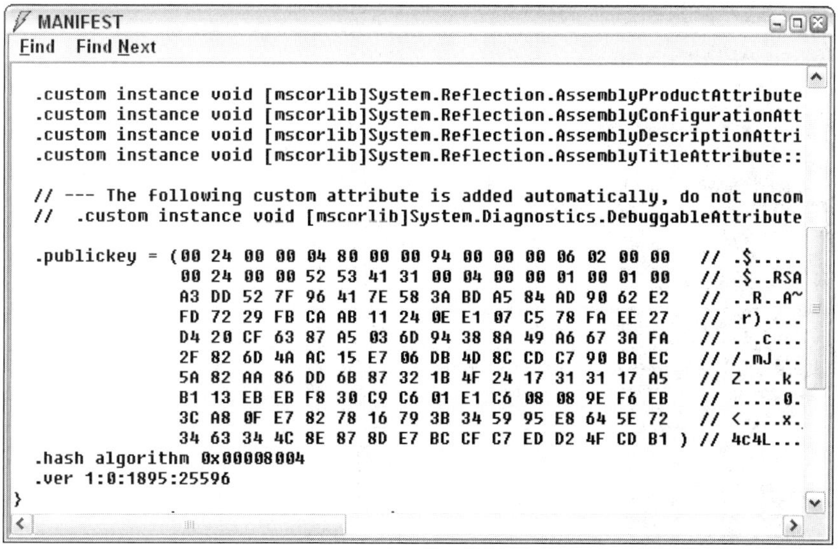

Figure 15-32

# Chapter 15

## Install the shared assembly

With a public key in the assembly, you can now install it in the global assembly cache using the global assembly cache tool gacutil with the /i option:

```
gacutil /i SharedDemo.dll
```

By configuring a post-build event command line with Visual Studio (see Figure 15-33), the assembly can be installed in the global assembly cache with each successful build.

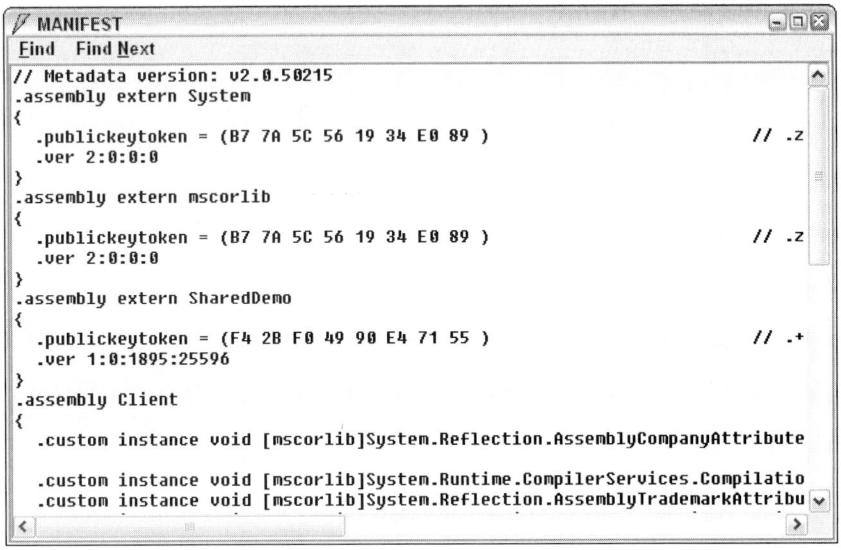

```
// Metadata version: v2.0.50215
.assembly extern System
{
  .publickeytoken = (B7 7A 5C 56 19 34 E0 89 )          // .z
  .ver 2:0:0:0
}
.assembly extern mscorlib
{
  .publickeytoken = (B7 7A 5C 56 19 34 E0 89 )          // .z
  .ver 2:0:0:0
}
.assembly extern SharedDemo
{
  .publickeytoken = (F4 2B F0 49 90 E4 71 55 )          // .+
  .ver 1:0:1895:25596
}
.assembly Client
{
  .custom instance void [mscorlib]System.Reflection.AssemblyCompanyAttribute
  .custom instance void [mscorlib]System.Runtime.CompilerServices.Compilatio
  .custom instance void [mscorlib]System.Reflection.AssemblyTrademarkAttribu
```

Figure 15-33

Then you can use the Global Assembly Cache Viewer to check the version of the shared assembly, and check if it is successfully installed.

## Using the shared assembly

To use the shared assembly, create a C# Console Application called Client. Change the name of the namespace to Wrox.ProCSharp.Assemblies.Sharing. The shared assembly can be referenced in the same way as a private assembly: using the Project ⇨ Add Reference menu.

> With shared assemblies the reference property Copy Local can be set to False. This way the assembly is not copied to the directory of the output files but will be loaded from the global assembly cache instead.

# Assemblies

Here's the code for the Client application:

```csharp
using System;
namespace Wrox.ProCSharp.Assemblies.Sharing
{
    class Program
    {
        static void Main(string[] args)
        {
            SharedDemo quotes =
                new SharedDemo(@"C:\ProCSharp\Assemblies\Quotes.txt");
            for (int i=0; i < 3; i++)
            {
                Console.WriteLine(quotes.GetQuoteOfTheDay());
                Console.WriteLine();
            }
        }
    }
}
```

Looking at the manifest in the client assembly using `ildasm` (see Figure 15-34), you can see the reference to the shared assembly SharedDemo: `.assembly extern SharedDemo`. Part of this referenced information is the version number discussed next, and the token of the public key.

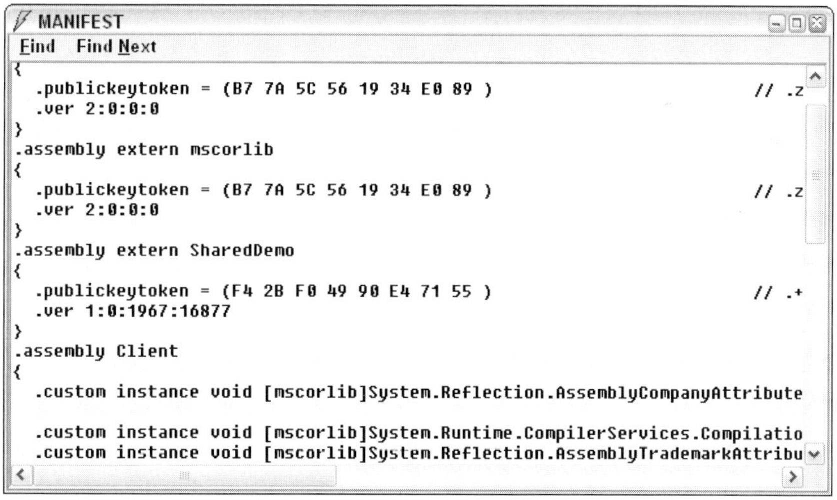

Figure 15-34

The token of the public key can also be seen within the shared assembly using the strong name utility: `sn -T` shows the token of the public key in the assembly, and `sn -Tp` shows the token and the public key. Pay attention to the use of the uppercase P!

The result of your program with a sample quotes file is shown in Figure 15-35.

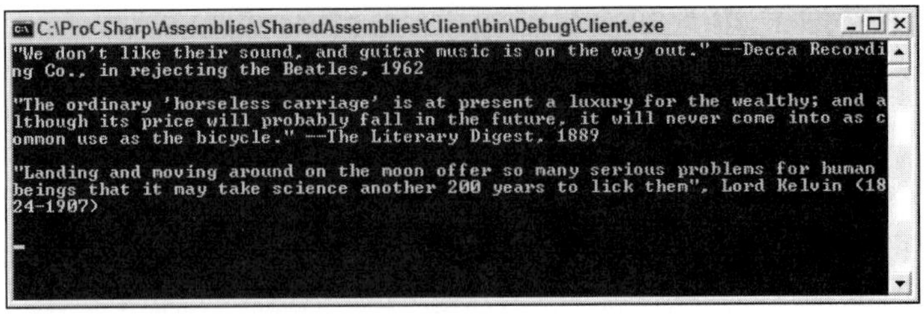

# Chapter 15

Figure 15-35

## *Delayed signing of assemblies*

The private key of a company should be safely stored. Most companies don't give all developers access to the private key; only a few security people have it. That's why the signature of an assembly can be added at a later date, such as before distribution. When the global assembly attribute `AssemblyDelaySign` is set to `true`, no signature is stored in the assembly, but enough free space is reserved so that it can be added later. However, without using a key, you cannot test the assembly and install it in the global assembly cache; but you can use a temporary key for testing purposes, and replace this key with the real company key later.

The following steps are required to delay signing of assemblies:

1. Create a public/private key pair with the strong name utility sn. The generated file `mykey.snk` includes both the public and private key.

   `sn -k mykey.snk`

2. Extract the public key to make it available to developers. The option `-p` extracts the public key of the keyfile. The file `mykeypub.snk` only holds the public key.

   `sn -p mykey.snk mykeypub.snk`

   All developers in the comp0061ny can use this keyfile `mykeypub.snk` and compile the assembly with the `/delaysign+` option. This way the signature is not added to the assembly, but it can be added afterward. In Visual Studio 2005 the delay sign option can be set with a checkbox in the Signing settings.

3. Turn off the verification of the signature, because the assembly doesn't have a signature.

   `sn -Vr SharedDemo.dll`

4. Before distribution the assembly can be re-signed with the sn utility. Use the `-R` option to re-sign previously signed or delayed signed assemblies.

   `sn -R MyAssembly.dll mykey.snk`

> The signature verification should only be turned off during the development process. Never distribute an assembly without verification, because it would be possible for this assembly to be replaced by a malicious one.

# Assemblies

## References

The Properties lists a reference count. This reference count is responsible for the fact that a cached assembly cannot be deleted if it is still needed by an application. For example, if a shared assembly is installed by a Microsoft installer package (MSI file), it can only be deleted by uninstalling the application, but not by deleting it from the global assembly cache. Trying to delete the assembly from the global assembly cache results in the error message "Assembly <name> could not be uninstalled because it is required by other applications."

A reference to the assembly can be set using the gacutil utility with the option /r. The option /r requires a reference type, a reference id, and a description. The type of the reference can be one of three options: UNINSTALL_KEY, FILEPATH, or OPAQUE. UNINSTALL_KEY is used by MSI where a registry key is defined that is also needed with the uninstallation. A directory can be specified with FILEPATH. A useful directory would be the root directory of the application. The OPAQUE reference type allows you to set any type of reference.

The command line

```
gacutil /i shareddemo.dll /r FILEPATH c:\ProCSharp\Assemblies\Client "Shared Demo"
```

installs the assembly `shareddemo` in the global assembly cache with a reference to the directory of the client application. Another installation of the same assembly can happen with a different path, or an OPAQUE id like in this command line:

```
gacutil /i shareddemo.dll /r OPAQUE 4711 "Opaque installation"
```

Now the assembly is in the global assembly cache only once, but it has two references. To delete the assembly from the global assembly cache, both references must be removed:

```
gacutil /u shareddemo /r OPAQUE 4711 "Opaque installation"
```

```
gacutil /u shareddemo /r FILEPATH c:\ProCSharp\Assemblies\Client "Shared Demo"
```

> To remove a shared assembly, the option /u requires the assembly name without the file extension dll. On the contrary, the option /i to install a shared assembly requires the complete file name including the file extension.

*Chapter 18, "Deployment," deals with deployment of assemblies, where the reference count is being dealt with in an MSI package.*

## Configuration

COM components used the registry to configure components. Configuration of .NET applications is done by using configuration files. With registry configurations, an xcopy-deployment is not possible. The configuration files use XML syntax to specify startup and runtime settings for applications.

This section explores the following:

- What you can configure using the XML base configuration files
- How you can redirect a strong named referenced assembly to a different version
- How you can specify the directory of assemblies to find private assemblies in subdirectories and shared assemblies in common directories or on a server

## *Configuration Categories*

The configuration can be grouped into these categories:

- **Startup settings** enable you to specify the version of the required runtime. It's possible that different versions of the runtime could be installed on the same system. The version of the runtime can be specified with the `<startup>` element.
- **Runtime settings** enable you to specify how garbage collection is performed by the runtime, and how the binding to assemblies works. You can also specify the version policy and the code base with these settings. You take a more detailed look into the runtime settings later in this chapter.
- **Remoting settings** are used to configure applications using .NET Remoting. You deal with these configurations in Chapter 29, ".NET Remoting."
- **Security settings** are introduced in Chapter 16, ".NET Security," and configuration for cryptography and permissions is done there.

These settings can be provided in three types of configuration files:

- **Application configuration files** include specific settings for an application, such as binding information to assemblies, configuration for remote objects, and so on. Such a configuration file is placed into the same directory as the executable; it has the same name as the executable with a `.config` extension appended. ASP.NET configuration files are named `web.config`.
- **Machine configuration files** are used for system-wide configurations. You can also specify assembly binding and remoting configurations here. During a binding process, the machine configuration file is consulted before the application configuration file. The application configuration can override settings from the machine configuration. The application configuration file should be the preferred place for application-specific settings so that the machine configuration file stays smaller and more manageable. A machine configuration file is located in `%runtime_install_path%\config\Machine.config`.
- **Publisher policy files** can be used by a component creator to specify that a shared assembly is compatible with older versions. If a new assembly version just fixes a bug of a shared component, it is not necessary to put application configuration files in every application directory that uses this component; the publisher can mark it as compatible by adding a publisher policy file instead. In case the component doesn't work with all applications it is possible to override the publisher policy setting in an application configuration file. In contrast to the other configuration files, publisher policy files are stored in the global assembly cache.

How are these configuration files used? How a client finds an assembly (also called *binding*) depends on whether the assembly is private or shared. Private assemblies must be in the directory of the application

# Assemblies

or in a subdirectory thereof. A process called *probing* is used to find such an assembly. If the assembly doesn't have a strong name, the version number is not used with probing.

Shared assemblies can be installed in the global assembly cache, placed in a directory, a network share, or on a Web site. You specify such a directory with the configuration of the codeBase shortly. The public key, version, and culture are all important aspects when binding to a shared assembly. The reference of the required assembly is recorded in the manifest of the client assembly, including the name, the version, and the public key token. All configuration files are checked to apply the correct version policy. The global assembly cache and code bases specified in the configuration files are checked, followed by the application directories, and probing rules are then applied.

## Versioning

For private assemblies, versioning is not important because the referenced assemblies are copied with the client. The client uses the assembly it has in its private directories.

This is, however, different for shared assemblies. This section looks at the traditional problems that can occur with sharing. With shared components, more than one client application can use the same component. The new version can break existing clients when updating a shared component with a newer version. You can't stop shipping new versions because new features are requested and introduced with new versions of existing components. You can try to program carefully to be backward compatible, but that's not always possible.

A solution to this dilemma could be an architecture that allows installation of different versions of shared components, with clients using the version that they referenced during the build process. This solves a lot of problems but not all of them. What happens if you detect a bug in a component that's referenced from the client? You would like to update this component and make sure that the client uses the new version instead of the version that was referenced during the build process.

Therefore, depending on the type in the fix of the new version, you sometimes want to use a newer version, and you also want to use the older referenced version as well. The .NET architecture enables both scenarios.

In .NET, the original referenced assembly is used by default. You can redirect the reference to a different version using configuration files. Versioning plays a key role in the binding architecture—how the client gets the right assembly where the components live.

### Version numbers

Assemblies have a four-part version number, for example, `1.0.400.3300`. The parts are

```
<Major>.<Minor>.<Build>.<Revision>
```

How these numbers are used depends on your application configuration.

> A good policy would be to change the major or minor number on changes incompatible with the previous version, but just the build or revision number with compatible changes. This way it can be assumed that redirecting an assembly to a new version where just the build and revision changed is safe.

The version number is specified in the assembly with the assembly attribute `AssemblyVersion`. In Visual Studio projects this attribute is in the file `AssemblyInfo.cs`:

```
[assembly: AssemblyVersion("1.0.*")]
```

The first two numbers specify the major and minor version, and the asterisk (*) means that the build and revision numbers are auto-generated. The build number is the number of days since January 1, 2000, and the revision is the number of seconds since midnight divided through two. Of course, you can also specify four values, but then you must be sure to change the version number when rebuilding the assembly manually. Before shipping, it is a good practice to define a specific version number.

This version is stored in the `.assembly` section of the manifest.

Referencing the assembly in the client application stores the version of the referenced assembly in the manifest of the client application.

## Getting the version programmatically

To make it possible to check the version of the assembly that is used from the client application, add the method `GetAssemblyFullName()` to the `SharedDemo` class created earlier to return the strong name of the assembly. For easy use of the `Assembly` class, you have to import the `System.Reflection` namespace:

```
public string GetAssemblyFullName()
{
    Assembly assembly = Assembly.GetExecutingAssembly();
    return assembly.FullName;
}
```

The `FullName` property of the `Assembly` class holds the name of the class, the version, the locality, and the public key token, as you see in the following output, when calling `GetAssemblyFullName()` in your client application.

In the client application, just add a call to `GetAssemblyFullName()` in the `Main()` method after creating the shared component:

```
static void Main(string[] args)
{
    SharedDemo quotes = new
        SharedDemo(@"C:\ProCSharp\Assemblies\Quotes.txt");

    Console.WriteLine(quotes.GetAssemblyFullName());
```

Be sure to register the new version of the shared assembly `SharedDemo` again in the global assembly cache using gacutil. If the referenced version cannot be found, you will get a `System.IO.FileLoadException`, because the binding to the correct assembly failed.

With a successful run, you can see the full name of the referenced assembly similar to Figure 15-36.

This client program can now be used to test different configurations of this shared component.

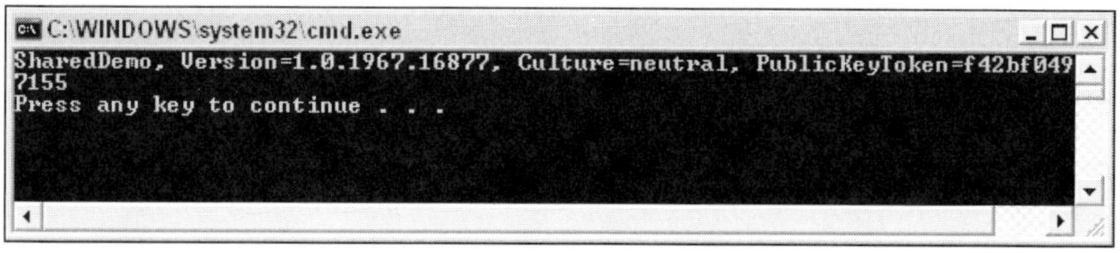
C:\WINDOWS\system32\cmd.exe
SharedDemo, Version=1.0.1967.16877, Culture=neutral, PublicKeyToken=f42bf049
7155
Press any key to continue . . .

Figure 15-36

## Application configuration files

With a configuration file you can specify that the binding should happen to a different version of a shared assembly. Assume you create a new version of the shared assembly `SharedDemo` with major and minor versions 1.1. Maybe you don't want to rebuild the client, but just the new version of the assembly should be used with the existing client instead. This is useful in cases where either a bug is fixed with the shared assembly, or you just want to get rid of the old version because the new version is compatible.

Figure 15-37 shows the Global Assembly Cache Viewer, where the versions 1.0.1967.16877 and 1.2.1967.17321 are installed for the `SharedDemo` assembly.

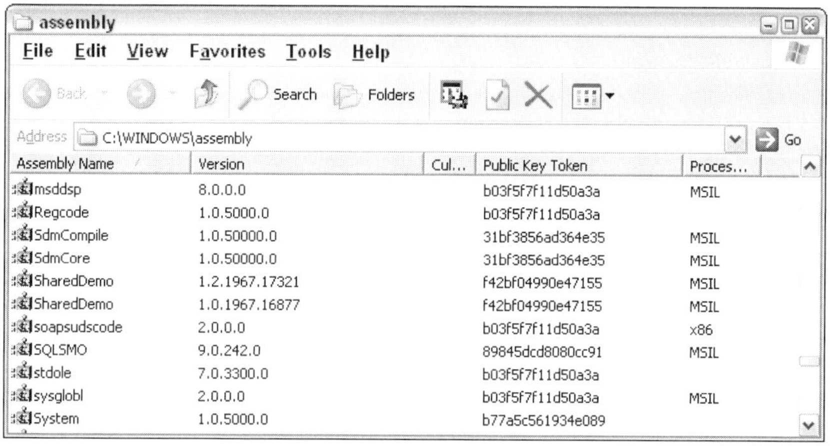
assembly
File Edit View Favorites Tools Help
Back Search Folders
Address C:\WINDOWS\assembly Go
Assembly Name Version Cul... Public Key Token Proces...
msddsp 8.0.0.0 b03f5f7f11d50a3a MSIL
Regcode 1.0.5000.0 b03f5f7f11d50a3a
SdmCompile 1.0.50000.0 31bf3856ad364e35 MSIL
SdmCore 1.0.50000.0 31bf3856ad364e35 MSIL
SharedDemo 1.2.1967.17321 f42bf04990e47155 MSIL
SharedDemo 1.0.1967.16877 f42bf04990e47155 MSIL
soapsudscode 2.0.0.0 b03f5f7f11d50a3a x86
SQLSMO 9.0.242.0 89845dcd8080cc91 MSIL
stdole 7.0.3300.0 b03f5f7f11d50a3a
sysglobl 2.0.0.0 b03f5f7f11d50a3a MSIL
System 1.0.5000.0 b77a5c561934e089

Figure 15-37

Figure 15-38 shows the manifest of the client application where the client references version 1.0.1967.16877 of the assembly `SharedDemo`.

Now an application configuration file is needed. It is not necessary to work directly with XML; the .NET Framework Configuration tool can create application and machine configuration files. Figure 15-39 shows the .NET Framework Configuration tool, which is an MMC Snap-in. You can start this tool from the Administrative Tools in the Control Panel.

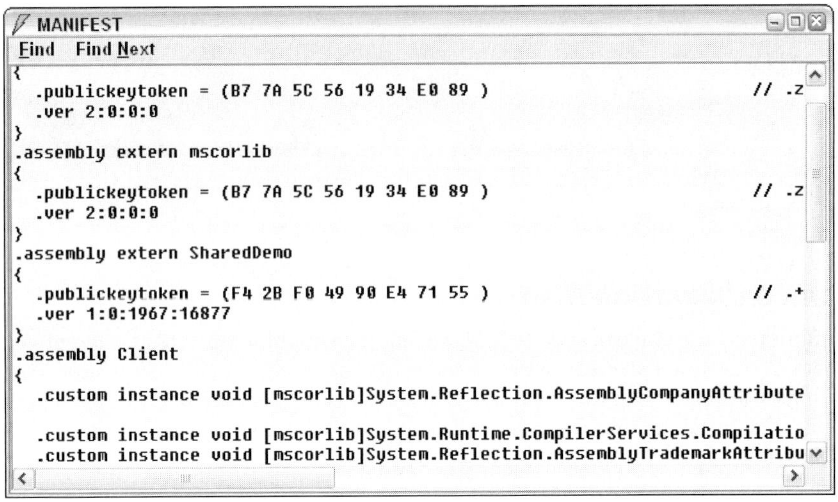

```
/ MANIFEST
Find  Find Next
{
  .publickeytoken = (B7 7A 5C 56 19 34 E0 89 )               // .z
  .ver 2:0:0:0
}
.assembly extern mscorlib
{
  .publickeytoken = (B7 7A 5C 56 19 34 E0 89 )               // .z
  .ver 2:0:0:0
}
.assembly extern SharedDemo
{
  .publickeytoken = (F4 2B F0 49 90 E4 71 55 )               // .+
  .ver 1:0:1967:16877
}
.assembly Client
{
  .custom instance void [mscorlib]System.Reflection.AssemblyCompanyAttribute
  .custom instance void [mscorlib]System.Runtime.CompilerServices.Compilatio
  .custom instance void [mscorlib]System.Reflection.AssemblyTrademarkAttribu
```

Figure 15-38

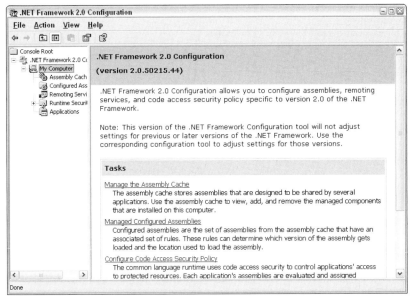

Figure 15-39

When you select Applications on the left side, and then select Action ➪ Add, you'll get a list that shows all .NET applications that have been previously started on this computer. Select the application Client.exe to create an application configuration file for this application. After adding the client application to the .NET Configuration utility, the assembly dependencies can be listed as is shown in Figure 15-40.

# Assemblies

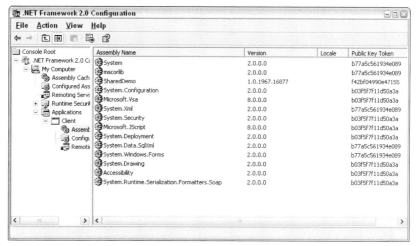

**Figure 15-40**

Select Configured Assemblies in the tree view and the menu Action ⇨ Add... to configure the dependency of the assembly `SharedDemo` from the dependency list. Select the Binding policy tab to define the version that should be used as is shown in Figure 15-41.

**Figure 15-41**

For the Requested Version, specify the version referenced in the manifest of the client assembly. New Version specifies the new version of the shared assembly. In Figure 15-41 it is defined that the version 1.2.1967.17321 should be used instead of any version in the range of 1.0.0.0 to 1.1.9999.99999.

# Chapter 15

Now you can find the application configuration file `Client.exe.config` in the directory of the `Client.exe` application that includes this XML code:

```xml
<?xml version="1.0"?>
<configuration>
   <runtime>
      <assemblyBinding xmlns="urn:schemas-microsoft-com:asm.v1">
         <dependentAssembly>
            <assemblyIdentity name="SharedDemo"
                  publicKeyToken="23f9b4bb8f65e63f" />
            <bindingRedirect oldVersion="1.0.0.0-1.0.999.99999"
                  newVersion="1.2.1967.17321" />
         </dependentAssembly>
      </assemblyBinding>
   </runtime>
</configuration>
```

Runtime settings can be configured with the `<runtime>` element. The subelement of `<runtime>` is `<assemblyBinding>`, which in turn has a subelement `<dependentAssembly>`. `<dependentAssembly>` has a required subelement `<assemblyIdentity>`. You specify the name of the referenced assembly with `<assemblyIdentity>`. `name` is the only mandatory attribute for `<assemblyIdentity>`. The optional attributes are `publicKeyToken` and `culture`. The other subelement of `<dependentAssembly>` that's needed for version redirection is `<bindingRedirect>`. The old and the new version of the dependent assembly is specified with this element.

When you start the client with this configuration file, you will get the new version of the referenced shared assembly.

## Publisher policy files

Using assemblies shared in the global assembly cache allows you to use publisher policies to override versioning issues. Assume that you have an assembly used by some applications. What can be done if a critical bug is found in the shared assembly? You have seen that it is not necessary to rebuild all the applications that use this shared assembly, because you can use configuration files to redirect to the new version of this shared assembly. Maybe you don't know all the applications that use this shared assembly, but you want to get the bug fix to all of them. In that case, you can create publisher policy files to redirect all applications to the new version of the shared assembly.

> **Publisher policy files only apply to shared assemblies installed into the global assembly cache.**

To set up publisher policies, you have to do the following:

- ❏   Create a publisher policy file.
- ❏   Create a publisher policy assembly.
- ❏   Add the publisher policy assembly to the global assembly cache.

## Create a publisher policy file

A publisher policy file is an XML file that redirects an existing version or version range to a new version. The syntax used here is the same as for application configuration files, so you can use the same file you created earlier to redirect the old versions 1.0.0.0 through 1.1.9999.99999 to the new version 1.1.1967.17321.

Rename the previously created file to `mypolicy.config` to use it as a publisher policy file:

```
<?xml version="1.0"?>
<configuration>
   <runtime>
      <assemblyBinding xmlns="urn:schemas-microsoft-com:asm.v1">
         <dependentAssembly>
            <assemblyIdentity name="SharedDemo"
                              publicKeyToken="23f9b4bb8f65e63f" />
            <bindingRedirect oldVersion="1.0.0.0-1.1.9999.99999"
                             newVersion="1.2.1967.17321" />
         </dependentAssembly>
      </assemblyBinding>
   </runtime>
</configuration>
```

## Create a publisher policy assembly

To associate the publisher policy file with the shared assembly it is necessary to create a publisher policy assembly, and to put it into the global assembly cache. The tool that can be used to create such files is the assembly linker al. The option `/linkresource` adds the publisher policy file to the generated assembly. The name of the generated assembly must start with policy, followed by the major and minor version number of the assembly that should be redirected, and the file name of the shared assembly. In this case the publisher policy assembly must be named `policy.1.0.SharedDemo.dll` to redirect the assemblies SharedDemo with the major version 1, and minor version 0. The key that must be added to this publisher key with the option `/keyfile` is the same key that was used to sign the shared assembly SharedDemo to guarantee that the version redirection is from the same publisher.

```
al /linkresource:mypolicy.config /out:policy.1.0.SharedDemo.dll
   /keyfile:..\..\mykey.snk
```

## Add the publisher policy assembly to the global assembly cache

The publisher policy assembly can now be added to the global assembly cache with the utility gacutil:

```
gacutil -i policy.1.0.SharedDemo.dll
```

Now remove the application configuration file that was placed in the directory of the client application, and start the client application. Although the client assembly references 1.0.1732.39307, you use the new version 1.2.1967.17321 of the shared assembly because of the publisher policy.

## Overriding publisher policies

With a publisher policy, the publisher of the shared assembly guarantees that a new version of the assembly is compatible with the old version. As you know, from changes of traditional DLLs, such guarantees don't always hold. Maybe all except one application is working with the new shared assembly. To fix the one application that has a problem with the new release, the publisher policy can be overridden by using an application configuration file.

With the .NET Framework configuration tool you can override the publisher policy by deselecting the Enable Publisher Policy check box, as shown in Figure 15-42.

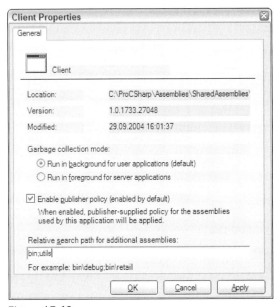

Figure 15-42

Disabling the publisher policy with the .NET Framework Configuration results in a configuration file with the XML element `<publisherPolicy>` and the attribute `apply="no"`.

```xml
<?xml version="1.0"?>
<configuration>
  <runtime>
    <assemblyBinding xmlns="urn:schemas-microsoft-com:asm.v1">
      <dependentAssembly>
        <assemblyIdentity name="SharedDemo" publicKeyToken="23f9b4bb8f65e63f" />
        <publisherPolicy apply="no" />
      </dependentAssembly>
    </assemblyBinding>
  </runtime>
</configuration>
```

By disabling the publisher policy, you can configure different version redirection in the application configuration file.

# Assemblies

## *Runtime version*

Installing and using multiple versions is not only possible with assemblies, but also with the .NET runtime. The versions 1.0, 1.1, and 2.0 (and later versions) of the .NET runtime can be installed on the same operating system side by side. Visual Studio 2005 targets applications running on .NET 2.0. .NET 2.0 is a major release following .NET 1.1. With this major release the assembly file format changed, so it is not possible to run .NET 2.0 applications with .NET 1.1.

If the application is built with .NET 1.1, it is possible to target systems that have only the .NET 1.0 runtime installed. The same can be expected about future minor releases in that they can target .NET 2.0 runtime versions.

An application that was built using .NET 1.0 may run without changes on .NET 1.1. If an operating system has both versions of the runtime installed, the application will use the version with which it was built. However, if only version 1.1 is installed with the operating system, and the application was built with version 1.0, it tries to run with the newer version. The registry key `HKEY_LOCAL_MACHINE\ Software\Microsoft\.NETFramework\policy` lists the ranges of the versions that will be used for a specific runtime.

If an application was built using .NET 1.1, it may run without changes on .NET 1.0, in case no classes or methods are used that are only available with .NET 1.1. Here an application configuration file is needed to make this possible.

In an application configuration file, it's not only possible to redirect versions of referenced assemblies; you can also define the required version of the runtime. Different .NET runtime versions can be installed on a single machine. You can specify the version that's required for the application in an application configuration file. The element `<supportedVersion>` marks the runtime versions that are supported by the application:

```xml
<?xml version="1.0"?>
<configuration>
   <startup>
      <supportedRuntime version="v1.1.4322" />
      <supportedRuntime version="v1.0.3512" />
   </startup>
</configuration>
```

There is one major point in case you still have .NET 1.0 applications that should run on .NET 1.1 runtime versions. The element `<supportedVersion>` was new with .NET 1.1. .NET 1.0 used the element `<requiredRuntime>` to specify the needed runtime. So for .NET 1.0 applications, both configurations must be done as shown here:

```xml
<?xml version="1.0"?>
<configuration>
   <startup>
    <supportedRuntime version="v1.1.4322"/>
    <supportedRuntime version="v1.0.3705"/>
      <requiredRuntime version="v1.0.3512" safeMode="true" />
   </startup>
</configuration>
```

# Chapter 15

`<requiredRuntime>` *does not overrule the configuration for* `<supportedRuntime>` *as it may look like, because* `<requiredRuntime>` *is used only with .NET 1.0, while* `<supportedRuntime>` *is used by .NET 1.1 and later versions.*

## Configuring Directories

You've already seen how to redirect referenced assemblies to a different version so that you can locate your assemblies, but there are more options to configure! For example, it's not necessary to install a shared assembly in the global assembly cache. It's also possible that shared assemblies can be found with the help of specific directory settings in configuration files. This feature can be used if you want to make the shared components available on a server. Another possible scenario arises if you want to share an assembly between your applications, but you don't want to make it publicly available in the global assembly cache, so you put it into a shared directory instead.

There are two ways to find the correct directory for an assembly: the `codeBase` element in an XML configuration file, or through probing. The `codeBase` configuration is available only for shared assemblies, and probing is done for private assemblies.

### <codeBase>

The `<codeBase>` can also be configured using the .NET Configuration utility. Codebases can be configured by selecting the properties of the configured application, `SimpleShared`, inside the Configured Assemblies in the Applications tree. Similar to the Binding Policy, you can configure lists of versions with the Codebases tab. Figure 15-43 shows that the version 1.0 should be loaded from the Web server `http://www.christiannagel.com/WroxUtils`.

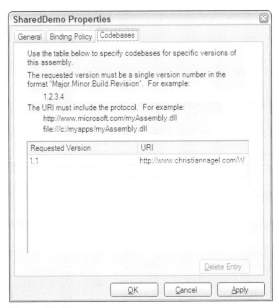

Figure 15-43

The .NET Configuration utility creates this application configuration file:

```xml
<?xml version="1.0"?>
<configuration>
  <runtime>
    <assemblyBinding xmlns="urn:schemas-microsoft-com:asm.v1">
      <dependentAssembly xmlns="">
        <assemblyIdentity name="SimpleShared"
                          publicKeyToken="23f9b4bb8f65e63f" />
        <codeBase version="1.1" href="http://www.christiannagel.com/WroxUtils" />
      </dependentAssembly>
    </assemblyBinding>
  </runtime>
</configuration>
```

The `<dependentAssembly>` element is the same used previously for the version redirection. The `<codeBase>` element has the attributes `version` and `href`. With `version`, the original referenced version of the assembly must be specified. With `href`, you can define the directory from where the assembly should be loaded. In the example, a path using the HTTP protocol is used. A directory on a local system or a share is specified using `href="file:C:/WroxUtils"`.

> *Using that assembly loaded from the network causes a* `System.Security.Permissions` *exception to occur. You must configure the required permissions for assemblies loaded from the network. In Chapter 16, ".NET Security," you learn how to configure security for assemblies.*

## *<probing>*

When the `<codeBase>` is not configured and the assembly is not stored in the global assembly cache, the runtime tries to find an assembly with probing. The .NET runtime tries to find an assembly with either a `.dll` or an `.exe` file extension in the application directory, or in one of its subdirectories, that has the same name as the assembly searched for. If the assembly is not found here, the search continues. You can configure search directories with the `<probing>` element in the `<runtime>` section of application configuration files. This XML configuration can also be done easily by selecting the properties of the application with the .NET Framework Configuration tool. You can configure the directories where the probing should occur by using the search path in the .NET Framework configuration (see Figure 15-44).

The XML file produced has these entries:

```xml
<?xml version="1.0"?>
<configuration>
  <runtime>
    <gcConcurrent enabled="enabled" />
    <assemblyBinding xmlns="urn:schemas-microsoft-com:asm.v1">
      <probing privatePath="bin;utils;" xmlns="" />
    </assemblyBinding>
  </runtime>
</configuration>
```

The `<probing>` element has just a single required attribute: `privatePath`. This application configuration file tells the runtime that assemblies should be searched for in the base directory of the application, followed by the `bin` and the `util` directory. Both directories are subdirectories of the application base directory. It's not possible to reference a private assembly outside the application base directory or a subdirectory thereof. An assembly outside of the application base directory must have a shared name and can be referenced using the `<codeBase>` element as you saw earlier.

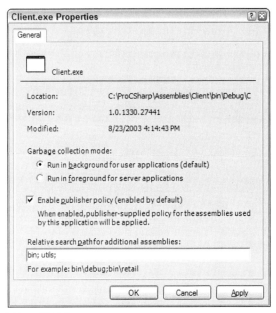

Figure 15-44

# Summary

Assemblies are the new installation unit for the .NET platform. Microsoft learned from problems with previous architectures and did a complete redesign to avoid the old problems. This chapter discussed the features of assemblies: they are self-describing and no type library and registry information is needed. Version dependencies are exactly recorded so that with assemblies, the DLL Hell we had with old DLLs no longer exists. Because of these features, not only development but also deployment and administration have become a lot easier.

The chapter also discussed cross-language support, and you created a C# class that derives from a Visual Basic class that makes use of a C++/CLI class and looked at the differences in the generated MSIL code.

You learned the differences between private and shared assemblies and saw how shared assemblies can be created. With private assemblies, you don't have to pay attention to uniqueness and versioning issues because these assemblies are copied and only used by a single application. Sharing assemblies has the requirement to use a key for uniqueness, and to define the version. You looked at the global assembly cache that can be used as an intelligent store for shared assemblies.

You looked at overriding versioning issues to use a version of an assembly different from the one that was used during development; this is done through publisher policies and application configuration files. Finally, you learned how probing works with private assemblies.

# 16

# .NET Security

You're sitting at your machine and you click a button on an application you're using. Behind the scenes, your application responds to the fact that you are attempting to use a feature for which it does not have the relevant module. It connects to the Internet, downloads the module into the Download Assembly Cache, and begins executing — all without prompting you.

This kind of behind-the-scenes upgrade functionality is already used with many .NET applications, but there is a concern here over the security implications relating to what is called *mobile code*. In clear terms, what evidence do you actually have that you can trust the code your computer is downloading? How do you know that the module you requested is, in fact, the one that you are receiving? What does the CLR do behind the scenes to ensure, for example, that a control on a Web site is not reading your private e-mails?

.NET enforces a security policy around assemblies. It uses the evidence it has about them — where they are from or by whom they are published — to group the assemblies with similar characteristics. For example, the runtime places all code from the local intranet into a specific group. It then uses the security policy (normally defined by a system administrator using the Code Access Security Policy Tool (caspol.exe) command-line utility, or the Microsoft Management Console) to decide what permissions the code should be granted at a very granular level. What do you have to do to enable security on a machine or for a specific application? Nothing — all code automatically runs within the security context of the CLR, although you can turn off security if necessary.

In addition to high levels of confidence that the code you are executing can be trusted, it is also important to allow the application users access to the features they need, but nothing more. By virtue of its role-based security, .NET facilitates effective management of users and roles.

This chapter looks through the features available in .NET to help you manage security, including how .NET protects you from malicious code, how to administer security policies, and how to access the security subsystem programmatically. It also looks at deploying .NET applications securely and provides a number of short example applications to solidify the concepts in this chapter for you.

# Chapter 16

# Code Access Security

Code access security is a feature of .NET that manages code, dependent on your level of trust. If the CLR trusts the code enough to allow it to run, it will begin executing the code. Depending on the permissions given to the assembly, however, it might run within a restricted environment. If the code is not trusted enough to run, or if it runs but then attempts to perform an action for which it does not have the relevant permissions, a security exception (of type SecurityException or a subclass of it) is thrown. The code access security system means that you can stop malicious code running, but you can also allow code to run within a protected environment where you are confident that it cannot do any damage.

For example, if a user attempted to run an application that attempted to execute code downloaded from the Internet, the default security policy would raise an exception and the application would fail to start. Similarly, if the user ran an application from a network drive it would begin executing, but if the application then attempted to access a file on the local drive, the runtime would raise an exception and, depending on the error handling in the application, it would either gracefully degrade or exit.

For most applications, .NET's code access security is a significant benefit, but one that sits at the back of the room quietly helping. It provides high levels of protection from malicious code, but generally, you needn't get involved. However, one area you will be involved in is the management of security policy, and this is especially the case when desktop applications are configured to trust code from the locations of software suppliers delivering applications to you.

Another area where code access security becomes very important is the building of an application that includes an element whose security you want to control closely. For example, if there is a database within your organization containing extremely sensitive data, you would use code access security to state what code is allowed to access that database, and what code must not access it.

It is important to realize that code access security is about protecting resources (local drive, network, and user interface) from malicious code; it is not primarily a tool for protecting software from users. For security in relation to users, you will generally use the built-in Windows user security subsystem, or make use of .NET role-based security, which is discussed later in this chapter.

Code access security is based on two high-level concepts: *code groups* and *permissions*. Let's look at them before we start since they both form the foundations of the sections that follow:

❑ **Code groups** bring together code with similar characteristics, although the most important property is usually where the code came from. Two examples for code groups are Internet and Intranet. The group Internet defines code that is sourced from the Internet, and the group Intranet defines code sourced from the LAN. The information used to place assemblies into code groups is called *evidence*. Other evidence is collected by the CLR, including the publisher of the code, the strong name, and (where applicable) the URI from which it was downloaded. Code groups are arranged in a hierarchy, and assemblies are nearly always matched to several code groups. The code group at the root of the hierarchy is called All Code and contains all other code groups. The hierarchy is used for deciding which code groups an assembly belongs to; if an assembly does not provide evidence that matches it to a group in the tree, no attempt is made to match it to code groups below.

❑ **Permissions** are the actions you allow each code group to perform. For example, permissions include "able to access the user interface" and "able to access local storage." The system administrator usually manages the permissions at the enterprise, machine, and user levels.

# .NET Security

The Virtual Execution System within the CLR loads and runs programs. It provides the functionality required to execute managed code and uses assembly metadata to connect modules together at runtime. When the VES loads an assembly, it matches the assembly to one or more of a number of code groups. Each code group is assigned to one or more permissions that specify what actions assemblies can do in that code group. For example, if the MyComputer code group is assigned the permission FileIOPermission, this means that assemblies from the local machine can read and write to the local file system.

## *Code Groups*

Code groups have an entry requirement called *membership condition*. For an assembly to be filed into a code group, it must match the group's membership condition. Membership conditions include "the assembly is from the site `www.microsoft.com`" or "the publisher of this software is Microsoft Corporation."

Each code group has one, and only one, membership condition. The following list provides the types of code group membership conditions available in .NET:

- **Zone** — The region from which the code originated.
- **Site** — The Web site from which the code originated.
- **Strong name** — A unique, verifiable name for the code. Strong names are discussed in Chapter 15, "Assemblies."
- **Publisher** — The publisher of the code.
- **URL** — The specific location from which the code originated.
- **Hash value** — The hash value for the assembly.
- **Skip verification** — This condition requests that it bypasses code verification checks. Code verification ensures the code accesses types in a well-defined and acceptable way. The runtime cannot enforce security on code that is not type safe.
- **Application directory** — The location of the assembly within the application.
- **All code** — All code fulfills this condition.
- **Custom** — A user-specified condition.

The first, and most commonly used, type of membership condition is the *Zone* condition. A zone is the region of origin of a piece of code and refers to one of the following: MyComputer, Internet, Intranet, Trusted, or Untrusted. These zones can be managed by using the security options in Internet Explorer. Zones are discussed in more detail in the section "Managing Security Policies." Although the settings are managed within Internet Explorer, they apply to the entire machine. Clearly, these configuration options are not available in non-Microsoft browsers and, in fact, in-page controls written using the .NET Framework will not work in browsers other than Internet Explorer.

Code groups are arranged hierarchically with the All Code membership condition at the root (see Figure 16-1). You can see that each code group has a single membership condition and specifies the permissions that the code group has been granted. Note that if an assembly does not match the membership condition in a code group, the CLR does not attempt to match code groups below it.

# Chapter 16

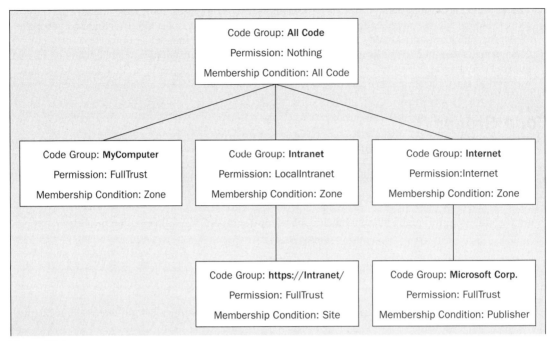

Figure 16-1

## caspol.exe — The Code Access Security Policy tool

This section spends a good deal of time looking at the command-line Code Access Security Policy tool. To get a list of options for the tool, just type the following at the command prompt:

    caspol.exe -?

To send the output to a text file, use:

    caspol.exe > output.txt

.NET also includes a snap-in for the Microsoft Management Console to manage code access security. However, this discussion is restricted to the command-line utility, because the examples are easier to follow, and you'll also be in a position to create scripts to alter the security policy, which is very useful when applying policies to large numbers of machines.

Let's look at the code groups on a machine using caspol.exe. The output of the command lists the hierarchical structure of the code groups on the machine, and next to each group there is a description of the code group. Type this command:

    caspol.exe -listdescription

Alternatively, the -listdescription parameter has a shortcut: -ld. You will see something like this:

```
Microsoft (R) .NET Framework CasPol 2.0.50727.7
Copyright (C) Microsoft Corporation. All rights reserved.

Security is ON
Execution checking is ON
Policy change prompt is ON

Level = Machine

Full Trust Assemblies:

1. All_Code: Code group grants no permissions and forms the root of the code
group tree.
    1.1. My_Computer_Zone: Code group grants full trust to all code originating
         on the local computer
        1.1.1. Microsoft_Strong_Name: Code group grants full trust to code signed
               with the Microsoft strong name.
        1.1.2. ECMA_Strong_Name: Code group grants full trust to code signed with
               the ECMA strong name.
    1.2. LocalIntranet_Zone: Code group grants the intranet permission set to
         code from the intranet zone. This permission set grants intranet code
         the right to use isolated storage, full UI access, some capability to do
         reflection, and limited access to environment variables.
        1.2.1. Intranet_Same_Site_Access: All intranet code gets the right to
               connect back to the site of its origin.
        1.2.2. Intranet_Same_Directory_Access: All intranet code gets the right to
               read from its install directory.
    1.3. Internet_Zone: Code group grants code from the Internet zone the
         Internet permission set. This permission set grants Internet code the right
         to use isolated storage and limited UI access.
        1.3.1. Internet_Same_Site_Access: All Internet code gets the right to
               connect back to the site of its origin.
    1.4. Restricted_Zone: Code coming from a restricted zone does not receive any
         permissions.
    1.5. Trusted_Zone: Code from a trusted zone is granted the Internet
         permission set. This permission set grants the right to use isolated
         storage and limited UI access.
        1.5.1. Trusted_Same_Site_Access: All Trusted Code gets the right to
               connect back to the site of its origin.
    1.6  Application_Security_Manager: Code group grants trust to ClickOnce
         applications.
        1.6.1. Intranet_Same_Site_Access: All intranet code gets the right
               to connect back to the site of its origin.
        1.6.2. Intranet_Same_Directory_Access: All intranet code gets the
               right to read from its install directory.
Success
```

The .NET security subsystem ensures that code from each code group is allowed to do only certain things. For example, code from the Internet zone will, by default, have much stricter limits than code from the local drive. Code from the local drive is normally granted access to data stored on the local drive, but assemblies from the Internet are not granted this permission by default.

## Chapter 16

Using caspol and its equivalent in the Microsoft Management Console, you can specify what level of trust you have for each code access group, as well as managing code groups and permissions in a more granular fashion.

Let's take another look at the code access groups, but this time in a slightly more compact view. Make sure you're logged in as a local administrator, go to a command prompt, and type this command:

**caspol.exe -listgroups**

You will see something like this:

```
Microsoft (R) .NET Framework CasPol 2.0.50727.7
Copyright (C) Microsoft Corporation. All rights reserved.

Security is ON
Execution checking is ON
Policy change prompt is ON

Level = Machine

Code Groups:

1.  All code: Nothing
    1.1.  Zone - MyComputer: FullTrust
        1.1.1.   StrongName - 00240000048000009400000006020000002400005253413100040
0000100010007D1FA57C4AED9F0A32E84AA0FAEFD0DE9E8FD6AEC8F87FB03766C834C99921EB23BE
79AD9D5DCC1DD9AD236132102900B723CF980957FC4E177108FC607774F29E8320E92EA05ECE4E82
1C0A5EFE8F1645C4C0C93C1AB99285D622CAA652C1DFAD63D745D6F2DE5F17E5EAF0FC4963D261C8
A12436518206DC093344D5AD293: FullTrust
        1.1.2.   StrongName - 00000000000000000400000000000000: FullTrust
    1.2.  Zone - Intranet: LocalIntranet
        1.2.1.   All code: Same site Web.
        1.2.2.   All code: Same directory FileIO - 'Read, PathDiscovery'
    1.3.  Zone - Internet: Internet
        1.3.1.   All code: Same site Web.
    1.4.  Zone - Untrusted: Nothing
    1.5.  Zone - Trusted: Internet
        1.5.1.   All code: Same site Web.
Success
```

You'll notice that near the start of the output it says Security is ON. Later in the chapter you see that it can be turned off and then turned on again.

The Execution Checking setting is on by default, which means that all assemblies must be granted the permission to execute before they can run. If execution checking is turned off using caspol (caspol.exe –execution on|off), assemblies that do not have the permission to run can execute, although they might cause security exceptions if they attempt to act contrary to the security policy later in their execution.

## .NET Security

The Policy change prompt option specifies whether you see an "Are you sure" warning message when you attempt to alter the security policy.

As code is broken down into these groups, you can manage security at a more granular level, and apply full trust to a much smaller percentage of code. Note that each group has a label (for example, 1.2). These labels are auto-generated by .NET, and can differ between machines. Generally, security is not managed for each assembly, but for using a code group instead.

When a machine has several side-by-side installations of .NET, the copy of caspol.exe that you run will only alter the security policy for the installation of .NET with which it is associated.

### Viewing an assembly's code groups

Assemblies are matched to code groups dependent on the membership conditions they match. If you go back to the code-groups example and load an assembly from the `https://intranet/` Web site, it would match the code groups shown in Figure 16-2. The assembly is a member of the root code group (All Code); because it came from the local network it is also a member of the Intranet code group. However, because it was loaded from the specific site `https://intranet`, it is also granted *FullTrust*, which means it can run unrestricted.

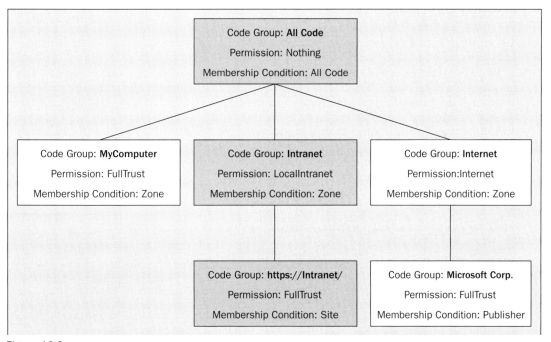

Figure 16-2

You can easily view the code groups that an assembly is a member of using this command:

```
caspol.exe -resolvegroup assembly.dll
```

469

## Chapter 16

Running this command on an assembly on the local drive produces the following output:

```
Microsoft (R) .NET Framework CasPol 2.0.50727.7
Copyright (C) Microsoft Corporation. All rights reserved.

Level = Enterprise

Code Groups:

1.  All code: FullTrust

Level = Machine

Code Groups:

1.  All code: Nothing
     1.1.  Zone - MyComputer: FullTrust

Level = User

Code Groups:

1.  All code: FullTrust

Success
```

You'll notice that code groups are listed on three levels — Enterprise, Machine, and User. For now, stay focused on the machine level. If you are curious about the relationship between the three, the effective permission given to an assembly is the intersection of the permissions from the three levels. For example, if you remove the FullTrust permission from the Internet zone at the enterprise-level policy, all permissions are revoked for code from the Internet zone, and the settings of the other two levels become irrelevant.

Now use this command once more with the same assembly to read the code groups. However, this time the assembly is accessed from a Web server using the HTTP protocol. You can see the assembly is a member of different groups that have much more restrictive permissions:

**caspol.exe -resolvegroup http://server/assembly.dll**

```
Microsoft (R) .NET Framework CasPol 2.0.50727.7
Copyright (C) Microsoft Corporation. All rights reserved.

Level = Enterprise

Code Groups:

1.  All code: FullTrust
Level = Machine

Code Groups:

1.  All code: Nothing
     1.1.  Zone - Internet: Internet
          1.1.1.  All code: Same site Web.
```

# .NET Security

```
Level = User

Code Groups:

1.  All code: FullTrust

Success
```

The assembly grants the Internet and the Same Site Web permissions. The intersection of the permissions allows the code limited UI access. It also permits the code to establish connections to the site it originated from.

The following section takes a closer look at permissions.

## Code Access Permissions and Permissions Sets

Imagine yourself administering security policy on a network of desktop machines in a large enterprise scenario. In this environment it's immensely useful for the CLR to collect evidence information on code before the code is allowed to execute. Likewise, you as the administrator must have the opportunity to control what code is allowed on the several hundred machines you manage once the CLR has identified its origin. This is where permissions start to act.

After an assembly has been matched to code groups, the CLR looks at the security policy to calculate the permissions it grants to an assembly. When managing permissions in Windows you generally don't want to apply permissions to users, but you apply permissions to user groups instead. This is also true with assemblies; permissions are applied to code groups rather than to individual assemblies, which makes the management of security policy in .NET a much easier task.

The security policy specifies what actions assemblies are allowed to perform in a code group. The following list shows a few of the code access permissions provided by the CLR; as you can see, you have big control of what code is permitted to do or not:

- **DirectoryServicesPermission** controls the ability to access Active Directory through the `System.DirectoryServices` classes.
- **DnsPermission** controls the ability to use the TCP/IP Domain Name System (DNS).
- **EnvironmentPermission** controls the ability to read and write environment variables.
- **EventLogPermission** controls the ability to read and write to the event log.
- **FileDialogPermission** controls the ability to access files that have been selected by the user in the Open dialog box. This permission is commonly used when `FileIOPermission` is not granted to allow limited access to files.
- **FileIOPermission** controls the ability to work with files (reading, writing, and appending to file, as well as creating and altering folders and accessing).
- **IsolatedStorageFilePermission** controls the ability to access private virtual file systems.
- **IsolatedStoragePermission** controls the ability to access isolated storage; storage that is associated with an individual user and with some aspect of the code's identity. Isolated storage is discussed in Chapter 34, "Manipulating Files and the Registry."

471

- **MessageQueuePermission** controls the ability to use message queues through the Microsoft Message Queue.
- **OleDbPermission** controls the ability to access databases with OLE DB providers.
- **PerformanceCounterPermission** controls the ability to make use of performance counters.
- **PrintingPermission** controls the ability to print.
- **ReflectionPermission** controls the ability to discover information about a type at runtime using `System.Reflection`.
- **RegistryPermission** controls the ability to read, write, create, or delete registry keys and values.
- **SecurityPermission** controls the ability to execute, assert permissions, call into unmanaged code, skip verification, and other rights.
- **ServiceControllerPermission** controls the ability to control Windows services.
- **SocketPermission** controls the ability to make or accept TCP/IP connections on a network transport address.
- **SQLClientPermission** controls the ability to access SQL Server databases with the .NET data provider for SQL Server.
- **UIPermission** controls the ability to access the user interface.
- **WebPermission** controls the ability to make or accept connections to or from the Web.

With each of these permission classes, it is often possible to specify an even deeper level of granularity. Later in this chapter you see an example of requesting not just file access but a specific level of file access.

In terms of best practice, you are well advised to ensure any attempts to make use of resources require that permissions are enclosed within `try/catch` error handling blocks, so that your application degrades gracefully should it be running under restricted permissions. The design of your application should specify how your application should act under these circumstances. Do not assume that it will be running under the same security policy under which it has been developed. For example, if your application cannot access the local drive, should it exit or operate in an alternative fashion?

An assembly is associated with several code groups; the effective permission of an assembly within the security policy is the union of all permissions from all the code groups to which it belongs. That is, each code group that an assembly matches extends what it is allowed to do. Note that code groups further down the tree are often assigned more relaxed permissions than those higher up.

Another set of permissions is assigned by the CLR on the basis of the identity of the code, which cannot be granted. These permissions relate to the evidence the CLR has collated about the assembly and are called *Identity Permissions*. Here are the names of the classes for the identity permissions:

- **PublisherIdentityPermission** refers to the software publisher's digital signature.
- **SiteIdentityPermission** refers to the name of the Web site from which the code originated.
- **StrongNameIdentityPermission** refers to the assembly's strong name.

# .NET Security

- **URLIdentityPermission** refers to the URL from which the code came (including the protocol, for example, `https://`).
- **ZoneIdentityPermission** refers to the zone from which the assembly originates.

By assigning the permission to code groups, there's no need to deal with every single permission. Instead, the permissions are applied in blocks, which is why .NET has the concept of permission sets. These are lists of code access permissions grouped into a named set. The following list explains the named permission sets you get out of the box:

- **FullTrust** means no permission restrictions.
- **SkipVerification** means that verification is not done.
- **Execution** grants the ability to run, but not to access any protected resources.
- **Nothing** grants no permissions and prevents the code from executing.
- **LocalIntranet** specifies the default policy for the local intranet, a subset of the full set of permissions. For example, file IO is restricted to read access on the share where the assembly originates.
- **Internet** specifies the default policy for code of unknown origin. This is the most restrictive policy listed. For example, code executing in this permission set has no file IO capability, cannot read or write event logs, and cannot read or write environment variables.
- **Everything** grants all the permissions that are listed under this set, except the permission to skip code verification. The administrator can alter any of the permissions in this permission set. This is useful where the default policy needs to be tighter.

   *Note that of these you can only change the definitions of the Everything permission set — the other sets are fixed and cannot be changed.*

Identity permissions cannot be included in permission sets because the CLR is the only body able to grant identity permissions to code. For example, if a piece of code is from a specific publisher, it would make little sense for the administrator to assign the identity permissions associated with another publisher. The CLR grants identity permissions where necessary, and if you want you can use them.

## Viewing an assembly's permissions

Imagine using a Microsoft application where you use a feature that you have not used before. The application does not have a copy of the code stored locally, so the code is requested from the Internet and downloaded into the Download Assembly Cache. Figure 16-3 illustrates what an assembly's code group membership might look like with code from the Internet published by a named organization that has signed the assembly with a certificate.

Although the All Code and Internet code groups bring only limited permissions according to the policy in this example, membership of the code group in the bottom right-hand corner grants the assembly the FullTrust permission. The overall effective permission is the *union* of permissions across the matching code groups. When the permissions are merged this way, the effective permission is that of all permissions granted, that is, each code group to which an assembly belongs brings additional permissions.

473

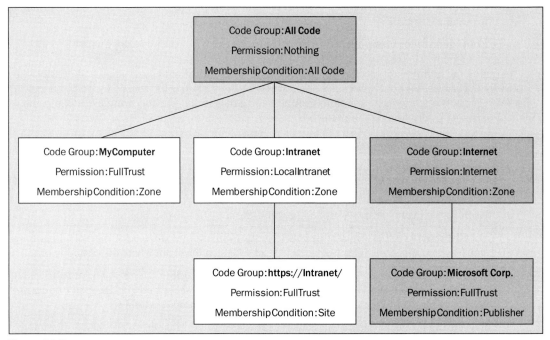

**Figure 16-3**

Just as you can check what code groups an assembly belongs to, it is also possible to look at the permissions assigned to the code groups. Doing this you'll see not only the code access permissions (what the code is allowed to do), but also the code identity permissions that will give you access to the evidence the code presented to the runtime. To see the permissions for an assembly's code groups, use a command like this:

```
caspol.exe -resolveperm assembly.dll
```

Try this on an assembly and look at the granted code access and identity permissions when the assembly is accessed over a local intranet. If you type the following command, you will see the code access permissions and then the three identity permissions at the end:

```
caspol.exe -resolveperm http://somehost/assembly.dll

Microsoft (R) .NET Framework CasPol 2.0.50727.7
Copyright (C) Microsoft Corporation. All rights reserved.

Resolving permissions for level = Enterprise
Resolving permissions for level = Machine
Resolving permissions for level = User

Grant =
<PermissionSet class="System.Security.PermissionSet"
```

```xml
      version="1">
<IPermission class="System.Security.Permissions.EnvironmentPermission,
      mscorlib, Version=2.0.0.0, Culture=neutral,
      PublicKeyToken=b77a5c561934e089" Version="1" Read="Username"/>
<IPermission class="System.Security.Permissions.FileDialogPermission,
      mscorlib, Version=2.0.0.0, Culture=neutral,
      PublicKeyToken=b77a5c561934e089"
      version="1" Unrestricted="true"/>
<IPermission class="System.Security.Permissions.IsolatedStorageFilePermission,
      mscorlib, Version=2.0.0.0, Culture=neutral,
      PublicKeyToken=b77a5c561934e089" version="1"
      Allowed="AssemblyIsolationByUser"
      UserQuota="9223372036854775807" Expiry="9223372036854775807"
      Permanent="True"/>
<IPermission class="System.Security.Permissions.ReflectionPermission,
      mscorlib, Version="2.0.0.0, Culture=neutral,
      PublicKeyToken= b77a5c561934e089" Version="1"
      Flags="ReflectionEmit" />
<IPermission class="System.Security.Permissions.SecurityPermission,
      mscorlib, Version=2.0.0.0, Culture=neutral,
      PublicKeyToken=b77a5c561934e089" version="1"
      Flags="Assertion, Execution, BindingRedirects"/>
<IPermission class="System.Security.Permissions.UIPermission,
      mscorlib, Version=2.0.0.0, Culture=neutral,
      PublicKeyToken=b77a5c561934e089" version="1"
      Unrestricted="true" />
<IPermission class="System.Security.Permissions.SiteIdentityPermission,
      mscorlib, Version=2.0.0.0, Culture=neutral,
      PublicKeyToken=b77a5c561934e089" version="1"
      Site="somehost" />
<IPermission class="System.Security.Permissions.UrlIdentityPermission,
      mscorlib, Version=2.0.0.0, Culture=neutral,
      PublicKeyToken=b77a5c561934e089" version="1"
      Url="http://somehost/assembly.dll" />
<IPermission class="System.Security.Permissions.ZoneIdentityPermission,
      mscorlib, Version=2.0.0.0, Culture=neutral,
      PublicKeyToken=b77a5c561934e089" version="1"
      Zone="Intranet" />
<IPermission class="System.Net.DnsPermission,
      System, Version=2.0.0.0, Culture=neutral,
      PublicKeyToken=b77a5c561934e089" version="1"
      Unrestricted="true" />
<IPermission class="System.Windows.Forms.WebBrowserPermission,
      System, Version=2.0.0.0, Culture=neutral,
      PublicKeyToken=b77a5c561934e089" version="1"
      Level="Restricted" />
<IPermission class="System.Drawing.Printing.PrintingPermission,
      System.Drawing, Version=2.0.0.0, Culture=neutral,
      PublicKeyToken=b03f5f7f11d50a3a" version="1"
      Level="DefaultPrinting" />
<IPermission class="System.Net.WebPermission,
      System, Version=2.0.0.0, Culture=neutral,
```

```
            PublicKeyToken=b77a5c561934e089" version="1">
        <ConnectAccess>
            <URI uri="(https|http)://somehost/.*[/]?"/>
        </ConnectAccess>
    </IPermission>
</PermissionSet>

Success
```

The output shows each of the permissions in XML, including the class defining the permission, the assembly containing the class, the permission version, and an encryption token. The output suggests that it is possible for you to create your own permissions. You can also see that each of the identity permissions includes more detailed information on, for example, the `UrlIdentityPermission` class, which provides access to the URL from which the code originated.

Note how at the start of the output, caspol.exe resolved the permissions at the enterprise, machine, and user levels and then listed the effective granted permissions, which is worth a closer look.

## Policy Levels: Machine, User, and Enterprise

Up to now, you have dealt with security in the context of a single machine. It's often necessary to specify security policies for specific users or for an entire organization, and that is why .NET provides not one but three policy levels:

- Machine
- Enterprise
- User

The code group levels are independently managed and exist in parallel, as shown in Figure 16-4.

If there are three security policies, how do you know which one applies? The effective permission is the *intersection* of the permissions from these three levels. Each of the three levels has the ability to veto the permissions allowed by another — this is really good news for administrators because their settings will override user settings.

To work with code groups and permissions on the user or enterprise levels using caspol.exe, add either the `-enterprise` or `-user` argument to change the command's mode. caspol.exe works at the machine level by default and that's how you've been using it until now. Use the following command to see the code groups listing at the user level:

```
caspol.exe -user -listgroups
```

# .NET Security

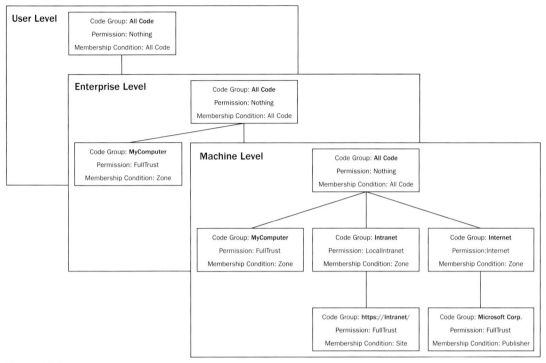

**Figure 16-4**

The output of the command on a default installation looks like this:

```
Security is ON
Execution checking is ON
Policy change prompt is ON

Level = User

Code Groups:

1.  All code: FullTrust
Success
```

Now run the same command but this time with the code groups at the enterprise level:

**caspol.exe -enterprise -listgroups**

## Chapter 16

The output of the command looks like this:

```
Security is ON
Execution checking is ON
Policy change prompt is ON

Level = Enterprise

Code Groups:

1.  All code: FullTrust
Success
```

As you can see, by default, both the user level and the enterprise level are configured to allow FullTrust for the single code group All Code. The result of this is that the default setting for .NET security places no restrictions at the enterprise or user levels, and the enforced policy is dictated solely by the machine-level policy. For example, if you were to assign a more restrictive permission or permission set to either the enterprise or user levels than FullTrust, those restrictions would restrict the overall permissions, and probably override permissions at the machine level. The effective permissions are intersected. If you want to apply FullTrust to a code group, this permission must be assigned to the code group on each of the three policy levels.

When you run caspol.exe as an administrator, it defaults to the machine level, but if you log out and log back in as a user who is not in the Administrator user group, caspol.exe will default to the user level instead. In addition, caspol.exe will not allow you to alter the security policy in a way that renders the caspol.exe utility itself inoperable.

You've had a high-level look at the security architecture in .NET; you now learn how to realize code access security features programmatically.

## Support for Security in the Framework

For .NET security to work, programmers must trust the CLR to enforce the security policy. When a call is made to a method that demands specific permissions (for example, accessing a file on the local drive) the CLR walks up the stack to ensure that every caller in the call chain has the permissions being demanded.

At this point the term *performance* is probably ringing in your mind, and clearly that is a concern, but to gain the benefits of a managed environment like .NET that is the price you pay. The alternative is that assemblies that are not fully trusted could make calls to trusted assemblies and your system is open to being attacked.

For reference, the parts of the .NET Framework library namespace most applicable to this chapter are:

- ❑    `System.Security.Permissions`
- ❑    `System.Security.Policy`
- ❑    `System.Security.Principal`

# .NET Security

Note that evidence-based code access security works in tandem with Windows logon security. If you attempt to run a .NET desktop application, the relevant .NET code access security permissions must be granted, but you as the logged-in user must use a Windows account that has the relevant permissions to execute the code. With desktop applications, the current user must have been granted the relevant rights to access the relevant assembly files on the drive. For Internet applications, the account under which Internet Information Server is running must be granted access to the assembly files.

## Demanding Permissions

To see how demanding permissions work, create a Windows Forms application that just contains a button. When the button is clicked, a file on the local file system is accessed. If the application does not have the relevant permission to access the local drive (`FileIOPermission`), the button will be marked as unavailable (dimmed).

If you import the namespace `System.Security.Permissions`, you can change the constructor of the class `Form1` to check for permissions by creating a `FileIOPermission` object, calling its `Demand()` method, and then acting on the result:

```
public Form1()
{
    InitializeComponent();

    try
    {
        FileIOPermission fileIOPermission = new
            FileIOPermission(FileIOPermissionAccess.AllAccess,@"c:\");
        fileIOPermission.Demand();
    }
    catch (SecurityException)
    {
        button1.Enabled = false;
    }
}
```

`FileIOPermission` is contained within the `System.Security.Permissions` namespace, which is the home to the full set of permissions and also provides classes for declarative permission attributes and enumerations for the parameters that are used to create permissions objects (for example creating a `FileIOPermission` specifying whether read-only or full access is needed).

If you run the application from the local drive where the default security policy allows access to local storage, you will see a dialog box that resembles the one in Figure 16-5.

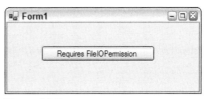

Figure 16-5

479

However, if you copy the executable to a network share and run it again, you are operating within the `LocalIntranet` permission set, which blocks access to local storage, and the button will be disabled as shown in Figure 16-6.

**Figure 16-6**

Within the implementation of the click event handler there's no need to check the required security because the relevant class in the .NET Framework already demands the file permission, and the CLR ensures that each caller up the stack has those permissions before proceeding. If you run the application from the intranet, and it attempts to open a file on the local disk, you will see an exception unless the security policy has been altered to grant access to the local drive.

If you want to catch exceptions thrown by the CLR when code attempts to act contrary to its granted permissions, you can catch the exception of the type `SecurityException`, which provides access to a number of useful pieces of information, including a human-readable stack trace (`SecurityException.StackTrace`) and a reference to the method that threw the exception (`SecurityException.TargetSite`). `SecurityException` even provides you with the `SecurityException.PermissionType` property, which returns the type of `Permission` object that caused the security exception to occur. If you have problems with security exceptions, this should be one of your first parts to diagnose. Simply remove the `try` and `catch` blocks from the previous code to see the security exception.

## *Requesting Permissions*

As discussed in the previous section, demanding permissions is where you state clearly what you need at runtime; however, you can configure an assembly so it makes a softer request for permissions right at the start of execution. The assembly can specify the required permissions before it begins executing.

You can request permissions in three ways:

- **Minimum** permissions specify the permissions your code must run.
- **Optional** permissions specify the permissions your code can use but is able to run effectively without.
- **Refused** permissions specify the permissions that you want to ensure are not granted to your code.

Why would you want to request permissions when your assembly starts? There are several reasons:

- If your assembly needs certain permissions to run, it makes sense to state this at the start of execution rather than during execution to ensure that the user does not experience a road block after beginning to work in your program.

❑ You will only be granted the permissions you request and nothing more. Without explicitly requesting permissions your assembly might be granted more permissions than it needs to execute. This increases the risk of your assembly being used for malicious purposes by other code.

❑ If you request only a minimum set of permissions, you are increasing the probability that your assembly will run, because you cannot predict the security policies that are effective at the user's location.

Requesting permissions is likely to be most useful if you're doing more complex deployment, and there is a higher risk that your application will be installed on a machine that does not grant the required permissions. It's usually preferable for the application to know right at the start if it will not be granted permissions, rather than halfway through execution.

In Visual Studio 2005, you can check the required permissions of an application by selecting the Security tab with the properties (see Figure 16-7). Clicking the Calculate Permissions button checks the code of the assembly and lists all required permissions.

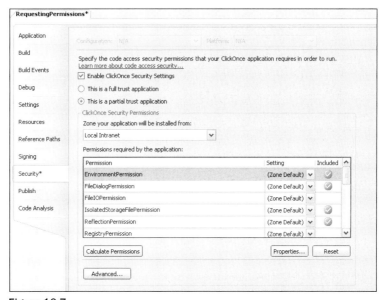

Figure 16-7

Instead of using Visual Studio, you can use the command line tool permcalc.exe to calculate the required permissions of an assembly. This tool is new with .NET 2.0.

The command line

```
permcalc.exe -show -stacks -cleancache DemandingPermissions.exe
```

creates an XML file that contains all required permissions. With the option –show the XML file is opened immediately. The option –stacks adds the stack information to the XML file, for you to see where the permissions demand originated from.

481

The required permissions can be added as attributes to the assembly. Following are three examples that demonstrate using attributes to request permissions. If you are following this with the code download, you can find these examples in the RequestingPermissions project. The first attribute requests that the assembly have `UIPermission` granted, which will allow the application access to the user interface. The request is for the minimum permissions, so if this permission is not granted, the assembly will fail to start:

```
using System.Security.Permissions;
[assembly:UIPermissionAttribute(SecurityAction.RequestMinimum, Unrestricted=true)]
```

Next, there is a request that the assembly is refused access to the C:\ drive. This attribute's setting means that the entire assembly will be blocked from accessing this drive:

```
[assembly:FileIOPermissionAttribute(SecurityAction.RequestRefuse, Read="C:/")]
```

Finally, here's an attribute that requests the assembly be optionally granted the permission to access unmanaged code:

```
[assembly:SecurityPermissionAttribute(SecurityAction.RequestOptional,
       Flags = SecurityPermissionFlag.UnmanagedCode)]
```

In this scenario, you want to add this attribute to an application that accesses unmanaged code in at least one place. In this case, it is specified that this permission is optional, which means that the application can run without the permission to access unmanaged code. If the assembly is not granted permission to access unmanaged code and attempts to do so, a `SecurityException` will be raised, which the application should expect and handle accordingly. The following table shows the full list of available `SecurityAction` enumeration values; some of these values are covered in more detail later on.

| SecurityAction Enumeration | Description |
| --- | --- |
| `Assert` | Allows code to access resources not available to the caller. |
| `Demand` | Requires all callers in the call stack to have the specified permission. |
| `DemandChoice` | Requires all callers in the stack to have one of the specified permissions. |
| `Deny` | Denies a permission by forcing any subsequent demand for the permission to fail. |
| `InheritanceDemand` | Requires derived classes to have the specified permission granted. |
| `LinkDemand` | Requires the immediate caller to have the specified permission. |
| `LinkDemandChoice` | Requires the immediate caller to have one of the specified permissions. |
| `PermitOnly` | Similar to `deny`, subsequent demands for resources not explicitly listed by `PermitOnly` are refused. |
| `RequestMinimum` | Applied at assembly scope; this contains a permission required for an assembly to operate correctly. |

## .NET Security

| SecurityAction Enumeration | Description |
|---|---|
| `RequestOptional` | Applied at assembly scope; this asks for permissions the assembly can use, if available, to provide additional features and functionality. |
| `RequestRefuse` | Applied at assembly scope when there is a permission you do not want your assembly to have. |

When you consider the permission requirements of your application, you have to decide between two options:

- Request all the permissions you need at the start of execution, and degrade gracefully or exit if those permissions are not granted.

- Avoid requesting permissions at the start of execution, but be prepared to handle security exceptions throughout your application.

After an assembly has been configured using permission attributes in this way, you can use the permcalc.exe utility to show the required permissions by aiming at the assembly file that contains the assembly manifest using the –assembly option of the permcalc.exe utility:

```
>permcalc.exe -show -assembly RequestingPermissions.exe
```

The output for an application using the three previously discussed attributes looks like this:

```
Microsoft (R) .NET Framework Permissions Calculator.
Copyright (C) Microsoft Corporation 2004. All rights reserved.

Analyzing...
|--------------------------------------------------------------------------|
..........................................................................

RequestingPermissions.exe
Minimal permission set:
<PermissionSet class="System.Security.PermissionSet"
version="1">
<IPermission class="System.Security.Permissions.UIPermission, mscorlib,
Version=2.0.0.0, Culture=neutral, PublicKeyToken=b77a5c561934e089" version="1"
Unrestricted="true"/>
</PermissionSet>

Optional permission set:
<PermissionSet class="System.Security.PermissionSet"
version="1">
<IPermission class="System.Security.Permissions.SecurityPermission, mscorlib,
Version=2.0.0.0, Culture=neutral, PublicKeyToken=b77a5c561934e089" version="1"
Flags="SecurityPermissionFlag.UnmanagedCode" />
</PermissionSet>

Refused permission set:
```

```
<PermissionSet class="System.Security.PermissionSet"
version="1">
<IPermission class="System.Security.Permissions.FileIOPermission, mscorlib,
Version=2.0.0.0, Culture=neutral, PublicKeyToken=b77a5c561934e089" version="1"
Read="C:"/>
</PermissionSet>

Generating output...
Writing file: permcalc.exe.PermCalc.xml...
```

In addition to requesting permissions, you can also request a complete permissions set; the advantage is that you don't have to deal with every single permission. However, you can only request permission sets that cannot be altered. The Everything permission set can be altered through the security policy while an assembly is running, so it cannot be requested.

Here's an example of how to request a built-in permission set:

```
[assembly:PermissionSetAttribute(SecurityAction.RequestMinimum,
                    Name = "FullTrust")]
```

In this example, the assembly requests that as a minimum it needs the FullTrust built-in permission set granted. If this set of permissions is not granted, the assembly will throw a security exception at runtime.

## Implicit Permission

When permissions are granted, there is often an implicit statement that you are also granted other permissions. For example, if you assign the `FileIOPermission` for C:\, there is an implicit assumption that there is also access to its subdirectories.

If you want to check whether a granted permission implicitly brings another permission as a subset, you can do this:

```
// Example ImplicitPermissions

    class Program
    {
        static void Main(string[] args)
        {
            CodeAccessPermission permissionA =
                new FileIOPermission(FileIOPermissionAccess.AllAccess, @"C:\");
            CodeAccessPermission permissionB =
                new FileIOPermission(FileIOPermissionAccess.Read, @"C:\temp");
            if (permissionB.IsSubsetOf(permissionA))
            {
                Console.WriteLine("PermissionB is a subset of PermissionA");
            }
        }
    }
```

## Denying Permissions

The output looks like this:

```
PermissionB is a subset of PermissionA
```

## Denying Permissions

Under certain circumstances, you might want to perform an action and be absolutely sure that the method that is called is acting within a protected environment. An assembly shouldn't be allowed to do anything unexpected. For example, say you want to make a call to a third-party class in a way that it will not access the local disk.

Create an instance of the permission you want to ensure the method is not granted, and then call its `Deny()` method before making the call to the class:

```
// Example DenyingPermissions

using System;
using System.IO;
using System.Security;
using System.Security.Permissions;
namespace Wrox.ProCSharp.Security
{
   class Program
   {
      static void Main(string[] args)
      {
         CodeAccessPermission permission =
            new FileIOPermission(FileIOPermissionAccess.AllAccess,@"C:\");
         permission.Deny();
         UntrustworthyClass.Method();
         CodeAccessPermission.RevertDeny();
      }
   }
   class UntrustworthyClass
   {
      public static void Method()
      {
         try
         {
            StreamReader din = File.OpenText(@"C:\textfile.txt");
         }
         catch
         {
            Console.WriteLine("Failed to open file");
         }
      }
   }
}
```

If you build this code the output will state *Failed to open file*, because the untrustworthy class does not have access to the local disk.

Note that the `Deny()` call is made on an instance of the `permission` object, whereas the `RevertDeny()` call is made statically. The reason for this is that the `RevertDeny()` call reverts all deny requests within the current stack frame; if you have made several calls to `Deny()`, you need only make one follow-up call to `RevertDeny()`.

## Asserting Permissions

Imagine that an assembly has been installed with full trust on a user's system. Within that assembly there is a method that saves auditing information to a text file on the local disk. If later an application is installed that wants to make use of the auditing feature, it will be necessary for the application to have the relevant `FileIOPermission` permissions to save the data to disk.

This seems excessive, however, because all you really want to do is perform a highly restricted action on the local disk. In these situations, it would be useful if assemblies with limiting permissions could make calls to more trusted assemblies that can temporarily increase the scope of the permissions on the stack, and perform operations on behalf of the caller. The caller doesn't need to have the permissions itself.

Assemblies with high enough levels of trust can assert permissions that they require. If the assembly has the permissions it needs to assert additional permissions, it removes the need for callers up the stack to have such wide-ranging permissions.

The code that follows contains a class called `AuditClass` that implements a method called `Save()`, which takes a string and saves audit data to `C:\audit.txt`. The `AuditClass` method asserts the permissions it needs to add the audit lines to the file. For testing it, the `Main()` method for the application explicitly denies the file permission that the `Audit` method needs:

```
// Example AssertingPermissions

using System;
using System.IO;
using System.Security;
using System.Security.Permissions;
namespace Wrox.ProCSharp.Security
{
    class Program
    {
        static void Main(string[] args)
        {
            CodeAccessPermission permission =
                new FileIOPermission(FileIOPermissionAccess.Append,
                                @"C:\audit.txt");
            permission.Deny();
            AuditClass.Save("some data to audit");
            CodeAccessPermission.RevertDeny();
        }
    }
    class AuditClass
    {
        public static void Save(string value)
        {
            try
```

## .NET Security

```
            {
                FileIOPermission permission =
                    new FileIOPermission(FileIOPermissionAccess.Append,
                                         @"C:\audit.txt");
                permission.Assert();
                FileStream stream = new FileStream(@"C:\audit.txt",
                    FileMode.Append, FileAccess.Write);

                // code to write to audit file here...
                CodeAccessPermission.RevertAssert();
                Console.WriteLine("Data written to audit file");
            }
            catch
            {
                Console.WriteLine("Failed to write data to audit file");
            }
        }
    }
}
```

When this code is executed, you'll find that the call to the `AuditClass` method does not cause a security exception, even though when it was called it did not have the required permissions to carry out the disk access.

Like `RevertDeny()`, `RevertAssert()` is a static method, and it reverts all assertions within the current frame.

It is important to be very careful when using assertions. You are explicitly assigning permissions to a method that has been called by code that might not have those permissions, and this could open a security hole. For example, in the auditing example, even if the security policy dictated that an installed application cannot write to the local disk, your assembly would be able to write to the disk when the auditing assembly asserts `FileIOPermissions` for writing.

However, to perform the assertion the auditing assembly must have been installed with permission for `FileIOAccess` and `SecurityPermission`. The `SecurityPermission` allows an assembly to perform an assert, and the assembly will need both the `SecurityPermission` and the permission being asserted to complete successfully.

An example in which this is used with the .NET Framework is with those classes that require unmanaged code access as they invoke Win32 API calls or COM components. The caller of these classes doesn't require unmanaged code access. The permissions that are required by the callers are verified by these classes.

## *Creating Code Access Permissions*

The .NET Framework implements code access security permissions that provide protection for the resources that it exposes. However, there might be occasions when you want to create your own permissions, which you can do by subclassing `CodeAccessPermission`. Deriving a custom permission class from the class `CodeAccessPermission` gives the benefits of the .NET code access security system, including stack walking and policy management.

Here are two examples of cases where you might want to roll your own code access permissions:

- **Protecting a resource not already protected by the Framework.** For example, you have developed a .NET application for home automation that is implemented by using an onboard hardware device. Creating your own code access permissions gives you a highly granular level of control over the access given to the home automation hardware.

- **Providing a finer degree of management than existing permissions.** For example, although the .NET Framework provides permissions that allow granular control over access to the local file system, you might have an application where you want to control access to a specific file or folder much more tightly. In this scenario, you might find it useful to create a code access permission that relates specifically to that file or folder; without that permission no managed code can access that area of the disk.

## Declarative Security

You can deny, demand, and assert permissions by calling classes in the .NET Framework. However, you can also use attributes and specify permission requirements declaratively.

The main benefit of using declarative security is that the settings are accessible through reflection. This can be of enormous benefit to system administrators, who often will want to view the security requirements of applications.

For example, you can specify that a method must have permission to read from C:\ to execute:

```
// Example DeclarativeSecurity

using System;
using System.Security.Permissions;
namespace Wrox.ProCSharp.Security
{
    class Program
    {
        static void Main(string[] args)
        {
            MyClass.Method();
        }
    }

    [FileIOPermission(SecurityAction.Assert, Read="C:/")]
    class MyClass
    {
        public static void Method()
        {
            // implementation goes here
        }
    }
}
```

Be aware that if you use attributes to assert or demand permissions, you cannot catch any exceptions that are raised if the action fails, because there is no imperative code around in which you can place a `try-catch-finally` clause.

# .NET Security

## Managing Security Policies

Although .NET's security features are wide ranging and far in advance of anything seen before on Windows, there are some limitations that you should be aware of:

- ❏ .NET security policy does not enforce security on unmanaged code (although it provides some protection against calls to unmanaged code).

- ❏ If a user copies an assembly to a local machine, the assembly has FullTrust and security policy is effectively bypassed. To work around this, you can limit the permissions granted to local code.

- ❏ .NET security policy provides very little help in dealing with script-based viruses and malicious Win32 `.exe` files, which Microsoft is dealing with in different ways. For example, recent versions of Outlook block executable files from e-mails.

However, .NET enormously assists the operating system in making intelligent decisions about how much trust to give to code, whether it originates from an intranet application, a control on a Web page, or a Windows Forms application downloaded from a software supplier on the Internet.

## *The Security Configuration File*

As you've already seen, the glue that connects code groups, permissions, and permission sets consists of three levels of security policy (enterprise, machine, and user). Security configuration information in .NET is stored in XML configuration files that are protected by Windows security. For example, the machine-level security policy is only writable to users in the Administrator, Power User, and SYSTEM Windows groups.

The files that store the security policy are located in the following paths:

- ❏ Enterprise policy configuration: `<windir>\Microsoft.NET\Framework\<version>\Config\enterprise.config`

- ❏ Machine policy configuration: `<windir>\Microsoft.NET\Framework\<version>\Config\security.config`

- ❏ User policy configuration: `%USERPROFILE%\application data\Microsoft\CLR Security Config\<version>\security.config`

The subdirectory `<version>` varies depending on the version of the .NET Framework you have on your machine. If necessary, it's possible to edit these configuration files manually, for example, if an administrator needs to configure policy for a user without logging into his account. However, in general it's recommended to use caspol.exe or the Runtime Security Policy node in the .NET Framework Configuration MMC snap-in to manage security policy.

Given everything you've read so far, create a simple application that accesses the local drive, the kind of behavior you're likely to want to manage carefully. The application is a C# Windows Forms application with a list box and a button (see Figure 16-8). If you click the button, the list box is populated from a file called `animals.txt` in the root of the C:\ drive.

# Chapter 16

Figure 16-8

The application was created by using Visual Studio 2005 and the only changes were to add the list box and Load Data button to the form and to add an event to the button that looks like this:

```
// Example from SimpleExample

private void OnLoadData(object sender, System.EventArgs e)
{
   StreamReader stream = File.OpenText("C:/animals.txt");
   string str;
   while ((str=stream.ReadLine()) != null)
   {
      listAnimals.Items.Add(str);
   }
}
```

It opens a simple text file `animals.txt` from the root of the C:\ drive, which contains a list of animals on separate lines, and loads each line into a string, which it then uses to create each item in the list box.

If you run the application from your local machine and click the button, you'll see the data loaded from the root of the C:\ drive and displayed in the list box (see Figure 16-9). Behind the scenes the runtime has granted the assembly the permission it needs to execute, access the user interface, and read data from the local disk.

Figure 16-9

As mentioned earlier, the permissions on the intranet zone code group are more restrictive than on the local machine; in particular, they do not allow access to the local disk. If you run the application again, but this time from a network share, it will run just as before because it is granted the permissions to execute and access the user interface; however, if you now click the Load Data button on the form, a security exception is thrown (see Figure 16-10). You'll see in the exception message text that it mentions the `System.Security.Permissions.FileIOPermission` object; this is the permission that the application was not granted and that was demanded by the class in the Framework that was used to load the data from the file on the local disk.

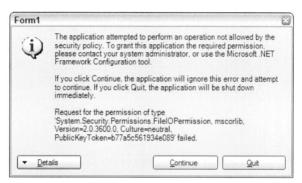

**Figure 16-10**

By default, the Intranet code group is granted the LocalIntranet permission set; change the permission set to FullTrust so any code from the intranet zone can run completely unrestricted.

First, you need to get the numeric label of the LocalIntranet code group. You can do this with the following command:

```
>caspol.exe -listgroups
```

This will output something like this:

```
Code Groups:

1.  All code: Nothing
   1.1.  Zone - MyComputer: FullTrust
      1.1.1.  StrongName -
0024000004800000940000000602000000240000525341310004000001000100007D1FA57C4AED9F0A32
E84AA0FAEFD0DE9E8FD6AEC8F87FB03766C834C99921EB23BE79AD9D5DCC1DD9AD236132102900B723C
F980957FC4E177108FC607774F29E8320E92EA05ECE4E821C0A5EFE8F1645C4C0C93C1AB99285D622CA
A652C1DFAD63D745D6F2DE5F17E5EAF0FC4963D261C8A12436518206DC093344D5AD293: FullTrust
      1.1.2.  StrongName - 0000000000000000400000000000000: FullTrust
   1.2.  Zone - Intranet: LocalIntranet
      1.2.1.  All code: Same site Web.
      1.2.2.  All code: Same directory FileIO - 'Read, PathDiscovery'
   1.3.  Zone - Internet: Internet
      1.3.1.  All code: Same site Web.
   1.4.  Zone - Untrusted: Nothing
   1.5.  Zone - Trusted: Internet
      1.5.1.  All code: Same site Web.
```

Notice the LocalIntranet group is listed as 1.2. You can use the following command to apply full trust:

```
>caspol.exe -chggroup 1.2 FullTrust
```

If you run the application from the network share again and click the button, you'll see that the list box is populated with the content of the file in the root of the C:\ drive and no exception occurs.

In scenarios like these where you're making use of resources governed by permissions, it is advisable to extend the code so that security exceptions are caught and the application can degrade gracefully. For example, in the sample application, you can add a `try-catch` block around the file access code, and if a `SecurityException` is thrown you display a line in the list box saying "Permission denied accessing file":

```
// Code from SimpleExample

private void OnLoadData(object sender, System.EventArgs e)
{
    try
    {
        StreamReader din = File.OpenText("C:/animals.txt");
        string str;
        while ((str=din.ReadLine()) != null)
        {
            listAnimals.Items.Add(str);
        }
    }
    catch (SecurityException ex)
    {
        MessageBox.Show(ex.Message);
    }
}
```

In reality, if you wanted to run a specific application from a network share, you'd most likely opt for a solution that didn't open up the client machine to all code on the intranet. Instead, code groups and membership conditions can be used to tightly control the requirements of the application — perhaps using its location on the intranet, a strong name, or a certificate proving the identity of the publisher.

## Managing Code Groups and Permissions

In managing security on .NET, if you find that an assembly is failing with a security exception, you usually have three choices:

- ❏ Ease the policy permissions
- ❏ Move the assembly
- ❏ Apply a strong name to the assembly

To make these kinds of decisions, you have to take into account your level of trust of the assembly.

## Turning Security On and Off

By default, .NET security is enabled. If, for any reason, you need to turn it off, you can do it like this:

```
>caspol.exe -security off
```

To turn security back on, use this:

```
>caspol.exe -security on
```

Generally, the security risks are too high when you turn off security. We recommend you do this only for testing and debugging purposes.

> Something you should be aware of is that the previous command does not need administrative privileges; this means any user (or a virus) could turn off .NET security. You are well advised to alter the Windows file security on the caspol utility to guard against malicious or misinformed usage.

## Resetting Security Policy

If you need to return the security configuration to its original state, you can type this command:

```
>caspol.exe -reset
```

This command resets the security policy to the installation default.

## Creating a Code Group

You can create your own code groups and then apply specific permissions to them. For example, you could specify that you want to trust all code from the Web site www.wrox.com and to give it full access to the system (without trusting code from any other Web site).

Earlier the tool caspol was used to display a list with the available group and number assignments. The zone Internet is labeled 1.3, so now type this command:

```
>caspol.exe -addgroup 1.3 -site www.wrox.com FullTrust
```

Note that this command will ask for confirmation, because this is an attempt to alter the security policy on the machine. If the command `caspol.exe -listgroups` is now run again, you'll see the new code group has been added and assigned FullTrust:

```
...
 1.2.  Zone - Intranet: LocalIntranet
    1.2.1.  All code: Same site Web.
    1.2.2.  All code: Same directory FileIO - Read, PathDiscovery
  1.3.  Zone - Internet: Internet
```

```
            1.3.1.  All code: Same site Web.
         1.3.2.  Site - www.wrox.com: FullTrust
   1.4.  Zone - Untrusted: Nothing
   1.5.  Zone - Trusted: Internet
      1.5.1.  All code: Same site Web.
```

Here's another example. Say you want to create a code group under the Intranet code group (1.2) that grants FullTrust to all applications running from a specific network share. To do so, you run the following command:

```
>caspol.exe -addgroup 1.2 -url file:\\intranetserver/sharename/* FullTrust
```

## Deleting a Code Group

To remove a code group that has been created, you can type a command like this:

```
>caspol.exe -remgroup 1.3.2
```

It will ask for confirmation that you want to alter the security policy, and if you give positive confirmation it will state that the group has been removed.

> Be aware that although you cannot delete the code group All Code, you can delete code groups at the level below it, including the Internet, MyComputer, and LocalIntranet groups.

## Changing a Code Group's Permissions

To ease or restrict the permissions assigned to a code group, you use caspol.exe again. Suppose you want to apply FullTrust to the Intranet zone; first you need to get the label that represents the Intranet code group:

```
>caspol.exe -listgroups
```

The output shows the Intranet code group:

```
Code Groups:

1.  All code: Nothing
   1.1.  Zone - MyComputer: FullTrust
      1.1.1.  StrongName -
002400000480000094000000060200000024000052534131000400000100010007D1FA57C4AED9F0A32
E84AA0FAEFD0DE9E8FD6AEC8F87FB03766C834C99921EB23BE79AD9D5DCC1DD9AD236132102900B72
3CF980957FC4E177108FC607774F29E8320E92EA05ECE4E821C0A5EFE8F1645C4C0C93C1AB99285D622
CAA652C1DFAD63D745D6F2DE5F17E5EAF0FC4963D261C8A12436518206DC093344D5AD293:
FullTrust
      1.1.2.  StrongName - 00000000000000000400000000000000: FullTrust
   1.2.  Zone - Intranet: LocalIntranet
      1.2.1.  All code: Same site Web.
```

```
            1.2.2.   All code: Same directory FileIO - Read, PathDiscovery
      1.3.  Zone - Internet: Internet
            1.3.1.   All code: Same site Web.
      1.4.  Zone - Untrusted: Nothing
      1.5.  Zone - Trusted: Internet
            1.5.1.   All code: Same site Web.
```

Once you have the Intranet code group's label, 1.2, you can enter a second command to alter the code group's permissions:

```
>caspol.exe -chggroup 1.2 FullTrust
```

The command asks to confirm the change to the security policy, and if you run the `caspol.exe -list-groups` command again, you can see that the permission on the end of the Intranet line has changed to FullTrust:

```
Code Groups:

1.  All code: Nothing
      1.1.  Zone - MyComputer: FullTrust
            1.1.1.   StrongName -
002400000480000094000000060200000024000052534131000400000100010007D1FA57C4AED9F0A32
E84AA0FAEFD0DE9E8FD6AEC8F87FB03766C834C99921EB23BE79AD9D5DCC1DD9AD236132102900B723C
F980957FC4E177108FC607774F29E8320E92EA05ECE4E821C0A5EFE8F1645C4C0C93C1AB99285D622CA
A652C1DFAD63D745D6F2DE5F17E5EAF0FC4963D261C8A12436518206DC093344D5AD293: FullTrust
            1.1.2.   StrongName - 00000000000000000400000000000000: FullTrust
      1.2.  Zone - Intranet: FullTrust
            1.2.1.   All code: Same site Web.
            1.2.2.   All code: Same directory FileIO - Read, PathDiscovery
      1.3.  Zone - Internet: Internet
            1.3.1.   All code: Same site Web.
      1.4.  Zone - Untrusted: Nothing
      1.5.  Zone - Trusted: Internet
            1.5.1.   All code: Same site Web.
```

## *Creating and Applying Permissions Sets*

You can create new permission sets using a command like this:

```
>caspol.exe -addpset MyCustomPermissionSet permissionset.xml
```

This command specifies that you are creating a new permission set called MyCustomPermissionSet, which is configured with the contents of the specified XML file. The XML file must contain a standard format that specifies a `PermissionSet`. For reference, here's the permission set file for the Everything permission set, which you can trim down to the permission set you want to create:

```
    <PermissionSet class="System.Security.NamedPermissionSet" version="1"
        Name="Everything"
        Description="Allows unrestricted access to all resources covered by
            built-in permissions">
      <IPermission class="System.Security.Permissions.EnvironmentPermission,
        mscorlib, Version=2.0.0.0, Culture=neutral,
```

```xml
        PublicKeyToken=b77a5c561934e089" version="1" Unrestricted="true" />
<IPermission class="System.Security.Permissions.FileDialogPermission,
    mscorlib, Version=2.0.0.0, Culture=neutral,
    PublicKeyToken=b77a5c561934e089" version="1" Unrestricted="true" />
<IPermission class="System.Security.Permissions.FileIOPermission,
    mscorlib, Version=2.0.0.0, Culture=neutral,
    PublicKeyToken=b77a5c561934e089" version="1" Unrestricted="true" />
<IPermission class="System.Security.Permissions.IsolatedStorageFilePermission,
    mscorlib, Version=2.0.0.0, Culture=neutral,
    PublicKeyToken=b77a5c561934e089" version="1" Unrestricted="true" />
<IPermission class="System.Security.Permissions.ReflectionPermission,
    mscorlib, Version=2.0.0.0, Culture=neutral,
    PublicKeyToken=b77a5c561934e089" version="1" Unrestricted="true" />
<IPermission class="System.Security.Permissions.RegistryPermission,
    mscorlib, Version=2.0.0.0, Culture=neutral,
    PublicKeyToken=b77a5c561934e089" version="1" Unrestricted="true" />
<IPermission class="System.Security.Permissions.SecurityPermission,
    mscorlib, Version=2.0.0.0, Culture=neutral,
    PublicKeyToken=b77a5c561934e089" version="1"
    Flags="Assertion, UnmanagedCode, Execution, ControlThread,
        ControlEvidence, ControlPolicy, SerializationFormatter,
        ControlDomainPolicy, ControlPrincipal, ControlAppDomain,
        RemotingConfiguration, Infrastructure, BindingRedirects" />
<IPermission class="System.Security.Permissions.UIPermission,
    mscorlib, Version=2.0.0.0, Culture=neutral,
    PublicKeyToken=b77a5c561934e089" version="1" Unrestricted="true" />
<IPermission class="System.Security.Permissions.KeyContainerPermission,
    mscorlib, Version=2.0.0.0, Culture=neutral,
    PublicKeyToken=b77a5c561934e089" version="1" Unrestricted="true" />
<IPermission class="System.Net.DnsPermission, System, Version=2.0.0.0,
    Culture=neutral, PublicKeyToken=b77a5c561934e089" version="1"
    Unrestricted="true" />
<IPermission class="System.Windows.Forms.WebBrowserPermission, System,
    Version=2.0.0.0, Culture=neutral,
    PublicKeyToken=b77a5c561934e089" version="1" Unrestricted="True" />
<IPermission class="System.Drawing.Printing.PrintingPermission,
    System.Drawing, Version=2.0.0.0, Culture=neutral,
    PublicKeyToken=b03f5f7f11d50a3a" version="1" Unrestricted="true" />
<IPermission class="System.Net.SocketPermission, System,
    Version=2.0.0.0, Culture=neutral,
    PublicKeyToken=b77a5c561934e089" version="1" Unrestricted="true" />
<IPermission class="System.Net.WebPermission, System,
    Version=2.0.0.0, Culture=neutral, PublicKeyToken=b77a5c561934e089"
    version="1" Unrestricted="true" />
<IPermission class="System.Diagnostics.EventLogPermission, System,
    Version=2.0.0.0, Culture=neutral,
    PublicKeyToken=b77a5c561934e089" version="1" Unrestricted="true" />
<IPermission class="System.Diagnostics.PerformanceCounterPermission,
    System, Version=2.0.0.0, Culture=neutral,
    PublicKeyToken=b77a5c561934e089" version="1" Unrestricted="true" />
<IPermission class="System.Data.OleDb.OleDbPermission,
    System.Data, Version=2.0.0.0, Culture=neutral,
    PublicKeyToken=b77a5c561934e089" version="1" Unrestricted="true" />
```

```
    <IPermission class="System.Data.SqlClient.SqlClientPermission,
        System.Data, Version=2.0.0.0, Culture=neutral,
        PublicKeyToken=b77a5c561934e089" version="1" Unrestricted="true" />
    <IPermission class="System.Security.Permissions.StorePermission,
        System.Security, Version=2.0.0.0, Culture=neutral,
        PublicKeyToken=b03f5f7f11d50a3a" version="1" Unrestricted="true" />
</PermissionSet>
```

To view all permission sets in XML format, you can use this command:

```
>caspol.exe -listpset
```

If you want to give a new definition to an existing permission set by applying an XML PermissionSet configuration file, you can use this command:

```
>caspol.exe -chgpset permissionset.xml MyCustomPermissionSet
```

## Distributing Code Using a Strong Name

.NET provides the ability to match an assembly to a code group when the assembly's identity and integrity have been confirmed using a strong name. This scenario is very common when assemblies are being deployed across networks (for example, distributing software over the Internet).

If you are a software company and you want to provide code to your customers via the Internet, you build an assembly and give it a strong name. The strong name ensures that the assembly can be uniquely identified, and also provides protection against tampering. Your customers can incorporate this strong name into their code access security policy; an assembly that matches this unique strong name can then be assigned permissions explicitly. As discussed in Chapter 15, "Assemblies," the strong name includes checksums for hashes of all the files within an assembly, so you have strong evidence that the assembly has not been altered since the publisher created the strong name.

Note that if your application uses an installer, the installer will install assemblies that have already been given a strong name. The strong name is generated once for each distribution before being sent to customers; the installer does not run these commands. The reason for this is that the strong name provides an assurance that the assembly has not been modified since it left your company; a common way to achieve this is to give your customer not only the application code, but also, separately, a copy of the strong name for the assembly. You might find it beneficial to pass the strong name to your customer using a secure form (perhaps fax or encrypted e-mail) to guard against the assembly being tampered with in the process.

Look at an example where an assembly with a strong name is created to distribute it in such a way that the recipient of the assembly can use the strong name to grant the FullTrust permission to the assembly.

First, a key pair is needed. Creating strong names has already been discussed in Chapter 15, so there's no need to repeat it here. Rebuilding the assembly with the key ensures that the hash is recalculated and the assembly is protected against malicious modifications. Also, the assembly can be uniquely identified with the strong name. This identification can be used with membership conditions of code groups. A membership condition can be based on the requirement to match a specific strong name.

The following command states that a new code group is created using the strong name from the specified assembly manifest file, that the code group is independent of the version number of the assembly, and that the code group has granted the FullTrust permissions:

```
>caspol.exe -addgroup 1 -strong -file SimpleExample.exe -noname -noversion
FullTrust
```

In this example, the application will now run from any zone, even the Internet zone, because the strong name provides powerful evidence that the assembly can be trusted. If you look at your code groups using `caspol.exe -listgroups`, you'll see the new code group (1.7 and its associated public key in hexadecimal):

```
Code Groups:

1.  All code: Nothing
    1.1.    Zone - MyComputer: FullTrust
        1.1.1.  StrongName -
002400000480000094000000060200000024000052534131000400000100010007D1FA57C4AED9F0A32
E84AA0FAEFD0DE9E8FD6AEC8F87FB03766C834C99921EB23BE79AD9D5DCC1DD9AD236132102900B723C
F980957FC4E177108FC607774F29E8320E92EA05ECE4E821C0A5EFE8F1645C4C0C93C1AB99285D622CA
A652C1DFAD63D745D6F2DE5F17E5EAF0FC4963D261C8A12436518206DC093344D5AD293: FullTrust
        1.1.2.  StrongName - 00000000000000000400000000000000: FullTrust
    1.2.    Zone - Intranet: LocalIntranet
        1.2.1.  All code: Same site Web
        1.2.2.  All code: Same directory FileIO - 'Read, PathDiscovery'
    1.3.    Zone - Internet: Internet
        1.3.1.  All code: Same site Web
    1.4.    Zone - Untrusted: Nothing
    1.5.    Zone - Trusted: Internet
        1.5.1.  All code: Same site Web
    1.6.    Application: Nothing
        1.6.1.  All code: Same site Web
        1.6.2.  All code: Same directory FileIO - 'Read'
    1.7.    StrongName -
002400000480000094000000060200000024000052534131000400000100010 0AD093685E490DC912EF
F4A3471E4024904E4EAA2367DB539E43D3ED287D954C531BFA51DDBE2D773C4CA8E3210776B0F4D1A8F
C3D2DC978F8CAEA951F29662F9879DC5D1D5755C990AA29DD73E4F4D4FDD223D26F3FBD8B17DEF878FF
DD2E42A0C9110B42D1E0C452ED8ABE62228A73F2CD9509E9D1631D88DF0238466785CCC: FullTrust
Success
```

If you want to access the strong name in an assembly you can use the secutil.exe tool against the assembly manifest file. You can use secutil.exe to view the strong name information for your assembly. Using the `-hex` option, the public key is shown in hexadecimal (like caspol.exe); the argument `-strongname` specifies that the strong name should be shown. Type this command, and you'll see a listing containing the strong name public key, the assembly name, and the assembly version:

```
>secutil.exe -hex -strongname SimpleExample.exe
Microsoft (R) .NET Framework SecUtil 2.0.50727.7
Copyright (C) Microsoft Corporation. All rights reserved.

Public Key =
0x002400000480000094000000060200000024000052534131000400000100010 0AD093685E490DC912
EFF4A3471E4024904E4EAA2367DB539E43D3ED287D954C531BFA51DDBE2D773C4CA8E3210776B0F4D1A
```

```
8FC3D2DC978F8CAEA951F29662F9879DC5D1D5755C990AA29DD73E4F4D4FDD223D26F3FBD8B17DEF878
FFDD2E42A0C9110B42D1E0C452ED8ABE62228A73F2CD9509E9D1631D88DF0238466785CCC
Name =
SimpleExample
Version =
1.0.1744.19477
Success
```

You may be surprised about the two strong name code groups that are installed by default and what they refer to. One is a strong name key for Microsoft code; the other strong name key is for the parts of .NET that have been submitted to the ECMA for standardization, which will give Microsoft much less control.

## Distributing Code Using Certificates

The preceding section discussed how a strong name can be applied to an assembly so that system administrators can explicitly grant permissions to assemblies that match that strong name using a code access group. Although this method of security policy management can be very effective, it's sometimes necessary to work at a higher level, where the administrator of the security policy grants permissions on the basis of the publisher of the software, rather than each individual software component. You probably have seen a similar method used before when you have downloaded executables from the Internet that have been Authenticode signed.

To provide information about the software publisher, you can make use of digital certificates and sign assemblies so that consumers of the software can verify the identity of the software publisher. In a commercial environment, you would obtain a certificate from a company such as Verisign or Thawte.

The advantage of buying a certificate from a supplier instead of creating your own is that it provides high levels of trust in its authenticity; the supplier acts as a trusted third party. For test purposes, however, .NET includes a command-line utility you can use to create a test certificate. The process of creating certificates and using them for publishing software is complex, but to give you an overview of what's involved this section walks you through a simple example.

The example will be made for the fictitious company called ABC Corporation. With this company the software product "ABC Suite" should be trusted. First off, create a test certificate by typing the following command:

```
>makecert -sk ABC -n "CN=ABC Corporation" abccorptest.cer
```

The command creates a test certificate under the name "ABC Corporation" and saves it to a file called `abccorptest.cer`. The `-sk ABC` argument creates a key container location, which is used by the public key cryptography.

To sign the assembly with the certificate, use the signcode.exe utility on the assembly file containing the assembly manifest. Often the easiest way to sign an assembly is to use the signtool.exe in its wizard mode; to start the wizard, just type `signtool.exe` with the parameter `signwizard`.

When you click Next, the program asks you to specify where the file is that should be signed. For an assembly, select the file containing the manifest, for example `SimpleExample.exe`, and click the Next button. On the Signing Options page, you have to select the Custom option to define the previously created certificate file.

In the next dialog box, you are asked to specify the certificate that should be used to sign the assembly. Click Select from File and browse to the file `abccorptest.cer`. You will now see the confirmation screen shown in Figure 16-11.

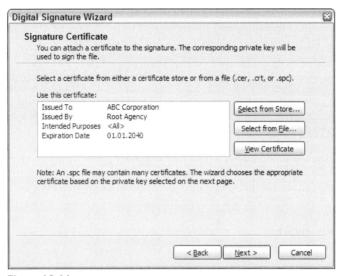

Figure 16-11

The next screen that appears asks for your private key. This key file was created by the makecert utility, so you can select the options as shown in Figure 16-12. The cryptographic service provider is an application that implements the cryptographic standards.

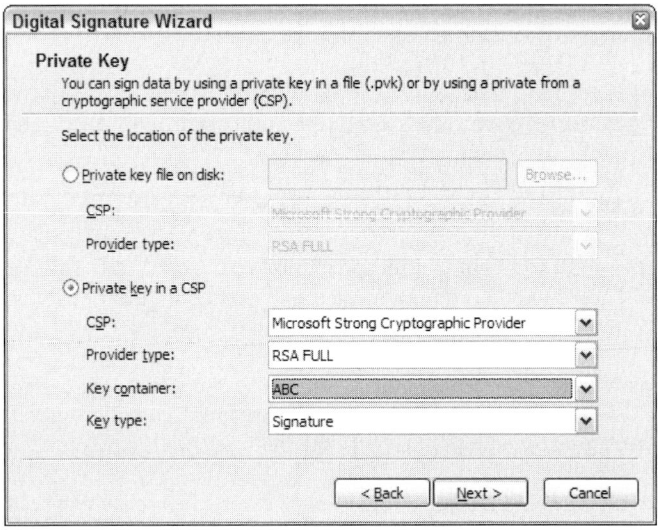

Figure 16-12

Next, you're asked a series of questions about the encryption algorithm that should be used for signing the assembly (md5 or sha1), the name and URL of the application, and shown a final confirmation dialog.

Because the executable is now signed with the certificate, a recipient of the assembly has access to strong evidence as to who published the software; the runtime can examine the certificate and match the publisher of the assembly to a code group with high levels of confidence as to the identity of the code, because the trusted third-party certifies the publisher's identity.

Let's look at the signed assembly in a bit more detail. Although a test certificate is used, you can temporarily configure .NET to treat test certificates more like trusted certificates issued by a trusted third party using the Set Registry Tool setreg.exe. This tool allows you to configure public key and certificate settings in the registry. If you enter the following command, the machine will be configured to trust the test root certificate, which gives a more meaningful test environment:

```
>setreg.exe 1 true
```

The utility setreg.exe can be used to configure that test certificates are accepted, to enable or disable expiration dates on certificates, and other certificate relevant options. When you are ready to reset the value, pass false as the last parameter. You can check out the assembly and verify its trust level using the Certification Verification Tool chktrust.exe utility:

```
>chktrust.exe SimpleExample.exe
```

This command pops up the window shown in Figure 16-13. Note that chktrust.exe has successfully confirmed the publisher of the software using the certificate, but also reminded you that, although the certificate has been verified, it is still a test certificate.

Figure 16-13

# Chapter 16

Now turn your attention to a machine that you want to configure in order to trust software from the ABC Corporation. You can create a new code access group that matches this software from ABC Corporation. You just have to grab a hexadecimal representation of the certificate from the assembly using the secutil.exe tool:

```
>secutil.exe -hex -x securityapp11.exe
```

This command results in the following output:

```
Microsoft (R) .NET Framework SecUtil 2.0.50727.7
Copyright (c) Microsoft Corp. All rights reserved.

X.509 Certificate =
0x308201BF30820169A003020102021044A1AF74BCB3F54BC4D1E30685397B68C300D06092A864886F70
D010104050030163114301206035504031305264F6F74204167656E6379301E170D3033313030353039
313733035A170D3339313233331323335393539A301A311830160603550403130F41424320436F72706
F726174696F6E30819F300D06092A864886F70D010101050003818D0030818902818100E537F563C230
4ECDA2DBEC892DED389C3C17E36500F381BD96E1C76185420F4EEA46051AD6972139AC7F0BCE3A473F7
B9E1DA0DB5F19CCB0A1774C7065DF9E56E4EC6E1F301FEEA899BD7D37A66F8150A987CD105059B402DE
641FB635A7E122F70A1F766D4A2B5030B32BA5189E1C918B0EF9E87151DACA49EB0160B051815902030
10001A34B304930470603551D010440303E801012E4092D061D1D4F008D6121DC166463A11830163114
30120603550403130B526F6F74204167656E6379821006376C00AA00648A11CFB8D4AA5C35F4300D060
92A864886F70D0101040500034100076FB204253DCA01C5B992DDCCC3CD26F0910E8EDA1C19552491492
8C1916FCD67E6093238152C50EDEBA9476983A9E660DD4849EFE3CFF3A5D2C09B7D4B9585E
Success
```

Now create the new code group and apply the FullTrust permission to assemblies published by the ABC Corporation using this (rather long) command:

```
>caspol -addgroup 1 -pub -hex 0 FullTrust
```

The parameters specify that the code group should be added at the top level (1.), and that the code group membership condition is of the type Publisher, and the last parameter specifies the permission set to grant (FullTrust). The command will ask for confirmation:

```
Microsoft (R) .NET Framework CasPol 2.0.50727.7
Copyright (C) Microsoft Corporation. All rights reserved.

The operation you are performing will alter security policy.
Are you sure you want to perform this operation? (yes/no)
y
Added union code group with "-pub" membership condition to the Machine level.
Success
```

The machine is now configured to fully trust all assemblies that have been signed with the certificate from ABC Corporation. To confirm that, you can run a `caspol.exe -lg` command, which lists the new code access group (1.7):

```
Security is ON
Execution checking is ON
Policy change prompt is ON

Level = Machine
```

```
Code Groups:

1.  All code: Nothing
    1.1.  Zone - MyComputer: FullTrust
       1.1.1.  StrongName -
002400000480000094000000060200000024000052534131000400000100010007D1FA57C4AED9F0A32
E84AA0FAEFD0DE9E8FD6AEC8F87FB03766C834C99921EB23BE79AD9D5DCC1DD9AD236132102900B723C
F980957FC4E177108FC607774F29E8320E92EA05ECE4E821C0A5EFE8F1645C4C0C93C1AB99285D622CA
A652C1DFAD63D745D6F2DE5F17E5EAF0FC4963D261C8A12436518206DC093344D5AD293: FullTrust
       1.1.2.  StrongName - 00000000000000000400000000000000: FullTrust
    1.2.  Zone - Intranet: LocalIntranet
       1.2.1.  All code: Same site Web.
       1.2.2.  All code: Same directory FileIO - Read, PathDiscovery
    1.3.  Zone - Internet: Internet
       1.3.1.  All code: Same site Web.
    1.4.  Zone - Untrusted: Nothing
    1.5.  Zone - Trusted: Internet
       1.5.1.  All code: Same site Web.
    1.6.  StrongName -
002400000480000094000000060200000024000052534131000400000100010000D51335D1B5B64BE976A
D8B08030F8E36A0DBBC3EEB5F8A18D0E30E8951DA059B440281997D760FFF61A6252A284061C1D714EF
EE5B329F410983A01DB324FA85BCE6C4E6384A2F3BC1FFA01E2586816B23888CFADD38D5AA5DF041ACE
2F81D9E8B591556852E83C473017A1785203B12F56B6D9DC23A8C9F691A0BC525D7B7EA: FullTrust
    1.7.  Publisher -
30818902818100E537F563C2304ECDA2DBEC892DED389C3C17E36500F381BD96E1C76185420F4EEA460
51AD6972139AC7F0BCE3A473F7B9E1DA0DB5F19CCB0A1774C7065DF9E56E4EC6E1F301FEEA899BD7D37
A66F8150A987CD105059B402DE641FB635A7E122F70A1F766D4A2B5030B32BA5189E1C918B0EF9E8715
1DACA49EB0160B05181590203010001: FullTrust: FullTrust
Success
```

As another check, ask caspol.exe to tell you what code groups your assembly matches:

```
>caspol.exe -resolvegroup securityapp11.exe
Level = Enterprise

Code Groups:

1.  All code: FullTrust


Level = Machine

Code Groups:
1.  All code: Nothing
    1.1.  Zone - MyComputer: FullTrust
    1.2.  Publisher -
30818902818100E537F563C2304ECDA2DBEC892DED389C3C17E36500F381BD96E1C76185420F4EEA460
51AD6972139AC7F0BCE3A473F7B9E1DA0DB5F19CCB0A1774C7065DF9E56E4EC6E1F301FEEA899BD7D37
A66F8150A987CD105059B402DE641FB635A7E122F70A1F766D4A2B5030B32BA5189E1C918B0EF9E8715
1DACA49EB0160B05181590203010001: FullTrust

Level = User
```

```
Code Groups:

1.   All code: FullTrust

Success
```

In the center of the results, you can see that the assembly has been successfully matched to your new code group and granted the FullTrust permission set.

## Managing Zones

Earlier, you learned about the zones that Windows provides and that you manage using Internet Explorer's security tools. The four zones that can be managed this way are:

- **Internet** specifies all Web sites that you haven't placed in other zones.
- **Intranet** specifies all Web sites that are on your organization's intranet.
- **Trusted Sites** specifies Web sites that you trust not to damage your data.
- **Restricted Sites** specifies Web sites that could potentially damage your computer.

These settings are managed either from within Internet Explorer or from the Windows Security Center that is new with Windows XP SP2.

Any user on a machine can alter the zone settings; however, the security settings for the zones that a user can specify only apply to his or her account. It is not possible for one user to alter another user's zone settings. There is a risk because users might alter the zone settings without understanding what they are doing and inadvertently open their machines up to attack.

To alter the settings associated with each zone, open the Windows Security Center and click the Internet Options. Select the Security tab as shown in Figure 16-14.

# .NET Security

Figure 16-14

At the top, you can see the four zones. When you select one of the zones, you can use the Sites button to specify sites that you want included in that zone. For example, if you want to configure the Local intranet zone, use the dialog box that is shown in Figure 16-15. The options here give you enough scope to accurately define what constitutes the intranet in your organization. In addition, the Advanced button gives you access to a dialog box in which you can specify URIs for particular sites you want to include in the Local intranet zone (see Figure 16-16).

Figure 16-15

505

Figure 16-16

Note the option at the bottom of this dialog box, which is provided for each of the zones except the Internet zone. It allows you to specify that you only trust sites in this zone when they are accessed over secure HTTP using Secure Sockets Layer (SSL) encryption. If you trust a site that is accessed over an unencrypted connection, you potentially risk an attack, because your traffic might be intercepted. If you want to verify that a site is held within a specific zone, visit the site and look at the bottom right-hand corner of the Internet Explorer window, which displays the name of the zone for the Web address you are currently viewing.

In addition to specifying the scope of the zone by detailing sites you either trust or do not, you can also specify what actions are permitted within each zone using the security-level settings. These settings enable you to specify whether a prompt should be given for ActiveX controls, and whether cookies are accepted.

# Role-Based Security

As you have seen, code access security gives the CLR the ability to make intelligent decisions behind the scenes as to whether code should run and with what permissions based on the evidence it presents. In addition, .NET provides role-based security that specifies whether code can perform actions on the basis of evidence about the user and their role, rather than just the code. You'll probably be glad to hear that this is done without walking the stack!

Role-based security is especially useful in situations where access to resources is an issue. A primary example is the finance industry, where employees' roles define what information they can access and what actions they can perform.

Role-based security is also ideal for use in conjunction with Windows accounts, Microsoft Passport, or a custom user directory to manage access to Web-based resources. For example, a Web site could restrict access to its content until a user registers with the site, and then additionally provide access to special content only, if the user is a paying subscriber. In many ways, ASP.NET makes role-based security easier because much of the code is based on the server.

For example, if you want to implement a Web service that requires authentication, you could use the account subsystem of Windows and write the Web method in such a way that it ensures the user is a member of a specific Windows user group before allowing access to the method's functionality.

## *The Principal*

.NET gives the current thread easy access to the application user, which it refers to as a *principal*. The principal is at the core of the role-based security that .NET provides, and through it, you can access the user's identity, which will usually map to a user account of one of these types:

- Windows account
- Passport account
- ASP.NET cookie-authenticated user

As an added bonus, the role-based security in .NET has been designed so that you can create your own principals by implementing the IPrincipal interface. If you are not relying on Windows authentication, Passport, or simple cookie authentication, you should look at creating your own using a custom principal class.

With access to the principal, you can make security decisions based on the principal's identity and roles. A role is a collection of users who have the same security permissions, and it is the unit of administration for users. For example, if Windows authentication is used to authenticate the users, you will use the WindowsIdentity type as the identity. You can use that type to find out whether the user is a member of a specific Windows user account group. You can then use that information to decide whether to grant or deny access to code and resources.

You'll generally find that it's much easier to manage security if you allow access to resources and functionality on the basis of roles rather than individual users. Imagine a scenario where you have three methods and each provides access to a feature over which you need tight control to ensure only authorized personnel can access it. Assume that the application has four users; you could quite easily specify within each method which users can and which users cannot access the method. However, imagine a time in the future where the number of features has extended to nine; to allow access to an additional user potentially requires changing every one of the nine methods even though this is an administrative task! Even worse, as users move between roles in the company you would have to change the code each time that happens. If you had implemented the system using roles instead, you could simply add users to and remove users from roles, rather than adding and removing individual users to and from the application. This simplifies the application because for each method you simply request that the user be a member of a specific role. It also simplifies the management of roles, because the administrator can do it rather than the application developer. The developer should be concerned with ensuring that, for example, managers but not secretaries can access a method.

.NET's role-based security builds on an idea that has been provided in MTS and COM+, and offers a flexible framework that can be used to build fences around sections of the application that have to be protected. If COM+ is installed on a machine, its role-based security will interoperate with .NET; however, COM is not required for .NET's role-based security to function.

# Chapter 16

## *Windows Principal*

In the following example, you create a console application that gives access to the principal in an application that, in turn, enables you to access the underlying Windows account. You need to import the `System.Security.Principal` and `System.Threading` namespaces. First of all, you must specify that .NET automatically hooks up the principal with the underlying Windows account, because .NET does not automatically populate the thread's `CurrentPrincipal` property for security reasons. You can do that like this:

```
// Example WindowsPrincipal

using System;
using System.Security.Principal;
using System.Security.Permissions;
using System.Threading;

namespace Wrox.ProCSharp.Security
{
    class Program
    {
        static void Main(string[] args)
        {
            AppDomain.CurrentDomain.SetPrincipalPolicy(
                PrincipalPolicy.WindowsPrincipal);
```

It's possible to use `WindowsIdentity.GetCurrent()` to access the Windows account details; however, that method is best used when you're only going to look at the principal once. If you want to access the principal a number of times it is more efficient to set the policy so that the current thread provides access to the principal for you. By using the `SetPrincipalPolicy` method it is specified that the principal in the current thread should hold a `WindowsIdentity` object. All identity classes, like `WindowsIdentity`, implement the `IIdentity` interface. The interface contains three properties (`AuthenticationType`, `IsAuthenticated`, and `Name`) for all derived identity classes to implement.

Add some code to access the principal's properties from the `Thread` object:

```
            WindowsPrincipal principal =
                (WindowsPrincipal)Thread.CurrentPrincipal;
            WindowsIdentity identity = (WindowsIdentity)principal.Identity;
            Console.WriteLine("IdentityType: " + identity.ToString());
            Console.WriteLine("Name: " + identity.Name);
            Console.WriteLine("'Users'?: " + principal.IsInRole("BUILTIN\\Users"));
            Console.WriteLine("'Administrators'?: " +
                principal.IsInRole(WindowsBuiltInRole.Administrator));
            Console.WriteLine("Authenticated: " + identity.IsAuthenticated);
            Console.WriteLine("AuthType: " + identity.AuthenticationType);
            Console.WriteLine("Anonymous?: " + identity.IsAnonymous);
            Console.WriteLine("Token: " + identity.Token);

            Console.ReadLine();
        }
    }
}
```

# .NET Security

The output from this console application looks similar to the following lines, depending on your machine configuration and the roles associated with the account under which you're signed in:

```
IdentityType:System.Security.Principal.WindowsIdentity
Name: cnagel\christian
'Users'?: True
'Administrators'?: True
Authenticated: True
AuthType: NTLM
Anonymous?: False
Token: 364
```

It is enormously beneficial to be able to easily access details about the current users and their roles. With this information you can make decisions about what actions should be permitted or denied. The ability to make use of roles and Windows user groups provides the added benefit that administration can be done by using standard user administration tools, and you can usually avoid altering the code when user roles change. The following section looks at roles in more detail.

## Roles

Imagine a scenario with an intranet application that relies on Windows accounts. The system has a group called `Manager` and one called `Assistant`; users are assigned to these groups dependent on their role within the organization. Say the application contains a feature that displays information about employees that should only be accessed by users in the `Managers` group. You can easily use code that checks whether the current user is a member of the `Managers` group and whether he is permitted or denied access.

However, if you decide later to rearrange the account groups and to introduce a group called `Personnel` that also has access to employee details, you will have a problem. You have to go through all the code and update it in order to include rules for this new group.

A better solution would be to create a permission called something like `ReadEmployeeDetails` and to assign it to groups where necessary. If the code applies a check for the `ReadEmployeeDetails` permission, updating the application to allow those in the `Personnel` group access to employee details is simply a matter of creating the group, placing the users in it, and assigning the `ReadEmployeeDetails` permission.

## Declarative Role-Based Security

Just as with code access security, you can implement role-based security requests ("the user must be in the Administrators group") using imperative requests (as you saw in the preceding section), or using attributes. You can state permission requirements declaratively at the class level like this:

```
// Example RoleBasedSecurity

using System;
using System.Security;
using System.Security.Principal;
using System.Security.Permissions;
```

```csharp
namespace Wrox.ProCSharp.Security
{
    class Program
    {
        static void Main(string[] args)
        {
            AppDomain.CurrentDomain.SetPrincipalPolicy(
                PrincipalPolicy.WindowsPrincipal);
            try
            {
                ShowMessage();
            }
            catch (SecurityException exception)
            {
                Console.WriteLine("Security exception caught (" +
                                  exception.Message + ")");
                Console.WriteLine("The current principal must be in the local"
                                  + "Users group");
            }
            Console.ReadLine();
        }

        [PrincipalPermissionAttribute(SecurityAction.Demand,
                                      Role = "BUILTIN\\Users")]
        static void ShowMessage()
        {
            Console.WriteLine("The current principal is logged in locally ");
            Console.WriteLine("(they are a member of the local Users group)");
        }
    }
}
```

The `ShowMessage()` method will throw an exception unless you execute the application in the context of a user in the Windows local Users group. For a Web application, the account under which the ASP.NET code is running must be in the group, although in a "real-world" example you would certainly avoid adding this account to the administrators group!

If you run the preceding code using an account in the local Users group, the output will look like this:

```
The current principal is logged in locally
(they are a member of the local Users group)
```

For more information on role-based security in .NET, your first stop should be the MSDN documentation for the `System.Security.Principal` namespace.

# Summary

This chapter covered how assemblies are matched to code groups, and how those code groups are assigned permissions by the security policy at the user, enterprise, and machine levels, and you saw how you can use tools to manage this policy. You learned how, for an assembly to execute, it must have the relevant permissions at the three policy levels, as well as the correct role-based permissions and the relevant Windows account permissions. You also looked at the options available to you in distributing code using strong names and digital certificates.

Clearly, there are more security checks in place with .NET than you have seen before on Windows, and much of the security comes "for free" because you needn't do much to make use of it at the basic level. However, when you want to extend it, you are provided with the classes and frameworks to do that.

Security is an ongoing challenge, and although Microsoft has not solved all the problems, the managed security environment provided by .NET is a significant step in the right direction because it provides a framework within which code is challenged before it executes. It's no coincidence that these developments are occurring at a time when Microsoft is moving toward distributing its products over the Web.

# 17
# Localization

NASA's Mars Climate Orbiter was lost on September 23, 1999, at a cost of $125 million because one engineering team used metric units, while another one used inches for a key spacecraft operation. When writing applications for international distribution, different cultures and regions must be kept in mind.

Different cultures have diverging calendars and use different number and date formats. Also, sorting strings may lead to various results because the order of A-Z is defined differently based on the culture. To make applications fit for global markets, you have to globalize and localize them.

*Globalization* is about internationalizing applications: preparing applications for international markets. With globalization, the application supports number and date formats depending on the culture, different calendars, and so on. *Localization* is about translating applications for specific cultures. For translations of strings, you can use resources.

.NET supports globalization and localization of Windows and Web applications. To globalize an application you can use classes from the namespace `System.Globalization`; to localize an application you can use resources that are supported by the namespace `System.Resources`.

This chapter covers the globalization and localization of .NET applications; more specifically, it discusses the following:

- Using classes that represent cultures and regions
- Internationalization of applications
- Localization of applications

# Chapter 17

# Namespace System.Globalization

The `System.Globalization` namespace holds all culture and region classes to support different date formats, different number formats, and even different calendars that are represented in classes such as `GregorianCalendar`, `HebrewCalendar`, `JapaneseCalendar`, and so on. By using these classes, you can display different representations depending on the user's locale.

This section looks at the following issues and considerations with using the `System.Globalization` namespace:

- Unicode issues
- Cultures and regions
- An example showing all cultures and their characteristics
- Sorting

## Unicode Issues

A Unicode character has 16 bits, so there is room for 65,536 characters. Is this enough for all languages currently used in information technology? In the case of the Chinese language, for example, more than 80,000 characters are needed. However, Unicode has been designed to deal with this issue. With Unicode you have to differentiate between base characters and combining characters. You can add multiple combining characters to a base character to build up a single display character or a text element.

Take, for example, the Icelandic character Ogonek. Ogonek can be combined by using the base character 0x006F (Latin small letter o) and the combining characters 0x0328 (combining Ogonek) and 0x0304 (combining Macron) as shown in Figure 17-1. Combining characters are defined within ranges from 0x0300 to 0x0345. For American and European markets, predefined characters exist to facilitate dealing with special characters. The character Ogonek is also defined with the predefined character 0x01ED.

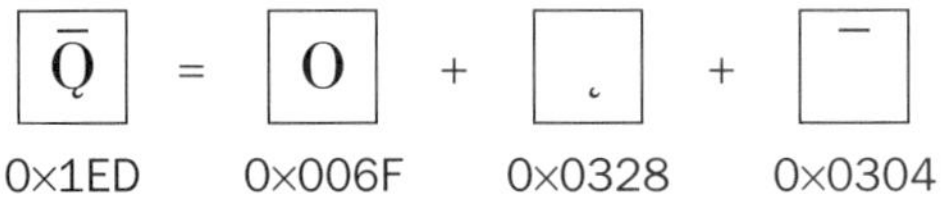

$$\bar{Q} = O + \, + \, $$

0x1ED    0x006F    0x0328    0x0304

**Figure 17-1**

For Asian markets, where more than 80,000 characters are necessary for Chinese alone, such predefined characters do not exist. In the case of Asian languages, you always have to deal with combining characters. The problem with this issue is getting the right number of display characters or text elements, and getting to the base characters instead of the combined characters. The namespace `System.Globalization` offers the class `StringInfo`, which you can use to deal with this issue.

The following table lists the static methods of the class `StringInfo` that help in dealing with combined characters.

| Method | Description |
| --- | --- |
| `GetNextTextElement` | Returns the first text element (base character and all combining characters) of a specified string. |
| `GetTextElementEnumerator` | Returns a `TextElementEnumerator` object that allows iterating all text elements of a string. |
| `ParseCombiningCharacters` | Returns an integer array referencing all base characters of a string. |

> A single display character can contain multiple Unicode characters. To address this issue, if you write applications that support international markets, don't use the data type char; use string instead. A string can hold a text element that contains both base characters and combining characters, whereas a char cannot.

## Cultures and Regions

The world is divided into multiple cultures and regions, and applications have to be aware of these cultural and regional differences. A culture is a set of preferences based on a user's language and cultural habits. RFC 1766 defines culture names that are used worldwide depending on a language and a country or region. Some examples are en-AU, en-CA, en-GB, and en-US for the English language in Australia, Canada, United Kingdom, and the United States, respectively.

Possibly the most important class in the `System.Globalization` namespace is the class `CultureInfo`. `CultureInfo` represents a culture and defines calendars, formatting of numbers and dates, and sorting strings used with the culture.

The class `RegionInfo` represents regional settings (such as the currency) and shows whether the region is using the metric system. Some regions can use multiple languages. One example is the region of Spain that has Basque (eu-ES), Catalan (ca-ES), Spanish (es-ES), and Galician (gl-ES) cultures. Similar to one region having multiple languages, one language can be spoken in different regions; for example, Spanish is spoken in Mexico, Spain, Guatemala, Argentina, and Peru, to name only a few.

Later in this chapter, you see a sample application that demonstrates these characteristics of cultures and regions.

### Specific, neutral, and invariant cultures

With the use of cultures in .NET Framework, you have to differentiate between three types: *specific*, *neutral*, and *invariant* cultures.

A specific culture is associated with a real, existing culture defined with RFC 1766 as you saw in the preceding section. A specific culture can be mapped to a neutral culture. For example, de is the neutral culture of the specific cultures de-AT, de-DE, de-CH, and others. de is the shorthand for the language German; AT, DE, CH are shorthands for the countries Austria, Germany, and Switzerland.

When translating applications, it is typically not necessary to do translations for every region; not much difference exists between the German language in the countries Austria and Germany. Instead of using specific cultures, you can use a neutral culture for localizing applications.

The invariant culture is independent of a real culture. Storing formatted numbers or dates into files, or sending them across a network to a server, using a culture that is independent of any user settings is the best option.

Figure 17-2 shows how the culture types relate to each other.

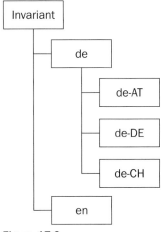

Figure 17-2

## *CurrentCulture and CurrentUICulture*

When you set cultures, you have to differentiate between a culture for the user interface and a culture for the number and date formats. Cultures are associated with a thread, and with these two culture types, two culture settings can be applied to a thread. The `Thread` class has the properties `CurrentCulture` and `CurrentUICulture`. The property `CurrentCulture` is for setting the culture that is used with formatting and sort options, whereas the property `CurrentUICulture` is used for the language of the user interface.

Users can change the default setting of the `CurrentCulture` using the Regional and Language options in the Windows Control Panel (see Figure 17-3). With this configuration, it is also possible to change the default number, the time, and the date format for the culture.

The `CurrentUICulture` does not depend on this configuration. The `CurrentUICulture` setting depends on the language of the operating system. There is one exception, though: If a multi-language user interface (MUI) is installed with Windows XP or Windows 2000, it is possible to change the language of the user interface with the regional configuration, and this influences the property `CurrentUICulture`.

# Localization

Figure 17-3

These settings make a very good default, and in many cases, there is no need to change the default behavior. If the culture should be changed, you can easily do this by changing both cultures of the thread to, say, the Spanish culture, as shown in this code snippet:

```
System.Globalization.CultureInfo ci = new
    System.Globalization.CultureInfo("es-ES");
System.Threading.Thread.CurrentThread.CurrentCulture = ci;
System.Threading.Thread.CurrentThread.CurrentUICulture = ci;
```

Now that you know about setting the culture, the following sections discuss number and date formatting, which are influenced by the `CurrentCulture` setting.

## Number formatting

The number structures `Int16`, `Int32`, `Int64`, and so on in the `System` namespace have an overloaded `ToString()` method. This method can be used to create a different representation of the number depending on the locale. For the `Int32` structure, `ToString()` is overloaded with these four versions:

```
public string ToString();
public string ToString(IFormatProvider);
public string ToString(string);
public string ToString(string, IFormatProvider);
```

`ToString()` without arguments returns a string without format options. You can also pass a string and a class that implements `IFormatProvider`.

517

The string specifies the format of the representation. The format can be a standard numeric formatting string or a picture numeric formatting string. For standard numeric formatting, strings are predefined, where C specifies the currency notation, D creates a decimal output, E creates scientific output, F creates fixed-point output, G creates general output, N creates number output, and X creates hexadecimal output. With a picture numeric format string, it is possible to specify the number of digits, section and group separators, percent notation, and so on. The picture numeric format string ###,### means two 3-digit blocks separated by a group separator.

The IFormatProvider interface is implemented by the NumberFormatInfo, DateTimeFormatInfo, and CultureInfo classes. This interface defines a single method, GetFormat(), that returns a format object.

NumberFormatInfo can be used to define custom formats for numbers. With the default constructor of NumberFormatInfo, a culture-independent or invariant object is created. Using the properties of NumberFormatInfo it is possible to change all the formatting options such as a positive sign, a percent symbol, a number group separator, a currency symbol, and a lot more. A read-only culture-independent NumberFormatInfo object is returned from the static property InvariantInfo. A NumberFormatInfo object where the format values are based on the CultureInfo of the current thread is returned from the static property CurrentInfo.

To create the next example you can start with a simple console project. In this code, the first example shows a number displayed in the format of the culture of the thread (here: English-US, the setting of the operating system). The second example uses the ToString() method with the IFormatProvider argument. CultureInfo implements IFormatProvider, so create a CultureInfo object using the French culture. The third example changes the culture of the thread. The culture is changed to German using the property CurrentCulture of the Thread instance:

```
using System;
using System.Globalization;
using System.Threading;

namespace Wrox.ProCSharp.Localization
{
    class Program
    {
        static void Main(string[] args)
        {
            int val = 1234567890;

            // culture of the current thread
            Console.WriteLine(val.ToString("N"));

            // use IFormatProvider
            Console.WriteLine(val.ToString("N",
                        new CultureInfo("fr-FR")));

            // change the culture of the thread
            Thread.CurrentThread.CurrentCulture =
                        new CultureInfo("de-DE");
            Console.WriteLine(val.ToString("N"));
        }
    }
}
```

# Localization

The output is shown in Figure 17-4. You can compare the outputs with the previously listed differences for U.S. English, French, and German.

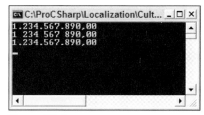

Figure 17-4

## *Date formatting*

The same support for numbers is here for dates. The `DateTime` structure has some methods for date-to-string conversions. The public instance methods `ToLongDateString()`, `ToLongTimeString()`, `ToShortDateString()`, and `ToShortTimeString()` create string representations using the current culture. You can use the `ToString()` method to assign a different culture:

```
public string ToString();
public string ToString(IFormatProvider);
public string ToString(string);
public string ToString(string, IFormatProvider);
```

With the string argument of the `ToString()` method, you can specify a predefined format character or a custom format string for converting the date to a string. The class `DateTimeFormatInfo` specifies the possible values. With the `IFormatProvider` argument, you can specify the culture. Using an overloaded method without the `IFormatProvider` argument implies that the culture of the current thread is used:

```
DateTime d = new DateTime(2005, 08, 09);

// current culture
Console.WriteLine(d.ToLongDateString());

// use IFormatProvider
Console.WriteLine(d.ToString("D", new CultureInfo("fr-FR")));

// use culture of thread
CultureInfo ci = Thread.CurrentThread.CurrentCulture;
Console.WriteLine(ci.ToString() + ": " + d.ToString("D"));

ci = new CultureInfo("es-ES");
Thread.CurrentThread.CurrentCulture = ci;
Console.WriteLine(ci.ToString() + ": " + d.ToString("D"));
```

The output of this example program shows `ToLongDateString()` with the current culture of the thread, a French version where a `CultureInfo` instance is passed to the `ToString()` method, and a Spanish version where the `CurrentCulture` property of the thread is changed to es-ES (see Figure 17-5).

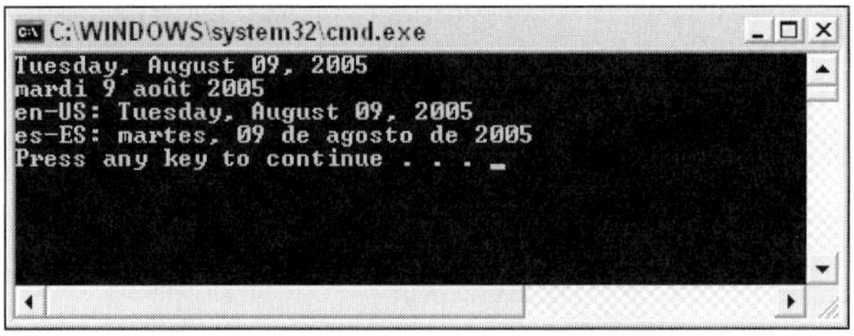

# Chapter 17

Figure 17-5

## Cultures in Action

To see all cultures in action, you can use a sample Windows Forms application that lists all cultures and demonstrates different characteristics of culture properties. Figure 17-6 shows the user interface of the application in the Visual Studio 2005 Forms Designer.

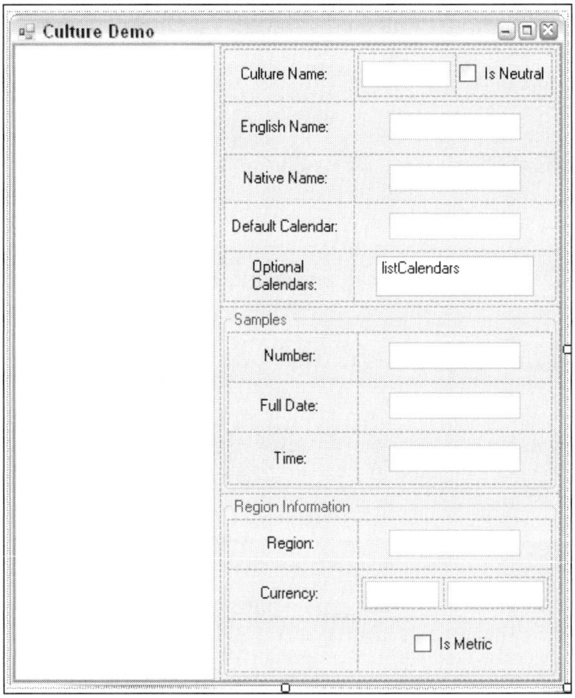

Figure 17-6

During initialization of the application, all available cultures are added to the tree view control that is placed on the left side of the application. This initialization happens in the method `AddCulturesToTree()` that is called in the constructor of the form class `CultureDemoForm`:

# Localization

```csharp
public CultureDemoForm()
{
   InitializeComponent();

   AddCulturesToTree();
}
```

In the method `AddCulturesToTree()`, you get all cultures from the static method `CultureInfo.GetCultures()`. Passing `CultureTypes.AllCultures` to this method returns an array of all available cultures. In the `foreach` loop every single culture is added to the tree view. A `TreeNode` object is created for every single culture, because the `TreeView` class uses `TreeNode` objects for display. The `Tag` property of the `TreeNode` object is set to the `CultureInfo` object, so that you can access the `CultureInfo` object at a later time from within the tree.

Where the `TreeNode` is added inside the tree depends on the culture type. If the culture is a neutral culture or an invariant culture, it is added to the root nodes of the tree. `TreeNodes` that represent specific cultures are added to their parent neutral culture node:

```csharp
// add all cultures to the tree view
public void AddCulturesToTree()
{
   // get all cultures
   CultureInfo[] cultures =
      CultureInfo.GetCultures(CultureTypes.AllCultures);
   Array.Sort(cultures, new CultureComparer());
   TreeNode[] nodes = new TreeNode[cultures.Length];

   int i = 0;
   TreeNode parent = null;
   foreach (CultureInfo ci in cultures)
   {
      nodes[i] = new TreeNode();
      nodes[i].Text = ci.DisplayName;
      nodes[i].Tag = ci;

      if (ci.IsNeutralCulture)
      {
         // remember neutral cultures as parent of the
         // following cultures
         parent = nodes[i];
         treeCultures.Nodes.Add(nodes[i]);
      }
      else if (ci.ThreeLetterISOLanguageName ==
         CultureInfo.InvariantCulture.ThreeLetterISOLanguageName)
      {
         // invariant cultures don't have a parent
         treeCultures.Nodes.Add(nodes[i]);
      }
      else
      {
         // specific cultures are added to the neutral parent
         parent.Nodes.Add(nodes[i]);
```

```
            }
            i++;
        }
    }
```

When the user selects a node inside the tree, the handler of the `AfterSelect` event of the `TreeView` will be called. Here the handler is implemented in the method `OnSelectCulture()`. Within this method all fields are cleared by calling the method `ClearTextFields()` before you get the `CultureInfo` object from the tree by selecting the `Tag` property of the `TreeNode`. Then some text fields are set using the properties `Name`, `NativeName`, and `EnglishName` of the `CultureInfo` object. If the `CultureInfo` is a neutral culture that can be queried with the `IsNeutralCulture` property, the corresponding check box will be set:

```
private void OnSelectCulture(object sender,
                System.Windows.Forms.TreeViewEventArgs e)
{
    ClearTextFields();

    // get CultureInfo object from tree
    CultureInfo ci = (CultureInfo)e.Node.Tag;

    textName.Text = ci.Name;
    textNativeName.Text = ci.NativeName;
    textEnglishName.Text = ci.EnglishName;

    checkIsNeutral.Checked = ci.IsNeutralCulture;
```

Then you get the calendar information about the culture. The `Calendar` property of the `CultureInfo` class returns the default `Calendar` object for the specific culture. Because the `Calender` class doesn't have a property to tell its name, you use the `ToString()` method of the base class to get the name of the class, and remove the namespace of this string to be displayed in the text field `textCalendar`.

Because a single culture might support multiple calendars, the `OptionalCalendars` property returns an array of additional supported `Calendar` objects. These optional calendars are displayed in the list box `listCalendars`. The `GregorianCalendar` class that derives from `Calendar` has an additional property called `CalendarType` that lists the type of the Gregorian calendar. This type can be a value of the enumeration `GregorianCalendarTypes`: `Arabic`, `MiddleEastFrench`, `TransliteratedFrench`, `USEnglish`, or `Localized` depending on the culture. With Gregorian calendars, the type is also displayed in the list box:

```
        // default calendar
        textCalendar.Text = ci.Calendar.ToString().Remove(0, 21);

        // fill optional calendars
        listCalendars.Items.Clear();
        foreach (Calendar optCal in ci.OptionalCalendars)
        {
            string calName = optCal.ToString().Remove(0, 21);

            // for GregorianCalendar add type information
            if (optCal is System.Globalization.GregorianCalendar)
```

# Localization

```
    {
        GregorianCalendar gregCal = optCal as GregorianCalendar;
        calName += " " + gregCal.CalendarType.ToString();
    }
    listCalendars.Items.Add(calName);
}
```

Next you check whether the culture is a specific culture (not a neutral culture) by using `!ci.IsNeutralCulture` in an `if` statement. The method `ShowSamples()` displays number and date samples. This method is implemented in the next code section. The method `ShowRegionInformation()` is used to display some information about the region. With the invariant culture, you can only display number and date samples, but no region information. The invariant culture is not related to any real language, and therefore it is not associated with a region:

```
// display number and date samples
if (!ci.IsNeutralCulture)
{
    groupSamples.Enabled = true;
    ShowSamples(ci);

    // invariant culture doesn't have a region
    if (ci.ThreeLetterISOLanguageName == "IVL")
    {
        groupRegionInformation.Enabled = false;
    }
    else
    {
        groupRegionInformation.Enabled = true;
        ShowRegionInformation(ci.LCID);
    }
}
else // neutral culture: no region, no number/date formatting
{
    groupSamples.Enabled = false;
    groupRegionInformation.Enabled = false;
}
```

To show some localized sample numbers and dates, the selected object of type `CultureInfo` is passed with the `IFormatProvider` argument of the `ToString()` method:

```
private void ShowSamples(CultureInfo ci)
{
    double number = 9876543.21;
    textSampleNumber.Text = number.ToString("N", ci);

    DateTime today = DateTime.Today;
    textSampleDate.Text = today.ToString("D", ci);

    DateTime now = DateTime.Now;
    textSampleTime.Text = now.ToString("T", ci);
}
```

# Chapter 17

To display the information associated with a `RegionInfo` object, in the method `ShowRegionInformation()` a `RegionInfo` object is constructed passing the selected culture identifier. Then you access the properties `DisplayName`, `CurrencySymbol`, `ISOCurrencySymbol`, and `IsMetric` properties to display this information:

```
private void ShowRegionInformation(int culture)
{
    RegionInfo ri = new RegionInfo(culture);
    textRegionName.Text = ri.DisplayName;
    textCurrency.Text = ri.CurrencySymbol;
    textCurrencyName.Text = ri.ISOCurrencySymbol;
    checkIsMetric.Checked = ri.IsMetric;
}
```

When you start the application, you can see all available cultures in the tree view, and selecting a culture lists the cultural characteristics as shown in Figure 17-7.

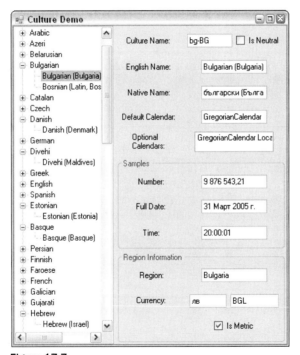

Figure 17-7

# Sorting

Sorting strings is dependent on the culture. Some cultures have different sorting orders. One example is Finnish, where the characters V and W are treated the same. The algorithms that compare strings for sorting by default use a culture-sensitive sort where the sort is dependent on the culture.

# Localization

To demonstrate this behavior of a Finnish sort, the following code creates a small sample console application where some U.S. states are stored unsorted inside an array. You are going to use classes from the namespaces `System.Collections`, `System.Threading`, and `System.Globalization`, so these namespaces must be declared. The method `DisplayNames()` shown here is used to display all elements of an array or of a collection on the console:

```
static void DisplayNames(IEnumerable e)
{
    foreach (string s in e)
        Console.Write(s + " - ");
    Console.WriteLine();
}
```

In the `Main()` method, after creating the array with some of the U.S. states, the thread property `CurrentCulture` is set to the Finnish culture, so that the following `Array.Sort()` uses the Finnish sort order. Calling the method `DisplayNames()` displays all the states on the console:

```
static void Main(string[] args)
{
    string[] names = {"Alabama", "Texas", "Washington",
                      "Virginia", "Wisconsin", "Wyoming",
                      "Kentucky", "Missouri", "Utah", "Hawaii",
                      "Kansas", "Lousiana", "Alaska", "Arizona"};

    Thread.CurrentThread.CurrentCulture =
        new CultureInfo("fi-FI");

    Array.Sort(names);
    Console.WriteLine("\nsorted...");
    DisplayNames(names);
```

After the first display of some U.S. states in the Finnish sort order, the array is sorted once again. If you want to have a sort that is independent of the users' culture, which would be useful when the sorted array is sent to a server or stored somewhere, you can use the invariant culture.

You can do this by passing a second argument to `Array.Sort()`. The `Sort()` method expects an object implementing `IComparer` with the second argument. The `Comparer` class from the `System.Collections` namespace implements `IComparer`. `Comparer.DefaultInvariant` returns a `Comparer` object that uses the invariant culture for comparing the array values for a culture-independent sort:

```
    // sort using the invariant culture
    Array.Sort(names, Comparer.DefaultInvariant);
    Console.WriteLine("\nsorted with invariant culture...");
    DisplayNames(names);
}
```

Figure 17-8 shows the output of this program: a sort with the Finnish culture and a culture-independent sort are shown. As you can see in this sort, Washington is listed before Virginia.

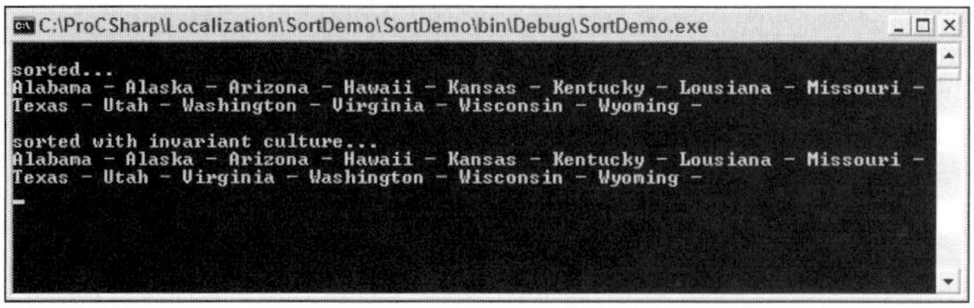

Figure 17-8

> If sorting a collection should be independent of a culture, the collection must be sorted with the invariant culture. This can be particularly useful when sending the sort result to a server or storing it inside a file.

In addition to a locale-dependent formatting and measurement system, text and pictures may differ depending on the culture. This is where resources come into play.

# Resources

Resources such as pictures or string tables can be put into resource files or satellite assemblies. Such resources can be very helpful when localizing applications, and .NET has built-in support to search for localized resources.

Before you see how to use resources to localize applications, the next sections discuss how resources can be created and read without looking at language aspects.

## Creating Resource Files

Resource files can contain such things as pictures and string tables. A resource file is created by using either a normal text file or a `.resX` file that utilizes XML. This section starts with a simple text file.

A resource that embeds a string table can be created by using a normal text file. The text file just assigns strings to keys. The key is the name that can be used from a program to get the value. Spaces are allowed in both keys and values.

This example shows a simple string table in the file `strings.txt`:

```
Title = Professional C#
Chapter = Localization
Author = Christian Nagel
Publisher = Wrox Press
```

# Localization

## Resource File Generator

The Resource File Generator (Resgen.exe) utility can be used to create a resource file out of `strings.txt`. Typing

```
resgen strings.txt
```

creates the file `strings.resources`. The resulting resource file can be added to an assembly either as an external file or embedded into the DLL or EXE. Resgen also supports the creation of XML-based .resX resource files. One easy way to build an XML file is by using Resgen itself:

```
resgen strings.txt strings.resX
```

This command creates the XML resource file `strings.resX`. You look at how to work with XML resource files in the section "Localization Sample with Visual Studio" later in this chapter.

In .NET 2.0, Resgen supports strongly typed resources. A strongly typed resource is represented by a class that accesses the resource. The class can be created with the `/str` option of the Resgen utility:

```
resgen /str:C#,DemoNamespace,DemoResource,DemoResource.cs strings.resX
```

With the option `/str`, the language, namespace, class name, and the file name for the source code are defined in that order.

The Resgen utility does not support adding pictures. With the .NET Framework SDK samples, you get a ResXGen sample with the tutorials. With ResXGen it is possible to reference pictures to a `.resX` file. Adding pictures can also be done programmatically by using the `ResourceWriter` or `ResXResourceWriter` classes, as you see next.

## ResourceWriter

Instead of using the Resgen utility to build resource files, a simple program can be written. The class `ResourceWriter` from the namespace `System.Resources` can be used to write binary resource files; `ResXResourceWriter` writes XML-based resource files. Both of these classes support pictures and any other object that is serializable. When you use the class `ResXResourceWriter`, the assembly System.Windows.Forms must be referenced.

In the following code example, you create a `ResXResourceWriter` object, rw, using a constructor with the file name `Demo.resx`. After creating an instance, you can add a number of resources of up to 2GB in total size using the `AddResource()` method of the `ResXResourceWriter` class. The first argument of `AddResource()` specifies the name of the resource and the second argument specifies the value. A picture resource can be added using an instance of the `Image` class. To use the `Image` class, you have to reference the assembly `System.Drawing`. You also add the `using` directive to open the namespace `System.Drawing`.

Create an `Image` object by opening the file `logo.gif`. You will have to copy the picture to the directory of the executable or specify the full path to the picture in the method argument of `Image.ToFile()`. The `using` statement specifies that the image resource should automatically be disposed at the end of the using block. Additional simple string resources are added to the `ResXResourceWriter` object. The `Close()` method of the `ResXResourceWriter` class automatically calls `ResXResourceWriter.Generate()` to finally write the resources to the file `Demo.resx`:

```csharp
using System;
using System.Resources;
using System.Drawing;

class Program
{
    static void Main()
    {
        ResXResourceWriter rw = new ResXResourceWriter("Demo.resx");
        using (Image image = Image.FromFile("logo.gif"))
        {
            rw.AddResource("WroxLogo", image);
            rw.AddResource("Title", "Professional C#");
            rw.AddResource("Chapter", "Localization");
            rw.AddResource("Author", "Christian Nagel");
            rw.AddResource("Publisher", "Wrox Press");
            rw.Close();
        }
    }
}
```

Starting this small program creates the resource file `Demo.resx` that embeds the image `logo.gif`. The resources will now be used in the next example with a Windows application.

## *Using Resource Files*

You can add resource files to assemblies with the command-line C# compiler csc.exe using the `/resource` option, or directly with Visual Studio 2005. To see how resource files can be used with Visual Studio 2005, create a C# Windows application and name it `ResourceDemo`.

Use the context menu of the Solution Explorer (Add ⇨ Add Existing Item) to add the previously created resource file `Demo.resources` to this project. By default, BuildAction of this resource is set to Embedded Resource so that this resource is embedded into the output assembly (see Figure 17-9).

After building the project, you can check the generated assembly with ildasm to see the attribute `.mresource` in the manifest (see Figure 17-10). `.mresource` declares the name for the resource in the assembly. If `.mresource` is declared `public` (as in the example), the resource is exported from the assembly and can be used from classes in other assemblies. `.mresource private` means that the resource is not exported and only available within the assembly.

# Localization

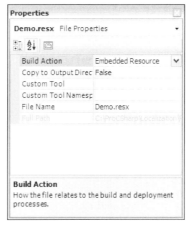

Figure 17-9

```
MANIFEST
File   Find Next

  .custom instance void [mscorlib]System.Reflection.AssemblyTitleAtt

  .hash algorithm 0x00008004
  .ver 1:0:1767:228
}
.mresource public ResourceDemo.Properties.Resources.resources
{
}
.mresource public ResourceDemo.Demo.resources
{
}
.module ResourceDemo.exe
// MVID: {B1597D46-96F7-4F1A-8CB5-FA2A19CDCE62}
.imagebase 0x00400000
.file alignment 0x00001000
```

Figure 17-10

When you add resources to the assembly using Visual Studio 2005, the resource is always public, as shown in Figure 17-10. If the assembly generation tool is used to create assemblies, you can use command-line options to differentiate between adding public and private resources. The option /embed:demo.resources,Y adds the resource as public, while /embed:demo.resources,N adds the resource as private.

> If the assembly was generated using Visual Studio 2005, you can change the visibility of the resources later. Use ilasm and select File ⇨ Dump to open the assembly and generate an MSIL source file. You can change the MSIL code with a text editor. Using the text editor, you can change .mresource public to .mresource private. Using the tool ilasm, you can then regenerate the assembly with the MSIL source code: ilasm /exe ResourceDemo.il.

529

## Chapter 17

In your Windows application, you add some text boxes and a picture by dropping Windows Forms elements from the Toolbox to the designer. The values from the resources will be displayed in these Windows Forms elements. Change the `Text` and `Name` properties of the text boxes and the labels to the values that you can see in the following code. The name property of the `PictureBox` control is changed to logo. Figure 17-11 shows the final form in the Forms Designer. The `PictureBox` control is shown as a rectangle without grid in the upper left-hand corner.

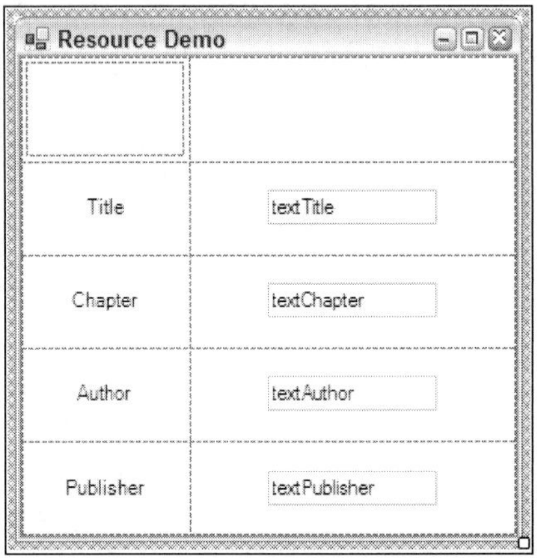

**Figure 17-11**

To access the embedded resource, use the `ResourceManager` class from the `System.Resources` namespace. You can pass the assembly that has the resources as an argument to the constructor of the `ResourceManager` class. In this example the resources are embedded in the executing assembly, so pass the result of `Assembly.GetExecutingAssembly()` as the second argument. The first argument is the root name of the resources. The root name consists of the namespace, with the name of the resource file but without the resources extension. As you saw earlier, ildasm shows the name. All you have to do is remove the file extension resources from the name shown. You can also get the name programmatically using the `GetManifestResourceNames()` method of the `System.Reflection.Assembly` class:

```
using System.Reflection;
using System.Resources;

//...

    partial class ResourceDemoForm : Form
    {
        private System.Resources.ResourceManager rm;

        public ResourceDemoForm()
        {
            InitializeComponent();

            Assembly assembly = Assembly.GetExecutingAssembly();

            rm = new ResourceManager("ResourceDemo.Demo", assembly);
```

# Localization

Using the `ResourceManager` instance `rm`, you can get all the resources by specifying the key to the methods `GetObject()` and `GetString()`:

```
        logo.Image = (Image)rm.GetObject("WroxLogo");
        textTitle.Text = rm.GetString("Title");
        textChapter.Text = rm.GetString("Chapter");
        textAuthor.Text = rm.GetString("Author");
        textPublisher.Text = rm.GetString("Publisher");
    }
```

When you run the code, you can see the string and picture resources (see Figure 17-12).

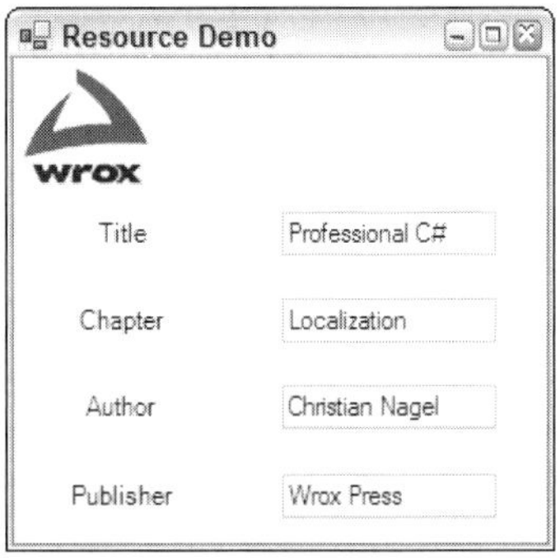

**Figure 17-12**

.NET 2.0 has a new feature of strongly typed resources, as mentioned earlier. With strongly typed resources, the code written earlier in the constructor of the class `ResourceDemoForm` can be simplified; there's no need to instantiate the `ResourceManager` and access the resources using indexers. Instead the names of the resources are accessed with properties:

```
        public ResourceDemoForm()
        {
            InitializeComponent();

            pictureLogo.Image = Demo.WroxLogo;
            textTitle.Text = Demo.Title;
            textChapter.Text = Demo.Chapter;
            textAuthor.Text = Demo.Author;
            textPublisher.Text = Demo.Publisher;
        }
```

To create a strongly typed resource, the Custom Tool property of the XML-based resource file must be set to `ResXFileCodeGenerator`. By setting this option, the class `Demo` (it has the same name as the resource) gets created. This class has static properties for all the resources to offer a strongly typed resource name. With the implementation of the static properties, a `ResourceManager` object is used that is instantiated on first access and then cached:

531

```csharp
/// <summary>
///     A strongly-typed resource class, for looking up localized strings, etc.
/// </summary>
// This class was auto-generated by the StronglyTypedResourceBuilder
// class via a tool like ResGen or Visual Studio.NET.
// To add or remove a member, edit your .ResX file then rerun ResGen
// with the /str option, or rebuild your VS project.
[global::System.CodeDom.Compiler.GeneratedCodeAttribute(
    "System.Resources.Tools.StronglyTypedResourceBuilder", "2.0.0.0")]
[global::System.Diagnostics.DebuggerNonUserCodeAttribute()]
[global::System.Runtime.CompilerServices.CompilerGeneratedAttribute()]
internal class Demo {
    
    private static global::System.Resources.ResourceManager resourceMan;
    
    private static global::System.Globalization.CultureInfo resourceCulture;
    
    [global::System.Diagnostics.CodeAnalysis.SuppressMessageAttribute(
        "Microsoft.Performance", "CA1811:AvoidUncalledPrivateCode")]
    internal Demo() {
    }
    
    /// <summary>
    ///     Returns the cached ResourceManager instance used by this class.
    /// </summary>
    [global::System.ComponentModel.EditorBrowsableAttribute(
        global::System.ComponentModel.EditorBrowsableState.Advanced)]
    internal static global::System.Resources.ResourceManager
        ResourceManager {
        get {
            if ((resourceMan == null)) {
                global::System.Resources.ResourceManager temp =
                    new global::System.Resources.ResourceManager(
                        "ResourceDemo.Demo", typeof(Demo).Assembly);
                resourceMan = temp;
            }
            return resourceMan;
        }
    }
    
    /// <summary>
    ///     Overrides the current thread's CurrentUICulture property for all
    ///     resource lookups using this strongly typed resource class.
    /// </summary>
    [global::System.ComponentModel.EditorBrowsableAttribute(
        global::System.ComponentModel.EditorBrowsableState.Advanced)]
    internal static System.Globalization.CultureInfo Culture {
        get {
            return resourceCulture;
        }
        set {
            resourceCulture = value;
        }
    }
    
    /// <summary>
    ///     Looks up a localized string similar to "Christian Nagel".
```

# Localization

```csharp
        /// </summary>
        internal static string Author {
            get {
                return ResourceManager.GetString("Author", resourceCulture);
            }
        }

        /// <summary>
        ///    Looks up a localized string similar to "Localization".
        /// </summary>
        internal static string Chapter {
            get {
                return ResourceManager.GetString("Chapter", resourceCulture);
            }
        }

        /// <summary>
        ///    Looks up a localized string similar to "Wrox Press".
        /// </summary>
        internal static string Publisher {
            get {
                return ResourceManager.GetString("Publisher", resourceCulture);
            }
        }

        /// <summary>
        ///    Looks up a localized string similar to "Professional C#".
        /// </summary>
        internal static string Title {
            get {
                return ResourceManager.GetString("Title", resourceCulture);
            }
        }

        internal static System.Drawing.Bitmap WroxLogo {
            get {
                return ((System.Drawing.Bitmap)(ResourceManager.GetObject(
                    "WroxLogo", rescourceCulture)));
            }
        }
    }
```

## The System.Resources Namespace

Before moving on to the next example, this section concludes with a review of the classes contained in the `System.Resources` namespace that deal with resources:

❑ The `ResourceManager` class can be used to get resources for the current culture from assemblies or resource files. Using the `ResourceManager`, you can also get a `ResourceSet` for a particular culture.

❑ A `ResourceSet` represents the resources for a particular culture. When a `ResourceSet` instance is created it enumerates over a class, implementing the interface `IResourceReader`, and stores all resources in a `Hashtable`.

## Chapter 17

- The interface `IResourceReader` is used from the `ResourceSet` to enumerate resources. The class `ResourceReader` implements this interface.

- The class `ResourceWriter` is used to create a resource file. `ResourceWriter` implements the interface `IResourceWriter`.

- `ResXResourceSet`, `ResXResourceReader`, and `ResXResourceWriter` are similar to `ResourceSet`, `ResourceReader`, and `ResourceWriter`; however, they are used to create an XML-based resource file `.resX` instead of a binary file. You can use `ResXFileRef` to make a link to a resource instead of embedding it inside an XML file.

# Localization Example Using Visual Studio

For this section, you create a simple Windows application that shows how to use Visual Studio 2005 for localization. This application does not use complex Windows Forms and does not have any real inner functionality, because the key feature it is intended to demonstrate here is localization. In the automatically generated source code, change the namespace to `Wrox.ProCSharp.Localization` and the class name to `BookOfTheDayForm`. The namespace is not only changed in the source file `BookOfTheDay Form.cs`, but also in the project settings, so that all generated resource files will get this namespace, too. You can change the namespace for all new items that are created by selecting Common Properties from the Project ➪ Properties menu.

> Windows Forms applications are covered in more detail in Chapter 23, "Windows Forms," Chapter 24, "Viewing .NET Data," and Chapter 25, "Graphics with GDI+."

To show some issues with localization, this program has a picture, some text, a date, and a number. The picture shows a flag that is also localized. Figure 17-13 shows this form of the application as seen in the Windows Forms Designer.

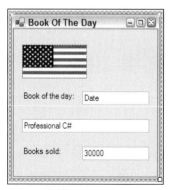

**Figure 17-13**

The following table lists the values for the `Name` and `Text` properties of the Windows Forms elements.

534

# Localization

| Name | Text |
|---|---|
| labelBookOfTheDay | Book of the day |
| labelItemsSold | Books sold |
| textDate | Date |
| textTitle | Professional C# |
| textItemsSold | 30000 |
| pictureFlag | |

In addition to this form, you might want a message box that displays a welcome message; this message might change depending on the current time of day. This example demonstrates that the localization for dynamically created dialogs must be done differently. In the method `WelcomeMessage()`, display a message box using `MessageBox.Show()`. Call the method `WelcomeMessage()` in the constructor of the form class `BookOfTheDayForm`, before the call to `InitializeComponent()`.

Here is the code for the method `WelcomeMessage()`:

```
public void WelcomeMessage()
{
   DateTime now = DateTime.Now;
   string message;
   if (now.Hour <= 12)
   {
      message = "Good Morning";
   }
   else if (now.Hour <= 19)
   {
      message = "Good Afternoon";
   }
   else
   {
      message = "Good Evening";
   }
   MessageBox.Show(message + "\nThis is a localization sample");
}
```

The number and date in the form should be set by using formatting options. Add a new method `SetDateAndNumber()` to set the values with the format option. In a real application, these values could be received from a Web Service or a database, but this example is just concentrating on localization. The date is formatted using the D option (to display the long date name). The number is displayed using the picture number format string ###,###,###, where # represents a digit and "," is the group separator:

```
public void SetDateAndNumber()
{
   DateTime today = DateTime.Today;
   textDate.Text = today.ToString("D");
   int itemsSold = 327444;
   textItemsSold.Text = itemsSold.ToString("###,###,###");
}
```

In the constructor of the `BookOfTheDayForm` class, both the `WelcomeMessage()` and `SetDateAndNumber()` methods are called:

```
public BookOfTheDayForm()
{
    WelcomeMessage();

    InitializeComponent();

    SetDateAndNumber();
}
```

A magic feature of the Windows Forms designer is started when you set the `Localizable` property of the form from `false` to `true`. This results in the creation of an XML-based resource file for the dialog box that stores all resource strings, properties (including the location and size of Windows Forms elements), embedded pictures, and so on. In addition, the implementation of the `InitializeComponent()` method is changed; an instance of the class `System.Resources.ResourceManager` is created, and to get to the values and positions of the text fields and pictures, the `GetObject()` method is used instead of writing the values directly into the code. `GetObject()` uses the `CurrentUICulture` property of the current thread for finding the correct localization of the resources.

Here is part of `InitializeComponent()` from the file `BookOfTheDayForm.Designer.cs` before the `Localizable` property is set to `true`, where all properties of `textboxTitle` are set:

```
private void InitializeComponent()
{
    //...
    this.textTitle = new System.Windows.Forms.TextBox();
    //...
    //
    // textTitle
    //
    this.textTitle.Location = new System.Drawing.Point(24, 152);
    this.textTitle.Name = "textTitle";
    this.textTitle.Size = new System.Drawing.Size(256, 20);
    this.textTitle.TabIndex = 2;
    this.textTitle.Text = "Professional C#";
```

The code for the `IntializeComponent()` method is automatically changed by setting the `Localizable` property set to `true`:

```
private void InitializeComponent()
{
    System.ComponentModel.ComponentResourceManager resources = new
        System.ComponentModel.ComponentResourceManager(
        typeof(BookOfTheDayForm));
    //...
    this.textTitle = new System.Windows.Forms.TextBox();
    //...
    resoures.ApplyResources(this.textTitle, "textTitle");
```

# Localization

Where does the resource manager get the data from? When the `Localizable` property is set to `true`, the resource file `BookOfTheDay.resX` is generated. In this file, you can find the scheme of the XML resource, followed by all elements in the form: `Type`, `Text`, `Location`, `TabIndex`, and so on.

The class `ComponentResourceManager` derives from `ResourceManager` and offers the method `ApplyResources()`. With `ApplyResources()` the resources that are defined with the second argument are applied to the object in the first argument.

The following XML segment shows a few of the properties of `textBoxTitle`: the `Location` property has a value of `13, 133`, the `TabIndex` property has a value of 2, the `Text` property is set to `Professional C#`, and so on. For every value, the type of the value is stored as well. For example, the `Location` property is of type `System.Drawing.Point`, and this class can be found in the assembly `System.Drawing`.

Why are the locations and sizes stored in this XML file? With translations, many strings have completely different sizes and no longer fit in to the original positions. When the locations and sizes are all stored inside the resource file, everything that is needed for localizations is stored in these files, separate from the C# code:

```
<data name="textTitle.Anchor" type="System.Windows.Forms.AnchorStyles,
   System.Windows.Forms">
   <value>Bottom, Left, Right</value>
</data>
<data name="textTitle.Location" type="System.Drawing.Point, System.Drawing">
   <value>13, 133</value>
</data>
<data name="textTitle.Size" type="System.Drawing.Size, System.Drawing">
   <value>196, 20</value>
</data>
<data name="textTitle.TabIndex" type="System.Int32, mscorlib">
   <value>2</value>
</data>
<data name="textTitle.Text">
   <value xml:space="preserve">Professional C#</value>
</data>
```

When changing some of these resource values, it is not necessary to work directly with the XML code. You can change these resources directly in the Visual Studio 2005 designer. Whenever you change the `Language` property of the form and the properties of some form elements, a new resource file is generated for the specified language. Create a German version of the form by setting the `Language` property to German, and a French version by setting the `Language` property to French. For every language, you get a resource file with the changed properties: `BookOfTheDayForm.de.resX` and `BookOfTheDayForm.fr.resX`.

The following table shows the changes needed for the German version.

| German Name | Value |
| --- | --- |
| `$this.Text` (title of the form) | Buch des Tages |
| `labelItemsSold.Text` | Bücher verkauft: |
| `labelBookOfTheDay.Text` | Buch des Tages: |

## Chapter 17

The following table lists the changes for the French version.

| French Name | Value |
|---|---|
| $this.Text (title of the form) | Le livre du jour |
| labelItemsSold.Text | Des livres vendus: |
| labelBookOfTheDay.Text | Le livre du jour: |

With .NET 2.0, images are no longer by default moved to the satellite assemblies. However, in the sample application the flag should be different depending on the country. To do this you have to add the image of the American flag to the file `Resources.resx`. You can find this file in the Properties section of the Visual Studio Solution Explorer. With the resource editor select the Images categories as shown in Figure 17-14, and add the file `americanflag.bmp`. To make localization with images possible, the image must have the same name with all languages. Here the image in the file `Resources.resx` has the name Flag. You can rename the image in the properties editor. Within the properties editor you can also change whether the image should be linked or embedded. For more performance with resources, Visual Studio 2005 changed the default behavior because here images are linked by default. With linked images, the image file must be delivered together with the application. If you want to embed the image within the assembly, you can change the `Persistence` property to `Embedded`.

**Figure 17-14**

The localized versions of the flags can be added by copying the file `Resource.resx` to `Resource.de.resx` and `Resource.fr.resx` and replacing the flags to `GermanFlag.bmp` and `FranceFlag.bmp`. Because a strongly typed resource class is only needed with the neutral resource, the property CustomTool can be cleared with the resource files of all specific languages.

Compiling the project now creates a *satellite assembly* for each language. Inside the debug directory (or the release, depending on your active configuration), language subdirectories like `de` and `fr` are created. In such a subdirectory, you will find the file `BookOfTheDay.resources.dll`. Such a file is a satellite assembly that only includes localized resources. Opening this assembly with ildasm (see Figure 17-15), you see a manifest with the embedded resources and a defined locale. The assembly has the locale `de` in the assembly attributes, and so it can be found in the `de` subdirectory. You can also see the name of the resource with `.mresource`; it is prefixed with the namespace name `Wrox.ProCSharp.Localization`, followed by the class name `BookOfTheDayForm` and the language code `de`.

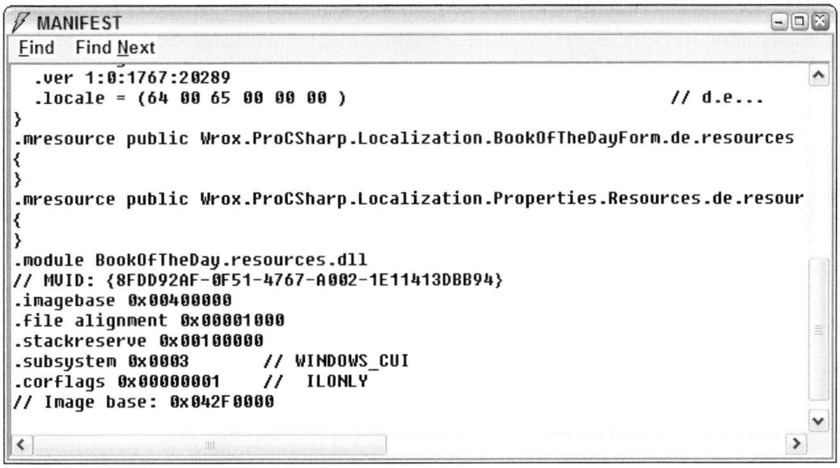

Figure 17-15

## Changing the Culture Programmatically

After translating the resources and building the satellite assemblies, you will get the correct translations depending on the configured culture for the user. The welcome message is not translated at this time. This needs to be done in a different way, as you see shortly.

In addition to the system configuration, it should be possible to send the language code as a command-line argument to your application for testing purposes. The `BookOfTheDayForm` constructor is changed to allow passing a culture string, and setting the culture depending on this string. A `CultureInfo` instance is created to pass it to the `CurrentCulture` and `CurrentUICulture` properties of the current thread. Remember that the `CurrentCulture` is used for formatting, and the `CurrentUICulture` is used for loading of resources:

```
public BookOfTheDayForm(string culture)
{
   if (culture != "")
   {
      CultureInfo ci = new CultureInfo(culture);
      // set culture for formatting
      Thread.CurrentThread.CurrentCulture = ci;
      // set culture for resources
      Thread.CurrentThread.CurrentUICulture = ci;
   }

   WelcomeMessage();

   InitializeComponent();
   SetDateAndNumber();
}
```

## Chapter 17

The `BookOfTheDayForm` is instantiated in the `Main` method that can be found in the file `Program.cs`. In this method, you pass the culture string to the `BookOfTheDayForm` constructor:

```
[STAThread]
static void Main(string[] args)
{
    string culture = "";
    if (args.Length == 1)
    {
        culture = args[0];
    }

    Application.EnableVisualStyles();
    Application.Run(new BookOfTheDayForm(culture));
}
```

Now you can start the application by using command-line options. With the running application you can see that the formatting options and the resources that were generated from the Windows Forms designer show up. Figures 17-16 and 17-17 show two localizations where the application is started with the command-line options `de-DE` and `fr-FR`.

Figure 17-16

Figure 17-17

# Localization

There is still a problem with the welcome message box: the strings are hard-coded inside the program. Because these strings are not properties of elements inside the form, the Forms Designer does not extract XML resources as it does from the properties for Windows controls when changing the `Localizable` property of the form. You have to change this code yourself.

## Using Custom Resource Messages

For the welcome message, you have to translate the hard-coded strings. The following table shows the translations for German and French. You can write custom resource messages directly in the file `Resources.resx` and the language-specific derivations. Of course, you can also create a new resource file.

| Name | English | German | French |
|---|---|---|---|
| Good Morning | Good Morning | Guten Morgen | Bonjour |
| Good Afternoon | Good Afternoon | Guten Tag | Bonjour |
| Good Evening | Good Evening | Guten Abend | Bonsoir |
| Message1 | This is a localization sample. | Das ist ein Beispiel mit Lokalisierung. | C'est un exemple avec la localisation. |

The source code of the method `WelcomeMessage()` must also be changed to use the resources. With strongly typed resources there's no need to instantiate the `ResourceManager` class. Instead the properties of the strongly typed resource can be used:

```
public void WelcomeMessage()
{
   DateTime now = DateTime.Now;
   string message;
   if (now.Hour <= 12)
   {
      message = Properties.Resources.Good_Morning;
   }
   else if (now.Hour <= 19)
   {
      message = Properties.Resources.Good_Afternoon;
   }
   else
   {
      message = Properties.Resources.Good_Evening;
   }
   MessageBox.Show(message + "\n" +
      Properties.Resources.Message1);
}
```

When the program is started using English, German, or French, you will get the message boxes shown in Figures 17-18, 17-19 and 17-20, respectively.

Figure 17-18

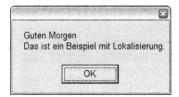

Figure 17-19

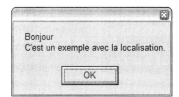

Figure 17-20

## *Automatic Fallback for Resources*

For the French and German versions, in the example all the resources are inside the satellite assemblies. If not all the values of labels or text boxes are changed, this is not a problem at all. You must have only the values that will change in the satellite assembly; the other values will be taken from the parent assembly. For example, for de-at (Austria) you could change the value for the *Good Afternoon* resource to *Grüß Gott* while leaving the other values intact. During runtime when looking for the value of the resource *Good Morning* that is not located in the de-at satellite assembly, the parent assembly would be searched. The parent for de-at is de. In cases where the de assembly does not have this resource either, the value would be searched for in the parent assembly of de, the neutral assembly. The neutral assembly does not have a culture code.

> **Keep in mind that with the culture code of the main assembly you shouldn't define any culture!**

# Localization

## *Outsourcing Translations*

It is an easy task to outsource translations using resource files. It is not necessary to install Visual Studio for translating resource files; a simple XML editor will suffice. The disadvantage of using an XML editor is that there is no real chance to rearrange Windows Forms elements and change the sizes if the translated text does not fit into the original borders of a label or button. Using a Windows Forms designer to do translations is a natural choice.

Microsoft provides a tool as part of the .NET Framework SDK that fulfills all these requirements: the Windows Resource Localization Editor winres.exe (see Figure 17-21). Users working with this tool do not need access to the C# source files; only binary or XML-based resource files are needed for translations. After these translations are completed, you can import the resource files to the Visual Studio project to build satellite assemblies.

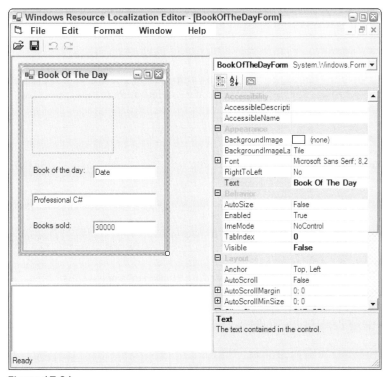

Figure 17-21

If you don't want your translation bureau to change sizes and locations of labels and buttons, and they cannot deal with XML files, you can send a simple text-based file. With the command-line utility resgen.exe you can create a text file from an XML file:

```
resgen myresource.resX myresource.txt
```

And after you've received the translation from the translation bureau you can create an XML file from the returned text file:

```
resgen myresource.es.txt myresource.es.resX
```

# Localization with ASP.NET

With ASP.NET applications, localization happens in a similar way to Windows applications. Chapter 26, "ASP.NET Pages," discusses the functionality of ASP.NET applications; this section discusses the localization issues of ASP.NET applications. ASP.NET 2.0 and Visual Studio 2005 have many new features to support localization. The basic concepts of localization and globalization are the same as discussed before. However, some specific issues are associated with ASP.NET.

As you've already learned, with ASP.NET you have to differentiate between the user interface culture and the culture used for formatting. Both of these cultures can be defined on a Web and page level, as well as programmatically.

To be independent of the Web server's operating system, the culture and user interface culture can be defined with the `<globalization>` element in the configuration file `web.config`:

```
<configuration>
    <system.web>
        <globalization culture="en-US" uiCulture="en-US" />
    </system.web>
</configuration>
```

If the configuration should be different for specific Web pages, the `Page` directive allows assigning the culture:

```
<%Page Language="C#" Culture="en-US" UICulture="en-US" %>
```

If the page language should be different depending on the language setting of the client, the culture of the thread can be set programmatically to the language setting that is received from the client. ASP.NET 2.0 has an automatic setting that does just that. Setting the culture to the value `Auto` sets the culture of the thread depending on the client's settings.

```
<%Page Language="C#" Culture="Auto" UICulture="Auto" %>
```

In dealing with resources, ASP.NET differentiates resources that are used for the complete Web site and resources that are only needed within a page.

If a resource is used within a page, you can create resources for the page by selecting the Visual Studio 2005 menu Tools ➪ Generate Local Resource in the design view. This way the subdirectory `App_Local Resources` is created where a resource file for every page is stored. These resources can be localized similarly to Windows applications. The association between the Web controls and the local resource files happen with a `meta:resourcekey` attribute as shown here with the ASP.NET `Label` control. `LabelResource1` is the name of the resource that can be changed in the local resource file:

# Localization

```
<asp:Label ID="Label1" Runat="server" Text="Label"
    meta:resourcekey="LabelResource1"></asp:Label>
```

For the resources that should be shared between multiple pages, you have to create a subdirectory, Application_Resources. In this directory you can add resource files, for example, Messages.resx with its resources. To associate the Web controls with these resources, you can use Expressions in the property editor. Clicking the Expressions button opens the Expressions dialog (see Figure 17-22). Here you can select the expression type Resources, add the name of the class (which is the name of the resource file—here, a strongly typed resource file is generated), and the name of the ResourceKey, which is the name of the resource.

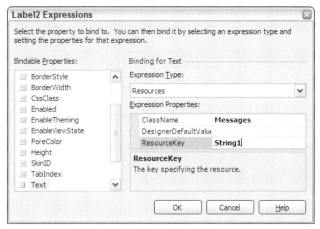

**Figure 17-22**

In the ASPX file, you can see the association to the resource with the binding expressions syntax <%$:

```
<asp:Label ID="Label1" Runat="server"
    Text="<%$ Resources:Messages, String1 %>">
</asp:Label>
```

# A Custom Resource Reader

With the resource readers that are part of .NET Framework 2.0, you can read resources from resource files and satellite assemblies. If you want to put the resources into a different store (such as a database), you can use a custom resource reader to read these resources.

To use a custom resource reader, you also need to create a custom resource set and a custom resource manager. However, doing this is not a hard task, because you can derive the custom classes from existing classes.

For the sample application, you have to create a simple database with just one table for storing messages that has one column for every supported language. The following table lists the columns and their corresponding values.

545

| Key | Default | de | es | fr | it |
|---|---|---|---|---|---|
| Welcome | Welcome | Willkommen | Recepción | Bienvenue | Benvenuto |
| Good Morning | Good Morning | Guten Morgen | Buonas díaz | Bonjour | Buona Mattina |
| Good Evening | Good Evening | Guten Abend | Buonas noches | Bonsoir | Buona sera |
| Thank you | Thank you | Danke | Gracias | Merci | Grazie |
| Goodbye | Goodbye | Auf Wiedersehen | Adiós | Au revoir | Arrivederci |

For the custom resource reader, you create a component library with three classes. The classes are `DatabaseResourceReader`, `DatabaseResourceSet`, and `DatabaseResourceManager`.

## Creating a DatabaseResourceReader

With the class `DatabaseResourceReader`, you define two fields: the data source name `dsn` that is needed to access the database and the language that should be returned by the reader. These fields are filled inside the constructor of this class. The field `language` is set to the name of the culture that is passed with the `CultureInfo` object to the constructor:

```
public class DatabaseResourceReader : IResourceReader
{
    private string dsn;
    private string language;

    public DatabaseResourceReader(string dsn, CultureInfo culture)
    {
        this.dsn = dsn;
        this.language = culture.Name;
    }
}
```

A resource reader has to implement the interface `IResourceReader`. This interface defines the methods `Close()` and `GetEnumerator()` to return an `IDictionaryEnumerator` that returns keys and values for the resources. In the implementation of `GetEnumerator()`, create a `Hashtable` where all keys and values for a specific language are stored. Next, you can use the `SqlConnection` class in the namespace `System.Data.SqlClient` to access the database in SQL Server. `Connection.CreateCommand()` creates a `SqlCommand()` object that you use to specify the SQL SELECT statement to access the data in the database. If the language is set to de, the SELECT statement is `SELECT [key], [de] FROM Messages`. Then you use a `SqlDataReader` object to read all values from the database, and put it into a `Hashtable`. Finally, the enumerator of the `Hashtable` is returned.

*For more information about accessing data with ADO.NET, see Chapter 19, "Data Access with .NET."*

```
public System.Collections.IDictionaryEnumerator GetEnumerator()
{
    Hashtable dict = new Hashtable();

    SqlConnection connection = new SqlConnection(dsn);
    SqlCommand command = connection.CreateCommand();
```

# Localization

```csharp
            if (language == "")
                language = "Default";

            command.CommandText = "SELECT [key], [" + language + "] " +
                                  "FROM Messages";

            try
            {
                connection.Open();

                SqlDataReader reader = command.ExecuteReader();
                while (reader.Read())
                {
                    if (reader.GetValue(1) != System.DBNull.Value)
                        dict.Add(reader.GetString(0), reader.GetString(1));
                }

                reader.Close();
            }
            catch    // ignore missing columns in the database
            {
            }
            finally
            {
                connection.Close();
            }
            return dict.GetEnumerator();
        }

        public void Close()
        {
        }
```

Because the interface `IResourceReader` derives from `IEnumerable` and `IDisposable`, the methods `GetEnumerator()`, which returns an `IEnumerator` interface, and `Dispose()` must be implemented, too:

```csharp
        IEnumerator IEnumerable.GetEnumerator()
        {
            return this.GetEnumerator();
        }

        void IDisposable.Dispose()
        {
        }
    }
```

## Creating a DatabaseResourceSet

The class `DatabaseResourceSet` can use nearly all implementations of the base class `ResourceSet`. You just need a different constructor that initializes the base class with our own resource reader, `DatabaseResourceReader`. The constructor of `ResourceSet` allows passing an object by implementing `IResourceReader`; this requirement is fulfilled by `DatabaseResourceReader`:

```csharp
public class DatabaseResourceSet : ResourceSet
{
    internal DatabaseResourceSet(string dsn, CultureInfo culture)
        : base(new DatabaseResourceReader(dsn, culture))
    {
    }

    public override Type GetDefaultReader()
    {
        return typeof(DatabaseResourceReader);
    }
}
```

## Creating a DatabaseResourceManager

The third class you have to create is the custom resource manager. `DatabaseResourceManager` derives from the class `ResourceManager`, and you only have to implement a new constructor and override the method `InternalGetResourceSet()`.

In the constructor, create a new `Hashtable` to store all queried resource sets and set it into the field `ResourceSets` defined by the base class:

```csharp
public class DatabaseResourceManager : ResourceManager
{
    private string dsn;

    public DatabaseResourceManager(string dsn)
    {
        this.dsn = dsn;
        ResourceSets = new Hashtable();
    }
```

The methods of the `ResourceManager` class that you can use to access resources (such as `GetString()` and `GetObject()`) invoke the method `InternalGetResourceSet()` to access a resource set where the appropriate values can be returned.

In the implementation of `InternalGetResourceSet()`, check first if the resource set for the culture queried for a resource is already in the hash table; if it already exists, return it to the caller. If the resource set is not available, create a new `DatabaseResourceSet` object with the queried culture, add it to the hash table, and return it to the caller:

```csharp
    protected override ResourceSet InternalGetResourceSet(
        CultureInfo culture, bool createIfNotExists, bool tryParents)
    {
        DatabaseResourceSet rs = null;

        if (ResourceSets.Contains(culture.Name))
        {
            rs = ResourceSets[culture.Name] as DatabaseResourceSet;
        }
```

# Localization

```
            else
            {
                rs = new DatabaseResourceSet(dsn, culture);
                ResourceSets.Add(culture.Name, rs);
            }
            return rs;
        }
    }
```

## Client Application for DatabaseResourceReader

How the class `ResourceManager` is used from the client application here does not differ a lot from the previous use of the `ResourceManager` class. The only difference is that the custom class `DatabaseResourceManager` is used instead of the class `ResourceManager`. The following code snippet demonstrates how you can use your own resource manager.

A new `DatabaseResourceManager` object is created by passing the database connection string to the constructor. Then you can invoke the `GetString()` method that is implemented in the base class as you did earlier, passing the key and an optional object of type `CultureInfo` to specify a culture. In turn, you get a resource value from the database, because this resource manager is using the classes `DatabaseResourceSet` and `DatabaseResourceReader`.

```
        DatabaseResourceManager rm = new DatabaseResourceManager(
    "server=localhost;database=LocalizationDemo;trusted_connection=true");

        string spanishWelcome = rm.GetString("Welcome",
                                            new CultureInfo("es-ES"));
        string italianThankyou = rm.GetString("Thank you",
                                            new CultureInfo("it"));
        string threadDefaultGoodMorning = rm.GetString("Good Morning");
```

# Creating Custom Cultures

.NET 2.0 has a new feature to create custom cultures. Custom cultures can be created for cultures that are not available with the .NET Framework. Some examples of where creating custom cultures can be useful are to support a minority within a region or to create subcultures for different dialects.

Custom cultures and regions can be created with the class `CultureAndRegionInfoBuilder` in the namespace `System.Globalization`. This class is in the assembly sysglobl in the file `sysglobl.dll`.

In the example, a new culture for a region inside Austira is defined: Styria. The new culture is based on the culture de-AT and on the region AT. With the constructor of the class `CultureAndRegionInfo Builder`, the name of the new culture is set to de-AT-ST. With the last argument of the constructor a prefix can also be assigned with the enumeration `CulturePrefix`. Here, no prefix is used, and the enumeration value `CulturePrefix.None` is passed. After the name of the new culture is defined, the default settings for the culture are loaded. The method `LoadDataFromCulture()` loads all the culture settings for the specified culture de-AT, and the method `LoadDataFromRegion()` loads all the region settings for the specified region AT.

# Chapter 17

After the `CultureAndRegionInfoBuilder` object is instantiated, it is possible to change some cultural behavior of the new culture by setting properties. Calling the method `Register()` registers the new culture with the operating system. Indeed, you can find the file that describes the culture in the directory `<windows>\Globalization`. Look for files with the extension nlp.

```
// Create a Styria culture
   CultureAndRegionInfoBuilder styria = new CultureAndRegionInfoBuilder(
      "de-AT-ST", CultureAndRegionModifiers.None);
   styria.LoadDataFromCulture(new CultureInfo("de-AT"));
   styria.LoadDataFromRegion(new RegionInfo("AT"));

   styria.Register();
```

The newly created culture now can be used like other cultures:

```
            CultureInfo ci = new CultureInfo("de-AT-ST");
            Thread.CurrentThread.CurrentCulture = ci;
            Thread.CurrentThread.CurrentUICulture = ci;
```

## Summary

This chapter discussed the globalization and localization of .NET applications.

In the context of globalization of applications, you learned about using the namespace `System.Globalization` to format culture-dependent numbers and dates. Furthermore, you learned that sorting strings by default depends on the culture, and you used the invariant culture for a culture-independent sort.

Localization of applications is accomplished by using resources. Resources can be packed into files, satellite assemblies, or a custom store such as a database. The classes used with localization are in the namespace `System.Resources`.

# 18

# Deployment

The development process does not end when the source code is compiled and testing is complete. At that stage, the job of getting the application into the user's hands begins. Whether it's an ASP.NET application, a smart client application, or an application built using the Compact Framework, the software must be deployed to a target environment. The .NET Framework has made deployment much easier than it was in the past. The pains of registering COM components and writing new hives to the registry are all gone.

This chapter looks at the options that are available for application deployment, both from an ASP.NET perspective and from the smart client perspective. The following topics are discussed:

- ❑ Deployment requirements
- ❑ Simple deployment scenarios
- ❑ Windows Installer based projects
- ❑ ClickOnce

## Designing for Deployment

Often, deployment is an afterthought in the development process that can lead to nasty, if not costly, surprises. To avoid grief in deployment scenarios, the deployment process should be planned out during the initial design stage. Any special deployment considerations — such as server capacity, desktop security, or where assemblies will be loaded from — should be built into the design from the start, resulting in a much smoother deployment process.

Another issue that must be addressed early in the development process is the environment in which to test the deployment. Whereas unit testing of application code and of deployment options can be done on the developer's system, the deployment must be tested in an environment that resembles the target system. This is important to eliminate the dependencies that don't exist on a

# Chapter 18

targeted computer. An example of this might be a third-party library that has been installed on the developer's computer early in the project. The target computer might not have this library on it. It can be easy to forget to include it in the deployment package. Testing on the developer's system would not uncover the error because the library already exists. Documenting dependencies can help in eliminating this potential problem.

Deployment processes can be very complex for a large application. Planning for the deployment can save time and effort when the deployment process is implemented.

## Deployment Options

This section provides an overview of the deployment options that are available to .NET developers. Most of these options are discussed in greater detail later in this chapter.

### Xcopy

The xcopy utility enables you to copy an assembly or group of assemblies to an application folder, cutting down on your development time. Because assemblies are self-discovering (that is, the metadata that describes the assembly is included in the assembly), there is no need to register anything in the registry. Each assembly keeps track of what other assemblies it requires to execute. By default, the assembly looks in the current application folder for the dependencies. The process of moving (or probing) assemblies to other folders is discussed later in this chapter.

### Copy Web Tool

If you are developing a Web project, using the Copy Web tool option on the Web site menu will copy the components needed to run the application to the server.

### Publishing Web Sites

When a Web site is published, the entire site is compiled and then copied to a specified location. By precompiling, all source code is removed from the final output and all compile errors can be found and dealt with.

### Deployment Projects

Visual Studio 2005 has the capability to create setup programs for an application. There are four options based on Microsoft Windows Installer technology: creating merge modules, creating a setup for client applications, creating a setup for Web applications, and creating a setup for Smart Device (Compact Framework) based applications. The ability to create cab files is also available. Deployment projects offer a great deal of flexibility and customization for the setup process. One of these deployment options will be useful for larger applications.

# Deployment

## ClickOnce

ClickOnce is a way to build self-updating Windows-based applications. ClickOnce allows an application to be published to a Web site, file share, or even a CD. As updates and new builds are made to the application they can be published to the same location or site by the development team. As the application is used by the end user, it will check the location and see if an update is available. If there is, an update is attempted.

# Deployment Requirements

It is instructive to look at the runtime requirements of a .NET-based application. The CLR does have certain requirements on the target platform before any managed application can execute.

The first requirement that must be met is the operating system. Currently, the following operating systems can run .NET-based applications:

- Windows 98
- Windows 98 Second Edition (SE)
- Windows Millennium Edition (ME)
- Windows NT 4.0 (Service Pack 6a)
- Windows 2000
- Windows XP Home
- Windows XP Professional
- Windows XP Professional TabletPC Edition

The following server platforms are supported:

- Windows 2000 Server and Advanced Server
- Windows 2003 Server Family

Other requirements are Windows Internet Explorer version 5.01 or later, MDAC version 2.6 or later (if the application is designed to access data), and Internet Information Services (IIS) for ASP.NET applications.

You also must consider hardware requirements when deploying .NET applications. The minimum requirements for hardware are as follows:

- Client: Pentium 90 MHz and 32MB RAM
- Server: Pentium 133 MHz and 128MB RAM

For best performance, increase the amount of RAM — the more RAM the better your .NET application runs. This is especially true for server applications.

# Chapter 18

# Simple Deployment

If deployment is part of an application's original design considerations, deployment can be as simple as copying a set of files to the target computer. For a Web application, it can be a simple menu choice in Visual Studio 2005. This section discusses these simple deployment scenarios.

To see how the various deployment options are set up, you must have an application to deploy. The sample download at www.wrox.com contains three projects: SampleClientApp, SampleWebApp, and AppSupport. SampleClientApp is a smart client application. SampleWebApp is a simple Web app. AppSupport is a class library that contains one simple class that returns a string with the current date and time. SampleClientApp and SampleWebApp use AppSupport to fill a label with the output of AppSupport. To use the examples, first load and build AppSupport. Then, in each of the other applications, set a reference to the newly built AppSupport dll.

Here is the code for the AppSupport assembly:

```
using System;

namespace AppSupport
{
  /// <summary>
  /// Simple assembly to return date and time string.
  /// </summary>
  public class Support
  {
    private Support()
    {
    }

    public static string GetDateTimeInfo()
    {
      DateTime dt = DateTime.Now;
      return string.Concat(dt.ToLongDateString(), " ", dt.ToLongTimeString());
    }
  }
}
```

This simple assembly suffices to demonstrate the deployment options available to you.

## *Xcopy*

Xcopy deployment is a term used for the process of copying a set of files to a folder on the target machine and then executing the application on the client. The term comes from the DOS command xcopy.exe. Regardless of the number of assemblies, if the files are copied into the same folder, the application will execute — rendering the task of editing the configuration settings or registry obsolete.

To see how an xcopy deployment works, open the SampleClientApp solution (SampleClientApp.sln) that is part of the sample download file. Change the target to Release and do a full compile. Next, use either My Computer or File Explorer to navigate to the project folder\SampleClientApp\ bin\ Release and double-click SampleClientApp.exe to run the application. Now click the button to

# Deployment

open another dialog. This verifies that the application functions properly. Of course this folder is where Visual Studio placed the output, so you would expect the application to work.

Create a new folder and call it ClientAppTest. Copy the two files from the release folder to this new folder and then delete the release folder. Again, double-click the `SampleClientApp.exe` file to verify that it's working.

That's all there is to it; xcopy deployment provides the ability to deploy a fully functional application simply by copying the assemblies to the target machine. Just because the example that is used here is simple does not mean that this process cannot work for more complex applications. There really is no limit to the size or number of assemblies that can be deployed using this method. The reason that you might not want to use xcopy deployment is the ability to place assemblies in the Global Assembly Cache (GAC) or the ability to add icons to the Start Menu. Also, if your application still relies on a COM library of some type, you will not be able to register the COM components easily.

## Xcopy and Web Applications

Xcopy deployment can also work with Web applications with the exception of the folder structure. You must establish the virtual directory of your Web application and configure the proper user rights. This process is generally accomplished with the IIS administration tool. After the virtual directory is set up, the Web application files can be copied to the virtual directory. Copying a Web application's files can be a bit tricky. A couple of configuration files need to be as accounted for as well as the images that the pages might be using.

## Copy Web Tool

A better way would be to use the Copy Web tool. The Copy Web tool is accessed from the Website ⇨ Copy Web Site menu choice in Visual Studio 2005. It is basically an FTP client for transferring files to and from a remote location. The remote location can be any FTP or Web site including local Web sites, IIS Web sites and Remote (Frontpage) Web sites. Another feature of the Copy Web tool is that it will synchronize files on the remote server with the source site. The source site will always be the site that is currently open in Visual Studio 2005. If the current project has multiple developers this tool can be used to keep changes in sync with the local development site. Changes can be synced back with a common server for testing.

## Publishing a Web Site

Another deployment option for Web projects is to publish the Web site. Publishing a Web site will pre-compile the entire site and place the compiled version into a specified location. The location can be a file share, FTP location, or any other location that can be accessed via HTTP. The compilation process strips all source code from the assemblies and creates the dlls for deployment. This also includes the mark-up contained in the `.ASPX` source files. Instead of containing the normal mark-up, the `.ASPX` files contain a pointer to an assembly. Each `.ASPX` file relates to an assembly. This process works regardless of the model, code behind or single file.

The advantages of publishing a Web site are speed and security. Speed is enhanced because all of the assemblies are already compiled. Otherwise, the first time a page is accessed there is a delay while the page and dependent code is compiled and cached. The security is enhanced because the source code is not deployed. Also, because everything is pre-compiled before deployment all compilation errors will be found.

You publish a Web site from the Website ⇨ Publish Web Site menu choice. You need to supply the location to publish to. Again, this can be a file share, FTP location, Web site, or local disk path. After the compilation is finished, the files are placed in the specified location. From there they can be copied to a staging server, test server, or the production server.

## Installer Projects

Xcopy deployment can be easy to use, but there are times when the lack of functionality becomes an issue. To overcome this shortcoming, Visual Studio 2005 has six installer project types. Four of these options are based on the Windows Installer technology. The following table lists the project types.

| Project Type | Description |
| --- | --- |
| Setup Project | Used for the installation of client applications, middle-tier applications, and applications that run as Windows Service. |
| Web Setup Project | Used for the installation of Web-based applications. |
| Merge Module Project | Creates merge modules that can be used with other Windows Installer–based setup applications. |
| Cab Project | Creates cab files for distribution through older deployment technologies. |
| Setup Wizard | Aids in the creation of a deployment project. |
| Smart Device CAB Project | CAB project for Pocket PC, Smartphone, and other CE-based applications. |

Setup and Web Setup Projects are very similar. The key difference is that with Web Setup the project is deployed to a virtual directory on a Web server, whereas with Setup Project it is deployed to a folder structure. Both project types are based on Windows Installer and have all of the features of a Windows Installer–based setup program. Merge Module Project is generally used when you have created a component or library of functionality that is included in a number of deployment projects. By creating a merge module you can set any configuration items specific to the component and without having to worry about them in the creation of the main deployment project. The Cab Project type simply creates cab files for the application. Cab files are used by older installation technologies as well as some Web-based installation processes. The Setup Wizard project type steps through the process of creating a deployment project, asking specific questions along the way. The following sections discuss how to create each of these deployment projects, what settings and properties can be changed, and what customization you can add.

### What Is Windows Installer?

Windows Installer is a service that manages the installation, update, repair, and removal of applications on most Windows operating systems. It is part of Windows ME, Windows 2000, and Windows XP and is available for Windows 95, Windows 98, and Windows NT 4.0. The current version of Windows Installer is 2.0.

Windows Installer tracks the installation of applications in a database. When an application has to be uninstalled, you can easily track and remove the registry settings that were added, the files that were copied to the hard drive, and the desktop and Start Menu icons that were added. If a particular file is

# Deployment

still referenced by another application, the installer will leave it on the hard drive so that the other application doesn't break. The database also makes it possible to perform repairs. If a registry setting or a dll associated with an application becomes corrupt or is accidentally deleted, you can repair the installation. During a repair, the installer reads the database from the last install and replicates that installation.

The deployment projects in Visual Studio 2005 give you the ability to create a Windows Installation package. The deployment projects give you access to most of what you will need to do in order to install a given application. However, if you need even more control, check out the Windows Installer SDK, which is part of the Platform SDK — it contains documentation on creating custom installation packages for your application. The following sections deal with creating these installation packages using the Visual Studio 2005 deployment projects.

## Creating Installers

Creating installation packages for client applications or for Web applications is not that difficult. One of the first tasks is to identify all of the external resources your application requires, including configuration files, COM components, third-party libraries, and controls and images. Including a list of dependencies in the project documentation was discussed earlier. This is where having that documentation can prove to be very useful. Visual Studio 2005 can do a reasonable job of interrogating an assembly and retrieving the dependencies for it, but you still have to audit the findings to make sure nothing is missing.

Another concern might be when in the overall process is the install package is created. If you have an automated build process set up, you can include the building of the installation package upon a successful build of the project. Automating the process greatly reduces the chance for errors in what can be a time-consuming and complicated process for large projects. What you can do is to include the deployment project with the project solution. The Solution Property Pages dialog box has a setting for Configuration Properties. You can use this setting to select the projects that will be included for your various build configurations. If you select the Build check box under Release builds but not for the Debug builds, the installation package will be created only when you are creating a release build. This is the process used in the following examples. Figure 18-1 shows the Solution Property Pages dialog box of the SampleClientApp solution. Notice that the Debug configuration is displayed and that the Build check box is unchecked for the setup project.

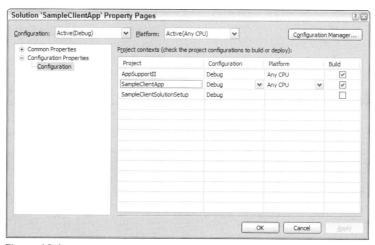

Figure 18-1

# Chapter 18

## Simple Client Application

In the following example, you create an installer for the SimpleClientApp solution (which is included in the sample download, together with the completed installer projects).

For the SimpleClientApp you create two deployment projects. One is done as a separate solution, the other is done in the same solution. This enables you to see the pros and cons of choosing either option.

The first example shows you how to create the deployment project in a separate solution. Before you get started on creating the deployment project, make sure that you have a release build of the application that will be deployed. Next, create a new project in Visual Studio 2005. In the New Project dialog box, select Setup and Deployment Projects on the left. On the right select Setup Project and assign it a name of your choice (for example, SampleClientStandaloneSetup). At this point, what you see on your screen resembles Figure 18-2.

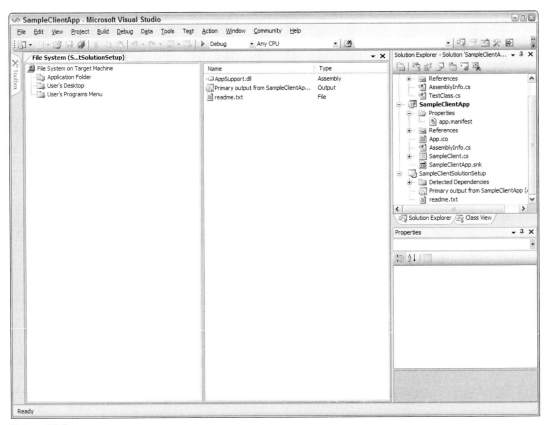

Figure 18-2

In the Solution Explorer window, click the project and then the Properties window. You will see a list of properties. These properties will be displayed during the setup of your application. Some of these properties are also displayed in the Add Remove Programs control panel applet. Because most of these properties are visible to the user during the installation process (or when they are looking at your installation in Add

# Deployment

Remove Programs), setting them correctly will add a professional touch to your application. The list of properties is important, especially if your application will be deployed commercially. The following table describes the properties and the values that you should enter.

| Project Property | Description |
| --- | --- |
| AddRemoveProgramsIcon | The icon that appears in the Add/Remove dialog box. |
| Author | The author of the application. Generally this property setting is the same as the manufacturer. It is displayed on the Summary page of the Properties dialog of the msi package, as well as the Contact field of the SupportInfo page on the Add/Remove dialog box. |
| Description | A freeform text field that describes the application or component that is being installed. This information is displayed on the Summary page of the Properties dialog of the msi package, as well as the Contact field of the SupportInfo page on the Add/Remove dialog box. |
| DetectNewerInstalledVersion | A Boolean value that, when set to true, will check to see if a newer version of the application is already installed. If so, the installation process will stop. |
| InstallAllUsers | Boolean value that, when set to true, will install that application for all users of the computer. If set to false, only the current user will have access. |
| Keywords | Keywords that can be used to search for the msi file on the target computer. This information is displayed on the Summary page of the Properties dialog of the msi package. |
| Localization | The locale used for string resources and registry settings. This affects the user interface of the installer. |
| Manufacturer | Name of the company that manufactured the application of component. Typically this is the same information as specified in the Author property. This information is displayed on the Summary page of the Properties dialog box of the msi package as well as the Publisher field of the SupportInfo page in the Add/Remove dialog box. It is used as part of the default installation path of the application. |
| ManufacturerURL | The URL for a Web site that relates to the application or component being installed. |
| PostBuildEvent | A command that is executed after the build ends. |
| PreBuildEvent | A command that is executed before the build begins. |
| ProductCode | A string GUID that is unique to this application or component. Windows Installer uses this property to identify the application for subsequent upgrades or installs. |
| ProductName | A name that describes the application. Used as the description of an application in the Add/Remove dialog box as well as part of the default install path: `C:\Program Files\Manufacturer\ProductName`. |

*Table continued on following page*

| Project Property | Description |
| --- | --- |
| RemovePrevious Versions | Boolean value that, if set to true, will check for a previous version of the application. If yes, the uninstall function of the previous version is called before installation continues. This property uses ProductCode and UpgradeCode to determine if uninstall should occur. UpgradeCode should be the same; ProductCode should be different. |
| RunPostBuildEvent | When the PostBuildEvent should be run. Options are On successful build or Always. |
| SearchPath | A string that represents the search path for dependent assemblies, files, or merge modules. Used when the installer package is built on the development machine. |
| Subject | Additional information regarding the application. This information is displayed on the Summary page of the Properties dialog box of the msi package. |
| SupportPhone | A phone number for support of the application or component. This information is displayed in the Support Information field of the SupportInfo page on the Add/Remove dialog box. |
| SupportURL | A URL for support of the application or component. This information is displayed in the Support Information field of the SupportInfo page in the Add/Remove dialog box. |
| TargetPlatform | Supports the 32-or 64-bit versions of Windows. |
| Title | The title of the installer. This is displayed on the Summary page of the Properties dialog box of the msi package. |
| UpgradeCode | A string GUID that represents a shared identifier of different versions of the same application. The UpgradeCode should not change for different versions or different language version of the application. Used by the DetectNewerInstalledVersion and RemovePreviousVersion. |
| Version | The version number of the installer, cab file, or merge module. Note that this is not the version of the application being installed. |

After you have set the properties, you can start to add assemblies. In this example, the only assembly you have to add is the main executable (`SampleClientApp.exe`). To do this you can either right-click the project in the Solution Explorer or select Add from the Project menu. You have four options:

- **Project Output.** You explore this option in the next example.
- **File.** This is used for adding a readme text file or any other file that is not part of the build process.
- **Merge Module.** A merge module that was created separately.
- **Assembly.** Use this option to select an assembly that is part of the installation.

Choose Assembly for this example. You will be presented with the Component Selector dialog box, which resembles the dialog box you use for adding references to a project. Browse to the \bin\release folder of your application. Select `SampleClientApp.exe` and then click OK in the Component Selector

# Deployment

dialog box. You can now see `SampleClientApp.exe` listed in the Solution Explorer of the deployment project. In the Detected Dependancies section, you can see that Visual Studio interrogated `SampleClientApp.exe` to find the assemblies on which it depends; in this case `AppSupport.dll` is included automatically. You would continue this process until all of the assemblies in your application are accounted for in the Solution Explorer of the deployment project.

Next, you have to determine where the assemblies will be deployed. By default the File System editor is displayed in Visual Studio 2005. The File System editor is split into two panes: The left pane shows the hierarchical structure of the file system on the target machine; the right pane provides a detail view of the selected folder. The folder names might not be what you expect to see, but keep in mind that these are for the target machine; for example, the folder labeled User's Programs Menu maps to the `C:\Documents` and `Settings\User Name\Start Menu\Programs` folder on the target client.

You can add other folders at this point, either special folders or a custom folder. To add a special folder make sure that File System on Target Machine is highlighted in the left pane, and select Action menu on the main menu. The Add Special Folder menu choice provides a list of folders that can be added. For example, if you want to add a folder under the Application folder, you can select the Application Folder folder in the left pane of the editor and then select the Action menu. This time there will be an Add menu that enables you to create the new folder. Rename the new folder and it will be created for you on the target machine.

One of the special folders that you might want to add is a folder for the GAC. `AppSupport.dll` can be installed to the GAC if it is used by several different applications. In order to add an assembly to the GAC it does have to have a strong name. The process for adding the assembly to the GAC is to add the GAC from the Special Folder menu as described previously and then drag the assembly that you want in the GAC from the current folder to the Global Assembly Cache Folder. If you try and do this with an assembly that is not strongly named, the deployment project will not compile.

If you select Application Folder, you will see on the right pane that the assemblies that you added are automatically added to the Application folder. You can move the assemblies to other folders, but keep in mind that the assemblies have to be able to find each other. (For more details on probing, see Chapter 15, "Assemblies.")

If you want to add a shortcut to the application on the user's desktop or to the Start Menu, drag the items to the appropriate folders. To create a desktop shortcut, go to the Application folder. On the right side of the editor select the application. Go to the Action menu and select the Create Shortcut item to create a shortcut to the application. After the shortcut is created, drag it to the User's Desktop folder. Now when the application is installed, the shortcut will appear on the desktop. Typically, it is up to the user to decide if he or she wants a desktop shortcut to your application. The process of asking the user for input and taking conditional steps is explored later in this chapter. The same process can be followed to create an item in the Start Menu. Also, if you look at the properties for the shortcut that you just created, you will see that you can configure the basic shortcut properties such as Arguments and what icon to use. The application icon is the default icon.

Before you build the deployment project you might have to check some project properties. If you select Project menu then SampleClientStandaloneSetup Properties you will see the project Property Pages dialog box. These are properties that are specific to a current configuration. After selecting the configuration in the Configuration drop-down, you can change the properties listed in the following table.

# Chapter 18

| Property | Description |
|---|---|
| Output file name | The name of the msi or msm file that is generated when the project is compiled. |
| Package files | This property enables you to specify how the files are packaged. Your options are: |
| | As loose uncompressed files. All of the deployment files are stored in the same directory as the .msi file. |
| | In setup file. Files are packaged in the .msi file (default setting). |
| | In cabinet file(s). Files are in one or more cab files in the same directory. When this is selected the CAB file size option becomes available. |
| Prerequisites URL | Allows you to specify where prerequisites such as the .NET Framework or Windows Installer 2.0 can be found. Clicking the Settings button will display a dialog that has the following technologies available to include in the setup: |
| | Windows Installer 2.0 |
| | .NET Framework |
| | Microsoft Visual J# .NET Redistributable Package 2.0 |
| | SQL Server 2005 Express Edition |
| | Microsoft Data Access Components 2.8 |
| | There is also an option to have the prerequisites downloaded from a predefined URL or to have them loaded from the same location as the setup. |
| Compression | This specifies the compression style for the files included. Your options are: |
| | Optimized for speed. Larger files but faster installation time (default setting). |
| | Optimized for size. Smaller files but slower installation time. |
| | None. No compression applied. |
| CAB size | This is enabled when the Package file setting is set to In cabinet files. Unlimited creates one single cabinet file; custom allows you to set the maximum size for each cab file. |
| Authenticode signature | When this is checked the deployment project output is signed using Authenticode; the default setting is unchecked. |
| Certificate file | The certificate used for signing. |
| Private key file | The private key that contains the digital encryption key for the signed files. |
| Timestamp server URL | URL for timestamp server. This is also used for Authenticode signing. |

After you have set the project properties, you should be able to build the deployment project and create the setup for the SampleClientApp application. After you build the project you can test the installation by right-clicking the project name in the Solution Explorer. This enables you to access an Install and

# Deployment

Uninstall choice in the context menu. If you have done everything correctly, you should be able to install and uninstall SampleClientApp successfully.

## Same solution project

The previous example works well for creating a deployment package but it does have a couple of downsides. For example, what happens when a new assembly is added to the original application? The deployment project will not automatically recognize any changes; you will have to add the new assemblies and verify that any new dependencies are covered. In smaller applications (like the example) this isn't that big of a deal. However, when you're dealing with an application that contains dozens or maybe hundreds of assemblies, this can become quite tedious to maintain. Visual Studio 2005 has a simple way of resolving this potential headache. Include the deployment project in your applications solution. You can then capture the output of the main project as your deployment assemblies. You can look at the SimpleClientApp as an example.

Open the SimpleClientApp solution in Visual Studio 2005. Add a new project using Solution Explorer. Select Deployment and Setup Projects and then select Setup Project, following the steps outlined in the previous section. You can name this project SimpleAppSolutionSetup. In the previous example, you added the assemblies by selecting Add ⇨ Assemblies from the Project menu. This time, select Add ⇨ Project Output from Project menu. This opens the Add Project Output Group dialog box (see Figure 18-3).

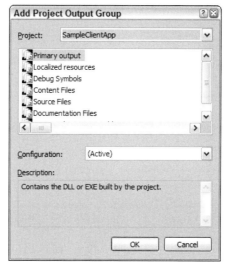

**Figure 18-3**

The top part of the dialog box has a drop-down list box that shows all projects in the current solution. Select the main startup project. Then select the items you want to include in your project from the list below. Your options are Documentation, Primary Output, Localized Resources, Debug Symbols, Content Files, and Source Files. First select Primary Output. This includes the output and all dependencies when the application is built. Another drop-down list box lists the valid configurations: Debug and Release plus any custom configurations you might have added. This also determines what outputs are picked up. For deployment you will most likely want to use the Release configuration.

After you make these selections, a new item is added to your deployment project in Solution Explorer. The name of the item is Primary output form SampleClientApp (Release .NET). You will also see the file `AppSupport.dll` listed under the dependencies. As before, no need to search for the dependant assemblies.

At this point all of the various project properties discussed in the previous section still apply. You can change the Name, Manufacturer, cab file size, and other properties. After setting the properties, do a Release build of the solution and test the installation. Everything should work as expected.

To see the advantage of adding the deployment package to the applications solution, add a new project to the solution. In the example it is called AppSupportII. In it is a simple test method that returns the string Hello World. Set a reference in SampleTestApp to the newly added project, and do another Release build of the solution. You should see that the deployment project picked up the new assembly without you having to do anything. If you go back and open up the standalone deployment project from the previous example, unless you specifically add the assembly it will not be picked up.

## *Simple Web application*

Creating an installation package for a Web application is not that different than creating a client install package. The download examples include a SimpleWebApp that also utilizes the `AppSupport.dll` assembly. You can create the deployment project the same way that the client deployment projects are created, either standalone or in the same solution. In this example, the deployment project is built in the same solution.

Start the SimpleWebApp solution and add a new Deployment and Setup Project. This time be sure to choose Web Setup Project in the Templates window. If you look at the properties view for the project you will see that all of the same properties exist for Web applications as did for client applications. The only addition is RestartWWWService. This is a Boolean value that will restart IIS during the install. If you're using ASP.NET components and not replacing any ATL or ISAPI dlls you shouldn't have to do this.

If you look at the File System editor, you will notice that there is only one folder. The Web Application folder is what will be your virtual directory. By default the name of the directory is the name of the deployment project, and it is located below the Web root directory. The following table explains the properties that can be set from the installer. The properties discussed in the previous section are not included.

| Property | Description |
| --- | --- |
| AllowDirectoryBrowsing | Boolean value that, if true, allows an HTML listing of the files and subfolders of the virtual directory. Maps to the Directory browsing property of IIS. |
| AllowReadAccess | Boolean value that, if true, allows users to read or download files. Maps to the Read property of IIS. |
| AllowScriptSourceAccess | Boolean value that, if true, allows users to access source code, including scripts. Maps to Script source access in IIS. |
| AllowWriteAccess | Boolean value that, if true, allows users to change content in write-enabled files. Maps to Write property of IIS. |

## Deployment

| Property | Description |
|---|---|
| ApplicationProtection | Determines the protection level of applications that are run on the server. The valid values are: |
| | Low. Applications run in the same process as Web Services. |
| | Medium. Applications run in same process but not the same as Web services. |
| | High. Application runs in its own process. |
| | Maps to the Application Protection property in IIS. Has no effect if the IsApplication property is false. |
| AppMappings | A list of application names and document or data files that are associated with the applications. Maps to the Application Mappings property of IIS. |
| Condition | A Windows Installer condition that must be met in order for the item to be installed. |
| DefaultDocument | The default or startup document when the user first browses to the site. |
| ExecutePermissions | The level of permissions that a user has to execute applications. The valid values are: |
| | None. Only static content can be accessed. |
| | ScriptsOnly. Only scripts can be accessed. Includes ASP. |
| | ScriptsAndExecutables. Any files can be accessed. |
| | Maps to Execute Permissions in IIS. |
| Index | Boolean value that, if true, would allow indexing of the content for Microsoft Indexing Service. Maps to the Index this resource property of IIS. |
| IsApplication | Boolean value that, if true, instructs IIS to create the application root for the folder. |
| LogVisits | Boolean value that, if true, logs visits to the Web site in a log file. Maps to the Log visits property of IIS. |
| Property | The named property that can be accessed at installation time. |
| VirtualDirectory | The virtual directory for the application. This is relative to the Web server. |

You might notice that most of these properties are properties of IIS and can be set in the IIS administrator tool. So the logical assumption is that in order to set these properties in the installer, the installer will need to run with administrator privileges. The settings made here can compromise security, so the changes should be well documented.

Other than these properties, the process of creating the deployment package is very similar to the previous client example. The main difference between the two projects is the ability to modify IIS from the installation process. As you can see, you have a great deal of control over the IIS environment.

# Chapter 18

## *Client from Web server*

Another installation scenario is either running the install program from a Web site or actually running the application from a Web site. Both of these are attractive options if you must deploy an application to a large number of users. By deploying from a Web site you eliminate the need for a distribution medium such as CD-ROM, DVD, or even floppy disks. By running the application from a Web site or even a network share, you eliminate the need to distribute a setup program at all.

Running an installer from a Web site is fairly simple. You use the Web Bootstrapper project compile option discussed earlier in this chapter. You will be asked to provide the URL of the setup folder. This is the folder in which the setup program is going to look for the msi and other files necessary for the setup to work. After you set this option and compile the deployment package you can copy it to the Web site that you specify in the Setup folder URL property. At this point when the user navigates to the folder, she will be able to either run the setup or download it and then run it. In both instances, the user must be able to connect to the same site to finish the installation.

## No Touch Deployment

You can also run the application from a Web site or network share. This process becomes a little more involved and is a prime reason that you should design the application with deployment in mind. This is sometimes referred to as *No Touch Deployment* (NTD).

To make this process work, the application code must be written in a way to support it. A couple of ways exist to architect the application to take advantage of NTD. One way is to write the majority of the application code into dll assemblies. The dlls will live on a Web server or file share on the network. Then you create a smaller application exe that will be deployed to the client pcs. This stub program will start the application by calling into one of the dll assemblies using the `LoadFrom` method. The only thing that the stub program will see is the main entry point in the dll. Once the dll assembly has been loaded, the application will continue loading other assemblies from the same URL or network share. Remember that an assembly first looks for dependant assemblies in the application directory (that is, the URL that was used to start the application). Here is the code used in the stub application on the user's client. This example calls the AppSupportII dll assembly and puts the output of the `TestMethod` call in `label1`:

```
Assembly testAssembly =
            Assembly.LoadFrom("http://localhost/AppSupport/AppSupportII.dll");
Type type = testAssembly.GetType("AppSupportII.TestClass");
object testObject = Activator.CreateInstance(type);
label1.Text = (string)type.GetMethod("TestMethod").Invoke(testObject,null);
```

This process uses Reflection to first load the assembly from the Web server. In this example the Web site is a folder on the local machine (localhost). Next, the type of the class is retrieved (here: `TestClass`). Now that you have type information the object can be created using the `Activator.CreateInstance` method. The last step is to get a `MethodInfo` object (the output of `GetMethod`) and call the `Invoke` method. In a more complex application this is the main entry point of the application. From this point on, the stub is not needed anymore.

Alternatively, you can also deploy the entire application to a Web site. For this method, create a simple Web page that contains a link to the application's setup executable or perhaps a shortcut on the user's desktop that has the Web site link. When the link is clicked, the application will be downloaded to the user's assembly download cache, which is located in the Global Assembly Cache. The application will run from the download cache. Each time a new assembly is requested, it will go to the download cache first to see if it exists; if not, it will go to the URL that the main application came from.

The advantage to deploying the application in this way is that when an update is made available for the application, it has to be deployed in only one place. You place the new assemblies in the Web folder and when the user starts the application, the runtime will actually look at the assemblies in the URL and the assemblies in the download cache to compare versions. If a new version is found at the URL, it is then downloaded to replace the current one in the download cache. This way, the user always has access to the most current version of the application.

For more control over the update process and over security, ClickOnce is probably a better choice.

# ClickOnce

ClickOnce is a deployment technology that allows applications to be self updating. Applications are published to a file share, Web site, or media such as a CD. Once published, ClickOnce apps can be automatically updated with minimal user input.

ClickOnce also solves the security permission problem. Normally, to install an application the user would need Administrative rights. With ClickOnce a user can install and run an application with only the absolute minimum permissions required to run the application.

## ClickOnce Operation

ClickOnce applications have two XML-based manifest files associated with them. One is the application manifest and the other is the deployment manifest. These two files describe everything that is required to know to deploy an application.

The application manifest contains information about the application such as permissions required, assemblies to include, and other dependencies. The deployment manifest is about the deployment of the app. Items such as the location of application manifest is contained in the deployment manifest. The complete schemas for the manifests are in the .NET SDK documentation.

ClickOnce has some limitations. Assemblies cannot be added to the GAC, for example. The following table compares ClickOnce and Windows Installer.

|  | ClickOnce | Windows Installer |
| --- | --- | --- |
| Application installation location | ClickOnce application cache | Program Files folder |
| Install for multiple users | No | Yes |
| Install Shared files | No | Yes |
| Install drivers | No | Yes |
| Install to the GAC | No | Yes |

*Table continued on following page*

|  | ClickOnce | Windows Installer |
|---|---|---|
| Add application to Startup group | No | Yes |
| Add application to the favorites menu | No | Yes |
| Register file types | No | Yes |
| Access registry | No. The HKLM can be accessed with Full Trust permissions. | Yes |
| Binary patching of files | Yes | No |
| Install assemblies on demand | Yes | No |

Some situations certainly exist where using Windows Installer is clearly a better choice; however, ClickOnce can be used for a large number of applications.

## *Publishing an Application*

Everything that ClickOnce needs to know is contained in the two manifest files. The process of publishing an application for ClickOnce deployment is simply generating the manifests and placing the files in the proper location. The manifest files can be generated in Visual Studio 2005. There is also a command-line tool (mage.exe) and a version with a gui (mageUI.exe).

You can create the manifest files in Visual Studio 2005 in two ways. At the bottom of the Publish tab on the Project Properties dialog are two buttons. One is the Publish Wizard and the other is Publish Now. The Publish Wizard asks several questions about the deployment of the application and then generates the manifest files and copies all of the needed files to the deployment location. The Publish Now button uses the values that have been set in the Publish tab to create the manifest files and copies the files to the deployment location.

In order to use the command-line tool mage.exe, the values for the various ClickOnce properties must be passed in. Manifest files can be both created and updated using mage.exe. Typing **mage.exe .help** at the command prompt will give the syntax for passing in the values required.

The gui version of mage.exe (mageUI.exe) is similar in appearance to the Publish tab in Visual Studio 2005. An application and deployment manifest file can be created and updated using the GUI tool.

ClickOnce applications appear in the Add/Remove control panel applet just like any other installed application. One big difference is that the user is presented with the choice of either uninstalling the application or rolling back to the previous version. ClickOnce keeps the previous version in the ClickOnce application cache.

## *ClickOnce Settings*

Several properties are available for both manifest files. The most important property is where the application should be deployed from. The dependencies for the application must be specified. The Publish tab has an Application Files button that shows a dialog for entering all of the assemblies required by the

# Deployment

application. The Prerequisite button displays a list of common prerequisites that can be installed along with application. You have the choice of installing the prerequisites from the same location that the application is being published to or you can optionally have the prerequisites installed from the vendor's web site.

The Update button displays a dialog that has the information about how the application should be updated. As new versions of an application are made available, ClickOnce can be used to update the application. Options include to check for updates every time the application starts or to check in the background. If the background option is selected, a specified period of time between checks can be entered. Options for allowing the user to be able to decline or accept the update are available. This can be used to force an update in the background so the user never is aware that the update is occurring. The next time the application is run, the new version will be used instead of the older version. A separate location for the update files can be used as well. This way the original installation package can be in one location and installed for new users and all of the updates can be staged in another location.

The application can be set up so that it will run in either online or offline mode. In offline mode the application can be run from the Start Menu and acts as if it were installed using the Windows Installer. Online mode means that the application will run only if the installation folder is available.

## *Application Cache*

Applications distributed with ClickOnce do not get installed in the Program Files folder. Instead, they are placed in an application cache that resides in the Local Settings folder under the current user's Document's and Settings folder. By controlling this aspect of the deployment, multiple versions of an application can reside on the client pc at the same time. If the application was set to run online, every version that the user has accessed is retained. For applications that are set to run locally, the current and previous versions are retained.

Because of this it is a very simple process to rollback a ClickOnce application to its previous version. If the user goes to the Add/Remove programs control panel applet, the dialog presented will have the choice of removing the ClickOnce application or rolling back to the previous version. An Administrator can change the manifest file to point to the previous version. By doing this the next time the user runs that application, a check will be made for an update. Instead of finding new assemblies to deploy, the application will restore the previous version without any interaction from the user.

## *Security*

Applications deployed over the Internet or intranet have a lower security or trust setting than applications that have been installed to the local drive have. For example, by default if an application is launched or deployed from the Internet it is in the Internet Security Zone. This means that it cannot access the file system, among other things. If the application is installed from a file share, it will run in the Intranet Zone.

If the application requires a higher level of trust than the default, the user will be prompted to grant the permissions required for the application to run. These permissions are set in the `trustInfo` element of the application manifest. Only the permissions asked for in this setting will be granted. So if an application asks for file access permissions, Full Trust will not be granted, only the specific permissions asked for.

Another option is to use Trusted Application Deployment. Trusted Application Deployment is a way to grant permissions on an enterprise-wide basis without having to prompt the user. A trust license issuer is identified to each client machine. This is done with public key cryptography. Typically an organization will have only one issuer. It is important to keep the private key for the issuer in a safe, secure location.

A trust license is requested from the issuer. The level of trust that is being requested is part of the trust license configuration. A public key used to sign the application must also be supplied to the license issuer. The license created contains the public key used to sign the application and the public key of the license issuer. This trust license is then embedded in the deployment manifest. The last step is to sign the deployment manifest with your own key pair. The application is now ready to deploy.

When the client opens the deployment manifest the Trust Manager will determine if the ClickOnce application has been given a higher trust. The issuer license is looked at first. If it is valid, the public key in the license is compared to the public key that was used to sign the application. If these match, the application is granted the requested permissions.

## *Advanced Options*

The installation processes discussed so far are very powerful and can do quite a bit. But there is much more that you can control in the installation process. For example, you can use the various editors in Visual Studio 2005 to build conditional installations, or add registry keys and custom dialog boxes. The SampleClientSetupSolution example has all of these advanced options enabled.

### *File System Editor*

The File System Editor enables you to specify where in the target the various files and assemblies that make up the application will be deployed. By default, a standard set of deployment folders is displayed. You can add any number of custom and special folders with the editor. This is also where you would add desktop and Start Menu shortcuts to the application. Any file that must be part of the deployment must be referenced in the File System Editor.

### *Registry Editor*

The Registry Editor allows you to add keys and data to the registry. When the editor is first displayed, a standard set of main keys is displayed:

- ❑ HKEY_CLASSES_ROOT
- ❑ HKEY_CURRENT_USER
- ❑ HKEY_LOCAL_MACHINE
- ❑ HKEY_USERS

HKEY_CURRENT_USER and HKEY_LOCAL_MACHINE contain additional entries in the Software/ [Manufacturer] key where Manufacturer is the information you entered in the Manufacturer property of the deployment project.

# Deployment

To add additional keys and values highlight one of the main keys on the left side of the editor. Select Action from the main menu and then select New. Select the key or the value type that you want to add. Repeat this step until you have all of the registry settings that you want. If you select the Registry on target Machine item on the left pane and then select the Action menu, you will see an Import option, which enables you to import an already defined *.reg file.

To create a default value for a key you must first enter value for the key. Then select the value name in the right or value pane. Select Rename from the File menu and delete the name. Press Enter and the value name is replaced with (Default).

You can also set some properties for the subkeys and values in the editor. The only one that hasn't been discussed already is the DeleteAtUninstall property. A well-designed application should remove all keys that have been added by the application at uninstall time. The default setting is not to delete the keys.

One thing to keep in mind is that the preferred method for maintaining application settings is to use XML-based configuration files. These files offer a great deal more flexibility and are much easier to restore and back up than registry entries.

## File Types Editor

The File Types Editor is used to establish associations between files and applications. For example, when you double-click a file with the .doc extension, the file is opened in Word. You can create these same associations for your application.

To add an association, select File Types on Target Machine from the Action menu. Then select Add File Type. In the properties window you can now set the name of the association. In the Extension property add the file extension that should be associated with the application. Do not enter the periods; you can separate multiple extensions with a semicolon like this: **ex1;ex2.** In the Command property select the ellipse button. Now select the file (typically an executable) that you want to associate with the specified file types. Keep in mind that any one extension should be associated with only one application.

By default, the editor shows &Open as the Document Action. You can add others. The order in which the actions appear in the editor is the order in which they will appear in the context menu when the user right-clicks the file type. Keep in mind that the first item is always the default action. You can set the Arguments property for the actions. This is the command-line argument used to start the application.

## User Interface Editor

Sometimes you might want to ask the user for more information during the installation process. The User Interface Editor is used to specify properties for a set of predefined dialog boxes. The editor is separated into two sections, Install and Admin. One is for the standard installation and the other is used for an administrator's installation. Each section is broken up into three subsections: Start, Progress, and End. These subsections represent the three basic stages of the installation process (see Figure 18-4).

# Chapter 18

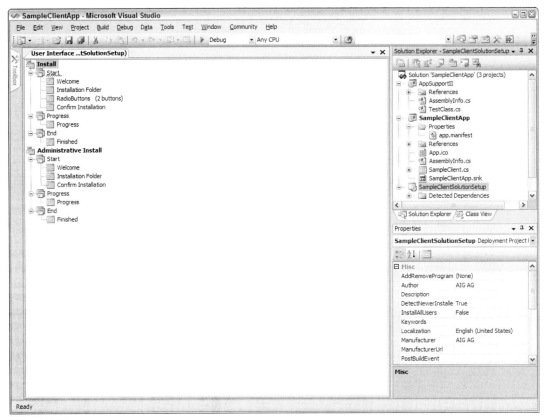

Figure 18-4

The following table lists the types of dialog boxes that you can add to the project.

| Dialog Box | Description |
| --- | --- |
| Checkboxes | Contains up to four check boxes. Each check box has a Label, Value, and Visible property. |
| Confirm Installation | Gives the user the ability to confirm the various settings before installation takes place. |
| Customer Information | Has edit fields for the collection name, organization name, and serial number. Organization name and serial number are optional. |
| Finished | Displayed at the end of the setup process. |
| Installation Address | For Web applications, displays a dialog box so users can choose an alternate installation URL. |
| Installation Folder | For client applications, displays a dialog box so users can select an alternate installation folder. |

| Dialog Box | Description |
| --- | --- |
| License Agreement | Displays the license agreement that is located in a file specified by the LicenseFile property. |
| Progress | Displays a progress indicator during the installation process that shows the current installation status. |
| RadioButtons | Contains up to four radio buttons. Each radio button has a Label and Value property. |
| Read Me | Shows the readme information contained in the file specified by the ReadMe property. |
| Register User | Executes an application that will guide the user through the registration process. This application must be supplied in the setup project. |
| Splash | Displays a bitmap image. |
| TextBoxes | Contains up to four text box fields. Each text box has a Label, Value, and Visible property. |
| Welcome | Contains two properties: the WelcomeText property and the Copyright-Warning. Both are string properties. |

Each of these dialog boxes also contains a property for setting the banner bitmap, and most have a property for banner text. You can also change the order in which the dialog boxes appear by dragging them up or down in the editor window.

Now that you can capture some of this information, the question is, how do you make use of it? This is where the Condition property that appears on most of the objects in the project comes in. The Condition property must evaluate to true for the installation step to proceed. For example, say the installation comes with three optional installation components. In this case, you would add a dialog box with three check boxes. The dialog should be somewhere after the Welcome and before the Confirm Installation dialog box. Change the Label property of each check box to describe the action. The first action could be "Install Component A," the second could be "Install Component B," and so on. In the File System Editor select the file that represents Component A. Assuming that the name of the check box on the dialog box is CHECKBOXA1, the Condition property of the file would be CHECKBOXA1=Checked — that is, if CHECKBOXA1 is checked, install the file; otherwise, don't install it.

## Custom Actions Editor

The Custom Actions Editor allows you to define custom steps that will take place during certain phases of the installation. Custom actions are created beforehand and consist of a DLL, EXE, script, or Installer class. The action would contain special steps to perform that can't be defined in the standard deployment project. The actions will be performed at four specific points in the deployment. When the editor is first started, you will see the four points in the project (see Figure 18-5):

## Chapter 18

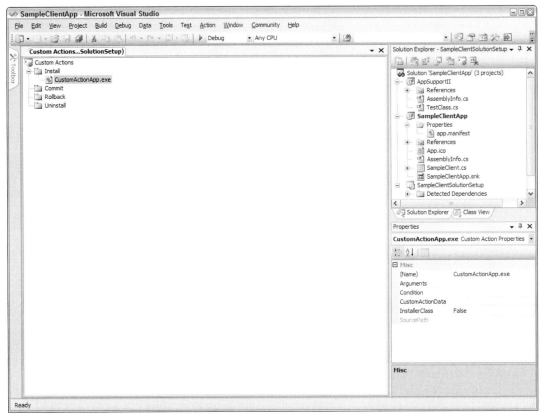

Figure 18-5

- **Install.** Actions will be executed at the end of the installation phase.
- **Commit.** Actions will be executed after the installation has finished and no errors have been recorded.
- **Rollback.** Actions occur after the rollback phase has completed.
- **Uninstall.** Actions occur after uninstall has completed.

To add an action you first select the phase of the installation in which you want the action to occur. Select the Add Custom Action menu selection from the Action menu to open the file system dialog box. This means that the component that contains the action must be part of the deployment project. Because it will be executing on the target machine it has to be deployed, therefore it should be listed in the File System editor.

After you have added the action, you can select one or more of the properties listed in the following table.

# Deployment

| Arguments | Command-Line Arguments |
|---|---|
| Condition | A Windows Installer condition that must be evaluated and result in true for the action to execute. |
| CustomDataAction | Custom data that will be available to the action. |
| EntryPoint | The entry point for the custom DLL that contains the action. If the Action is contained in an executable, this property does not apply. |
| InstallerClass | A Boolean value that, if true, specifies that the action is a .NET `Project Installer` class. |
| Name | Name of the action. Defaults to the file name of the action. |
| SourcePath | The path to action on the development machine. |

Because the action is code that you develop outside of the deployment project, you have the freedom to add just about anything that adds a professional touch to your application. The thing to remember is that these actions happen after the phase it is associated with is complete. If you select the Install phase, the action will not execute until after the install phase has completed. If you want to make determinations before the process, you will want to create a launch condition.

## Launch Conditions Editor

The Launch Conditions Editor allows you to specify that certain conditions must be met before installation can continue. Launch conditions are organized into types of conditions. The basic launch conditions are File Search, Registry Search, and Windows Installer Search. When the editor is first started you see two groups (see Figure 18-6): Search Target Machine and Launch Conditions. Typically, a search is conducted, and, based on the success or failure of that search, a condition is executed. This happens by setting the `Property` property of the search. The `Property` property can be accessed by the installation process. It can be checked in the `Condition` property of other actions, for example. You can also add a Launch Condition in the editor. In this condition you set the `Condition` property to the value of the `Property` property in the search. In the condition you can specify a URL that will download the file, registry key, or installer component that was being search for. Notice in Figure 18-6 that a .NET Framework condition is added by default.

File Search will search for a file or type of file. You can set many different file-related properties that determine how files are searched, including file name, folder location, various date values, version information, and size. You can also set the number of subfolders that are searched.

The Registry Search allows you to search for keys and values. It also allows you to set the root key for searching.

The Windows Installer Search looks for the specified Installer component. The search is conducted by GUID.

The Launch Conditions Editor provides two pre-packaged launch conditions: the .NET Framework Launch Condition, which allows you to search for a specific version of the runtime, and a search for a specific version of MDAC, which uses the registry search to find the relevant MDAC registry entries.

## Chapter 18

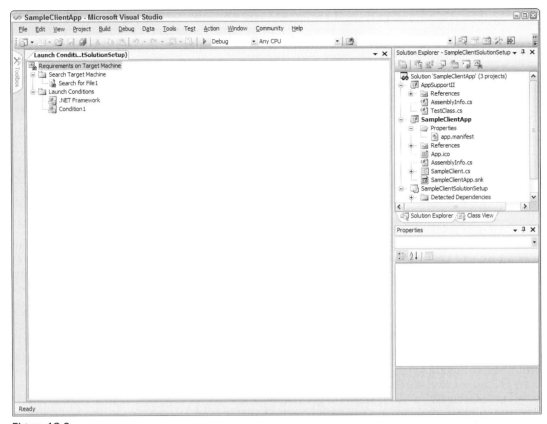

Figure 18-6

## Summary

Deploying software has been difficult for developers of desktop software. As Web sites grew more complex, the ease of deployment for server-based software has become nearly as difficult. This chapter looked at the options and capabilities that Visual Studio 2005 and version 2.0 of the .NET Framework have to help make deployment easier and less error prone.

After reading this chapter, you should be able to create a deployment package that solves almost any deployment issue that you might have. Client applications can be deployed locally or via the Internet or intranet. The extensive features of deployment projects and on the ways that deployment projects can be configured were covered. You can also use No Touch Deployment and ClickOnce to deploy applications. The security features of ClickOnce will make this a secure and efficient way of deploying client applications. Using deployment projects to install Web applications can make the process of configuring IIS much easier as well. Publishing a Web site gives the added benefit if pre-compiling the application.

# Part III
# Data

**Chapter 19:** Data Access with .NET

**Chapter 20:** .NET Programming with SQL Server 2005

**Chapter 21:** Manipulating XML

**Chapter 22:** Working with Active Directory

# 19
# Data Access with .NET

This chapter discusses how to get at data from your C# programs using ADO.NET and covers the following details:

- Connecting to the database — You learn how to use the `SqlConnection` and `OleDbConnection` classes to connect to and disconnect from the database.

- Executing commands — ADO.NET has command objects, which can execute SQL commands or issue a stored procedure with return values. You learn the various command object options and see how commands can be used for each of the options presented by the `Sql` and `OleDB` classes.

- Stored procedures — You learn how to call stored procedures with command objects, and how the results of those stored procedures can be integrated into the data cached on the client.

- The ADO.NET object model — This is significantly different from the objects available with ADO, and the `DataSet`, `DataTable`, `DataRow`, and `DataColumn` classes are discussed as well as the relationships between tables and constraints that are part of `DataSet`. The class hierarchy has changed significantly with version 2 of the .NET framework, and some of these changes are also described.

- Using XML and XML schemas — You examine the XML framework on which ADO.NET is built.

As is the case with the other chapters, you can download the code for the examples used in this chapter from the Wrox Web site at www.wrox.com. The chapter begins with a brief tour of ADO.NET.

# Chapter 19

# ADO.NET Overview

ADO.NET is more than just a thin veneer over some existing API. The similarity to ADO is fairly minimal — the classes and methods of accessing data are completely different.

ADO (ActiveX Data Objects) is a library of COM components that has had many incarnations over the last few years. Currently at version 2.7, ADO consists primarily of the `Connection`, `Command`, `Recordset`, and `Field` objects. Using ADO, a connection is opened to the database, some data is selected into a record set consisting of fields, that data is then manipulated and updated on the server, and the connection is closed. ADO also introduced a so-called disconnected record set, which is used when keeping the connection open for long periods of time is not desirable.

There were several problems that ADO did not address satisfactorily, most notably the unwieldiness (in physical size) of a disconnected record set. This support was more necessary than ever with the evolution of Web-centric computing, so a fresh approach was required. A number of similarities exist between ADO.NET programming and ADO (not only the name), so upgrading from ADO shouldn't be too difficult. What's more, if you're using SQL Server, there's a fantastic new set of managed classes that are tuned to squeeze maximum performance out of the database. This alone should be reason enough to migrate to ADO.NET.

ADO.NET ships with four database client namespaces: one for SQL Server, another for Oracle, the third for ODBC datasources, and the fourth for any database exposed through OLEDB. If your database of choice is not SQL Server or Oracle, the OLEDB route should be taken unless you have no other choice than to use ODBC.

## Namespaces

All of the examples in this chapter access data in one way or another. The following namespaces expose the classes and interfaces used in .NET data access:

- `System.Data` — All generic data access classes
- `System.Data.Common` — Classes shared (or overridden) by individual data providers
- `System.Data.Odbc` — ODBC provider classes
- `System.Data.OleDb` — OLE DB provider classes
- `System.Data.ProviderBase` — New base classes and connection factory classes
- `System.Data.Oracle` — Oracle provider classes
- `System.Data.Sql` — New generic interfaces and classes for SQL Server data access
- `System.Data.SqlClient` — SQL Server provider classes
- `System.Data.SqlTypes` — SQL Server data types

The main classes in ADO.NET are listed in the following subsections.

# Data Access with .NET

## Shared Classes

ADO.NET contains a number of classes that are used regardless of whether you are using the SQL Server classes or the OLE DB classes.

The following classes are contained in the `System.Data` namespace:

- `DataSet` — This object is designed for disconnected use and can contain a set of `DataTables` and include relationships between these tables.
- `DataTable` — A container of data that consists of one or more `DataColumns` and, when populated, will have one or more `DataRows` containing data.
- `DataRow` — A number of values, akin to a row from a database table, or a row from a spreadsheet.
- `DataColumn` — This object contains the definition of a column, such as the name and data type.
- `DataRelation` — A link between two `DataTable` classes within a `DataSet` class. Used for foreign key and master/detail relationships.
- `Constraint` — This class defines a rule for a `DataColumn` class (or set of data columns), such as unique values.

The following classes can be found in the `System.Data.Common` namespace:

- `DataColumnMapping` — Maps the name of a column from the database with the name of a column within a `DataTable`.
- `DataTableMapping` — Maps a table name from the database to a `DataTable` within a `DataSet`.

## Database-Specific Classes

In addition to the shared classes introduced in the previous section, ADO.NET contains a number of database-specific classes. These classes implement a set of standard interfaces defined within the `System.Data` namespace, allowing the classes to be used in a generic manner if necessary. For example, both the `SqlConnection` and `OleDbConnection` classes implement the `IDbConnection` interface.

- `SqlCommand, OleDbCommand, OracleCommand,` and `ODBCCommand` — Used as wrappers for SQL statements or stored procedure calls.
- `SqlCommandBuilder, OleDbCommandBuilder, OracleCommandBuilder,` and `ODBCCommandBuilder` — Used to generate SQL commands (such as `INSERT`, `UPDATE`, and `DELETE` statements) from a `SELECT` statement.
- `SqlConnection, OleDbConnection, OracleConnection, ODBCConnection` — Used to connect to the database. Similar to an ADO `Connection`.
- `SqlDataAdapter, OleDbDataAdapter, OracleDataAdapter, ODBCDataAdapter` — Used to hold select, insert, update, and delete commands, which are then used to populate a `DataSet` and update the `Database`.

- `SqlDataReader`, `OleDbDataReader`, `OracleDataReader`, `ODBCDataReader` — Used as a forward only, connected data reader.
- `SqlParameter`, `OleDbParameter`, `OracleParameter`, `ODBCParameter` — Used to define a parameter to a stored procedure.
- `SqlTransaction`, `OleDbTransaction`, `OracleTransaction`, `ODBCTransaction` — Used for a database transaction, wrapped in an object.

As you can see from the previous list, there are four classes for each type of object — one for each of the providers that are part of .NET version 1.1. In the rest of this chapter, unless otherwise stated, the prefix <provider> is used to indicate that the particular class used is dependent on the database provider in use. With version 2.0 of .NET, the designers have updated the class hierarchy for these classes significantly. In 1.1, all that was common between the various connection classes was the implementation of the IConnection interface. This has changed in .NET 2.0 because now both share a common base class. Similarly the other classes such as Commands, DataAdapters, DataReaders, and so on also share common base classes.

The most important feature of the ADO.NET classes is that they are designed to work in a disconnected manner, which is important in today's highly Web-centric world. It is now common practice to architect a service (such as an online bookshop) to connect to a server, retrieve some data, and then work on that data on the client before reconnecting and passing the data back for processing. The disconnected nature of ADO.NET enables this type of behavior.

ADO 2.1 introduced the disconnected record set, which would permit data to be retrieved from a database, passed to the client for processing, and then reattached to the server. This used to be cumbersome to use, because disconnected behavior was not part of the original design. The ADO.NET classes are different — in all but one case (the <provider>`DataReader`) they are designed for use offline from the database.

> *The classes and interfaces used for data access in the .NET Framework are introduced in the course of this chapter. The focus is mainly on the SQL classes when connecting to the database, because the Framework SDK samples install an MSDE database (SQL Server). In most cases, the OleDb, Oracle and ODBC classes mimic exactly the SQL code.*

## Using Database Connections

To access the database, you need to provide connection parameters, such as the machine that the database is running on, and possibly your login credentials. Anyone who has worked with ADO will be familiar with the .NET connection classes, `OleDbConnection` and `SqlConnection`. Figure 19-1 shows two of the connection classes and includes the class hierarchy.

This is a significant change from that in .NET versions 1.0 and 1.1; however, in practice, using the connection class (and other classes in ADO.NET) is backwardly compatible.

# Data Access with .NET

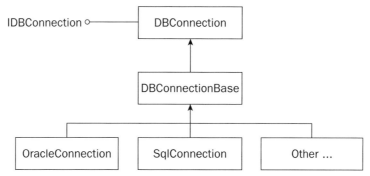

Figure 19-1

The examples in this chapter use the Northwind database, which is installed with the .NET Framework SDK samples. The following code snippet illustrates how to create, open, and close a connection to the Northwind database:

```
using System.Data.SqlClient;

string source = "server=(local);" +
                "integrated security=SSPI;" +
                "database=Northwind";
SqlConnection conn = new SqlConnection(source);
conn.Open();

// Do something useful

conn.Close();
```

The connection string should be very familiar to you if you've used ADO or OLE DB before—indeed, you should be able to cut and paste from your old code if you use the `OleDb` provider. In the example connection string, the parameters used are as follows (the parameters are delimited by a semicolon in the connection string):

- `server=(local)` —This denotes the database server to connect to. SQL Server permits a number of separate database server instances to be running on the same machine, and here you're connecting to the default SQL Server instance.

- `integrated security=SSPI` —This uses Windows Authentication to connect to the database, which is highly recommended over using a username and password within the source code.

- `database=Northwind` —This describes the database instance to connect to; each SQL Server process can expose several database instances.

The example opens a database connection using the defined connection string and then closes that connection. Once the connection has been opened, you can issue commands against the data source, and when you're finished, the connection can be closed.

SQL Server has another mode of authentication—it can use Windows-integrated security, so that the credentials supplied at logon are passed to SQL Server. This is accomplished by removing the `uid` and `pwd` portions of the connection string, and adding in `Integrated Security=SSPI`.

In the download code available for this chapter, you will find the file `Login.cs` that simplifies the examples in this chapter. It is linked to all the example code, and includes database connection information used for the examples; you can alter this to supply your own server name, user, and password as appropriate. This by default uses Windows-integrated security; however, you can change the username and password as appropriate.

## *Managing Connection Strings*

In the previous .NET releases it was up to the developer to manage the database connection strings, often done by storing a connection string in the application configuration file, or more commonly hard-coded somewhere within the application itself.

With .NET 2.0, you now have a predefined way to store connection strings, and even use database connections in a type agnostic manner—for example, it would now be possible to write an application and then plug in various database providers, all without altering the main application.

To define a database connection string you should use the new `<connectionStrings>` section of the configuration file. Here you can specify a name for the connection, the actual database connection string parameters, and in addition you need to specify the provider for this connection type. Here is an example:

```
<configuration>
  ...
  <connectionStrings>
    <add name="Northwind"
         providerName="System.Data.SqlClient"
         connectionString="server=(local);integrated security=SSPI;
                           database=Northwind" />
  </connectionStrings>
</configuration>
```

You use this same connection string in the other examples in this chapter.

Once the database connection information has been defined within the configuration file, you then need to utilize this within the application. You'll most likely want to create a method such as the following to retrieve a database connection based on the name of the connection:

```
private DbConnection GetDatabaseConnection ( string name )
{
  ConnectionStringSettings settings =
    ConfigurationSettings.ConnectionStrings[name];

  DbProviderFactory factory = DbProviderFactories.GetFactory
    ( settings.ProviderName ) ;

  DbConnection conn = factory.CreateConnection ( ) ;
  conn.ConnectionString = settings.ConnectionString ;
```

# Data Access with .NET

```
        return conn ;
    }
```

This code reads the named connection string section (using the new `ConfigurationStringSettings` class), and then requests a provider factory from the generic `DbProviderFactories` class. This uses the `ProviderName` property, which was set to `"System.Data.SqlClient"` in the application configuration file. You might be wondering how this maps to the actual factory class used to generate a database connection for SQL Server — in this case it should utilize the `SqlClientFactory` class from `System.Data.SqlClient`.

If you look into the `machine.config` file for .NET 2.0, you may notice the `DbProviderFactories` section — this maps the alias names (such as `'System.Data.SqlClient'`) to the factory object for that type of database. The following shows an abridged copy of the information I have on my system:

```
<system.data>
  <DbProviderFactories>
    ...
    <add name="SqlClient Data Provider"
         invariant="System.Data.SqlClient" support="FF"
         description=".Net Framework Data Provider for SqlServer"
         type="System.Data.SqlClient.SqlClientFactory, System.Data,
           Version=2.0.3600.0, Culture=neutral,
           PublicKeyToken=b77a5c561934e089" />
    ...
  </DbProviderFactories>
</system.data>
```

This just shows the entry for the SqlClient provider — there are other entries for Odbc, OleDb, Oracle, and also the SqlCE.

So, in the example, the `DbProviderFactory` class just looks up the factory class from the machine configuration settings, and uses that concrete factory class to instantiate the connection object. In the case of the `SqlClientFactory` class, all this does is construct an instance of `SqlConnection` and return this to the caller.

This may seem like a lot of unnecessary work to obtain a database connection, and indeed it is if your application is never going to run on any other database than the one it was designed for. If, however, you use the preceding factory method and also use the generic Db* classes (such as `DbConnection`, `DbCommand`, and `DbDataReader`), you'll future-proof the application and any move in the future to another database system will be fairly simple.

## Using Connections Efficiently

In general, when using *scarce* resources in .NET, such as database connections, windows, or graphics objects, it is good practice to ensure that each resource is closed after use. Although the designers of .NET have implemented automatic garbage collection, which will tidy up eventually, it is necessary to release resources as early as possible to avoid starvation of resources.

This is all too apparent when writing code that accesses a database, because keeping a connection open for slightly longer than necessary can affect other sessions. In extreme circumstances, not closing a connection can lock other users out of an entire set of tables, considerably hurting application performance. Closing database connections should be considered mandatory, so this section shows how to structure your code so as to minimize the risk of leaving a resource open.

You have two main ways to ensure that database connections and the like are released after use.

## Option One: try...catch...finally

The first option to ensure that resources are cleaned up is to use try...catch...finally blocks, and ensure that you close any open connections within the finally block. Here's a short example:

```
try
{
    // Open the connection
    conn.Open();
    // Do something useful
}
catch ( SqlException ex )
{
    // Do something about the exception
}
finally
{
    // Ensure that the connection is freed
    conn.Close ( ) ;
}
```

Within the finally block, you can release any resources you have used. The only trouble with this method is that you have to ensure that you close the connection — it is all too easy to forget to add in the finally clause, so something less prone to vagaries in coding style might be worthwhile.

Also, you might find that you open a number of resources (say two database connections and a file) within a given method, so the cascading of try...catch...finally blocks can sometimes become less easy to read. There is, however, another way to guarantee resource cleanup — the using statement.

## Option Two: The using block statement

During development of C#, the debate on how .NET uses nondeterministic destruction became very heated.

In C++, as soon as an object went out of scope, its destructor would be automatically called. This was great news for designers of resource-based classes, because the destructor was the ideal place to close the resource if the user had forgotten to do so. A C++ destructor is called whenever an object goes out of scope — so, for instance, if an exception was raised and not caught, all destructors would be called.

With C# and the other managed languages, there is no concept of automatic, deterministic destruction. Instead there is the garbage collector, which disposes of resources at some point in the future. What makes this nondeterministic is that you have little say over when this process actually happens. Forgetting to close a database connection could cause all sorts of problems for a .NET executable.

# Data Access with .NET

Luckily, help is at hand. The following code demonstrates how to use the `using` clause to ensure that objects that implement the `IDisposable` interface (see Chapter 7, "Memory Management and Pointers") are cleared up immediately after the block exits:

```
string source = "server=(local);" +
                "integrated security=SSPI;" +
                "database=Northwind";


using ( SqlConnection conn = new SqlConnection ( source ) )
{
   // Open the connection
   conn.Open ( ) ;

   // Do something useful
}
```

In this instance, the `using` clause ensures that the database connection is closed, regardless of how the block is exited.

Looking at the IL code for the `Dispose()` method of the connection classes, all of them check the current state of the connection object, and if open will call the `Close()` method. A great tool for browsing .NET assemblies is Reflector (available at http://www.aisto.com/roeder/dotnet/). This tool permits you to view the IL code for any .NET method, and will also reverse-engineer the IL into C# source code so you can easily see what a given method is doing.

When programming, you should use at least one of these methods, and probably both. Wherever you acquire resources it is good practice to use the `using` statement; even though we all mean to write the `Close()` statement, sometimes we forget, and in the face of exceptions the `using` clause does the right thing. There is no substitute for good exception handling either, so in most instances I would suggest you use both methods together as in the following example:

```
try
{
   using (SqlConnection conn = new SqlConnection ( source ))
   {
      // Open the connection
      conn.Open ( ) ;

      // Do something useful

      // Close it myself
      conn.Close ( ) ;
   }
}
catch (SqlException e)
{
   // Do something with the exception here...
}
```

Note that this example called `Close()`, which isn't strictly necessary, because the `using` clause will ensure that this is done anyway. However, you should ensure that any resources such as this are released as soon as possible — you might have more code in the rest of the block and there's no point locking a resource unnecessarily.

In addition, if an exception is raised within the `using` block, the `IDisposable.Dispose` method will be called on the resource guarded by the `using` clause, which in this example ensures that the database connection is always closed. This produces easier-to-read code than having to ensure you close a connection within an exception clause. You might also note that the exception is defined as a `SqlException` rather than the catch-all `Exception` type — always try to catch as specific an exception as possible and let all others that are not explicitly handled rise up the execution stack.

In conclusion, if you are writing a class that wraps a resource, whatever that resource may be, always implement the `IDisposable` interface to close the resource. That way anyone coding with your class can use the `using()` statement and guarantee that the resource will be cleared up.

## Transactions

Often when there is more than one update to be made to the database, these updates must be performed within the scope of a transaction. A transaction in ADO.NET is initiated by calling one of the `BeginTransaction()` methods on the database connection object. These methods return an object that implements the `IDbTransaction` interface, defined within `System.Data`.

The following sequence of code initiates a transaction on a SQL Server connection:

```
string source = "server=(local);" +
                "integrated security=SSPI;" +
                "database=Northwind";
SqlConnection conn = new SqlConnection(source);
conn.Open();
SqlTransaction tx = conn.BeginTransaction();

// Execute some commands, then commit the transaction

tx.Commit();
conn.Close();
```

When you begin a transaction, you can choose the isolation level for commands executed within that transaction. The level determines how changes made in one database session are viewed by another. Not all database engines support all of the four levels presented in the following table.

| Isolation Level | Description |
| --- | --- |
| ReadCommitted | The default for SQL Server. This level ensures that data written by one transaction will only be accessible in a second transaction after the first transaction commits. |

# Data Access with .NET

| Isolation Level | Description |
|---|---|
| ReadUncommitted | This permits your transaction to read data within the database, even data that has not yet been committed by another transaction. For example, if two users were accessing the same database, and the first inserted some data without concluding their transaction (by means of a Commit or Rollback), then the second user with their isolation level set to ReadUncommitted could read the data. |
| RepeatableRead | This level, which extends the ReadCommitted level, ensures that if the same statement is issued within the transaction, regardless of other potential updates made to the database, the same data will always be returned. This level does require extra locks to be held on the data, which could adversely affect performance. |
| | This level guarantees that, for each row in the initial query, no changes can be made to that data. It does, however, permit "phantom" rows to show up — these are completely new rows that another transaction might have inserted while your transaction was running. |
| Serializable | This is the most "exclusive" transaction level, which in effect serializes access to data within the database. With this isolation level, phantom rows can never show up, so a SQL statement issued within a serializable transaction will always retrieve the same data. The negative performance impact of a Serializable transaction should not be underestimated — if you don't absolutely need to use this level of isolation, stay away from it. |

The SQL Server default isolation level, ReadCommitted, is a good compromise between data coherence and data availability, because fewer locks are required on data than in RepeatableRead or Serializable modes. However, situations exist where the isolation level should be increased, and so within .NET you can simply begin a transaction with a different level from the default. There are no hard-and-fast rules as to which levels to pick — that comes with experience.

> *If you are currently using a database that does not support transactions, it is well worth changing to a database that does. Once I was working as a trusted employee and had been given complete access to the bug database. I typed what I thought was delete from bug where id=99999, but in fact had typed a < rather than an =. I deleted the entire database of bugs (except the one I wanted to!). Luckily for me our I.S team backed up the database on a nightly basis and we could restore this, but a rollback command would have been much easier.*

## Commands

The "Using Database Connections" section briefly touched on the idea of issuing commands against a database. A command is, in its simplest form, a string of text containing SQL statements that is to be issued to the database. A command could also be a stored procedure, or the name of a table that will return all columns and all rows from that table (in other words, a SELECT *-style clause).

# Chapter 19

A command can be constructed by passing the SQL clause as a parameter to the constructor of the `Command` class, as shown in this example:

```
string source = "server=(local);" +
                "integrated security=SSPI;" +
                "database=Northwind";
string select = "SELECT ContactName,CompanyName FROM Customers";
SqlConnection conn = new SqlConnection(source);
conn.Open();

SqlCommand cmd = new SqlCommand(select, conn);
```

The `<provider>Command` classes have a property called `CommandType`, which is used to define whether the command is a SQL clause, a call to a stored procedure, or a full table statement (which simply selects all columns and rows from a given table). The following table summarizes the `CommandType` enumeration.

| CommandType | Example |
| --- | --- |
| `Text` (default) | String select = "SELECT ContactName FROM Customers";<br>SqlCommand cmd = new SqlCommand(select , conn); |
| `StoredProcedure` | SqlCommand cmd = new SqlCommand("CustOrderHist", conn);<br>cmd.CommandType = CommandType.StoredProcedure;<br>cmd.Parameters.AddWithValue("@CustomerID", "QUICK"); |
| `TableDirect` | OleDbCommand cmd = new OleDbCommand("Categories", conn);<br>cmd.CommandType = CommandType.TableDirect; |

When executing a stored procedure, it might be necessary to pass parameters to that procedure. The previous example sets the `@CustomerID` parameter directly, although there are other ways of setting the parameter value, which you look at later in the chapter. Note that in .NET 2.0, the `AddWithValue` method has been added to the command parameters collection — and the `Add ( name, value)` member has been attributed as Obsolete. If like me you have used this original method of constructing parameters for calling a stored procedure, you'll receive compiler warnings when you recompile your code. I would suggest altering your code now because I think it likely that Microsoft will remove the older method in a subsequent release of .NET.

> The `TableDirect` command type is only valid for the OleDb provider; other providers will throw an exception if you attempt to use this command type with them.

## Executing Commands

After you have defined the command, you need to execute it. A number of ways exist to issue the statement, depending on what you expect to be returned (if anything) from that command. The `<provider>Command` classes provide the following execute methods:

- ❑ `ExecuteNonQuery()` — Executes the command but does not return any output
- ❑ `ExecuteReader()` — Executes the command and returns a typed `IDataReader`
- ❑ `ExecuteScalar()` — Executes the command and returns a single value

# Data Access with .NET

In addition to these methods, the `SqlCommand` class exposes the following method:

- `ExecuteXmlReader()` — Executes the command and returns an `XmlReader` object, which can be used to traverse the XML fragment returned from the database.

As with the other chapters, you can download the sample code from the Wrox Web site at www.wrox.com.

## ExecuteNonQuery()

This method is commonly used for `UPDATE`, `INSERT`, or `DELETE` statements, where the only returned value is the number of records affected. This method can, however, return results if you call a stored procedure that has output parameters:

```
using System;
using System.Data.SqlClient;
public class ExecuteNonQueryExample
{
   public static void Main(string[] args)
   {
      string source = "server=(local);" +
                      "integrated security=SSPI;" +
                      "database=Northwind";
      string select = "UPDATE Customers " +
                      "SET ContactName = 'Bob' " +
                      "WHERE ContactName = 'Bill'";
      SqlConnection  conn = new SqlConnection(source);
      conn.Open();
      SqlCommand cmd = new SqlCommand(select, conn);
      int rowsReturned = cmd.ExecuteNonQuery();
      Console.WriteLine("{0} rows returned.", rowsReturned);
      conn.Close();
   }
}
```

`ExecuteNonQuery()` returns the number of rows affected by the command as an `int`.

## ExecuteReader()

This method executes the command and returns a typed data reader object, depending on the provider in use. The object returned can be used to iterate through the record(s) returned, as shown in the following code:

```
using System;
using System.Data.SqlClient;
public class ExecuteReaderExample
{
   public static void Main(string[] args)
   {
      string source = "server=(local);" +
                      "integrated security=SSPI;" +
                      "database=Northwind";
      string select = "SELECT ContactName,CompanyName FROM Customers";
      SqlConnection conn = new SqlConnection(source);
```

## Chapter 19

```
      conn.Open();
      SqlCommand cmd = new SqlCommand(select, conn);
      SqlDataReader reader = cmd.ExecuteReader();
      while(reader.Read())
      {
         Console.WriteLine("Contact : {0,-20} Company : {1}" ,
                           reader[0] , reader[1]);
      }
   }
}
```

Figure 19-2 shows the output of this code.

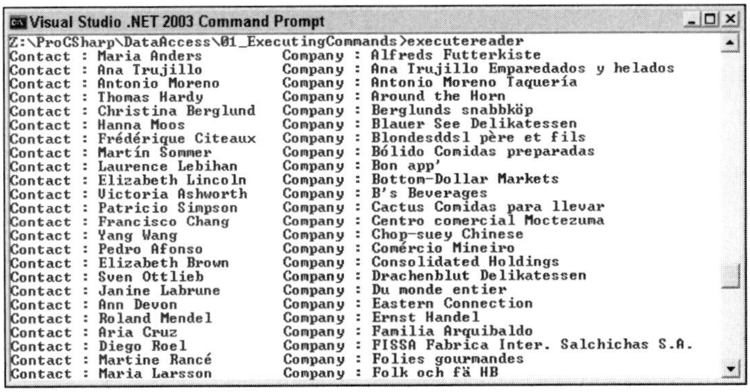

**Figure 19-2**

The <provider>DataReader objects are discussed later in this chapter.

## ExecuteScalar()

On many occasions, it is necessary to return a single result from a SQL statement, such as the count of records in a given table, or the current date/time on the server. The ExecuteScalar method can be used in such situations:

```
using System;
using System.Data.SqlClient;
public class ExecuteScalarExample
{
   public static void Main(string[] args)
   {
      string source = "server=(local);" +
                      "integrated security=SSPI;" +
                      "database=Northwind";
      string select = "SELECT COUNT(*) FROM Customers";
      SqlConnection conn = new SqlConnection(source);
      conn.Open();
      SqlCommand cmd = new SqlCommand(select, conn);
      object o = cmd.ExecuteScalar();
      Console.WriteLine ( o ) ;
   }
}
```

# Data Access with .NET

The method returns an object, which you can cast to the appropriate type if required. If the SQL you are calling only returns one column, it is preferable to use `ExecuteScalar` over any other method of retrieving that column. That also applies to stored procedures that return a single value.

## ExecuteXmlReader() (SqlClient Provider Only)

As its name implies, this method executes the command and returns an `XmlReader` object to the caller. SQL Server permits a SQL `SELECT` statement to be extended with a `FOR XML` clause. This clause can take one of three options:

- `FOR XML AUTO`—Builds a tree based on the tables in the `FROM` clause
- `FOR XML RAW`—Maps result set rows to elements, with columns mapped to attributes
- `FOR XML EXPLICIT`—Requires that you specify the shape of the XML tree to be returned

*Professional SQL Server 2000 XML* (Wrox Press, ISBN 1-861005-46-6) includes a complete description of these options. For this example use `AUTO`:

```
using System;
using System.Data.SqlClient;
using System.Xml;
public class ExecuteXmlReaderExample
{
   public static void Main(string[] args)
   {
      string source = "server=(local);" +
                      "integrated security=SSPI;" +
                      "database=Northwind";
      string select = "SELECT ContactName,CompanyName " +
                      "FROM Customers FOR XML AUTO";
      SqlConnection conn = new SqlConnection(source);
      conn.Open();
      SqlCommand cmd = new SqlCommand(select, conn);
      XmlReader xr = cmd.ExecuteXmlReader();
      xr.Read();
      string s;
      do
      {
         s = xr.ReadOuterXml();
         if (s!="")
            Console.WriteLine(s);
      } while (s!= "");
      conn.Close();
   }
}
```

Note that you have to import the `System.Xml` namespace in order to output the returned XML. This namespace and further XML capabilities of .NET Framework are explored in more detail in Chapter 21, "Manipulating XML."

Here you include the `FOR XML AUTO` clause in the SQL statement, then call the `ExecuteXmlReader()` method. Figure 19-3 shows the output of this code.

593

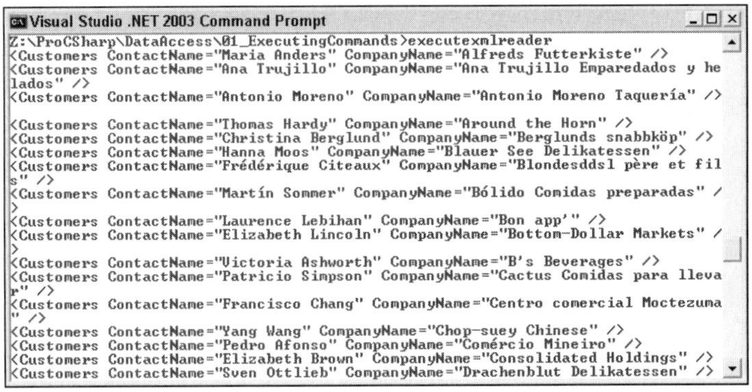

# Chapter 19

**Figure 19-3**

In the SQL clause, you specified `FROM Customers`, so an element of type Customers is shown in the output. To this are added attributes, one for each column selected from the database. This builds up an XML fragment for each row selected from the database.

## Calling Stored Procedures

Calling a stored procedure with a command object is just a matter of defining the name of the stored procedure, adding a definition for each parameter of the procedure, then executing the command with one of the methods presented in the previous section.

To make the examples in this section more useful, a set of stored procedures has been defined that can be used to insert, update, and delete records from the Region table in the Northwind sample database. Despite its small size this is a good candidate to choose for the example, because it can be used to define examples for each of the types of stored procedures you will commonly write.

### Calling a stored procedure that returns nothing

The simplest example of calling a stored procedure is one that returns nothing to the caller. Two such procedures are defined in the following two subsections: one for updating a pre-existing Region record and one for deleting a given Region record.

#### Record update

Updating a `Region` record is fairly trivial, because there is only one column that can be modified (assuming primary keys cannot be updated). You can type these examples directly into the SQL Server Query Analyzer, or run the `StoredProcs.sql` file that is part of the downloadable code for this chapter. This file installs each of the stored procedures in this section:

```
CREATE PROCEDURE RegionUpdate (@RegionID INTEGER,
                               @RegionDescription NCHAR(50)) AS
    SET NOCOUNT OFF
    UPDATE Region
        SET RegionDescription = @RegionDescription
        WHERE RegionID = @RegionID
GO
```

An update command on a more real-world table might need to re-select and return the updated record in its entirety. This stored procedure takes two input parameters (`@RegionID` and `@RegionDescription`), and issues an `UPDATE` statement against the database.

To run this stored procedure from within .NET code, you need to define a SQL command and execute it:

```
SqlCommand aCommand = new SqlCommand("RegionUpdate", conn);

aCommand.CommandType = CommandType.StoredProcedure;
aCommand.Parameters.Add(new SqlParameter ("@RegionID",
                                          SqlDbType.Int,
                                          0,
                                          "RegionID"));
aCommand.Parameters.Add(new SqlParameter("@RegionDescription",
                                          SqlDbType.NChar,
                                          50,
                                          "RegionDescription"));
aCommand.UpdatedRowSource = UpdateRowSource.None;
```

This code creates a new `SqlCommand` object named `aCommand`, and defines it as a stored procedure. You then add each parameter in turn, and finally set the expected output from the stored procedure to one of the values in the `UpdateRowSource` enumeration, which is discussed later in this chapter.

The stored procedure takes two parameters: the unique primary key of the `Region` record being updated, and the new description to be given to this record. After the command has been created, it can be executed by issuing the following commands:

```
aCommand.Parameters[0].Value = 999;
aCommand.Parameters[1].Value = "South Western England";
aCommand.ExecuteNonQuery();
```

Here the value of each parameter is set; then the stored procedure is executed. Because the procedure returns nothing, `ExecuteNonQuery()` will suffice. Command parameters can be set by ordinal numbers (as shown in the previous example) or by name.

## Record deletion

The next stored procedure required is one that can be used to delete a Region record from the database:

```
CREATE PROCEDURE RegionDelete (@RegionID INTEGER) AS
    SET NOCOUNT OFF
    DELETE FROM Region
    WHERE      RegionID = @RegionID
GO
```

This procedure requires only the primary key value of the record. The code uses a `SqlCommand` object to call this stored procedure as follows:

```
SqlCommand aCommand = new SqlCommand("RegionDelete" , conn);
aCommand.CommandType = CommandType.StoredProcedure;
aCommand.Parameters.Add(new SqlParameter("@RegionID" , SqlDbType.Int , 0 ,
                                          "RegionID"));
aCommand.UpdatedRowSource = UpdateRowSource.None;
```

This command only accepts a single parameter as shown in the following code, which will execute the `RegionDelete` stored procedure; here you see an example of setting the parameter by name:

```
aCommand.Parameters["@RegionID"].Value= 999;
aCommand.ExecuteNonQuery();
```

## Calling a stored procedure that returns output parameters

Both of the previous examples execute stored procedures that return nothing. If a stored procedure includes output parameters, these need to be defined within the .NET client so that they can be filled when the procedure returns. The following example shows how to insert a record into the database, and return the primary key of that record to the caller.

### Record insertion

The Region table only consists of a primary key (`RegionID`) and description field (`RegionDescription`). To insert a record, this numeric primary key needs to be generated, and then a new row needs to be inserted into the database. The primary key generation in this example has been simplified by creating one within the stored procedure. The method used is exceedingly crude, which is why there is a section on key generation later in this chapter. For now this primitive example suffices:

```
CREATE PROCEDURE RegionInsert(@RegionDescription NCHAR(50),
                              @RegionID INTEGER OUTPUT)AS
   SET NOCOUNT OFF
   SELECT @RegionID = MAX(RegionID)+ 1
   FROM Region
   INSERT INTO Region(RegionID, RegionDescription)
   VALUES(@RegionID, @RegionDescription)
GO
```

The insert procedure creates a new Region record. As the primary key value is generated by the database itself, this value is returned as an output parameter from the procedure (`@RegionID`). This is sufficient for this simple example, but for a more complex table (especially one with default values), it is more common not to utilize output parameters, and instead select the entire inserted row and return this to the caller. The .NET classes can cope with either scenario.

```
SqlCommand   aCommand = new SqlCommand("RegionInsert" , conn);
aCommand.CommandType = CommandType.StoredProcedure;
aCommand.Parameters.Add(new SqlParameter("@RegionDescription" ,
                                  SqlDbType.NChar ,
                                  50 ,
                                  "RegionDescription"));
aCommand.Parameters.Add(new SqlParameter("@RegionID" ,
                                  SqlDbType.Int,
                                  0 ,
                                  ParameterDirection.Output ,
                                  false ,
                                  0 ,
                                  0 ,
                                  "RegionID" ,
                                  DataRowVersion.Default ,
                                  null));
aCommand.UpdatedRowSource = UpdateRowSource.OutputParameters;
```

# Data Access with .NET

Here, the definition of the parameters is much more complex. The second parameter, `@RegionID`, is defined to include its parameter direction, which in this example is `Output`. In addition to this flag, on the last line of the code, the `UpdateRowSource` enumeration is used to indicate that data will be returned from this stored procedure via output parameters. This flag is mainly used when issuing stored procedure calls from a `DataTable` (which is discussed later in this chapter).

Calling this stored procedure is similar to the previous examples, except in this instance the output parameter is read after executing the procedure:

```
aCommand.Parameters["@RegionDescription"].Value = "South West";
aCommand.ExecuteNonQuery();
int newRegionID = (int) aCommand.Parameters["@RegionID"].Value;
```

After executing the command, the value of the `@RegionID` parameter is read and cast to an integer.

You might be wondering what to do if the stored procedure you call returns output parameters and a set of rows. In this instance, define the parameters as appropriate, and rather than calling `ExecuteNonQuery()`, call one of the other methods (such as `ExecuteReader()`) that will permit you to traverse any record(s) returned.

## Fast Data Access: The Data Reader

A data reader is the simplest and fastest way of selecting some data from a data source, but also the least capable. You cannot directly instantiate a data reader object—an instance is returned from the appropriate database's command object (such as `SqlCommand`) after having called the `ExecuteReader()` method.

The following code demonstrates how to select data from the Customers table in the Northwind database. The example connects to the database, selects a number of records, loops through these selected records, and outputs them to the console.

This example utilizes the OLE DB provider as a brief respite from the SQL provider. In most cases the classes have a one-to-one correspondence with their `SqlClient` cousins; for example, there is the `OleDbConnection` object, which is similar to the `SqlConnection` object used in the previous examples.

To execute commands against an OLE DB data source, the `OleDbCommand` class is used. The following code shows an example of executing a simple SQL statement and reading the records by returning an `OleDbDataReader` object.

Note the second `using` directive below that makes available the `OleDb` classes:

```
using System;
using System.Data.OleDb;
```

Most of the data providers currently available are shipped within the same assembly, so it is only necessary to reference the `System.Data.dll` assembly to import all classes used in this section. The only exception is the Oracle classes, which reside in `System.Data.Oracle.dll`.

```csharp
public class DataReaderExample
{
  public static void Main(string[] args)
  {
    string source = "Provider=SQLOLEDB;" +
                    "server=(local);" +
                    "integrated security=SSPI;" +
                    "database=northwind";
    string select = "SELECT ContactName,CompanyName FROM Customers";
    OleDbConnection conn = new OleDbConnection(source);
    conn.Open();
    OleDbCommand cmd = new OleDbCommand(select , conn);
    OleDbDataReader aReader = cmd.ExecuteReader();
    while(aReader.Read())
       Console.WriteLine("'{0}' from {1}" ,
                         aReader.GetString(0) , aReader.GetString(1));
    aReader.Close();
    conn.Close();
  }
}
```

The preceding code includes many familiar aspects of C# already covered in this chapter. To compile the example, issue the following command:

**csc /t:exe /debug+ DataReaderExample.cs /r:System.Data.dll**

The following code from the previous example creates a new OLE DB .NET database connection, based on the source connection string:

```csharp
OleDbConnection conn = new OleDbConnection(source);
conn.Open();
OleDbCommand cmd = new OleDbCommand(select, conn);
```

The third line creates a new `OleDbCommand` object, based on a particular SELECT statement, and the database connection to be used when the command is executed. When you have a valid command, you need to execute it, which returns an initialized `OleDbDataReader`:

```csharp
OleDbDataReader aReader = cmd.ExecuteReader();
```

An `OleDbDataReader` is a forward-only "connected" cursor. In other words, you can only traverse through the records returned in one direction, and the database connection used is kept open until the data reader has been closed.

> **An OleDbDataReader keeps the database connection open until explicitly closed.**

The `OleDbDataReader` class cannot be instantiated directly — it is always returned by a call to the `ExecuteReader()` method of the `OleDbCommand` class. Once you have an open data reader, there are various ways to access the data contained within the reader.

# Data Access with .NET

When the `OleDbDataReader` object is closed (via an explicit call to `Close()`, or the object being garbage collected), the underlying connection may also be closed, depending on which of the `ExecuteReader()` methods is called. If you call `ExecuteReader()` and pass `CommandBehavior.CloseConnection`, you can force the connection to be closed when the reader is closed.

The `OleDbDataReader` class has an indexer that permits access (although not type-safe access) to any field using the familiar array style syntax:

```
object o = aReader[0];
```
or
```
object o = aReader["CategoryID"];
```

Assuming that the `CategoryID` field was the first in the `SELECT` statement used to populate the reader, these two lines are functionally equivalent, although the second is slower than the first; to verify this, a test application was written that performed a million iterations of accessing the same column from an open data reader, just to get some numbers that were big enough to read. You probably don't read the same column a million times in a tight loop, but every (micro) second counts, and you might as well write code that is as close to optimal as possible.

As an aside, the numeric indexer took on average 0.09 seconds for the million accesses, and the textual one 0.63 seconds. The reason for this difference is that the textual method looks up the column number internally from the schema and then accesses it using its ordinal. If you know this information beforehand you can do a better job of accessing the data.

So, should you use the numeric indexer? Maybe, but there is a better way.

In addition to the indexers just presented, `OleDbDataReader` has a set of type-safe methods that can be used to read columns. These are fairly self-explanatory, and all begin with `Get`. There are methods to read most types of data, such as `GetInt32`, `GetFloat`, `GetGuid`, and so on.

The million iterations using `GetInt32` took 0.06 seconds. The overhead in the numeric indexer is incurred while getting the data type, calling the same code as `GetInt32`, then boxing (and in this instance unboxing) an integer. So, if you know the schema beforehand, are willing to use cryptic numbers instead of column names, and you can be bothered to use a type-safe function for each and every column access, you stand to gain somewhere in the region of a ten-fold speed increase over using a textual column name (when selecting those million copies of the same column).

Needless to say, there is a tradeoff between maintainability and speed. If you must use numeric indexers, define constants within class scope for each of the columns that you will be accessing. The preceding code can be used to select data from any OLE DB database; however, there are a number of SQL Server–specific classes that can be used with the obvious portability tradeoff.

The following example is the same as the previous one, except in this instance the OLE DB provider and all references to OLE DB classes have been replaced with the SQL counterparts. The changes in the code from the previous example have been highlighted. The example is in the `04_DataReaderSql` directory:

```
using System;
using System.Data.SqlClient;
public class DataReaderSql
{
```

```csharp
public static int Main(string[] args)
{
    string source = "server=(local);" +
                    "integrated security=SSPI;" +
                    "database=northwind";
    string select = "SELECT ContactName,CompanyName FROM Customers";
    SqlConnection conn = new SqlConnection(source);
    conn.Open();
    SqlCommand cmd = new SqlCommand(select , conn);
    SqlDataReader aReader = cmd.ExecuteReader();
    while(aReader.Read())
        Console.WriteLine("'{0}' from {1}" , aReader.GetString(0) ,
                            aReader.GetString(1));
    aReader.Close();
    conn.Close();
    return 0;
}
}
```

Notice the difference? If you're typing this, do a global replace on OleDb with Sql, change the data source string, and recompile. It's that easy!

The same performance tests were run on the indexers for the SQL provider, and this time the numeric indexers were both exactly the same at 0.13 seconds for the million accesses, and the string-based indexer ran at about 0.65 seconds. You would expect the native SQL Server provider to be faster than going through OleDb, which up until this was tested under the release version of .NET it was. This might be an anomaly due to the simplistic test approach used in the example (selecting the same value 1,000,000 times); a real-world test should show better performance from the managed SQL provider.

# Managing Data and Relationships: The DataSet Class

The DataSet class has been designed as an offline container of data. It has no notion of database connections. In fact, the data held within a DataSet doesn't necessarily need to have come from a database — it could just as easily be records from a CSV file, or points read from a measuring device.

A DataSet class consists of a set of data tables, each of which will have a set of data columns and data rows (see Figure 19-4). In addition to defining the data, you can also define *links* between tables within the DataSet class. One common scenario would be when defining a parent-child relationship (commonly known as master/detail). One record in a table (say Order) links to many records in another table (say Order_Details). This relationship can be defined and navigated within the DataSet.

The following sections describe the classes that are used with a DataSet class.

# Data Access with .NET

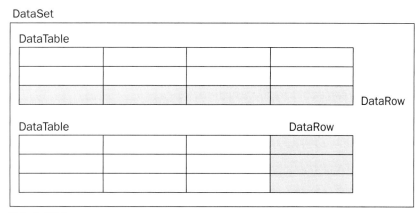

Figure 19-4

## Data Tables

A data table is very similar to a physical database table — it consists of a set of columns with particular properties, and might have zero or more rows of data. A data table might also define a primary key, which can be one or more columns, and might also contain constraints on columns. The generic term for this information used throughout the rest of the chapter is *schema*.

Several ways exist to define the schema for a particular data table (and indeed the DataSet class as a whole). These are discussed after introducing data columns and data rows. Figure 19-5 shows some of the objects that are accessible through the data table.

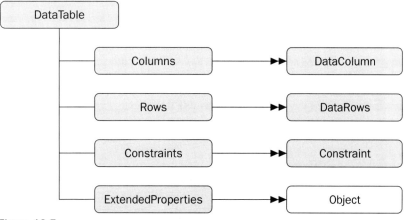

Figure 19-5

601

A `DataTable` object (and also a `DataColumn`) can have an arbitrary number of extended properties associated with it. This collection can be populated with any user-defined information pertaining to the object. For example, a given column might have an input mask used to validate the contents of that column—a typical example is the U.S. Social Security number. Extended properties are especially useful when the data is constructed within a middle tier and returned to the client for some processing. You could, for example, store validation criteria (such as `min` and `max`) for numeric columns in extended properties and use this in the UI tier when validating user input.

When a data table has been populated—by selecting data from a database, reading data from a file, or manually populating within code—the `Rows` collection will contain this retrieved data.

The `Columns` collection contains `DataColumn` instances that have been added to this table. These define the schema of the data, such as the data type, nullability, default values, and so on. The `Constraints` collection can be populated with either unique or primary key constraints.

One example of where the schema information for a data table is used is when displaying that data in a `DataGrid` (which is discussed in Chapter 24, "Viewing .NET Data"). The `DataGrid` control uses properties such as the data type of the column to decide what control to use for that column. A bit field within the database will be displayed as a check box within the `DataGrid`. If a column is defined within the database schema as `NOT NULL`, this fact will be stored within the `DataColumn` so that it can be tested when the user attempts to move off a row.

## Data Columns

A `DataColumn` object defines properties of a column within the `DataTable`, such as the data type of that column, whether the column is read-only, and various other facts. A column can be created in code, or it can be automatically generated by the runtime.

When creating a column, it is also useful to give it a name; otherwise the runtime will generate a name for you in the form `Column`*n* where *n* is an incrementing number.

The data type of the column can be set either by supplying it in the constructor or by setting the `DataType` property. Once you have loaded data into a data table you cannot alter the type of a column—you'll just receive an `ArgumentException`.

Data columns can be created to hold the following .NET Framework data types:

| Boolean  | Decimal | Int64  | TimeSpan |
|----------|---------|--------|----------|
| Byte     | Double  | Sbyte  | UInt16   |
| Char     | Int16   | Single | UInt32   |
| DateTime | Int32   | String | UInt64   |

Once created, the next thing to do with a `DataColumn` object is to set up other properties, such as the nullability of the column or the default value. The following code fragment shows a few of the more common options to set on a `DataColumn` object:

# Data Access with .NET

```
DataColumn customerID = new DataColumn("CustomerID" , typeof(int));
customerID.AllowDBNull = false;
customerID.ReadOnly = false;
customerID.AutoIncrement = true;
customerID.AutoIncrementSeed = 1000;
DataColumn name = new DataColumn("Name" , typeof(string));
name.AllowDBNull = false;
name.Unique = true;
```

The following table shows the properties that can be set on a `DataColumn` object.

| Property | Description |
|---|---|
| AllowDBNull | If `true`, permits the column to be set to `DBNull`. |
| AutoIncrement | Defines that this column value is automatically generated as an incrementing number. |
| AutoIncrementSeed | Defines the initial seed value for an `AutoIncrement` column. |
| AutoIncrementStep | Defines the step between automatically generated column values, with a default of one. |
| Caption | Can be used for displaying the name of the column on screen. |
| ColumnMapping | Defines how a column is mapped into XML when a `DataSet` class is saved by calling `DataSet.WriteXml`. |
| ColumnName | The name of the column. This is auto-generated by the runtime if not set in the constructor. |
| DataType | Defines the `System.Type` value of the column. |
| DefaultValue | Can define a default value for a column. |
| Expression | Defines the expression to be used in a computed column. |

## Data rows

This class makes up the other part of the `DataTable` class. The columns within a data table are defined in terms of the `DataColumn` class. The actual data within the table is accessed using the `DataRow` object. The following example shows how to access rows within a data table. First, the connection details:

```
string source = "server=(local);" +
                " integrated security=SSPI;" +
                "database=northwind";
string select = "SELECT ContactName,CompanyName FROM Customers";
SqlConnection  conn = new SqlConnection(source);
```

The following code introduces the `SqlDataAdapter` class, which is used to place data into a `DataSet` class. `SqlDataAdapter` issues the SQL clause and fills a table in the `DataSet` class called `Customers` with the output of the following query. (For more details on the `SqlDataAdapter` class see the section "Populating a DataSet" later in the chapter.)

```
SqlDataAdapter da = new SqlDataAdapter(select, conn);
DataSet ds = new DataSet();
da.Fill(ds , "Customers");
```

In the following code, you might notice the use of the `DataRow` indexer to access values from within that row. The value for a given column can be retrieved using one of the several overloaded indexers. These permit you to retrieve a value knowing the column number, name, or `DataColumn`:

```
foreach(DataRow row in ds.Tables["Customers"].Rows)
    Console.WriteLine("'{0}' from {1}" , row[0] ,row[1]);
```

One of the most appealing aspects of `DataRow` is that it is versioned. This permits you to receive various values for a given column in a particular row. The versions are described in the following table.

| DataRow Version Value | Description |
| --- | --- |
| `Current` | The value existing at present within the column. If no edit has occurred, this will be the same as the original value. If an edit (or edits) have occurred, the value will be the last valid value entered. |
| `Default` | The default value (in other words, any default set up for the column). |
| `Original` | The value of the column when originally selected from the database. If the `DataRow`'s `AcceptChanges` method is called, this value will update to the `Current` value. |
| `Proposed` | When changes are in progress for a row, it is possible to retrieve this modified value. If you call `BeginEdit()` on the row and make changes, each column will have a proposed value until either `EndEdit()` or `CancelEdit()` is called. |

The version of a given column could be used in many ways. One example is when updating rows within the database, in which instance it is common to issue a SQL statement such as the following:

```
UPDATE Products
SET    Name = Column.Current
WHERE  ProductID = xxx
AND    Name = Column.Original;
```

Obviously, this code would never compile, but it shows one use for original and current values of a column within a row.

To retrieve a versioned value from the `DataRow` indexer, use one of the indexer methods that accept a `DataRowVersion` value as a parameter. The following snippet shows how to obtain all values of each column in a `DataTable` object:

```
foreach (DataRow row in ds.Tables["Customers"].Rows )
{
  foreach ( DataColumn dc in ds.Tables["Customers"].Columns )
  {
```

```
        Console.WriteLine ("{0} Current  = {1}" , dc.ColumnName ,
                                                  row[dc,DataRowVersion.Current]);
        Console.WriteLine ("    Default  = {0}" , row[dc,DataRowVersion.Default]);
        Console.WriteLine ("    Original = {0}" , row[dc,DataRowVersion.Original]);
    }
}
```

The whole row has a state flag called `RowState`, which can be used to determine what operation is needed on the row when it is persisted back to the database. The `RowState` property is set to keep track of all the changes made to the `DataTable`, such as adding new rows, deleting existing rows, and changing columns within the table. When the data is reconciled with the database, the row state flag is used to determine what SQL operations should occur. The following table provides an overview of the flags that are defined by the `DataRowState` enumeration.

| DataRowState Value | Description |
| --- | --- |
| `Added` | Indicates that the row has been newly added to a `DataTable`'s `Rows` collection. All rows created on the client are set to this value, and will ultimately issue SQL `INSERT` statements when reconciled with the database. |
| `Deleted` | Indicates that the row has been marked as deleted from the `DataTable` by means of the `DataRow.Delete()` method. The row still exists within the `DataTable`, but will not normally be viewable onscreen (unless a `DataView` has been explicitly set up). `DataViews` are discussed in the next chapter. Rows marked as deleted in the `DataTable` will be deleted from the database when reconciled. |
| `Detached` | Indicates that a row is in this state immediately after it is created, and can also be returned to this state by calling `DataRow.Remove()`. A detached row is not considered to be part of any data table, and as such no SQL for rows in this state will be issued. |
| `Modified` | Indicates that a row will be `Modified` if the value in any column has been changed. |
| `Unchanged` | Indicates that the row has not been changed since the last call to `AcceptChanges()`. |

The state of the row depends also on what methods have been called on the row. The `AcceptChanges()` method is generally called after successfully updating the data source (that is, after persisting changes to the database).

The most common way to alter data in a `DataRow` is to use the indexer; however, if you have a number of changes to make you also need to consider the `BeginEdit()` and `EndEdit()` methods.

When an alteration is made to a column within a `DataRow`, the `ColumnChanging` event is raised on the row's `DataTable`. This permits you to override the `ProposedValue` property of the `DataColumn ChangeEventArgs` class, and change it as required. This is one way of performing some data validation on column values. If you call `BeginEdit()` before making changes, the `ColumnChanging` event will not be raised. This permits you to make multiple changes and then call `EndEdit()` to persist these changes. If you want to revert to the original values, call `CancelEdit()`.

A `DataRow` can be linked in some way to other rows of data. This permits the creation of navigable links between rows, which is common in master/detail scenarios. The `DataRow` contains a `GetChildRows()` method that will return an array of associated rows from another table in the same `DataSet` as the current row. These are discussed in the "Data Relationships" section later in this chapter.

## Schema generation

You can create the schema for a `DataTable` in three ways:

- Let the runtime do it for you.
- Write code to create the table(s).
- Use the XML schema generator.

### Runtime schema generation

The `DataRow` example shown earlier presented the following code for selecting data from a database and populating a `DataSet` class:

```
SqlDataAdapter da = new SqlDataAdapter(select , conn);
DataSet ds = new DataSet();
da.Fill(ds , "Customers");
```

This is obviously easy to use, but it has a few drawbacks as well. For example, you have to make do with the default column names, which might work for you, but in certain instances you might want to rename a physical database column (say `PKID`) to something more user-friendly.

You could naturally alias columns within your SQL clause, as in `SELECT PID AS PersonID FROM PersonTable`; I would always recommend not renaming columns within SQL, because a column only really needs to have a "pretty" name onscreen.

Another potential problem with automated `DataTable`/`DataColumn` generation is that you have no control over the column types that the runtime chooses for your data. It does a fairly good job of deciding the correct data type for you, but as usual there are instances where you need more control. For example, you might have defined an enumerated type for a given column, so as to simplify user code written against your class. If you accept the default column types that the runtime generates, the column will likely be an integer with a 32-bit range, as opposed to an `enum` with your predefined options.

Lastly, and probably most problematic, is that when using automated table generation, you have no type-safe access to the data within the `DataTable`—you are at the mercy of indexers, which return instances of `object` rather than derived data types. If you like sprinkling your code with typecast expressions, skip the following sections.

### Hand-coded schema

Generating the code to create a `DataTable`, replete with associated `DataColumns`, is fairly easy. The examples within this section access the Products table from the Northwind database shown in Figure 19-6.

**Products**

| | Column Name | Data Type | Length | Allow Nulls |
|---|---|---|---|---|
| 🔑 | ProductID | int | 4 | |
| | ProductName | nvarchar | 40 | |
| | SupplierID | int | 4 | ✓ |
| | CategoryID | int | 4 | ✓ |
| | QuantityPerUnit | nvarchar | 20 | ✓ |
| | UnitPrice | money | 8 | ✓ |
| | UnitsInStock | smallint | 2 | ✓ |
| | UnitsOnOrder | smallint | 2 | ✓ |
| | ReorderLevel | smallint | 2 | ✓ |
| | Discontinued | bit | 1 | |

**Figure 19-6**

The following code manufactures a `DataTable`, which corresponds to the schema shown in Figure 19-6 (but doesn't cover the nullability of columns):

```
public static void ManufactureProductDataTable(DataSet ds)
{
   DataTable   products = new DataTable("Products");
   products.Columns.Add(new DataColumn("ProductID", typeof(int)));
   products.Columns.Add(new DataColumn("ProductName", typeof(string)));
   products.Columns.Add(new DataColumn("SupplierID", typeof(int)));
   products.Columns.Add(new DataColumn("CategoryID", typeof(int)));
   products.Columns.Add(new DataColumn("QuantityPerUnit", typeof(string)));
   products.Columns.Add(new DataColumn("UnitPrice", typeof(decimal)));
   products.Columns.Add(new DataColumn("UnitsInStock", typeof(short)));
   products.Columns.Add(new DataColumn("UnitsOnOrder", typeof(short)));
   products.Columns.Add(new DataColumn("ReorderLevel", typeof(short)));
   products.Columns.Add(new DataColumn("Discontinued", typeof(bool)));
   ds.Tables.Add(products);
}
```

You can alter the code in the `DataRow` example to utilize this newly generated table definition as follows:

```
string source = "server=(local);" +
                "integrated security=sspi;" +
                "database=Northwind";
string select = "SELECT * FROM Products";
SqlConnection conn = new SqlConnection(source);
SqlDataAdapter cmd = new SqlDataAdapter(select, conn);
DataSet ds = new DataSet();
ManufactureProductDataTable(ds);
cmd.Fill(ds, "Products");
foreach(DataRow row in ds.Tables["Products"].Rows)
   Console.WriteLine("'{0}' from {1}", row[0], row[1]);
```

The `ManufactureProductDataTable()` method creates a new `DataTable`, adds each column in turn, and finally appends this to the list of tables within the `DataSet`. The `DataSet` has an indexer that takes the name of the table and returns that `DataTable` to the caller.

The previous example is still not really type-safe, because indexers are being used on columns to retrieve the data. What would be better is a class (or set of classes) derived from `DataSet`, `DataTable`, and

# Chapter 19

`DataRow` that define type-safe accessors for tables, rows, and columns. You can generate this code yourself; it's not particularly tedious and you end up with truly type-safe data access classes.

If you don't like generating these type-safe classes yourself, help is at hand. The .NET Framework includes support for using XML schemas to define a `DataSet` class, a `DataTable` class, and the other classes that have been described in this section. (For more details on this method see the section "XML Schemas" later in this chapter.)

## Data Relationships

When writing an application, it is often necessary to obtain and cache various tables of information. The `DataSet` class is the container for this information. With regular OLE DB it was necessary to provide a strange SQL dialect to enforce hierarchical data relationships, and the provider itself was not without its own subtle quirks.

The `DataSet` class, on the other hand, has been designed from the start to establish relationships between data tables with ease. The code in this section shows how to generate manually and populate two tables with data. So, if you don't have access to SQL Server or the Northwind database, you can run this example anyway:

```
DataSet ds = new DataSet("Relationships");
ds.Tables.Add(CreateBuildingTable());
ds.Tables.Add(CreateRoomTable());
ds.Relations.Add("Rooms",
                 ds.Tables["Building"].Columns["BuildingID"],
                 ds.Tables["Room"].Columns["BuildingID"]);
```

The tables used in this example are shown in Figure 19-7. They contain a primary key and name field, with the `Room` table having `BuildingID` as a foreign key.

**Figure 19-7**

These tables have been kept deliberately simple. The following code shows how to iterate through the rows in the Building table and traverse the relationship to list all of the child rows from the room table:

```
foreach(DataRow theBuilding in ds.Tables["Building"].Rows)
{
    DataRow[] children = theBuilding.GetChildRows("Rooms");
    int roomCount = children.Length;
    Console.WriteLine("Building {0} contains {1} room{2}",
                      theBuilding["Name"],
                      roomCount,
                      roomCount > 1 ? "s" : "");
    // Loop through the rooms
    foreach(DataRow theRoom in children)
        Console.WriteLine("Room: {0}", theRoom["Name"]);
}
```

# Data Access with .NET

The key difference between the `DataSet` class and the old-style hierarchical `Recordset` object is in the way the relationship is presented. In a hierarchical `Recordset` object, the relationship was presented as a pseudo-column within the row. This column itself was a `Recordset` object that could be iterated through. Under ADO.NET, however, a relationship is traversed simply by calling the `GetChildRows()` method:

```
DataRow[] children = theBuilding.GetChildRows("Rooms");
```

This method has a number of forms, but the preceding simple example just uses the name of the relationship to traverse between parent and child rows. It returns an array of rows that can be updated as appropriate by using the indexers as shown in earlier examples.

What's more interesting with data relationships is that they can be traversed both ways. Not only can you go from a parent to the child rows, but you can also find a parent row (or rows) from a child record simply by using the `ParentRelations` property on the `DataTable` class. This property returns a `DataRelationCollection`, which can be indexed using the `[]` array syntax (for example, `ParentRelations["Rooms"]`), or as an alternative the `GetParentRows()` method can be called as shown here:

```
foreach(DataRow theRoom in ds.Tables["Room"].Rows)
{
    DataRow[] parents = theRoom.GetParentRows("Rooms");
    foreach(DataRow theBuilding in parents)
        Console.WriteLine("Room {0} is contained in building {1}",
                          theRoom["Name"],
                          theBuilding["Name"]);
}
```

Two methods with various overrides are available for retrieving the parent row(s): `GetParentRows()` (which returns an array of zero or more rows) and `GetParentRow()` (which retrieves a single parent row given a relationship).

## Data Constraints

Changing the data type of columns created on the client is not the only thing a `DataTable` is good for. ADO.NET permits you to create a set of constraints on a column (or columns), which are then used to enforce rules within the data.

The following table lists the constraint types that are currently supported by the runtime, embodied as classes in the `System.Data` namespace.

| Constraint | Description |
| --- | --- |
| `ForeignKeyConstraint` | Enforces a link between two `DataTables` within a `DataSet`. |
| `UniqueConstraint` | Ensures that entries in a given column are unique. |

## Chapter 19

### Setting a primary key

As is common for a table in a relational database, you can supply a primary key, which can be based on one or more columns from the `DataTable`.

The following code creates a primary key for the Products table, whose schema was constructed by hand earlier.

Note that a primary key on a table is just one form of constraint. When a primary key is added to a `DataTable`, the runtime also generates a unique constraint over the key column(s). This is because there isn't actually a constraint type of `PrimaryKey`—a primary key is simply a unique constraint over one or more columns.

```
public static void ManufacturePrimaryKey(DataTable dt)
{
    DataColumn[] pk = new DataColumn[1];
    pk[0] = dt.Columns["ProductID"];
    dt.PrimaryKey = pk;
}
```

Because a primary key can contain several columns, it is typed as an array of `DataColumns`. A table's primary key can be set to those columns simply by assigning an array of columns to the property.

To check the constraints for a table, you can iterate through the `ConstraintCollection`. For the auto-generated constraint produced by the preceding code, the name of the constraint is `Constraint1`. That's not a very useful name, so to avoid this problem it is always best to create the constraint in code first, then define which column(s) make up the primary key.

The following code names the constraint before creating the primary key:

```
DataColumn[] pk = new DataColumn[1];
pk[0] = dt.Columns["ProductID"];
dt.Constraints.Add(new UniqueConstraint("PK_Products", pk[0]));
dt.PrimaryKey = pk;
```

Unique constraints can be applied to as many columns as you want.

### Setting a foreign key

In addition to unique constraints, a `DataTable` class can also contain foreign key constraints. These are primarily used to enforce master/detail relationships, but can also be used to replicate columns between tables if you set the constraint up correctly. A master/detail relationship is one where there is commonly one parent record (say an order) and many child records (order lines), linked by the primary key of the parent record.

A foreign key constraint can only operate over tables within the same `DataSet`, so the following example uses the Categories table from the Northwind database (shown in Figure 19-8), and assigns a constraint between it and the Products table.

# Data Access with .NET

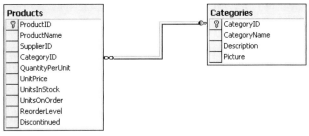

Figure 19-8

The first step is to generate a new data table for the Categories table:

```
DataTable categories = new DataTable("Categories");
categories.Columns.Add(new DataColumn("CategoryID", typeof(int)));
categories.Columns.Add(new DataColumn("CategoryName", typeof(string)));
categories.Columns.Add(new DataColumn("Description", typeof(string)));
categories.Constraints.Add(new UniqueConstraint("PK_Categories",
                         categories.Columns["CategoryID"]));
categories.PrimaryKey = new DataColumn[1]
                         {categories.Columns["CategoryID"]};
```

The last line of this code creates the primary key for the Categories table. The primary key in this instance is a single column; however, it is possible to generate a key over multiple columns using the array syntax shown.

Then the constraint can be created between the two tables:

```
DataColumn parent = ds.Tables["Categories"].Columns["CategoryID"];
DataColumn child = ds.Tables["Products"].Columns["CategoryID"];
ForeignKeyConstraint fk =
    new ForeignKeyConstraint("FK_Product_CategoryID", parent, child);
fk.UpdateRule = Rule.Cascade;
fk.DeleteRule = Rule.SetNull;
ds.Tables["Products"].Constraints.Add(fk);
```

This constraint applies to the link between `Categories.CategoryID` and `Products.CategoryID`. There are four different `ForeignKeyConstraint` — use those that permit you to name the constraint.

## *Setting Update and Delete constraints*

In addition to defining that there is some type of constraint between parent and child tables, you can define what should happen when a column in the constraint is updated.

The previous example sets the update rule and the delete rule. These rules are used when an action occurs to a column (or row) within the parent table, and the rule is used to decide what should happen to row(s) within the child table that could be affected. Four different rules can be applied through the `Rule` enumeration:

# Chapter 19

- `Cascade` — If the parent key has been updated, copy the new key value to all child records. If the parent record has been deleted, delete the child records also. This is the default option.
- `None` — No action whatsoever. This option leaves orphaned rows within the child data table.
- `SetDefault` — Each child record affected has the foreign key column(s) set to its default value, if one has been defined.
- `SetNull` — All child rows have the key column(s) set to `DBNull`. (Following the naming convention that Microsoft uses, this should really be `SetDBNull`).

> **Constraints are enforced only within a `DataSet` class if the `EnforceConstraints` property of the `DataSet` is true.**

This covers the main classes that make up the constituent parts of the `DataSet` class, and has shown how to generate manually each of these classes in code. You can also define a `DataTable`, `DataRow`, `DataColumn`, `DataRelation`, and `Constraint` using the XML schema file(s) and the XSD tool that ships with .NET. The following section describes how to set up a simple schema and generate type-safe classes to access your data.

# XML Schemas

XML is firmly entrenched in ADO.NET — indeed, the remoting format for passing data between objects is now XML. With the .NET runtime, it is possible to describe a `DataTable` class within an XML schema definition file (XSD). What's more, you can define an entire `DataSet` class, with a number of `DataTable` classes, a set of relationships between these tables, and include various other details to fully describe the data.

When you have defined an XSD file, there is a new tool in the runtime that will convert this schema to the corresponding data access class(es), such as the type-safe product `DataTable` class shown earlier. Let's start with a simple XSD file (`Products.xsd`) that describes the same information as the Products sample discussed earlier and then extend it to include some extra functionality:

```xml
<?xml version="1.0" encoding="utf-8" ?>
<xs:schema id="Products" targetNamespace="http://tempuri.org/XMLSchema1.xsd"
  xmlns:mstns="http://tempuri.org/XMLSchema1.xsd"
  xmlns:xs="http://www.w3.org/2001/XMLSchema"
  xmlns:msdata="urn:schemas-microsoft-com:xml-msdata">
  <xs:element name="Product">
    <xs:complexType>
      <xs:sequence>
        <xs:element name="ProductID" msdata:ReadOnly="true"
          msdata:AutoIncrement="true" type="xs:int" />
        <xs:element name="ProductName" type="xs:string" />
        <xs:element name="SupplierID" type="xs:int" minOccurs="0" />
        <xs:element name="CategoryID" type="xs:int" minOccurs="0" />
        <xs:element name="QuantityPerUnit" type="xs:string" minOccurs="0" />
        <xs:element name="UnitPrice" type="xs:decimal" minOccurs="0" />
```

```
            <xs:element name="UnitsInStock" type="xs:short" minOccurs="0" />
            <xs:element name="UnitsOnOrder" type="xs:short" minOccurs="0" />
            <xs:element name="ReorderLevel" type="xs:short" minOccurs="0" />
            <xs:element name="Discontinued" type="xs:boolean" />
          </xs:sequence>
        </xs:complexType>
    </xs:element>
</xs:schema>
```

These options are covered in detail in Chapter 21, "Manipulating XML"; for now, this file basically defines a schema with the `id` attribute set to `Products`. A complex type called `Product` is defined, which contains a number of elements, one for each of the fields within the `Products` table.

These items map to data classes as follows. The `Products` schema maps to a class derived from `DataSet`. The `Product` complex type maps to a class derived from `DataTable`. Each subelement maps to a class derived from `DataColumn`. The collection of all columns maps to a class derived from `DataRow`.

Thankfully, there is a tool within the .NET Framework that produces the code for these classes with the help of the input XSD file. Because its sole job in life is to perform various functions on XSD files, the tool itself is called XSD.EXE.

## Generating Code with XSD

Assuming you save the preceding file as `Product.xsd`, you would convert the file into code by issuing the following command in a command prompt:

```
xsd Product.xsd /d
```

This creates the file `Product.cs`.

Various switches can be used with XSD to alter the output generated. Some of the more commonly used are shown in the following table.

| Switch | Description |
| --- | --- |
| /dataset (/d) | Enables you to generate classes derived from `DataSet`, `DataTable`, and `DataRow`. |
| /language:<language> | Permits you to choose which language the output file will be written in. C# is the default, but you can choose VB for a Visual Basic .NET file. |
| /namespace:<namespace> | Enables you to define the namespace that the generated code should reside within. The default is no namespace. |

The following is an abridged version of the output from XSD for the Products schema. The output has been altered slightly to fit into a format appropriate for the book. To see the complete output, run XSD.EXE on the Products schema (or one of your own making) and take a look at the `.cs` file generated.

The example includes the entire source code plus the `Product.xsd` file. (Note that this output is part of the downloadable code file at www.wrox.xom):

```
//------------------------------------------------------------------------------
// <autogenerated>
//     This code was generated by a tool.
//     Runtime Version:2.0.40426.16
//
//     Changes to this file may cause incorrect behavior and will be lost if
//     the code is regenerated.
// </autogenerated>
//------------------------------------------------------------------------------

using System;

//
// This source code was auto-generated by xsd, Version=2.0.40426.16.
//


[Serializable()]
[System.ComponentModel.DesignerCategoryAttribute("code")]
[System.Diagnostics.DebuggerStepThrough()]
[System.ComponentModel.ToolboxItem(true)]
[System.Xml.Serialization.XmlSchemaProviderAttribute("GetTypedDataSetSchema")]
[System.Xml.Serialization.XmlRootAttribute("Products")]
public partial class Products : System.Data.DataSet {
{
    private ProductDataTable tableProduct;
    public Products()
    public ProductDataTable Product
    public override DataSet Clone()
    public delegate void ProductRowChangeEventHandler ( object sender,
                                                 ProductRowChangeEvent e);

    [System.Diagnostics.DebuggerStepThrough()]
    public partial class ProductDataTable : DataTable, IEnumerable

    [System.Diagnostics.DebuggerStepThrough()]
    public class ProductRow : DataRow
}
```

All private and protected members have been removed to concentrate on the public interface. The emboldened `ProductDataTable` and `ProductRow` definitions show the positions of two nested classes, which will be implemented next. You review the code for these classes after a brief explanation of the `DataSet`-derived class.

The `Products()` constructor calls a private method, `InitClass()`, which constructs an instance of the `DataTable`-derived class `ProductDataTable`, and adds the table to the `Tables` collection of the `DataSet` class. The Products data table can be accessed by the following code:

```
DataSet ds = new Products();
DataTable products = ds.Tables["Products"];
```

# Data Access with .NET

Or, more simply by using the property `Product`, available on the derived `DataSet` object:

```
DataTable products = ds.Product;
```

Because the `Product` property is strongly typed, you could naturally use `ProductDataTable` rather than the `DataTable` reference shown in the previous code.

The `ProductDataTable` class includes far more code (note this is an abridged version of the code):

```
[System.Serializable()]
[System.Diagnostics.DebuggerStepThrough()]
[System.Xml.Serialization.XmlSchemaProviderAttribute("GetTypedTableSchema")]
public partial class ProductDataTable : DataTable, System.Collections.IEnumerable
{
    private DataColumn columnProductID;
    private DataColumn columnProductName;
    private DataColumn columnSupplierID;
    private DataColumn columnCategoryID;
    private DataColumn columnQuantityPerUnit;
    private DataColumn columnUnitPrice;
    private DataColumn columnUnitsInStock;
    private DataColumn columnUnitsOnOrder;
    private DataColumn columnReorderLevel;
    private DataColumn columnDiscontinued;

    public ProductDataTable()    {
        this.TableName = "Product";
        this.BeginInit();
        this.InitClass();
        this.EndInit();     }
```

The `ProductDataTable` class, derived from `DataTable` and implementing the `IEnumerable` interface, defines a private `DataColumn` instance for each of the columns within the table. These are initialized again from the constructor by calling the private `InitClass()` member. Each column is given an internal accessor, which is used by the `DataRow` class (which is described shortly):

```
[System.ComponentModel.Browsable(false)]
public int Count
{
    get { return this.Rows.Count; }
}
internal DataColumn ProductIDColumn
{
    get { return this.columnProductID; }
}
// Other row accessors removed for clarity -- there is one for each of the columns
```

Adding rows to the table is taken care of by the two overloaded (and significantly different) `AddProductRow()` methods. The first takes an already constructed `DataRow` and returns a void. The second takes a set of values, one for each of the columns in the `DataTable`, constructs a new row, sets the values within this new row, adds the row to the `DataTable` object, and returns the row to the caller. Such widely different functions shouldn't really have the same name!

```csharp
public void AddProductRow(ProductRow row)
{
   this.Rows.Add(row);
}

public ProductRow AddProductRow ( string ProductName , int SupplierID ,
                                  int CategoryID , string QuantityPerUnit ,
                                  System.Decimal UnitPrice , short UnitsInStock ,
                                  short UnitsOnOrder , short ReorderLevel ,
                                  bool Discontinued )
{
   ProductRow rowProductRow = ((ProductRow)(this.NewRow()));
   rowProductRow.ItemArray = new object[]
   {
      null,
      ProductName,
      SupplierID,
      CategoryID,
      QuantityPerUnit,
      UnitPrice,
      UnitsInStock,
      UnitsOnOrder,
      ReorderLevel,
      Discontinued
   };
   this.Rows.Add(rowProductRow);
   return rowProductRow;
}
```

Just like the `InitClass()` member in the `DataSet`-derived class, which added the table into the `DataSet` class, the `InitClass()` member in `ProductDataTable` adds columns to the `DataTable` class. Each column's properties are set as appropriate, and the column is then appended to the columns collection:

```csharp
private void InitClass()
{
   this.columnProductID = new DataColumn ( "ProductID",
                                           typeof(int),
                                           null,
                                           System.Data.MappingType.Element);
   this.columnProductID.ExtendedProperties.Add
      ("Generator_ChangedEventName", "ProductIDChanged");
   this.columnProductID.ExtendedProperties.Add
      ("Generator_ChangingEventName", "ProductIDChanging");
   this.columnProductID.ExtendedProperties.Add
      ("Generator_ColumnPropNameInRow", "ProductID");
   this.columnProductID.ExtendedProperties.Add
      ("Generator_ColumnPropNameInTable", "ProductIDColumn");
   this.columnProductID.ExtendedProperties.Add
      ("Generator_ColumnVarNameInTable", "columnProductID");
   this.columnProductID.ExtendedProperties.Add
      ("Generator_DelegateName", "ProductIDChangeEventHandler");
   this.columnProductID.ExtendedProperties.Add
      ("Generator_EventArgName", "ProductIDChangeEventArg");
```

# Data Access with .NET

```
    this.Columns.Add(this.columnProductID);
    // Other columns removed for clarity

    this.columnProductID.AutoIncrement = true;
    this.columnProductID.AllowDBNull = false;
    this.columnProductID.ReadOnly = true;
    this.columnProductName.AllowDBNull = false;
    this.columnDiscontinued.AllowDBNull = false;
}

public ProductRow NewProductRow()
{
    return ((ProductRow)(this.NewRow()));
}
```

`NewRowFromBuilder()` is called internally from the `DataTable` class's `NewRow()` method. Here, it creates a new strongly typed row. The `DataRowBuilder` instance is created by the `DataTable` class, and its members are accessible only within the `System.Data` assembly:

```
protected override DataRow NewRowFromBuilder(DataRowBuilder builder)
{
    return new ProductRow(builder);
}
```

The last class to discuss is the `ProductRow` class, derived from `DataRow`. This class is used to provide type-safe access to all fields in the data table. It wraps the storage for a particular row, and provides members to read (and write) each of the fields in the table.

In addition, for each nullable field, there are functions to set the field to `null`, and check if the field is `null`. The following example shows the functions for the `SupplierID` column:

```
[System.Diagnostics.DebuggerStepThrough()]
public class ProductRow : DataRow
{
    private ProductDataTable tableProduct;

    internal ProductRow(DataRowBuilder rb) : base(rb)
    {
        this.tableProduct = ((ProductDataTable)(this.Table));
    }

    public int ProductID
    {
        get { return ((int)(this[this.tableProduct.ProductIDColumn])); }
        set { this[this.tableProduct.ProductIDColumn] = value; }
    }
    // Other column accessors/mutators removed for clarity

    public bool IsSupplierIDNull()
    {
        return this.IsNull(this.tableProduct.SupplierIDColumn);
    }
```

```
        public void SetSupplierIDNull()
        {
            this[this.tableProduct.SupplierIDColumn] = System.Convert.DBNull;
        }
    }
}
```

The following code utilizes the classes ouptut from the XSD tool to retrieve data from the Products table and display that data to the console:

```
using System;
using System.Data;
using System.Data.SqlClient;

public class XSD_DataSet
{
    public static void Main()
    {
        string source = "server=(local);" +
                        " integrated security=SSPI;" +
                        "database=northwind";
        string select = "SELECT * FROM Products";
        SqlConnection conn = new SqlConnection(source);
        SqlDataAdapter da = new SqlDataAdapter(select , conn);
        Products ds = new Products();
        da.Fill(ds , "Product");
        foreach(Products.ProductRow row in ds.Product )
            Console.WriteLine("'{0}' from {1}" ,
                              row.ProductID ,
                              row.ProductName);
    }
}
```

The main areas of interest are highlighted. The output of the XSD file contains a class derived from `DataSet`, `Products`, which is created and then filled by the use of the data adapter. The `foreach` statement uses the strongly typed `ProductRow` and also the `Product` property, which returns the `Product` data table.

To compile this example, issue the following commands:

**xsd product.xsd /d**

and

**csc /recurse:*.cs**

The first generates the `Products.cs` file from the `Products.XSD` schema, and then the `csc` command utilizes the `/recurse:*.cs` parameter to go through all files with the extension `.cs` and add these to the resulting assembly.

# Data Access with .NET

## Populating a DataSet

After you have defined the schema of your data set, replete with `DataTable`, `DataColumn`, and `Constraint` classes, and whatever else is necessary, you need to be able to populate the `DataSet` class with some information. You have two main ways to read data from an external source and insert it into the `DataSet` class:

- Use a data adapter.
- Read XML into the `DataSet` class.

### Populating a DataSet Class with a Data Adapter

The section on data rows briefly introduced the `SqlDataAdapter` class, as shown in the following code:

```
string select = "SELECT ContactName,CompanyName FROM Customers";
SqlConnection conn = new SqlConnection(source);
SqlDataAdapter da = new SqlDataAdapter(select , conn);
DataSet ds = new DataSet();
da.Fill(ds , "Customers");
```

The two highlighted lines show the `SqlDataAdapter` class in use; the other data adapter classes are again virtually identical in functionality to the `Sql` equivalent.

To retrieve data into a `DataSet`, it is necessary to have some form of command that is executed to select that data. The command in question could be a SQL `SELECT` statement, a call to a stored procedure, or for the OLE DB provider, a `TableDirect` command. The preceding example uses one of the constructors available on `SqlDataAdapter` that converts the passed SQL `SELECT` statement into a `SqlCommand`, and issues this when the `Fill()` method is called on the adapter.

In the stored procedures example earlier in this chapter, the `INSERT`, `UPDATE`, and `DELETE` procedures were defined but the `SELECT` procedure was not. That gap is filled in the next section, which also shows how to call a stored procedure from a `SqlDataAdapter` class to populate data in a `DataSet` class.

#### Using a stored procedure in a data adapter

The first step in this example is to define the stored procedure. The stored procedure to `SELECT` data is as follows:

```
CREATE PROCEDURE RegionSelect AS
  SET NOCOUNT OFF
  SELECT * FROM Region
GO
```

This stored procedure can be typed directly into the SQL Server Query Analyzer, or you can run the `StoredProc.sql` file that is provided for use by this example.

619

Next, the `SqlCommand` that executes this stored procedure needs to be defined. Again the code is very simple, and most of it was already presented in the earlier section on issuing commands:

```
private static SqlCommand GenerateSelectCommand(SqlConnection conn )
{
    SqlCommand  aCommand = new SqlCommand("RegionSelect" , conn);
    aCommand.CommandType = CommandType.StoredProcedure;
    aCommand.UpdatedRowSource = UpdateRowSource.None;
    return aCommand;
}
```

This method generates the `SqlCommand` that calls the `RegionSelect` procedure when executed. All that remains is to hook up this command to a `SqlDataAdapter` class, and call the `Fill()` method:

```
DataSet ds = new DataSet();
// Create a data adapter to fill the DataSet
SqlDataAdapter da = new SqlDataAdapter();
// Set the data adapter's select command
da.SelectCommand = GenerateSelectCommand (conn);
da.Fill(ds , "Region");
```

Here, the `SqlDataAdapter` class is created, and the generated `SqlCommand` is then assigned to the `SelectCommand` property of the data adapter. Subsequently `Fill()` is called, which will execute the stored procedure and insert all rows returned into the Region `DataTable` (which in this instance is generated by the runtime).

There's more to a data adapter than just selecting data by issuing a command, as discussed in the upcoming section "Persisting DataSet Changes."

## *Populating a DataSet from XML*

In addition to generating the schema for a given `DataSet` and associated tables and so on, a `DataSet` class can read and write data in native XML, such as a file on disk, a stream, or a text reader.

To load XML into a `DataSet` class, simply call one of the `ReadXML()` methods to read data from a disk file, as shown in this example:

```
DataSet ds = new DataSet();
ds.ReadXml(".\\MyData.xml");
```

The `ReadXml()` method attempts to load any inline schema information from the input XML, and if found, uses this schema in the validation of any data loaded from that file. If no inline schema is found, the `DataSet` will extend its internal structure as data is loaded. This is similar to the behavior of `Fill()` in the previous example, which retrieves the data and constructs a `DataTable` based on the data selected.

# **Persisting DataSet Changes**

After editing data within a `DataSet`, it is usually necessary to persist these changes. The most common example would be selecting data from a database, displaying it to the user, and returning those updates to the database.

# Data Access with .NET

In a less "connected" application, changes might be persisted to an XML file, transported to a middle-tier application server, and then processed to update several data sources.

A `DataSet` class can be used for either of these examples; what's more, it's really easy to do.

## Updating with Data Adapters

In addition to the `SelectCommand` that a `SqlDataAdapter` most likely includes, you can also define an `InsertCommand`, `UpdateCommand`, and `DeleteCommand`. As these names imply, these objects are instances of the command object appropriate for your provider such as `SqlCommand` and `OleDbCommand`.

With this level of flexibility, you are free to tune the application by judicious use of stored procedures for frequently used commands (say `SELECT` and `INSERT`), and use straight SQL for less commonly used commands such as `DELETE`. In general it is recommended to provide stored procedures for all database interaction, because it is faster and easier to tune.

This example uses the stored procedure code from the "Calling Stored Procedures" section for inserting, updating, and deleting `Region` records, coupled with the `RegionSelect` procedure written above, which produces an example that utilizes each of these commands to retrieve and update data in a `DataSet` class. The main body of code is shown in the following section.

### Inserting a new row

You can add a new row to a `DataTable` in two ways. The first way is to call the `NewRow()` method, which returns a blank row that you then populate and add to the `Rows` collection, as follows:

```
DataRow r = ds.Tables["Region"].NewRow();
r["RegionID"]=999;
r["RegionDescription"]="North West";
ds.Tables["Region"].Rows.Add(r);
```

The second way to add a new row would be to pass an array of data to the `Rows.Add()` method as shown in the following code:

```
DataRow r = ds.Tables["Region"].Rows.Add
            (new object [] { 999 , "North West" });
```

Each new row within the `DataTable` will have its `RowState` set to `Added`. The example dumps out the records before each change is made to the database, so after adding a row (either way) to the `DataTable`, the rows will look something like the following. Note that the right-hand column shows the row state:

```
New row pending inserting into database
  1   Eastern                                    Unchanged
  2   Western                                    Unchanged
  3   Northern                                   Unchanged
  4   Southern                                   Unchanged
999   North West                                 Added
```

To update the database from the `DataAdapter`, call one of the `Update()` methods as shown here:

```
da.Update(ds , "Region");
```

For the new row within the `DataTable`, this executes the stored procedure (in this instance `RegionInsert`). The example then dumps the state of the data so you can see that changes have been made to the database.

```
New row updated and new RegionID assigned by database
    1    Eastern                                              Unchanged
    2    Western                                              Unchanged
    3    Northern                                             Unchanged
    4    Southern                                             Unchanged
    5    North West                                           Unchanged
```

Look at the last row in the `DataTable`. The `RegionID` had been set in code to 999, but after executing the `RegionInsert` stored procedure the value has been changed to 5. This is intentional — the database will often generate primary keys for you, and the updated data in the `DataTable` is due to the fact that the `SqlCommand` definition within the source code has the `UpdatedRowSource` property set to `UpdateRowSource.OutputParameters`:

```
SqlCommand aCommand = new SqlCommand("RegionInsert" , conn);

aCommand.CommandType = CommandType.StoredProcedure;
aCommand.Parameters.Add(new SqlParameter("@RegionDescription" ,
                        SqlDbType.NChar ,
                        50 ,
                        "RegionDescription"));
aCommand.Parameters.Add(new SqlParameter("@RegionID" ,
                        SqlDbType.Int,
                        0 ,
                        ParameterDirection.Output ,
                        false ,
                        0 ,
                        0 ,
                        "RegionID" ,    // Defines the SOURCE column
                        DataRowVersion.Default ,
                        null));
aCommand.UpdatedRowSource = UpdateRowSource.OutputParameters;
```

What this means is that whenever a data adapter issues this command, the output parameters should be mapped to the source of the row, which in this instance was a row in a `DataTable`. The flag states what data should be updated — the stored procedure has an output parameter that is mapped to the `DataRow`. The column it applies to is `RegionID`, because this is defined within the command definition.

The following table shows the values for `UpdateRowSource`.

| UpdateRowSource Value | Description |
| --- | --- |
| Both | A stored procedure might return output parameters and also a complete database record. Both of these data sources are used to update the source row. |

# Data Access with .NET

| UpdateRowSource Value | Description |
|---|---|
| FirstReturnedRecord | This infers that the command returns a single record, and that the contents of that record should be merged into the original source DataRow. This is useful where a given table has a number of default (or computed) columns, because after an INSERT statement these need to be synchronized with the DataRow on the client. An example might be 'INSERT (columns) INTO (table) WITH (primarykey)', then 'SELECT (columns) FROM (table) WHERE (primarykey)'. The returned record would then be merged into the original row. |
| None | All data returned from the command is discarded. |
| OutputParameters | Any output parameters from the command are mapped onto the appropriate column(s) in the DataRow. |

## Updating an existing row

Updating an existing row within the DataTable is just a case of utilizing the DataRow class's indexer with either a column name or column number, as shown in the following code:

```
r["RegionDescription"]="North West England";
r[1] = "North East England";
```

Both of these statements are equivalent (in this example):

```
Changed RegionID 5 description
   1    Eastern                              Unchanged
   2    Western                              Unchanged
   3    Northern                             Unchanged
   4    Southern                             Unchanged
   5    North West England                   Modified
```

Prior to updating the database, the row updated has its state set to Modified as shown.

## Deleting a row

Deleting a row is a matter of calling the Delete() method:

```
r.Delete();
```

A deleted row has its row state set to Deleted, but you cannot read columns from the deleted DataRow, because they are no longer valid. When the adaptor's Update() method is called, all deleted rows will use the DeleteCommand, which in this instance executes the RegionDelete stored procedure.

# Writing XML Output

As you have seen already, the DataSet class has great support for defining its schema in XML, and just like you can read data from an XML document, you can also write data to an XML document.

623

The `DataSet.WriteXml()` method enables you to output various parts of the data stored within the `DataSet`. You can elect to output just the data, or the data and the schema. The following code shows an example of both for the Region example shown earlier:

```
ds.WriteXml(".\\WithoutSchema.xml");
ds.WriteXml(".\\WithSchema.xml" , XmlWriteMode.WriteSchema);
```

The first file, `WithoutSchema.xml`, is shown here:

```xml
<?xml version="1.0" standalone="yes"?>
<NewDataSet>
   <Region>
      <RegionID>1</RegionID>
      <RegionDescription>Eastern                                           </RegionDescription>
   </Region>
   <Region>
      <RegionID>2</RegionID>
      <RegionDescription>Western                                           </RegionDescription>
   </Region>
   <Region>
      <RegionID>3</RegionID>
      <RegionDescription>Northern                                          </RegionDescription>
   </Region>
   <Region>
      <RegionID>4</RegionID>
      <RegionDescription>Southern                                          </RegionDescription>
   </Region>
</NewDataSet>
```

The closing tag on `RegionDescription` is over to the right of the page, because the database column is defined as `NCHAR(50)`, which is a 50-character string padded with spaces.

The output produced in the `WithSchema.xml` file includes the XML schema for the `DataSet` as well as the data itself:

```xml
<?xml version="1.0" standalone="yes"?>
<NewDataSet>
   <xs:schema id="NewDataSet" xmlns=""
              xmlns:xs="http://www.w3.org/2001/XMLSchema"
              xmlns:msdata="urn:schemas-microsoft-com:xml-msdata">
      <xs:element name="NewDataSet" msdata:IsDataSet="true">
         <xs:complexType>
            <xs:choice maxOccurs="unbounded">
               <xs:element name="Region">
                  <xs:complexType>
                     <xs:sequence>
                        <xs:element name="RegionID"
                                    msdata:AutoIncrement="true"
                                    msdata:AutoIncrementSeed="1"
                                    type="xs:int" />
                        <xs:element name="RegionDescription"
                                    type="xs:string" />
                     </xs:sequence>
```

```
                </xs:complexType>
              </xs:element>
            </xs:choice>
          </xs:complexType>
        </xs:element>
    </xs:schema>
    <Region>
        <RegionID>1</RegionID>
        <RegionDescription>Eastern                                   </RegionDescription>
    </Region>
    <Region>
        <RegionID>2</RegionID>
        <RegionDescription>Western                                   </RegionDescription>
    </Region>
    <Region>
        <RegionID>3</RegionID>
        <RegionDescription>Northern                                  </RegionDescription>
    </Region>
    <Region>
        <RegionID>4</RegionID>
        <RegionDescription>Southern                                  </RegionDescription>
    </Region>
</NewDataSet>
```

Note the use in this file of the `msdata` schema, which defines extra attributes for columns within a `DataSet`, such as `AutoIncrement` and `AutoIncrementSeed` — these attributes correspond directly with the properties definable on a `DataColumn` class.

# Working with ADO.NET

This section addresses some common scenarios when developing data access applications with ADO.NET.

## Tiered Development

Producing an application that interacts with data is often done by splitting up the application into tiers. A common model is to have an application tier (the front end), a data services tier, and the database itself.

One of the difficulties with this model is deciding what data to transport between tiers, and the format that it should be transported in. With ADO.NET you'll be pleased to learn that these wrinkles have been ironed out, and support for this style of architecture is part of the design.

One of the things that's much better in ADO.NET than OLE DB is the support for copying an entire Recordset. In .NET it's easy to copy a `DataSet`:

```
DataSet source = {some dataset};
DataSet dest = source.Copy();
```

This creates an exact copy of the source `DataSet`—each `DataTable`, `DataColumn`, `DataRow`, and `Relation` will be copied, and all data will be in exactly the same state as it was in the source. If all you want to copy is the schema of the `DataSet`, you can use the following code:

```
DataSet source = {some dataset};
DataSet dest = source.Clone();
```

This again copies all tables, relations, and so on. However, each copied `DataTable` will be empty. This process really couldn't be more straightforward.

A common requirement when writing a tiered system, whether based on Win32 or the Web, is to be able to ship as little data as possible between tiers. This reduces the amount of resources consumed.

To cope with this requirement, the `DataSet` class has the `GetChanges()` method. This simple method performs a huge amount of work, and returns a `DataSet` with only the changed rows from the source data set. This is ideal for passing data between tiers, because only a minimal set of data has to be passed along.

The following example shows how to generate a "changes" `DataSet`:

```
DataSet source = {some dataset};
DataSet dest = source.GetChanges();
```

Again, this is trivial. Under the hood, things are a little more interesting. There are two overloads of the `GetChanges()` method. One overload takes a value of the `DataRowState` enumeration, and returns only rows that correspond to that state (or states). `GetChanges()` simply calls `GetChanges(Deleted | Modified | Added)`, and first checks to ensure that there are some changes by calling `HasChanges()`. If no changes have been made, `null` is returned to the caller immediately.

The next operation is to clone the current `DataSet`. Once done, the new `DataSet` is set up to ignore constraint violations (`EnforceConstraints = false`), and then each changed row for every table is copied into the new `DataSet`.

When you have a `DataSet` that just contains changes, you can then move these off to the data services tier for processing. After the data has been updated in the database, the "changes" `DataSet` can be returned to the caller (for example, there might be some output parameters from the stored procedures that have updated values in the columns). These changes can then be merged into the original `DataSet` using the `Merge()` method. Figure 19-9 depicts this sequence of operations.

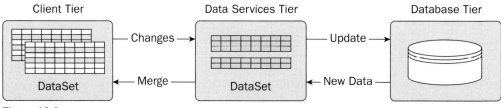

Figure 19-9

# Data Access with .NET

## Key Generation with SQL Server

The `RegionInsert` stored procedure presented earlier in this chapter is one example of generating a primary key value on insertion into the database. The method for generating the key in this particular example is fairly crude and wouldn't scale well, so for a real application you should use some other strategy for generating keys.

Your first instinct might be to define an identity column, and return the `@@IDENTITY` value from the stored procedure. The following stored procedure shows how this might be defined for the Categories table in the Northwind example database. Type this stored procedure into SQL Query Analyzer, or run the `StoredProcs.sql` file that is part of the code download:

```
CREATE PROCEDURE CategoryInsert(@CategoryName NVARCHAR(15),
                                @Description NTEXT,
                                @CategoryID INTEGER OUTPUT) AS
    SET NOCOUNT OFF
    INSERT INTO Categories (CategoryName, Description)
        VALUES(@CategoryName, @Description)
    SELECT @CategoryID = @@IDENTITY
GO
```

This inserts a new row into the Category table, and returns the generated primary key to the caller (the value of the CategoryID column). You can test the procedure by typing in the following SQL in Query Analyzer:

```
DECLARE @CatID int;
EXECUTE CategoryInsert 'Pasties' , 'Heaven Sent Food' , @CatID OUTPUT;
PRINT @CatID;
```

When executed as a batch of commands, this inserts a new row into the Categories table, and returns the identity of the new record, which is then displayed to the user.

Suppose that some months down the line, someone decides to add a simple audit trail, which will record all insertions and modifications made to the category name. In that case, you define a table similar to the one shown in Figure 19-10, which will record the old and new value of the category.

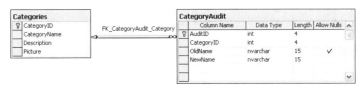

Figure 19-10

The script for this table is included in the `StoredProcs.sql` file. The AuditID column is defined as an IDENTITY column. You then construct a couple of database triggers that will record changes to the CategoryName field:

627

# Chapter 19

```
CREATE TRIGGER CategoryInsertTrigger
    ON Categories
    AFTER UPDATE
AS
    INSERT INTO CategoryAudit(CategoryID , OldName , NewName )
        SELECT old.CategoryID, old.CategoryName, new.CategoryName
        FROM Deleted AS old,
             Categories AS new
        WHERE old.CategoryID = new.CategoryID;
GO
```

If you are used to Oracle stored procedures, SQL Server doesn't exactly have the concept of OLD and NEW rows; instead for an insert trigger there is an in memory table called Inserted, and for deletes and updates the old rows are available within the Deleted table.

This trigger retrieves the CategoryID of the record(s) affected, and stores this together with the old and new value of the CategoryName column.

Now, when you call your original stored procedure to insert a new CategoryID, you receive an identity value; however, this is no longer the identity value from the row inserted into the Categories table, it is now the new value generated for the row in the CategoryAudit table. Ouch!

To view the problem first hand, open a copy of SQL Server Enterprise manager, and view the contents of the Categories table (see Figure 19-11).

| CategoryID | CategoryName | Description | Picture |
|---|---|---|---|
| 1 | Beverages | Soft drinks, coffees, teas, beers, and ales | <Binary> |
| 2 | Condiments | Sweet and savory sauces, relishes, spreads, and seasonings | <Binary> |
| 3 | Confections | Desserts, candies, and sweet breads | <Binary> |
| 4 | Dairy Products | Cheeses | <Binary> |
| 5 | Grains/Cereals | Breads, crackers, pasta, and cereal | <Binary> |
| 6 | Meat/Poultry | Prepared meats | <Binary> |
| 7 | Produce | Dried fruit and bean curd | <Binary> |
| 8 | Seafood | Seaweed and fish | <Binary> |

**Figure 19-11**

This lists all the categories in the Northwind database.

The next identity value for the Categories table should be 9, so a new row can be inserted by executing the following code, to see what ID is returned:

```
DECLARE @CatID int;
EXECUTE CategoryInsert 'Pasties' , 'Heaven Sent Food' , @CatID OUTPUT;
PRINT @CatID;
```

The output value of this on a test PC was 1. If you look at the CategoryAudit table shown in Figure 19-12, you will find that this is the identity of the newly inserted audit record, not the identity of the category record created.

| AuditID | CategoryID | OldName | NewName |
|---|---|---|---|
| 1 | 9 | <NULL> | Pasties |

**Figure 19-12**

# Data Access with .NET

The problem lies in the way that @@IDENTITY actually works. It returns the LAST identity value created by your session, so as shown in Figure 19-12 it isn't completely reliable.

Two other identity functions can be used instead of @@IDENTITY, but neither are free from possible problems. The first, SCOPE_IDENTITY(), returns the last identity value created within the current *scope*. SQL Server defines scope as a stored procedure, trigger, or function. This may work most of the time, but if for some reason someone adds another INSERT statement into the stored procedure, then you can receive this value rather than the one you expected.

The other identity function, IDENT_CURRENT(), returns the last identity value generated for a given table in any scope. For example, if two users were accessing SQL Server at exactly the same time, it might be possible to receive the other user's generated identity value.

As you might imagine, tracking down a problem of this nature isn't easy. The moral of the story is to beware when utilizing IDENTITY columns in SQL Server.

## *Naming Conventions*

The following tips and conventions are not directly .NET related. However, they are worth sharing and following, especially when naming constraints. Feel free to skip this section if you already have your own views on this subject.

### *Conventions for database tables*

- ❑ Always use singular names—Product rather than Products. This one is largely due to having to explain to customers a database schema; it's much better grammatically to say "The Product table contains products" than "The Products table contains products." Check out the Northwind database to see an example of how not to do this.

- ❑ Adopt some form of naming convention for the fields that go into a table—Ours is <Table>_Id for the primary key of a table (assuming that the primary key is a single column), Name for the field considered to be the user-friendly name of the record, and Description for any textual information about the record itself. Having a good table convention means you can look at virtually any table in the database and instinctively know what the fields are used for.

### *Conventions for database columns*

- ❑ Use singular rather than plural names.

- ❑ Any columns that link to another table should be named the same as the primary key of that table. For example, a link to the Product table would be Product_Id, and to the Sample table Sample_Id. This isn't always possible, especially if one table has multiple references to another. In that case use your own judgment.

- ❑ Date fields should have a suffix of _On, as in Modified_On and Created_On. Then it's easy to read some SQL output and infer what a column means just by its name.

- ❑ Fields that record the user should be suffixed with _By, as in Modified_By and Created_By. Again, this aids legibility.

# Chapter 19

### *Conventions for constraints*

- ❏ If possible, include in the name of the constraint the table and column name, as in `CK_<Table>_<Field>`. For example, `CK_Person_Sex` for a check constraint on the `Sex` column of the `Person` table. A foreign key example would be `FK_Product_Supplier_Id`, for the foreign key relationship between product and supplier.

- ❏ Show the type of constraint with a prefix, such as `CK` for a check constraint and `FK` for a foreign key constraint. Feel free to be more specific, as in `CK_Person_Age_GT0` for a constraint on the age column indicating that the age should be greater than zero.

- ❏ If you have to trim the length of the constraint, do it on the table name part rather than the column name. When you get a constraint violation, it's usually easy to infer which table was in error, but sometimes not so easy to check which column caused the problem. Oracle has a 30-character limit on names, which is easy to surpass.

## *Stored procedures*

Just like the obsession many have fallen into over the past few years of putting a C in front of each and every class they have declared (you know you have!), many SQL Server developers feel compelled to prefix every stored procedure with `sp_` or something similar. This is not a good idea.

SQL Server uses the `sp_` prefix for all (well, most) system stored procedures. So, on the one hand, you risk confusing your users into thinking that `sp_widget` is something that comes as standard with SQL Server. In addition, when looking for a stored procedure, SQL Server will treat procedures with the `sp_` prefix differently from those without.

If you use this prefix, and do not qualify the database/owner of the stored procedure, SQL Server will look in the current scope and then jump into the master database and look up the stored procedure there. Without the `sp_` prefix your users would get an error a little earlier. What's worse, and also possible to do, is to create a local stored procedure (one within your database) that has the same name and parameters as a system stored procedure. Avoid this at all costs — if in doubt, don't prefix.

When calling stored procedures, always prefix with the owner of the procedure, as in `dbo.selectWidgets`. This is slightly faster than not using the prefix as SQL Server has less work to do to find the stored proc. Something like this is not likely to have a huge impact on the execution speed of your application, but it is a tuning trick that is essentially available for free.

Above all, when naming entities, whether within the database or within code, *be consistent*.

# Summary

The subject of data access is a large one, especially in .NET, because there is an abundance of new material to cover. This chapter has provided an outline of the main classes in the ADO.NET namespaces, and shown how to use the classes when manipulating data from a data source.

First, the `Connection` object was explored, through the use of both the `SqlConnection` (SQL Server–specific) and `OleDbConnection` (for any OLE DB data sources). The programming model for these two classes is so similar that one can normally be substituted for the other and the code will continue to run. With the advent of .NET version 1.1, you can now use an Oracle provider and also an ODBC provider.

# Data Access with .NET

This chapter also discussed how to use connections properly, so that these scarce resources could be closed as early as possible. All of the connection classes implement the `IDisposable` interface, called when the object is placed within a `using` clause. If there's one thing you should take away from this chapter, it is the importance of closing database connections as early as possible.

Furthermore, this chapter discussed database commands by way of examples that executed with no returned data to calling stored procedures with input and output parameters. It described various execute methods, including the `ExecuteXmlReader` method available only on the SQL Server provider. This vastly simplifies the selection and manipulation of XML-based data.

The generic classes within the `System.Data` namespace were all described in detail, from the `DataSet` class through `DataTable`, `DataColumn`, `DataRow` and on to relationships and constraints. The `DataSet` class is an excellent container of data, and various methods make it ideal for cross-tier data flow. The data within a `DataSet` is represented in XML for transport, and in addition, methods are available that pass a minimal amount of data between tiers. The ability of having many tables of data within a single `DataSet` can greatly increase its usability; being able to maintain relationships automatically between master/details rows is expanded upon in the next chapter.

Having the schema stored within a `DataSet` is one thing, but .NET also includes the data adapter that, next to various `Command` objects, can be used to select data into a `DataSet` and subsequently update data in the data store. One of the beneficial aspects of a data adapter is that a distinct command can be defined for each of the four actions: `SELECT`, `INSERT`, `UPDATE`, and `DELETE`. The system can create a default set of commands based on database schema information and a `SELECT` statement, but for the best performance, a set of stored procedures can be used, with the `DataAdapter`'s commands defined appropriately to pass only the necessary information to these stored procedures.

The XSD tool (XSD.EXE) was described, using an example that shows how to work with classes based on an XML schema from within .NET. The classes produced are ready to be used within an application, and their automatic generation can save many hours of laborious typing.

Finally, this chapter discussed some best practices and naming conventions for database development.

Armed with this knowledge, you're now in a good position to move on to Chapter 20, which explores programming SQL Server 2005 with .NET.

# 20
# .NET Programming with SQL Server 2005

.NET 2.0 is a simultaneous release with the new version of SQL Server. SQL Server 2005 is a new host of the .NET runtime, and therefore it allows running .NET assemblies in the SQL Server process. It enables you to create stored procedures, functions, and data types with a .NET programming language such as C# and Visual Basic.

This chapter looks at the following:

- Hosting the .NET runtime with SQL Server
- Classes from the namespace `System.Data.SqlServer`
- Creating user-defined types
- Creating user-defined aggregates
- Stored procedures
- User-defined functions
- Triggers
- XML data types

> SQL Server 2005 also has many new features that are not directly associated with the CLR, such as many T-SQL improvements, but they are not covered in this book. To get more information about these features you can read Wrox's *SQL Server 2005 Express Edition Starter Kit* (Wiley Publishing, Inc., ISBN 0-7645-8923-7).

Chapter 20

# .NET Runtime Host

SQL Server 2005 is a new host of the .NET runtime. In versions prior to .NET 2.0, the .NET runtime can be hosted with Web applications from ASP.NET and Windows Forms controls can run in the Internet Explorer runtime host.

SQL Server 2005 allows running a .NET assembly inside the SQL Server process, where it is possible to create stored procedures, functions, data types, and triggers with CLR code.

Every database that makes use of CLR code creates its own *application domain*. This guarantees that CLR code from one database doesn't have any influence on any other database.

> *You can read more about application domains in Chapter 15, "Assemblies."*

.NET 1.0 already had a well-thought-out security environment with evidence-based security. This security environment was not enough for mission-critical databases — .NET needed some extensions. SQL Server 2005 as a .NET runtime host defines additional permission levels: *safe, external,* and *unsafe*.

> *You can read more about evidence-based security in Chapter 16, ".NET Security."*

With the safety level *safe*, only computational CLR classes can be used. The functionality of these classes is similar to a T-SQL stored procedure. The code access security defines that the only .NET permission is execution of CLR code. With the safety level *external* it is possible to access the file system or other databases with client-side ADO.NET. The safety level *unsafe* means that everything can happen, because this safety level allows you to invoke native code. Assemblies with the unsafe permission level can only be installed by a database administrator.

To enable custom .NET code to be run within SQL Server 2005, the CLR must be enabled with the `sp_configure` stored procedure:

```
sp_configure "clr enabled", 1
reconfigure
```

With .NET 2.0, the attribute class `HostProtectionAttribute` in the namespace `System.Security.Permissions` was invented for better protection of the hosting environment. With this attribute it is possible to define if a method uses shared state, exposes synchronization, or controls the hosting environment. Because such behavior is usually not needed within SQL Server code (and could influence the performance of the SQL Server), assemblies that have these settings applied are not allowed to be loaded in SQL Server with safe and external safety levels.

For using assemblies with SQL Server 2005, the assembly can be installed with the CREATE ASSEMBLY command. With this command, the name of the assembly used in SQL Server, the path to the assembly, and the safety level can be applied:

```
CREATE ASSEMBLY mylibrary FROM c:/ProCSharp/SqlServer2005/Demo.dll
   WITH PERMISSION SET = SAFE
```

With Visual Studio 2005, the permission level of the generated assembly can be defined with the Database properties of the project, as shown in Figure 20-1.

# .NET Programming with SQL Server 2005

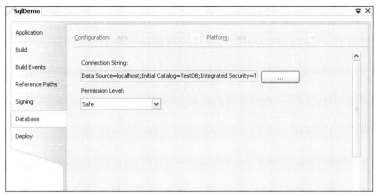

Figure 20-1

## Microsoft.SqlServer.Server

Chapter 19, "Data Access with .NET," discussed classes from the namespace `System.Data.SqlClient`. For adding functionality to the SQL Server 2005, the `Microsoft.SqlServer.Server` namespace has been defined, which includes classes to be used within SQL Server. Many of the `System.Data.SqlClient` classes can be used together with classes from the namespace `Microsoft.SqlServer.Server`, with the big difference that a connection is not newly initiated, but an already opened connection from the client is used instead.

The following table lists major classes from the `Microsoft.SqlServer.Server` namespace and their functionality.

| Class | Description |
| --- | --- |
| SqlContext | Like an HTTP context, the SQL context is associated with the request of a client. With static members of the `SqlContext` class, `SqlPipe`, `SqlTriggerContext`, and `WindowsIdentitiy` can be accessed. |
| SqlPipe | With the `SqlPipe` class results or information can be sent to the client. This class offers the methods `ExecuteAndSend()`, `Send()`, and `SendResultsRow()`. The `Send()` method has different overloads to either send a `SqlDataReader`, `SqlDataRecord`, and `string`. |
| SqlTriggerContext | The `SqlTriggerContext` class is used within triggers. |

You see these classes in action later in this chapter when writing stored procedures and user-defined functions is discussed, but first, the following section looks into creating user-defined types with C#.

635

# Chapter 20

# User-Defined Types

User-defined types (UDTs) can be used similarly to normal SQL Server data types to define the type of a column in a table. With older versions of SQL Server it was already possible to define UDTs. Of course, these UDTs could only be based on SQL types, such as the ZIP type shown in the following code. The stored procedure sp_addtype allows you to create user-defined types. Here the user-defined type ZIP is based on the CHAR data type with a length of 5. NOT NULL defines that NULL is not allowed with the ZIP data type. By using ZIP as a data type, it is no longer necessary to remember that it should be 5 char long and not null:

```
EXEC sp_addtype ZIP 'CHAR(5)', 'NOT NULL'
```

With SQL Server 2005, UDTs can be defined with CLR classes. However, this feature is not meant to create a `Person` class to have a `Person` data type. SQL Server is a relational data store, and this is still true with UDTs. You cannot create a class hierarchy of UDTs, and it is not possible to reference a part of a UDT type with a SELECT statement. If parts of a person must be accessed or sorted (for example, the `Firstname` or `Lastname`), it is still better to define columns for first name or last name or to use the XML data type.

UDTs are meant for very simple data types. Before .NET, it was also possible to create custom data types, for example, the ZIP data type. With UDTs it is not possible to create a class hierarchy, and they are not meant to get complex data types to the database. One requirement of a UDT is that it must be convertible to a string, because the string representation is used to display the value. How the data is stored within SQL Server can be defined: either an automatic mechanism can be used to store the data in a native format, or you can convert the data to a byte stream to define how the data should be stored.

## Creating UDTs

Here you look at how to create a user-defined type with Visual Studio 2005. Using the database project and the template for a User-Defined Type with Visual Studio 2005, the base functionality of a custom type is already defined:

```
using System;
using System.Data;
using System.Data.Sql;
using System.Data.SqlTypes;
using Microsoft.SqlServer.Server;

[Serializable]
[Microsoft.SqlServer.Server.SqlUserDefinedType(Format.Native)]
public struct Type1 : INullable
{
   public override string ToString()
   {
      // Replace the following code with your code
      return "";
   }

   public bool IsNull
   {
      get
      {
```

```
            // Put your code here
            return m_Null;
        }
    }

    public static Type1 Null
    {
        get
        {
            Type1 h = new Type1();
            h.m_Null = true;
            return h;
        }
    }

    public static Type1 Parse(SqlString s)
    {
        if (s.IsNull)
            return Null;
        Type1 u = new Type1();
        // Put your code here
        return u;
    }

    // This is a place-holder method
    public string Method1()
    {
        //Insert method code here
        return "Hello";
    }

    // This is a place-holder static method
    public static SqlString Method2()
    {
        // Insert method code here
        return new SqlString("Hello");
    }

    // This is a place-holder field member
    public int var1;
    // Private member
    private bool m_Null;
}
```

You change the implementation to represent the type Coordinate. Coordinate is used to represent the world coordinates longitude and latitude.

The struct Coordinate implements the interface INullable. The interface INullable is required for UDTs because database types can also be null. The attribute [SqlUserDefinedType] is used for automatic deployment with Visual Studio for UDTs. The argument Format.Native defines the serialization format to be used. Two serialization formats are possible: Format.Native and Format.UserDefined. Format.Native is the simple serialization format where the engine performs serialization and deserialization of instances. This serialization allows only blittable data types. With the Coordinate class the data types to serialize are of type int and bool, which are blittable data types. A string is not a blittable data type. Using `Format.UserDefined` requires the interface `IBinarySerialize` to be implemented. With this interface `Read()` and `Write()` methods must be implemented for serialization of the data to a `BinaryReader` and a `BinaryWriter`.

*Blittable data types have the same memory representation in both managed and unmanaged memory. Conversion is not needed with blittable data types. Blittable data types are byte, sbyte, short, ushort, int, uint, long, ulong, and combinations of these data types such as arrays and structs that only contain these data types.*

> **If wrong data types are used with the native format, you will not get an error during compile time; instead you will get an error during deployment.**

```
[Serializable]
[SqlUserDefinedType(Format.Native)]
public struct Coordinate : INullable
{
    private int longitude;
    private int latitude;
    private bool isNull;
```

The attribute `[SqlUserDefinedType]` allows setting several properties, which are shown in the following table.

| SqlUserDefined-TypeAttribute Property | Description |
| --- | --- |
| `Format` | The property `Format` defines how the data type is stored within SQL Server. Currently supported formats are `Format.Native` and `Format.UserDefined`. |
| `IsByteOrdered` | If the property `IsByteOrdered` is set to `true`, it is possible to create an index for the data type, and it can be used with `GROUP BY` and `ORDER BY` SQL statements. The disk representation will be used for binary comparisons.<br><br>The default is `false`. |
| `IsFixedLength` | If the disk representation of all instances is of the same size, `IsFixedLength` can be set to `true`. |
| `MaxByteSize` | The maximum number of bytes needed to store the data is set with `MaxByteSize`. This property is specified only with a user-defined serialization. |
| `Name` | With the `Name` property, a different name of the type can be set. By default the name of the class is used. |
| `ValidationMethodName` | With the `ValidationMethodName` property a method name can be defined to validate instances when the deserialization takes place. |

To represent the direction of the coordinate, the enumeration `Orientation` is defined:

```
public enum Orientation
{
   NorthEast,
   NorthWest,
   SouthEast,
   SouthWest
}
```

This enumeration can only be used within methods of the struct `Coordinate`, not as a member field because enumerations are not blittable.

The struct `Coordinate` specifies some constructors to initialize the `longitude`, `latitude`, and `isNull` variables. The variable `isNull` is set to `true` if no values are assigned to `longitude` and `latitude`, which is the case in the default constructor. A default constructor is needed with UDTs.

With the worldwide coordination system, longitude and latitude are defined with degrees, minutes, and seconds. Vienna, Austria has the coordinates 48° 14′ longitude and 16° 20′ latitude. The symbols °, ′, and ″ represent degrees, minutes, and seconds, respectively.

With the variables `longitude` and `latitude`, the longitude and latitude values are stored using seconds. The constructor with seven integer parameters converts degrees, minutes, and seconds to seconds, and sets the longitude and latitude to negative values if the coordinate is based in the South or West:

```
public Coordinate(int longitude, int latitude)
{
   isNull = false;
   this.longitude = longitude;
   this.latitude = latitude;
}

public Coordinate(int longitudeDegrees, int longitudeMinutes,
      int longitudeSeconds, int latitudeDegrees, int latitudeMinutes,
      int latitudeSeconds, Orientation orientation)
{
   isNull = false;
   this.longitude = longitudeSeconds + 60 * longitudeMinutes + 3600 *
         longitudeDegrees;
   this.latitude = latitudeSeconds + 60 * latitudeMinutes + 3600 *
         latitudeDegrees;
   switch (orientation)
   {
      case Orientation.SouthWest:
         longitude = -longitude;
         latitude = -latitude;
         break;
      case Orientation.SouthEast:
         longitude = -longitude;
         break;
      case Orientation.NorthWest:
         latitude = -latitude;
         break;
   }
}
```

The `INullable` interface defines the property `IsNull`, which must be implemented to support nullability. The static property `Null` is used to create an object that represents a null value. In the `get` accessor a `Coordinate` object is created, and the `isNull` field is set to `true`:

```
public bool IsNull
{
   get
   {
      return isNull;
   }
}

public static Coordinate Null
{
   get
   {
      Coordinate c = new Coordinate();
      c.isNull = true;
      return c;
   }
}
```

A UDT must be converted from and to a string. For conversion to a string, the `ToString()` method of the `Object` class must be overridden. Here the variables `longitude` and `latitude` are converted for a string representation to show the degrees, minutes, and seconds notation:

```
public override string ToString()
{
   string s;
   if (isNull)
      s = null;
   else
   {
      char northSouth;
      char eastWest;
      if (longitude > 0)
         northSouth = 'N';
      else
         northSouth = 'S';
      if (latitude > 0)
         eastWest = 'E';
      else
         eastWest = 'W';

      int longitudeDegrees = Math.Abs(longitude) / 3600;
      int remainingSeconds = Math.Abs(longitude) % 3600;
      int longitudeMinutes = remainingSeconds / 60;
      int longitudeSeconds = remainingSeconds % 60;

      int latitudeDegrees = Math.Abs(latitude) / 3600;
      remainingSeconds = Math.Abs(latitude) % 3600;
      int latitudeMinutes = remainingSeconds / 60;
      int latitudeSeconds = remainingSeconds % 60;
```

```
            s = longitudeDegrees + "°" + longitudeMinutes + "\'" +
                longitudeSeconds + "\"" + northSouth + "," +
                latitudeDegrees + "°" + latitudeMinutes + "\'" +
                latitudeSeconds + "\"" + eastWest;
    }
    return s;
}
```

The string that is entered from the user is represented in the `SqlString` parameter of the static method `Parse()`. First the `Parse()` method checks if the string represents a null value, in which case the `Null` property is invoked to return an empty `Coordinate` object. If the `SqlString` s does not represent a null value, the text of the string is converted to pass the longitude and latitude values to the `Coordinate` constructor:

```
public static Coordinate Parse(SqlString s)
{
    if (s.IsNull)
        return Null;

    try
    {
        string[] coordinates = s.Value.Split(',');
        char[] separators = { '°', '\'', '\"' };
        string[] longitudeVals = coordinates[0].Split(separators);
        string[] latitudeVals = coordinates[1].Split(separators);

        Orientation orientation;
        if (longitudeVals[3] == "N" && latitudeVals[3] == "E")
            orientation = Orientation.NorthEast;
        else if (longitudeVals[3] == "S" && latitudeVals[3] == "W")
            orientation = Orientation.SouthWest;
        else if (longitudeVals[3] == "S" && latitudeVals[3] == "E")
            orientation = Orientation.SouthEast;
        else
            orientation = Orientation.NorthWest;

        Coordinate coordinate = new Coordinate(
            int.Parse(longitudeVals[0]), int.Parse(longitudeVals[1]),
            int.Parse(longitudeVals[2]),
            int.Parse(latitudeVals[0]), int.Parse(latitudeVals[1]),
            int.Parse(latitudeVals[2]), orientation);

        return coordinate;
    }
    catch (Exception ex)
    {
        throw new ArgumentException(
            "Argument has a wrong syntax. " +
            "This syntax is required: 37°47\'0\"N,122°26\'0\"W",
            ex);
    }
}
```

## Chapter 20

## Using UDTs

After building the assembly, it can be deployed with SQL Server 2005. Configuration of the UDT in SQL Server 2005 can either be done with Visual Studio 2005 using the Build ➪ Deploy Project menu, or using these SQL commands:

```
CREATE ASSEMBLY SampleTypes FROM 'c:\ProCSharp\SQL2005\SampleTypes\SampleTypes.dll'
CREATE TYPE Coordinate EXTERNAL NAME SampleTypes.Coordinate
```

Now it is possible to create a table called `Cities` that contains the data type `Coordinate` as shown in Figure 20-2 and Figure 20-3.

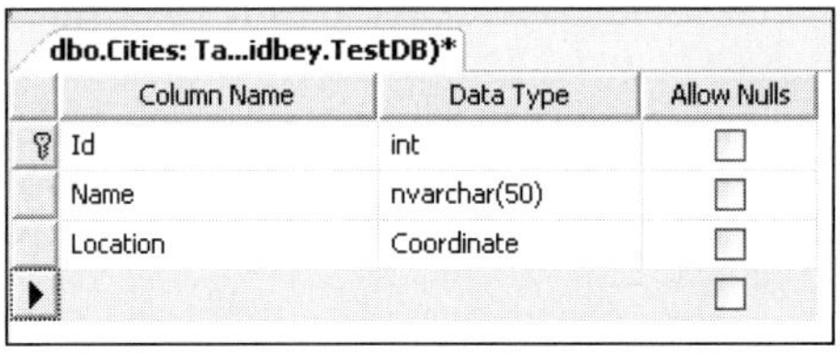

**Figure 20-2**

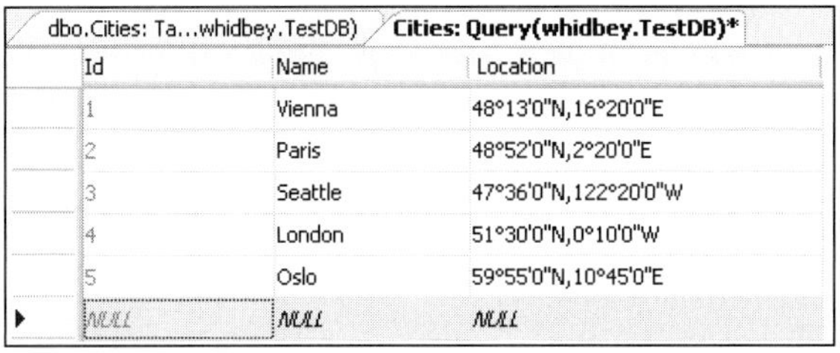

**Figure 20-3**

## Using UDTs from Client-Side Code

The assembly of the UDT must be referenced to use the UDT from client-side code. Then it can be used like any other type on the client.

In the sample code, the `SELECT` statement of the `SqlCommand` object references the columns of the `Cities` table that contains the `Location` column, which is of type `Coordinate`. Calling the method `ToString()` invokes the `ToString()` method of the `Coordinate` class to display the coordinate value in a string format:

```
using System;
using System.Data;
using System.Data.SqlClient;

class Program
{
    static void Main(string[] args)
```

```
    {
        string dsn = @"server=localhost;database=MyTest;trusted_connection=true";
        SqlConnection connection = new SqlConnection(dsn);
        SqlCommand command = connection.CreateCommand();
        command.CommandText = "SELECT Id, Name, Location FROM Cities";
        connection.Open();

        SqlDataReader reader =
            command.ExecuteReader(CommandBehavior.CloseConnection);
        while (reader.Read())
        {
           Console.WriteLine("{0}: {1}", reader[1].ToString(), reader[2].ToString());
        }
        reader.Close();

        Console.ReadLine();
    }
}
```

Of course, it is also possible to cast the returned object from the `SqlDataReader` to a `Coordinate` type for using any other implemented methods of the `Coordinate` type:

```
Coordinate c = (Coordinate)reader[2];
```

# User-Defined Aggregates

An aggregate is a function that returns a single value based on multiple rows. Examples of built-in aggregates are COUNT, AVG, and SUM. COUNT returns the record count of all selected records, AVG returns the average of values from a column of selected rows, and SUM returns the sum of all values of a column. All built-in aggregates work only with built-in value types.

A simple usage of the built-in aggregate AVG is shown here to return the average unit price of all products from the Northwind database by passing the UnitPrice column to the AVG aggregate in the SELECT statement:

```
SELECT AVG(UnitPrice) AS 'average unit price'
FROM dbo.Products
```

The SELECT statement just returns a single value that represents the average of all UnitPrice column values. Aggregates can also work with groups. In the next example the AVG aggregate is combined with the GROUP BY clause to return the average unit price of every supplier:

```
SELECT SupplierID, AVG(UnitPrice) AS 'average unit price'
FROM dbo.Products
GROUP BY SupplierID
```

For custom value types, and if you want to do a specific calculation based on a selection of rows, you can create a user-defined aggregate.

# Chapter 20

## Creating User-Defined Aggregates

To write a user-defined aggregate with CLR code, a simple class with the methods `Init()`, `Accumulate()`, `Merge()`, and `Terminate()` must be implemented. The functionality of these methods is shown in the following table.

| UDT Method | Description |
| --- | --- |
| `Init()` | The `Init()` method is invoked for every group of rows to be processed. In this method, initialization can be done for calculation of every row group. |
| `Accumulate()` | The method `Accumulate()` is invoked for every value in all groups. The parameter of this method must be of the correct type that is accumulated; this can also be the class of a user-defined type. |
| `Merge()` | The method `Merge()` is invoked when the result of one aggregation must be combined with another aggregation. |
| `Terminate()` | After the last row of every group is processed, the method `Terminate()` is invoked. Here the result of the aggregate must be returned with the correct data type. |

The code sample shows how to implement a simple user-defined aggregate to calculate the sum of all rows in every group. For deployment with Visual Studio, the attribute `[SqlUserDefinedAggregate]` is applied to the class `SampleSum`. As with the user-defined type, with user-defined aggregates the format for storing the aggregate must be defined with a value from the `Format` enumeration. Again, `Format.Native` is for using the automatic serialization with blittable data types.

The variable `sum` is used for accumulation of all values of a group. In the `Init()` method, the variable `sum` is initialized for every new group to accumulate. The method `Accumulate()` that is invoked for every value adds the value of the parameter to the `sum` variable. With the `Merge()` method, one aggregated group is added to the current group. Finally, the method `Terminate()` returns the result of a group:

```
[Serializable]
[SqlUserDefinedAggregate(Format.Native)]
public struct SampleSum
{
    private int sum;

    public void Init()
    {
        sum = 0;
    }

    public void Accumulate(SqlInt32 Value)
    {
        sum += Value.Value;
    }

    public void Merge(SampleSum Group)
    {
```

```
        sum += Group.sum;
    }

    public SqlInt32 Terminate()
    {
        return new SqlInt32(sum);
    }
}
```

## *Using User-Defined Aggregates*

The user-defined aggregate can be deployed either with Visual Studio 2005 or with the CREATE AGGREGATE statement:

```
CREATE AGGREGATE [SampleSum] (@value int) RETURNS [int] EXTERNAL NAME
[Demo].[SampleSum]
```

After the user-defined aggregate has been installed, it can be used as shown in the following SELECT statement, where the number of ordered products is returned by joining the Products and Order Details tables. For the user-defined aggregate, the Quantity column of the Order Details table is defined as an argument:

```
SELECT DISTINCT dbo.[Order Details].ProductID AS 'Id', dbo.Products.ProductName,
   dbo.SampleSum(dbo.[Order Details].Quantity) AS 'Sum'
FROM dbo.Products INNER JOIN
    dbo.[Order Details] ON dbo.Products.ProductID = dbo.[Order Details].ProductID
GROUP BY dbo.[Order Details].ProductID, dbo.Products.ProductName
ORDER BY dbo.[Order Details].ProductID
```

# Stored Procedures

SQL Server 2005 allows creating stored procedures with C#. However, this isn't a replacement for T-SQL. T-SQL still has an advantage when the procedure is mainly data-driven.

Take a look at the T-SQL stored procedure CustOrdersOrders that is part of the Northwind database. This stored procedure returns orders from the customer that is specified with the parameter CustomerID:

```
CREATE PROCEDURE CustOrdersOrders @CustomerID nchar(5)
AS
SELECT OrderID, OrderDate, RequiredDate, ShippedDate FROM Orders
   WHERE CustomerID = @CustomerID
   ORDER BY OrderID
```

## *Creating Stored Procedures*

As you can see in the following code listing, implementing the same stored procedure with C# has more complexity. The attribute [SqlProcedure] is used to mark a stored procedure for deployment. With the implementation, a SqlCommand object is created. With the constructor of the SqlConnection object the string `"Context Connection=true"` is passed to use the connection that was already opened by the client calling the stored procedure. Very similar to the code you saw in Chapter 19, the SQL SELECT statement is set and one parameter is added. The `ExecuteReader()` method returns a `SqlDataReader` object. This reader object is returned to the client by invoking the `Send()` method of the `SqlPipe`:

```
using System;
using System.Data;
using System.Data.Sql;
using System.Data.SqlTypes;
using Microsoft.SqlServer.Server;
using System.Data.SqlClient;

public partial class StoredProcedures
{
   [SqlProcedure]
   public static void GetCustomersOrders(string customerId)
   {
      SqlConnection connection = new SqlConnection("Context Connection=true");
      SqlCommand command = new SqlCommand();
      command.Connection = connection;
      command.CommandText = "SELECT OrderID, OrderDate, RequiredDate, " +
         "ShippedDate FROM Orders " +
         "WHERE CustomerId = @CustomerID ORDER BY OrderID";
      command.Parameters.Add("@CustomerID", SqlDbType.NChar, 5);
      command.Parameters["@CustomerID"].Value = customerId;

      SqlDataReader reader = command.ExecuteReader();
      SqlPipe pipe = SqlContext.Pipe;
      pipe.Send(reader);
   }
};
```

CLR stored procedures are deployed with SQL Server either using Visual Studio or with the CREATE PROCEDURE statement. With this SQL statement the parameters of the stored procedure are defined, as well as the name of the assembly, class, and method:

```
CREATE PROCEDURE GetCustomersOrders
(
   @CustomerID nchar(5)
)
AS EXTERNAL NAME Demo.StoredProcedures.GetCustomersOrders
```

## Using Stored Procedures

The CLR stored procedure can be invoked just like a normal stored procedure by using classes from the namespace `System.Data.SqlClient`. First, a `SqlConnection` object is created. The `CreateCommand()` method returns a `SqlCommand` object. With the command object, the name of the stored procedure is defined. `GetCustomerOrders` is the name of the previously created stored procedure. The method `ExecuteReader()` returns a `SqlDataReader` object to read record by record:

# .NET Programming with SQL Server 2005

```csharp
using System.Data.SqlClient;

//...

    string dsn =
        @"server=localhost;database=Northwind;trusted_connection=true";
    SqlConnection connection = new SqlConnection(dsn);
    SqlCommand command = connection.CreateCommand();
    command.CommandText = "GetCustomersOrders";
    command.CommandType = CommandType.StoredProcedure;
    SqlParameter param = new SqlParameter("@customerId", "ALFKI");
    command.Parameters.Add(param);
    connection.Open();
    SqlDataReader reader =
            command.ExecuteReader(CommandBehavior.CloseConnection);
    while (reader.Read())
    {
        Console.WriteLine("{0} {1}", reader["OrderID"], reader["OrderDate"]);
    }
    reader.Close();
    Console.ReadLine();
```

*The classes from the namespace* `System.Data.SqlClient` *are discussed in Chapter 19.*

As you've seen, mainly data-driven stored procedures are better done with T-SQL. Writing stored procedures with the CLR has the advantage if you need some specific data-processing, for example, by using the .NET cryptography classes.

## User-Defined Functions

User-defined functions are somewhat similar to stored procedures. However, the big difference is that user-defined functions can be invoked within SQL statements.

### *Creating User-Defined Functions*

A CLR user-defined function can be defined with the attribute `[SqlFunction]`. The sample function `CalcHash()` converts the string that is passed to a hashed string. The MD5 algorithm that is used for hashing the string is implemented with the class `MD5CryptoServiceProvider` from the namespace `System.Security.Cryptography`:

```csharp
using System;
using System.Data;
using System.Data.Sql;
using System.Data.SqlTypes;
using Microsoft.SqlServer.Server;
using System.Text;
using System.Security.Cryptography;
```

```
public partial class UserDefinedFunctions
{
   [SqlFunction]
   public static SqlString CalcHash(SqlString value)
   {
      byte[] source;
      byte[] hash;

      source = ASCIIEncoding.ASCII.GetBytes(value.ToString());
      hash = new MD5CryptoServiceProvider().ComputeHash(source);

      StringBuilder output = new StringBuilder(hash.Length);

      for (int i = 0; i < hash.Length - 1; i++)
      {
         output.Append(hash[i].ToString("X2"));
      }

      return new SqlString(output.ToString());
   }
}
```

## *Using User-Defined Functions*

A user-defined function can be deployed with SQL Server 2005 very similar to the other .NET extensions: either with Visual Studio 2005 or with the CREATE FUNCTION statement:

```
CREATE FUNCTION CalcHash
(
   @value nvarchar
)
RETURNS nvarchar
AS EXTERNAL NAME Demo.UserDefinedFunctions.CalcHash
```

A sample usage of the CalcHash() function is shown with this SELECT statement:

```
SELECT dbo.CalcHash(ColumnName) AS Hash
FROM Table
```

# Triggers

A trigger is a special kind of stored procedure invoked when a table is modified (for example, when a row is inserted, updated, or deleted). Triggers are associated with tables and the action that should activate them (for example, on insert/update/delete of rows).

With triggers, changes of rows can be cascaded through related tables or more complex data integrity can be enforced.

# .NET Programming with SQL Server 2005

Within a trigger you have access to the current data of a row and the original data, so it is possible to reset the change to the earlier state. Triggers are automatically associated with the same transaction as the command that fires the trigger, so you get a correct transactional behavior.

The trigger `CategoryDelete` that follows can be used with the Northwind database. This trigger is fired when a row in the Categories table is deleted. If a category is deleted, with all products from the Products table that have the same CategoryId, the column Discontinued is set to 1.

Of course, this trigger can only be used if there is no constraint between the Category and Products tables that checks for referential integrity:

```
CREATE TRIGGER CategoryDelete
ON Categories
FOR DELETE AS
UPDATE Products SET Discontinued = 1
   FROM Products INNER JOIN Deleted ON
       Products.CategoryId = Deleted.CategoryId
```

## Creating Triggers

The example shown here demonstrates implementing data integrity with triggers when new records are inserted to the `Users` table. To create a trigger with the CLR, a simple class must be defined that includes static methods that have the attribute `[SqlTrigger]` applied. The attribute `[SqlTrigger]` defines the table that is associated with the trigger and the event when the trigger should occur. In the example, the associated table is `Users` which is indicated by the `Target` property. The `Event` property defines when the trigger should occur; here the event string is set to `FOR INSERT`, which means the trigger is started when a new row is inserted in the `Users` table.

The property `SqlContext.TriggerContext` returns the trigger context in an object of type `SqlTriggerContext`. The `SqlTriggerContext` class offers three properties: `ColumnsUpdated` returns a Boolean array to flag every column that was changed, `EventData` contains the new and the original data of an update in an XML format, and `TriggerAction` returns an enumeration of type `TriggerAction` to mark the reason for the trigger. In the example, it is compared if the `TriggerAction` of the trigger context is set to `TriggerAction.Insert` before continuing.

Triggers can access temporary tables; for example, here the table `INSERTED` is accessed. With `INSERT`, `UPDATE`, and `DELETE` SQL statements, temporary tables are created. The `INSERT` statement creates an `INSERTED` table; the `DELETE` statement creates a `DELETED` table. With the `UPDATE` statement both `INSERTED` and `DELETED` tables are used. The temporary tables have the same columns as the table that is associated with the trigger. The SQL statement `SELECT Username, Email FROM INSERTED` is used to access username and e-mail, and to check the e-mail address for a correct syntax. `SqlCommand.ExecuteReader()` returns a reader object that is used to read the inserted record. Username and e-mail are read from the data record. Using the regular expression class `RegEx` the expression used with the `IsMatch()` method checks if the e-mail address conforms to valid e-mail syntax. If it doesn't conform, an exception is thrown and the record is not inserted, because a rollback occurs with the transaction:

```
using System;
using System.Data;
using System.Data.Sql;
using Microsoft.SqlServer.Server;
```

```csharp
using System.Data.SqlClient;
using System.Data.SqlTypes;
using System.Text.RegularExpressions;

public partial class Triggers
{
   [SqlTrigger(Name ="InsertUser", Target="Users", Event="FOR INSERT")]
   public static void InsertUserRegistration()
   {
      SqlTriggerContext triggerContext = SqlContext.TriggerContext;

      if (triggerContext.TriggerAction == TriggerAction.Insert)
      {
         SqlConnection connection = new SqlConnection("Context Connection=true");
         SqlCommand command = new SqlCommand();
         command.Connection = connection;
         command.CommandText = "SELECT Username, Email FROM INSERTED";
       connection.Open();
         SqlDataReader reader =
         command.ExecuteReader(CommandBehavior.Close Connection);
         reader.Read();
         string username = (string)reader["Username"];
         string email = (string)reader["Email"`];
         reader.Close();
         if (!Regex.IsMatch(email, @"^.+@[*\.[a@@hyz]{2,}$"))
         {
            throw new Exception("Invalid email");
         }
      }
   }
}
```

## Using Triggers

Using deployment of Visual Studio 2005, the trigger can be deployed to the database. You can use the CREATE TRIGGER command to create the trigger manually:

```
CREATE TRIGGER InsertUser ON Users
FOR INSERT
AS EXTERNAL NAME Demo.UserRegistrationTriggers.InsertUser
```

Trying to insert rows to the Users table with an incorrect e-mail throws an exception, and the insert is not done.

# XML Data Type

One of the major new features of SQL Server 2005 is the XML data type. With older versions of SQL Server, XML data have been stored inside a string or a blob. Now XML is a supported data type that allows combining SQL queries with XQuery expressions to search within XML data.

# .NET Programming with SQL Server 2005

With Office 2003, it is possible to store Word and Excel documents as XML. Word and Excel also support using custom XML schemas, where only the content (and not the presentation) is stored with XML. The output of Office applications can be stored directly in SQL Server 2005, where it is possible to search within this data. Of course custom XML data can also be used for storing in SQL Server.

> Don't use XML types for relational data. If you do a search for some of the elements and if the schema is clearly defined for the data, by storing these elements in a relational fashion, the data can be accessed faster. If the data is hierarchical and some elements are optional and may change over time, storing XML data has many advantages.

## Tables with XML Data

Creating tables with XML data is as simple as selecting the Xml data type with a column. The following CREATE TABLE SQL command creates the Events table with the column Id that is also the primary key and the column Event, which is of type `xml`:

```
CREATE TABLE [dbo].[Events](
    [Id] [int] IDENTITY(1,1) NOT NULL,
    [Number] [nchar] (10) NOT NULL,
    [Info] [xml] NOT NULL,
 CONSTRAINT [PK_Exams] PRIMARY KEY CLUSTERED
(
    [Id] ASC
) ON [PRIMARY]
) ON [PRIMARY]
```

For a simple test, the table is filled with these data:

```
INSERT INTO Exams values('70-315,
  <Exam Number="70-315">
    <Title>Developing and Implementing Web Applications with Microsoft Visual C#</Title>
    <Certification Name="MCAD" Status="Elective" />
    <Certification Name="MCSD" Status="Core" />
    <Course>2310</Course>
    <Course>2389</Course>
    <Course>2640</Course>
    <Topic>Creating User Services</Topic>
    <Topic>Creating and Managing Components and .NET Assemblies</Topic>
    <Topic>Consuming and Manipulating Data</Topic>
    <Topic>Testing and Debugging</Topic>
    <Topic>Deploying a Web Application</Topic>
    <Topic>Maintaining and Supporting a Web Application</Topic>
    <Topic>Configuring and Securing a Web Application</Topic>
  </Exam>')

INSERT INTO Exams values(70-316,
  <Exam Number="70-316">
    <Title>Developing and Implementing Windows-based Applications with Microsoft Visual C#</Title>
```

```
          <Certification Name="MCAD" Status="Elective" />
          <Certification Name="MCSD" Status="Core" />
          <Course>2555</Course>
          <Course>2389</Course>
          <Topic>Creating User Services</Topic>
          <Topic>Creating and Managing Components and .NET Assemblies</Topic>
          <Topic>Consuming and Manipulating Data</Topic>
          <Topic>Testing and Debugging</Topic>
          <Topic>Deploying a Windows-based Application</Topic>
          <Topic>Maintaining and Supporting a Windows-based Application</Topic>
          <Topic>Configuring and Securing a Windows-based Application</Topic>
    </Exam>')

INSERT INTO Exams values('70-320,
    <Exam Number="70-320">
        <Title>Developing XML Web Services and Server Components with Microsoft Visual C#</Title>
        <Certification Name="MCAD" Status="Core" />
        <Certification Name="MCSD" Status="Core" />
        <Course>2524</Course>
        <Course>2389</Course>
        <Course>2557</Course>
        <Course>2663</Course>
        <Topic>Creating and Managing Microsoft Windows Services, Serviced Components,
.NET Remoting Objects and XML Web Services</Topic>
        <Topic>Consuming and Manipulating Data</Topic>
        <Topic>Testing and Debugging</Topic>
        <Topic>Deploying Windows Services, Serviced Components, .NET Remoting Objects,
and XML Web Services</Topic>
    </Exam>')
```

You can read the XML data with ADO.NET using a `SqlDataReader` object. The `SqlDataReader` method `GetSqlXml()` returns a `SqlXml` object. The `SqlXml` class has a property `Value` that returns the complete XML representation and a `CreateReader()` method that returns a `XmlReader` object.

*Using the `XmlReader` class is discussed in Chapter 21, "Manipulating XML."*

```
using System;
using System.Data;
using System.Data.SqlClient;
using System.Data.SqlTypes;
using System.Xml;

    class Program
    {
        static void Main(string[] args)
        {
            string dsn =
                @"server=localhost;database=WroxDemo;trusted_connection=true";
            SqlConnection connection = new SqlConnection(dsn);
            SqlCommand command = connection.CreateCommand();
            command.CommandText = "SELECT Id, Number, Info FROM Exams";
            connection.Open();
```

```
            SqlDataReader reader = command.ExecuteReader(
                CommandBehavior.CloseConnection);
            while (reader.Read())
            {
                SqlXml xml = reader.GetSqlXml(2);
                Console.WriteLine(xml.Value);

                XmlReader xmlReader = xml.CreateReader();
                // use the reader

            }
            reader.Close();
        }
    }
}
```

## Query of Data

Until now, you haven't seen the really cool features of the XML data type. SQL SELECT statements can be combined with XML XQuery.

A SELECT statement combined with an XQuery expression to read into the XML value is shown here:

```
SELECT Id, Number, Info.query('/Exam/Course') AS Course FROM Exams
```

The XQuery expression /Exam/Course accesses the Course elements that are children of the Exam element. The result of this query returns the ids, exam numbers, and courses:

```
1  70-315  <Course>2310</Course><Course>2389</Course><Course>2640</Course>
2  70-316  <Course>2555</Course><Course>2389</Course>
3  70-320  <Course>2524</Course><Course>2389</Course><Course>2557</Course>
            <Course>2663</Course>
```

With an XQuery expression you can create more complex statements to query data within the XML content of a cell. The next example converts the XML from the exam information to XML that lists information about courses:

```
SELECT Info.query('
    for $course in /Exam/Course
    return
<Course>
    <Exam>{ data(/Exam[1]/@Number) }</Exam>
    <Number>{ data($course) }</Number>
</Course>')
AS Course
FROM Exams
WHERE Id=1
```

Here just a single row is selected with SELECT Info... FROM Exams WHERE Id = 1. With the result of this SQL query, the for and return statements of an XQuery expression are used. for $course in /Exam/Course iterates through all Course elements. $course declares a variable that is set with every iteration (similar to a C# `foreach` statement). Following the `return` statement the result of the query for every row is defined. The result for every course element is surrounded with the `<Course>` element. Embedded inside the `<Course>` element are `<Exam>` and `<Number>`. The text within the `<Exam>` element is defined with `data(/Exam[1]/@Number)`. `data()` is an XQuery function that returns the value of the node specified with the argument. The node `/Exam[1]` is used to access the first `<Exam>` element; `@Number` specifies the XML attribute `Number`. The text within the element `<Number>` is defined from the variable `$course`.

> *Contrary to C#, where the first element in a collection is accessed with an index of 0, with XPath the first element in a collection is accessed with an index of 1.*

The result of this query is shown here:

```
<Course>
   <Exam>70-315</Exam>
   <Number>2310></Number>
</Course>
<Course>
   <Exam>70-315</Exam>
   <Number>2389</Number>
</Course>
<Course
   <Exam>70-315</Exam>
   <Number>2640</Number>
</Course>
```

XQuery in SQL Server allows using several other XQuery functions for getting minimum, maximum, or summary values, working with strings, numbers, checking for positions within collections, and so on.

## XML Data Modification Language (XML DML)

XQuery as it is defined by the W3C (http://www.w3c.org) only allows querying of data. Because of this XQuery restriction, Microsoft defined an extension to XQuery that has the name XML Data Modification Language (XML DML). With XML DML it is possible to modify XML data. For this the following keywords extend XQuery: `insert`, `delete`, and `replace value of`.

This section looks at some examples to insert, delete, and modify XML contents within a cell.

You can use the `insert` keyword to insert some XML content within an XML column without replacing the complete XML cell. Here `<Course>2555</Course>` is inserted as the last child-element of the first `Exam` element:

```
UPDATE Exams
SET Info.modify('
    insert <Course>2555</Course> as last into Exam[1]')
WHERE id=3
```

XML content can be deleted with the `delete` keyword. Within the first `Exam` element, the fifth `Course` element is deleted:

```
UPDATE Exams
SET Info.modify('
    delete /Exam[1]/Course[5])
FROM Exams WHERE id=3
```

It is also possible to change XML content. Here, the keyword `replace value of` is used. The expression `/Exam/Course[text() = 2310]` accesses only the children-elements Course where the text content contains the string 2310. From these elements, only the text content is accessed for replacement. `with 2644` specifies that the new course number is 2644:

```
UPDATE Exams
SET Info.modify('
    replace value of /Exam/Course[text() = 2310]/text()[1] with 2644')
FROM Events
```

## XML Indexes

Indexes can also be set to XML types. With XML indexes, these index types must be distinguished between a primary and a secondary XML index. A primary XML index is created for the complete persisted representation of the XML value.

The following SQL command `CREATE PRIMARY XML INDEX` creates the index `idx_events` on the Event column:

```
CREATE PRIMARY XML INDEX idx_exams on Exams (Info)
```

Primary indexes don't help if the query contains an XPath expression to directly access XML elements of the XML type. For XPath and XQuery expressions, XML secondary indexes can be used. If an XML secondary index is created, the primary index must already exist. With secondary indexes, these index types must be distinguished:

- PATH index
- VALUE index
- PROPERTY index

A PATH index is used if `exists()` or `query()` functions are used and XML elements are accessed with an XPath expression. Using the XPath expression `/Event/Location` it might be useful to do a PATH index:

```
CREATE XML INDEX idx_examNumbers on Exams (Info)
    USING XML INDEX idx_exams FOR PATH
```

The PROPERTY index is used if properties are fetched from elements with the `value()` function. The FOR PROPERTY statement with the index creation defines a PROPERTY index:

```
CREATE XML INDEX idx_examsNumbers on Exams (Info)
    USING XML INDEX idx_exams FOR PROPERTY
```

If elements are searched through the tree with an XPath descendant-or-self axis expression, the best performance might be achieved with a VALUE index. The XPath expression //Certification searches all Certification elements with the descendant-or-self axis. The expression [@Name="MCAD"] returns only the elements where the attribute Name has the value MCAD:

```
SELECT Info FROM Exams
   WHERE Info.exists('//Certification[@Name="MCAD"]') = 1
```

The VALUE index is created with the FOR VALUE statement:

```
CREATE XML INDEX idx_examNumbers on Exams (Info)
   USING XML INDEX idx_exams FOR VALUE
```

## Strongly Typed XML

The XML data type in SQL Server can also be strongly typed with XML schemas. With a strongly typed XML column it is verified if the data conforms to the schema when XML data is inserted.

A XML schema can be created with the CREATE XML SCHEMA COLLECTION statement. The statement shown here creates the XML schema CourseSchema that defines the element Course with the child elements Number and Title:

```
CREATE XML SCHEMA COLLECTION CourseSchema AS
'<?xml version="1.0" encoding="UTF-8"?>
<xs:schema id="Courses" targetNamespace="http://thinktecture.com/Courses.xsd"
   elementFormDefault="qualified" xmlns="http://thinktecture.com/Courses.xsd"
   xmlns:mstns="http://thinktecture.com/Courses.xsd"
   xmlns:xs="http://www.w3.org/2001/XMLSchema">
     <xs:complexType name="CourseElt">
       <xs:sequence>
         <xs:element name="Number" type="xs:string" maxOccurs="1" minOccurs="1" />
         <xs:element name="Title" type="xs:string" maxOccurs="1" minOccurs="1" />
         <xs:element name="Any" type="xs:anyType"
             maxOccurs="unbounded" minOccurs="0" />
       </xs:sequence>
     </xs:complexType>
     <xs:element name="Course" type="CourseElt">
     </xs:element>
</xs:schema>'
```

With the Visual Studio 2005 Database project type, there's no support to add a schema to the database. This feature is not available from the GUI by Visual Studio 2005 but must be done manually. For creating an XML schema with Visual Studio 2005, you can use an empty Visual Studio project type. You can copy the XML syntax of the schema and copy it to the CREATE XML SCHEMA statement.

Besides using Visual Studio you can copy the XML syntax to the SQL Server Management Studio to create and view the XML schemas (see Figure 20-4). The object explorer lists the XML schemas below the Types entry.

## .NET Programming with SQL Server 2005

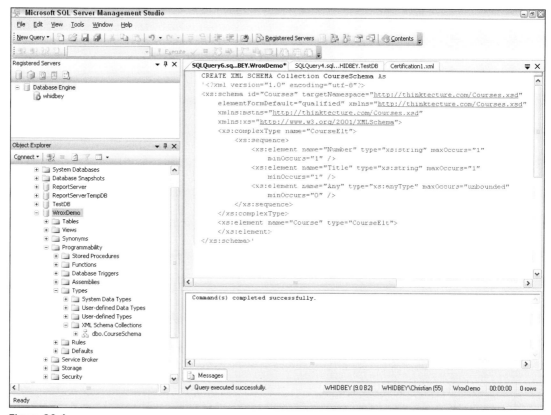

Figure 20-4

The XML schema can be assigned to a column by setting it with the xml data type:

```
CREATE TABLE Courses
(
[Id] [int] IDENTITY(1,1) NOT NULL,
[Course] [xml]([dbo].[CourseSchema]) NOT NULL
)
```

By creating the table with Visual Studio 2005 or with the SQL Server Management Studio, the XML schema can be assigned to a column by setting the property XML schema namespace.

# Summary

This chapter discussed the new features of SQL Server 2005 as they are related with CLR functionality. The CLR is hosted by SQL Server, so it is possible to create user-defined types, aggregates, stored procedures, functions, and triggers with C#.

# Chapter 20

User-defined types have some strict requirements to the .NET class for conversion to and from a string. How the data is stored internally in SQL Server depends on the format that is defined with the type. User-defined aggregates make it possible to do a custom accumulation using .NET classes. With stored procedures and functions it is possible to make use of CLR classes for server-side code.

Using CLR with SQL Server doesn't mean that T-SQL is obsolete. You've seen that T-SQL has advantages because of less code if just data-intensive queries are done. CLR classes can add advantages to data-processing if .NET features such as cryptography come into play.

You've also seen a glance into the XML data type of SQL Server to combine XQuery expressions with T-SQL statements.

# 21
# Manipulating XML

XML plays a significant role in the .NET Framework. Not only does the .NET Framework allow you to use XML in your application, but the .NET Framework itself uses XML for configuration files and source code documentation, as do SOAP, Web services, and ADO.NET, just to name a few.

To accommodate this extensive use of XML, the .NET Framework includes the `System.Xml` namespace. This namespace is loaded with classes that can be used for the processing of XML, and many of these classes are discussed in this chapter.

This chapter discusses how to use the `XmlDocument` class, which is the implementation of the document object model (DOM), as well as what .NET offers as a replacement for SAX (the `XmlReader` and `XmlWriter` classes). It also discusses the class implementations of XPath and XSLT and demonstrates how XML and ADO.NET work together, as well as how easy it is to transform one to the other. You also learn how you can serialize your objects to XML and create an object from (or deserialize) an XML document using classes in the `System.Xml.Serialization` namespace. More to the point, you learn how you can incorporate XML into your C# applications.

You should note that the XML namespace allows you to get similar results in a number of different ways. It is impossible to include all these variations in one chapter, so while exploring one possible way of doing things we'll try our best to mention alternative routes that will yield the same or similar results.

Because there's not space here to teach you XML from scratch, we are assuming that you are already somewhat familiar with XML technology. For example, you should be familiar with elements, attributes, and nodes, and you should also know what is meant by a well-formed document. You should also be familiar with SAX and DOM. If you want to find out more about XML, Wrox's *Beginning XML* (Wiley Publishing, Inc., ISBN 0-7645-7077-3) is a great place to start.

This chapter covers the following:

- ❑ XML Standards
- ❑ XmlReader and XmlWriter

- XmlDocument
- XPathDocument
- XmlNavigator

The discussion begins with a brief overview of the current status of XML standards.

# XML Standards Support in .NET

The World Wide Web Consortium (W3C) has developed a set of standards that give XML its power and potential. Without these standards, XML would not have the impact on the development world that it does. The W3C Web site (www.w3.org) is a valuable source of all things XML.

As of August 2003, the .NET Framework supports the following W3C standards:

- XML 1.0 (www.w3.org/TR/1998/REC-xml-19980210), including DTD support
- XML Namespaces (www.w3.org/TR/REC-xml-names), both stream-level and DOM
- XML Schemas (www.w3.org/2001/XMLSchema)
- XPath expressions (www.w3.org/TR/xpath)
- XSLT transformations (www.w3.org/TR/xslt)
- DOM Level 1 Core (www.w3.org/TR/REC-DOM-Level-1/)
- DOM Level 2 Core (www.w3.org/TR/DOM-Level-2-Core/)
- SOAP 1.1 (www.w3.org/TR/SOAP)

The level of standards support will change as the framework matures and the W3C updates the recommended standards. Because of this, you need to make sure you stay up-to-date with the standards and the level of support provided by Microsoft.

# Introducing the System.Xml Namespace

Support for processing XML is provided by the classes in the `System.Xml` namespace in .NET. This section looks (in no particular order) at some of the more important classes that the `System.Xml` namespace provides. The following table lists the main XML reader and writer classes.

| Class Name | Description |
| --- | --- |
| XmlReader | An abstract reader class that provides fast, non-cached XML data. XmlReader is forward-only, like the SAX parser. |
| XmlWriter | An abstract writer class that provides fast, non-cached XML data in stream or file format. |

# Manipulating XML

| Class Name | Description |
| --- | --- |
| `XmlTextReader` | Extends `XmlReader`. Provides fast forward-only stream access to XML data. |
| `XmlTextWriter` | Extends `XmlWriter`. Fast forward-only generation of XML streams. |

The following table lists some other useful classes for handling XML.

| Class Name | Description |
| --- | --- |
| `XmlNode` | An abstract class that represents a single node in an XML document. Base class for several classes in the XML namespace. |
| `XmlDocument` | Extends `XmlNode`. This is the W3C DOM implementation. It provides a tree representation in memory of an XML document, enabling navigation and editing. |
| `XmlDataDocument` | Extends `XmlDocument`. This is a document that can be loaded from XML data or from relational data in an ADO.NET `DataSet`. Allows the mixing of XML and relational data in the same view. |
| `XmlResolver` | An abstract class that resolves external XML-based resources such as DTD and schema references. Also used to process `<xsl:include>` and `<xsl:import>` elements. |
| `XmlUrlResolver` | Extends `XmlResolver`. Resolves external resources named by a uniform resource identifier (URI). |

Many of the classes in the `System.Xml` namespace provide a means to manage XML documents and streams, whereas others (such as the `XmlDataDocument` class) provide a bridge between XML data stores and the relational data stored in `DataSets`.

> It is worth noting that the XML namespace is available to any language that is part of the .NET family. This means that all of the examples in this chapter could also be written in Visual Basic .NET, managed C++, and so on.

## Using MSXML in .NET

What if you have a ton of code developed using the latest Microsoft parser (currently MSXML 4.0)? Do you have to toss it away and start over if you want to use it with .NET? What if you are comfortable using the MSXML 4.0 DOM? Do you have to switch to .NET right away?

The answer is no. XML 4.0, 3.0, or 2.0 can be used directly in your applications. When you add a reference to msxml4.DLL to your solution, you can start writing some code.

The following examples use `books.xml` as the source of data. You can download this file from the Wrox Web site (www.wrox.com), but it is also included in several examples in the .NET SDK. The `books.xml` file is a book catalog for an imaginary bookstore. It includes book information such as genre, author name, price, and ISBN number. As with the other chapters, you can download all code examples in this chapter from the Wrox Web site.

This is what the `books.xml` file looks like:

```xml
<?xml version='1.0'?>
<!-- This file represents a fragment of a book store inventory database -->
<bookstore>
    <book genre="autobiography" publicationdate="1981" ISBN="1-861003-11-0">
        <title>The Autobiography of Benjamin Franklin</title>
        <author>
            <first-name>Benjamin</first-name>
            <last-name>Franklin</last-name>
        </author>
        <price>8.99</price>
    </book>
    <book genre="novel" publicationdate="1967" ISBN="0-201-63361-2">
        <title>The Confidence Man</title>
        <author>
            <first-name>Herman</first-name>
            <last-name>Melville</last-name>
        </author>
        <price>11.99</price>
    </book>
    <book genre="philosophy" publicationdate="1991" ISBN="1-861001-57-6">
        <title>The Gorgias</title>
        <author>
            <name>Plato</name>
        </author>
        <price>9.99</price>
    </book>
</bookstore>
```

Let's look at some code that uses MSXML 4.0 to load a list box with the ISBNs from `books.xml`. You'll find the full code in the MSXML_Sample folder of the download. You can copy this code into the Visual Studio IDE or create a new Windows Form from scratch. This form contains a list box and a button that use the default names of `listBox1` and `button1`, with the Text property of `button1` set to Load XML.

One thing that should be pointed out is that because MSXML 4 is a COM-based component, you will need to create the interop assembly. The easiest way is to select Add Reference from the Project menu in the Visual Studio IDE. Go to the COM tab and select Microsoft XML, v4.0 (or v3.0, v2.6). You will see MSXML2 as the added namespace in Solution Explorer. Why is it MSXML2? When you import a COM component the namespace that is given to the new assembly is the typelib name for the COM component. In this case it is MSXML2. If you use `TLBIMP` you can change the namespace to something else if you want to.

Next, you take a closer look at the most important lines from the MSXML_sample example code.

Because you now have the reference, you add the line:

```
using MSXML2;
```

# Manipulating XML

You also need a class-level variable:

```
private DOMDocument40 doc;
```

Now you are ready to use MSXML in your application.

You want to take the ISBN from the list box and, using a simple XPath search, find the book node that it matches and display the node text (the book title and book price) in a message box. XML Path Language (XPath) is an XML notation that can be used for querying and filtering text in an XML document. You look more closely at how to use XPath in .NET later in the chapter.

Here is the event handler code for selecting an entry in the list box:

```
protected void listBox1_SelectedIndexChanged (
                        object sender, System.EventArgs e)
{
    string srch=listBox1.SelectedItem.ToString();
    IXMLDOMNode nd=doc.selectSingleNode(
                        "bookstore/book[@ISBN='" + srch + "']");
    MessageBox.Show(nd.text);
}
```

Next is the event handler for clicking the button. First, you load the `books.xml` file—note that if you're running the executable from somewhere that isn't the `bin/debug` or `bin/release` folder, you'll need to adjust the path appropriately:

```
protected void button1_Click (object sender, System.EventArgs e)
{
    doc=new DOMDocument40 ();
    doc.load("..\\..\\..\\books.xml");
```

The next lines declare that `nodes` is a `NodeList` of book nodes. In this case there are three `book` nodes:

```
    IXMLDOMNodeList nodes;
    nodes = doc.selectNodes("bookstore/book");
    IXMLDOMNode node=nodes.nextNode();
```

Then you loop through the nodes and add the text value of the `ISBN` attribute to `listBox1`:

```
    while(node!=null)
    {
        listBox1.Items.Add(node.attributes.getNamedItem("ISBN").text);
            node=nodes.nextNode ();
    }
}
```

## Using System.Xml Classes

If you have done any work with MSXML 3.0 or 4.0, the preceding code will look pretty familiar. So why would you want to do this if the .NET Framework is supposed to have all of these wonderful XML classes to use?

Although the `System.Xml` namespace is powerful and relatively easy to use, it is different from the MSXML 3.0 model. If you are comfortable using MSXML 3.0, then use it until you become familiar with the `System.Xml` namespace.

However, `System.Xml` classes have several advantages over MSXML classes. First, `System.Xml` is managed code, so by using it you will gain all of the code security and type safety of using managed code. Also, using COM interop incurs some overhead. Most importantly, however, the `System.Xml` namespace is easy to use and offers a great deal of flexibility. By the end of this chapter, this will have become very evident to you.

Note that the `books.xml` file is used for several examples in this chapter, and the code sample you just looked at is the basis for many examples too.

# Reading and Writing Streamed XML

The `XmlReader` and `XmlWriter` classes will feel familiar if you have ever used SAX. `XmlReader`-based classes provide a very fast, forward-only, read-only cursor that streams the XML data for processing. Because it is a streaming model, the memory requirements are not very demanding. However, you don't have the navigation flexibility and the read or write capabilities that would be available from a DOM-based model. `XmlWriter`-based classes produce an XML document that conforms to the W3C's XML 1.0 Namespace Recommendations.

`XmlReader` and `XmlWriter` are both abstract classes. The following classes are derived from XmlReader:

- XmlNodeReader
- XmlTextReader
- XmlValidatingReader

The following classes are derived from XmlWriter:

- XmlTextWriter
- XmlQueryOutput

`XmlTextReader` and `XmlTextWriter` work with either a stream-based object from the `System.IO` namespace or `TextReader`/`TextWriter` objects. `XmlNodeReader` uses an `XmlNode` as its source instead of a stream. The `XmlValidatingReader` adds DTD and schema validation and therefore offers data validation. You look at these a bit more closely later in this chapter.

## *Using the XmlReader Class*

As mentioned previously, `XmlReader` is a lot like SAX. One of the biggest differences, however, is that whereas SAX is a *push* type of model (that is, it pushes data out to the application, and the developer has to be ready to accept it), the `XmlReader` has a *pull* model, where data is pulled into an application requesting it. This provides an easier and more intuitive programming model. Another advantage to this is that a pull model can be selective about the data that is sent to the application: if you don't want all of the data, you don't need to process it. In a push model, all of the XML data has to be processed by the application, whether it is needed or not.

# Manipulating XML

The following is a very simple example of reading XML data, and later you take a closer look at the `XmlReader` class. You'll find the code in the XmlReaderSample folder. Here is the code for reading in the `books.xml` document. As each node is read, the `NodeType` property is checked. If the node is a text node, the value is appended to the text box:

```
using System.Xml;

private void button3_Click(object sender, EventArgs e)
{
  richTextBox1.Clear();
  XmlReader rdr = XmlReader.Create("books.xml");
  while (rdr.Read())
  {
    if (rdr.NodeType == XmlNodeType.Text)
      richTextBox1.AppendText(rdr.Value + "\r\n");
  }
}
```

Earlier it was mentioned that `XmlReader` is an abstract class. So in order to use the `XmlReader` class directly, a `Create` static method has been added. The create method returns an `XmlReader` object. The overload list for the `Create` method contains nine entries. In the preceding example, a string that represents the file name of the `XmlDocument` is passed in as a parameter. Stream-based objects and `TextReader`-based objects can also be passed in.

Another object that can be used is an `XmlReaderSettings` object. `XmlReaderSettings` specifies the features of the reader. For example, a schema can be used to validate the stream. Set the `Schemas` property to a valid `XmlSchemaSet` object, which is a cache of XSD schemas. Then the `XsdValidate` property on the `XmlReaderSettings` object can be set to `true`.

Several `Ignore` properties exist that can be used to control the way the reader processes certain nodes and values. These properties include `IgnoreComments`, `IgnoreIdentityConstraints`, `IgnoreInlineSchema`, `IgnoreProcessingInstructions`, `IgnoreSchemaLocation`, and `IgnoreWhitespace`. These properties can be used to strip certain items from the document.

## Read methods

Several ways exist to move through the document. As shown in the previous example, `Read()` takes you to the next node. You can then verify whether the node has a value (`HasValue()`) or, as you see shortly, whether the node has any attributes (`HasAttributes()`). You can also use the `ReadStartElement()` method, which verifies whether the current node is the start element, and then positions you on to the next node. If you are not on the start element, an `XmlException` is raised. Calling this method is the same as calling the `IsStartElement()` method followed by a `Read()` method.

`ReadElementString()` is similar to `ReadString()`, except that you can optionally pass in the name of an element. If the next content node is not a start tag, or if the `Name` parameter does not match the current node `Name`, an exception is raised.

Here is an example of how `ReadElementString()` can be used. Notice that this example uses `FileStreams`, so you will need to make sure that you include the `System.IO` namespace via a `using` statement:

```csharp
private void button6_Click(object sender, EventArgs e)
{
    FileStream fs = new FileStream("books.xml", FileMode.Open);
    XmlReader tr = XmlReader.Create(fs);
    while (!tr.EOF)
    {
        //if we hit an element type, try and load it in the listbox
        if (tr.MoveToContent() == XmlNodeType.Element && tr.Name == "title")
        {
            richTextBox1.AppendText(tr.ReadElementString() + "\r\n");
        }
        else
        {
            //otherwise move on
            tr.Read();
        }
    }
}
```

In the `while` loop, you use `MoveToContent()` to find each node of type `XmlNodeType.Element` with the name `title`. You use the `EOF` property of the `XmlTextReader` as the loop condition. If the node is not of type `Element` or not named `title`, the `else` clause will issue a `Read()` method to move to the next node. When you find a node that matches the criteria, you add the result of a `ReadElementString()` to the list box. This should leave you with just the book titles in the list box. Note that you don't have to issue a `Read()` call after a successful `ReadElementString()`. This is because `ReadElementString()` consumes the entire `Element` and positions you on the next node.

If you remove `&& tr.Name=="title"` from the `if` clause, you will have to catch the `XmlException` when it is thrown. If you look at the data file, you will see that the first element that `MoveToContent()` will find is the `<bookstore>` element. Because it is an element, it will pass the check in the `if` statement. However, Because it does not contain a simple text type, it will cause `ReadElementString()` to raise an `XmlException`. One way to work around this is to put the `ReadElementString()` call in a function of its own. Then, if the call to `ReadElementString()` fails inside this function, you can deal with the error and return to the calling function.

Go ahead and do this; call this new method `LoadTextBox()` and pass in the `XmlTextReader` as a parameter. This is what the `LoadTextBox()` method looks like with these changes:

```csharp
private void LoadTextBox(XmlReader reader)
{
    try
    {
        richTextBox1.AppendText (reader.ReadElementString() + "\r\n");
    }
    // if an XmlException is raised, ignore it.
    catch(XmlException er){}
}
```

This section from the previous example

# Manipulating XML

```
if (tr.MoveToContent() == XmlNodeType.Element && tr.Name == "title")
{
  richTextBox1.AppendText(tr.ReadElementString() + "\r\n");
}
else
{
  //otherwise move on
  tr.Read();
}
```

will have to change to the following:

```
if (tr.MoveToContent() == XmlNodeType.Element)
{
  LoadTextBox(tr);
}
else
{
  //otherwise move on
  tr.Read();
}
```

After running this example, the results should be the same as before. What you are seeing is that there is more than one way to accomplish the same goal. This is where the flexibility of the classes in the System.Xml namespace starts to become apparent.

The XmlReader can also read strongly typed data. There are several ReadValueAs methods, such as ReadValueAsDouble, ReadValueAsBoolean, and so on. The following example shows how to read in the values as a decimal and do some math on the value. In this case, the value from the price element is increased by 25%:

```
private void button5_Click(object sender, EventArgs e)
{
  richTextBox1.Clear();
  XmlReader rdr = XmlReader.Create("books.xml");
  while (rdr.Read())
  {
    if (rdr.NodeType == XmlNodeType.Element)
    {
      if (rdr.Name == "price")
      {
        decimal price = rdr.ReadValueAsDecimal();
        richTextBox1.AppendText("Current Price = " + price + "\r\n");
        price += price * (decimal).25;
        richTextBox1.AppendText("New Price = " + price + "\r\n\r\n");
      }
      else if(rdr.Name== "title")
        richTextBox1.AppendText(rdr.ReadValueAsString() + "\r\n");
    }
  }
}
```

If the value cannot be converted to a decimal value, a FormatException is raised. This is a much more efficient method than reading the value as a string and casting it to the proper data type.

## Chapter 21

### *Retrieving attribute data*

As you play with the sample code, you might notice that when the nodes are read in, you don't see any attributes. This is because attributes are not considered part of a document's structure. When you are on an element node, you can check for the existence of attributes and optionally retrieve the attribute values.

For example, the `HasAttributes` property returns `true` if there are any attributes; otherwise, it returns `false`. The `AttributeCount` property tells you how many attributes there are, and the `GetAttribute()` method gets an attribute by name or by index. If you want to iterate through the attributes one at a time, you can use `MoveToFirstAttribute()` and `MoveToNextAttribute()` methods.

Here is an example of iterating through the attributes of the `books.xml` document:

```
private void button7_Click(object sender, EventArgs e)
{
  richTextBox1.Clear();
  XmlReader tr = XmlReader.Create("books.xml");
  //Read in node at a time
  while (tr.Read())
  {
    //check to see if it's a NodeType element
    if (tr.NodeType == XmlNodeType.Element)
    {
      //if it's an element, then let's look at the attributes.
      for (int i = 0; i < tr.AttributeCount; i++)
      {
        richTextBox1.AppendText(tr.GetAttribute(i) + "\r\n");
      }
    }
  }
}
```

This time you are looking for element nodes. When you find one, you loop through all of the attributes and, using the `GetAttribute()` method, you load the value of the attribute into the list box. In this example, those attributes would be `genre`, `publicationdate`, and `ISBN`.

### *Validating with XmlReader*

Sometimes it's important to not only know that the document is well-formed, but also that the document is valid. An `XmlReader` can validate the XML to an XSD schema by using the `XmlReaderSettings` class. The XSD schema is added to the `XmlSchemaSet` that is exposed through the `Schemas` property. The `XsdValidate` property must also be set to `true`; the default for this property is `false`.

The following example demonstrates the use of the `XmlReaderSettings` class. The following is the XSD schema that will be used to validate the `books.xml` document:

```
<?xml version="1.0" encoding="utf-8"?>
<xs:schema attributeFormDefault="unqualified"
           elementFormDefault="qualified" xmlns:xs="http://www.w3.org/2001/XMLSchema">
  <xs:element name="bookstore">
    <xs:complexType>
```

## Manipulating XML

```xml
      <xs:sequence>
        <xs:element maxOccurs="unbounded" name="book">
          <xs:complexType>
            <xs:sequence>
              <xs:element name="title" type="xs:string" />
              <xs:element name="author">
                <xs:complexType>
                  <xs:sequence>
                    <xs:element minOccurs="0" name="name" type="xs:string" />
                    <xs:element minOccurs="0" name="first-name" type="xs:string" />
                    <xs:element minOccurs="0" name="last-name" type="xs:string" />
                  </xs:sequence>
                </xs:complexType>
              </xs:element>
              <xs:element name="price" type="xs:decimal" />
            </xs:sequence>
            <xs:attribute name="genre" type="xs:string" use="required" />
            <!-- <xs:attribute name="publicationdate"
                                type="xs:unsignedShort" use="required" /> -->
            <xs:attribute name="ISBN" type="xs:string" use="required" />
          </xs:complexType>
        </xs:element>
      </xs:sequence>
    </xs:complexType>
  </xs:element>
</xs:schema>
```

This schema was generated from the `books.xml` in Visual Studio. Notice that the `publicationdate` attribute has been commented out. This will cause the validation to fail at that point.

The following is the code that uses the schema to validate the `books.xml` document:

```csharp
private void button8_Click(object sender, EventArgs e)
{
  richTextBox1.Clear();

  XmlReaderSettings settings = new XmlReaderSettings();
  settings.Schemas.Add(null, "books.xsd");
  settings.XsdValidate = true;
  settings.ValidationEventHandler +=
     new System.Xml.Schema.ValidationEventHandler(settings_ValidationEventHandler);
  XmlReader rdr = XmlReader.Create("books.xml", settings);
  while (rdr.Read())
  {
    if (rdr.NodeType == XmlNodeType.Text)
      richTextBox1.AppendText(rdr.Value + "\r\n");
  }
}

void settings_ValidationEventHandler(object sender,
                                     System.Xml.Schema.ValidationEventArgs e)
{
  MessageBox.Show(e.Message);
}
```

After the `XmlReaderSettings` object setting is created, the schema `books.xsd` is added to the `XmlSchemaSet` object. The `Add` method for `XmlSchemaSet` has four overloads. One takes an `XmlSchema` object. The `XmlSchema` object can be used to create a schema on the fly without having to create the schema file on disk. Another overload takes another `XmlSchemaSet` object as a parameter. Another takes two string values: The first is the target namespace and the other is the URL for the XSD document. If the target namespace parameter is null, the `targetNamespace` of the schema will be used. The last overload takes the `targetNamespace` as the first parameter as well, but it used an `XmlReader`-based object to read in the schema. The `XmlSchemaSet` preprocesses the schema before the document to be validated is processed.

After the schema is referenced, the `XsdValidate` property is set to true. This must be done or else validation will not occur.

Because the `XmlReader` object is being used, if there is a validation problem with the document it will not be found until that attribute or element is read by the reader. When the validation failure does occur, an `XmlSchemaValidationException` is raised. This exception can be handled in a `catch` block; however, handling exceptions can make controlling the flow of the data difficult. To help with this, a `ValidationEvent` is available in the `XmlReaderSettings` class. This way the validation failure can be handled without having to use exception handling. The event is also raised by validation warnings, something that does not raise an exception. The `ValidationEvent` passes in a `ValidationEventArgs` object that contains a `Severity` property. This property determines whether the event was raised by an error or a warning. If the event was raised by an error, the exception that caused the event to be raised is passed in as well. There is also a message property. In the example, the message is displayed in a `MessageBox`.

## Using the XmlWriter Class

The `XmlWriter` class allows you write XML to a stream, a file, a `StringBuilder`, a `TextWriter` or another `XmlWriter` object. Like `XmlTextReader`, it does so in a forward-only, non-cached manner. `XmlWriter` is highly configurable, allowing you to specify such things as whether or not to indent content, the amount to indent, what quote character to use in attribute values, and whether namespaces are supported. Like the `XmlReader` this configuration is done using an `XmlWriterSettings` object.

Here's a simple example that shows how the `XmlTextWriter` class can be used:

```
private void button9_Click(object sender, EventArgs e)
{
    XmlWriterSettings settings = new XmlWriterSettings();
    settings.Indent = true;
    settings.NewLineOnAttributes = true;
    XmlWriter writer = XmlWriter.Create("booknew.xml", settings);
    writer.WriteStartDocument();
    //Start creating elements and attributes
    writer.WriteStartElement("book");
    writer.WriteAttributeString("genre", "Mystery");
    writer.WriteAttributeString("publicationdate", "2001");
    writer.WriteAttributeString("ISBN", "123456789");
    writer.WriteElementString("title", "Case of the Missing Cookie");
    writer.WriteStartElement("author");
    writer.WriteElementString("name", "Cookie Monster");
    writer.WriteEndElement();
    writer.WriteElementString("price", "9.99");
```

# Manipulating XML

```
    writer.WriteEndElement();
    writer.WriteEndDocument();
    //clean up
    writer.Flush();
    writer.Close();
}
```

Here you are writing to a new XML file called `booknew.xml`, adding the data for a new book. Note that `XmlWriter` will overwrite an existing file with a new one. You look at inserting a new element or node into an existing document later in this chapter. You are instantiating the `XmlWriter` object using the `Create` static method. In this example a string representing a file name is passed as a parameter along with an instance of an `XmlWriterSetting` class.

The `XmlWriterSettings` class has properties that control the way that the xml is generated. The `CheckedCharacters` property is a Boolean that will raise an exception if a character in the xml does not conform to the W3C XML 1.0 recommendation. The `Encoding` class sets the encoding used for the xml being generated; the default is Encoding.UTF8. The `Indent` property is a Boolean value that determines if elements should be indented. The `IndentChars` property is set to the character string that is used to indent. The default is two spaces. The `NewLine` property is used to determine the characters for line breaks. In the preceding example, the `NewLineOnAttribute` is set to `true`. This will put each attribute in a separate line, which can make the xml generated a little easier to read.

`WriteStartDocument()` adds the document declaration. Now you start writing data. First comes the `book` element, then you add the `genre`, `publicationdate`, and `ISBN` attributes, and then you write the `title`, `author`, and `price` elements. Note that the `author` element has a child element name.

When you click the button, you produce the `booknew.xml` file, which looks like this:

```xml
<?xml version="1.0" encoding="utf-8"?>
<book
  genre="Mystery"
  publicationdate="2001"
  ISBN="123456789">
  <title>Case of the Missing Cookie</title>
  <author>
    <name>Cookie Monster</name>
  </author>
  <price>9.99</price>
</book>
```

The nesting of elements is controlled by paying attention to when you start and finish writing elements and attributes. You can see this when you add the `name` child element to the `authors` element. Note how the `WriteStartElement()` and `WriteEndElement()` method calls are arranged, and how that arrangement produces the nested elements in the output file.

To go along with the `WriteElementString()` and `WriteAttributeString()` methods, there are several other specialized write methods. `WriteCData()` outputs a CData section (`<![CDATA[...]]>`), writing out the text it takes as a parameter. `WriteComment()` writes out a comment in proper XML format. `WriteChars()` writes out the contents of a char buffer. This works in a similar fashion to the `ReadChars()` method that you looked at earlier; they both use the same type of parameters. `WriteChars()` needs a buffer (an array of characters), the starting position for writing (an integer), and the number of characters to write (an integer).

# Chapter 21

Reading and writing XML using the `XmlReader`- and `XmlWriter`-based classes is surprisingly flexible and simple to use. Next, you learn how the DOM is implemented in the `System.Xml` namespace, through the `XmlDocument` and `XmlNode` classes.

## Using the DOM in .NET

The DOM implementation in .NET supports the W3C DOM Level 1 and Core DOM Level 2 specifications. The DOM is implemented through the `XmlNode` class, which is an abstract class that represents a node of an XML document.

There is also an `XmlNodeList` class, which is an ordered list of nodes. This is a live list of nodes, and any changes to any node are immediately reflected in the list. `XmlNodeList` supports indexed access or iterative access. Another abstract class, `XmlCharacterData`, extends `XmlLinkedNode` and provides text manipulation methods for other classes.

The `XmlNode` and `XmlNodeList` classes make up the core of the DOM implementation in the .NET Framework. The following table lists some of the classes that are based on `XmlNode`.

| Class Name | Description |
|---|---|
| XmlLinkedNode | Returns the node immediately before or after the current node. Adds `NextSibling` and `PreviousSibling` properties to `XmlNode`. |
| XmlDocument | Represents the entire document. Implements the DOM Level 1 and Level 2 specifications. |
| XmlDocumentFragment | Represents a fragment of the document tree. |
| XmlAttribute | Represents an attribute object of an `XmlElement` object. |
| XmlEntity | Represents a parsed or unparsed entity node. |
| XmlNotation | Contains a notation declared in a DTD or schema. |

The following table lists classes that extend `XmlCharacterData`.

| Class Name | Description |
|---|---|
| XmlCDataSection | Represents a `CData` section of a document. |
| XmlComment | Represents an XML comment object. |
| XmlSignificantWhitespace | Represents a node with whitespace. Nodes are created only if the `PreserveWhiteSpace` flag is `true`. |
| XmlWhitespace | Represents whitespace in element content. Nodes are created only if the `PreserveWhiteSpace` flag is `true`. |
| XmlText | Represents the textual content of an element or attribute. |

# Manipulating XML

The following table lists classes that extend the XmlLinkedNode.

| Class Name | Description |
| --- | --- |
| XmlDeclaration | Represents the declaration node (<?xml version='1.0'...>). |
| XmlDocumentType | Represents data relating to the document type declaration. |
| XmlElement | Represents an XML element object. |
| XmlEntityReferenceNode | Represents an entity reference node. |
| XmlProcessingInstruction | Contains an XML processing instruction. |

As you can see, .NET makes available a class to fit just about any XML type that you might encounter. Because of this, you end up with a very flexible and powerful tool set. This section won't look at every class in detail, but you will see several examples to give you an idea of what you can accomplish. Figure 21-1 illustrates what the inheritance diagram looks like.

## Using the XmlDocument Class

XmlDocument and its derived class XmlDataDocument (discussed later in this chapter) are the classes that you will be using to represent the DOM in .NET. Unlike XmlReader and XmlWriter, XmlDocument gives you read and write capabilities as well as random access to the DOM tree. XmlDocument resembles the DOM implementation in MSXML. If you have experience programming with MSXML, you will feel comfortable using XmlDocument.

This section introduces an example that creates an XmlDocument object, loads a document from disk, and loads a list box with data from the title elements. This is similar to one of the examples that you constructed in the XmlReader section. The difference here is that you will be selecting the nodes you want to work with, instead of going through the entire document as in the XmlReader-based example.

Here is the code. Notice how simple it looks in comparison to the XmlReader example (you can find the file in the DOMSample1 folder of the download):

```
private void button1_Click(object sender, System.EventArgs e)
{
    //doc is declared at the module level
    //change path to math your path structure
    _doc.Load("books.xml");
    //get only the nodes that we want.
    XmlNodeList nodeLst = _doc.GetElementsByTagName("title");
    //iterate through the XmlNodeList
    foreach (XmlNode node in nodeLst)
      listBox1.Items.Add(node.InnerText);
}
```

Note that you also add the following declaration at the module level for the examples in this section:

```
private XmlDocument doc=new XmlDocument();
```

# Chapter 21

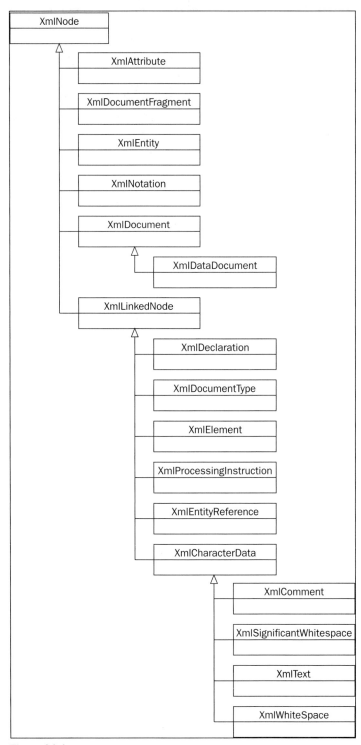

Figure 21-1

# Manipulating XML

If this is all that you wanted to do, using the `XmlReader` would have been a much more efficient way to load the list box, because you just go through the document once and then you are finished with it. This is exactly the type of work that `XmlReader` was designed for. However, if you wanted to revisit a node, using `XmlDocument` is a better way. Extend the previous example by adding another event handler:

```
private void listBox1_SelectedIndexChanged(object sender, EventArgs e)
    {
      //create XPath search string
      string srch="bookstore/book[title='" + listBox1.SelectedItem.ToString() + "']";
      //look for the extra data
      XmlNode foundNode = _doc.SelectSingleNode(srch);
      if (foundNode != null)
        MessageBox.Show(foundNode.OuterXml);
      else
        MessageBox.Show("Not found");
    }
```

In this example, you load the list box with the titles from the `books.xml` document, as in the previous example. When you click on the list box, it triggers the `SelectedIndexChanged()` event handler. In this case, you take the text of the selected item in the list box (the book title), create an XPath statement, and pass it to the `SelectSingleNode()` method of the `doc` object. This returns the `book` element that the `title` is part of (`foundNode`). Then you display the `OuterXml` of the node in a message box. You can keep clicking items in the list box as many times as you want, because the document is loaded and stays loaded until you release it.

A quick comment regarding the `SelectSingleNode()` method: This is an XPath implementation in the `XmlDocument` class. Both `SelectSingleNode()` and `SelectNodes()` methods are defined in `XmlNode`, which `XmlDocument` in based on. `SelectSingleNode()` returns an `XmlNode` and `SelectNodes()` returns an `XmlNodeList`. However, the `System.Xml.XPath` namespace contains a richer XPath implementation, and you look at that in a later section.

## *Inserting nodes*

Earlier, you looked at an example using `XmlTextWriter` that created a new document. The limitation was that it would not insert a node into a current document. With the `XmlDocument` class you can do just that. Change the `button1_Click()` event handler from the last example to the following (`DOMSample3` in the download code):

```
private void button1_Click(object sender, System.EventArgs e)
{
    //change path to match your structure
    doc.Load("..\\..\\..\\books.xml");
    //create a new 'book' element
    XmlElement newBook=doc.CreateElement("book");
    //set some attributes
    newBook.SetAttribute("genre","Mystery");
    newBook.SetAttribute("publicationdate","2001");
    newBook.SetAttribute("ISBN","123456789");
    //create a new 'title' element
    XmlElement newTitle=doc.CreateElement("title");
    newTitle.InnerText="The Case of the Missing Cookie";
    newBook.AppendChild(newTitle);
    //create new author element
    XmlElement newAuthor=doc.CreateElement("author");
    newBook.AppendChild(newAuthor);
```

```
    //create new name element
    XmlElement newName=doc.CreateElement("name");
    newName.InnerText="C. Monster";
    newAuthor.AppendChild(newName);
    //create new price element
    XmlElement newPrice=doc.CreateElement("price");
    newPrice.InnerText="9.95";
    newBook.AppendChild(newPrice);
    //add to the current document
    doc.DocumentElement.AppendChild(newBook);
    //write out the doc to disk
    XmlTextWriter tr=new XmlTextWriter("..\\..\\..\\booksEdit.xml",null);
    tr.Formatting=Formatting.Indented;
    doc.WriteContentTo(tr);
    tr.Close();
    //load listBox1 with all of the titles, including new one
    XmlNodeList nodeLst=doc.GetElementsByTagName("title");
    foreach(XmlNode node in nodeLst)
        listBox1.Items.Add(node.InnerText);
}
```

After executing this code, you end up with the same functionality as in the previous example, but there is one additional book in the list box, *The Case of the Missing Cookie* (a soon-to-be classic). Clicking on the cookie caper title will show all of the same info as the other titles. Breaking down the code, you can see that this is actually a fairly simple process. The first thing that you do is create a new book element:

```
XmlElement newBook = doc.CreateElement("book");
```

CreateElement() has three overloads that allow you to specify the following:

- ❑ The element name
- ❑ The name and namespace URI
- ❑ The prefix, localname, and namespace

Once the element is created you need to add attributes:

```
newBook.SetAttribute("genre","Mystery");
newBook.SetAttribute("publicationdate","2001");
newBook.SetAttribute("ISBN","123456789");
```

Now that you have the attributes created, you need to add the other elements of a book:

```
XmlElement newTitle = doc.CreateElement("title");
newTitle.InnerText = "The Case of the Missing Cookie";
newBook.AppendChild(newTitle);
```

Once again, you create a new XmlElement-based object (newTitle). Then you set the InnerText property to the title of our new classic, and append the element as a child to the book element. You repeat this for the rest of the elements in this book element. Note that you add the name element as a child to the author element. This will give you the proper nesting relationship as in the other book elements.

Finally, you append the newBook element to the doc.DocumentElement node. This is the same level as all of the other book elements. You have now updated an existing document with a new element.

# Manipulating XML

The last thing to do is to write the new XML document to disk. In this example, you create a new `XmlTextWriter` and pass it to the `WriteContentTo()` method. `WriteContentTo()` and `WriteTo()` both take an `XmlTextWriter` as a parameter. `WriteContentTo()` saves the current node and all of its children to the `XmlTextWriter`, whereas `WriteTo()` just saves the current node. Because `doc` is an `XmlDocument`-based object, it represents the entire document and so that is what is saved. You could also use the `Save()` method. It will always save the entire document. `Save()` has four overloads. You can specify a string with the file name and path, a `Stream`-based object, a `TextWriter`-based object, or an `XmlWriter`-based object.

You also call the `Close()` method on `XmlTextWriter` to flush the internal buffers and close the file.

Figure 21-2 shows what you get when you run this example. Notice the new entry at the bottom of the list.

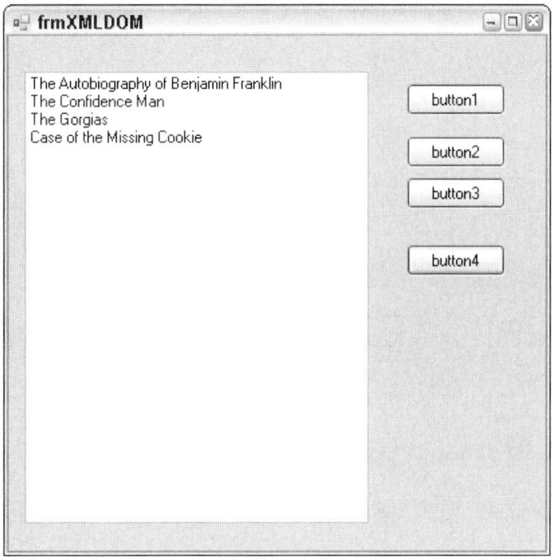

**Figure 21-2**

If you wanted to create a document from scratch, you could use the `XmlTextWriter`, which you saw in action earlier in the chapter. You can also use `XmlDocument`. Why would you use one in preference to the other? If the data that you want streamed to XML is available and ready to write, then the `XmlTextWriter` class would be the best choice. However, if you need to build the XML document a little at a time, inserting nodes into various places, then creating the document with `XmlDocument` might be the better choice. You can accomplish this by changing the following line:

```
doc.Load("books.xml");
```

to this code (example `DOMSample4`):

```
//create the declaration section
XmlDeclaration newDec = doc.CreateXmlDeclaration("1.0",null,null);
doc.AppendChild(newDec);
//create the new root element
XmlElement newRoot = doc.CreateElement("newBookstore");
doc.AppendChild(newRoot);
```

First, you create a new `XmlDeclaration`. The parameters are the version (always `1.0` for now), the encoding, and the standalone flag. The encoding parameter should be set to a string that is part of the `System.Text.Encoding` class if `null` isn't used. (`null` defaults to UTF-8). The standalone flag can be either `yes`, `no`, or `null`. If it is `null`, the attribute is not used and will not be included in the document.

The next element that is created will become the `DocumentElement`. In this case, it is called `newBookstore` so that you can see the difference. The rest of the code is the same as in the previous example and works in the same way. This is `booksEdit.xml`, which is generated from the code:

```xml
<?xml version="1.0"?>
<newBookstore>
    <book genre="Mystery" publicationdate="2001" ISBN="123456789">
        <title>The Case of the Missing Cookie</title>
        <author>
            <name>C. Monster</name>
        </author>
        <price>9.95</price>
    </book>
</newBookstore>
```

You will want to use the `XmlDocument` class when you want to have random access to the document, or the `XmlReader`-based classes when you want a streaming type model instead. Remember that there is a cost for the flexibility of the `XmlNode`-based `XmlDocument` class — memory requirements are higher and the performance of reading the document is not as good as using `XmlReader`. There is another way to traverse an xml document: the XPathNavigator.

# Using XPathNavigators

An XPathNavigator is used to select, iterate, and sometimes edit data from an xml document. An XPathNavigator can be created from an XmlDocument to allow editing capabilities or from an XPathDocument for read-only use. Since the XPathDocument is read-only it performs very well. Unlike the XmlReader, the XPathNavigator isn't a streaming model, so the same document can be used without having to re-read and parse.

The XPathNavigaor is part of the System.Xml.XPath namespace. XPath is a query language used to select specific nodes or elements from an xml document for processing.

## The System.Xml.XPath Namespace

The `System.Xml.XPath` namespace is built for speed. It provides a read-only view of your XML documents, so there are no editing capabilities. Classes in this namespace are built to do fast iteration and selections on the XML document in a cursor fashion.

The following table lists the key classes in `System.Xml.XPath` and gives a short description of the purpose of each class.

# Manipulating XML

| Class Name | Description |
|---|---|
| XPathDocument | Provides a view of the entire XML document. Read-only. |
| XPathNavigator | Provides the navigation capabilities to an XPathDocument. |
| XPathNodeIterator | Provides iteration capabilities to a node set. |
| XPathExpression | Represents a compiled XPath expression. Used by SelectNodes, SelectSingleNodes, Evaluate, and Matches. |
| XPathException | An XPath exception class. |

## XPathDocument

XPathDocument doesn't offer any of the functionality of the XmlDocument class. Its sole purpose is to create XPathNavigators. As a matter of fact, that is the only method available on the XPathDocument class (other then those provided by Object).

An XPathDocument can be created a number of different ways. You can pass in an XmlReader, a file name of an xml document or a Stream based object ti the constructor. This allows a great deal of flexibility. For example, you could use the XmlValidatingReader to validate the xml and the use that same object to create the XPathDocument.

## XPathNavigator

XPathNavigator contains all of the methods for moving and selecting elements that you need. The following table lists some of the "move" methods defined in this class.

| Method Name | Description |
|---|---|
| MoveTo() | Takes XPathNavigator as a parameter. Moves the current position to be the same as that passed in to XPathNavigator. |
| MoveToAttribute() | Moves to the named attribute. Takes the attribute name and namespace as parameters. |
| MoveToFirstAttribute() | Moves to the first attribute in the current element. Returns true if successful. |
| MoveToNextAttribute() | Moves to the next attribute in the current element. Returns true if successful. |
| MoveToFirst() | Moves to the first sibling in the current node. Returns true if successful; otherwise it returns false. |
| MoveToLast() | Moves to the last sibling in the current node. Returns true if successful. |
| MoveToNext() | Moves to the next sibling in the current node. Returns true if successful. |

*Table continued on following page*

| Method Name | Description |
|---|---|
| `MoveToPrevious()` | Moves to the previous sibling in the current node. Returns `true` if successful. |
| `MoveToFirstChild()` | Moves to the first child of the current element. Returns `true` if successful. |
| `MoveToId()` | Moves to the element with the ID supplied as a parameter. There needs to be a schema for the document, and the data type for the element must be of type `ID`. |
| `MoveToParent()` | Moves to the parent of the current node. Returns `true` if successful. |
| `MoveToRoot()` | Moves to the root node of the document. |

In order to select a subset of the document you can use one of the Select methods:

| Method Name | Description |
|---|---|
| `Select()` | Select a node set using an XPath expression. |
| `SelectAncestors`()` | Selects all of the ancestors of the current node based on an XPath expression. |
| `SelectChildren()` | Select all of the children of the current node based on an XPath expression. |
| `SelectDescendants()` | Select all of the descendants of the current node based on an XPath expression. |
| `SelectSingleNode()` | Select one node based on an XPath expression. |

If the XPathNavigator was created from an XPathDocument, it is read-only. If it is created from an XmlDocument, the XPathNavigator can be used to edit the document. This can be verified by checking the CanEdit property. If true, you can use one of the Insert methods. InsertBefore and InsertAfter will create a new node either before or after the current node. The source of the new node can be from an XmlReader or a string. Optionally an XmlWriter can be returned and used to write the new node information.

Strongly typed values can be read form the nods using the ValueAs properties. Notice that this is different from XmReader, which used ReadValue methods.

## *XPathNodeIterator*

`XPathNodeIterator` can be thought of as the equivalent of a `NodeList` or a `NodeSet` in `XPath`. This object has three properties and two methods:

- `Clone` — Creates a new copy of itself
- `Count` — Number of nodes in the `XPathNodeIterator` object

# Manipulating XML

- `Current` — Returns an `XPathNavigator` pointing to the current node
- `CurrentPosition()` — Returns an integer with the current position
- `MoveNext()` — Moves to the next node that matches the XPath expression that created the `XPathNodeIterator`

The XPathNodeIterator is returned by the XPathNavigators select methods. You use it to iterate over the set of nodes returned by a Select method of the XPathNavigator. Using the MoveNext method of the XPathNodeIterator does not change the location of the XPathNavigator that created it.

## Using classes from the XPath namespace

The best way to see how these classes are used is to look at some code that iterates through the `books.xml` document. This will allow you to see how the navigation works. In order to use the examples, you first add a reference to the `System.Xml.Xsl` and `System.Xml.XPath` namespaces:

```
using System.Xml.XPath;
using System.Xml.Xsl;
```

For this example, you are using the file `booksxpath.xml`. It is similar to the `books.xml` that you have been using, except there are a couple of extra books added. Here's the form code, which is part of the XmlSample project:

```
private void button1_Click(object sender, EventArgs e)
{
  //modify to match your path structure
  XPathDocument doc = new XPathDocument("books.xml");
  //create the XPath navigator
  XPathNavigator nav = ((IXPathNavigable)doc).CreateNavigator();
  //create the XPathNodeIterator of book nodes
  // that have genre attribute value of novel
  XPathNodeIterator iter = nav.Select("/bookstore/book[@genre='novel']");

  while (iter.MoveNext())
  {
     XPathNodeIterator newIter =
iter.Current.SelectDescendants(XPathNodeType.Element, false);
     while(newIter.MoveNext())
        listView1.Items.Add(newIter.Current.Name + ": " + newIter.Current.Value);
  }
}
```

The first thing you do in the `button1_Click()` method is to create the `XPathDocument` (called doc), passing in the file and path string of the document you want opened. The next line is where the `XPathNavigator` is created:

```
XPathNavigator nav = doc.CreateNavigator();
```

In the example, you can see that you use the `Select()` method to retrieve a set of nodes that all have `novel` as the value of the `genre` attribute. You then use the `MoveNext()` method to iterate through all of the novels in the book list.

681

## Chapter 21

To load the data into the list box, you use the `XPathNodeIterator.Current` property. This creates a new `XPathNavigator` object based on just the node that the `XPathNodeIterator` is pointing to. In this case, you are creating an `XPathNavigator` for one `book` node in the document.

The next loop takes this `XPathNavigator` and creates another `XPathNodeIterator` by issuing another type of select method, the `SelectDescendants()` method. This gives you an `XPathNodeIterator` of all of the child nodes and children of the child nodes of the `book` node.

Then you do another `MoveNext()` loop on the `XPathNodeIterator` and load the list box with the element names and element values.

Figure 21-3 shows what the screen looks like after running the code. Note that novels are the only books listed now.

**Figure 21-3**

What if you wanted to add up the cost of these books? `XPathNavigator` includes the `Evaluate()` method for just this reason. `Evaluate()` has three overloads. The first one contains a string that is the XPath function call. The second overload uses the `XPathExpression` object as a parameter, and the third uses `XPathExpression` and an `XPathNodeIterator` as parameters. The following code is similar to the previous example, except this time all of the nodes in the document are iterated. The `Evaluate` at the end totals up the cost of all of the books:

```
private void button2_Click(object sender, EventArgs e)
{
    //modify to match your path structure
    XPathDocument doc = new XPathDocument("books.xml");
    //create the XPath navigator
    XPathNavigator nav = ((IXPathNavigable)doc).CreateNavigator();
    //create the XPathNodeIterator of book nodes
    // that have genre attribute value of novel
    XPathNodeIterator iter = nav.Select("/bookstore/book");
    while (iter.MoveNext())
    {
```

# Manipulating XML

```
      XPathNodeIterator newIter =
   iter.Current.SelectDescendants(XPathNodeType.Element, false);
      while (newIter.MoveNext())
         listView1.Items.Add(newIter.Current.Name + ": " + newIter.Current.Value);
   }
   listView1.Items.Add("=========================");
   listView1.Items.Add("Total Cost = " +
nav.Evaluate("sum(/bookstore/book/price)"));
}
```

This time, you see the total cost of the books evaluated in the list box (see Figure 21-4).

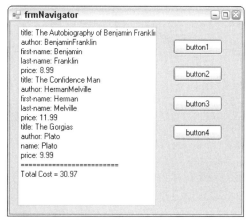

**Figure 21-4**

Now let's say that you need to add a node for discount. Using the InsertAfter method can get this done fairly easily. Here is the code:

```
private void button3_Click(object sender, EventArgs e)
{
  XmlDocument doc = new XmlDocument();
  doc.Load("books.xml");
  XPathNavigator nav = doc.CreateNavigator();
  if (nav.CanEdit)
  {
    XPathNodeIterator iter = nav.Select("/bookstore/book/price");
    while (iter.MoveNext())
    {
       iter.Current.InsertAfter("<disc>5</disc>");
    }
  }
  doc.Save("newbooks.xml");
}
```

Here we add the <disc>5</disc> element after the price elements. First all of the price nodes are selected. The XPathNodeIterator is used to iterate over the nodes and the new node is inserted. The modified document is saved with a new name, newbooks.xml. Here is what the new version looks like:

**683**

```xml
<?xml version="1.0"?>
<!-- This file represents a fragment of a book store inventory database -->
<bookstore>
  <book genre="autobiography" publicationdate="1991" ISBN="1-861003-11-0">
    <title>The Autobiography of Benjamin Franklin</title>
    <author>
      <first-name>Benjamin</first-name>
      <last-name>Franklin</last-name>
    </author>
    <price>8.99</price>
    <disc>5</disc>
  </book>
  <book genre="novel" publicationdate="1967" ISBN="0-201-63361-2">
    <title>The Confidence Man</title>
    <author>
      <first-name>Herman</first-name>
      <last-name>Melville</last-name>
    </author>
    <price>11.99</price>
    <disc>5</disc>
  </book>
  <book genre="philosophy" publicationdate="1991" ISBN="1-861001-57-6">
    <title>The Gorgias</title>
    <author>
      <name>Plato</name>
    </author>
    <price>9.99</price>
    <disc>5</disc>
  </book>
</bookstore>
```

Nodes can be inserted before or after a selected node. The nodes can also be changed and they can be deleted. If you have changes that have to be done to large numbers of nodes, using the XPathNavigator created from an XmlDocument may be your best choice.

## The System.Xml.Xsl Namespace

The `System.Xml.Xsl` namespace contains the classes that the .NET Framework uses to support XSL Transforms. The contents of this namespace are available to any store whose classes implement the `IXPathNavigable` interface. In the .NET Framework that would currently include `XmlDocument`, `XmlDataDocument`, and `XPathDocument`. Again, just as with `XPath`, use the store that makes the most sense. If you plan to create a custom store, such as one using the file system and you want to be able to do transforms, be sure to implement the `IXPathNavigable` interface in your class.

XSLT is based on a streaming pull model. Because of this, you can chain several transforms together. You could even apply a custom reader between transforms if needed. This allows a great deal of flexibility in design.

### Transforming XML

The first example you look at takes the `books.xml` document and transforms it into a simple HTML document for display using the XSLT file `books.xsl`. (This code is in the `XPathXSLSample3` folder.) You will need to add the following `using` statements:

# Manipulating XML

```
using System.IO;
using System.Xml.Xsl;
using System.Xml.XPath;
```

Here is the code to perform the transform:

```
private void transformtoHTMLToolStripButton_Click(object sender, EventArgs e)
{
  XslTransform trans = new XslTransform();
  trans.Load("books.xsl");
  trans.Transform("books.xml", "out.html");
  webBrowser1.Url = AppDomain.CurrentDomain.BaseDirectory + "//out.html";
}
```

A transform doesn't get any simpler than this. First a new XmlTransform object is created. It loads the books.xsl transform document and then performs the transform. In this example, a string with the file name is used as the input. The output is out.html. This file is then loaded into the web browser control used on the form. Instead of the file name books.xml as the input document, you can also use an IXPathNavigable based object. This would be any object that can create an XPathNavigator. An XPathNavigator can also be used as the source of the transform.

If this were an ASP.NET application, you would have used a `TextWriter` object and passed it to the `HttpResponse` object instead. If you were transforming to another XML document, you would have used an `XmlWriter`-based object.

After the `XslTransform` object is ready, you create the `XPathNavigator` on the `XPathDocument`, and pass the `XPathNavigator` and the `FileStream` into the `Transform()` method of the `XslTransform` object. `Transform()` has several overloads, passing in combinations of navigators, `XsltArgumentList` (more on this shortly), IO streams, and `XmlResolvers`. The navigator parameter can be `XPathNavigator` or anything that implements the `IXPathNavigable` interface. The IO streams can be a `TextWriter`, `Stream`, or `XmlWriter`-based object. The `XmlResolver` is used to manage the process of getting a resource from an external source. The `XmlResolver` handles the security, opening the data source and returning the data or stream. In the .Net Framework 1.0 the `XmlResolver` parameter was not a requirement. All of those versions of the `Transform` method have been deprecated and now the `XmlResolver` parameter is required; however, you can pass null if the features of an `XmlResolver`, namely security and credential management, are not needed.

The `books.xsl` document is a fairly straightforward style sheet. The document looks like this:

```
<xsl:stylesheet version="1.0"
                xmlns:xsl="http://www.w3.org/1999/XSL/Transform">
<xsl:template match="/">
   <html>
      <head>
         <title>Price List</title>
      </head>
      <body>
         <table>
            <xsl:apply-templates/>
         </table>
      </body>
   </html>
```

685

```
      </xsl:template>
    <xsl:template match="bookstore">
        <xsl:apply-templates select="book"/>
    </xsl:template>
    <xsl:template match="book">
       <tr><td>
           <xsl:value-of select="title"/>
        </td><td>
           <xsl:value-of select="price"/>
        </td></tr>
    </xsl:template>
</xsl:stylesheet>
```

## Using XsltArgumentList

XsltArgumentList was mentioned earlier. This is a way that you can bind an object with methods to a namespace. Once this is done, you can invoke the methods during the transform. Here's an example:

```
private void button3_Click(object sender, EventArgs e)
{
  //new XPathDocument
  XPathDocument doc = new XPathDocument("books.xml");
  //new XslTransform
  XslCompiledTransform trans = new XslCompiledTransform();
  trans.Load("booksarg.xsl");
  //new XmlTextWriter since we are creating a new xml document
  XmlWriter xw = new XmlTextWriter("argSample.xml", null);
  //create the XslArgumentList and new BookUtils object
  XsltArgumentList argBook = new XsltArgumentList();
  BookUtils bu = new BookUtils();
  //this tells the argumentlist about BookUtils
  argBook.AddExtensionObject("urn:XslSample", bu);
  //new XPathNavigator
  XPathNavigator nav = doc.CreateNavigator();
  //do the transform
  trans.Transform(nav, argBook, xw);
  xw.Close();
  webBrowser1.Navigate(AppDomain.CurrentDomain.BaseDirectory + "//argSample.xml");
}
```

This is the code for the BooksItil class. This is the class that will be called from the transform.

```
namespace XslSample
{
  class BookUtils
    {
      public BookUtils() { }

      public string ShowText()
      {
        return "This came from the ShowText method!";
      }
    }
}
```

# Manipulating XML

This is what the output of the transform looks like; the output has been formatted for easier viewing (`argSample.xml`):

```xml
<books>
    <discbook>
        <booktitle>The Autobiography of Benjamin Franklin</booktitle>
        <showtext>This came from the ShowText method!</showtext>
    </discbook>
    <discbook>
        <booktitle>The Confidence Man</booktitle>
        <showtext>This came from the ShowText method!</showtext>
    </discbook>
    <discbook>
        <booktitle>The Gorgias</booktitle>
        <showtext>This came from the ShowText method!</showtext>
    </discbook>
    <discbook>
        <booktitle>The Great Cookie Caper</booktitle>
        <showtext>This came from the ShowText method!</showtext>
    </discbook>
    <discbook>
        <booktitle>A Really Great Book</booktitle>
        <showtext>This came from the ShowText method!</showtext>
    </discbook>
</books>
```

In this example, you define a new class, `BookUtils`. In this class you have one rather useless method that returns the string "This came from the ShowText method!" In the `button1_Click()` event, you create the `XPathDocument` and `XslTransform` objects. Before we loaded the xml document and the transform document directly into the XslComiledTransform object. This time you will use the XPathNavigator to load the documents.

Next you need to do the following:

```
XsltArgumentList argBook=new XsltArgumentList();
BookUtils bu=new BookUtils();
argBook.AddExtensionObject("urn:XslSample",bu);
```

This is where you create the `XsltArgumentList` object. You create an instance of the `BookUtils` object, and when you call the `AddExtensionObject()` method, you pass in a namespace for your extension and the object that you want to be able to call methods from. When you make the `Transform()` call, you pass in the `XsltArgumentList` (`argBook`) along with the `XPathNavigator` and the `XmlWriter` object you made.

Here is the `booksarg.xsl` document (based on `books.xsl`):

```xml
<xsl:stylesheet version="1.0" xmlns:xsl="http://www.w3.org/1999/XSL/Transform"
                              xmlns:bookUtil="urn:XslSample">
    <xsl:output method="xml" indent="yes"/>

    <xsl:template match="/">
        <xsl:element name="books">
            <xsl:apply-templates/>
```

```
            </xsl:element>
        </xsl:template>
        <xsl:template match="bookstore">
            <xsl:apply-templates select="book"/>
        </xsl:template>
        <xsl:template match="book">
            <xsl:element name="discbook">
                <xsl:element name="booktitle">
                    <xsl:value-of select="title"/>
                </xsl:element>
                <xsl:element name="showtext">
                    <xsl:value-of select="bookUtil:ShowText()"/>
                </xsl:element>
            </xsl:element>
        </xsl:template>
</xsl:stylesheet>
```

The two important new lines are highlighted. First, you add the namespace that you created when you added the object to `XsltArgumentList`. Then when you want to make the method call, you use standard XSLT namespace prefixing syntax and make the method call.

Another way you could have accomplished this is with XSLT scripting. You can include C#, Visual Basic, and JavaScript code in the style sheet. The great thing about this is that unlike current non-.NET implementations, the script is compiled at the `XslTransform.Load()` call; this way, you are executing already compiled scripts.

Go ahead and modify the previous XSLT file in this way. First, you add the script to the style sheet. You can see the following changes in `booksscript.xsl`:

```
<xsl:stylesheet version="1.0" xmlns:xsl="http://www.w3.org/1999/XSL/Transform"
                              xmlns:msxsl="urn:schemas-microsoft-com:xslt"
                              xmlns:user="http://wrox.com">

    <msxsl:script language="C#" implements-prefix="user">

        string ShowText()
        {
            return "This came from the ShowText method!";

        }
    </msxsl:script>

    <xsl:output method="xml" indent="yes"/>
        <xsl:template match="/">
    <xsl:element name="books">
        <xsl:apply-templates/>
    </xsl:element>
        </xsl:template>
    <xsl:template match="bookstore">
        <xsl:apply-templates select="book"/>
    </xsl:template>
        <xsl:template match="book">
```

```
        <xsl:element name="discbook">
        <xsl:element name="booktitle">
           <xsl:value-of select="title"/>
        </xsl:element>
        <xsl:element name="showtext">
           <xsl:value-of select="user:ShowText()"/>
        </xsl:element>
     </xsl:element>
   </xsl:template>
</xsl:stylesheet>
```

Once again, the changes are highlighted. You set the scripting namespace, add the code (which was copied and pasted in from the Visual Studio .NET IDE), and make the call in the style sheet. The output looks the same as that of the previous example.

To summarize, the key thing to keep in mind when performing transforms is to remember to use the proper XML data store. Use `XPathDocument` if you don't need edit capabilities, `XmlDataDocument` if you're getting your data from ADO.NET, and `XmlDocument` if you need to be able to edit the data. In each case you are dealing with the same process.

# XML and ADO.NET

XML is the glue that binds ADO.NET to the rest of the world. ADO.NET was designed from the ground up to work within the XML environment. XML is used to transfer the data to and from the data store and the application or Web page. Because ADO.NET uses XML as the transport in remoting scenarios, data can be exchanged with applications and systems that are not even aware of ADO.NET. Because of the importance of XML in ADO.NET, there are some powerful features in ADO.NET that allow the reading and writing of XML documents. The `System.Xml` namespace also contains classes that can consume or utilize ADO.NET relational data.

## Converting ADO.NET Data to XML

The first example uses ADO.NET, streams, and XML to pull some data from the Northwind database into a `DataSet`, load an `XmlDocument` object with the XML from the `DataSet`, and load the XML into a list box. To run the next few examples, you need to add the following `using` statements:

```
using System.Data;
using System.Xml;
using System.Data.SqlClient;
using System.IO;
```

Because you will be using `XmlDocument`, you also need to add the following at the module level:

```
private XmlDocument doc = new XmlDocument();
```

Also, the ADO.NET samples have a `DataGrid` object added to the forms. This will allow you to see the data in the ADO.NET `DataSet` because it is bound to the grid, as well as the data from the generated XML documents that you load in the list box. Here is the code for the first example:

```csharp
private void button1_Click(object sender, EventArgs e)
{
  listBox1.SelectedIndexChanged += new EventHandler(example1_SelectedIndexChanged);

  //create a dataset
  DataSet ds = new DataSet("XMLAuthors");
  //connect to the northwind database and
  SqlConnection conn = new SqlConnection(_connectString);
  SqlDataAdapter da = new SqlDataAdapter("SELECT * FROM authors", conn);
```

After you create the `SqlDataAdapter`, da, and the `DataSet`, ds, you instantiate a `MemoryStream` object, a `StreamReader` object, and a `StreamWriter` object. The `StreamReader` and `StreamWriter` objects will use the `MemoryStream` to move the XML around:

```csharp
MemoryStream memStrm=new MemoryStream();
StreamReader strmRead=new StreamReader(memStrm);
StreamWriter strmWrite=new StreamWriter(memStrm);
```

You use a `MemoryStream` so that you don't have to write anything to disk; however, you could have used any object that was based on the `Stream` class, such as `FileStream`. Next, you fill the `DataSet` and bind it to the `DataGrid`. The data in the `DataSet` will now be displayed in the `DataGrid`:

```csharp
da.Fill(ds, "Authors");
//load data into grid
dataGridView1.DataSource = ds.Tables[0];
```

This next step is where the XML is generated. You call the `WriteXml()` method from the `DataSet` class. This method generates an XML document. `WriteXml()` has two overloads: one takes a string with the file path and name, and the other adds a mode parameter. This mode is an `XmlWriteMode` enumeration, with the following possible values:

- ❏ `IgnoreSchema`
- ❏ `WriteSchema`
- ❏ `DiffGram`

`IgnoreSchema` is used if you don't want `WriteXml()` to write an inline schema at the start of your XML file; use the `WriteSchema` parameter if you do want one. You look at `DiffGrams` later in this section.

```csharp
    ds.WriteXml(strmWrite,XmlWriteMode.IgnoreSchema);
    memStrm.Seek(0,SeekOrigin.Begin);
    //read from the memory stream to an XmlDocument object
    doc.Load(strmRead);
      XmlNodeList nodeLst = doc.SelectNodes("//au_lname");   //load them into the
list box
    foreach(XmlNode nd in nodeLst)
      listBox1.Items.Add(nd.InnerText);
}
void example1_SelectedIndexChanged(object sender, EventArgs e)
{
  //when you click on the listbox.
  //a message box with the XML of the selected node
```

# Manipulating XML

```
    string srch = "XMLAuthors/Authors[au_lname=" + '"' +
                                listBox1.SelectedItem.ToString() + '"' + "]";
    XmlNode foundNode = doc.SelectSingleNode(srch);
    if (foundNode != null)
      MessageBox.Show(foundNode.OuterXml);
    else
      MessageBox.Show("Not found");
}
```

Figure 21-5 shows the data in the list as well as the bound data grid.

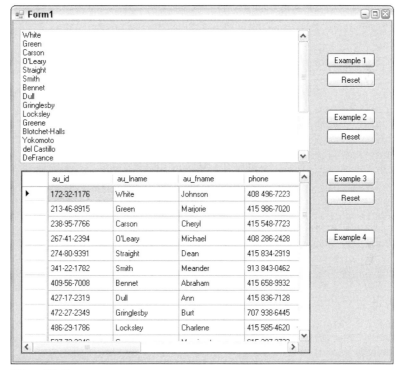

**Figure 21-5**

If you had only wanted the schema, you could have called `WriteXmlSchema()` instead of `WriteXml()`. This method has four overloads. One takes a string, which is the path and file name of where to write the XML document. The second overload uses an object that is based on the `XmlWriter` class. The third overload uses an object based on the `TextWriter` class. The fourth overload is derived from the `Stream` class.

Also, if you wanted to persist the XML document to disk, you would have used something like this:

```
string file = "c:\\test\\product.xml";
ds.WriteXml(file);
```

This would give you a well-formed XML document on disk that could be read in by another stream, or by `DataSet`, or used by another application or Web site. Because no `XmlMode` parameter is specified, this

691

`XmlDocument` would have the schema included. In this example, you use the stream as a parameter to the `XmlDocument.Load()` method.

Once the `XmlDocument` is prepared, you load the list box using the same XPath statement that you used before. If you look closely, you'll see that you changed the `listBox1_SelectedIndexChanged()` event slightly. Instead of showing the `InnerText` of the element, you do another XPath search using `SelectSingleNode()` to get the authors last name element. So now every time you select an author in the list box, a `MessageBox` pops up with the xml of the element. You now have two views of the data, but more importantly, you can manipulate the data using two different models. You can use the `System.Data` namespace to use the data or you can use the `System.Xml` namespace on the data. This can lead to some very flexible designs in your applications, because now you are not tied to just one object model to program with. This is the real power to the ADO.NET and `System.Xml` combination. You have multiple views of the same data and multiple ways to access the data.

The following example simplifies the process by eliminating the three streams and by using some of the ADO capabilities built into the `System.Xml` namespace. You will need to change the module-level line of code

```
private XmlDocument doc = new XmlDocument();
```

to

```
private XmlDataDocument doc;
```

You need this because you are now using the `XmlDataDocument`. Here is the code (which you can find in the `ADOSample2` folder):

```
private void button3_Click(object sender, EventArgs e)
{
    listBox1.SelectedIndexChanged += new EventHandler(example1_SelectedIndexChanged);

    //create a dataset
    DataSet ds = new DataSet("XMLAuthors");
    //connect to the northwind database and
    //select all of the rows from products table
    SqlConnection conn = new SqlConnection(_connectString);
    SqlDataAdapter da = new SqlDataAdapter("SELECT * FROM authors", conn);
    //fill the dataset
    da.Fill(ds, "Authors");
    ds.WriteXml("sample.xml", XmlWriteMode.WriteSchema);
    //load data into grid
    dataGridView1.DataSource = ds.Tables[0];
    doc = new XmlDataDocument(ds);
    //get all of the products elements
    XmlNodeList nodeLst = doc.GetElementsByTagName("au_lname");
    //load them into the list box
    for (int ctr = 0; ctr < nodeLst.Count; ctr++)
        //foreach(XmlNode node in nodeLst)
        // listBox1.Items.Add(node.InnerText);
        listBox1.Items.Add(nodeLst[ctr].InnerText);
```

# Manipulating XML

As you can see, the code to load the `DataSet` object into the XML document has been simplified. Instead of using the `XmlDocument` class, you are using the `XmlDataDocument` class. This class was built specifically for using data with a `DataSet` object.

The `XmlDataDocument` is based on the `XmlDocument` class, so it has all of the functionality that the `XmlDocument` class has. One of the main differences is the overloaded constructor that the `XmlDataDocument` has. Note the line of code that instantiates `XmlDataDocument` (doc):

```
doc = new XmlDataDocument(ds);
```

It passes in the `DataSet` object that you created, `ds`, as a parameter. This creates the XML document from the `DataSet`, and you don't have to use the `Load()` method. In fact, if you instantiate a new `XmlDataDocument` object without passing in a `DataSet` as the parameter, it will contain a `DataSet` with the name `NewDataSet` that has no `DataTables` in the `tables` collection. There is also a `DataSet` property that you can set after an `XmlDataDocument`-based object is created.

Suppose you add the following line of code after the `DataSet.Fill()` call:

```
ds.WriteXml("c:\\test\\sample.xml", XmlWriteMode.WriteSchema);
```

In this case, the following XML file, `sample.xml`, is produced in the folder `c:\test`:

```xml
?xml version="1.0" standalone="yes"?>
<XMLAuthors>
  <xs:schema id="XMLAuthors" xmlns="" xmlns:xs=http://www.w3.org/2001/XMLSchema
                        xmlns:msdata="urn:schemas-microsoft-com:xml-msdata">
    <xs:element name="XMLAuthors" msdata:IsDataSet="true"
                                          msdata:UseCurrentLocale="true">
      <xs:complexType>
        <xs:choice minOccurs="0" maxOccurs="unbounded">
          <xs:element name="Authors">
            <xs:complexType>
              <xs:sequence>
                <xs:element name="au_id" type="xs:string" minOccurs="0" />
                <xs:element name="au_lname" type="xs:string" minOccurs="0" />
                <xs:element name="au_fname" type="xs:string" minOccurs="0" />
                <xs:element name="phone" type="xs:string" minOccurs="0" />
                <xs:element name="address" type="xs:string" minOccurs="0" />
                <xs:element name="city" type="xs:string" minOccurs="0" />
                <xs:element name="state" type="xs:string" minOccurs="0" />
                <xs:element name="zip" type="xs:string" minOccurs="0" />
                <xs:element name="contract" type="xs:boolean" minOccurs="0" />
              </xs:sequence>
            </xs:complexType>
          </xs:element>
        </xs:choice>
      </xs:complexType>
    </xs:element>
  </xs:schema>
  <Authors>
    <au_id>172-32-1176</au_id>
    <au_lname>White</au_lname>
    <au_fname>Johnson</au_fname>
```

```
            <phone>408 496-7223</phone>
            <address>10932 Bigge Rd.</address>
            <city>Menlo Park</city>
            <state>CA</state>
            <zip>94025</zip>
            <contract>true</contract>
    </Authors>
```

Only the first `products` element is shown. The actual XML file would contain all of the products in the Products table of Northwind database.

## Converting relational data

This looks simple enough for a single table, but what about relational data, such as multiple `DataTables` and `Relations` in the `DataSet`? It all still works the same way. Make the following changes to the code that you've been using (this version is in `ADOSample3`):

```
private void button5_Click(object sender, EventArgs e)
{
    listBox1.SelectedIndexChanged += new EventHandler(example1_SelectedIndexChanged);

    //create a dataset
    DataSet ds = new DataSet("XMLAuthors");
    //connect to the pubs database and
    //select all of the rows from authors table and from titleauthors table
    //make sure you connect string matches you server configuration
    SqlConnection conn = new SqlConnection(_connectString);
    SqlDataAdapter daProd = new SqlDataAdapter("SELECT * FROM authors", conn);
    SqlDataAdapter daSup = new SqlDataAdapter("SELECT * FROM titleauthor", conn);
    //Fill DataSet from both SqlAdapters
    daProd.Fill(ds, "Authors");
    daSup.Fill(ds, "Titles");
    //Add the relation
    ds.Relations.Add(ds.Tables["Authors"].Columns["au_id"],
        ds.Tables["Titles"].Columns["au_id"]);
    //Write the Xml to a file so we can look at it later
    ds.WriteXml("AuthorTitle.xml", XmlWriteMode.WriteSchema);
    //load data into grid
    dataGridView1.DataSource = ds.Tables[0];
    //create the XmlDataDocument
    doc = new XmlDataDocument(ds);
    //Select the productname elements and load them in the grid
    XmlNodeList nodeLst = doc.SelectNodes("//au_lname");

    foreach (XmlNode nd in nodeLst)
        listBox1.Items.Add(nd.InnerXml);

}
```

In this sample you are creating two `DataTables` in the `XMLAuthors DataSet`: `Authors` and `Titles`. You create a new relation on the au_id column in both tables.

By making the same `WriteXml()` method call that you did in the previous example, you will get the following XML file (`SuppProd.xml`):

# Manipulating XML

```xml
<?xml version="1.0" standalone="yes"?>
<XMLAuthors>
  <xs:schema id="XMLAuthors" xmlns="" xmlns:xs="http://www.w3.org/2001/XMLSchema" xmlns:msdata="urn:schemas-microsoft-com:xml-msdata">
    <xs:element name="XMLAuthors" msdata:IsDataSet="true" msdata:UseCurrentLocale="true">
      <xs:complexType>
        <xs:choice minOccurs="0" maxOccurs="unbounded">
          <xs:element name="Authors">
            <xs:complexType>
              <xs:sequence>
                <xs:element name="au_id" type="xs:string" minOccurs="0" />
                <xs:element name="au_lname" type="xs:string" minOccurs="0" />
                <xs:element name="au_fname" type="xs:string" minOccurs="0" />
                <xs:element name="phone" type="xs:string" minOccurs="0" />
                <xs:element name="address" type="xs:string" minOccurs="0" />
                <xs:element name="city" type="xs:string" minOccurs="0" />
                <xs:element name="state" type="xs:string" minOccurs="0" />
                <xs:element name="zip" type="xs:string" minOccurs="0" />
                <xs:element name="contract" type="xs:boolean" minOccurs="0" />
              </xs:sequence>
            </xs:complexType>
          </xs:element>
          <xs:element name="Titles">
            <xs:complexType>
              <xs:sequence>
                <xs:element name="au_id" type="xs:string" minOccurs="0" />
                <xs:element name="title_id" type="xs:string" minOccurs="0" />
                <xs:element name="au_ord" type="xs:unsignedByte" minOccurs="0" />
                <xs:element name="royaltyper" type="xs:int" minOccurs="0" />
              </xs:sequence>
            </xs:complexType>
          </xs:element>
        </xs:choice>
      </xs:complexType>
      <xs:unique name="Constraint1">
        <xs:selector xpath=".//Authors" />
        <xs:field xpath="au_id" />
      </xs:unique>
      <xs:keyref name="Relation1" refer="Constraint1">
        <xs:selector xpath=".//Titles" />
        <xs:field xpath="au_id" />
      </xs:keyref>
    </xs:element>
  </xs:schema>
  <Authors>
    <au_id>213-46-8915</au_id>
    <au_lname>Green</au_lname>
    <au_fname>Marjorie</au_fname>
    <phone>415 986-7020</phone>
    <address>309 63rd St. #411</address>
    <city>Oakland</city>
    <state>CA</state>
```

```
      <zip>94618</zip>
      <contract>true</contract>
   </Authors>
   <Titles>
      <au_id>213-46-8915</au_id>
      <title_id>BU1032</title_id>
      <au_ord>2</au_ord>
      <royaltyper>40</royaltyper>
   </Titles>
   <Titles>
      <au_id>213-46-8915</au_id>
      <title_id>BU2075</title_id>
      <au_ord>1</au_ord>
      <royaltyper>100</royaltyper>
   </Titles>
</XMLAuthors>
```

The schema includes both `DataTables` that were in the `DataSet`. In addition, the data includes all of the data from both tables. For the sake of brevity, only the first author and title records are shown here. As before, you could have saved just the schema or just the data by passing in the correct `XmlWriteMode` parameter.

## Converting XML to ADO.NET Data

Suppose that you have an XML document that you would like to get into an ADO.NET `DataSet`. You would want to do this so you could load the XML into a database, or perhaps bind the data to a .NET data control such as `DataGrid`. This way, you could actually use the XML document as your data store and eliminate the overhead of the database altogether. If your data is reasonably small in size, this is an attractive possibility. Here is some code to get you started (ADOSample5):

```
private void button1_Click(object sender, System.EventArgs e)
{
    //create a new DataSet
    DataSet ds=new DataSet("XMLAuthors");
    //read in the XML document to the Dataset
    ds.ReadXml("sample.xml");
    //load data into grid
    dataGridView1.DataSource = ds;
        //create the new XmlDataDocument
    Doc = new XmlDataDocument(ds);
    //load the product names into the listbox
    XmlNodeList nodeLst=doc.SelectNodes("//au_lname");
    foreach(XmlNode nd in nodeLst)
        listBox1.Items.Add(nd.InnerXml);
}
```

It is that easy. You instantiate a new `DataSet` object. Then you call the `ReadXml()` method, and you have XML in a `DataTable` in your `DataSet`. As with the `WriteXml()` methods, `ReadXml()` has an `XmlReadMode` parameter. `ReadXml()` has a few more options in the `XmlReadMode`, as shown in the following table.

## Manipulating XML

| Value | Description |
|---|---|
| Auto | Sets the `XmlReadMode` to the most appropriate setting. If data is in `DiffGram` format, `DiffGram` is selected. If a schema has already been read, or an inline schema is detected, then `ReadSchema` is selected. If no schema has been assigned to the `DataSet`, and none is detected inline, then `IgnoreSchema` is selected. |
| DiffGram | Reads in the `DiffGram` and applies the changes to the `DataSet`. `DiffGrams` are described later in the chapter. |
| Fragment | Reads documents that contain XDR schema fragments, such as the type created by SQL Server. |
| IgnoreSchema | Ignores any inline schema that may be found. Reads data into the current `DataSet` schema. If data does not match `DataSet` schema it is discarded. |
| InferSchema | Ignores any inline schema. Creates the schema based on data in the XML document. If a schema exists in the `DataSet`, that schema is used, and extended with additional columns and tables if needed. An exception is thrown if a column exists but is of a different data type. |
| ReadSchema | Reads the inline schema and loads the data. Will not overwrite a schema in the `DataSet`, but will throw an exception if a table in the inline schema already exists in the `DataSet`. |

There is also the `ReadXmlSchema()` method. This reads in a standalone schema and creates the tables, columns, and relations. You would use this if your schema is not inline with your data. `ReadXmlSchema()` has the same four overloads: a string with file and path name, a `Stream`-based object, a `TextReader`-based object, and an `XmlReader`-based object.

To show that the data tables are getting created properly, load the XML document that contains the `Products` and `Suppliers` tables that you used in an earlier example. This time, however, load the list box with the `DataTable` names and the `DataColumn` names and data types. You can look at this and compare it to the original Northwind database to see that all is well. Here is the code for this example (ADOSample5):

```
private void button7_Click(object sender, EventArgs e)
{
  //create the DataSet
  DataSet ds = new DataSet("XMLAuthors");
  //read in the xml document
  ds.ReadXml("AuthorTitle.xml");

  //load data into grid
  dataGridView1.DataSource = ds.Tables[0];
  //load the listbox with table, column and datatype info
  foreach (DataTable dt in ds.Tables)
  {
    listBox1.Items.Add(dt.TableName);
    foreach (DataColumn col in dt.Columns)
    {
```

```
            listBox1.Items.Add
                ('\t' + col.ColumnName + " - " + col.DataType.FullName);
          }
       }
    }
```

Note the addition of the two `foreach` loops. The first loop gets the table name from each table in the `Tables` collection of the `DataSet`. Inside the inner `foreach` loop you get the name and data type of each column in the `DataTable`. You load this data into the list box, allowing you to display it. Figure 21-6 shows the output.

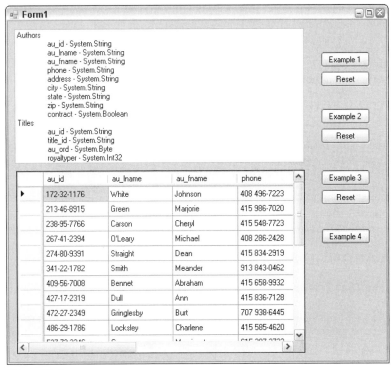

Figure 21-6

Looking at the list box you can check that the data tables were created with the columns all having the correct names and data types.

Something else you might want to note is that because the previous two examples didn't transfer any data to or from a database, no `SqlDataAdapter` or `SqlConnection` was defined. This shows the real flexibility of both the `System.Xml` namespace and ADO.NET: you can look at the same data in multiple formats. If you need to do a transform and show the data in HTML format, or if you need to bind the data to a grid, you can take the same data and, with just a method call, have it in the required format.

# Manipulating XML

## Reading and Writing a DiffGram

A `DiffGram` is an XML document that contains the before and after data of an edit session. This can include any combination of data changes, additions, and deletions. A `DiffGram` can be used as an audit trail or for a commit/rollback process. Most DBMS systems today have this built in, but if you happen to be working with a DBMS that does not have these features or if XML is your data store and you do not have a DBMS, you can implement commit or rollback features yourself.

The beginning part of this code should look familiar. You define and set up a new `DataSet`, ds, a new `SqlConnection`, conn, and a new `SqlDataAdapter`, da. You connect to the database, select all of the rows from the `authors` table, create a new `DataTable` named `authors`, and load the data from the database into the `DataSet`:

```
private void button1_Click(object sender, EventArgs e)
{
   string connectString = "data source=(local)\\sqlexpress;initial catalog=pubs;integrated security=SSPI;";
   //create a dataset
   DataSet ds = new DataSet("XMLAuthors");
   //connect to the pubs database and
   //select all of the rows from products table

   SqlConnection conn = new SqlConnection(connectString);
   SqlDataAdapter da = new SqlDataAdapter("SELECT * FROM authors", conn);
   da.Fill(ds, "Authors");
```

In this next code block, you do two things. First, you modify the au_lame column in the first row to NewName. Second, you create a new row in the `DataTable`, set the column values, and finally add the new data row to the `DataTable`:

```
   ds.Tables[0].Rows[0]["au_lname"] = "NewName";
   DataRow dr = ds.Tables[0].NewRow();
   dr["au_id"] = "123-123-1234";
   dr["au_lname"] = "Bunny";
   dr["au_fname"] = "Bugs";
   dr["contract"]= true;
```

The next block is the interesting part of the code. First, you write out the schema with `WriteXmlSchema()`. This is important because you cannot read back in a `DiffGram` without the schema. `WriteXml()` with the `XmlWriteMode.DiffGram` parameter passed to it actually creates the `DiffGram`. The next line accepts the changes that you made. It is important that the `DiffGram` is created before calling `AcceptChanges()`; otherwise there would not appear to be any modifications to the data:

```
   ds.Tables[0].Rows.Add(dr);
   ds.WriteXmlSchema("author.xdr");
   ds.WriteXml("authdiff.xml", XmlWriteMode.DiffGram);
   ds.AcceptChanges();
}
```

To get the data back into a `DataSet`, you can do the following:

## Chapter 21

```
DataSet dsNew=new DataSet();
dsNew.ReadXmlSchema("author.xsd");
dsNew.XmlRead("authdiff.xml",XmlReadMode.DiffGram);
```

Here you are creating a new `DataSet`, dsNew. The call to the `ReadXmlSchema()` method creates a new `DataTable` based on the schema information. In this case it would be a clone of the `products` `DataTable`. Now you can read in the `DiffGram`. The `DiffGram` does not contain schema information, so it is important that the `DataTable` be created and ready before you call the `ReadXml()` method.

Here is a sample of what the `DiffGram` (diffgram.xml) looks like:

```
?xml version="1.0" standalone="yes"?>
<diffgr:diffgram xmlns:msdata="urn:schemas-microsoft-com:xml-msdata"
                 xmlns:diffgr="urn:schemas-microsoft-com:xml-diffgram-v1">
  <XMLAuthors>
    <Authors diffgr:id="Authors1" msdata:rowOrder="0" diffgr:hasChanges="modified">
      <au_id>172-32-1176</au_id>
      <au_lname>NewName</au_lname>
      <au_fname>Johnson</au_fname>
      <phone>408 496-7223</phone>
      <address>10932 Bigge Rd.</address>
      <city>Menlo Park</city>
      <state>CA</state>
      <zip>94025</zip>
      <contract>true</contract>
    </Authors>
    <Authors diffgr:id="Authors2" msdata:rowOrder="1">
      <au_id>213-46-8915</au_id>
      <au_lname>Green</au_lname>
      <au_fname>Marjorie</au_fname>
      <phone>415 986-7020</phone>
      <address>309 63rd St. #411</address>
      <city>Oakland</city>
      <state>CA</state>
      <zip>94618</zip>
      <contract>true</contract>
    </Authors>
<diffgr:before>
    <Authors diffgr:id="Authors1" msdata:rowOrder="0">
      <au_id>172-32-1176</au_id>
      <au_lname>White</au_lname>
      <au_fname>Johnson</au_fname>
      <phone>408 496-7223</phone>
      <address>10932 Bigge Rd.</address>
      <city>Menlo Park</city>
      <state>CA</state>
      <zip>94025</zip>
      <contract>true</contract>
    </Authors>
  </diffgr:before>
</diffgr:diffgram>
```

# Manipulating XML

Note that each `DataTable` row is repeated and that there is a `diffgr:id` attribute for each `<Authors>` element (only the first and last of the `<Authors>` elements is shown in order to save space). `diffgr` is the namespace prefix for `urn:schemas-microsoft-com:xml-diffgram-v1`. For rows that were modified or inserted, ADO.NET adds a `diffgr:hasChanges` attribute. There'salso a `<diffgr:before>` element after the `<XMLAuthors>` element, which contains an `<Authors>` element indicating the previous contents of any modified rows. Obviously the inserted row didn't have any previous contents, so this doesn't have an element in `<diffgr:before>`.

After the `DiffGram` has been read into the `DataTable`, it is in the state that it would be in after changes were made to the data but before `AcceptChanges()` is called. At this point, you can actually roll back changes by calling the `RejectChanges()` method. By looking at the `DataRow.Item` property and passing in either `DataRowVersion.Original` or `DataRowVersion.Current`, you can see the before and after values in the `DataTable`.

If you keep a series of `DiffGrams`, it is important that you are able to reapply them in the proper order. You probably would not want to try to roll back changes for more than a couple of iterations. You could, however, use the `DiffGrams` as a form of logging or for auditing purposes if the DBMS that is being used does not offer these facilities.

## Serializing Objects in XML

Serializing is the process of persisting an object to disk. Another part of your application, or even a separate application, can deserialize the object and it will be in the same state it was in prior to serialization. The .NET Framework includes a couple of ways to do this.

This section looks at the `System.Xml.Serialization` namespace, which contains classes used to serialize objects into XML documents or streams. This means that an object's public properties and public fields are converted into XML elements or attributes or both.

The most important class in the `System.Xml.Serialization` namespace is `XmlSerializer`. To serialize an object, you first need to instantiate an `XmlSerializer` object, specifying the type of the object to serialize. Then you need to instantiate a stream/writer object to write the file to a stream/document. The final step is to call the `Serialize()` method on the `XMLSerializer`, passing it the stream/writer object and the object to serialize.

Data that can be serialized can be primitive types, fields, arrays, and embedded XML in the form of `XmlElement` and `XmlAttribute` objects.

To deserialize an object from an XML document, you reverse the process in the previous example. You create a stream/reader and an `XmlSerializer` object and then pass the stream/reader to the `Deserialize()` method. This method returns the deserialized object, although it needs to be cast to the correct type.

> The XML serializer cannot convert private data, only public data, and it cannot serialize object graphs.

However, these should not be serious limitations; by carefully designing your classes, they should be easily avoided. If you do need to be able to serialize public and private data as well as an object graph containing many nested objects, you will want to use the `System.Runtime.Serialization.Formatters.Binary` namespace.

Some of the other tasks that you can accomplish with `System.Xml.Serialization` classes are

- Determine if the data should be an attribute or element
- Specify the namespace
- Change the attribute or element name

The links between your object and the XML document are the custom C# attributes that annotate your classes. These attributes are what are used to inform the serializer how to write out the data. The xsd.exe tool, which is included with the .NET Framework, can help create these attributes for you. xsd.exe can do the following:

- Generate an XML schema from an XDR schema file
- Generate an XML schema from an XML file
- Generate `DataSet` classes from an XSD schema file
- Generate runtime classes that have the custom attributes for `XmlSerialization`
- Generate an XSD file from classes that you have already developed
- Limit which elements are created in code
- Determine which programming language the generated code should be in (C#, Visual Basic .NET, or JScript .NET)
- Create schemas from types in compiled assemblies

You should refer to the framework documentation for details of command-line options for xsd.exe.

Despite these capabilities, you don't *have* to use xsd.exe to create the classes for serialization. The process is quite simple. The following is a simple application that serializes a class. At the beginning of the example you have very simple code that creates a new `Product` object, pd, and fills it with some data:

```
private void button1_Click(object sender, EventArgs e)
{
    //new products object
    Product pd = new Product();
    //set some properties
    pd.ProductID = 200;
    pd.CategoryID = 100;
    pd.Discontinued = false;
    pd.ProductName = "Serialize Objects";
    pd.QuantityPerUnit = "6";
    pd.ReorderLevel = 1;
    pd.SupplierID = 1;
    pd.UnitPrice = 1000;
```

```
      pd.UnitsInStock = 10;
      pd.UnitsOnOrder = 0;

}
```

The `Serialize()` method of the `XmlSerializer` class actually performs the serialization, and it has nine overloads. One of the parameters required is a stream to write the data to. It can be a `Stream`, `TextWriter`, or an `XmlWriter` parameter. In the example, you create a `TextWriter`-based object, `tr`. The next thing to do is to create the `XmlSerializer`-based object, `sr`. The `XmlSerializer` needs to know type information for the object that it is serializing, so you use the `typeof` keyword with the type that is to be serialized. After the `sr` object is created, you call the `Serialize()` method, passing in the `tr` (`Stream`-based object) and the object that you want serialized, in this case `pd`. Be sure to close the stream when you are finished with it:

```
//new TextWriter and XmlSerializer
TextWriter tr = new StreamWriter("serialprod.xml");
XmlSerializer sr = new XmlSerializer(typeof(Product));
//serialize object
sr.Serialize(tr, pd);
tr.Close();
webBrowser1.Navigate(AppDomain.CurrentDomain.BaseDirectory + "//serialprod.xml");
```

Next is the `Products` class, the class to be serialized. The only differences between this and any other class that you may write are the C# attributes that have been added. The `XmlRootAttribute` and `XmlElementAttribute` classes in the attributes inherit from the `System.Attribute` class. Don't confuse these attributes with the attributes in an XML document. A C# attribute is simply some declarative information that can be retrieved at runtime by the CLR (see Chapter 6, "Delegates and Events," for more details). In this case, the attributes describe how the object should be serialized:

```
//class that will be serialized.
//attributes determine how object is serialized
[System.Xml.Serialization.XmlRootAttribute()]
  public class Product {
    private int prodId;
    private string prodName;
    private int suppId;
    private int catId;
    private string qtyPerUnit;
    private Decimal unitPrice;
    private short unitsInStock;
    private short unitsOnOrder;
    private short reorderLvl;
    private bool discont;
    private int disc;

    //added the Discount attribute
    [XmlAttributeAttribute(AttributeName="Discount")]
    public int Discount {
      get {return disc;}
      set {disc=value;}
    }

    [XmlElementAttribute()]
```

```csharp
      public int  ProductID {
        get {return prodId;}
        set {prodId=value;}
      }
      [XmlElementAttribute()]
      public string ProductName {
        get {return prodName;}
        set {prodName=value;}
      }
      [XmlElementAttribute()]
      public int SupplierID {
        get {return suppId;}
        set {suppId=value;}
      }

      [XmlElementAttribute()]
      public int CategoryID {
        get {return catId;}
        set {catId=value;}
      }

      [XmlElementAttribute()]
      public string QuantityPerUnit {
        get {return qtyPerUnit;}
        set {qtyPerUnit=value;}
      }

      [XmlElementAttribute()]
      public Decimal UnitPrice {
        get {return unitPrice;}
        set {unitPrice=value;}
      }

      [XmlElementAttribute()]
      public short UnitsInStock {
        get {return unitsInStock;}
        set {unitsInStock=value;}
      }

      [XmlElementAttribute()]
      public short UnitsOnOrder {
        get {return unitsOnOrder;}
        set {unitsOnOrder=value;}
      }

      [XmlElementAttribute()]
      public short ReorderLevel {
        get {return reorderLvl;}
        set {reorderLvl=value;}
      }

      [XmlElementAttribute()]
      public bool Discontinued {
        get {return discont;}
```

## Manipulating XML

```
        set {discont=value;}
      }
  }
```

The `XmlRootAttribute()` invocation in the attribute above the `Products` class definition identifies this class as a root element (in the XML file produced upon serialization). The attribute containing `XmlElementAttribute()` identifies that the member below the attribute represents an XML element.

If you take a look at the XML document created during serialization, you will see that it looks like any other XML document that you might have created, which is the point of the exercise. Here's the document:

```
<?xml version="1.0" encoding="utf-8"?>
<Products xmlns:xsi=http://www.w3.org/2001/XMLSchema-instance
                    xmlns:xsd="http://www.w3.org/2001/XMLSchema" Discount="0">
  <ProductID>200</ProductID>
  <ProductName>Serialize Objects</ProductName>
  <SupplierID>1</SupplierID>
  <CategoryID>100</CategoryID>
  <QuantityPerUnit>6</QuantityPerUnit>
  <UnitPrice>1000</UnitPrice>
  <UnitsInStock>10</UnitsInStock>
  <UnitsOnOrder>0</UnitsOnOrder>
  <ReorderLevel>1</ReorderLevel>
  <Discontinued>false</Discontinued>
</Products>
```

There is nothing out of the ordinary here. You could use this any way that you would use an XML document. You could transform it and display it as HTML, load into a `DataSet` using ADO.NET, load an `XmlDocument` with it, or, as you can see in the example, deserialize it and create an object in the same state that pd was in prior to serializing it (which is exactly what you're doing with the second button).

Next, you add another button event handler to deserialize a new `Products`-based object, `newPd`. This time you use a `FileStream` object to read in the XML:

```
private void button2_Click(object sender, EventArgs e)
    {
        //create a reference to producst type
        Product newPd;
        //new filestream to open serialized object
        FileStream f = new FileStream("serialprod.xml", FileMode.Open);
```

Once again, you create a new `XmlSerializer`, passing in the type information of `Product`. You can then make the call to the `Deserialize()` method. Note that you still need to do an explicit cast when you create the `newPd` object. At this point `newPd` is in exactly the same state as pd was:

```
    //new serializer
        XmlSerializer newSr = new XmlSerializer(typeof(Product));
        //deserialize the object
        newPd = (Product)newSr.Deserialize(f);
        f.Close();
    }
```

What about situations where you have derived classes and possibly properties that return an array? `XmlSerializer` has that covered as well. Here's a slightly more complex example that deals with these issues.

First you define three new classes, `Product`, `BookProduct` (derived from `Product`), and `Inventory` (which contains both of the other classes):

```csharp
public class BookProduct : Product
{
    private string isbnNum;
    public BookProduct() {}
    public string ISBN
    {
        get {return isbnNum;}
        set {isbnNum=value;}
    }
}
public class Inventory
{
    private Product[] stuff;
    public Inventory() {}
    //need to have an attribute entry for each data type
    [XmlArrayItem("Prod",typeof(Product)),
    XmlArrayItem("Book",typeof(BookProduct))]
    public Product[] InventoryItems
    {
        get {return stuff;}
        set {stuff=value;}
    }
}
```

The `Inventory` class is the one of interest here. If you are to serialize this class, you need to insert an attribute containing `XmlArrayItem` constructors for each type that can be added to the array. You should note that `XmlArrayItem` is the name of the .NET attribute represented by the `XmlArrayItemAttribute` class.

The first parameter supplied to these constructors is what you would like the element name to be in the XML document that is created during serialization. If you leave off the `ElementName` parameter, the elements will be given the same name as the object type (`Product` and `BookProduct` in this case). The second parameter that must be specified is the type of the object.

There is also an `XmlArrayAttribute` class that you would use if the property were returning an array of objects or primitive types. Because you are returning different types in the array, you use `XmlArrayItemAttribute`, which allows the higher level of control.

In the `button4_Click()` event handler, you create a new `Product` object and a new `BookProduct` object (newProd and newBook). You add data to the various properties of each object, and add the objects to a `Product` array. You then create a new `Inventory` object and pass in the array as a parameter. You can then serialize the `Inventory` object to re-create it at a later time:

# Manipulating XML

```csharp
private void button4_Click(object sender, EventArgs e)
{
  //create the XmlAttributes boject
  XmlAttributes attrs = new XmlAttributes();
  //add the types of the objects that will be serialized
  attrs.XmlElements.Add(new XmlElementAttribute("Book", typeof(BookProduct)));
  attrs.XmlElements.Add(new XmlElementAttribute("Product", typeof(Product)));
  XmlAttributeOverrides attrOver = new XmlAttributeOverrides();
  //add to the attributes collection
  attrOver.Add(typeof(Inventory), "InventoryItems", attrs);
  //create the Product and Book objects
  Product newProd = new Product();
  BookProduct newBook = new BookProduct();
  newProd.ProductID = 100;
  newProd.ProductName = "Product Thing";
  newProd.SupplierID = 10;
  newBook.ProductID = 101;
  newBook.ProductName = "How to Use Your New Product Thing";
  newBook.SupplierID = 10;
  newBook.ISBN = "123456789";
  Product[] addProd ={ newProd, newBook };
  Inventory inv = new Inventory();
  inv.InventoryItems = addProd;
  TextWriter tr = new StreamWriter("inventory.xml");
  XmlSerializer sr = new XmlSerializer(typeof(Inventory), attrOver);
  sr.Serialize(tr, inv);
  tr.Close();
  webBrowser1.Navigate(AppDomain.CurrentDomain.BaseDirectory + "//inventory.xml");
}
}
```

This is what the XML document looks like:

```xml
<?xml version="1.0" encoding="utf-8"?>
<Inventory xmlns:xsi="http://www.w3.org/2001/XMLSchema-instance"
xmlns:xsd="http://www.w3.org/2001/XMLSchema">
  <Product Discount="0">
    <ProductID>100</ProductID>
    <ProductName>Product Thing</ProductName>
    <SupplierID>10</SupplierID>
    <CategoryID>0</CategoryID>
    <UnitPrice>0</UnitPrice>
    <UnitsInStock>0</UnitsInStock>
    <UnitsOnOrder>0</UnitsOnOrder>
    <ReorderLevel>0</ReorderLevel>
    <Discontinued>false</Discontinued>
  </Product>
  <Book Discount="0">
    <ProductID>101</ProductID>
    <ProductName>How to Use Your New Product Thing</ProductName>
    <SupplierID>10</SupplierID>
    <CategoryID>0</CategoryID>
    <UnitPrice>0</UnitPrice>
    <UnitsInStock>0</UnitsInStock>
    <UnitsOnOrder>0</UnitsOnOrder>
```

```
            <ReorderLevel>0</ReorderLevel>
            <Discontinued>false</Discontinued>
            <ISBN>123456789</ISBN>
        </Book>
    </Inventory>
```

The `button2_Click()` event handler implements deserialization of the `Inventory` object. Note that you iterate through the array in the newly created `newInv` object to show that it is the same data:

```
private void button2_Click(object sender, System.EventArgs e)
{
    Inventory newInv;
    FileStream f=new FileStream("order.xml",FileMode.Open);
    XmlSerializer newSr=new XmlSerializer(typeof(Inventory));
    newInv=(Inventory)newSr.Deserialize(f);
    foreach(Product prod in newInv.InventoryItems)
        listBox1.Items.Add(prod.ProductName);
    f.Close();
}
```

## Serialization without Source Code Access

Well, this all works great, but what if you don't have access to the source code for the types that are being serialized? You can't add the attribute if you don't have the source. There is another way. You can use the `XmlAttributes` class and the `XmlAttributeOverrides` class. Together these classes enable you to accomplish exactly what you have just done, but without adding the attributes. This section looks at an example of how this works.

For this example, imagine that the `Inventory`, `Product`, and the derived `BookProduct` classes are in a separate DLL, and that you don't have the source. The `Product` and `BookProduct` classes are the same as in the previous example, but you should note that there are now no attributes added to the `Inventory` class:

```
public class Inventory
{
    private Product[] stuff;
    public Inventory() {}
    public Product[] InventoryItems
    {
        get {return stuff;}
        set {stuff=value;}
    }
}
```

Next, you deal with the serialization in the `button1_Click()` event handler:

```
private void button1_Click(object sender, System.EventArgs e)
{
```

The first step in the serialization process is to create an `XmlAttributes` object and an `XmlElementAttribute` object for each data type that you will be overriding:

# Manipulating XML

```
        XmlAttributes attrs=new XmlAttributes();
        attrs.XmlElements.Add(new XmlElementAttribute("Book",typeof(BookProduct)));
        attrs.XmlElements.Add(new XmlElementAttribute("Product",typeof(Product)));
```

Here you can see that you are adding new `XmlElementAttribute` objects to the `XmlElements` collection of the `XmlAttributes` class. The `XmlAttributes` class has properties that correspond to the attributes that can be applied; `XmlArray` and `XmlArrayItems`, which you looked at in the previous example, are just a few of these. You now have an `XmlAttributes` object with two `XmlElementAttribute`-based objects added to the `XmlElements` collection.

The next thing you have to do is create an `XmlAttributeOverrides` object:

```
        XmlAttributeOverrides attrOver=new XmlAttributeOverrides();
        attrOver.Add(typeof(Inventory),"InventoryItems",attrs);
```

The `Add()` method of this class has two overloads. The first one takes the type information of the object to override and the `XmlAttributes` object that you created earlier. The other overload, which is the one you are using, also takes a string value that is the member in the overridden object. In this case, you want to override the `InventoryItems` member in the `Inventory` class.

When you create the `XmlSerializer` object, you add the `XmlAttributeOverrides` object as a parameter. Now the `XmlSerializer` knows which types you want to override and what you need to return for those types:

```
        //create the Product and Book objects
        Product newProd=new Product();
        BookProduct newBook=new BookProduct();
        newProd.ProductID=100;
        newProd.ProductName="Product Thing";
        newProd.SupplierID=10;
        newBook.ProductID=101;
        newBook.ProductName="How to Use Your New Product Thing";
        newBook.SupplierID=10;
        newBook.ISBN="123456789";
        Product[] addProd={newProd,newBook};

        Inventory inv=new Inventory();
        inv.InventoryItems=addProd;
        TextWriter tr=new StreamWriter("inventory.xml");
        XmlSerializer sr=new XmlSerializer(typeof(Inventory),attrOver);
        sr.Serialize(tr,inv);
        tr.Close();
    }
```

If you execute the `Serialize()` method, you get this XML output:

```
<?xml version="1.0" encoding="utf-8"?>
<Inventory xmlns:xsi="http://www.w3.org/2001/XMLSchema-instance"
xmlns:xsd="http://www.w3.org/2001/XMLSchema">
  <Product Discount="0">
    <ProductID>100</ProductID>
    <ProductName>Product Thing</ProductName>
    <SupplierID>10</SupplierID>
```

```xml
        <CategoryID>0</CategoryID>
        <UnitPrice>0</UnitPrice>
        <UnitsInStock>0</UnitsInStock>
        <UnitsOnOrder>0</UnitsOnOrder>
        <ReorderLevel>0</ReorderLevel>
        <Discontinued>false</Discontinued>
    </Product>
    <Book Discount="0">
        <ProductID>101</ProductID>
        <ProductName>How to Use Your New Product Thing</ProductName>
        <SupplierID>10</SupplierID>
        <CategoryID>0</CategoryID>
        <UnitPrice>0</UnitPrice>
        <UnitsInStock>0</UnitsInStock>
        <UnitsOnOrder>0</UnitsOnOrder>
        <ReorderLevel>0</ReorderLevel>
        <Discontinued>false</Discontinued>
        <ISBN>123456789</ISBN>
    </Book>
</Inventory>
```

As you can see, you get the same XML as you did with the earlier example. To deserialize this object and re-create the `Inventory`-based object that you started out with, you need to create all of the same `XmlAttributes`, `XmlElementAttribute`, and `XmlAttributeOverrides` objects that you created when you serialized the object. Once you do that, you can read in the XML and re-create the `Inventory` object just as you did before. Here is the code to deserialize the `Inventory` object:

```csharp
private void button2_Click(object sender, System.EventArgs e)
{
    //create the new XmlAttributes collection
    XmlAttributes attrs=new XmlAttributes();
    //add the type information to the elements collection
    attrs.XmlElements.Add(new XmlElementAttribute("Book",typeof(BookProduct)));
    attrs.XmlElements.Add(new XmlElementAttribute("Product",typeof(Product)));
    XmlAttributeOverrides attrOver=new XmlAttributeOverrides();
    //add to the Attributes collection
    attrOver.Add(typeof(Inventory),"InventoryItems",attrs);
    //need a new Inventory object to deserialize to
    Inventory newInv;
    //deserialize and load data into the listbox from deserialized object
    FileStream f=new FileStream("..\\..\\..\\inventory.xml",FileMode.Open);
    XmlSerializer newSr=new XmlSerializer(typeof(Inventory),attrOver);
    newInv=(Inventory)newSr.Deserialize(f);
    if(newInv!=null)
    {
        foreach(Product prod in newInv.InventoryItems)
            listBox1.Items.Add(prod.ProductName);
    }
    f.Close();
}
```

Note that the first few lines of code are identical to the code you used to serialize the object.

The `System.Xml.XmlSerialization` namespace provides a very powerful tool set for serializing objects to XML. By serializing and deserializing objects to XML instead of to binary format, you are given the option of doing something else with this XML, greatly adding to the flexibility of your designs.

## Summary

In this chapter, you explored many of the corners of the `System.Xml` namespace of the .NET Framework. You looked at how to read and write XML documents using the very fast `XmlReader`- and `XmlWriter`-based classes. You looked at how the DOM is implemented in .NET, and how to use the power of DOM. You saw that XML and ADO.NET are indeed very closely related. A `DataSet` and an XML document are just two different views of the same underlying architecture. And, of course, you visited XPath and XSL Transforms.

Finally, you serialized objects to XML, and were able to bring them back with just a couple of method calls.

XML will be an important part of your application development for years to come. The .NET Framework has made available a very rich and powerful tool set for working with XML. In Chapter 22, you look at how to handle files and the registry using C# classes.

# 22

# Working with Active Directory

A major (maybe the most important) feature introduced with Windows 2000 is *Active Directory*. Active Directory is a *directory service* that provides a central, hierarchical store for user information, network resources, services, and so on. It is also possible to extend the information in this directory service in order to store custom data that is of interest for the enterprise.

For example, Microsoft Exchange Server 2003 and Microsoft CRM use Active Directory intensively to store public folders and other items.

Before the release of Active Directory, Exchange Server used its own private store for its objects. It was necessary for a system administrator to configure two user IDs for a single person: a user account in the Windows NT domain to enable a logon, and a user in Exchange Directory. This was necessary for the additional information required by users (such as e-mail addresses, phone numbers, and so on), and the user information for the NT domain was not extensible to add the required information. Now the system administrator just has to configure a single user for a person in Active Directory; the information for a `user` object can be extended so that it fits the requirements of Exchange Server. You can also extend this information.

If you require the user information to be extended with a skills list, storing user information in the Active Directory makes this possible. Here it would easily be possible to track down a C# developer by searching for the required C# skill.

This chapter looks at how you can use the .NET Framework to access and manipulate the data in a directory service using classes from the `System.DirectoryServices` namespace.

> *This chapter uses Windows Server 2003 with Active Directory configured. You can also use Windows 2000 Server or other directory services with small modifications to the code presented here.*

# Chapter 22

This chapter covers the following:

- The architecture of Active Directory, including features and basic concepts
- Some of the tools available for administration of Active Directory, and their benefit to programming
- How to read and modify data in Active Directory
- Searching for objects in Active Directory
- Accessing a DSML Web service to search for objects

After discussing the architecture and how to program Active Directory, you create a Windows application where you can specify properties and a filter to search for `user` objects. Similar to other chapters, you can also download the code for the examples in this chapter from the Wrox Web site at www.wrox.com.

# The Architecture of Active Directory

Before starting to program Active Directory, you have to know how it works, what it is used for, and what data can be stored there.

## Features

The features of Active Directory can be summarized as follows:

- The data in Active Directory is grouped *hierarchically*. Objects can be stored inside other container objects. Instead of having a single, large list of users, users can be grouped inside organizational units. An organizational unit can contain other organizational units, so you can build a tree.

- Active Directory uses a *multimaster replication*. With the Active Directory every *domain controller* (DC) is a master. With multiple masters, updates can be applied to any DC. This model is much more scalable compared to a single-master model, because updates can be made to different servers concurrently. The disadvantage of this model is a more complex replication. Replication issues are discussed later in this chapter.

- The *replication topology* is flexible, to support replications across slow links in WANs. How often data should be replicated is configurable by the domain administrators.

- Active Directory supports *open standards*. The *Lightweight Directory Access Protocol* (LDAP) is one of the standards that can be used to access the data in Active Directory. LDAP is an Internet standard that can be used to access a lot of different directory services. With LDAP a programming interface, LDAP API, is also defined. The LDAP API can be used to access the Active Directory with the C language. Microsoft's preferred programming interface to directory services is the *Active Directory Service Interface* (ADSI). This, of course, is not an open standard. In contrast to the LDAP API, ADSI makes it possible to access all features of Active Directory. Another standard used within Active Directory is *Kerberos*, which is used for authentication. The Windows 2000 Kerberos service can also be used to authenticate Unix clients.

- With Active Directory, a fine-grained security is available. Every object stored in Active Directory can have an associated access-control list that defines who can do what with that object.

# Working with Active Directory

The objects in the directory are *strongly typed*, which means that the type of an object is exactly defined; no attributes that are not specified may be added to an object. In the *schema*, the object types as well as the parts of an object (attributes) are defined. Attributes can be mandatory or optional.

## Active Directory Concepts

Before programming Active Directory, you need to know some basic terms and definitions.

### Objects

Active Directory stores objects. An object refers to something concrete such as a user, a printer, or a network share. Objects have mandatory and optional attributes that describe them. Some examples of the attributes of a `user` object are the first name, last name, e-mail address, phone number, and so on.

Figure 22-1 shows a container object called `Wrox Press` that contains some other objects; two user objects, a contact object, a printer object, and a user group object.

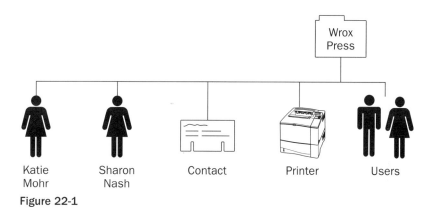

Figure 22-1

### Schema

Every object is an instance of a class defined in the *schema*. The schema *defines the types* and is itself stored in objects in Active Directory. You have to differentiate between `classSchema` and `attributeSchema`. The types of objects are defined in `classSchema`, as well as detailing what mandatory and optional attributes an object has. `attributeSchema` defines what an attribute looks like and what the allowed syntax for a specific attribute is.

You can define custom types and attributes and add these to the schema. Be aware, however, that a new schema type cannot be removed from Active Directory. You can mark it as inactive so that new objects cannot be created anymore, but there can be existing objects of that type, so it's not possible to remove classes or attributes defined in the schema.

The user group Administrator doesn't have enough rights to create new schema entries; the group Enterprise Admins is needed here.

## Configuration

In addition to objects and class definitions stored as objects, the configuration of Active Directory itself is stored in Active Directory. The configuration of Active Directory stores the information about all sites, such as the replication interval, that is set up by the system administrator. Because the configuration itself is stored in Active Directory, you can access the configuration information like all other objects in Active Directory.

## The Active Directory domain

A domain is a security boundary of a Windows network. In the Active Directory domain, the objects are stored in a hierarchical order. Active Directory itself is made up of one or more domains. Figure 22-2 shows the hierarchical order of objects in a domain; the domain is represented by a triangle. Container objects such as Users, Computers, and Books can store other objects. Each oval in the picture represents an object, with the lines between the objects representing parent-child relationships. For example, Books is the parent of .NET and Java, and Pro C#, Beg C#, and ASP.NET are child objects of the .NET object.

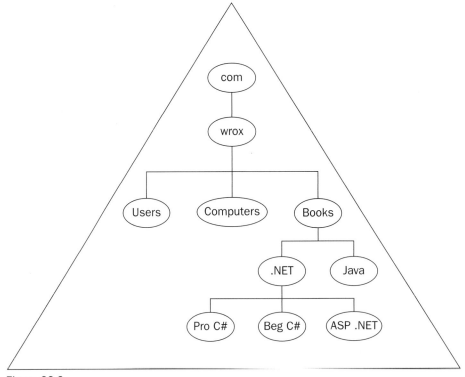

Figure 22-2

## Domain controller

A single domain can have multiple domain controllers, each of which stores all of the objects in the domain. There is no master server, and all DCs are treated equally; you have a multimaster model. The objects are replicated across the servers inside the domain.

# Working with Active Directory

### Site

A *site* is a location in the network that holds at least one DC. If you have multiple locations in the enterprise, which are connected with slow network links, you can use multiple sites for a single domain. For backup or scalability reasons, each site can have one or more DCs running. Replication between servers in a site can happen at shorter intervals due to the faster network connection. Replication is configured to occur at larger time intervals between servers across sites, depending on the speed of the network. Of course, replication intervals can be configured by the domain administrator.

### Domain tree

Multiple domains can be connected by trust relationships. These domains share a *common schema*, a *common configuration*, and a *global catalog* (more on global catalogs shortly). A common schema and a common configuration imply that this data is replicated across domains. Domain trees share the same class and attribute schema. The objects themselves are not replicated across domains.

Domains connected in such a way form a domain tree. Domains in a domain tree have a *contiguous, hierarchical namespace*. This means that the domain name of the child domain is the name of that child domain appended to the name of the parent domain. Between domains, trusts using the Kerberos protocol are established.

For example, you have the root domain `wrox.com`, which is the *parent domain* of the *child domains* `india.wrox.com` and `uk.wrox.com`. A trust is set up between the parent and the child domains, so that accounts from one domain can be authenticated by another domain.

### Forest

Multiple domain trees that are connected by using a common schema, a common configuration, and a global catalog without a contiguous namespace are called a *forest*. A forest is a set of domain trees; it can be used if the company has a subcompany where a different domain name should be used. Here's one example: `wrox.com` should be relatively independent of the domain `wiley.com`, but it should be possible to have a common management, and be possible for users from `wrox.com` to access resources from the `wiley.com` domain and vice versa. With a forest you can have trusts between multiple domain trees.

### Global catalog

A search for an object can span multiple domains. If you look for a specific `user` object with some attributes, you have to search every domain. Starting with `wrox.com`, the search continues to `uk.wrox.com` and `india.wrox.com`; across slow links such a search could take a while.

To make searches faster, all objects are copied to the *global catalog* (GC). The GC is replicated in every domain of a forest. There's at least one server in every domain holding a GC. For performance and scalability reasons, you can have more than one GC server in a domain. Using a GC, a search through all the objects can happen on a single server.

The GC is a *read-only cache* of all the objects that can only be used for searches; the domain controllers must be used to do updates.

Not all attributes of an object are stored in the GC. You can define whether or not an attribute should be stored with an object. The decision whether to store an attribute in the GC depends on how the attribute is used. If the attribute is frequently used in searches, putting it into the GC makes the search faster. A picture of a user isn't useful in the GC, because you would never search for a picture. Conversely, a phone number would be a useful addition to the store. You can also define that an attribute should be indexed so that a query for it is faster.

## Replication

As a programmer you are unlikely ever to configure replication, but because it affects the data you store in Active Directory, you have to know how it works. Active Directory uses a *multimaster* server architecture. Updates happen to every domain controller in the domain. The *replication latency* defines how long it takes until an update starts:

- ❏ The configurable *change notification* happens, by default, every 5 minutes inside a site if some attributes change. The DC where a change occurred informs one server after the other with 30-second intervals, so the fourth DC can get the change notification after 7 minutes. The default change notification across sites is set to 180 minutes. Intra- and intersite replication can each be configured to other values.
- ❏ If no changes occurred, the *scheduled replication* occurs every 60 minutes inside a site. This is to ensure that a change notification wasn't missed.
- ❏ For security-sensitive information, such as account lockout, *immediate notification* can occur.

With a replication, only the changes are copied to the DCs. With every change of an attribute a version number (update sequence number or USN) and a time stamp are recorded. These are used to help resolve conflicts if updates happened to the same attribute on different servers.

Here's an example. The mobile phone attribute of the user John Doe has the USN number 47. This value is already replicated to all DCs. One system administrator changes the phone number. The change occurs on the server DC1; the new USN of this attribute on the server DC1 is now 48, whereas the other DCs still have the USN 47. For someone still reading the attribute, the old value can be read until the replication to all domain controllers has occurred.

Now the rare case can happen that another administrator changes the phone number attribute, and here a different DC is selected because this administrator received a faster response from the server DC2. The USN of this attribute on the server DC2 is also changed to 48.

At the notification intervals, notification happens because the USN for the attribute changed, and the last time replication occurred was with a USN value of 47. The replication mechanism now detects that the servers DC1 and DC2 both have a USN of 48 for the phone number attribute. Which server is the winner is not really important, but one server must definitely win. To resolve this conflict the time stamp of the change is used. Because the change happened later on DC2, the value stored in the DC2 domain controller gets replicated.

> **When reading objects, you have to be aware that the data is not necessarily current. The currency of the data depends on replication latencies. When updating objects, another user can still read some old values after the update. It's also possible that different updates can happen at the same time.**

# Working with Active Directory

## Characteristics of Active Directory Data

Active Directory doesn't replace a relational database or the registry, so what kind of data would you store in it?

- With Active Directory you get *hierarchical data*. You can have containers that store further containers and objects, too. Containers themselves are objects as well.

- The data should be used for *read-mostly*. Because of replication occurring at certain time-intervals, you cannot be sure that you will read up-to-date data. You must be aware that in applications the information you read is possibly not the current up-to-date information.

- Data should be of *global interest* to the enterprise; this is because adding a new data type to the schema replicates it to all the servers in the enterprise. For data types of interest only to a small number of users, the domain enterprise administrator normally wouldn't install new schema types.

- The data stored should be of *reasonable size* because of replication issues. For a data size of 100K, it is fine to store it in the directory, if the data changes only once a week. However, if the data changes every hour, then the data of this size is too large. Always think about replicating the data to different servers: where the data gets transferred to and at what intervals. If you have larger data it's possible to put a link into Active Directory and store the data itself in a different place.

To summarize, the data you store in Active Directory should be hierarchically organized, of reasonable size, and of importance to the enterprise.

## Schema

Active Directory objects are strongly typed. The schema defines the types of the objects, mandatory and optional attributes, and the syntax and constraints of these attributes. In the schema it is necessary to differentiate between class-schema and attribute-schema objects. A class is a collection of attributes. With the classes, single inheritance is supported. As you can see in Figure 22-3, the user class derives from the organizationalPerson class, organizationalPerson is a subclass of person, and the base class is top. The classSchema that defines a class describes the attributes with the systemMayContain attribute.

Figure 22-3 shows only a few of all the systemMayContain values. Using the ADSI Edit tool, you can easily see all the values; you look at this tool in the next section. In the root class top you can see that every object can have common name (cn), displayName, objectGUID, whenChanged, and whenCreated attributes. The person class derives from top. A person object also has a userPassword and a telephoneNumber. OrganizationalPerson derives from person. In addition to the attributes of person it has a manager, department, and company; and a user has extra attributes needed to log on to a system.

719

# Chapter 22

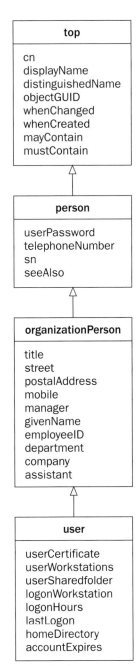

Figure 22-3

# Working with Active Directory

## Administration Tools for Active Directory

Looking into some of the Active Directory administration tools can help to give you an idea of Active Directory, what data is in there, and what can be done programmatically.

The system administrator has a lot of tools to enter new data, update data, and configure Active Directory:

- ❑ The **Active Directory Users and Computers** MMC snap-in is used to enter new users and update user data.

- ❑ The **Active Directory Sites and Services** MMC snap-in is used to configure sites in a domain and replication between these sites.

- ❑ The **Active Directory Domains and Trusts** MMC snap-in can be used to build up a trust relationship between domains in a tree.

- ❑ **ADSI Edit** is the editor of Active Directory, where every object can be viewed and edited.

### *Active Directory Users and Computers*

The Active Directory Users and Computers snap-in is the tool that system administrators use to manage users. Select Start ➪ Programs ➪ Administrative Tools ➪ Active Directory Users and Computers to start this program (see Figure 22-4).

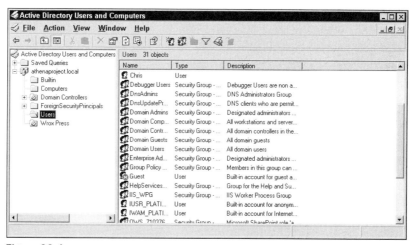

Figure 22-4

With this tool you can add new users, groups, contacts, organizational units, printers, shared folders, or computers, and modify existing ones. Figure 22-5 shows the attributes that can be entered for a user object: office, phone numbers, e-mail addresses, Web pages, organization information, addresses, groups, and so on.

721

# Chapter 22

**Figure 22-5**

Active Directory Users and Computers can also be used in big enterprises with millions of objects. It's not necessary to look through a list with a thousand objects, because you can select a custom filter to display only some of the objects. You can also perform an LDAP query to search for the objects in the enterprise. You explore these possibilities later in this chapter.

## ADSI Edit

ADSI Edit is the editor of Active Directory. This tool is not installed automatically; on the Windows 2000 Server or Windows Server 2003 CD you can find a directory named Supporting Tools. When the supporting tools are installed you can access ADSI Edit by invoking the program `adsiedit.msc`.

ADSI Edit offers greater control than the Active Directory Users and Computers tool (see Figure 22-6); with ADSI Edit everything can be configured, and you can also look at the schema and the configuration. This tool is not very intuitive to use, however, and it is very easy to enter wrong data.

By opening the Properties window of an object, you can view and change every attribute of an object in Active Directory. With this tool you can see mandatory and optional attributes, with their types and values (see Figure 22-7).

## Working with Active Directory

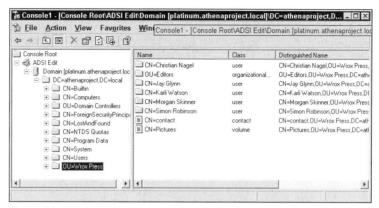

Figure 22-6

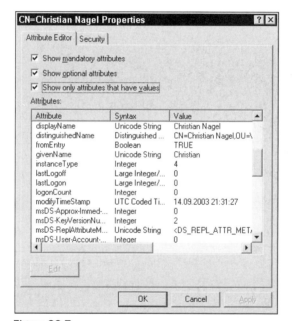

Figure 22-7

## Programming Active Directory

To develop programs for Active Directory, you can either use the classes from the `System.Directory Services` or the `System.DirectoryServices.Protocols` namespaces. In the namespace `System.DirectoryServices` you can find classes that wrap *Active Directory Service Interfaces* (ADSI) COM objects to access the Active Directory.

# Chapter 22

ADSI is a programmatic interface to directory services. It defines some COM interfaces that are implemented by ADSI providers. This means that the client can use different directory services with the same programmatic interfaces. The .NET Framework classes in the System.DirectoryServices namespace make use of ADSI.

Figure 22-8 shows some ADSI Providers (LDAP, WinNT, and NDS) that implement COM interfaces such as IADs and IUnknown. The assembly System.DirectoryServices makes use of the ADSI providers.

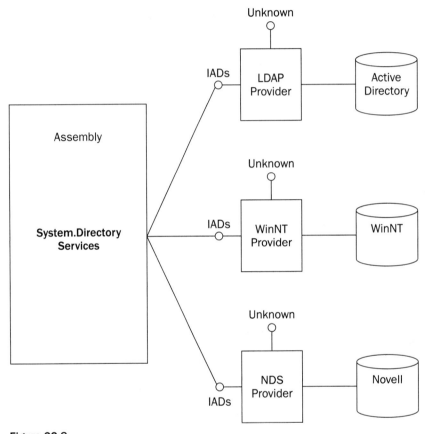

Figure 22-8

Classes from the namespace System.DirectoryServices.Protocols make use of Directory Services Markup Language (DSML) Services for Windows. With DSML, standardized Web service interfaces are defined by the OASIS group (http://www.oasis-open.org/committees/dsml).

To use the classes from the System.DirectoryServices namespace, you have to reference the System.DirectoryServices assembly. With the classes in this assembly you can query objects, view and update properties, search for objects, and move objects to other container objects. In the code segments that follow a little later in this section, you use a simple C# console application that demonstrates the functionality of the classes in the System.DirectoryServices namespace.

# Working with Active Directory

This section covers the following:

- Classes in the `System.DirectoryServices` namespace
- The process of connecting to the Active Directory (binding)
- Getting directory entries and creating new objects and updating existing entries
- Searching Active Directory

## Classes in System.DirectoryServices

The following table shows the major classes in the `System.DirectoryServices` namespace.

| Class | Description |
| --- | --- |
| `DirectoryEntry` | This class is the main class of the `System.DirectoryServices` namespace. An object of this class represents an object in the Active Directory store. This class is used to bind to an object and to view and to update properties. The properties of the object are represented in a `PropertyCollection`. Every item in the `PropertyCollection` has a `PropertyValueCollection`. |
| `DirectoryEntries` | `DirectoryEntries` is a collection of `DirectoryEntry` objects. The `Children` property of a `DirectoryEntry` object returns a list of objects in a `DirectoryEntries` collection. |
| `DirectorySearcher` | This class is the main class used for searching for objects with specific attributes. To define the search the `SortOption` class and the enumerations `SearchScope`, `SortDirection`, and `ReferalChasingOption` can be used. The search results in a `SearchResult` or a `SearchResultCollection`. You also get `ResultPropertyCollection` and `ResultPropertyValueCollection` objects. |

## Binding

To get the values of an object in Active Directory, you have to connect to the Active Directory service. This connecting process is called *binding*. The binding path can look like this:

```
LDAP://dc01.thinktecture.com/OU=Development, DC=Thinktecture, DC=Com
```

With the binding process, you can specify these items:

- The **protocol** specifies the provider to be used
- The **server name** of the domain controller
- The **port number** of the server process
- The **distinguished name** of the object; this identifies the object you want to access

725

❑ The **username and password**, if the user who is allowed to access the Active Directory is different from the current logged-on user

❑ An **authentication** type can also be specified if encryption is needed

The following subsections discuss these options in more detail.

## Protocol

The first part of a binding path specifies the ADSI provider. The provider is implemented as a COM server; for identification a `progID` can be found in the registry directly under `HKEY_CLASSES_ROOT`. The providers that are available with Windows XP are listed in the following table.

| Provider | Description |
| --- | --- |
| LDAP | LDAP Server, such as the Exchange directory and Windows 2000 Server or Windows Server 2003 Active Directory Server. |
| GC | GC is used to access the global catalog in Active Directory. It can be used for fast queries. |
| IIS | With the ADSI provider for IIS it's possible to create new Web sites and to administer them in the IIS catalog. |
| WinNT | To access the user database of old Windows NT 4 domains you can use the ADSI provider for WinNT. The fact that NT 4 users only have a few attributes remains unchanged. It is also possible to use this protocol to bind to a Windows 2000 domain, but here you are also restricted to the attributes available with NT 4. |
| NDS | This progid is used to communicate with Novell Directory Services. |
| NWCOMPAT | With NWCOMPAT you can access old Novell directories, such as Novell Netware 3.x. |

## Server name

The *server name* follows the protocol in the binding path. The server name is optional if you are logged on to an Active Directory domain. Without a server name, *serverless binding* occurs; this means that Windows Server 2003 tries to get the "best" domain controller in the domain that's associated with the user doing the bind. If there's no server inside a site, the first domain controller that can be found will be used.

A serverless binding might look like this: `LDAP://OU=Sales, DC=Thinktecture, DC=Local`.

## Port number

After the server name, you can specify the *port number* of the server process by using the syntax `:xxx`. The default port number for the LDAP server is port 389: `LDAP://dc01.sentinel.net:389`. The Exchange server uses the same port number as the LDAP server. If the Exchange server is installed on the same system — for example, as a domain controller of Active Directory — a different port can be configured.

# Working with Active Directory

## Distinguished name

The fourth part that you can specify in the path is the *distinguished name* (DN). The distinguished name is a unique name that identifies the object you want to access. With Active Directory you can use LDAP syntax that is based on X.500 to specify the name of the object.

This is an example of a distinguished name:

```
CN=Christian Nagel, OU=Consultants, DC=Thinktecture, DC=local
```

This distinguished name specifies the common name (`CN`) of `Christian Nagel` in the organizational unit (`OU`) called `Consultants` in the domain component (`DC`) called `Thinktecture` of the domain `Thinktecture.local`. The part specified to the right is the root object of the domain. The name has to follow the hierarchy in the object tree.

You can find the LDAP specification for the string representation of distinguished names in RFC 2253 at www.ietf.org/rfc/rfc2253.txt.

## Relative distinguished name

A *relative distinguished name* (RDN) is used to reference objects within a container object. With an RDN the specification of `OU` and `DC` is not needed, because a common name is enough. `CN=Christian Nagel` is the relative distinguished name inside the organizational unit. A relative distinguished name can be used if you already have a reference to a container object and if you want to access child objects.

## Default naming context

If a distinguished name is not specified in the path, the binding process will be made to the default naming context. You can read the default naming context with the help of `rootDSE`. LDAP 3.0 defines `rootDSE` as the root of a directory tree on a directory server. For example:

```
LDAP://rootDSE
```

or

```
LDAP://servername/rootDSE
```

By enumerating all properties of the `rootDSE`, you can get the information about the `defaultNamingContext` that will be used when no name is specified. `schemaNamingContext` and `configurationNamingContext` specify the required names to be used to access the schema and the configuration in the Active Directory store.

The following code is used to get all properties of `rootDSE`:

```csharp
using (DirectoryEntry de = new DirectoryEntry())
{
    de.Path = "LDAP://treslunas/rootDSE";
    de.Username = @"explorer\christian";
    de.Password = "password";
```

# Chapter 22

```csharp
        PropertyCollection props = de.Properties;
        foreach (string prop in props.PropertyNames)
        {
            PropertyValueCollection values = props[prop];
            foreach (string val in values)
            {
                Console.Write(prop + ": ");
                Console.WriteLine(val);
            }
        }
    }
}
```

This program shows the default naming context (`defaultNamingContext DC=explorer, DC=local`), the context that can be used to access the schema (`CN=Schema, CN=Configuration, DC=explorer, DC=local`), and the naming context of the configuration (`CN=Configuration, DC=explorer, DC=local`), as shown in Figure 22-9.

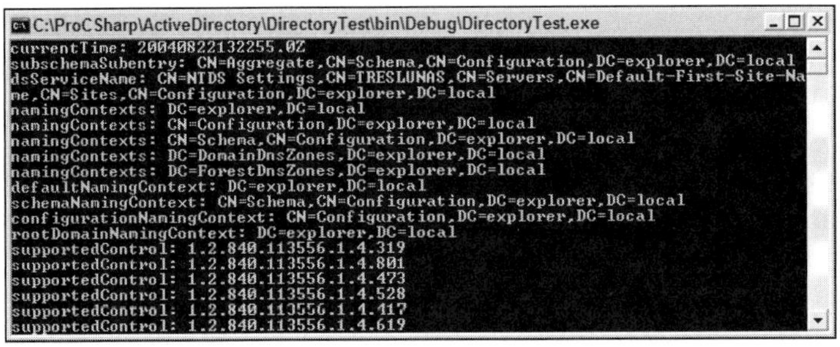

Figure 22-9

## Object identifier

Every object has a *globally unique identifier* (GUID). A GUID is a unique 128-bit number as you may already know from COM development. You can bind to an object using the GUID. This way you always get to the same object, regardless of whether the object was moved to a different container. The GUID is generated at object creation and always remains the same.

You can get to a GUID string representation with `DirectoryEntry.NativeGuid`. This string representation can then be used to bind to the object.

This example shows the path name for a serverless binding to bind to a specific object represented by a GUID:

```
LDAP://<GUID=14abbd652aae1a47abc60782dcfc78ea>
```

## User name

If a different user from the one of the current process must be used for accessing the directory (maybe this user doesn't have the required permissions to access Active Directory), explicit *user credentials* must be specified for the binding process. Active Directory has multiple ways to specify the user name.

# Working with Active Directory

### Downlevel logon

With a downlevel logon the user name can be specified with the pre-Windows 2000 domain name:

    domain\username

### Distinguished name

The user can also be specified by a distinguished name of a `user` object, for example:

    CN=Administrator, CN=Users, DC=thinktecture, DC=local

### User principal name

The *user principal name* (UPN) of an object is defined with the `userPrincipalName` attribute. The system administrator specifies this with the logon information in the Account tab of the User properties with the Active Directory Users and Computers tool. Note that this is not the e-mail address of the user.

This information also uniquely identifies a user and can be used for a logon:

    Nagel@thinktecture.local

## *Authentication*

For secure encrypted authentication, the *authentication* type can also be specified. The authentication can be set with the `AuthenticationType` property of the `DirectoryEntry` class. The value that can be assigned is one of the `AuthenticationTypes` enumeration values. Because the enumeration is marked with the `[Flags]` attribute, multiple values can be specified. Some of the possible values are where the data sent is encrypted; `ReadonlyServer`, where you specify that you need only read access; and `Secure` for secure authentication.

## *Binding with the DirectoryEntry class*

The `System.DirectoryServices.DirectoryEntry` class can be used to specify all the binding information. You can use the default constructor and define the binding information with the properties `Path`, `Username`, `Password`, and `AuthenticationType`, or pass all the information in the constructor:

```
DirectoryEntry de = new DirectoryEntry();
de.Path = "LDAP://platinum/DC=thinktecture, DC=local";
de.Username = "nagel@thinktecture.local";
de.Password = "password";

// use the current user credentials
DirectoryEntry de2 = new DirectoryEntry(
                "LDAP://DC=thinktecture, DC=local");
```

Even if constructing the `DirectoryEntry` object is successful, this doesn't mean that the binding was a success. Binding will happen the first time a property is read to avoid unnecessary network traffic. At the first access of the object, you can see if the object exists and if the specified user credentials are correct.

# Chapter 22

## Getting Directory Entries

Now that you know how to specify the binding attributes to an object in Active Directory, you can move on to read the attributes of an object. In the following example, you read the properties of user objects.

The `DirectoryEntry` class has some properties to get information about the object: the `Name`, `Guid`, and `SchemaClassName` properties. The first time a property of the `DirectoryEntry` object is accessed, the binding occurs and the cache of the underlying ADSI object is filled. (This is discussed in more detail shortly.) Additional properties are read from the cache, and communication with the server isn't necessary for data from the same object.

In the following example, the `user` object with the common name `Christian Nagel` in the organizational unit `Wrox Press` is accessed:

```
using (DirectoryEntry de = new DirectoryEntry())
{
    de.Path = "LDAP://treslunas/CN=Christian Nagel, " +
              "OU=Thinktecture, DC=explorer, DC=local";

    Console.WriteLine("Name: " + de.Name);
    Console.WriteLine("GUID: " + de.Guid);
    Console.WriteLine("Type: " + de.SchemaClassName);
    Console.WriteLine();

    //...
}
```

*To have this code running on your machine, you must change the path to the object to access including the server name.*

An Active Directory object holds much more information, with the information available depending on the type of the object; the `Properties` property returns a `PropertyCollection`. Each property is a collection itself, because a single property can have multiple values; for example, the `user` object can have multiple phone numbers. In this case, you go through the values with an inner `foreach` loop. The collection returned from `properties[name]` is an `object` array. The attribute values can be strings, numbers, or other types. Here, just the `ToString()` method is used to display the values.

```
Console.WriteLine("Properties: ");
PropertyCollection properties = de.Properties;
foreach (string name in properties.PropertyNames)
{
    foreach (object o in properties[name])
    {
        Console.WriteLine(name + ": " + o.ToString());
    }
}
```

In the resulting output, you can see all attributes of the `user` object `Christian Nagel` (see Figure 22-10). `otherTelephone` is a multivalue property that has many phone numbers. Some of the property values just display the type of the object, `System.__ComObject`; for example `lastLogoff`, `lastLogon`, and `nTSecurityDescriptor`. To get the values of these attributes, you have to use the ADSI COM interfaces directly from the classes in the `System.DirectoryServices` namespace.

# Working with Active Directory

Chapter 33, "COM Interoperability," explains how to work with COM objects and interfaces.

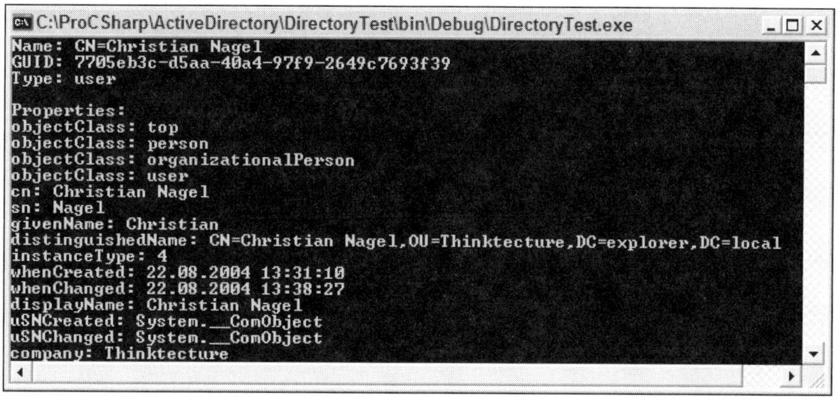

```
C:\ProCSharp\ActiveDirectory\DirectoryTest\bin\Debug\DirectoryTest.exe
Name: CN=Christian Nagel
GUID: 7705eb3c-d5aa-40a4-97f9-2649c7693f39
Type: user

Properties:
objectClass: top
objectClass: person
objectClass: organizationalPerson
objectClass: user
cn: Christian Nagel
sn: Nagel
givenName: Christian
distinguishedName: CN=Christian Nagel,OU=Thinktecture,DC=explorer,DC=local
instanceType: 4
whenCreated: 22.08.2004 13:31:10
whenChanged: 22.08.2004 13:38:27
displayName: Christian Nagel
uSNCreated: System.__ComObject
uSNChanged: System.__ComObject
company: Thinktecture
```

Figure 22-10

### Access a property directly by name

With `DirectoryEntry.Properties` you can access all properties. If a property name is known, you can access the values directly:

```
foreach (string homePage in de.Properties["wWWHomePage"])
    Console.WriteLine("Home page: " + homePage);
```

## *Object Collections*

Objects are stored hierarchically in the Active Directory. Container objects contain children. You can enumerate these child objects with the `Children` property of the class `DirectoryEntry`. In the other direction, you can get the container of an object with the `Parent` property.

A `user` object doesn't have children, so you use an organizational unit in the following example (see Figure 22-11). Non-container objects return an empty collection with the `Children` property. Get all `user` objects from the organizational unit `Wrox Press` in the domain `thinktecture.local`. The `Children` property returns a `DirectoryEntries` collection that collects `DirectoryEntry` objects. You iterate through all `DirectoryEntry` objects to display the name of the child objects:

```
using (DirectoryEntry de = new DirectoryEntry())
{
    de.Path = "LDAP://platinum/OU=Thinktecture, " +
              "DC=explorer, DC=local";

    Console.WriteLine("Children of " + de.Name);
    foreach (DirectoryEntry obj in de.Children)
    {
        Console.WriteLine(obj.Name);
    }
}
```

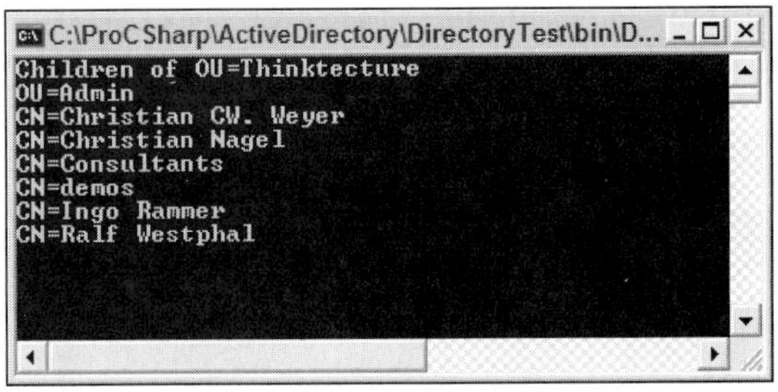

# Chapter 22

**Figure 22-11**

In this example you see all the objects in the organizational unit: users, contacts, printers, shares, and others. If you want to display only some object types, you can use the SchemaFilter property of the DirectoryEntries class. The SchemaFilter property returns a SchemaNameCollection. With this SchemaNameCollection you can use the Add() method to define the object types you want to see. Here you are just interested in seeing the user objects, so user is added to this collection:

```
using (DirectoryEntry de = new DirectoryEntry())
{
    de.Path = "LDAP://treslunas/OU=Thinktecture, " +
              "DC=explorer, DC=local";

    Console.WriteLine("Children of " + de.Name);
    de.Children.SchemaFilter.Add("user");
    foreach (DirectoryEntry obj in de.Children)
    {
        Console.WriteLine(obj.Name);
    }
}
```

As a result you see only the user objects in the organizational unit in Figure 22-12.

**Figure 22-12**

## Cache

To reduce the network transfers, ADSI uses a cache for the object properties. As mentioned earlier, the server isn't accessed when a DirectoryEntry object is created; instead with the first reading of a value from the directory store all the properties are written into the cache, so that a round trip to the server isn't necessary when the next property is accessed.

# Working with Active Directory

Writing any changes to objects changes only the cached object; setting properties doesn't generate network traffic. You must use `DirectoryEntry.CommitChanges()` to flush the cache and to transfer any changed data to the server. To get the newly written data from the directory store, you can use `DirectoryEntry.RefreshCache()` to read the properties. Of course, if you change some properties without calling `CommitChanges()` and do a `RefreshCache()`, all your changes will be lost, because you read the values from the directory service again using `RefreshCache()`.

It is possible to turn off this property cache by setting the `DirectoryEntry.UsePropertyCache` property to `false`. However, unless you are debugging your code, it's better not to turn off the cache because of the extra round trips to the server that will be generated.

## Creating New Objects

When you want to create new Active Directory objects — such as users, computers, printers, contacts, and so on — you can do this programmatically with the `DirectoryEntries` class.

To add new objects to the directory, first you have to bind to a container object, such as an organizational unit, where new objects can be inserted — you cannot use objects that are not able to contain other objects. The following example uses the container object with the distinguished name CN=Users, DC=thinktecture, DC=local:

```
DirectoryEntry de = new DirectoryEntry();
de.Path = "LDAP://treslunas/CN=Users, DC=explorer, DC=local";
```

You can get to the `DirectoryEntries` object with the `Children` property of a `DirectoryEntry`:

```
DirectoryEntries users = de.Children;
```

The class `DirectoryEntries` offers methods to add, remove, and find objects in the collection. Here a new user object is created. With the `Add()` method, the name of the object and a type name are required. You can get to the type names directly using ADSI Edit.

```
DirectoryEntry user = users.Add("CN=John Doe", "user");
```

The object now has the default property values. To assign specific property values, you can add properties with the `Add()` method of the `Properties` property. Of course, all of the properties must exist in the schema for the `user` object. If a specified property doesn't exist, you'll get a `COMException`: "The specified directory service attribute or value doesn't exist":

```
user.Properties["company"].Add("Some Company");
user.Properties["department"].Add("Sales");
user.Properties["employeeID"].Add("4711");
user.Properties["samAccountName"].Add("JDoe");
user.Properties["userPrincipalName"].Add("JDoe@explorer.local");
user.Properties["givenName"].Add("John");
user.Properties["sn"].Add("Doe");
user.Properties["userPassword"].Add("someSecret");
```

Finally, to write the data to Active Directory, you have to flush the cache:

```
user.CommitChanges();
```

# Chapter 22

## Updating Directory Entries

Objects in the Active Directory service can be updated as easily as they can be read. After reading the object, you can change the values. To remove all values of a single property, you can call the method `PropertyValueCollection.Clear()`. You can add new values to a property with `Add()`. `Remove()` and `RemoveAt()` remove specific values from a property collection.

You can change a value simply by setting it to the specified value. The following example uses an indexer for `PropertyValueCollection` to set the mobile phone number to a new value. With the indexer a value can only be changed if it exists. Therefore, you should always check with `DirectoryEntry.Properties.Contains()` to see if the attribute is available:

```
using (DirectoryEntry de = new DirectoryEntry())
{
    de.Path = "LDAP://treslunas/CN=Christian Nagel, " +
              "OU=Thinktecture, DC=explorer, DC=local";

    if (de.Properties.Contains("mobile"))
    {
        de.Properties["mobile"][0] = "+43(664)3434343434";
    }
    else
    {
        de.Properties["mobile"].Add("+43(664)3434343434");
    }

    de.CommitChanges();
}
```

The `else` part in this example uses the method `PropertyValueCollection.Add()` to add a new property for the mobile phone number, if it doesn't exist already. If you use the `Add()` method with already existing properties, the resulting effect would depend on the type of the property (single-value or multi-value property). Using the `Add()` method with a single-value property that already exists results in a `COMException`: "A constraint violation occurred." Using `Add()` with a multivalue property, however, succeeds, and an additional value is added to the property.

The `mobile` property for a `user` object is defined as a single-value property, so additional mobile phone numbers cannot be added. However, a user can have more than one mobile phone number. For multiple mobile phone numbers, the `otherMobile` property is available. `otherMobile` is a multivalue property that allows setting multiple phone numbers, and so calling `Add()` multiple times is allowed. Note that multivalue properties are checked for uniqueness. In case the second phone number is added to the same user object again, you get a `COMException`: "The specified directory service attribute or value already exists."

> Remember to call `DirectoryEntry.CommitChanges()` after creating or updating new directory objects. Otherwise, only the cache gets updated, and the changes are not sent to the directory service.

# Working with Active Directory

## Accessing Native ADSI Objects

Often, it is a lot easier to call methods of predefined ADSI interfaces instead of searching for the names of object properties. Some ADSI objects also support methods that cannot be used directly from the `DirectoryEntry` class. One example of a practical use is the `IADsServiceOperations` interface that has methods to start and stop Windows services. (For more details on Windows services see Chapter 36, "Windows Services.")

The classes of the `System.DirectoryServices` namespace use the underlying ADSI COM objects as mentioned earlier. The `DirectoryEntry` class supports calling methods of the underlying objects directly by using the `Invoke()` method.

The first parameter of `Invoke()` requires the method name that should be called in the ADSI object; the `params` keyword of the second parameter allows a flexible number of additional arguments that can be passed to the ADSI method:

```
public object Invoke(string methodName, params object[] args);
```

You can find the methods that can be called with the `Invoke()` method in the ADSI documentation. Every object in the domain supports the methods of the `IADs` interface. The `user` object that you created previously also supports the methods of the `IADsUser` interface.

In the following example, the method `IADsUser.SetPassword()` changes the password of the previously created `user` object:

```
using (DirectoryEntry de = new DirectoryEntry())
{
   de.Path = "LDAP://treslunas/CN=John Doe, " +
             "CN=Users, DC=explorer, DC=local";

   de.Invoke("SetPassword", "anotherSecret");
   de.CommitChanges();
}
```

It is also possible to use the underlying ADSI object directly instead of using `Invoke()`. To use these objects choose Project ⇨ Add Reference to add a reference to the Active DS Type Library (see Figure 22-13). This creates a wrapper class where you can access these objects in the namespace `ActiveDs`.

The native object can be accessed with the `NativeObject` property of the `DirectoryEntry` class. In the following example, the object `de` is a `user` object, so it can be cast to `ActiveDs.IADsUser`. `SetPassword()` is a method documented in the `IADsUser` interface, so you can call it directly instead of using the `Invoke()` method. By setting the `AccountDisabled` property of `IADsUser` to `false`, you can enable the account. As in the previous examples, the changes are written to the directory service by calling `CommitChanges()` with the `DirectoryEntry` object:

```
ActiveDs.IADsUser user = (ActiveDs.IADsUser)de.NativeObject;
user.SetPassword("someSecret");
user.AccountDisabled = false;
de.CommitChanges();
```

# Chapter 22

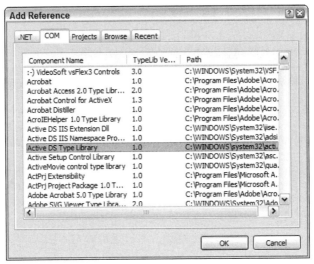

Figure 22-13

## Searching in Active Directory

Because Active Directory is a data store optimized for *read-mostly* access, you will generally search for values. To search in Active Directory, the .NET Framework provides the `DirectorySearcher` class.

> *You can only use* `DirectorySearcher` *with the LDAP provider; it doesn't work with the other providers such as NDS or IIS.*

In the constructor of the `DirectorySearcher` class, you can define four important parts for the search. You can also use a default constructor and define the search options with properties.

### SearchRoot

The search root specifies where the search should start. The default of `SearchRoot` is the root of the domain you're currently using. `SearchRoot` is specified with the `Path` of a `DirectoryEntry` object.

### Filter

The filter defines the values where you want to get hits. The filter is a string that must be enclosed in parentheses.

Relational operators such as <=, =, and >= are allowed in expressions. (objectClass=contact) searches all objects of type contact; (lastName>=Nagel) searches all objects alphabetically where the lastName property is equal to or larger than Nagel.

Expressions can be combined with the & and | prefix operators. For example, (&(objectClass=user) (description=Auth*)) searches all objects of type user where the property description starts with the string Auth. Because the & and | operators are at the beginning of the expressions, it's possible to combine more than two expressions with a single prefix operator.

# Working with Active Directory

The default filter is (objectClass=*) so all objects are valid.

*The filter syntax is defined in RFC 2254, "The String Representation of LDAP Search Filters." You can find this RFC at* http://www.ietf.org/rfc/rfc2254.txt.

## PropertiesToLoad

With PropertiesToLoad you can define a StringCollection of all the properties that you are interested in. Objects can have a lot of properties, most of which will not be important for your search request. You define the properties that should be loaded into the cache. The default properties that are returned if nothing is specified are the path and the name of the object.

## SearchScope

SearchScope is an enumeration that defines how deep the search should extend:

- SearchScope.Base searches only the attributes in the object where the search started, so at most one object is found.

- With SearchScope.OneLevel the search continues in the child collection of the base object. The base object itself is not searched for a hit.

- SearchScope.Subtree defines that the search should go down the complete tree.

The default value of the SearchScope property is SearchScope.Subtree.

## Search limits

A search for specific objects in a directory service can span multiple domains. To limit the search to the number of objects or the time taken, you have some additional properties to define, as shown in the following table.

| Property | Description |
| --- | --- |
| ClientTimeout | The maximum time the client waits for the server to return a result. If the server does not respond, no records are returned. |
| PageSize | With a *paged search* the server returns a number of objects defined with the PageSize instead of the complete result. This reduces the time for the client to get a first answer and the memory needed. The server sends a cookie to the client, which is sent back to the server with the next search request so that the search can continue at the point where it finished. |
| ServerPageTimeLimit | For paged searches this value defines the time a search should continue to return a number of objects that are defined with the PageSize value. If the time is reached before the PageSize value, the objects that were found up to that point are returned to the client. The default value is -1, which means infinite. |

*Table continued on following page*

| Property | Description |
|---|---|
| ServerTimeLimit | Defines the maximum time the server will search for objects. When this time is reached, all objects that are found up to this point are returned to the client. The default is 120 seconds, and you cannot set the search to a higher value. |
| ReferalChasing | A search can cross multiple domains. If the root that's specified with SearchRoot is a parent domain or no root was specified, the search can continue to child domains. With this property you can specify if the search should continue on different servers.<br>ReferalChasingOption.None means that the search does not continue on other servers.<br>The value ReferalChasingOption.Subordinate specifies that the search should go on to child domains. When the search starts at DC=Wrox, DC=com the server can return a result set and the referral to DC=France, DC=Wrox, DC=COM. The client can continue the search in the subdomain.<br>ReferalChasingOption.External means that the server can refer the client to an independent server that is not in the subdomain. This is the default option.<br>With ReferalChasingOption.All both external and subordinate referrals are returned. |
| Tombstone | If the property Tombstone is set to true, all deleted objects that match the search are returned, too. |
| VirtualListView | If large results are expected with the search, the property Virtual ListView can be used to define a subset that should be returned from the search. The subset is defined with the class DirectoryVirtual Listview. |

In the search example all user objects with a property description value of Author are searched in the organizational unit Thinktecture.

First, bind to the organizational unit Thinktecture. This is where the search should start. Create a DirectorySearcher object where the SearchRoot is set. The filter is defined as (&(objectClass=user)(description=Auth*)), so that the search spans all objects of type user with a description of Auth followed by something else. The scope of the search should be a subtree so that child organizational units within Thinktecture are searched, too:

```
using (DirectoryEntry de =
    new DirectoryEntry("LDAP://OU=Thinktecture, DC=explorer, DC=local"))
using (DirectorySearcher searcher = new DirectorySearcher())
{
    searcher.SearchRoot = de;
    searcher.Filter = "(&(objectClass=user)(description=Auth*))";
    searcher.SearchScope = SearchScope.Subtree;
```

## Working with Active Directory

The properties that should be in the result of the search are `name`, `description`, `givenName`, and `wWWHomePage`:

```
searcher.PropertiesToLoad.Add("name");
searcher.PropertiesToLoad.Add("description");
searcher.PropertiesToLoad.Add("givenName");
searcher.PropertiesToLoad.Add("wWWHomePage");
```

You are ready to do the search. However, the result should also be sorted. `DirectorySearcher` has a `Sort` property, where you can set a `SortOption`. The first argument in the constructor of the `SortOption` class defines the property that will be used for a sort; the second argument defines the direction of the sort. The `SortDirection` enumeration has `Ascending` and `Descending` values.

To start the search you can use the `FindOne()` method to find the first object, or `FindAll()`. `FindOne()` returns a simple `SearchResult`, whereas `FindAll()` returns a `SearchResultCollection`. Here all authors should be returned, so `FindAll()` is used:

```
searcher.Sort = new SortOption("givenName", SortDirection.Ascending);

SearchResultCollection results = searcher.FindAll();
```

With a `foreach` loop every `SearchResult` in the `SearchResultCollection` is accessed. A `SearchResult` represents a single object in the search cache. The `Properties` property returns a `ResultPropertyCollection`, where you access all properties and values with the property name and the indexer:

```
SearchResultCollection results = searcher.FindAll();

foreach (SearchResult result in results)
{
   ResultPropertyCollection props = result.Properties;
   foreach (string propName in props.PropertyNames)
   {
      Console.Write(propName + ": ");
      Console.WriteLine(props[propName][0]);
   }
   Console.WriteLine();
}
```

It is also possible to get the complete object after a search: `SearchResult` has a `GetDirectoryEntry()` method that returns the corresponding `DirectoryEntry` of the found object.

The resulting output shows the beginning of the list of all `Thinktecture` associates with the properties that have been chosen (see Figure 22-14).

739

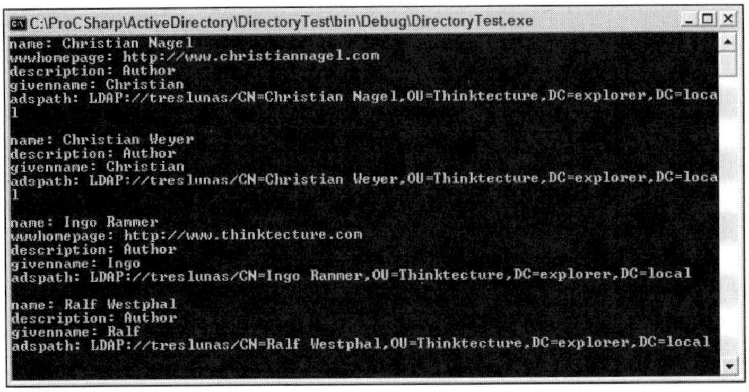

[Screenshot of DirectoryTest.exe console output]

Figure 22-14

# Searching for User Objects

In the final section of this chapter you build a Windows Forms application called `UserSearch`. This application is flexible insofar as a specific domain controller, username, and password to access the Active Directory can be entered; otherwise, the user of the running process is used. In this application you access the schema of the Active Directory service to get the properties of a `user` object. The user can enter a filter string to search all `user` objects of a domain. It's also possible to set the properties of the `user` objects that should be displayed.

## User Interface

The user interface shows numbered steps to indicate how to use the application (see Figure 22-15):

1. In the first step, `Username`, `Password`, and the `Domain Controller` can be entered. All this information is optional. If no domain controller is entered, the connection works with serverless binding. If the user name is missing, the security context of the current user is taken.

2. A button allows all the property names of the `user` object to be loaded dynamically in the `listBoxProperties` list box.

3. After the property names are loaded, the properties to be displayed can be selected. The `SelectionMode` of the list box is set to `MultiSimple`.

4. The filter to limit the search can be entered. The default value set in this dialog box searches for all `user` objects: `(objectClass=user)`.

5. Now the search can start.

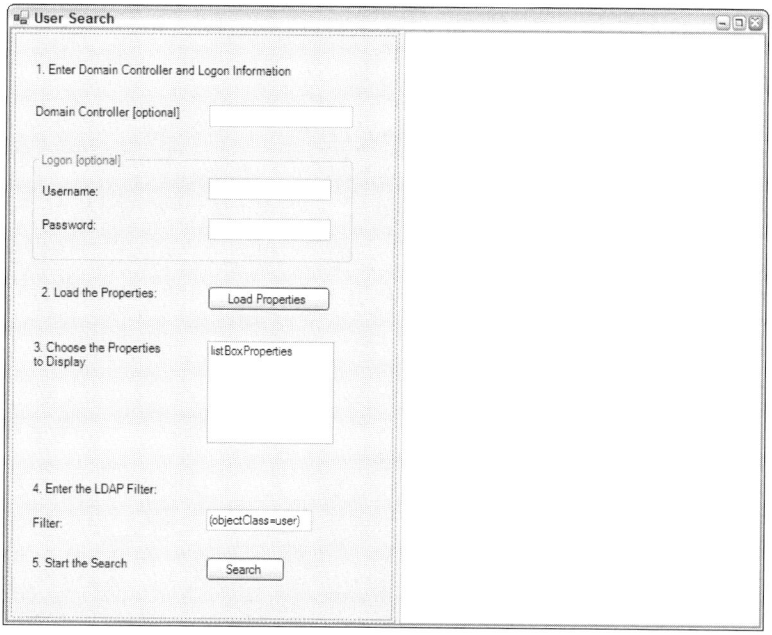

# Working with Active Directory

Figure 22-15

## Get the Schema Naming Context

This application has only two handler methods: one method for the button to load the properties and one to start the search in the domain. First, you read the properties of the user class dynamically from the schema to display it in the user interface.

In the handler `buttonLoadProperties_Click()` method, `SetLogonInformation()` reads the user name, password, and host name from the dialog box and stores them in members of the class. Next, the method `SetNamingContext()` sets the LDAP name of the schema and the LDAP name of the default context. This schema LDAP name is used in the call to set the properties in the list box: `SetUserProperties()`.

```
private void OnLoadProperties(object sender, System.EventArgs e)
{
    try
    {
        SetLogonInformation();
        SetNamingContext();

        SetUserProperties(schemaNamingContext);
    }
    catch (Exception ex)
    {
        MessageBox.Show("Check your inputs! " + ex.Message);
```

```
        }
    }
    protected void SetLogonInformation()
    {
        username = (textBoxUsername.Text == "" ? null : textBoxUsername.Text);
        password = (textBoxPassword.Text == "" ? null : textBoxPassword.Text);
        hostname = textBoxHostname.Text;
        if (hostname != "") hostname += "/";
    }
```

In the helper method `SetNamingContext()`, you are using the root of the directory tree to get the properties of the server. You are interested only in the value of two properties: `schemaNamingContext` and `defaultNamingContext`.

```
    protected void SetNamingContext()
    {
        using (DirectoryEntry de = new DirectoryEntry())
        {
            string path = "LDAP://" + hostname + "rootDSE";
            de.Username = username;
            de.Password = password;
            de.Path = path;
            schemaNamingContext = de.Properties["schemaNamingContext"][0].ToString();
            defaultNamingContext =
                        de.Properties["defaultNamingContext"][0].ToString();
        }
    }
```

## Get the Property Names of the User Class

You have the LDAP name to access the schema. You can use this to access the directory and read the properties. You are not only interested in the properties of the `user` class but also those of the base classes of `user`: `Organizational-Person`, `Person`, and `Top`. In this program, the names of the base classes are hard-coded. You could also read the base class dynamically with the `subClassOf` attribute. `GetSchemaProperties()` returns a string array with all property names of the specific object type. All the property names are collected in the `StringCollection` properties:

```
    protected void SetUserProperties(string schemaNamingContext)
    {
        List<string> properties = new List<string>();
        string[] data = GetSchemaProperties(schemaNamingContext, "User");
        properties.AddRange(GetSchemaProperties(schemaNamingContext,
                        "Organizational-Person"));
        properties.AddRange(GetSchemaProperties(schemaNamingContext, "Person"));
        properties.AddRange(GetSchemaProperties(schemaNamingContext, "Top"));

        listBoxProperties.Items.Clear();
        foreach (string s in properties)
        {
            listBoxProperties.Items.Add(s);
        }
    }
```

# Working with Active Directory

In `GetSchemaProperties()` you are accessing the Active Directory service again. This time `rootDSE` is not used but rather the LDAP name to the schema that you discovered earlier. The property `systemMay Contain` holds a collection of all attributes that are allowed in the class `objectType`:

```csharp
protected string[] GetSchemaProperties(string schemaNamingContext,
                                      string objectType)
{
   string[] data;
   using (DirectoryEntry de = new DirectoryEntry())
   {
      de.Username = username;
      de.Password = password;

      de.Path = "LDAP://" + hostname + "CN=" + objectType + "," +
                schemaNamingContext;

      DS.PropertyCollection properties = de.Properties;
      DS.PropertyValueCollection values = properties["systemMayContain"];

      data = new String[values.Count];
      values.CopyTo(data, 0);
   }
   return data;
}
```

Note the presence of `DS.PropertyCollection` in the preceding code; this is because in a Windows Forms application, the `PropertyCollection` class of the `System.DirectoryServices` namespace has a naming conflict with `System.Data.PropertyCollection`, and to avoid long names like `System.DirectoryServices.PropertyCollection`, the namespace name can be shortened as follows:

```csharp
using DS = System.DirectoryServices;
```

Step 2 in the application is completed. The `listbox` control has all the property names of the `user` objects.

## Search for User Objects

The handler for the search button calls only the helper method `FillResult()`:

```csharp
private void OnSearch(object sender, System.EventArgs e)
{
   try
   {
      FillResult();
   }
   catch (Exception ex)
   {
      MessageBox.Show("Check your input: " + ex.Message);
   }
}
```

In `FillResult()` you do a normal search in the complete Active Directory Domain as you saw earlier. `SearchScope` is set to `Subtree`, the `Filter` to the string you get from a `TextBox` object, and the properties that should be loaded into the cache are set by the values the user selected in the list box. The method `GetProperties()` that is used to pass an array of properties to the method `searcher.PropertiesToLoad.AddRange()` is a helper method that reads the selected properties from the list box into an array. After setting the properties of the `DirectorySearcher` object, the properties are searched by calling the `SearchAll()` method. The result of the search inside the `SearchResultCollection` is used to generate summary information that is written to the text box `textBoxResults`:

```csharp
protected void FillResult()
{
    using (DirectoryEntry root = new DirectoryEntry())
    {
        root.Username = username;
        root.Password = password;
        root.Path = "LDAP://" + hostname + defaultNamingContext;

        using (DirectorySearcher searcher = new DirectorySearcher())
        {
            searcher.SearchRoot = root;
            searcher.SearchScope = SearchScope.Subtree;
            searcher.Filter = textBoxFilter.Text;
            searcher.PropertiesToLoad.AddRange(GetProperties());

            SearchResultCollection results = searcher.FindAll();
            StringBuilder summary = new StringBuilder();
            foreach (SearchResult result in results)
            {
                foreach (string propName in
                    result.Properties.PropertyNames)
                {
                    foreach (string s in result.Properties[propName])
                    {
                        summary.Append(" " + propName + ": " + s + "\r\n");
                    }
                }
                summary.Append("\r\n");
            }
            textBoxResults.Text = summary.ToString();
        }
    }
}
```

Starting the application gives you a list of all objects where the filter is valid (see Figure 22-16).

# Working with Active Directory

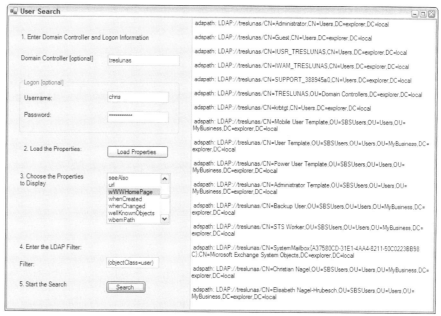

Figure 22-16

# DSML

With the new .NET 2.0 namespace `System.DirectoryServices.Protocols` you can access the Active Directory through DSML (Directory Services Markup Language). DSML is a standard defined by the OASIS group (http://www.oasis-open.org) that allows you to access directory services through a Web service.

To make Active Directory available through DSML, you must either have Windows Server 2003 R2 or you have to install DSML Services for Windows. You can download DSML Services for Windows from the Microsoft Web site: http://www.microsoft.com/windowsserver2003/downloads/feature packs/default.mspx.

Figure 22-17 shows a configuration scenario with DSML. A system that offers DSML services accesses the Active Directory via LDAP. On the client system the DSML classes from the namespace `System.DirectoryServices.Protocols` are used to make SOAP requests to the DSML service.

# Chapter 22

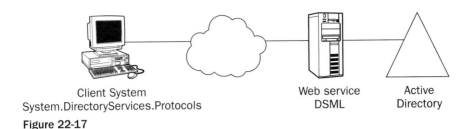

Client System  
System.DirectoryServices.Protocols  

Web service  
DSML  

Active  
Directory  

**Figure 22-17**

## Classes in System.DirectoryServices.Protocols

The following table shows the major classes in the `System.DirectoryServices.Protocols` namespace.

| Class | Description |
| --- | --- |
| DirectoryConnection | DirectoryConnection is the base class of all the connection classes that can be used to define the connection to the directory service. The classes that derive from DirectoryConnection are LdapConnection (for using the LDAP protocol), DsmlSoapConnection, and DsmlSoapHttpConnection.<br>With the method SendRequest a message is sent to the directory service. |
| DirectoryRequest | A request that can be sent to the directory service is defined by a class that derives from the base class DirectoryRequest. Depending on the request type, classes such as SearchRequest, AddRequest, DeleteRequest, and ModifyRequest can be used to send a request. |
| DirectoryResponse | The result that is returned with a SendRequest is of a type that derives from the base class DirectoryResponse. Examples for derived classes are SearchResponse, AddResponse, DeleteResponse, and ModifyResponse. |

## Searching for Active Directory Objects with DSML

This section looks at an example of how a search for directory services objects can be performed. As you can see in the code that follows, first a `DsmlSoapHttpConnection` object is instantiated that defines the connection to the DSML service. The connection is defined with the class `DsmlDirectoryIdentifier` that contains an `Uri` object. Optionally, the user credentials can be set with the connection:

```
Uri uri = new Uri("http://dsmlserver/dsml");
DsmlDirectoryIdentifier identifier = new DsmlDirectoryIdentifier(uri);

NetworkCredential credentials = new NetworkCredential();
credentials.UserName = "cnagel";
credentials.Password = "password";
credentials.Domain = "explorer";

DsmlSoapHttpConnection dsmlConnection =
    new DsmlSoapHttpConnection(identifier, credentials);
```

# Working with Active Directory

After the connection is defined, the search request can be configured. The search request consists of the directory entry where the search should start, an LDAP search filter, and the definition of what property values should be returned from the search. Here the filter is set to (objectClass=user), so that all user objects are returned from the search. attributesToReturn is set to null, and you can read all attributes that have values. SearchScope is an enumeration in the namespace System.Directory Services.Protocols that is similar to the SearchScope enumeration in the namespace System.DirectoryServices to define how deep the search should go. Here the SearchScope is set to Full to walk through the complete Active Directory tree.

The search filter can be defined with an LDAP string or by using an XML document contained in the XmlDocument class:

```
string distinguishedName = null;
string ldapFilter = "(objectClass=user)";
string[] attributesToReturn = null;// return all attributes

SearchRequest searchRequest = new SearchRequest(distinguishedName,
     ldapFilter, SearchScope.Full, attributesToReturn);
```

After the search is defined with the SearchRequest object, the search is sent to the Web service by calling the method SendRequest. SendRequest is a method of the DsmlSoapHttpConnection class. SendRequest returns a SearchResponse object where the returned objects can be read.

Instead of invoking the synchronous SendRequest method, the DsmlSoapHttpConnection class also offers the asynchronous methods BeginSendRequest and EndSendRequest.

```
SearchResponse searchResponse =
     (SearchResponse)dsmlConnection.SendRequest(searchRequest);
```

The returned Active Directory objects can be read within the SearchResponse. SearchResponse.Entries contains a collection of all entries that are wrapped with the type SearchResultEntry. The SearchResultEntry class has the Attributes property that contains all attributes. Each attribute can be read with help of the DirectoryAttribute class.

In the code example the distinguished name of each object is written to the console. Next, the attribute values for the organizational unit (ou) are accessed, and the name of the organizational unit is written to the console. After this, all values of the DirectoryAttribute objects are written to the console:

```
Console.WriteLine("\r\nSearch matched " + searchResponse.Entries.Count +
    " entries:");
foreach (SearchResultEntry entry in searchResponse.Entries)
{
   Console.WriteLine(entry.DistinguishedName);

   // retrieve a specific attribute
   DirectoryAttribute attribute = entry.Attributes["ou"];
   Console.WriteLine(attribute.Name + "=" + attribute[0]);

   // retrieve all attributes
   foreach (DirectoryAttribute attr in entry.Attributes.Values)
   {
      Console.Write(attr.Name + "=");
```

# Chapter 22

```
            // retrieve all values for the attribute
            // the type of the value can be one of string, byte[] or Uri
            foreach (object value in attr)
            {
               Console.Write(value + "   ");
            }
         }
      }
   }
```

Adding, modifying, and deleting objects can be done similarly to searching objects. Depending on the action you want to do, you can use the corresponding classes.

# Summary

This chapter discussed the architecture of Active Directory: the important concepts of domains, trees, and forests. You can access information in the complete enterprise. When writing applications that access Active Directory services, you must be aware that the data you read might not be up-to-date because of the replication latency.

The classes in the `System.DirectoryServices` namespaces give you easy ways to access Active Directory services by wrapping to the ADSI providers. The `DirectoryEntry` class makes it possible to read and write objects directly in the data store.

With the `DirectorySearcher` class you can do complex searches and define filters, timeouts, properties to load, and a scope. By using the global catalog, you can speed up the search for objects in the complete enterprise, because it stores a read-only version of all objects in the forest.

# Part IV
# Windows Applications

Chapter 23: Windows Forms

Chapter 24: Viewing .NET Data

Chapter 25: Graphics with GDI+

# 23

# Windows Forms

Web-based applications have become very popular over the past several years. The ability to have all of your application logic reside on a centralized server is very appealing from an administrator's viewpoint. Deploying client-based software can be very difficult, especially COM-based client software. The downside of Web-based applications is that they cannot provide that rich user experience. The .NET Framework has given developers the ability to create rich, smart client applications and eliminate the deployment problems and "DLL Hell" that existed before. The new deployment services that .NET provides, coupled with the System.Windows.Forms and System.Windows.Forms.Design namespaces that make up Windows Forms, promise to make client applications popular again.

Windows Forms has already made an impact on Windows development. Now when an application is in the initial design phase, the decision between building a Web-based application or a client application has become a little more difficult. Windows client applications can be developed quickly and efficiently, and they can provide users with the rich experience that they expect.

Windows Forms will seem somewhat familiar if you are a Visual Basic developer. You create new forms (also known as windows or dialogs) in the same fashion of dragging and dropping controls from a toolbox onto the form designer. However, if your background is in the classic C style of windows programming where you create the message pump and monitor messages, or if you're an MFC programmer, you will find that you're able to get to the lower-level internals if you need to. You can override the wndproc and catch those messages, but you might be surprised that you really won't need to very often.

This chapter looks at the following aspects of Windows Forms:

- ❑ The Form class
- ❑ The class hierarchy of Windows Forms
- ❑ The controls and components that are part of the System.Windows.Forms namespace

## Chapter 23

- Menus and toolbars
- Creating controls
- Creating user controls

# Creating a Windows Form Application

The first thing you need to do is create a Windows Form application. For the following example, create a blank form and show it on the screen. This example does not use Visual Studio .NET. It has been entered in a text editor and compiled using the command-line compiler. Here is the code listing:

```
using System;
using System.Windows.Forms;
namespace NotepadForms
{
  public class MyForm : System.Windows.Forms.Form
  {
    public MyForm()
    {
    }

    [STAThread]
    static void Main()
    {
      Application.Run(new MyForm());
    }
  }
}
```

When you compile and run this example, you will get a small blank form without a caption. Not real functional, but it is a Windows Form.

Looking at the code, two items deserve attention. The first is the fact that you have used inheritance to create the `MyForm` class. The following line declares that `MyForm` is derived from `System.Windows.Forms`.

```
public class MyForm : System.Windows.Forms.Form
```

The Form class is one of the main classes in the `System.Windows.Forms` namespace. The other section of code that you want to look at is:

```
[STAThread]
static void Main()
{
  Application.Run(new MyForm());
}
```

# Windows Forms

`Main` is the default entry point into any C# client application. Typically in larger applications, the `Main()` method would not be in a form, but in a class that is responsible for any startup processing that needs to be done. In this case, you would set the startup class name in the project properties dialog box. Notice the attribute `[STAThread]`. This sets the COM threading model to single-threaded apartment (STA). The STA threading model is required for COM interop and is added by default to a Windows Form project.

The `Application.Run()` method is responsible for starting the standard application message loop. `ApplicationRun()` has three overloads: The first takes no parameter; the second takes an `ApplicationContext` object as a parameter; and the one you see in the example takes a form object as a parameter. In the example, the `MyForm` object will become the main form of the application. This means that when this form is closed, the application ends. By using the `ApplicationContext` class, you can gain a little more control over when the main message loop ends and the application exits.

The `Application` class contains some very useful functionality. It provides a handful of static methods and properties for controlling the application's starting and stopping process and to gain access to the Windows messages that are being processed by the application. The following table lists some of the more useful of these methods and properties.

| Method/Property | Description |
| --- | --- |
| `CommonAppDataPath` | The path for the data that is common for all users of the application. Typically this is `BasePath\Company Name\Product Name\Version` where `BasePath` is `C:\Documents and Settings\username\ApplicationData`. If it does not exist, the path will be created. |
| `ExecutablePath` | This is the path and file name of the executable file that starts the application. |
| `LocalUserAppDataPath` | Similar to `CommonAppDataPath` with the exception that this property supports roaming. |
| `MessageLoop` | True or false if a message loop exists on the current thread. |
| `StartupPath` | Similar to `ExecutablePath`, except the file name is not returned. |
| `AddMessageFilter` | Used to pre-process messages. By implementing an `IMessageFilter`-based object, the messages can be filtered from the message loop or special processing can take place prior to the message being passed to the loop. |
| `DoEvents` | Similar to the Visual Basic `DoEvents` statement. Allows messages in the queue to be processed. |
| `EnableVisualStyles` | Enables XP visual styles for the various visual elements of the application. There are two overloads that will accept manifest information. One is a stream of the manifest and the other is the full name and path of where the manifest exists. |
| `Exit` and `ExitThread` | `Exit` ends all currently running message loops and exits the application. `ExitThread` ends the message loop and closes all windows on the current thread. |

Now what does this sample application look like when it is generated in Visual Studio 2005? The first thing to notice is that two files are created. The reason for this is that Visual Studio 2005 takes advantage of the partial class feature of the framework and separates all of the designer-generated code into a separate file. Using the default name of Form1, the two files are `Form1.cs` and `Form1.Designer.cs`. Unless you have the Show All Files option checked on the Project menu you won't see `Form1.Designer.cs` in the Solution Explorer. Following is the code that Visual Studio generates for the two files. First is `Form1.cs`:

```csharp
#region Using directives

using System;
using System.Collections.Generic;
using System.ComponentModel;
using System.Data;
using System.Drawing;
using System.Windows.Forms;

#endregion

namespace VisualStudioForm
{
    partial class Form1 : Form
    {
        public Form1()
        {
            InitializeComponent();
        }
    }
}
```

This is pretty simple, a handful of using statements and a simple constructor. Here is the code in `Form1.Designer.cs`:

```csharp
namespace VisualStudioForm
{
    partial class Form1
    {
        /// <summary>
        /// Required designer variable.
        /// </summary>
        private System.ComponentModel.IContainer components = null;

        /// <summary>
        /// Clean up any resources being used.
        /// </summary>
        protected override void Dispose(bool disposing)
        {
            if (disposing && (components != null))
            {
                components.Dispose();
            }
            base.Dispose(disposing);
        }
```

```
    #region Windows Form Designer generated code

    /// <summary>
    /// Required method for Designer support - do not modify
    /// the contents of this method with the code editor.
    /// </summary>
    private void InitializeComponent()
    {
      this.components = new System.ComponentModel.Container();
      this.Text = "Form1";
    }

    #endregion
  }
}
```

The designer file of a form should rarely be edited directly. The only exception would be if there is any special processing that needs to take place in the `Dispose` method. The `InitializeComponent` method is discussed later in this chapter.

Looking at the code as a whole for this sample application, you can see it is much longer than the simple command-line example. There are several `using` statements at the start of the class; most are not necessary for this example. There is no penalty for keeping them there. The class `Form1` is derived from `System.Windows.Forms` just like the earlier notepad example, but things start to get different at this point. First there is this line in the `Form1.Designer` file:

```
private System.ComponentModel.IContainer components = null;
```

In the example, this line of code doesn't really do anything. When you add a component to a form, you can also add it to the components object, which is a container. The reason for adding to this container has to do with disposing of the form. The form class supports the `IDisposable` interface because it is implemented in the `Component` class. When a component is added to the components container, the container will make sure that the components are tracked properly and disposed of when the form is disposed of. You can see this if you look at the `Dispose` method in the code:

```
protected override void Dispose(bool disposing)
{
  if (disposing && (components != null))
  {
    components.Dispose();
  }
  base.Dispose(disposing);
}
```

Here you can see that when the `Dispose` method is called, the `Dispose` method of the components object is also called and because the component object contains the other components, they are also disposed.

The constructor of the `Form1` class, which is in the `Form1.cs` file, looks like this:

```
public Form1()
{
  InitializeComponent();
}
```

Notice the call to `InitializeComponent()`. `InitializeComponent()` is located in `Form1.Designer.cs` and does pretty much what it describes, and that is to initialize any controls that might have been added to the form. It also initializes the form properties. This is what `InitializeComponent()` looks like for this simple example:

```csharp
private void InitializeComponent()
{
  this.components = new System.ComponentModel.Container();
  this.Text = "Form1";
}
```

As you can see it is basic initialization code. This method is tied to the Designer in Visual Studio. When you make changes to the form by using the Designer, the changes are reflected in `InitializeComponent()`. If you make any type of code change in `InitializeComponent()`, the next time you make a change in the designer, your changes will be lost. `InitializeComponent()` gets regenerated after each change in the designer. If you need to add additional initialization code for the form or controls and components on the form, be sure to add it after `InitializeComponent()` is called. `InitializeComponent()` is also responsible for instantiating the controls so any call that references a control prior to `InitializeComponent()` will fail with a null reference exception.

To add a control or component to the form, press Ctrl+Alt-X or select Toolbox from the View menu in Visual Studio .NET. `Form1` should be in design mode. Right-click `Form1.cs` in Solution Explorer and select View Designer from the context menu. Select the Button control and drag it to the form in the designer. You can also double-click the control and it will be added to the form. Do the same with the TextBox control.

Now that you have added a `TextBox` control and a `Button` control to the form, `InitializeComponent()` expands to include the following code:

```csharp
private void InitializeComponent()
{
  this.button1 = new System.Windows.Forms.Button();
  this.textBox1 = new System.Windows.Forms.TextBox();
  this.SuspendLayout();
  //
  // button1
  //
  this.button1.Location = new System.Drawing.Point(96, 56);
  this.button1.Name = "button1";
  this.button1.TabIndex = 0;
  this.button1.Text = "button1";
  //
  // textBox1
  //
  this.textBox1.Location = new System.Drawing.Point(88, 104);
  this.textBox1.Name = "textBox1";
  this.textBox1.TabIndex = 1;
  this.textBox1.Text = "textBox1";
  //
  // Form1
  //
```

# Windows Forms

```
        this.AutoScaleBaseSize = new System.Drawing.Size(5, 13);
        this.ClientSize = new System.Drawing.Size(292, 271);
        this.Controls.Add(this.textBox1);
        this.Controls.Add(this.button1);
        this.Name = "Form1";
        this.Text = "Form1";
        this.ResumeLayout(false);

    }
```

If you look at the first three lines of code in the method, you can see the Button and TextBox controls are instantiated. Notice the names given to the controls, `textBox1` and `button1`. By default the designer uses the name of the control and adds an integer value to the name. When you add another button, the designer adds the name `button2`, and so on. The next line is part of the `SuspendLayout` and `ResumeLayout` pair. `SuspendLayout()` temporarily suspends the layout events that take place when a control is first initialized. At the end of the method the `ResumeLayout()` method is called to set things back to normal. In a complex form with many controls, the `InitializeComponent()` method can get quite large.

To change a property value of a control, either press F4 or select Properties Window from the View menu. The Properties Window enables you to modify most of the properties for a control or component. By making a change in the Properties Window, the `InitializeComponent()` method will be rewritten to reflect the new property value. For example, if the Text property is changed to My Button in the Property Window, `InitializeComponent()` will contain this code:

```
//
// button1
//
this.button1.Location = new System.Drawing.Point(96, 56);
this.button1.Name = "button1";
this.button1.TabIndex = 0;
this.button1.Text = "My Button";
```

If you are using an editor other than Visual Studio .NET, you will want to include an `Initialize Component()` type function in your designs. Keeping all of this initialization code in one spot will help keep the constructor cleaner, not to mention that if you have multiple constructors you can make sure the initialization code is called from each constructor.

## Class Hierarchy

The importance of understanding the hierarchy becomes apparent during the design and construction of custom controls. If your custom control is a derivative of a current control, for example a text box with some added properties and methods, you will want to inherit from the text box control and then override and add the properties and methods to suit your needs. However, if you are creating a control that doesn't match up to any of the controls included with the .NET Framework, you will have to inherit from one of the three base control classes — `Control` or `ScrollableControl` if you need autoscrolling capabilities, and `ContainerControl` if your control needs to be a container of other controls.

Figure 23-1 shows the relationship between the classes of the `System.Windows.Forms` namespace.

# Chapter 23

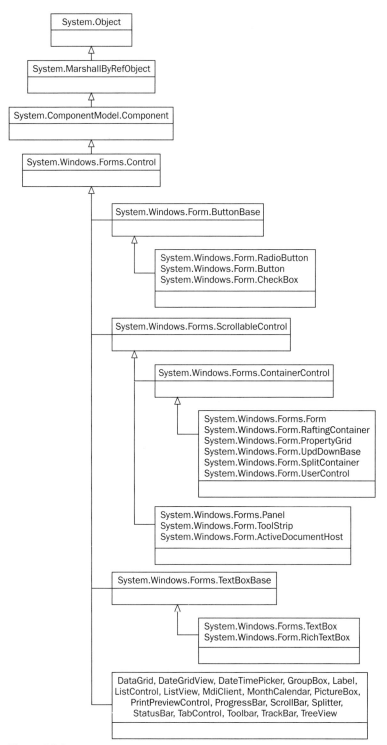

Figure 23-1

# Windows Forms

The rest of this chapter is devoted to looking at many of these classes—how they work together and how they can be used to build professional-looking client applications.

# Control Class

The `System.Windows.Forms` namespace has one particular class that is the base class for virtually every control and form that is created. This class is the `System.Windows.Forms.Control` class. The `Control` class implements the core functionality to create the display that the user sees. The `Control` class is derived from the `System.ComponentModel.Component` class. The `Component` class provides the `Control` class with the necessary infrastructure required to be dropped on a design surface and to be contained by another object. The `Control` class provides a large list of functionality to the classes that are derived from it. The list is too long to itemize here, so this section looks at the more important items that are provided by the `Control` class. Later in the chapter when you look at the specific controls based on the `Control` class you will see the properties and methods in some example code. The following subsections group the methods and properties by functionality, so related items can be looked at together.

## Size and Location

The size and location of a control are determined by the properties `Height`, `Width`, `Top`, `Bottom`, `Left`, and `Right` along with the complementary properties `Size` and `Location`. The difference is that `Height`, `Width`, `Top`, `Bottom`, `Left`, and `Right` all take single integers as their value. `Size` takes a `Size` structure and `Location` takes a `Point` structure as their values. The `Size` and `Point` structures are a contained version of XY coordinates. `Point` generally relates to a location and `Size` is the height and width of an object. `Size` and `Point` are in the `System.Drawing` namespace. Both are very similar in that they provide an XY coordinate pair but also have overridden operators for easy comparison and conversion. You can, for example, add two `Size` structures together. In the case of the `Point` structure the `Addition` operator is overridden so that you can add a `Size` structure to a `Point` and get a new `Point` in return. This has the effect of adding distance to a location and getting a new location. This is very handy if you're in the situation of having to dynamically create forms or controls.

The `Bounds` property returns a `Rectangle` object that represents the area of a control. This area includes scroll bars and title bars. `Rectangle` is also part of the `System.Drawing` namespace. The `ClientSize` property is a `Size` structure that represents the client area of the control, minus the scroll bars and title bar.

The `PointToClient` and `PointToScreen` methods are handy conversion methods that take a `Point` and return a `Point`. The `PointToClient` takes a `Point` that represents screen coordinates and translates them to coordinates based on the current client object. This is handy for drag-and-drop actions. The `PointToScreen` does just the opposite—it takes coordinates of a client object and translates them to screen coordinates. The `RectangleToScreen` and `ScreenToRectangle` methods perform the same functionality with Rectangle structures instead of Points.

The `Dock` property determines which edge of the parent control the control will be docked to. A `DockStyle` enumeration value is used as the property's value. This value can be `Top`, `Bottom`, `Right`, `Left`, `Fill`, and `None`. `Fill` sets the control's size to match the client area of the parent control.

The `Anchor` property anchors an edge of the control to the edge of the parent control. This is different from docking in that it does not set the edge to the parent control, but sets the current distance from the edge to be constant. For example, if you anchor the right edge of the control to the right edge of the parent and the parent is resized, the right edge of the control will maintain the same distance from the parent's right edge. The `Anchor` property takes a value of the `AnchorStyles` enumeration. The values are `Top`, `Bottom`, `Left`, `Right`, and `None`. By setting the values you can make control resize dynamically with the parent as the parent is resized. This way, buttons and text boxes will not be cut off or hidden as the form is resized by the user.

The `Dock` and `Anchor` properties used in conjunction with the `Flow` and `Table` layout controls (discussed later in this chapter) allow you to create very sophisticated user windows. Window resizing can be difficult with complex forms with many controls. These tools help make that process much easier.

## Appearance

Properties that relate to the appearance of the control are `BackColor` and `ForeColor`, which take a `System.Drawing.Color` object as a value. The `BackGroundImage` property takes an Image-based object as a value. The `System.Drawing.Image` class is an abstract class that is used as the base for the `Bitmap` and `Metafile` classes. The `BackgroundImageLayout` property uses the `ImageLayout` enumeration to set how the image is displayed on the control. Valid values are `Center`, `Tile`, `Stretch`, `Zoom`, or `None`.

The `Font` and `Text` properties deal with displaying the written word. In order to change the `Font` you will need to create a `Font` object. When you create the `Font` object you specify the font name, size, and style.

## User Interaction

User interaction is best described as the various events that a control creates and responds to. Some of the more common events are `Click`, `DoubleClick`, `KeyDown`, `KeyPress`, `Validating`, and `Paint`.

The Mouse events — `Click`, `DoubleClick`, `MouseDown`, `MouseUp`, `MouseEnter`, `MouseLeave`, and `MouseHover` — deal with the interaction of the mouse and the control. If you are handling both the `Click` and the `DoubleClick` events, every time you catch a `DoubleClick` event the `Click` event is raised as well. This can result in undesired results if not handled properly. Also the `Click` and `DoubleClick` receive an `EventArgs` as an argument, whereas the `MouseDown` and `MouseUp` events receive a `MouseEventArgs`. The `MouseEventArgs` contain several pieces of useful information such as the button that was clicked, the number of times the button was clicked, the number of mouse wheel detents (notches in the mouse wheel), and the current X and Y coordinates of the mouse. If you have access to any of this information, you will have to handle either the `MouseDown` or `MouseUp` events, not the `Click` or `DoubleClick` events.

The keyboard events work in a similar fashion: The amount of information needed determines the event that is handled. For simple situations the `KeyPress` event receives a `KeyPressEventArgs`. This contains the `KeyChar`, which is a char value that represents the key pressed. The `Handled` property is used to determine whether or not the event was handled. By setting the `Handled` property to `true`, the event is not passed on for default handling by the operating system. If you need more information about the key that was pressed, the `KeyDown` or `KeyUp` event is more appropriate to handle. They both receive a `KeyEventArgs`. Properties in `KeyEventArgs` include whether the Ctrl, Alt, or Shift key was pressed. The `KeyCode` property returns a `Keys` enumeration value that identifies the key that was pressed. Unlike the `KeyPressEventArgs.KeyChar` property, the `KeyCode` property tells you about every key on the keyboard, not just the alphanumeric keys. The `KeyData` property returns a Keys value and will also set the modifier. The modifiers are ORd with the value. This tells you that the Shift key or the Ctrl key was pressed as well. The `KeyValue` property is the int value of the `Keys` enumeration. The `Modifiers` property contains a `Keys` value that represents the modifier keys that were pressed. If more than one has been selected, the values are ORd together. The key events are raised in the following order:

1. `KeyDown`
2. `KeyPress`
3. `KeyUp`

The `Validating`, `Validated`, `Enter`, `Leave`, `GotFocus`, and `LostFocus` events all deal with a control gaining focus (or becoming active) or losing focus. This happens when the user tabs into a control or selects the control with the mouse. `Enter`, `Leave`, `GotFocus`, and `LostFocus` seem to be very similar in what they do. The `GotFocus` and `LostFocus` events are lower-level events that are tied to the `WM_SETFOCUS` and the `WM_KILLFOCUS` Windows messages. Generally you should use the Enter and Leave events if possible. The Validating and Validated events are raised when the control is validating. These events receive a `CancelEventArgs`. With this you can cancel the following events by setting the `Cancel` property to `true`. If you have custom validation code, and validation fails, you can set `Cancel` to `true` and the control will not lose focus. `Validating` occurs during validation; `Validated` occurs after validation. The order in which these events are raised is as follows:

1. `Enter`
2. `GotFocus`
3. `Leave`
4. `Validating`
5. `Validated`
6. `LostFocus`

Understanding the order of these events is important so that you don't inadvertently create a recursive situation. For example, trying to set the focus of a control from the control's LostFocus event creates a message deadlock and the application stops responding.

## *Windows Functionality*

The `System.Windows.Forms` namespace is one of the few namespaces that relies on Windows functionality. The `Control` class is a good example of that. If you were to do a disassembly of the `System.Windows.Forms.dll`, you would see a list of references to the `UnsafeNativeMethods` class. The .NET Framework uses this class to wrap all of the standard Win32 API calls. By using interop to the Win32 API, the look and feel of a standard Windows application can still be achieved with the `System.Windows.Forms` namespace.

Functionality that supports the interaction with Windows includes the Handle and IsHandleCreated properties. Handle returns an IntPtr that contains the HWND (windows handle) for the control. The window handle is an HWND that uniquely identifies the window. A control can be considered a window, so it has a corresponding HWND. You can use the Handle property to call any number of Win32 API calls.

To gain access to the windows messages you can override the `WndProc` method. The `WindProc` method takes a `Message` object as a parameter. The `Message` object is a simple wrapper for a windows message. It contains the `HWnd`, `LParam`, `WParam`, `Msg`, and `Result` properties. If you want to have the message processed by the system, you must make sure that you pass the message to the base.`WndProc(msg)` method. If you want to handle the message, you don't want to pass the message on.

## Miscellaneous Functionality

Some items that are a little more difficult to classify are the data-binding capabilities. The `Binding Context` property returns a `BindingManagerBase` object. The `DataBindings` collection maintains a `ControlBindingsCollection`, which is a collection of binding objects for the control. Data-binding is discussed in Chapter 24, "Viewing .NET Data."

The `CompanyName`, `ProductName`, and `Product` versions provide data on the origination of the control and its current version.

The `Invalidate` method allows you to invalidate a region of the control for repainting. You can invalidate the entire control or specify a region or rectangle to invalidate. This causes a paint message to be sent to the control's `WindProc`. You also have the option to invalidate any child controls at the same time.

Dozens of other properties, methods, and events make up the `Control` class. This list represents some of the more commonly used ones and is meant to give you an idea of the functionality available.

# Standard Controls and Components

The previous section covered some of the common methods and properties for controls. This section looks at the various controls that ship with the .NET Framework, and explains what each of them offers in added functionality. The sample download (www.wrox.com) includes a sample application called `FormExample`. This sample application is an MDI application (discussed later in the chapter) and includes a form named `frmControls` that contains many controls with basic functionality enabled. Figure 23-2 shows what `frmControls` looks like.

## Button

The `Button` class represents the simple command button and is derived from `ButtonBase` class. The most common thing to do is to write code to handle the `Click` event of the button. The following code snippet implements an event handler for the `Click` event. When the button is clicked, a message box pops up that displays the button's name:

```
private void btnTest_Click(object sender, System.EventArgs e)
{
    MessageBox.Show(((Button)sender).Name + " was clicked.");
}
```

# Windows Forms

Figure 23-2

With the `PerformClick` method, you can simulate the `Click` event on a button without the user actually clicking the button. The `NotifyDefault` method takes a Boolean value as a parameter and tells the button to draw itself as the default button. Typically the default button on a form has a slightly thicker border. To identify the button as default, you set the AcceptButton property on the form to the button. Then, when the user presses the Enter key, the button `Click` event for the default button is raised. Figure 23-3 shows that the button with the caption Default is the default button (notice the dark border).

Figure 23-3

Buttons can have images as well as text. Images are supplied by way of an `ImageList` object or the `Image` property. `ImageList` objects are exactly what they sound like: a list of images managed by a component placed on a form. They are explained in detail later in this chapter.

Both `Text` and `Image` have an `Align` property to align the text or image on the `Button`. The `Align` property takes a `ContentAlignment` enumeration value. The text or image can be aligned in combinations of left and right and top and bottom.

763

Chapter 23

## *CheckBox*

The `CheckBox` control is also derived from `ButtonBase` and is used to accept a two-state or three-state response from the user. If you set the `ThreeState` property to `true`, the `CheckBox`'s `CheckState` property can be one of these three `CheckState` enum values:

| | |
|---|---|
| Checked | The `CheckBox` has a check mark. |
| Unchecked | The `CheckBox` does not have a check mark. |
| Indeterminate | In this state the `CheckBox` becomes gray. |

The `Indeterminate` value can be set only in code and not by a user. This is useful if you need to convey to the user that an option has not been set. You can also check the `Checked` property if you want a Boolean value.

The `CheckedChanged` and `CheckStateChanged` events occur when the `CheckState` or `Checked` properties change. Catching these events can be useful for setting other values based on the new state of the `CheckBox`. In the `frmControls` form class, the `CheckedChanged` event for several `CheckBoxes` is handled by the following method:

```
private void checkBoxChanged(object sender, EventArgs e)
{
  CheckBox checkBox = (CheckBox)sender;
  MessageBox.Show(checkBox.Name + " new value is " + checkBox.Checked.ToString());
}
```

As the checked state of each check box changes, a message box is displayed with the name of the check box that was changed along with the new value.

## *RadioButton*

The last control derived from `ButtonBase` is the `radio` button. Radio buttons are generally used as a group. Sometimes referred to as option buttons, radio buttons allow the user to choose one of several options. When you have multiple `RadioButton` controls in the same container, only one at a time may be selected. So if you have three options — for example, `Red`, `Green`, and `Blue` — if the `Red` option is selected and the user clicks the `Blue` option, the `Red` is automatically deselected.

The `Appearance` property takes an `Appearance` enumeration value. This can be either `Button` or `Normal`. When choosing `Normal`, the radio button looks like a small circle with a label beside it. Selecting the button fills the circle; selecting another button deselects the currently selected button and makes the circle look empty. When choosing `Button`, the control looks like a standard button, but it works like a toggle — selected is the in position, deselected is the normal or out position.

The `CheckedAlign` property determines where the circle is in relation to the label text. It could be on top of the label, on either side, or below.

The `CheckedChanged` event is raised whenever the value of the Checked property changes. This way you can perform other actions based on the new value of the control.

# Windows Forms

## ComboBox, ListBox, and CheckedListBox

`ComboBox`, `ListBox`, and `CheckedListBox` are all derived from the `ListControl` class. This class provides some of the basic list management functionality. The most important things about using list controls are adding and selecting data to the list. Which list is used is generally determined by how the list is used and the type of data that is going to be in the list. If there is a need to have multiple selections or the user needs to be able to see several items in the list at any time, the `ListBox` or `CheckedListBox` is going to be the best choice. If only a single item is ever selected in the list at any time, a `ComboBox` may be a good choice.

Data must be added to a list box before it can be useful. This is done by adding objects to the `ListBox.ObjectCollection`. This collection is exposed by the list's `Items` property. Because the collection stores objects, any valid .NET type can be added to the list. In order to identify the items, two important properties need to be set. The first is the `DisplayMember` property. This setting tells the `ListControl` what property of your object should be displayed in the list. The other is `ValueMember`, which is the property of your object that you want to return as the value. If strings have been added to the list, by default the string value is used for both of these properties. The `frmLists` form in the sample application shows how both objects and strings (which are of course objects) can be loaded into a list box. The example uses `Vendor` objects for the list data. The `Vendor` object contains just two properties: `Name` and `PhoneNo`. The `DisplayMember` property is set to the `Name` property. This tells the list control to display the value from the `Name` property in the list to the user.

A couple of ways exist to access the data in the list control, as shown in the following code example. The list is loaded with the `Vendor` objects. The DisplayMember and ValueMember properties are set. You can find this code in the `frmLists` form class in the sample application.

First is the `LoadList` method. This method loads the list with either `Vendor` objects or a simple string containing the vendor name. An option button is checked to see which values should be loaded in the list:

```
private void LoadList(Control ctrlToLoad)
{
    ListBox tmpCtrl = null;

    if (ctrlToLoad is ListBox)
      tmpCtrl = (ListBox)ctrlToLoad;

    tmpCtrl.Items.Clear();
    tmpCtrl.DataSource = null;

    if (radioButton1.Checked)
    {
      //load objects
      tmpCtrl.Items.Add(new Vendor("XYZ Company", "555-555-1234"));
      tmpCtrl.Items.Add(new Vendor("ABC Company", "555-555-2345"));
      tmpCtrl.Items.Add(new Vendor("Other Company", "555-555-3456"));
      tmpCtrl.Items.Add(new Vendor("Another Company", "555-555-4567"));
      tmpCtrl.Items.Add(new Vendor("More Company", "555-555-6789"));
      tmpCtrl.Items.Add(new Vendor("Last Company", "555-555-7890"));
      tmpCtrl.DisplayMember = "Name";
    }
    else
    {
```

# Chapter 23

```
            tmpCtrl.Items.Clear();
            tmpCtrl.Items.Add("XYZ Company");
            tmpCtrl.Items.Add("ABC Company");
            tmpCtrl.Items.Add("Other Company");
            tmpCtrl.Items.Add("Another Company");
            tmpCtrl.Items.Add("More Company");
            tmpCtrl.Items.Add("Last Company");
        }
    }
```

Once the data is loaded in the list the `SelectedItem` and `SelectedIndex` properties can be used to get at the data. The `SelectedItem` returns the object that is currently selected. If the list is set to allow multiple selections, there is no guarantee which of the selected items will be returned. In this case, the SelectObject collection should be used. This contains a list of all of the currently selected items in the list.

If the item at a specific index is needed, the Items property can be used to access the `ListBox.ObjectCollection`. Because this is a standard .NET collection class, the items in the collection can be accessed in the same way as any other collection class.

If DataBinding is used to populate the list, the SelectedValue property will return the property value of the selected object that was set to the `ValueMember` property. If Phone is set to `ValueMember`, the `SelectedValue` will return the Phone value from the selected item. In order to use `ValueMember` and `SelectValue` the list must be loaded by way of the `DataSource` property. An ArrayList or any other `IList`-based collection must be loaded with the objects first, then the list can be assigned to the `DataSource` property. This short example demonstrates this:

```
listBox1.DataSource = null;
System.Collections.ArrayList lst = new System.Collections.ArrayList();
lst.Add(new Vendor("XYZ Company", "555-555-1234"));
lst.Add(new Vendor("ABC Company", "555-555-2345"));
lst.Add(new Vendor("Other Company", "555-555-3456"));
lst.Add(new Vendor("Another Company", "555-555-4567"));
lst.Add(new Vendor("More Company", "555-555-6789"));
lst.Add(new Vendor("Last Company", "555-555-7890"));
listBox1.Items.Clear();
listBox1.DataSource = lst;
listBox1.DisplayMember = "Name";
listBox1.ValueMember = "Phone";
```

Using `SelectedValue` without using DataBinding will result in a `NullException` error.

The following lines of code show the syntax of accessing the data in the list:

```
//obj is set to the selected Vendor object
obj = listBox1.SelectedItem;

//obj is set to the Vendor object with index of 3 (4th object)
obj = listBox.Items[3];

//obj is set to the values of the Phone property of the selected vendor object
//This example assumes that databinding was used to populate the list
listBox1.ValuesMember = "Phone";
obj = listBox1.SelectValue;
```

# Windows Forms

The thing to remember is that all of these methods return object as the type. A cast to the proper data type will need to be done in order to use the value of obj.

The `Items` property of the `ComboBox` returns `ComboBox.ObjectCollection`. A `ComboBox` is a combination of an edit control and a list box. You set the style of the `ComboBox` by passing a `DropDownStyle` enumeration value to the `DropDownStyle` property. The following table lists the various `DropDownStyle` values.

| Value | Description |
| --- | --- |
| DropDown | The text portion of the combo box is editable and users can enter a value. They also must click the arrow button to show the list. |
| DropDownList | The text portion is not editable. Users must make a selection from the list. |
| Simple | This is similar to DropDown except that the list is always visible. |

If the values in the list are wide you can change the width of the drop-down portion of the control with the `DropDownWidth` property. The `MaxDropDownItems` property sets the number of items to show when the drop-down portion of the list is displayed.

The `FindString` and `FindStringExact` methods are two other useful methods of the list controls. `FindString` finds the first string in the list that starts with the passed-in string. `FindStringExact` finds the first string that matches the passed-in string. Both return the index of the value that is found or -1 if the value is not found. They can also take an integer that is the starting index to search from.

## DateTimePicker

The `DateTimePicker` allows users to select a date or time value (or both) in a number of different formats. You can display the `DateTime`-based value in any of the standard time and date formats. The Format property takes a `DateTimePickerFormat` enumeration that sets the format to Long, Short, Time, or Custom. If the Format property is set to `DateTiemePickerFormat.Custom`, you can set the `CustomFormat` property to a string that represents the format.

There is both a `Text` property and a `Value` property. The `Text` property returns a text representation of the `DateTime` value whereas the `Value` property returns the `DateTime` object. You can also set the maximum and minimum allowable date values with the `MinDate` and `MaxDate` properties.

When users click the down arrow, a calendar is displayed allowing the users to select a date in the calendar. Properties are available that allow you to change the appearance of the calendar by setting the title and month background colors as well as the foreground colors.

The `ShowUpDown` property determines whether an `UpDown` arrow is displayed on the control. The currently highlighted value can be changed by clicking the up or down arrow.

## ErrorProvider

`ErrorProvider` is actually not a control but a component. When you drag a component to the designer, it shows in the component tray under the designer. What the `ErrorProvider` does is flash an icon next to a control when an error condition or validation failure exists. Suppose that you have a `TextBox` entry for an age. Your business rules say that the age value cannot be greater than 65. If users try to enter an age greater than that you must inform them that the age is greater than the allowable value and that they need to change the entered value. The check for a valid value takes place in the `Validated` event of the text box. If the validation fails, you call the `SetError` method, passing in the control that caused the error and a string that informs the user what the error is. An icon starts flashing indicating that an error has occurred, and when the user hovers over the icon the error text is displayed. Figure 23-4 shows the icon that is displayed when an invalid entry is made in the text box.

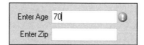

**Figure 23-4**

You can create an `ErrorProvider` for each control that produces errors on a form, but if you have a large number of controls this can become unwieldy. Another option is to use one error provider and in the validate event call the `IconLocation` method with the control that is causing the validation and one of the ErrorIconAlignment enumeration values. This value sets where the icon is aligned near the control. Then you call the `SetError` method. If no error condition exists, you can clear the `ErrorProvider` by calling `SetError` with an empty string as the error string. The following example shows how this works:

```
private void txtAge_Validating(object sender,
                                      System.ComponentModel.CancelEventArgs e)
{
   if(txtAge.TextLength > 0 && Convert.ToInt32(txtAge.Text) > 65)
   {
      errMain.SetIconAlignment((Control)sender,
                                      ErrorIconAlignment.MiddleRight);
      errMain.SetError((Control)sender, "Value must be less then 65.");
      e.Cancel = true;
   }
   else
   {
      errMain.SetError((Control)sender, "");
   }
}

private void txtZipCode_Validating(object sender,
                                      System.ComponentModel.CancelEventArgs e)
{
   if(txtZipCode.TextLength > 0 && txtZipCode.Text.Length != 5)
   {
      errMain.SetIconAlignment((Control)sender,
                                      ErrorIconAlignment.MiddleRight);
      errMain.SetError((Control)sender, "Must be 5 charactors..");
      e.Cancel = true;

   }
   else
   {
      errMain.SetError((Control)sender, "");
   }
}
```

# Windows Forms

If the validation fails (the age is over 65 in `txtAge`, for example), then the `SetIcon` method of the ErrorProvider `errMain` is called. It will set the icon next to the control that failed validation. The error is set next so that when users hover over the icon, the message informs them of what is responsible for the failed validation.

## HelpProvider

`HelpProvider`, like `ErrorProvider`, is a component and not a control. `HelpProvider` allows you to hook up controls to help topics. To associate a control with the help provider you call the `SetShowHelp` method, passing the control and a `Boolean` value that determines whether help will be shown. The `HelpNamespace` property allows you to set a help file. When the `HelpNamespace` property is set, the help file is displayed anytime you select F1 and a control that you have registered with the `HelpProvider` is in focus. You can set a keyword to the help file with the `SetHelpKeyword` method. `SetHelpNavigator` takes a `HelpNavigator` enumeration value to determine which element in the help file should be displayed. You can set it for a specific topic, the index, the table of contents, or the search page. The `SetHelpString` associates a string value of help-related text to a control. If the `HelpNamespace` property has not been set, pressing F1 will show this text in a pop-up window. Go ahead and add a `HelpProvider` to the previous example:

```
helpProvider1.SetHelpString(txtAge,"Enter an age that is less than 65");
helpProvider1.SetHelpString(txtZipCode,"Enter a 5 digit zip code");
```

## ImageList

An `ImageList` component is exactly what the name implies — a list of images. Typically, this component is used for holding a collection of images that are used as toolbar icons or icons in a `TreeView` control. Many controls have an `ImageList` property. The `ImageList` property typically comes with an `ImageIndex` property. The `ImageList` property is set to an instance of the `ImageList` component and the `ImageIndex` property is set to the index in the `ImageList` that represents the image that should be displayed on the control. You add images to the `ImageList` component by using the `Add` method of the `ImageList.Images` property. The `Images` property returns an `ImageCollection`.

The two most commonly used properties are `ImageSize` and `ColorDepth`. `ImageSize` uses a `Size` structure as its value. The default value is 16×16 but it can be any value from 1 to 256. The `ColorDepth` uses a `ColorDepth` enumeration as its value. The color depth values go from 4 bit to 32 bit. For .NET Framework 1.1, the default is `ColorDepth.Depth8Bit`.

## Label

`Label`s are generally used to provide descriptive text to the user. The text might be related to other controls or the current system state. You usually see a label together with a text box. The label provides the user with a description of the type of data to be entered in the text box. The `Label` control is always read-only — the user cannot change the string value of the `Text` property. However, you can change the `Text` property in your code. The `UseMnemonic` property allows you to enable the access key functionality. When you precede a character in the `Text` property with the ampersand (&), that letter will appear underlined in the label control. Pressing the Alt key in combination with the underlined letter puts the focus on the next control in the tab order. If the `Text` property contains an ampersand in the text, add a second one and it will not underline the next letter. For example, if the label text is "Nuts & Bolts," set the property to "Nuts && Bolts." Because the `Label` control is read-only, it cannot gain focus; that's why focus is sent to the next control. Because of this, it is important to remember that if you enable mnemonics, you must be certain to set the tab order properly on your form.

The `AutoSize` property is a `Boolean` value that specifies whether the `Label` will resize itself based on the contents of the `Label`. This can be useful for multilanguage applications where the length of the `Text` property can change based on the current language.

## ListView

The `ListView` control allows you to display items in one of four different ways. You can display text with an optional large icon, text with an optional small icon, or text and small icons in a vertical list or in detail view, which allows you to display the item text plus any sub items in columns. If this sounds familiar it should, because this is what the right side of File Explorer uses to display the contents of folders. `ListView` contains a collection of `ListViewItems`. `ListViewItems` allows you to set a `Text` property used for the display. `ListViewItem` has a property called `SubItems` that contains the text that appears in detail view.

The following example demonstrates how you might use `ListView`. This example includes a short list of countries. Each `CountryList` object contains a property for the country name, country abbreviation, and currency. Here is the code for the `CountryList` class:

```csharp
using System;

namespace FormsSample
{
  public class CountryItem   : System.Windows.Forms.ListViewItem
  {
    string _cntryName = "";
    string _cntryAbbrev = "";

    public CountryItem(string countryName,
                       string countryAbbreviation, string currency)
    {
      _cntryName = countryName;
      _cntryAbbrev = countryAbbreviation;
      base.Text = _cntryName;
      base.SubItems.Add(currency);
    }

    public string CountryName
    {
      get {return _cntryName;}
    }

    public string CountryAbbreviation
    {
      get {return _cntryAbbrev;}
    }
  }
}
```

# Windows Forms

Notice that you are deriving the `CountryList` class from `ListViewItem`. This is because you can add only `ListViewItem`-based objects to the `ListView` control. In the constructor, you pass the country name to the `base.Text` property and add the currency value to the `base.SubItems` property. This displays the country name in the list and the currency in a separate column when in details view.

Next, you need to add a couple of the `CountryItem` objects to the `ListView` control in the code of the form:

```
lvCountries.Items.Add(new CountryItem("United States","US","Dollar"));
lvCountries.Items[0].ImageIndex = 0;
lvCountries.Items.Add(new CountryItem("Great Britain", "GB", "Pound"));
lvCountries.Items[1].ImageIndex = 1;
lvCountries.Items.Add(new CountryItem("Canada", "CA", "Dollar"));
lvCountries.Items[2].ImageIndex = 2;
lvCountries.Items.Add(new CountryItem("Japan", "JP", "Yen"));
lvCountries.Items[3].ImageIndex = 3;
lvCountries.Items.Add(new CountryItem("Germany", "GM", "Deutch Mark"));
lvCountries.Items[4].ImageIndex = 4;
```

Here you add a new `CountryItem` to the `Items` collection of the `ListView` control (`lvCountries`). Notice that you set the `ImageIndex` property of the item after you add it to the control. There are two `ImageIndex` objects, one for large icons and one for small icons (`SmallImageList` and `LargeImageList` properties). The trick with having two `ImageLists` with differing image sizes is to make sure you add the items to the `ImageList` in the same order. This way the index of each `ImageList` represents the same image, just different sizes. In the example, the `ImageLists` contain icons of the flags for each country added.

On top of the form, there is a `ComboBox` (`cbView`) that lists the four different `View` enumeration values. You add the items to the `cbView` like this:

```
cbView.Items.Add(View.LargeIcon);
cbView.Items.Add(View.SmallIcon);
cbView.Items.Add(View.List);
cbView.Items.Add(View.Details);
cbView.SelectedIndex = 0;
```

In the `SelectedIndexChanged` event of `cbView`, you add the single line of code:

```
lvCountries.View = (View)cbView.SelectedItem;
```

This sets the `View` property of `lvCountries` to the new value selected in the `ComboBox` control. Notice that you need to cast to the `View` type because `object` is returned from the `SelectedItem` property of the `cbView`.

Last, but hardly least, you have to add columns to the `Columns` collection. The columns are for details view. In this case you are adding two columns: Country Name and Currency. The order of the columns is as follows: the `Text` of the `ListViewItem`, then each item in the `ListViewItem.SubItem` collection, in the order it appears in the collection. You can add columns either by creating a `ColumnHeader` object and setting the `Text` property and optionally the `Width` and `Alignment` properties. After creating the `ColumnHeader` object you can add it to the `Columns` property. The other way to add columns is to use an override of the `Columns.Add` method. It allows you to pass in the `Text`, `Width`, and `Alignment` values. Here is an example:

# Chapter 23

```
lvCountries.Columns.Add("Country",100, HorizontalAlignment.Left);
lvCountries.Columns.Add("Currency",100, HorizontalAlignment.Left);
```

If you set the `AllowColumnReorder` property to `true`, the user can drag the column headers around and rearrange the column order.

The `CheckBoxes` property on the `ListView` shows check boxes next to the items in the `ListView`. This allows the user to easily select multiple items in the `ListView` control. You can check which items are selected by checking the `CheckedItems` collection.

The `Alignment` property sets the alignment of icons in Large and Small icon view. The value can be any of the `ListViewAlignment` enumeration values. They are `Default`, `Left`, `Top`, and `SnapToGrid`. The `Default` value allows the user to arrange the icons in any position that they want. When choosing `Left` or `Top`, the items are aligned with the left or top of the `ListView` control. When choosing `SnapToGrid`, the items snap to an invisible grid on the `ListView` control. The `AutoArrange` property can be set to a `Boolean` value and will automatically align the icons based on the `Alignment` property.

## PictureBox

The `PictureBox` control is used to display an image. The image can be a BMP, JPEG, GIF, PNG, metafile, or icon. The `SizeMode` property uses the `PictureBoxSizeMode` enumeration to determine how the image is sized and positioned in the control. The `SizeMode` property can be `AutoSize`, `CenterImage`, `Normal`, and `StretchImage`.

You can change the size of the display of the `PictureBox` by setting the `ClientSize` property. You load the `PictureBox` by first creating an `Image`-based object. For example, to load a JPEG file into a `PictureBox` you would do the following:

```
Bitmap myJpeg = new Bitmap("mypic.jpg");
pictureBox1.Image = (Image)myJpeg;
```

Notice that you will need to cast back to an `Image` type because that is what the `Image` property expects.

## ProgressBar

The `ProgressBar` control is a visual clue to the status of a lengthy operation. It indicates to users that there is something going on and that they should wait. The `ProgressBar` control works by setting the `Minimum` and `Maximum` properties. These properties correspond to the progress indicator being all the way to the left (`Minimum`) or all the way to the right (`Maximum`). You set the `Step` property to determine the number that the value is incremented each time the `PerformStep` method is called. You can also use the `Increment` method and increment the value by the value passed in the method call. The `Value` property returns the current value of the `ProgressBar`.

You can use the `Text` property to inform the user of the percentage of the operation that has been completed or the number of items left to process. There is also a `BackgroundImage` property to customize the look of the progress bar.

# Windows Forms

## TextBox, RichTextBox and MaskedTextBox

The `TextBox` control is one of the most used controls in the `Toolbox`. The `TextBox`, `RichTextBox`, and `MaskedTextBox` controls are all derived from `TextBoxBase`. `TextBoxBase` provides properties such as `MultiLine` and `Lines`. `MultiLine` is a `Boolean` value that allows the `TextBox` control to display text in more than one line. Each line in a text box is a part of an array of strings. This array is exposed through the `Lines` property. The `Text` property returns the entire text box contents as a single string. `TextLength` is the total length of the string that text would return. The `MaxLength` property will limit the length of the text to the specified amount.

`SelectedText`, `SelectionLength`, and `SelectionStart` all deal with the currently selected text in the text box. The selected text is highlighted when the control has focus.

The `TextBox` control adds a couple of interesting properties. `AcceptsReturn` is a `Boolean` value that will allow the `TextBox` to accept the `Enter` key as a new line or whether it activates the default button on the form. When set to `true`, pressing the `Enter` key creates a new line in the `TextBox`. `CharacterCasing` determines the casing of the text in the text box. The `CharacterCasing` enumeration contains three values, `Lower`, `Normal`, and `Upper`. `Lower` lowercases all text regardless of how it is entered, `Upper` renders all text in uppercase letters, and `Normal` displays the text as it is entered. The `PasswordChar` property takes a char that represents what is displayed to the users when they type text in the text box. This is typically used for entering passwords and PINs. The `text` property will return the actual text that was entered; only the display is affected by this property.

The `RichTextBox` is a text editing control that can handle special formatting features. As the name implies, the `RichTextBox` control uses Rich Text Format (RTF) to handle the special formatting. You can make formatting changes by using the `Selection` properties: `SelectionFont`, `SelectionColor`, and `SelectionBullet`, and paragraph formatting with `SelectionIndent`, `SelectionRightIndent`, and `SelectionHangingIndent`. All of the `Selection` properties work in the same way. If there is a section of text highlighted, a change to a `Selection` property affects the selected text. If no text is selected, the change takes effect with any text that is inserted to the right of the current insertion point.

The text of the control can be retrieved by using the `Text` property or the `Rtf` property. The `Text` property returns just the text of the control whereas the `Rtf` property returns the formatted text.

The `LoadFile` method can load text from a file in a couple of different ways. It can use either a string that represents the path and file name or it can use a stream object. You can also specify the `RichTextBoxStreamType`. The following table lists the values of `RichTextBoxStreamType`.

| Value | Description |
| --- | --- |
| `PlainText` | No formatting information. In places that contained OLE objects, spaces are used. |
| `RichNoOleObjs` | Rich text formatting, but spaces where the OLE objects would have been. |
| `RichText` | Formatted RTF with OLE objects in place. |
| `TextTextOleObjs` | Plain text with text replacing the OLE objects. |
| `UnicodePlainText` | Same as `PlainText` but Unicode encoded. |

The `SaveFile` method works with the same parameters, saving the data from the control to a specified file. If a file by that name already exists, it will be overwritten.

The `MaskedTextBox` supplies the ability to limit what the user may input into the control. It also allows for automatic formatting of the data entered. Several properties are used in order to validate or format the user's input. `Mask` is the property that contains the mask string. The mask string is similar to a format string. The number of characters allowed, the data type of allowed characters, and the format of the data are all set using the `Mask` string. A `MaskedTextProvider`-based class can also provide the formatting and validation information needed. The `MaskedTextProvider` can only be set by passing it in on one of the constrictors.

Three different properties will return the text of the `MaskedTextControl`. The `Text` property returns the text of the control at the current moment. This could be different depending on whether or not the control has focus, which depends on the value of the `HidePromptOnLeave` property. The prompt is a string that users see to guide them on what should be entered. The `InputText` property always returns just the text that the user entered. The `OutputText` property returns the text formatted based on the `IncludeLiterals` and `IncludePrompt` properties. If, for example, the mask is for a phone number, the Mask string would possibly include parentheses and a couple of dashes. These would be the literal characters and would be included in the `OutputText` property if the `IncludeLiteral` property is set to true.

A couple of extra events also exist for the `MaskedTextBox` control. `OutputTextChanged` and `InputTextChanged` are raised when `InputText` or `OutputText` changes.

## *Panel*

A `Panel` is simply a control that contains other controls. By grouping controls together and placing them in a panel, it is a little easier to manage the controls. For example, you can disable all of the controls in the panel by disabling the panel. Because the `Panel` control is derived from `ScrollableControl`, you also can get the advantage of the `AutoScroll` property. If you have too many controls to display in the available area, place them in a `Panel` and set `AutoScroll` to true — now you can scroll through all of the controls.

Panels do not show a border by default, but by setting the `BorderStyle` property to something other than none, you can use the `Panel` to visually group related controls. This makes the user interface more user-friendly.

`Panel` is the base class for the `FlowLayoutPanel`, `TableLayoutPanel`, `TabPage`, and `SplitterPanel`. By using these controls, a very sophisticated and professional-looking form or window can be created. The `FlowLayoutPanel` and `TableLayoutPanel` are especially useful for creating forms that resize properly.

## *FlowLayoutPanel and TableLayoutPanel*

`FlowLayoutPanel` and `TableLayoutPanel` are new additions to the .NET Framework. As the names might suggest, the panels offer the ability to lay out a form using the same paradigm as a Web Form. `FlowLayoutPanel` is a container that allows the contained controls to flow in either the horizontal or vertical directions. Instead of flowing, clipping of the controls can be done. Flow direction is set using the

`FlowDirection` property and the `FlowDirection` enumeration. The `WrapContents` property determines if controls flow to the next row or column when the form is resized or if the control is clipped.

`TableLayoutPanel` uses a grid structure to control the layout of controls. Any Windows Forms control can be a child of the `TableLayoutPanel`, including another `TableLayoutPanel`. This allows for a very flexible and dynamic window design. When a control is added to a `TableLayoutPanel`, four additional properties are added to the Layout category of the property page. They are `Column`, `ColumnSpan`, `Row`, and `RowSpan`. Much like an html table on a Web page, column and row spans can be set for each control. By default the control will be centered in the cell of the table, but this can be changed by using the Anchor and Dock properties.

The default style of the rows and columns can be changed using `RowStyles` and `ColumnsStyles` collections. These collections contain `RowStyle` and `ColumnsStyle` objects, respectively. The Style objects have a common property, `SizeType`. SizeType uses the SizeType enumeration to determine how the column width or row height should be sized. Values include AutoSize, Absolute, and Percent. AutoSize shares the space with other peer controls. Absolute allows a set number of pixels for the size and Percent tells the control to size the column or width as a percentage of the parent control.

Rows, columns, and child controls can be added or removed at runtime. The `GrowStyle` property takes a `TableLayoutPanelGrowStyle` enumeration value that sets the table to add a column, a row, or stay fixed size when a new control is added to a full table. If the value is `FixedSized`, an `AurgumentException` is thrown when there is an attempt to add another control. If a cell in the table is empty, the control will be placed in the empty cell. This property only has an effect when the table is full and a control is added.

The `frmPanel` form in the sample application has `FlowLayoutPanels` and `TableLayoutPanels` with a variety of controls set in them. Experimenting with the controls, especially the `Dock` and `Anchor` properties of the controls placed in the layout panels, is the best way to understand how they work.

## *SplitContainer*

The `SplitContainer` control is really three controls in one. It has two panel controls with a bar or splitter between them. The user is able to move the bar and resize the panels. As the panels resize, the controls in the panels also can be resized. The best example of a `SplitContainer` would be File Explorer. The left panel contains a `TreeView` of folders and the right side contains a ListView of folder contents. When the user moves the mouse over the splitter bar, the cursor changes showing that the bar can be moved. The `SplitContainer` can contain any control including layout panels and other `SplitContainers`. This allows the creation of very complex and sophisticated forms.

The movement and position of the splitter bar can be controlled with the `SplitterDistance` and `SplitterIncrement` properties. The `SplitterDistance` property determines where the splitter starts in relation to the left or top of the control. The `SplitterIncrement` determines the number of pixels the splitter moves when being dragged. The panels can have their minimum size set with the `Panel1MinSize` and `Panel2MinSize` properties. These properties are also in pixels.

The Splitter control raises two events that relate to moving: the `SplitterMoving` event and the `SplitterMoved` event. One takes place during the move and the other takes place after the move has happened. They both receive a `SplitterEventArgs`. The `SplitterEventArgs` contains properties for the X and Y coordinates of the upper-left corner of the Splitter (`SplitX` and `SplitY`) and the X and Y coordinates of the mouse pointer (X and Y).

## Chapter 23

## *TabControl and TabPages*

`TabControl` allows you to group related controls onto a series of tab pages. `TabControl` manages the collection of `TabPages`. Several properties control the appearance of `TabControl`. The `Appearance` property uses the `TabAppearance` enumeration to determine what the tabs look like. The values are `FlatButtons`, `Buttons`, or `Normal`. The `Multiline` property is a `Boolean` that determines if more than one row of tabs is shown. If the `Multiline` property is set to `false` and there are more tabs than can fit in the display, a set of arrows appears that allow the user to scroll and see the rest of the tabs.

The `TabPage Text` property is what is displayed on the tab. The `Text` property is a parameter in a constructor override as well.

Once you create a `TabPage` control, it is basically a container control for you to place other controls. The designer in Visual Studio .NET makes it easy to add `TabPage` controls to a `TabControl` control by using the collection editor. You can set the various properties as you add each page. Then you can drag the other child controls to each `TabPage` control.

You can determine the current tab by looking at the `SelectedTab` property. The `SelectedIndex` event is raised each time a new tab is selected. By listening to the `SelectedIndex` property and then confirming the current tab with `SelectedTab`, you can do special processing based on each tab.

## *ToolStrip*

The `ToolStrip` control is a container control used to create toolbars, menu structures, and status bars. The `ToolStrip` is used directly for toolbars, and serves as the base class for the `MenuStrip` and `StatusStrip` controls.

When used as a toolbar, the `ToolStrip` control uses a set of controls based on the abstract `ToolStripItem` class. `ToolStripItem` adds the common display and layout functionality as well as managing most of the events used by the controls. `ToolStripItem` is derived from the `System.ComponentModel.Component` class and not from the `Control` class. `ToolStripItem`-based classes must be contained in a `ToolStrip`-based container.

`Image` and `Text` are probably the most common properties that will be set. Images can be set with either the `Image` property or by using the `ImageList` control and setting it to the `ImageList` property of the `ToolStrip` control. The `ImageIndex` property of the individual controls can then be set.

Formatting of the text on a `ToolStripItem` is handled with the `Font`, `TextAlign`, and `TextDirection` properties. `TextAlign` sets the alignment of the text in relation to the control. This can be any on the `ControlAlignment` enumeration values. The default is `MiddleRight`. The `TextDirection` property sets the orientation of the text. Values can be any of the `ToolStripTextDirection` enumeration values, which include `Horizontal`, `Inherit`, `Vertical270`, and `Vertical90`. `Vertical270` rotates the text 270 degrees and `Vertical90` rotates the text 90 degrees.

The `DisplayStyle` property controls whether text, image, text and image, or nothing is displayed on the control. When `AutoSize` is set to `true`, the `ToolStripItem` will resize itself so only the minimum amount of space is used.

The controls that are derived directly from `ToolStripItem` are listed in the following table.

# Windows Forms

| Tool Strip Items | Description |
|---|---|
| ToolStripButton | Represents a button that the user can select. |
| ToolStripLabel | Displays non-selectable text or image on the ToolStrip. The ToolStripLabel can also display one or more hyperlinks. |
| ToolStripSeparator | Used to separate and group other ToolStripItems. Items can be grouped according to functionality. |
| ToolStripDropDownItem | Displays drop-down items. Base class for ToolStripDropDownButton, ToolStripMenuItem, and ToolStripSplitButton. |
| ToolStripControlHost | Hosts other non-ToolStripItem derived controls on a ToolStrip. Base class for ToolStripComboBox, ToolStripProgressBar, and ToolStripTextBox. |

The first two items in the list, `ToolStripDropDownItem` and `ToolStripControlHost`, deserve a little more discussion. `ToolStripDropDownItem` is the base class for `ToolStripMenuItems`, which are used to build the menu structure. `ToolStripMenuItems` are added to `MenuStrip` controls. As mentioned earlier, `MenuStrips` are derived from `ToolStrip` controls. This is important when it comes time to manipulate or extend menu items. Because toolbars and menus are derived from the same classes, creating a framework for managing and executing commands becomes much easier.

`ToolStripControlHost` can be used to host other controls that do not derive from `ToolStripItem`. Remember that the only controls that can be directly hosted by a `ToolStrip` are those that derive from `ToolStripItem`. The following example shows how to host a `DateTimePicker` control on a `ToolStrip`:

```
public mdiParent()
{
   InitializeComponent();

   ToolStripControlHost _dateTimeCtl;
  _dateTimeCtl = new ToolStripControlHost(new DateTimePicker());
   ((DateTimePicker)_dateTimeCtl.Control).ValueChanged +=
         delegate {
                 toolStripLabel1.Text =
 ((DateTimePicker)_dateTimeCtl.Control).Value.Subtract(DateTime.Now).ToString();
                 };

  _dateTimeCtl.Width = 200;
  _dateTimeCtl.DisplayStyle = ToolStripItemDisplayStyle.Text;
   toolStrip1.Items.Add(_dateTimeCtl);
}
```

This is the constructor from the `frmMain` form in the code sample. First, a `ToolStripControlHost` is declared and instantiated. Notice that when the control is instantiated that the control that is to be hosted is passed in on the constructor. The next line is setting up the `ValueChanged` event of the `DateTimePicker` control. The control can be accessed through the `Control` property of the `ToolStripHostControl`. This will return a `Control` object, so it will need to be cast back to the proper type of control. Once that is done, the properties and methods of the hosted control are available to use.

Another way to do this that would perhaps enforce encapsulation a little better would be to create a new class derived from `ToolStripControlHost`. The following code is another version of the tool strip version of the `DateTimePicker` called `ToolStripDateTimePicker`:

```
namespace FormsSample.SampleControls
{
  public class ToolStripDateTimePicker: System.Windows.Forms.ToolStripControlHost
  {
    //need to declare the event that will be exposed
    public event EventHandler ValueChanged;

    public ToolStripDateTimePicker ()   : base(new DateTimePicker())
    {
    }
    //create strong typed Control property.
    public new DateTimePicker Control
    {
      get{return (DateTimePicker)base.Control;}
    }
    //create a striong typed Value property
    public DateTime Value
    {
      get { return Control.Value; }
    }

    protected override void OnSubscribeControlEvents(Control control)
    {
      base.OnSubscribeControlEvents(control);
      ((DateTimePicker)control).ValueChanged +=
                                    new EventHandler(HandleValueChanged;
    }

    protected override void OnUnsubscribeControlEvents(Control control)
    {
      base.OnSubscribeControlEvents(control);
      ((DateTimePicker)control).ValueChanged -=
                                    new EventHandler(HandleValueChanged);
    }

    private void HandleValueChanged (object sender, EventArgs e)
    {
      if (ValueChanged != null)
        ValueChanged(this, e);
    }
  }
}
```

Most of what this class is doing is exposing selected properties, methods, and events of the `DateTimePicker`. This way a reference to the underlying control doesn't have to be maintained by the hosting application. The process of exposing events is a bit involved. The `OnSubscribecontrolEvents` method is used to synchronize the events of the hosted control, in this case `DateTimePicker`, to the `ToolStripControlHost`-based class, which is `ToolStripDateTimePicker` in the example. In this example, the `ValueChanged` event is being passed up to the `ToolStripDateTimePicker`. What this effectively does is allow the user of the control to set up the event in the host application as if `ToolStripDate TimePicker` was derived from `DateTimePicker` instead of `ToolStripControlHost`. The following code example shows this. This is the code to use `ToolStripDateTimePicker`:

```
public mdiParent()
{
   ToolStripDateTimePicker otherDateTimePicker = new ToolStripDateTimePicker ();
   otherDateTimePicker.Width = 200;
   otherDateTimePicker.ValueChanged +=
                              new EventHandler(otherDateTimePicker_ValueChanged);
   toolStrip1.Items.Add(otherDateTimePicker);
}
```

Notice that when the `ValueChanged` event handler is set up that the reference is to the `ToolStrip DateTimePicker` class and not to the `DateTimePicker` control as in the previous example. Notice how much cleaner the code in this example looks as compared to the first example. Not only that, because the `DateTimePicker` is wrapped up in another class, encapsulation has improved dramatically and `ToolStripDateTimePicker` is now much easier to use in other parts of the application or in other projects.

## MenuStrip

The `MenuStrip` control is the container for the menu structure of an application. As mentioned earlier, `MenuStrip` is derived form the `ToolStrip` class. The menu system is built by adding `ToolStripMenu` objects to the `MenuStrip`. This can be done in code or in the designer of Visual Studio. Drag a `MenuStrip` control onto a form in the designer and the `MenuStrip` will allow the entry of the menu text directly on the menu items.

The `MenuStrip` control has only a couple of additional properties. `GripStyle` uses the `ToolStripGrip Style` enumeration to set the grip as visible or hidden. The `MdiWindowListItem` property takes or returns a `ToolStripMenuItem`. This `ToolStripMenuItem` will be the menu that shows all open windows in an MDI application.

## ContextMenuStrip

To show a context menu, or a menu displayed when the user right-clicks the mouse, the `ContextMenu Strip` class is used. Like `MenuStrip`, `ContextMenuStrip` is a container for `ToolStripMenuItems` objects. However, it is derived from `ToolStripDropDownMenu`. A `ContextMenu` is created the same as a `MenuStrip`. `ToolStripMenuItems` are added and the Click event of each item is defined to perform a specific task. Context menus are assigned to specific controls. This is done by setting the `ContextMenu Strip` property of the control. When the user right-clicks the control, the menu will be displayed.

## ToolStripMenuItem

`ToolStripMenuItem` is the class that builds the menu structures. Each `ToolStripMenuItem` object represents a single menu choice on the menu system. Each `ToolStripMenuItem` has a `ToolStrip ItemCollection` that maintains the child menus. This functionality is inherited from `ToolStrip DropDownItem`.

Because `ToolStripMenuItem` is derived from `ToolStripItem`, all of the same formatting properties apply. Images appear as small icons to the right of the menu text. Menu items can have check marks show up next to them with the `Checked` and `CheckState` properties.

Shortcut keys can be assigned to each menu item. Shortcut keys are generally two key chords such as Ctrl+C (common shortcut for Copy). When a shortcut key is assigned it can optionally be displayed on the menu by setting the `ShowShortCutKey` property to `true`.

To be useful, the menu item has to do something when the user clicks it or uses the defined shortcut keys. The most common way is to handle the Click event. If the `Checked` property is being used, the `CheckStateChanged` and `CheckedChanged` events can be used to determine a change in the checked state.

## ToolStripManager

Menu and toolbar structures can become large and cumbersome to manage. The `ToolStripManager` class provides the ability to create smaller, more manageable pieces of a menu or toolbar structure and then combine them when needed. An example of this is if a form has several different controls on it. Each control must display a context menu. Several menu choices will be available for all of the controls, but each control will also have a couple of unique menu choices. The common choices can be defined on one `ContextMenuStrip`. Each of the unique menu items can be predefined or created at runtime. For each control that needs a context menu assigned to it, the common menu is cloned and the unique choices are merged with the common menu using the `ToolStripManager.Merge` method. The resulting menu is assigned to the `ContextMenuStrip` property of the control.

## ToolStripContainer

The `ToolStripContainer` control is used for docking of `ToolStrip` based controls. Adding a `ToolStripContainer` and setting the `Docked` property to `Fill`, a `ToolStripPanel` is added to each side of the form and a `ToolStripContainerPanel` is added to middle of the form. Any `ToolStrip` (`ToolStrip`, `MenuStrip`, or `StatusStrip`) can be added to any of the `ToolStripPanels`. The user can move the `ToolStrips` by grabbing the `ToolStrip` and dragging it to either side or bottom of the form. By setting the `Visible` property to false on any of the `ToolStripPanels`, a `ToolStrip` can no longer be placed in the panel. The `ToolStripContainerPanel` in the center of the form can be used to place the other controls the form may need.

# Forms

Earlier in this chapter, you learned how to create a simple Windows application. The example contained one class derived from the `System.Windows.Forms.Form` class. According to the .NET Framework documentation, "a Form is a representation of any window in your application." If you come from a Visual Basic background, the term *form* will seem familiar. If your background is C++ using MFC, you're probably used to calling a form a window, dialog box, or maybe a frame. Regardless, the form is the basic means of interacting with the user. Earlier, the chapter covered some of the more common and useful properties, methods, and events of the `Control` class, and because the `Form` class is a descendant of the `Control` class, all of the same properties, methods, and events exist in the `Form` class. The `Form` class adds considerable functionality to what the `Control` class provides, and that's what this section discusses.

# Windows Forms

## Form Class

A Windows client application can contain one form or hundreds of forms. They can be an SDI-based (Single Document Interface) or MDI-based (Multiple Document Interface) application. Regardless, the `System.Windows.Forms.Form` class is the heart of the Windows client. The `Form` class is derived from `ContainerControl`, which is derived from `ScrollableControl`, which is derived from Control. Because of this you can assume that a form is capable of being a container for other controls, capable of scrolling when the contained controls do not fit the client area, and has many of the same properties, methods, and events that other controls have. Because of this, it also makes the `Form` class rather complex. This section looks at much of that functionality.

### Form instantiation and destruction

The process of form creation is important to understand. What you want to do depends on where you write the initialization code. For instantiation, the events occur in the following order:

- Constructor
- Load
- Activated
- Closing
- Closed
- Deactivate

The first three events are of concern during initialization. Depending on what type of initialization you want to do could determine which event you would hook into. The constructor of a class occurs during the object instantiation. The `Load` event occurs after object instantiation, but just before the form becomes visible. The difference between this and the constructor is the viability of the form. When the Load event is raised, the form exists but isn't visible. During constructor execution, the form is in the process of existing. The Activated event occurs when the form becomes visible and current.

There is a situation where this order can be altered slightly. If during the constructor execution of the form the `Visible` property is set to `true` or the `Show` method is called (which sets the `Visible` property to `true`), the `Load` event fires immediately. Because this also makes the form visible and current, the `Activate` event is also raised. If there is code after the `Visible` property has been set, it will execute. So the startup event might look something like this:

- Constructor, up to `Visible = true`
- Load
- Activate
- Constructor, after `Visible = true`

This could potentially lead to some unexpected results. From a best practices standpoint, it would seem that doing as much initialization as possible in the constructor might be a good idea.

Now what happens when the form is closed? The `Closing` event gives you the opportunity to cancel the process. The `Closing` event receives the `CancelEventArgs` as a parameter. This has a `Cancel` property that if set to `true` cancels the event and the form remains open. The `Closing` event happens as the form is being closed, whereas the `Closed` event happens after the form has been closed. Both allow you to do any cleanup that might have to be done. Notice that the `Deactivate` event occurs after the form has been closed. This is another potential source of difficult-to-find bugs. Be sure that you don't have anything in `Deactivate` that could keep the form from being properly garbage-collected. For example, setting a reference to another object would cause the form to remain alive.

If you call the `Application.Exit()` method and you have one or more forms currently open, the `Closing` and `Closed` events will not be raised. This is an important consideration if you have open files or database connections that you were going to clean up. The `Dispose` method is called, so perhaps another best practice would be to put most of your cleanup code in the `Dispose` method.

Some properties that relate to the startup of a form are `StartPosition`, `ShowInTaskbar`, and `TopMost`. `StartPosition` can be any of the `FormStartPosition` enumeration values. They are:

- `CenterParent` — The form is centered in the client area of the parent form.
- `CenterScreen` — The form is centered in the current display.
- `Manual` — The form's location is based on the values in the `Location` property.
- `WindowsDefaultBounds` — The form is located at the default Windows position and uses the default size.
- `WindowsDefaultLocation` — The Windows default location is used, but the size is based on the `Size` property.

The `ShowInTaskbar` property determines if the form should be available in the taskbar. This is only relevant if the form is a child form and you only want the parent form to show in the taskbar. The `TopMost` property tells the form to start in the topmost position in the Z-order of the application. This is true even of the form does not immediately have focus.

In order for users to interact with the application, they must be able to see the form. The `Show` and `ShowDialog` methods accomplish this. The `Show` method just makes the form visible to the user. The following code segment demonstrates how to create a form and show it to the user. Assume that the form you want to display is called `MyFormClass`.

```
MyFormClass myForm = new MyFormClass();
myForm.Show();
```

That's the simple way. The one drawback to this is that there isn't any notification back to the calling code that `myForm` is finished and has been exited. Sometimes this isn't a big deal and the `Show` method will work fine. If you do need some type of notification, the `ShowDialog` is a better option.

When the `Show` method is called, the code that follows the `Show` method is executed immediately. When `ShowDialog` is called, the calling code is blocked and will wait until the form that `ShowDialog` called is closed. Not only will the calling code be blocked, but the form will optionally return a `DialogResult` value. The `DialogResult` enumeration is a list of identifiers that describe the reason for the dialog being closed. These include `OK`, `Cancel`, `Yes`, `No`, and several others. In order for the form to return a

DialogResult, the form's DialogResult property must be set or the DialogResult property on one of the form's buttons must be set.

For example, suppose that part of application asks for the phone number of a client. The form has a text box for the phone number and two buttons; one is labeled OK and the other is labeled Cancel. If you set the DialogResult of the OK button to DialogResult.OK and the DialogResult property on the Cancel button to DialogResult.Cancel, then when either of these buttons is selected, the form becomes invisible and returns to the calling form the appropriate DialogResult value. Now notice that the form does not get destroyed; only the Visible property is set to false. That's because you still must get values from the form. For this example, you need to phone number. By creating a property on the form for the phone number, the parent form can now get the value and call the Close method on the form. This is what the code for the child form looks like:

```
namespace FormsSample.DialogSample
{
  partial class Phone : Form
  {
    public Phone()
    {
      InitializeComponent();

      btnOK.DialogResult = DialogResult.OK;
      btnCancel.DialogResult = DialogResult.Cancel;

    }


    public string PhoneNumber
    {
      get { return textBox1.Text; }
      set { textBox1.Text = value; }
    }
  }
}
```

The first thing to notice is that there isn't code to handle the click events of the buttons. Because the DialogResult property is set for each of the buttons, the form disappears after either the OK or Cancel button is clicked. The only property added is the PhoneNumber property. The following code shows the method in the parent form that calls the Phone dialog:

```
Phone frm = new Phone();

frm.ShowDialog();
if (frm.DialogResult == DialogResult.OK)
{
  label1.Text = "Phone number is " + frm.PhoneNumber;
}
else if (frm.DialogResult == DialogResult.Cancel)
{
  label1.Text = "Form was canceled.";
}

frm.Close();
```

This looks simple enough. Create the new `Phone` object (`frm`). When the `frm.ShowDialog()` method is called, the code in this method will stop and wait for the `Phone` form to return. You can then check the `DialogResult` property of the `Phone` form. Because it has not been destroyed yet, just made invisible, you can still access the public properties, one of them being the `PhoneNumber` property. Once you get the data you need, you can call the `Close` method on the form.

This works well, but what if the returned phone number is not formatted correctly? If you put the `ShowDialog` inside of the loop, you can just recall it and have the user re-enter the value. This way, you get a proper value. Remember that you must also handle the `DialogResult.Cancel` if the user clicks the Cancel button.

```
Phone frm = new Phone();

while (true)
{
   frm.ShowDialog();
   if (frm.DialogResult == DialogResult.OK)
   {
      label1.Text = "Phone number is " + frm.PhoneNumber;
      if (frm.PhoneNumber.Length == 8 | frm.PhoneNumber.Length == 12)
      {
         break;
      }
      else
      {
         MessageBox.Show("Phone number was not formatted correctly.
                                                 Please correct entry.");
      }
   }
   else if (frm.DialogResult == DialogResult.Cancel)
   {
      label1.Text = "Form was canceled.";
      break;
   }
}
frm.Close();
```

Now if the phone number does not pass a simple test for length, the `Phone` form appears so the user can correct the error. The `ShowDialog` box does not create a new instance of the form. Any text entered on the form will still be there, so if the form has to be reset, it will be up to you to do that.

## Appearance

The first thing that the user sees is the form for the application. It should be first and foremost functional. If the application doesn't solve a business problem, it really doesn't matter how it looks. This is not to say that the form and application's overall GUI design should not be pleasing to the eye. Simple things like color combinations, font sizing, and window sizing can make an application much easier for the user.

Sometimes you don't want the user to have access to the system menu. This is the menu that appears when you click the icon on the top-left corner of a window. Generally it has items such as `Restore`, `Minimize`, `Maximize`, and `Close` on it. The `ControlBox` property allows you to set the visibility of the system menu. You can also set the visibility of the `Maximize` and `Minimize` buttons with the

# Windows Forms

`MaximizeBox` and `MinimizeBox` properties. If you remove all of the buttons and then set the `Text` property to an empty string (""), the title bar disappears completely.

If you set the `Icon` property of a form and you don't set the `ControlBox` property to `false`, the icon will appear in the top-left corner of the form. It's common to set this to the app.ico. This makes each form's icon the same as the application icon.

The `FormBorderStyle` property sets the type of border that appears around the form. This uses the `FormBorderStyle` enumeration. The values can be as follows:

- `Fixed3D`
- `FixedDialog`
- `FixedSingle`
- `FixedToolWindow`
- `None`
- `Sizable`
- `SizableToolWindow`

Most of these are self-explanatory, with the exception of the two tool window borders. A `Tool` window will not appear in the taskbar, regardless of how `ShowInTaskBar` is set. Also a `Tool` window will not show in the list of windows when the user presses Alt+Tab. The default setting is Sizable.

Unless a requirement dictates otherwise, colors for most GUI elements should be set to system colors and not to specific colors. This way if some users like to have all of their buttons green with purple text, the application will follow along with the same colors. To set a control to use a specific system color, you must call the `FromKnownColor` method of the `System.Drawing.Color` class. The `FromKnownColor` method takes a `KnownColor` enumeration value. Many colors are defined in the enumeration, as well as the various GUI element colors, such as `Control`, `ActiveBorder`, and `Desktop`. So, for example, if the `Background` color of the form should always match the `Desktop` color, the code would look like this:

```
myForm.BackColor = Color.FromKnownColor(KnownColor.Desktop);
```

Now if users change the color of their desktops, the background of the form changes as well. This is a nice, friendly touch to add to an application. Users might pick out some strange color combinations for their desktops, but it is their choice.

Windows XP introduced a feature called visual styles. Visual styles change the way buttons, text boxes, menus, and other controls look and react when the mouse pointer is either hovering or clicking. You can enable visual styles for your application by calling the `Application.EnableVisualStyles` method. This method has to be called before any type of GUI is instantiated. Because of this, it is generally called in the `Main` method, as demonstrated in this example:

```
[STAThread]
static void Main()
{
  Application.EnableVisualStyles();
  Application.Run(new Form1());
}
```

This code allows the various controls that support visual styles to take advantage of them. Because of an issue with the `EnableVisualStyles` method, you might have to add an `Application.DoEvents()` method right after the call to `EnableVisualStyles`. This should resolve the problem if icons on toolbars begin to disappear at runtime. Also, `EnableVisualStyles` is available only in .NET Framework 1.1.

You have to accomplish one more task pertaining to the controls. Most controls expose `FlatStyle` property that takes a `FlatStyle` enumeration as its value. This property can take one of four different values:

- `Flat`—Similar to flat, except that when the mouse pointer hovers over the control, it appears in 3D.
- `Standard`—The control appears in 3D.
- `System`—The look of the control is controlled by the operating system.

To enable visual styles, the control's `FlatStyle` property should be set to `FlatStyle.System`. The application will now take on the XP look and feel and will support XP themes.

## Multiple Document Interface (MDI)

MDI-type applications are used when you have an application that can show either multiple instances of the same type of form or different forms that must be contained in some way. An example of multiple instances of the same type of form is a text editor that can show multiple edit windows at the same time. An example of the second type of application is Microsoft Access. You can have query windows, design windows, and table windows all open at the same time. The windows never leave the boundaries of the main Access application.

The project that contains the examples for this chapter is an example of an MDI application. The form `mdiParent` in the project is the MDI parent form. Setting the `IsMdiContainer` to `true` will make any form an MDI parent form. If you have the form in the designer you'll notice that the background turns a dark gray color. This is to let you know that this is an MDI parent form. You can still add controls to the form, but it is generally not recommended.

For the child forms to behave like MDI children, the child form needs to know what form the parent is. This is done by setting the `MdiParent` property to the parent form. In the example, all children forms are created using the `ShowMdiChild` method. It takes a reference to the child form that is to be shown. After setting the `MdiParent` property to this, which is referencing the `mdiParent` form, the form is shown. Here is the code for the `ShowMdiParent` method:

```
private void ShowMdiChild(Form childForm)
{
   childForm.MdiParent = this;
   childForm.Show();
}
```

One of the issues with MDI applications is that there may be several child forms open at any given time. A reference to the current active child can be retrieved by using the `ActiveMdiChild` property on the

# Windows Forms

parent form. This is demonstrated on the `Current Active` menu choice on the Window menu. This will show a message box with the form's name and text value.

The child forms can be arranged by calling the `LayoutMdi` method. The `LayoutMdi` method takes an `MdiLayout` enumeration value as a parameter. The possible values include `Cascade`, `TileHorizontal`, and `TileVertical`.

## Custom Controls

Using controls and components is a big part of what makes developing with a forms package such as Windows Forms so productive. The ability to create your own controls, components, and user controls makes it even more productive. By creating controls, functionality can be encapsulated into packages that can be reused over and over.

You can create a control in a number of ways. You can start from scratch, deriving your class from either `Control`, `ScrollableControl`, or `ContainerControl`. You will have to override the `Paint` event and do all of your drawing, not to mention adding the functionality that your control is supposed to provide. If the control is supposed to be an enhanced version of a current control, the thing to do is to derive from the control that is being enhanced. For example, if a `TextBox` control is needed that changes background color if the `ReadOnly` property is set, creating a completely new `TextBox` control would be a waste of time. Derive from the `TextBox` control and override the `ReadOnly` property. Because the `ReadOnly` property of the `TextBox` control is not marked override, you have to use the new clause. The following code shows the new `ReadOnly` property:

```
public new bool ReadOnly
{
  get  { return base.ReadOnly;}
  set  {
    if(value)
       this.BackgroundColor = Color.Red;
    else
       this.BackgroundColor = Color.FromKnowColor(KnownColor.Window);

    base.ReadOnly = value;
  }
}
```

For the property `get`, you return what the base object is set to. The way that the property handles the process of making a text box read-only is not relevant here, so you just pass that functionality to the base object. In the property set, check to see if the passed-in value is `true` or `false`. If it is `true`, change the color to the read-only color (Red in this case); if it is `false`, set the `BackgroundColor` to the default. Finally, pass the value down to the base object so that the text box actually does become read-only. As you can see, by overriding one simple property, you can add new functionality to a control.

### Control attributes

You can add attributes to the custom control that will enhance the design-time capabilities of the control. The following table describes some of the more useful attributes.

| Attribute Name | Description |
|---|---|
| `BindableAttribute` | Used at design time to determine if the property supports two-way data binding. |
| `BrowsableAttribute` | Determines if the property is shown in the visual designer. |
| `CategoryAttribute` | Determines under what category the property is displayed in the Property window. Use on predefined categories or create new ones. Default is Misc. |
| `DefaultEventAttribute` | Specifies the default event for a class. |
| `DefaultPropertyAttribute` | Specifies the default property for a class. |
| `DefaultValueAttribute` | Specifies the default value for a property. Typically, this is the initial value. |
| `DecriptionAttribute` | This is the text that appears at the bottom of the designer window when the property is selected. |
| `DesignOnlyAttribute` | This marks the property as being editable in design mode only. |

Other attributes are available that relate to the editor that the property uses in design time and other advanced design-time capabilities. The `Category` and `Description` attributes should almost always be added. This helps other developers who use the control to better understand the property's purpose. To add IntelliSense support, you should add XML comments for each property, method, and event. When the control is compiled with the `/doc` option, the XML file of comments that is generated will provide IntelliSense for the control.

## *TreeView-based custom control*

This section shows you how to develop a custom control based on the `TreeView` control. This control displays the file structure of a drive. You'll add properties that set the base or root folder and determine whether files and folders will be displayed. You also use the various attributes discussed in the previous section.

As with any new project, requirements for the control have to be defined. Here is a list of basic requirements that have to be implemented:

- ❏ Read folders and files and display to user.
- ❏ Display folder structure in a tree-like hierarchical view.
- ❏ Optionally hide files from view.
- ❏ Define what folder should be the base or root folder.
- ❏ Return the currently selected folder.
- ❏ Provide the ability to delay loading of the file structure.

This should be a good starting point. One requirement has been satisfied by the fact the `TreeView` control will be the base of the new control.

# Windows Forms

The `TreeView` control displays data in a hierarchical format. It displays text describing the object in the list and optionally an icon. This list can be expanded and contracted by clicking an object or using the arrows keys.

Create a new Windows Control Library project in Visual Studio .NET named `FolderTree`, and delete the class `UserControl1`. Add a new class and call it `FolderTree`. Because `FolderTree` will be derived from `TreeView`, change the class declaration from

```
public class FolderTree
```

to

```
public class FolderTree  :  System.Windows.Forms.TreeView
```

At this point, you actually have a fully functional and working `FolderTree` control. It will do everything that the `TreeView` can do, and nothing more.

The `TreeView` control maintains a collection of `TreeNode` objects. You can't load files and folders directly into the control. You have a couple of ways to map the `TreeNode` that is loaded into the `Nodes` collection of the `TreeView` and the file or folder that it represents.

For example, when each folder is processed, a new `TreeNode` object is created, and the text property is set to the name of the file or folder. If at some point additional information about the file or folder is needed, you have to make another trip to the disk to gather that information or store additional data regarding the file or folder in the `Tag` property.

Another method is to create a new class that is derived from `TreeNode`. New properties and methods can be added and the base functionality of the `TreeNode` is still there. This is the path that you use in this example. It allows for a more flexible design. If you need new properties, you can add them easily without breaking the existing code.

You must load two types of objects into the control: folders and files. Each has its own characteristics. For example, folders have a `DirectoryInfo` object that contains additional information, and files have a `FileInfo` object. Because of these differences you use two separate classes to load the `TreeView` control: `FileNode` and `FolderNode`. You add these two classes to the project; each is derived from `TreeNode`. This is the listing for `FileNode`:

```
namespace FormsSample.SampleControls
{
  public class FileNode : System.Windows.Forms.TreeNode
  {
    string _fileName = "";
    FileInfo _info;

    public FileNode(string fileName)
    {
      _fileName = fileName;
      _info = new FileInfo(_fileName);
      base.Text = _info.Name;
      if (_info.Extension.ToLower() == ".exe")
        this.ForeColor = System.Drawing.Color.Red;
```

```
      }

      public string FileName
      {
        get { return _fileName; }
        set { _fileName = value; }
      }


      public FileInfo FileNodeInfo
      {
        get { return _info; }
      }

    }
  }
```

The name of the file being processed is passed into the constructor of `FileNode`. In the constructor the `FileInfo` object for the file is created and set to the member variable `_info`. The `base.Text` property is set to the name of the file. Because you are deriving from `TreeNode`, this sets the `TreeNode`'s `Text` property. This is the text displayed in the `TreeView` control.

Two properties are added to retrieve the data. `FileName` returns the name of the file and `FileNodeInfo` returns the `FileInfo` object for the file.

Here is the code for the `FolderNode` class. It is very similar in structure to the `FileNode` class. The differences are that you have a `DirectoryInfo` property instead of `FileInfo`, and instead of `FileName` you have `FolderPath`:

```
namespace FormsSample.SampleControls
{
  public class FolderNode : System.Windows.Forms.TreeNode
  {
    string _folderPath = "";
    DirectoryInfo _info;

    public FolderNode(string folderPath)
    {
      _folderPath = folderPath;
      _info = new DirectoryInfo(folderPath);
      this.Text = _info.Name;
    }

    public string FolderPath
    {
      get { return _folderPath; }
      set { _folderPath = value; }
    }

    public DirectoryInfo FolderNodeInfo
    {
      get { return _info; }
```

           }
        }
}

Now you can construct the `FolderTree` control. Based on the requirements, you need a property to read and set the `RootFolder`. You also need a `ShowFiles` property for determining if files should be shown in the tree. A `SelectedFolder` property returns the currently highlighted folder in the tree. This is what the code looks like so far for the `FolderTree` control:

```
using System;
using System.Windows.Forms;
using System.IO;
using System.ComponentModel;

namespace FolderTree
{
   /// <summary>
   /// Summary description for FolderTreeCtrl.
   /// </summary>
   public class FolderTree :   System.Windows.Forms.TreeView
   {
      string _rootFolder = "";
      bool _showFiles = true;
      bool _inInit = false;

      public FolderTree()
      {

      }

      [Category("Behavior"),
         Description("Gets or sets the base or root folder of the tree"),
         DefaultValue("C:\\")]
      public string RootFolder
      {
        get {return _rootFolder;}
        set
        {
          _rootFolder = value;
          if(!_inInit)
            InitializeTree();


        }
      }



      [Category("Behavior"),
         Description("Indicates whether files will be seen in the list."),
         DefaultValue(true)]
      public bool ShowFiles
      {
```

```csharp
      get {return _showFiles;}
      set {_showFiles = value;}
    }


    [Browsable(false)]
    public string SelectedFolder
    {
      get
      {
        if(this.SelectedNode is FolderNode)
          return ((FolderNode)this.SelectedNode).FolderPath;

        return "";
      }
    }
  }
}
```

Three properties were added: `ShowFiles`, `SelectedFolder`, and `RootFolder`. Notice the attributes that have been added. You set `Category`, `Description`, and `DefaultValues` for the `ShowFiles` and `RootFolder`. These two properties will appear in the property browser in design mode. The `SelectedFolder` really has no meaning at design time, so you select the `Browsable=false` attribute. `SelectedFolder` does not appear in the property browser. However, because it is a public property, it will appear in IntelliSense and is accessible in code.

Next, you have to initialize the loading of the file system. Initializing a control can be tricky. Both design time and runtime initializing must be well thought out. When a control is sitting on a designer, it is actually running. If there is a call to a database in the constructor, for example, this call will execute when you drop the control on the designer. In the case of the `FolderTree` control, this can be an issue.

Here's a look at the method that is actually going to load the files:

```csharp
private void LoadTree(FolderNode folder)
{
  string[] dirs = Directory.GetDirectories(folder.FolderPath);
  foreach(string dir in dirs)
  {
    FolderNode tmpfolder = new FolderNode(dir);
    folder.Nodes.Add(tmpfolder);
    LoadTree(tmpfolder);
  }
  if(_showFiles)
  {

    string[] files = Directory.GetFiles(folder.FolderPath);
    foreach(string file in files)
    {
      FileNode fnode = new FileNode(file);
      folder.Nodes.Add(fnode);
    }

  }
}
```

# Windows Forms

showFiles is a `Boolean` member variable that is set from the `ShowFiles` property. If `true`, files are also shown in the tree. The only question now is when `LoadTree` should be called. You have several options. It can be called when the `RootFolder` property is set. That is desirable in some situations, but not at design time. Remember that the control is "live" on the designer so when the `RootNode` property is set, the control will attempt to load the file system.

What you can do to solve this is to check the `DesignMode` property. This returns `true` if the control is in the designer. Now you can write the code to initialize the control:

```
private void InitializeTree()
{
   if(!this.DesignMode && _rootFolder != "")
   {
      FolderNode rootNode = new FolderNode(_rootFolder);
      LoadTree(rootNode);
      this.Nodes.Clear();
      this.Nodes.Add(rootNode);
   }
}
```

If the control is not in design mode and `_rootFolder` is not an empty string, the loading of the tree will begin. The `Root` node is created first and this is passed into the `LoadTree` method.

Another option is to implement a public `Init` method. In the `Init` method the call to `LoadTree` can happen. The problem with this option is that the developer who uses your control is required to make the `Init` call. Depending on the situation, this might be an acceptable solution.

For added flexibility the `ISupportInitialize` interface can be implemented. `ISupportInitialize` has two methods, `BeginInit` and `EndInit`. When a control implements `ISupportInitialize` the `BeginInit` and `EndInit` methods are called automatically in the generated code in `Initialize Component`. This allows the initialization process to be delayed until all of the properties are set. `ISupportInitialize` allows the code in the parent form to delay initialization as well. If the `RootNode` property is being set in code, a call to `BeginInit` first will allow the `RootNode` property as well as other properties to be set or actions to be performed before the control loads the file system. When `EndInit` is called, the control initializes. This is what `BeginInit` and `EndInit` look like:

```
#region ISupportInitialize Members

void ISupportInitialize.BeginInit()
{
   _inInit = true;
}

void ISupportInitialize.EndInit()
{

   if(_rootFolder != "")
   {
      InitializeTree();
   }

   _inInit = false;
```

```
    }

    #endregion
```

In the `BeginInit` method, all that is done is that a member variable `_inInit` is set to `true`. This flag is used to determine if the control is in the initialization process and is used in the `RootFolder` property. If the `RootFolder` property is set outside of the `InitializeComponent` class, the tree will need to be reinitialized. In the `RootFolder` property you check to see if `_inInit` is `true` or `false`. If it is `true`, then you don't want to go through the initialization process. If `inInit` is `false`, you call `InitializeTree`. You could also have a public `Init` method and accomplish the same task.

In the `EndInit` method you check to see if the control is in design mode and if `_rootFolder` has a valid path assigned to it. Only then is `InitializeTree` called.

To add a final professional-looking touch, you have to add a bitmap image. This is the icon that shows up in the Toolbox when the control is added to a project. The bitmap image should be 16×16 pixels and 16 colors. You can create this image file with any graphics editor as long as the size and color depth are set properly. You can even create this file in Visual Studio .NET: right-click the project and select Add New Item. From the list select Bitmap File to open the graphics editor. After you have created the bitmap file, add it to the project, making sure it is in the same namespace and has the same name as the control. Finally, set the Build Action of the bitmap to Embedded Resource: Right-click the bitmap file in the Solution Explorer and select Properties. Select Embedded Resource form the Build Action property.

To test the control, create a `TestHarness` project in the same solution. The `TestHarness` is a simple Windows Forms application with a single form. In the references section add a reference to the `FolderTreeCtl` project. In the Toolbox window, add a reference to the `FolderTreeCtl.DLL`. `FolderTreeCtl` should now show up in the toolbox with the bitmap added as the icon. Click the icon and drag it to the `TestHarness` form. Set the `RootFolder` to an available folder and run the solution.

This is by no means a complete control. Several things could be enhanced to make this a full-featured, production-ready control. For example, you could add the following:

- **Exceptions** — If the control tries to load a folder that the user does not have access to, an exception is raised.
- **Background loading** — Loading a large folder tree can take a long time. Enhancing the initialization process to take advantage of a background thread for loading is a good idea.
- **Color codes** — You can make the text of certain file types a different color.
- **Icons** — You can add an `ImageList` control and add an icon to each file or folder as it is loaded.

## User control

User controls are one of the more powerful features of Windows Forms. They allow encapsulating user interface designs into nice reusable packages that can be plugged into project after project. It is not uncommon for an organization to have a couple of libraries of frequently used user controls. Not only can user interface functionality be contained in user controls, but common data validation can be incorporated in them as well, such as formatting phone numbers or id numbers. A predefined list of items can be in the user control for fast loading of a list box or combo box. State codes or country codes fit into this category. Incorporating as much functionality that does not depend on the current application as possible into a user control makes the control that much more useful in the organization.

## Windows Forms

In this section, you create a simple address user control. You also will add the various events that make the control ready for data binding. The address control will have text entry for two address lines, city, state, and zip code.

To create a user control in a current project, just right-click the project in Solution Explorer and select Add, and then select Add New User Control. You can also create a new Control Library project and add user controls to it. After a new user control has been started, you will see a form without any borders on the designer. This is where you drop the controls that make up the user control. Remember that a user control is actually one or more controls added to a container control, so it is somewhat like creating a form. For the address control there are five `TextBox` controls and three `Label` controls. The controls can be arranged any way that seems appropriate (see Figure 23-5).

The `TextBox` controls in this example are named as follows:

- ❑ txtAddress1
- ❑ txtAddress2
- ❑ txtCity
- ❑ txtState
- ❑ txtZip

Figure 23-5

795

After the `TextBox` controls are in place and have valid names, add the public properties. You might be tempted to set the visibility of the `TextBox` controls to public instead of private. However, this is not a good idea, because it defeats the purpose of encapsulating the functionality that you might want to add to the properties. Here is a listing of the properties that must be added:

```
public string AddressLine1
{
  get{return txtAddress1.Text;}
  set{
    if(txtAddress1.Text != value)
    {
      txtAddress1.Text = value;
      if(AddressLine1Changed != null)
        AddressLine1Changed(this, PropertyChangedEventArgs.Empty);
    }
  }
}

public string AddressLine2
{
  get{return txtAddress2.Text;}
  set{
    if(txtAddress2.Text != value)
    {
      txtAddress2.Text = value;
      if(AddressLine2Changed != null)
        AddressLine2Changed(this, PropertyChangedEventArgs.Empty);
    }
  }
}

public string City
{
  get{return txtCity.Text;}
  set{
    if(txtCity.Text != value)
    {
      txtCity.Text = value;
      if(CityChanged != null)
        CityChanged(this, PropertyChangedEventArgs.Empty);
    }
  }
}

public string State
{
  get{return txtState.Text;}
  set{
    if(txtState.Text != value)
    {
      txtState.Text = value;
      if(StateChanged != null)
```

```
            StateChanged(this, PropertyChangedEventArgs.Empty);
        }
    }
}

public string Zip
{
  get{return txtZip.Text;}
  set{
    if(txtZip.Text != value)
    {
      txtZip.Text = value;
      if(ZipChanged != null)
        ZipChanged(this, PropertyChangedEventArgs.Empty);
    }
  }
}
```

The property `get`s are fairly straightforward. They return the value of the corresponding `TextBox` control's text property. The property `set`s, however, are doing a bit more work. All of the property `set`s work the same way. A check is made to see whether or not the value of the property is actually changing. If the new value is the same as the current value, then a quick escape can be made. If there is a new value sent in, set the text property of the `TextBox` to the new value and test to see if an event has been instantiated. The event to look for is the changed event for the property. It has a specific naming format, *propertyname*Changed where *propertyname* is the name of the property. In the case of the `AddressLine1` property, this event is called `AddressLine1Changed`. The properties are declared as follows:

```
public event EventHandler AddressLine1Changed;
public event EventHandler AddressLine2Changed;
public event EventHandler CityChanged;
public event EventHandler StateChanged;
public event EventHandler ZipChanged;
```

The purpose of the events is to notify binding that the property has changed. Once validation occurs, binding will make sure that the new value makes its way back to the object that the control is bound to. One other step should be done to support binding. A change to the text box by the user will not set the property directly. So the `propertynameChanged` event must be raised when the text box changes as well. The easiest way to do this is to monitor the `TextChanged` event of the `TextBox` control. This example has only one `TextChanged` event handler and all of the text boxes use it. The control name is checked to see which control raised the event and the appropriate `propertynameChanged` event is raised. Here is the code for the event handler:

```
private void TextBoxControls_TextChanged(
                              object sender, System.EventArgs e)
{
  switch(((TextBox)sender).Name)
  {
    case "txtAddress1" :
       if(AddressLine1Changed != null)
         AddressLine1Changed(this, EventArgs.Empty);
```

```
            break;

        case "txtAddress2" :
          if(AddressLine2Changed != null)
             AddressLine2Changed(this, EventArgs.Empty);

          break;

        case "txtCity" :
          if(CityChanged != null)
             CityChanged(this, EventArgs.Empty);

          break;

        case "txtState" :
            if(StateChanged != null)
              StateChanged(this, EventArgs.Empty);

            break;

        case "txtZip" :
            if(ZipChanged != null)
              ZipChanged(this, EventArgs.Empty);

            break;

    }
}
```

This example uses a simple `switch` statement to determine which text box raised the `TextChanged` event. Then a check is made to verify that the event is valid and not equal to null. Then the `Changed` event is raised. One thing to note is that an empty `EventArgs` is sent (`EventArgs.Empty`). Because these events have been added to the properties to support data binding does not mean that the only way to use the control is with data binding. The properties can be set in and read from code without using data binding. They have been added so that the user control is able to use binding if it is available. This is just one way of making the user control as flexible as possible so that it might be used in as many situations as possible.

Remembering that a user control is essentially a control with some added features, all of the design-time issues discussed in the previous section apply here as well. Initializing user controls can bring on the same issues that you saw in the `FolderTree` example. Care must be taken in the design of user controls so that access to data stores that might not be available to other developers using your control is avoided.

The other thing that is similar to the control creation is the attributes that can be applied to user controls. The public properties and methods of the user control are displayed in the Properties Window when the control is placed on the designer. In the example of the address user control it is a good idea to add `Category`, `Description`, and `DefaultValue` attributes to the address properties. A new `AddressData` category can be created and the default values would all be "". Here is an example of these attributes applied to the `AddressLine1` property:

```csharp
[Category("AddressData"),
      Description("Gets or sets the AddressLine1 value"),
      DefaultValue("")]
public string AddressLine1
{
  get{return txtAddress1.Text;}
  set{
    if(txtAddress1.Text != value)
    {
      txtAddress1.Text = value;
      if(AddressLine1Changed != null)
        AddressLine1Changed(this, EventArgs.Empty);
    }
  }
}
```

As you can see, all that needs to be done to add a new category is to set the text in the `Category` attribute. The new category is automatically added.

There still is a lot of room for improvement. For example, you could include a list of state names and abbreviations in the control. Instead of just the state property, the user control could expose both the state name and state abbreviation properties. Exception handling should also be added. You could also add validation for the address lines. Making sure the casing is correct, you might ask yourself whether AddressLine1 could be optional or whether apartment and suite numbers should be entered on AddressLine2 and not on AddressLine1.

# Summary

This chapter has given you the basics for building Windows client-based applications. It explained each of the basic controls by discussing the hierarchy of the Windows.Forms namespace and examining the various properties and methods of the controls.

The chapter also showed you how to create a basic custom control as well as a basic user control. The power and flexibility of creating your own controls cannot be emphasized enough. By creating your own toolbox of custom controls, Windows-based client application will become easier to develop and to test, because you will be reusing the same tested components over and over again.

# 24

# Viewing .NET Data

This chapter builds on the content of Chapter 19, "Data Access with .NET," which covers various ways of selecting and changing data, showing you how to present data to the user by binding to various Windows controls. More specifically, this chapter discusses:

- Displaying data using the `DataGridView` control — new with Visual Studio 2005
- The .NET data-binding capabilities and how they work
- How to use the Server Explorer to create a connection and generate a `DataSet` class (all without writing a line of code)
- How to use hit testing and reflection on rows in the `DataGrid`

You can download the source code for the examples in this chapter from the Wrox Web site at www.wrox.com.

## The DataGridView Control

The `DataGrid` control that has been available from the initial release of .NET was functional, but had many areas that made it unsuitable for use in a commercial application — such as an inability to display images, drop-down controls, or lock columns, to name but a few. The control always felt half completed, so many control vendors provided custom grid controls that overcame these deficiencies and also provided much more functionality.

With .NET 2.0, you now have an additional `Grid` control — the `DataGridView`. This addresses many of the deficiencies of the original control, and adds significant functionality that has to this point only been available with add-on products.

The new control has similar binding capabilities as the old `DataGrid`, so it can bind to an `Array`, `DataTable`, `DataView`, or `DataSet` class, or a component that implements either the

# Chapter 24

`IListSource` or `IList` interface. The `DataGridView` control gives you a variety of views of the same data. In its simplest guise, data can be displayed (as in a `DataSet` class) by setting the `DataSource` and `DataMember` properties — note that this new control is not a plug-in replacement for the `DataGrid`, so the programmatic interface to it is entirely different than that of the `DataGrid`. This control also provides more complex capabilities, which are discussed in the course of this chapter.

## Displaying Tabular Data

Chapter 19 introduced numerous ways of selecting data and reading it into a data table, although the data was displayed in a very basic fashion using `Console.WriteLine()`.

The following example demonstrates how to retrieve some data and display it in a `DataGridView` control. For this purpose, you'll build a new application, `DisplayTabularData`, shown in Figure 24-1.

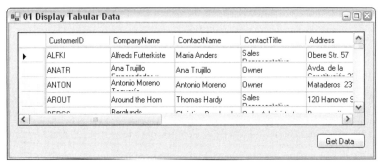

**Figure 24-1**

This simple application selects every record from the Customer table in the Northwind database, and displays these records to the user in the `DataGridView` control. The following snippet shows the code for this example (excluding the form and control definition code):

```
#region Using directives

using System;
using System.Configuration;
using System.Data;
using System.Data.Common;
using System.Data.SqlClient;
using System.Windows.Forms;

#endregion

namespace DisplayTabularData
{
    partial class Form1: Form
    {
        public Form1()
        {
            InitializeComponent();
        }
```

# Viewing .NET Data

```csharp
        private void getData_Click(object sender, EventArgs e)
        {
          string customers = "SELECT * FROM Customers";

          using (SqlConnection con =
                  new SqlConnection (ConfigurationSettings.
                    ConnectionStrings["northwind"].ConnectionString))
          {
            DataSet ds = new DataSet();

            SqlDataAdapter da = new SqlDataAdapter(customers, con);

            da.Fill(ds, "Customers");

            dataGridView.AutoGenerateColumns = true;
            dataGridView.DataSource = ds;
            dataGridView.DataMember = "Customers";
          }
        }
      }
    }
```

The form consists of the getData button, which when clicked calls the getData_Click method shown in the example code.

This constructs a `SqlConnection` object, using the new `ConnectionStrings` property of the `ConfigurationSettings` class. Subsequently a dataset is constructed, and filled from the database table using a `DataAdapter` object. The data is then displayed by the `DataGridView` control by setting the `DataSource` and `DataMember` properties. Note that the AutoGenerateColumns property is also set to `true`, because this ensures that something is displayed to the user. If this flag is not specified, you need to create all columns yourself.

## Data Sources

The `DataGridView` control provides a flexible way to display data; in addition to setting the DataSource to a `DataSet` and the DataMember to the name of the table to display, the DataSource property can be set to any of the following sources:

- An array (the grid can bind to any one-dimensional array)
- `DataTable`
- `DataView`
- `DataSet` or `DataViewManager`
- Components that implement the `IListSource` interface
- Components that implement the `IList` interface
- Any generic collection class or object derived from a generic collection class

The following sections give an example of each of these data sources.

# Chapter 24

## Displaying data from an array

At first glance this seems to be easy. Create an array, fill it with some data, and set the DataSource property on the `DataGridView` control. Here's some example code:

```
string[] stuff = new string[] {"One", "Two", "Three"};
dataGridView.DataSource = stuff;
```

If the data source contains multiple possible candidate tables (such as when using a `DataSet` or `DataViewManager`), you need also to set the DataMember property.

You could replace the code in the previous examples `getData_Click` event handler with the preceding array code. The problem with this code is the resulting display (see Figure 24-2).

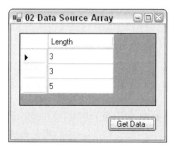

**Figure 24-2**

Instead of displaying the strings defined within the array, the grid displays the length of those strings. The reason for this is that when using an array as the source of data for a `DataGridView` control, the grid looks for the first public property of the object within the array and displays this value rather than the string value. The first (and only) public property of a string is its length, so that is what is displayed. The list of properties for any class can be obtained using the `GetProperties` method of the `TypeDescriptor` class. This returns a collection of `PropertyDescriptor` objects, which can then be used when displaying data. The .NET PropertyGrid control uses this method when displaying arbitrary objects.

One way to rectify the problem with displaying strings in the DataGridView is to create a wrapper class:

```
protected class Item
{
    public Item(string text)
    {
        _text = text;
    }
    public string Text
    {
        get{return _text;}
    }
    private string _text;
}
```

Figure 24-3 shows the output when an array of this `Item` class (which could just as well be a `struct` for all the processing that it does) is added to your data source array code.

# Viewing .NET Data

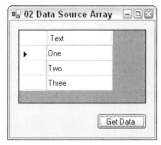

Figure 24-3

## *DataTable*

You can display a `DataTable` within a `DataGridView` control in two ways:

- ❑ If your `DataTable` is standalone, simply set the DataSource property of the control to the table.

- ❑ If your `DataTable` is contained within a `DataSet`, you need to set the DataSource to the dataset, and the DataMember property should be set to the name of the DataTable within the dataset.

Figure 24-4 shows the result of running the `DataSourceDataTable` sample code.

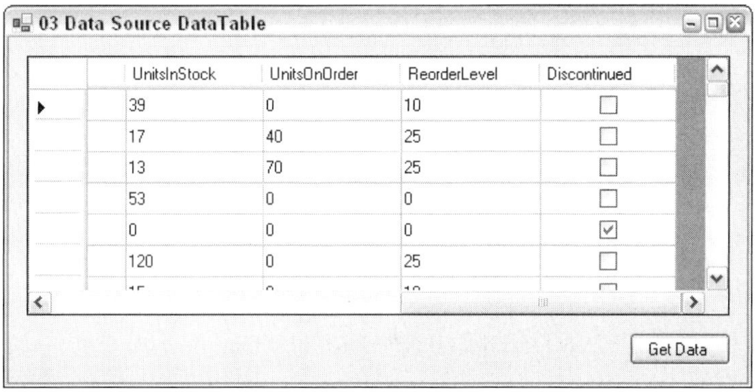

Figure 24-4

Note the display of the last column; it shows a check box instead of the more common edit control. The `DataGridView` control, in the absence of any other information, will read the schema from the data source (which in this case is the Products table), and infer from the column types what control is to be displayed. Unlike the original `DataGrid` control, the `DataGridView` control has built-in support for image columns, buttons, and combo boxes.

The data in the database does not change when fields are altered in the data grid, because the data is stored only locally on the client computer — there is no active connection to the database. Updating data in the database is discussed later in this chapter.

805

# Chapter 24

## Displaying data from a DataView

A `DataView` provides a means to filter and sort data within a `DataTable`. When data has been selected from the database, it is common to permit the user to sort that data, such as by clicking on column headings. In addition, the user might want to filter the data to show only certain rows, such as all those that have been altered. A `DataView` can be filtered so that only selected rows are shown to the user; however, it does not limit the columns from the `DataTable`.

> A `DataView` **does not permit filtering of columns, only rows.**

An example of how to limit the columns shown is provided in the section "DataGridTableStyle and DataGridColumnStyle" later in this chapter.

To create a `DataView` based on an existing `DataTable` use the following code:

```
DataView dv = new DataView(dataTable);
```

Once created, further settings can be altered on the `DataView`, which affect the data and operations permitted on that data when it is displayed within the data grid. For example:

- Setting `AllowEdit = false` disables all column edit functionality for rows
- Setting `AllowNew = false` disables the new row functionality
- Setting `AllowDelete = false` disables the delete row capability
- Setting the `RowStateFilter` displays only rows of a given state
- Setting the `RowFilter` enables you to filter rows

The next section explains how to use the `RowStateFilter` setting; the other options are fairly self-explanatory.

## Filtering rows by data

After the `DataView` has been created, the data displayed by that view can be altered by setting the `RowFilter` property. This property, typed as a string, is used as a means of filtering based on certain criteria defined by the value of the string. Its syntax is similar to a WHERE clause in regular SQL, but it is issued against data already selected from the database.

The following table shows some examples of filter clauses.

| Clause | Description |
| --- | --- |
| `UnitsInStock > 50` | Shows only those rows where the `UnitsInStock` column is greater than 50. |
| `Client = 'Smith'` | Returns only the records for a given client. |
| `County LIKE 'C*'` | Returns all records where the `County` field begins with a C — in this example, the rows for Cornwall, Cumbria, Cheshire, and Cambridgeshire would be returned. The `%` character can be used as a single-character wildcard, whereas the `*` denotes a general wildcard that will match zero or more characters. |

# Viewing .NET Data

The runtime will do its best to coerce the data types used within the filter expression into the appropriate types for the source columns. As an example, it is perfectly legal to write `"UnitsInStock > '50'"` in the earlier example, even though the column is an integer. If an invalid filter string is provided, an `EvaluateException` will be thrown.

## Filtering rows on state

Each row within a `DataView` has a defined row state, which has one of the values shown in the following table. This state can also be used to filter the rows viewed by the user.

| DataViewRowState | Description |
| --- | --- |
| Added | Lists all rows that have been newly created. |
| CurrentRows | Lists all rows except those that have been deleted. |
| Deleted | Lists all rows that were originally selected and have been deleted; does not show newly created rows that have been deleted. |
| ModifiedCurrent | Lists all rows that have been modified, and shows the current value of each column. |
| ModifiedOriginal | Lists all rows that have been modified, but shows the original value of the column and not the current value. |
| OriginalRows | Lists all rows that were originally selected from a data source. Does not include new rows. Shows the original values of the columns (that is, not the current values if changes have been made). |
| Unchanged | Lists all rows that have not changed in any way. |

Figure 24-5 shows a grid that can have rows added, deleted, or amended and a second grid that lists rows in one of the preceding states.

The filter not only applies to the visible rows but also to the state of the columns within those rows. This is evident when choosing the `ModifiedOriginal` or `ModifiedCurrent` selections. These states are described in Chapter 19, and are based on the `DataRowVersion` enumeration. For example, when the user has updated a column in the row, the row will be displayed when either `ModifiedOriginal` or `ModifiedCurrent` are chosen; however, the actual value will either be the `Original` value selected from the database (if `ModifiedOriginal` is chosen) or the current value in the `DataColumn` (if `ModifiedCurrent` is chosen).

## Sorting rows

Apart from filtering data, you might also have to sort the data within a `DataView`. To sort data in ascending or descending order, simply click the column header in the `DataGridView` control (see Figure 24-6). The only trouble is that the control can sort by only one column, whereas the underlying `DataView` control can sort by multiple columns.

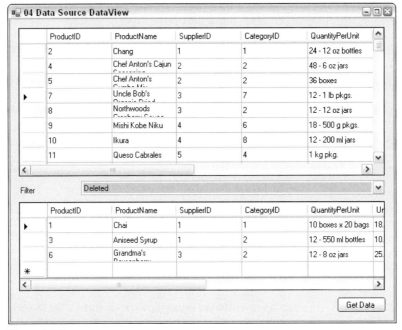

Figure 24-5

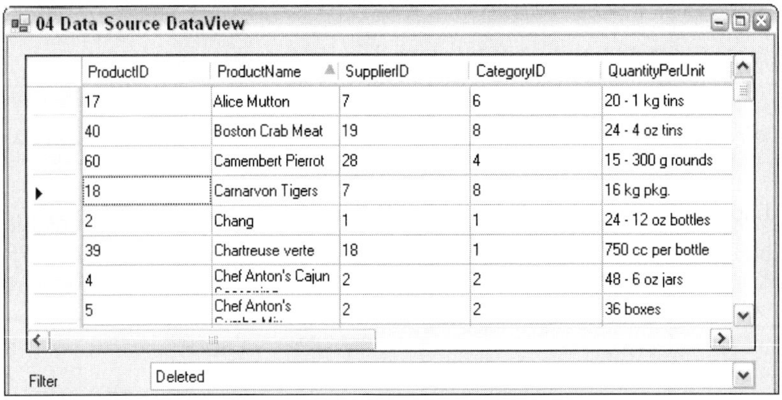

Figure 24-6

When a column is sorted, either by clicking the header (as shown on the ProductName column) or in code, the `DataGrid` displays an arrow bitmap to indicate which column the sort has been applied to.

To set the sort order on a column programmatically, use the `Sort` property of the `DataView`:

```
dataView.Sort = "ProductName";
dataView.Sort = "ProductName ASC, ProductID DESC";
```

# Viewing .NET Data

The first line sorts the data based on the ProductName column, as shown in Figure 24-6. The second line sorts the data in ascending order, based on the ProductName column, then in descending order of ProductID.

The `DataView` supports both ascending (default) and descending sort orders on columns. If more than one column is sorted in code in the `DataView`, the `DataGridView` will cease to display any sort arrows.

Each column in the grid can be strongly typed, so its sort order is not based on the string representation of the column but instead is based on the data within that column. The upshot is that if there is a date column in the `DataGrid`, the user can sort numerically on the date rather than on the date string representation.

## Displaying data from a DataSet class

There is one feature of `DataSets` that the `DataGridView` cannot match the `DataGrid` in — this is where a `DataSet` is defined that includes relationships between tables. As with the preceding `DataGridView` examples, the `DataGrid` can only display a single `DataTable` at a time. However, as shown in the following example, `DataSourceDataSet`, it is possible to navigate relationships within the `DataSet` onscreen. The following code can be used to generate such a `DataSet` based on the Customers and Orders tables in the Northwind database. This example loads data from these two `DataTables` and then creates a relationship between these tables called `CustomerOrders`:

```
string orders = "SELECT * FROM Orders";
string customers = "SELECT * FROM Customers";
SqlConnection conn = new SqlConnection(source);
SqlDataAdapter da = new SqlDataAdapter(orders, conn);
DataSet ds = new DataSet();
da.Fill(ds, "Orders");
da = new SqlDataAdapter(customers , conn);
da.Fill(ds, "Customers");
ds.Relations.Add("CustomerOrders",
            ds.Tables["Customers"].Columns["CustomerID"],
            ds.Tables["Orders"].Columns["CustomerID"]);
```

Once created, the data in the `DataSet` is bound to the `DataGrid` simply by calling `SetDataBinding()`:

```
dataGrid1.SetDataBinding(ds, "Customers");
```

This produces the output shown in Figure 24-7.

Unlike the `DataGridView` examples shown in this chapter, there is now a + sign to the left of each record. This reflects the fact that the `DataSet` has a navigable relationship between customers and orders. Any number of such relationships can be defined in code.

When the user clicks the + sign, the list of relationships is shown (or hidden if already visible). Clicking the name of the relationship enables you to navigate to the linked records (see Figure 24-8); in this example, listing all orders placed by the selected customer.

# Chapter 24

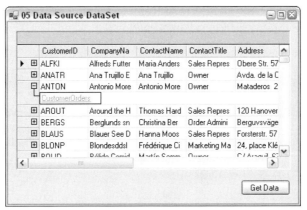

Figure 24-7

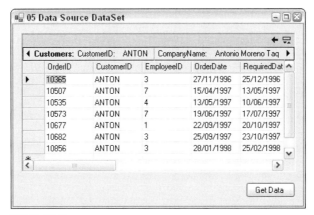

Figure 24-8

The `DataGrid` control also includes a couple of new icons in the top-right corner. The arrow permits the user to navigate to the parent row, and will change the display to that on the previous page. The header row showing details of the parent record can be shown or hidden by clicking the other button.

## Displaying data in a DataViewManager

The display of data in a `DataViewManager` is the same as that for the `DataSet` shown in the previous section. However, when a `DataViewManager` is created for a `DataSet`, an individual `DataView` is created for each `DataTable`, which then permits the code to alter the displayed rows based on a filter or the row state as shown in the `DataView` example. Even if the code doesn't need to filter data, it is good practice to wrap the `DataSet` in a `DataViewManager` for display, because it provides more options when revising the source code.

The following creates a `DataViewManager` based on the `DataSet` from the previous example, and then alters the `DataView` for the `Customers` table to show only customers from the United Kingdom:

# Viewing .NET Data

```
DataViewManager dvm = new DataViewManager(ds);
dvm.DataViewSettings["Customers"].RowFilter = "Country='UK'";
dataGrid.SetDataBinding(dvm, "Customers");
```

Figure 24-9 shows the output of the `DataSourceDataViewManager` sample code.

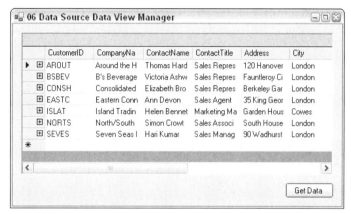

**Figure 24-9**

## IListSource and IList interfaces

The `DataGridView` also supports any object that exposes one of the interfaces `IListSource` or `IList`. `IListSource` only has one method, `GetList()`, which returns an `IList` interface. `IList`, on the other hand, is somewhat more interesting and is implemented by a large number of classes in the runtime. Some of the classes that implement this interface are `Array`, `ArrayList`, and `StringCollection`.

When using `IList`, the same caveat for the object within the collection holds true as for the `Array` implementation shown earlier — if a `StringCollection` is used as the data source for the `DataGrid`, the length of the strings is displayed within the grid, not within the text of the item as expected.

## Displaying generic collections

In addition to the types already described, the `DataGridView` also supports binding to generic collections. The syntax is just as in the other examples already provided in this chapter — simply set the `DataSource` property to the collection and the control will generate an appropriate display.

Once again, the columns displayed are based on the properties of the object — all public readable fields are displayed in the `DataGridView`. The following example shows the display for a list class defined as follows:

```
class PersonList : List < Person >
{
}

class Person
{
    public Person( string name, Sex sex, DateTime dob )
```

811

```csharp
        {
            _name = name;
            _sex = sex;
            _dateOfBirth = dob;
        }

        public string Name
        {
            get { return _name; }
            set { _name = value; }
        }

        public Sex Sex
        {
            get { return _sex; }
            set { _sex = value; }
        }

        public DateTime DateOfBirth
        {
            get { return _dateOfBirth; }
            set { _dateOfBirth = value; }
        }

        private string _name;
        private Sex _sex;
        private DateTime _dateOfBirth;
    }

    enum Sex
    {
        Male,
        Female
    }
```

The display shows several instances of the `Person` class that were constructed within the `PersonList` class. See Figure 24-10.

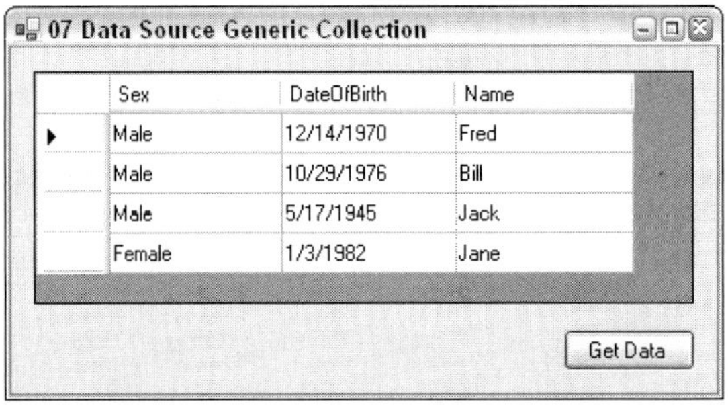

**Figure 24-10**

# Viewing .NET Data

In some circumstances it might be necessary to hide certain properties from the grid display — for this you can utilize the `Browsable` attribute as shown in the following code snippet. Any properties marked as non-browsable are not displayed in the property grid.

```
[Browsable(false)]
public bool IsEmployed
{
    ...
}
```

The `DataGridView` uses this property to determine whether to display the property or hide it. In the absence of the attribute, the default is to display the property. If a property is read-only, the grid control will display the values from the object, but it will be read-only within the grid.

Any changes made in the grid view are reflected in the underlying objects — so for example if in the previous code the name of a person was changed within the user interface, the setter method for that property would be called.

## DataGridView Class Hierarchy

The class hierarchy for the main parts of the `DataGridView` control is shown in Figure 24-11.

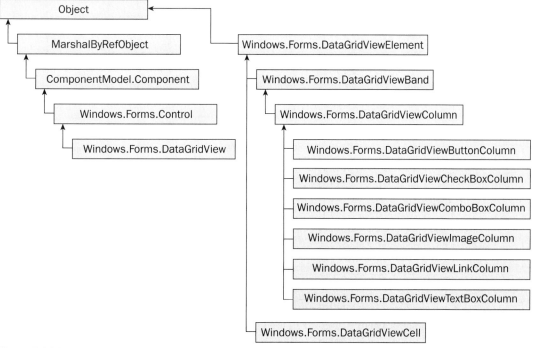

Figure 24-11

The control utilizes objects derived from `DataGridViewColumn` when displaying data—as you can see from Figure 24-11, there are now far more options for displaying data than there were with the original `DataGrid`. One major omission was the display of drop-down columns within the `DataGrid`—this functionality has now been provided for the `DataGridView` in the form of the `DataGridViewComboBoxColumn`.

When you specify a data source for the `DataGridView`, by default it will construct columns for you automatically. These will be created based on the data types in the data source, so for example any Boolean field will be mapped to the `DataGridViewCheckBoxColumn`. If you would rather handle the creation of columns yourself, you can set the `AutoGenerateColumns` property to `false` and construct the columns yourself.

The following example shows how to construct columns and includes an image and also a `ComboBox` column. The code utilizes a `DataSet` and retrieves data into two data tables. The first `DataTable` contains the employee information from the Northwind database. The second table consists of the EmployeeID column and a generated Name column, which is used when rendering the `ComboBox`:

```
using (SqlConnection con =
  new SqlConnection (
    ConfigurationSettings.ConnectionStrings["northwind"].ConnectionString ) )
{
    string select = "SELECT EmployeeID, FirstName, LastName, Photo,
                    IsNull(ReportsTo,0) as ReportsTo FROM Employees";

    SqlDataAdapter da = new SqlDataAdapter(select, con);

    DataSet ds = new DataSet();

    da.Fill(ds, "Employees");

    select = "SELECT EmployeeID, FirstName + ' ' + LastName as Name
              FROM Employees UNION SELECT 0,'(None)'";

    da = new SqlDataAdapter(select, con);
    da.Fill(ds, "Managers");

    // Construct the columns in the grid view
    SetupColumns(ds);

    // Set the default height for a row
    dataGridView.RowTemplate.Height = 100 ;

    // Then setup the datasource
    dataGridView.AutoGenerateColumns = false;
    dataGridView.DataSource = ds.Tables["Employees"];
}
```

Here there are two things to note. The first select statement replaces NULL values in the ReportsTo column with the value zero. There is one row in the database that contains a NULL value in this field, indicating that the individual has no manager. However, when data binding, the `ComboBox` needs a value in this column, otherwise an exception will be raised when the grid is displayed. In the example, the value zero is chosen because it does not exist within the table—this is commonly termed a *sentinel value* because it has special meaning to the application.

# Viewing .NET Data

The second SQL clause selects data for the `ComboBox` and includes a manufactured row where the values Zero and (None) are created. In Figure 24-12, the second row displays the (None) entry.

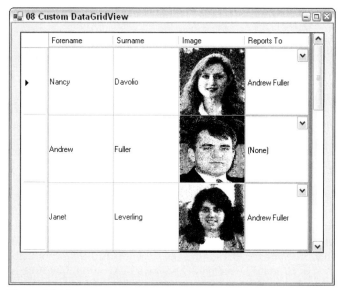

**Figure 24-12**

The custom columns are created by the following function:

```
private void SetupColumns(DataSet ds)
{
    DataGridViewTextBoxColumn forenameColumn = new DataGridViewTextBoxColumn();
    forenameColumn.DataPropertyName = "FirstName";
    forenameColumn.HeaderText = "Forename";
    forenameColumn.ValueType = typeof(string);
    forenameColumn.Frozen = true;
    dataGridView.Columns.Add(forenameColumn);

    DataGridViewTextBoxColumn surnameColumn = new DataGridViewTextBoxColumn();
    surnameColumn.DataPropertyName = "LastName";
    surnameColumn.HeaderText = "Surname";
    surnameColumn.Frozen = true;
    surnameColumn.ValueType = typeof(string);
    dataGridView.Columns.Add(surnameColumn);

    DataGridViewImageColumn photoColumn = new DataGridViewImageColumn();
    photoColumn.DataPropertyName = "Photo";
    photoColumn.Width = 100;
    photoColumn.HeaderText = "Image";
    photoColumn.ReadOnly = true;
    photoColumn.ImageLayout = DataGridViewImageCellLayout.Normal;
    dataGridView.Columns.Add(photoColumn);
```

815

# Chapter 24

```
        DataGridViewComboBoxColumn reportsToColumn = new DataGridViewComboBoxColumn();
        reportsToColumn.HeaderText = "Reports To";
        reportsToColumn.DataSource = ds.Tables["Managers"];
        reportsToColumn.DisplayMember = "Name";
        reportsToColumn.ValueMember = "EmployeeID";
        reportsToColumn.DataPropertyName = "ReportsTo";
        dataGridView.Columns.Add(reportsToColumn);
    }
```

The `ComboBox` is created last in this example—and uses the Managers table in the passed data set as its data source. This contains Name and EmployeeID columns, and these are assigned to the `DisplayMember` and `ValueMember` properties, respectively. These properties define where the data is coming from for the `ComboBox`.

The `DataPropertyName` is set to the column in the main data table that the combo box links to—this provides the initial value for the column, and if the user chooses another entry from the combo box, this value would be updated.

The only other thing this example needs to do is handle null values correctly when updating the database. At present, it will attempt to write the value zero into any row if you were to choose the (None) item onscreen. This would cause an exception from SQL Server because this would violate the foreign key constraint on the ReportsTo column. To overcome this, you would need to preprocess the data before sending it back to SQL Server, and set to NULL the ReportsTo column for any rows where this value was zero.

# Data Binding

The previous examples have used the `DataGrid` and `DataGridView` controls, which form only a small part of the controls in the .NET runtime that can be used to display data. The process of linking a control to a data source is called *data binding*.

In MFC the process of linking data from class variables to a set of controls was termed *Dialog Data Exchange* (DDX). The facilities available within .NET for binding data to controls are substantially easier to use and also more capable. For example, in .NET you can bind data to most properties of a control, not just the text property. You can also bind data in a similar manner to ASP.NET controls (see Chapter 26, "ASP.NET Pages").

## Simple Binding

A control that supports single binding typically displays only a single value at once, such as a text box or radio button. The following example shows how to bind a column from a `DataTable` to a `TextBox`:

```
DataSet ds = CreateDataSet();
textBox.DataBindings.Add("Text", ds , "Products.ProductName");
```

# Viewing .NET Data

After retrieving some data from the Products table and storing it in the returned DataSet with the CreateDataSet() method as shown here, the second line binds the Text property of the control (textBox1) to the Products.ProductName column. Figure 24-13 shows the result of this type of data binding.

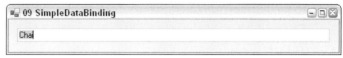

**Figure 24-13**

The text box displays a string from the database. Figure 24-14 shows how the SQL Server Query Analyzer tool could be used to verify the contents of the Products table to verify that it is the right column and value.

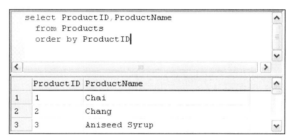

**Figure 24-14**

Having a single text box onscreen with no way to scroll to the next or the previous record and no way to update the database is not very useful, so the following section shows a more realistic example, and introduces the other objects that are necessary for data binding to work.

## Data-Binding Objects

Figure 24-15 shows a class hierarchy for the objects that are used in data binding. This section discusses the BindingContext, CurrencyManager, and PropertyManager classes of the System.Windows.Forms namespace, and shows how they interact when data is bound to one or more controls on a form. The shaded objects are those used in binding.

In the previous example, the DataBindings property of the TextBox control was used to bind a column from a DataSet to the Text property of the control. The DataBindings property is an instance of the ControlBindingsCollection shown in Figure 24-15:

```
textBox1.DataBindings.Add("Text", ds, "Products.ProductName");
```

This line adds a Binding object to the ControlBindingsCollection.

817

# Chapter 24

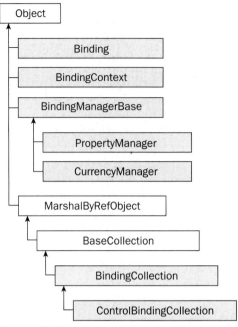

**Figure 24-15**

## BindingContext

Each Windows Form has a `BindingContext` property. Incidentally, `Form` is derived from `Control`, which is where this property is actually defined, so most controls have this property. A `Binding Context` object has a collection of `BindingManagerBase` instances (see Figure 24-16). These instances are created and added to the binding manager object when a control is data-bound.

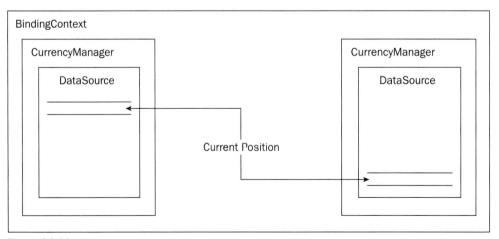

**Figure 24-16**

# Viewing .NET Data

The `BindingContext` might contain several data sources, wrapped in either a `CurrencyManager` or a `PropertyManager`. The decision on which class is used is based on the data source itself.

If the data source contains a list of items, such as a `DataTable`, `DataView`, or any object that implements the `IList` interface, a `CurrencyManager` will be used. A `CurrencyManager` can maintain the current position within that data source. If the data source returns only a single value, a `PropertyManager` will be stored within the `BindingContext`.

A `CurrencyManager` or `PropertyManager` is only created once for a given data source. If two text boxes are bound to a row from a `DataTable`, only one `CurrencyManager` will be created within the binding context.

Each control added to a form is linked to the form's binding manager, so all controls share the same instance. When a control is initially created, its `BindingContext` property is `null`. When the control is added to the `Controls` collection of the form, the `BindingContext` is set to that of the form.

To bind a control to a form, an entry needs to be added to its `DataBindings` property, which is an instance of `ControlBindingsCollection`. The following code shown creates a new binding:

```
textBox.DataBindings.Add("Text", ds, "Products.ProductName");
```

Internally, the `Add()` method of `ControlBindingsCollection` creates a new instance of a `Binding` object from the parameters passed to this method, and adds this to the bindings collection represented in Figure 24-17.

Figure 24-17 illustrates roughly what is going on when a `Binding` object is added to a `Control`. The binding links the control to a data source, which is maintained within the `BindingContext` of the `Form` (or control itself). Changes within the data source are reflected into the control, as are changes in the control.

## Binding

This class links a property of the control to a member of the data source. When that member changes, the control's property is updated to reflect this change. The opposite is also true — if the text in the text box is updated, this change is reflected in the data source.

Bindings can be set up from any column to any property of the control. For example, you can not only bind the text of a text box, but also the color of that text box. It is possible to bind properties of a control to completely different data sources; for example, the color of the cell might be defined in a colors table, and the actual data might be defined in another table.

# Chapter 24

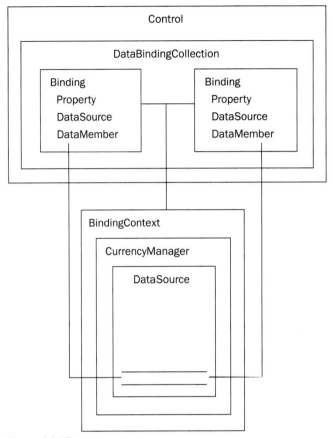

Figure 24-17

## CurrencyManager and PropertyManager

When a `Binding` object is created, a corresponding `CurrencyManager` or `PropertyManager` object is also created, provided this is the first time that data from the given source has been bound. The purpose of this class is to define the position of the current record within the data source, and to coordinate all list bindings when this current record is changed. Figure 24-18 displays two fields from the Products table, and includes a way to move between records by means of a `TrackBar` control.

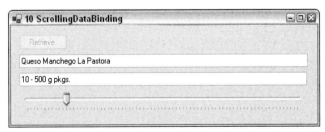

Figure 24-18

# Viewing .NET Data

The following example shows the main `ScrollingDataBinding` code:

```csharp
namespace ScrollingDataBinding
{
  partial class Form1: Form
  {
    public Form1()
    {
      InitializeComponent();
    }

    private DataSet CreateDataSet()
    {
      string customers = "SELECT * FROM Products";
      DataSet ds = new DataSet();

      using (SqlConnection con = new SqlConnection (
              ConfigurationSettings.
              ConnectionStrings["northwind"].ConnectionString))
      {
        SqlDataAdapter da = new SqlDataAdapter(customers, con);

        da.Fill(ds, "Products");
      }

      return ds;
    }

    private void trackBar_Scroll(object sender, EventArgs e)
    {
        this.BindingContext[ds, "Products"].Position = trackBar.Value;
    }

    private void retrieveButton_Click(object sender, EventArgs e)
    {
      retrieveButton.Enabled = false;

      ds = CreateDataSet();

      textName.DataBindings.Add("Text", ds, "Products.ProductName");
      textQuan.DataBindings.Add("Text", ds, "Products.QuantityPerUnit");

      trackBar.Minimum = 0;
      trackBar.Maximum = this.BindingContext[ds, "Products"].Count - 1;

      textName.Enabled = true;
      textQuan.Enabled = true;
      trackBar.Enabled = true;

    }

    private DataSet ds;
  }
}
```

# Chapter 24

The scrolling mechanism is provided by the `trackBar_Scroll` event handler, which sets the position of the `BindingContext` to the current position of the track bar thumb—altering the binding context here updates the data displayed on the screen.

Data is bound to the two text boxes in the `retrieveButton_Click` event by adding a data binding expression—here the `Text` properties of the controls are set to fields from the data source. It is possible to bind any simple property of a control to an item from the data source; for example, you could bind the text color, enabled, or other properties as appropriate.

When the data is originally retrieved, the maximum position on the track bar is set to be the number of records. Then, in the scroll method, the position of the `BindingContext` for the products `DataTable` is set to the position of the scroll bar thumb. This changes the current record from the `DataTable`, so all controls bound to the current row (in this example, the two text boxes) are updated.

Now that you know how to bind to various data sources, such as arrays, data tables, data views, and various other containers of data, and how to sort and filter that data, the next section discusses how Visual Studio has been extended to permit data access to be better integrated with the application.

## Visual Studio .NET and Data Access

This section discusses some of the new ways that Visual Studio allows data to be integrated into the GUI. More specifically, it discusses how to create a connection, select some data, generate a `DataSet`, and use all of the generated objects to produce a simple application. The available tools enable you to create a database connection with the `OleDbConnection` or `SqlConnection` classes. The class you use depends on the type of database you are using. After a connection has been defined, you can create a `DataSet` and populate it from within Visual Studio .NET. This generates an XSD file for the `DataSet` (similar to the file that was created manually in Chapter 19) and the .cs code. The result is a type-safe `DataSet`.

### Creating a Connection

First, create a new Windows application and then create a new database connection. Using the Server Explorer (see Figure 24-19), you can manage various aspects of data access.

**Figure 24-19**

For this example, create a connection to the Northwind database. Select the Add Connection option from the context menu available on the Data Connections item to launch a wizard that enables you to choose a database provider. Select the .NET Framework Provider for SQL Server. Figure 24-20 shows the second page of the Connection Properties dialog box.

# Viewing .NET Data

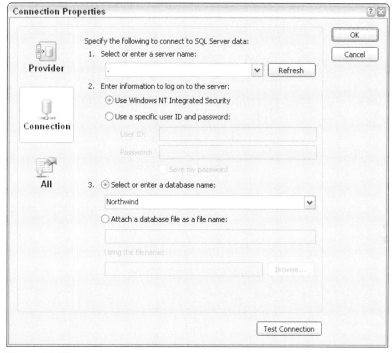

Figure 24-20

Depending on your .NET Framework installation, the sample databases might be located in SQL Server, MSDE (Microsoft SQL Server Data Engine), or both.

To connect to the local MSDE database, if it exists, type **(local)\\NETSDK** for the name of the server. To connect to a regular SQL Server instance, type **(local)** or '.' to select a database on the current machine, or the name of the desired server on the network. You may need to enter a username and password to access the database.

Select the Northwind database from the drop-down list of databases, and to ensure everything is set up correctly, click the Test Connection button. If everything is set up properly, you should see a message box with a confirmation message.

Visual Studio 2005 has numerous changes when accessing data, and these are available from several places in the user interface. I prefer to use the new Data menu, which permits you to view any data sources already added to the project, add a new data source, and preview data from the underlying database (or other data source).

The following example uses the Northwind database connection to generate a user interface for selecting data from the Employees table. The first step is to choose Add New Data Source from the Data menu, which begins a wizard that walks you through the process. You can also configure the data sources for your application with the new Data Sources window shown in Figure 24-21 which is available from the Data menu in the IDE.

# Chapter 24

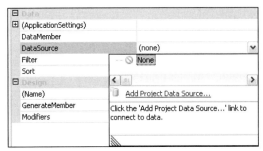

Figure 24-21

As you progress through the wizard you can choose the data source, which can be a database, local database file (such as an .mdb file), a WebService, or an object. You'll then be prompted for further information based on the type of data source chosen. For a database connection this includes the name of the connection (which is subsequently stored in the application configuration file shown in the following code), and you can then select the table, view, or stored procedure that supplies the data. Ultimately, this generates a strongly typed DataSet within your application.

```xml
<?xml version="1.0" encoding="utf-8"?>
<configuration>
  <connectionStrings>
    <add name="SimpleApp.Properties.Settings.NorthwindConnection"
        connectionString="Server=.;Integrated Security=True;Database=Northwind"
        providerName="System.Data.SqlClient" />
  </connectionStrings>
</configuration>
```

This includes the name of the connection, the connection string itself, and a provider name, which is used when generating the connection object. You can manually edit this information as necessary. To display a user interface for the employee data, you can simply drag the chosen data from the Data Sources window onto your form. This will generate one of two styles of User Interface for you — a grid style UI that utilizes the DataGridView control described earlier, or a Details view that presents just the data for a single record at a time. Figure 24-22 shows the Details view.

Dragging the data source onto the form generates a number of objects, both visual and non-visual. The non-visual objects are created within the tray area of the form, and comprise a DataConnector, a strongly typed DataSet, and a TableAdapter, which contains the SQL used to select/update the data. The visual objects created depend on whether you have chosen the DataGridView or the Details view. Both include a DataNavigator control that can be used to page through the data. Figure 24-23 shows the user interface generated using the DataGridView control — one of the goals of Visual Studio 2005 was to simplify data access to the point where you could generate functional forms without writing a single line of code.

When the data source is created, it adds a number of files to your solution — to view these click the Show All Files button in the Solution Explorer. You'll then be able to expand the dataset node and view the extra files added. The main one of interest is the .Designer file, which includes the C# source code used to populate the dataset.

# Viewing .NET Data

Figure 24-22

![Figure 24-23 - SimpleApp window showing Employees data grid]

| | EmployeeID | LastName | FirstName | Title | TitleOfCourtesy |
|---|---|---|---|---|---|
| ▶ | 1 | Davolio | Nancy | Sales... | Ms. |
| | 2 | Fuller | Andrew | Vice President,... | Dr. |
| | 3 | Leverling | Janet | Sales... | Ms. |
| | 4 | Peacock | Margaret | Sales... | Mrs. |
| | 5 | Buchanan | Steven | Sales Manager | Mr. |
| | 6 | Suyama | Michael | Sales... | Mr. |
| | 7 | King | Robert | Sales... | Mr. |
| | 8 | Callahan | Laura | Inside Sales... | Ms. |
| | 9 | Dodsworth | Anne | Sales... | Ms. |

Figure 24-23

You'll find two classes and one interface in the `.Designer` file. The interface exposes methods to select, insert, update, and delete data. The classes represent the strongly typed dataset and an object that implements the defined interface, which acts in a similar way to the standard `DataAdapter` class. This class internally uses the `DataAdapter` to fill the `DataSet`.

## Selecting Data

The table adapter generated contains commands for SELECT, INSERT, UPDATE, and DELETE. Needless to say, these can (and probably should) be tailored to call stored procedures rather than using straight SQL. The wizard-generated code will do for now, however. Visual Studio .NET adds the following code to the `.Designer` file:

825

```
private System.Data.SqlClient.SqlCommand m_DeleteCommand;
private System.Data.SqlClient.SqlCommand m_InsertCommand;
private System.Data.SqlClient.SqlCommand m_UpdateCommand;
private System.Data.SqlClient.SqlDataAdapter m_adapter;
```

An object is defined for each of the SQL commands with the exception of the Select command, and also a `SqlDataAdapter`. Further down the file, in the `InitializeComponent()` method, the wizard has generated code to create each one of these commands as well as the data adapter. Strangely, the code emitted to set up the DataAdapter doesn't use the commands defined within this class. Presumably, this and the omission of the Select command are beta issues that will be resolved before the software is formally released.

In previous versions of Visual Studio .NET, the commands generated for Insert and Update also included a select clause — this was used as a way to resynchronize the data with that on the server, just in case any fields within the database were calculated (such as identity columns and/or computed fields). Visual Studio 2005 only generates the Insert/Update clauses, so you may need to manually resynchronize the data if appropriate.

I think that generation of an additional Select clause wasn't necessary in most circumstances, so I am glad that the product group has altered this feature.

The wizard-generated code works but is less than optimal. For a production system, all the generated SQL should probably be replaced with calls to stored procedures. If the INSERT or UPDATE clauses didn't have to resynchronize the data, the removal of the redundant SQL clause would speed up the application a little.

## Updating the Data Source

So far, the applications have selected data from the database. This section discusses how to persist changes to the database. If you followed the steps in the previous section, you should have an application that contains everything needed for a rudimentary application. The one change necessary is to enable the Save button on the generated toolbar and write an event handler that will update the database.

From the IDE, select the Save button from the data navigator control, and change the Enabled property to `true`. Then double-click the button to generate an event handler. Within this handler, save the changes made onscreen to the database:

```
private void dataNavigatorSaveItem_Click(object sender, EventArgs e)
{
    employeesTableAdapter.Update(employeesDataset.Employees);
}
```

Because Visual Studio 2005 has done the donkeywork for you, all that's needed is to use the Update method of the table adapter class that was generated. Six Update methods are available on the table adapter — this example uses the override that takes a `DataTable` as the parameter.

# Viewing .NET Data

## Building a Schema

Chapter 19 showed you how to define an XSD schema. Visual Studio .NET includes an editor for creating XSD schemas, which you can access by choosing Add New Item from the Project menu and selecting the XML Schema item (see Figure 24-24). Name your schema `TestSchema.xsd`.

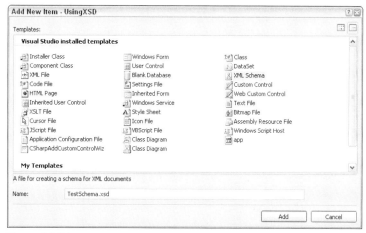

**Figure 24-24**

This adds two new files to the project: an .xsd file and a corresponding .xsx file (which is used by the designer to store layout information for the schema elements that are designed). To create a corresponding set of code for the schema, choose the Generate Dataset option from the Schema menu (see Figure 24-25).

**Figure 24-25**

Choosing this option adds an extra C# file to the project, which is displayed below the XSD file in Solution Explorer. This file is automatically generated whenever changes are made to the XSD schema and should not be edited manually; it is generated with the xsd.exe tool.

827

# Chapter 24

The Visual Studio .NET editor has two views of an XSD file: Schema view and XML view. Clicking the XML tab displays the raw schema template:

```xml
<?xml version="1.0" encoding="utf-8" ?>
<xs:schema id="TestSchema"
        targetNamespace="http://tempuri.org/TestSchema.xsd"
        elementFormDefault="qualified"
        xmlns="http://tempuri.org/TestSchema.xsd"
        xmlns:mstns="http://tempuri.org/TestSchema.xsd"
        xmlns:xs="http://www.w3.org/2001/XMLSchema">
</xs:schema>
```

This XSD script generates the following C# in the file `TestSchema.cs`. In the following code some of the bodies of the methods have been omitted and/or formatted for easier reading; you can inspect the code generated as you work through the example:

```csharp
using System;
using System.Data;
using System.Xml;
using System.Runtime.Serialization;

[Serializable()]
[System.ComponentModel.DesignerCategoryAttribute("code")]
[System.Diagnostics.DebuggerStepThrough()]
[System.ComponentModel.ToolboxItem(true)]
[System.Xml.Serialization.XmlSchemaProviderAttribute("GetTypedDataSetSchema")]
[System.Xml.Serialization.XmlRootAttribute("TestSchema")]
public class TestSchema : DataSet
{
    public TestSchema() { ... }

    protected TestSchema(SerializationInfo info, StreamingContext context)
    { ... }
    public override DataSet Clone() { ... }
    protected override bool ShouldSerializeTables() { ... }
    protected override bool ShouldSerializeRelations() { ... }
    protected override void ReadXmlSerializable(XmlReader reader) { ... }
    protected override System.Xml.Schema.XmlSchema GetSchemaSerializable()
    { ... }
    internal void InitVars() { ... }
    private void InitClass() { ... }
    private void SchemaChanged(object sender,
                System.ComponentModel.CollectionChangeEventArgs e)
    { ... }
}
```

This code provides the starting point for this section, so that the code changes can be described as items are added into the XSD schema. The two main things to note are that an XSD schema is mapped to a `DataSet`, and that this `DataSet` is serializable—note the protected constructor that can be used by an `ISerializable` implementation. Serialization is covered in greater depth in Chapter 21, "Manipulating XML."

# Viewing .NET Data

## Adding an element

To add a new top-level element, right-click inside your workspace and choose Add ⇨ New Element from the context menu. This displays in a new, unnamed element. Figure 24-26 shows the attributes for this example's product element.

**Figure 24-26**

When the XSD file is saved, the C# file is modified and a number of new classes are generated, as shown in the following code. The most pertinent aspects of the code generated in the file `TestSchema.Designer.cs` are discussed in the next section.

```
public class TestSchema : DataSet
{
  private ProductDataTable tableProduct ;

  [Browsable(false)]
  [DesignerSerializationVisibility(DesignerSerializationVisibility.Content)]
  public ProductDataTable Product
  {
    get
    {
      return this.tableProduct ;
    }
  }
}
```

A new member variable of the class `ProductDataTable` is created. This object is returned by the `Product` property and is constructed within the updated `InitClass()` method. From this small section of code, it's evident that the user of these classes can construct a `DataSet` from the class in this file and use `DataSet.Products` to return the products `DataTable`.

## Generated DataTable

The following code is generated for the `DataTable` (`Product`) that was added to the schema template:

```
public delegate void ProductRowChangeEventHandler
                (object sender, ProductRowChangeEvent e);
public class ProductDataTable : DataTable, System.Collections.IEnumerable
{
   internal ProductDataTable() : base("Product")
   {
      this.InitClass();
   }
   [System.ComponentModel.Browsable(false)]
   public int Count
```

829

```
    {
        get { return this.Rows.Count;}
    }
    public ProductRow this[int index]
    {
        get { return ((ProductRow)(this.Rows[index]));}
    }
    public event ProductRowChangeEventHandler ProductRowChanged;
    public event ProductRowChangeEventHandler ProductRowChanging;
    public event ProductRowChangeEventHandler ProductRowDeleted;
    public event ProductRowChangeEventHandler ProductRowDeleting;
```

The generated `ProductDataTable` class is derived from `DataTable`, and includes an implementation of the `IEnumerable` interface. Four events are defined that use the delegate defined above the class when raised. This delegate is passed an instance of the `ProductRowChangeEvent` class, again defined by Visual Studio .NET.

The generated code includes a class derived from `DataRow`, which permits type-safe access to columns within the table. A new row can be created in one of two ways:

- ❑ Call the `NewRow()` (or generated `NewProductRow()`) method to return a new instance of the row class. Pass this new row to the `Rows.Add()` method (or the type-safe `AddProductRow()`).
- ❑ Call the `Rows.Add()` (or generated `AddProductRow()`) method and pass an array of objects, one for each column in the table.

The following code demonstrates the `AddProductRow()` methods:

```
public void AddProductRow(ProductRow row)
{
    this.Rows.Add(row);
}
public ProductRow AddProductRow ( string Name, string SKU, string Description,
                                  decimal Price )
{
    ProductRow rowProductRow = ((ProductRow)(this.NewRow()));
    rowProductRow.ItemArray = new Object[0] {
                    Name,
                    SKU,
                    Description,
                    Price};   this.Rows.Add(rowProductRow);
    return rowProductRow;
}
```

As you can see, the second method creates a new row, inserts that row in the `Rows` collection of the `DataTable`, and then returns this object to the caller. The bulk of the other methods on the `DataTable` are for raising events.

## Generated DataRow

The following code shows the `ProductRow` class:

```
public class ProductRow : DataRow
{
  private ProductDataTable tableProduct;
  internal ProductRow(DataRowBuilder rb) : base(rb)
  {
    this.tableProduct = ((ProductDataTable)(this.Table));
  }
  public string Name { ... }
  // Other accessors/mutators omitted for clarity
}
```

When attributes are added to an element, a property is added to the generated `DataRow` class as shown in the preceding code. The property has the same name as the attribute; in this example, the `Product` row has properties for `Name`, `SKU`, `Description`, and `Price`.

For each attribute added, several changes are made to the `.cs` file. In the following example, suppose there is an attribute called `ProductId` of type `int`.

At first a private member is added to the `ProductDataTable` class (derived from `DataTable`), which is the new `DataColumn`:

```
private DataColumn columnProductId;
```

This is joined by a property named `ProductIDColumn`. This property is defined as `internal`:

```
internal DataColumn ProductIdColumn
{
   get { return this.columnProductId; }
}
```

The `AddProductRow()` method shown previously is also modified; it now takes an integer `ProductID` and stores the value entered in the newly created column:

```
public ProductRow AddProductRow ( ... , int ProductId)
{
   ProductRow rowProductRow = ((ProductRow)(this.NewRow()));
   rowProductRow.ItemArray = new Object[] { ... , ProductId};
   this.Rows.Add(rowProductRow);
   return rowProductRow;
}
```

Finally, in the `ProductDataTable`, there is a modification to the `InitClass()` method:

```
private void InitClass()
{
   ...
   this.columnProductID = new DataColumn("ProductID", typeof(int), null,
                          System.Data.MappingType.Attribute);
   this.Columns.Add(this.columnProductID);
   this.columnProductID.Namespace = "";
}
```

This creates the new `DataColumn` and adds it to the `Columns` collection of the `DataTable`. The final parameter to the `DataColumn` constructor defines how this column is mapped to XML; this is of use when the `DataSet` is saved to an XML file, for example.

The `ProductRow` class is updated to add an accessor for this column:

```
public int ProductId
{
   get { return ((int)(this[this.tableProduct.ProductIdColumn])); }
   set { this[this.tableProduct.ProductIdColumn] = value; }
}
```

## Generated EventArgs

The final class added to the source code is a derivation of `EventArgs`, which provides methods for directly accessing the row that has changed (or is changing), and for the action that is applied to that row. This code has been omitted for brevity.

## Other Common Requirements

A common requirement when displaying data is to provide a pop-up menu for a given row. You can do this in numerous ways. The example in this section focuses on one approach that can simplify the code required, especially if the display context is a `DataGrid`, where a `DataSet` with some relations is displayed. The problem here is that the context menu depends on the row that is selected, and that row could be part of any source `DataTable` in the `DataSet`.

Because the context menu functionality is likely to be general-purpose in nature, the implementation here uses a base class (`ContextDataRow`) that supports the menu-building code, and each data row class that supports a pop-up menu derives from this base class.

When the user right-clicks any part of a row in the `DataGrid`, the row is looked up to check if it derives from `ContextDataRow`, and if so, `PopupMenu()` can be called. This could be implemented using an interface; however, in this instance a base class provides a simpler solution.

This example demonstrates how to generate `DataRow` and `DataTable` classes that can be used to provide type-safe access to data in much the same way as the previous XSD sample. However, this time you write the code yourself to show how to use custom attributes and reflection in this context.

Figure 24-27 illustrates the class hierarchy for this example.

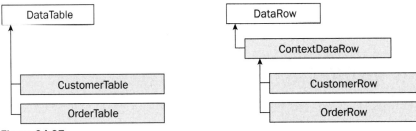

Figure 24-27

Here is the code for this example:

```csharp
using System;
using System.Windows.Forms;
using System.Data;
using System.Data.SqlClient;
using System.Reflection;

public class ContextDataRow : DataRow
{
    public ContextDataRow(DataRowBuilder builder) : base(builder)
    {
    }
    public void PopupMenu(System.Windows.Forms.Control parent, int x, int y)
    {

        // Use reflection to get the list of popup menu commands
        MemberInfo[] members = this.GetType().FindMembers (MemberTypes.Method,
                             BindingFlags.Public | BindingFlags.Instance ,
                             new System.Reflection.MemberFilter(Filter),
                             null);
        if (members.Length > 0)
        {

            // Create a context menu

            ContextMenu menu = new ContextMenu();

            // Now loop through those members and generate the popup menu
            // Note the cast to MethodInfo in the foreach
            foreach (MethodInfo meth in members)
            {

                // Get the caption for the operation from the
                // ContextMenuAttribute

                ContextMenuAttribute[] ctx = (ContextMenuAttribute[])
                   meth.GetCustomAttributes(typeof(ContextMenuAttribute), true);
                MenuCommand callback = new MenuCommand(this, meth);
                MenuItem item = new MenuItem(ctx[0].Caption, new
                                EventHandler(callback.Execute));
                item.DefaultItem = ctx[0].Default;
                menu.MenuItems.Add(item);
            }
            System.Drawing.Point pt = new System.Drawing.Point(x,y);
            menu.Show(parent, pt);
        }
    }

    private bool Filter(MemberInfo member, object criteria)
    {
        bool bInclude = false;

        // Cast MemberInfo to MethodInfo
```

```
            MethodInfo meth = member as MethodInfo;
            if (meth != null)
            {
                if (meth.ReturnType == typeof(void))
                {
                    ParameterInfo[] parms = meth.GetParameters();
                    if (parms.Length == 0)
                    {
                        // Lastly check if there is a ContextMenuAttribute on the
                        // method...

                        object[] atts = meth.GetCustomAttributes
                                    (typeof(ContextMenuAttribute), true);
                        bInclude = (atts.Length == 1);
                    }
                }
            }
            return bInclude;
    }
}
```

The `ContextDataRow` class is derived from `DataRow`, and contains just two member functions: `PopupMenu` and `Filter()`. `PopupMenu` uses reflection to look for methods that correspond to a particular signature, and it displays a pop-up menu of these options to the user. `Filter()` is used as a delegate by `PopupMenu` when enumerating methods. It simply returns `true` if the member function does correspond to the appropriate calling convention:

```
MemberInfo[] members = this.GetType().FindMembers(MemberTypes.Method,
            BindingFlags.Public | BindingFlags.Instance,
            new System.Reflection.MemberFilter(Filter),
            null);
```

This single statement is used to filter all methods on the current object and return only those that match the following criteria:

- ❏  The member must be a method
- ❏  The member must be a public instance method
- ❏  The member must return `void`
- ❏  The member must accept zero parameters
- ❏  The member must include the `ContextMenuAttribute`

The last of these criteria refers to a custom attribute, written specifically for this example. (It's discussed after discussing the `PopupMenu` method.)

```
ContextMenu menu = new ContextMenu();
foreach (MethodInfo meth in members)
{
    // ... Add the menu item
}
```

# Viewing .NET Data

```
System.Drawing.Point pt = new System.Drawing.Point(x,y);
menu.Show(parent, pt);
```

A context menu instance is created, and a pop-up menu item is added for each method that matches the preceding criteria. The menu is subsequently displayed as shown in Figure 24-28.

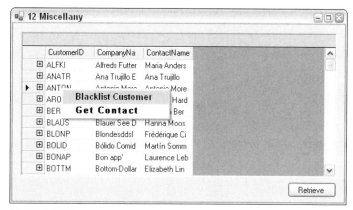

Figure 24-28

The main area of difficulty with this example is the following section of code, repeated once for each member function to be displayed on the pop-up menu:

```
System.Type ctxtype = typeof(ContextMenuAttribute);
ContextMenuAttribute[] ctx = (ContextMenuAttribute[])
                    meth.GetCustomAttributes(ctxtype, true);
MenuCommand callback = new MenuCommand(this, meth);
MenuItem item = new MenuItem(ctx[0].Caption,
            new EventHandler(callback.Execute));
item.DefaultItem = ctx[0].Default;
menu.MenuItems.Add(item);
```

Each method that should be displayed on the context menu is attributed with the `ContextMenuAttribute`. This defines a user-friendly name for the menu option, because a C# method name cannot include spaces, and it's wise to use real English on pop-up menus rather than some internal code. The attribute is retrieved from the method, and a new menu item is created and added to the menu items collection of the pop-up menu.

This sample code also shows the use of a simplified `Command` class (a common design pattern). The `MenuCommand` class used in this instance is triggered by the user choosing an item on the context menu, and it forwards the call to the receiver of the method — in this case the object and method that was attributed. This also helps keep the code in the receiver object more isolated from the user interface code. This code is explained in the following sections.

## Manufactured tables and rows

The XSD example earlier in the chapter showed the code produced when the Visual Studio .NET editor is used to generate a set of data access classes. The following class shows the required methods for a `DataTable`, which are fairly minimal (and they all have been generated manually):

# Chapter 24

```csharp
public class CustomerTable : DataTable
{
    public CustomerTable() : base("Customers")
    {
        this.Columns.Add("CustomerID", typeof(string));
        this.Columns.Add("CompanyName", typeof(string));
        this.Columns.Add("ContactName", typeof(string));
    }
    protected override System.Type GetRowType()
    {
        return typeof(CustomerRow);
    }
    protected override DataRow NewRowFromBuilder(DataRowBuilder builder)
    {
        return(DataRow) new CustomerRow(builder);
    }
}
```

The first prerequisite of a `DataTable` is to override the `GetRowType()` method. This is used by the .NET internals when generating new rows for the table. The type used to represent each row should be returned from this method.

The next prerequisite is to implement `NewRowFromBuilder()`, which is called by the runtime when creating new rows for the table. That's enough for a minimal implementation. The corresponding `CustomerRow` class is fairly simple. It implements properties for each of the columns within the row, and then implements the methods that ultimately are displayed on the context menu:

```csharp
public class CustomerRow : ContextDataRow
{
    public CustomerRow(DataRowBuilder builder) : base(builder)
    {
    }
    public string CustomerID
    {
        get { return (string)this["CustomerID"];}
        set { this["CustomerID"] = value;}
    }

    // Other properties omitted for clarity

    [ContextMenu("Blacklist Customer")]
    public void Blacklist()
    {
        // Do something
    }
    [ContextMenu("Get Contact",Default=true)]
    public void GetContact()
    {
        // Do something else
    }
}
```

# Viewing .NET Data

The class simply derives from `ContextDataRow`, including the appropriate getter/setter methods on properties that are named the same as each field, and then a set of methods may be added that are used when reflecting on the class:

```
[ContextMenu("Blacklist Customer")]
public void Blacklist()
{

    // Do something
}
```

Each method that is to be displayed on the context menu has the same signature and includes the custom `ContextMenu` attribute.

## Using an attribute

The idea behind writing the `ContextMenu` attribute is to be able to supply a free text name for a given menu option. The following example also adds a `Default` flag, which is used to indicate the default menu choice. The entire attribute class is presented here:

```
[AttributeUsage(AttributeTargets.Method,AllowMultiple=false,Inherited=true)]
public class ContextMenuAttribute : System.Attribute
{
    public ContextMenuAttribute(string caption)
    {
        Caption = caption;
        Default = false;
    }
    public readonly string Caption;
}
```

The `AttributeUsage` attribute on the class marks `ContextMenuAttribute` as only being usable on a method, and it also defines that there can only be one instance of this object on any given method. The `Inherited=true` clause defines whether the attribute can be placed on a superclass method and still reflected on by a subclass.

A number of other members could be added to this attribute, including the following:

- ❏ A hotkey for the menu option
- ❏ An image to be displayed
- ❏ Some text to be displayed in the toolbar as the mouse pointer rolls over the menu option
- ❏ A help context ID

## Dispatching methods

When a menu is displayed in .NET, each menu option is linked to the processing code for that option by means of a delegate. In implementing the mechanism for connecting menu choices to code, you have two options:

## Chapter 24

- Implement a method with the same signature as the `System.EventHandler`. This is defined as shown in this snippet:

```
public delegate void EventHandler(object sender, EventArgs e);
```

- Define a proxy class, which implements the preceding delegate, and forwards calls to the received class. This is known as the Command pattern and is what has been chosen for this example.

The Command pattern separates the sender and the receiver of the call by means of a simple intermediate class. This may be overkill for such an example, but it makes the methods on each `DataRow` simpler (because they don't need the parameters passed to the delegate), and it is more extensible:

```
public class MenuCommand
{
    public MenuCommand(object receiver, MethodInfo method)
    {
        Receiver = receiver;
        Method = method;
    }
    public void Execute(object sender, EventArgs e)
    {
        Method.Invoke(Receiver, new object[] {} );
    }
    public readonly object Receiver;
    public readonly MethodInfo Method;
}
```

The class simply provides an `EventHandler` delegate (the `Execute` method), which invokes the desired method on the receiver object. This example handles two different types of row: rows from the `Customers` table and rows from the `Orders` table. Naturally, the processing options for each of these types of data are likely to differ. Figure 24-28 shows the operations available for a `Customer` row, whereas Figure 24-29 shows the options available for an `Order` row.

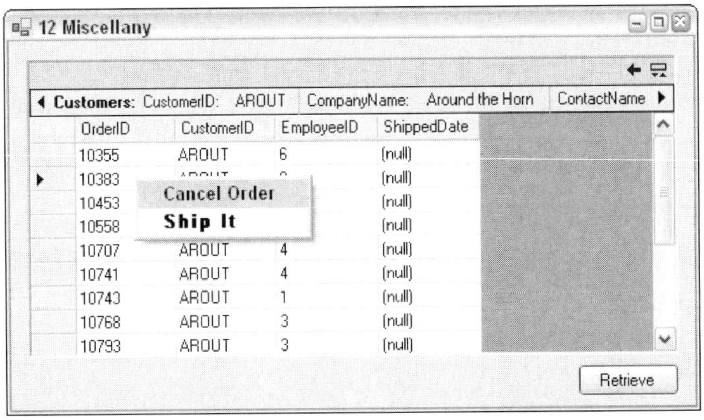

Figure 24-29

# Viewing .NET Data

## Getting the selected row

The last piece of the puzzle for this example is how to work out which row within the `DataSet` the user has selected. You might think that it must be a property on the `DataGrid`. However, this control is not available in this context. The hit test information obtained from within the `MouseUp()` event handler might also be a likely candidate to look at, but that only helps if the data displayed is from a single `DataTable`.

Remember how the grid is filled:

```
dataGrid.SetDataBinding(ds,"Customers");
```

This method adds a new `CurrencyManager` to the `BindingContext`, which represents the current `DataTable` and the `DataSet`. Now, the `DataGrid` has two properties, `DataSource` and `DataMember`, which are set when the `SetDataBinding()` is called. `DataSource` in this instance refers to a `DataSet` and `DataMember` are `Customers`.

Given the data source, a data member, and the binding context of the form, the current row can be located with the following code:

```
protected void dataGrid_MouseUp(object sender, MouseEventArgs e)
{
   // Perform a hit test
   if(e.Button == MouseButtons.Right)
   {
      // Find which row the user clicked on, if any
      DataGrid.HitTestInfo hti = dataGrid.HitTest(e.X, e.Y);

      // Check if the user hit a cell
      if(hti.Type == DataGrid.HitTestType.Cell)
      {
         // Find the DataRow that corresponds to the cell
         //the user has clicked upon
```

After calling `dataGrid.HitTest()` to calculate where the user has clicked the mouse, the `BindingManagerBase` instance for the data grid is retrieved:

```
BindingManagerBase bmb = this.BindingContext[ dataGrid.DataSource,
                                              dataGrid.DataMember];
```

This uses the `DataGrid`'s `DataSource` and `DataMember` to name the object to be returned. All that is left now is to find the row the user clicked and display the context menu. With a right-click on a row, the current row indicator doesn't normally move, but that's not good enough. The row indicator should be moved and then the pop-up menu should be displayed. The `HitTestInfo` object includes the row number, so the `BindingManagerBase` object's current position can be changed as follows:

```
bmb.Position = hti.Row;
```

# Chapter 24

This changes the cell indicator, and at the same time means that when a call is made into the class to get the `Row`, the current row is returned, not the previous one selected:

```
            DataRowView drv = bmb.Current as DataRowView;
            if(drv != null)
            {
                ContextDataRow ctx = drv.Row as ContextDataRow;
                if(ctx != null) ctx.PopupMenu(dataGrid,e.X,e.Y);
            }
         }
      }
   }
```

Because the `DataGrid` is displaying items from a `DataSet`, the `Current` object within the `Binding ManagerBase` collection is a `DataRowView`, which is tested by an explicit cast in the previous code. If this succeeds, the actual row that the `DataRowView` wraps can be retrieved by performing another cast to check if it is indeed a `ContextDataRow`, and finally pop up a menu.

In this example, you'll notice that two data tables, `Customers` and `Orders`, have been created, and a relationship has been defined between these tables, so that when users click `CustomerOrders` they see a filtered list of orders. When the user clicks, the `DataGrid` changes the `DataMember` from `Customers` to `Customers.CustomerOrders`, which just so happens to be the correct object that the `BindingContext` indexer uses to retrieve the data being shown.

## Summary

This chapter has introduced some of the methods of displaying data under .NET. `System.Windows.Forms` includes large number of classes to be explored, and this chapter used the `DataGridView` and `DataGrid` controls to display data from many different data sources, such as an `Array`, `DataTable`, or `DataSet`.

Because it is not always appropriate to display data in a grid, this chapter also discussed how to link a column of data to a single control in the user interface. The binding capabilities of .NET make this type of user interface very easy to support, because it's generally just a case of binding a control to a column and letting .NET do the rest of the work.

Furthermore, this chapter explored the integration of Visual Studio .NET and XML schemas. It discussed XSD and automatic code generation, and presented a minimal implementation of XSD using a hand-crafted example. Using an XSD schema to generate `DataSet` code can save you a lot of time (and typing), because this tool takes care of all of the underlying code.

Chapter 25 explores in more detail how you can use XML in Visual Studio .NET, and how well it has been integrated into the .NET Framework.

# 25
# Graphics with GDI+

This is the third of the three chapters that deal with user interaction and the .NET Framework. Chapter 23, "Windows Forms," focused on Windows Forms and discussed how to display a dialog box or SDI or MDI window, and how to place various controls such as buttons, text boxes, and list boxes. Chapter 24, "Viewing .NET Data," looked at working with data in Windows Forms using a number of the Windows Forms controls that work with the disparate data sources that you might encounter.

Although these standard controls are powerful and, by themselves, quite adequate for the complete user interface for many applications, there are some situations in which you need more flexibility. For example, you might want to draw text in a given font in a precise position in a window, display images without using a picture box control, or draw simple shapes or other graphics. None of this can be done with the controls discussed in Chapter 23. To display that kind of output, the application must instruct the operating system what to display and where in its window to display it.

Therefore, this chapter shows you how to draw a variety of items including:

- Lines and simple shapes
- .BMP images and other image files
- Text

In the process, you'll need to use a variety of helper objects, including pens (to define the characteristics of lines), brushes (to define how areas are filled in), and fonts (to define the shape of the characters of text). The chapter also goes into some detail on how devices interpret and display different colors.

The chapter starts, however, by discussing a technology called *GDI+*. GDI+ consists of the set of .NET base classes that are available to control custom drawing on the screen. These classes arrange for the appropriate instructions to be sent to graphics device drivers to ensure the correct output is placed on the screen (or printed to a hard copy).

# Chapter 25

# Understanding Drawing Principles

This section examines the basic principles that you need to understand to start drawing to the screen. It starts by giving an overview of GDI, the underlying technology on which GDI+ is based, and shows how GDI and GDI+ are related. Then you move on to a couple of simple examples.

## *GDI and GDI+*

In general, one of the strengths of Windows—and indeed of modern operating systems in general—lies in its ability to abstract the details of particular devices without input from the developer. For example, you don't need to understand anything about your hard drive device driver in order to programmatically read and write files to disk; you simply call the appropriate methods in the relevant .NET classes (or in pre-.NET days, the equivalent Windows API functions). This principle is also true when it comes to drawing. When the computer draws anything to the screen, it does so by sending instructions to the video card. However, many hundreds of different video cards are on the market, most of which have different instruction sets and capabilities. If you had to take that into account and write specific code for each video driver, writing any such application would be an almost impossible task. This is why the Windows *graphical device interface* (GDI) has been around because the earliest versions of Windows.

GDI provides a layer of abstraction, hiding the differences between the different video cards. You simply call the Windows API function to do the specific task, and internally the GDI figures out how to get the client's particular video card to do whatever it is you want when they run your particular piece of code. Not only this, but if the client has several display devices—for example, monitors and printers—GDI achieves the remarkable feat of making the printer look the same as the screen as far as the application is concerned. If the client wants to print something instead of displaying it, your application will simply inform the system that the output device is the printer and then call the same API functions in exactly the same way.

As you can see, the device-context (DC) object is a very powerful object and you won't be surprised to learn that under GDI *all* drawing had to be done through a device context. The DC was even used for operations that don't involve drawing to the screen or to any hardware device, such as modifying images in memory.

Although GDI exposes a relatively high-level API to developers, it is still an API that is based on the old Windows API, with C-style functions. *GDI+* to a large extent sits as a layer between GDI and your application, providing a more intuitive, inheritance-based object model. Although GDI+ is basically a wrapper around GDI, Microsoft has been able through GDI+ to provide new features and some performance improvements to some of the older features of GDI as well.

The GDI+ part of the .NET Base Class Library is huge, and this chapter scarcely scratches the surface of its features. That's a deliberate decision, because trying to cover more than a tiny fraction of the library would have turned this chapter into a huge reference guide that simply listed classes and methods. It's more important to understand the fundamental principles involved in drawing, so that you are in a good position to explore the available classes. Full lists of all the classes and methods available in GDI+ are of course available in the SDK documentation.

# Graphics with GDI+

*Visual Basic 6 developers are likely to find the concepts involved in drawing quite unfamiliar, because Visual Basic 6 focuses on controls that handle their own painting. C++/MFC developers are likely to be in more familiar territory because MFC does require developers to take control of more of the drawing process, using GDI. However, even if you have a strong background in the classic GDI, you'll find a lot of the material presented in this chapter is new.*

## GDI+ namespaces

The following table provides an overview of the main namespaces you'll need to explore to find the GDI+ base classes.

| Namespace | Description |
| --- | --- |
| `System.Drawing` | Contains most of the classes, structs, enums, and delegates concerned with the basic functionality of drawing |
| `System.Drawing.Drawing2D` | Provides most of the support for advanced 2D and vector drawing, including anti-aliasing, geometric transformations, and graphics paths |
| `System.Drawing.Imaging` | Contains various classes that assist in the manipulation of images (bitmaps, GIF files, and so on) |
| `System.Drawing.Printing` | Contains classes to assist when specifically targeting a printer or print preview window as the "output device" |
| `System.Drawing.Design` | Contains some predefined dialog boxes, property sheets, and other user interface elements concerned with extending the design-time user interface |
| `System.Drawing.Text` | Contains classes to perform more advanced manipulation of fonts and font families |

You should note that almost all of the classes and structs used in this chapter are taken from the `System.Drawing` namespace.

## Device contexts and the Graphics object

In GDI, the way that you identify which device you want your output to go to is through an object known as the *device context* (DC). The DC stores information about a particular device and is able to translate calls to the GDI API functions into whatever instructions need to be sent to that device. You can also query the device context to find out what the capabilities of the corresponding device are (for example, whether a printer prints in color or only in black and white), so the output can be adjusted accordingly. If you ask the device to do something it's not capable of, the DC will normally detect this and take appropriate action (which, depending on the situation, might mean throwing an error or modifying the request to get the closest match that the device is actually capable of using).

However, the DC doesn't only deal with the hardware device. It acts as a bridge to Windows and is able to take account of any requirements or restrictions placed on the drawing by Windows. For example, if Windows knows that only a portion of your application's window needs to be redrawn, the DC can trap and nullify attempts to draw outside that area. Due to the DC's relationship with Windows, working through the device context can simplify your code in other ways.

For example, hardware devices need to be told where to draw objects, and they usually want coordinates relative to the top-left corner of the screen (or output device). Usually, however, your application will be thinking of drawing something at a certain position within the client area (the area reserved for drawing) of its own window, possibly using its own coordinate system. Because the window might be positioned anywhere on the screen, and a user might move it at any time, translating between the two coordinate systems is potentially a difficult task. However, the DC always knows where your window is and is able to perform this translation automatically.

With GDI+, the device context is wrapped up in the .NET base class `System.Drawing.Graphics`. Most drawing is done by calling methods on an instance of `Graphics`. In fact, because the `Graphics` class is the class that is responsible for handling most drawing operations, very little gets done in GDI+ that doesn't involve a `Graphics` instance somewhere, so understanding how to manipulate this object is the key to understanding how to draw to display devices with GDI+.

## Drawing Shapes

To show this at work, this section starts off with a short example, `DisplayAtStartup`, to illustrate drawing to an application's main window. The examples in this chapter are all created in Visual Studio 2005 as C# Windows Applications. Recall that for this type of project the code wizard gives you a class called `Form1`, derived from `System.Windows.Form`, which represents the application's main window. Also generated for you is a class called `Program` (found in the `Program.cs` file), which represents the application's main starting point. Unless otherwise stated, in all code samples, new or modified code means code that you've added to the wizard-generated code. (You can download the sample code from the Wrox Web site at www.wrox.com.)

> *In .NET usage, when we are talking about applications that display various controls, the terminology "form" has largely replaced "window" to represent the rectangular object that occupies an area of the screen on behalf of an application. In this chapter, we've tended to stick to the term window, because in the context of manually drawing items it's rather more meaningful. We'll also talk about the form when we're referring to the .NET class used to instantiate the form/window. Finally, we'll use the terms "drawing" and "painting" interchangeably to describe the process of displaying some item on the screen or other display device.*

The first example simply creates a form and draws to it in the constructor when the form starts up. Note that this is not actually the best or the correct way to draw to the screen — you'll quickly find that this example has a problem in that it is unable to redraw anything after starting up. However, this example illustrates quite a few points about drawing without your having to do very much work.

For this example, start Visual Studio 2005 and create a Windows Application. First, set the background color of the form to white. In the example this line is after the `InitializeComponent()` method so that Visual Studio 2005 recognizes the line and is able to alter the design view appearance of the form. You can find the `InitializeComponent()` method by first clicking the Show All Files button in the Visual

# Graphics with GDI+

Studio Solution Explorer and then expanding the plus sign next to the `Form1.cs` file. Here you will find the `Form1.Designer.cs` file. It is here in this file where you will find the `InitializeComponent()` method. You could have used the design view to set the background color, but this would have resulted in pretty much the same line being added automatically:

```
        private void InitializeComponent()
        {
//
// Form1
//
            this.AutoScaleBaseSize = new System.Drawing.Size(5, 13);
            this.BackColor = System.Drawing.Color.White;
            this.ClientSize = new System.Drawing.Size(292, 266);
            this.Name = "Form1";
            this.Text = "Form1";
```

Then you add code to the `Form1` constructor. You create a `Graphics` object using the form's `CreateGraphics()` method. This `Graphics` object contains the Windows DC you need to draw with. The device context created is associated with the display device, and also with this window:

```
        public Form1()
        {
            InitializeComponent();

            Graphics dc = this.CreateGraphics();
            this.Show();
            Pen bluePen = new Pen(Color.Blue, 3);
            dc.DrawRectangle(bluePen, 0,0,50,50);
            Pen redPen = new Pen(Color.Red, 2);
            dc.DrawEllipse(redPen, 0, 50, 80, 60);
        }
```

As you can see, you then call the `Show()` method to display the window. This is really done to force the window to display immediately, because you can't actually do any drawing until the window has been displayed. If the window isn't displayed, there's nothing for you to draw onto.

Finally, you display a rectangle at coordinates (0,0) and with width and height 50, and an ellipse with coordinates (0,50) and with width 80 and height 50. Note that coordinates (x,y) translate to x pixels to the right and y pixels down from the top-left corner of the client area of the window — and these coordinates start from the top-left corner of the shape to be displayed.

The overloads that you are using of the `DrawRectangle()` and `DrawEllipse()` methods each take five parameters. The first parameter of each is an instance of the class `System.Drawing.Pen`. A `Pen` is one of a number of supporting objects to help with drawing — it contains information about how lines are to be drawn. Your first pen instructs that lines should be the color blue with a width of 3 pixels; the second pen instructs that lines should be red and have a width of 2 pixels. The final four parameters are coordinates and size. For the rectangle, they represent the (x,y) coordinates of the top left-hand corner of the rectangle in addition to its width and height. For the ellipse, these numbers represent the same thing, except that you are talking about a hypothetical rectangle that the ellipse just fits into, rather than the ellipse itself. Figure 25-1 shows the result of running this code. Of course, because this is not a color book, you cannot see the colors.

# Chapter 25

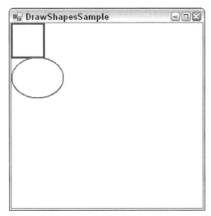

Figure 25-1

Figure 25-1 demonstrates a couple of points. First, you can see clearly where the client area of the window is located. It's the white area — the area that has been affected by setting the `BackColor` property. And notice that the rectangle nestles up in the corner of this area, as you'd expect when you specified coordinates of (0,0) for it. Second, notice that the top of the ellipse overlaps the rectangle slightly, which you wouldn't expect from the coordinates given in the code. The culprit here is Windows itself and where it places the lines that border the rectangle and ellipse. By default, Windows will try to center the line on the border of the shape — that's not always possible to do exactly, because the line has to be drawn on pixels (obviously), but normally the border of each shape theoretically lies between two pixels. The result is that lines that are 1 pixel thick will get drawn just *inside* the top and left sides of a shape, but just *outside* the bottom and right sides — which means that shapes that strictly speaking are next to each other will have their borders overlap by one pixel. You've specified wider lines; therefore the overlap is greater. It is possible to change the default behavior by setting the `Pen.Alignment` property, as detailed in the SDK documentation, but for these purposes the default behavior is adequate.

Unfortunately, if you actually run the sample you'll notice the form behaves a bit strangely. It's fine if you just leave it there, and it's fine if you drag it around the screen with the mouse. If you try minimizing the window and then restoring it, then your carefully drawn shapes just vanish! The same thing happens if you drag another window across the sample. If you drag another window across it so that it only obscures a portion of your shapes, then drag the other window away again, you'll find the temporarily obscured portion has disappeared and you're left with half an ellipse or half a rectangle!

So what's going on? The problem arises when part of a window is hidden, because Windows usually discards immediately all the information concerning exactly what has been displayed. This is something Windows has to do or else the memory usage for storing screen data would be astronomical. A typical computer might be running with the video card set to display 1024×768 pixels, perhaps in a 24-bit color mode, which implies that each pixel on the screen occupies 3 bytes — 2.25MB to display the screen. (What 24-bit color means is covered later in this chapter.) However, it's not uncommon for a user to work with 10 or 20 minimized windows in the taskbar. In a worst-case scenario, you might have 20 windows, each of which would occupy the whole screen if it wasn't minimized. If Windows actually stored the visual information those windows contained, ready for when the user restores them, that would amount to some 45MB! These days, a good graphics card might have 64MB of memory and be able to cope with that, but it was only a couple of years ago that 4MB was considered generous in a graphics card — and the excess

# Graphics with GDI+

would need to be stored in the computer's main memory. A lot of people still have old machines, some of them with only 4MB graphic cards. Clearly it wouldn't be practical for Windows to manage its user interface like that.

The moment any part of a window is hidden, the "hidden" pixels get lost, because Windows frees the memory that was holding those pixels. It does, however, note that a portion of the window is hidden, and when it detects that it is no longer hidden, it asks the application that owns the window to redraw its contents. There are a couple of exceptions to this rule — generally for cases in which a small portion of a window is hidden very temporarily (a good example is when you select an item from the main menu and that menu item drops down, temporarily obscuring part of the window below). In general, however, you can expect that if part of your window is hidden, your application will need to redraw it later.

That's the source of the problem for the sample application. You placed your drawing code in the `Form1` constructor, which is called just once when the application starts up, and you can't call the constructor again to redraw the shapes when required later on.

When working with Windows Forms server controls, there is no need to know anything about how to accomplish this task. This is because the standard controls are pretty sophisticated and they are able to redraw themselves correctly whenever Windows asks them to. That's one reason why when programming controls you don't need to worry about the actual drawing process at all. If you are taking responsibility for drawing to the screen in your application, you also need to make sure your application will respond correctly whenever Windows asks it to redraw all or part of its window. In the next section, you modify the sample to do just that.

## *Painting Shapes Using OnPaint()*

If the preceding explanation has made you worried that drawing your own user interface is going to be terribly complicated, don't worry. Getting your application to redraw itself when necessary is actually quite easy.

Windows notifies an application that some repainting needs to be done by raising a `Paint` event. Interestingly, the `Form` class has already implemented a handler for this event, so you don't need to add one yourself. The `Form1` handler for the `Paint` event will at some point in its processing call up a virtual method, `OnPaint()`, passing to it a single `PaintEventArgs` parameter. This means that all you need to do is override `OnPaint()` to perform your painting.

Although for this example you work by overriding `OnPaint()`, it's equally possible to achieve the same results by simply adding your own event handler for the `Paint` event (a `Form1_Paint()` method, say) — in much the same way as you would for any other Windows Forms event. This other approach is arguably more convenient, because you can add a new event handler through the Visual Studio 2005 properties window, saving yourself from typing some code. However, the approach of overriding `OnPaint()` is slightly more flexible in terms of letting you control when the call to the base class window processing occurs, and is the approach recommended in the documentation. We suggest you use this approach for consistency.

In this section, you create a new Windows Application called `DrawShapes` to do this. As before, you set the background color to white using the Properties Window. You'll also change the form's text to `DrawShapes Sample`. Then you add the following code to the generated code for the `Form1` class:

```
        protected override void OnPaint( PaintEventArgs e )
        {
            base.OnPaint(e);
            Graphics dc = e.Graphics;
            Pen bluePen = new Pen(Color.Blue, 3);
            dc.DrawRectangle(bluePen, 0,0,50,50);
            Pen redPen = new Pen(Color.Red, 2);
            dc.DrawEllipse(redPen, 0, 50, 80, 60);
        }
```

Notice that `OnPaint()` is declared as `protected`, because it is normally used internally within the class, so there's no reason for any other code outside the class to know about its existence.

`PaintEventArgs` is a class that is derived from the `EventArgs` class normally used to pass in information about events. `PaintEventArgs` has two additional properties, of which the more important one is a `Graphics` instance, already primed and optimized to paint the required portion of the window. This means that you don't have to call `CreateGraphics()` to get a DC in the `OnPaint()` method — you've already been provided with one. You look at the other additional property soon; it contains more detailed information about which area of the window actually needs repainting.

In your implementation of `OnPaint()`, you first get a reference to the `Graphics` object from `Paint EventArgs`, then you draw your shapes exactly as you did before. At the end you call the base class's `OnPaint()` method. This step is important. You've overridden `OnPaint()` to do your own painting, but it's possible that Windows may have some additional work of its own to do in the painting process — any such work will be dealt with in an `OnPaint()` method in one of the .NET base classes.

> *For this example, you'll find that removing the call to `base.OnPaint()` doesn't seem to have any effect, but don't ever be tempted to leave this call out. You might be stopping Windows from doing its work properly and the results could be unpredictable.*

`OnPaint()` will also be called when the application first starts up and your window is displayed for the first time, so there is no need to duplicate the drawing code in the constructor.

Running this code gives the same results initially as for the previous example, except that now your application behaves itself properly when you minimize it or hide parts of the window.

## Using the Clipping Region

The `DrawShapes` sample from the previous section illustrates the main principles involved with drawing to a window, although it's not very efficient. The reason is that it attempts to draw everything in the window, irrespective of how much needs to be drawn. Figure 25-2 shows the result of running the `DrawShapes` example and opening another window and moving it over the DrawShapes form so part of it is hidden.

So far, so good. However, when you move the overlapping window so that the DrawShapes window is fully visible again, Windows will as usual send a `Paint` event to the form, asking it to repaint itself. The rectangle and ellipse both lie in the top-left corner of the client area, and so were visible all the time; therefore, there's actually nothing that needs to be done in this case apart from repainting the white background area. However, Windows doesn't know that, so it thinks it should raise the `Paint` event, resulting in your `OnPaint()` implementation being called. `OnPaint()` will then unnecessarily attempt to redraw the rectangle and ellipse.

# Graphics with GDI+

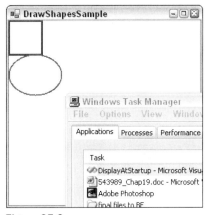

Figure 25-2

Actually, in this case, the shapes will not get repainted because of the device context. Windows has pre-initialized the device context with information concerning what area actually needed repainting. In the days of GDI, the region marked for repainting used to be known as the *invalidated region*, but with GDI+ the terminology has largely changed to *clipping region*. The device context knows what this region is; therefore, it will intercept any attempts to draw outside this region and not pass the relevant drawing commands on to the graphics card. That sounds good, but there's still a potential performance hit here. You don't know how much processing the device context had to do before it figured out that the drawing was outside the invalidated region. In some cases it might be quite a lot, because calculating which pixels need to be changed to what color can be very processor-intensive (although a good graphics card will provide hardware acceleration to help with some of this).

The bottom line to this is that asking the `Graphics` instance to do some drawing outside the invalidated region is almost certainly wasting processor time and slowing your application down. In a well-designed application, your code will help out the device context by carrying out a few simple checks, to see if the proposed drawing work is likely to be needed before it calls the relevant `Graphics` instance methods. In this section you code a new example, `DrawShapesWithClipping`, by modifying the `DisplayShapes` example to do just that. In your `OnPaint()` code, you'll do a simple test to see whether the invalidated region intersects the area you need to draw in and only call the drawing methods if it does.

First, you need to obtain the details of the clipping region. This is where an extra property, `ClipRectangle`, on `PaintEventArgs` comes in. `ClipRectangle` contains the coordinates of the region to be repainted, wrapped up in an instance of a struct, `System.Drawing.Rectangle`. `Rectangle` is quite a simple struct — it contains four properties of interest: `Top`, `Bottom`, `Left`, and `Right`. These respectively contain the vertical coordinates of the top and bottom of the rectangle and the horizontal coordinates of the left and right edges.

Next, you need to decide what test you'll use to determine whether drawing should take place. You'll go for a simple test here. Notice that in your drawing, the rectangle and ellipse are both entirely contained within the rectangle that stretches from point (0,0) to point (80,130) of the client area; actually, point (82,132) to be on the safe side, because you know that the lines might stray a pixel or so outside this area. So you'll check whether the top-left corner of the clipping region is inside this rectangle. If it is, you'll go ahead and redraw. If it isn't, you won't bother.

849

Here is the code to do this:

```
protected override void OnPaint( PaintEventArgs e )
{
    base.OnPaint(e);
    Graphics dc = e.Graphics;

    if (e.ClipRectangle.Top < 132 && e.ClipRectangle.Left < 82)
    {
        Pen bluePen = new Pen(Color.Blue, 3);
        dc.DrawRectangle(bluePen, 0,0,50,50);
        Pen redPen = new Pen(Color.Red, 2);
        dc.DrawEllipse(redPen, 0, 50, 80, 60);
    }
}
```

Note that what gets displayed is exactly the same as before. However, performance is improved now by the early detection of some cases in which nothing needs to be drawn. Notice also that the example uses a fairly crude test of whether to proceed with the drawing. A more refined test might be to check separately whether the rectangle or the ellipse needs to be redrawn. However, there's a balance here. You can make your tests in OnPaint() more sophisticated, improving performance, but you'll also make your own OnPaint() code more complex. It's almost always worth putting some test in, because you've written the code so you understand far more about what is being drawn than the Graphics instance, which just blindly follows drawing commands.

## Measuring Coordinates and Areas

In the previous example, you encountered the base struct, Rectangle, which is used to represent the coordinates of a rectangle. GDI+ actually uses several similar structures to represent coordinates or areas. The following table lists the structs that are defined in the System.Drawing namespace.

| Struct | Main Public Properties |
|---|---|
| Point | X, Y |
| PointF | |
| Size | Width, Height |
| SizeF | |
| Rectangle | Left, Right, Top, Bottom, Width, Height, X, Y, Location, Size |
| RectangleF | |

Note that many of these objects have a number of other properties, methods, or operator overloads not listed here. This section just discusses some of the most important ones.

# Graphics with GDI+

## Point and PointF

Point is conceptually the simplest of these structs. Mathematically, it's completely equivalent to a 2D vector. It contains two public integer properties, which represent how far you move horizontally and vertically from a particular location (perhaps on the screen), as shown in Figure 25-3.

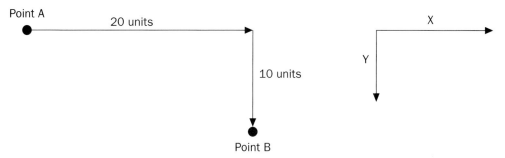

Figure 25-3

To get from point A to point B, you move 20 units across and 10 units down, marked as x and y on the diagram because this is how they are commonly referred to. The following Point struct would represent that line:

```
Point ab = new Point(20, 10);
Console.WriteLine("Moved {0} across, {1} down", ab.X, ab.Y);
```

X and Y are read-write properties, which means you can also set the values in a Point like this:

```
Point ab = new Point();
ab.X = 20;
ab.Y = 10;
Console.WriteLine("Moved {0} across, {1} down", ab.X, ab.Y);
```

Note that although conventionally horizontal and vertical coordinates are referred to as x and y coordinates (lowercase), the corresponding Point properties are X and Y (uppercase) because the usual convention in C# is for public properties to have names that start with an uppercase letter.

PointF is essentially identical to Point, except that X and Y are of type float instead of int. PointF is used when the coordinates are not necessarily integer values. A cast has been defined so that you can implicitly convert from Point to PointF. (Note that because Point and PointF are structs, this cast involves actually making a copy of the data.) There is no corresponding reverse case — to convert from PointF to Point you have to copy the values across, or use one of three conversion methods, Round(), Truncate(), and Ceiling():

```
PointF abFloat = new PointF(20.5F, 10.9F);

// converting to Point
Point ab = new Point();
ab.X = (int)abFloat.X;
ab.Y = (int)abFloat.Y;
```

# Chapter 25

```
Point ab1 = Point.Round(abFloat);
Point ab2 = Point.Truncate(abFloat);
Point ab3 = Point.Ceiling(abFloat);

// but conversion back to PointF is implicit
PointF abFloat2 = ab;
```

You might be wondering what a unit is measured in. By default, GDI+ interprets units as pixels along the screen (or printer, whatever the graphics device is); that's how the `Graphics` object methods will view any coordinates that they get passed as parameters. For example, the point new Point(20,10) represents 20 pixels across the screen and 10 pixels down. Usually these pixels are measured from the top-left corner of the client area of the window, as has been the case in the examples up to now. However, that won't always be the case. For example, on some occasions you might want to draw relative to the top-left corner of the whole window (including its border), or even to the top-left corner of the screen. In most cases, however, unless the documentation tells you otherwise, you can assume you're talking pixels relative to the top-left corner of the client area.

You learn more on this subject later on, after scrolling is examined, when the three different coordinate systems in use—world, page, and device coordinates— are discussed.

## *Size and SizeF*

Like `Point` and `PointF`, sizes come in two varieties. The `Size` struct is for when you are using `int` types; `SizeF` is available if you need to use `float` types. Otherwise `Size` and `SizeF` are identical. This section focuses on the `Size` struct.

In many ways, the `Size` struct is identical to the `Point` struct. It has two integer properties that represent a distance horizontally and a distance vertically. The main difference is that instead of X and Y, these properties are named `Width` and `Height`. You can represent the earlier diagram using this code:

```
Size ab = new Size(20,10);
Console.WriteLine("Moved {0} across, {1} down", ab.Width, ab.Height);
```

Although strictly speaking, `Size` mathematically represents exactly the same thing as `Point`; conceptually it is intended to be used in a slightly different way. `Point` is used when you are talking about where something is, and `Size` is used when you are talking about how big it is. However, because `Size` and `Point` are so closely related, there are even supported conversions between these two:

```
Point point = new Point(20, 10);
Size size = (Size) point;
Point anotherPoint = (Point) size;
```

As an example, think about the rectangle you drew earlier, with top-left coordinate (0,0) and size (50,50). The size of this rectangle is (50,50) and might be represented by a `Size` instance. The bottom-right corner is also at (50,50), but that would be represented by a `Point` instance. To see the difference, suppose you draw the rectangle in a different location, so its top-left coordinate is at (10,10):

```
dc.DrawRectangle(bluePen, 10,10,50,50);
```

Now the bottom-right corner is at coordinate (60,60), but the size is unchanged at (50,50).

# Graphics with GDI+

The addition operator has been overloaded for Point and Size structs, so that it is possible to add a Size to a Point struct, resulting in another Point struct:

```
static void Main(string[] args)
{
    Point topLeft = new Point(10,10);
    Size rectangleSize = new Size(50,50);
    Point bottomRight = topLeft + rectangleSize;
    Console.WriteLine("topLeft = " + topLeft);
    Console.WriteLine("bottomRight = " + bottomRight);
    Console.WriteLine("Size = " + rectangleSize);
}
```

This code, running as a simple console application called PointsAndSizes, produces the output shown in Figure 25-4.

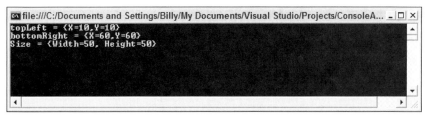

Figure 25-4

Note that this output also shows how the ToString() method has been overridden in both Point and Size to display the value in {X, Y} format.

It is also possible to subtract a Size from a Point struct to give a Point struct, and you can add two Size structs together, giving another Size. It is not possible, however, to add a Point struct to another Point. Microsoft decided that adding Point structs doesn't conceptually make sense, and so chose not supply any overload to the + operator that would have allowed that.

You can also explicitly cast a Point to a Size struct and vice versa:

```
Point topLeft = new Point(10,10);
Size s1 = (Size)topLeft;
Point p1 = (Point)s1;
```

With this cast s1.Width is assigned the value of topLeft.X, and s1.Height is assigned the value of topLeft.Y. Hence, s1 contains (10,10). p1 will end up storing the same values as topLeft.

## Rectangle and RectangleF

These structures represent a rectangular region (usually of the screen). Just as with Point and Size, only the Rectangle struct is considered here. RectangleF is basically identical except that those of its properties that represent dimensions all use float, whereas those of Rectangle use int.

853

A `Rectangle` struct can be thought of as composed of a point, representing the top-left corner of the rectangle, and a `Size` struct, which represents how large it is. One of its constructors actually takes a `Point` struct and a `Size` struct as its parameters. You can see this by rewriting the earlier code from the `DrawShapes` sample that draws a rectangle:

```
Graphics dc = e.Graphics;
Pen bluePen = new Pen(Color.Blue, 3);
Point topLeft = new Point(0,0);
Size howBig = new Size(50,50);
Rectangle rectangleArea = new Rectangle(topLeft, howBig);
dc.DrawRectangle(bluePen, rectangleArea);
```

This code also uses an alternative override of `Graphics.DrawRectangle()`, which takes a `Pen` and a `Rectangle` struct as its parameters.

You can also construct a `Rectangle` struct by supplying the top-left horizontal coordinate, top-left vertical coordinate, width, and height separately, and in that order, as individual numbers:

```
Rectangle rectangleArea = new Rectangle(0, 0, 50, 50);
```

`Rectangle` makes quite a few read-write properties available to set or extract its dimensions in different combinations. See the following table for details.

| Property | Description |
| --- | --- |
| int Left | x-coordinate of left-hand edge |
| int Right | x-coordinate of right-hand edge |
| int Top | y-coordinate of top |
| int Bottom | y-coordinate of bottom |
| int X | Same as Left |
| int Y | Same as Top |
| int Width | Width of rectangle |
| int Height | Height of rectangle |
| Point Location | Top-left corner |
| Size Size | Size of rectangle |

Note that these properties are not all independent. For example, setting `Width` also affects the value of `Right`.

## Region

`Region` represents an area of the screen that has some complex shape. For example, the shaded area in Figure 25-5 could be represented by `Region`.

# Graphics with GDI+

Figure 25-5

As you can imagine, the process of initializing a `Region` instance is itself quite complex. Broadly speaking, you can do it by indicating either what component simple shapes make up the region or what path you take as you trace round the edge of the region. If you do need to start working with areas like this, it's worth looking up the `Region` class in the SDK documentation.

# A Note about Debugging

You're just about ready to do some more advanced types of drawing now. First, however, I just want to say a few things about debugging. If you have tried setting break points in the examples of this chapter you will have noticed that debugging drawing routines isn't quite as simple as debugging other parts of your program. This is because entering and leaving the debugger often causes `Paint` messages to be sent to your application. The result can be that setting a break point in your `OnPaint()` override simply causes your application to keep painting itself over and over again, so it's basically unable to do anything else.

A typical scenario is as follows. You want to find out why your application is displaying something incorrectly, so you set a break point within the `OnPaint()` event. As expected, the application hits your break point and the debugger comes in, at which point your developer environment MDI window comes to the foreground. If you're anything like me, you probably have the developer environments set to full screen display so you can more easily view all the debugging information, which means it always completely hides the application you are debugging.

Moving on, you examine the values of some variables and hopefully find out something useful. Then you press F5 to tell the application to continue, so that you can go on to see what happens when the application displays something else after some processing. Unfortunately, the first thing that happens is that the application comes to the foreground and Windows efficiently detects that the form is visible again and promptly sends it a `Paint` event. This means, of course, that your break point is hit again. If that's what you want, fine. More commonly, what you really want is to hit the break point *later*, when the application is drawing something more interesting, perhaps after you've selected some menu option to read in a file or in some other way changed what gets displayed. It looks like you're stuck. Either you don't have a break point in `OnPaint()` at all, or your application can never get beyond the point where it's displaying its initial startup window.

There is a workaround to this problem.

If you have a big screen the easiest way is simply to keep your developer environment window tiled rather than maximized and keep it well away from your application window, so your application never is hidden in the first place. Unfortunately, in most cases that is not a practical solution, because that would make your developer environment window too small. An alternative that uses the same principle is to have your application declare itself as the topmost application while you are debugging. You do this by setting a property in the `Form` class, `TopMost`, which you can easily do in the `InitializeComponent()` method:

```
private void InitializeComponent()
{
    this.TopMost = true;
```

You can also set this property through the Properties window in Visual Studio 2005.

Being a `TopMost` window means your application can never be hidden by other windows (except other topmost windows). It always remains above other windows even when another application has the focus. This is how the Task Manager behaves.

Even with this technique you have to be careful, because you can never be certain when Windows might decide for some reason to raise a `Paint` event. If you really want to trap some problem that occurs in `OnPaint()` in some specific circumstance (for example, the application draws something after you select a certain menu option, and something goes wrong at that point), then the best way to do this is to place some dummy code in `OnPaint()` that tests some condition, which will only be `true` in the specified circumstances — and then place the break point inside the `if` block, like this:

```
protected override void OnPaint( PaintEventArgs e )
{
    // Condition() evaluates to true when we want to break
    if ( Condition() == true)
    {
        int ii = 0;     // <-- SET BREAKPOINT HERE!!!
    }
```

This is a quick-and-easy way of setting a conditional break point.

## Drawing Scrollable Windows

The earlier `DrawShapes` example worked very well, because everything you needed to draw fit into the initial window size. This section looks at what you need to do if that's not the case.

For this example, you expand the `DrawShapes` sample to demonstrate scrolling. To make things a bit more realistic, you start by creating an example, `BigShapes`, in which you make the rectangle and ellipse a bit bigger. Also, while you're at it, you'll see how to use the `Point`, `Size`, and `Rectangle` structs by using them to assist in defining the drawing areas. With these changes, the relevant part of the `Form1` class looks like this:

# Graphics with GDI+

```
        // member fields
        private Point rectangleTopLeft = new Point(0, 0);
        private Size rectangleSize = new Size(200,200);
        private Point ellipseTopLeft = new Point(50, 200);
        private Size ellipseSize = new Size(200, 150);
        private Pen bluePen = new Pen(Color.Blue, 3);
        private Pen redPen = new Pen(Color.Red, 2);

        protected override void OnPaint( PaintEventArgs e )
        {
           base.OnPaint(e);
           Graphics dc = e.Graphics;

           if (e.ClipRectangle.Top < 350 || e.ClipRectangle.Left < 250)
           {
              Rectangle rectangleArea =
                 new Rectangle (rectangleTopLeft, rectangleSize);
              Rectangle ellipseArea =
                 new Rectangle (ellipseTopLeft, ellipseSize);
              dc.DrawRectangle(bluePen, rectangleArea);
              dc.DrawEllipse(redPen, ellipseArea);
           }
        }
```

Note that you've also turned the `Pen`, `Size`, and `Point` objects into member fields — this is more efficient than creating a new `Pen` every time you need to draw anything, as you have been doing up to now.

The result of running this example looks like Figure 25-6.

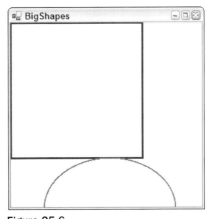

**Figure 25-6**

You can see a problem instantly. The shapes don't fit in your 300×300 pixel drawing area.

Normally, if a document is too large to display, an application will add scroll bars to let you scroll the window and look at a chosen part of it. This is another area in which if you were building Windows

Forms using standard controls, then you'd just let the .NET runtime and the base classes handle everything for you. If your form has various controls attached to it, the Form instance will normally know where these controls are and it will therefore know if its window becomes so small that scroll bars are necessary. The Form instance also automatically adds the scroll bars for you, and it is also able to draw correctly whichever portion of the screen you've scrolled to. In that case there is nothing you need to do in your code. In this chapter, however, you're taking responsibility for drawing to the screen; therefore, you're going to have to help the Form instance out when it comes to scrolling.

Getting the scroll bars added is actually very easy. The Form can still handle all that for you, because it doesn't know how big an area you will want to draw in. (The reason it hasn't in the earlier BigShapes example is that Windows doesn't know they are needed.) What you need to figure out is the size of a rectangle that stretches from the top-left corner of the document (or equivalently, the top-left corner of the client area before you've done any scrolling), and which is just big enough to contain the entire document. In this chapter, this area is referred to as the document area. As shown in Figure 25-7, for this example the document area is (250, 350) pixels.

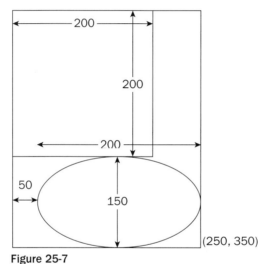

**Figure 25-7**

It is easy to tell the form how big the document is. You use the relevant property, Form .AutoScrollMinSize. Therefore you can add this code to either the InitializeComponent() method or the Form1 constructor:

```
private void InitializeComponent()
{
    this.AutoScaleBaseSize = new System.Drawing.Size(5, 13);
    this.ClientSize = new System.Drawing.Size(292, 266);
    this.Name = "Form1";
    this.Text = "BigShapes";
    this.BackColor = Color.White;
    this.AutoScrollMinSize = new Size(250, 350);
}
```

# Graphics with GDI+

Alternatively, the `AutoScrollMinSize` property can be set using the Visual Studio 2005 Properties window.

Setting the minimum size at application startup and leaving it thereafter is fine in this particular example, because you know that is how big the screen area will always be. Your document never changes size while this particular application is running. Keep in mind, however, that if your application does things like display contents of files or something else for which the area of the screen might change, you will need to set this property at other times (and in that case you'll have to sort out the code manually — the Visual Studio 2005 Properties window can only help you with the initial value that a property has when the form is constructed).

Setting `AutoScrollMinSize` is a start, but it's not yet quite enough. Figure 25-8 shows what the sample application looks like now — initially you get the screen that correctly displays the shapes.

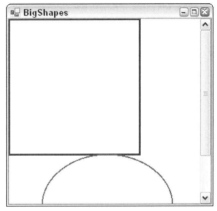

Figure 25-8

Notice that not only has the form correctly set the scroll bars, but it has also correctly sized them to indicate what proportion of the document is currently displayed. You can try resizing the window while the sample is running — you'll find the scroll bars respond properly, and even disappear if you make the window big enough so that they are no longer needed.

However, look at what happens when you actually use one of the scroll bars and scroll down a bit (see Figure 25-9). Clearly, something has gone wrong!

What's wrong is that you haven't taken into account the position of the scroll bars in the code in your `OnPaint()` override. You can see this very clearly if you force the window to repaint itself completely by minimizing and restoring it (see Figure 25-10).

The shapes have been painted, just as before, with the top-left corner of the rectangle nestled into the top-left corner of the client area — just as if you hadn't moved the scroll bars at all.

859

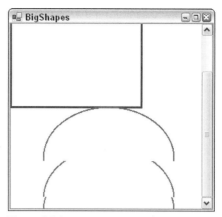

**Figure 25-9**

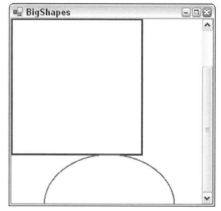

**Figure 25-10**

Before you see how to correct this problem, take a closer look at precisely what is happening in these screenshots.

Start with the BigShapes sample, shown in Figure 25-8. In this example, the entire window has just been repainted. Reviewing your code you learn that it instructs the graphics instance to draw a rectangle with top-left coordinates (0,0) — relative to the top-left corner of the client area of the window — which is what has been drawn. The problem is that the graphics instance by default interprets coordinates as relative to the client window and is unaware of the scroll bars. Your code as yet does not attempt to adjust the coordinates for the scroll bar positions. The same goes for the ellipse.

Now, you can tackle the screenshot in Figure 25-9. After you scroll down, you notice that the top half of the window looks fine. That's because it was drawn when the application first started up. When you scroll windows, Windows doesn't ask the application to redraw what was already on the screen. Windows is smart enough to figure out for itself which bits of what's currently being displayed on the screen can be smoothly moved around to match where the scroll bars now are located. That's a much more efficient process, because it may be able to use some hardware acceleration to do that too. The bit in this screenshot that's wrong is the bottom third of the window. This part of the window didn't get drawn when the application first appeared, because before you started scrolling it was outside the client area. This means that Windows asks your `BigShapes` application to draw this area. It'll raise a `Paint` event passing in just this area as the clipping rectangle. And that's exactly what your `OnPaint()` override has done.

One way of looking at the problem is that you are at the moment expressing your coordinates relative to the top-left corner of the start of the document — you need to convert them to express them relative to the top-left corner of the client area instead (see Figure 25-11).

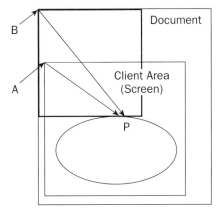

Figure 25-11

To make the diagram clearer, the document is actually extended further downward and to the right, beyond the boundaries of the screen, but this doesn't change our reasoning. It also assumes a small horizontal scroll as well as a vertical one.

In Figure 25-11 the thin rectangles mark the borders of the screen area and of the entire document. The thick lines mark the rectangle and ellipse that you are trying to draw. P marks some arbitrary point that you are drawing and which is being used as an example. When calling the drawing methods the graphics instance was supplied with the vector from point B to (say) point P, expressed as a `Point` instance. You actually need to give it the vector from point A to point P.

The problem is that you don't know what the vector from A to P is. You know what B to P is — that's just the coordinates of P relative to the top-left corner of the document — the position where you want to draw point P in the document. You also know the vector from B to A is just the amount you've scrolled by; this is stored in a property of the `Form` class called `AutoScrollPosition`. However, you don't know the vector from A to P.

Now, if you remember your high school math, you will know how to solve this problem — you subtract the one vector from the other. Say, for example, to get from B to P you move 150 pixels across and 200 pixels down, whereas to get from B to A you have to move 10 pixels across and 57 pixels down. That means to get from A to P you have to move 140 (=150 minus 10) pixels across and 143 (=200 minus 57) pixels down. To make it even simpler, the `Graphics` class actually implements a method that will do

# Chapter 25

these calculations for you. It's called `TranslateTransform()`. You pass it the horizontal and vertical coordinates that say where the top left of the client area is relative to the top-left corner of the document (your `AutoScrollPosition` property, that is, the vector from B to A in the diagram). The `Graphics` device will now work out all its coordinates, taking into account where the client area is relative to the document.

Translating this long explanation into code, all you typically need to do is add this line to your drawing code:

```
dc.TranslateTransform(this.AutoScrollPosition.X, this.AutoScrollPosition.Y);
```

However in this example, it's a little more complicated because you are also separately testing whether you need to do any drawing by looking at the clipping region. You need to adjust this test to take the scroll position into account too. When you've done that, the full drawing code for the sample looks like this:

```
protected override void OnPaint( PaintEventArgs e )
{
    base.OnPaint(e);
    Graphics dc = e.Graphics;
    Size scrollOffset = new Size(this.AutoScrollPosition);

    if (e.ClipRectangle.Top+scrollOffset.Width < 350 ||
        e.ClipRectangle.Left+scrollOffset.Height < 250)
    {
        Rectangle rectangleArea = new Rectangle
            (rectangleTopLeft+scrollOffset, rectangleSize);
        Rectangle ellipseArea = new Rectangle
            (ellipseTopLeft+scrollOffset, ellipseSize);
        dc.DrawRectangle(bluePen, rectangleArea);
        dc.DrawEllipse(redPen, ellipseArea);
    }
}
```

Now you have your scroll code working perfectly; you can at last obtain a correctly scrolled screenshot (see Figure 25-12).

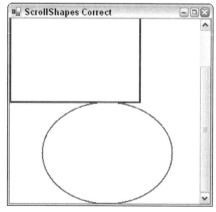

**Figure 25-12**

# Graphics with GDI+

## World, Page, and Device Coordinates

The distinction between measuring position relative to the top-left corner of the document and measuring it relative to the top-left corner of the screen (desktop) is so important that GDI+ has special names for these coordinate systems:

- ❑ **World coordinates** specify the position of a point measured in pixels from the top-left corner of the document.

- ❑ **Page coordinates** specify the position of a point measured in pixels from the top-left corner of the client area.

*Developers familiar with GDI will note that world coordinates correspond to what in GDI were known as logical coordinates. Page coordinates correspond to what used to be known as device coordinates. As a developer familiar with GDI you should also note that the way you code conversion between logical and device coordinates has changed in GDI+. In GDI, conversions took place via the device context, using the* `LPtoDP()` *and* `DPtoLP()` *Windows API functions. In GDI+, it's the* `Control` *class, from which both* `Form` *and all the various Windows Forms controls derive, that maintains the information needed to carry out the conversion.*

GDI+ also distinguishes a third coordinate system, which is now known as *device coordinates*. Device coordinates are similar to page coordinates, except that you do not use pixels as the unit of measurement. Instead you use some other unit that can be specified by the user by calling the `Graphics.PageUnit` property. Possible units, besides the default of pixels, include inches and millimeters. Although you won't use the `PageUnit` property in this chapter, you might find it useful as a way of getting around the different pixel densities of devices. For example, 100 pixels on most monitors will occupy something like an inch. However, laser printers can have 1,200 or more dpi (dots per inch), which means that a shape specified to be 100 pixels wide will look a lot smaller when printed on it. By setting the units to, say, inches and specifying that the shape should be 1 inch wide, you can ensure that the shape will look the same size on the different devices.

## Colors

This section discusses the ways that you can specify what color you want something to be drawn in.

Colors in GDI+ are represented by instances of the `System.Drawing.Color` struct. Generally, once you've instantiated this struct, you won't do much with the corresponding `Color` instance — you just pass it to whatever other method you are calling that requires a `Color`. You've encountered this struct before, when you set the background color of the client area of the window in each of the examples, as well as when you set the colors of the various shapes you were displaying. The `Form.BackColor` property actually returns a `Color` instance. This section looks at this struct in more detail. In particular, it examines several different ways that you can construct a `Color`.

### Red-Green-Blue (RGB) Values

The total number of colors that can be displayed by a monitor is huge — more than 16 million. To be exact the number is 2 to the power 24, which works out to 16,777,216. Obviously you need some way of indexing those colors so you can indicate which of these is the color you want to display at any given pixel.

The most common way of indexing colors is by dividing them into the red, green, and blue components. This idea is based on the theory that any color that the human eye can distinguish can be constructed from a certain amount of red light, a certain amount of the green light, and a certain amount of blue light. These colors are known as *components*. In practice, it's found that if you divide the amount of each component light into 256 possible intensities, then that gives a sufficiently fine gradation to be able to display images that are perceived by the human eye to be of photographic quality. You therefore specify colors by giving the amounts of these components on a scale of 0 to 255 where 0 means that the component is not present and 255 means that it is at its maximum intensity.

> You can now see where the quoted figure of 16,777,216 colors comes from, because that number is just 256 cubed.

This gives you your first way of telling GDI+ about a color. You can indicate a color's red, green, and blue values by calling the static function `Color.FromArgb()`. Microsoft has chosen not to supply a constructor to do this task. The reason is that there are other ways, besides the usual RGB components, to indicate a color. Because of this, Microsoft felt that the meaning of parameters passed to any constructor they defined would be open to misinterpretation:

```
Color redColor = Color.FromArgb(255,0,0);
Color funnyOrangyBrownColor = Color.FromArgb(255,155,100);
Color blackColor = Color.FromArgb(0,0,0);
Color whiteColor = Color.FromArgb(255,255,255);
```

The three parameters are, respectively, the quantities of red, green, and blue. This function has a number of other overloads, some of which also allow you to specify something called an alpha-blend (that's the A in the name of the method, `FromArgb()`). Alpha blending is beyond the scope of this chapter, but it allows you to paint a color semi-transparently by combining it with whatever color was already on the screen. This can give some beautiful effects and is often used in games.

## *The Named Colors*

Constructing a `Color` using `FromArgb()` is the most flexible technique, because it literally means you can specify any color that the human eye can see. However, if you want a simple, standard, well-known color such as red or blue, it's a lot easier to just be able to name the color you want. Hence, Microsoft has also provided a large number of static properties in `Color`, each of which returns a named color. It was one of these properties that you used when you set the background color of your windows to white in the examples:

```
        this.BackColor = Color.White;

        // has the same effect as:
        // this.BackColor - Color.FromArgb(255, 255 , 255);
```

Several hundred such colors exist. The full list is given in the SDK documentation. They include all the simple colors: `Red`, `White`, `Blue`, `Green`, `Black`, and so on, as well as such delights as `MediumAquamarine`, `LightCoral`, and `DarkOrchid`. There is also a `KnownColor` enumeration, which lists the named colors.

# Graphics with GDI+

*Incidentally, although it might look that way, these named colors have not been chosen at random. Each one represents a precise set of RGB values, and they were originally chosen many years ago for use on the Internet. The idea was to provide a useful set of colors right across the spectrum whose names would be recognized by Web browsers, thus saving you from having to write explicit RGB values in your HTML code. A few years ago these colors were also important because early browsers couldn't necessarily display very many colors accurately, and the named colors were supposed to provide a set of colors that would be displayed correctly by most browsers. These days, that aspect is less important because modern Web browsers are quite capable of displaying any RGB value correctly. Web-safe color palettes are also available that provide developers with a comprehensive list of colors that work with most browsers.*

## Graphics Display Modes and the Safety Palette

Although in principle monitors can display any of the more than 16 million RGB colors, in practice this depends on how you've set the display properties on your computer. In Windows, there are traditionally three main color options (although some machines might provide other options depending on the hardware): true color (24-bit), high color (16-bit), and 256 colors. (On some graphics cards these days, true color is actually marked as 32-bit. This has to do with optimizing the hardware, though in that case only 24 bits of the 32 bits are used for the color itself.)

Only true-color mode allows you to display all of the RGB colors simultaneously. This sounds like the best option, but it comes at a cost: 3 bytes are needed to hold a full RGB value, which means 3 bytes of graphics card memory are needed to hold each pixel that is displayed. If graphics card memory is at a premium (a restriction that's less common now than it used to be) you might want to choose one of the other modes. High-color mode gives you 2 bytes per pixel. That's enough to give 5 bits for each RGB component. So instead of 256 gradations of red intensity you just get 32 gradations; the same for blue and green, which gives a total of 65,536 colors. That is just about enough to give apparent photographic quality on a casual inspection, though areas of subtle shading tend to be broken up a bit.

The 256-color mode gives you even fewer colors. However, in this mode, you get to choose which colors. What happens is that the system sets up something known as a *palette*. This is a list of 256 colors chosen from the 16 million RGB colors. Once you've specified the colors in the palette, the graphics device will be able to display just those colors. The palette can be changed at any time, but the graphics device can only display 256 different colors on the screen at any one time. The 256-color mode is only used when high performance and video memory is at a premium. Most computer games will use this mode, and they can still achieve decent-looking graphics because of a very careful choice of palette.

In general, if a display device is in high-color or 256-color mode and a particular RGB color is requested, it will pick the nearest mathematical match from the pool of colors that it is able to display. It's for this reason that it's important to be aware of the color modes. If you are drawing something that involves subtle shading or photographic-quality images, and the user does not have 24-bit color mode selected, she might not see the image the same way you intended it. So if you're doing that kind of work with GDI+, you should test your application in different color modes. (It is also possible for your application to programmatically set a given color mode, though that is not discussed this in this chapter for lack of space.)

## The Safety Palette

For reference, this section quickly mentions the safety palette, which is a very commonly used default palette. The way it works is that you set six equally spaced possible values for each color component: 0, 51, 102, 153, 204, and 255. In other words, the red component can have any of these values. So can the green component. So can the blue component. So possible colors from the safety palette include (0,0,0), black; (153,0,0), a fairly dark shade of red; (0, 255,102), green with a smattering of blue added; and so on. This gives you a total of 6 cubed = 216 colors. The idea is that this gives you an easy way of having a palette that contains colors from right across the spectrum and of all degrees of brightness, although in practice this doesn't actually work that well because equal mathematical spacing of color components doesn't mean equal perception of color differences by the human eye. Because the safety palette used to be widely used, however, you'll still find that a fair number of applications and images exclusively use colors from the safety palette.

If you set Windows to 256-color mode, you'll find the default palette you get is the safety palette, with 20 Windows-standard colors added to it, and 20 spare colors.

# Pens and Brushes

This section reviews two helper classes that are needed in order to draw shapes. You've already encountered the Pen class, which you used to instruct the graphics instance how to draw lines. A related class is System.Drawing.Brush, which instructs the graphics instance how to fill regions. For example, the Pen is needed to draw the outlines of the rectangle and ellipse in the previous examples. If you had needed to draw these shapes as solid, you would have used a brush to specify how to fill them in. One aspect of both of these classes is that you will hardly ever call any methods on them. You simply construct a Pen or Brush instance with the required color and other properties, and then pass it to drawing methods that require a Pen or Brush.

> *If you've programmed using GDI before, you have noticed from the first couple of examples that pens are used in a different way in GDI+. In GDI the normal practice was to call a Windows API function,* SelectObject(), *which actually associated a pen with the device context. That pen was then used in all drawing operations that required a pen until you informed the device context otherwise, by calling* SelectObject() *again. The same principle held for brushes and other objects such as fonts or bitmaps. With GDI+ Microsoft has opted for a stateless model in which there is no default pen or other helper object. Rather, you simply specify with each method call the appropriate helper object to be used for that particular method.*

## Brushes

GDI+ has several different kinds of brushes — more than there is space to go into in this chapter, so this section just explains the simpler ones to give you an idea of the principles. Each type of brush is represented by an instance of a class derived from the abstract class System.Drawing.Brush. The simplest brush, System.Drawing.SolidBrush, indicates that a region is to be filled with solid color:

```
Brush solidBeigeBrush = new SolidBrush(Color.Beige);
Brush solidFunnyOrangyBrownBrush =
                    new SolidBrush(Color.FromArgb(255,155,100));
```

# Graphics with GDI+

Alternatively, if the brush is one of the Web-safe colors you can construct the brush using another class, `System.Drawing.Brushes`. `Brushes` is one of those classes that you never actually instantiate (it has a private constructor to stop you from doing that). It simply has a large number of static properties, each of which returns a brush of a specified color. You can use `Brushes` like this:

```
Brush solidAzureBrush = Brushes.Azure;
Brush solidChocolateBrush = Brushes.Chocolate;
```

The next level of complexity is a hatch brush, which fills a region by drawing a pattern. This type of brush is considered more advanced, so it's in the `Drawing2D` namespace, represented by the class `System.Drawing.Drawing2D.HatchBrush`. The `Brushes` class can't help you with hatch brushes — you'll need to construct one explicitly by supplying the hatch style and two colors, the foreground color followed by the background color (you can omit the background color, in which case it defaults to black). The hatch style comes from an enumeration, `System.Drawing.Drawing2D.HatchStyle`. You can choose from a large number of `HatchStyle` values (see the SDK documentation for the full list). To give you an idea, typical styles include `ForwardDiagonal`, `Cross`, `DiagonalCross`, `SmallConfetti`, and `ZigZag`. Examples of constructing a hatch brush include:

```
Brush crossBrush = new HatchBrush(HatchStyle.Cross, Color.Azure);

// background color of CrossBrush is black

Brush brickBrush = new HatchBrush(HatchStyle.DiagonalBrick,
                        Color.DarkGoldenrod, Color.Cyan);
```

Solid and hatch brushes are the only brushes available under GDI. GDI+ has added a couple of new styles of brushes:

- ❑ `System.Drawing.Drawing2D.LinearGradientBrush` fills in an area with a color that varies across the screen.
- ❑ `System.Drawing.Drawing2D.PathGradientBrush` is similar, but in this case the color varies along a path around the region to be filled.

Note that both brushes can render some spectacular effects if used carefully.

## Pens

Unlike brushes, pens are represented by just one class: `System.Drawing.Pen`. However, the pen is slightly more complex than the brush, because it needs to indicate how thick lines should be (how many pixels wide) and, for a wide line, how to fill the area inside the line. Pens can also specify a number of other properties, which are beyond the scope of this chapter, but which include the `Alignment` property mentioned earlier. This property indicates where in relation to the border of a shape a line should be drawn, as well as what shape to draw at the end of a line (whether to round off the shape).

The area inside a thick line can be filled with solid color, or it can be filled using a brush. Hence, a `Pen` instance might contain a reference to a `Brush` instance. This is quite powerful, because it means you can draw lines that are colored in by using, say, hatching or linear shading. You have four different ways to construct a `Pen` instance that you have designed yourself. You can do it by passing a color, or you can do it by passing in a brush. Both of these constructors will produce a pen with a width of one pixel.

Alternatively, you can pass in a color or a brush, and additionally a `float`, which represents the width of the pen. (It needs to be a `float` in case you are using non-default units such as millimeters or inches for the `Graphics` object that will do the drawing, so you can, for example, specify fractions of an inch.) For example, you can construct pens like this:

```
Brush brickBrush = new HatchBrush(HatchStyle.DiagonalBrick,
                                  Color.DarkGoldenrod, Color.Cyan);

Pen solidBluePen = new Pen(Color.FromArgb(0,0,255));
Pen solidWideBluePen = new Pen(Color.Blue, 4);
Pen brickPen = new Pen(brickBrush);
Pen brickWidePen = new Pen(brickBrush, 10);
```

Additionally, for the quick construction of pens, you can use the class `System.Drawing.Pens`, which, like the `Brushes` class, contains a number of stock pens. These pens all have one-pixel width and come in the usual sets of Web-safe colors. This allows you to construct pens in this way:

```
Pen solidYellowPen = Pens.Yellow;
```

## Drawing Shapes and Lines

You've almost finished the first part of the chapter, and you've seen all the basic classes and objects required in order to draw specified shapes and so on to the screen. This section starts off by reviewing some of the drawing methods the `Graphics` class makes available and presents a short example that illustrates the use of several brushes and pens.

`System.Drawing.Graphics` has a large number of methods that allow you to draw various lines, outline shapes, and solid shapes. Once again there are too many to provide a comprehensive list here, but the following table lists the main ones and should give you some idea of the variety of shapes you can draw.

| Method | Typical Parameters | What it Draws |
|---|---|---|
| DrawLine | Pen, start and end points | A single straight line |
| DrawRectangle | Pen, position, and size | Outline of a rectangle |
| DrawEllipse | Pen, position, and size | Outline of an ellipse |
| FillRectangle | Brush, position, and size | Solid rectangle |
| FillEllipse | Brush, position, and size | Solid ellipse |
| DrawLines | Pen, array of points | Series of lines, connecting each point to the next one in the array |
| DrawBezier | Pen, 4 points | A smooth curve through the two end points, with the remaining two points used to control the shape of the curve |
| DrawCurve | Pen, array of points | A smooth curve through the points |

# Graphics with GDI+

| Method | Typical Parameters | What it Draws |
|---|---|---|
| DrawArc | Pen, rectangle, two angles | Portion of circle within the rectangle defined by the angles |
| DrawClosedCurve | Pen, array of points | Like DrawCurve but also draws a straight line to close the curve |
| DrawPie | Pen, rectangle, two angles | Wedge-shaped outline within the rectangle |
| FillPie | Brush, rectangle, two angles | Solid wedge-shaped area within the rectangle |
| DrawPolygon | Pen, array of points | Like DrawLines but also connects first and last points to close the figure drawn |

Before leaving the subject of drawing simple objects, this section rounds off with a simple example that demonstrates the kinds of visual effects you can achieve using brushes. The example is called ScrollMoreShapes, and it's essentially a revision of ScrollShapes. Besides the rectangle and ellipse, you'll add a thick line and fill in the shapes with various custom brushes. You've already learned the principles of drawing, so the code speaks for itself. First, because of your new brushes, you need to indicate you are using the System.Drawing.Drawing2D namespace:

```
using System;
using System.Collections.Generic;
using System.ComponentModel;
using System.Data;
using System.Drawing;
using System.Drawing.Drawing2D;
using System.Text;
using System.Windows.Forms;
```

Next are some extra fields in your Form1 class, which contain details of the locations where the shapes are to be drawn, as well as various pens and brushes you will use:

```
private Rectangle rectangleBounds = new Rectangle(new Point(0,0),
                                                  new Size(200,200));
private Rectangle ellipseBounds = new Rectangle(new Point(50,200),
                                                new Size(200,150));
private Pen bluePen = new Pen(Color.Blue, 3);
private Pen redPen = new Pen(Color.Red, 2);
private Brush solidAzureBrush = Brushes.Azure;
private Brush solidYellowBrush = new SolidBrush(Color.Yellow);
static private Brush brickBrush = new HatchBrush(HatchStyle.DiagonalBrick,
                                      Color.DarkGoldenrod, Color.Cyan);
private Pen brickWidePen = new Pen(brickBrush, 10);
```

The brickBrush field has been declared as static, so that you can use its value to initialize the brickWidePen field. C# won't let you use one instance field to initialize another instance field, because it's not defined which one will be initialized first. However, declaring the field as static solves the problem. Because only one instance of the Form1 class will be instantiated, it is immaterial whether the fields are static or instance fields.

# Chapter 25

Here is the `OnPaint()` override:

```
protected override void OnPaint( PaintEventArgs e )
{
   base.OnPaint(e);
   Graphics dc = e.Graphics;
   Point scrollOffset = this.AutoScrollPosition;
   dc.TranslateTransform(scrollOffset.X, scrollOffset.Y);

   if (e.ClipRectangle.Top+scrollOffset.X < 350 ||
       e.ClipRectangle.Left+scrollOffset.Y < 250)
   {
      dc.DrawRectangle(bluePen, rectangleBounds);
      dc.FillRectangle(solidYellowBrush, rectangleBounds);
      dc.DrawEllipse(redPen, ellipseBounds);
      dc.FillEllipse(solidAzureBrush, ellipseBounds);
      dc.DrawLine(brickWidePen, rectangleBounds.Location,
                       ellipseBounds.Location+ellipseBounds.Size);
   }
}
```

As before, you also set the `AutoScrollMinSize` to (250,350). Figure 25-13 shows the new results.

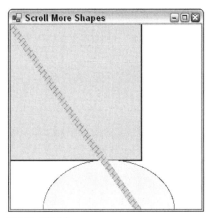

**Figure 25-13**

Notice that the thick diagonal line has been drawn on top of the rectangle and ellipse, because it was the last item to be painted.

# Displaying Images

One of the most common things you might want to do with GDI+ is display an image that already exists in a file. This is actually a lot simpler than drawing your own user interface, because the image is already

# Graphics with GDI+

pre-drawn. Effectively, all you have to do is load the file and instruct GDI+ to display it. The image can be a simple line drawing, an icon, or a complex image such as a photograph. You can also manipulate the image by stretching or rotating it, or simply displaying only a portion of it.

This section, just for a change, presents the sample first. Then it discusses some of the issues you need to be aware of when displaying images. Presenting it this way is possible because the code needed to display an image is so simple.

The class you need is the .NET base class, `System.Drawing.Image`. An instance of `Image` represents one image. Reading in an image simply takes one line of code:

```
Image myImage = Image.FromFile("FileName");
```

`FromFile()` is a static member of `Image` and is the usual way of instantiating an image. The file can be any of the commonly supported graphics file formats, including `.bmp`, `.jpg`, `.gif`, and `.png`.

Displaying an image is also very simple, assuming you have a suitable `Graphics` instance at hand — a call to either `Graphics.DrawImageUnscaled()` or `Graphics.DrawImage()` suffices. There are quite a few overloads of these methods, allowing you a lot of flexibility in the information you supply in terms of where the image is located and how big it is to be drawn. But this example uses `DrawImage()`, like this:

```
dc.DrawImage(myImage, points);
```

In this line of code, `dc` is assumed to be a `Graphics` instance, and `myImage` is the `Image` to be displayed. `points` is an array of `Point` structs, where `points[0]`, `points[1]`, and `points[2]` are the coordinates of top-left, top-right, and bottom-left corner of the image.

> *Images are probably the area in which developers familiar with GDI will notice the biggest difference between GDI and GDI+. In GDI, displaying an image involved several nontrivial steps. If the image was a bitmap, loading it was reasonably simple. But if it was any other file type, loading it would involve a sequence of calls to OLE objects. Actually getting a loaded image onto the screen involved getting a handle to it, selecting it into a memory device context, and then performing a block transfer between device contexts. Although the device contexts and handles are still there behind the scenes, and will be needed if you want to start doing sophisticated editing of the images from your code, simple tasks have now been extremely well wrapped up in the GDI+ object model.*

The process of displaying an image is illustrated with an example called `DisplayImage`. The example simply displays a `.jpg` file in the application's main window. To keep things simple, the path of the `.jpg` file is hard-coded into the application (so if you run the example you'll need to change it to reflect the location of the file in your system). The `.jpg` file you'll display is a sunset picture in London.

As with the other examples, the `DisplayImage` project is a standard C# Visual Studio 2005 generated Windows application. You add the following fields to your `Form1` class:

```
Image piccy;
private Point [] piccyBounds;
```

871

You then load the file in the `Form1()` constructor:

```
public Form1()
{
   InitializeComponent();

   piccy =
       Image.FromFile(@"C:\ProCSharp\GdiPlus\Images\London.jpg");
   this.AutoScrollMinSize = piccy.Size;
   piccyBounds = new Point[3];
   piccyBounds[0] = new Point(0,0);              // top left
   piccyBounds[1] = new Point(piccy.Width,0);    // top right
   piccyBounds[2] = new Point(0,piccy.Height);   // bottom left
}
```

Note that the size in pixels of the image is obtained as its `Size` property, which you use to set the document area. You also set up the `piccyBounds` array, which is used to identify the position of the image on the screen. You have chosen the coordinates of the three corners to draw the image in its actual size and shape here, but if you'd wanted the image to be resized, stretched, or even sheared into a non-rectangular parallelogram, you could do so simply by changing the values of the `Points` in the `piccyBounds` array.

The image is displayed in the `OnPaint()` override:

```
protected override void OnPaint(PaintEventArgs e)
{
   base.OnPaint(e);
   Graphics dc = e.Graphics;
   dc.ScaleTransform(1.0f, 1.0f);
   dc.TranslateTransform(this.AutoScrollPosition.X, this.AutoScrollPosition.Y);
   dc.DrawImage(piccy, piccyBounds);
}
```

Finally, note the modification made to the code wizard-generated `Form1.Dispose()` method:

```
        protected override void Dispose(bool disposing)
        {
           piccy.Dispose();
           if( disposing )
           {
              if (components != null)
              {
                 components.Dispose();
              }
           }
           base.Dispose( disposing );
        }
```

Disposing of the image as soon as possible when it's no longer needed is important, because images generally take up a lot of memory while in use. After `Image.Dispose()` has been called, the `Image` instance no longer refers to any actual image, and so it can no longer be displayed (unless you load a new image).

Figure 25-14 shows the result of running this code.

# Graphics with GDI+

Figure 25-14

## Issues When Manipulating Images

Although displaying images is very simple, it still pays to have some understanding of what's going on behind the scenes.

The most important point to understand about images is that they are always rectangular. That's not just a convenience, it's because of the underlying technology. All modern graphics cards have hardware built in that can efficiently copy blocks of pixels from one area of memory to another area of memory, provided that the block of pixels represents a rectangular region. This hardware-accelerated operation can occur virtually as one single operation, and as such is extremely fast. Indeed, it is the key to modern high-performance graphics. This operation is known as a *bitmap block transfer* (or *BitBlt*). `Graphics .DrawImageUnscaled()` internally uses a `BitBlt`, which is why you can see a huge image, perhaps containing as many as a million pixels, appearing almost instantly. If the computer had to copy the image to the screen pixel by pixel, you'd see the image gradually being drawn over a period of up to several seconds.

`BitBlt`s are very efficient; therefore almost all drawing and manipulation of images is carried out using them. Even some editing of images will be done by manipulating portions of images with `BitBlt`s between DCs that represent areas of memory. In the days of GDI, the Windows 32 API function `BitBlt()` was arguably the most important and widely used function for image manipulation, though with GDI+ the `BitBlt` operations are largely hidden by the GDI+ object model.

It's not possible to `BitBlt` areas of images that are not rectangular, although similar effects can be easily simulated. One way is to mark a certain color as transparent for the purposes of a `BitBlt`, so that areas

873

of that color in the source image will not overwrite the existing color of the corresponding pixel in the destination device. It is also possible to specify that in the process of a `BitBlt`, each pixel of the resultant image will be formed by some logical operation (such as a bitwise AND) on the colors of that pixel in the source image and in the destination device before the `BitBlt`. Such operations are supported by hardware acceleration and can be used to give a variety of subtle effects. Note that the `Graphics` object implements another method, `DrawImage()`. This is similar to `DrawImageUnscaled()` but comes in a large number of overloads that allow you to specify more complex forms of `BitBlt` to be used in the drawing process. `DrawImage()` also allows you to draw (using `BitBlt`) only a specified part of the image, or to perform certain other operations on it such as scaling it (expanding or reducing it in size) as it is drawn.

## Drawing Text

The very important topic of displaying text is left until this late in the chapter because drawing text to the screen is (in general) more complex than drawing simple graphics. Although displaying a line or two of text when you're not that bothered about the appearance is extremely easy — it takes one single call to the `Graphics.DrawString()` method; if you are trying to display a document that has a fair amount of text in it, you rapidly find that things become a lot more complex. This is for two reasons:

❑   If you're concerned about getting the appearance just right, you must understand fonts. Whereas shape drawing requires brushes and pens as helper objects, the process of drawing text requires fonts as helper objects. And understanding fonts is not a trivial task.

❑   Text needs to be very carefully laid out in the window. Users generally expect words to follow naturally from one word to another and to be lined up with clear spaces in between. Doing that is harder than you might think. For starters, you don't usually know in advance how much space on the screen a word is going to take up. That has to be calculated (using the `Graphics.MeasureString()` method). Also, the space a word occupies on the screen affects where in the document every subsequent word is placed. If your application does any line wrapping, it'll need to assess word sizes carefully before deciding where to place the line break. The next time you run Microsoft Word, look carefully at the way Word is continually repositioning text as you do your work: there's a lot of complex processing going on there. Chances are that any GDI+ application you work on won't be nearly as complex as Word. However, if you need to display any text, many of the same considerations apply.

In short, high-quality text processing is tricky to get right. However, putting a line of text on the screen, assuming you know the font and where you want it to go, is actually very simple. Therefore, the next section presents a quick example that shows how to display some text, followed by a short review of the principles of fonts and font families and a more realistic (and involved) text-processing example, `CapsEditor`.

## Simple Text Example

This example, `DisplayText`, is your usual Windows Forms effort. This time you override `OnPaint()` and add member fields as follows:

# Graphics with GDI+

```
    private System.ComponentModel.Container components = null;
    private Brush blackBrush = Brushes.Black;
    private Brush blueBrush = Brushes.Blue;
    private Font haettenschweilerFont = new Font("Haettenschweiler", 12);
    private Font boldTimesFont = new Font("Times New Roman", 10, FontStyle.Bold);
    private Font italicCourierFont = new Font("Courier", 11, FontStyle.Italic |
       FontStyle.Underline);

    protected override void OnPaint(PaintEventArgs e)
    {
       base.OnPaint(e);
       Graphics dc = e.Graphics;
       dc.DrawString("This is a groovy string", haettenschweilerFont, blackBrush,
                  10, 10);
       dc.DrawString("This is a groovy string " +
                  "with some very long text that will never fit in the box",
                  boldTimesFont, blueBrush,
                  new Rectangle(new Point(10, 40), new Size(100, 40)));
       dc.DrawString("This is a groovy string", italicCourierFont, blackBrush,
                  new Point(10, 100));
    }
```

Figure 25-15 shows the result of running this example.

**Figure 25-15**

The example demonstrates the use of the `Graphics.DrawString()` method to draw items of text. The method `DrawString()` comes in a number of overloads, three of which are demonstrated here. The different overloads require parameters that indicate the text to be displayed, the font that the string should be drawn in, and the brush that should be used to construct the various lines and curves that make up each character of text. A couple of alternatives exist for the remaining parameters. In general, however, it is possible to specify either a `Point` (or equivalently, two numbers) or a `Rectangle`.

If you specify a `Point`, the text will start with its top-left corner at that `Point` and simply stretch out to the right. If you specify a `Rectangle`, then the `Graphics` instance will lay out the string inside that rectangle. If the text doesn't fit within the boundaries of the rectangle, it'll be cut off (see the fourth line of text in Figure 25-15). Passing a rectangle to `DrawString()` means that the drawing process will take longer, because `DrawString()` will need to figure out where to put line breaks, but the result may look nicer, provided the string fits in the rectangle!

This example also shows a couple of ways of constructing fonts. You always need to include the name of the font and its size (height). You can also optionally pass in various styles that modify how the text is to be drawn (bold, underline, and so on).

# Fonts and Font Families

We all think intuitively that we have a fairly good understanding of fonts; after all, we look at them almost all the time. A font describes exactly how each letter should be displayed. Selection of the appropriate font and providing a reasonable variety of fonts within a document are important factors in improving readability.

Oddly, our intuitive understanding usually isn't quite correct. Most people, if asked to name a font, might mention Arial or Times New Roman (if they are Windows users) or Times or Helvetica (if they are Mac OS users). In fact, these are not fonts at all — they are *font families*. The font family tells you in generic terms the visual style of the text and is a key factor in the overall appearance of your application. Most of us will have become used to recognizing the styles of the most common font families, even if we're not consciously aware of it.

An actual *font* would be something like Arial 9-point italic. In other words, the size and other modifications to the text are specified as well as the font family. These modifications might include whether it is **bold**, *italic*, underlined, or displayed in SMALL CAPS or as a $_{subscript}$; this is technically referred to as the *style*, though in some ways the term is misleading, because the visual appearance is determined as much by the font family.

The way the size of the text is measured is by specifying its height. The height is measured in *points* — a traditional unit that represents 1/72 of an inch (0.351 mm). So letters in a 10-point font are roughly 1/7" or 3.5 mm high. However, you won't get seven lines of 10-point text into one inch of vertical screen or paper space, because you need to allow for the spacing between the lines as well.

> *Strictly speaking, measuring the height isn't quite as simple as that, because there are several different heights that you must consider. For example, there is the height of tall letters like the A or F (this is the measurement that we are referring to when we talk about the height), the additional height occupied by any accents on letters like Å or Ñ (the internal leading), and the extra height below the baseline needed for the tails of letters like y and g (the descent). However, for this chapter we won't worry about that. Once you specify the font family and the main height, these subsidiary heights are determined automatically.*

When you're dealing with fonts, you might also encounter some other terms commonly used to describe certain font families:

❑   **Serif** font families have little tick marks at the ends of many of the lines that make up the characters (these ticks are known as serifs). Times New Roman is a classic example of this.

# Graphics with GDI+

- **Sans serif** font families, by contrast, don't have these ticks. Good examples of sans serif fonts are Arial and Verdana. The lack of tick marks often gives text a blunt, in-your-face appearance, so sans serif fonts are often used for important text.

- A **True Type** font family is one that is defined by expressing the shapes of the curves that make up the characters in a precise mathematical manner. This means that that the same definition can be used to calculate how to draw fonts of any size within the family. These days, virtually all the fonts you might use are true type fonts. Some older font families from the days of Windows 3.1 were defined by individually specifying the bitmap for each character separately for each font size, but the use of these fonts is now discouraged.

Microsoft has provided two main classes that you need to deal with when selecting or manipulating fonts:

- `System.Drawing.Font`
- `System.Drawing.FontFamily`

You have already seen the main use of the `Font` class. When you want to draw text you instantiate an instance of `Font` and pass it to the `DrawString()` method to indicate how the text should be drawn. A `FontFamily` instance is used to represent a family of fonts.

One use of the `FontFamily` class is if you know you want a font of a particular type (Serif, Sans Serif or Monospace), but don't mind which font. The static properties `GenericSerif`, `GenericSansSerif`, and `GenericMonospace` return default fonts that satisfy these criteria:

```
FontFamily sansSerifFont = FontFamily.GenericSansSerif;
```

Generally speaking, however, if you're writing a professional application, you will want to choose your font in a more sophisticated way. Most likely, you will implement your drawing code so that it checks the font families available and selects the appropriate one, perhaps by taking the first available one on a list of preferred fonts. And if you want your application to be very user-friendly, the first choice on the list will probably be the one that users selected the last time they ran your software. Usually, if you're dealing with the most popular font families, such as Arial and Times New Roman, you'll be safe. However, if you do try to display text using a font that doesn't exist, the results aren't always predictable and you're quite likely to find that Windows just substitutes the standard system font, which is very easy for the system to draw but it doesn't look very pleasant — and if it does appear in your document it's likely to give the impression of software that is of poor quality.

You can find out what fonts are available on your system using a class called `InstalledFontCollection`, which is in the `System.Drawing.Text` namespace. This class implements a property, `Families`, which is an array of all the fonts that are available to use on your system:

```
InstalledFontCollection insFont = new InstalledFontCollection();
FontFamily [] families = insFont.Families;
foreach (FontFamily family in families)
{

   // do processing with this font family


}
```

877

# Example: Enumerating Font Families

In this section, you work through a quick example, `EnumFontFamilies`, which lists all the font families available on the system and illustrates them by displaying the name of each family using an appropriate font (the 10-point regular version of that font family). Figure 25-16 shows the result of running `EnumFontFamilies`.

Figure 25-16

Of course, the results that you get will depend on the fonts you have installed on your computer.

For this example you as usual create a standard C# Windows Application, `EnumFontFamilies`. You start off by adding an extra namespace to be searched. You will be using the `InstalledFontCollection` class, which is defined in `System.Drawing.Text`.

```
using System;
using System.Drawing;
using System.Drawing.Text;
```

You then add the following constant to the `Form1` class:

```
private const int margin = 10;
```

`margin` is the size of the left and top margin between the text and the edge of the document — it stops the text from appearing right at the edge of the client area.

## Graphics with GDI+

This is designed as a quick-and-easy way of showing off font families; therefore the code is crude and in many instances doesn't do things the way you ought to in a real application. For example, here you hard-code an estimated value for the document size of (200,1500) and set the `AutoScrollMinSize` property to this value using the Visual Studio 2005 Properties window. Normally you would have to examine the text to be displayed to work out the document size. You do that in the next section.

Here is the `OnPaint()` method:

```
protected override void OnPaint(PaintEventArgs e)
{
    base.OnPaint(e);
    int verticalCoordinate = margin;
    Point topLeftCorner;
    InstalledFontCollection insFont = new InstalledFontCollection();
    FontFamily [] families = insFont.Families;
    e.Graphics.TranslateTransform(AutoScrollPosition.X,
                                  AutoScrollPosition.Y);
    foreach (FontFamily family in families)
    {
        if (family.IsStyleAvailable(FontStyle.Regular))
        {
            Font f = new Font(family.Name, 12);
            topLeftCorner = new Point(margin, verticalCoordinate);
            verticalCoordinate += f.Height;
            e.Graphics.DrawString (family.Name, f,
                                   Brushes.Black,topLeftCorner);
            f.Dispose();
        }
    }
}
```

In this code you start off by using an `InstalledFontCollection` object to obtain an array that contains details of all the available font families. For each family, you instantiate a 12-point `Font`. You use a simple constructor for `Font` — there are many more that allow additional options to be specified. The constructor takes two parameters, the name of the family and the size of the font:

```
Font f = new Font(family.Name, 12);
```

This constructor builds a font that has the regular style. To be on the safe side, however, you first check that this style is available for each font family before attempting to display anything using that font. This is done using the `FontFamily.IsStyleAvailable()` method. This check is important, because not all fonts are available in all styles:

```
if (family.IsStyleAvailable(FontStyle.Regular))
```

`FontFamily.IsStyleAvailable()` takes one parameter, a `FontStyle` enumeration. This enumeration contains a number of flags that might be combined with the bitwise `OR` operator. The possible flags are `Bold`, `Italic`, `Regular`, `Strikeout`, and `Underline`.

Finally, note that you use a property of the `Font` class, `Height`, which returns the height needed to display text of that font, in order to work out the line spacing:

```
            Font f = new Font(family.Name, 12);
            topLeftCorner = new Point(margin, verticalCoordinate);
            verticalCoordinate += f.Height;
```

Again, to keep things simple, this version of `OnPaint()` reveals some bad programming practices. For a start, you haven't bothered to check what area of the document actually needs drawing — you just try to display everything. Also, instantiating a `Font` is, as remarked earlier, a computationally intensive process, so you really ought to save the fonts rather than instantiating new copies every time `OnPaint()` is called. As a result of the way the code has been designed, you might note that this example actually takes a noticeable time to paint itself. To try to conserve memory and help the garbage collector out you do, however, call `Dispose()` on each font instance after you have finished with it. If you didn't, after 10 or 20 paint operations, there'd be a lot of wasted memory storing fonts that are no longer needed.

# Editing a Text Document: The CapsEditor Sample

You now come to the extended example in this chapter. The `CapsEditor` example is designed to demonstrate how the principles of drawing that you've learned so far have to be applied in a more realistic context. The `CapsEditor` example does not require any new material, apart from responding to user input via the mouse, but it shows how to manage the drawing of text so that the application maintains performance while ensuring that the contents of the client area of the main window are always kept up to date.

The `CapsEditor` program is functionally quite simple. It allows the user to read in a text file, which is then displayed line by line in the client area. If the user double-clicks any line, that line will be changed to all uppercase. That's literally all the example does. Even with this limited set of features, you'll find that the work involved in making sure everything is displayed in the right place while considering performance issues is quite complex. In particular, you have a new element here: the contents of the document can change — either when the user selects the menu option to read a new file, or when she double-clicks to capitalize a line. In the first case you need to update the document size so the scroll bars still work correctly, and you have to redisplay everything. In the second case, you need to check carefully whether the document size has changed, and what text needs to be redisplayed.

This section starts by reviewing the appearance of `CapsEditor`. When the application is first run, it has no document loaded and resembles Figure 25-17.

The File menu has two options: Open, which evokes `OpenFileDialog` when selected and reads in whatever file the user clicks, and Exit, which closes the application when clicked. Figure 25-18 shows `CapsEditor` displaying its own source file, `Form1.cs`. (A couple of lines have been double-clicked to convert them to uppercase.)

The sizes of the horizontal and vertical scroll bars are correct. The client area will scroll just enough to view the entire document. `CapsEditor` doesn't try to wrap lines of text — the example is already complicated enough as is. It just displays each line of the file exactly as it is read in. There are no limits to the size of the file, but you are assuming it is a text file and doesn't contain any non-printable characters.

# Graphics with GDI+

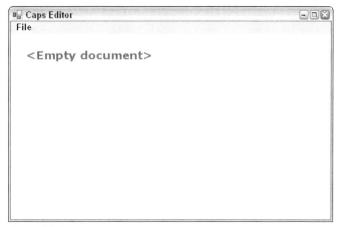

Figure 25-17

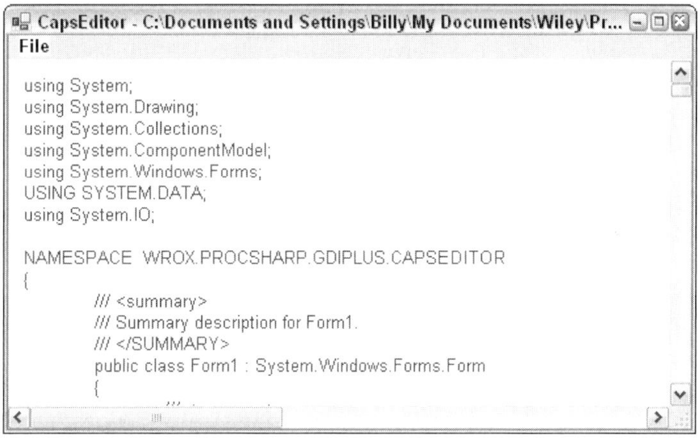

Figure 25-18

Begin by adding a `using` command:

```
using System;
using System.Collections.Generic;
using System.ComponentModel;
using System.Data;
using System.Drawing;
using System.Text;
using System.Windows.Forms;
using System.IO;
```

This is because you'll be using the `StreamReader` class, which is in the `System.IO` namespace. Next, you add some fields to the `Form1` class:

```
#region Constant fields
private const string standardTitle = "CapsEditor";
                                          // default text in titlebar
private const uint margin = 10;
                    // horizontal and vertical margin in client area
#endregion

#region Member fields
private ArrayList documentLines = new ArrayList();   // the 'document'
private uint lineHeight;          // height in pixels of one line
private Size documentSize;        // how big a client area is needed to
                                  // display document
private uint nLines;              // number of lines in document
private Font mainFont;            // font used to display all lines
private Font emptyDocumentFont;   // font used to display empty message
private Brush mainBrush = Brushes.Blue;
                                  // brush used to display document text
private Brush emptyDocumentBrush = Brushes.Red;
                    // brush used to display empty document message
private Point mouseDoubleClickPosition;
        // location mouse is pointing to when double-clicked
private OpenFileDialog fileOpenDialog = new OpenFileDialog();
        // standard open file dialog
private bool documentHasData = false;
        // set to true if document has some data in it
#endregion
```

Most of these fields should be self-explanatory. The `documentLines` field is an `ArrayList` that contains the actual text of the file that has been read in. In a real sense, this is the field that contains the data in the document. Each element of `documentLines` contains information for one line of text that has been read in. Because it's an `ArrayList`, rather than a plain array, you can dynamically add elements to it as you read in a file. Note also that you've used `#region` preprocessor directives to block bits of the program to make it easier to edit.

As previously mentioned, each `documentLines` element contains information about a line of text. This information is actually an instance of another class, `TextLineInformation`:

```
class TextLineInformation
{
    public string Text;
    public uint Width;
}
```

`TextLineInformation` looks like a classic case where you'd normally use a struct rather than a class because it's just there to group a couple of fields. However, its instances are always accessed as elements of an `ArrayList`, which expects its elements to be stored as reference types, so declaring `TextLineInformation` as a class makes things more efficient by saving a lot of boxing and unboxing operations.

Each `TextLineInformation` instance stores a line of text—and that can be thought of as the smallest item that is displayed as a single item. In general, for each similar item in a GDI+ application, you'd probably want to store the text of the item, as well as the world coordinates of where it should be displayed and its size (the page coordinates will change frequently, whenever the user scrolls, whereas world coordinates will normally only change when other parts of the document are modified in some way). In this case you've only stored the `Width` of the item. The reason is because the height in this case is just the height of whatever your selected font is. It's the same for all lines of text so there's no point storing it separately for each one; you store it once, in the `Form1.lineHeight` field. As for the position, well, in this case, the x coordinate is just equal to the margin, and the y coordinate is easily calculated as:

```
margin + lineHeight*(however many lines are above this one)
```

If you'd been trying to display and manipulate, say, individual words instead of complete lines, then the x position of each word would have to be calculated using the widths of all the previous words on that line of text, but the intent is to keep it simple here, which is why you're treating each line of text as one single item.

Let's turn to the main menu now. This part of the application is more the realm of Windows Forms (see Chapter 23) than of GDI+. Add the menu options using the design view in Visual Studio 2005, but rename them as `menuFile`, `menuFileOpen`, and `menuFileExit`. Next add event handlers for the File Open and File Exit menu options using the Visual Studio 2005 Properties window. The event handlers have their Visual Studio 2005–generated names of `menuFileOpen_Click()` and `menuFileExit_Click()`.

Add some extra initialization code in the `Form1()` constructor:

```
public Form1()
{
    InitializeComponent();

    CreateFonts();
    fileOpenDialog.FileOk += new
        System.ComponentModel.CancelEventHandler(
        this.OpenFileDialog_FileOk);
    fileOpenDialog.Filter =
        "Text files (*.txt)|*.txt|C# source files (*.cs)|*.cs";
}
```

The event handler added here is for when the user clicks OK in the File Open dialog box. You have also set the filter for the Open File dialog box, so that you can only load text files—the example opted for .txt files as well as C# source files, so you can use the application to examine the source code for the samples.

`CreateFonts()` is a helper method that sorts out the fonts you intend to use:

```
        private void CreateFonts()
        {
            mainFont = new Font("Arial", 10);
            lineHeight = (uint)mainFont.Height;
            emptyDocumentFont = new Font("Verdana", 13, FontStyle.Bold);
        }
```

883

The actual definitions of the handlers are pretty standard stuff:

```
protected void OpenFileDialog_FileOk(object Sender, CancelEventArgs e)
{
   this.LoadFile(fileOpenDialog.FileName);
}

protected void menuFileOpen_Click(object sender, EventArgs e)
{
   fileOpenDialog.ShowDialog();
}

protected void menuFileExit_Click(object sender, EventArgs e)
{
   this.Close();
}
```

Next, take a look the `LoadFile()` method. It's the method that handles the opening and reading of a file (as well as ensuring a `Paint` event is raised to force a repaint with the new file):

```
private void LoadFile(string FileName)
{
   StreamReader sr = new StreamReader(FileName);
   string nextLine;
   documentLines.Clear();
   nLines = 0;
   TextLineInformation nextLineInfo;
   while ( (nextLine = sr.ReadLine()) != null)
   {
      nextLineInfo = new TextLineInformation();
      nextLineInfo.Text = nextLine;
      documentLines.Add(nextLineInfo);
      ++nLines;
   }
   sr.Close();
   documentHasData = (nLines>0) ? true : false;

   CalculateLineWidths();
   CalculateDocumentSize();

   this.Text = standardTitle + " - " + FileName;
   this.Invalidate();
}
```

Most of this function is just standard file-reading stuff (see Chapter 34, "Manipulating Files and the Registry"). Note that as the file is read, you progressively add lines to `documentLines ArrayList`, so this array ends up containing information for each of the lines in order. After you've read in the file, you set the `documentHasData` flag, which indicates whether there is actually anything to display. Your next task is to work out where everything is to be displayed, and, having done that, how much client area you need to display the file—the document size that will be used to set the scroll bars. Finally, you set the title bar text and call `Invalidate()`. `Invalidate()` is an important method supplied by Microsoft, so the next section discusses its use first, before examining the code for the `CalculateLineWidths()` and `CalculateDocumentSize()` methods.

## *The Invalidate() Method*

`Invalidate()` is a member of `System.Windows.Forms.Form`. It marks an area of the client window as invalid and, therefore, in need of repainting, and then makes sure a `Paint` event is raised. `Invalidate()` has a couple of overrides: you can pass it a rectangle that specifies (in page coordinates) precisely which area of the window needs repainting, or if you don't pass any parameters it'll just mark the entire client area as invalid.

You might wonder why you would do it this way. If you know that something needs painting, why don't you just call `OnPaint()` or some other method to do the painting directly? The answer is that in general, calling painting routines directly is regarded as bad programming practice — if your code decides it wants some painting done, you should call `Invalidate()`. Here's why:

- ❑ Drawing is almost always the most processor-intensive task a GDI+ application will carry out, so doing it in the middle of other work holds up the other work. With the example, if you'd directly called a method to do the drawing from the `LoadFile()` method, then the `LoadFile()` method wouldn't return until that drawing task was complete. During that time, your application can't respond to any other events. On the other hand, by calling `Invalidate()` you are simply getting Windows to raise a `Paint` event before immediately returning from `LoadFile()`. Windows is then free to examine the events that are in line to be handled. How this works internally is that the events sit as what are known as *messages* in a *message queue*. Windows periodically examines the queue, and if there are events in it, it picks one and calls the corresponding event handler. Although the `Paint` event might be the only one sitting in the queue (so `OnPaint()` gets called immediately anyway), in a more complex application there might be other events that ought to get priority over your `Paint` event. In particular, if the user has decided to quit the application, this will be marked by a message known as `WM_QUIT`.

- ❑ Related to the previous point, if you have a more complicated, multithreaded application, you'll probably want just one thread to handle all the drawing. Using `Invalidate()` to route all drawing through the message queue provides a good way of ensuring that the same thread (whatever thread is responsible for the message queue, this will be the thread that called `Application.Run()`) does all the drawing, no matter what other thread requested the drawing operation.

- ❑ There's an additional performance-related reason. Suppose a couple of different requests to draw part of the screen come in at about the same time. Maybe your code has just modified the document and wants to ensure the updated document is displayed, while at the same time the user has just moved another window that was covering part of the client area out of the way. By calling `Invalidate()`, you are giving Windows a chance to notice that this has occurred. Windows can then merge the `Paint` events if appropriate, combining the invalidated areas, so that the painting is only done once.

- ❑ Finally, the code to do the painting is probably going to be one of the most complex parts of the code in your application, especially if you have a very sophisticated user interface. The guys who have to maintain your code in a couple of years time will thank you for having kept your painting code all in one place and as simple as you reasonably can — something that's easier to do if you don't have too many pathways into it from other parts of the program.

The bottom line from all this is that it is good practice to keep all your painting in the `OnPaint()` routine, or in other methods called from that method. However, you have to strike a balance; if you want to replace just one character on the screen and you know perfectly well that it won't affect anything else that you've

# Chapter 25

drawn, then you might decide that it's not worth the overhead of going through Invalidate() and just write a separate drawing routine.

> *In a very complicated application, you might even write a full class that takes responsibility for drawing to the screen. A few years ago when MFC was the standard technology for GDI-intensive applications, MFC followed this model, with a C++ class,* C<ApplicationName>View, *that was responsible for painting. However, even in this case, this class had one member function,* OnDraw(), *which was designed to be the entry point for most drawing requests.*

## Calculating Item Sizes and Document Size

This section returns to the CapsEditor example and examines the CalculateLineWidths() and CalculateDocumentSize() methods called from LoadFile():

```
private void CalculateLineWidths()
{
    Graphics dc = this.CreateGraphics();
    foreach (TextLineInformation nextLine in documentLines)
    {
        nextLine.Width = (uint)dc.MeasureString(nextLine.Text, mainFont).Width;
    }
}
```

This method simply runs through each line that has been read in and uses the Graphics.MeasureString() method to work out and store how much horizontal screen space the string requires. You store the value because MeasureString() is computationally intensive. If the CapsEditor sample hadn't been simple enough to easily work out the height and location of each item, this method would almost certainly have needed to be implemented in such a way as to compute all those quantities too.

Now that you know how big each item on the screen is and you can calculate where each item goes, you are in a position to work out the actual document size. The height is basically the number of lines multiplied by the height of each line. The width will need to be worked out by iterating through the lines to find the longest. For both height and width, you will also want to make an allowance for a small margin around the displayed document to make the application look more attractive.

Here's the method that calculates the document size:

```
private void CalculateDocumentSize()
{
    if (!documentHasData)
    {
        documentSize = new Size(100, 200);
    }
    else
    {
        documentSize.Height = (int)(nLines*lineHeight) + 2*(int)margin;
        uint maxLineLength = 0;
        foreach (TextLineInformation nextWord in documentLines)
        {
            uint tempLineLength = nextWord.Width + 2*margin;
            if (tempLineLength > maxLineLength)
```

# Graphics with GDI+

```
                maxLineLength = tempLineLength;
      }
      documentSize.Width = (int)maxLineLength;
   }
   this.AutoScrollMinSize = documentSize;
}
```

This method first checks whether there is any data to be displayed. If there isn't, you cheat a bit and use a hard-coded document size, which is big enough to display the big red <Empty Document> warning. If you'd wanted to really do it properly, you'd have used `MeasureString()` to check how big that warning actually is.

Once you've worked out the document size, you tell the `Form` instance what the size is by setting the `Form.AutoScrollMinSize` property. When you do this, something interesting happens behind the scenes. In the process of setting this property, the client area is invalidated and a `Paint` event is raised, for the very sensible reason that changing the size of the document means scroll bars will need to be added or modified and the entire client area will almost certainly be repainted. Why is that interesting? If you look back at the code for `LoadFile()`, you'll realize that the call to `Invalidate()` in that method is actually redundant. The client area will be invalidated anyway when you set the document size. The explicit call to `Invalidate()` was left in the `LoadFile()` implementation to illustrate how in general you should normally do things. In fact in this case, all calling `Invalidate()` again will do is needlessly request a duplicate `Paint` event. However, this in turn illustrates how `Invalidate()` gives Windows the chance to optimize performance. The second `Paint` event won't in fact get raised: Windows will see that there's a `Paint` event already sitting in the queue and will compare the requested invalidated regions to see if it needs to do anything to merge them. In this case, both `Paint` events will specify the entire client area, so nothing needs to be done, and Windows will quietly drop the second `Paint` request. Of course, going through that process will take up a little bit of processor time, but it'll be a negligible amount of time compared to how long it takes to actually do some painting.

## OnPaint()

Now that you've seen how `CapsEditor` loads the file, it's time to look at how the painting is done:

```
protected override void OnPaint(PaintEventArgs e)
{
   base.OnPaint(e);
   Graphics dc = e.Graphics;
   int scrollPositionX = this.AutoScrollPosition.X;
   int scrollPositionY = this.AutoScrollPosition.Y;
   dc.TranslateTransform(scrollPositionX, scrollPositionY);

   if (!documentHasData)
   {
      dc.DrawString("<Empty document>", emptyDocumentFont,
         emptyDocumentBrush, new Point(20,20));
      base.OnPaint(e);
      return;
   }

   // work out which lines are in clipping rectangle
   int minLineInClipRegion =
```

```
                        WorldYCoordinateToLineIndex(e.ClipRectangle.Top -
                                                    scrollPositionY);
    if (minLineInClipRegion == -1)
        minLineInClipRegion = 0;
    int maxLineInClipRegion =
                WorldYCoordinateToLineIndex(e.ClipRectangle.Bottom -
                                                    scrollPositionY);
    if (maxLineInClipRegion >= this.documentLines.Count ||
        maxLineInClipRegion == -1)
    maxLineInClipRegion = this.documentLines.Count-1;

    TextLineInformation nextLine;
    for (int i=minLineInClipRegion; i<=maxLineInClipRegion ; i++)
    {
        nextLine = (TextLineInformation)documentLines[i];
        dc.DrawString(nextLine.Text, mainFont, mainBrush,
                    this.LineIndexToWorldCoordinates(i));
    }
}
```

At the heart of this `OnPaint()` override is a loop that goes through each line of the document, calling `Graphics.DrawString()` to paint each one. The rest of this code is mostly to do with optimizing the painting — the usual stuff about figuring out what exactly needs painting instead of rushing in and telling the graphics instance to redraw everything.

You begin by checking if there is any data in the document. If there isn't, you draw a quick message saying so, call the base class's `OnPaint()` implementation, and exit. If there is data, then you start looking at the clipping rectangle. The way you do this is by calling another method, `WorldYCoordinateToLineIndex()`. This method is examined next, but essentially it takes a given y position relative to the top of the document, and works out what line of the document is being displayed at that point.

The first time you call the `WorldYCoordinateToLineIndex()` method, you pass it the coordinate value `(e.ClipRectangle.Top - scrollPositionY)`. This is just the top of the clipping region, converted to world coordinates. If the return value is –1, you play safe and assume you need to start at the beginning of the document (this is the case if the top of the clipping region is within the top margin).

Once you've done all that, you essentially repeat the same process for the bottom of the clipping rectangle, in order to find the last line of the document that is inside the clipping region. The indices of the first and last lines are respectively stored in `minLineInClipRegion` and `maxLineInClipRegion`, so then you can just run a `for` loop between these values to do your painting. Inside the painting loop, you actually need to do roughly the reverse transformation to the one performed by `WorldYCoordinateToLineIndex()`. You are given the index of a line of text, and you need to check where it should be drawn. This calculation is actually quite simple, but you've wrapped it up in another method, `LineIndexToWorldCoordinates()`, which returns the required coordinates of the top-left corner of the item. The returned coordinates are world coordinates, but that's fine, because you have already called `TranslateTransform()` on the `Graphics` object so that you need to pass it world, rather than page, coordinates when asking it to display items.

## Graphics with GDI+

## *Coordinate Transforms*

This section examines the implementation of the helper methods that are written in the `CapsEditor` sample to help you with coordinate transforms. These are the `WorldYCoordinateToLineIndex()` and `LineIndexToWorldCoordinates()` methods referred to in the previous section, as well as a couple of other methods.

First, `LineIndexToWorldCoordinates()` takes a given line index, and works out the world coordinates of the top-left corner of that line, using the known margin and line height:

```
private Point LineIndexToWorldCoordinates(int index)
{
    Point TopLeftCorner = new Point(
        (int)margin, (int)(lineHeight*index + margin));
    return TopLeftCorner;
}
```

You also use a method that roughly does the reverse transform in `OnPaint()`. `WorldYCoordinateToLineIndex()` works out the line index, but it only takes into account a vertical world coordinate. This is because it is used to work out the line index corresponding to the top and bottom of the clip region:

```
private int WorldYCoordinateToLineIndex(int y)
{
    if (y < margin)
        return -1;
    return (int)((y-margin)/lineHeight);
}
```

There are three more methods, which will be called from the handler routine that responds to the user double-clicking the mouse. First, you have a method that works out the index of the line being displayed at given world coordinates. Unlike `WorldYCoordinateToLineIndex()`, this method takes into account the x and y positions of the coordinates. It returns –1 if there is no line of text covering the coordinates passed in:

```
private int WorldCoordinatesToLineIndex(Point position)
{
    if (!documentHasData)
       return -1;
    if (position.Y < margin || position.X < margin)
       return -1;
    int index = (int)(position.Y-margin)/(int)this.lineHeight;
    // check position isn't below document
    if (index >= documentLines.Count)
       return -1;
    // now check that horizontal position is within this line
    TextLineInformation theLine =
                       (TextLineInformation)documentLines[index];
    if (position.X > margin + theLine.Width)
       return -1;

    // all is OK. We can return answer
    return index;
}
```

889

Finally, on occasions you also need to convert between line index and page, rather than world, coordinates. The following methods achieve this:

```
        private Point LineIndexToPageCoordinates(int index)
        {
           return LineIndexToWorldCoordinates(index) +
                                       new Size(AutoScrollPosition);
        }

        private int PageCoordinatesToLineIndex(Point position)
        {
           return WorldCoordinatesToLineIndex(position - new
                                       Size(AutoScrollPosition));
        }
```

Note that when converting *to* page coordinates, you add the `AutoScrollPosition`, which is negative.

Although these methods by themselves don't look particularly interesting, they do illustrate a general technique that you'll probably need to use often. With GDI+, you'll often find yourself in a situation where you have been given specific coordinates (for example the coordinates of where the user has clicked the mouse) and you'll need to figure out what item is being displayed at that point. Or it could happen the other way around — given a particular display item, whereabouts should it be displayed? Hence, if you are writing a GDI+ application, you'll probably find it useful to write methods that do the equivalent of the coordinate transformation methods illustrated here.

## *Responding to User Input*

So far, with the exception of the File menu in the `CapsEditor` sample, everything you've done in this chapter has been one way: the application has talked to the user by displaying information on the screen. Almost all software of course works both ways: the user can talk to the software as well. You're now going to add that facility to `CapsEditor`.

Getting a GDI+ application to respond to user input is actually a lot simpler than writing the code to draw to the screen (Chapter 23 covers how to handle user input). Essentially, you override methods from the `Form` class that get called from the relevant event handler, in much the same way that `OnPaint()` is called when a `Paint` event is raised.

The following table lists the methods you might want to override when the user clicks or moves the mouse.

| Method | Called when... |
|---|---|
| OnClick(EventArgs e) | Mouse is clicked. |
| OnDoubleClick(EventArgs e) | Mouse is double-clicked. |
| OnMouseDown(MouseEventArgs e) | Left mouse button pressed. |
| OnMouseHover(MouseEventArgs e) | Mouse stays still somewhere after moving. |
| OnMouseMove(MouseEventArgs e) | Mouse is moved. |
| OnMouseUp(MouseEventArgs e) | Left mouse button is released. |

## Graphics with GDI+

If you want to detect when the user types in any text, you'll probably want to override the methods listed in the following table.

| Method | Called When... |
| --- | --- |
| OnKeyDown(KeyEventArgs e) | A key is pressed. |
| OnKeyPress(KeyPressEventArgs e) | A key is pressed and released. |
| OnKeyUp(KeyEventArgs e) | A pressed key is released. |

Note that some of these events overlap. For example, if the user presses a mouse button this will raise the MouseDown event. If the button is immediately released again, this will raise the MouseUp event and the Click event. Also, some of these methods take an argument that is derived from EventArgs rather than an instance of EventArgs itself. These instances of derived classes can be used to give more information about a particular event. MouseEventArgs has two properties, X and Y, which give the device coordinates of the mouse at the time it was pressed. Both KeyEventArgs and KeyPressEventArgs have properties that indicate which key or keys the event concerns.

That's all there is to it. It's up to you to think about the logic of precisely what you want to do. The only point to note is that you'll probably find yourself doing a bit more logic work with a GDI+ application than you would have with a Windows.Forms application. That's because in a Windows.Forms application you are typically responding to high-level events (TextChanged for a text box, for example). By contrast with GDI+, the events tend to be more elementary — user clicks the mouse or presses the H key. The action your application takes is likely to depend on a sequence of events rather than a single event. For example, say your application works like Word for Windows, where in order to select some text the user clicks the left mouse button, then moves the mouse and releases the left mouse button. Your application receives the MouseDown event, but there's not much you can do with this event except record that the mouse was clicked with the cursor in a certain position. Then, when the MouseMove event is received, you'll want to check from the record whether the left button is currently down, and if so highlight text as the user selects it. When the user releases the left mouse button, your corresponding action (in the OnMouseUp() method) will need to check whether any dragging took place while the mouse button was down and act accordingly. Only at this point is the sequence complete.

Another point to consider is that, because certain events overlap, you will often have a choice of which event you want your code to respond to.

The golden rule really is to think carefully about the logic of every combination of mouse movement or click and keyboard event that the user might initiate, and ensure that your application responds in a way that is intuitive and in accordance with the expected behavior of applications in *every* case. Most of your work here will be in thinking rather than in coding, though the coding you do will be tricky because you might need to take into account a lot of combinations of user input. For example, what should your application do if the user starts typing in text while one of the mouse buttons is held down? It might sound like an improbable combination, but sooner or later some user is going to try it!

The CapsEditor example keeps things very simple, so you don't really have any combinations to think about. The only thing you are going to respond to is when the user double-clicks, in which case you capitalize whatever line of text the mouse pointer is hovering over.

This should be a fairly simple task, but there is one snag. You need to trap the `DoubleClick` event, but the previous table shows that this event takes an `EventArgs` parameter, not a `MouseEventArgs` parameter. The trouble is that you'll need to know where the mouse is when the user double-clicks if you are to identify correctly the line of text to be capitalized — and you need a `MouseEventArgs` parameter to do that. There are two workarounds. One is to use a static method implemented by the `Form1` object, `Control.MousePosition`, to find out the mouse position:

```
protected override void OnDoubleClick(EventArgs e)
{
   Point MouseLocation = Control.MousePosition;
   // handle double click
}
```

In most cases, this will work. However, there could be a problem if your application (or even some other application with a high priority) is doing some computationally intensive work at the moment the user double-clicks. It just might happen in that case that the `OnDoubleClick()` event handler doesn't get called until perhaps half a second or so *after* the user has double-clicked. You don't really want delays like that, because they usually annoy users intensely, but even so, occasionally it does happen and sometimes for reasons beyond the control of your app (a slow computer, for instance). Trouble is, half a second is easily enough time for the mouse to get moved halfway across the screen, in which case your call to `Control.MousePosition` will return the completely wrong location!

A better way here is to rely on one of the many overlaps between mouse-event meanings. The first part of double-clicking a mouse involves pressing the left button down. This means that if `OnDoubleClick()` is called, you know that `OnMouseDown()` has also just been called, with the mouse at the same location. You can use the `OnMouseDown()` override to record the position of the mouse, ready for `OnDoubleClick()`. This is the approach taken in `CapsEditor`:

```
protected override void OnMouseDown(MouseEventArgs e)
{
    base.OnMouseDown(e);
    this.mouseDoubleClickPosition = new Point(e.X, e.Y);
}
```

Now look at the `OnDoubleClick()` override. There's quite a bit more work to do here:

```
protected override void OnDoubleClick(EventArgs e)
{
    int i = PageCoordinatesToLineIndex(this.mouseDoubleClickPosition);
    if (i >= 0)
    {
        TextLineInformation lineToBeChanged =
                        (TextLineInformation)documentLines[i];
        lineToBeChanged.Text = lineToBeChanged.Text.ToUpper();
        Graphics dc = this.CreateGraphics();
        uint newWidth =(uint)dc.MeasureString(lineToBeChanged.Text,
                                        mainFont).Width;
        if (newWidth > lineToBeChanged.Width)
            lineToBeChanged.Width = newWidth;
        if (newWidth+2*margin > this.documentSize.Width)
        {
            this.documentSize.Width = (int)newWidth;
            this.AutoScrollMinSize = this.documentSize;
```

```
            }
            Rectangle changedRectangle = new Rectangle(
                                        LineIndexToPageCoordinates(i),
                                        new Size((int)newWidth,
                                        (int)this.lineHeight));
            this.Invalidate(changedRectangle);
        }
        base.OnDoubleClick(e);
    }
```

You start off by calling `PageCoordinatesToLineIndex()` to work out which line of text the mouse pointer was hovering over when the user double-clicked. If this call returns -1, then you weren't over any text, so there's nothing to do; except, of course, call the base class version of `OnDoubleClick()` to let Windows do any default processing.

Assuming you've identified a line of text, you can use the `string.ToUpper()` method to convert it to uppercase. That was the easy part. The hard part is figuring out what needs to be redrawn where. Fortunately, because this example is simple, there aren't too many combinations. You can assume for a start that converting to uppercase will always either leave the width of the line on the screen unchanged or increase it. Capital letters are bigger than lowercase letters; therefore, the width will never go down. You also know that because you are not wrapping lines, your line of text won't overflow to the next line and push out other text below. Your action of converting the line to uppercase won't, therefore, actually change the locations of any of the other items being displayed. That's a big simplification!

The next thing the code does is use `Graphics.MeasureString()` to work out the new width of the text. There are now just two possibilities:

❑   The new width might make your line the longest line, and cause the width of the entire document to increase. If that's the case you'll need to set `AutoScrollMinSize` to the new size so that the scroll bars are correctly placed.

❑   The size of the document might be unchanged.

In either case, you need to get the screen redrawn by calling `Invalidate()`. Only one line has changed; therefore, you don't want to have the entire document repainted. Rather, you need to work out the bounds of a rectangle that contains just the modified line, so that you can pass this rectangle to `Invalidate()`, ensuring that just that line of text will be repainted. That's precisely what the previous code does. Your call to `Invalidate()` initiates a call to `OnPaint()` when the mouse event handler finally returns. Keeping in mind the earlier comments about the difficulty in setting a break point in `OnPaint()`, if you run the sample and set a break point in `OnPaint()` to trap the resultant painting action, you'll find that the `PaintEventArgs` parameter to `OnPaint()` does indeed contain a clipping region that matches the specified rectangle. And because you've overloaded `OnPaint()` to take careful account of the clipping region, only the one required line of text will be repainted.

## Printing

So far, the chapter has focused exclusively on drawing to the screen. However, at some point you will probably also want to be able to produce a hard copy of the data. That's the topic of this section. You're going to extend the `CapsEditor` sample so that it is able to print preview and print the document that is being edited.

Unfortunately, there's not enough space to go into too much detail about printing here, so the printing functionality you will implement is very basic. Usually, if you are implementing the ability for an application to print data, you will need to add three items to the application's main File menu:

- Page Setup, which allows the user to choose options such as which pages to print, which printer to use, and so on.
- Print Preview, which opens a new Form that displays a mock-up of what the printed copy should look like.
- Print, which prints the document.

In this case, to keep things simple, you won't implement a Page Setup menu option. Printing will only be possible using default settings. Note, however, that, if you do want to implement Page Setup, Microsoft has already written a page setup dialog class for you to use: `System.Windows.Forms.PrintDialog`. You will normally want to write an event handler that displays this form and saves the settings chosen by the user.

In many ways, printing is just the same as displaying to a screen. You will be supplied with a device context (`Graphics` instance) and call all the usual display commands against that instance. Microsoft has written a number of classes to assist you in doing this; the two main ones that you need to use are `System.Drawing.Printing.PrintDocument` and `System.Drawing.Printing.PrintPreviewDialog`. These two classes handle the process of making sure that drawing instructions passed to a device context are handled appropriately for printing, leaving you to think about the logic of what to print where.

Some important differences exist between printing or print previewing on the one hand, and displaying to the screen on the other hand. Printers cannot scroll; instead they turn out pages. So you'll need to make sure you find a sensible way of dividing your document into pages, and draw each page as requested. Among other things that means calculating how much of your document will fit onto a single page, and therefore how many pages you'll need, and which page each part of the document needs to be written to.

Despite these complications, the process of printing is quite simple. Programmatically, the steps you need to go through look roughly like this:

- **Printing.** You instantiate a `PrintDocument` object and call its `Print()` method. This method signals the `PrintPage` event to print the first page. `PrintPage` takes a `PrintPageEventArgs` parameter, which supplies information concerning paper size and setup, as well as a `Graphics` object used for the drawing commands. You should therefore have written an event handler for this event, and have implemented this handler to print a page. This event handler should also set a Boolean property of the `PrintPageEventArgs`, `HasMorePages` to either `true` or `false` to indicate whether there are more pages to be printed. The `PrintDocument.Print()` method will repeatedly raise the `PrintPage` event until it sees that `HasMorePages` has been set to `false`.
- **Print Previewing.** In this case, you instantiate both a `PrintDocument` object and a `PrintPreviewDialog` object. You attach the `PrintDocument` to the `PrintPreviewDialog` (using the property `PrintPreviewDialog.Document`) and then call the dialog's `ShowDialog()` method. This method modally displays the dialog, which turns out to be a standard Windows print preview form, and which displays pages of the document. Internally, the pages are displayed once again by repeatedly raising the `PrintPage` event until the `HasMorePages` property is `false`.

# Graphics with GDI+

There's no need to write a separate event handler for this; you can use the same event handler as used for printing each page because the drawing code ought to be identical in both cases. (After all, whatever is print previewed ought to look identical to the printed version!)

## Implementing Print and Print Preview

Now that this process has been outlined in broad strokes, in this section you see how this works in code terms. You can download the code as the `PrintingCapsEdit` project at www.wrox.com; it consists of the `CapsEditor` project with the changes highlighted in the following snippet.

You begin by using the Visual Studio 2005 design view to add two new items to the `File` menu: Print and Print Preview. You also use the properties window to name these items `menuFilePrint` and `menuFilePrintPreview`, and to set them to be disabled when the application starts up (you can't print anything until a document has been opened!). You arrange for these menu items to be enabled by adding the following code to the main form's `LoadFile()` method, which is responsible for loading a file into the `CapsEditor` application:

```
private void LoadFile(string FileName)
{
    StreamReader sr = new StreamReader(FileName);
    string nextLine;
    documentLines.Clear();
    nLines = 0;
    TextLineInformation nextLineInfo;
    while ( (nextLine = sr.ReadLine()) != null)
    {
        nextLineInfo = new TextLineInformation();
        nextLineInfo.Text = nextLine;
        documentLines.Add(nextLineInfo);
        ++nLines;
    }
    sr.Close();
    if (nLines > 0)
    {
        documentHasData = true;
        menuFilePrint.Enabled = true;
        menuFilePrintPreview.Enabled = true;
    }
    else
    {
        documentHasData = false;
        menuFilePrint.Enabled = false;
        menuFilePrintPreview.Enabled = false;
    }

    CalculateLineWidths();
    CalculateDocumentSize();

    this.Text = standardTitle + " - " + FileName;
    this.Invalidate();
}
```

The highlighted code is the new code added to this method. Next, you add a member field to the `Form1` class:

```
public class Form1 : System.Windows.Forms.Form
{
    private int pagesPrinted = 0;
```

This field will be used to indicate which page you are currently printing. You are making it a member field, because you will need to remember this information between calls to the `PrintPage` event handler.

Next, the event handlers that handle the selection of the Print or Print Preview menu options:

```
private void menuFilePrintPreview_Click(object sender, System.EventArgs e)
{
    this.pagesPrinted = 0;
    PrintPreviewDialog ppd = new PrintPreviewDialog();
    PrintDocument pd = new PrintDocument();
    pd.PrintPage += new PrintPageEventHandler
        (this.pd_PrintPage);
    ppd.Document = pd;
    ppd.ShowDialog();
}

private void menuFilePrint_Click(object sender, System.EventArgs e)
{
    this.pagesPrinted = 0;
    PrintDocument pd = new PrintDocument();
    pd.PrintPage += new PrintPageEventHandler
        (this.pd_PrintPage);
    pd.Print();
}
```

You've already seen the steps involved in printing, and you can see that these event handlers are simply implementing that procedure. In both cases, you are instantiating a `PrintDocument` object and attaching an event handler to its `PrintPage` event. In the case of printing, you call `PrintDocument.Print()`, whereas for print previewing, you attach the `PrintDocument` object to a `PrintPreviewDialog` and call the preview dialog box object's `ShowDialog()` method. The real work to the `PrintPage` event is done in the event handler. Here is what this handler looks like:

```
private void pd_PrintPage(object sender, PrintPageEventArgs e)
{
    float yPos = 0;
    float leftMargin = e.MarginBounds.Left;
    float topMargin = e.MarginBounds.Top;
    string line = null;

    // Calculate the number of lines per page.
    int linesPerPage = (int)(e.MarginBounds.Height /
        mainFont.GetHeight(e.Graphics));
    int lineNo = this.pagesPrinted * linesPerPage;
```

# Graphics with GDI+

```
   // Print each line of the file.
   int count = 0;
   while(count < linesPerPage && lineNo < this.nLines)
   {
      line = ((TextLineInformation)this.documentLines[lineNo]).Text;
      yPos = topMargin + (count * mainFont.GetHeight(e.Graphics));
      e.Graphics.DrawString(line, mainFont, Brushes.Blue,
         leftMargin, yPos, new StringFormat());
      lineNo++;
      count++;
   }

   // If more lines exist, print another page.
   if(this.nLines > lineNo)
      e.HasMorePages = true;
   else
      e.HasMorePages = false;
   pagesPrinted++;
}
```

After declaring a couple of local variables, the first thing you do is work out how many lines of text can be displayed on one page, which will be the height of a page divided by the height of a line and rounded down. The height of the page can be obtained from the `PrintPageEventArgs.MarginBounds` property. This property is a `RectangleF` struct that has been initialized to give the bounds of the page. The height of a line is obtained from the `Form1.mainFont` field, which is the font used for displaying the text. There is no reason here for not using the same font for printing too. Note that for the `PrintingCaps Editor` sample, the number of lines per page is always the same, so you arguably could have cached the value the first time you calculated it. However, the calculation isn't too hard, and in a more sophisticated application the value might change, so it's not bad practice to recalculate it every time you print a page.

You also initialize a variable called `lineNo`. This gives the zero-based index of the line of the document that will be the first line of this page. This information is important because in principle, the `pd_PrintPage()` method could have been called to print any page, not just the first page. `lineNo` is computed as the number of lines per page times the number of pages that have so far been printed.

Next, you run through a loop, printing each line. This loop will terminate either when you find that you have printed all the lines of text in the document, or when you find that you have printed all the lines that will fit on this page, whichever condition occurs first. Finally, you check whether there is any more of the document to be printed, and set the `HasMorePages` property of your `PrintPageEventArgs` accordingly, and also increment the `pagesPrinted` field, so that you know to print the correct page the next time the `PrintPage` event handler is invoked.

One point to note about this event handler is that you do not worry about where the drawing commands are being sent. You simply use the `Graphics` object that was supplied with the `PrintPage EventArgs`. The `PrintDocument` class that Microsoft has written will internally take care of making sure that, if you are printing, the `Graphics` object will have been hooked up to the printer; if you are print previewing, the `Graphics` object will have been hooked up to the print preview form on the screen.

Finally, you need to ensure the `System.Drawing.Printing` namespace is searched for type definitions:

```
using System;
using System.Collections.Generic;
using System.ComponentModel;
using System.Data;
using System.Drawing;
using System.Drawing.Printing;
using System.Text;
using System.Windows.Forms;
using System.IO;
```

All that remains is to compile the project and check that the code works. Figure 25-19 shows what happens when you run `CapsEdit`, load a text document (as before, you've picked the C# source file for the project), and select Print Preview.

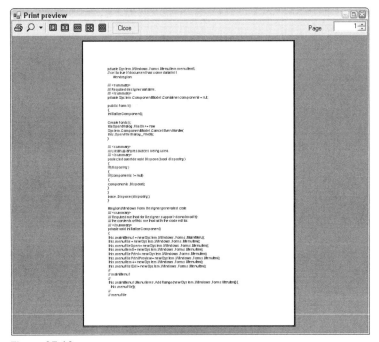

Figure 25-19

In Figure 25-19, the document is scrolled to page 5 and the preview is set to display normal size. The `PrintPreviewDialog` has supplied quite a lot of features, as you can see by looking at the toolbar at the top of the form. The options available include printing the document, zooming in or out, and displaying two, three, four, or six pages together. These options are all fully functional, without your having to do any work. Figure 25-20 shows the result of changing the zoom to auto and clicking to display four pages (third toolbar button from the right).

# Graphics with GDI+

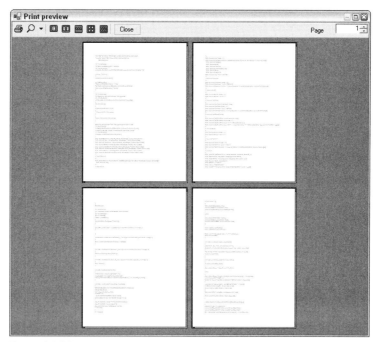

Figure 25-20

## Summary

This chapter covered the area of drawing to a display device, where the drawing is done by your code rather than by some predefined control or dialog box — the realm of GDI+. GDI+ is a powerful tool, and there are many .NET base classes available to help you draw to a device. You've seen that the process of drawing is actually relatively simple — in most cases you can draw text or sophisticated figures or display images with just a couple of C# statements. However, managing your drawing — the behind-the-scenes work involving working out what to draw, where to draw it, and what does or doesn't need repainting in any given situation — is far more complex and requires careful algorithm design. For this reason, it is also important to have a good understanding of how GDI+ works, and what actions Windows takes in order to get something drawn. In particular, because of the architecture of Windows, it is important that, where possible, drawing should be done by invalidating areas of the window and relying on Windows to respond by issuing a `Paint` event.

Many more .NET classes can be used for drawing than there is space to cover in this chapter. However, if you've worked through it and understood the principles involved in drawing, you'll be in an excellent position to explore them by looking at their lists of methods in the SDK documentation and instantiating instances of them to see what they do. In the end, drawing, like almost any other aspect of programming, requires logic, careful thought, and clear algorithms if you want to go beyond the standard controls. Your software will benefit in both user-friendliness and visual appearance if it is well thought out. Many applications out there rely entirely on controls for their user interface. Although this can be effective, such applications very quickly end up resembling each other. By adding some GDI+ code to do some custom drawing you can mark out your software as distinct and make it appear more original, which can only help increase your sales!

# Part V
# Web Applications

Chapter 26: ASP.NET Pages

Chapter 27: ASP.NET Development

# 26

# ASP.NET Pages

If you are new to the world of C# and .NET, you might wonder why a chapter on ASP.NET has been included in this book. It's a whole new language, right? Well, not really. In fact, as you will see, you can use C# to create ASP.NET pages.

ASP.NET is part of the .NET Framework and is a technology that allows for the dynamic creation of documents on a Web server when they are requested via HTTP. This mostly means HTML documents, although it is equally possible to create WML documents for consumption on WAP browsers, or anything else that supports MIME types.

In some ways ASP.NET is similar to many other technologies — such as PHP, ASP, or ColdFusion. There is, however, one key difference: ASP.NET, as its name suggests, has been designed to be fully integrated with the .NET Framework, part of which includes support for C#.

Perhaps you are familiar with Active Server Pages (ASP) technology, which enables you to create dynamic content. If this is the case, you will probably know that programming in this technology used scripting languages such as VBScript or JScript. The result was not always perfect, at least not for those of us used to "proper," compiled programming languages, and it certainly resulted in a loss of performance.

One major difference related to the use of more advanced programming languages is the provision of a complete server-side object model for use at runtime. ASP.NET provides access to all of the controls on a page as objects, in a rich environment. On the server side you also have access to other .NET classes, allowing for the integration of many useful services. Controls used on a page expose a lot of functionality; in fact you can do almost as much as with Windows Forms classes, which provide plenty of flexibility. For this reason, ASP.NET pages that generate HTML content are often called *Web Forms*.

This chapter takes a more detailed look at ASP.NET, including how it works, what you can do with it, and how C# fits in.

# Chapter 26

# ASP.NET Introduction

ASP.NET works with Internet Information Server (IIS) to deliver content in response to HTTP requests. ASP.NET pages are found in .aspx files. Figure 26-1 illustrates the technology's basic architecture.

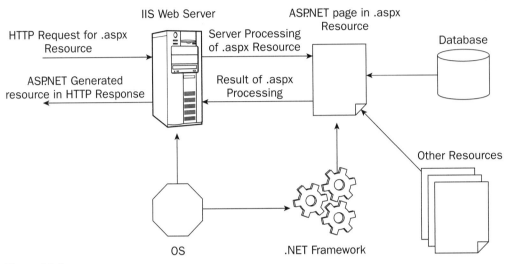

**Figure 26-1**

During ASP.NET processing you have access to all .NET classes, custom components created in C# or other languages, databases, and so on. In fact, you have as much power as you would have running a C# application; using C# in ASP.NET is in effect running a C# application.

An ASP.NET file can contain any of the following:

- Processing instructions for the server
- Code in C#, Visual Basic .NET, JScript .NET, or any other language that the .NET Framework supports
- Content in whatever form is appropriate for the generated resource, such as HTML
- Client-side script code
- Embedded ASP.NET server controls

So, in fact you could have an ASP.NET file as simple as this:

```
Hello!
```

This would simply result in an HTML page being returned (as HTML is the default output of ASP.NET pages) containing just this text.

As you see later in this chapter, it is also possible to split certain portions of the code into other files, which can provide a more logical structure.

## State Management in ASP.NET

One of the key properties of ASP.NET pages is that they are effectively stateless. By default, no information is stored on the server between user requests (although there are methods for doing this, as you see later in this chapter). At first glance this seems a little strange, because state management is something that seems essential for user-friendly interactive sessions. However, ASP.NET provides a workaround to this problem, such that session management becomes almost transparent.

In short, information such as the state of controls on a Web Form (including data entered in text boxes or selections from drop-down lists) is stored in a hidden *viewstate* field that is part of the page generated by the server and passed to the user. Subsequent actions, such as triggering events that require server-side processing like submitting form data, result in this information being sent back to the server, known as *postback*. On the server this information is used to repopulate the page object model allowing you to operate on it as if the changes had been made locally.

You'll see this in action shortly and examine the details.

# ASP.NET Web Forms

As mentioned earlier, much of the functionality in ASP.NET is achieved using Web Forms. Before long you'll dive in and create a simple Web Form to give you a starting point to explore this technology. First, however, this section reviews some key points pertinent to Web Form design. It should be noted that some ASP.NET developers simply use a text editor such as Notepad to create files. I wouldn't advocate this myself, because the benefits you get via an IDE such as Visual Studio or Web Developer Express are substantial, but it's worth mentioning because it is a possibility. However, if you do take this route you have a great deal of flexibility as to which parts of a Web application you put where. This enables you, for example, to combine all your code in one file. You can achieve this by enclosing code in `<script>` elements, using two attributes on the opening `<script>` tag:

```
<script language="c#" runat="server">
   // Server-side code goes here.
</script>
```

The `runat="server"` attribute here is crucial, because it instructs the ASP.NET engine to execute this code on the server rather than sending it to the client, thus giving you access to the rich environment hinted at earlier. You can place your functions, event handlers, and so on, in server-side script blocks.

If you omit the `runat="server"` attribute, you are effectively providing client-side code, which will fail if it uses any of the server-side style coding that is discussed in this chapter. However, there might be times when you want to provide client-side code (indeed, ASP.NET generates some itself sometimes, depending on browser capabilities and what Web Form code is used). Unfortunately you can't use C# here; to do so would require the .NET Framework to be installed on the client, which might not always be the case. JavaScript is probably the next best option, because it is supported on the widest variety of client browsers. To change the language, you simply change the value of the `language` attribute as follows:

```
<script language="JavaScript" type="text/JavaScript">
   // Client-side code goes here; you can also use "vbscript".
</script>
```

905

*Note that the* `type` *attribute here is optional, but necessary if you want XHTML compliance.*

It is equally possible to create ASP.NET files in Visual Studio, which is great for you as you're already familiar with this environment for C# programming. However, the default project setup for Web applications in this environment has a slightly more complex structure than a single `.aspx` file. This isn't a problem for you though, and does make things a bit more logical (more programmer-like and less Web developer-like). For this reason, you'll use Visual Studio throughout this chapter for your ASP.NET programming (instead of Notepad).

The `.aspx` files can also include code in blocks enclosed by `<%` and `%>` tags. However, function definitions and variable declarations cannot go here. Instead you can insert code that is executed as soon as the block is reached, which is useful when outputting simple HTML content. This behavior is similar to that of old-style ASP pages, with one important difference: the code is compiled, not interpreted. This results in far better performance.

Now it's time for an example. In Visual Studio you create a new Web application by using the File ➪ New ➪ Web Site menu option. From the dialog that appears, select the Visual C# language type and the ASP.NET Web Site template. At this point, you have a choice to make. Visual Studio can create Web sites in a number of different locations:

- On your local IIS Web server
- On your local disk, configured to use the built-in Visual Web Developer Web server
- At any location accessible via FTP
- On a remote Web server that supports Front Page Server Extensions

Without worrying about the latter two choices, which use remote servers, you are left with the first two choices. In general IIS is the best place to install ASP.NET Web sites, because it is likely to be closest to the configuration required when you deploy a Web site. The alternative, using the built-in Web server, is fine for testing but has certain limitations:

- Only the local computer can see the Web site
- Access to services such as SMTP is restricted
- The security model is different to IIS — the application runs in the context of the current user rather than an ASP.NET-specific account.

This last point requires clarification, because security is very important when it comes to accessing databases or anything else that requires authentication. By default, Web applications running on IIS do so in an account called ASPNET on Windows XP or 2000 Web servers, or in an account called NETWORK SERVICES on Windows Server 2003. This is configurable if you are using IIS, but not if you use the built-in Web server.

For the purposes of illustration, though, and because you may not have IIS installed on your computer, you can use the built-in Web server. You aren't worried about security at this stage, so you can go with simplicity.

Create a new ASP.NET Web Site called PCSWebApp1 using the File System option, at `C:\ProCSharp\Chapter26` as shown in Figure 26-2.

# ASP.NET Pages

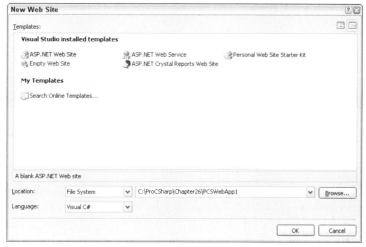

Figure 26-2

After a few moments, Visual Studio .NET should have set up the following:

- ❑ `PCSWebApp1`, a new solution containing the C# Web Application PCSWebApp1
- ❑ A reserved folder called `App_Data` for containing data files, such as XML files or database files
- ❑ `Default.aspx`, the first ASP.NET page in the Web application
- ❑ `Default.aspx.cs`, a "code-behind" class file for `Default.aspx`

You can see all of this in the Solution Explorer, as shown in Figure 26-3.

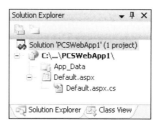

Figure 26-3

You can view `.aspx` files in design or source (HTML) view. This is the same as for Windows Forms (as discussed in Part III). The initial view in Visual Studio is either the design or source view for `Default.aspx` (you can toggle between the views using the buttons in the bottom left). The design view is shown in Figure 26-4.

**Figure 26-4**

Underneath the (currently empty) form, you can see where in the HTML for the form the cursor is currently positioned. Here the cursor is in a `<div>` element inside the `<body>` element of the page. The source view for the page shows you the code generated inside the .aspx file:

```
<%@ Page Language="C#" AutoEventWireup="true" CodeFile="Default.aspx.cs"
   Inherits="_Default" %>
<!DOCTYPE html PUBLIC "-//W3C//DTD XHTML 1.1//EN"
  "http://www.w3.org/TR/xhtml11/DTD/xhtml11.dtd">
<html xmlns="http://www.w3.org/1999/xhtml">
<head runat="server">
  <title>Untitled Page</title>
</head>
<body>
  <form id="form1" runat="server">
    <div>
    </div>
  </form>
</body>
</html>
```

If you know any HTML syntax, this will look familiar to you. You are presented with the basic code required for an HTML page following the XHTML schema, with a few extra bits of code. The most important extra is the `<form>` element, which will contain your ASP.NET code. The most important thing to note here is the `runat` attribute. Just as with the server-side code blocks you saw at the start of this section this is set to `server`, meaning that the processing of the form will take place on the server. If you don't include this reference, then no server-side processing will be performed and the form won't do anything. There can only be one server-side `<form>` element in an ASP.NET page.

The other interesting thing about this code is the `<%@ Page %>` tag at the top. This tag defines page characteristics that are important to you as a C# Web application developer. There is a Language attribute that specifies that you will use C# throughout your page, as you saw earlier with `<script>` blocks (the default for Web applications is Visual Basic .NET, although this can be changed using a `Web.config` file, which you'll see later in this chapter). The other three attributes, AutoEventWireup, CodeFile, and Inherits, are used to associate the Web Form with a class in a code-behind code file, in this case the partial class Default_aspx in the file Default.aspx.cs. This leads straight into a necessary discussion about the ASP.NET code model.

# ASP.NET Pages

## The ASP.NET Code Model

In ASP.NET a combination of layout (HTML) code, ASP.NET controls, and C# code is used to generate the HTML that users see. The layout and ASP.NET code is stored in an .aspx file, such as the one you looked at in the preceding section. The C# code that you add to customize the behavior of the form is contained either in the .aspx file or, as in the preceding example, in a separate .aspx.cs file.

When an ASP.NET Web Form is processed, typically when a user requests the page, although sites can be precompiled, several things happen:

- ❑ The ASP.NET process examines the page, and determines what objects must be created in order to instantiate the page object model.
- ❑ A base class for the base is dynamically created, including members for the controls on the page as well as event handlers for these controls (such as button click events).
- ❑ Additional code contained in the .aspx page, as well as any additional code files for the page, is combined with this base class to complete the object model—hence the need for a partial class in the code-behind file as noted earlier.
- ❑ The complete code is compiled and cached ready to process subsequent requests.
- ❑ HTML is generated and returned to the user.

The code-behind file generated for you in the PCSWebApp1 Web site for Default.aspx is initially very sparse. First, you see the default set of namespace references required for basic usage:

```
using System;
using System.Data;
using System.Configuration;
using System.Web;
using System.Web.Security;
using System.Web.UI;
using System.Web.UI.WebControls;
using System.Web.UI.WebControls.WebParts;
using System.Web.UI.HtmlControls;
```

Below these references you see an almost completely empty partial class definition for Default_aspx:

```
public partial class _Default : System.Web.UI.Page
{
    protected void Page_Load(object sender, EventArgs e)
    {

    }
}
```

Here the Page_Load() event handler can be used to add any code that is required when the page is loaded. As you add more event handlers and so on this class file will become increasingly full of code. Note that you don't see the code that wires up this event handler to the page—this is inferred by the ASP.NET runtime as noted earlier. This is due to the AutoEventWireUp attribute—setting this to false will mean that you'll have to associate the event handlers in your code with events on your own.

# Chapter 26

## *ASP.NET Server Controls*

Your generated code doesn't do very much as yet, so next you need to add some content. You can do this in Visual Studio using the Web Form designer, which supports drag-and-drop in just the same way as the Windows Forms designer.

You can add three types of controls to your ASP.NET pages:

- **HTML server controls** — These controls mimic HTML elements, which will be familiar to HTML developers.

- **Web server controls** — This is a new set of controls, some of which have the same functionality as HTML controls. These controls have a common naming scheme for properties and other elements to ease development, and provide consistency with analogous Windows Forms controls. There are also some completely new and very powerful controls as you see later. Several types of Web server controls exist, including the standard ones such as buttons, validation controls for validating user input, login controls to simplify user management, and more complicated controls for dealing with data sources.

- **Custom and user controls** — These controls are defined by the developer, which can be created in a number of ways as discussed in Chapter 27, "ASP.NET Development."

*The next section provides a list of many of the frequently used Web server controls, along with usage notes. Some additional controls are examined in the next chapter. HTML controls will not be covered in this book. These controls don't do anything more than the Web server controls, and the Web server controls provide a richer environment for developers more familiar with programming than HTML design. Learning how to use the Web server controls provides enough knowledge to use HTML server controls. For more information, check out* Professional ASP.NET 1.1 *(Wiley Publishing Inc., ISBN 0-7645-5890-0).*

Now you add a couple of Web server controls to the PCSWebApp1 Web site you created in the last section. All Web server controls are used in the following XML element-type form:

```
<asp:X runat="server" attribute="value">Contents</asp:X>
```

X is the name of the ASP.NET server control, `attribute="value"` is one or more attribute specifications, and `Contents` specifies the control content, if any. Some controls allow properties to be set using attributes and control element content, such as `Label` (used for simple text display), where `Text` can be specified in either way. Other controls might use an element containment scheme to define their hierarchy, for example `Table` (which defines a table), which can contain `TableRow` elements in order to specify table rows declaratively.

Because the syntax for controls is based on XML (although the controls may be used embedded in non-XML code such as HTML), it is an error to omit the closing tags and `/>` for empty elements, or overlap controls.

Finally, you once again see the `runat="server"` attribute on the Web server controls. It is just as essential here as it is elsewhere, and it is a common mistake to miss this attribute, resulting in Web Forms that don't function.

# ASP.NET Pages

This first example is simple. Change the HTML design view for `Default.aspx` as follows:

```
<%@ Page Language="C#" AutoEventWireup="true" CodeFile="Default.aspx.cs"
Inherits="_Default" %>

<!DOCTYPE html PUBLIC "-//W3C//DTD XHTML 1.1//EN"
"http://www.w3.org/TR/xhtml11/DTD/xhtml11.dtd">
<html xmlns="http://www.w3.org/1999/xhtml">
<head runat="server">
  <title>Untitled Page</title>
</head>
<body>
  <form id="form1" runat="server">
    <div>
      <asp:Label runat="server" ID="resultLabel" /><br />
      <asp:Button runat="server" ID="triggerButton" Text="Click Me" />
    </div>
  </form>
</body>
</html>
```

Here you have added two Web Form controls: a label and a button.

*Note that as you do this, Visual Studio .NET IntelliSense predicts your code entry just like in the C# code editor.*

Going back to the design screen you can see that your controls have been added, and named using their `ID` attributes. As with Windows Forms, you have full access to properties, events, and so on through the Properties window and get instant feedback in code or design whenever you make changes.

Any server controls you add will automatically become part of the object model for the form that you are building. This is an instant bonus for Windows Forms developers — the similarities are beginning to emerge!

To make this application do something, you can add an event handler for clicking the button. Here you can either enter a method name in the Properties window for the button or just double-click the button to get the default event handler. If you double-click the button, you'll automatically add an event-handling method as follows:

```
    void triggerButton_Click(object sender, EventArgs e)
    {

    }
```

This is hooked up to the button by some code added to the source of `Default.aspx`:

```
    <div>
      <asp:Label Runat="server" ID="resultLabel" /><br />
      <asp:Button Runat="server" ID="triggerButton" Text="Click Me"
        OnClick="triggerButton_Click" />
    </div>
```

Here the `OnClick` attribute lets the ASP.NET runtime know to wire up the click event of the button to the `triggerButton_Click()` method when it generates the code model for the form.

Modify the code in `triggerButton_Click()` as follows:

```
void triggerButton_Click(object sender, EventArgs e)
{
   resultLabel.Text = "Button clicked!";
}
```

Now you're ready to make it go. There is no need to build the project; you simply need to make sure everything is saved and then point a Web browser at the location of the Web site. If you had used IIS this would be simple, because you'd know the URL to point at. However, because you are using the built-in Web server for this example you need to start things running. The quickest way to do this is to press Ctrl+F5, which will start the server and open a browser pointing at the required URL.

When the built-in Web server is running an icon will appear in your system tray. If you double-click this icon, you can see what the Web server is doing, and stop it if required. This is shown in Figure 26-5.

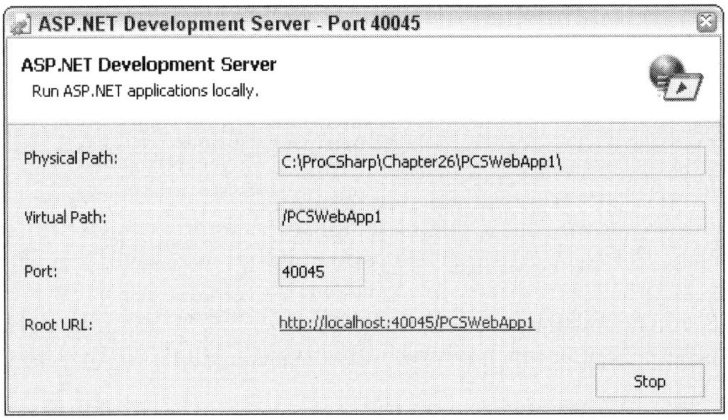

**Figure 26-5**

In Figure 26-5 you can see the port that the Web server is running on and the URL required to see the Web site you have created.

The browser that has opened should display the Click Me button on a Web page. Before pressing the button, take a quick look at the code received by the browser using View ⇨ Source (in IE). The `<form>` section should look something like this:

```
<form method="post" action="Default.aspx" id="form1">
   <div>
      <input type="hidden" name="__VIEWSTATE" id="__VIEWSTATE"
         value="/wEPDwUKLTE2MjY5MTY1NWRkQw+7xydPDuBqgjPjjMHnYk872ZE=" />
   </div>
   <div>
      <span id="resultLabel"></span><br />
      <input type="submit" name="triggerButton" value="Click Me"
```

# ASP.NET Pages

```
        id="triggerButton" />
   </div>
</form>
```

The Web server controls have generated straight HTML, `<span>` and `<input>` for `<asp:Label>` and `<asp:Button>`, respectively. There is also a `<input type="hidden">` field with the name __VIEWSTATE. This encapsulates the state of the form as mentioned earlier. This information is used when the form is posted back to the server to re-create the user interface, keeping track of changes and so on. Note that the `<form>` element has been configured for this; it will post data back to `Default.aspx` (specified in `action`) via an HTTP POST operation (specified in `method`). It has also been assigned the name `form1`.

After clicking the button and seeing the text appear, check out the source HTML again (spacing has been added for clarity):

```
<form method="post" action="Default.aspx" id="form1">
  <div>
    <input type="hidden" name="__VIEWSTATE" id="__VIEWSTATE"
      value="/wEPDwUKLTE2MjY5MTY1NQ9kFgICAw9kFgICAQ8PFgIeBFRleHQFD0J1dHRvbiB
        jbGlja2VkIWRkZDidaqI09bI1Bj6+MlyIDO4yAtb1" />
  </div>
  <div>
    <span id="resultLabel">Button clicked!</span><br />
    <input type="submit" name="triggerButton" value="Click Me"
      id="triggerButton" />
  </div>
</form>
```

This time the value of the view state contains more information, because the HTML result relies on more than the default output from the ASP.NET page. In complex forms this can be a very long string indeed, but you shouldn't complain, because so much is done for you behind the scenes. You can almost forget about state management, keeping field values between posts, and so on.

To convince yourself that you don't have to perform any compilation manually, try changing the text "Button clicked!" in `Default.aspx.cs` to something else, saving the file, and clicking the button again. The text on the Web page should change appropriately.

## *The control palette*

This section takes a quick look at some of the available controls before you put more of them together into a full, and more interesting, application. This section is divided into topics that correspond to the divisions in the Toolbox you can see when editing ASP.NET pages, as shown in Figure 26-6.

Figure 26-6

913

# Chapter 26

Note that the control descriptions refer to properties — in all cases, the corresponding attribute for use in ASP.NET code is identically named. Note that this section isn't an attempt to provide a complete reference, so many controls and properties are omitted. Only the most frequently used controls and properties are shown here.

## Crystal Reports Web server controls

These Web server controls enable Crystal Report information to be presented on Web pages. Because this is quite a specialized area, they will not be covered in this book.

## Standard Web server controls

Almost all the Web server controls (in this and other categories) inherit from `System.Web.UI.WebControls.WebControl`, which in turn inherits from `System.Web.UI.Control`. Those that don't use this inheritance instead derive either directly from `Control` or from a more specialized base class that derives (eventually) from `Control`. As such the Web server controls have many common properties and events that you can use if required. There are quite a few of these, so I won't attempt to cover them all, just as with the properties and events of the Web server controls themselves.

Many of the frequently used inherited properties are those that deal with display style. This can be controlled simply, using properties such as `ForeColor`, `BackColor`, `Font`, and so on, but can also be controlled using cascading style sheet (CSS) classes. This is achieved by setting the string property `CssClass` to the name of a CSS class in a separate file. Other notable properties include `Width` and `Height` to size a control, `AccessKey` and `TabIndex` to ease user interaction, and `Enabled` to set whether the control's functionality is activated in the Web Form.

Some controls can contain other controls, building up a control hierarchy on a page. You can get access to the controls contained by a given control using its `Controls` property, or to the container of a control via `Parent`.

You are likely to use the inherited `Load` event most often, to perform initialization on a control, and `PreRender` to perform last-minute modifications before HTML is output by the control.

Plenty more events and properties exist, and you see many of these in more detail in the next chapter. In particular, the next chapter deals with more advanced styling and skinning techniques. The following table describes the standard Web server controls in more detail.

| Control | Description |
|---------|-------------|
| Label | Simple text display; use the `Text` property to set and programmatically modify displayed text. |
| TextBox | Provides a text box that users can edit. Use the `Text` property to access the entered data, and the `TextChanged` event to act on selection changes on postback. If automatic postback is required (as opposed to using a button), set the `AutoPostBack` property to `true`. |
| Button | Adds a standard button for the user to click. Use the `Text` property for text on the button, and the `Click` event to respond to clicks (server postback is automatic). You can also use the `Command` event to respond to clicks, which gives access to additional `CommandName` and `CommandArgument` properties on receipt. |

## ASP.NET Pages

| Control | Description |
|---|---|
| LinkButton | Is identical to Button, but displays button as a hyperlink. |
| ImageButton | Displays an image that doubles as a clickable button. Properties and events are inherited from Button and Image. |
| HyperLink | Adds an HTML hyperlink. Set the destination with NavigateUrl and the text to display with Text. You can also use ImageUrl to specify an image for the link and Target to specify the browser window to use. This control has no non-standard events, so use a LinkButton instead if additional processing is required when the link is followed. |
| DropDownList | Allows the user to select one of a list of choices, either by choosing it directly from a list or typing the first letter or two. Use the Items property to set the item list (this is a ListItemCollection class containing ListItem objects) and the SelectedItem and SelectedIndex properties to determine what is selected. The SelectedIndexChanged event can be used to determine whether the selection has changed, and this control also has an AutoPostBack property so that this selection change will trigger a postback operation. |
| ListBox | Allows the user to make one or more selections from a list. Set SelectionMode to Multiple or Single to specify how many items can be selected at once, and Rows to determine how many items to display. Other properties and events are as for DropDownList. |
| CheckBox | Displays a box that can be checked or unchecked. The state is stored in the Boolean property Checked, and the text associated with the check box in Text. The AutoPostBack property can be used to initiate automatic postback and the CheckedChanged event to act on changes. |
| CheckBoxList | Creates a group of check boxes. Properties and events are identical to other list controls, such as DropDownList. |
| RadioButton | Displays a button that can be turned on or off. Generally these are grouped such that only one in the group is active at any time. Use the GroupName property to link RadioButton controls into a group. Other properties and events are as per CheckBox. |
| RadioButtonList | Creates a group of radio buttons where only one button in the group can be selected at a time. Properties and events are as per other list controls. |
| Image | Displays an image. Use ImageUrl for the image reference, and AlternateText to provide text if the image fails to load. |
| ImageMap | Like Image, but allows you to specify specific actions to trigger if users click one or more hot spots in the image. The action to take can either be a postback or a redirection to another URL. Hot spots are supplied by embedded controls that derive from HotSpot, such as RectangleHotSpot and CircleHotSpot. |
| Table | Specifies a table. Use this in conjunction with TableRow and TableCell at design time or programmatically assign rows using the Rows property of type TableRowCollection. You can also use this property for runtime modifications. This control has several styling properties unique to tables, as do TableRow and TableCell. |

*Table continued on following page*

| Control | Description |
| --- | --- |
| BulletedList | Formats a list of items as a bulleted list. Unlike the other list controls, this one has a Click event that you can use to determine what item a user has clicked during a postback. Other properties and events are as for DropDownList. |
| HiddenField | Used to provide a hidden field, to store non-displayed values for any reason. These can be very useful to store settings that would otherwise need an alternative storage mechanism to function. Use the Value property to access the stored value. |
| Literal | Performs the same function as Label, but has no styling properties, just a Text one (because it derives from Control, not WebControl). |
| Calendar | Allows the user to select a date from a graphical calendar display. This control has many style-related properties, but essential functionality can be achieved using the SelectedDate and VisibleDate properties (of type System.DateTime) to get access to the date selected by the user and the month to display (which will always contain VisibleDate). The key event to hook up to is SelectionChanged. Postback from this control is automatic. |
| AdRotator | Displays several images in succession, with a different one displayed after each server round trip. Use the AdvertisementFile property to specify the XML file describing the possible images and the AdCreated event to perform processing before each image is sent back. You can also use the Target property to name a window to open when an image is clicked. |
| FileUpload | This control presents the user with a text box and a Browse button, such that a file to be uploaded can be selected. Once the user has done this, you can look at the HasFile property to determine if a file has been selected, then use the SaveAs() method from code behind to perform the file upload. |
| Wizard | An advanced control used to simplify the common task of getting several pages of user input in one go. You can add multiple steps to a wizard which can be presented to a user sequentially or non-sequentially, and rely on this control to maintain state and so on. |
| Xml | A more complicated text display control, used for displaying XML content, which may be transformed using an XSLT style sheet. The XML content is set using one of the Document, DocumentContent, or DocumentSource properties (depending on the format of the original XML), and the XSLT style sheet (optional) using either Transform or TransformSource. |
| MultiView | A control that contains one or more View controls, where only one View is rendered at a time. The currently displayed view is specified using ActiveViewIndex, and you can detect if the view changes (perhaps due to a Next link on the currently displayed view or similar) using the ActiveViewChanged event. |
| Panel | Adds a container for other controls. You can use HorizontalAlign and Wrap to specify how the contents are arranged. |
| PlaceHolder | This control doesn't render any output, but can be handy for grouping other controls together, or for adding controls programmatically to a given location. Contained controls can be accessed using the Controls property. |

# ASP.NET Pages

| Control | Description |
|---|---|
| View | A container for controls, much like `PlaceHolder`, but designed for use as a child of `MultiView`. You can tell if a given `View` is being displayed using `Visible`, or use the `Activate` and `Deactivate` events to detect changes in activation state. |
| Substitution | Specifies a section of a Web page that isn't cached along with other output. This is an advanced topic related to ASP.NET caching behavior, which you won't be looking at in this book. |

## Data Web server controls

The data Web server controls are divided into two types:

- Data source controls (`SqlDataSource`, `AccessDataSource`, `ObjectDataSource`, `XmlDataSource`, and `SiteMapDataSource`)
- Data display controls (`GridView`, `DataList`, `DetailsView`, `FormView`, `Repeater`, and `ReportViewer`)

In general, you will place one of the (non-visual) data source controls on a page to link to a data source; then you'll add a data display control that binds to a data source control to display that data. Some of the more advanced data display controls, such as `GridView`, also allow you to edit data.

All the data source controls derive from either `System.Web.UI.DataSource` or `System.Web.UI.HierarchicalDataSource`. These classes expose methods such as `GetView()` (or `GetHierarchicalView()`) to give access to internal data views and skinning capabilities.

The following table describes the various data source controls. Note that there is less detail about properties in this section than in others — mainly because configuration of these controls is best done graphically or through wizards. Later in this chapter you see some of these controls in action to give you a better understanding about how they work.

| Control | Description |
|---|---|
| SqlDataSource | Acts as a conduit for data stored in a SQL Server database. By placing this control on a page you can manipulate SQL Server data using a data display control. You see this control in action later in the chapter. |
| AccessDataSource | As `SqlDataSource`, but works with data stored in a Microsoft Access database. |
| ObjectDataSource | This control allows you to manipulate data stored in objects that you have created, which may be grouped in a collection class. This can be a very quick way to expose custom object models to an ASP.NET page. |
| XmlDataSource | Similar to `DataSetDataSource`, but works with hierarchical data. This works well in binding to, for example, a `TreeView` control (one of the Navigation controls). You can also transform XML data using and XSL style sheet using this control if desired. |

*Table continued on following page*

| Control | Description |
|---|---|
| `SiteMapDataSource` | Allows binding to hierarchical site map data. See the section on navigation Web server controls later in this chapter for more information. |

Next, you have the data display controls, shown in the following table. Several of these are available to suit various needs. Some are more fully functional than others, but often you can go with simplicity (for example, when you don't need to be able to edit data items).

| Control | Description |
|---|---|
| `GridView` | Displays multiple data items (such as rows in a database) in the form of rows, where each row has columns reflecting data fields. By manipulating the properties of this control you can select, sort, and edit data items. |
| `DataList` | Displays multiple data items where you can supply templates for each item to display data fields in any way you choose. As with `GridView`, you can select, sort, and edit data items. |
| `DetailsView` | Displays a single data item in tabular form, with each row of the table relating to a data field. This control enables you to add, edit, and delete data items. |
| `FormView` | Displays a single data item using a template. As with `DetailsView`, this control enables you to add, edit, and delete data items. |
| `Repeater` | Like `DataList`, but without selecting or editing capabilities. |
| `ReportViewer` | An advanced control for displaying reporting services data, that we won't be looking at in this book. |

## Validation Web server controls

Validation controls provide a method of validating user input without (in most cases) writing any code at all. Whenever postback is initiated each validation control checks the control it is validating and changes its `IsValid` property accordingly. If this property is `false`, the user input for the validated control has failed validation. The page containing all the controls also has an `IsValid` property — if any of the validation controls has its version of this property set to `false`, this will be `false` also. You can check this property from your server-side code and act on it.

Validation controls also have another function. Not only do they validate controls at runtime; they can also output helpful hints to users. Simply setting the `ErrorMessage` property to the text you want means users will see it when they attempt to post back invalid data.

The text stored in `ErrorMessage` may be output at the point where the validation control is located, or at a separate point, along with the messages from all other validation controls on a page. This latter behavior is achieved using the `ValidationSummary` control, which displays all error messages along with additional text as required.

# ASP.NET Pages

On browsers that support it, these controls even generate client-side JavaScript functions to streamline their validation behavior. This means that in some cases postback won't even occur, because the validation controls can prevent this under certain circumstances and output error messages without involving the server.

All validation controls inherit from `BaseValidator`, and thus share several important properties. Perhaps the most important is the `ErrorMessage` property discussed earlier, with the `ControlTo Validate` property coming in a close second. This property specifies the programmatic ID of the control that is being validated. Another important property is `Display`, which determines whether to place text at the validation summary position (if set to `none`), or at the validator position. You also have the choice to make space for the error message even when it's not being displayed (set `Display` to `Static`) or to dynamically allocate space when required, which might shift page contents around slightly (set `Display` to `Dynamic`). The following table describes the validation controls.

| Control | Description |
| --- | --- |
| `RequiredField Validator` | Used to check if the user has entered data in a control such as `TextBox`. |
| `CompareValidator` | Used to check that data entered fulfills simple requirements, by use of an operator set using the `Operator` property and a `ValueToCompare` property to validate against. `Operator` can be `Equal`, `GreaterThan`, `GreaterThanEqual`, `LessThan`, `LessThanEqual`, `NotEqual`, and `DataTypeCheck`. `DataTypeCheck` simply compares the data type of `ValueToCompare` with the data in the control to be validated. `ValueTo Compare` is a string property but is interpreted as different data types based on its contents. To further control the comparison to make, you can set the `Type` property to `Currency`, `Date`, `Double`, `Integer`, or `String`. |
| `RangeValidator` | Validates that data in the control falls between `MaximumValue` and `MinimumValue` property values. Has a Type property as per `Compare Validator`. |
| `RegularExpression Validator` | Validates the contents of a field based on a regular expression stored in `ValidationExpression`. This can be useful for known sequences such as zip codes, phone numbers, IP numbers, and so on. |
| `CustomValidator` | Used to validate data in a control using a custom function. `Client ValidationFunction` is used to specify a client-side function used to validate a control (which means, unfortunately, that you can't use C#). This function should return a Boolean value indicating whether validation was successful. Alternatively, you can use the `ServerValidate` event to specify a server-side function to use for validation. This function is a `bool` type event handler that receives a string containing the data to validate instead of an `EventArgs` parameter. Returns `true` if validation succeeds, otherwise `false`. |

*Table continued on following page*

| Control | Description |
| --- | --- |
| `ValidationSummary` | Displays validation errors for all validation controls that have an `ErrorMessage` set. The display can be formatted by setting the `DisplayMode` (`BulletList`, `List`, or `SingleParagraph`) and `Header Text` properties. The display can be disabled by setting `ShowSummary` to `false`, and displayed in a pop-up message box by setting `ShowMessage Box` to `true`. |

### Navigation and Login Web server controls

These Web server controls are examined in Chapter 27.

### WebParts Web server controls

These Web server controls enable users to customize page layout as they use your sites. They can choose content regions from a list of available controls, position them on pages, and customize their layout. Unfortunately, this subject could fill a chapter on its own, so it won't be covered in this book.

> *One place where WebPart controls are used a great deal is in SharePoint Web sites. If you have ever used these, you will know that the sort of editing mentioned here is used to great effect to supply users with full customization ability. If you are interested, log into the demo site at* `http://www.utopia systems.com/spdemo.html` *and click the Modify My Page link in the top right.*

## *Server control example*

In this example, you create the framework for a Web application, a meeting room booking tool. (As with the other examples in this book, you can download the sample application and code from the Wrox Web site at `www.wrox.com`.) At first you will include only the front end and simple event processing; later you extend this example with ADO.NET and data binding to include server-side business logic.

The Web Form you are going to create contains fields for user name, event name, meeting room, and attendees, along with a calendar to select a date (you're assuming for the purposes of this example that you are dealing with all-day events). You will include validation controls for all fields except the calendar, which you will validate on the server side, and provide a default date in case none has been entered.

For user interface (UI) testing, you will also have a `Label` control on the form that you can use to display submission results.

For starters, create a new Web site in Visual Studio .NET in the `C:\ProCSharp\Chapter26\` directory, and call it PCSWebApp2. Next, design the form, which is generated using the following code in `Default.aspx` (with auto-generated code not highlighted):

```
<%@ Page Language="C#" AutoEventWireup="true" CodeFile="Default.aspx.cs"
    Inherits="_Default" %>

<!DOCTYPE html PUBLIC "-//W3C//DTD XHTML 1.1//EN"
    "http://www.w3.org/TR/xhtml11/DTD/xhtml11.dtd">

<html xmlns="http://www.w3.org/1999/xhtml">
```

# ASP.NET Pages

```
<head runat="server">
  <title>Meeting Room Booker</title>
</head>
<body>
  <form id="form1" runat="server">
    <div>
      <h1 style="text-align: center;">
        Enter details and set a day to initiate an event.
      </h1>
    </div>
```

After the title of the page (which is enclosed in HTML `<h1>` tags to get large, title-style text), the main body of the form is enclosed in an HTML `<table>`. You could use a Web server control table, but this introduces unnecessary complexity because you are using a table purely for formatting the display, not to be a dynamic UI element (an important point to bear in mind when designing Web Forms—don't add Web server controls unnecessarily). The table is divided into three columns: the first column holds simple text labels; the second column holds UI fields corresponding to the text labels (along with validation controls for these); and the third column contains a calendar control for date selection, which spans four rows. The fifth row contains a submission button spanning all columns, and the sixth row contains a `ValidationSummary` control to display error messages when required (all the other validation controls have `Display="None"`, because they will use this summary for display). Beneath the table is a simple label that you can use to display results for now, before you add database access later:

```
<div style="text-align: center;">
  <table style="text-align: left; border-color: #000000; border-width: 2px;
    background-color: #fff99e;" cellspacing="0" cellpadding="8" rules="none"
    width="540">
    <tr>
      <td valign="top">
        Your Name:</td>
      <td valign="top">
        <asp:TextBox ID="nameBox" Runat="server" Width="160px" />
        <asp:RequiredFieldValidator ID="validateName" Runat="server"
          ErrorMessage="You must enter a name."
          ControlToValidate="nameBox" Display="None" />
      </td>
      <td valign="middle" rowspan="4">
        <asp:Calendar ID="calendar" Runat="server" BackColor="White" />
      </td>
    </tr>
    <tr>
      <td valign="top">
        Event Name:</td>
      <td valign="top">
        <asp:TextBox ID="eventBox" Runat="server" Width="160px" />
        <asp:RequiredFieldValidator ID="validateEvent" Runat="server"
          ErrorMessage="You must enter an event name."
          ControlToValidate="eventBox" Display="None" />
      </td>
    </tr>
```

Most of the ASP.NET code in this file is remarkably simple, and much can be learned simply by reading through it. Of particular note in this code is the way in which list items are attached to the controls for selecting a meeting room and multiple attendees for the event:

```
<tr>
  <td valign="top">
    Meeting Room:</td>
  <td valign="top">
    <asp:DropDownList ID="roomList" Runat="server" Width="160px">
      <asp:ListItem Value="1">The Happy Room</asp:ListItem>
      <asp:ListItem Value="2">The Angry Room</asp:ListItem>
      <asp:ListItem Value="3">The Depressing
        Room</asp:ListItem>
      <asp:ListItem Value="4">The Funked Out
        Room</asp:ListItem>
    </asp:DropDownList>
    <asp:RequiredFieldValidator ID="validateRoom" Runat="server"
      ErrorMessage="You must select a room."
      ControlToValidate="roomList" Display="None" />
  </td>
</tr>
<tr>
  <td valign="top">
    Attendees:</td>
  <td valign="top">
    <asp:ListBox ID="attendeeList" Runat="server" Width="160px"
      SelectionMode="Multiple" Rows="6">
      <asp:ListItem Value="1">Bill Gates</asp:ListItem>
      <asp:ListItem Value="2">Monica Lewinsky</asp:ListItem>
      <asp:ListItem Value="3">Vincent Price</asp:ListItem>
      <asp:ListItem Value="4">Vlad the Impaler</asp:ListItem>
      <asp:ListItem Value="5">Iggy Pop</asp:ListItem>
      <asp:ListItem Value="6">William
        Shakespeare</asp:ListItem>
    </asp:ListBox>
```

Here you are associating `ListItem` objects with the two Web server controls. These objects are not Web server controls in their own right (they simply inherit from `System.Object`), which is why you don't need to use `Runat="server"` on them. When the page is processed, the `<asp:ListItem>` entries are used to create `ListItem` objects, which are added to the `Items` collection of their parent list control. This makes it easier for you to initialize lists than having to write code for this yourself (you'd have to create a `ListItemCollection` object, add `ListItem` objects, and then pass the collection to the list control). Of course, you can still do all of this programmatically if you want.

```
        <asp:RequiredFieldValidator ID="validateAttendees" Runat="server"
          ErrorMessage="You must have at least one attendee."
          ControlToValidate="attendeeList" Display="None" />
      </td>
    </tr>
    <tr>
      <td align="center" colspan="3">
        <asp:Button ID="submitButton" Runat="server" Width="100%"
          Text="Submit meeting room request" />
```

```
          </td>
        </tr>
        <tr>
          <td align="center" colspan="3">
            <asp:ValidationSummary ID="validationSummary" Runat="server"
              HeaderText="Before submitting your request:" />
          </td>
        </tr>
      </table>
    </div>
    <div>
      <p>
        Results:
        <asp:Label Runat="server" ID="resultLabel" Text="None." />
      </p>
    </div>
  </form>
</body>
</html>
```

In Design view, the form you have created looks like Figure 26-7. This is a fully functioning UI, which maintains its own state between server requests, and validates user input. Considering the brevity of the preceding code, this is quite something. In fact, it leaves you with very little to do, at least for this example; you just have to specify the button click event for the submission button.

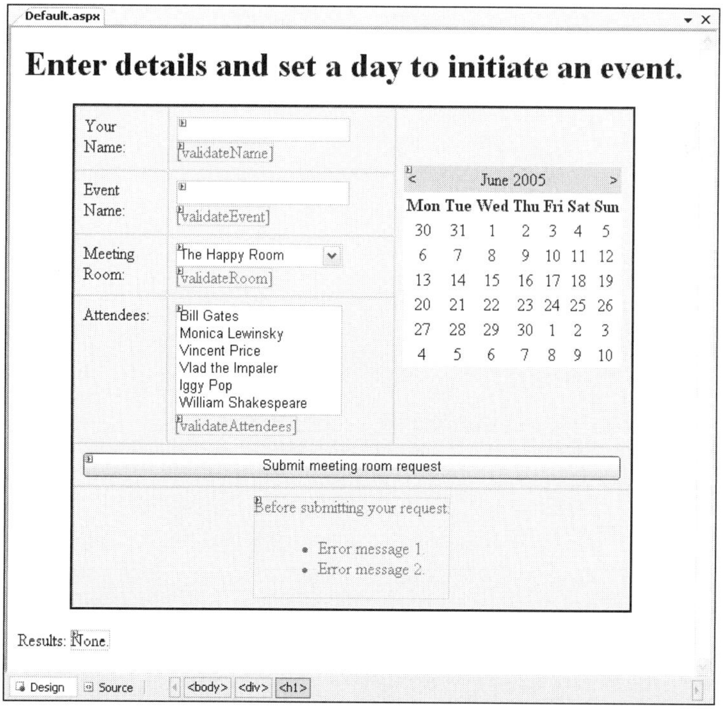

Figure 26-7

Actually, that's not quite true. So far you have no validation for the calendar control. All you have to do is give it an initial value. You can do this in the `Page_Load()` event handler for your page in the code-behind file:

```csharp
private void Page_Load(object sender, EventArgs e)
{
    if (!this.IsPostBack)
    {
        calendar.SelectedDate = System.DateTime.Now;
    }
}
```

Here you just select today's date as a starting point. Note that you first check to see if `Page_Load()` is being called as the result of a postback operation by checking the `IsPostBack` property of the page. If a postback is in progress, this property will be `true` and you leave the selected date alone (you don't want to lose the user's selection, after all).

To add the button click handler, simply double-click the button and add the following code:

```csharp
private void submitButton_Click(object sender, EventArgs e)
{
    if (this.IsValid)
    {
        resultLabel.Text = roomList.SelectedItem.Text +
            " has been booked on " +
            calendar.SelectedDate.ToLongDateString() +
            " by " + nameBox.Text + " for " +
            eventBox.Text + " event. ";
        foreach (ListItem attendee in attendeeList.Items)
        {
            if (attendee.Selected)
            {
                resultLabel.Text += attendee.Text + ", ";
            }
        }
        resultLabel.Text += " and " + nameBox.Text +
            " will be attending.";
    }
}
```

Here you just set the `resultLabel` control `Text` property to a result string, which will then appear below the main table. In IE the result of such a submission might look something like Figure 26-8, unless there are errors, in which case the `ValidationSummary` will activate instead, as shown in Figure 26-9.

# ASP.NET Pages

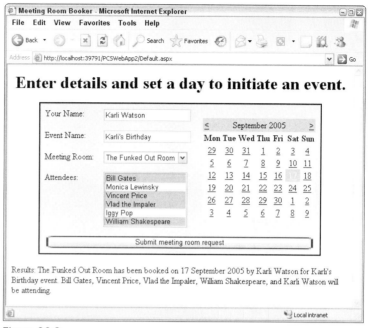

Figure 26-8

Figure 26-9

Chapter 26

# ADO.NET and Data Binding

The Web Form application you created in the previous section is perfectly functional, but only contains static data. In addition, the event booking process does not include persisting event data. To solve both of these problems, you can make use of ADO.NET to access data stored in a database, so that you can store and retrieve event data along with the lists of rooms and attendees.

Data binding makes the process of retrieving data even easier. Controls such as list boxes (and some of the more specialized controls you'll look at a bit later) come enabled for this technique. They can be bound to any object that exposes an `IEnumerable`, `ICollection`, or `IListSource` interface, as well as any of the data source Web server controls.

In this section you start by updating your event-booking application to be data-aware, and then move on to take a look at some of the other results you can achieve with data binding, using some of the other data-aware Web controls.

## *Updating the Event-Booking Application*

To keep things separate from the last example, create a new Web site called `PCSWebApp3` in the directory `C:\ProCSharp\Chapter26\` and copy the code from the `PCSWebApp2` application created earlier into the new application. Before you start on your new code, take a look at the database you'll be accessing.

### *The database*

For the purposes of this example, you will use a Microsoft SQL Server Express database called `Meeting RoomBooker.mdf`, which is part of the downloadable code for this book. For an enterprise-scale application it would make more sense to use a full SQL Server database, but the techniques involved are practically identical and SQL Server Express makes life a bit easier for testing. The code will also be identical.

> *If you are adding your own version of this database you will need to add a new database to the App_Data folder in the Solution Explorer. You can do this by right clicking on the App_Data folder, selecting Add New Item, selecting a database, naming it MeetingRoomBooker, and clicking on Add. This will also configure a data connection in the Server Explorer window ready for you to use. Next you can add the tables required as shown in the next sections and supply your own data. Alternatively, to use the downloadable database with your own code, simply copy it to the App_Data directory for your Web site.*

The database provided contains three tables:

- `Attendees`, which contains a list of possible event attendees
- `Rooms`, which contains a list of possible rooms for events
- `Events`, which contains a list of booked events

#### Attendees

The `Attendees` table contains the columns shown in the following table.

# ASP.NET Pages

| Column | Type | Notes |
|---|---|---|
| ID | Identity, primary key | Attendee identification number |
| Name | varchar, required, 50 chars | Name of attendee |
| Email | varchar, optional, 50 chars | E-mail address of attendee |

The supplied database includes entries for 20 attendees, all with their own (fictional) e-mail addresses. You can envision that in a more developed application e-mails could automatically be sent to attendees when a booking is made, but this is left to you as an optional exercise using techniques found elsewhere in this book.

## Rooms

The `Rooms` table contains the columns shown in the following table.

| Column | Type | Notes |
|---|---|---|
| ID | Identity, primary key | Room identification number |
| Room | varchar, required, 50 chars | Name of room |

Twenty records are supplied in the database.

## Events

The `Events` table contains the columns shown in the following table.

| Column | Type | Notes |
|---|---|---|
| ID | Identity, primary key | Event identification number |
| Name | varchar, required, 255 chars | Name of event |
| Room | int, required | ID of room for event |
| AttendeeList | text, required | List of attendee names |
| EventDate | datetime, required | Date of event |

A few events are supplied in the downloadable database.

## Binding to the database

The two controls you are going to bind to data are `attendeeList` and `roomList`. Before you do this you have to add `SqlDataSource` Web server controls that map to the tables you want to access in the `MeetingRoomBooker.mdf` database. The quickest way to do this is to drag them from the toolbox onto the `Default.aspx` Web Form and configure them via the configuration wizard. Figure 26-10 shows how to access this wizard for a `SqlDataSource` control called `MRBAttendeeData`.

927

# Chapter 26

Figure 26-10

From the first page of the data source configuration wizard, you need to select the connection to the database created earlier. Next, choose to save the connection string as MRBConnectionString; then choose to select * (all fields) from the Attendees table in the database.

You also need to do this for two more SqlDataSource controls, MRBRoomData and MRBEventData. For these subsequent controls you can use the saved MRBConnectionString for your connection.

Once you've added these data sources, you'll see in the code for the form that the syntax is very simple:

```
<asp:SqlDataSource ID="MRBAttendeeData" runat="server"
    ConnectionString="<%$ ConnectionStrings:MRBConnectionString %>"
    SelectCommand="SELECT * FROM [Attendees]"></asp:SqlDataSource>
<asp:SqlDataSource ID="MRBRoomData" runat="server"
    ConnectionString="<%$ ConnectionStrings:MRBConnectionString %>"
    SelectCommand="SELECT * FROM [Rooms]"></asp:SqlDataSource>
<asp:SqlDataSource ID="MRBEventData" runat="server"
    ConnectionString="<%$ ConnectionStrings:MRBConnectionString %>"
    SelectCommand="SELECT * FROM [Events]"></asp:SqlDataSource>
```

The definition of the connection string in use is found in the web.config file, which we'll look at in more details later in this chapter.

Next, you need to set the databinding properties of the roomList and attendeeList controls. For roomList the settings required are as follows:

- DataSourceID — MRBRoomData
- DataTextField — Room
- DataValueField — ID

And, similarly, for attendeeList:

- DataSourceID — MRBAttendeeData
- DataTextField — Name
- DataValueField — ID

Running the application now will result in the full attendee and room data being available from your data-bound controls. You'll use the MRBEventData control shortly.

## Customizing the calendar control

Before discussing the addition of events to the database, you need to modify your calendar display. It would be nice to display any day where a booking has previously been made in a different color, and prevent such days from being selectable. This requires modifying the way you set dates in the calendar and the way day cells are displayed.

You'll start with date selection. You need to check three places for dates where events are booked and modify the selection accordingly: when you set the initial date in `Page_Load()`, when the user attempts to select a date from the calendar, and when an event is booked and you want to set a new date to prevent the user form booking two events on the same day before selecting a new date. Because this is going to be a common feature you might as well create a private method to perform this calculation. This method should accept a trial date as a parameter and return the date to use, which will either be the same date as the trial date, or the next available day after the trial date.

Before adding this method, you need to give your code access to data in the `Events` table. You can use the `MRBEventData` control to do this, because this control is capable of populating a `DataView`. To facilitate this, add the following private member and property:

```
private DataView eventData;

private DataView EventData
{
    get
    {
        if (eventData == null)
        {
            eventData =
                MRBEventData.Select(new DataSourceSelectArguments()) as DataView;
        }
        return eventData;
    }
    set
    {
        eventData = value;
    }
}
```

The `EventData` property populated the `eventData` member with data as it is required, with the results cached for subsequent use. Here you use the `SqlDataSource.Select()` method to obtain a `DataView`.

Next, add this method, `GetFreeDate()`, to the code-behind file:

```
private System.DateTime GetFreeDate(System.DateTime trialDate)
{
    if (EventData.Count > 0)
    {
        System.DateTime testDate;
        bool trialDateOK = false;
        while (!trialDateOK)
        {
            trialDateOK = true;
            foreach (DataRowView testRow in EventData)
            {
                testDate = (System.DateTime)testRow["EventDate"];
                if (testDate.Date == trialDate.Date)
                {
```

```
                    trialDateOK = false;
                    trialDate = trialDate.AddDays(1);
                }
            }
        }
    }
    return trialDate;
}
```

This simple code uses the `EventData DataView` to extract event data. First, you check for the trivial case where no events have been booked, in which case you can just confirm the trial date by returning it. Next you iterate through the dates in the `Event` table, comparing them with the trial date. If you find a match you add one day to the trial date and perform another search.

Extracting the date from the `DataTable` is remarkably simple:

```
testDate = (System.DateTime)testRow["EventDate"];
```

Casting the column data into `System.DateTime` works fine.

The first place you will use `getFreeDate()`, then, is back in `Page_Load()`. This simply means making a minor modification to the code that sets the calendar `SelectedDate` property:

```
if (!this.IsPostBack)
{
    System.DateTime trialDate = System.DateTime.Now;
    calendar.SelectedDate = GetFreeDate(trialDate);
}
```

Next, you need to respond to date selection on the calendar. To do this, simply add an event handler for the `SelectionChanged` event of the calendar, and force the date to be checked against existing events. Double-click the calendar in the Designer and add this code:

```
void calendar_SelectionChanged(object sender, EventArgs e)
{
    System.DateTime trialDate = calendar.SelectedDate;
    calendar.SelectedDate = GetFreeDate(trialDate);
}
```

The code here is practically identical to that in `Page_Load()`.

The third place that you must perform this check is in response to the pressed booking button. You'll come back to this shortly, because you have several changes to make here.

Next, you need to color the day cells of the calendar to signify existing events. To do this you add an event handler for the `DayRender` event of the calendar object. This event is raised each time an individual day is rendered, and gives you access to the cell object being displayed and the date of this cell through the `Cell` and `Date` properties of the `DayRenderEventArgs` parameter you receive in the handler function. You simply compare the date of the cell being rendered to the dates in the `eventTable` object and color the cell using the `Cell.BackColor` property if there is a match:

```
void calendar_DayRender(object sender, DayRenderEventArgs e)
{
   if (EventData.Count > 0)
   {
      System.DateTime testDate;
      foreach (DataRowView testRow in EventData)
      {
         testDate = (System.DateTime)testRow["EventDate"];
         if (testDate.Date == e.Day.Date)
         {
            e.Cell.BackColor = System.Drawing.Color.Red;
         }
      }
   }
}
```

Here you are using red, which will give you a display along the lines of Figure 26-11, where June 12, 15, and 22 all contain events, and the user has selected June 24.

**Figure 26-11**

With the addition of the date-selection logic it is now impossible to select a day that is shown in red; if an attempt is made, a later date is selected instead (for example, selecting June 15 results in the selection of June 16).

## Adding events to the database

The `submitButton_Click()` event handler currently assembles a string from the event characteristics and displays it in the `resultLabel` control. To add an event to the database, you simply reformat the string created into a SQL `INSERT` query and execute it.

> Note that in the development environment you are using you don't have to worry too much about security. Adding a SQL Server 2005 Express database via a Web site solution and configuring `SqlDataSource` controls to use it automatically gives you a connection string that you can use to write to the database. In more advanced situations you might want to access resources using other accounts, for example a domain account used to access a SQL Server instance elsewhere on a network. The capability to do this (via impersonation, COM+ Services, or other means) exists in ASP.NET, but is beyond the scope of this book. In most cases, configuring the connection string appropriately is as complicated as things need to get.

Much of the following code will therefore look familiar:

```csharp
void submitButton_Click(object sender, EventArgs e)
{
    if (this.IsValid)
    {
        string attendees = "";
        foreach (ListItem attendee in attendeeList.Items)
        {
            if (attendee.Selected)
            {
                attendees += attendee.Text + " (" + attendee.Value
                    + "), ";
            }
        }
        attendees += " and " + nameBox.Text;

        try
        {
            System.Data.SqlClient.SqlConnection conn =
                new System.Data.SqlClient.SqlConnection(
                    ConfigurationManager.ConnectionStrings["MRBConnectionString"]
                    .ConnectionString);
            System.Data.SqlClient.SqlCommand insertCommand =
                new System.Data.SqlClient.SqlCommand("INSERT INTO [Events] "
                    + "(Name, Room, AttendeeList, EventDate) VALUES (@Name, "
                    + "@Room, @AttendeeList, @EventDate)", conn);
            insertCommand.Parameters.Add(
                "Name", SqlDbType.VarChar, 255).Value = eventBox.Text;
            insertCommand.Parameters.Add(
                "Room", SqlDbType.Int, 4).Value = roomList.SelectedValue;
            insertCommand.Parameters.Add(
                "AttendeeList", SqlDbType.Text, 16).Value = attendees;
            insertCommand.Parameters.Add(
                "EventDate", SqlDbType.DateTime, 8).Value = calendar.SelectedDate;
```

The most interesting thing here is how you access the connection string you created earlier, using the following syntax:

```
ConfigurationManager.ConnectionStrings["MRBConnectionString"].ConnectionString
```

The `ConfigurationManager` class gives you access to all manner of configuration information, all stored in the `Web.Config` configuration file for your Web application. You look at this in more detail later in this chapter.

After you have created your SQL command, you can use it to insert the new event:

```csharp
conn.Open();
int queryResult = insertCommand.ExecuteNonQuery();
conn.Close();
```

# ASP.NET Pages

`ExecuteNonQuery()` returns an integer representing how many table rows were affected by the query. If this is equal to 1, you know that your insertion was successful. If so, then you put a success message in `resultLabel`, clear `EventData` because it is now out of date, and change the calendar selection to a new, free, date. Because `GetFreeDate()` involves using `EventData` and the `EventData` property automatically refreshes itself if it has no data, the event data stored will be refreshed:

```
if (queryResult == 1)
{
    resultLabel.Text = "Event Added.";
    EventData = null;
    calendar.SelectedDate =
        GetFreeDate(calendar.SelectedDate.AddDays(1));
}
```

If `ExecuteNonQuery()` returns a number other than 1, you know that there has been a problem. For this example you won't worry too much about this, and simply throw an exception that is caught in the general catch block that is wrapped around the database access code. This catch block simply displays a general failure notification in `resultLabel`:

```
                else
                {
                    throw new System.Data.DataException("Unknown data error.");
                }
            }
            catch
            {
                resultLabel.Text = "Event not added due to DB access "
                                 + "problem.";
            }
        }
    }
```

This completes your data-aware version of the event booking application.

## More on Data Binding

As mentioned earlier in this chapter, the available Web server controls include several that deal with data display (`GridView`, `DataList`, `DetailsView`, `FormView`, and `Repeater`). These are all extremely useful when it comes to outputting data to a Web page, because they perform many tasks automatically that would otherwise require a fair amount of coding.

For starters, you'll look at how easy using these controls can be by adding an event list display to the bottom of the display of PCSWebApp3.

Drag a `GridView` control from the toolbox to the bottom of `Default.aspx`, and select the `MRBEventData` data source you added earlier for it as shown in Figure 26-12.

933

# Chapter 26

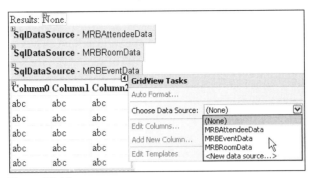

Figure 26-12

This is in fact all you need to do to display a list of events under the form — try viewing the Web site now and you should see the events, as shown in Figure 26-13.

| ID | Name | Room | AttendeeList | EventDate |
|---|---|---|---|---|
| 1 | My Birthday | 4 | Iggy Pop (5), Sean Connery (7), Albert Einstein (10), George Clooney (14), Jules Verne (18), Robin Hood (20), and Karli Watson | 17/09/2005 00:00:00 |
| 2 | Dinner | 1 | Bill Gates (1), Monika Lewinsky (2), and Bruce Lee | 05/08/2005 00:00:00 |
| 3 | Discussion of darkness | 6 | Vlad the Impaler (4), Myra Hindley (13), and Beelzebub | 29/10/2005 00:00:00 |
| 4 | Christmas with Pals | 9 | Dr Frank N Furter (11), Bobby Davro (15), John F Kennedy (16), Stephen King (19), and Karli Watson | 25/12/2005 00:00:00 |
| 5 | Escape | 17 | Monika Lewinsky (2), Stephen King (19), and Spartacus | 10/05/2005 00:00:00 |
| 6 | Planetary Conquest | 14 | Bill Gates (1), Albert Einstein (10), Dr Frank N Furter (11), Bobby Davro (15), and Darth Vader | 15/06/2005 00:00:00 |
| 7 | Homecoming Celebration | 7 | William Shakespeare (6), Christopher Columbus (12), Robin Hood (20), and Ulysses | 22/06/2005 00:00:00 |
| 8 | Dalek Reunion Ball | 12 | Roger Moore (8), George Clooney (14), Bobby Davro (15), and Davros | 12/06/2005 00:00:00 |
| 9 | Romantic meal for two | 13 | George Clooney (14), and Donna Watson | 29/03/2006 00:00:00 |

Figure 26-13

You can also make one further modification in `submitButton_Click()` to ensure that this data is updated when new records are added:

```
if (queryResult == 1)
{
    resultLabel.Text = "Event Added.";
    EventData = null;
    calendar.SelectedDate =
        GetFreeDate(calendar.SelectedDate.AddDays(1));
    GridView1.DataBind();
}
```

All data-bindable controls support this method, which is normally called by the form if you call the top-level (`this`) `DataBind()` method.

# ASP.NET Pages

One thing you'll probably have noticed in Figure 26-13 is that the date/time display for the `EventDate` field is a little messy. Because you are only looking at dates, the time is always 00:00:00 — information that it isn't really necessary to display. In the next sections, you see how this date information can be displayed in a more user-friendly fashion in the context of a `DataList` control. As you might expect, the `DataGrid` control contains many properties that you can use to format the displayed data, but I'll leave these for you to discover.

## Data display with templates

Many of the data display controls allow you to use templates to format data for display. Templates, in an ASP.NET sense, are parameterized sections of HTML that are used as elements of output in certain controls. They enable you to customize exactly how data is output to the browser, and can result in professional-looking displays without too much effort.

Several templates are available to customize various aspects of list behavior, but the one template that is essential for both `Repeater` and `DataList` is `<ItemTemplate>`, which is used in the display of each data item. You declare this template (and all the others) inside the control declaration, for example:

```
<asp:DataList Runat="server" ... >
   <ItemTemplate>
      ...
   </ItemTemplate>
</asp:DataList>
```

Within template declarations you will normally want to output sections of HTML along with parameters from the data that is bound to the control. You can use a special syntax to output such parameters:

```
<%# expression %>
```

The *expression* placeholder might be simply an expression binding the parameter to a page or control property, but is more likely to consist of an `Eval()` or `Bind()` expression. These functions can be used to output data from a table bound to a control simply by specifying the column. The following syntax is used for `Eval()`:

```
<%# Eval("ColumnName") %>
```

There is also an optional second parameter that allows you to format the data returned, which has identical syntax to string formatting expressions used elsewhere. This can be used, for example, to format date strings into a more readable format — something that was lacking in the earlier example.

The `Bind()` expression is identical but allows you to insert data into attributes of server controls, for example:

```
<asp:Label RunAt="server" ID="ColumnDisplay" Text='<%# Bind("ColumnName") %>' />
```

Note that because double quotes are used here in the `Bind()` parameter, single quotes are required to enclose the attribute value.

The following table provides a list of available templates and when they are used.

| Template | Applies To | Description |
|---|---|---|
| `<ItemTemplate>` | `DataList, Repeater` | Used for list items. |
| `<HeaderTemplate>` | `DataList, DetailsView, FormView, Repeater` | Used for output before items(s). |
| `<FooterTemplate>` | `DataList, DetailsView, FormView, Repeater` | Used for output after item(s). |
| `<SeparatorTemplate>` | `DataList, Repeater` | Used between items in list. |
| `<AlternatingItemTemplate>` | `DataList` | Used for alternate items; can aid visibility. |
| `<SelectedItemTemplate>` | `DataList` | Used for selected items in the list. |
| `<EditItemTemplate>` | `DataList, FormView` | Used for items being edited. |
| `<InsertItemTemplate>` | `FormView` | Used for items being inserted. |
| `<EmptyDataTemplate>` | `GridView, DetailsView, FormView` | Used to display empty items, for example when no records are available in a `GridView`. |
| `<PagerTemplate>` | `GridView, DetailsView, FormView` | Used to format pagination. |

The easiest way to understand how to use these is by way of an example.

## Using templates

You'll extend the table at the top of the `Default.aspx` page of PCSWebApp3 to contain a `DataList` displaying each of the events stored in the database. You'll make these events selectable such that details of any event can be displayed by clicking on its name, in a `FormView` control.

First, you need to create new data sources for the data-bound controls. It is good practice (and strongly recommended) to have separate data sources for each data-bound control.

The `SqlDataSource` control required for the `DataList` control, `MRBEventData2`, is much like `MRBEventData`, except that it needs only to return `Name` and `ID` data. The required code is as follows:

```
<asp:SqlDataSource ID="MRBEventData2" Runat="server"
    SelectCommand="SELECT [ID], [Name] FROM [Events]"
    ConnectionString="<%$ ConnectionStrings:MRBConnectionString %>">
</asp:SqlDataSource>
```

The data source for the `FormView` control, `MRBEventDetailData`, is more complicated, although you can build it easily enough through the data source configuration wizard. This data source uses the selected item of the `DataList` control, which you'll call `EventList`, to get only the selected item data. This is achieved using a parameter in the SQL query, as follows:

```
<asp:SqlDataSource ID="MRBEventDetailData" Runat="server"
   SelectCommand="SELECT dbo.Events.Name, dbo.Rooms.Room, dbo.Events.AttendeeList,
               dbo.Events.EventDate FROM dbo.Events INNER JOIN dbo.Rooms
               ON dbo.Events.ID = dbo.Rooms.ID WHERE dbo.Events.ID = @ID"
   ConnectionString="<%$ ConnectionStrings:MRBConnectionString %>">
   <SelectParameters>
      <asp:ControlParameter Name="ID" DefaultValue="-1" ControlID="EventList"
         PropertyName="SelectedValue" />
   </SelectParameters>
</asp:SqlDataSource>
```

Here the `ID` parameter results in a value being inserted in place of `@ID` in the select query. The `ControlParameter` entry takes this value from the `SelectedValue` property of `EventList`, or uses -1 if there is no selected item. At first glance this syntax seems a little odd, but it is very flexible, and once you've generated a few of these using the wizard you won't have any trouble assembling your own.

Next, you need to add the `DataList` and `FormView` controls. The changes to the code in `Default.aspx` in the PCSWebApp3 project are shown in the shaded area:

```
<tr>
   <td align="center" colspan="3">
      <asp:ValidationSummary ID="validationSummary" Runat="server"
         HeaderText="Before submitting your request:" />
   </td>
</tr>
<tr>
   <td align="left" colspan="3" style="width: 40%;">
      <table cellspacing="4" style="width: 100%;">
         <tr>
            <td colspan="2" style="text-align: center;">
               <h2>Event details</h2>
            </td>
         </tr>
         <tr>
            <td style="width: 40%; background-color: #ccffcc;" valign="top">
               <asp:DataList ID="EventList" Runat="server"
                  DataSourceID="MRBEventData2" DataKeyField="ID"
                  OnSelectedIndexChanged="EventList_SelectedIndexChanged">
                  <HeaderTemplate>
                     <ul>
                  </HeaderTemplate>
                  <ItemTemplate>
                     <li>
                        <asp:LinkButton Text='<%# Bind("Name") %>' Runat="server"
                           ID="NameLink" CommandName="Select"
                           CommandArgument='<%# Bind("ID") %>'
                           CausesValidation="false" />
                     </li>
                  </ItemTemplate>
                  <SelectedItemTemplate>
                     <li>
                        <b><%# Eval("Name") %></b>
                     </li>
                  </SelectedItemTemplate>
```

```
            <FooterTemplate>
              </ul>
            </FooterTemplate>
          </asp:DataList>
        </td>
        <td valign="top">
          <asp:FormView ID="FormView1" Runat="server"
            DataSourceID="MRBEventDetailData">
            <ItemTemplate>
              <h3><%# Eval("Name") %></h3>
              <b>Date:</b>
              <%# Eval("EventDate", "{0:D}") %>
              <br />
              <b>Room:</b>
              <%# Eval("Room") %>
              <br />
              <b>Attendees:</b>
              <%# Eval("AttendeeList") %>
            </ItemTemplate>
          </asp:FormView>
        </td>
      </tr>
    </table>
  </td>
</tr>
</table>
```

Here you have added a new table row containing a table with a `DataList` control in one column and a `FormView` control in the other.

The `DataList` uses `<HeaderTemplate>` and `<FooterTemplate>` to output header and footer HTML and `<ItemTemplate>` and `<SelectedItemTemplate>` to display event details. To facilitate selection, you raise a `Select` command from the event name link rendered in `<ItemTemplate>`, which automatically changes the selection. You also use the `OnSelectedIndexChanged` event, triggered when the `Select` command changes the selection, to ensure that the list display updates itself to display the selected item in a different style. The event handler for this is shown in the following code.

```
void EventList_SelectedIndexChanged(object sender, EventArgs e)
{
    EventList.DataBind();
}
```

You also need to ensure new events are added to the list:

```
            if (queryResult == 1)
            {
                resultLabel.Text = "Event Added.";
                EventData = null;
                calendar.SelectedDate =
                    GetFreeDate(calendar.SelectedDate.AddDays(1));
                GridView1.DataBind();
                EventList.DataBind();
            }
```

# ASP.NET Pages

Now selectable event details are available in the table, as shown in Figure 26-14.

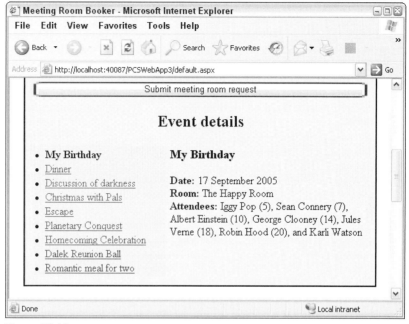

Figure 26-14

There is *much* more that you can do with templates and data-bound controls in general, enough in fact to fill a whole book. However, this should be enough to get you started with your experimentation.

## Application Configuration

One thing alluded to throughout this chapter is the existence of a conceptual application containing Web pages and configuration settings. This is an important concept to grasp, especially when configuring your Web site for multiple concurrent users.

A few notes on terminology and application lifetime are necessary here. An *application* is defined as all files in your project, and is configured by the Web.Config file. An Application object is created when an application is started for the first time, which will be when the first HTTP request arrives. Also at this time the Application_Start event is triggered and a pool of HttpApplication instances is created. Each incoming request receives one of these instances, which performs request processing. Note that this means HttpApplication objects do not need to cope with concurrent access, unlike the global Application object. When all HttpApplication instances finish their work the Application_End event fires and the application terminates, destroying the Application object.

The event handlers for the events mentioned earlier (along with handlers for all other events discussed in this chapter) can be defined in a Global.asax file, which you can add to any Web site project. The generated file contains blanks for you to fill in; for example:

```
protected void Application_Start(Object sender, EventArgs e)
{
}
```

When an individual user accesses the Web application a *session* is started. Similar to the application, this involves the creation of a user-specific `Session` object, along with the triggering of a `Session_Start` event. Within a session individual *requests* trigger `Application_BeginRequest` and `Application_EndRequest` events. These can occur several times over the scope of a session as different resources within the application are accessed. Individual sessions can be terminated manually, or will time out if no further requests are received. Session termination triggers a `Session_End` event and the destruction of the `Session` object.

Against the background of this process, you can do several things to streamline your application. If all instances of your application use a single, resource-heavy object, for example, you might consider instantiating it at the application level. This could improve performance and reduce memory usage with multiple users, because in most requests no such instantiation will be required.

Another technique you can use is to store session-level information for use by individual users across requests. This might include user-specific information extracted from a data store when the user first connects, and available until the user ceases to submit requests or logs out.

These techniques are beyond the scope of this book (and you might want to consult *Professional ASP.NET 1.1* [Wiley, ISBN 0-7645-5890-0] for details), but it helps to have a broad understanding of the processes.

Finally, you need to look at `Web.Config` files. A Web site will usually have one of these in its root directory (although it is not created for you by default), and may have additional ones in subdirectories to configure directory-specific settings (such as security). The PCSWebApp3 Web site developed in this chapter received an auto-generated `Web.Config` file when you added a stored database connection string, which you can see in the file:

```
<connectionStrings>
   <add name="MRBConnectionString" connectionString="Data Source=.\SQLEXPRESS;
      AttachDbFilename=|DataDirectory|\MeetingRoomBooker.mdf;
      Integrated Security=True;User Instance=True"
      providerName="System.Data.SqlClient" />
</connectionStrings>
```

If you ran the project in debug mode you'll also see some additional settings in the `Web.Config` file.

You can edit `Web.Config` files manually, but you can also configure Web sites (and their underlying configuration files) using a tool. This tool is accessible on the Visual Studio Website menu, under ASP.NET Configuration. The display for this tool is shown in Figure 26-15.

As you can see from the text, this tool lets you configure a number of settings, including security. You see a lot more of this tool in the next chapter.

# ASP.NET Pages

Figure 26-15

# Summary

This chapter has provided an overview of Web application creation with ASP.NET. You have seen how you can use C# in combination with Web server controls to provide a truly rich development environment. You have developed an event booking sample application to illustrate many of the techniques available, such as the variety of server controls that exist, and data binding with ADO.NET.

Specifically, you've looked at:

- An introduction to ASP.NET and how it fits in with .NET development in general.
- How the basic syntax of ASP.NET works, how state management is achieved, and how to integrate C# code with ASP.NET pages.
- How to create an ASP.NET Web application using Visual Studio, and what options exist for hosting and testing of Web sites.
- A summary of the Web controls available to ASP.NET developers, and how they work together to deliver dynamic and/or data-driven content.
- How to work with event handlers to both detect and act on user interaction with controls and customize controls via page and rendering events.
- How to bind data to Web controls, and format the data displayed using templates and data binding expressions.
- How to put all this together to build a meeting room booker application.

Using this information you are already at a point where you could assemble powerful Web applications of your own. However, so far you've only scratched the surface of what's possible. So, before you put down this book and dive into your own Web development, I'd beg your indulgence to read a little more. In Chapter 27, you expand your knowledge of ASP.NET by looking at some more important Web topics, including master pages, skinning, and personalization. And I promise you — the results are worth it!

# 27
# ASP.NET Development

It has often been the case with Web development that the tools available, however powerful, don't quite match up with your requirements for a specific project. Perhaps a given control doesn't quite work as you'd like it to, or perhaps one section of code, intended for reuse on several pages, is too complex in the hands of multiple developers. In cases such as these, there is a strong argument for building your own controls. Such controls can, at their simplest, wrap multiple existing controls together, perhaps with additional properties specifying layout. They can also be completely unlike any existing control. Using a control you have built yourself can be as simple as using any other control in ASP.NET (if you have written them well), which can certainly ease Web site coding.

In the first part of this chapter, you examine the options available to control developers, and assemble some simple user controls of your own. You also look at the basics of more advanced control construction, although you won't see these in any great depth; whole books are devoted to the subject.

Next, you look at master pages, a technique new to ASP.NET 2.0 that enables you to provide templates for your Web sites. Using master pages you can implement complex layouts on Web pages throughout a Web site with a great deal of code reuse. You also see how you can use the navigation Web server controls in combination with a master page to provide consistent navigation across a Web site.

Site navigation can be made user specific, such that only certain users (those that are registered with the site, or site administrators, say) can access certain sections. You also look at site security and logging in to Web sites in this chapter — something that is made extremely easy via the login Web server controls.

Finally, you look at some more advanced styling techniques, namely providing and choosing themes for Web sites, which separate the presentation of your Web pages from their functionality. You can supply alternative CSS style sheets for your sites as well as different skins for Web server controls.

# Chapter 27

Throughout this chapter you refer to one large example application that includes all the techniques you've seen in this and the last chapter. This application, `PCSDemoSite`, is available in the downloadable code for this chapter. It's a little too large to include all the code here, but you don't need to have it running in front of you to learn about the techniques it illustrates. The relevant sections of code are examined as and when necessary, and the additional code (mostly dummy content or simple code you've already seen) is left for you to examine at your convenience.

## Custom Controls

In the past it has been tricky to implement custom-built controls, especially on large-scale systems where complex registration procedures might be required in order to use them. Even on simple systems, the coding required to create a custom control could become a very involved process. The scripting capabilities of older Web languages also suffered by not giving the perfect access to your cunningly crafted object models, and resulted in poor performance all around.

The .NET Framework provides an ideal setting for the creation of custom controls, using simple programming techniques. Every aspect of ASP.NET server controls is exposed for you to customize, including such capabilities as templating and client-side scripting. However, there is no need to write code for all of these eventualities; simpler controls can be a lot easier to create.

In addition, the dynamic discovery of assemblies that is inherent in a .NET system makes installation of Web applications on a new Web server as simple as copying the directory structure containing your code. To make use of the controls you have created you simply copy the assemblies containing those controls along with the rest of the code. You can even place frequently used controls in an assembly located in the global assembly cache (GAC) on the Web server, so that all Web applications on the server have access to them.

This chapter discusses two different kinds of controls:

- ❑ **User controls** (and how to convert existing ASP.NET pages into controls)
- ❑ **Custom controls** (and how to group the functionality of several controls, extend existing controls, and create new controls from scratch)

User controls are illustrated with a simple control that displays a card suit (club, diamond, heart, or spade), so that you can embed it in other ASP.NET pages with ease. In the case of custom controls, you won't go into too much depth, although you will see the basic principles and be pointed to where you can find out more.

### User Controls

User controls are controls that you create using ASP.NET code, just as you would in standard ASP.NET Web pages. The difference is that after you have created a user control you can reuse it in multiple ASP.NET pages with a minimum of difficulty.

For example, say that you have created a page that displays some information from a database, perhaps information about an order. Instead of creating a fixed page that does this, it is possible to place the relevant code into a user control, and then insert that control into as many different Web pages as you want.

# ASP.NET Development

In addition, it is possible to define properties and methods for user controls. For example, you can specify a property for the background color for displaying your database table in a Web page, or a method to re-run a database query to check for changes.

To start with, you create a simple user control. As is the case with the other chapters, you can download the code for the sample projects in this chapter from the Wrox Web site at www.wrox.com.

## A simple user control

In Visual Studio .NET, create a new Web site called PCSUserCWebApp1 in the directory C:\ProCSharp\Chapter27. After the standard files have been generated, select the Website ➪ Add New Item... menu option and add a Web User Control called PCSUserC1.ascx as shown in Figure 27-1.

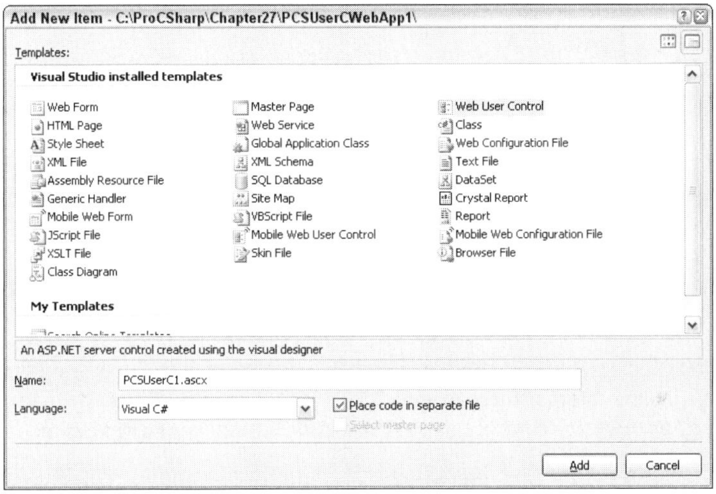

**Figure 27-1**

The files added to your project, with the extensions .ascx and .ascx.cs, work in a very similar way to the .aspx files you've seen already. The .ascx file contains your ASP.NET code and looks very similar to a normal .aspx file. The .ascx.cs file is your code-behind file, which defines custom code for the user control, much in the same way that forms are extended by .aspx.cs files.

The .ascx files can be viewed in Design or HTML view just like .aspx files. Looking at the file in HTML view reveals an important difference: there is no HTML code present, and in particular no <form> element. This is because user controls are inserted inside ASP.NET forms in other files and so don't need a <form> tag of their own. The generated code is as follows:

```
<%@ Control Language="C#" AutoEventWireup="true" CodeFile="PCSUserC1.ascx.cs"
    Inherits="PCSUserC1" %>
```

This is very similar to the <%@ Page %> directive generated in .aspx files, except that Control is specified rather than Page. It specifies the additional code-behind file and the class name that will be generated. The generated code in the .ascx.cs file is, like in auto-generated .aspx.cs files, empty.

Your simple control will be one that displays a graphic corresponding to one of the four standard suits in cards (club, diamond, heart, or spade). The graphics required for this are shipped as part of Visual Studio .NET; you can find them in the directory `C:\Program Files\Microsoft Visual Studio 8\Common7\Graphics\bitmaps\assorted`, with the file names `CLUB.BMP`, `DIAMOND.BMP`, `HEART.BMP`, and `SPADE.BMP`. Copy these files into a new `Images` subdirectory of your project's directory so that you can use them in a moment.

> *Note that unlike earlier versions of Visual Studio, changes you make to the Web site structure outside of Visual Studio are automatically reflected in the IDE. You have to hit the refresh button in the Solution Explorer window, but you should see the new `Images` directory and bitmap files appear automatically.*

Now add some code to your new control. In the HTML view of `PCSUserC1.ascx` add the following:

```
<%@ Control Language="C#" AutoEventWireup="true" CodeFile="PCSUserC1.ascx.cs"
    Inherits="PCSUserC1" %>
<table cellspacing="4">
  <tr valign="middle">
    <td>
      <asp:Image Runat="server" ID="suitPic" ImageURL="~/Images/club.bmp"/>
    </td>
    <td>
      <asp:Label Runat="server" ID="suitLabel">Club</asp:Label>
    </td>
  </tr>
</table>
```

This defines a default state for your control, which is a picture of a club along with a label. The ~ in the path to the image means "start at the root directory of the Web site." Before you add functionality, you'll test this default by adding this control to your project Web page `webForm1.aspx`.

To use a custom control in an `.aspx` file, you first need to specify how you will refer to it, that is, the name of the tag that will represent the control in your HTML. To do this you use the `<%@ Register %>` directive at the top of the code in `Default.aspx` as follows:

```
<%@ Register TagPrefix="pcs" TagName="UserC1" Src="PCSUserC1.ascx" %>
```

The `TagPrefix` and `TagName` attributes specify the tag name to use (in the form `<TagPrefix:TagName>`), and you use the `Src` attribute to point to the file containing your user control. Now you can use the control by adding the following element:

```
<form id="Form1" method="post" runat="server">
  <div>
    <pcs:UserC1 Runat="server" ID="myUserControl"/>
  </div>
</form>
```

This is all you need to do to test your user control. Figure 27-2 shows the results of running this code.

As it stands, this control groups two existing controls, an image and a label, in a table layout. As such, it falls into the category of a composite control.

# ASP.NET Development

Figure 27-2

To gain control over the displayed suit, you can use an attribute on the `<PCS:UserC1>` element. Attributes on user control elements are automatically mapped to properties on user controls, so all you have to do to make this work is add a property to the code behind your control, `PCSUserC1.ascx.cs`. Call this property `Suit`, and let it take any suit value. To make it easier for you to represent the state of the control, you define an enumeration to hold the four suit names. The best way to do this is to add an `App_Code` directory to your Web site (`App_Code` is another "special" directory, like `App_Data`, whose functionality is defined for you — in this case it holds additional code files for your Web application), then add a `.cs` file called `suit.cs` in this directory with code as follows:

```
using System;

public enum suit
{
   club, diamond, heart, spade
}
```

The `PCSUserC1` class needs a member variable to hold the suit type, `currentSuit`:

```
public partial class PCSUserC1 : System.Web.UI.UserControl
{
    protected suit currentSuit;
```

And a property to access this member variable, `Suit`:

```
    public suit Suit
    {
      get
      {
         return currentSuit;
      }
      set
      {
         currentSuit = value;
         suitPic.ImageUrl = "~/Images/" + currentSuit.ToString() + ".bmp";
         suitLabel.Text = currentSuit.ToString();
      }
    }
```

947

The set accessor here sets the URL of the image to one of the files you copied earlier, and the text displayed to the suit name.

Next, you must add code to `Default.aspx` so you can access this new property. You could simply specify the suit using the property you have just added:

```
<PCS:UserC1 Runat="server" id="myUserControl" Suit="diamond"/>
```

The ASP.NET processor is intelligent enough to get the correct enumeration item from the string provided. To make things a bit more interesting and interactive, though, you'll use a radio button list to select a suit:

```
<form id="form1" runat="server">
  <div>
    <pcs:UserC1 id="myUserControl" runat="server" />
    <asp:RadioButtonList Runat="server" ID="suitList" AutoPostBack="True">
      <asp:ListItem Value="club" Selected="True">Club</asp:ListItem>
      <asp:ListItem Value="diamond">Diamond</asp:ListItem>
      <asp:ListItem Value="heart">Heart</asp:ListItem>
      <asp:ListItem Value="spade">Spade</asp:ListItem>
    </asp:RadioButtonList>
  </div>
</form>
```

You also need to add an event handler for the `SelectedIndexChanged` event of the list, which you can do simply by double-clicking the radio button list control in Design view.

*Note that you have set the `AutoPostBack` property of this list to `True`, because the `suitList_SelectedIndexChanged()` event handler won't be executed on the server unless a postback is in operation, and this control doesn't trigger a postback by default.*

The `suitList_SelectedIndexChanged()` method requires the following code in `Default.aspx.cs`:

```
public partial class Default
{
    protected void suitList_SelectedIndexChanged(object sender, EventArgs e)
    {
        myUserControl.Suit = (suit)Enum.Parse(typeof(suit),
                                      suitList.SelectedItem.Value);
    }
}
```

You know that the `Value` attributes on the `<ListItem>` elements represent valid values for the suit enumeration you defined earlier, so you simply parse these as enumeration types and use them as values of the `Suit` property of your user control. You cast the returned object type to `suit` using simple casing syntax, as this can't be achieved implicitly.

Now you can change the suit when you run your Web application (see Figure 27-3).

# ASP.NET Development

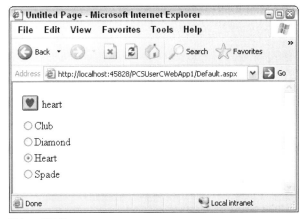

Figure 27-3

Next, you'll give your control some methods. Again, this is very simple; you just add methods to the `PCSUserC1` class:

```
public void Club()
{
   Suit = suit.club;
}

public void Diamond()
{
   Suit = suit.diamond;
}

public void Heart()
{
   Suit = suit.heart;
}

public void Spade()
{
   Suit = suit.spade;
}
```

These four methods — `Club()`, `Diamond()`, `Heart()`, and `Spade()` — change the suit displayed on the screen to the respective suit clicked.

You'll call these functions from four `ImageButton` controls in your .aspx page:

```
      </asp:RadioButtonList>
      <asp:ImageButton Runat="server" ID="clubButton"
        ImageUrl="~/Images/CLUB.BMP" OnClick="clubButton_Click" />
      <asp:ImageButton Runat="server" ID="diamondButton"
        ImageUrl="~/Images/DIAMOND.BMP" OnClick="diamondButton_Click" />
```

## Chapter 27

```
        <asp:ImageButton Runat="server" ID="heartButton"
           ImageUrl="~/Images/HEART.BMP" OnClick="heartButton_Click" />
        <asp:ImageButton Runat="server" ID="spadeButton"
           ImageUrl="~/Images/SPADE.BMP" OnClick="spadeButton_Click" />
      </div>
    </form>
```

You'll use the following event handlers:

```
    protected void clubButton_Click(object sender, ImageClickEventArgs e)
    {
       myUserControl.Club();
       suitList.SelectedIndex = 0;
    }

    protected void diamondButton_Click(object sender, ImageClickEventArgs e)
    {
       myUserControl.Diamond();
       suitList.SelectedIndex = 1;
    }

    protected void heartButton_Click(object sender, ImageClickEventArgs e)
    {
       myUserControl.Heart();
       suitList.SelectedIndex = 2;
    }

    protected void spadeButton_Click(object sender, ImageClickEventArgs e)
    {
       myUserControl.Spade();
       suitList.SelectedIndex = 3;
    }
```

*Note that you could use a single event handler for all four buttons, because they have identical method signatures, and detect which button had been pressed and so which method of* `myUserControl` *to call and index to set dynamically. In this case, though, there wouldn't be a huge difference in the amount of code required, so for simplicity things are kept separate.*

Now you have four new buttons you can use to change the suit, as shown in Figure 27-4.

Now that you've created your user control, you can use it in any other Web page simply by using the `<%@ Register %>` directive and the two source code files (`PCSUserC1.ascx` and `PCSUserC1.ascx.cs`) you have created for the control.

## User Controls in PCSDemoSite

In the PCSDemoSite the Meeting Room Booker application from the last chapter has been converted into a user control for ease of reuse. To see the control, you have to log into the site as User1, with password User1!! (you see how the logging in system works later in the chapter), and navigate to the Meeting Room Booker page as shown in Figure 27-5.

# ASP.NET Development

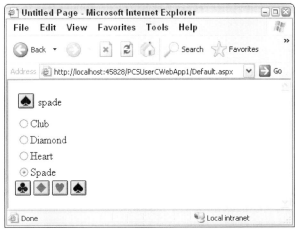

Figure 27-4

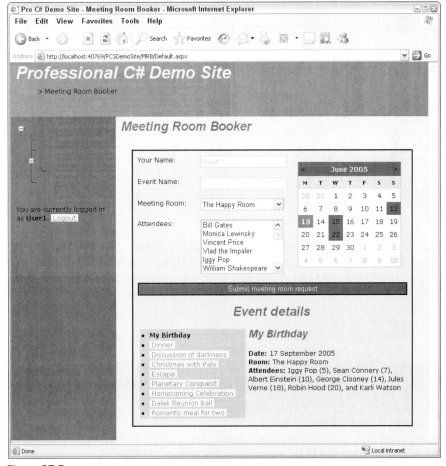

Figure 27-5

Apart from the obvious change in style, which is achieved by themes as you see later in this chapter, the major modifications are as follows:

- The username is automatically taken from user details.
- There is no extra data display at the bottom of the page, and corresponding `DataBind()` calls are removed from the code-behind.
- There is no result label beneath the control — the user gets enough feedback by seeing events added to the calendar and event list without being told that event addition was successful.
- The page containing the user control uses a master page.

The code modifications to achieve all this are remarkably simple, and you won't look at them here. You'll come back to this control later in the chapter, when you look at logging in.

## Custom Controls

Custom controls go a step beyond user controls in that they are entirely self-contained in C# assemblies, requiring no separate ASP.NET code. This means that you don't need to go through the process of assembling a user interface (UI) in an `.ascx` file. Instead, you have complete control over what is written to the output stream, that is, the exact HTML generated by your control.

In general, it will take longer to develop custom controls than user controls, because the syntax is more complex and you often have to write significantly more code to get results. A user control may be as simple as a few other controls grouped together as you've seen, whereas a custom control can do just about anything short of making you a cup of coffee.

To get the most customizable behavior for your custom controls you can derive a class from `System.Web.UI.WebControls.WebControl`. If you do this, you are creating a full custom control. Alternatively, you can extend the functionality of an existing control, creating a derived custom control. Finally, you can group existing controls together, much like you did in the last section but with a more logical structure, to create a composite custom control.

Whatever you create can be used in ASP.NET pages in pretty much the same way. All you need to do is to place the generated assembly in a location where the Web application that will use it can find it, and register the element names to use with the `<%@ Register %>` directive. For this location, you have two options: you can either put the assembly in the bin directory of the Web application, or place it in the GAC if you want all Web applications on the server to have access to it. Alternatively, if you are just using a user control on a single Web site you can just put the .cs file for the control in the `App_Code` directory for the site.

The `<%@ Register %>` directive takes a slightly different syntax for custom controls:

```
<%@ Register TagPrefix="PCS" Namespace="PCSCustomWebControls"
        Assembly="PCSCustomWebControls"%>
```

You use the `TagPrefix` option in the same way as before, but you don't use the `TagName` or `Src` attributes. This is because the custom control assembly you use may contain several custom controls, and each of these will be named by its class, so `TagName` is redundant. In addition, because you can use the dynamic discovery capabilities of the .NET Framework to find your assembly you simply have to name it and the namespace in it that contains your controls.

# ASP.NET Development

In the previous line of code, you are instructing the program to use an assembly called PCSCustomWeb Controls.dll with controls in the PCSCustomWebControls namespace, and use the tag prefix PCS. If you have a control called Control1 in this namespace, you could use it with the ASP.NET code:

```
<PCS:Control1 Runat="server" ID="MyControl1"/>
```

The Assembly attribute is optional — if you have custom controls in the App_Code directory of your site, you can omit this, and the Web site will look at code here for controls. One thing though — the Namespace attribute is *not* optional. You must include a namespace in code files for custom controls, or the ASP.NET runtime will not be able to find them.

With custom controls it is also possible to reproduce some of the control nesting behavior that exists in list controls:

```
<asp:DropDownList ID="roomList" Runat="server" Width="160px">
   <asp:ListItem Value="1">The Happy Room</asp:ListItem>
   <asp:ListItem Value="2">The Angry Room</asp:ListItem>
   <asp:ListItem Value="3">The Depressing Room</asp:ListItem>
   <asp:ListItem Value="4">The Funked Out Room</asp:ListItem>
</asp:DropDownList>
```

You can create controls that should be interpreted as being children of other controls in a very similar way to this. This is one of the more advanced techniques that you won't be looking at in this book.

## Custom control sample

Now it's time to put some of this theory into practice. You'll use a single Web site called PCSCustomCWebApp1 in the C:\ProCSharp\Chapter27\ directory, with a custom control in its App_Code directory to illustrate a simple custom control. The control here will be a multicolored version of the existing Label control, with the ability to cycle through a set of colors for each letter in its text.

The code for the control, RainbowLabel, in the file App_Code\Rainbow.cs, starts with the following using statements:

```
using System;
using System.Web.UI;
using System.Web.UI.WebControls;
using System.Drawing;
```

These are fairly standard, giving you access to the library of Web types as well as the System.Drawing namespace for the Color enumeration. The class maintains an array of colors to use for letters in its text in a private Color array called colors:

```
namespace PCSCustomWebControls
{
   public class RainbowLabel : Label
   {
      private Color[] colors = new Color[] {Color.Red, Color.Orange,
                                   Color.Yellow,
                                   Color.GreenYellow,
                                   Color.Blue, Color.Indigo,
                                   Color.Violet};
```

953

To enable color cycling, you also store an integer offset value in a private `offset` property:

```
private int offset
{
    get
    {
        object rawOffset = ViewState["_offset"];
        if (rawOffset != null)
        {
            return (int)rawOffset;
        }
        else
        {
            ViewState["_offset"] = 0;
            return 0;
        }
    }
    set
    {
        ViewState["_offset"] = value;
    }
}
```

Note that this property isn't as simple as just storing a value in a member field. This is down to the way ASP.NET maintains state, as discussed in the previous chapter. Controls are instantiated on each postback operation, so to store values you must make use of view state. This is easy to access—you simply use the `ViewState` collection, which can store any object that is serializable. Without doing this, offset would revert to its initial value between each postback.

To modify offset, you use a method called `Cycle()`:

```
public void Cycle()
{
    offset = ++offset;
}
```

This simply increments the value stored in the view state for `offset`.

Finally, you come to perhaps the most important method override for any custom control—`Render()`. This is where you output HTML, and as such it can be a very complicated method to implement. If you were to take into account all the browsers that may view your controls, and all the variables that could affect rendering, this method could get very big. Fortunately, for this example it's quite simple:

```
protected override void Render(HtmlTextWriter output)
{
    string text = Text;
    for (int pos = 0; pos < text.Length; pos++)
    {
        int rgb = colors[(pos + offset) % colors.Length].ToArgb()
                                                        & 0xFFFFFF;
        output.Write("<font color='#" + rgb.ToString("X6") + "'>"
                        + text[pos] + "</font>");
```

# ASP.NET Development

```
            }
        }
    }
}
```

This method gives you access to the output stream to display your control content. There are only two cases where you don't need to implement this method:

❑   When you are designing a control that has no visual representation (usually known as a component).

❑   When you are deriving from an existing control and don't need to change its display characteristics.

Custom controls can also expose custom methods, raise custom events, and respond to child controls (if any). In the case of `RainbowLabel`, you don't have to worry about any of this.

Next, you need to modify `Default.aspx` to view the control and provide access to `Cycle()`, as follows:

```
<%@ Page Language="C#" AutoEventWireup="true" CodeFile="Default.aspx.cs"
  Inherits="_Default" %>

<%@ Register TagPrefix="pcs" Namespace="PCSCustomWebControls" %>
<!DOCTYPE html PUBLIC "-//W3C//DTD XHTML 1.1//EN"
    "http://www.w3.org/TR/xhtml11/DTD/xhtml11.dtd">
<html xmlns="http://www.w3.org/1999/xhtml">
<head runat="server">
  <title>Untitled Page</title>
</head>
<body>
  <form id="form1" runat="server">
    <div>
      <pcs:RainbowLabel runat="server" ID="rainbowLabel1"
        Text="Multicolored label!" />
      <asp:Button Runat="server" ID="cycleButton" Text="Cycle colors"
        OnClick="cycleButton_Click" />
    </div>
  </form>
</body>
</html>
```

The required code in `Default.aspx.cs` is simply:

```
public partial class _Default : System.Web.UI.Page
{
    protected void cycleButton_Click(object sender, EventArgs e)
    {
        rainbowLabel1.Cycle();
    }
}
```

Now you can view the sample and cycle the colors in the sample text, as shown in Figure 27-6.

# Chapter 27

Figure 27-6

You can do a lot more with custom controls; indeed, the possibilities are practically limitless, but you'll have to experiment on your own to find out more.

# Master Pages

Master pages provide an excellent way to make your Web sites easier to design. By putting all (or at least most) of your page layout in a single file, you can concentrate on the more important things for the individual Web pages of your site.

Master pages are created in files with the extension `.master`, and can be added via the Website ➪ Add New Item... menu item like any other site content. At first glance, the code generated for a master page is much like that for a standard `.aspx` page:

```
<%@ Master Language="C#" AutoEventWireup="true" CodeFile="MyMasterPage.master.cs"
    Inherits="MyMasterPage" %>
<!DOCTYPE html PUBLIC "-//W3C//DTD XHTML 1.1//EN"
    "http://www.w3.org/TR/xhtml11/DTD/xhtml11.dtd">
<html xmlns="http://www.w3.org/1999/xhtml">
<head runat="server">
  <title>Untitled Page</title>
</head>
<body>
  <form id="form1" runat="server">
    <div>
      <asp:ContentPlaceHolder ID="ContentPlaceHolder1" Runat="server">
      </asp:ContentPlaceHolder>
    </div>
  </form>
</body>
</html>
```

# ASP.NET Development

The differences are as follows:

- A `<%@ Master %>` directive is used instead of a `<%@ Page %>` directive, although the attributes are the same.
- A `ContentPlaceHolder` control with an ID of `ContentPlaceHolder1` is placed on the page.

It is the `ContentPlaceHolder` control that makes master pages so useful. You can have any number of these on a page, and they are used by .aspx pages using the master page to "plug in" content. You can put default content inside a `ContentPlaceHolder` control, but .aspx pages can override this content.

For an .aspx page to use a master page, you need to modify the `<%@ Page %>` directive as follows:

```
<%@ Page Language="C#" AutoEventWireup="true" CodeFile="Default.aspx.cs"
   Inherits="_Default" MasterPageFile="~/MyMasterPage.master"
   Title="Page Title" %>
```

Here you've added two new attributes: a `MasterPageFile` attribute saying which master page to use and a `Title` attribute that sets the content of the `<title>` element in the master page.

When you add an .aspx page to a Web site you can choose to select a master page, as shown in Figure 27-7.

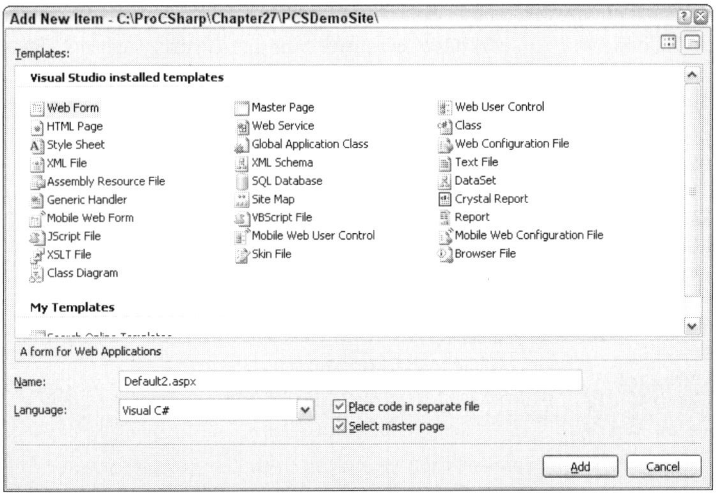

**Figure 27-7**

If you do this, you can navigate through your site structure to find the master page you want, as shown in Figure 27-8.

957

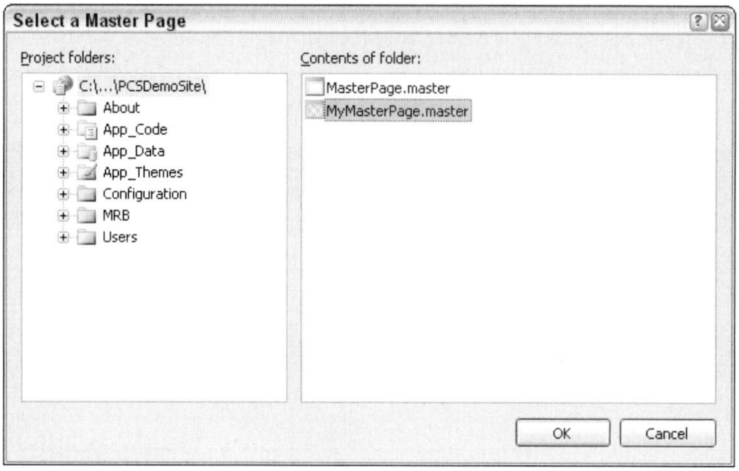

**Figure 27-8**

The .aspx page doesn't have to contain any other code if you want to use the default master page content. In fact, it is an error to include a Form control, because a page may only have one of these.

.aspx pages that use a master page can contain no root-level content other than directives, script elements, and Content controls. You can have as many Content controls as you like, where each one inserts content into one of the ContentPlaceHolder controls in the master page. The only thing to look out for is to make sure that the ContentPlaceHolderID attribute of the Content control matches the ID of the ContentPlaceHolder control where you want to insert content. So, to add content into the master page shown earlier, you'd simply need the following:

```
<%@ Page Language="C#" MasterPageFile="~/MyMasterPage.master"
AutoEventWireup="true"
   CodeFile="Default2.aspx.cs" Inherits="Default2" Title="Untitled Page" %>

<asp:Content ID="Content1" ContentPlaceHolderID="ContentPlaceHolder1"
   runat="Server">
   Custom content!
</asp:Content>
```

The true power of master pages comes when you wrap your ContentPlaceHolder controls in other page content, such as navigation controls, site logos, and other HTML. You could supply multiple ContentPlaceHolder controls for main content, sidebar content, footer text, and so on.

## Master Pages in PCSDemoSite

In PCSDemoSite the single master page MasterPage.master (the default name for a master page) is used, with code as follows:

```
<%@ Master Language="C#" AutoEventWireup="true" CodeFile="MasterPage.master.cs"
   Inherits="MasterPage" %>
<!DOCTYPE html PUBLIC "-//W3C//DTD XHTML 1.1//EN"
   "http://www.w3.org/TR/xhtml11/DTD/xhtml11.dtd">
```

# ASP.NET Development

```
<html xmlns="http://www.w3.org/1999/xhtml">
<head runat="server">
  <link rel="stylesheet" href="StyleSheet.css" type="text/css" />
  <title></title>
</head>
<body>
  <form id="form1" runat="server">
    <div id="header">
      <h1><asp:literal ID="Literal1" runat="server"
        text="<%$ AppSettings:SiteTitle %>" /></h1>
      <asp:SiteMapPath ID="SiteMapPath1" Runat="server" CssClass="breadcrumb" />
    </div>
    <div id="nav">
      <div class="navTree">
        <asp:TreeView ID="TreeView1" runat="server"
          DataSourceID="SiteMapDataSource1" ShowLines="True" />
      </div>
      <br />
      <br />
      <asp:LoginView ID="LoginView1" Runat="server">
        <LoggedInTemplate>
          You are currently logged in as
          <b><asp:LoginName ID="LoginName1" Runat="server" /></b>.
          <asp:LoginStatus ID="LoginStatus1" Runat="server" />
        </LoggedInTemplate>
      </asp:LoginView>
    </div>
    <div id="body">
      <asp:ContentPlaceHolder ID="ContentPlaceHolder1" Runat="server" />
    </div>
  </form>
  <asp:SiteMapDataSource ID="SiteMapDataSource1" Runat="server" />
</body>
</html>
```

Many of the controls here are ones that you haven't looked at yet, and you'll come back to those shortly. The important things to note here are the `<div>` elements that hold the various content sections (header, navigation bar, and body), and the use of `<%$ AppSettings:SiteTitle %>` to obtain the site title from the `Web.config` file:

```
<appSettings>
  <add key="SiteTitle" value="Professional C# Demo Site"/>
</appSettings>
```

There is also a style sheet link to `StyleSheet.css`:

```
<link rel="stylesheet" href="StyleSheet.css" type="text/css" />
```

This CSS style sheet contains the basic layout information for the `<div>` elements on this page, as well as for a section of the meeting room booker control:

```
div#header
{
    position: absolute;
```

```css
        top: 0px;
        left: 0px;
        height: 80px;
        width: 780px;
        padding: 10px;
    }

    div#nav
    {
        position: absolute;
        left: 0px;
        top: 100px;
        width: 180px;
        height: 580px;
        padding: 10px;
    }

    div#body
    {
        position: absolute;
        left: 200px;
        top: 100px;
        width: 580px;
        height: 580px;
        padding: 10px;
    }

    .mrbEventList
    {
        width: 40%;
    }
```

Note that none of this style information includes colors, fonts, and so on. This is achieved by style sheets within themes, which you see later in this chapter. The only information here is layout information, such as `<div>` sizes.

> Note that Web site best practices have been adhered to in this chapter wherever possible. Using CSS for layout rather than tables is fast becoming the industry standard for Web site layout and is well worth learning about. In the preceding code, # symbols are used to format `<div>` elements with specific id attributes, while .mrbEventList will format an HTML element with a specific class attribute.

# Site Navigation

The three navigation Web server controls, `SiteMapPath`, `Menu` and `TreeView`, can work with an XML sitemap that you provide for your Web site, or a site map provided in a different format if you implement an alternative site map provider. Once you have created such a data source, these navigation Web server controls are able to automatically generate location and navigation information for users.

You can also use a `TreeView` control to display other structured data, but it really comes into its own with site maps, and gives you an alternative view of navigation information.

# ASP.NET Development

The navigation Web server controls are shown in the following table.

| Control | Description |
| --- | --- |
| SiteMapPath | Displays breadcrumb-style information allowing users to see where they are in the structure of a site and navigate to parent areas. You can supply various templates, such as `NodeStyle` and `CurrentNodeStyle` to customize the appearance of the breadcrumb trail. |
| Menu | Links to site map information via a `SiteMapDataSource` control, and enables a view of the complete site structure, appearance customized by templates. |
| TreeView | Allows the display of hierarchical data, such as a table of contents, in a tree structure. Tree nodes are stored in a `Nodes` property, with the selected node stored in `SelectedNode`. Several events allow for server-side processing of user interaction, including `SelectedNodeChanged` and `TreeNodeCollapsed`. This control is typically data bound. |

To provide a site map XML file for your site you can add a site map file (`.sitemap`) using the Web site — Add New Item menu item. You link to site maps via providers. The default XML provider looks for a file called `Web.sitemap` in the root of your site, so unless you are going to use a different provider you should accept the default file name supplied.

A site map XML file contains a root `<siteMap>` element containing a single `<siteMapNode>` element, which in turn can contain any number of nested `<siteMapNode>` elements.

Each `<siteMapNode>` element uses the attributes shown in the following table.

| Attribute | Description |
| --- | --- |
| title | Page title, used as the text for links in site map displays. |
| url | Page location, used as the hyperlink location in site map displays. |
| roles | The user roles that are allowed to see this site map entry in menus and so on. |
| description | Optional text used for tooltip pop-ups for site map displays. |

Once a site has a `Web.sitemap` file, adding a breadcrumb trail is as simple as putting the following code on your page:

```
<asp:SiteMapPath ID="SiteMapPath1" Runat="server" />
```

This will use the default provider and the current URL location to format a list of links to parent pages.

Adding a menu or tree view menu requires a `SiteMapDataSource` control, but again this can be very simple:

```
<asp:SiteMapDataSource ID="SiteMapDataSource1" Runat="server" />
```

If you are using a custom provider, the only difference is that you can supply the provider ID via a `SiteMapProvider` attribute. You can also remove upper levels of the menu data (such as the root `Home` item) using `StartingNodeOffset`, remove just the top-level link using `ShowStartingNode="False"`, start from the current location using `StartFromCurrentNode="True"`, and override the root node using `StrtingNodeUrl`.

The data from this data source is consumed by `Menu` and `TreeView` controls simply by setting their `DataSourceID` to the ID of the `SiteMapDataSource`. Both controls include numerous styling properties and can be themed as you see later in this chapter.

## Navigation in PCSDemoSite

The site map for PCSDemoSite is as follows:

```xml
<?xml version="1.0" encoding="utf-8" ?>
<siteMap>
  <siteMapNode url="~/Default.aspx" title="Home">
    <siteMapNode url="~/About/Default.aspx" title="About" />
    <siteMapNode url="~/MRB/Default.aspx" title="Meeting Room Booker"
      roles="RegisteredUser,SiteAdministrator" />
    <siteMapNode url="~/Configuration/Default.aspx" title="Configuration"
      roles="RegisteredUser,SiteAdministrator">
      <siteMapNode url="~/Configuration/Themes/Default.aspx" title="Themes"
        roles="RegisteredUser,SiteAdministrator"/>
    </siteMapNode>
    <siteMapNode url="~/Users/Default.aspx" title="User Area"
      roles="SiteAdministrator" />
    <siteMapNode url="~/Login.aspx" title="Login Details" />
  </siteMapNode>
</siteMap>
```

The PCSDemoSite Web site uses a custom provider to obtain information form `Web.sitemap`—necessary because the default provider ignores the `roles` attributes. The provider is defined in the `Web.config` file for the Web site as follows:

```xml
<configuration xmlns="http://schemas.microsoft.com/.NetConfiguration/v2.0">
  ...
  <system.Web>
    ...
    <siteMap defaultProvider="CustomProvider">
      <providers>
        <add name="CustomProvider"
          description="SiteMap provider which reads in .sitemap XML files."
          type="System.Web.XmlSiteMapProvider, System.Web, Version=2.0.3600.0,
            Culture=neutral, PublicKeyToken=b03f5f7f11d50a3a"
          siteMapFile="Web.sitemap" securityTrimmingEnabled="true" />
      </providers>
    </siteMap>
    ...
```

# ASP.NET Development

The only difference between this and the default provider is the addition of `securityTrimming Enabled="true"`, which instructs the provider to supply data for just those nodes that this current user is allowed to see. This visibility is determined by the role membership of the user, as you see in the next section.

The `MasterPage.master` page in PCSDemoSite includes `SiteMapPath` and `TreeView` navigation displays along with a data source as follows:

```
<div id="header">
  <h1><asp:literal ID="Literal1" runat="server"
    text="<%$ AppSettings:SiteTitle %>" /></h1>
  <asp:SiteMapPath ID="SiteMapPath1" Runat="server" CssClass="breadcrumb" />
</div>
<div id="nav">
  <div class="navTree">
    <asp:TreeView ID="TreeView1" runat="server"
      DataSourceID="SiteMapDataSource1" ShowLines="True" />
  </div>
  <br />
  <br />
  <asp:LoginView ID="LoginView1" Runat="server">
    <LoggedInTemplate>
      You are currently logged in as
      <b><asp:LoginName ID="LoginName1" Runat="server" /></b>.
      <asp:LoginStatus ID="LoginStatus1" Runat="server" />
    </LoggedInTemplate>
  </asp:LoginView>
</div>
<div id="body">
  <asp:ContentPlaceHolder ID="ContentPlaceHolder1" Runat="server" />
</div>
</form>
<asp:SiteMapDataSource ID="SiteMapDataSource1" Runat="server" />
```

The only point to note here is that CSS classes are supplied for both `SiteMapPath` and `TreeView`, to facilitate theming.

# Security

Security and user management has often been seen as quite a complicated thing to implement in Web sites and with good reason. You have to take a number of factors into consideration, including:

- ❑ What sort of user management system will I implement? Will users map to Windows user accounts, or will I implement something independent?
- ❑ How do I implement a login system?
- ❑ Do I let users register on the site, and if so how?

# Chapter 27

- ❑ How do I let some users see and do only some things, while supplying some users with additional privileges?
- ❑ What happens in the case of forgotten passwords?

With ASP.NET 2.0 you have a whole suite of tools at your disposal for dealing with questions such as these, and it can in fact take only a matter of minutes to implement a user system on your site. You have three types of authentication at your disposal:

- ❑ Windows authentication, where users have Windows accounts, typically used with intranet sites or WAN portals
- ❑ Forms authentication, where the Web site maintains its own list of users and handles its own authentication
- ❑ Passport authentication, where Microsoft provides a centralized authentication service for you to use

A full discussion of security in ASP.NET would take up at least a full chapter, but there are plenty of things you can look at quickly to get an idea about how things work. You'll concentrate on Forms authentication here, because it is the most versatile system and very quick to get up and running.

The quickest way to implement Forms authentication is via the Website — ASP.NET Configuration tool, which you saw briefly in the last chapter. This tool has a Security tab, and on it a security wizard. This wizard lets you choose an authentication type, add roles, add users, and secure areas of your site.

## *Adding Forms Authentication Using the Security Wizard*

For the purposes of this explanation, create a new Web site called PCSAuthenticationDemo in the directory C:\ProCSharp\Chapter27\, and once the site has been created open the Website — ASP.NET Configuration tool. Navigate to the Security tab, then click the "Use the security setup wizard to configure security step by step." link. Click Next on the first step after reading the information there. On the second step, select "From the internet" as shown in Figure 27-9.

# ASP.NET Development

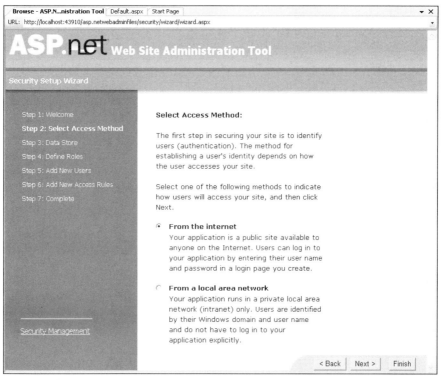

Figure 27-9

Click Next, and then Next again after confirming that you will be using the default "Advanced provider settings" provider to store security information. This provider information is configurable via the Provider tab, where you can choose to store information elsewhere, such as in a SQL Server database, but an access database is fine for illustrative purposes.

# Chapter 27

Next, check the "Enable roles for this Web site." option as shown in Figure 27-10 and click Next.

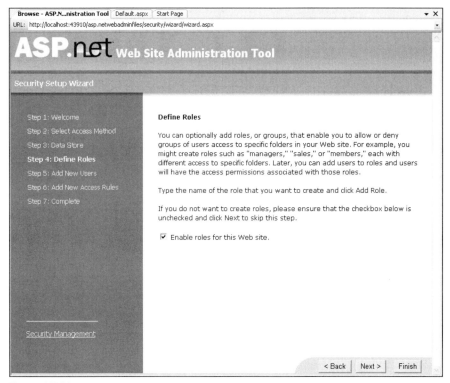

**Figure 27-10**

Next, add some roles as shown in Figure 27-11.

# ASP.NET Development

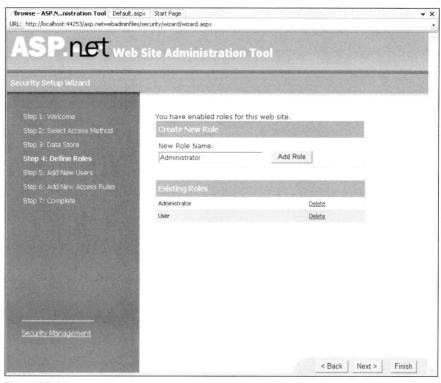

Figure 27-11

Next, add some users as shown in Figure 27-12. Note that the default security rules for passwords (defined in `machine.config`) are quite strong; there is a 7 character minimum, including at least 1 symbol character and a mix of uppercase and lowercase.

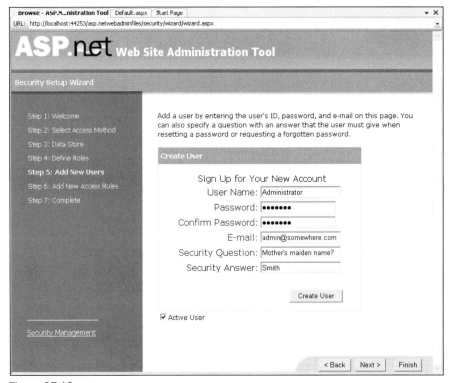

**Figure 27-12**

On the Next tab you can define access rules for your site. By default, all users and roles will have access to all areas of your site. From this dialog you can restrict areas by role, by user, or for anonymous users. You can do this for each directory in your site, because this is achieved via `Web.config` files in directories as you see shortly. For now, skip this step, and complete authentication setup.

The last step is to assign users to roles, which you can do via the Manage users link on the Security tab. From here you can edit user roles, as shown in Figure 27-13.

Once you have done all this, you're pretty much there. You have a user system in place, as well as roles and users.

Now you have to add a few controls to your Web site to make things work.

# ASP.NET Development

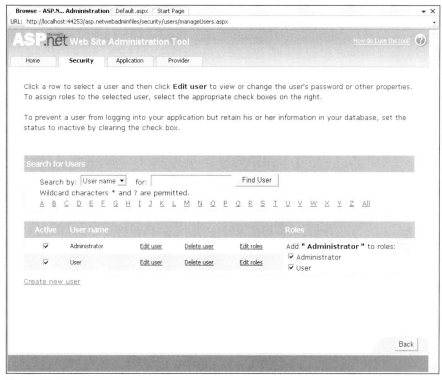

Figure 27-13

## Implementing a Login System

If you refresh the Solution Explorer display after running the security wizard you'll see that a `Web.config` file has been added to your project with the following content:

```
<?xml version="1.0" encoding="utf-8"?>
<configuration>
  <system.web>
    <roleManager enabled="true" />
    <authentication mode="Forms" />
  </system.web>
</configuration>
```

This doesn't seem like a lot for the work you've put in, but remember that a lot of information is stored in a SQL Express database, which you can see in the `App_Data` directory, called `ASPNETDB.MDF`. You can inspect the data that has been stored in this file using any standard database management tool, including Visual Studio. You can even add users and roles directly to this database if you are careful.

By default, logging in is achieved via a page called `Login.aspx` in the root of your Web site. If users attempt to navigate to a location that they don't have permission to access, they will automatically be redirected to this page and returned to the desired location after successfully logging in.

# Chapter 27

Add a Web Form called `Login.aspx` to the PCSAuthenticationDemo site and drag a `Login` control onto the form from the toolbox.

This is all you need to do to enable users to log in to your Web site. Open the site in a browser and navigate to `Login.aspx`; then enter the details for a user you added in the wizard, as shown in Figure 27-14.

**Figure 27-14**

Once you have logged in, you will be sent back to `Default.aspx`, currently a blank page.

## Login Web Server Controls

The Login section of the toolbox contains several controls, as shown in the following table.

| Control | Description |
| --- | --- |
| `Login` | As you have seen, this control allows users to log in to your Web site. Most of the properties of this control are for styling the supplied template. You can also use `DestinationPageUrl` to force redirection to a specific location on logging in, `VisibleWhenLoggedIn` to determine whether the control is visible to logged in users, and various text properties such as `CreateUserText` to output helpful messages to users. |
| `LoginView` | This control enables you to display content that varies depending on whether users are logged in, or what roles users are in. You can put content in `<AnonymousTemplate>` and `<LoggedInTemplate>`, as well as `<Role Groups>` to control the output of this control. |
| `PasswordRecovery` | This control enables users to have their password mailed to them, and can use the password recovery question defined for a user. Again, most properties are for display formatting, but there are properties such as `Mail Definition-Subject` for configuring the e-mail to be sent to the user's address, and `SuccessPageUrl` to redirect the users after they have requested a password. |

# ASP.NET Development

| Control | Description |
|---|---|
| `LoginStatus` | Displays a Login or Logout link, with customizable text and images, to users depending on whether they are logged in. |
| `LoginName` | Outputs the username for the currently logged-in user. |
| `CreateUserWizard` | Displays a form that users can use to register with your site and be added to the user list. As with other login controls, there are a large number of properties relating to layout formatting, but the default is perfectly serviceable. |
| `ChangePassword` | Enables users to change their passwords. There are three fields, one for the old password, and two for new password and confirmation. There are many styling properties. |

You see some of these in action in PCSDemoSite shortly.

## Securing Directories

One final thing to discuss is how to restrict access to directories. You can do this via the Site Configuration tool as noted earlier, but it's actually quite easy to do this yourself.

Add a directory to PCSAuthenticationDemo called `SecureDirectory`, as well as a `Default.aspx` Web page in this directory, and a new `Web.config` file. Replace the contents of `Web.config` with the following:

```
<?xml version="1.0" ?>
<configuration xmlns="http://schemas.microsoft.com/.NetConfiguration/v2.0">
  <system.web>
    <authorization>
      <deny users="?" />
      <allow roles="Administrator"/>
      <deny roles="User" />
    </authorization>
  </system.web>
</configuration>
```

The `<authorization>` element can contain one or more `<deny>` or `<allow>` elements representing permission rules, each of which can have a `users` or `roles` attribute saying what the rule applies to. The rules are applied from top to bottom, so more specific rules should generally be near the top if the membership of rules overlaps. In this example, `?` refers to anonymous users, who will be denied access to this directory, along with users in the `User` role. Note that users in both the `User` and `Administrator` roles will only be allowed access if the `<allow>` rule shown here comes before the `<deny>` rule for the `User` role—all of a users' roles are taken into account, but the rule order still applies.

Now when you log in to the Web site and try to navigate to `SecureDirectory/Default.aspx` you will only be permitted if you are in the `Admin` role. Other users, or users that aren't authenticated, will be redirected to the login page.

971

# Chapter 27

## Security in PCSDemoSite

The PCSDemoSite site uses the `Login` control you've already seen, as well as a `LoginView` control, a `LoginStatus` control, a `LoginName` control, a `PasswordRecovery` control, and a `ChangePassword` control.

One difference is that a Guest role is included, and one consequence of this is that guest users shouldn't be able to change their password—an ideal use for `LoginView`, as illustrated by `Login.aspx`:

```
<asp:Content ID="Content1" ContentPlaceHolderID="ContentPlaceHolder1"
  Runat="server">
  <h2>Login Page</h2>
  <asp:LoginView ID="LoginView1" Runat="server">
    <RoleGroups>
      <asp:RoleGroup Roles="Guest">
        <ContentTemplate>
          You are currently logged in as <b>
          <asp:LoginName ID="LoginName1" Runat="server" /></b>.
          <br />
          <br />
          <asp:LoginStatus ID="LoginStatus1" Runat="server" />
        </ContentTemplate>
      </asp:RoleGroup>
      <asp:RoleGroup Roles="RegisteredUser,SiteAdministrator">
        <ContentTemplate>
          You are currently logged in as <b>
          <asp:LoginName ID="LoginName2" Runat="server" /></b>.
          <br />
          <br />
          <asp:ChangePassword ID="ChangePassword1" Runat="server">
          </asp:ChangePassword>
          <br />
          <br />
          <asp:LoginStatus ID="LoginStatus2" Runat="server" />
        </ContentTemplate>
      </asp:RoleGroup>
    </RoleGroups>
    <AnonymousTemplate>
      <asp:Login ID="Login1" Runat="server">
      </asp:Login>
      <asp:PasswordRecovery ID="PasswordRecovery1" Runat="Server" />
    </AnonymousTemplate>
  </asp:LoginView>
</asp:Content>
```

The view here displays one of several pages:

- ❏ For anonymous users a `Login` and a `PasswordRecovery` control are shown.
- ❏ For Guest users `LoginName` and `LoginStatus` controls are shown, giving the logged-in user name and the facility to log out if required.
- ❏ For RegisteredUser and SiteAdministrator users `LoginName`, `LoginStatus`, and `ChangePassword` controls are shown.

# ASP.NET Development

The site also includes various `Web.config` files in various directories to limit access, and the navigation is also restricted by role.

*Note that the configured users for the site are shown on the about page, or you can add your own.*

One point to note here is that while the root of the site denies anonymous users, the Themes directory (described in the next section) overrides this setting by permitting anonymous users. This is necessary because without this, anonymous users would see a themeless site, because the theme files wouldn't be accessible. In addition, the full security specification in the root `Web.config` file is as follows:

```
<configuration xmlns="http://schemas.microsoft.com/.NetConfiguration/v2.0">
  ...
  <location path="StyleSheet.css">
    <system.web>
      <authorization>
        <allow users="?"/>
      </authorization>
    </system.web>
  </location>
  <system.web>
    <authorization>
      <deny users="?" />
    </authorization>
    ...
  </system.web>
</configuration>
```

Here a `<location>` element is used to override the default setting for a specific file specified using a `path` attribute, in this case for the file `StyleSheet.css`. `<location>` elements can be used to apply any `<system.web>` settings to specific files or directories, and can be used to centralize all directory-specific settings in one place if desired (as an alternative to multiple `Web.config` files). In the preceding code, permission is given for anonymous users to access the root style sheet for the Web site, necessary because this file defines the layout of the `<div>` elements in the master page. Without this, the HTML shown on the login page for anonymous users would be difficult to read.

Another point to note is in the code-behind file for the meeting room booker user control, in the `Page_Load()` event handler:

```
void Page_Load(object sender, EventArgs e)
{
   if (!this.IsPostBack)
   {
      nameBox.Text = Context.User.Identity.Name;
      System.DateTime trialDate = System.DateTime.Now;
      calendar.SelectedDate = GetFreeDate(trialDate);
   }
}
```

Here the username is extracted from the current context. Note that in your code-behind files you will probably also use `Context.User.IsInRole()` frequently to check access.

# Chapter 27

# Themes

By combining ASP.NET pages with master pages and CSS style sheets, you can go a long way in separating form and function, where the look and feel of your pages is defined separately from their operation. With themes you can take this a step further and dynamically apply this look and feel from one of several themes that you supply yourself.

A theme consists of the following:

- A name for the theme
- An optional CSS style sheet
- Skin (.skin) files allowing individual control types to be styled

These can be applied to pages in two different ways: as a `Theme` or as a `StyleSheetTheme`:

- **Theme** — All skin properties are applied to controls, overriding any properties the controls on the page may already have.
- **StyleSheetTheme** — Existing control properties take precedence over properties defined in skin files.

CSS style sheets work in the same way whichever method is used, because they are applied in the standard CSS way.

## Applying Themes to Pages

You can apply a theme to a page in several ways, declaratively or programmatically. The simplest declarative way to apply a theme is via the `<%@ Page %>` directive, using the `Theme` or `StyleSheetTheme` attribute:

```
<%@ Page Theme="myTheme" ... %>
```

Or:

```
<%@ Page StyleSheetTheme="myTheme" ... %>
```

Here `myTheme` is the name defined for the theme.

Alternatively, you can specify a theme to use for all pages in a site using an entry in the `Web.config` file for your Web site:

```
<configuration xmlns="http://schemas.microsoft.com/.NetConfiguration/v2.0">
  <system.web>
    <pages Theme="myTheme" />
  </system.web>
</configuration>
```

# ASP.NET Development

Again, you can use `Theme` or `StyleSheetTheme` here. You can also be more specific by using `<location>` elements to override this setting for individual pages or directories, in the same way as this element was used in the previous section for security information.

Programmatically, you can apply themes in the code-behind file for a page. There is only one place where you are allowed to do this — in the `Page_PreInit()` event handler, which is triggered very early on in the life cycle of the page. In this event you simply have to set the `Page.Theme` or `Page.StyleSheetTheme` property to the name of the theme you want to apply, for example:

```
protected override void OnPreInit(EventArgs e)
{
   Page.Theme = "myTheme";
}
```

Because you are using code to do this, you can dynamically apply a theme file from a selection of themes. This technique is used in PCSDemoSite, as you see shortly.

## Defining Themes

Themes are defined in yet another of the "special" directories in ASP.NET — in this case `App_Themes`. The `App_Themes` directory can contain any number of subdirectories, one per theme, where the name of the subdirectory defines the name of the theme.

Defining a theme involves putting the required files for the theme in the theme subdirectory. For CSS style sheets you don't have to worry about the file name; the theme system simply looks for a file with a `.css` extension. Similarly, `.skin` files can have any file name, although it is recommended that you use multiple `.skin` files, one for each control type you want to skin, and each named after the control it skins.

Skin files contain server control definitions in exactly the same format as you'd use in standard ASP.NET pages. The difference is that the controls in skin files are never added to your page, they are simply used to extract properties. A definition for a button skin, typically placed in a file called `Button.skin`, might be as follows:

```
<asp:Button Runat="server" BackColor="#444499" BorderColor="#000000"
   ForeColor="#ccccff" />
```

This skin is actually taken from the `DefaultTheme` theme in PCSDemoSite, and is responsible for the look of the button on the Meeting Room Booker page you saw earlier in this chapter.

## Themes in PCSDemoSite

The PCSDemoSite Web site includes three themes that you can select on the `/Configuration/Themes/Default.aspx` page — as long as you are logged in as a member of the RegisteredUser or SiteAdministrator roles. This page is shown in Figure 27-15.

# Chapter 27

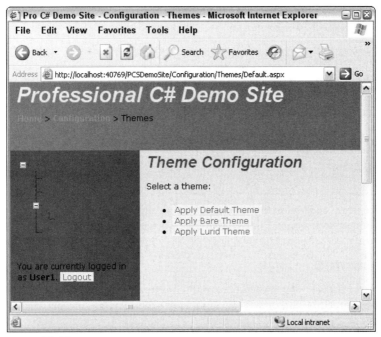

**Figure 27-15**

The theme in use here is `DefaultTheme`, but you can select from the other options on this page. Figure 27-16 shows the `BareTheme` theme.

This sort of theme is useful in, for example, printable versions of Web pages. The `BareTheme` directory actually consists of no files at all — the only file in use here is the root `StyleSheet.css` style sheet.

Figure 27-17 shows the `LuridTheme` theme.

This brightly colored and difficult to read theme is just a bit of fun really but does show how the look of a site can be dramatically changed using themes. On a more serious note, themes similar to this can be used to provide high contrast or large text versions of Web sites for accessibility purposes.

# ASP.NET Development

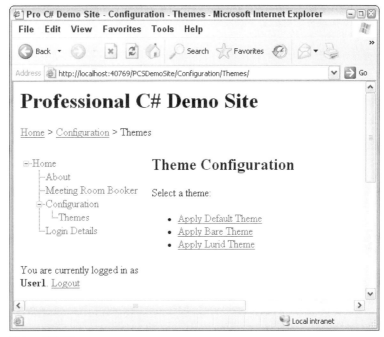

Figure 27-16

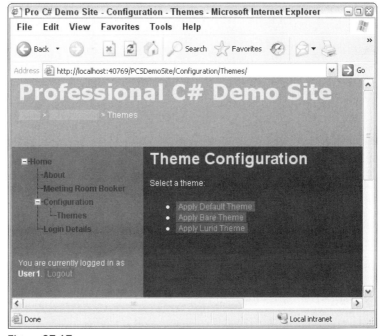

Figure 27-17

## Chapter 27

In PCSDemoSite the currently selected theme is stored in session state, so the theme is maintained when you navigate around the site. The code-behind file for `/Configuration/Themes/Default.aspx` is as follows:

```
public partial class _Default : MyPageBase
{
    private void ApplyTheme(string themeName)
    {
        if (Session["SessionTheme"] != null)
        {
            Session.Remove("SessionTheme");
        }
        Session.Add("SessionTheme", themeName);
        Response.Redirect("~/Configuration/Themes", true);
    }

    void applyDefaultTheme_Click(object sender, EventArgs e)
    {
        ApplyTheme("DefaultTheme");
    }

    void applyBareTheme_Click(object sender, EventArgs e)
    {
        ApplyTheme("BareTheme");
    }

    void applyLuridTheme_Click(object sender, EventArgs e)
    {
        ApplyTheme("LuridTheme");
    }
}
```

The key functionality here is in `ApplyTheme()`, which puts the name of the selected theme into session state, using the key `SessionTheme`. It also checks to see if there is already an entry here and if so removes it.

As mentioned earlier, themes must be applied in the `Page_PreInit()` event handler. This isn't accessible from the master page that all pages use, so if you want to apply a selected theme to all pages you are left with two options:

- ❏ Override the `Page_PreInit()` event handler in all pages where you want themes to be applied.
- ❏ Provide a common base class for all pages where you want themes to be applied, and override the `Page_PreInit()` event handler in this base class.

PCSDemoSite uses the second option, with a common page base class provided in `Code/MyPageBase.cs`:

```
public class MyPageBase : Page
{
    protected override void OnPreInit(EventArgs e)
    {
```

# ASP.NET Development

```
        // theming
        if (Session["SessionTheme"] != null)
        {
            Page.Theme = Session["SessionTheme"] as string;
        }
        else
        {
            Page.Theme = "DefaultTheme";
        }

        // base call
        base.OnPreInit(e);
    }
}
```

This event handler checks the session state for an entry in `SessionTheme` and applies the selected theme if there is one, otherwise `DefaultTheme` is used.

Note also that this class inherits from the usual page base class `Page`. This is necessary or else the page wouldn't function as an ASP.NET Web page.

The other thing necessary for this to work is to specify this base class for all Web pages. There are several ways of doing this, the most obvious being either in the <@ Page %> directive for a page or in the code behind a page. The former strategy is fine for simple pages but precludes the use of custom code behind for a page, since the page will no longer use the code in its own code behind file. The other alternative is to change the class that the page inherits from in the code behind file. By default, new pages inherit from Page, but you can change this. In the code behind file for the theme selection page shown earlier, you may have noticed the following code:

```
    public partial class _Default : MyPageBase
    {
        ...
    }
```

Here `MyPageBase` is specified as the base of the `_Default` class, and thus the method override in `MyPageBase.cs` is used.

## Summary

In this chapter you have looked at the several more advanced techniques for creating ASP.NET pages and Web sites, and saw these techniques in action in a demonstration Web site called PCSDemoSite.

First, you looked at how you can create reusable ASP.NET server controls using C#. You have seen how to create simple user controls from existing ASP.NET pages, as well as how to create custom controls from scratch. You also saw how the meeting room booker sample from the previous chapter can be reformatted as a user control.

# Chapter 27

Next you looked at master pages, and how you can provide a template for the pages of your Web site; another way to reuse code and simplify your development. In PCSDemoSite you saw a master page that included navigation Web server controls to enable users to move around the site, and laid the framework for themes. The themes you looked at later in the chapter are an excellent way to separate functionality from design, and can be a powerful accessibility technique.

You also took a brief look at security and saw how you can implement forms-based authentication on your Web sites with the minimum of effort.

You have only scratched the surface of what is possible in ASP.NET 2.0. For example, you can do a whole lot more with custom controls. It would have been interesting to discuss templates and data-binding, and how to create controls with this in mind. However, with the information in this chapter you should be able to start building (and experimenting with) your own custom controls, as well as all the other techniques discussed. For more details on ASP.NET, check out *Professional ASP.NET 1.1* (Wiley Publishing, Inc., ISBN: 0-7645-5890-0).

# Part VI
# Communication

Chapter 28: Web Services

Chapter 29: .NET Remoting

Chapter 30: Enterprise Services

Chapter 31: Message Queuing

Chapter 32: Future of Distributed Programming

# 28

# Web Services

*Web services* are a new way of performing remote method calls over HTTP that can make use of *Simple Object Access Protocol* (SOAP). In the past this issue has been fraught with difficulty, as anyone who has any DCOM (Distributed COM) experience knows. The act of instantiating an object on a remote server, calling a method, and obtaining the result was far from simple, and the necessary configuration was even trickier.

SOAP simplifies matters immensely. This technology is an XML-based standard that details how method calls can be made over HTTP in a reproducible manner. A remote SOAP server is capable of understanding these calls and performing all the hard work for you, such as instantiating the required object, making the call, and returning a SOAP-formatted response to the client.

The .NET Framework makes it very easy for you to make use of all this. As with ASP.NET, you are able to use the full array of C# and .NET techniques on the server, but (perhaps more importantly) the simple consumption of Web services can be achieved from any platform with HTTP access to the server. In other words, it is conceivable that Linux code could, for example, use .NET Web Services, or even Internet-enabled fridges. To quote a real-world example, in the past I have had great success combining Web services with Macromedia Flash to create data-enabled flash content.

In addition, Web services can be completely described using *Web Service Description Language* (WSDL), allowing dynamic discovery of Web services at runtime. WSDL provides descriptions of all methods (along with the types required to call them) using XML with XML schemas. A wide variety of types are available to Web services, which range from simple primitive types to full `DataSet` objects, such that full in-memory databases can be marshaled to a client, which can result in a dramatic reduction in load on a database server.

In this chapter, you do the following:

- Look at the syntax of SOAP and WSDL, then move on to see how they are used by Web services.

- Learn how to expose and consume Web services.

## Chapter 28

❑ Work through a complete example building on the meeting room booking application from Chapter 26, "ASP.NET Pages," and Chapter 27, "ASP.NET Development," to illustrate the use of Web services.

❑ Learn how to exchange data using SOAP Headers.

# SOAP

As mentioned, one method used to exchange data with Web services is SOAP. This technology has had a lot of press, especially since Microsoft decided to adopt it for use in the .NET Framework. Now, though, the excitement seems to be dying down a bit as the SOAP specification is finalized. When you think about it, finding out exactly how SOAP works is a bit like finding out about how HTTP works—interesting, but not essential. Most of the time you don't have to worry about the format of the exchanges made with Web services; they just happen, you get the results you want, and everyone is happy.

For this reason, this section won't go into a huge amount of depth, but you will see some simple SOAP requests and responses so you can get a feel for what is going on under the hood.

Imagine that you want to call a method in a Web service with the following signature:

```
int DoSomething(string stringParam, int intParam)
```

The SOAP headers and body required for this are shown in the following code, with the address of the Web service (more on this later) at the top:

```
POST /SomeLocation/myWebService.asmx HTTP/1.1
Host: hostname
Content-Type: text/xml; charset=utf-8
Content-Length: length
SOAPAction: "http://tempuri.org/DoSomething"
<?xml version="1.0" encoding="utf-8"?>
<soap:Envelope xmlns:xsi="http://www.w3.org/2001/XMLSchema-instance"
               xmlns:xsd="http://www.w3.org/2001/XMLSchema"
               xmlns:soap="http://schemas.xmlsoap.org/soap/envelope/">
   <soap:Body>
      <DoSomething xmlns="http://tempuri.org/">
         <stringParam>string</stringParam>
         <intParam>int</intParam>
      </DoSomething>
   </soap:Body>
</soap:Envelope>
```

The `length` parameter here specifies the total byte size of the content and will vary depending on the values sent in the `string` and `int` parameters. `Host` will also vary, depending on where the Web service is located.

The `soap` namespace referenced here defines various elements that you use to build your message. When you send this over HTTP, the actual data sent is slightly different (but related). For example, you could call the preceding method using the simple GET method:

```
GET /SomeLocation/myWebService.asmx/DoSomething?stringParam=string&intParam=int
   HTTP/1.1
Host: hostname
```

The SOAP response of this method is as follows:

```
HTTP/1.1 200 OK
Content-Type: text/xml; charset=utf-8
Content-Length: length
<?xml version="1.0" encoding="utf-8"?>
<soap:Envelope xmlns:xsi="http://www.w3.org/2001/XMLSchema-instance"
               xmlns:xsd="http://www.w3.org/2001/XMLSchema"
               xmlns:soap="http://schemas.xmlsoap.org/soap/envelope/">
   <soap:Body>
      <DoSomethingResponse xmlns="http://tempuri.org/">
         <DoSomethingResult>int</DoSomethingResult>
      </DoSomethingResponse>
   </soap:Body>
</soap:Envelope>
```

where `length` varies depending on to the contents, in this case int.

The actual response over HTTP is simpler, as shown in this example:

```
HTTP/1.1 200 OK
Content-Type: text/xml; charset=utf-8
Content-Length: length
<?xml version="1.0"?>
<int xmlns="http://tempuri.org/">int</int>
```

This is a far simpler XML format.

As discussed at the start of this section, the beauty of all this is that you can ignore it completely. Only if you want to do something really odd does the exact syntax become important.

# WSDL

WSDL completely describes Web services, the methods available, and the various ways of calling these methods. The exact details of this process won't really benefit you that much, but a general understanding is useful.

WSDL is another fully XML-compliant syntax, and specifies Web services by the methods available, the types used by these methods, the formats of request and response messages sent to and from methods via various protocols (pure SOAP, HTTP GET, and so on), and various bindings between these specifications. WSDL is understood by a variety of clients — not just .NET ones, but others such as Macromedia Flash, as mentioned in the introduction to this chapter.

Perhaps the most important part of a WSDL file is the type-definition section. This section uses XML schemas to describe the format for data exchange with the XML elements that can be used and their relationships.

For example, the Web service method used as an example in the last section:

```
int DoSomething(string stringParam, int intParam)
```

would have types declared for the request as follows:

```xml
<?xml version="1.0" encoding="utf-8"?>
<definitions xmlns:http="http://schemas.xmlsoap.org/wsdl/http/"
             xmlns:soap="http://schemas.xmlsoap.org/wsdl/soap/"
             xmlns:s="http://www.w3.org/2001/XMLSchema"
             xmlns:wsdl="http://schemas.xmlsoap.org/wsdl"
             ...other namespaces...>
   <wsdl:types>
      <s:schema elementFormDefault="qualified"
                targetNamespace="http://tempuri.org/">
         <s:element name="DoSomething">
            <s:complexType>
               <s:sequence>
                  <s:element minOccurs="0" maxOccurs="1" name="stringParam"
                             type="s:string" />
                  <s:element minOccurs="1" maxOccurs="1" name="intParam"
                             type="s:int" />
               </s:sequence>
            </s:complexType>
         </s:element>
         <s:element name="DoSomethingResponse">
            <s:complexType>
               <s:sequence>
                  <s:element minOccurs="1" maxOccurs="1" name="DoSomethingResult"
                             type="s:int" />
               </s:sequence>
            </s:complexType>
         </s:element>
      </s:schema>
   </wsdl:types>
   ...other definitions...
</definitions>
```

These types are all that are required for the SOAP and HTTP requests and responses you saw earlier, and are bound to these operations later in the file. All the types are specified using standard XML schema syntax, for example:

```xml
            <s:element name="DoSomethingResponse">
               <s:complexType>
                  <s:sequence>
                     <s:element minOccurs="1" maxOccurs="1" name="DoSomethingResult"
                                type="s:int" />
                  </s:sequence>
               </s:complexType>
            </s:element>
```

This specifies that an element called `DoSomethingResponse` has a child element called `DoSomethingResult` that contains an integer. This integer must occur between 1 or 1 times, meaning that it must be included.

# Web Services

If you have access to the WSDL for a Web service, you can use it. As you see shortly, this isn't that difficult to do.

After this brief look at SOAP and WSDL it's time to move on to discuss how you create and consume Web services.

## Web Services

The information about Web services in this chapter is divided into two subsections:

❏ "Exposing Web Services," which concerns writing Web services and placing them on Web Servers.

❏ "Consuming Web Services," which concerns using the services you design on a client.

### Exposing Web Services

Web services are exposed by placing code either directly into .asmx files or by referencing Web service classes from these files. As with ASP.NET pages, creating a Web service in Visual Studio .NET uses the latter method, and you will too for demonstration purposes.

Create a Web service project (via File ➪ New ➪ Web Site...) in the C:\ProCSharp\Chapter28 directory and call it PCSWebService1 (see Figure 28-1). Creating a Web service project generates a similar set of files as creating a Web application project, and you have the same location options for creating the project. In fact, the only difference is that instead of a file called Default.aspx, a file called Service.asmx is created, with code-behind in App_Code/Service.cs.

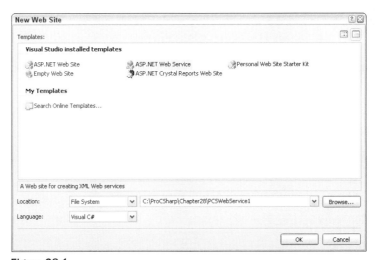

Figure 28-1

The code in `Service.asmx` is as follows:

```
<%@ WebService Language="C#" CodeBehind="~/App_Code/Service.cs" Class="Service" %>
```

This references the code file `/App_Code/Service.cs`. The following listing shows the generated code:

```csharp
using System;
using System.Web;
using System.Web.Services;
using System.Web.Services.Protocols;

[WebService(Namespace = "http://tempuri.org/")]
[WebServiceBinding(ConformsTo = WsiProfiles.BasicProfile1_1)]
public class Service : System.Web.Services.WebService
{
    public Service()
    {

    }

    [WebMethod]
    public string HelloWorld()
    {
        return "Hello World";
    }
}
```

This code contains several standard namespace references, and defines the Web service class `Service` (which is referenced in `Service.asmx`), which inherits from `System.Web.Services.WebService`. The `WebService` attribute specifies the namespace for the web service, which enables client applications to differentiate between web service methods with the same name, but on different web services. The `WebServiceBinding` attribute relates to Web service interoperability, as defined in the WS-I Basic Profile 1.1 specification. Put simply, this attribute can declare that a Web service supports a standard WSDL description for one or more of its Web methods, or, as is the case here, defines a new set of WSDL definitions. It is now up to you to provide additional methods on this Web service class.

Adding a method accessible through the Web service simply requires defining the method as `public` and giving it the `WebMethod` attribute. This attribute simply labels the methods you want to be accessible through the Web service. You look at the types you can use for the return type and parameters shortly, but for now replace the autogenerated `HelloWorld()` method with the following one:

```csharp
[WebMethod]
public string CanWeFixIt()
{
    return "Yes we can!";
}
```

Now compile the project.

To see whether everything works, run the application with Ctrl+F5 and you'll be taken straight to the test interface for the Web service, as shown in Figure 28-2.

# Web Services

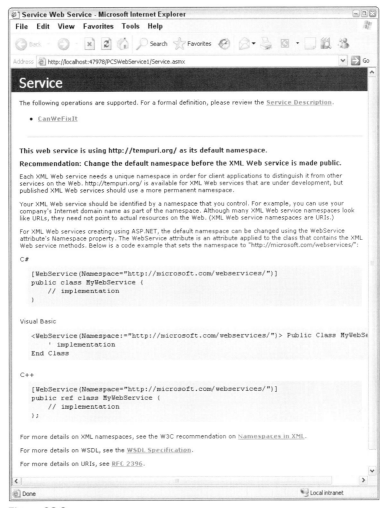

Figure 28-2

Most of the text shown in the browser concerns the fact that the Web service namespace is set to `http://tempuri.org/`. This isn't a problem during development, although (as the text says) it should be changed later on. This can be done using the `WebService` attribute as shown. For now, though, you'll leave things as they are.

Clicking the method name gives you information about the SOAP request and response, as well as examples of how the request and response will look using the HTTP GET and HTTP POST methods. You can also test the method by clicking the Invoke button. If the method requires simple parameters, you can enter these on this form as well (for more complex parameters this form won't allow you to test the method in this way). If you do this you, will see the XML returned by the method call:

```
<?xml version="1.0" encoding="utf-8"?>
<string xmlns="http://tempuri.org/">Yes we can!</string>
```

This demonstrates that your method is working perfectly.

Following the Service Description link from the browser screen shown in Figure 28-2 allows you to view the WSDL description of the Web service. The most important part is the description of the element types for requests and responses:

```
<wsdl:types>
  <s:schema elementFormDefault="qualified" targetNamespace="http://tempuri.org/">
    <s:element name="CanWeFixIt">
      <s:complexType />
    </s:element>
    <s:element name="CanWeFixItResponse">
      <s:complexType>
        <s:sequence>
          <s:element minOccurs="0" maxOccurs="1" name="CanWeFixItResult"
                     type="s:string" />
        </s:sequence>
      </s:complexType>
    </s:element>
  </s:schema>
</wsdl:types>
```

The description also contains descriptions of the types required for requests and responses, as well as various bindings for the service, making it quite a long file.

## Types available for Web services

Web services can be used to exchange any of the following types:

| | | |
|---|---|---|
| String | Char | Byte |
| Boolean | Int16 | Int32 |
| Int64 | UInt16 | UInt32 |
| UInt64 | Single | Double |
| Guid | Decimal | DateTime |
| XmlQualifiedName | Class | struct |
| XmlNode | DataSet | enum |

Arrays of all these types are also allowed, as are generic collection types such as `List<string>`. Note also that only public properties and fields of `Class` and `struct` types are marshaled.

# Consuming Web Services

Now that you know how to create Web services, in this section you look at how to use them. To do this, you need to generate a proxy class in your code that knows how to communicate with a given Web service. Any calls from your code to the Web service will go through this proxy, which looks identical to the Web service, giving your code the illusion that you have a local copy of it. In actual fact there is a lot of

# Web Services

HTTP communication going on, but you are shielded from the details. There are two ways of doing this. You can either use the WSDL.exe command line tool or the Add Web Reference menu option in Visual Studio .NET.

Using WSDL.exe from the command line generates a `.cs` file containing a proxy class, based on the WSDL description of the Web service. You specify this using the URL of the Web service, for example:

```
WSDL http://localhost:61968/PCSWebService1/Service.asmx?WSDL
```

*Note that both here and in the example that follows you are using the default file system hosting for Web applications. In order for the preceding URL to work the Visual Web Developer Web Server for the Web service must be running. There is also no guarantee that the port number for the Web service (in this case 61968) will stay the same. While this is fine for illustration, typically you will want your Web services to reside on a fixed Web server such as IIS — otherwise you'll have to continually remake proxy classes. One way to make sure the Web service is available for testing is to include multiple Web sites in one solution.*

This generates a proxy class for the example from the previous section in a file called `Service.cs`. The class will be named after the Web service, in this case `Service`, and contain methods that call identically named methods of the service. To use this class you simply add the `.cs` file generated to a project and use code along the lines of:

```
Service myService = new Service();
string result = myService.CanWeFixIt();
```

By default, the class generated is placed in the root namespace, so no `using` statement is necessary, but you can specify a different namespace to use with the `/n:<namespace>` command-line option of WSDL.exe.

This technique works fine but can be annoying to continually redo if the service is being developed and changing continuously. Of course, it could be executed in the build options for a project in order to automatically update the generated proxy before each compile, but there is a better way.

This better way is illustrated by creating a client for the example in the previous section, in a new Web site called PCSWebClient1 (in the C:\ProCSharp\Chapter 28 directory). Create this project now and add the following code to `Default.aspx`:

```
<form id="form1" runat="server">
  <div>
    <asp:Label Runat="server" ID="resultLabel" />
    <br />
    <asp:Button Runat="server" ID="triggerButton" Text="Invoke CanWeFixIt()"
      OnClick="triggerButton_Click" />
  </div>
</form>
```

You'll bind the button-click event handler to the Web service shortly. First, you must add a reference to the Web service to your project. To do this, right-click the new client project in the Solution Explorer and select the Add Web Reference... option. In the window that appears, type the URL of the Web service `Service.asmx` file, or use the "Web services on the local machine" link to find it automatically, as shown in Figure 28-3.

991

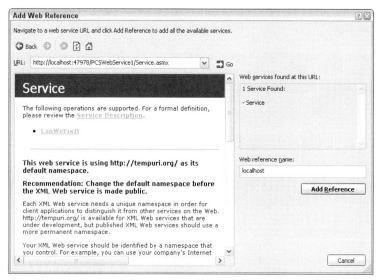

**Figure 28-3**

From here you can add a reference with the Add Reference button. First, though, change the default entry for Web reference name from `localhost` to `myWebService`. Pressing the Add Reference button now adds `myWebService` to the `WebReferences` folder of the project in Solution Explorer. If you examine this folder in the Solution Explorer widow, you can see that the files `Service.disco`, `Service.discomap`, and `Service.wsdl` have been added to the project.

The Web reference name, `myWebService`, is also the namespace you need to reference to use the proxy class that has been created for you. Add the following using statement to your code in `Default.aspx.cs`:

```
using myWebService;
```

Now you can use the service in your class without fully qualifying its name.

Add an event handler to the button on the form with the following code:

```
protected void triggerButton_Click(object sender, EventArgs e)
{
    Service myService = new Service();
    resultLabel.Text = myService.CanWeFixIt();
}
```

Running the application and clicking the button displays the result of `CanWeFixIt()` in the browser window.

> *Note that if you are using the ASP.NET Development Server (that is, your web applications are hosted on the local file system not IIS) you may get a 401: Unauthorized error. This is because this server is configured to require NTLM authentication by default. To fix this you can either disable this setting by unchecking the NTLM Authentication box on the Start Options page of the property pages for PCSWebService1 or pass default credentials when calling the web service method. This latter option*

# Web Services

*requires the code* `myService.Credentials = System.Net.CredentialCache.DefaultCredentials;`.

This Web service might change later, but with this method you can simply right-click the `WebReference` folder in the Server Explorer and select Update Web Reference. This generates a new proxy class for you to use.

# Extending the Event-Booking Example

Now that you know the basics of creating and consuming Web services, you can apply your knowledge to extending the meeting room booker application from the previous two chapters. Specifically, you extract the database access aspects from the application and place them into a Web service. This Web service has two methods:

- `GetData()`, which returns a `DataSet` object containing all three tables in the `PCSWebApp3` database.
- `AddEvent()`, which adds an event and returns the number of rows affected so the client application can check that a change has been made.

In addition, you'll design the Web service with load-reducing in mind. Specifically, you'll store a `DataSet` containing the meeting room booker data at the application level in the Web service application. This means that multiple requests for the data won't require additional database requests. The data in this application-level `DataSet` object will only be refreshed when new data is added to the database. This means that changes made to the database by other means, such as manual editing, will *not* be reflected in the `DataSet`. Still, as long as you know that your Web service is the only application with direct access to the data you have nothing to worry about.

## The Event-Booking Web Service

Create a new Web service project in Visual Studio in the C:\ProCSharp\Chapter28 directory and call it PCSWebService2. The first thing to do is to copy the database files (`MeetingRoomBooker.mdf` and `MeetingRoomBooker_log.ldf`) from PCSWebApp3 (or PCSDemoSite). Next you need to add a `Global.asax` file to the project, then modify the code in its `Application_Start()` event handler. You want to load all the data in the MeetingRoomBooker database into a data set and store it. This mostly involves code that you've already seen, because getting the database into a `DataSet` is something you've already done. You'll also use a connection string stored in `Web.config` as you've seen in earlier chapters. The code for the `Web.config` is as follows (the connection string should be placed on a single line):

```xml
<?xml version="1.0" ?>
<configuration xmlns="http://schemas.microsoft.com/.NetConfiguration/v2.0">
  <appSettings />
  <connectionStrings>
    <add name="MRBConnectionString"
      connectionString="Data Source=.\SQLExpress;Integrated
        Security=True;AttachDBFilename=|DataDirectory|MeetingRoomBooker.mdf"
      providerName="System.Data.SqlClient"/>
  </connectionStrings>
</configuration>
```

And the code for the `Application_Start()` event handler in `Global.asax` is as follows:

```csharp
void Application_Start(Object sender, EventArgs e)
{
    System.Data.DataSet ds;
    System.Data.SqlClient.SqlConnection sqlConnection1;
    System.Data.SqlClient.SqlDataAdapter daAttendees;
    System.Data.SqlClient.SqlDataAdapter daRooms;
    System.Data.SqlClient.SqlDataAdapter daEvents;

    sqlConnection1 = new System.Data.SqlClient.SqlConnection();
    sqlConnection1.ConnectionString =
        ConfigurationManager.ConnectionStrings["MRBConnectionString"]
          .ConnectionString;

    sqlConnection1.Open();

    ds = new System.Data.DataSet();
    daAttendees = new System.Data.SqlClient.SqlDataAdapter(
                    "SELECT * FROM Attendees", sqlConnection1);
    daRooms = new System.Data.SqlClient.SqlDataAdapter(
                    "SELECT * FROM Rooms", sqlConnection1);
    daEvents = new System.Data.SqlClient.SqlDataAdapter(
                    "SELECT * FROM Events", sqlConnection1);

    daAttendees.Fill(ds, "Attendees");
    daRooms.Fill(ds, "Rooms");
    daEvents.Fill(ds, "Events");

    sqlConnection1.Close();

    Application["ds"] = ds;
}
```

The important code to note here is in the last line. `Application` objects (like `Session` objects) have a collection of name-value pairs that you can use to store data. Here you are creating a name in the `Application` store called `ds`, which takes the serialized value of `ds` containing the `Attendees`, `Rooms`, and `Events` tables from your database. This value will be accessible to all instances of the Web service at any time.

This technique is very useful for read-only data because multiple threads will be able to access it, reducing the load on your database. Note, however, that the `Events` table is likely to change, and you'll have to update the application-level `DataSet` class when this happens. You look at this shortly.

Next you can replace the default `Service` service with a new service, called `MRBService`. To do this, delete the existing `Service.asmx` and `Service.cs` files and add a new Web service to the project called `MRBService`. You can then add the `GetData()` method to your service in `MRBService.cs`:

```csharp
[WebMethod]
public DataSet GetData()
{
    return (DataSet) Application["ds"];
}
```

# Web Services

This uses the same syntax as `Application_Load()` to access the stored `DataSet`, which you simply cast to the correct type and return.

Note that for this to work, and to make life easier in the other Web method you'll be adding, you can add the following `using` statements:

```
using System;
using System.Configuration;
using System.Data;
using System.Web;
using System.Collections;
using System.Web.Services;
using System.Web.Services.Protocols;
```

The `AddEvent()` method is slightly more complicated. Conceptually, you need to do the following:

- ❏ Accept event data from the client.
- ❏ Create a SQL `INSERT` command using this data.
- ❏ Connect to the database and execute the SQL statement.
- ❏ Refresh the data in `Application["ds"]` if the addition is successful.
- ❏ Return a success or failure notification to the client (you'll leave it up to the client to refresh its `DataSet` if required).

Starting from the top, you'll accept all fields in their correct data types:

```
[WebMethod]
public int AddEvent(string eventName, int eventRoom,
                    string eventAttendees, DateTime eventDate)
{
    ...
}
```

Next, you declare the objects you'll need for database access, connect to the database, and execute your query, all using similar code to that in PCSWebApp3 (remember, you need the connection string here, taken from `Web.config`):

```
[WebMethod]
public int AddEvent(string eventName, int eventRoom,
                    string eventAttendees, DateTime eventDate)
{
    System.Data.SqlClient.SqlConnection sqlConnection1;
    System.Data.SqlClient.SqlDataAdapter daEvents;
    DataSet ds;

    sqlConnection1 = new System.Data.SqlClient.SqlConnection();
    sqlConnection1.ConnectionString =
       ConfigurationManager.ConnectionStrings["MRBConnectionString"]
          .ConnectionString;

    System.Data.SqlClient.SqlCommand insertCommand =
```

995

```
            new System.Data.SqlClient.SqlCommand("INSERT INTO [Events] (Name, Room, "
                + "AttendeeList, EventDate) VALUES   (@Name, @Room, @AttendeeList, "
                + "@EventDate)", sqlConnection1);
        insertCommand.Parameters.Add("Name", SqlDbType.VarChar, 255).Value
            = eventName;
        insertCommand.Parameters.Add("Room", SqlDbType.Int, 4).Value
            = eventRoom;
        insertCommand.Parameters.Add("AttendeeList", SqlDbType.Text, 16).Value
            = eventAttendees;
        insertCommand.Parameters.Add("EventDate", SqlDbType.DateTime, 8).Value
            = eventDate;

        sqlConnection1.Open();

        int queryResult = insertCommand.ExecuteNonQuery();
    }
```

You use `queryResult` to store the number of rows affected by the query as before. You can check this to see whether it is 1 to gauge your success. If you are successful, you execute a new query on the database to refresh the `Events` table in your `DataSet`. It is vital to lock the application data while you perform updates to ensure that no other threads can access `Application["ds"]` while you update it. You can do this using the `Lock()` and `UnLock()` methods of the `Application` object:

```
[WebMethod]
public int AddEvent(string eventName, int eventRoom,
                    string eventAttendees, DateTime eventDate)
{
    ...
    int queryResult = insertCommand.ExecuteNonQuery();
    if (queryResult == 1)
    {
        daEvents = new System.Data.SqlClient.SqlDataAdapter(
                    "SELECT * FROM Events", sqlConnection1);
        ds = (DataSet)Application["ds"];
        ds.Tables["Events"].Clear();
        daEvents.Fill(ds, "Events");
        Application.Lock();
        Application["ds"] = ds;
        Application.UnLock();
    }

    sqlConnection1.Close();
}
```

Finally, you return `queryResult`, allowing the client to know if the query was successful:

```
[WebMethod]
public int AddEvent(string eventName, int eventRoom,
                    string eventAttendees, DateTime eventDate)
{
    ...
    return queryResult;
}
```

# Web Services

And with that, you have completed your Web service. As before, you can test this service out simply by viewing the `.asmx` file in a Web browser, so you can add records and look at the XML representation of the `DataSet` returned by `GetData()` without writing any client code.

Before moving on, it's worth discussing the use of `DataSet` objects with Web services. At first glance this seems like a fantastic way of exchanging data, and indeed it is an extremely powerful technique. However, the fact that the `DataSet` class is so versatile does have implications. If you examine the WSDL generated for the `GetData()` method, you'll see the following:

```xml
<s:element name="GetDataResponse">
  <s:complexType>
    <s:sequence>
      <s:element minOccurs="0" maxOccurs="1" name="GetDataResult">
        <s:complexType>
          <s:sequence>
            <s:element ref="s:schema" />
            <s:any />
          </s:sequence>
        </s:complexType>
      </s:element>
    </s:sequence>
  </s:complexType>
</s:element>
```

As you can see, this is very generic code, which allows the `DataSet` object passed to contain any data specified with an inline schema. Unfortunately, this does mean that the WSDL is not completely describing the Web service. For .NET clients this isn't a problem, and things progress as naturally as they did when passing a simple string in the earlier example, the only difference being that you exchange a `DataSet` object. However, non-.NET clients must have prior knowledge of the data that will be passed or some equivalent of a `DataSet` class in order to access the data.

A workaround to this requirement is to repackage the data into a different format — an array of structs, for example. If you were to do this, you could customize the XML produced in any way you want, and the XML could be completely described by the schema for the Web service. This can also have an impact in terms of performance, because passing a `DataSet` object can result in an awful lot of XML — far more than is necessary in most cases. The overhead resulting from repackaging data is likely to be much less than that associated with sending the data over the Web, and because there'll probably be less data the serialization and deserialization is also likely to be quicker, so if performance is an issue you probably should avoid using `DataSet` objects in this way — unless of course you will be making use of the additional functionality that `DataSet` objects make available to you.

For the purposes of this example, though, using a `DataSet` object is not a problem and greatly simplifies other code.

## *The Event-Booking Client*

The client you use in this section is a development of the PCSDemoSite Web site from the previous chapter. Call this application PCSDemoSite2, in the directory C:\ProCSharp\Chapter28, and use the code from PCSDemoSite as a starting point.

You'll make two major modifications to the project. First, you'll remove all direct database access from this application and use the Web service instead. Second, you'll introduce an application-level store of the `DataSet` object returned from the Web service that is updated only when necessary, meaning that even less of a load is placed on the database.

The first thing to do to your new Web application is to add a Web reference to the `PCSWebService2/MRBService.asmx` service. You can do this in the same way you saw earlier in this chapter through right-clicking on the project in Server Explorer, locating the `.asmx` file, calling the Web reference `MRBService`, and clicking Add Reference. Because you aren't using the local database anymore you can also delete that from the `App_Data` directory, and remove the `MRBConnectionString` entry from `Web.config`. All the rest of the modifications are to `MRB.ascx` and `MRB.ascx.cs`.

To start with, you can delete all the data sources on `MRB.ascx`, and remove the `DataSourceID` entries on all the currently data-bound controls. This is because you'll be handling the data binding yourself from the code-behind file.

> Note that when you change or remove the `DataSourceID` property of a Web server control you may be asked if you want to remove the templates you have defined, because there is no guarantee that the data the control will work with will be valid for those templates. In this case you'll be using the same data, just from a different source, so make sure you keep the templates. If you do delete them the HTML layout of the result will revert to the default, which won't look very nice, so you'd have to add them again from scratch or rewrite them.

Next, you'll need to add a property to `MRB.ascx.cs` to store the `DataSet` returned by the Web service. This property will actually use Application state storage, in much the same way as `Global.asax` in the Web service. The code is as follows:

```
public DataSet MRBData
{
   get
   {
      if (Application["mrbData"] == null)
      {
         Application.Lock();
         MRBService.MRBService service = new MRBService.MRBService();
         service.Credentials = System.Net.CredentialCache.DefaultCredentials;
         Application["mrbData"] = service.GetData();
         Application.UnLock();
      }
      return Application["mrbData"] as DataSet;
   }
   set
   {
      Application.Lock();
      if (value == null && Application["mrbData"] != null)
      {
         Application.Remove("mrbData");
      }
      else
      {
         Application["mrbData"] = value;
      }
      Application.UnLock();
   }
}
```

# Web Services

Note that you need to lock and unlock the Application state, also just like in the Web service. Also, note that the `Application["mrbData"]` storage is filled only when necessary, that is, when it is empty. This `DataSet` object is now available to all instances of PCSDemoSite2, meaning that multiple users can read data without any calls to the Web service or indeed to the database. The credentials are also set here, which as noted earlier is necessary for using Web services hosted using the ASP.NET Development Server. You can comment out this line if you don't need it.

To bind to the controls on the Web page, you can supply `DataView` properties that map to data stored in this property, as follows:

```
private DataView EventData
{
   get
   {
      return MRBData.Tables["Events"].DefaultView;
   }
}

private DataView RoomData
{
   get
   {
      return MRBData.Tables["Rooms"].DefaultView;
   }
}

private DataView AttendeeData
{
   get
   {
      return MRBData.Tables["Attendees"].DefaultView;
   }
}

private DataView EventDetailData
{
   get
   {
      if (EventList != null && EventList.SelectedValue != null)
      {
         return new DataView(MRBData.Tables["Events"], "ID=" +
            EventList.SelectedValue.ToString(), "",
            DataViewRowState.CurrentRows);
      }
      else
      {
         return null;
      }
   }
}
```

You can also remove the existing `eventData` field and `EventData` property.

Most of these properties are simple; it's only the last that does anything new. In this case, you are filtering the data in the `Events` table to obtain just one event—ready to display in the detail view `FormView` control.

Now that you aren't using data source controls, you have to bind data yourself. A call to the `DataBind()` method of the page will achieve this, but you also need to set the data source `DataView` properties for the various data-bound controls on the page. One good way to do this is to do it during an override of the `OnDataBinding()` event handler, as follows:

```
protected override void OnDataBinding(EventArgs e)
{
   roomList.DataSource = RoomData;
   attendeeList.DataSource = AttendeeData;
   EventList.DataSource = EventData;
   FormView1.DataSource = EventDetailData;
   base.OnDataBinding(e);
}
```

Here you are just setting the `DataSource` properties of `roomList`, `attendeeList`, `EventList`, and `FormView1` to the properties defined earlier. Next, you can add the `DataBind()` call to `Page_Load()`:

```
void Page_Load(object sender, EventArgs e)
{
   if (!this.IsPostBack)
   {
      nameBox.Text = Context.User.Identity.Name;
      System.DateTime trialDate = System.DateTime.Now;
      calendar.SelectedDate = GetFreeDate(trialDate);
      DataBind();
   }
}
```

Also, you must change `submitButton_Click()` to use the Web service `AddData()` method. Again, much of the code can remain unchanged; only the data addition code needs changing:

```
void submitButton_Click(object sender, EventArgs e)
{
   if (Page.IsValid)
   {
      string attendees = "";
      foreach (ListItem attendee in attendeeList.Items)
      {
         if (attendee.Selected)
         {
            attendees += attendee.Text + " (" + attendee.Value
                     + "), ";
         }
      }
      attendees += " and " + nameBox.Text;

      try
      {
```

# Web Services

```
            MRBService.MRBService service = new MRBService.MRBService();
            if (service.AddEvent(eventBox.Text, int.Parse(roomList.SelectedValue),
               attendees, calendar.SelectedDate) == 1)
            {
               MRBData = null;
               DataBind();
               calendar.SelectedDate =
                  GetFreeDate(calendar.SelectedDate.AddDays(1));
            }
         }
      }
      catch
      {
      }
   }
}
```

In fact, all you've really done here is simplify things a great deal. This is often the case when using well-designed Web services — you can forget about much of the workings and instead concentrate on the user experience.

There isn't a huge amount to comment on in this code. Continuing to make use of `queryResult` is a bonus, and locking the application is essential as already noted.

One final modification is required: `EventList_SelectedIndexChanged()`:

```
void EventList_SelectedIndexChanged(object sender, EventArgs e)
{
    FormView1.DataSource = EventDetailData;
    EventList.DataSource = EventData;
    EventList.DataBind();
    FormView1.DataBind();
}
```

This is simply to make sure that the data sources for the event list and detail views are refreshed properly.

The meeting room booker in the PCSDemoSite2 Web site should look and function exactly like the one in PCSDemoSite, but perform substantially better. You can also use the same Web service very easily for other applications — simply displaying events on a page, for example, or even editing events, attendee names, and rooms if you add some more methods. Doing this won't break PCSDemoSite2 because it will simply ignore any new methods created. You will, however, have to introduce some kind of trigger mechanism to update the data cached in the event list, because modifying this data elsewhere will cause data to go out of date.

# Exchanging Data Using SOAP Headers

One final topic to look at in this chapter is using SOAP headers to exchange information, rather than including information in method parameters. The reason for covering it is that it is a very nice system to use for maintaining a user login. This section won't go into detail about setting up your server for SSL connections, or the various methods of authentication that can be configured using IIS, because these do not affect the Web service code you need to get this behavior.

# Chapter 28

Say you have a service that contains a simple authentication method with a signature as follows:

```
AuthenticationToken AuthenticateUser(string userName, string password);
```

where `AuthenticationToken` is a type you define that can be used by the user in later method calls, for example:

```
void DoSomething(AuthenticationToken token, OtherParamType param);
```

After logging in, the user has access to other methods using the token received from `AuthenticateUser()`. This technique is typical of secure Web systems, although it is often implemented in a far more complex way.

You can simplify this process further by using a SOAP header to exchange tokens (or any other data). You can restrict methods so that they can only be called if a specified SOAP header is included in the method call. This simplifies their structure as follows:

```
void DoSomething(OtherParamType param);
```

The advantage here is that, after you have set the header on the client, it persists. After an initial bit of setting up, you can ignore authentication tokens in all further Web method calls.

To see this in action create a new Web service project called PCSWebService3 in the directory C:\ProCSharp\Chapter28\, and add a new class to the `App_Code` directory called `AuthenticationToken` as follows:

```
using System;
using System.Web.Services.Protocols;

public class AuthenticationToken : SoapHeader
{
    public Guid InnerToken;
}
```

You'll use a GUID to identify the token, a common procedure, because you can be sure that it is unique.

To declare that the Web service can have a custom SOAP header you simply add a public member to the service class of your new type:

```
public class Service : System.Web.Services.WebService
{
    public AuthenticationToken AuthenticationTokenHeader;
```

You will also need to use the `System.Web.Services.Protocols.SoapHeaderAttribute` attribute to mark those Web methods that require the extra SOAP header in order work. However, before you add such a method, you can add a very simple `Login()` method that clients can use to obtain an authentication token:

```
[WebMethod(true)]
public Guid Login(string userName, string password)
{
```

```csharp
        if ((userName == "Karli") && (password == "Cheese"))
        {
            Guid currentUser = Guid.NewGuid();
            Session["currentUser"] = currentUser;
            return currentUser;
        }
        else
        {
            Session["currentUser"] = null;
            return Guid.Empty;
        }
    }
```

If the correct username and password are used, then a new `Guid` object is generated, stored in a session-level variable, and returned to the user. If authentication fails, an empty `Guid` instance is returned and stored at the session level. The `true` parameter enables session state for this Web method, because it is disabled by default in Web services and it is required for this functionality.

Next you have a method that accepts the header, as specified by the `SoapHeaderAttribute` attribute:

```csharp
    [WebMethod(true)]
    [SoapHeaderAttribute("AuthenticationTokenHeader",
                         Direction = SoapHeaderDirection.In)]
    public string DoSomething()
    {
        if (Session["currentUser"] != null &&
            AuthenticationTokenHeader != null &&
            AuthenticationTokenHeader.InnerToken
            == (Guid)Session["currentUser"])
        {
            return "Authentication OK.";
        }
        else
        {
            return "Authentication failed.";
        }
    }
```

This returns one of two strings, depending on whether the `AuthenticationTokenHeader` header exists, isn't an empty `Guid` and matches the one stored in `Session["currentUser"]` (if this `Session` variable exists).

Next you must create a quick client to test this service. Add a new Web site called PCSWebClient2 to the solution, with the following simple code for the user interface:

```aspx
    <form id="form1" runat="server">
      <div>
        User Name:
        <asp:TextBox Runat="server" ID="userNameBox" /><br />
        Password:
        <asp:TextBox Runat="server" ID="passwordBox" /><br />
        <asp:Button Runat="server" ID="loginButton" Text="Log in" /><br />
```

```
            <asp:Label Runat="server" ID="tokenLabel" /><br />
            <asp:Button Runat="server" ID="invokeButton"
              Text="Invoke DoSomething()" /><br />
            <asp:Label Runat="server" ID="resultLabel" /><br />
        </div>
    </form>
```

Add the `PCSWebService3` service as a Web reference (because the Web service is local to the solution you can click on the "Web services in this solution" link to get a reference quickly) with the name `authenticateService`, and add the following `using` statements to `Default.aspx.cs`:

```
using System.Net;
using authenticateService;
```

You need to use the `System.Net` namespace because it includes the `CookieContainer` class. This is used to store a reference to a cookie, and you require this if you are working with Web services that use session state. This is because you need someway for the Web service to retrieve the correct session state across multiple calls from the client, where the proxy for the service is re-created on each postback. By retrieving the cookie used by the Web service to store session state, storing it between Web service calls, and then using it in later calls, you can maintain the correct session state in the Web service. Without doing this, the Web service would lose its session state, and therefore the login information required in this scenario.

Back to the code, where you use a protected member to store the Web reference proxy, and another to store a Boolean value indicating whether the user is authenticated or not:

```
    public partial class _Default : System.Web.UI.Page
    {
        protected Service myService;
        protected bool authenticated;
```

`Page_Load()` starts by initializing the `myService` service, as well as preparing a `CookieContainer` instance for use with the service:

```
        protected void Page_Load(object sender, EventArgs e)
        {
            myService = new Service();
            myService.Credentials = CredentialCache.DefaultCredentials;
            CookieContainer serviceCookie;
```

Next, you check for a stored `CookieContainer` instance or create a new one. Either way you assign the `CookieContainer` to the Web service proxy, ready to receive the cookie information from the Web service after a call is made. The storage used here is the `ViewState` collection of the form (a useful way to persist information between postbacks, which works in a similar way to storing information at the application or session level):

```
            if (ViewState["serviceCookie"] == null)
            {
                serviceCookie = new CookieContainer();
            }
            else
```

# Web Services

```
    {
        serviceCookie = (CookieContainer)ViewState["serviceCookie"];
    }
    myService.CookieContainer = serviceCookie;
```

`Page_Load()` then looks to see if there is a stored header and assigns the header to the proxy accordingly (assigning the header in this way is the only step you must take for the data to be sent as a SOAP header). This way any event handlers that are being called (such as the one for the Web method–invoking button) don't have to assign a header — that step has already been taken:

```
    AuthenticationToken header = new AuthenticationToken();
    if (ViewState["AuthenticationTokenHeader"] != null)
    {
        header.InnerToken = (Guid)ViewState["AuthenticationTokenHeader"];
    }
    else
    {
        header.InnerToken = Guid.Empty;
    }
    myService.AuthenticationTokenValue = header;
}
```

Next, you add an event handler for the Log in button by double-clicking it in the designer:

```
    protected void loginButton_Click(object sender, EventArgs e)
    {
        Guid authenticationTokenHeader = myService.Login(userNameBox.Text,
                                                         passwordBox.Text);
        tokenLabel.Text = authenticationTokenHeader.ToString();
        if (ViewState["AuthenticationTokenHeader"] != null)
        {
            ViewState.Remove("AuthenticationTokenHeader");
        }
        ViewState.Add("AuthenticationTokenHeader", authenticationTokenHeader);
        if (ViewState["serviceCookie"] != null)
        {
            ViewState.Remove("serviceCookie");
        }
        ViewState.Add("serviceCookie", myService.CookieContainer);
    }
```

This handler uses any data entered in the two text boxes to call `Login()`, displays the `Guid` returned, and stores the `Guid` in the `ViewState` collection. It also updates the `CookieContainer` stored in the `ViewState` collection, ready for reuse.

Finally, you have to add a handler in the same way for the Invoke DoSomething() button:

```
    protected void invokeButton_Click(object sender, EventArgs e)
    {
        resultLabel.Text = myService.DoSomething();
        if (ViewState["serviceCookie"] != null)
        {
```

# Chapter 28

```
        ViewState.Remove("serviceCookie");
    }
    ViewState.Add("serviceCookie", myService.CookieContainer);
}
```

This handler simply outputs the text returned by `DoSomething()` and updates the `CookieContainer` storage just like `loginButton_Click()`.

When you run this application you can press the Invoke DoSomething() button straight away, because `Page_Load()` has assigned a header for you to use (if no header is assigned, an exception will be thrown because you have specified that the header is required for this method). This results in a failure message, returned from `DoSomething()`, as shown in Figure 28-4.

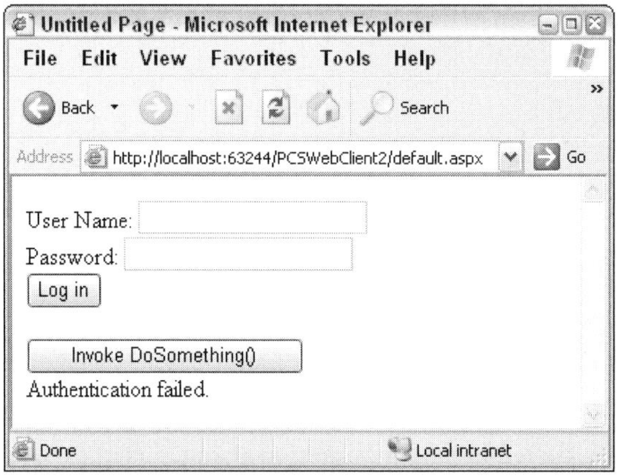

**Figure 28-4**

If you try to log in with any user name and password except "Karli" and "Cheese" you will get the same result. If, on the other hand, you log in using these credentials and then call `DoSomething()`, you get the success message, as shown in Figure 28-5.

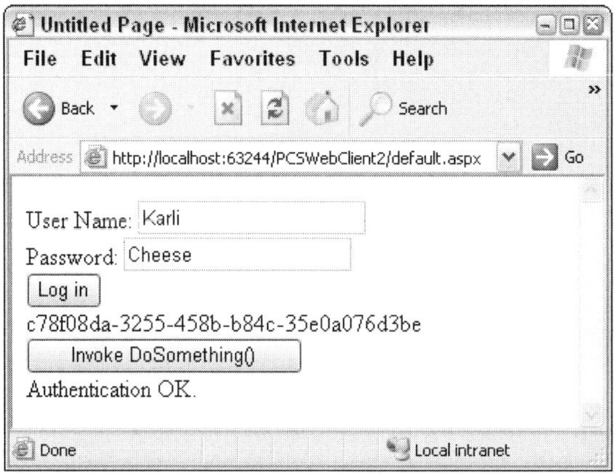

**Figure 28-5**

1006

You can also see a string representation of the `Guid` used for validation.

Of course, applications that use this technique of exchanging data via SOAP headers are likely to be far more complicated. You may decide to store login tokens in a more scalable way than just session storage, perhaps in a database. For completeness you can also implement your own expiration scheme for these tokens when a certain amount of time has passed and provide the option for users to log out, which would simply mean removing the token. Session state does expire after a certain amount of time (20 minutes by default), but more complicated and powerful schemes are possible. You could even validate the token against the IP address used by the user for further security. The key points here though are that the username and password of the user are only sent once, and that using a SOAP header simplifies later method calls.

## Summary

In this chapter you have seen how to create and consume Web services using C# and the Visual Studio .NET development platform. Doing this is perhaps surprisingly simple, but is instantly recognizable as something that could prove to be incredibly useful. There have already been many announcements about new Web services, and I suspect that they will be everywhere before long.

It has also been pointed out that Web services may be accessed from any platform. This is due to the SOAP protocol, which doesn't limit you to .NET.

The main example developed in this chapter illustrates how you can create .NET-distributed applications with ease. I have assumed here that you are using a single server to test things out, but there is no reason why the Web service shouldn't be completely separate from the client. It may even be on a separate server from the database if an additional data tier is required.

The use of data caching throughout is another important technique to master for use in large-scale applications, which might have thousands of users connecting simultaneously.

Exchanging data via SOAP headers, introduced in the last example, is another useful technique that can be worked into your applications. The example uses the exchange of a login token, but there is no reason why more complex data shouldn't be exchanged in this way. Perhaps this could be used for simple password protection of Web services, without having to resort to imposing more complex security.

Finally, remember that Web service consumers don't necessarily have to be Web applications. There is no reason why you can't use Web services from Windows Forms applications — which certainly seems like an attractive option for a corporate intranet. One added bonus concerning Web services in ASP.NET 2.0 is the ability to call Web services asynchronously, using a simple, event-driven system. This fits in perfectly with Windows Forms applications, and means that you can keep your applications responsive while complicated Web services carry out hard work for you.

All in all, the potential of Web services certainly astounds me, and I hope you're impressed too!

# 29
# .NET Remoting

This chapter explores .NET Remoting. .NET Remoting can be used for accessing objects in another application domain (for example, on another server). .NET Remoting provides a faster format for communication between .NET applications on both the client and the server side.

In this chapter you develop .NET Remoting objects, clients, and servers by using the HTTP, TCP, and IPC channels. First, you configure the client and server programmatically before you change the application to use configuration files instead, where only a few .NET Remoting methods are required. You also write small programs to use .NET Remoting asynchronously and for calling event handlers in the client application.

The .NET Remoting classes can be found in the namespace `System.Runtime.Remoting` and its sub-namespaces. Many of these classes are in the core assembly mscorlib, and some needed only for cross-network communication are available in the assembly `System.Runtime.Remoting`.

The .NET Remoting topics covered in this chapter include the following:

- An overview of .NET Remoting
- Contexts, which are used to group objects with similar execution requirements
- Implementing a simple remote object, client, and server
- The .NET Remoting architecture
- .NET Remoting configuration files
- Hosting .NET Remoting objects in ASP.NET
- Using Soapsuds to access the metadata of remote objects
- Calling .NET Remoting methods asynchronously

# Chapter 29

- ❑ Calling methods in the client with the help of events
- ❑ Using the `CallContext` to automatically pass data to the server

The chapter starts with a discussion of what .NET Remoting really is.

# What Is .NET Remoting?

.NET Remoting is a technology for communication between different application domains. Application domains are discussed in Chapter 15, "Assemblies." Using .NET Remoting for communication between application domains can happen inside the same process, between processes on a single system, or between processes on different systems.

Different technologies can be used for communication with a client and a server application. You can program your application by using sockets, or you can use some helper classes from the `System.Net` namespace that make it easier to deal with protocols, IP addresses, and port numbers (see Chapter 35, "Accessing the Internet," for details). Using this technology you always have to send data across the network. The data you send can be your own custom protocol where the packet is interpreted by the server, so that the server knows what methods should be invoked. You not only have to deal with the data that is sent but also have to create threads yourself.

Using XML Web services you can send messages across the network. With XML Web services you get platform independence. XML Web services do not only have the advantage of platform independence, but you also get a loose coupling between client and server, which means that it's easier to deal with versioning issues.

With .NET Remoting you have a tight coupling between client and server, because the same object types are shared. .NET Remoting brings CLR object functionality to methods that are invoked across different application domains.

The functionality of .NET Remoting can be described with the application types and protocols that are supported, and by looking at the term *CLR Object Remoting*.

> *Although SOAP is offered by .NET Remoting, don't assume that this can be used for interoperability between different platforms. The SOAP Document style is not available with .NET Remoting. .NET Remoting is designed for .NET applications on both sides. If you want to have interoperability, use Web services instead.*

## Application Types and Protocols

.NET Remoting is an extremely flexible architecture that can be used in *any application type* over *any transport*, using *any payload encoding*.

Using SOAP and HTTP is just one way to call remote objects. The transport channel is pluggable and can be replaced. With .NET 2.0 you get HTTP, TCP, and IPC channels represented by the classes `HttpChannel`, `TcpChannel`, and `IpcChannel`, respectively. You can build transport channels to use UDP, IPX, SMTP, a shared memory mechanism, or message queuing — the choice is entirely yours.

# .NET Remoting

*The term pluggable is often used with .NET Remoting. Pluggable means that a specific part is designed so that it can be replaced by a custom implementation.*

The payload is used to transport the parameters of a method call. This payload encoding can also be replaced. Microsoft delivers SOAP and binary encoding mechanisms. You can use either the SOAP formatter with the HTTP channel or HTTP with the binary formatter. Of course, both of these formatters can also be used with the TCP channel.

*Although SOAP is used with .NET Remoting, you should be aware that .NET Remoting only supports the SOAP RPC style, whereas ASP.NET Web services supports both the DOC style (default) and the RPC style.*

.NET Remoting not only enables you to use server functionality in every .NET application. You can use .NET Remoting anywhere — regardless of whether you are building a console or a Windows application, a Windows Service, or a COM+ component. .NET Remoting is also a good technology for peer-to-peer communication.

## CLR Object Remoting

CLR Object Remoting is an importing aspect of .NET Remoting. All of the language constructs (such as constructors, delegates, interfaces, methods, properties, and fields) can be used with remote objects. .NET Remoting extends the CLR object functionality across the network. CLR Object Remoting deals with activation, distributed identities, lifetimes, and call contexts.

This is a major difference to XML Web services. With XML Web services, the objects are abstracted and the client doesn't need to know the object types of the server. Unlike .NET Remoting, XML Web services are platform independent.

## .NET Remoting Overview

.NET Remoting can be used for accessing objects in another application domain. .NET Remoting can always be used whether the two objects live inside a single process, in separate processes, or on separate systems.

Remote assemblies can be configured to work locally in the application domain or as part of a remote application. If the assembly is part of the remote application, the client receives a proxy to talk to instead of the real object. The proxy is a representative of the remote object in the client process, used by the client application to call methods. When the client calls a method in the proxy, the proxy sends a message into the channel that is passed on to the remote object.

.NET applications work within an application domain. An application domain can be seen as a subprocess within a process. Traditionally, processes were used as an isolation boundary. An application running in one process cannot access and destroy memory in another process. Cross-process communication is needed for applications to communicate with each other. With .NET, the application domain is the new safety boundary inside a process, because the MSIL code is type-safe and verifiable. As discussed in Chapter 15, different applications can run inside the same process but within different application domains. Objects inside the same application domain can interact directly; a proxy is needed to access objects in a different application domain.

# Chapter 29

The following list provides an overview of the key elements of this architecture:

- A *remote object* is an object that's running on the server. The client doesn't call methods on this object directly, but uses a proxy instead. With .NET it's easy to distinguish remote objects from local objects: every class that's derived from `MarshalByRefObject` never leaves its application domain. The client can call methods of the remote object via a proxy.

- A *channel* is used for communication between the client and the server. There are client and server parts of the channel. .NET Framework 2.0 offers channel types that communicate via TCP, HTTP, or IPC. You can also create a custom channel that communicates by using a different protocol.

- *Messages* are sent into the channel; they are created for communication between the client and the server. These messages hold the information about the remote object, the method name called, and all of the arguments.

- The *formatter* defines how messages are transferred into the channel. .NET 2.0 has SOAP and binary formatters. The SOAP formatter can be used to communicate with Web services that are not based on the .NET Framework. Binary formatters are much faster and can be used efficiently in an intranet environment. Of course, you also have the option to create a custom formatter.

- A *formatter provider* is used to associate a formatter with a channel. By creating a channel, you can specify the formatter provider to be used, and this in turn defines the formatter that is used to transfer the data into the channel.

- The client calls methods on a *proxy* instead of the remote object. Two types of proxies exist: the *transparent proxy* and the *real proxy*. For the client, the transparent proxy looks like the remote object. On the transparent proxy, the client can call the methods implemented by the remote objects. In turn, the transparent proxy calls the `Invoke()` method on the real proxy. The `Invoke()` method uses the message sink to pass the message to the channel.

- A *message sink*, or *sink* for short, is an interceptor object. Interceptors are used on both the client and the server. A sink is associated with the channel. The real proxy uses the message sink to pass the message into the channel, so the sink can do some interception before the message goes into the channel. Depending on where the sink is used, it is known as an envoy sink, a server context sink, an object context sink, and so on.

- The client can use an *activator* to create a remote object on the server or to get a proxy of a server-activated object.

- `RemotingConfiguration` is a utility class to configure remote servers and clients. This class can be used either to read configuration files or to configure remote objects dynamically.

- `ChannelServices` is a utility class to register channels and then to dispatch messages to them.

Figure 29-1 shows a conceptual picture of how these pieces fit together.

When the client calls methods on a remote object, it actually calls them on a transparent proxy instead. The transparent proxy looks like the real object — it implements the public methods of the real object. The transparent proxy knows about the public methods of the real object by using the reflection mechanism to read the metadata from the assembly.

# .NET Remoting

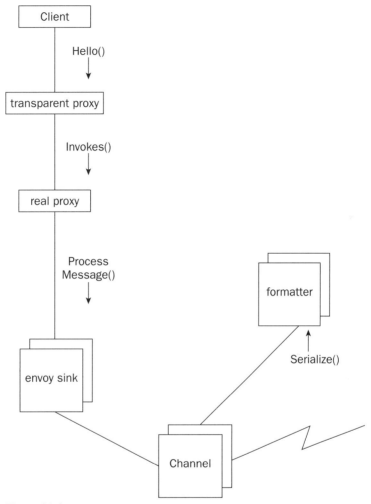

**Figure 29-1**

In turn, the transparent proxy calls the real proxy. The real proxy is responsible for sending the message to the channel. This proxy is pluggable: it can be replaced with a custom implementation. Such a custom implementation can be used to write a log, or to use another way to find a channel, and so on. The default implementation of the real proxy locates the collection (or chain) of envoy sinks and passes the message to the first envoy sink. An envoy sink can intercept and change the message. Examples of such sinks are debugging sinks, security sinks, and synchronization sinks.

The last envoy sink sends the message into the channel. The formatter defines how the messages are sent over the wire. As previously stated, SOAP and binary formatters are available with .NET Framework

2.0. The formatter, however, is also pluggable. The channel is responsible for either connecting to a listening socket on the server or sending the formatted data. With a custom channel you can do something different; you just have to implement the code and to do what's necessary to transfer the data to the other side.

Let's continue with the server side as shown in Figure 29-2:

❑   The channel receives the formatted messages from the client and uses the formatter to unmarshal the SOAP or binary data into messages. Then the channel calls server-context sinks.

❑   The server-context sinks are a chain of sinks, where the last sink in the chain continues the call to the chain of object-context sinks.

❑   The last object-context sink then calls the method in the remote object.

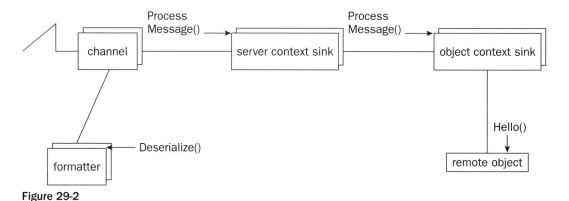

**Figure 29-2**

Note that the object context sinks are confined to the object context, and the server context sinks are confined to the server context. A single server-context sink can be used to access a number of object sinks.

> .NET Remoting is extremely customizable: You can replace the real proxy, add sink objects, or replace the formatter and channel. Of course, you can also use what's already provided.

Going through these layers you may be wondering about the overhead, but there's not much overhead left if nothing is happening in there. If you add your own functionality, the overhead will depend on that.

# Contexts

Before you look at using .NET Remoting to build servers and clients that communicate across a network, this section turns to the cases where a channel is needed inside an application domain: calling objects across contexts.

If you've previously written COM+ components, you already know about COM+ contexts. Contexts in .NET are very similar. A context is a boundary containing a collection of objects. Likewise, with a COM+ context, the objects in such a collection require the same usage rules that are defined by the context attributes.

# .NET Remoting

As you already know, a single process can have multiple application domains. An application domain is something like a subprocess with security boundaries. Application domains are discussed in Chapter 15.

An application domain can have different contexts. A context is used to group objects with similar execution requirements. Contexts are composed from a set of properties and are used for interception: when a *context-bound object* is accessed by a different context, an *interceptor* can do some work before the call reaches the object. Examples where this can be used are for thread synchronization, transactions, and security management.

A class derived from `MarshalByRefObject` is bound to the application domain. Outside the application domain a proxy is needed to access the object. A class derived from `ContextBoundObject` that itself derives from `MarshalByRefObject` is bound to a context. Outside the context, a proxy is needed to access the object.

Context-bound objects can have *context attributes*. A context-bound object without context attributes is created in the context of the creator. A context-bound object with context attributes is created in a new context or in the creator's context if the attributes are compatible.

To further understand contexts, you must be familiar with these terms:

- Creating an application domain creates the *default context* in this application domain. If a new object is instantiated that needs different context properties, a new context is created.
- *Context attributes* can be assigned to classes derived from `ContextBoundObject`. You can create a custom attribute class by implementing the interface `IContextAttribute`. The .NET Framework has one context attribute class in the namespace `System.Runtime.Remoting.Contexts: SynchronizationAttribute`.
- Context attributes define *context properties* that are needed for an object. A context property class implements the interface `IContextProperty`. Active properties contribute message sinks to the call chain. The class `ContextAttribute` implements both `IContextProperty` and `IContextAttribute`, and can be used as a base class for custom attributes.
- A *message sink* is an interceptor for a method call. With a message sink, method calls can be intercepted. Properties can contribute to message sinks.

## Activation

A new context is created if an instance of a class that's created needs a context different from the calling context. The attribute classes that are associated with the target class are asked if all the properties of the current context are acceptable. If any of these properties are unacceptable, the runtime asks for all property classes associated with the attribute class and creates a new context. The runtime then asks the property classes for the sinks they want to install. A property class can implement one of the `IContributeXXXSink` interfaces to contribute sink objects. Several of these interfaces are available to go with the variety of sinks.

## Attributes and Properties

The properties of a context are defined with context attributes. A context attribute class primarily is an attribute — you can find out more about attributes in Chapter 11, "Reflection." Context attribute classes must implement the interface `IContextAttribute`. A custom context attribute class can derive from the class `ContextAttribute`, because this class already has a default implementation of this interface.

.NET Framework 2.0 includes two context attribute classes: `System.Runtime.Remoting.Contexts.SynchronizationAttribute` and `System.Runtime.Remoting.Activation.UrlAttribute`. The `Synchronization` attribute defines synchronization requirements; it specifies the synchronization property that is needed by the object. With this attribute you can specify that multiple threads cannot access the object concurrently, but the thread accessing the object can change.

With the constructor of this attribute, you can set one of four values:

- `NOT_SUPPORTED` defines that the class should not be instantiated in a context where the synchronization is set.
- `REQUIRED` specifies that a synchronization context is required.
- `REQUIRES_NEW` always creates a new context.
- `SUPPORTED` means that it doesn't matter what context you get; the object can live in it.

## Communication between Contexts

How does the communication between contexts happen? The client uses a proxy instead of the real object. The proxy creates a message that is transferred to a channel, and sinks can do interception. Does this sound familiar? It ought to. The same mechanism is used for communication across different application domains or different systems. A TCP or HTTP channel is not required for the communication across contexts, but a channel is used here too. `CrossContextChannel` can use the same virtual memory in both the client and server sides of the channel, and formatters are not required for crossing contexts.

# Remote Objects, Clients, and Servers

Before stepping into the details of the .NET Remoting architecture, this section looks briefly at a remote object and a very small, simple client-server application that uses this remote object. After that the required steps and options are discussed in more detail.

Figure 29-3 shows the major .NET Remoting classes in the client and server application. The remote object that will be implemented is called `Hello`. `HelloServer` and is the main class of the application on the server, and `HelloClient` is for the client.

# .NET Remoting

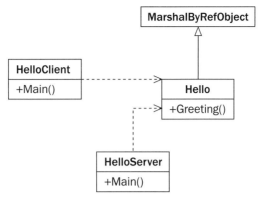

Figure 29-3

## Remote Objects

Remote objects are required for distributed computing. An object that should be called remotely from a different system must be derived from System.MarshalByRefObject. MarshalByRefObject objects are *confined to the application domain* in which they were created. This means that they are never passed across application domains; instead, a proxy object is used to access the remote object from another application domain. The other application domain can live inside the same process, in another process, or on another system.

A remote object has *distributed identity*. Because of this, a reference to the object can be passed to other clients, and they will still access the same object. The proxy knows about the identity of the remote object.

The MarshalByRefObject class has, in addition to the inherited methods from the Object class, methods to initialize and to get the lifetime services. The lifetime services define how long the remote object lives. Lifetime services and leasing features are dealt with later in this chapter.

To see .NET Remoting in action, create a Class Library for the remote object. The class Hello derives from System.MarshalByRefObject. In the constructor and destructor, a message is written to the console that provides information about the object's lifetime. In addition, add the method Greeting() that will be called from the client.

To distinguish easily between the assembly and the class in the following sections, give them different names in the arguments of the method calls used. The name of the assembly is RemoteHello, and the class is named Hello:

```
using System;

namespace Wrox.ProCSharp.Remoting
{
    public class Hello : System.MarshalByRefObject
    {
        public Hello()
        {
```

1017

```
            Console.WriteLine("Constructor called");
        }
        ~Hello()
        {
            Console.WriteLine("Destructor called");
        }

        public string Greeting(string name)
        {
            Console.WriteLine("Greeting called");
            return "Hello, " + name;
        }
    }
}
```

## A Simple Server

For the server, create a new C# console application called `HelloServer`. To use the `TcpServerChannel` class, you have to reference the `System.Runtime.Remoting` assembly. It's also required that you reference the `RemoteHello` assembly that was created earlier.

In the `Main()` method, an object of type `System.Runtime.Remoting.Channels.Tcp.TcpServerChannel` is created with the port number `8086`. This channel is registered with the `System.Runtime.Remoting.Channels.ChannelServices` class to make it available for remote objects. The second argument of this method is set to false to disable security. The remote object type is registered using `System.Runtime.Remoting.RemotingConfiguration.RegisterWellKnownServiceType`. In the example, the type of the remote object class, the URI used by the client, and a mode are specified. The mode `WellKnownObject.SingleCall` means that a new instance is created for every method call; in the sample application no state is held in the remote object.

> .NET Remoting allows creating stateless and stateful remote objects. In the first example, well-known single-call objects that don't hold state are used. The other object type is called client-activated. Client-activated objects hold state. Later in this chapter, when looking at the object activation sequence, you learn more details about these differences and how these object types can be used.

After registration of the remote object, it is necessary to keep the server running until a key is pressed:

```
using System;
using System.Runtime.Remoting;
using System.Runtime.Remoting.Channels;
using System.Runtime.Remoting.Channels.Tcp;

namespace Wrox.ProCSharp.Remoting
{
    class Program
    {
        static void Main(string[] args)
        {
            TcpServerChannel channel = new TcpServerChannel(8086);
            ChannelServices.RegisterChannel(channel,false);
            RemotingConfiguration.RegisterWellKnownServiceType(
```

```
            typeof(Hello), "Hi", WellKnownObjectMode.SingleCall);
         System.Console.WriteLine("press return to exit");
         System.Console.ReadLine();
      }
   }
}
```

## A Simple Client

The client is again a C# console application: `HelloClient`. With this project you also have to reference the `System.Runtime.Remoting` assembly so that the `TcpClientChannel` class can be used. In addition, you have to reference the `RemoteHello` assembly. Although the object will be created on the remote server, the assembly is needed on the client for the proxy to read the type information during runtime.

In the client program create a `TcpClientChannel` object that's registered in `ChannelServices`. For the `TcpChannel` you can use the default constructor, so a free port is selected. Next, the `Activator` class is used to return a proxy to the remote object. The proxy is of type `System.Runtime.Remoting.Proxies.__TransparentProxy`. This object looks like the real object because it offers the same methods. The transparent proxy uses the real proxy to send messages to the channel:

```
using System;
using System.Runtime.Remoting.Channels;
using System.Runtime.Remoting.Channels.Tcp;

namespace Wrox.ProCSharp.Remoting
{
   class Program
   {
      static void Main(string[] args)
      {
         ChannelServices.RegisterChannel(new TcpClientChannel(),false);
         Hello obj = (Hello)Activator.GetObject(
                              typeof(Hello), "tcp://localhost:8086/Hi");
         if (obj == null)
         {
            Console.WriteLine("could not locate server");
            return;
         }
         for (int i=0; i< 5; i++)
         {
            Console.WriteLine(obj.Greeting("Christian"));
         }
      }
   }
}
```

*A proxy is an object used by the client application in place of the remote object. Proxies that are used in Chapter 28, "Web Services," have a similar functionality to the proxies in this chapter. The implementation of proxies for Web services and proxies for .NET Remoting is very different.*

# Chapter 29

Now you can start the server and then the client program. Within the client console, the text `Hello, Christian` appears five times. With your server console window you can see the output shown in Figure 29-4: With every method call a new instance gets created because the `WellKnownObjectMode.SingleCall` activation mode was selected. Depending on timing and resources needed, you might also see some calls to the destructor. If you start the client a few times, you are sure to see some destructor calls.

Figure 29-4

# .NET Remoting Architecture

Now that you've seen a simple client and server in action, this section discusses an overview of the .NET Remoting architecture before we dive into the details. Based on the previously created program, you look at the details of the architecture and the mechanisms for extensibility.

This section explores the following topics:

- The functionality of a channel and how a channel can be configured
- Formatters and how they are used
- The utility classes `ChannelServices` and `RemotingConfiguration`
- Different ways to activate remote objects, and how stateless and stateful objects can be used with .NET Remoting
- Functionality of message sinks
- How to pass objects by value and by reference
- Lifetime management of stateful objects with .NET Remoting leasing mechanisms

## Channels

A channel is used to communicate between a .NET client and a server. .NET Framework 2.0 ships with channel classes that communicate using TCP, HTTP, or IPC. You can create custom channels for other protocols.

# .NET Remoting

The *HTTP channel* is used by most Web services. It uses the HTTP protocol for communication. Because firewalls usually have port 80 opened so that the clients can access Web servers, .NET Remoting Web services can listen to port 80 so that they can easily be used by these clients.

It's also possible to use the *TCP channel* on the Internet, but here the firewalls must be configured so that clients can access a specified port that's used by the TCP channel. The TCP channel can be used to communicate more efficiently in an intranet environment compared to the HTTP channel.

The IPC channel is best for communication on a single system across different processes. It uses the Windows interprocess communication mechanism and thus it is faster than the other channels.

Performing a method call on the remote object causes the client channel object to send a message to the remote channel object.

Both the server and the client application must create a channel. This code shows how a `TcpServerChannel` can be created on the server side:

```
using System.Runtime.Remoting.Channels.Tcp;
    ...
TcpServerChannel channel = new TcpServerChannel(8086);
```

The port on which the TCP socket is listening is specified in the constructor argument. The server channel must specify a well-known port, and the client must use this port when accessing the server. For creating a `TcpClientChannel` on the client, however, it isn't necessary to specify a well-known port. The default constructor of `TcpClientChannel` chooses an available port, which is passed to the server at connection-time so that the server can return data back to the client.

Creating a new channel instance immediately switches the socket to the listening state, which can be verified by typing **netstat –a** at the command line.

> *A very useful tool for testing to see what data is sent across the network is tcpTrace. tcpTrace can be downloaded from* http://www.pocketsoap.com/tcptrace.

The HTTP channels can be used similarly to the TCP channels. You can specify the port where the server can create the listening socket.

A server can listen to multiple channels. This code creates HTTP, TCP, and IPC channels in the file `HelloServer.cs`:

```
using System;
using System.Runtime.Remoting;
using System.Runtime.Remoting.Channels;
using System.Runtime.Remoting.Channels.Tcp;
using System.Runtime.Remoting.Channels.Http;
using System.Runtime.Remoting.Channels.Ipc;

namespace Wrox.ProCSharp.Remoting
{

    public class HelloServer
    {
```

```csharp
public static void Main(string[] args)
{
    TcpServerChannel tcpChannel = new TcpServerChannel(8086);
    HttpServerChannel httpChannel = new HttpServerChannel(8085);
    IpcServerChannel ipcChannel = new IpcServerChannel("myIPCPort");

    // register the channels
    ChannelServices.RegisterChannel(tcpChannel, false);
    ChannelServices.RegisterChannel(httpChannel, false);
    ChannelServices.RegisterChannel(ipcChannel, false);
    //...
}
```

A channel class must implement the `IChannel` interface. The `IChannel` interface has these two properties:

- `ChannelName` is a read-only property that returns the name of the channel. The name of the channel depends on the type; for example, the HTTP channel is named HTTP.

- `ChannelPriority` is a read-only property. More than one channel can be used for communication between a client and a server. The priority defines the order of the channel. On the client the channel with the higher priority is chosen first to connect to the server. The bigger the priority value, the higher the priority. The default value is 1, but negative values are allowed to create lower priorities.

Additional interfaces are implemented depending on whether the channel is a client channel or a server channel. The server versions of the channels implement the `IChannelReceiver` interface; the client versions implement the `IChannelSender` interface.

The `HttpChannel`, `TcpChannel`, and `IPCChannel` classes can be used for both the client and the server. They implement `IChannelSender` and `IChannelReceiver`. These interfaces derive from `IChannel`.

The client-side `IChannelSender` has, in addition to `IChannel`, a single method called `CreateMessageSink()`, which returns an object that implements `IMessageSink`. The `IMessageSink` interface can be used for putting synchronous as well as asynchronous messages into the channel. With the server-side interface `IChannelReceiver`, the channel can be put into listening mode using `StartListening()`, and stopped again with `StopListening()`. The property `ChannelData` can be used to access the received data.

You can get information about the configuration of the channels using properties of the channel classes. For both channels, the properties `ChannelName`, `ChannelPriority`, and `ChannelData` are offered. The `ChannelData` property can be used to get information about the URIs that are stored in the `ChannelDataStore` class. With the `HttpServerChannel` there's also a `Scheme` property. The following code shows a helper method, `ShowChannelProperties()`, in the file `HelloServer.cs` that displays this information:

```csharp
static void ShowChannelProperties(IChannelReceiver channel)
{
    Console.WriteLine("Name: " + channel.ChannelName);
    Console.WriteLine("Priority: " + channel.ChannelPriority);
    if (channel is HttpServerChannel)
    {
```

# .NET Remoting

```
      HttpServerChannel httpChannel = channel as HttpServerChannel;
      Console.WriteLine("Scheme: " + httpChannel.ChannelScheme);
   }
   ChannelDataStore data = (ChannelDataStore)channel.ChannelData;
   if (data != null)
   {
      foreach (string uri in data.ChannelUris)
      {
         Console.WriteLine("URI: " + uri);
      }
   }
   Console.WriteLine();
}
```

The method `ShowChannelProperties()` is called after creating the channels in the `Main()` method. When you start the server you will get the console output that is shown in Figure 29-5. As you can see here, the default name for the `TcpServerChannel` is *tcp*, the HTTP channel is called *http server*, and the IPC channel is called *ipc server*. The HTTP and TCP channels have a default priority of 1, whereas the IPC channel has the default priority 20. The IPC channel is faster than the other channels because it has a higher priority. The ports that have been set with the constructors are seen in the URI. The URI of the channels shows the protocol, IP address, and port number:

```
TcpServerChannel tcpChannel = new TcpServerChannel(8086);
ShowChannelProperties(tcpChannel);
HttpServerChannel httpChannel = new HttpServerChannel(8085);
ShowChannelProperties(httpChannel);
IpcServerChannel ipcChannel = new IpcServerChannel("myIPCPort");
ShowChannelProperties(ipcChannel);
```

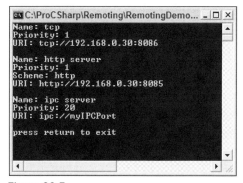

Figure 29-5

## *Setting channel properties*

You can set all the properties of a channel in a list using the constructor `HttpServerChannel (IDictionary, IServerChannelSinkProvider)`. The generic `Dictionary` class implements `IDictionary`, so you can set the `Name`, `Priority`, and `Port` property with the help of this class. To use the `Dictionary` class you have to import the `System.Collections.Generic` namespace.

1023

With the constructor of the class HttpServerChannel, you can pass an object that implements the interface IServerChannelSinkProvider in addition to the IDictionary parameter. In the example, a BinaryServerFormatterSinkProvider is set instead of the SoapServerFormatterSinkProvider, which is the default of the HttpServerChannel. The default implementation of the BinaryServerFormatterSinkProvider class associates a BinaryServerFormatterSink class with the channel that uses a BinaryFormatter object to convert the data for the transfer:

```
Dictionary<string, string> properties = new Dictionary<string, string>();
properties["name"] = "HTTP Channel with a Binary Formatter";
properties["priority"] = "15";
properties["port"] = "8085";
BinaryServerFormatterSinkProvider sinkProvider =
                new BinaryServerFormatterSinkProvider();
HttpServerChannel httpChannel =
                new HttpServerChannel(properties, sinkProvider);
ShowChannelProperties(httpChannel);
```

The new output from the server console shows the new properties of the HTTP channel (see Figure 29-6).

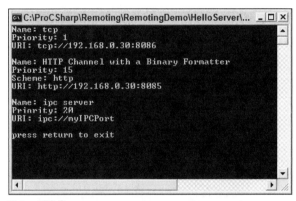

**Figure 29-6**

Depending on the channel types, different properties can be specified. Both the TCP and the HTTP channel support the name and priority channel property used in the example. These channels also support other properties such as bindTo, which specifies an IP address for binding that can be used if the computer has multiple IP addresses configured. rejectRemoteRequests is supported by the TCP server channel to allow client connections only from the local computer.

## Pluggability of a channel

A custom channel can be created to send the messages by using a transport protocol other than HTTP, TCP, or IPC, or the existing channels can be extended to offer more functionality:

❑ The sending part must implement the IChannelSender interface. The most important part is the CreateMessageSink() method, with which the client sends a URL, and here a connection to the server can be instantiated. A message sink must be created, which is then used by the proxy to send messages to the channel.

# .NET Remoting

❑ The receiving part must implement the `IChannelReceiver` interface. You have to start the listening in the `ChannelData get` property. Then you can wait in a separate thread to receive data from the client. After unmarshaling the message, you can use `ChannelServices.SyncDispatchMessage()` to dispatch the message to the object.

## Formatters

The .NET Framework delivers two formatter classes:

❑ `System.Runtime.Serialization.Formatters.Binary.BinaryFormatter`

❑ `System.Runtime.Serialization.Formatters.Soap.SoapFormatter`

Formatters are associated with channels through formatter sink objects and formatter sink providers.

Both of these formatter classes implement the interface `System.Runtime.Remoting.Messaging.IRemotingFormatter`, which defines the methods `Serialize()` and `Deserialize()` to transfer the data to and from the channel.

The formatter is also pluggable. When you're writing a custom formatter class, an instance must be associated with the channel you want to use. This is done by using a formatter sink and a formatter sink provider. The formatter sink provider, for example, `SoapServerFormatterSinkProvider`, can be passed as an argument when creating a channel as shown earlier. A formatter sink provider implements the interface `IServerChannelSinkProvider` for the server and `IClientChannelSinkProvider` for the client. Both of these interfaces define a `CreateSink()` method where a formatter sink must be returned. The `SoapServerFormatterSinkProvider` returns an instance of the class `SoapServerFormatterSink`.

On the client side, the `SoapClientFormatterSink` class uses the `SyncProcessMessage()` and `AsyncProcessMessage()` methods of the `SoapFormatter` class to serialize the message. The `SoapServerFormatterSink` class deserializes the message, again using the `SoapFormatter` class.

All these sink and provider classes can be extended and replaced with custom implementations.

## ChannelServices and RemotingConfiguration

The `ChannelServices` utility class is used to register channels into the .NET Remoting runtime. With this class, you can also access all registered channels. This is extremely useful if configuration files are used to configure the channel, because here the channel is created implicitly, as you see later.

A channel is registered using the static method `ChannelServices.RegisterChannel()`.

Here you can see the server code to register the HTTP, TCP, and IPC channels:

```
TcpChannel tcpChannel = new TcpChannel(8086);
HttpChannel httpChannel = new HttpChannel(8085);
IpcChannel ipcChannel = new IpcChannel("myIPCPort");
ChannelServices.RegisterChannel(tcpChannel,false);
ChannelServices.RegisterChannel(httpChannel,false);
ChannelServices.RegisterChannel(ipcChannel,false);
```

# Chapter 29

The `ChannelServices` utility class can now be used to dispatch synchronous and asynchronous messages, and to unregister specific channels. The `RegisteredChannels` property returns an `IChannel` array of all the channels you registered. You can also use the `GetChannel()` method to get to a specific channel by its name. With the help of `ChannelServices` you can write a custom administration utility that manages your channels. Here is a small example to show how the server channel can be stopped from listening to incoming requests:

```
HttpServerChannel channel = (HttpServerChannel)ChannelServices.GetChannel("http");
channel.StopListening(null);
```

The `RemotingConfiguration` class is another .NET Remoting utility class. On the server side it's used to register remote object types for server-activated objects, and to marshal remote objects to a marshaled object reference class `ObjRef`. `ObjRef` is a serializable representation of an object that's sent over the wire. On the client side, `RemotingServices` is used to unmarshal a remote object in order to create a proxy from the object reference.

## Server for well-known objects

Here is the server-side code to register a well-known remote object type to the `RemotingServices`:

```
RemotingConfiguration.RegisterWellKnownServiceType(
                        typeof(Hello),                      // Type
                        "Hi",                               // URI
                        WellKnownObjectMode.SingleCall);    // Mode
```

The first argument of `RegisterWellKnownServiceType()`, `typeof(Hello)`, specifies the type of the remote object. The second argument, `"Hi"`, is the uniform resource identifier of the remote object, used by the client to access the remote object. The last argument is the mode of the remote object. The mode can be a value of the `WellKnownObjectMode` enumeration: `SingleCall` or `Singleton`.

- ❏ *SingleCall* means that the object holds no state. With every call to the remote object a new instance is created. A single-call object is created from the server with the `RemotingConfiguration.RegisterWellKnownServiceType()` method and a `WellKnownObjectMode.SingleCall` argument. This is very efficient on the server, because it means that you needn't hold any resources for maybe thousands of clients.

- ❏ With a *Singleton* the object is shared for all clients of the server; typically, such object types can be used if you want to share some data between all clients. This shouldn't be a problem for read-only data, but with read-write data you have to be aware of locking issues and scalability. A singleton object is created by the server with the `RemotingConfiguration.RegisterWellKnownServiceType()` method and a `WellKnownObjectMode.Singleton` argument. You have to pay attention to the locking of resources held by the singleton object; you have to make sure that data can't be corrupted when clients are accessing the singleton object concurrently, but you also have to check that the locking is done efficiently enough to reach the required scalability.

## Server for client-activated objects

If a remote object should hold state for a specific client, you can use client-activated objects. The next section looks at how to call server-activated or client-activated objects on the client side. On the server side, client-activated objects must be registered in a different way from server-activated objects.

# .NET Remoting

Instead of calling `RemotingConfiguration.RegisterWellKnownServiceType()`, you have to call `RemotingConfiguration.RegisterActivatedServiceType()`. With this method, only the type is specified, not the URI. The reason for this is that for client-activated objects, the clients can instantiate different object types with the same URI. The URI for all client-activated objects must be defined using `RemotingConfiguration.ApplicationName`:

```
RemotingConfiguration.ApplicationName = "HelloServer";
RemotingConfiguration.RegisterActivatedServiceType(typeof(Hello));
```

## Object Activation

Clients can use and create a remote `Activator` class. You can get a proxy to a server-activated or well-known remote object by using the `GetObject()` method. The `CreateInstance()` method returns a proxy to a client-activated remote object.

Instead of using the `Activator` class, the `new` operator can also be used to activate remote objects. To make this possible, the remote object must also be configured within the client using the `RemotingConfiguration` class.

### Application URL

In all activation scenarios, you have to specify a URL to the remote object. This URL is the same one you'd use when browsing with a Web browser. The first part specifies the protocol followed by the server name or IP address, the port number, and a URI that was specified when registering the remote object on the server in this form:

```
protocol://server:port/URI
```

In the code samples, three URL examples are used continuously in the code. With the URL, the protocol is specified with `http`, `tcp`, or `ipc`. With the HTTP and TCP channels the server name is `localhost` and the port numbers are `8085` and `8086`. With the IPC channel there's no need to define a hostname because IPC is possible only on a single system. With all protocols the URI is `Hi`, as follows.

```
http://localhost:8085/Hi
tcp://localhost:8086/Hi
ipc://myIPCPort/Hi
```

### Activating well-known objects

In the previous simple client example, well-known objects have been activated. Here, you take a more detailed look at the activation sequence:

```
using System;
using System.Runtime.Remoting;
using System.Runtime.Remoting.Channels;
using System.Runtime.Remoting.Channels.Tcp;

// ...
TcpClientChannel channel = new TcpClientChannel();
ChannelServices.RegisterChannel(channel);
```

```csharp
Hello obj = (Hello)Activator.GetObject(typeof(Hello),
                         "tcp://localhost:8086/Hi");
```

`GetObject()` is a static method of the class `System.Activator` that calls `RemotingServices.Connect()` to return a proxy object to the remote object. The first argument of this method specifies the type of the remote object. The proxy implements all public and protected methods and properties, so that the client can call these methods as it would do on the real object. The second argument is the URL to the remote object. Here the string `tcp://localhost:8086/Hi` is used. `tcp` is the protocol, `localhost:8086` is the hostname and the port number, and finally `Hi` is the URI of the object that is specified using `RemotingConfiguration.RegisterWellKnownServiceType()`.

Instead of using `Activator.GetObject()`, you can also use `RemotingServices.Connect()` directly:

```csharp
Hello obj = (Hello)RemotingServices.Connect(typeof(Hello),
                         "tcp://localhost:8086/Hi");
```

If you prefer to use the `new` operator to activate well-known remote objects, the remote object can be registered on the client using `RemotingConfiguration.RegisterWellKnownClientType()`. The arguments are similar: the type of the remote object and the URI. `new` doesn't really create a new remote object, it returns a proxy similar to `Activator.GetObject()` instead. If the remote object is registered with a flag, `WellKnownObjectMode.SingleCall`, the rule always stays the same — the remote object is created with every method call:

```csharp
RemotingConfiguration.RegisterWellKnownClientType(typeof(Hello),
                         "tcp://localhost:8086/Hi");
Hello obj = new Hello();
```

## Activating client-activated objects

Remote objects can hold state for a client. `Activator.CreateInstance()` creates a client-activated remote object. Using the `Activator.GetObject()` method, the remote object is created on a method call, and is destroyed when the method is finished. The object doesn't hold state on the server. The situation is different with `Activator.CreateInstance()`. With the static `CreateInstance()` method an activation sequence is started to create the remote object. This object lives until the lease time is expired and a garbage collection occurs. The leasing mechanism is discussed later in this chapter.

Some of the overloaded `Activator.CreateInstance()` methods can only be used to create local objects. To create remote objects a method is needed where it's possible to pass activation attributes. One of these overloaded methods is used in the example. This method accepts two string parameters and an array of objects. The first parameter is the name of the assembly, and the second is the type of the remote object class. With the third parameter it is possible to pass arguments to the constructor of the remote object class. The channel and the object name are specified in the object array with the help of an `UrlAttribute`. To use the `UrlAttribute` class, the namespace `System.Runtime.Remoting.Activation` must be specified.

```csharp
object[] attrs = {new UrlAttribute("tcp://localhost:8086/HelloServer") };
ObjectHandle handle = Activator.CreateInstance(
            "RemoteHello", "Wrox.ProCSharp.Remoting.Hello", attrs);
if (handle == null)
{
```

# .NET Remoting

```
      Console.WriteLine("could not locate server");
      return;
   }
   Hello obj = (Hello)handle.Unwrap();
   Console.WriteLine(obj.Greeting("Christian"));
```

Of course, for client-activated objects, it's again possible to use the new operator instead of the Activator class, but then you have to register the client-activated object using RemotingConfiguration. RegisterActivatedClientType(). In the architecture of client-activated objects the new operator not only returns a proxy but also creates the remote object:

```
   RemotingConfiguration.RegisterActivatedClientType(typeof(Hello),
                                  "tcp://localhost:8086/HelloServer");
   Hello obj = new Hello();
```

## Proxy objects

The Activator.GetObject() and Activator.CreateInstance() methods return a proxy to the client. Actually, two proxies are used: the transparent proxy and the real proxy. The transparent proxy looks like the remote object — it implements all public methods of the remote object. These methods just call the Invoke() method of the RealProxy, where a message containing the method to call is passed. The real proxy sends the message to the channel with the help of message sinks.

With RemotingServices.IsTransparentProxy(), you can check if your object is really a transparent proxy. You can also get to the real proxy using RemotingServices.GetRealProxy(). Using the Visual Studio debugger, it's now easy to see all the properties of the real proxy:

```
   ChannelServices.RegisterChannel(new TCPChannel());
   Hello obj = (Hello)Activator.GetObject(typeof(Hello),
                                  "tcp://localhost:8086/Hi");
   if (obj == null)
   {
      Console.WriteLine("could not locate server");
      return;
   }
   if (RemotingServices.IsTransparentProxy(obj))
   {
      Console.WriteLine("Using a transparent proxy");
      RealProxy proxy = RemotingServices.GetRealProxy(obj);

      // proxy.Invoke(message);
   }
```

## Pluggability of a proxy

The real proxy can be replaced with a custom proxy. A custom proxy can extend the base class System.Runtime.Remoting.Proxies.RealProxy. The type of the remote object is received in the constructor of the custom proxy. Calling the constructor of the RealProxy creates a transparent proxy in addition to the real proxy. In the constructor, the registered channels can be accessed with the ChannelServices class to create a message sink, IChannelSender.CreateMessageSink(). Besides implementing the constructor, a custom channel has to override the Invoke() method. In Invoke() a message is received that can be analyzed and sent to the message sink.

# Chapter 29

## Messages

The proxy sends a message into the channel. On the server side, a method call can be made after analyzing the message. This section takes a closer look at the messages.

The .NET Framework has some message classes for method calls, responses, return messages, and so on. What all the message classes have in common is that they implement the `IMessage` interface. This interface has a single property: `Properties`. This property represents a dictionary with the `IDictionary` interface, which packages the `URI` to the object, `MethodName`, `MethodSignature`, `TypeName`, `Args`, and `CallContext`.

Figure 29-7 shows the hierarchy of the message classes and interfaces. The message that is sent to the real proxy is an object of type `MethodCall`. With the interfaces `IMethodCallMessage` and `IMethodMessage`, you can have easier access to the properties of the message than through the `IMessage` interface. Instead of using the `IDictionary` interface, you have direct access to the method name, the URI, the arguments, and so on. The real proxy returns a `ReturnMessage` to the transparent proxy.

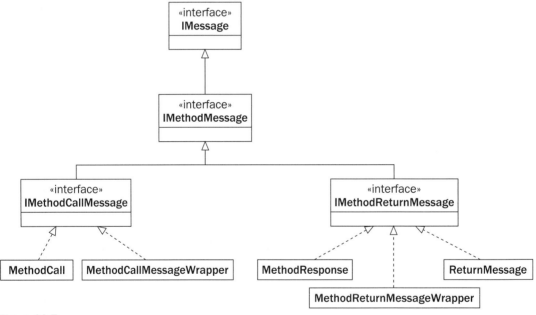

Figure 29-7

## Message Sinks

The `Activator.GetObject()` method calls `RemotingServices.Connect()` to connect to a well-known object. In the `Connect()` method, an `Unmarshal()` happens where not only the proxy, but also envoy sinks are created. The proxy uses a chain of envoy sinks to pass the message to the channel. All the sinks are interceptors that can change the messages and perform some additional actions such as creating a lock, writing an event, performing security checking, and so on.

# .NET Remoting

All message sinks implement the interface `IMessageSink`. This interface defines one property and two methods:

- The property `NextSink` is used by a sink to get to the next sink and pass the message along.
- For synchronous messages, `SyncProcessMessage()` is invoked by a previous sink or by the remoting infrastructure. It has an `IMessage` parameter to send a message and to return a message.
- For asynchronous messages, `AsyncProcessMessage()` is invoked by a previous sink in the chain, or by the remoting infrastructure. `AsyncProcessMessage()` has two parameters: a message and a message sink that receives the reply.

The following sections look at the three different message sinks available for use.

### Envoy sink

You can get to the chain of envoy sinks using the `IEnvoyInfo` interface. The marshaled object reference `ObjRef` has the `EnvoyInfo` property, which returns the `IEnvoyInfo` interface. The envoy list is created from the server context, so the server can inject functionality into the client. Envoys can collect identity information about the client and pass that information to the server.

### Server context sink

When the message is received on the server side of the channel, it is passed to the server context sinks. The last of the server context sinks routes the message to the object sink chain.

### Object sink

The object sink is associated with a particular object. If the object class defines particular context attributes, context sinks are created for the object.

## Passing Objects in Remote Methods

The parameter types of remote method calls aren't limited only to basic data types but can also be classes that you define yourself. For remoting, three types of classes must be differentiated:

- **Marshal-by-value classes** — These classes are serialized through the channel. Classes that should be marshaled must be marked with the `[Serializable]` attribute. Objects of these classes don't have a remote identity, because the complete object is marshaled through the channel, and the object that is serialized to the client is independent of the server object (or the other way around). Marshal-by-value classes are also called *unbound classes* because they don't have data that depends on the application domain. Serialization is discussed in detail in Chapter 34, "Manipulating Files and the Registry."

- **Marshal-by-reference classes** — These classes do have a remote identity. The objects are not passed across the wire, but a proxy is returned instead. A class marshaled by reference must derive from `MarshalByRefObject`. `MarshalByRefObjects` are known as *application domain–bound objects*. A specialized version of `MarshalByRefObject` is `ContextBoundObject`: the abstract class `ContextBoundObject` is derived from `MarshalByRefObject`. If a class is derived from `ContextBoundObject`, a proxy is needed even in the same application domain when context boundaries are crossed. Such objects are called *context-bound objects*, and they are only valid in the creation context.

❑ **Not-remotable classes** — These classes are not serializable and don't derive from `MarshalByRefObject`. Classes of these types cannot be used as parameters in a remote object's public methods. These classes are bound to the application domain where they are created. Non-remotable classes should be used if the class has a data member that is only valid in the application domain, such as a Win32 file handle.

To see marshaling in action, change the remote object to send two objects to the client: the class `MySerialized` will be sent marshal-by-value, and the class `MyRemote` will be sent marshal-by-reference. In the methods a message is written to the console so that you can verify if the call was made on the client or on the server. In addition, the `Hello` class is extended to return a `MySerialized` and a `MyRemote` instance:

```csharp
using System;

namespace Wrox.ProCSharp.Remoting
{
   [Serializable]
   public class MySerialized
   {
      public MySerialized(int val)
      {
         a = val;
      }
      public void Foo()
      {
         Console.WriteLine("MySerialized.Foo called");
      }
      public int A
      {
         get
         {
            Console.WriteLine("MySerialized.A called");
            return a;
         }
         set
         {
            a = value;
         }
      }
      protected int a;
   }
   public class MyRemote : System.MarshalByRefObject
   {
      public MyRemote(int val)
      {
         a = val;
      }
      public void Foo()
      {
```

```csharp
            Console.WriteLine("MyRemote.Foo called");
        }
        public int A
        {
            get
            {
                Console.WriteLine("MyRemote.A called");
                return a;
            }
            set
            {
                a = value;
            }
        }
        protected int a;
    }

    public class Hello : System.MarshalByRefObject
    {
        public Hello()
        {
            Console.WriteLine("Constructor called");
        }
        ~Hello()
        {
            Console.WriteLine("Destructor called");
        }
        public string Greeting(string name)
        {
            Console.WriteLine("Greeting called");
            return "Hello, " + name;
        }
        public MySerialized GetMySerialized()
        {
            return new MySerialized(4711);
        }
        public MyRemote GetMyRemote()
        {
            return new MyRemote(4712);
        }
    }
}
```

The client application also needs to be changed to see the effects when using marshaled-by-value and marshaled-by-reference objects. Invoke the methods `GetMySerialized()` and `GetMyRemote()` to retrieve the new objects. Also make use of the method `RemotingServices.IsTransparentProxy()` to check whether or not the returned object is a proxy:

```csharp
ChannelServices.RegisterChannel(new TcpClientChannel(),false);
Hello obj = (Hello)Activator.GetObject(typeof(Hello),
    "tcp://localhost:8086/Hi");
if (obj == null)
{
```

```
            Console.WriteLine("could not locate server");
            return;
        }
        MySerialized ser = obj.GetMySerialized();
        if (!RemotingServices.IsTransparentProxy(ser))
        {
            Console.WriteLine("ser is not a transparent proxy");
        }
        ser.Foo();
        MyRemote rem = obj.GetMyRemote();
        if (RemotingServices.IsTransparentProxy(rem))
        {
            Console.WriteLine("rem is a transparent proxy");
        }
        rem.Foo();
```

In the client console window (see Figure 29-8), you can see that the `ser` object is called on the client. This object is not a transparent proxy because it's serialized to the client. In contrast, the `rem` object on the client is a transparent proxy. Methods called on this object are transferred to the server.

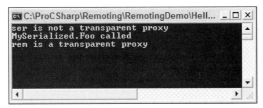

Figure 29-8

The server output (see Figure 29-9) reveals that the `Foo()` method is called with the remote object `MyRemote`.

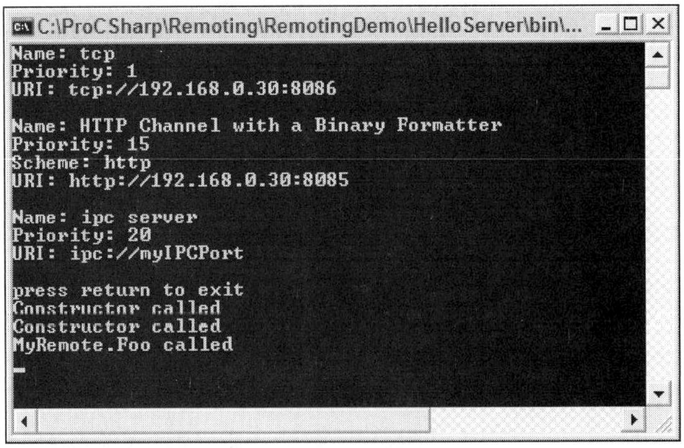

Figure 29-9

# .NET Remoting

## Security and serialized objects

One important difference with .NET Remoting and ASP.NET Web services is how objects are marshaled. With ASP.NET Web services, only the public fields and properties are transferred across the wire. .NET Remoting uses a different serialization mechanism to serialize all data, including all private data. Malicious clients could use the serialization and deserialization phases to harm the application.

To take this problem into account, two automatic deserialization levels are defined when passing objects across .NET Remoting boundaries: low and full.

By default, low-level deserialization is used. With low-level deserialization it is not possible to pass `ObjRef` objects and objects that implement the `ISponsor` interface. To make this possible, you can change the deserialization level to full. You can do this programmatically by creating a formatter sink provider, and assign the property `TypeFilterLevel`. For the binary formatter, the provider class is `BinaryServerFormatterSinkProvider`, whereas for the SOAP formatter the provider class is `SoapServerFormatterSinkProvider`.

The following code shows how you can create a TCP channel with full serialization support:

```
BinaryServerFormatterSinkProvider serverProvider =
   new BinaryServerFormatterSinkProvider();
serverProvider.TypeFilterLevel = TypeFilterLevel.Full;

BinaryClientFormatterSinkProvider clientProvider =
   new BinaryClientFormatterSinkProvider();

Dictionary<string, string> properties = new Dictionary<string, string>();
properties["port"] = 6789;

TcpChannel channel = new TcpChannel(properties, clientProvider, serverProvider);
```

At first, a `BinaryServerFormatterSinkProvider` is created where the property `TypeFilterLevel` is set to `TypeFilterLevel.Full`. The enumeration `TypeFilterLevel` is defined in the namespace `System.Runtime.Serialization.Formatters`, so you have to declare this namespace. For the client side of the channel, a `BinaryClientFormatterSinkProvider` is created. Both the client-side and the server-side formatter sink provider instances are passed to the constructor of the `TcpChannel`, as well as the `IDictionary` properties that define the attributes of the channel.

## Directional attributes

Remote objects are never transferred over the wire, whereas value types and serializable classes are transferred. Sometimes the data should be sent in one direction only. This can be especially important when the data is transferred over the network. For example, if you want to send data in a collection to the server for the server to perform some calculation on this data and return a simple value to the client, it would not be very efficient to send the collection back to the client. With COM it was possible to declare the directional attributes `[in]`, `[out]`, and `[in, out]` to the arguments if the data should be sent to the server, to the client, or in both directions.

C# has similar attributes as part of the language: `ref` and `out` method parameters. The `ref` and `out` method parameters can be used for value types and for reference types that are serializable. Using the `ref` parameter, the argument is marshaled in both directions, and with the `out` parameter the data is sent from the server to the client. With no parameters the data is sent to the server.

*You can read more about the `out` and `ref` keywords in Chapter 3, "Objects and Types."*

# Lifetime Management

How do a client and a server detect if the other side is not available anymore, and what are the problems you might get into?

For a client the answer can be simple. As soon as the client does a call to a method on the remote object you get an exception of type `System.Runtime.Remoting.RemotingException`. You just have to handle this exception and do what's necessary; for example, perform a retry, write to a log, inform the user, and so on.

What about the server? When does the server detect if the client is not around anymore, meaning that the server can go ahead and clean up any resources it's holding for the client? You could wait until the next method call from the client—but maybe it will never arrive. In the COM realm, the DCOM protocol used a ping mechanism. The client sent a ping to the server with the information about the object referenced. A client can have hundreds of objects referenced on the server, and so the information in the ping can be very large. To make this mechanism more efficient, DCOM didn't send all the information about all objects, but just the difference from the previous ping.

This ping mechanism was efficient on a LAN, but it is not suitable for scalable solutions—imagine thousands of clients sending ping information to the server! .NET Remoting has a much more scalable solution for lifetime management: the *Leasing Distributed Garbage Collector* (LDGC).

This lifetime management is only active for *client-activated objects* and well-known singleton objects. Single-call objects can be destroyed after every method call because they don't hold state. Client-activated objects do have state and you should be aware of the resources used. A lease is created for client-activated objects that are referenced outside the application domain. A lease has a lease time, and when the lease time reaches zero, the lease expires and the remote object is disconnected and, finally, it is garbage-collected.

## Lease renewals

If the client calls a method on the object when the lease has expired, an exception is thrown. If you have a client where the remote object could be needed for more than 300 seconds (the default value for lease times), you have three ways to renew a lease:

- ❑ **Implicit renewal**—This renewal of the lease is automatically done when the client calls a method on the remote object. If the current lease time is less than the `RenewOnCallTime` value, the lease is set to `RenewOnCallTime`.

- ❑ **Explicit renewal**—With this renewal, the client can specify the new lease time. This is done with the `Renew()` method of the `ILease` interface. You can get to the `ILease` interface by calling the `GetLifetimeService()` method of the transparent proxy.

- ❑ **Sponsoring renewal**—In the case of this renewal the client can create a sponsor that implements the `ISponsor` interface and registers the sponsor in the leasing services using the

# .NET Remoting

`Register()` method of the `ILease` interface. The sponsor defines the lease extension time. When a lease expires the sponsor is asked for an extension of the lease. The sponsoring mechanism can be used if you want long-lived remote objects on the server.

## Leasing configuration values

Here are the values that can be configured:

- `LeaseTime` defines the time until a lease expires.
- `RenewOnCallTime` is the time the lease is set on a method call if the current lease time has a lower value.
- If a sponsor is not available within the `SponsorshipTimeout`, the remoting infrastructure looks for the next sponsor. If there are no more sponsors, the lease expires.
- The `LeaseManagerPollTime` defines the time interval at which the lease manager checks for expired objects.

The default values are listed in the following table.

| Lease Configuration | Default Value (seconds) |
| --- | --- |
| LeaseTime | 300 |
| RenewOnCallTime | 120 |
| SponsorshipTimeout | 120 |
| LeaseManagerPollTime | 10 |

## Classes used for lifetime management

The `ClientSponsor` class implements the `ISponsor` interface. It can be used on the client side for lease extension. With the `ILease` interface you can get all information about the lease, all the lease properties, and the current lease time and state. The state is specified with the `LeaseState` enumeration. With the `LifetimeServices` utility class, you can get and set the properties for the lease of all remote objects in the application domain.

## Getting lease information example

In this small code example, the lease information is accessed by calling the `GetLifetimeService()` method of the transparent proxy. For the `ILease` interface, you have to declare the namespace `System.Runtime.Remoting.Lifetime`.

The leasing mechanism can only be used with stateful (client-activated and singleton) objects. Single-call objects are instantiated with every method call anyway, so the leasing mechanism doesn't apply. To offer client-activated objects with the server you can change the remoting configuration to a call to `RegisterActivatedServiceType()` in the file `HelloServer.cs`:

```
RemotingConfiguration.ApplicationName = "Hello";
RemotingConfiguration.RegisterActivatedServiceType(typeof(Hello));
```

1037

# Chapter 29

In the client application, the instantiation of the remote object must be changed, too. Instead of using the method `Activator.GetObject()`, `Activator.CreateInstance()` is used to invoke client-activated objects:

```
ChannelServices.RegisterChannel(new TcpClientChannel());

object[] attrs = {new UrlAttribute("tcp://localhost:8086/Hello") };
Hello obj = (Hello)Activator.CreateInstance(typeof(Hello), null, attrs);
```

To show the leasing time, you can use the `ILease` interface returned by calling `GetLifetimeService()` from the proxy object:

```
ILease lease = (ILease)obj.GetLifetimeService();
if (lease != null)
{
    Console.WriteLine("Lease Configuration:");
    Console.WriteLine("InitialLeaseTime: " +
                      lease.InitialLeaseTime);
    Console.WriteLine("RenewOnCallTime: " +
                      lease.RenewOnCallTime);
    Console.WriteLine("SponsorshipTimeout: " +
                      lease.SponsorshipTimeout);
    Console.WriteLine(lease.CurrentLeaseTime);
}
```

Figure 29-10 shows the output in the client console window.

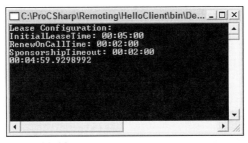

**Figure 29-10**

## Changing default lease configurations

The server itself can change the default lease configuration for all remote objects of the server using the `System.Runtime.Remoting.Lifetime.LifetimeServices` utility class:

```
LifetimeServices.LeaseTime = TimeSpan.FromMinutes(10);
LifetimeServices.RenewOnCallTime = TimeSpan.FromMinutes(2);
```

If you want different default lifetimes depending on the type of the remote object, you can change the lease configuration of the remote object by overriding the `InitializeLifetimeService()` method of the base class `MarshalByRefObject`:

```csharp
public class Hello : System.MarshalByRefObject
{
   public Hello()
   {
      Console.WriteLine("Constructor called");
   }
   ~Hello()
   {
      Console.WriteLine("Destructor called");
   }
   public override Object InitializeLifetimeService()
   {
      ILease lease = (ILease)base.InitializeLifetimeService();
      lease.InitialLeaseTime = TimeSpan.FromMinutes(10);
      lease.RenewOnCallTime = TimeSpan.FromSeconds(40);
      return lease;
   }
}
```

The lifetime services configuration can also be done by using a configuration file that is discussed next.

# Miscellaneous .NET Remoting Features

The final section of this chapter explores the following .NET Remoting features:

- How application configuration files can be used to define remoting channels
- Hosting .NET Remoting Servers in an IIS Server by using the ASP.NET runtime
- Different ways to get the type information of the server for building the client with the utility `Soapsuds`
- Calling .NET Remoting methods asynchronously
- Implementing events to callback methods in the client
- Using call contexts to pass some data automatically to the server behind the scenes

## Configuration Files

Instead of writing the channel and object configuration in the source code, you can use configuration files. This way the channel can be reconfigured, additional channels can be added, and so on, without changing the source code. Like all the other configuration files on the .NET platform, XML is used. The same application and configuration files that you read about in Chapter 15 and in Chapter 16, ".NET Security," are used here, too. For .NET Remoting, there are some more XML elements and attributes to configure the channel and the remote objects. The difference with the remoting configuration file is that this configuration needn't be in the application configuration file itself; the file can have any name. To make the build process easier, in this chapter the Remoting configuration is written inside the application configuration files named with a `.config` file extension after the file name of the executable.

The code download (from www.wrox.xom) contains the following example configuration files in the root directory of the client and the server examples: `clientactivated.config` and `wellknown.config`.

With the client example, you will also find the file `wellknownhttp.config` that specifies an HTTP channel to a well-known remote object. To use these configurations, the files must be renamed to the name that is used with the parameter of the `RemotingConfiguration.Configure()` method and placed in the directory containing the executable file.

Here is just one example of how such a configuration file might look:

```
<configuration>
    <system.runtime.remoting>
        <application name="Hello">
            <service>
                <wellknown mode="SingleCall"
                    type="Wrox.ProCSharp.Remoting.Hello, RemoteHello"
                        objectUri="Hi" />
            </service>
            <channels>
                <channel ref="tcp" port="6791" />
                <channel ref="http" port="6792" />
                <channel ref="ipc" portName="myIPCPort" />
            </channels>
        </application>
    </system.runtime.remoting>
</configuration>
```

`<configuration>` is the XML root element for all .NET configuration files. All the remoting configurations can be found in the subelement `<system.runtime.remoting>`. `<application>` is a subelement of `<system.runtime.remoting>`.

The following list describes the main elements and attributes of the parts within `<system.runtime.remoting>`:

- With the `<application>` element you can specify the name of the application using the attribute name. On the server side, this is the name of the server, and on the client side it's the name of the client application. As an example for a server configuration, `<application name="Hello">` defines the remote application name `Hello`, which is used as part of the URL by the client to access the remote object.

- On the server, the element `<service>` is used to specify a collection of remote objects. It can have `<wellknown>` and `<activated>` subelements to specify the type of the remote object as well-known or client-activated.

- The client part of the `<service>` element is `<client>`. Like the `<service>` element, it can have `<wellknown>` and `<activated>` subelements to specify the type of the remote object. Unlike the `<service>` counterpart, `<client>` has a `url` attribute to specify the URL to the remote object.

- `<wellknown>` is an element that's used on the server and the client to specify well-known remote objects. The server part could look like this:

```
<wellknown mode="SingleCall"
    type="Wrox.ProCSharp.Remoting.Hello, RemoteHello"
        objectURI="Hi" />
```

# .NET Remoting

- While the `mode` attribute `SingleCall` or `Singleton` can be specified, the type is the type of the remote class, including the namespace `Wrox.ProCSharp.Remoting.Hello`, followed by the assembly name RemoteHello. `objectURI` is the name of the remote object that's registered in the channel.

- On the client, the `type` attribute is the same as it is for the server version. `mode` and `objectURI` are not needed, but the `url` attribute is used to define the path to the remote object instead: protocol, hostname, port number, application name, and the object URI:

    ```
    <wellknown type="Wrox.ProCSharp.Remoting.Hello, RemoteHello"
               url="tcp://localhost:6791/Hello/Hi" />
    ```

- The `<activated>` element is used for client-activated objects. With the `type` attribute the type and the assembly must be defined for both the client and the server application:

    ```
    <activated type="Wrox.ProCSharp.Remoting.Hello, RemoteHello" />
    ```

- To specify the channel, the `<channel>` element is used. It's a subelement of `<channels>` so that a collection of channels can be configured for a single application. Its use is similar for clients and servers. With the XML attribute `ref` you reference a preconfigured channel name. For the server channel you have to set the port number with the XML attribute `port`. The XML attribute `displayName` is used to specify a name for the channel that is used from the .NET Framework Configuration tool, as discussed later in this chapter.

    ```
    <channels>
        <channel ref="tcp" port="6791" displayName="TCP Channel" />
        <channel ref="http" port="6792" displayName="HTTP Channel" />
        <channel ref="ipc" portName="myIPCPort" displayName="IPC Channel" />
    </channels>
    ```

## *Predefined channels*

You can use predefined channels instead of defining the channel types with the configuration file. Prior to .NET 2.0, you can read predefined channels in the `machine.config` configuration file, which is in the directory `<windir>\Microsoft.NET\Framework\<version>\CONFIG`. With .NET 2.0 the predefined channels are defined by the `RemotingConfiguration` class to get a better performance.

In the following XML file extract you can see the predefined channels. The `<channel>` element is used as a subelement of `<channels>` to define channels. Here the attribute `id` specifies a name of a channel that can be referenced with the `ref` attribute. With the `type` attribute the class of the channel is specified followed by the assembly; for example, the channel class `System.Runtime.Remoting.Channels.Http.HttpChannel` can be found in the assembly `System.Runtime.Remoting`. Because the `System.Runtime.Remoting` assembly is shared, the strong name of the assembly must be specified with `Version`, `Culture`, and `PublicKeyToken`:

```
<system.runtime.remoting>
  <!-- ... -->
  <channels>
    <channel id="http" type="System.Runtime.Remoting.Channels.Http.HttpChannel,
        System.Runtime.Remoting, Version=2.0.0.0, Culture=neutral,
        PublicKeyToken=b77a5c561934e089"/>
    <channel id="http client"
      type="System.Runtime.Remoting.Channels.Http.HttpClientChannel,
```

```xml
          System.Runtime.Remoting, Version=2.0.0.0, Culture=neutral,
          PublicKeyToken=b77a5c561934e089"/>
      <channel id="http server"
        type="System.Runtime.Remoting.Channels.Http.HttpServerChannel,
          System.Runtime.Remoting, Version=2.0.0.0, Culture=neutral,
          PublicKeyToken=b77a5c561934e089"/>
      <channel id="tcp" type="System.Runtime.Remoting.Channels.Tcp.TcpChannel,
          System.Runtime.Remoting, Version=2.0.0.0, Culture=neutral,
          PublicKeyToken=b77a5c561934e089"/>
      <channel id="tcp client"
        type="System.Runtime.Remoting.Channels.Tcp.TcpClientChannel,
          System.Runtime.Remoting, Version=2.0.0.0, Culture=neutral,
          PublicKeyToken=b77a5c561934e089"/>
      <channel id="tcp server"
        type="System.Runtime.Remoting.Channels.Tcp.TcpServerChannel,
          System.Runtime.Remoting, Version=2.0.0.0, Culture=neutral,
          PublicKeyToken=b77a5c561934e089"/>
      <channel id="ipc" type="System.Runtime.Remoting.Channels.Ipc.IpcChannel,
          System.Runtime.Remoting, Version=2.0.0.0, Culture=neutral,
          PublicKeyToken=b77a5c561934e089"/>
      <channel id="ipc client"
        type="System.Runtime.Remoting.Channels.Ipc.IpcClientChannel,
          System.Runtime.Remoting, Version=2.0.0.0, Culture=neutral,
          PublicKeyToken=b77a5c561934e089"/>
      <channel id="ipc server"
        type="System.Runtime.Remoting.Channels.Ipc.IpcServerChannel,
          System.Runtime.Remoting, Version=2.0.0.0, Culture=neutral,
          PublicKeyToken=b77a5c561934e089"/>
    </channels>
  <!-- ... -->
<system.runtime.remoting>
```

## *Server configuration for well-known objects*

This example file, `Wellknown_Server.config`, has the value `Hello` for the `name` property. In the following configuration file, the TCP channel is set to listen on port 6791 and the HTTP channel is set to listen on port 6792. The IPC channel is configured with the port name `myIPCPort`. The remote object class is `Wrox.ProCSharp.Remoting.Hello` in the assembly `RemoteHello`, the object is called `Hi` in the channel, and the object mode is `SingleCall`:

```xml
<configuration>
  <system.runtime.remoting>
    <application name="Hello">
      <service>
        <wellknown mode="SingleCall"
                   type="Wrox.ProCSharp.Remoting.Hello, RemoteHello"
                   objectUri="Hi" />
      </service>
      <channels>
        <channel ref="tcp" port="6791"
            displayName="TCP Channel (HelloServer)" />
        <channel ref="http" port="6792"
            displayName="HTTP Channel (HelloServer)" />
```

```
                <channel ref="ipc" portName="myIPCPort"
                    displayName="IPC Channel (HelloServer)" />
            </channels>
        </application>
    </system.runtime.remoting>
</configuration>
```

## Client configuration for well-known objects

For well-known objects, you have to specify the assembly and the channel in the client configuration file `Wellknown_Client.config`. The types for the remote object are in the `RemoteHello` assembly, `Hi` is the name of the object in the channel, and the URI for the remote type `Wrox.ProCSharp.Remoting.Hello` is `ipc://myIPCPort/Hello/Hi`. In the client, an IPC channel is used as well, but no port is specified, so a free port is selected. The channel that is selected with the client must correspond to the URL:

```
<configuration>
    <system.runtime.remoting>
        <application name="Client">
            <client displayName="Hello client for well-known objects">
                <wellknown type = "Wrox.ProCSharp.Remoting.Hello, RemoteHello"
                           url="ipc://myIPCPort/Hello/Hi" />
            </client>
            <channels>
                <channel ref="ipc" displayName="IPC Channel (HelloClient)" />
            </channels>
        </application>
    </system.runtime.remoting>
</configuration>
```

After a small change in the configuration file, you're using the HTTP channel (as you can see in `WellknownHttp_Client.config`):

```
<client>
    <wellknown type="Wrox.ProCSharp.Remoting.Hello, RemoteHello"
               url="http://localhost:6792/Hello/Hi" />
</client>
<channels>
    <channel ref="http" displayName="HTTP Channel (HelloClient)" />
</channels>
```

## Server configuration for client-activated objects

By changing only the configuration file (located in `ClientActivated_Server.config`), you can change the server configuration from server-activated to client-activated objects. Here the `<activated>` subelement of the `<service>` element is specified. With the `<activated>` element for the server configuration, just the `type` attribute must be specified. The `name` attribute of the `application` element defines the URI:

```
<configuration>
    <system.runtime.remoting>
        <application name="HelloServer">
            <service>
                <activated type="Wrox.ProCSharp.Remoting.Hello, RemoteHello" />
            </service>
```

## Chapter 29

```xml
            <channels>
               <channel ref="http" port="6788"
                        displayName="HTTP Channel (HelloServer)" />
               <channel ref="tcp" port="6789"
                  displayName="TCP Channel (HelloServer)" />
               <channel ref="ipc" portName="myIPCPort"
                        displayName="IPC Channel (HelloServer)" />
            </channels>
         </application>
      </system.runtime.remoting>
</configuration>
```

### Client configuration for client-activated objects

The `ClientActivated_Client.config` file defines the client-activated remote object using the `url` attribute of the `<client>` element and the `type` attribute of the `<activated>` element:

```xml
<configuration>
   <system.runtime.remoting>
      <application>
         <client url="http://localhost:6788/HelloServer"
                 displayName="Hello client for client-activated objects">
            <activated type="Wrox.ProCSharp.Remoting.Hello, RemoteHello" />
         </client>
         <channels>
            <channel ref="http" displayName="HTTP Channel (HelloClient)" />
            <channel ref="tcp" displayName="TCP Channel (HelloClient)" />
            <channel ref="ipc" displayName="IPC Channel (HelloClient)" />
         </channels>
      </application>
   </system.runtime.remoting>
</configuration>
```

### Server code using configuration files

In the server code, you have to configure remoting using the static method `Configure()` from the `RemotingConfiguration` class. Here all channels that are defined in the configuration file are created and configured with the .NET Remoting runtime. Maybe you also want to know about the channel configurations from the server application—that's why the static methods `ShowActivatedServiceTypes()` and `ShowWellKnownServiceTypes()` were created; they are called after loading and starting the remoting configuration:

```csharp
public static void Main(string[] args)
{
    RemotingConfiguration.Configure("HelloServer.exe.config",false);
    Console.WriteLine("Application: " + RemotingConfiguration.ApplicationName);
    ShowActivatedServiceTypes();
    ShowWellKnownServiceTypes();
    System.Console.WriteLine("press return to exit");
    System.Console.ReadLine();
    return;
}
```

# .NET Remoting

These two functions show configuration information of well-known and client-activated types:

```
public static void ShowWellKnownServiceTypes()
{
   WellKnownServiceTypeEntry[] entries =
   RemotingConfiguration.GetRegisteredWellKnownServiceTypes();
   foreach (WellKnownServiceTypeEntry entry in entries)
   {
      Console.WriteLine("Assembly: " + entry.AssemblyName);
      Console.WriteLine("Mode: " + entry.Mode);
      Console.WriteLine("URI: " + entry.ObjectUri);
      Console.WriteLine("Type: " + entry.TypeName);
   }
}
public static void ShowActivatedServiceTypes()
{
   ActivatedServiceTypeEntry[] entries =
   RemotingConfiguration.GetRegisteredActivatedServiceTypes();
   foreach (ActivatedServiceTypeEntry entry in entries)
   {
      Console.WriteLine("Assembly: " + entry.AssemblyName);
      Console.WriteLine("Type: " + entry.TypeName);
   }
}
```

## *Client code using configuration files*

In the client code, it is only necessary to configure the remoting services using the configuration file `client.exe.config`. After that, you can use the `new` operator to create new instances of the remote class `Hello`, no matter whether you work with server-activated or client-activated remote objects. However, there's a small difference — with client-activated objects it's now possible to use *non-default constructors* with the `new` operator. This isn't possible for server-activated objects: single-call objects can have no state because they are destroyed with every call; singleton objects are created just once. Calling non-default constructors is only possible with client-activated objects because this is the only type where by invoking the `new` operator the remote object the object is instantiated.

In the `Main()` method of the file `HelloClient.cs`, you can now change the remoting code to use the configuration file with `RemotingConfiguration.Configure()` and create the remote object with the `new` operator:

```
RemotingConfiguration.Configure("HelloClient.exe.config",false);
Hello obj = new Hello();
if (obj == null)
{
   Console.WriteLine("could not locate server");
   return;
}
for (int i=0; i < 5; i++)
{
   Console.WriteLine(obj.Greeting("Christian"));
}
```

## Delayed loading of client channels

With the configuration file `machine.config`, three channels are configured that can be used automatically if the client doesn't configure a channel:

```
<system.runtime.remoting>
   <application>
      <channels>
         <channel ref="http client" displayName="http client (delay loaded)"
                  delayLoadAsClientChannel="true" />
         <channel ref="tcp client" displayName="tcp client (delay loaded)"
                  delayLoadAsClientChannel="true" />
         <channel ref="ipc client" displayName="ipc client (delay loaded)"
                  delayLoadAsClientChannel="true" />
      </channels>
   </application>
</system.runtime.remoting>
```

The XML attribute `delayLoadAsClientChannel` with a value `true` defines that the channel should be used from a client that doesn't configure a channel. The runtime tries to connect to the server using the delay-loaded channels. So it is not necessary to configure a channel in the client configuration file, and a client configuration file for the well-known object you have used earlier can look as simple as this:

```
<configuration>
   <system.runtime.remoting>
      <application name="Client">
         <client url="tcp:/localhost:6791/Hello">
            <wellknown type = "Wrox.ProCSharp.Remoting.Hello, RemoteHello"
                       url="tcp://localhost:6791/Hello/Hi" />
         </client>
      </application>
   </system.runtime.remoting>
</configuration>
```

## Debugging Configuration

If you have a misconfigured server configuration file (for example, by specifying the wrong name of the remote assembly), the error is not detected when the server starts. Instead, the error is detected when the client instantiates a remote object and invokes a method. The client will get the exception that the remote object assembly cannot be found. By specifying the configuration <debug loadTypes="true" />, the remote object is loaded and instantiated on the server when the server starts up. This way you will get an error on the server if the configuration file is misconfigured:

```
<configuration>
   <system.runtime.remoting>
      <application name="Hello">
         <service>
            <wellknown mode="SingleCall"
                       type="Wrox.ProCSharp.Remoting.Hello, RemoteHello"
                       objectUri="Hi" />
         </service>
         <channels>
```

# .NET Remoting

```
            <channel ref="tcp" port="6791"
                displayName="TCP Channel (HelloServer)" />
         </channels>
      </application>
      <debug loadTypes="true" />
   </system.runtime.remoting>
</configuration>
```

## Lifetime services in configuration files

Leasing configuration for remote servers can also be done with the application configuration files. The `<lifetime>` element has the attributes `leaseTime`, `sponsorshipTimeOut`, `renewOnCallTime`, and `pollTime` as shown in this example:

```
<configuration>
   <system.runtime.remoting>
      <application>
         <lifetime leaseTime = "15M" sponsorshipTimeOut = "4M"
                   renewOnCallTime = "3M" pollTime = "30s"/>
      </application>
   </system.runtime.remoting>
</configuration>
```

Using configuration files, it is possible to change the remoting configuration by editing files instead of working with source code. You can easily change the channel to use HTTP instead of TCP, change a port, the name of the channel, and so on. With the addition of a single line the server can listen to two channels instead of one.

## Formatter providers

Earlier, this chapter discussed where properties of the formatter provider need to be changed to support marshaling all objects across the network. Instead of doing this programmatically, as was done earlier, you can configure the properties of a formatter provider in a configuration file.

The following server configuration file is changed within the `<channel>` element, insofar as `<serverProviders>` and `<clientProviders>` are defined as child elements. With the `<serverProviders>`, the built-in providers `wsdl`, `soap`, and `binary` are referenced, and with the soap and binary providers the property `typeFilterLevel` is set to `Full`:

```
<configuration>
   <system.runtime.remoting>
      <application name="HelloServer">
         <service>
            <activated type="Wrox.ProCSharp.Remoting.Hello, RemoteHello" />
         </service>
         <channels>
            <channel ref="tcp" port="6789"
                     displayName="TCP Channel (HelloServer)">
               <serverProviders>
                  <provider ref="wsdl" />
                  <provider ref="soap" typeFilterLevel="Full" />
```

1047

# Chapter 29

```
                <provider ref="binary" typeFilterLevel="Full" />
            </serverProviders>
            <clientProviders>
                <provider ref="binary" />
            </clientProviders>
        </channel>
      </channels>
    </application>
  </system.runtime.remoting>
</configuration>
```

## .NET Framework Configuration tool

The System Administrator can use the .NET Framework Configuration tool (see Figure 29-11) to reconfigure existing configuration files. This tool is part of the Administrative Tools, which can be accessed by using the Control Panel.

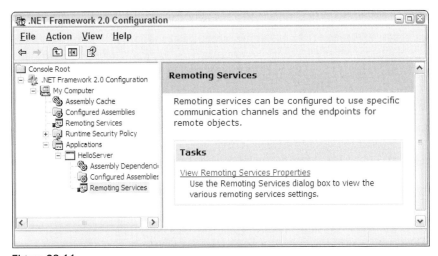

**Figure 29-11**

By adding the application `HelloClient.exe` where you used the client configuration file to the configured applications in this tool, you can configure the URL of the remote object by selecting the hyperlink View Remoting Services Properties.

As shown in Figure 29-12, for the client application you can see the value of the `displayName` attribute in the combo box. This combo box allows you to select the remote application so you can change the URL of the remote object.

By adding the server application to this tool, the configuration of the remote object and the channels can be changed as shown in Figure 29-13 and Figure 29-14.

# .NET Remoting

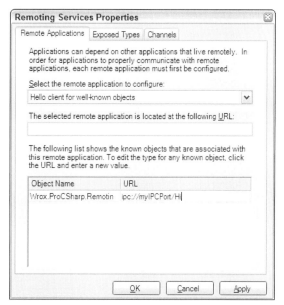

Figure 29-12

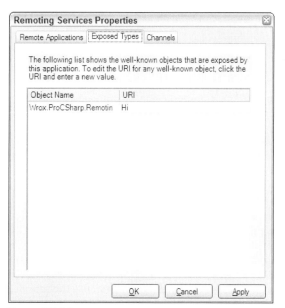

Figure 29-13

# Chapter 29

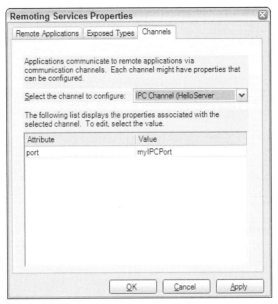

Figure 29-14

## Hosting Servers in ASP.NET

Up to this point, all the sample servers were running in self-hosted .NET servers. A self-hosted server must be launched manually. A .NET Remoting server can also be started in a lot of other application types. In a Windows Service the server can be automatically started at boot-time, and in addition the process can run with the credentials of the system account. For more details on Windows Services, see Chapter 36, "Windows Services."

There's special support for .NET Remoting servers for ASP.NET. ASP.NET can be used for the automatic startup of remote servers. Contrary to EXE-hosted applications, ASP.NET-hosted Remoting uses a different file for configuration, but it has the same syntax.

To use the infrastructure from the Internet Information Server and ASP.NET, you have to create a class that derives from `System.MarshalByRefObject` and has a default constructor. The code used earlier for the server to create and register the channel is no longer necessary; that's done by the ASP.NET runtime. You have to create only a virtual directory on the Web server that maps a directory into which you put the configuration file `web.config`. The assembly of the remote class must reside in the bin subdirectory.

To configure a virtual directory on the Web server, you can use the Internet Information Services MMC. Selecting the Default Web site and opening the Action menu creates a new Virtual Directory.

The configuration file `web.config` on the Web server must be put in the home directory of the virtual Web site. With the default IIS configuration, the channel that will be used listens to port 80:

```xml
<configuration>
   <system.runtime.remoting>
      <application>
         <service>
            <wellknown mode="SingleCall"
               type="Wrox.ProCSharp.Remoting.Hello, RemoteHello"
               objectUri="HelloService.soap" />
         </service>
      </application>
   </system.runtime.remoting>
</configuration>
```

> If the remoting object is hosted within IIS, the name of the remote object must end either with .soap, or .rem, depending on the type of formatter that is used (SOAP or the binary).

The client can now connect to the remote object using the following configuration file. The URL that must be specified for the remote object here is the Web server localhost, followed by the Web application name RemoteHello (specified when creating the virtual Web site), and the URI of the remote object HelloService.soap that is defined in the file web.config. It's not necessary to specify the port number 80, because that's the default port for the HTTP protocol. Not specifying a <channels> section means that the delay-loaded HTTP channel from the configuration file machine.config is used:

```xml
<configuration>
   <system.runtime.remoting>
      <application>
         <client url="http:/localhost/RemoteHello">
            <wellknown type="Wrox.ProCSharp.Remoting.Hello, RemoteHello"
                       url="http://localhost/RemoteHello/HelloService.soap" />
         </client>
      </application>
   </system.runtime.remoting>
</configuration>
```

> Hosting remote objects in ASP.NET only supports well-known objects.

## Classes, Interfaces, and Soapsuds

In the .NET Remoting samples you have seen until now, you have always copied the assembly of the remote object not only to the server, but also to the client application. This way the MSIL code of the remote object is on both the client and the server system, although in the client application only the metadata is needed. However, copying the remoting object assembly means that it's not possible for the client and the server to be programmed independently. A much better way to use just the metadata is to use interfaces or the Soapsuds.exe utility instead.

# Chapter 29

## *Interfaces*

You get a cleaner separation of the client and server code by using interfaces. An interface simply defines the methods without implementation. This way the contract (the interface) is separated from the implementation, and just the contract is needed on the client system. Here are the necessary steps for using an interface:

1. Define an interface that will be placed in a separate assembly.
2. Implement the interface in the remote object class. To do this, the assembly of the interface must be referenced.
3. On the server side no more changes are required. The server can be programmed and configured in the usual ways.
4. On the client side, reference the assembly of the interface instead of the assembly of the remote class.
5. The client can now use the interface of the remote object rather than the remote object class. The object can be created using the `Activator` class as it was done earlier. You can't use the `new` operator in this way, because the interface itself cannot be instantiated.

The interface defines the contract between the client and server. The two applications can now be developed independently of each other. If you also stick to the old COM rules about interfaces (that interfaces should never be changed), you will not have any versioning problems.

## *Soapsuds*

You can also use the Soapsuds utility to get the metadata from an assembly if an HTTP channel and the SOAP formatter are used. Soapsuds can convert assemblies to XML Schemas, XML Schemas to wrapper classes, and also works in the other directions.

The following command converts the type `Hello` from the assembly `RemoteHello` to the assembly `HelloWrapper` where a transparent proxy is generated that calls the remote object:

```
soapsuds -types:Wrox.ProCSharp.Remoting.Hello,RemoteHello -oa:HelloWrapper.dll
```

With Soapsuds you can also get the type information directly from a running server, if the HTTP channel and the SOAP formatter are used:

```
soapsuds -url:http://localhost:6792/hello/hi?wsdl -oa:HelloWrapper.dll
```

In the client, you can now reference the generated assembly instead of the original one. Some of the Soapsuds options are listed in the following table.

| Option | Description |
| --- | --- |
| `-url` | Retrieve schema from the specified URL |
| `-proxyurl` | If a proxy server is required to access the server, specify the proxy with this option |
| `-types` | Specify a type and assembly to read the schema information from it |

# .NET Remoting

| Option | Description |
| --- | --- |
| -is | Input schema file |
| -ia | Input assembly file |
| -os | Output schema file |
| -oa | Output assembly file |

## Asynchronous Remoting

If server methods take some time to complete and the client needs to do some different work at the same time, it isn't necessary to start a separate thread to do the remote call. By doing an asynchronous call, the method starts but returns immediately to the client. Asynchronous calls can be made on a remote object as they are made on a local object with the help of a delegate. With methods that don't return a value, you can also use the `OneWay` attribute.

### Using delegates with .NET Remoting

To make an asynchronous method, you create a delegate, `GreetingDelegate`, with the same argument and return value as the `Greeting()` method of the remote object. With the `delegate` keyword a new class `GreetingDelegate` that derives from `MulticastDelegate` is created. You can verify this by using ildasm and checking the assembly. The argument of the constructor of this delegate class is a reference to the `Greeting()` method. You start the `Greeting()` call using the `BeginInvoke()` method of the delegate class. The second argument of `BeginInvoke()` is an `AsyncCallback` instance that defines the method `HelloClient.Callback()`, which is called when the remote method is finished. In the `Callback()` method, the remote call is finished using `EndInvoke()`:

```
using System;
using System.Runtime.Remoting;
namespace Wrox.ProCSharp.Remoting
{
    public class HelloClient
    {
        private delegate String GreetingDelegate(String name);
        private static string greeting;

        public static void Main(string[] args)
        {
            RemotingConfiguration.Configure("HelloClient.exe.config",false);
            Hello obj = new Hello();
            if (obj == null)
            {
                Console.WriteLine("could not locate server");
                return;
            }
            // synchronous version
            // string greeting = obj.Greeting("Christian");
            // asynchronous version

            GreetingDelegate d = new GreetingDelegate(obj.Greeting);
```

```
            IAsyncResult ar = d.BeginInvoke("Christian", null, null);

            // do some work and then wait
            ar.AsyncWaitHandle.WaitOne();
            if (ar.IsCompleted)
            {
                greeting = d.EndInvoke(ar);
            }

            Console.WriteLine(greeting);
        }
    }
}
```

You can find more information about delegates and events in Chapter 6, "Delegates and Events."

## OneWay attribute

A method that has a void return and only input parameters can be marked with the OneWay attribute. The OneWay attribute (defined within the namespace System.Runtime.Remoting.Messaging) makes a method automatically asynchronous, regardless of how the client calls it. Adding the method TakeAWhile() to your remote object class RemoteHello creates a fire-and-forget method. If the client calls it by the proxy, the proxy immediately returns to the client. On the server, the method finishes some time later:

```
[OneWay]
public void TakeAWhile(int ms)
{
    Console.WriteLine("TakeAWhile started");
    System.Threading.Thread.Sleep(ms);
    Console.WriteLine("TakeAWhile finished");
}
```

## Security with .NET Remoting

A complete new feature with .NET 2.0 is security support with .NET Remoting. With .NET 1.1, security was only available when the remote object was hosted within IIS and ASP.NET. .NET 2.0 supports confidentiality of the data that is transferred across the wire as well as authentication of the user.

Security for .NET Remoting is a new feature of .NET 2.0. Every channel that implements the interface ISecurableChannel supports security. With .NET 2.0, the TCP and IPC channels support security. However, the TcpClientChannel and TcpServerChannel classes don't support security. You have to use the TcpChannel class on both the client and server. For using security with the HTTP channel, the remoting object must be configured within IIS.

Let's start with the server configuration. The following extract of the configuration file shows how the security can be defined for the server.

With the XML attribute protectionLevel you can specify if the server requires encrypted data to be sent across the network. The possible values that can be set with the protectionLevel attribute are None, Sign, and EncryptAndSign. With the value Sign a signature is created that is used to verify if the data that is sent didn't change on its way across the network. However, it is still possible to read the data with a sniffer that reads all the data on the network. With the value `EncryptAndSign`, the data that is sent is also encrypted to make it impossible that systems not officially participating with the message transfer can read the data.

The attribute `impersonate` can be set to `true` or `false`. If `impersonate` is set to `true`, the server can impersonate the user of the client to access resources in its name.

```
<channels>
    <channel ref="tcp" port="9001"
        secure="true"
        protectionLevel="EncryptAndSign"
        impersonate="false" />
</channels>
```

Configuring a secure channel, you should also enable security with `RemotingConfiguration.Configure()`. The second parameter of this method has a Boolean value, where you can enable security by passing the value `true`. This way all configured channels must support security, otherwise an exception is thrown.

With the client configuration, the capabilities of the network communication are defined. If the capabilities don't fulfil the server requirements, the communication fails. You can see `protectionLevel` and `TokenImpersonationLevel` configured in the following sample configuration.

`protectionLevel` can be set to the same options as you have seen with the server configuration file.

The `TokenImpersonationLevel` can be set to `Anonymous`, `Identification`, `Impersonation` and `Delegation`. With the `Anonymous` value, the server cannot identify the user of the client. If the value is set to `Identification`, the server can find out the user identity of the server. In case the server is configured with `impersonate` set to `true`, the communication fails if the client is only configured with `Anonymous` or `Identification`. `TokenImpersonationLevel` set to `Impersonation` allows the server to impersonate the client. `TokenImpersonationLevel` set to `Delegation` allows the server to impersonate the client not only to access resources local on the server, but also to use the user identification to access resources on other servers. Delegation is only possible if Kerberos is used for logon of the user as is possible with the Active Directory.

```
<channels>
    <channel ref="tcp"
        secure="true"
        protectionLevel="EncryptAndSign"
        TokenImpersonationLevel="Impersonation" />
</channels>
```

If you create the channel programmatically instead of using configuration files, you can define the security setting programmatically as well. A collection that contains all security settings can be passed to the constructor of the channel as shown. The requirement for the collection class is to implement the interface `IDictionary`, for example the generic `Dictionary` class or the `Hashtable` class.

```
Dictionary<string, string> dict;
         = new Dictionary<string, string>();
dict.Add("secure", "true");

TcpChannel clientChannel =
         new TcpChannel(dict, null, null);
```

# Chapter 29

Configuring a secure channel, with the method `ChannelServices.RegisterChannel()` the second parameter must be set to `true`.

You can read more about security in Chapter 16.

## Remoting and Events

Not only can the client invoke methods on the remote object across the network; the server can do the same: invoking methods in the client. For this, a mechanism that you already know from the basic language features is used: *delegates and events*.

In principle, the architecture is simple. The server has a remotable object that the client can call, and the client has a remotable object that the server can call:

- ❑ The remote object in the server must declare an external function (a delegate) with the signature of the method that the client will implement in a handler.
- ❑ The arguments that are passed with the handler function to the client must be marshalable, so all the data sent to the client must be serializable.
- ❑ The remote object must also declare an instance of the delegate function modified with the `event` keyword; the client will use this to register a handler.
- ❑ The client must create a sink object with a handler method that has the same signature as the delegate defined, and it has to register the sink object with the event in the remote object.

Take a look at an example. To see all the parts of event handling with .NET Remoting, create five classes: `Server`, `Client`, `RemoteObject`, `EventSink`, and `StatusEventArgs`. The dependencies of these classes are shown in Figure 29-15.

The `Server` class is a remoting server such as the one you already are familiar with. The `Server` class will create a channel based on information from a configuration file and register the remote object that's implemented in the `RemoteObject` class in the remoting runtime. The remote object declares the arguments of a delegate and fires events in the registered handler functions. The argument that's passed to the handler function is of type `StatusEventArgs`. The class `StatusEventArgs` must be serializable so it can be marshaled to the client.

The `Client` class represents the client application. This class creates an instance of the `EventSink` class and registers the `StatusHandler()` method of this class as a handler for the delegate in the remote object. `EventSink` must be remotable like the `RemoteObject` class, because this class will also be called across the network.

### Remote object

The remote object class is implemented in the file `RemoteObject.cs`. The remote object class must be derived from `MarshalByRefObject`, as you already know from the previous examples. To enable the client to register an event handler that can be called from within the remote object, you have to declare an external function with the `delegate` keyword. Declare the delegate `StatusEvent()` with two arguments: the `sender` (so the client knows about the object that fired the event) and a variable of type `StatusEventArgs`. Into the argument class you can put all the additional information that you want to send to the client.

# .NET Remoting

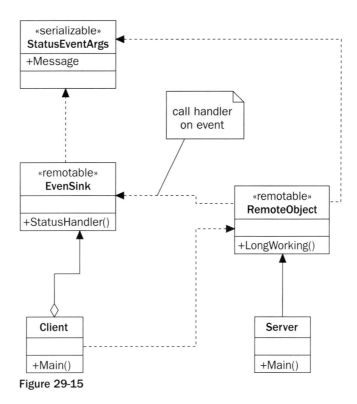

Figure 29-15

The method that will be implemented in the client has some strict requirements. It can only have input parameters — return types, ref, and out parameters are not allowed — and the argument types must be either [Serializable] or remotable (derived from MarshalByRefObject). These requirements are fulfilled by the parameters that are defined with this StatusEvent delegate:

```
public delegate void StatusEvent(object sender, StatusEventArgs e);

public class RemoteObject : MarshalByRefObject
{
```

Within the RemoteObject class, declare an event name Status of type StatusEvent, which is the delegate. The client must add an event handler to the Status event to receive status information from the remote object:

```
public class RemoteObject : MarshalByRefObject
{
    public RemoteObject()
    {
        Console.WriteLine("RemoteObject constructor called");
    }
    public event StatusEvent Status;
```

The `LongWorking()` method checks if an event handler is registered before the event is fired by calling `Status(this, e)`. To verify that the event is fired asynchronously, fire an event at the start of the method before doing the `Thread.Sleep()` and after the sleep:

```
public void LongWorking(int ms)
{
   Console.WriteLine("RemoteObject: LongWorking() Started");
   StatusEventArgs e = new StatusEventArgs(
                       "Message for Client: LongWorking() Started");
   // fire event
   if (Status != null)
   {
      Console.WriteLine("RemoteObject: Firing Starting Event");
      Status(this, e);
   }
   System.Threading.Thread.Sleep(ms);
   e.Message = "Message for Client: LongWorking() Ending";
   // fire ending event
   if (Status != null)
   {
      Console.WriteLine("RemoteObject: Firing Ending Event");
      Status(this, e);
   }
   Console.WriteLine("RemoteObject: LongWorking() Ending");
}
```

## Event arguments

As you've seen in the `RemoteObject` class, the class `StatusEventArgs` is used as an argument for the delegate. With the `[Serializable]` attribute an instance of this class can be transferred from the server to the client. Here is a simple property of type `string` to send a message to the client:

```
[Serializable]
public class StatusEventArgs
{
   public StatusEventArgs(string m)
   {
      message = m;
   }
   public string Message
   {
      get
      {
         return message;
      }
      set
      {
         message = value;
      }
   }
   private string message;
}
```

# .NET Remoting

## Server

The server is implemented within a console application. With `RemotingConfiguration.Configure()`, the configuration file is read and thus the channel and remote objects are set up. With the Console.ReadLine() the server waits until the user stops the application:

```
using System;
using System.Runtime.Remoting;
namespace Wrox.ProCSharp.Remoting
{
   class Server
   {
      static void Main(string[] args)
      {
         RemotingConfiguration.Configure("Server.exe.config",false);
         Console.WriteLine("press return to exit");
         Console.ReadLine();
      }
   }
}
```

## Server configuration file

The server configuration file, `Server.exe.config`, is also created as already discussed. There is just one important point: the remote object must keep state for the client because the client at first registers the event handler and calls the remote method afterward. You cannot use single-call objects with events, so the `RemoteObject` class is configured as a client-activated type. Also, to support delegates, you have to enable full serialization by specifying the `typeFilterLevel` attribute with the `<provider>` element:

```
<configuration>
   <system.runtime.remoting>
      <application name="CallbackSample">
         <service>
            <activated type="Wrox.ProCSharp.Remoting.RemoteObject,
                            RemoteObject" />
         </service>
         <channels>
            <channel ref="http" port="6791">
               <serverProviders>
                  <provider ref="binary" typeFilterLevel="Full" />
               </serverProviders>
            </channel>
         </channels>
      </application>
   </system.runtime.remoting>
</configuration>
```

## Event sink

An event sink library is required for use by the client and is invoked by the server. The event sink implements the handler `StatusHandler()` that's defined with the delegate. As previously noted, the method can only have input parameters and only a void return. The `EventSink` class must also inherit from the class `MarshalByRefObject` to make it remotable, because it will be called remotely from the server:

# Chapter 29

```csharp
using System;
using System.Runtime.Remoting.Messaging;
namespace Wrox.ProCSharp.Remoting
{
   public class EventSink : MarshalByRefObject
   {
      public EventSink()
      {
      }
      public void StatusHandler(object sender, StatusEventArgs e)
      {
         Console.WriteLine("EventSink: Event occurred: " + e.Message);
      }
   }
}
```

## Client

The client reads the client configuration file with the `RemotingConfiguration` class, which is not different from the clients that have been discussed so far. The client creates an instance of the remotable sink class `EventSink` locally. The method that should be called from the remote object on the server is passed to the remote object:

```csharp
using System;
using System.Runtime.Remoting;
namespace Wrox.ProCSharp.Remoting
{
   class Client
   {
      static void Main(string[] args)
      {
         RemotingConfiguration.Configure("Client.exe.config");
```

The differences start here. You have to create an instance of the remotable sink class `EventSink` locally. Because this class will not be configured with the `<client>` element, it's instantiated locally. Next, the remote object class `RemoteObject` is instantiated. This class is configured in the `<client>` element, so it's instantiated on the remote server:

```csharp
         EventSink sink = new EventSink();
         RemoteObject obj = new RemoteObject();
```

Now you can register the handler method of the `EventSink` object in the remote object. `StatusEvent` is the name of the delegate that was defined in the server. The `StatusHandler()` method has the same arguments as defined in the `StatusEvent`.

By calling the `LongWorking()` method, the server will call back into the method `StatusHandler()` at the beginning and at the end of the method:

```csharp
         // register client sink in server - subscribe to event

         obj.Status += new StatusEvent(sink.StatusHandler);
         obj.LongWorking(5000);
```

# .NET Remoting

Now you are no longer interested in receiving events from the server and so you are unsubscribing from the event. The next time you call `LongWorking()`, no events will be received:

```
        // unsubscribe from event

        obj.Status -= new StatusEvent(sink.StatusHandler);
        obj.LongWorking(5000);

        Console.WriteLine("press return to exit");
        Console.ReadLine();
      }
   }
}
```

## Client configuration file

The configuration file for the client, `client.exe.config`, is nearly the same configuration file for client-activated objects that we've already seen. The difference is in defining a port number for the channel. Because the server must reach the client with a known port, you have to define the port number for the channel as an attribute of the `<channel>` element. It isn't necessary to define a `<service>` section for your `EventSink` class, because this class will be instantiated from the client with the `new` operator locally. The server does not access this object by its name; it will receive a marshaled reference to the instance instead:

```
<configuration>
   <system.runtime.remoting>
      <application name="Client">
         <client url="http://localhost:6791/CallbackSample">
            <activated type="Wrox.ProCSharp.Remoting.RemoteObject,
                          RemoteObject" />
         </client>
         <channels>
            <channel ref="http" port="0">
               <serverProviders>
                  <provider ref="binary" typeFilterLevel="Full" />
               </serverProviders>
            </channel>
         </channels>
      </application>
   </system.runtime.remoting>
</configuration>
```

## *Running programs*

Figure 29-16 shows the resulting output of the server. The constructor of the remote object is called once because you have a client-activated object. Next, you can see the call to `LongWorking()` has started and an event is fired to the client. The next start of the `LongWorking()` method doesn't fire events, because the client has already unregistered its interest in the event.

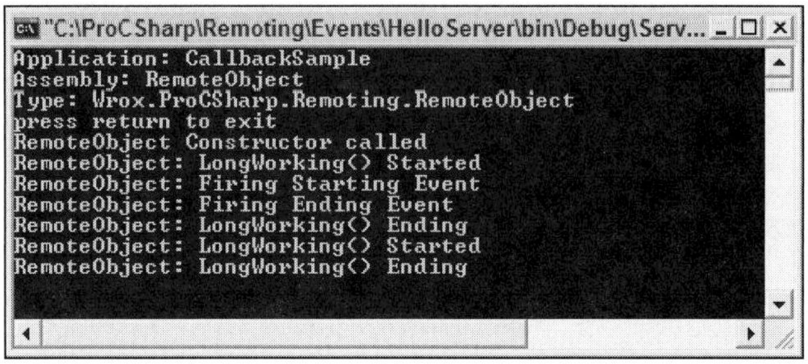

Figure 29-16

Figure 29-17 shows the client output of the events that made it across the network.

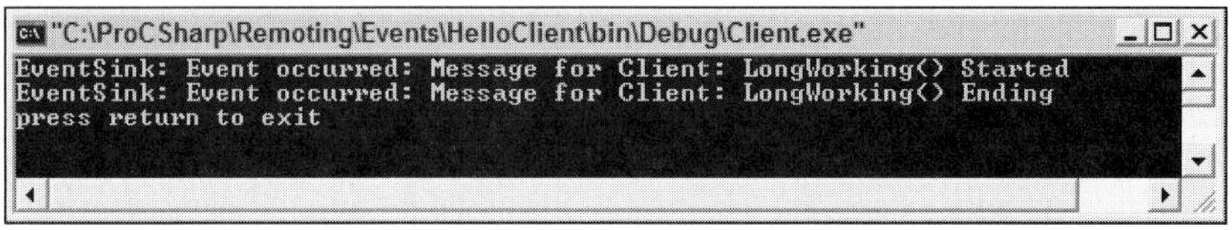

Figure 29-17

## *Call Contexts*

Client-activated objects can hold state for a specific client. With client-activated objects the server allocates resources for every client. With server-activated SingleCall objects, a new instance is created for every instance call, and no resources are held on the server; these objects can't hold state for a client. For state management you can keep state on the client side; the state information is sent with every method call to the server. To implement such a state management, it is not necessary to change all method signatures to include an additional parameter that passes the state to the server; this is automatically done by the *call context*.

A call context flows with a logical thread and is passed with every method call. A *logical thread* is started from the calling thread and flows through all method calls that are started from the calling thread, passing through different contexts, different application domains, and different processes.

You can assign data to the call context using CallContext.SetData(). The class of the object that's used as data for the SetData() method must implement the interface ILogicalThreadAffinative. You can get this data again in the same logical thread (but possibly a different physical thread) using CallContext.GetData().

For the data of the call context, create a new C# Class Library with the class CallContextData. This class will be used to pass some data from the client to the server with every method call. The class that's passed with the call context must implement the System.Runtime.Remoting.Messaging. ILogicalThreadAffinative interface. This interface doesn't have a method; it's just a markup for the runtime to define that instances of this class should flow with a logical thread. The CallContextData class must also be marked with the Serializable attribute so it can be transferred through the channel:

```csharp
using System;
using System.Runtime.Remoting.Messaging;
namespace Wrox.ProCSharp.Remoting
{
   [Serializable]
   public class CallContextData : ILogicalThreadAffinative
   {
      public CallContextData()
      {
      }
      public string Data
      {
         get
         {
            return data;
         }
         set
         {
            data = value;
         }
      }
      protected string data;
   }
}
```

In the remote object class Hello, change the Greeting() method to access the call context. For the use of the CallContextData class you have to reference the previously created assembly CallContextData in the file CallContextData.dll. To work with the CallContext class, the namespace System.Runtime.Remoting.Messaging must be opened. The variable cookie holds the data that is sent from the client to the server. The name "cookie" is chosen because the context works similar to a browser-based cookie, where the client automatically sends data to the Web server:

```csharp
public string Greeting(string name)
{
   Console.WriteLine("Greeting started");
   CallContextData cookie =
      (CallContextData)CallContext.GetData("mycookie");
   if (cookie != null)
   {
      Console.WriteLine("Cookie: " + cookie.Data);
   }
   Console.WriteLine("Greeting finished");
   return "Hello, " + name;
}
```

In the client code, the call context information is set by calling CallContext.SetData(). With this method an instance of the class CallContextData is assigned to be passed to the server. Now every time the method Greeting() is called in the for loop, the context data is automatically passed to the server:

```csharp
CallContextData cookie = new CallContextData();
cookie.Data = "information for the server";
CallContext.SetData("mycookie", cookie);
```

```
        for (int i=0; i < 5; i++)
        {
            Console.WriteLine(obj.Greeting("Christian"));
        }
```

You can use such a call context to send information about the user, the name of the client system, or simply a unique identifier used on the server side to get some state information from a database.

# Summary

In this chapter, you've seen that .NET Remoting facilitates the task of invoking methods across the network: A remote object has to inherit form `MarshalByRefObject`. In the server application only a single method is needed to load the configuration file so that the channels and remote objects are both set up and running. Within the client, you load the configuration file and can use the `new` operator to instantiate the remote object.

You also used .NET Remoting without the help of configuration files. On the server, you simply created a channel and registered a remote object. On the client, you created a channel and used the remote object.

Furthermore, you learned that the .NET Remoting architecture is flexible and can be extended. All parts of this technology such as channels, proxies, formatters, message sinks, and so on are pluggable and can be replaced with custom implementations.

You used HTTP, TCP, and IPC channels for the communication across the network, and SOAP and binary formatters to format the parameters before sending them.

You learned about the stateless and stateful object types that are used by well-known and client-activated objects. With client-activated objects you have seen how the leasing mechanism is used to specify the lifetime of remote objects.

You have also seen that .NET Remoting is very well integrated in other parts of the .NET Framework, such as calling asynchronous methods, performing callbacks using the delegate and event keywords, and so on.

# 30

# Enterprise Services

*Enterprise Services* is the name of the Microsoft application server technology that offers services for distributed solutions. Enterprise Services is based on the COM+ technology that has already been in use for many years. However, instead of wrapping .NET objects as COM objects to use these services, .NET offers extensions for .NET components to take direct advantage of these services. With .NET you get easy access to COM+ services for .NET components.

This chapter covers the following topics:

- ❑ When to use Enterprise Services
- ❑ What services you get with this technology
- ❑ How to create a serviced component to use Enterprise Services
- ❑ How to deploy COM+ applications
- ❑ How to use transactions with Enterprise Services
- ❑ How to use Services without components

## Overview

The complexity of Enterprise Services and the different configuration options (many of them are not needed if all the components of the solution are developed with .NET) can be more easily understood if you know the history of Enterprise Services. That's why this section starts with the history of Enterprise Services. After that, you get an overview of the different services offered by this technology so you will know what feature could be useful for your application.

# Chapter 30

The topics of this section are as follows:

- History
- Where to use Enterprise Services
- Contexts
- Automatic transactions
- Distributed transactions
- Object pooling
- Role-based security
- Queued components
- Loosely coupled events
- Services without components

## History

Enterprise Services can be traced back to Microsoft Transaction Server (MTS), which was released as an option pack for Windows NT 4.0. MTS extended COM by offering services such as transactions for COM objects. The services could be used by configuring metadata: the configuration of the component defined whether or not a transaction was required. With MTS it was no longer necessary to deal with transactions programmatically. However, MTS had a big disadvantage. COM was not designed to be extensible, so MTS made extensions by overwriting the COM component registry configuration to direct the instantiation of the component to MTS, and some special MTS API calls have been required to instantiate COM objects within MTS. This problem was solved with Windows 2000.

One of the most important features of Windows 2000 was the integration of MTS and COM in a new technology with the name COM+. With Windows 2000, COM+ base services are aware of the context that is needed by COM+ services (previously MTS services), and so the special MTS API calls are no longer needed. With COM+ services some new service functionality is offered in addition to distributed transactions.

Windows 2000 includes COM+ 1.0. COM+ 1.5 is available with Windows XP and Windows Server 2003. COM+ 1.5 adds more features to increase scalability and availability, including application pooling and recycling, and configurable isolation levels.

.NET Enterprise Services allows you to use COM+ services from within .NET components. Support is offered for Windows 2000 and later. When .NET components are run within COM+ applications, no COM callable wrapper is used (see Chapter 33, "COM Interoperability"); it runs as a .NET component instead. When you install the .NET runtime on an operating system, some runtime extensions are added to COM+ Services. If two .NET components are installed with Enterprise Services, and component A is using component B, COM marshaling is not used; instead the .NET components can invoke each other directly.

# Enterprise Services

## Where to Use Enterprise Services

Business applications can be logically separated into presentation, business, and data service layers. The *presentation service layer* is responsible for user interaction. Here the user can interact with the application to enter and view data. Technologies used with this layer are Windows Forms and ASP.NET Web Forms. The *business service layer* consists of business rules and data rules. The *data service layer* interacts with persistent storage. Here you can use components that make use of ADO.NET. Enterprise Services fits both to the business service layer and to the data service layer.

Figure 30-1 shows two typical application scenarios. Enterprise Services can be used directly from a rich client using Windows Forms or from a Web application that is running ASP.NET.

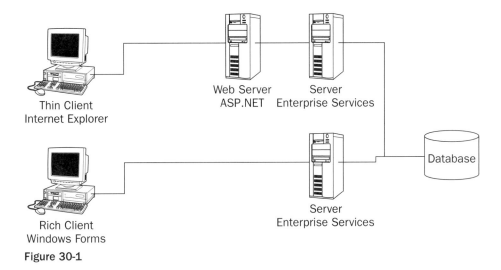

Figure 30-1

Enterprise Services is also a scalable technology. Using *component load balancing* makes it possible to distribute the load of the clients across different systems. Component load balancing requires the Microsoft Application Center Server. You can read more information abut the Microsoft Application Center Server at http://www.microsoft.com/applicationcenter.

You can also use Enterprise Services on the client system, because this technology is included in Windows XP.

## Contexts

The base functionality behind the services offered by Enterprise Services is the context. The context makes it possible to intercept a method call, and some service functionality can be carried out before the expected method call is invoked.

Contexts are discussed in Chapter 29, ".NET Remoting." .NET Remoting contexts also play an important role with Enterprise Services, because these contexts are used for intercepting .NET objects configured with Enterprise Services. However, because COM components can be configured with Enterprise

1067

Services in a similar way as with .NET components, the COM+ context exists in conjunction with the .NET Remoting context. This way, a COM component and a .NET component can participate in the same transaction.

## Automatic Transactions

The most commonly used feature of Enterprise Services is *automatic transactions*. With automatic transactions, you needn't start and commit a transaction in the code; an attribute can be applied to a class instead. By using the [Transaction] attribute with the options Required, Supported, RequiresNew, and NotSupported, you can mark a class with the requirements it has for transactions. If you mark the class with the option Required, a transaction is created automatically when a method starts and is committed to or aborted when the root component of the transaction is finished.

Such a declarative way to program is of particular advantage when a complex object model is developed. Here automatic transactions have a big advantage instead of programming transactions manually. Assume you have a Person object with multiple Address and Document objects that are associated with the Person, and you want to store the Person object together with all associated objects in a single transaction. Doing transactions programmatically would mean passing a transaction object to all the related objects so that they can participate in the same transaction. Using transactions declaratively means there is no need to pass the transaction object, because this happens behind the scenes by using the context.

## Distributed Transactions

Enterprise Services not only offers automatic transactions, but the transactions can also be distributed across multiple databases. Enterprise Services transactions are enlisted with the *Distributed Transaction Coordinator* (DTC). The DTC supports databases that make use of the XA protocol, which is a two-phase commit protocol, and is supported by SQL Server and Oracle. A single transaction can span writing data to both a SQL Server and an Oracle database.

Distributed transactions are not only useful with databases, but a single transaction can also span writing data to a database and writing data to a message queue. If one of these two actions fails, a rollback is done with the other action. You can read more about message queuing in Chapter 31, "Message Queuing."

Later in this chapter, you see how to create a component that requires transactions.

## Object Pooling

Pooling is another feature offered by Enterprise Services. These services use a pool of threads to answer requests from clients. Object pooling can be used for objects with a long initialization time. With object pooling, objects are created in advance so that clients don't have to wait until the object is initialized.

## Role-based Security

Using *role-based security* allows you to define roles declaratively and define what methods or components can be used from what roles. The system administrator assigns users or user groups to these roles. In the program there is no need to deal with access control lists; instead, roles that are simple strings can be used.

# Enterprise Services

## Queued Components

*Queued components* is an abstraction layer to message queuing. Instead of sending messages to a message queue, the client can invoke methods with a recorder that offers the same methods as a .NET class configured in Enterprise Services. The recorder in turn creates messages that are transferred via a message queue to the server application.

Queued components and message queuing are useful if the client application is running in a disconnected environment (for example, on a laptop that does not always has a connection to the server), or if the request that is sent to the server should be cached before it is forwarded to a different server (for example, to a server of a partner company).

## Loosely Coupled Events

Chapter 29 discussed how to use events with .NET Remoting. Chapter 33 describes how to use events in a COM environment. With both of these event mechanisms, the client and the server do have a tight connection. This is different with *loosely coupled events* (LCE). With LCE the COM+ facility is inserted between client and server (see Figure 30-2). The publisher registers the events it will offer with COM+ by defining an event class. Instead of sending the events directly to the client, the publisher sends events to the event class that is registered with the LCE service. The LCE service forwards the events to the subscriber, which is the client application that registered a subscription for the event.

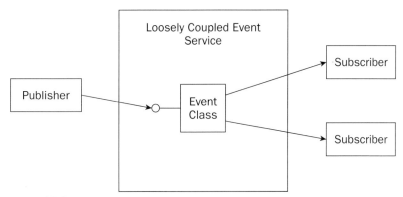

Figure 30-2

## Services without Components

Services without Components is a new feature of COM+ 1.5. With this service it is possible to create a context without the need of configuring a component. By using some classes from the namespace System.EnterpriseServices, the context can be created within a method. Such a context can have transactional requirements associated to automatically deal with transactions that are managed by the DTC.

At the end of this chapter you see how Services without Components can be used from a .NET application.

1069

# Chapter 30

# Creating a Simple COM+ Application

To create a .NET class that can be configured with Enterprise Services, you have to reference the assembly `System.EnterpriseServices` and add the namespace `System.EnterpriseServices` to the using declarations. The most important class to use is `ServicedComponent`.

The first example shows the basic requirements to create a serviced component. You start by creating a C# library application. All COM+ applications must be written as library applications regardless whether they will run in their own process or in the process of the client. Name the library `SimpleServer`. Reference the assembly `System.EnterpriseServices` and add the declaration `using System.EnterpriseServices;` to the `assmblyinfo.cs` and `class1.cs` files.

## Class ServicedComponent

Every serviced component class must derive from the base class `ServicedComponent`. `ServicedComponent` itself derives from the class `ContextBoundObject`, so an instance is bound to a .NET Remoting context.

The class `ServicedComponent` has some protected methods that can be overridden, as shown in the following table.

| Protected Method | Description |
| --- | --- |
| Activate()<br>Deactivate() | The Activate() and Deactivate() methods are called if the object is configured to use object pooling. When the object is taken from the pool, the Activate() method is called. Before the object is returned to the pool, Deactivate() is called. |
| CanBePooled() | This is another method for object pooling. If the object is in an inconsistent state, you can return false in your overridden implementation of CanBePooled(). This way the object is not put back into the pool, but destroyed instead. A new object will be created for the pool. |
| Construct() | This method is called at instantiation time, where a construction string can be passed to the object. The construction string can be modified by the system administrator. Later in this chapter, you use the construction string to define the database connection string. |

## Sign the Assembly

Libraries configured with Enterprise Services need a strong name. For some Enterprise Services features it is also necessary to install the assembly in the global assembly cache. Strong names and the global assembly cache are discussed in Chapter 15, "Assemblies."

# Enterprise Services

## *Assembly Attributes*

Some Enterprise Services attributes are also needed. The attribute `ApplicationName` defines the name of the application as it will be seen in the Component Services explorer. The value of the `Description` attribute shows up as a description within the application configuration tool.

`ApplicationActivation` allows you to define whether the application should be configured as a library application or a server application, using the options `ActivationOption.Library` or `ActivationOption.Server`. With a library application, the application is loaded inside the process of the client. In that case the client might be the ASP.NET runtime. With a server application, a process for the application is started. The name of the process is dllhost.exe. With the attribute `ApplicationAccessControl` you can turn off security so that every user is allowed to use the component.

You can add these attributes to the file `class1.cs` outside the namespace declaration:

```
[assembly: ApplicationName("Wrox EnterpriseDemo")]
[assembly: Description("Wrox Sample Application for Professional C#")]
[assembly: ApplicationActivation(ActivationOption.Server)]
[assembly: ApplicationAccessControl(false)]
```

The following table lists the most important assembly attributes that can be defined with Enterprise Services applications.

| Attribute | Description |
| --- | --- |
| [ApplicationName] | The attribute [ApplicationName] defines the name for the COM+ application that shows up in the Component Services explorer after the component is configured. |
| [ApplicationActivation] | The attribute [ApplicationActivation] defines if the application should run as a library within the client application, or if a separate process should be started. The options to configure are defined with the enumeration ActivationOption. ActivationOption.Library defines to run the application inside the process of the client; ActivationOption.Server starts its own process, dllhost.exe. |
| [ApplicationAccessControl] | The attribute [ApplicationAccessControl] defines the security configuration of the application. Using a Boolean value you can set whether access control should be enabled or disabled. With the Authentication property you can set privacy levels — whether the client should be authenticated with every method call or just with the connection, and whether the data sent should be encrypted. |

1071

## Creating the Component

In the `class1.cs` file you can create your serviced component class. With serviced components it is best to define interfaces that are used as the contract between the client and the component. This is not a strict requirement, but some of the Enterprise Services features (such as setting role-based security on a method or interface level) do require interfaces. Create the interface `IGreeting` with the method `Welcome()`:

```csharp
using System;
using System.EnterpriseServices;

namespace Wrox.ProCSharp.EnterpriseServices
{
   public interface IGreeting
   {
      string Welcome(string name);
   }
```

The class `SimpleComponent` derives from the base class `ServicedComponent` and implements the interface `IGreeting`. The class `ServicedComponent` acts as a base class of all serviced component classes, and offers some methods for the activation and construction phases. Applying the attribute `[EventTrackingEnabled]` to this class makes it possible to monitor the objects with the Component Services explorer. By default monitoring is disabled because using this feature reduces performance. The attribute `[Description]` only specifies text that shows up in the explorer:

```csharp
[EventTrackingEnabled(true)]
[Description("Simple Serviced Component Sample")]
public class SimpleComponent : ServicedComponent, IGreeting
{
   public SimpleComponent()
   {
   }
```

The method `Welcome()` only returns `"Hello, "` with the name that is passed to the argument. So you can see some visible result in the Component Services explorer while the component is running, `Thread.Sleep()` simulates some processing time:

```csharp
      public string Welcome(string name)
      {
         // simulate some processing time
         System.Threading.Thread.Sleep(1000);
         return "Hello, " + name;
      }
   }
}
```

Other than applying some attributes and deriving the class from `ServicedComponent`, there's nothing special to do with classes that should use Enterprises Services features. All that is left to do is building and deploying a client application.

With the first sample component the attribute `[EventTrackingEnabled]` was set. Some more commonly used attributes that influence the configuration of serviced components are described in the following table.

# Enterprise Services

| Attribute Class | Description |
|---|---|
| [EventTrackingEnabled] | Setting the attribute [EventTrackingEnabled] allows monitoring the component with the Component Services explorer. Setting this attribute to true has some additional overhead associated; that's why by default event tracking is turned off. |
| [JustInTimeActivation] | With this attribute the component can be configured to not activate when the caller instantiates the class, but instead when the first method is invoked. Also, with this attribute the component can deactivate itself. |
| [ObjectPooling] | If the initialization time of a component is long compared to the time of a method call, an object pool can be configured with the attribute [ObjectPooling]. With this attribute minimum and maximum values can be defined that influence the number of objects in the pool. |
| [Transaction] | The attribute [Transaction] defines transactional characteristics of the component. Here the component defines whether a transaction is required, supported, or not supported. |

# Deployment

Assemblies with serviced components must be configured with COM+. This configuration can be done automatically or by registering the assembly manually.

## Automatic Deployment

If a .NET client application that uses the serviced component is started, the COM+ application is configured automatically. This is true for all classes that derive from the class ServicedComponent. Application and class attributes such as [EventTrackingEnabled] define the characteristics of the configuration.

Automatic deployment has an important drawback. For automatic deployment to work, the client application needs administrative rights. If the client application that invokes the serviced component is ASP.NET, the ASP.NET runtime usually doesn't have administrative rights. With this drawback, automatic deployment is useful only during development time. However, during development automatic deployment is an extremely advantageous feature because it is not necessary to do manual deployment after every build.

## Manual Deployment

You can deploy the assembly manually with the command-line utility .NET Services Installation Tool regsvcs.exe. Starting the command

```
regsvcs SimpleServer.dll
```

registers the assembly `SimpleServer` as a COM+ application and configures the included components according to their attributes, and also creates a type library that can be used by COM clients accessing the .NET component.

After you've configured the assembly, you can start the Component Services explorer by selecting Administrative Tools ➪ Component Services from the Windows menu. In the left tree view of this application, you can select Component Services ➪ Computers ➪ My Computer ➪ COM+ Applications to verify that the application was configured.

## Creating an Installer Package

With the Component Services explorer, you can create Windows installer packages for server or client systems. An installer package for the server includes the assemblies and configuration settings to install the application on a different server. If the serviced component is invoked from applications running on different systems, a proxy must be installed on the client system. The installer package for the client includes assemblies and configuration for proxies.

To create an installer package, you can start the Component Services explorer, select the COM+ application, select the menu Action ➪ Export, and click the Next button with the first dialog. Then the dialog shown in Figure 30-3 is opened. With this dialog you can export either a Server application or an Application proxy. With the option Server application you can also configure to export user identities with roles. This option should only be selected if the target system is in the same domain as the system where the package is created, as the configured user identities are put into the installer package. With the option Application proxy, an installer package for the client system is created.

**Figure 30-3**

*The option to create an Application proxy is not available if the application is configured as a library application.*

# Enterprise Services

To install the proxy, you just have to start the setup.exe from the installer package. Be aware that an application proxy cannot be installed on the same system where the application is installed. After installation of the application proxy, you can see an entry in Component Services explorer that represents the application proxy. With the application proxy the only option that can be configured is the name of the server in the Activation tab as discussed in the next section.

## Component Services Explorer

After a successful configuration, you can see Wrox EnterpriseDemo as an application name in the tree view of the Component Services explorer. This name was set by the attribute [ApplicationName]. Selecting Action ⇨ Properties opens the dialog box shown in Figure 30-4. Both the name and the description have been configured by using attributes. When you select the Activation tab, you can see that the application is configured as a server application because this has been defined with the [ApplicationActivation] attribute, and selecting the Security tab shows that the Enforce access checks for this application option is not selected because the attribute [ApplicationAccessControl] was set to false.

Figure 30-4

The following is a list of some more options that can be set with this application:

❑ **Security.** With the security configuration, you can enable or disable access checks. If security is enabled, you can set access checks to the application level, the component, the interface, and to the method level. It is also possible to encrypt messages that are sent across the network using packet privacy as an authentication level for calls. Of course, this also increases the overhead.

# Chapter 30

- **Identity.** With server applications you can use the Identity tab to configure the user account that will be used for the process that hosts the application. By default this is the interactive user. This setting is very useful while debugging the application but cannot be used on a production system if the application is running on a server, because there might not be anybody logged on. The configuration can be changed for a specific user.

- **Activation.** The Activation tab allows you to configure the application either as a library or as a server application. Two new options with COM+ 1.5 are the option to run the application as a Windows Service and to use SOAP to access the application. Windows Services are discussed in Chapter 36, "Windows Services." Selecting the SOAP option uses .NET Remoting configured within Internet Information Server to access the component. .NET Remoting is discussed in Chapter 29, ".NET Remoting."

  With an application proxy, the option Remote server name is the only option that can be configured. With this option the name of the server is set. By default, the DCOM protocol is used as the network protocol. However, if SOAP is selected with the server configuration, the communication happens through .NET Remoting.

- **Queuing.** The Queuing configuration is required for service components that make use of Message Queuing.

- **Advanced.** With the Advanced tab you can specify whether the application should be shut down after a certain period of client inactivity. You can also specify whether to lock a certain configuration so no one can change it accidentally.

- **Dump.** If the application crashes, you can specify the directory where the dumps should be stored. This is useful for components developed with C++.

- **Pooling & Recycling.** Pooling and recycling is a new option with COM+ 1.5. With this option you can configure whether the application should be restarted (recycled) depending on application lifetime, memory needs, number of calls, and so on.

With the Component Services explorer you can also view and configure the component itself. When opening child elements of the application, you can view the component `Wrox.ProCSharp.Enterprise Services.SimpleComponent`. Selecting Action ⇨ Properties opens the dialog box shown in Figure 30-5.

Using this dialog box, you can configure these options:

- **Transactions.** With the Transactions tab you can specify whether the component requires transactions. You use this feature in the next example.

- **Security.** If security is enabled with the application, you can define with this configuration what roles are allowed to use the component.

- **Activation.** The Activation configuration enables you to set object pooling and to assign a construction string.

- **Concurrency.** If the component is not thread-safe, concurrency can be set to Required or Requires New. This way the COM+ runtime only allows one thread at a time to access the component.

# Enterprise Services

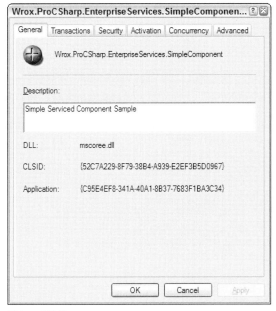

Figure 30-5

# Client Application

After building the serviced component library, you can create a client application. This can be as simple as a C# console application. After you've created the project for the client, you have to reference both the assembly from the serviced component, `SimpleServer`, and the assembly `System.EnterpriseServices`. Then you can write the code to instantiate a new `SimpleComponent` instance, and invoke the method `Welcome()`. In the following code the `Welcome()` method is called 10 times. The `using` statement helps to release the resources allocated with the instance before the garbage collector takes action. With the `using` statement, the `Dispose()` method of the serviced component is called when the scope of the `using` statement ends.

```
using System;

namespace Wrox.ProCSharp.EnterpriseServices
{
   class Program
   {
      static void Main(string[] args)
      {
         using (SimpleComponent obj = new SimpleComponent())
         {
            for (int i = 0; i < 10; i++)
            {
               Console.WriteLine(obj.Welcome("Kathie"));
            }
```

```
            }
        }
    }
}
```

If you start the client application before configuring the server, the server will be configured automatically. The automatic configuration of the server is done with the values that you've specified using attributes. For a test you can unregister the serviced component and start the client again. If the serviced component is configured during the start of the client application, the startup needs more time. Remember that this feature is only useful during development time.

While the application is running, you can monitor the serviced component with the Component Services explorer. By selecting Components in the tree view and choosing View ➪ Detail, you can view the number of instantiated objects if the attribute [EventTrackingEnabled] is set.

As you've seen, creating serviced components is just a matter of deriving the class from the base class ServicedComponent and setting some attributes to configure the application. Next you see how transactions can be used with serviced components.

# Transactions

*Automatic transactions* are the most frequently used feature of Enterprise Services. What are transactions? Think about ordering a book from a Web site. The book order process removes the book you want to buy from the stock and puts it in your order box, and the cost of your book is charged to your credit card. With these two actions, either both actions should complete successfully or neither of these actions should happen.

Such a scenario can be solved with transactions. A transaction has some specific requirements; for example, a valid state must be the result of a transaction. Valid state is also required if the server has a power failure. The characteristics of transactions can be defined with the term "ACID," as described in the following section.

## *ACID Properties*

ACID is a four-letter acronym for *atomicity, consistency, isolation,* and *durability*:

- **Atomicity.** Atomicity represents one unit of work. With a transaction, either the complete unit of work succeeds or nothing is changed.

- **Consistency.** The state of the database must be a valid, consistent state after the transaction committed.

- **Isolation.** Isolation means that transactions that happen concurrently are isolated from state that is changed during a transaction. Transaction A cannot see the changed state of transaction B until the transaction is completed.

- **Durability.** After the transaction is completed, it must be stored in a durable way. This means that if the power goes down or the server crashes, the state must be recovered at reboot.

# Enterprise Services

## Transaction Attributes

Serviced components can be marked with the `[Transaction]` attribute to define if and how transactions are required with the component.

| TransactionOption Value | Description |
| --- | --- |
| `Required` | Setting the `[Transaction]` attribute to `TransactionOption.Required` means that the component runs inside a transaction. If a transaction has been created already, the component will run in the same transaction. If no transaction exists, a transaction will be created. |
| `RequiresNew` | `TransactionOption.RequiresNew` always results in a newly created transaction. The component never participates in the same transaction as the caller. |
| `Supported` | With `TransactionOption.Supported`, the component doesn't need transactions itself. However, the transaction will span the caller and the called component, if these components require transactions. |
| `NotSupported` | The option `TransactionOption.NotSupported` means that the component never runs in a transaction, regardless of whether the caller has a transaction. |
| `Disabled` | `TransactionOption.Disabled` means that a possible transaction of the current context is ignored. |

Figure 30-6 shows multiple components with different transactional configurations. The client invokes component A. Because component A is configured with Transaction Required and no transaction existed previously, the new transaction 1 is created. Component A invokes component B, which in turn invokes component C. Because component B is configured with Transaction Supported, and the configuration of component C is set to Transaction Required, all three components A, B, and C do use the same transaction context. If component B were configured with the transaction setting NotSupported, component C would get a new transaction. Component D is configured with the setting New Transaction Required, so a new transaction is created when it is called by component A.

## Transaction Results

A transaction can be influenced by setting the *consistent* and the *done* bit of the context. If the consistent bit is set to `true`, the component is happy with the outcome of the transaction. The transaction can be committed if all components participating with the transaction are similarly successful. If the consistent bit is set to `false`, the component is not happy with the outcome of the transaction, and the transaction will be aborted when the root object that started the transaction is finished. If the done bit is set, the object can be deactivated after the method call ends. A new instance will be created with the next method call.

# Chapter 30

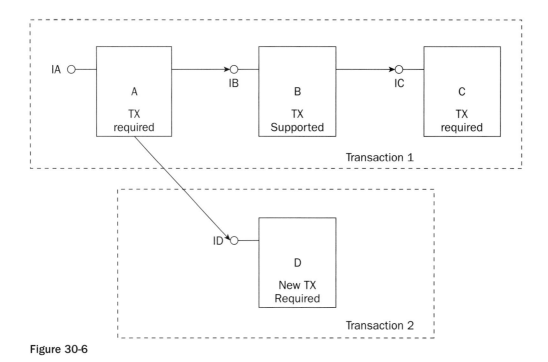

**Figure 30-6**

The consistent and done bits can be set using four methods of the `ContextUtil` class with the results that you can see in the following table.

| ContextUtil Method | Consistent Bit | Done Bit |
|---|---|---|
| SetComplete | true | true |
| SetAbort | false | true |
| EnableCommit | true | false |
| DisableCommit | false | false |

With .NET it is also possible to set the consistent and done bit by applying the attribute `[AutoComplete]` to the method instead of calling the `ContextUtil` methods. With this attribute the method `ContextUtil.SetComplete()` will be called automatically if the method is successful. If the method fails and an exception is thrown, with `[AutoComplete]` the method `ContextUtil.SetAbort()` will be called.

# Sample Application

This sample application simulates a simplified scenario that writes new orders to the Northwind sample database. As shown in Figure 30-7, multiple components are used with the COM+ application. The class `OderControl` is called from the client application to create new orders. `OrderControl` uses the

OrderData component. OrderData has the responsibility of creating a new entry in the Order table of
the Northwind database. The OrderData component uses the OrderLineData component to write
Order Detail entries to the database. Both OrderData and OrderLineData must participate in the same
transaction.

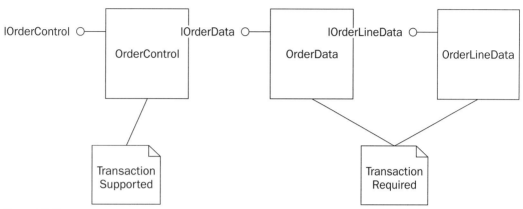

Figure 30-7

Start by creating a C# Component library with the name NorthwindComponent. Sign the assembly with
a keyfile, and define the Enterprise Services application attributes as shown in the following code:

```
[assembly: ApplicationName("Wrox.NorthwindDemo")]
[assembly: ApplicationActivation(ActivationOption.Library)]
[assembly: ApplicationAccessControl(false)]
```

## *Entity Classes*

Next add some entity classes that represent the columns in the Northwind database tables Order and
Order Details. The class Order has a static method Create() that creates and returns a new instance
of the class Order, and initializes this instance with the arguments passed to this method. Also, the
class Order has some read-only properties to access the fields oderId, customerId, orderData,
shipAddress, shipCity, and shipCountry. OrderId is not known at creation time of the class Order,
but because the Order table in the Northwind database has an auto-increment attribute, OrderId is just
known after the order is written to the database. The method SetOrderId() is used to set the corresponding id after the order has been written to the database. Because this method is called by a class
inside the same assembly, the access level of this method is set to internal. The method
AddOrderLine() adds order details to the order:

```
using System;
using System.Collections.Generic;

namespace Wrox.ProCSharp.EnterpriseServices
{
    [Serializable]
    public class Order
    {
```

# Chapter 30

```csharp
public static Order Create(string customerId, DateTime orderDate,
            string shipAddress, string shipCity, string shipCountry)
{
   Order o = new Order();
   o.customerId = customerId;
   o.orderDate = orderDate;
   o.shipAddress = shipAddress;
   o.shipCity = shipCity;
   o.shipCountry = shipCountry;
   return o;
}

public Order()
{
}

internal void SetOrderId(int orderId)
{
   this.orderId = orderId;
}

public void AddOrderLine(OrderLine orderLine)
{
   orderLines.Add(orderLine);
}

private int orderId;
private string customerId;
private DateTime orderDate;
private string shipAddress;
private string shipCity;
private string shipCountry;
private List<OrderLine> orderLines = new List<OrderLine>();

public int OrderId
{
   get
   {
      return orderId;
   }
}
public string CustomerId
{
   get
   {
      return customerId;
   }
}
public DateTime OrderDate
{
   get
   {
      return orderDate;
   }
```

```
         }
         public string ShipAddress
         {
            get
            {
               return shipAddress;
            }
         }
         public string ShipCity
         {
            get
            {
               return shipCity;
            }
         }
         public string ShipCountry
         {
            get
            {
               return shipCountry;
            }
         }
         public OrderLine[] OrderLines
         {
            get
            {
               OrderLine[] ol = new OrderLine[orderLines.Count];
               orderLines.CopyTo(ol);
               return ol;
            }
         }
      }
   }
```

The second entity class is OrderLine. OrderLine has a static Create() method similar to the one of the Order class. Other than that, the class only has some properties for the fields productId, unitPrice, and quantity:

```
using System;

namespace Wrox.ProCSharp.EnterpriseServices
{
   [Serializable]
   public class OrderLine
   {
      public static OrderLine Create(int productId, float unitPrice, int quantity)
      {
         OrderLine detail = new OrderLine();
         detail.productId = productId;
         detail.unitPrice = unitPrice;
         detail.quantity = quantity;
         return detail;
      }
      public OrderLine()
```

```csharp
        {
        }

        private int productId;
        private float unitPrice;
        private int quantity;

        public int ProductId
        {
            get
            {
                return productId;
            }
            set
            {
                productId = value;
            }
        }
        public float UnitPrice
        {
            get
            {
                return unitPrice;
            }
            set
            {
                unitPrice = value;
            }
        }
        public int Quantity
        {
            get
            {
                return quantity;
            }
            set
            {
                quantity = value;
            }
        }
    }
}
```

## The OrderControl Component

The class `OrderControl` represents a simple business services component. In this example, just one method, `NewOrder()`, is defined in the interface `IOrderControl`. The implementation of `NewOrder()` does nothing more than instantiate a new instance of the data services component `OrderData` and call the method `Insert()` to write an `Order` object to the database. In a more complex scenario, this method could be extended to write a log entry to a database or to invoke a queued component to send the `Order` object to a message queue:

```csharp
using System;
using System.EnterpriseServices;
using System.Data;
using System.Data.SqlClient;
using System.Collections.Generic;

namespace Wrox.ProCSharp.EnterpriseServices
{
   public interface IOrderControl
   {
      void NewOrder(Order order);
   }

   [Transaction(TransactionOption.Supported)]
   [EventTrackingEnabled(true)]
   public class OrderControl : ServicedComponent, IOrderControl
   {
      [AutoComplete()]
      public void NewOrder(Order order)
      {
         OrderData data = new OrderData();
         data.Insert(order);
      }
   }
}
```

## The OrderData Component

The `OrderData` class is responsible for writing the values of `Order` objects to the database. The interface `IOrderUpdate` defines the `Insert()` method. You can extend this interface to also support an `Update()` method where an existing entry in the database gets updated:

```csharp
using System;
using System.EnterpriseServices;
using System.Data;
using System.Data.SqlClient;

namespace Wrox.ProCSharp.EnterpriseServices
{
   public interface IOrderUpdate
   {
      void Insert(Order order);
   }
```

The class `OrderData` has the attribute `[Transaction]` with the value `TransactionOption.Required` applied. This means that the component will run in a transaction in any case. Either a transaction is created by the caller and `OrderData` uses the same transaction, or a new transaction is created. Here a new transaction will be created because the calling component `OrderControl` doesn't have a transaction.

With serviced components you can only use default constructors. However, you can use the Component Services explorer to configure a construction string that is sent to a component (see Figure 30-8). Selecting the Activation tab of the component configuration enables you to change the construction string. The

## Chapter 30

option "Enable object construction" is turned on when the attribute [ConstructionEnabled] is set, as it is with the class OrderData. The Default property of the [ConstructionEnabled] attribute defines the default connection string shown in the Activation settings after registration of the assembly. Setting this attribute also requires you to overload the method Construct() from the base class ServicedComponent. This method is called by the COM+ runtime at object instantiation, and the construction string is passed as an argument. The construction string is set to the variable connectionString that is used later to connect to the database:

```
[Transaction(TransactionOption.Required)]
[EventTrackingEnabled(true)]
[ConstructionEnabled(true, Default="server=localhost;
                     database=northwind;trusted_connection=true")]
public class OrderData : ServicedComponent, IOrderUpdate
{
   private string connectionString = null;

   protected override void Construct(string s)
   {
      connectionString = s;
   }
}
```

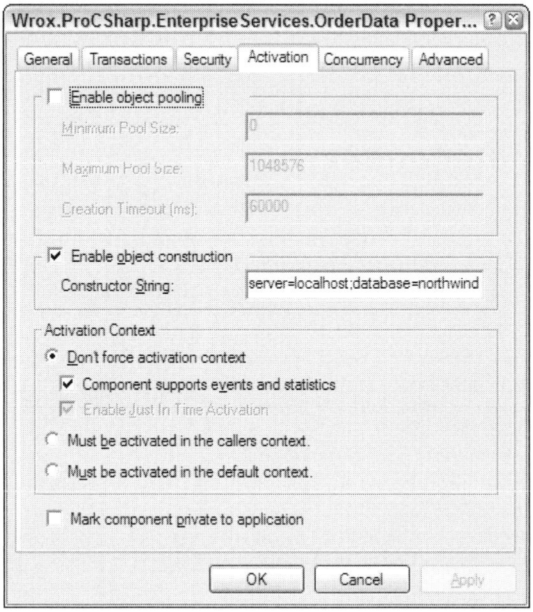

**Figure 30-8**

The method Insert() is at the heart of the component. Here you use ADO.NET to write the Order object to the database. (ADO.NET is discussed in more detail in Chapter 19, "Data Access with .NET.") For this example, you create a SqlConnection object where the connection string that was set with the Construct() method is used to initialize the object.

# Enterprise Services

The attribute `[AutoComplete()]` is applied to the method to get automatic transaction handling as discussed earlier:

```
[AutoComplete()]
public void Insert(Order order)
{
    SqlConnection connection = new SqlConnection(connectionString);
```

The method `connection.CreateCommand()` creates a `SqlCommand` object where the `CommandText` property is set to a SQL `INSERT` statement to add a new record to the Orders table. The method `ExecuteNonQuery()` executes the SQL statement:

```
try
{
    SqlCommand command = connection.CreateCommand();
    command.CommandText = "INSERT INTO Orders (CustomerId, OrderDate, " +
        "ShipAddress, ShipCity, ShipCountry)" +
        "VALUES(@CustomerId, @OrderDate, @ShipAddress, @ShipCity, " +
        "@ShipCountry)";
    command.Parameters.AddWithValue("@CustomerId", order.CustomerId);
    command.Parameters.AddWithValue("@OrderDate", order.OrderDate);
    command.Parameters.AddWithValue("@ShipAddress", order.ShipAddress);
    command.Parameters.AddWithValue("@ShipCity", order.ShipCity);
    command.Parameters.AddWithValue("@ShipCountry", order.ShipCountry);

    connection.Open();

    command.ExecuteNonQuery();
```

Because `OrderId` is defined as an auto-increment value in the database, and this id is needed for writing the Order Details to the database, `OrderId` is read by using `@@IDENTITY`. Then it is set to the `Order` object by calling the method `SetOrderId()`:

```
    command.CommandText = "SELECT @@IDENTITY AS 'Identity'";
    object identity = command.ExecuteScalar();
    order.SetOrderId(Convert.ToInt32(identity));
```

After the order is written to the database, all order lines of the order are written by using the `OrderLineData` component:

```
    OrderLineData updateOrderLine = new OrderLineData();
    foreach (OrderLine orderLine in order.OrderLines)
    {
        updateOrderLine.Insert(order.OrderId, orderLine);
    }
}
```

Finally, regardless of whether the code in the `try` block was successful or an exception occurred, the connection is closed:

```
                finally
                {
                    connection.Close();
                }
            }
        }
    }
}
```

## The OrderLineData Component

The `OrderLineData` component is implemented similar to the `OrderData` component. You use the attribute `[ConstructionEnabled]` to define the database connection string:

```
using System;
using System.EnterpriseServices;
using System.Data;
using System.Data.SqlClient;

namespace Wrox.ProCSharp.EnterpriseServices
{
    public interface IOrderLineUpdate
    {
        void Insert(int orderId, OrderLine orderDetail);
    }

    [Transaction(TransactionOption.Required)]
    [EventTrackingEnabled(true)]
    [ConstructionEnabled(true, Default="server=localhost;database=northwind;" +
        "trusted_connection=true")]
    public class OrderLineData : ServicedComponent, IOrderLineUpdate
    {
        private string connectionString = null;

        protected override void Construct(string s)
        {
            connectionString = s;
        }
```

With the `Insert()` method of the `OrderLineData` class in this example, the `[AutoComplete]` attribute isn't used to demonstrate a different way to define the transaction outcome. It shows how to set the consistent and done bit with the `ContextUtil` class instead. The method `SetComplete()` is called at the end of the method, depending on whether inserting the data in the database was successful. In case of an error where an exception is thrown, the method `SetAbort()` sets the consistent bit to `false` instead, so that the transaction is undone with all components participating in the transaction:

```
        public void Insert(int orderId, OrderLine orderDetail)
        {
            SqlConnection connection = new SqlConnection(connectionString);
            try
            {
                SqlCommand command = connection.CreateCommand();
                command.CommandText = "INSERT INTO [Order Details] (OrderId, " +
```

```
            "ProductId, UnitPrice, Quantity)" +
            "VALUES(@OrderId, @ProductId, @UnitPrice, @Quantity)";
        command.Parameters.AddWithValue("@OrderId", orderId);
        command.Parameters.AddWithValue("@ProductId", orderDetail.ProductId);
        command.Parameters.AddWithValue("@UnitPrice", orderDetail.UnitPrice);
        command.Parameters.AddWithValue("@Quantity", orderDetail.Quantity);

        connection.Open();

        command.ExecuteNonQuery();
      }
      catch (Exception)
      {
        ContextUtil.SetAbort();
        throw;
      }
      finally
      {
        connection.Close();
      }
      ContextUtil.SetComplete();
    }
  }
}
```

## Client Application

Having built the component, you can create a client application. For testing purposes, a console application serves the purpose. After referencing the assembly NorthwindComponent and the assembly System.EnterpriseServices, you can create a new Order with the static method Order.Create(). order.AddOrderLine() adds an order line to the order. OrderLine.Create() accepts product ids, the price, and quantity to create an order line. With a real application it would be useful to add a Product class instead of using product ids, but the purpose of this example is to demonstrate transactions in general.

Finally, the serviced component class OrderControl is created to invoke the method NewOrder():

```
Order order = Order.Create("PICCO", DateTime.Today, "Georg Pipps",
                           "Salzburg", "Austria");
order.AddOrderLine(OrderLine.Create(16, 17.45F, 2));
order.AddOrderLine(OrderLine.Create(67, 14, 1));

using (OrderControl orderControl = new OrderControl())
{
    orderControl.NewOrder(order);
}
```

You can try to write products that don't exist to the `OrderLine` (using a product id that is not listed in the table Products). In this case, the transaction will be aborted, and no data will be written to the database.

While a transaction is active you can see the transaction in the Component Services explorer by selecting Distributed Transaction Coordinator in the tree view (see Figure 30-9).

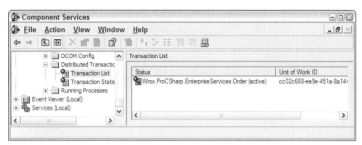

Figure 30-9

> If you are debugging the serviced component while it is running inside a transaction, be aware that the default transaction timeout is 60 seconds for serviced components. You can change the default for the complete system in the Component Services explorer by clicking My Computer, selecting Action ⇨ Properties, and opening the Options tab. Instead of changing the value for the complete system, the transaction timeout can also be configured on a component-by-component level with the Transaction options of the component.

## Services without Components

Starting with Windows Server 2003 and Windows XP (with Windows XP you either need SP2 or SP1 with the Windows XP hotfix 828741) you can create a COM+ context without a component configuration. This makes it easy to make use of transaction and synchronization services without deriving from the base class `ServicedComponent` and without the need to configure the assembly. The context can be created within a method, there's no need to define context requirements with a class because different methods can have different context requirements, and the class can have any base class.

The heart of Services without Components are the `ServiceConfig` and the `ServiceDomain` classes. The `ServiceConfig` class is used to configure the context that is required for the actions that should be done. The `ServiceDomain` class is used to create a context that is described with the `ServiceConfig` class.

The following table lists some of the properties of the `ServiceConfig` class.

| ServiceConfig Property | Description |
| --- | --- |
| Inheritance | With the `Inheritance` property you can define if the newly created context should be based on the existing context, or if a completely new context should be created. By default the new context is based on the existing context with the enumeration value `InheritanceOption.Inherit`. If the `Inheritance` property is set to `InheritanceOption.Ignore`, the existing context is not used. |
| Transaction | With the `Transaction` property you can define the transactional requirements with the `TransactionOption` enumeration. |
| TransactionDescription | With the `TransactionDescription` property you can set a descriptive string for the transaction. |
| TransactionTimeout | With the `TransactionTimeout` property you can configure how long a transaction may last before a timeout occurs. |
| IsolationLevel | With the `IsolationLevel` property you can set a value from the enumeration `TransactionIsolationLevel`. |

By using the `ServiceDomain` and `ServiceConfig` classes the previously created `OrderControl` class can be changed as shown in the following code. The class `OrderControl` no longer derives from the base class `ServicedComponent`, and there are no attributes defined with the class. Instead, within the method `NewOrder()` the requirements of the context are defined with the `ServiceConfig` class. Here the requirements are set that a new transaction is required by setting the `Transaction` property to `TransactionOption.RequiresNew`. Next, `ServiceDomain.Enter()` creates a new context that includes a transaction. You can read the transaction and context ids by reading the values with `ContextUtil.TransactionId` and `ContextUtil.ContextId`. The transactional outcome is defined with the help of the class `ContextUtil`, as was already shown with serviced components. `ServiceDomain.Leave` exits the context:

```
public class OrderControl
{
   public void NewOrder(Order order)
   {
      ServiceConfig serviceConfig = new ServiceConfig();
      serviceConfig.Transaction = TransactionOption.RequiresNew;
      ServiceDomain.Enter(serviceConfig);
      try
      {
         OrderData data = new OrderData();
         data.Insert(order);
         ContextUtil.SetComplete();
      }
      catch (Exception)
      {
         ContextUtil.SetAbort();
         throw;
      }
```

```
            finally
            {
                ServiceDomain.Leave();
            }
        }
    }
}
```

The class `OrderData` from before is also changed, so that it is uses Services without Components. The database connection string can no longer be read from the construction string, because the `Construct` method is available only with serviced components. Instead, the construction string is read from an application configuration file:

```
public class OrderData : IOrderUpdate
{
    private string connectionString = null;

    public OrderData()
    {
        this.connectionString =
            ConfigurationSettings.AppSettings["NorthwindConnection"];
    }
```

The `Insert()` method of the class `OrderData` shows that the transactional outcome can not only be defined with the `ContextUtil` class; instead, the `[AutoComplete]` attribute is used. This is similar to serviced components. When an exception occurs, the consistent bit is set to `false`; without an exception the consistent bit is set to `true`.

Within the `Insert()` method again a context is created with `ServiceDomain.Enter()`. Here the transactional requirements are set to `TransactionOption.Required` with the `ServiceConfig` class. Because the method `Insert()` is invoked from the method `NewOrder()` where a transaction already existed, here the same transaction is used:

```
    [AutoComplete()]
    public void Insert(Order order)
    {
        ServiceConfig serviceConfig = new ServiceConfig();
        serviceConfig.Transaction = TransactionOption.Required;
        serviceConfig.TransactionDescription = "Demo Transaction";
        ServiceDomain.Enter(serviceConfig);

        SqlConnection connection = new SqlConnection(connectionString);
        try
        {
            SqlCommand command = connection.CreateCommand();
            command.CommandText = "INSERT INTO Orders (CustomerId, OrderDate, " +
                "ShipAddress, ShipCity, ShipCountry)" +
                "VALUES(@CustomerId, @OrderDate, @ShipAddress, @ShipCity, " +
                "@ShipCountry)";
            command.Parameters.AddWithValue("@CustomerId", order.CustomerId);
            command.Parameters.AddWithValue("@OrderDate", order.OrderDate);
            command.Parameters.AddWithValue("@ShipAddress", order.ShipAddress);
            command.Parameters.AddWithValue("@ShipCity", order.ShipCity);
```

```
                command.Parameters.AddWithValue("@ShipCountry", order.ShipCountry);

                connection.Open();
                command.ExecuteNonQuery();

                command.CommandText = "SELECT @@IDENTITY AS 'Identity'";
                object identity = command.ExecuteScalar();
                order.SetOrderId(Convert.ToInt32(identity));

                OrderLineData updateOrderLine = new OrderLineData();
                foreach (OrderLine orderLine in order.OrderLines)
                {
                    updateOrderLine.Insert(order.OrderId, orderLine);
                }
            }
            catch
            {
                throw;
            }
            finally
            {
                connection.Close();
                ServiceDomain.Leave();
            }
        }
    }
```

The class `OrderControl` can now be used like a simple .NET class — without the need to configure the application as is required with serviced components. Of course, not all features of Enterprise Services are available with Services without Components.

## Summary

This chapter discussed the rich features offered by Enterprise Services, such as automatic transactions, object pooling, queued components, and loosely coupled events.

To create serviced components, you have to reference the assembly `System.EnterpriseServices`. The base class of all serviced components is `ServicedComponent`. With this class the context makes it possible to intercept method calls. You can use attributes to specify the interception that will be used. You also learned how to configure an application and its components using attributes, as well as how to manage transactions and specify transactional requirements of components using the `[Transaction]` attribute.

Instead of using attributes with the class, Services without Components allows you to define transaction requirements within a method. Services without Components don't have the requirement to configure the class.

# Message Queuing

`System.Messaging` is a namespace that includes classes for reading and writing messages with the Message Queuing facility of the Windows operating system. Messaging can be used in a disconnected scenario where the client and server needn't be running at the same time.

This chapter looks at the following topics:

- An overview of Message Queuing
- Message Queuing architecture
- Message queue administrative tools
- Programming Message Queuing
- Course order sample application

## Overview

Before diving in to programming Message Queuing, this section discusses the basic concepts of messaging and compares it to synchronous and asynchronous programming. With synchronous programming, when a method is invoked the caller has to wait until the method is completed. With asynchronous programming the calling thread starts the method that runs concurrently. Asynchronous programming can be done with delegates, class libraries that already support asynchronous methods (for example, Web service proxies, `System.Net`, `System.IO` classes), or by using custom threads (see Chapter 13, "Threading"). With both synchronous and asynchronous programming the client and the server must be running at the same time.

Although Message Queuing operates asynchronously, because the client (sender) does not wait for the server (receiver) to read the data sent to it, there is a crucial difference between Messaging

# Chapter 31

Queuing and asynchronous programming: Message Queuing can be done in a disconnected environment. At the time data is sent, the receiver can be offline. Later, when the receiver goes online, it receives the data without the sending application to intervene.

You can compare connected and disconnected programming with talking to someone on the phone and sending an e-mail. When talking to someone on the phone, both participants must be connected at the same time. The communication is synchronous. With an e-mail, the sender isn't sure when the e-mail will be dealt with. People using this technology are working in a disconnected mode. Of course the e-mail may never be dealt with — it may be ignored. That's in the nature of disconnected communication. To avoid this problem it is possible to ask for a reply to confirm that the e-mail has been read. If the answer doesn't arrive within a time limit, you may be required to deal with this "exception." This is also possible with Message Queuing.

In some ways Message Queuing is e-mail for application-to-application communication, instead of person-to-person communication. However, this gives you a lot of features that are not available with mailing services, such as guaranteed delivery, transactions, confirmations, express mode using memory, and so on. As you see in the next section, Message Queuing has a lot of features useful for communication between applications.

With Message Queuing you can send, receive, and route messages in a connected or disconnected environment. Figure 31-1 shows a very simple way of using messages. The sender sends messages to the message queue, and the receiver receives messages from the queue.

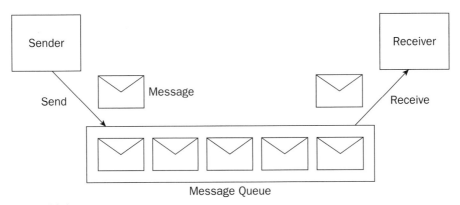

Figure 31-1

## When to Use Message Queuing

One case where Messaging Queuing is useful is when the client application is often disconnected from the network (for example with a salesperson visiting customers onsite). The salesperson can enter order data directly at the customer's site. The application sends a message for each order to the message queue that is located on the client's system (see Figure 31-2). As soon as the salesperson is back in the office, the order is automatically transferred from the message queue of the client system to the message queue of the target system where the message is processed.

# Message Queuing

In addition to using a laptop, the salesperson could use a Pocket Windows device where Message Queuing is available.

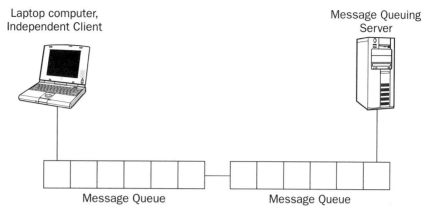

**Figure 31-2**

Message Queuing can also be useful in a connected environment. Imagine an e-commerce site (see Figure 31-3) where the server is fully loaded with order transactions at certain times, for example early evening and weekends, but the load is low at night time. A solution would be to buy a faster server or to add additional servers to the system so that the peaks can be handled. But there's a cheaper solution: Flatten the peak loads by moving transactions from the times with higher loads to the times with lower loads. In this scheme, orders are sent to the message queue, and the receiving side reads the orders at the rates that are useful for the database system. The load of the system is now flattened over time so that the server dealing with the transactions can be less expensive than an upgrade of the database server(s).

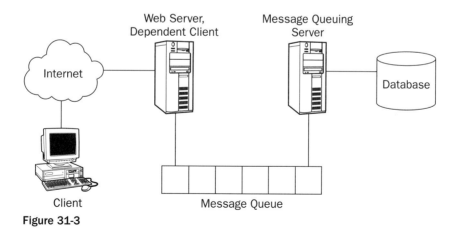

**Figure 31-3**

# Chapter 31

## *Message Queuing Features*

Message Queuing is part of the Windows operating system. The main features of this service are as follows:

- Messages can be sent in a disconnected environment. It is not necessary for the sending and receiving application to run at the same time.
- With express mode, messages can be sent very fast. Express mode messages are just stored in memory.
- For a recoverable mechanism, messages can be sent using guaranteed delivery. Recoverable messages are stored within files. They are delivered even in cases when the server reboots.
- Message queues can be secured with access control lists to define which users can send or receive messages from a queue. Messages can also be encrypted to avoid network sniffers reading the data.
- Messages can be sent with priorities to handle high-priority items faster.
- Message Queuing 3.0 supports sending multicast messages.
- With transactional message queues, messages can take part in a DTC transaction (see Chapter 30, "Enterprise Services," for transactions with the DTC).

*Because Message Queuing is part of the operating system, you cannot install Message Queuing 3.0 on a Windows 2000 system. Message Queuing 3.0 is part of Windows Server 2003 and Windows XP.*

The reminder of this chapter discusses how these features can be used.

# Message Queuing Products

Message Queuing 3.0 is part of Windows XP and Windows Server 2003. Windows 2000 was delivered with Message Queuing 2.0, which didn't have support for the HTTP protocol and multicast messages. Message Queuing 3.0 can be installed as part of the operating system. With Windows XP using Add or Remove Programs, a separate section within Windows Components exists where Message Queuing options can be selected. With the Message Queuing options, the following components can be selected:

- **Common:** The Common subcomponent is required for base functionality with Message Queuing.
- **Active Directory Integration:** With the Active Directory Integration message queue names are written to the Active Directory. With this option it is possible to find queues with the Active Directory integration, and to secure queues with Windows users and groups.
- **MSMQ HTTP Support:** The MSMQ HTTP Support allows you to send and receive messages using the HTTP protocol.
- **Triggers:** With Triggers applications can be instantiated on the arrival of a new message.

When Message Queuing is installed, the Message Queuing service (see Figure 31-4) must be started. This service reads and writes messages and communicates with other Message Queuing servers to route messages across the network.

# Message Queuing

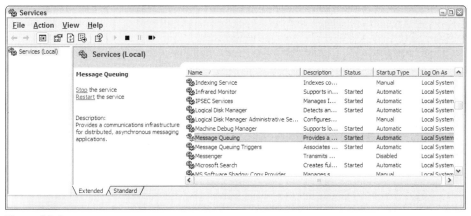

Figure 31-4

## Message Queuing Architecture

With Message Queuing, messages are written and read from a message queue. Messages and message queues have several attributes that must be further elaborated.

### Messages

A message is sent to a message queue. The message includes a body containing the data that is sent and a label that is the title of the message. Any information can be put into the body of the message. With .NET, several formatters convert data to be put into the body. In addition to the label and the body, the message includes more information about the sender, timeout configuration, transaction id, or priority.

Message queues have several types of messages:

- A **normal message** is sent by an application.
- An **acknowledgement message** reports the status of a normal message. Acknowledgement messages are sent to administration queues to report success or failure of sending normal messages.
- **Response messages** are sent by receiving applications when the original sender requires some special answer.
- A **report message** is generated by the Message Queuing system. Test messages and route-tracking messages belong to this category.

A message can have a priority that defines the order in which the messages will be read from the queue. The messages are sorted in the queue according to their priority; so the next message read in the queue is the one with the highest priority.

Messages have two delivery modes: express and recoverable. Express messages are delivered very fast because memory is only used for the message store. Recoverable messages are stored in files at every step along the route until the message is delivered. This way delivery of the message is assured, even with a computer reboot or network failure.

Transactional messages are a special version of recoverable messages. With transactional messaging it is guaranteed that messages arrive only once and in the same order that they were sent. Priorities cannot be used with transactional messages.

## *Message Queue*

A message queue is a message store. Messages that are stored on-disk can be found in the `<windir>\system32\msmq\storage` directory.

Public or private queues are usually used for sending messages, but other queue types also exist:

- A **public queue** is published in the Active Directory. Information about these queues is replicated across Active Directory domains. You can use browse and search features to get information about these queues. A public queue can be accessed without knowing the name of the computer where it is placed. It is also possible to move such a queue from one system to another without the client knowing it. It's not possible to create public queues in a Workgroup environment because the Active Directory is needed. The Active Directory is discussed in Chapter 22, "Working with Active Directory."

- **Private queues** are not published in the Active Directory. These queues can be accessed only when the full path name to the queue is known. Private queues can be used in a Workgroup environment.

- **Journal queues** are used to keep copies of messages after they have been received or sent. Enabling journaling for a public or a private queue automatically creates a journal queue. With journal queues, two different queue types are possible: source journaling and target journaling. **Source journaling** is turned on with the properties of a message; the journal messages are stored with the source system. **Target journaling** is turned on with the properties of a queue; these messages are stored in the journal queue of the target system.

- Contrary to synchronous programming where errors are immediately detected, errors must be dealt with differently using Message Queuing. If a message doesn't arrive at the target system before a specified timeout is reached, the message is stored in the **dead-letter queue.** The dead-letter queue can be checked for messages that didn't arrive.

- **Administration queues** contain acknowledgments for messages sent. The sender can specify an administration queue from which it receives notification of whether the message was sent successfully.

- If more than a simple acknowledgment is needed as an answer from the receiving side, a **response queue** can be used. The receiving application can send response messages back to the original sender.

- A **report queue** is used for test messages. Report queues can be created by changing the type (or category) of a public or private queue to the predefined id {55EE8F33-CCE9-11CF-B108-0020AFD61CE9}. Report queues are useful as a testing tool to track messages on their route.

# Message Queuing

❑ **System queues** are private and are used by the Message Queuing system. These queues are used for administrative messages, storing of notification messages, and to guarantee the correct order of transactional messages.

## Message Queuing Administrative Tools

Before looking at how to deal with Message Queuing programmatically, this section looks at the administrative tools that are part of the Windows operating system to create and manage queues and messages. The tools shown here are not only used with Message Queuing. The Message Queuing features of these tools are only available if Message Queuing is installed.

### Creating Message Queues

Message queues can be created with the Computer Management MMC snap-in. On a Windows XP System you can start the Computer Management MMC snap-in with the Start ➪ Control Panel ➪ Administrative Tools ➪ Computer Management menu. In the tree view pane Message Queuing is located below the Services and Applications entry. By selecting Private Queues or Public Queues, new queues can be created from the Action menu (see Figure 31-5). Public queues are available only if Message Queuing is configured in Active Directory mode.

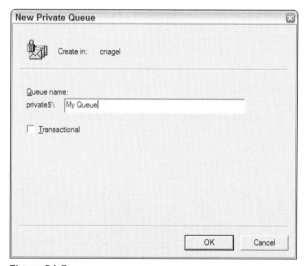

Figure 31-5

### Message Queue Properties

After a queue is created, you can modify the queue's properties with the Computer Management snap-in by selecting the queue in the tree pane and selecting the Action ➪ Properties menu (see Figure 31-6).

1101

# Chapter 31

Figure 31-6

Several options can be configured:

- The label is the name of the queue that can be used to search for the queue.

- The type id that is by default set to {00000000-0000-0000-0000-000000000000} to map multiple queues to a single category or type. Report queues use a specific type id, as discussed earlier. A type id is a universal unique id (uuid) or GUID.

  *Custom type identifiers can be created with the uuidgen.exe or guidgen.exe utilities. uuidgen.exe is a command-line utility to create unique ids, and guidgen.exe is a graphical version to create uuids.*

- The maximum size of all messages of a queue can be limited to not fill up the disk. Message Queuing 2.0 had a limit of 2GB for the message store, which no longer exists with Message Queuing 3.0.

- The Authenticated option can be checked to allow only authenticated users to write and read messages from the queue.

- With the privacy level option, the content of the message can be encrypted. The possible values to set are None, Optional, or Body. None means that no encrypted messages are accepted, Body accepts only encrypted messages, and the default Optional value accepts both.

- Target journaling can be configured with the journal settings. With this option, copies of the messages received are stored into the journal. The maximum size of disk space that is occupied can be configured for the journal messages of a queue. When the maximum size is reached, target journaling is ceased.

- Message Queuing 3.0 has a new configuration option, *Multicast*, to define a multicast IP address for the queue. The same multicast IP address can be used with different nodes in the network, so that a message sent to a single address is received with multiple queues.

# Programming Message Queuing

Now that you understand the architecture of Message Queuing, you can look into the programming. In the next sections, you see how to create and control queues, and how to send and receive messages.

You also build a small course order application that consists of a sending and receiving part.

## Creating a Message Queue

You've already seen how to create message queues with the Computer Management utility. Message queues can be created programmatically with the `Create()` method of the `MessageQueue` class.

With the `Create()` method, the path of the new queue must be passed. The path consists of the host name where the queue is located and the name of the queue. In the example the queue `MyNewPublicQueue` is created on the local host. To create a private queue the path name must include `Private$`; for example, `\Private$\MyNewPrivateQueue`.

After the `Create()` method is invoked, properties of queue can be changed. For example, using the `Label` property, the label of the queue is set to `Demo Queue`. The sample program writes the path of the queue and the format name to the console. The format name is automatically created with a UUID that can be used to access the queue without the name of the server:

```
using System;
using System.Messaging;

namespace Wrox.ProCSharp.Messaging
{
   class Program
   {
      static void Main(string[] args)
      {
         using (MessageQueue queue = MessageQueue.Create(@".\MyNewPublicQueue"))
         {
            queue.Label = "Demo Queue";
            Console.WriteLine("Queue created:");
            Console.WriteLine("Path: {0}", queue.Path);
            Console.WriteLine("FormatName: {0}", queue.FormatName);
         }
      }
   }
}
```

*Administrative privileges are required to create a queue. Usually you cannot expect the user of your application to have administrative privileges. That's why queues usually are created with installation programs. Later in this chapter you see how message queues can be created with the `MessageQueueInstaller` class.*

## Finding a Queue

The path name and the format name can be used to identify queues. To find queues, you must differentiate between public and private queues. Public queues are published in the Active Directory. For these queues it is not necessary to know the system where they are located. Private queues can be found only if the name of the system where the queue is located is known.

You can find public queues in the Active Directory domain by searching for the queue's label, category, or format name. You can also get all queues on a machine. The class `MessageQueue` has static methods to search for queues: `GetPublicQueuesByLabel()`, `GetPublicQueuesByCategory()`, and `GetPublicQueuesByMachine()`. The method `GetPublicQueues()` returns an array of all public queues in the domain:

```
using System;
using System.Messaging;

namespace Wrox.ProCSharp.Messaging
{
   class Program
   {
      static void Main(string[] args)
      {
         foreach (MessageQueue queue in MessageQueue.GetPublicQueues())
         {
            Console.WriteLine(queue.Path);
         }
      }
   }
}
```

The method `GetPublicQueues()` is overloaded. One version allows passing an instance of the `MessageQueueCriteria` class. With this class you can search for queues created or modified before or after a certain time, and you can also look for a category, label, or machine name.

Private queues can be searched with the static method `GetPrivateQueuesByMachine()`. This method returns all private queues from a specific system.

## Opening Known Queues

If the name of the queue is known, it is not necessary to search for it. Queues can be opened by using the path or format name. They both can be set in the constructor of the `MessageQueue` class.

### Path name

The path specifies the machine name and the queue name to open the queue. This code example opens the queue `MyPublicQueue` on the local host. To be sure that the queue exists, you use the static method `MessageQueue.Exists()`:

```
using System;
using System.Messaging;

namespace Wrox.ProCSharp.Messaging
{
   class Program
   {
      static void Main(string[] args)
```

# Message Queuing

```
      {
         if (MessageQueue.Exists(@".\MyPublicQueue"))
         {
            MessageQueue queue = new MessageQueue(@".\MyPublicQueue");
            //...
         }
         else
         {
            Console.WriteLine("Queue .\MyPublicQueue not existing");
         }
      }
   }
}
```

Depending on the queue type, different identifiers are required when queues are opened. The following table shows the syntax of the queue name for specific types.

| Queue Type | Syntax |
| --- | --- |
| Public queue | `MachineName\QueueName` |
| Private queue | `MachineName\Private$\QueueName` |
| Journal queue | `MachineName\QueueName\Journal$` |
| Machine journal queue | `MachineName\Journal$` |
| Machine dead-letter queue | `MachineName\DeadLetter$` |
| Machine transactional dead-letter queue | `MachineName\XactDeadLetter$` |

When you use the path name to open public queues it is necessary to pass the machine name. If the machine name is not known, the format name can be used instead. The path name for private queues can only be used on the local system. The format name must be used to access private queues remotely.

## Format name

Instead of the path name, you can use the format name to open a queue. The format name is used for searching the queue in the Active Directory to get the host where the queue is located. In a disconnected environment where the queue cannot be reached at the time the message is sent, it is necessary to use the format name:

```
           MessageQueue queue = new MessageQueue(
               @"FormatName:PUBLIC=09816AFF-3608-4c5d-B892-69754BA151FF");
```

The format name has some different uses. It can be used to open private queues and to specify a protocol that should be used:

- ❏ For accessing a private queue, the string that has to be passed to the constructor is `FormatName:PRIVATE=MachineGUID\QueueNumber`. The queue number for private queues is generated when the queue is created. You can see the queue numbers in the `<windows>\System32\msmq\storage\lqs` directory.

1105

## Chapter 31

- With `FormatName:DIRECT=Protocol:MachineAddress\QueueName` you can specify the protocol that should be used to send the message. The HTTP protocol is supported with Message Queuing 3.0.

- `FormatName:DIRECT=OS:MachineName\QueueName` is another way to specify a queue using the format name. This way you don't have to specify the protocol but still can use the machine name with the format name.

# Sending a Message

You can use the `Send` method of the `MessageQueue` class to send a message to the queue. The object passed as an argument of the `Send()` method is serialized to the associated queue. The `Send()` method is overloaded so that a label and a `MessageQueueTransaction` object can be passed. Transactional behavior of Message Queuing is discussed later.

The code example first checks if the queue exists. If it doesn't exist, a queue is created. Then the queue is opened and the message `Sample Message` is sent to the queue using the `Send()` method.

The path name specifies "." for the server name, which is the local system. Path names to private queues only work locally.

```csharp
using System;
using System.Messaging;

namespace Wrox.ProCSharp.Messaging
{
    class Program
    {
        static void Main(string[] args)
        {
            try
            {
                if (!MessageQueue.Exists(@".\Private$\MyPrivateQueue"))
                {
                    MessageQueue.Create(@".\Private$\MyPrivateQueue");
                }
                MessageQueue queue = new MessageQueue(@".\Private$\MyPrivateQueue");

                queue.Send("Sample Message", "Label");
            }
            catch (MessageQueueException ex)
            {
                Console.WriteLine(ex.Message);
            }
        }
    }
}
```

Figure 31-7 shows the Computer Management admin tool where you can see the message that arrived in the queue.

# Message Queuing

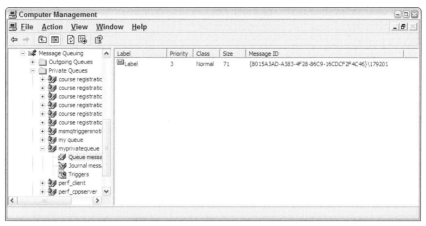

Figure 31-7

By opening the message and selecting the Body tab (see Figure 31-8) of the dialog, you can see that the message was formatted using XML. How the message is formatted is the function of the formatter that's associated with the message queue.

Figure 31-8

## Message formatter

The format in which messages are transferred to the queue depends on the formatter. The `MessageQueue` class has a `Formatter` property through which a formatter can be assigned. The default formatter, `XmlMessageFormatter`, will format the message in XML syntax as shown in the previous example.

1107

## Chapter 31

A message formatter implements the interface `IMessageFormatter`. Three message formatters are available with the namespace `System.Messaging`:

- The `XmlMessageFormatter` is the default formatter. It serializes objects using XML. See Chapter 21, "Manipulating XML," for more on XML formatting.

- With the `BinaryMessageFormatter`, messages are serialized in a binary format. These messages are shorter than the messages formatted using XML.

- The `ActiveXMessageFormatter` is a binary formatter, so messages can be read or written with COM Objects. Using this formatter it is possible to write a message to the queue with a .NET class and to read the message from the queue with a COM object or vice versa.

The sample message shown in Figure 31-8 with XML is formatted with the `BinaryMessageFormatter` in Figure 31-9.

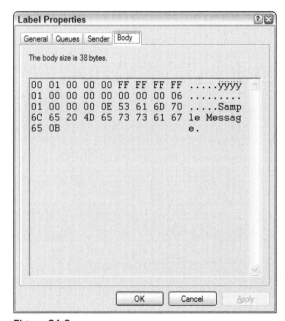

Figure 31-9

### Sending complex messages

Instead of passing strings, it is possible to pass objects to the `Send()` method of the `MessageQueue` class. The type of the class must fulfill some specific requirements, but they depend on the formatter.

For the binary formatter the class must be serializable with the `[Serializable]` attribute. With the .NET runtime serialization all fields are serialized (this includes private fields). Custom serialization can be defined by implementing the interface `ISerializable`. You can read more about the .NET runtime serialization in Chapter 34, "Manipulating Files and the Registry."

# Message Queuing

XML serialization takes place with the XML formatter. With XML serialization all public fields and properties are serialized. The XML serialization can be influenced by using attributes from the `System.Xml.Serialization` namespace. You can read more about XML serialization in Chapter 21.

## Receiving Messages

To read messages, again the `MessageQueue` class can be used. With the `Receive()` method a single message is read and removed from the queue. If messages are sent with different priorities, the message with the highest priority is read. Reading messages with the same priority may mean that the first message sent is not the first message read because the order of messages across the network is not guaranteed. For a guaranteed order, transactional message queues can be used.

In the following example a message is read from the private queue `MyPrivateQueue`. Previously a simple string was passed to the message. When you read a message using the `XmlMessageFormatter`, you have to pass the types of the objects that are read to the constructor of the formatter. In the example the type `System.String` is passed to the argument array of the `XmlMessageFormatter` constructor. This constructor allows either a `String` array that contains the types as strings to be passed or a `Type` array.

The message is read with the `Receive()` method and then the message body is written to the console:

```
using System;
using System.Messaging;

namespace Wrox.ProCSharp.Messaging
{
   class Program
   {
      static void Main(string[] args)
      {
         MessageQueue queue = new MessageQueue(@".\Private$\MyPrivateQueue");
         queue.Formatter = new XmlMessageFormatter(
               new string[] {"System.String"});

         Message message = queue.Receive();
         Console.WriteLine(message.Body);
      }
   }
}
```

The `Receive()` message behaves synchronously and waits until a message is in the queue if there is none.

### Enumerating messages

Instead of reading message-by-message with the `Receive()` method, an enumerator can be used to walk through all messages. The `MessageQueue` class implements the interface `IEnumerable` and thus can be used with a `foreach` statement. Here the messages are not removed from the queue, but you get just a peek at the messages to get their content:

```
MessageQueue queue = new MessageQueue(@".\Private$\MyPrivateQueue");
queue.Formatter = new XmlMessageFormatter(
      new string[] {"System.String"});
```

```
            foreach (Message message in queue)
            {
                Console.WriteLine(message.Body);
            }
```

Instead of using the `IEnumerable` interface, the class `MessageEnumerator` can be used. `MessageEnumerator` implements the interface `IEnumerator`, but has some more features. With the `IEnumerable` interface, the messages are not removed from the queue. The method `RemoveCurrent()` of the `MessageEnumerator` removes the message from the current cursor position of the enumerator.

In the example the `MessageQueue` method `GetMessageEnumerator2()` is used to access the `MessageEnumerator`. With the `MessageEnumerator` the method `MoveNext()` takes a peek message by message. The `MoveNext()` method is overloaded to allow a time span as an argument. This is one of the big advantages when using this enumerator. Here the thread can wait until a message arrives in the queue, but only for the specified time span. The `Current` property, which is defined by the `IEnumerator` interface, returns a reference to a message:

```
        MessageQueue queue = new MessageQueue(@".\Private$\MyPrivateQueue");
        queue.Formatter = new XmlMessageFormatter(
            new string[] {"System.String"});
```

```
        using (MessageEnumerator messages = queue.GetMessageEnumerator2())
        {
            while (messages.MoveNext(TimeSpan.FromMinutes(30)))
            {
                Message message = messages.Current;
                Console.WriteLine(message.Body);
            }
        }
```

## *Asynchronous read*

The `Receive` method of the `MessageQueue` class waits until a message from the queue can be read. To avoid blocking the thread a timeout can be specified in an overloaded version of the `Receive` method. To read the message from the queue after the timeout, `Receive()` must be invoked again. Instead of polling for messages, the asynchronous method `BeginReceive()` can be called. Before starting the asynchronous read with `BeginReceive()`, the event `ReceiveCompleted` should be set. The `ReceiveCompleted` event requires a `ReceiveCompletedEventHandler` delegate that references the method that is invoked when a message arrives with the queue and can be read. In the example the method `MessageArrived` is passed to the `ReceivedCompletedEventHandler` delegate:

```
        MessageQueue queue = new MessageQueue(@".\Private$\MyPrivateQueue");
        queue.Formatter = new XmlMessageFormatter(
            new string[] {"System.String"});
```

```
        queue.ReceiveCompleted +=
            new ReceiveComletedEventHandler(MessageArrived);
        queue.BeginReceive();
        // thread does not wait
```

The handler method `MessageArrived` requires two parameters. The first parameter is the origin of the event, the `MessageQueue`. The second parameter is of type `ReceiveCompletedEventArgs` that

# Message Queuing

contains the message and the async result. In the example the method `EndReceive()` from the queue is invoked to get the result of the asynchronous method, the message:

```
public static void MessageArrived(object source,
    ReceiveCompletedEventArgs e)
{
    MessageQueue queue = (MessageQueue)source;
    Message message = queue.EndReceive(e.AsyncResult);
    Console.WriteLine(message.Body);
}
```

If the message should not be removed from the queue, the `BeginPeek()` and `EndPeek()` methods can be used with asynchronous I/O.

## Course Order Application

To demonstrate the use of Message Queuing, in this section you create a sample solution to order courses. The sample solution is made up of three assemblies:

- A component library (`CourseOrder`) that includes entity classes for the messages that are transferred
- A Windows Forms application (`CourseOrderSender`) that sends messages to the message queue
- A Windows Forms application (`CourseOrderReceiver`) that receives messages from the message queue

### Course Order Class Library

Both the sending and the receiving application need the order information. For this reason, the entity classes are put into a separate assembly. The `CourseOrder` assembly includes three entity classes: `CourseOrder`, `Course`, and `Customer`. With the sample application not all properties are implemented as they would be in a real application, but just enough properties to show the concept.

In the file `Course.cs` the class `Course` is defined. This class just has a one property for the title of the course:

```
using System;

namespace Wrox.ProCSharp.Messaging
{
    public class Course
    {
        public Course()
        {
        }

        public Course(string title)
        {
```

1111

```
            this.title = title;
        }

        private string title;
        public string Title
        {
            get
            {
                return title;
            }
            set
            {
                title = value;
            }
        }
    }
}
```

The file `Customer.cs` includes the class `Customer` that includes properties for the company and contact names:

```
using System;

namespace Wrox.ProCSharp.Messaging
{
    public class Customer
    {
        public Customer()
        {
        }

        public Customer(string company, string contact)
        {
            this.company = company;
            this.contact = contact;
        }

        private string company;
        public string Company
        {
            get
            {
                return company;
            }
            set
            {
                company = value;
            }
        }

        private string contact;
        public string Contact
```

```
            {
               get
               {
                  return contact;
               }
               set
               {
                  contact = value;
               }
            }
         }
      }
```

The class `CourseOrder` in the file `CourseOrder.cs` maps a customer and a course inside an order:

```
using System;

namespace Wrox.ProCSharp.Messaging
{
   public class CourseOrder
   {
      public CourseOrder()
      {
      }

      private Customer customer;
      public Customer Customer
      {
         get
         {
            return customer;
         }
         set
         {
            customer = value;
         }
      }

      private Course course;
      public Course Course
      {
         get
         {
            return course;
         }
         set
         {
            course = value;
         }
      }
   }
}
```

# Chapter 31

## Course Order Message Sender

The second part of the solution is a Windows application called `CourseOrderSender`. With this application, course orders are sent to the message queue. The assemblies `System.Messaging` and `CourseOrder` must be referenced.

The user interface of this application is shown in Figure 31-10. The items of the combo box `comboBoxCourses` include several courses such as "Advanced .NET Programming," "Web Services," and "ADO.NET."

**Figure 31-10**

When the Submit the Order button is clicked, the handler method `OnSubmitCourseOrder()` is invoked. With this method a `CourseOrder` object is created and filled with the content from the `TextBox` and `ComboBox` controls. Then a `MessageQueue` instance is created to open a public queue with a format name. The format name is used to send the message even in the case the queue cannot be reached currently. You can get the format name by using the Computer Management snap-in to read the id of the message queue. With the `Send()` method the `CourseOrder` object is passed to serialize it with the default `XmlMessageFormatter` and to write it to the queue:

```
private void OnSubmitCourseOrder(object sender, EventArgs e)
{
    CourseOrder order = new CourseOrder();
    order.Course = new Course(comboBoxCourses.SelectedItem.ToString());
    order.Customer = new Customer(textCompany.Text, textContact.Text);

    using (MessageQueue queue = new MessageQueue(
        "FormatName:Public=D99CE5F3-4282-4a97-93EE-E9558B15EB13"))
    {
        queue.Send(order, "Course Order {" + order.Customer.Company + "}");
    }
    MessageBox.Show("Course Order submitted");
}
```

# Message Queuing

## Sending Priority and Recoverable Messages

Messages can be prioritized by setting the `Priority` property of the `Message` class. If messages are specially configured, a `Message` object must be created where the body of the message is passed in the constructor.

In the example the priority is set to `MessagePriority.High` if the `checkBoxPriority` check box is checked. `MessagePriority` is an enumeration that allows you to set values from `Lowest` (0) to `Highest` (7). The default value `Normal` has a priority value of 3.

To make the message recoverable, the property `Recoverable` is set to `true`:

```
private void OnSubmitCourseOrder(object sender, EventArgs e)
{
   CourseOrder order = new CourseOrder();
   order.Course = new Course(comboBoxCourses.SelectedItem.ToString());
   order.Customer = new Customer(textCompany.Text, textContact.Text);

   using (MessageQueue queue = new MessageQueue(
         "FormatName:Public=D99CE5F3-4282-4a97-93EE-E9558B15EB13"))
   using (System.Messaging.Message message =
         new System.Messaging.Message(order))
   {
      if (checkBoxPriority.Checked)
         message.Priority = MessagePriority.High;
      message.Recoverable = true;
      queue.Send(message, "Course Order {" + order.Customer.Company + "}");
   }
   MessageBox.Show("Course Order submitted");
}
```

By running the application, you can add course orders to the message queue (see Figure 31-11).

Figure 31-11

1115

# Chapter 31

## Course Order Message Receiver

The design view of the Course Order receiving application that reads messages from the queue is shown in Figure 31-12. This application displays labels of every order in the `listOrders` list box. When an order is selected, the content of the order is displayed with the controls on the right side of the application.

Figure 31-12

In the constructor of the form class `CourseOrderReceiverForm`, the `MessageQueue` object is created that references the same queue that was used with the sending application. For reading messages, the `XmlMessageFormatter` with the types that are read is associated with the queue using the `Formatter` property.

For displaying the available messages in the list, a new thread is created that peeks at messages in the background. The thread's main method is `PeekMessages`.

> *You can read more about threads in Chapter 13, "Threading."*

```
using System;
using System.ComponentModel;
using System.Drawing;
using System.Windows.Forms;
using System.Threading;
using System.Messaging;
using Wrox.ProCSharp.Messaging;

namespace CourseOrderReceiver
{
    public partial class CourseOrderReceiverForm : Form
    {
        private MessageQueue orderQueue;

        public CourseOrderReceiverForm()
```

# Message Queuing

```
{
    InitializeComponent();

    orderQueue = new MessageQueue(
        "FormatName:Public=D99CE5F3-4282-4a97-93EE-E9558B15EB13");
    System.Type[] types = new Type[3];
    types[0] = typeof(CourseOrder);
    types[1] = typeof(Customer);
    types[2] = typeof(Course);
    orderQueue.Formatter = new XmlMessageFormatter(types);

    // start the thread that fills the ListBox with orders
    Thread t1 = new Thread(new ThreadStart(PeekMessages));
    t1.IsBackground = true;
    t1.Start();
}
```

The thread's main method `PeekMessages()` uses the enumerator of the message queue to display all messages. Within the `while` loop it is continuously checked if there is a new message in the queue. If there is no message in the queue, the thread waits three hours for the next message to arrive before it exits.

To display every message from the queue in the list box, the thread has to forward writing to the list box to the list box's creator thread. Because Windows Forms controls are bound to a single thread, only the creator thread is allowed to access methods and properties. The `Invoke()` method forwards the request to the creator thread:

```
private delegate void MethodInvoker(LabelIdMapping labelIdMapping);

private void PeekMessages()
{
    using (MessageEnumerator messageEnum = orderQueue.GetMessageEnumerator2())
    {
        while (messageEnum.MoveNext(TimeSpan.FromHours(3)))
        {
            Invoke(new MethodInvoker(AddListItem),
                new LabelIdMapping(messageEnum.Current.Label,
                    messageEnum.Current.Id));
        }
    }
    MessageBox.Show("No orders in the last 3 hours. Exiting thread");
}

private void AddListItem(LabelIdMapping labelIdMapping)
{
    listOrders.Items.Add(labelIdMapping);
}
```

The `ListBox` control contains elements of the `LabelIdMapping` class. This class is used to display the labels of the messages in the list box, but to keep the id of the message hidden. The id of the message can be used to read the message at a later time:

```csharp
            private class LabelIdMapping
            {
                private string label;
                private string id;

                public LabelIdMapping(string label, string id)
                {
                    this.label = label;
                    this.id = id;
                }

                public override string ToString()
                {
                    return label;
                }

                public string Id
                {
                    get
                    {
                        return id;
                    }
                }
            }
```

The `ListBox` control has the `SelectedIndexChanged` event associated with the method `OnOrderSelectionChanged()`. This method gets the `LabelIdMapping` object from the current selection, and uses the id to peek at the message once more with the `PeekById()` method. Then the content of the message is displayed in the `TextBox` controls:

```csharp
            private void OnOrderSelectionChanged(object sender, EventArgs e)
            {
                LabelIdMapping labelId = (LabelIdMapping)listOrders.SelectedItem;

                if (labelId == null)
                    return;

                System.Messaging.Message message = orderQueue.PeekById(labelId.Id);

                CourseOrder order = message.Body as CourseOrder;
                if (order != null)
                {
                    textCourse.Text = order.Course.Title;
                    textCompany.Text = order.Customer.Company;
                    textContact.Text = order.Customer.Contact;
                    buttonProcessOrder.Enabled = true;

                    if (message.Priority > MessagePriority.Normal)
                    {
                        labelPriority.Visible = true;
                    }
                    else
                    {
                        labelPriority.Visible = false;
```

# Message Queuing

```
            }
        }
        else
        {
            MessageBox.Show("The selected item is not a course order");
        }
    }
}
```

When the Process Order button is clicked, the handler method `OnProcessOrder()` is invoked. Here again, the currently selected message from the list box is referenced, and the message is removed from the queue by calling the method `ReceiveById()`:

```
private void OnProcessOrder(object sender, EventArgs e)
{
    LabelIdMapping labelId = (LabelIdMapping)listOrders.SelectedItem;
    System.Messaging.Message message =
        orderQueue.ReceiveById(labelId.Id);

    listOrders.Items.Remove(labelId);
    listOrders.SelectedIndex = -1;
    buttonProcessOrder.Enabled = false;
    textCompany.Text = "";
    textContact.Text = "";
    textCourse.Text = "";

    MessageBox.Show("Course order processed");
}
```

Figure 31-13 shows the running receiving application that lists three orders in the queue, and one order is currently selected.

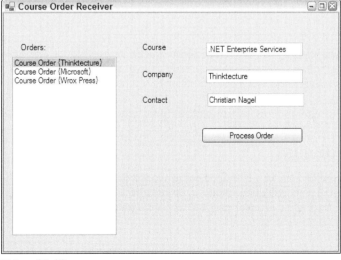

Figure 31-13

Chapter 31

# Receiving Results

With the current version of the sample application, the sending application never knows if the message is ever dealt with. To get results from the receiver, acknowledgement queues or response queues can be used.

## Acknowledgement Queues

With an acknowledgement queue, the sending application can get information about the status of the message. With the acknowledgements you can define if you would like to receive an answer, if everything went OK, or if something went wrong. For example, acknowledgements can be sent when the message reaches the destination queue or when the message is read or if it didn't reach the destination queue or was not read before a timeout elapsed.

In the example the `AdministrationQueue` of the `Message` class is set to the `CourseOrderAck` queue. This queue must be created similar to a normal queue. This queue is just used the other way around: the original sender receives acknowledgements. The `AcknowledgementType` property is set to `AcknowledgementTypes.FullReceive` to get an acknowledgement when the message is read:

```
Message message = new Message(order);

message.AdministrationQueue =
    new MessageQueue(@".\CourseOrderAck");
message.AcknowledgementType = AcknowledgementTypes.FullReceive;

queue.Send(message, "Course Order {" +
    order.Customer.Company + "}");

string id = message.Id;
```

The *correlation id* is used to determine what acknowledgement message belongs to which message sent. Every message that is sent has an id, and the acknowledgement message that is sent in response to that message holds the id of the originating message as its correlation id. The messages from the acknowledgement queue can be read using `MessageQueue.ReceiveByCorrelationId()` to receive the associated acknowledgement.

Instead of using acknowledgements, the dead-letter queue can be used for messages that didn't arrive at their destination. By setting the `UseDeadLetterQueue` property of the `Message` class to `true`, the message is copied to the dead-letter queue if it didn't arrive at the target queue before the timeout was reached.

Timeouts can be set with the `Message` properties `TimeToReachQueue` and `TimeToBeReceived`.

## Response Queues

If more information than an acknowledgement is needed from the receiving application, a response queue can be used. A response queue is like a normal queue, but the original sender uses the queue as a receiver and the original receiver uses the response queue as a sender.

# Message Queuing

The sender must assign the response queue with the `ResponseQueue` property of the `Message` class. The sample code here shows how the receiver uses the response queue to return a response message. With the response message `responseMessage` the property `CorrelationId` is set to the id of the original message. This way the client application knows what message the answer belongs to. This is similar to acknowledgement queues. The response message is sent with the `Send()` method of the `MessageQueue` object that is returned from the `ResponseQueue` property:

```
public void ReceiveMessage(Message message)
{
    Message responseMessage = new Message("response");
    responseMessage.CorrelationId = message.Id;

    message.ReesponseQueue.Send(responseMessage);
}
```

## Transactional Queues

With recoverable messages it is not guaranteed that the message will arrive in order and just once. Failures on the network can cause messages to arrive multiple times; this happens also if both the sender and receiver have multiple network protocols installed that are used by Message Queuing.

Transactional queues can be used where these guarantees are required:

- ❏ Messages arrive in the same order they have been sent
- ❏ Messages arrive only once

With transactional queues, a single transaction doesn't span the sending and receiving of messages. The nature of Message Queuing is that the time between send and receive can be quite long. In contrast, transactions should be short. With Message Queuing the first transaction is used to send the message into the queue, the second transaction forwards the message on the network, and the third transaction is used to receive the messages.

The next example shows how to create a transactional message queue and how to send messages using a transaction.

A transactional message queue is created by passing `true` with the second parameter of the `MessageQueue.Create()` method.

If you would like to write multiple messages to a queue within a single transaction, you have to instantiate a `MessageQueueTransaction` object and invoke the `Begin()` method. When you are finished with sending all messages that belong to the transaction, the `Commit()` method of the `MessageQueueTransaction` object must be called. To cancel a transaction (and no messages are written to the queue), the `Abort()` method must be called as you can see within the `catch` block:

```
using System;
using System.Messaging;

namespace Wrox.ProCSharp.Messaging
```

```csharp
{
    class Program
    {
        static void Main(string[] args)
        {
            if (!MessageQueue.Exists(@".\MyTransactionalQueue"))
            {
                MessageQueue.Create(@".\MyTransactionalQueue", true);
            }
            MessageQueue queue = new MessageQueue(@".\MyTransactionalQueue");
            MessageQueueTransaction transaction =
                    new MessageQueueTransaction();
            try
            {
                transaction.Begin();
                queue.Send("a", transaction);
                queue.Send("b", transaction);
                queue.Send("c", transaction);
                transaction.Commit();
            }
            catch
            {
                transaction.Abort();
            }
        }
    }
}
```

## Message Queue Installation

Message queues can be created with the `MessageQueue.Create()` method. However, the user running an application usually doesn't have the administrative privileges that are required to create message queues.

Usually message queues are created with an installation program. For installation programs, the class `MessageQueueInstaller` can be used. If an installer class is part of an application, the command-line utility installutil.exe (or a Windows Installation Package) invokes the `Install()` method of the installer.

Visual Studio 2005 has a special support for using the `MessageQueueInstaller` with Windows Forms applications. If a `MessageQueue` component is dropped from the toolbox onto the form, the smart tag of the component allows you to add an installer with the menu entry Add Installer. The `MessageQueueInstaller` object can be configured with the properties editor to define transactional queues, journal queues, the type of the formatter, the base priority, and so on.

*Installers are discussed in Chapter 36, "Windows Services."*

## Summary

In this chapter you've seen how Message Queuing can be used. Message Queuing is an important technology to offer not only asynchronous but also disconnected communication. The sender and receiver can be running at different times, which makes Message Queuing an option for smart clients and also useful to distribute the load on the server over time.

The most important classes with Message Queuing are `Message` and `MessageQueue`. The `MessageQueue` class allows sending, receiving, and peeking at messages, and the `Message` class defines the content that is sent.

# 32

# Future of Distributed Programming

In the last four chapters, you learned several different ways of using services across the network: Web services using ASP.NET, .NET Remoting, Message Queuing and Enterprise Services with DCOM as the native communication protocol. Every technology has its advantages and disadvantages. Writing Web services using ASP.NET, the services can be used from different platforms, while .NET Remoting and DCOM are bound to the Microsoft platform; comparing performance with these communication technologies, DCOM often is the fastest, followed by .NET Remoting and ASP.NET. The extension mechanisms are very different in that ASP.NET Web services can be extended by using SOAP headers, whereas .NET Remoting uses sinks. Extending DCOM is not supported. You get some overlapping features, but using them in tandem is often the best choice. For example, with many applications Web services are used as a front-end to serviced components. All these technologies have a different programming model, which requires many skills from the developer. What's the future?

This chapter shows the future of communication technology, Windows Communication Foundation (WCF). WCF will offer features that are available today with ASP.NET Web services, .NET Remoting, Message Queuing, and Enterprise Services. There's something good and bad with the existing solutions. WCF combines the best of these technologies to form a new technology. However, instead of rewriting applications for WCF, WCF will also support the integration of the existing technologies.

Because WCF is not released at the time of this writing, the focus of this chapter is to give ideas on how this technology can replace existing communication technologies, and to give you guidance on how to use today's technologies so that you can easily make use of the new technology when it is ready.

Particularly, this chapter discusses the following topics:

- Problems today
- Web services specifications
- WCF overview

# Chapter 32

- Programming with WCF
- Preparing for WCF

## Problems Today

In previous chapters, you learned several options that .NET offers for higher-level network communication. One option is .NET Remoting, which uses an object-oriented approach. With .NET Remoting, .NET objects can be used across application domains, and that also includes using the objects across the network. Using object fidelity has the disadvantage that the types are shared and it's not only hard to use different platforms, but it's also difficult to keep the clients and the servers in contact as new versions of remote objects are developed — new versions of the remote object assemblies must be distributed to the client.

The client system usually needs the assembly of the remote object. The requirement of deriving the remote object class from the base class `MarshalByRefObject` probably was not the best design decision because it is not possible to derive it from a different class, too. Security was added late with .NET Remoting, but .NET 2.0 now offers security. A really good feature of this technology is its customizability. It is possible to replace channels using other transport protocols, develop different formatters, and extend the call flow by using message sinks.

DCOM is the protocol that is used by Enterprise Services to flow the context across the wire. DCOM is a very fast protocol, but there's no support for extending it with custom interceptors. With DCOM, Microsoft technologies must be available on both the client and the server, and a proxy must be installed on the client system. Enterprise Services makes it easy to use services such as transactions, object pooling, and so forth on the server side. With this technology, attributes are used to define the requirements of a serviced component. Because installation of a client proxy is often not easy to do in a large scale solution, Web services are used as a front-end.

ASP.NET is the technology used today for developing Web services. They not only make it possible to use clients and servers on different platforms, but it is also possible to plan ahead for version changes by defining a good WSDL contract and not breaking existing clients and servers. The issues with ASP.NET Web services are the use of the HTTP protocol (using WSE 2.0 a TCP channel is available, too), that XML serialization with the SOAP protocol is not fast enough with all scenarios, and some extension features are hard to use. Besides a clear contract that's the only shared item between the client and the server, ASP.NET Web services can be easily developed by using attributes. Derivation of a specific base class is not required.

## Web Services

More issues exist with Web services and ASP.NET. Web services caused a big hype in past years with offering services across different platforms. What we've seen in the past has just been a first step into the possibilities that this technology can offer. To build great interoperable services where licensing is involved, guaranteed message delivery is needed, platform-independent authentication, authorization and confidentiality is needed, some more features of Web services are required.

# Future of Distributed Programming

Here's one example in more detail. As many departments of bigger companies are thinking about opening applications for their partners to allow better integration and faster business processes, company policies might soon get put into place that do not allow departments to control who is authorized to access what data. Of course, not every department would want to manage users and deal with authentication issues. On the other hand, with big companies it is not possible to centrally control applications that are designed with department support in mind.

What's needed in such a scenario is a federation server. With federation, identities are shared across extranets. The federation server uses policies that define who is allowed to access what services offered by the enterprise.

Figure 32-1 shows a federation scenario where a security token from the requestor is used to acquire a security token from the resources realm (which may be a partner company) to access the resources. A trust is set up between the requestor and the resource realms—the security token service from the resource realm trusts the identity provider from the requestor realm. The security token from the requestor is checked by the security token service of the resource realm to determine if the requestor is allowed to access the resource.

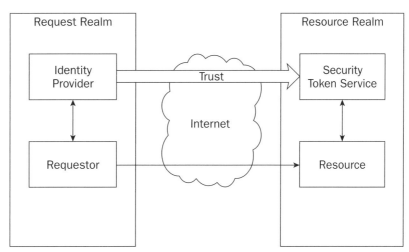

Figure 32-1

> Federation is defined with the specification WS-Federation. You can find the Web services specifications at http://msdn.microsoft.com/webserivces.

Some requirements of Web services in progressing stages are listed here:

- ❑ Security
- ❑ Reliability
- ❑ Transactions
- ❑ Performance

These requirements and current proceedings are discussed in the next sections.

# Chapter 32

# *Security*

The WS-Security specification defines a framework for building security protocols. WS-Federation is based on many security specifications. The base features of Web services security must include these requirements:

- ❑ Message authentication
- ❑ Message integrity
- ❑ Message confidentiality

Authentication defines that the caller must be identified. With an identified caller it can be verified if the caller is allowed to use the resource (authorization). For authentication, the WS-Security specification defines how to pass security tokens with a SOAP request.

A simple example of passing a username is shown with the following SOAP header segment. The username is defined within the `<wsse:UsernameToken>` element. The element `<wsse:Username>` is defined as an extensible element that allows additional attributes:

```
<S:Header>
...
  <wsse:Security>
    <wsse:UsernameToken>
      <wsse:Username>Christian</wsse:Username>
    </wsse:UsernameToken>
  </wsse:Security>
</S:Header>
```

Security tokens can also be defined as binary with the element `<wsse:BinarySecurityToken>` or in XML format.

The specification WS-SecureConversation defines how messages can be transferred in a secure way. The next example shows the use of a security context token. Here a connection is already established between the client and the server, and a security key is also negotiated. The security key is used to encrypt the message body:

```
<S:Envelope xmlns:S="http://www.w3.org/2003/05/soap-envelope"
    xmlns:ds="http://www.w3.org/2000/09/xmldsig#"
    xmlns:wsse=
"http://docs.oasis-open.org/wss/2004/01/oasis-200401-wss-wssecurity-secext-1.0.xsd"
    xmlns:wst="http://schemas.xmlsoap.org/ws/2004/04/trust"
    xmlns:wsc="http://schemas.xmlsoap.org/ws/2004/04/sc">
  <S:Header>
    ...
    <wsse:Security>
      <wsc:SecurityContextToken wsu:Id="MyID">
        <wsc:Identifier>
          uuid:09190A0B-9C3D-4a61-944C-164A9E385D4E
        </wsc:Identifier>
      </wsc:SecurityContextToken>
```

# Future of Distributed Programming

```
      <ds:Signature>
        ...
        <ds:KeyInfo>
          <wsse:SecurityTokenReference>
            <wsse:Reference URI="#MyID"/>
          </wsse:SecurityTokenReference>
        </ds:KeyInfo>
      </ds:Signature>
    </wsse:Security>
  </S:Header>
  <S:Body wsu:Id="MsgBody">
    <tru:StockSymbol
        xmlns:tru="http://fabrikam123.com/payloads">
      QQQ
    </tru:StockSymbol>
  </S:Body>
</S:Envelope>
```

## *Reliability*

The HTTP protocol is not reliable: messages might be lost, duplicated, or reordered. The WS-ReliableMessaging specification defines an interoperability protocol that can be used to guarantee that a message is delivered.

WS-ReliableMessaging defines sequence and message numbers so that messages can be sent and received exactly once and in order. To guarantee delivery, acknowledgements are returned from the destination — if many messages and acknowledgements are sent this would cause a very high volume of traffic. It is also possible that NACKs (not acknowledged or negative acknowledgements) would be returned in case a message was missed.

WS-ReliableMessaging uses the following mechanisms to guarantee reliable message transfers:

- **Sequences:** When messages are sent from the source to the destination, a unique identifier is used to define a sequence of messages. Several messages can belong to one sequence.

- **Message Numbers:** The messages are numbered within a sequence. Every message has a unique number within the sequence. With every message, the number of messages is also sent so that the receiver knows when all messages of a sequence have been received. When messages are received out of order the client can cache and reorder them.

- **Acknowledgements:** Acknowledgements are sent to indicate the successful receipt of the message. To increase performance, acknowledgments are sent with acknowledgement ranges (for example, messages 1–5 have been received successfully). To increase performance the receiver can also send a negative acknowledgement (NACK) instead of ACK to indicate that a message must be sent once more.

Figure 32-2 shows how the reliable messaging mechanism is disconnected from the job of the application and how it is dealt with the RM (reliable messaging) source and destination facilities. The application just sends a message to the RM source, where the message is forwarded to the RM destination receive.

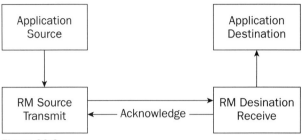

Figure 32-2

An example of a SOAP message that contains an RM sequence is shown in the following SOAP envelope. You can see the RM sequence with the `wsrm` prefix. The identifier `http://wrox.com/ab4711` defines a unique identifier for a sequence created by the source. This identifier is sent with every message of the sequence, so the RM destination receive can map the messages into the correct sequence. The message number is sent inside the `<wsrm:MessageNumber>` element. With the last message of a sequence, an empty `<LastMessage />` element is sent. With the last message, the receiver must return a response with information about what messages have been received:

```
<S:Envelope xmlns:S="http://www.w3.org/2003/05/soap-envelope"
    xmlns:xsi="http://www.w3.org/2001/XMLSchema-instance"
    xmlns:wsu="http://schemas.xmlsoap.org/ws/2002/07/utility"
    xmlns:wsp="http://schemas.xmlsoap.org/ws/2002/12/policy"
    xmlns:wsrm="http://schemas.xmlsoap.org/ws/2004/03/rm"
    xmlns:wsa="http://schemas.xmlsoap.org/ws/2003/03/addressing">
  <S:Header>
    <wsa:MessageID>
      http://thinktecture.com/guid/9BEF0F9B-459F-462a-B9EE-0ADBA4BEDB13
    </wsa:MessageID>
    <wsa:To>http://thinktecture.com/training</wsa:To>
    <wsa:From>
      <wsa:Address>http://wrox.com/services/books</wsa:Address>
    </wsa:From>
    <wsrm:Sequence>
      <wsu:Identifier>http://wrox.com/ab4711</wsu:Identifier>
      <wsrm:MessageNumber>10</wsrm:MessageNumber>
      <wsrm:LastMessage/>
    </wsrm:Sequence>
  </S:Header>
  <S:Body>
    ...
  </S:Body>
</S:Envelope>
```

If the receiver didn't receive all messages, the response may look like the following sequence. Here, the receiver acknowledges the receipt of messages 2 to 5 and 7 to 10, so messages 1 and 6 are missing:

```
<wsrm:SequenceAcknowledgement>
  <wsu:Identifier> http://wrox.com/ab4711</wsu:Identifier>
  <wsrm:AcknowledgementRange Upper="5" Lower="2"/>
  <wsrm:AcknowledgementRange Upper="10" Lower="7"/>
</wsrm:SequenceAcknowledgement>
```

# Future of Distributed Programming

Instead of responding with acknowledgements about the messages received, the following is an example of returning negative acknowledgements about missing messages 1 and 6:

```
<wsrm:SequenceAcknowledgement>
   <wsu:Identifier> http://wrox.com/ab4711</wsu:Identifier>
   <wsrm:Nack>1</wsrm:Nack>
   <wsrm:Nack>6</wsrm:Nack>
</wsrm:SequenceAcknowledgement>
```

> **Persistence is not defined with the WS-ReliableMessaging specification. An implementation of the reliable messaging functionality can add a persistence mechanism to guarantee message delivery in case of system failures. This can be compared to Message Queuing as shown in Chapter 31, "Message Queuing."**

## Transactions

In Chapter 30, "Enterprise Services," transactions were used with Enterprise Services. With transactions the result is all or nothing; either all actions occurred, or nothing happened. For Web services three specifications exist to bring transactions to Web services: WS-Coordination, WS-AtomicTransactions, and WS-BusinessActivity. WS-Coordination is a base specification extended by the other specifications.

The WS-Coordination specification defines a framework to coordinate the actions of distributed applications. This specification enables coordination of multiple Web services, for example, coordination for transaction processing and workflow management that spans different Web services.

The WS-AtomicTransactions specification is an extension of WS-Coordination to support transactions across Web services. The functionality of WS-AtomicTransactions is somewhat similar to atomic transactions with database development.

Figure 32-3 shows a two-phase commit scenario of Web services that use WS-AtomicTransaction. The coordinator sends a Prepare message to all participating Web services, where all participants must respond with a Prepared message if the transaction is okay from their viewpoint. Then the coordinator can send a Commit message that must be committed by all participants.

In case a participant cannot prepare the transaction successfully, the message Aborted is sent to the coordinator. Then the coordinator sends a Rollback message to the remaining participants, as shown in Figure 32-4.

WS-AtomicTransactions should not be used across company boundaries because such a transaction will have locks with the resources held. WS-AtomicTransaction is good only for short-lived transactions without user activity.

For long-running transactions where user activity and other businesses may participate, the specification WS-BusinessActivity is the right way to go. With this specification, no resources are locked, and business activities may span a long time. Instead of committing and aborting transactions, the actions can be compensated. If one of the participants fails the transaction, a Compensate message is sent so that all participants can undo their actions.

1131

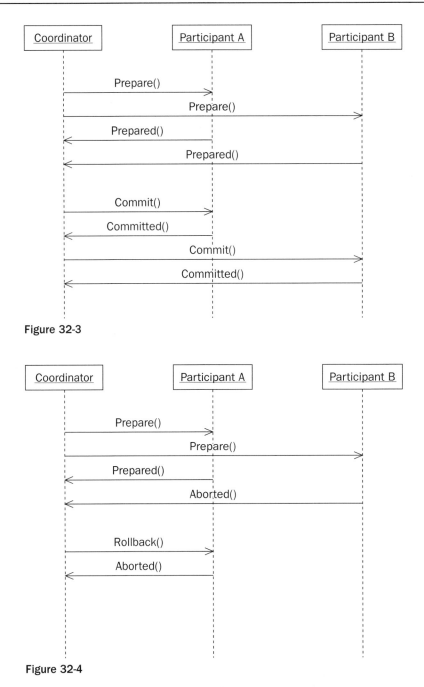

Figure 32-3

Figure 32-4

Figure 32-5 shows a sequence of a business activity with two participants. Participant A sends a Completed message to the coordinator when it has done the activity successfully. Participant B cannot fulfill its activity successfully, so a Fault message is sent. Because of the erroneous outcome of participant B, participant A is sent the Compensate message by the coordinator to undo the action done.

# Future of Distributed Programming

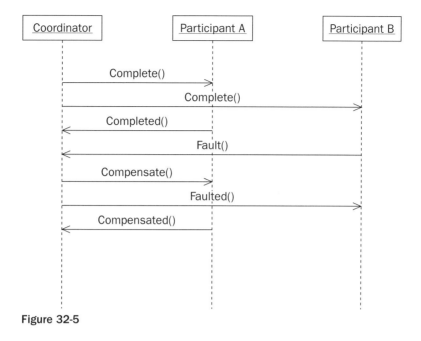

Figure 32-5

## *Performance*

Some services need higher performance (particularly smaller network packets) than is possible with the HTTP and SOAP protocols. SOAP 1.2 no longer depends on the HTTP protocol.

Smaller network packets can be created by using the fact that SOAP is based on the XML infoset instead of the XML structural information items. This makes it possible for a binary SOAP variant where less data can be transmitted.

Another issue is the HTTP protocol in regard to performance. WSE 2.0 already supports Web services with the TCP protocol, which makes them a lot faster.

The UDP protocol has no guaranteed delivery; packets can be lost very easily. The advantage of this protocol is the possibility of sending messages to multiple receivers at once instead of talking to every receiver. Looking at the companies that define the SOAP-over-UDP specification, it becomes immediately clear what systems will use this specification. The authors of the specification are from Lexmark, Ricoh, BEA, and Microsoft. You can expect printers to send the status of the printer supplies to Print Manager Web services in the network.

With SOAP-over-UDP, the following message patterns are defined:

- **Unicast one-way:** A unicast one-way message is sent to a single node where no response message is sent.
- **Multicast one-way:** A multicast one-way message is sent to a group of nodes. Again, no response message is sent.

# Chapter 32

- **Unicast request, unicast response:** With a unicast request and a unicast response the message is sent to a single node and a response is sent back.

- **Multicast request, unicast response:** The multicast request, unicast response message pattern defines that the request is sent to a group of nodes, and every node that receives the request answers with a response message. The response must not be a multicast because this could very easily lead to a saturated network when every receiver sends a response to all nodes. Of course, the original sender can receive multiple response messages from every node in the multicast group.

> For multicast groups, a special IP address range is defined. Every node of a group that participates in a multicasting session must register the multicast address of the group.

*You can read more about the multicast protocol in the book* Pro .NET 1.1 Network Programming *by Christian Nagel et al., published by APress, ISBN 1590593456.*

An example of a multicast one-way message is shown in the following SOAP envelope. The specification WS-Addressing is used with the SOAP-over-UDP specification to address the target nodes as can be seen with the `wsa` prefix. Although the `http` scheme is used with the specification of the destination, the message is transmitted with UDP:

```
<S:Envelope xmlns:S="http://www.w3.org/2003/05/soap-envelope"
       xmlns:wsa="http://schemas.xmlsoap.org/ws/2004/08/addressing" >
  <S:Header>
    <wsa:To>http://MulticastAddress</wsa:To>
    <wsa:Action>http://MulticastAddress/Status</wsa:Action>
    <wsa:MessageId>
       uuid:3613EEA6-1D77-4db8-8C78-A3D6019CD0BD
    </wsa:MessageId>
  </S:Header>
  <S:Body>
    ...
  </S:Body>
</S:Envelope>
```

Now that you've seen some of the specifications that will enhance your life with Web services, the next section looks into the WCF architecture that will offer implementations of many of these specifications.

# WCF Overview

WCF combines the functionality from ASP.NET Web services, .NET Remoting, Message Queuing, and Enterprise Services. What you get from WCF is:

- **Hosting for components and services:** Just as you can use custom hosts with .NET Remoting and WSE, you can host a WCF service in the ASP.NET runtime, a Windows service, a COM+ process, or just a Windows Forms application for peer-to-peer computing.

# Future of Distributed Programming

- **Declarative behavior:** Instead of the requirement to derive from a base class (this requirement exists with .NET Remoting and Enterprise Services), attributes can be used to define the services. This is similar to Web services developed with ASP.NET.

- **Communication channels:** Although to .NET Remoting is very flexible with changing the communication channel, WCF is a good alternative because it offers the same flexibility. WCF will offer multiple channels to communicate using HTTP, TCP, or an IPC channel. Maybe a UDP channel (SOAP over UDP is discussed earlier) will be available, too.

- **Security infrastructure:** For implementing platform-independent Web services, a standardized security environment must be used. The proposed standards are implemented with WSE 2.0, and this will continue with WCF.

- **Extensibility:** .NET Remoting has a rich extensibility story. It is not only possible to create custom channels, formatters, and proxies; it is also possible to inject functionality inside the message flow on the client and on the server. WCF will offer similar extensibilities, however here the extensions are created by using SOAP headers.

- **Support of today's technologies:** Instead of rewriting a distributed solution completely to make use of WCF, WCF can integrate with existing technology. A channel offered by WCF is communicating with a serviced components using DCOM. Web services developed with ASP.NET can be integrated.

WCF has a very flexible layered architecture. Distributed applications can be written using a high-level API or a low-level API. The high-level API or service layer can be used to invoke methods and events. The service layer converts these high-level abstractions into messages to use channels and ports from the lower-level API.

Figure 32-6 shows the layers of a WCF application. The application can use messaging services such as queuing, routing, eventing, and discovery. Examples of service behaviors offered to distributed applications are automatic transactions, concurrency management, error handling, and instance creation. The messaging block is divided into two areas: transport channels, which are adapters that connect to transport protocol (for example, HTTP, TCP, UDP, and IPC), and channels that add additional functionality such as security, reliability, and eventing. Transport channels can be combined with other channels. The hosting environment section shows that WCF can be hosted in any application type. WCF services can be offered from ASP.NET, Windows Services, COM+, or in custom executables. This is very similar to .NET Remoting.

Figure 32-7 shows how different parts of a WCF application interact. A message is sent to a named port. The transport channel associated with the transport protocol forwards the message to the channel where the message is dispatched to the service.

Sending messages can be done in three different ways:

- **Datagram Messaging:** datagram messages are sent in a "fire-and-forget" way. The message is sent and no answer is expected from the receiver. For the sender there's no need to wait for an answer from the receiver. Of course with such operations the methods may only have input parameters.

- **Request-Reply Messaging:** request-reply messaging is the mostly used scenario. The sender sends a request message to the receiver, and the receiver returns a reply message.

- **Duplex Messaging:** with duplex messaging both sides on the network act as a sender and receiver.

# Chapter 32

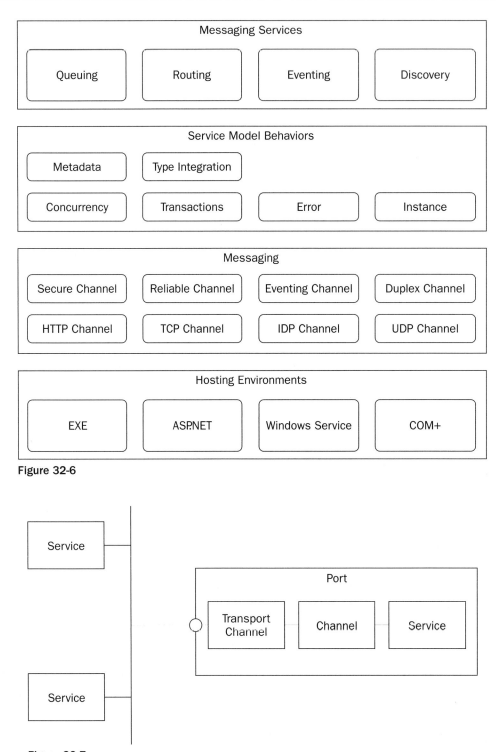

Figure 32-6

Figure 32-7

# Future of Distributed Programming

## Programming with WCF

Programming WCF clients and services you will see many concepts that are known from other technologies. Nothing is really new, but all the different programming models are combined that you just have to learn one model instead of multiple when using different communication techniques.

Next, we look into:

- Contracts
- Service Implementation
- Binding
- Hosting
- Clients

## *Contracts*

A contract defines what functionality a service offers and what functionality can be used by the client. The contract can be completely independent of the implementation of the service.

The contract of Web services is the WSDL document. Developing Web services with ASP.NET, the contract doesn't have the big role as it should have. With ASP.NET contracts are done implicitly by specifying attributes with the Web service methods. Of course you can also use a tool such as WSCF from Thinktecture (http://www.thinktecture.com) to explicitly design a contract.

WCF has a greater focus on designing contracts. The contracts defined by WCF can be grouped into three different contract types: service contracts, data contracts, and message contracts. The contracts can be specified (this is similar to ASP.NET) by using .NET attributes.

- **Service contract:** The service contract is used to define the WSDL that describes the service. This contract is defined with interfaces or classes.
- **Data contract:** The data contract defines the data received and returned from the service. The classes used for sending and receiving messages have data contract attributes associated.
- **Message contract:** If complete control over the SOAP message is needed, a message contract can specify what data should go into the SOAP header, and what belongs to the SOAP body.

WSDL was discussed in Chapter 28, "Web Services."

Let's get into contracts in more detail.

### *Service contract*

The service contract defines the operations the service can perform. The attribute `[ServiceContract]` is used with interfaces or classes to define a service contract. The methods that are offered by the service have the attribute `[OperationContract]` applied as you can see with the `ICourseRegistration` service.

```
[ServiceContract]
public interface ICourseRegistration
{
    [OperationContract]
    public bool RegisterForCourse(Course course, Attendee attendee);
}
```

With the service contract, you can also define the requirements that the service has from the transport with the attribute `[BindingRequirements]`. The property `RequireOrderedDelivery` defines that the messages sent must arrive in the same order. With the property `QueuedDeliveryRequirements` you can define that the message is sent in a disconnected mode, e.g. by using Message queuing. With the property `TransactionFlowRequirements` you can define transactional requirements as known from Enterprise Services.

## *Data contract*

With the data contract, CLR types are mapped to XML schemas.

The data contract is different from other serialization mechanisms; with runtime serialization, all fields are serialized (including private fields), with XML serialization only the public fields and properties are serialized. The data contract requires explicit marking of the fields that should be serialized with the `[DataMember]` attribute. This attribute can be used no matter if the field is private or public.

```
[DataContract(Namespace="http://www.thinktecture.com")]
public class Course
{
    [DataMember] public string Number;
    [DataMember] public string Title;
    [DataMember] public DateTime StartDate;
}
```

The data contract supports versioning. With the named property `VersionAdded`, you can specify additional elements that are added with newer versions as shown with the `LocationCode`. The property `IsOptional` specifies that messages from earlier versions of the contract are still accepted, as the `LocationCode` is an optional field.

```
[DataContract(Namespace="http://www.thinktecture.com")]
public class Course
{
    [DataMember] public string Number;
    [DataMember] public string Title;
    [DataMember] public DateTime StartDate;
    [DataMember(VersionAdded=2 IsOptional=true]
    public string LocationCode;
}
```

For being platform- and version-independent, using data contracts is the best way to define what data should be sent. However, you can also make use of XML serialization and runtime serialization. XML serialization was the mechanism used by ASP.NET Web services, .NET Remoting makes use of runtime serialization.

# Future of Distributed Programming

## Message contract

A message contract is used if complete control over the SOAP message is needed. With the message contract you can specify what part of the message should go into the SOAP header, and what belongs to the SOAP body. The following example shows a message contract for the class `ProcessPersonRequestMessage`. The message contract is specified with the attribute `[MessageContract]`. The header and body of the SOAP message are specified with the attributes `[MessageHeader]` and `[MessageBody]`. By specifying the `Position` property, the element order within the body can be defined.

```
[MessageContract]
public class ProcessPersonRequestMessage
{
    [MessageHeader]
    public int employeeId;

    [MessageBody(Position=0)]
    public Person person;
}
```

The class `ProcessPersonRequestMessage` is used with the service contract that is defined with the interface `IProcessPerson`:

```
[ServiceContract]
public interface IProcessPerson
{
    [OperationContract]
    public PersonResponseMessage ProcessPerson(
        ProcessPersonRequestMessage message);
}
```

## Service Implementation

The implementation of the service is marked with the attribute `[ServiceBehavior]` as shown with the class `CourseRegistrationService`:

```
[ServiceBehavior]
public class CourseRegistrationService : ICourseRegistration
{
    public bool RegisterForCourse(Course course, Attendee attendee)
    {
        // implementation
    }
}
```

The attribute `[ServiceBehavior]` is used to describe behavior as is offered by WCF services to intercept the code for required functionality as shown in the following table.

| ServiceBehavior Property | Description |
| --- | --- |
| `AllowConcurrentTransactions` | If incoming transactions should be allowed, you can set the property AllowConcurrentTransactions to true. |
| `TransactionIsolationLevel` | To define the isolation level of the transaction within the service, the property `TransactionIsolationLevel` can be set to one value of the `IsolationLevel` enumeration (`Serializable, Repeatable, ReadCommitted, ReadUncommitted, Snapshot, Chaos, Unspecified`). |
| `AutomaticSessionShutdown` | If the session should not be closed when the client closes the connection, you can set the property `AutomaticSessionShutdown` to `false`. By default, the session is closed. |
| `InstanceMode` | With the property `InstanceMode` you can define if stateful or stateless objects should be used. The default setting is `InstanceMode.PerCall` to create a new object with every method call. You can compare this with .NET Remoting well-known `SingleCall` objects. Other possible settings are `PrivateSession` and `SharedSession`. With both of these settings stateful objects are used. However, with `PrivateSession` a new object is created for every client. `SharedSession` allows sharing the same object with multiple clients. |
| `ConcurrencyMode` | Because stateful objects can be used by multiple clients (or multiple threads of a single client), you must pay attention to concurrency issues with such object types. If the property `ConcurrencyMode` is set to `Multiple`, multiple threads can access the object, and you have to deal with synchronization. If you set the option to `Single`, only one thread accesses the object at a time. Here you don't have to do synchronization; however scalability problems can occur with a higher client number. |
| | For stateless objects, this setting doesn't have any meaning as new objects are instantiated with every method call and thus no state is shared. |
| `ReturnUnknownExceptionsAsFaults` | With .NET, errors face up as exceptions. SOAP defines that a SOAP fault is returned to the client in case the server has a problem. For security reasons it's not a good idea to return details of server side exceptions to the client. Thus, by default exceptions are converted to unknown faults. To return specific faults, exceptions of type `Fault<string>` can be thrown. |

# Future of Distributed Programming

| ServiceBehavior Property | Description |
|---|---|
| | For debugging purposes, it can be very helpful to return the real exception information. This is the case when changing the setting of `ReturnUnknownExceptionsAsFaults` to `true`. |
| `RunOnUIThread` | If the service is offered by a Windows Forms application, invoking methods of UI controls always the same thread is needed. This is done automatically if you set the property `RunOnUIThread` to `true`. |
| `ValidateMustUnderstand` | The property `ValidateMustUnderstand` set to `true` means that the SOAP headers must be understood (which is the default). |

## *Binding*

A binding describes how a service wants to communicate. With binding, you can specify the following features.

- Transport protocol
- Security requirements
- Encoding format
- Transaction requirements

A binding is composed of multiple binding elements that describe all binding requirements. You can create a custom binding or use one of the predefined bindings that are shown in the following table.

| Standard Binding | Description |
|---|---|
| BasicProfile | BasicProfile is the binding for the broadest interoperability, the first-generation Web services. Transport protocols used are HTTP or HTTPS; security is available only from the protocol. |
| WSProfile | WSProfile is the binding for the next-generation Web services, platforms that implement SOAP extensions for security, reliability, and transactions. The transports used are HTTP or HTTPS; for security the WS-Security specification is implemented; transactions are supported as has been described with the WS-Coordination; WS-AtomicTransaction and WS-BusinessActivity specifications; reliable messaging is supported with an implementation of WS-ReliableMessaging. WSProfile also supports MTOM encoding for sending attachments. |
| WSProfileDualHttp | The binding WSProfileDualHttp in contrast to WSProfile supports duplex messaging. |

*Table continued on following page*

| Standard Binding | Description |
| --- | --- |
| NetProfileTcp | All standard bindings prefixed with the name Net use a binary encoding used for communication between .NET applications. This encoding faster than the text encoding with WSxxx bindings. The binding NetProfileTcpBinding uses the TCP/IP protocol. |
| NetProfileDualTcp | Contrary to NetProfileTcp, NetProfileDualTcp supports duplex messaging. |
| NetProfileNamedPipe | For communication between different processes on the same system, the NetProfileNamedPipe binding is the fastest binding. |
| NetProfileMsmq | The binding NetProfileMsmq brings queued communication to WCF. Here the messages are sent to the message queue. |
| MsmqIntegration | MsmqIntegration is the binding for existing applications that make use of message queuing. The binding NetProfileMsmq requires WCF applications both on the client and server. |
| Intermediary | The Intermediary binding is for intermediaries that sit between client and the service. HTTP, TCP, and named pipes are supported transport protocols. |

Along with defining the binding, the service must define an endpoint. The endpoint is dependent on the contract, the address of the service, and the binding. In the following code, sample a `ServiceHost` object is instantiated, and the address `http://localhost:9200/CourseRegistrationService` as well as a `WsProfileBinding` instance is added to an endpoint of the service.

```
using (ServiceHost<CourseRegistrationService> serviceHost = new
ServiceHost<CourseRegistrationService>())
{
   // add a WSProfile endpoint to the service
   Uri address1 = new Uri("http://localhost:9200/CourseRegistrationService");
   WsProfileBinding binding1 = new WsProfileBinding();
   serviceHost.AddEndpoint(typeof(ICourseRegistration), binding, address);
   //...
}
```

Besides defining the binding programmatically, you can also define it with the application configuration file. The configuration for WCF is placed inside the element <system.serviceModel>. The <service> element defines the services offered. Similar as you've seen in code, the service needs an endpoint, and the endpoint contains address, binding, and contract information.

```
<?xml version="1.0" encoding="utf-8" ?>
<configuration xmlns="http://schemas.microsoft.com/.NetConfiguration/v2.0">
   <system.serviceModel>
      <services>
         <service serviceType="Wrox.ProCSharp.Indigo.CourseRegistrationService">
            <endpoint address="http://localhost:9200/CourseRegistrationService"
               bindingConfiguration="CourseRegistrationConfiguration"
               bindingSectionName="wsProfileBinding"
               contractType="Wrox.ProCSharp.Indigo.ICourseRegistration" />
```

```xml
            </service>
        </services>
        <bindings>
            <wsProfileBinding>
                <binding configurationName="CourseRegistrationConfiguration"
                    securityMode="WSSecurityOverHttp"
                    reliableSessionEnabled="true">
            </wsProfileBinding>
        </bindings>
    </system.serviceModel>
</configuration>
```

## Hosting

WCF is very flexible in choosing a host to run the service. The host can be a Windows service, a COM+ application, ASP.NET, a Windows application, or just a simple console application. Creating a custom host with Windows Forms, you can easily create a peer-to-peer solution.

The sample code shows hosting of a service within a console application. In the `Main()` method, a `ServiceHost<>` instance is created. After the `ServiceHost<>` instance is created, the application configuration file is read to define the bindings. You can also define the bindings programmatically as shown earlier. Next the `Open()` method of the `ServiceHost<>` class is invoked, so the service accepts client calls. With a console application, you have to pay attention not to close the main thread until the service should be closed. Here the user is asked to end the service.

```csharp
using System;
using System.ServiceModel;

public class Program
{
    public static void Main()
    {
        using (ServiceHost<CourseRegistrationService> serviceHost =
            new ServiceHost<CourseRegistrationService>())
        {
            serviceHost.Open();

            Console.WriteLine("The service started. Press return to exit");
            Console.ReadLine();

            serviceHost.Close();
        }
    }
}
```

> If you start the service from within a Windows Forms application and the service code invokes methods of Windows Forms controls, you must pay attention that only the control's creator thread is allowed to access the methods and properties of the control. With WCF this behavior can be reached easily by setting the `RunOnUIThread` **property of the attribute** `[ServiceBehavior]`.

With ASP.NET hosting you get the features from the ASP.NET worker process like automatic activation of the service, health monitoring, and process recycling.

For using ASP.NET hosting, you just have to create a .svc file with the `Service` declaration that includes the language and the name of the service class (here the class is `Wrox.ProCSharp.WCF.CourseRegistrationService`). In addition, you must specify the assembly that contains the class. Instead of specifying the assembly it is also possible to specify the source file for compilation on demand.

```
<%@Service language="C#" class="Wrox.ProCSharp.Indigo.CourseRegistrationService" %>
<%@Assembly name="CourseRegistrationService" %>
```

## Clients

A client application needs a proxy to access a service. There are two ways to create a proxy for the client:

- **Svcutil.exe:** You can create a proxy class with the SvcUtil utility. This utility reads metadata from the service to create the proxy class.

- **ChannelFactory class:** This class is used by the proxy generated from Svcutil; however, it can also be used to create a proxy programmatically.

The Svcutil utility needs metadata to create the proxy class. You've seen similar utilities wsdl.exe with Web services and soapsuds with .NET Remoting. The Svcutil utility can create a proxy from the mex metadata endpoint, the metadata of the assembly or the WSDL and XSD documentation:

```
svcutil http://localhost:9200/CourseRegistrationService /language:C# /out:proxy.cs
svcutil CourseRegistration.dll
svcutil CourseRegistration.wsdl CourseRegistration.xsd
```

The generated proxy class just needs to be instantiated, methods called, and finally the `Close()` method must be invoked:

```
CourseRegistrationProxy proxy = new CourseRegistrationProxy();
proxy.RegisterForCourse(courseRegistration);
proxy.Close();
```

Instead of using a generated proxy class, the static method `CreateChannel()` of the `ChannelFactory` class can be used instead. Creating the proxy this way is useful if metadata for creating the proxy are not available at compile time. Within the generated proxy class shown earlier, the `ChannelFactory.CreateChannel()` method is invoked within the constructor. The `CreateChannel()` method returns a channel object that implements the service contract requested with the address and binding information.

```
EndpointAddress address =
    new EndpointAddress("http://localhost:9200/CourseRegistrationService");
WsProfileBinding binding = new WsProfileBinding();
ICourseRegistration proxy =
    ChannelFactory.CreateChannel<ICourseRegistration>(address, binding);
proxy.RegisterForCourse(course);
((IChannel)proxy).Close();
```

# Future of Distributed Programming

## Preparing for WCF

Now you've seen how WCF services can be created and used. However, WCF is not ready with the release date of .NET 2.0. You can be best prepared for WCF by using today's technologies if you use them carefully with WCF in mind.

By using ASP.NET to develop Web services you have a great path to WCF. You can use Web Services Enhancements (WSE) if more Web service features are needed than are available with ASP.NET. WSE offers security, custom hosting of services, and the use of the TCP channel.

If services such as automatic transactions, object pooling, or separate processes are needed, Enterprise Services is a good option. You will see soon how Enterprise Services can be integrated with WCF.

For disconnected scenarios, where the client and server may run at different times (for example, with a notebook system), you should use `System.Messaging`.

For a fast communication between .NET applications, .NET Remoting with a binary formatter can be a good option. Be aware that .NET Remoting should only be used for communication between .NET applications on both sides of the channel. .NET Remoting is not a choice for platform-independent services.

Let's look at how these technologies can be integrated with WCF.

## *.NET Remoting*

The major features of .NET Remoting are that you can use any application as a host, with the binary formatter faster communication than with ASP.NET Web services is possible, and you can have stateful and stateless objects. In this chapter, you've already seen that WCF supports any host and fast communication with NetProfileXXX bindings.

With .NET Remoting you can create stateless and stateful components. The .NET Remoting terms are well-known single-call and client-activated objects for stateless and stateful components. With well-known-singleton just a single object is shared for all clients. Using WCF, the behavior of instantiating objects is defined with the attribute [ServiceBehavior]. The InstanceMode property can have the values PerCall, PrivateSession, SharedSession, and Singleton. PerCall means that a new instance is created with every method call, PrivateSession defines that the same object is used within a session, setting the value to SharedSession allows sharing the same object across different sessions. With the value Singleton, just one instance is shared for all clients.

| Object Type | .NET Remoting | WCF |
| --- | --- | --- |
| Stateful objects | Client-Activated Objects | InstanceMode.PrivateSession |
|  |  | InstanceMode.SharedSession |
| Stateless objects | Wellknown, SingleCall | InstanceMode.PerCall |
| Singleton | Wellknown, Singleton | InstanceMode.Singleton |

```
[ServiceBehavior(InstanceMode=InstanceMode.PerCall)]
public class CourseRegistration : ICourseRegistration
{
```

How can you decide about using .NET Remoting or ASP.NET Web services today? .NET Remoting should only be used for communication between .NET applications on both sides of the channel. .NET Remoting is not a choice for platform-independent services.

As of today, there's no plan to offer accessing direct interop between .NET Remoting and WCF applications. You have to rewrite your .NET Remoting services for using WCF's features. If you factor the functionality of your service-code to separate classes, it shouldn't be a big issue to do that. With the service class you just have to remove the derivation from the base class `MarshalByRefObject`, and add the required attributes. The .NET Remoting configuration files can be replaced by WCF configuration. It also helps if you are using interfaces for the service classes.

There will be more issues if you extend .NET Remoting by using sinks. There's no easy way to change the sink code to create WCF interception code. Here the programming model is very different. However, the functionality of many sinks that you might implement today can be readily available with WCF. There wouldn't be the need to migrate these sinks. For the other sinks where you don't find corresponding functionality with WCF you should factor the functionality of the sinks to separate classes to make it easy for reusing at least part of your code.

If there's no need to use the new features of WCF with .NET Remoting applications, .NET Remoting and WCF can run side by side.

## ASP.NET Web Services

With ASP.NET Web services, you can create platform-independent services today. Using ASP.NET to create Web services is a good option for being prepared for WCF in the future: ASP.NET Web services and WCF can interoperate directly. A WCF client can access an ASP.NET Web service, and a .NET 2.0 Web services proxy can access an WCF service. For this interoperability, the binding BasicProfile is used with WCF.

Porting the ASP.NET Web service to WCF is not a big deal, too. WCF can be hosted in ASP.NET; you just have to create a .svc file as shown earlier. The attributes `[WebMethod]` need to be changed to `[OperationContract]`. Other attributes can be added as needed, and you can get the additional WCF features for your service.

## Enterprise Services

If you write serviced components today, there's a great migration path to WCF. Without changing the serviced components, you can create a WCF front-end that offers Web services access to the serviced components. Also, with the WCF service moniker, a COM client can access WCF services.

With the ComSvcConfig utility, you can create a WCF front-end to an Enterprise Services application:

```
ComSvcConfig add /application:OrderControlComponent
/interface:Wrox.ProCSharp.EnterpriseServices.OrderControl, IOrderControl
/hosting:was /webDirectory:OrderControl /mex
```

# Future of Distributed Programming

The option /application specifies the COM+ application, /interface the interface of the application that should be made available as a Web service. The option /hosting defines the process where the service should be hosted. The possible values for the /hosting option are was and complus. was uses a virtual directory of IIS, with complus the COM+ application process itself is used as the hosting process. The setting for /webDirectory specifies the virtual directory of the service. This directory must be configured with IIS before the WCF service is created. With the option /mex a metadata endpoint is created that can be used by WCF clients to read the metadata of the service.

The other way around, using COM clients to access WCF services, can be done too. In such a scenario, proxy code for the client must be created with the svcutil utility:

```
svcutil "http://localhost/OrderControl/OrderControl.svc" /language:c# /out:proxy.cs
```

The resulting proxy.cs file must be put into an assembly that is strongly signed and has the assembly attribute [ComVisible] applied:

```
[assembly: ComVisible(true)]
```

For this assembly, a COM Callable Wrapper (CCW) must be created and configured with the regasm utility (see Chapter 33, "COM Interoperability"), and the assembly must be installed into the GAC (see Chapter 15, "Assemblies"). When this is done, the COM client can access the service using a WCF service moniker. The code is an example of a VBScript client application using the service moniker:

```
Set proxy = GetObject(
    "service:address=http://localhost/OrderControl/OrderControl.svc,
    binding=wsProfileBinding, contract={05AFF608-AA50-444a-B85B-D5E4248956DA}")
```

As you've seen, WCF and Enterprise Services has a great interoperability features. The same can be said about Message queuing.

## Message Queuing

Message Queuing is the technology that can be used in a disconnected environment. It's not necessary that the client and server applications are running during the same time (as it is necessary with asynchronous programming). Here the sending application writes messages to a queue, and the receiving application that can run on different times reads messages from the queue.

Using WCF, the WCF client application can write messages to the queue that are read from applications that make use of the System.Messaging namespace (see Chapter 31, Message Queuing). The other way around, using WCF as a service and classes from the System.Messaging namespace for the client application, can be done similarly. With both scenarios, the binding MsmqIntegration is used. This binding doesn't support authentication.

If both the sending and receiving applications are using WCF, the binding NetProfileMsmq can be used that also offers security integration with Message Queuing.

Chapter 32

# Summary

In this chapter, you've learned how to prepare for upcoming technologies in the communication area. With Web services, security, reliability, transactions, and performance are required features for many business solutions. WCF is the technology that implements these features.

WCF combines the features of .NET Remoting, ASP.NET Web services, Enterprise Services, and Message Queuing. It offers the same programming model for using all these features. Also, WCF can be easily integrated with existing technologies.

# Part VII
# Interop

**Chapter 33: COM Interoperability**

# 33

# COM Interoperability

If you have Windows programs written prior to .NET, you probably don't have the time and resources to rewrite everything for .NET. There should not be a reason to rewrite old code just because a new technology is available. You might have thousands of lines of existing, running code, which would require too much effort to rewrite just to move it into the managed environment.

The same applies to Microsoft. With the namespace System.DirectoryServices, Microsoft hasn't rewritten the COM objects accessing the hierarchical data store; the classes inside this namespace are wrappers accessing the ADSI COM objects instead. The same thing happens with System.Data.OleDb, where the OLE DB providers that are used by classes from this namespace do have quite complex COM interfaces.

The same issue may apply for your own solutions. If you have existing COM objects that should be used from .NET applications, or the other way around if you want to write .NET components that should be used in old COM clients, this chapter will be a starter for using COM interoperability.

If you don't have existing COM components you want to integrate with your application, or old COM clients that should use some .NET components, you can skip this chapter.

This chapter discusses the following:

- COM and .NET technologies
- Using COM objects from within .NET applications
- Using .NET components from within COM clients

Like all other chapters, you can download the sample code for this chapter from the Wrox Web site at www.wrox.com.

# Chapter 33

# .NET and COM

COM is the predecessor technology to .NET. COM defines a component model where components can be written in different programming languages. A component written with C++ can be used from a Visual Basic client. Components can also be used locally inside a process, across processes, or across the network. Does this sound familiar? Of course, .NET has similar goals. However, the way in which these goals are achieved is different. The COM concepts became more and more complex to use and turned out not to be extensible enough. .NET fulfills similar goals as COM had, but introduces new concepts to make your job easier.

Even today, when using COM Interop the prerequisite is to know COM. It doesn't matter if .NET components are used by COM clients or COM components are used by .NET applications, you must know COM. So this section compares COM and .NET functionality.

If you already have a good grasp of COM technologies, this section may be a refresher to your COM knowledge. Otherwise it introduces you to the concepts of COM — now using .NET — that you can be happy not to deal with anymore in your daily business. However, all the problems that came with COM still apply when COM technology is integrated in .NET applications.

COM and .NET do have many similar concepts with very different solutions, including the following:

- Metadata
- Freeing memory
- Interfaces
- Method binding
- Data types
- Registration
- Threading
- Error handling
- Event handling

## *Metadata*

With COM, all information about the component is stored inside the type library. The type library includes information such as names and ids of interfaces, methods, and arguments. With .NET all this information can be found inside the assembly itself, as you saw in Chapter 11, "Reflection," and Chapter 15, "Assemblies." The problem with COM is that the type library is not extensible. With C++, IDL (interface definition language) files have been used to describe the interfaces and methods. Some of the IDL modifiers cannot be found inside the type library, because Visual Basic (and the Visual Basic team was responsible for the type library) couldn't use these IDL modifiers. With .NET this problem doesn't exist because the .NET metadata is extensible using custom attributes.

As a result of this behavior, some COM components have a type library and others don't. Where no type library is available, a C++ header file can be used that describes the interfaces and methods. With .NET it is easier using COM components that do have a type library, but it is also possible to use COM components without a type library. In that case it is necessary to redefine the COM interface by using C# code.

# COM Interoperability

## Freeing Memory

With .NET, memory is released by the garbage collector. This is completely different with COM. COM relies on reference counts.

The interface `IUnknown`, which is the interface that is required to be implemented by every COM object, offers three methods. Two of these methods are related to reference counts. The method `AddRef()` must be called by the client if another interface pointer is needed; this method increments the reference count. The method `Release()` decrements the reference count, and if the resulting reference count is 0, the object destroys itself to free memory.

## Interfaces

Interfaces are the heart of COM. They distinguish between a contract used between the client and the object, and the implementation. The interface (the contract) defines the methods that are offered by the component and that can be used by the client. With .NET, interfaces play an important part, too.

COM distinguishes between three interface types: *custom*, *dispatch*, and *dual* interfaces.

### Custom interfaces

Custom interfaces derive from the interface `IUnknown`. A custom interface defines the order of the methods in a virtual table (vtable), so that the client can access the methods of the interface directly. This also means that the client needs to know the vtable during development time, because binding to the methods happens by using memory addresses. As a conclusion, custom interfaces cannot be used by scripting clients. Figure 33-1 shows the vtable of the custom interface `IMath` that offers the methods `Add()` and `Sub()` in addition to the methods of the `IUnknown` interface.

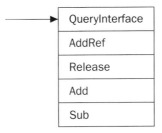

Figure 33-1

### Dispatch interfaces

Because a scripting client (and earlier Visual Basic clients) doesn't support custom interfaces, a different interface type is needed. With dispatch interfaces, the interface available for the client is always the `IDispatch` interface. `IDispatch` derives from `IUnknown` and offers four methods in addition to the `IUnknown` methods. The two most important methods are `GetIDsOfNames()` and `Invoke()`. As shown in Figure 33-2, with a dispatch interface two tables are needed. The first one maps the method or property name to a dispatch id; the second one maps the dispatch id to the implementation of the method or property.

1153

# Chapter 33

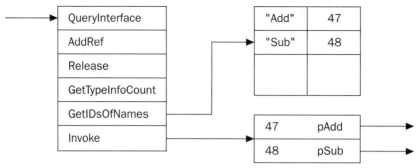

Figure 33-2

When the client invokes a method in the component, at first it calls the method `GetIDsOfNames()`, passing the name of the method it wants to call. `GetIDsOfNames()` makes a lookup into the name-to-id table to return the dispatch id. This id is used by the client to call the `Invoke()` method.

*Usually, the two tables for the `IDispatch` interface are stored inside the type library, but this is not a requirement, and some components have the tables on other places.*

## Dual interfaces

As you can imagine, dispatch interfaces are a lot slower compared to custom interfaces. On the other hand, custom interfaces cannot be used by scripting clients. A dual interface can solve this dilemma. As you can see in Figure 33-3, a dual interface derives from `IDispatch` but offers the additional methods of the interface directly in the vtable. Scripting clients can use the `IDispatch` interface to invoke the methods, whereas clients aware of the vtable can call the methods directly.

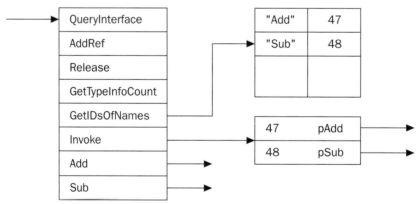

Figure 33-3

## Casting and QueryInterface

If a .NET class implements multiple interfaces, casts can be done to get one interface or another. With COM, the interface `IUnknown` offers a similar mechanism with the method `QueryInterface()`. As

1154

# COM Interoperability

discussed in the previous section, the interface `IUnknown` is the base interface of every interface, so `QueryInterface()` is available anyway.

## Method Binding

How a client maps to a method is defined with the terms *early* and *late binding*. Late binding means that the method to invoke is looked for during runtime. .NET uses the `System.Reflection` namespace to make this possible (see Chapter 11).

COM uses the `IDispatch` interface discussed earlier for late binding. Late binding is possible with dispatch and dual interfaces.

With COM, early binding has two different options. One way of early binding, also known as vtable binding, is using the vtable directly — this is possible with custom and dual interfaces. The second option of early binding is also known as id binding. Here the dispatch id is stored inside the client code, so during runtime only a call to `Invoke()` is necessary. `GetIdsOfNames()` is called during design time. With such clients it is important to remember that the dispatch id must not be changed.

## Data Types

For dual and dispatch interfaces, the data types that can be used with COM are restricted to a list of automation-compatible data types. The `Invoke()` method of the `IDispatch` interface accepts an array of `VARIANT` data types. The `VARIANT` is a union of many different data types such as `BYTE`, `SHORT`, `LONG`, `FLOAT`, `DOUBLE`, `BSTR`, `IUnknown*`, `IDispatch*`, and so on. `VARIANT`s have been easy to use from Visual Basic, but it was complex to use them from C++. .NET has the `Object` class instead of `VARIANT`s.

With custom interfaces, all data types available with C++ can be used with COM. However, this also restricts the clients that can use this component to certain programming languages.

## Registration

.NET distinguishes between private and shared assemblies, as discussed in Chapter 15. With COM, all components are globally available by a registry configuration.

All COM objects have a unique identifier that consists of a 128-bit number and is also known as class id (CLSID). The COM API call to create COM objects, `CoCreateInstance()`, just looks into the registry to find the CLSID and the path to the DLL or EXE to load the DLL or launch the EXE and instantiate the component.

Because such a 128-bit number cannot be easily remembered, many COM objects also have a prog id. The prog id is an easy-to-remember name, such as `Excel.Application`, that just maps to the CLSID.

In addition to the CLSID, COM objects also have a unique identifier for each interface (IID) and for the type library (typelib id).

Information in the registry is discussed in more detail later in the chapter.

# Chapter 33

# Threading

COM uses apartment models to relieve the programmer from threading issues. However, this also adds some more complexity. Different apartment types have been added with different releases of the operating system. This section discusses the single-threaded apartment and the multi-threaded apartment.

*Threading with .NET is discussed in Chapter 13, "Threading."*

## Single-threaded apartment

The single-threaded apartment (STA) was introduced with Windows NT 3.51. With an STA, only one thread (the thread that created the instance) is allowed to access the component. However, it is legal to have multiple STAs inside one process, as shown in Figure 33-4.

In this figure, the inner rectangles with the lollipop represent COM components. Components and threads (curved arrows) are surrounded by apartments. The outer rectangle represents a process.

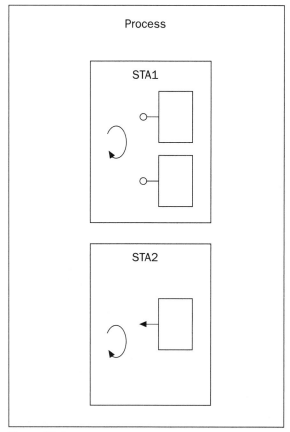

Figure 33-4

# COM Interoperability

With STAs there's no need to protect instance variables from multiple thread access because this protection is provided by a COM facility, and only one thread accesses the component.

A COM object that is not programmed with thread safety marks the requirements for an STA in the registry with the registry key `ThreadingModel` set to `Apartment`.

## Multi-threaded apartment

Windows NT 4.0 introduced the concept of a multi-threaded apartment (MTA). With an MTA, multiple threads can access the component simultaneously. Figure 33-5 shows a process with one MTA and two STAs.

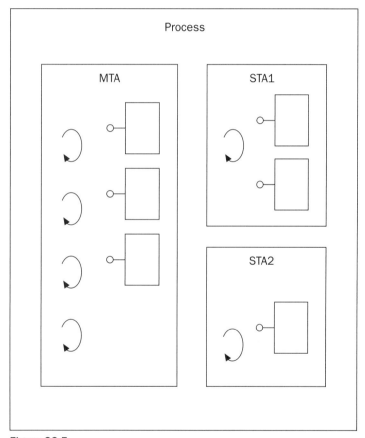

**Figure 33-5**

A COM object programmed with thread-safety in mind marks the requirement for an MTA in the registry with the key `ThreadingModel` set to `Free`. The value `Both` is used for thread-safe COM objects that don't mind the apartment type.

*Visual Basic 6.0 didn't offer support for multi-threaded apartments.*

# Chapter 33

## *Error Handling*

With .NET, errors are generated by throwing exceptions. With the older COM technology, errors are defined by returning HRESULT values with the methods. An HRESULT value of S_OK means that the method was successful.

If a more detailed error message is offered by the COM component, the COM component implements the interface ISupportErrorInfo, where not only an error message but also a link to a help file and the source of the error is returned with an error information object on the return of the method. Objects that implement ISupportErrorInfo are automatically mapped to more detailed error information with an exception in .NET.

## *Event Handling*

.NET offers an event-handling mechanism with the C# keywords event and delegate (see Chapter 6, "Delegates and Events"). Chapter 29, ".NET Remoting," discussed that the same mechanism is also available with .NET Remoting.

Figure 33-6 shows the COM event-handling architecture. With COM events, the component has to implement the interface IConnectionPointContainer and one or more connection point objects (CPOs) that implement the interface IConnectionPoint. The component also defines an outgoing interface—ICompletedEvents in Figure 33-6—that is invoked by the CPO. The client must implement this outgoing interface in the sink object, which itself is a COM object. During runtime, the client queries the server for the interface IConnectionPointContainer. With the help of this interface, the client asks for a CPO with the method FindConnectionPoint() to get a pointer to IConnectionPoint returned. This interface pointer is used by the client to call the Advise() method, where a pointer to the sink object is passed to the server. In turn, the component can invoke methods inside the sink object of the client.

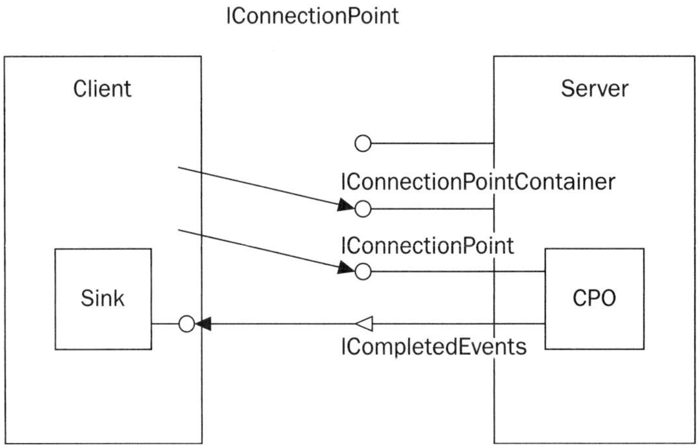

**Figure 33-6**

Later in this chapter, you learn how the .NET events and the COM events can be mapped so that COM events can be handled by a .NET client and vice versa.

# COM Interoperability

## Marshaling

Data passed from .NET to the COM component and the other way around must be converted to the corresponding representation. This mechanism is also known as *marshaling*. What happens here depends on the data type of the data that is passed: you have to differentiate between *blittable* and *non-blittable* data types.

Blittable data types have a common representation with both .NET and COM, and no conversion is needed. Simple data types such as `byte`, `short`, `int`, `long`, and classes and arrays that only contain these simple data types belong to the blittable data types. Arrays must be one-dimensional to be blittable.

A conversion is needed with non-blittable data types. The following table lists some of the non-blittable COM data types with their .NET-related data types. Non-blittable types have a higher overhead because of the conversion.

| COM Data Type | .NET Data Type |
| --- | --- |
| SAFEARRAY | Array |
| VARIANT | Object |
| BSTR | String |
| IUnknown*, IDispatch* | Object |

## Using a COM Component from a .NET Client

To see how a .NET application can use a COM component, you first have to create a COM component. Creating COM components is not possible with C# or Visual Basic 2005; you need either Visual Basic 6 or C++ (or any other language that supports COM). This chapters uses the Active Template Library (ATL) and C++.

> *A short note about building COM components with Visual Basic 2005 and C#: With Visual Basic 2005 and C# it is possible to build .NET components that can be used as COM objects by using a wrapper that is the real COM component. It would make no sense that a .NET component that is wrapped from a COM component is used by a .NET client with COM interop.*
>
> *Because this is not a COM book, it does not discuss all aspects of the code but only what you need to build the sample.*

### Creating a COM Component

To create a COM component with ATL and C++, create a new ATL Project. You can find the ATL Project Wizard within the Visual C++ Projects group when you select File ➪ New ➪ Project. Set the name to COMServer. With the Application Settings, select Attributed and Dynamic Link Library and click Finish.

> *Since Visual Studio .NET 2002, the ATL offers attributes that make it easier to build a COM server. These attributes have nothing in common with the .NET attributes; instead, they are used only with ATL. Instead of writing a separate IDL file and a C++ file defining the interface, only a C++ file is needed that also has attributes required by COM.*

# Chapter 33

The ATL Project Wizard just creates the foundation for the server. A COM object is still needed. Add a class in Solution Explorer and select ATL Simple Object. In the dialog that starts up, enter **COMDemo** in the field for the Short name. The other fields will be filled automatically, but change the interface name to **IWelcome** (see Figure 33-7).

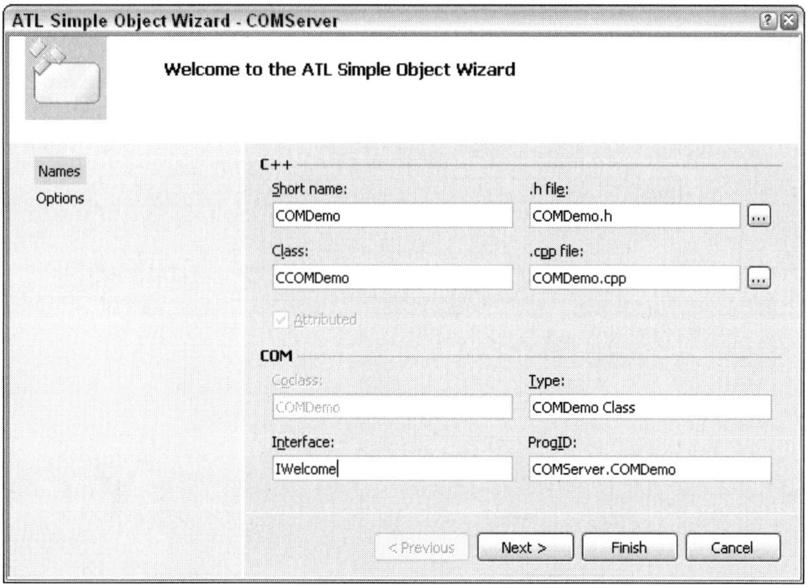

**Figure 33-7**

The COM component offers two interfaces, so that you can see how `QueryInterface()` is mapped from .NET, and just three simple methods, so that you can see how the interaction takes place. In the Class View, select the interface `IWelcome` and add the method `Greeting()` (see Figure 33-7) with these parameters:

```
HRESULT Greeting([in] BSTR name, [out, retval] BSTR* message);
```

Your wizard-generated code from the file `COMDemo.h` should look similar to the following code. The unique identifiers (`uuid`s) will differ. The interface `IWelcome` defines the `Greeting()` methods. The brackets before the keyword `__interface` define some attributes for the interface. `uuid` defines the interface id and `dual` marks the type of the interface:

```
// COMDemo.h : Declaration of the CCOMDemo

#pragma once
#include "resource.h"       // main symbols

// IWelcome
[
  object,
  uuid("015ED275-3DE6-4716-A6FA-4EBC71E4A8EA"),
  dual, helpstring("IWelcome Interface"),
  pointer_default(unique)
```

```
]
__interface IWelcome : IDispatch
{
  [id(1), helpstring("method Greeting")] HRESULT Greeting([in] BSTR name,
      [out, retval] BSTR* message);
};
```

The class `CCOMDemo` is also in the file `COMDemo.h`. The attribute `uuid()` in the header section of the class defines the CLSID. The attributes `vi_progid` and `progid` name the prog id that will be written into the registry:

```
// CCOMDemo

[
 coclass,
 threading(apartment),
 vi_progid("COMServer.COMDemo"),
 progid("COMServer.COMDemo.1"),
 version(1.0),
 uuid("2388AAA8-AD72-4022-948D-555316F708E8"),
 helpstring("COMDemo Class")
]
class ATL_NO_VTABLE CCOMDemo :
 public IWelcome
{
public:
  CCOMDemo()
  {
  }


  DECLARE_PROTECT_FINAL_CONSTRUCT()

  HRESULT FinalConstruct()
  {
    return S_OK;
  }

  void FinalRelease()
  {
  }

public:

  STDMETHOD(Greeting)(BSTR name, BSTR* message);
};
```

> With custom attributes, it is possible to change the name of the class and interfaces that are generated by a .NET wrapper class. You just have to add the attribute `custom` with the identifier 0F21F359-AB84-41e8-9A78-36D110E6D2F9, and the name under which it should appear within .NET.

Add the custom attribute with the same identifier and the name `Wrox.ProCSharp.COMInterop.Server.IWelcome` to the header section of the `IWelcome` interface. Add the same attribute with a corresponding name to the class `CCOMDemo`:

```
// IWelcome
[
  object,
  uuid("015ED275-3DE6-4716-A6FA-4EBC71E4A8EA"),
  dual, helpstring("ICOMDemo Interface"),
  pointer_default(unique),
  custom(0F21F359-AB84-41e8-9A78-36D110E6D2F9,
     "Wrox.ProCSharp.COMInterop.Server.IWelcome")
]
__interface IWelcome : IDispatch
{
    [id(1)] HRESULT Greeting([in] BSTR name, [out, retval] BSTR* message);
};
```

Now add a second interface to the file `COMDemo.h`. You can copy the header section of the `IWelcome` interface to the header section of the new `IMath` interface, but be sure to change the unique identifier that is defined with the `uuid` keyword. You can generate such an id with the guidgen utility. The interface `IMath` offers the methods `Add()` and `Sub()`:

```
// IMath
[
  object,
  uuid("2158751B-896E-461d-9012-EF1680BE0628"),
  dual,
  helpstring("IMath Interface"),
  pointer_default(unique),
  custom(0F21F359-AB84-41e8-9A78-36D110E6D2F9,
     "Wrox.ProCSharp.COMInterop.Server.IMath")
]
__interface IMath : IDispatch
{
    [id(1)] HRESULT Add([in] LONG val1, [in] LONG val2, [out, retval] LONG* result);
    [id(2)] HRESULT Sub([in] LONG val1, [in] LONG val2, [out, retval] LONG* result);
};
```

The class `CCOMDemo` must also be changed so that it implements both interfaces `IWelcome` and `IMath`:

```
[
  coclass,
  threading(apartment),
  vi_progid("COMServer.COMDemo"),
  progid("COMServer.COMDemo.1"),
  version(1.0),
  custom(0F21F359-AB84-41e8-9A78-36D110E6D2F9,
     "Wrox.ProCSharp.COMInterop.Server.COMDemo"),
  uuid("2388AAA8-AD72-4022-948D-555316F708E8"),
  helpstring("COMDemo Class")
]
```

# COM Interoperability

```
class ATL_NO_VTABLE CCOMDemo :
    public IWelcome, public IMath
{
```

Now you can implement the three methods in the file `COMDemo.cpp` with the following code. The `CComBSTR` is an ATL class that makes it easier to deal with `BSTR`s. In the `Greeting()` method just a welcome message is returned that adds the name passed in the first argument to the message that is returned. The `Add()` method just does a simple addition of two values and the `Sub()` method does a subtraction, and returns the result:

```
STDMETHODIMP CCOMDemo::Greeting(BSTR name, BSTR* message)
{
    CComBSTR tmp("Welcome, ");
    tmp.Append(name);
    *message = tmp;
    return S_OK;
}

STDMETHODIMP CCOMDemo::Add(LONG val1, LONG val2, LONG* result)
{
    *result = val1 + val2;
    return S_OK;
}

STDMETHODIMP CCOMDemo::Sub(LONG val1, LONG val2, LONG* result)
{
    *result = val1 -- val2;
    return S_OK;
}
```

Now you can build the component. The build process also configures the component in the registry.

## Creating a Runtime Callable Wrapper

You can now use the COM component from within .NET. To make this possible, you must create a runtime callable wrapper (RCW). Using the RCW, the .NET client sees a .NET object instead of the COM component; there is no need to deal with the COM characteristics because this is done by the wrapper. An RCW hides `IUnknown` and `IDispatch` interfaces (see Figure 33-8) and deals itself with the reference counts of the COM object.

The RCW can be created by using the command-line utility tlbimp or by using Visual Studio. Starting the command

```
tlbimp COMServer.dll /out: Interop.COMServer.dll
```

creates the file `Interop.COMServer.dll` including a .NET assembly with the wrapper class. In this generated assembly you can find the namespace `COMWrapper` with the class `CCOMDemoClass` and the interfaces `CCOMDemo`, `IMath`, and `IWelcome`. The name of the namespace can be changed by using options of the tlbimp utility. The option `/namespace` allows you to specify a different namespace, and with `/asmversion` you can define the version number of the assembly.

1163

## Chapter 33

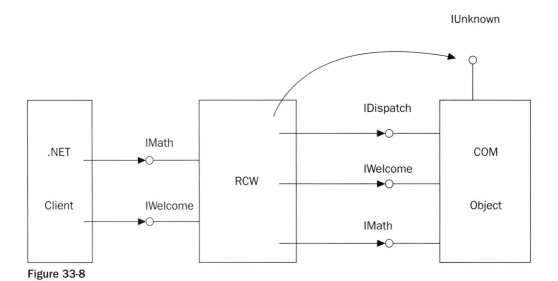

Figure 33-8

*Another important option of this command-line utility is /keyfile, which is used for assigning a strong name to the generated assembly. Strong names are discussed in Chapter 15.*

An RCW can also be created by using Visual Studio. To create a simple sample application, create a C# console project. In Solution Explorer, add a reference to the COM server by selecting the COM tab and scroll down to the entry `COMServer 1.0 Type Library` (see Figure 33-9). Here all COM objects are listed that are configured in the registry. Selecting a COM component from the list creates an assembly with an RCW class.

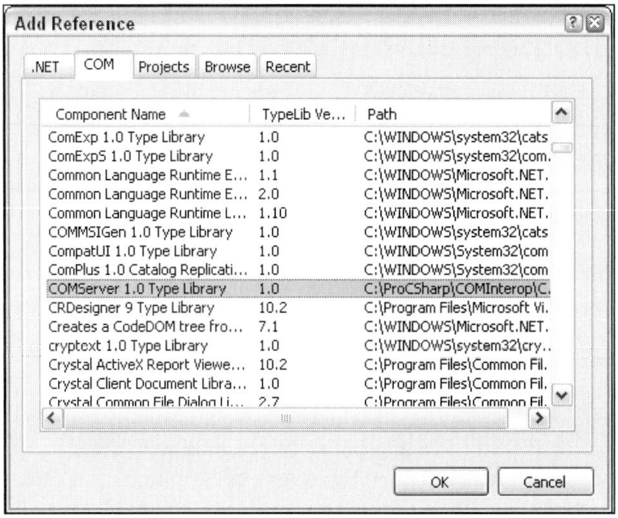

Figure 33-9

# COM Interoperability

After creating the wrapper class you can write the code for the application to instantiate and access the component. Because of the custom attributes in the C++ file, the generated namespace of the RCW class is `Wrox.ProCSharp.COMInterop.Server`. Add this namespace as well as the namespace `System.Runtime.InteropServices` to the declarations. From the namespace `System.Runtime.InteropServices` the `Marshal` class will be used to release the COM object:

```
using System;
using System.Runtime.InteropServices;
using Wrox.ProCSharp.COMInteorp.Server

namespace Wrox.ProCSharp.COMInterop.Client
{
   class Program
   {
      [STAThread]
      static void Main(string[] args)
      {
```

Now the COM component can be used similar to a .NET class. `obj` is a variable of type `COMDemo`. `COMDemo` is a .NET interface that offers the methods of both the `IWelcome` and the `IMath` interfaces. However, it is also possible to cast to a specific interface such as `IWelcome`. With a variable that is declared of type `IWelcome`, the method `Greeting()` can be called.

> *Although* `COMDemo` *is an interface, you can instantiate new objects of type* `COMDemo`. *Contrary to normal interfaces, you can do this with wrapped COM interfaces.*

```
COMDemo obj = new COMDemo();
IWelcome welcome = (IWelcome)obj;
Console.WriteLine(welcome.Greeting("Christian"));
```

If the object — as in this case — offers multiple interfaces, a variable of the other interface can be declared, and by using a simple assignment with the cast operator, the wrapper class does a `QueryInterface()` with the COM object to return the second interface pointer. With the `math` variable, the methods of the `IMath` interface can be called:

```
IMath math;
math = (IMath)obj;
int x = math.Add(4, 5);
Console.WriteLine(x);
```

If the COM object should be released before the garbage collector cleans up the object, the static method `Marshal.ReleaseComObject()` invokes the `Release()` method of the component, so that the component can destroy itself and free memory:

```
         Marshal.ReleaseComObject(math);
      }
   }
}
```

As you can see, with a runtime callable wrapper, a COM component can be used similar to a .NET object.

A special case of a runtime callable wrapper is a primary interop assembly, which is discussed next.

## Primary interop assemblies

A *primary interop assembly* is an assembly that is already prepared by the vendor of the COM component. This makes it easier to use the COM component. A primary interop assembly is a runtime-callable wrapper that might differ from an automatically generated RCW.

You can find primary interop assemblies in the directory `<program files>\Microsoft .NET\Primary Interop Assemblies`. A primary interop assembly already exists for the use of ADO from within .NET. If you add a reference to the COM library Microsoft ActiveX Data Objects 2.7 Library, no wrapper class is created because a primary interop assembly already exists; the primary interop assembly is referenced instead.

# Threading Issues

As discussed earlier in this chapter, a COM component marks the apartment (STA or MTA) it wants to live in, based on whether it is implemented thread-safe or not. However, the thread has to join an apartment. What apartment the thread should join can be defined with the `[STAThread]` and `[MTAThread]` attributes, which can be applied to the `Main()` method of an application. The attribute `[STAThread]` means that the thread joins an STA, whereas the attribute `[MTAThread]` means that the thread joins an MTA. Joining an MTA is the default if no attribute is applied.

It is also possible to set the apartment state programmatically with the `ApartmentState` property of the `Thread` class. The `ApartmentState` property allows you to set a value from the `ApartmentState` enumeration. `ApartmentState` has the possible values `STA` and `MTA` (and `Unknown` if it wasn't set). Be aware that the apartment state of a thread can only be set once. If it is set a second time, the second setting is ignored.

> **What happens if the thread chooses a different apartment from the apartments supported by the component?** The correct apartment for the COM component is created automatically by the COM runtime. However, the performance decreases if the apartment boundaries are crossed while calling the methods of a component.

# Adding Connection Points

To see how COM events can be handled in a .NET application, first the COM component must be extended. Implementing a COM event in an ATL class using attributes looks very similar to the events in .NET, although the functionality is different.

First you have to add another interface to the header file `COMDemo.h`. The interface `_ICompletedEvents` is implemented by the client, which is the .NET application, and called by the component. In this example, the method `Completed()` is called by the component when the calculation is ready. Such an interface is also known as an outgoing interface. An outgoing interface must either be a dispatch or a custom interface. Dispatch interfaces are supported by all clients. The custom attribute with the id `0F21F359-AB84-41e8-9A78-36D110E6D2F9` defines the name of this interface that will be created in the RCW:

```
// _ICompletedEvents
[
    dispinterface,
    uuid("B2CBBCD3-2993-4148-8EF4-356EACFD834B"),
    custom(0F21F359-AB84-41e8-9A78-36D110E6D2F9,
```

```
        "Wrox.ProCSharp.COMInterop.Server.ICompletedEvents"),
      helpstring("_ICompletedEvents Interface")
    ]
    __interface _ICompletedEvents
    {
     [id(1)] void Completed(void);
    };
```

Apply the attribute event_source(com) to the class CCOMDemo to create a connection point object, and add the __event keyword to the public section of this class as shown in the following code. This keyword __event creates a helper class for all methods of the defined interface that fires events to the client. The event is fired using the __raise keyword inside the method FireCompleted():

```
    [
      coclass,
      threading(apartment),
      vi_progid("COMServer.COMDemo"),
      progid("COMServer.COMDemo.1"),
      version(1.0),
      custom(0F21F359-AB84-41e8-9A78-36D110E6D2F9,
        "Wrox.ProCSharp.COMInterop.Server.COMDemo"),
      uuid("2388AAA8-AD72-4022-948D-555316F708E8"),
      event_source(com),
      helpstring("COMDemo Class")
    ]
    class ATL_NO_VTABLE CCOMDemo :
        public IWelcome, public IMath
    {
    public:
        CCOMDemo()
        {
        }

        __event __interface _ICompletedEvents;
        void FireCompleted()
        {
            __raise Completed();
        }
```

Finally, the method FireCompleted() can be called inside the methods Add() and Sub() in the file COMDemo.cpp:

```
    STDMETHODIMP CCOMDemo::Add(LONG val1, LONG val2, LONG* result)
    {
        *result = val1 + val2;
        FireCompleted();
        return S_OK;
    }

    STDMETHODIMP CCOMDemo::Sub(LONG val1, LONG val2, LONG* result)
    {
        *result = val1 - val2;
        FireCompleted();
        return S_OK;
    }
```

After rebuilding the COM DLL, you can change the .NET client to use these COM events:

```
static void Main(string[] args)
{
    COMDemo obj = new COMDemo();

    IWelcome welcome = (IWelcome)obj;
    Console.WriteLine(welcome.Greeting("Christian"));

    obj.Completed +=
        new ICompletedEvents_CompletedEventHandler(Completed);

    IMath math = (IMath)welcome;
    int result = math.Add(3, 5);
    Console.WriteLine(result);

    Marshal.ReleaseComObject(math);
}

private static void Completed()
{
    Console.WriteLine("Calculation completed");
}
```

As you can see, the RCW offers automatic mapping from COM events to .NET events. COM events can be used similar to .NET events in a .NET client.

## *Using ActiveX Controls in Windows Forms*

ActiveX controls are COM objects with a user interface and many optional COM interfaces to deal with the user interface and the interaction with the container. ActiveX controls can be used by many different containers such as Internet Explorer, Word, Excel, and applications written using Visual Basic 6, MFC (Microsoft Foundation Classes), or ATL (Active Template Library). A Windows Forms application is another container that can manage ActiveX controls. ActiveX controls can be used similar to Windows Forms controls as you see shortly.

### *ActiveX Control Importer*

Similar to runtime callable wrappers, you can also create a wrapper for ActiveX controls. A wrapper for an ActiveX control is created by using the command-line utility *Windows Forms ActiveX Control Importer*, aximp.exe. This utility creates a class that derives from the base class System.Windows.Forms.AxHost that acts as a wrapper to use the ActiveX control.

You can enter this command to create a wrapper class from the Web Forms Control:

```
aximp c:\windows\system32\shdocvw.dll
```

ActiveX controls can also be imported directly using Visual Studio. If the ActiveX control is configured within the toolbox, it can be dragged and dropped to a Windows Forms control that creates the wrapper.

# COM Interoperability

## Creating a Windows Forms application

To see ActiveX controls running inside a Windows Forms application, create a simple Windows Forms application project. With this application, you will build a simple Internet browser that uses the Web Browser control, which comes as part of the operating system.

Create a form as shown in Figure 33-10. The form should include a text box that is used to enter a URL with the name `textUrl`, three buttons with the names `buttonNavigate`, `buttonBack`, and `buttonForward` to navigate Web pages, and a status bar with the name `statusBar`.

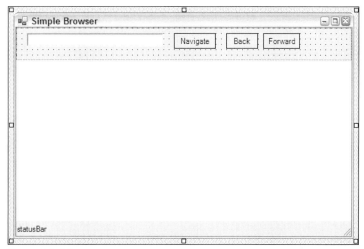

**Figure 33-10**

Using Visual Studio, you can add ActiveX controls to the toolbar to use it in the same way as a Windows Forms control. In the Customize Toolbox context menu, select the Add/Remove Items menu entry and select the Microsoft Web Browser control in the COM Components category (see Figure 33-11).

This way, an icon will show up in the toolbox. Similar to other Windows controls, you can drag and drop this icon to the Windows Forms designer to create (with the aximp utility) a wrapper assembly hosting the ActiveX control. You can see the wrapper assemblies with the references in the project: AxSHDocVw and SHDocVw. Now you can invoke methods of the control by using the generated variable axWebBrowser1 as shown in the following code. Add a Click event handler to the button buttonNavigate in order to navigate the browser to a Web page. The method Navigate() used for this purpose requires a URL string with the first argument that you get by accessing the Text property of the text field textUrl. The following four arguments are all optional with the Navigate() method. Because C# doesn't support optional arguments, you have to pass values. However, passing null values with the noArg variable is good enough:

```
private void OnNavigate(object sender, System.EventArgs e)
{
   object noArg = null;
   axWebBrowser1.Navigate(textUrl.Text, ref noArg, ref noArg, ref noArg,
                 ref noArg);
}
```

# Chapter 33

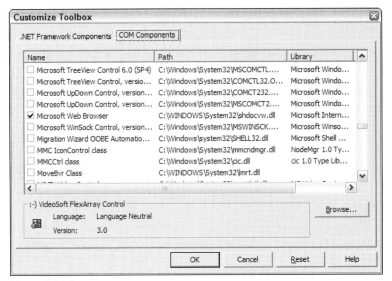

Figure 33-11

With the Click event handler of the Back and Forward buttons, call the GoBack() and GoForward() methods of the browser control:

```
private void OnBack(object sender, System.EventArgs e)
{
   try
   {
      axWebBrowser1.GoBack();
   }
   catch
   {
   }
}

private void OnForward(object sender, System.EventArgs e)
{
   try
   {
      axWebBrowser1.GoForward();
   }
   catch
   {
   }
}
```

The Web control also offers some events that can be used just like a .NET event. Add the event handler OnStatusChange() to the event StatusTextChange to set the status that is returned by the control to the status bar in the Windows Forms application:

# COM Interoperability

```
private void OnStatusChange(object sender,
            AxSHDocVw.DWebBrowserEvents2_StatusTextChangeEvent e)
{
    statusBar.Text = e.text;
}
```

Now you have a simple browser that you can use to navigate to Web pages (see Figure 33-12).

Figure 33-12

## Using COM Objects from within ASP.NET

COM objects can be used in a similar way to what you have seen before from within ASP.NET. However, there is one important distinction. The ASP.NET runtime by default runs in an MTA. If the COM object is configured with the threading model value `Apartment` (as all COM object that have been written with Visual Basic 6 are), an exception is thrown. Because of performance and scalability reasons, it is best to avoid STA objects within ASP.NET. If you really want to use an STA object with ASP.NET, you can set the `AspCompat` attribute with the `Page` directive as shown in the following snippet. Be aware that the Web site performance might suffer when you are using this option:

```
<%@ Page AspCompat="true" Language="C#" %>
```

## Using a .NET Component from a COM Client

So far you have seen how to access a COM component from a .NET client. Equally interesting is to find a solution for accessing .NET components in an old COM client that is using Visual Basic 6, MFC, or ATL.

# Chapter 33

## COM Callable Wrapper

If you want to access a COM component with a .NET client, you have to work with an RCW. To access a .NET component from a COM client application, you must use a COM Callable Wrapper (CCW). Figure 33-13 shows a CCW that wraps a .NET class, and offers COM interfaces that a COM client expects to use. The CCW offers interfaces such as `IUnknown`, `IDispatch`, `ISupportErrorInfo`, and others. It also offers interfaces such as `IConnectionPointContainer` and `IConnectionPoint` for events. A COM client gets what it expects from a COM object — although a .NET component is behind the scenes. The wrapper deals with methods such as `AddRef()`, `Release()`, and `QueryInterface()` from the `IUnknown` interface, whereas in the .NET object you can count on the garbage collector without the need to deal with reference counts.

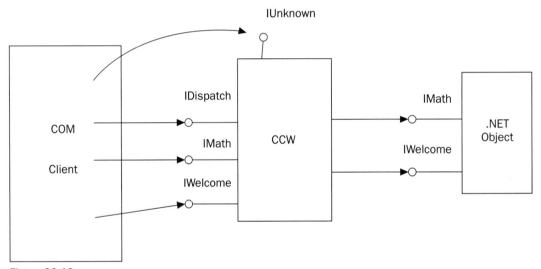

**Figure 33-13**

## Creating a .NET Component

In the following example, you build the same functionality into a .NET class that you have previously built into a COM component. Start by creating a C# class library, and name it `DotNetComponent`. Then add the interfaces `IWelcome` and `IMath`, and the class `NetComponent` that implements these interfaces:

```
using System;
using System.Runtime.InteropServices;

namespace Wrox.ProCSharp.COMInterop.Server
{
    public interface IWelcome
    {
        string Greeting(string name);
    }

    public interface IMath
```

# COM Interoperability

```
    {
        int Add(int val1, int val2);
        int Sub(int val1, int val2);
    }

    public class DotnetComponent : IWelcome, IMath
    {
        public DotnetComponent()
        {
        }

        public string Greeting(string name)
        {
            return "Hello " + name;
        }

        public int Add(int val1, int val2)
        {
            return val1 + val2;
        }

        public int Sub(int val1, int val2)
        {
            return val1 - val2;
        }
    }
}
```

After building the project, you can create a type library.

## Creating a Type Library

A type library can be created by using the command-line utility tlbexp. The command

```
tlbexp DotnetComponent.dll
```

creates the type library `DotnetComponent.tlb`. You can view the type library with the utility *OLE/COM Object Viewer*. To access this utility in Visual Studio, select Tools ➪ OLE/COM Object Viewer. Next, select File ➪ View TypeLib to open the type library. Now you can see the interface definition shown in the following code. The unique ids will differ.

The name of the type library is created from the name of the assembly. The header of the type library also defines the full name of the assembly in a custom attribute, and all the interfaces are forward-declared before they are defined:

```
// Generated .IDL file (by the OLE/COM Object Viewer)
//
// typelib filename: <could not determine filename>

[
  uuid(0AA0953A-B2A0-32CB-A5AC-5DA0DF698EB8),
  version(1.0),
```

1173

```
    custom(90883F05-3D28-11D2-8F17-00A0C9A6186D, DotNetComponent,
            Version=1.0.1321.19165, Culture=neutral, PublicKeyToken=null)
]
library DotnetComponent
{
    // TLib : Common Language Runtime Library :
    // {BED7F4EA-1A96-11D2-8F08-00A0C9A6186D}
    importlib("mscorlib.tlb");
    // TLib : OLE Automation : {00020430-0000-0000-C000-000000000046}
    importlib("stdole2.tlb");

    // Forward declare all types defined in this typelib
    interface IWelcome;
    interface IMath;
    interface _Settings;
    interface _DotnetComponent;
```

In the following generated code, you can see that the interfaces `IWelcome` and `IMath` are defined as COM dual interfaces. You can see all methods that have been declared in the C# code are listed here in the type library definition. The parameters changed: the .NET types are mapped to COM types (such as the `String` class to the `BSTR` type), and the signature is changed, so that a `HRESULT` is returned. Because the interfaces are dual, dispatch ids are also generated:

```
    [
        odl,
        uuid(F39A4143-F88D-321E-9A33-8208E256A2DF),
        version(1.0),
        dual,
        oleautomation,
        custom(0F21F359-AB84-41E8-9A78-36D110E6D2F9,
               Wrox.ProCSharp.COMInterop.Server.IWelcome)
    ]
    interface IWelcome : IDispatch {
        [id(0x60020000)]
        HRESULT Greeting([in] BSTR name, [out, retval] BSTR* pRetVal);
    };

    [
        odl,
        uuid(EF596F3F-B69B-3657-9D48-C906CBF12565),
        version(1.0),
        dual,
        oleautomation,
        custom(0F21F359-AB84-41E8-9A78-36D110E6D2F9,
               Wrox.ProCSharp.COMInterop.Server.IMath)
    ]
    interface IMath : IDispatch {
        [id(0x60020000)] HRESULT Add([in] long val1, [in] long val2,
                                     [out, retval] long* pRetVal);
        [id(0x60020001)] HRESULT Sub([in] long val1, [in] long val2,
                                     [out, retval] long* pRetVal);
    };
```

# COM Interoperability

The `coclass` section marks the COM object itself. The `uuid` in the header is the CLSID used to instantiate the object. The class `DotnetComponent` supports the interfaces `_DotnetComonent`, `_Object`, `IWelcome`, and `IMath`. `_Object` is defined in the file `mscorlib.tlb` included in an earlier code section and offers the methods of the base class `Object`. The default interface of the component is `_DotnetComponent`, which is defined after the `coclass` section as a dispatch interface. In the interface declaration it is marked as dual, but because no methods are included, it is a dispatch interface. With this interface it is possible to access all methods of the component using late binding:

```
[
  uuid(5BCD9C26-D68D-38C2-92E3-DA0C1741A8CD),
  version(1.0),
  custom(0F21F359-AB84-41E8-9A78-36D110E6D2F9,
         Wrox.ProCSharp.COMInterop.Server.DotnetComponent)
]
coclass DotnetComponent {
   [default] interface _DotnetComponent;
   interface _Object;
   interface IWelcome;
   interface IMath;
};

[
  odl,
  uuid(884C59C6-B3C2-3455-BB74-52753C409097),
  hidden,
  dual,
  oleautomation,
  custom(0F21F359-AB84-41E8-9A78-36D110E6D2F9,
         Wrox.ProCSharp.COMInterop.Server.DotnetComponent)
]
interface _DotnetComponent : IDispatch {
};
};
```

There are quite a few defaults for generating the type library. However, often it is advantageous to change some of the default .NET to COM mappings. This can be done with several attributes in the `System.Runtime.InteropServices` namespaces.

## COM Interop Attributes

Applying attributes from the namespace `System.Runtime.InteropServices` to classes, interfaces, or methods allows you to change the implementation of the CCW. The following table lists these attributes and a description.

| Attribute | Description |
|---|---|
| Guid | This attribute can be assigned to the assembly, interfaces, and classes. Using the Guid as an assembly attribute defines the type-library id, applying it to interfaces defines the interface id (IID), and setting the attribute to a class defines the class id (CLSID). |

*Table continued on following page*

| Attribute | Description |
|---|---|
|  | The unique ids needed to be defined with this attribute can be created with the utility guidgen.

The CLSID and type-library ids are changed automatically with every build. If you don't want to change it with every build, you can fix it by using this attribute. The IID is only changed if the signature of the interface changes, for example, a method is added or removed, or some parameters changed. Because with COM the IID should change with every new version of this interface, this is a very good default behavior, and usually there's no need to apply the IID with the `Guid` attribute. The only time you want to apply a fixed IID for an interface is when the .NET interface is an exact representation of an existing COM interface, and the COM client already expects this identifier. |
| `ProgId` | This attribute can be applied to a class to specify what name should be used when the object is configured into the registry. |
| `ComVisible` | This attribute enables you to hide classes, interfaces, and delegates from COM when set to `false`. This prevents a COM representation from being created. |
| `InterfaceType` | This attribute, if set to a `ComInterfaceType` enumeration value, enables you to modify the default dual interface type that is created for .NET interfaces. `ComInterfaceType` has the values `InterfaceIsDual`, `InterfaceIsIDispatch`, and `InterfaceIsIUnknown`. If you want to apply a custom interface type to a .NET interface, set the attribute like this: `[InterfaceType(ComInterfaceType.InterfaceIsIUnkwnown)]` |
| `ClassInterface` | This attribute enables you to modify the default dispatch interface that is created for a class. `ClassInterface` accepts an argument of a `ClassInterfaceType` enumeration. The possible values are `AutoDispatch`, `AutoDual`, and `None`. In the previous example you have seen that the default is `AutoDispatch`, since a dispatch interface is created. If the class should only be accessible by the defined interfaces, apply the attribute `[ClassInterface(ClassInterfaceType.None)]` to the class. |
| `DispId` | This attribute can be used with dual and dispatch interfaces to define the dispid of methods and properties. |
| `In` `Out` | COM allows specifying attributes to parameter types if the parameter should be sent to the component `[In]`, from the component to the client `[Out]`, or in both directions `[In, Out]`. |
| `Optional` | Parameters of COM methods may be optional. Parameters that should be optional can be marked with the `Optional` attribute. |

Now you can change the C# code to specify a dual interface type for the `IWelcome` interface and a custom interface type for the `IMath` interface. With the class `DotnetComponent` the attribute `ClassInterface` with the argument `ClassInterfaceType.None` defines that no separate COM interface will be generated. The attributes ProgId and Guid specifiy a prog id and a guid:

# COM Interoperability

```csharp
[InterfaceType(ComInterfaceType.InterfaceIsDual)]
public interface IWelcome
{
   [DispId(60040)] string Greeting(string name);
}

[InterfaceType(ComInterfaceType.InterfaceIsIUnknown)]
public interface IMath
{
  int Add(int val1, int val2);
  int Sub(int val1, int val2);
}

[ClassInterface(ClassInterfaceType.None)]
[ProgId("Wrox.DotnetComponent")]
[Guid("77839717-40DD-4876-8297-35B98A8402C7")]
public class DotnetComponent : IWelcome, IMath
{
   public DotnetComponent()
   {
   }
}
```

Rebuilding the class library and the type library changes the interface definition. You can verify this with OleView.exe. As you can see in the following IDL code, the interface `IWelcome` is still a dual interface, whereas the `IMath` interface now is a custom interface that derives from `IUnknown` instead of `IDispatch`. In the `coclass` section, the interface `_DotnetComponent` is removed, and now the `IWelcome` is the new default interface, because it was the first interface in the inheritance list of the class `DotnetComponent`:

```
// Generated .IDL file (by the OLE/COM Object Viewer)
//
// typelib filename: <could not determine filename>

[
 uuid(11E86506-EA54-3611-A55C-6830C48A554B),
 version(1.0),
 custom(90883F05-3D28-11D2-8F17-00A0C9A6186D, DotNetComponent,
        Version=1.0.1321.28677, Culture=neutral, PublicKeyToken=null)
]
library DotnetComponent
{
   // TLib : Common Language Runtime Library :
   // {BED7F4EA-1A96-11D2-8F08-00A0C9A6186D}
   importlib("mscorlib.tlb");
   // TLib : OLE Automation : {00020430-0000-0000-C000-000000000046}
   importlib("stdole2.tlb");

   // Forward declare all types defined in this typelib
   interface IWelcome;
   interface IMath;
   interface _Settings;

   [
     odl,
     uuid(F39A4143-F88D-321E-9A33-8208E256A2DF),
```

```
        version(1.0),
        dual,
        oleautomation,
        custom(0F21F359-AB84-41E8-9A78-36D110E6D2F9,
                Wrox.ProCSharp.COMInterop.Server.IWelcome)
    ]
    interface IWelcome : IDispatch {
        [id(0x0000ea88)]
        HRESULT Greeting([in] BSTR name, [out, retval] BSTR* pRetVal);
    };

    [
        odl,
        uuid(EF596F3F-B69B-3657-9D48-C906CBF12565),
        version(1.0),
        oleautomation,
        custom(0F21F359-AB84-41E8-9A78-36D110E6D2F9,
                Wrox.ProCSharp.COMInterop.Server.IMath)
    ]
    interface IMath : IUnknown {
        HRESULT _stdcall Add([in] long val1, [in] long val2,
                            [out, retval] long* pRetVal);
        HRESULT _stdcall Sub([in] long val1, [in] long val2,
                            [out, retval] long* pRetVal);
    };

    [
        uuid(77839717 40DD-4876-8297-35B98A8402C7),
        version(1.0),
        custom(0F21F359-AB84-41E8-9A78-36D110E6D2F9,
                Wrox.ProCSharp.COMInterop.Server.DotnetComponent)
    ]
    coclass DotnetComponent {
        interface _Object;
        [default] interface IWelcome;
        interface IMath;
    };
};
```

## COM Registration

Before the .NET component can be used as a COM object, it is necessary to configure it in the registry. Also, if you don't want to copy the assembly into the same directory as the client application, it is necessary to install the assembly in the global assembly cache. The global assembly cache itself is discussed in Chapter 15.

For installing the assembly into the global assembly cache, you must sign it with a strong name (using Visual Studio 2005 you can define a strong name within properties of the solution). Then you can register the assembly in the global assembly cache:

```
gacutil -i dotnetcomponent.dll
```

# COM Interoperability

Now you can use the regasm utility to configure the component inside the registry. The option /tlb extracts the type library, and also configures the type library in the registry:

```
regasm dotnetcomponent.dll /tlb
```

The information for the .NET component that is written to the registry is as follows. All COM configuration is in the hive HKEY_CLASSES_ROOT (HKCR). The key of the prog id (in the case of this example, it is Wrox.DotnetComponent) is written directly to this hive, along with the CLSID.

The key HKCR\CLSID\{CLSID}\InProcServer32 has the following entries:

- **mscoree.dll:** mscoree.dll represents the CCW. This is a real COM object that is responsible for hosting the .NET component. This COM object accesses the .NET component to offer COM behavior for the client. The file mscoree.dll is loaded and instantiated from the client via the normal COM instantiation mechanism.
- **ThreadingModel=Both:** This is an attribute of the mscoree.dll COM object. This component is programmed in a way to offer support both for STA and MTA.
- **Assembly=DotnetComponent, Version=1.0.1321.33886, Culture=neutral, PublicKeyToken= 5cd57c93b4d9c41a:** The value of the Assembly stores the assembly full name including the version number and the public key token, so that the assembly can be uniquely identified. The assembly registered here will be loaded by mscoree.dll.
- **Class=Wrox.ProCSharp.COMInterop.Server.DotnetComponent:** The name of the class will also be used by mscoree.dll. This is the class that will be instantiated.
- **RuntimeVersion=v2.0.50110:** The registry entry RuntimeVersion specifies the version of the .NET runtime that will be used to host the .NET assembly.

In addition to the configurations shown here, all the interfaces and the type library are configured with their identifiers, too.

## Creating a COM Client

Now it's time to create a COM client. Start by creating a simple C++ Win32 Console Application Project, and name it COMClient. You can leave the default options selected, and click Finish in the project wizard.

In the beginning of the file COMClient.cpp, add a preprocessor command to include the <iostream> header file and to import the type library that you created for the .NET component. The import statement creates a "smart pointer" class that makes it easier to deal with COM objects. During a build process, the import statement creates .tlh and .tli files that you can find in the debug directory of your project, which includes the smart pointer class. Then add using namespace directives to open the namespace std that will be used for writing output messages to the console, and the namespace DotnetComponent that is created inside the smart pointer class:

```
// COMClient.cpp : Defines the entry point for the console application.
//

#include "stdafx.h"
#include <iostream>
```

1179

```
#import "../DotNetComponent/bin/debug/DotnetComponent.tlb"

using namespace std;
using namespace DotnetComponent;
```

In the `_tmain()` method, the first thing to do before any other COM call is initialization of COM with the API call `CoInitialize()`. `CoIntialize()` creates and enters an STA for the thread. The variable `spWelcome` is of type `IWelcomePtr`, which is a smart pointer. The smart pointer method `CreateInstance()` accepts the prog id as an argument to create the COM object by using the COM API `CoCreateInstance()`. The operator `->` is overridden with the smart pointer, so that you can invoke the methods of the COM object such as `Greeting()`:

```
int _tmain(int argc, _TCHAR* argv[])
{
  HRESULT hr;
  hr = CoInitialize(NULL);

  try
  {
    IWelcomePtr spWelcome;
    hr = spWelcome.CreateInstance("Wrox.DotnetComponent");   // CoCreateInstance()

    cout << spWelcome->Greeting("Bill") << endl;
```

The second interface supported by your .NET component is `IMath`, and there is also a smart pointer that wraps the COM interface: `IMathPtr`. You can directly assign one smart pointer to another as in `spMath = spWelcome;`. In the implementation of the smart pointer (the – operator is overridden), the `QueryInterface()` method is called. With a reference to the `IMath` interface you can call the `Add()` method.

```
    IMathPtr spMath;
    spMath = spWelcome; // QueryInterface()

    long result = spMath->Add(4, 5);
    cout << "result:" << result << endl;
  }
```

In case an `HRESULT` error value is returned by the COM object (this is done by the CCW that returns `HRESULT` errors if the .NET component generates exceptions), the smart pointer wraps the `HRESULT` errors and generates `_com_error` exceptions instead. Errors are handled in the catch block. At the end of the program, the COM DLLs are closed and unloaded using `CoUninitialize()`:

```
  catch (_com_error& e)
  {
    cout << e.ErrorMessage() << endl;
  }

  CoUninitialize();
  return 0;
}
```

# COM Interoperability

Now you can run the application, and you will get outputs from the `Greeting()` and the `Add()` methods to the console. You can also try to debug into the smart pointer class, where you can see the COM API calls directly.

> In case you get an exception that the component cannot be found, check if the same version of the assembly that is configured in the registry is installed in the global assembly cache.

## Adding Connection Points

Adding support for COM events to the .NET components requires some changes to the implementation of your .NET class. Offering COM events is not a simple usage of the event and delegate keywords, it is necessary to add some more COM interop attributes.

First, you have to add an interface to the .NET project: `IMathEvents`. This interface is the source or outgoing interface for the component, and will be implemented by the sink object in the client. A source interface must be either a dispatch or a custom interface. A scripting client supports only dispatch interfaces. Dispatch interfaces are usually preferred as source interfaces:

```
[InterfaceType(ComInterfaceType.InterfaceIsIDispatch)]
public interface IMathEvents
{
    [DispId(46200)] void CalculationCompleted();
}
```

Next, you have to add a delegate. The delegate must have the same signature and return type as the method in the outgoing interface. If you have multiple methods in your source interface, for each one that differs with the arguments, you have to specify a separate delegate. Because the COM client does not have to access this delegate directly, the delegate can be marked with the attribute `[ComVisible(false)]`:

```
[ComVisible(false)]
public delegate void CalculationCompletedDelegate();
```

With the class `DotnetComponent`, a source interface must be specified. This can be done with the attribute `[ComSourceInterfaces]`. Add the attribute `[ComSourceInterfaces]` and specify the outgoing interface declared earlier. You can add more than one source interface with different constructors of the attribute class; however, the only client language that supports more than one source interface is C++. Visual Basic 6 clients only support one source interface.

```
[ClassInterface(ClassInterfaceType.None)]
[ProgId("Wrox.DotnetComponent")]
[Guid("77839717-40DD-4876-8297-35B98A8402C7")]
[ComSourceInterfaces(typeof(IMathEvents))]
public class DotnetComponent : IWelcome, IMath
{
    public DotnetComponent()
    {
    }
```

Inside the class `DotnetComponent`, you have to declare an event for every method of the source interface. The type of the method must be the name of the delegate, and the name of the event must be exactly the name of the method inside the source interface. You can add the event calls to the `Add()` and `Sub()` methods. This step is the normal .NET way to invoke events, as discussed in Chapter 6.

```csharp
        public event CalculationCompletedDelegate CalculationCompleted;

    public int Add(int val1, int val2)
    {
        int result = val1 + val2;
        if (CalculationCompleted != null)
            CalculationCompleted();
        return result;
    }

    public int Sub(int val1, int val2)
    {
        int result = val1 - val2;
        if (CalculationCompleted != null)
            CalculationCompleted();
        return result;
    }
}
```

> The name of the event must be the same as the name of the method inside the source interface. Otherwise, the events cannot be mapped for COM clients.

## Creating a Client with a Sink Object

After you've built and registered the .NET assembly, and installed it into the global assembly cache, you can build a client application by using the event sources. This time you will write a client with Visual Basic 6 that uses the events.

Start Visual Basic 6 and create a Standard EXE file. Select Project ⇨ References, browse for the type library of the .NET component, and add the type library. Next add a button to the form and add the following code. Using Visual Basic 6, the `WithEvents` keyword automatically creates a sink object by implementing the default source interface of the component. With this example, the source interface is `IMathEvents`. The handler method that is invoked when the event is fired from the component is `obj_CalcuationCompleted()`, which consists of the variable name of the object and the name of the method that is defined with the source interface. You can start the application, and you will see that the event gets fired:

```vb
Dim WithEvents obj As DotnetComponent.DotnetComponent
Dim math As DotnetComponent.IMath

Private Sub Command1_Click()
    Dim greeting As String
    Set obj = New DotnetComponent.DotnetComponent
```

```
    greeting = obj.greeting("Bill")
    MsgBox (greeting)

    Set math = obj
    Dim result As Integer
    result = math.Add(4, 5)
    MsgBox (result)
End Sub

Private Sub obj_CalculationCompleted()
    MsgBox "calculation ready"
End Sub
```

## Running Windows Forms Controls in Internet Explorer

Windows Forms controls can be hosted in Internet Explorer as ActiveX controls. Because there are many different ActiveX control containers, and all these containers do have different requirements on the ActiveX controls. Hosting Windows Forms controls in any container is not supported by Microsoft. Supported containers are Internet Explorer and MFC containers (MFC containers were supported first with Visual Studio .NET 2003). With MFC containers, however, you have to manually change the code to host ActiveX controls from an MFC application.

For hosting a Windows Forms control inside Internet Explorer, you have to copy the assembly file to your Web server, and add some information about the control inside the HTML page. For the support of Windows Forms controls, the syntax of the `<object>` tag has been extended. With the attribute `classid`, you can add the assembly file and the name of the class separated by a # sign: `classid="<assembly file>#class name"`.

With the assembly file `ControlDemo.dll` and the class `UserControl1` in the namespace `Wrox.ProCSharp.COMInterop`, the syntax looks like this:

```
<object id="myControl"
  classid="ControlDemo.dll#Wrox.ProCSharp.COMInterop.UserControl1"
  height="400" width="400">
</object>
```

As soon as a user opens the HTML page, the assembly is downloaded to the client system. The assembly is stored in the download assembly cache, and every time the user accesses the page, the version numbers are rechecked. In case the version number didn't change, the assembly will be used from the local cache.

> As a requirement to use Windows Forms control in a Web page, the client must have the .NET runtime installed, Internet Explorer 5.5 or higher must be used, and the security setting must allow downloading assemblies. The default security setting with .NET 1.1 doesn't allow downloading assemblies from the Internet.

# Chapter 33

# Summary

In this chapter, you have seen how the different generations of COM and .NET applications can interact. Instead of rewriting applications and components, a COM component can be used from a .NET application just like a .NET class. The tool that makes this possible is tlbimp, which creates a runtime callable wrapper (RCW) that hides the COM object behind a .NET façade.

Likewise, tlbexp creates a type library from a .NET component that is used by the COM callable wrapper (CCW). The CCW hides the .NET component behind a COM façade. Using .NET classes as COM components makes it necessary to use some attributes from the namespace System.Runtime.InteropServices to define specific COM characteristics that are needed by the COM client.

# Part VIII
# Windows Base Services

Chapter 34: Manipulating Files and the Registry

Chapter 35: Accessing the Internet

Chapter 36: Windows Services

# 34

# Manipulating Files and the Registry

This chapter examines how to perform tasks involving reading from and writing to files and the system registry in C#. In particular, it covers the following:

- ❑ Exploring the directory structure, finding out what files and folders are present, and checking their properties
- ❑ Moving, copying, and deleting files and folders
- ❑ Reading and writing text in files
- ❑ Reading and writing keys in the registry

Microsoft has provided very intuitive object models covering these areas, and in this chapter you learn how to use .NET base classes to perform the tasks mentioned in the preceding list. In the case of file system operations, the relevant classes are almost all found in the `System.IO` namespace, whereas registry operations are dealt with by a classes in the `Microsoft.Win32` namespace.

> *The .NET base classes also include a number of classes and interfaces in the* `System.Runtime.Serialization` *namespace concerned with serialization — that is, the process of converting data (for example, the contents of a document) into a stream of bytes for storage. This chapter doesn't focus on these classes; it focuses on the classes that give you direct access to files.*

Note that security is particularly important when modifying files or registry entries. The whole area of security is covered separately in Chapter 16, ".NET Security." In this chapter, however, we assume that you have sufficient access rights to run all the examples that modify files or registry entries, which should be the case if you are running from an account with administrator privileges.

Chapter 34

# Managing the File System

The classes that are used to browse around the file system and perform operations such as moving, copying, and deleting files are shown in Figure 34-1. The namespace of each class is shown in brackets beneath the class name.

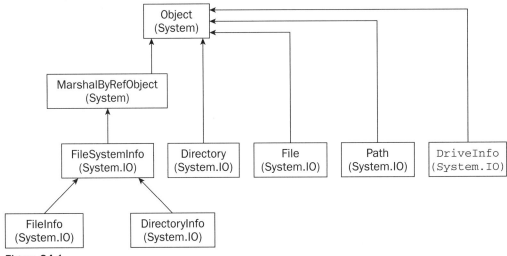

**Figure 34-1**

The following list explains the function of these classes:

- `System.MarshalByRefObject` — Base object class for .NET classes that are remotable; permits marshaling of data between application domains.
- `FileSystemInfo` — Base class that represents any file system object.
- `FileInfo` and `File` — These classes represent a file on the file system.
- `DirectoryInfo` and `Directory` — These classes represent a folder on the file system.
- `Path` — This class contains static members that you can use to manipulate pathnames.
- `DriveInfo` — This class provides properties and methods that provide information on a selected drive.

> *On Windows, the objects that contain files and are used to organize the file system are termed folders. For example, in the path C:\My Documents\ReadMe.txt, ReadMe.txt is a file and My Documents is a folder. Folder is a very Windows-specific term: On virtually every other operating system the term directory is used in place of folder, and in accordance with Microsoft's goal to design .NET as a platform-independent technology, the corresponding .NET base classes are called Directory and DirectoryInfo. However, due to the potential for confusion with LDAP directories (as discussed in Chapter 22, "Working with the Active Directory"), and because this is a Windows book, we'll stick to the term folder in this discussion.*

## .NET Classes That Represent Files and Folders

You will notice from the previous list that two classes are used to represent a folder and two classes for a file. Which one of these classes you use depends largely on how many times you need to access that folder or file:

- ❑ `Directory` and `File` contain only static methods and are never instantiated. You use these classes by supplying the path to the appropriate file system object whenever you call a member method. If you only want to do one operation on a folder or file, then using these classes is more efficient because it saves the overhead of instantiating a .NET class.

- ❑ `DirectoryInfo` and `FileInfo` implement roughly the same public methods as `Directory` and `File`, as well as some public properties and constructors, but they are stateful and the members of these classes are not static. You need to instantiate these classes before each instance is associated with a particular folder or file. This means that these classes are more efficient if you're performing multiple operations using the same object, because they read in the authentication and other information for the appropriate file system object on construction, and then do not need to read that information again no matter how many methods and so on you call against each object (class instance). In comparison, the corresponding stateless classes need to check the details of the file or folder again with every method you call.

In this section you will be mostly using the `FileInfo` and `DirectoryInfo` classes, but it so happens that many (though not all) of the methods called are also implemented by `File` and `Directory` (although in those cases these methods require an extra parameter — the pathname of the file system object, and a couple of the methods have slightly different names). For example

```
FileInfo myFile = new FileInfo(@"C:\Program Files\My Program\ReadMe.txt");
myFile.CopyTo(@"D:\Copies\ReadMe.txt");
```

has the same effect as

```
File.Copy(@"C:\Program Files\My Program\ReadMe.txt", @"D:\Copies\ReadMe.txt");
```

The first code snippet will take slightly longer to execute, because of the need to instantiate a `FileInfo` object, `myFile`, but it leaves `myFile` ready for you to perform further actions on the same file. By using the second example, there is no need to instantiate an object to copy the file.

You can instantiate a `FileInfo` or `DirectoryInfo` class by passing to the constructor a string containing the path to the corresponding file system. You've just seen the process for a file. For a folder the code looks similar:

```
DirectoryInfo myFolder = new DirectoryInfo(@"C:\Program Files");
```

If the path represents an object that does not exist, an exception will not be thrown at construction, but will instead be thrown the first time that you call a method that actually requires the corresponding file system object to be there. You can find out whether the object exists and is of the appropriate type by checking the `Exists` property, which is implemented by both of these classes:

```
FileInfo test = new FileInfo(@"C:\Windows");
Console.WriteLine(test.Exists.ToString());
```

Note that for this property to return `true`, the corresponding file system object must be of the appropriate type. In other words, if you instantiate a `FileInfo` object supplying the path of a folder, or you instantiate a `DirectoryInfo` object, giving it the path of a file, `Exists` will have the value `false`. On the other hand, most of the properties and methods of these objects will return a value if at all possible — they won't necessarily throw an exception just because the wrong type of object has been called, unless they are asked to do something that really is impossible. For example, the preceding code snippet might first display `false` (because `C:\Windows` is a folder). However, it still displays the time the folder was created because a folder still has that information. But if you tried to open the folder as if it were a file, using the `FileInfo.Open()` method, you'd get an exception.

After you have established whether the corresponding file system object exists, you can (if you are using the `FileInfo` or `DirectoryInfo` class) find out information about it using of the properties in the following table.

| Name | Description |
| --- | --- |
| `CreationTime` | Time file or folder was created |
| `DirectoryName` (`FileInfo` only) | Full pathname of the containing folder |
| `Parent` (`DirectoryInfo` only) | The parent directory of a specified subdirectory |
| `Exists` | Whether file or folder exists |
| `Extension` | Extension of the file; returns blank for folders |
| `FullName` | Full pathname of the file or folder |
| `LastAccessTime` | Time file or folder was last accessed |
| `LastWriteTime` | Time file or folder was last modified |
| `Name` | Name of the file or folder |
| `Root` (`DirectoryInfo` only) | The root portion of the path |
| `Length` (`FileInfo` only) | The size of the file in bytes |

You can also perform actions on the file system object using the methods in the following table.

| Name | Purpose |
| --- | --- |
| `Create()` | Creates a folder or empty file of the given name. For a `FileInfo` this also returns a stream object to let you write to the file. (Streams are covered later in the chapter.) |
| `Delete()` | Deletes the file or folder. For folders there is an option for the `Delete` to be recursive. |
| `MoveTo()` | Moves and/or renames the file or folder. |

# Manipulating Files and the Registry

| Name | Purpose |
|---|---|
| `CopyTo()` | (`FileInfo` only) Copies the file. Note that there is no copy method for folders. If you're copying complete directory trees you'll need to individually copy each file and create new folders corresponding to the old folders. |
| `GetDirectories()` | (`DirectoryInfo` only) Returns an array of `DirectoryInfo` objects representing all folders contained in this folder. |
| `GetFiles()` | (`DirectoryInfo` only) Returns an array of `FileInfo` objects representing all files contained in this folder. |
| `GetFileSystemInfos()` | (`DirectoryInfo` only) Returns `FileInfo` and `DirectoryInfo` objects representing all objects contained in this folder, as an array of `FileSystemInfo` references. |

Note that these tables list the main properties and methods and are not intended to be exhaustive.

*The preceding tables do not list most of the properties or methods that allow you to write to or read the data in files. This is actually done using stream objects, which are covered later in this chapter.* `FileInfo` *also implements a number of methods,* `Open()`, `OpenRead()`, `OpenText()`, `OpenWrite()`, `Create()`, *and* `CreateText()`, *that return stream objects for this purpose.*

Interestingly, the creation time, last access time, and last write time are all writable:

```
// displays the creation time of a file,
// then changes it and displays it again
FileInfo test = new FileInfo(@"C:\MyFile.txt");
Console.WriteLine(test.Exists.ToString());
Console.WriteLine(test.CreationTime.ToString());
test.CreationTime = new DateTime(2001, 1, 1, 7, 30, 0);
Console.WriteLine(test.CreationTime.ToString());
```

Running this application produces results similar to the following:

```
True
6/5/2005 2:59:32 PM
1/1/2001 7:30:00 AM
```

Being able to manually modify these properties might seem strange at first, but it can be quite useful. For example, if you have a program that effectively modifies a file by simply reading it in, deleting it and creating a new file with the new contents, you'd probably want to modify the creation date to match the original creation date of the old file.

## *The Path Class*

The `Path` class is not a class that you would instantiate. Rather, it exposes some static methods that make operations on pathnames easier. For example, suppose you want to display the full pathname for a file, `ReadMe.txt` in the folder `C:\My Documents`. You could find the path to the file using the following code:

1191

```
Console.WriteLine(Path.Combine(@"C:\My Documents", "ReadMe.txt"));
```

Using the `Path` class is a lot easier than trying to fiddle about with separation symbols manually, especially because the `Path` class is aware of different formats for pathnames on different operating systems. At the time of writing, Windows is the only operating system supported by .NET. However, if .NET were later ported to Unix, `Path` would be able to cope with Unix paths, in which /, rather than \, is used as a separator in pathnames. `Path.Combine()` is the method of this class that you are likely to use most often, but `Path` also implements other methods that supply information about the path or the required format for it.

The following section presents an example that illustrates how to browse directories and view the properties of files.

## Example: A File Browser

This section presents a sample C# application called `FileProperties` that presents a simple user interface that allows you to browse around the file system, and view the creation time, last access time, last write time, and size of files. (You can download the sample code for this application from the Wrox Web site at www.wrox.com.)

The `FileProperties` application works like this. You type in the name of a folder or file in the main text box at the top of the window and click the Display button. If you type in the path to a folder, its contents are listed in the list boxes. If you type in the path to a file, its details are displayed in the text boxes at the bottom of the form and the contents of its parent folder are displayed in the list boxes. Figure 34-2 shows the `FileProperties` sample application in action.

Figure 34-2

# Manipulating Files and the Registry

The user can very easily navigate around the file system by clicking any folder in the right-hand list box to move down to that folder or by clicking the Up button to move up to the parent folder. Figure 34-2 shows the contents of the My Documents folder. The user can also select a file by clicking its name in the list box. This displays the file's properties in the text boxes at the bottom of the application (see Figure 34-3).

Figure 34-3

Note that if you wanted, you could also display the creation time, last access time, and last modification time for folders using the `DirectoryInfo` property. You are going to display these properties only for a selected file to keep things simple.

You create the project as a standard C# Windows application in Visual Studio 2005, and add the various text boxes and the list box from the Windows Forms area of the toolbox. You've also renamed the controls with the more intuitive names of `textBoxInput`, `textBoxFolder`, `buttonDisplay`, `buttonUp`, `listBoxFiles`, `listBoxFolders`, `textBoxFileName`, `textBoxCreationTime`, `textBoxLastAccessTime`, `textBoxLastWriteTime`, and `textBoxFileSize`.

Next, you need to indicate that you will be using the `System.IO` namespace:

```
using System;
using System.Collections.Generic;
using System.ComponentModel;
using System.Data;
using System.Drawing;
```

# Chapter 34

```csharp
using System.Text;
using System.Windows.Forms;
using System.IO;
```

You need to do this for all the file system-related examples in this chapter, but this part of the code won't be explicitly shown in the remaining examples. You then add a member field to the main form:

```csharp
partial class Form1 : Form
{
    private string currentFolderPath;
```

`currentFolderPath` stores the path of the folder whose contents are displayed in the list boxes.

Next, you need to add event handlers for the user-generated events. The possible user inputs are:

- **User clicks the Display button.** In this case you need to figure out whether what the user has typed in the main text box is the path to a file or folder. If it's a folder you list the files and subfolders of this folder in the list boxes. If it is a file, you still do this for the folder containing that file, but you also display the file properties in the lower text boxes.

- **User clicks on a file name in the Files list box.** In this case you display the properties of this file in the lower text boxes.

- **User clicks on a folder name in the Folders list box.** In this case you clear all the controls and then display the contents of this subfolder in the list boxes.

- **User clicks on the Up button.** In this case you clear all the controls and then display the contents of the parent of the currently selected folder.

Before you see the code for the event handlers, here is the code for the methods that do all the work. First, you need to clear the contents of all the controls. This method is fairly self-explanatory:

```csharp
protected void ClearAllFields()
{
    listBoxFolders.Items.Clear();
    listBoxFiles.Items.Clear();
    textBoxFolder.Text = "";
    textBoxFileName.Text = "";
    textBoxCreationTime.Text = "";
    textBoxLastAccessTime.Text = "";
    textBoxLastWriteTime.Text = "";
    textBoxFileSize.Text = "";
}
```

Next, you define a method, `DisplayFileInfo()`, that handles the process of displaying the information for a given file in the text boxes. This method takes one parameter, the full pathname of the file as a `String`, and it works by creating a `FileInfo` object based on this path:

```csharp
protected void DisplayFileInfo(string fileFullName)
{
    FileInfo theFile = new FileInfo(fileFullName);
    if (!theFile.Exists)
        throw new FileNotFoundException("File not found: " + fileFullName);
```

```csharp
        textBoxFileName.Text = theFile.Name;
        textBoxCreationTime.Text = theFile.CreationTime.ToLongTimeString();
        textBoxLastAccessTime.Text = theFile.LastAccessTime.ToLongDateString();
        textBoxLastWriteTime.Text = theFile.LastWriteTime.ToLongDateString();
        textBoxFileSize.Text = theFile.Length.ToString() + " bytes";
    }
```

Note that you take the precaution of throwing an exception if there are any problems locating a file at the specified location. The exception itself will be handled in the calling routine (one of the event handlers). Finally, you define a method, `DisplayFolderList()`, which displays the contents of a given folder in the two list boxes. The full pathname of the folder is passed in as a parameter to this method:

```csharp
    protected void DisplayFolderList(string folderFullName)
    {
        DirectoryInfo theFolder = new DirectoryInfo(folderFullName);
        if (!theFolder.Exists)
            throw new DirectoryNotFoundException("Folder not found: " + folderFullName);
        ClearAllFields();
        textBoxFolder.Text = theFolder.FullName;
        currentFolderPath = theFolder.FullName;

        // list all subfolders in folder
        foreach(DirectoryInfo nextFolder in theFolder.GetDirectories())
            listBoxFolders.Items.Add(nextFolder.Name);

        // list all files in folder
        foreach(FileInfo nextFile in theFolder.GetFiles())
            listBoxFiles.Items.Add(nextFile.Name);
    }
```

Next, you examine the event handlers. The event handler that manages the event that is triggered when the user clicks the Display button is the most complex, because it needs to handle three different possibilities for the text the user enters in the text box. For instance, it could be the pathname of a folder, the pathname of a file, or neither of these:

```csharp
    protected void OnDisplayButtonClick(object sender, EventArgs e)
    {
        try
        {
            string folderPath = textBoxInput.Text;
            DirectoryInfo theFolder = new DirectoryInfo(folderPath);
            if (theFolder.Exists)
            {
                DisplayFolderList(theFolder.FullName);
                return;
            }
            FileInfo theFile = new FileInfo(folderPath);
            if (theFile.Exists)
            {
                DisplayFolderList(theFile.Directory.FullName);
                int index = listBoxFiles.Items.IndexOf(theFile.Name);
                listBoxFiles.SetSelected(index, true);
                return;
            }
```

```csharp
        throw new FileNotFoundException("There is no file or folder with "
                                    + "this name: " + textBoxInput.Text);
    }
    catch(Exception ex)
    {
        MessageBox.Show(ex.Message);
    }
}
```

In this code, you establish if the supplied text represents a folder or file by instantiating `DirectoryInfo` and `FileInfo` instances and examining the `Exists` property of each object. If neither exists, then you throw an exception. If it's a folder, you call `DisplayFolderList()` to populate the list boxes. If it's a file, you need to populate the list boxes and sort out the text boxes that display the file properties. You handle this case by first populating the list boxes. You then programmatically select the appropriate file name in the Files list box. This has exactly the same effect as if the user had selected that item — it raises the item-selected event. You can then simply exit the current event handler, knowing that the selected item event handler will immediately be called to display the file properties.

The following code is the event handler that is called when an item in the Files list box is selected, either by the user or, as indicated previously, programmatically. It simply constructs the full pathname of the selected file, and passes this to the `DisplayFileInfo()` method presented earlier:

```csharp
protected void OnListBoxFilesSelected(object sender, EventArgs e)
{
    try
    {
        string selectedString = listBoxFiles.SelectedItem.ToString();
        string fullFileName = Path.Combine(currentFolderPath, selectedString);
        DisplayFileInfo(fullFileName);
    }
    catch(Exception ex)
    {
        MessageBox.Show(ex.Message);
    }
}
```

The event handler for the selection of a folder in the Folders list box is implemented in a very similar way, except that in this case you call `DisplayFolderList()` to update the contents of the list boxes:

```csharp
protected void OnListBoxFoldersSelected(object sender, EventArgs e)
{
    try
    {
        string selectedString = listBoxFolders.SelectedItem.ToString();
        string fullPathName = Path.Combine(currentFolderPath, selectedString);
        DisplayFolderList(fullPathName);
    }
    catch(Exception ex)
    {
        MessageBox.Show(ex.Message);
    }
}
```

# Manipulating Files and the Registry

Finally, when the Up button is clicked, `DisplayFolderList()` must also be called, except that this time you need to obtain the path of the parent of the folder currently being displayed. This is done with the `FileInfo.DirectoryName` property, which returns the parent folder path:

```
protected void OnUpButtonClick(object sender, EventArgs e)
{
    try
    {
        string folderPath = new FileInfo(currentFolderPath).DirectoryName;
        DisplayFolderList(folderPath);
    }
    catch(Exception ex)
    {
        MessageBox.Show(ex.Message);
    }
}
```

# Moving, Copying, and Deleting Files

As already mentioned, moving and deleting files or folders is done by the `MoveTo()` and `Delete()` methods of the `FileInfo` and `DirectoryInfo` classes. The equivalent methods on the `File` and `Directory` classes are `Move()` and `Delete()`. The `FileInfo` and `File` classes also implement the methods `CopyTo()` and `Copy()`, respectively. However, no methods exist to copy complete folders — you need to do that by copying each file in the folder.

Use of all these methods is quite intuitive — you can find detailed descriptions in the SDK documentation. This section illustrates their use for the particular cases of calling the static `Move()`, `Copy()`, and `Delete()` methods on the `File` class. To do this you will build on the previous `FileProperties` example and call its iteration `FilePropertiesAndMovement`. This example will have the extra feature that whenever the properties of a file are displayed, the application gives you the option of deleting that file or moving or copying the file to another location.

## Example: FilePropertiesAndMovement

Figure 34-4 shows the user interface of the new sample application.

As you can see, `FilePropertiesAndMovement` is similar in appearance to `FileProperties`, except for the group of three buttons and a text box at the bottom of the window. These controls are only enabled when the example is actually displaying the properties of a file; at all other times, they are disabled. The existing controls are also squashed up a bit to stop the main form from getting too big. When the properties of a selected file are displayed, `FilePropertiesAndMovement` automatically places the full pathname of that file in the bottom text box for the user to edit. Users can then click any of the buttons to perform the appropriate operation. When they do, a message box is displayed that confirms the action taken by the user (see Figure 34-5).

1197

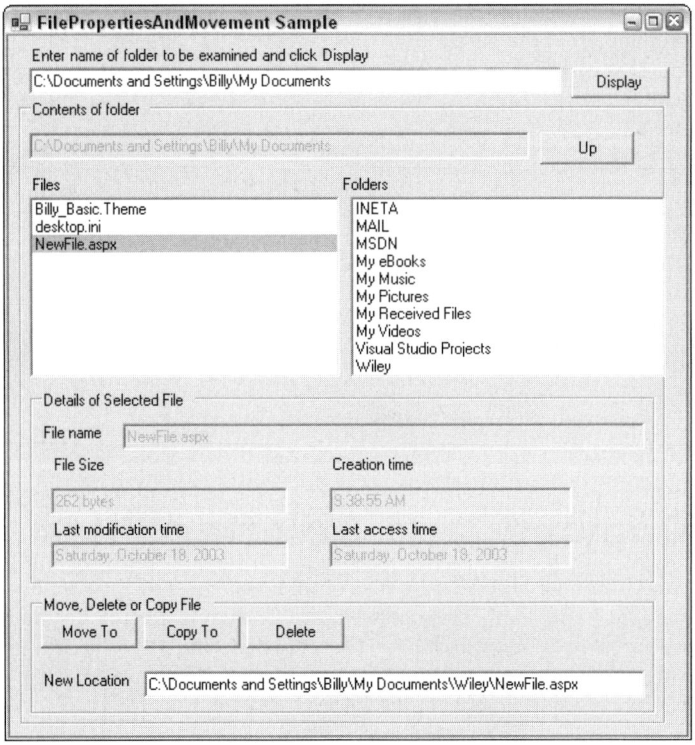

# Chapter 34

Figure 34-4

When the user clicks the Yes button, the action will be initiated. There are some actions in the form that the user can take that will then cause the display to be incorrect. For instance, if the user moves or deletes a file, you obviously cannot continue to display the contents of that file in the same location. Also, if you change the name of a file in the same folder, your display will also be out of date. In these cases, `FilePropertiesAndMovement` resets its controls to display only the folder where the file resides after the file operation.

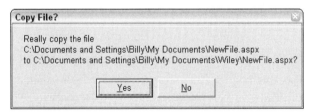

Figure 34-5

## Looking at the Code for FilePropertiesAndMovement

To code this process, you need to add the relevant controls, as well as their event handlers, to the code for the `FileProperties` example. The new controls are given the names `buttonDelete`, `buttonCopyTo`, `buttonMoveTo`, and `textBoxNewPath`.

## Manipulating Files and the Registry

First, look at the event handler that gets called when the user clicks the Delete button:

```
protected void OnDeleteButtonClick(object sender, EventArgs e)
{
   try
   {
      string filePath = Path.Combine(currentFolderPath,
                                    textBoxFileName.Text);
      string query = "Really delete the file\n" + filePath + "?";
      if (MessageBox.Show(query,
          "Delete File?", MessageBoxButtons.YesNo) == DialogResult.Yes)
      {
         File.Delete(filePath);
         DisplayFolderList(currentFolderPath);
      }
   }
   catch(Exception ex)
   {
      MessageBox.Show("Unable to delete file. The following exception"
                      + " occurred:\n" + ex.Message, "Failed");
   }
}
```

The code for this method is contained in a `try` block because of the obvious risk of an exception being thrown if, for example, you don't have permission to delete the file, or the file is moved by another process after it has been displayed but before the user presses the Delete button. You construct the path of the file to be deleted from the `CurrentParentPath` field, which contains the path of the parent folder, and the text in the `textBoxFileName` text box, which contains the name of the file.

The methods to move and copy the file are structured in a very similar manner:

```
protected void OnMoveButtonClick(object sender, EventArgs e)
{
   try
   {
      string filePath = Path.Combine(currentFolderPath,
                                    textBoxFileName.Text);
      string query = "Really move the file\n" + filePath + "\nto "
             + textBoxNewPath.Text + "?";
      if (MessageBox.Show(query,
          "Move File?", MessageBoxButtons.YesNo) == DialogResult.Yes)
      {
         File.Move(filePath, textBoxNewPath.Text);
         DisplayFolderList(currentFolderPath);
      }
   }
   catch(Exception ex)
   {
      MessageBox.Show("Unable to move file. The following exception"
                      + " occurred:\n" + ex.Message, "Failed");
   }
}

protected void OnCopyButtonClick(object sender, EventArgs e)
```

1199

## Chapter 34

```csharp
{
    try
    {
        string filePath = Path.Combine(currentFolderPath,
                                       textBoxFileName.Text);
        string query = "Really copy the file\n" + filePath + "\nto "
                       + textBoxNewPath.Text + "?";
        if (MessageBox.Show(query,
            "Copy File?", MessageBoxButtons.YesNo) == DialogResult.Yes)
        {
            File.Copy(filePath, textBoxNewPath.Text);
            DisplayFolderList(currentFolderPath);
        }
    }
    catch(Exception ex)
    {
        MessageBox.Show("Unable to copy file. The following exception"
                        + " occurred:\n" + ex.Message, "Failed");
    }
}
```

You're not quite done yet. You also need to make sure the new buttons and text box are enabled and disabled at the appropriate times. To enable them when you are displaying the contents of a file, you add the following code to `DisplayFileInfo()`:

```csharp
protected void DisplayFileInfo(string fileFullName)
{
    FileInfo theFile = new FileInfo(fileFullName);
    if (!theFile.Exists)
        throw new FileNotFoundException("File not found: " + fileFullName);

    textBoxFileName.Text = theFile.Name;
    textBoxCreationTime.Text = theFile.CreationTime.ToLongTimeString();
    textBoxLastAccessTime.Text = theFile.LastAccessTime.ToLongDateString();
    textBoxLastWriteTime.Text = theFile.LastWriteTime.ToLongDateString();
    textBoxFileSize.Text = theFile.Length.ToString() + " bytes";

    // enable move, copy, delete buttons
    textBoxNewPath.Text = theFile.FullName;
    textBoxNewPath.Enabled = true;
    buttonCopyTo.Enabled = true;
    buttonDelete.Enabled = true;
    buttonMoveTo.Enabled = true;
}
```

You also need to make one change to `DisplayFolderList`:

```csharp
protected void DisplayFolderList(string folderFullName)
{
    DirectoryInfo theFolder = new DirectoryInfo(folderFullName);
    if (!theFolder.Exists)
        throw new DirectoryNotFoundException("Folder not found: " + folderFullName);

    ClearAllFields();
```

# Manipulating Files and the Registry

```
      DisableMoveFeatures();
      textBoxFolder.Text = theFolder.FullName;
      currentFolderPath = theFolder.FullName;

      // list all subfolders in folder
      foreach(DirectoryInfo nextFolder in theFolder.GetDirectories())
         listBoxFolders.Items.Add(NextFolder.Name);

      // list all files in folder
      foreach(FileInfo nextFile in theFolder.GetFiles())
         listBoxFiles.Items.Add(NextFile.Name);
   }
```

`DisableMoveFeatures` is a small utility function that disables the new controls:

```
      void DisableMoveFeatures()
      {
         textBoxNewPath.Text = "";
         textBoxNewPath.Enabled = false;
         buttonCopyTo.Enabled = false;
         buttonDelete.Enabled = false;
         buttonMoveTo.Enabled = false;
      }
```

You also need to add extra code to `ClearAllFields()` to clear the extra text box:

```
      protected void ClearAllFields()
      {
         listBoxFolders.Items.Clear();
         listBoxFiles.Items.Clear();
         textBoxFolder.Text = "";
         textBoxFileName.Text = "";
         textBoxCreationTime.Text = "";
         textBoxLastAccessTime.Text = "";
         textBoxLastWriteTime.Text = "";
         textBoxFileSize.Text = "";
         textBoxNewPath.Text = "";
      }
```

With that, the code is complete.

# Reading and Writing to Files

Reading and writing to files is in principle very simple; however, it is not done through the `DirectoryInfo` or `FileInfo` objects. Instead, using the .NET Framework 2.0, you can now do it through the `File` object. Later in this chapter, you see how to accomplish this through the use of a number of other classes that represent a generic concept called a *stream*.

Before the .NET Framework 2.0, it took a bit of wrangling to read and write to files. It was possible using the available classes from the framework, but it wasn't really that straightforward. The .NET Framework 2.0 has expanded upon the `File` class to make it as simple as just one line of code to read or write to a file.

# Chapter 34

## Reading a File

For an example of reading a file, create a Windows Form application that contains a regular text box, a button, and a multi-line text box. In the end, your form should appear something like Figure 34-6.

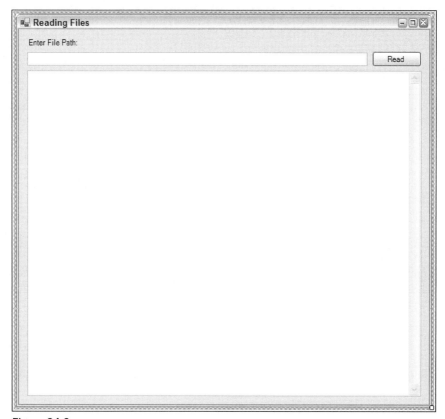

**Figure 34-6**

The idea of this form is that the end user will enter in the path of a specific file in the first text box and click the Read button. From here, the application will read the specified file and display the file's contents in the multi-lined text box. This is illustrated in the following code example:

```
using System;
using System.Collections.Generic;
using System.ComponentModel;
using System.Data;
using System.Drawing;
using System.Text;
using System.Windows.Forms;
using System.IO;

namespace ReadingFiles
{
```

# Manipulating Files and the Registry

```
partial class Form1 : Form
{
    public Form1()
    {
        InitializeComponent();
    }

    private void button1_Click(object sender, EventArgs e)
    {
        textBox2.Text = File.ReadAll(textBox1.Text);
    }
}
```

In building this example, the first step is to add the `using` statement to bring in the `System.IO` namespace. From there, simply use the `button1_Click` event for the Send button on the form to populate the text box with what comes back from the file. You can now get at the file's contents by using the `File.ReadAll` method. Now with the .NET Framework 2.0, you can read files with a single statement. The `ReadAll` method opens the specified file, reads the contents, and then closes the file. The return value of the `ReadAll` method is a string containing the entire contents of the file specified. The end result would be something similar to what is shown in Figure 34-7.

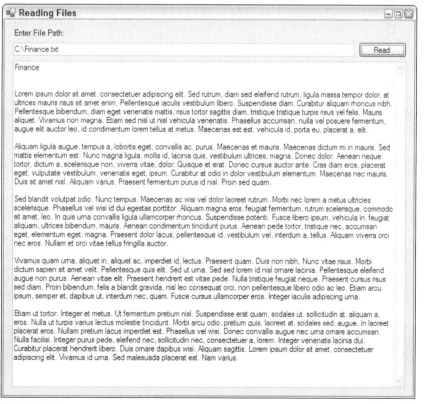

Figure 34-7

1203

# Chapter 34

The `File.ReadAll` signature shown in the preceding example is of the following construction:

```
File.ReadAll(FilePath);
```

The other option is to also specify the encoding of the file being read:

```
File.ReadAll(FilePath, Encoding);
```

Using this signature allows you to specify the encoding to use when opening and reading the contents of the file. So this means that you could do something like the following:

```
File.ReadAll(textBox1.Text, Encoding.ASCII);
```

Some of the other options for opening and working with files include using the `ReadAllBytes` and the `ReadAllLines` methods. The `ReadAllBytes` method allows you to open up a binary file and read the contents into a byte array. The `ReadAll` method shown earlier gives you the entire contents of the specified file in a single string instance. This might not be something that you are interested in. You might instead be interested in working with what comes back from the file in a line-by-line fashion. In this case, you will want to use the `ReadAllLines` method because it will allow for this kind of functionality.

## Writing to a File

Besides making reading from files an extremely simple process under the .NET Framework 2.0 umbrella, writing to files is just as easy. Just as the Base Class Library (BCL) gives you the `ReadAll`, `ReadAllLines`, and `ReadAllBytes` methods to read files in a couple of different ways, to write to files the BCL gives you the `WriteAll`, `WriteAllBytes`, and `WriteAllLines` methods.

For an example of how to write to a file, use the same Windows Form application, but instead, use the multi-line text box in the form to input data into a file. The code for the `button1_Click` event handler should appear as shown here:

```
private void button1_Click(object sender, EventArgs e)
{
    File.WriteAll(textBox1.Text, textBox2.Text);
}
```

Build and start the form, type `C:\Testing.txt` in the first text box, type some random content in the second text box, and then click the button. Nothing will happen visually, but if you look in your root C drive, you will see the `Testing.txt` file with the content you specified.

The `WriteAll` method went to the specified location, created a new text file, and provided the file the specified contents before saving and closing the file. Not bad for just one line of code!

If you run the application again, and specify the same file (`Testing.txt`) but with some new content, pressing the button again will cause the application to go out and perform the same task again. This time though, as it is important to note, the new content is not added to the previous content you specified, but instead, the new content completely overrides the previous content. In fact, the `WriteAll`, `WriteAllBytes`, and `WriteAllLines` all override any previous files, so you have to be careful when using these methods.

# Manipulating Files and the Registry

The `WriteAll` method in the previous example is using the following signature:

```
File.WriteAll(FilePath, Content)
```

You can also specify the encoding of the new file:

```
File.WriteAll(FilePath, Content, Encoding)
```

The `WriteAllBytes` method allows you to write content to a file using a byte array and the `WriteAllLines` method allows you to write a string array to a file. An example of this is illustrated in the following event handler:

```csharp
private void button1_Click(object sender, EventArgs e)
{
    string[] movies =
        {"Grease",
         "Close Encounters of the Third Kind",
         "The Day After Tomorrow"};

    File.WriteAllLines("C:\Testing.txt", movies);
}
```

Now clicking the button for such an application will give you a `Testing.txt` file with the following contents:

```
Grease
Close Encounters of the Third Kind
The Day After Tomorrow
```

The `WriteAllLines` method writes out the string array with each array item taking its own line in the file.

Because of the fact that data may not only be written to disk, but to other places as well (such as named pipes or to memory), it is also important to understand how to deal with File I/O in .NET using streams as a means of moving file contents around. This is shown in the following section.

## Streams

The idea of a stream has been around for a very long time. A stream is an object used to transfer data. The data can be transferred in one of two directions:

- ❏ If the data is being transferred from some outside source into your program, it is called *reading* from the stream.
- ❏ If the data is being transferred from your program to some outside source, it is called *writing* to the stream.

Very often, the outside source will be a file, but that is not necessarily the case. Other possibilities include

- ❏ Reading or writing data on the network using some network protocol, where the intention is for this data to be picked up by or sent from another computer

1205

## Chapter 34

- Reading or writing to a named pipe
- Reading or writing to an area of memory

Of these examples, Microsoft has supplied a .NET base class for writing to or reading from memory, `System.IO.MemoryStream`. `System.Net.Sockets.NetworkStream` handles network data. There are no base stream classes for writing to or reading from pipes, but there is a generic stream class, `System.IO.Stream`, from which you would inherit if you wanted to write such a class. `Stream` does not make any assumptions about the nature of the external data source.

The outside source might even be a variable within your own code. This might sound paradoxical, but the technique of using streams to transmit data between variables can be a useful trick for converting data between data types. The C language used something like this to convert between integer data types and strings or to format strings using a function, `sprintf`.

The advantage of having a separate object for the transfer of data, rather than using the `FileInfo` or `DirectoryInfo` classes to do this, is that by separating the concept of transferring data from the particular data source, it makes it easier to swap data sources. Stream objects themselves contain a lot of generic code that concerns the movement of data between outside sources and variables in your code, and by keeping this code separate from any concept of a particular data source, you make it easier for this code to be reused (through inheritance) in different circumstances. For example, the `StringReader` and `StringWriter` classes are part of the same inheritance tree as two classes that you will be using later on to read and write text files, `StreamReader` and `StreamWriter`. The classes will almost certainly share a substantial amount of code behind the scenes.

Figure 34-8 illustrates the actual hierarchy of stream-related classes in the `System.IO` namespace.

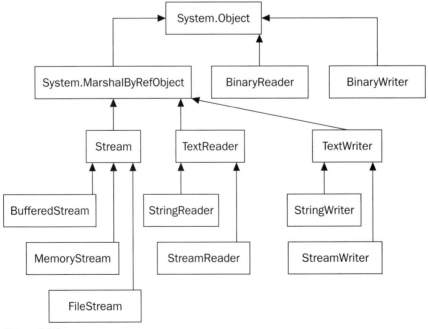

**Figure 34-8**

# Manipulating Files and the Registry

As far as reading and writing files is concerned, the classes that concern us most are:

- `FileStream` — This class is intended for reading and writing binary data in a binary file. However, you can also use it to read from or write to any file.
- `StreamReader` and `StreamWriter` — These classes are designed specifically for reading from and writing to text files.

You might also find the `BinaryReader` and `BinaryWriter` classes useful, although they are not used in the examples here. These classes do not actually implement streams themselves, but they are able to provide wrappers around other stream objects. `BinaryReader` and `BinaryWriter` provide extra formatting of binary data, which allows you to directly read or write the contents of C# variables to the relevant stream. Think of the `BinaryReader` and `BinaryWriter` as sitting between the stream and your code, providing extra formatting (see Figure 34-9).

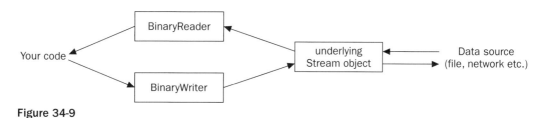

**Figure 34-9**

The difference between using these classes and directly using the underlying stream objects is that a basic stream works in bytes. For example, suppose as part of the process of saving some document you want to write the contents of a variable of type `long` to a binary file. Each `long` occupies 8 bytes, and if you used an ordinary binary stream you would have to explicitly write each of those 8 bytes of memory. In C# code that would mean you'd have to perform some bitwise operations to extract each of those 8 bytes from the `long` value. Using a `BinaryWriter` instance, you can encapsulate the entire operation in an overload of the `BinaryWriter.Write()` method that takes a `long` as a parameter, and which will place those 8 bytes into the stream (and hence if the stream is directed to a file, into the file). A corresponding `BinaryReader.Read()` method will extract 8 bytes from the stream and recover the value of the `long`.

For more information on the `BinaryReader` and `BinaryWriter` classes refer to the SDK documentation.

## *Buffered Streams*

For performance reasons, when you read or write to a file, the output is buffered. This means that if your program asks for the next 2 bytes of a file stream, and the stream passes the request on to Windows, then Windows will not go through the trouble of connecting to the file system and then locating and reading the file off the disk, just to get 2 bytes. Instead, Windows will retrieve a large block of the file in one go, and store this block in an area of memory known as a *buffer*. Subsequent requests for data from the stream will be satisfied from the buffer until the buffer runs out, at which point Windows grabs another block of data from the file. Writing to files works in the same way. For files this is done automatically by the operating system, but you might have to write a stream class to read from some other device that isn't buffered. If so, you can derive your class from `BufferedStream`, which implements a buffer itself. (Note, however, that `BufferedStream` is not designed for the situation in which an application frequently alternates between reading and writing data.)

# Chapter 34

# Reading and Writing to Binary Files Using FileStream

Reading and writing to binary files can be done using the `FileStream` class (note that if you are working with the .NET Framework 1.x, this will most likely be the case).

## The FileStream class

A `FileStream` instance is used to read or write data to or from a file. In order to construct a `FileStream`, you need four pieces of information:

- The **file** you want to access.
- The **mode**, which indicates how you want to open the file. For example, are you intending to create a new file or open an existing file? And if you are opening an existing file, should any write operations be interpreted as overwriting the contents of the file or appending to the file?
- The **access**, which indicates how you want access to file. For example, do you want to read or write to the file or do both?
- The **share** access, which specifies whether you want exclusive access to the file. Or, are you willing for other streams to be able to access this file simultaneously? If so, should other streams have access to read the file, to write to it, or to do both?

The first of these pieces of information is usually represented by a string that contains the full pathname of the file, and this chapter only considers those constructors that require a string here. Besides those constructors, however, there are some additional ones that take an old Windows-API-style Windows handle to a file instead. The remaining three pieces of information are represented by three .NET enumerations called `FileMode`, `FileAccess`, and `FileShare`. The values of these enumerations are listed in the following table; they should be self-explanatory.

| Enumeration | Values |
| --- | --- |
| FileMode | Append, Create, CreateNew, Open, OpenOrCreate, or Truncate |
| FileAccess | Read, ReadWrite, or Write |
| FileShare | Inheritable, None, Read, ReadWrite, or Write |

Note that in the case of `FileMode`, exceptions can be thrown if you request a mode that is inconsistent with the existing status of the file. `Append`, `Open`, and `Truncate` will throw an exception if the file does not already exist, and `CreateNew` will throw an exception if it does. `Create` and `OpenOrCreate` will cope with either scenario, but `Create` will delete any existing file to replace it with a new, initially empty, one. The `FileAccess` and `FileShare` enumerations are bitwise flags, so values can be combined with the C# bitwise OR operator, `|`.

There are a large number of constructors for the `FileStream`. The three simplest ones work as follows:

```
// creates file with read-write access and allows other streams read access
FileStream fs = new FileStream(@"C:\C# Projects\Project.doc",
                   FileMode.Create);
// as above, but we only get write access to the file
```

# Manipulating Files and the Registry

```
FileStream fs2 = new FileStream(@"C:\C# Projects\Project2.doc",
                FileMode.Create, FileAccess.Write);
// as above but other streams don't get access to the file while
// fs3 is open
FileStream fs3 = new FileStream(@"C:\C# Projects\Project3.doc",
                FileMode.Create, FileAccess.Write, FileShare.None);
```

As this code reveals, the overloads of these constructors have the effect of providing default values of `FileAccess.ReadWrite` and `FileShare.Read` to the third and fourth parameters. It is also possible to create a file stream from a `FileInfo` instance in various ways:

```
FileInfo myFile4 = new FileInfo(@"C:\C# Projects\Project4.doc");
FileStream fs4 = myFile4.OpenRead();
FileInfo myFile5= new FileInfo(@"C:\C# Projects\Project5doc");
FileStream fs5 = myFile5.OpenWrite();
FileInfo myFile6= new FileInfo(@"C:\C# Projects\Project6doc");
FileStream fs6 = myFile6.Open(FileMode.Append, FileAccess.Write,
                FileShare.None);
FileInfo myFile7 = new FileInfo(@"C:\C# Projects\Project7.doc");
FileStream fs7 = myFile7.Create();
```

`FileInfo.OpenRead()` supplies a stream that gives you read-only access to an existing file, whereas `FileInfo.OpenWrite()` gives you read-write access. `FileInfo.Open()` allows you to specify the mode, access, and file share parameters explicitly.

Of course, after you've finished with a stream, you should close it:

```
fs.Close();
```

Closing the stream frees up the resources associated with it, and allows other applications to set up streams to the same file. In between opening and closing the stream, you'll want to read data from it and/or write data to it. `FileStream` implements a number of methods to do this.

`ReadByte()` is the simplest way of reading data. It grabs one byte from the stream, and casts the result to an `int` having a value between 0 and 255. If you have reached the end of the stream, it returns -1:

```
int NextByte = fs.ReadByte();
```

If you prefer to read a number of bytes at a time, you can call the `Read()` method, which reads a specified number of bytes into an array. `Read()` returns the number of bytes actually read — if this value is zero, you know you're at the end of the stream. Here's an example where you read into a byte array called `ByteArray`:

```
int nBytesRead = fs.Read(ByteArray, 0, nBytes);
```

The second parameter to `Read()` is an offset, which you can use to request that the `Read` operation starts populating the array at some element other than the first, and the third parameter is the number of bytes to read into the array.

If you want to write data to a file, two parallel methods are available, `WriteByte()` and `Write()`. `WriteByte()` writes a single byte to the stream:

# Chapter 34

```
        byte NextByte = 100;
        fs.WriteByte(NextByte);
```

`Write()`, on the other hand, writes out an array of bytes. For instance, if you initialized the `ByteArray` mentioned before with some values, you could use the following code to write out the first `nBytes` of the array:

```
        fs.Write(ByteArray, 0, nBytes);
```

As with `Read()`, the second parameter allows you to start writing from some point other than the beginning of the array. Both `WriteByte()` and `Write()` return `void`.

In addition to these methods, `FileStream` implements various other methods and properties to do with bookkeeping tasks such as determining how many bytes are in the stream, locking the stream, or flushing the buffer. These other methods aren't usually required for basic reading and writing, and if you need them, full details are in the SDK documentation.

## Example: BinaryFileReader

The use of the `FileStream` class is illustrated by writing an example, `BinaryFileReader`, which reads in and displays any file. Create the project in Visual Studio 2005 as a Windows application. It has one menu item, which brings up a standard `OpenFileDialog` asking what file to read in, then displays the file as binary code. As you are reading in binary files, you need to be able to display non-printable characters. You will do this is by displaying each byte of the file individually, showing 16 bytes on each line of a multi-line text box. If the byte represents a printable ASCII character, you'll display that character; otherwise, you'll display the value of the byte in a hexadecimal format. In either case, you pad out the displayed text with spaces so that each byte displayed occupies four columns so the bytes line up nicely under each other.

Figure 34-10 shows what the `BinaryFileReader` application looks like when viewing a text file (because `BinaryFileReader` can view any file, it's quite possible to use it on text files as well as binary ones). In this case, the application has read in a basic ASP.NET page (`.aspx`).

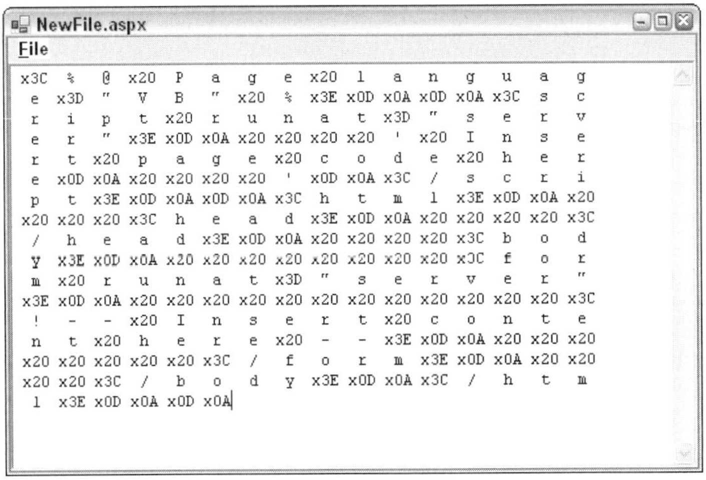

**Figure 34-10**

# Manipulating Files and the Registry

Clearly, this format is more suited to looking at the values of individual bytes rather than displaying text! Later in this chapter, you develop an example that is specifically designed to read text files; then you will be able to see what this file really says. On the other hand, the advantage of this example is that you can look at the contents of any file.

This example won't demonstrate writing to files because you don't want to get bogged down in the complexities of trying to translate the contents of a text box like the one shown in Figure 34-10 into a binary stream! You see how to write to files later on when you develop an example that can read or write, but only to text files.

Here's at the code used to get these results. First, you need to make sure that you have brought in the `System.IO` namespace through the use of the using statement:

```
using System.IO;
```

Next, you add a couple of fields to the main form class — one representing the file dialog and a string that gives the path of the file currently being viewed:

```
partial class Form1 : Form
{
    private OpenFileDialog chooseOpenFileDialog = new OpenFileDialog();
    private string chosenFile;
```

You also need to add some standard Windows Forms code to deal with the handlers for the menu and the file dialog:

```
    public Form1()
    {
        InitializeComponent();
        menuFileOpen.Click += new EventHandler(OnFileOpen);
        chooseOpenFileDialog.FileOk += new
            CancelEventHandler(OnOpenFileDialogOK);
    }

    void OnFileOpen(object Sender, EventArgs e)
    {
        chooseOpenFileDialog.ShowDialog();
    }

    void OnOpenFileDialogOK(object Sender, CancelEventArgs e)
    {
        chosenFile = chooseOpenFileDialog.FileName;
        this.Text = Path.GetFileName(chosenFile);
        DisplayFile();
    }
```

As this code demonstrates, when the user clicks OK to select a file in the file dialog, you call the `DisplayFile()` method, which does the work of reading in the selected file:

```
    void DisplayFile()
    {
        int nCols = 16;
```

```csharp
        FileStream inStream = new FileStream(chosenFile, FileMode.Open,
                                                         FileAccess.Read);
    long nBytesToRead = inStream.Length;
    if (nBytesToRead > 65536/4)
        nBytesToRead = 65536/4;

    int nLines = (int)(nBytesToRead/nCols) + 1;
    string [] lines = new string[nLines];
    int nBytesRead = 0;

    for (int i=0 ; i<nLines ; i++)
    {
        StringBuilder nextLine = new StringBuilder();
        nextLine.Capacity = 4*nCols;

        for (int j = 0 ; j<nCols ; j++)
        {
            int nextByte = inStream.ReadByte();
            nBytesRead++;
            if (nextByte < 0 || nBytesRead > 65536)
                break;
            char nextChar = (char)nextByte;
            if (nextChar < 16)
                nextLine.Append(" x0" + string.Format("{0,1:X}",
                                                     (int)nextChar));
            else if
                (char.IsLetterOrDigit(nextChar) ||
                                char.IsPunctuation(nextChar))
                nextLine.Append("  " + nextChar + " ");
            else
                nextLine.Append(" x" + string.Format("{0,2:X}",
                                                    (int)nextChar));
        }
        lines[i] = nextLine.ToString();
    }
    inStream.Close();
    this.textBoxContents.Lines = lines;
}
```

There's quite a lot going on in this method, so here's a breakdown. You instantiate a `FileStream` object for the selected file, which specifies that you want to open an existing file for reading. You then work out how many bytes there are to read in and how many lines should be displayed. The number of bytes will normally be the number of bytes in the file. However, text boxes can display only a maximum of 65,536 characters and with the chosen display format, you are displaying four characters for every byte in the file, so you will need to cap the number of bytes shown in the text box if the selected file is longer than 65,536/4 = 16,384 bytes.

> If you want to display longer files in this sort of environment, you might want to look up the `RichTextBox` class in the `System.Windows.Forms` namespace. `RichTextBox` is similar to a text box, but has many more advanced formatting facilities and does not have a limit on how much text it can display. `TextBox` is used here to keep the example simple and focused on the process of reading in files.

The bulk of the method is given over to two nested `for` loops that construct each line of text to be displayed. You use a `StringBuilder` class to construct each line for performance reasons: You are appending suitable text for each byte to the string that represents each line 16 times. If on each occasion you allocate a new string and take a copy of the half-constructed line, you are not only going to be spending a lot of time allocating strings, but will be wasting a lot of memory on the heap. Notice that the definition of *printable* characters is anything that is a letter, digit, or punctuation, as indicated by the relevant static `System.Char` methods. You've excluded any character with a value less than 16 from the printable list, however, which means you'll trap the carriage return (13) and line feed (10) as binary characters (a multi-line text box isn't able to display these characters properly if they occur individually within a line).

Furthermore, using the Properties Window, you changed the Font property for the text box to a fixed width font. In this case, you chose `Courier New 9pt regular`, and also set the text box to have vertical and horizontal scroll bars.

Upon completion, you close the stream and set the contents of the text box to the array of strings that you've built up.

## Reading and Writing to Text Files

Theoretically, it's perfectly possible to use the `FileStream` class to read in and display text files. You have, after all, just done that. The format in which the `NewFile.aspx` file is displayed in the preceding example isn't particularly user-friendly, but that has nothing to do with any intrinsic problem with the `FileStream` class, only with how you chose to display the results in the text box.

Having said that, if you know that a particular file contains text, you will usually find it more convenient to read and write it using the `StreamReader` and `StreamWriter` classes instead of the `FileStream` class. That's because these classes work at a slightly higher level and are specifically geared to reading and writing text. The methods that they implement are able to automatically detect where convenient points to stop reading text are, based on the contents of the stream. In particular:

- ❑ These classes implement methods to read or write one line of text at a time, `StreamReader.ReadLine()` and `StreamWriter.WriteLine()`. In the case of reading, this means that the stream will automatically figure out for you where the next carriage return is and stop reading at that point. In the case of writing, it means that the stream will automatically append the carriage return-line feed combination to the text that it writes out.

- ❑ By using the `StreamReader` and `StreamWriter` classes you don't need to worry about the encoding (the text format) used in the file. Possible encodings include ASCII (1 byte for each character), or any or the Unicode-based formats, UNICODE, UTF7, UTF8, and UTF32. Text files on Windows 9x systems are always in ASCII, because Windows 9x doesn't support Unicode, but Windows NT, 2000, XP, and 2003 all do support Unicode, and so text files might theoretically contain Unicode, UTF7, UTF8, or UTF32 data instead of ASCII data. The convention is that if the file is in ASCII format, it will simply contain the text. If it is in any Unicode format, this will be indicated by the first two or three bytes of the file, which are set to particular combinations of values to indicate the format used in the file.

These bytes are known as the *byte code markers*. When you open a file using any of the standard Windows applications, such as Notepad or WordPad, you don't need to worry about this because these applications are aware of the different encoding methods and will automatically read the file correctly. This is also the case for the `StreamReader` class, which will correctly read in a file in any of these formats, while the `StreamWriter` class is capable of formatting the text it writes out using whatever encoding technique you request. On the other hand, if you wanted to read in and display a text file using the `FileStream` class, you would have to handle all this yourself.

## The StreamReader class

`StreamReader` is used to read text files. Constructing a `StreamReader` is in some ways easier than constructing a `FileStream` instance, because some of the `FileStream` options are not required when using `StreamReader`. In particular, the mode and access types are not relevant to `StreamReader`, because the only thing you can do with a `StreamReader` is read! Furthermore, there is no direct option to specify the sharing permissions. However, there are a couple of new options:

- You need to specify what to do about the different encoding methods. You can instruct the `StreamReader` to examine the byte code markers in the beginning of the file to determine the encoding method, or you can simply tell the `StreamReader` to assume that the file uses a specified encoding method.

- Instead of supplying a file name to be read from, you can supply a reference to another stream.

This last option deserves a bit more discussion, because it illustrates another advantage of basing the model for reading and writing data on the concept of streams. Because the `StreamReader` works at a relatively high level, you might find it useful if you are in the situation in which you have another stream that is there to read data from some other source, but you would like to use the facilities provided by `StreamReader` to process that other stream as if it contained text. You can do so by simply passing the output from this stream to a `StreamReader`. In this way, `StreamReader` can be used to read and process data from any data source—not only files. This is essentially the situation discussed earlier with regard to the `BinaryReader` class. However, in this book you will only use `StreamReader` to connect directly to files.

The result of these possibilities is that `StreamReader` has a large number of constructors. Not only that, but there are a couple of `FileInfo` methods that return `StreamReader` references too: `OpenText()` and `CreateText()`. The following just illustrates some of the constructors.

The simplest constructor takes just a file name. This `StreamReader` will examine the byte order marks to determine the encoding:

```
StreamReader sr = new StreamReader(@"C:\My Documents\ReadMe.txt");
```

Alternatively, if you prefer to specify that UTF8 encoding should be assumed:

```
StreamReader sr = new StreamReader(@"C:\My Documents\ReadMe.txt",
                        Encoding.UTF8);
```

You specify the encoding by using one of several properties on a class, `System.Text.Encoding`. This class is an abstract base class, from which a number of classes are derived and which implements methods that actually perform the text encoding. Each property returns an instance of the appropriate class, and the possible properties you can use here are as follows:

- ASCII
- Unicode
- UTF7

# Manipulating Files and the Registry

- UTF8
- UTF32
- BigEndianUnicode

The following example demonstrates hooking up a `StreamReader` to a `FileStream`. The advantage of this is that you can specify whether to create the file and the share permissions, which you cannot do if you directly attach a `StreamReader` to the file:

```
FileStream fs = new FileStream(@"C:\My Documents\ReadMe.txt",
                  FileMode.Open, FileAccess.Read, FileShare.None);
StreamReader sr = new StreamReader(fs);
```

For this example, you specify that the `StreamReader` will look for byte code markers to determine the encoding method used, as it will do in the following examples, in which the `StreamReader` is obtained from a `FileInfo` instance:

```
FileInfo myFile = new FileInfo(@"C:\My Documents\ReadMe.txt");
StreamReader sr = myFile.OpenText();
```

Just as with a `FileStream`, you should always close a `StreamReader` after use. Failure to do so will result in the file remaining locked to other processes (unless you used a `FileStream` to construct the `StreamReader` and specified `FileShare.ShareReadWrite`):

```
sr.Close();
```

Now that you've gone to the trouble of instantiating a `StreamReader`, you can do something with it. As with the `FileStream`, you'll simply see the various ways to read data, and the other, less commonly used `StreamReader` methods are left to the SDK documentation.

Possibly the easiest method to use is `ReadLine()`, which keeps reading until it gets to the end of a line. It does not include the carriage return–line feed combination that marks the end of the line in the returned string:

```
string nextLine = sr.ReadLine();
```

Alternatively, you can grab the entire remainder of the file (or strictly, the remainder of the stream) in one string:

```
string restOfStream = sr.ReadToEnd();
```

You can read a single character:

```
int nextChar = sr.Read();
```

This overload of `Read()` casts the returned character to an `int`. This is so that it has the option of returning a value of `-1` if the end of the stream has been reached.

Finally, you can read a given number of characters into an array, with an offset:

```
        // to read 100 characters in.

        int nChars = 100;
        char [] charArray = new char[nChars];
        int nCharsRead = sr.Read(charArray, 0, nChars);
```

`nCharsRead` will be less than `nChars` if you have requested to read more characters than are left in the file.

## The StreamWriter class

This works in basically the same way as the `StreamReader`, except that you can only use `StreamWriter` to write to a file (or to another stream). Possibilities for constructing a `StreamWriter` include:

```
        StreamWriter sw = new StreamWriter(@"C:\My Documents\ReadMe.txt");
```

This will use UTF8 Encoding, which is regarded by .NET as the default encoding method. If you want, you can specify an alternative encoding:

```
        StreamWriter sw = new StreamWriter(@"C:\My Documents\ReadMe.txt", true,
            Encoding.ASCII);
```

In this constructor, the second parameter is a `Boolean` that indicates whether the file should be opened for appending. There is, oddly, no constructor that takes only a file name and an encoding class.

Of course, you may want to hook up `StreamWriter` to a file stream to give you more control over the options for opening the file:

```
        FileStream fs = new FileStream(@"C:\My Documents\ReadMe.txt",
            FileMode.CreateNew, FileAccess.Write, FileShare.Read);
        StreamWriter sw = new StreamWriter(fs);
```

`FileStream` does not implement any methods that return a `StreamWriter` class.

Alternatively, if you want to create a new file and start writing data to it, you'll find this sequence useful:

```
        FileInfo myFile = new FileInfo(@"C:\My Documents\NewFile.txt");
        StreamWriter sw = myFile.CreateText();
```

Just as with all other stream classes it is important to close a `StreamWriter` class when you have finished with it:

```
        sw.Close();
```

Writing to the stream is done using any of four overloads of `StreamWriter.Write()`. The simplest writes out a string and appends it with a carriage return–line feed combination:

```
        string nextLine = "Groovy Line";
        sw.Write(nextLine);
```

It is also possible to write out a single character:

# Manipulating Files and the Registry

```
char nextChar = 'a';
sw.Write(nextChar);
```

An array of characters is also possible:

```
char [] charArray = new char[100];

// initialize these characters

sw.Write(charArray);
```

It is even possible to write out a portion of an array of characters:

```
int nCharsToWrite = 50;
int startAtLocation = 25;
char [] charArray = new char[100];

// initialize these characters

sw.Write(charArray, startAtLocation, nCharsToWrite);
```

## Example: ReadWriteText

The `ReadWriteText` example displays the use of the `StreamReader` and `StreamWriter` classes. It is similar to the earlier `ReadBinaryFile` example, but it assumes the file to be read in is a text file and displays it as such. It is also capable of saving the file (with any modifications you've made to the text in the text box). It will save any file in Unicode format.

The screenshot in Figure 34-11 shows `ReadWriteText` displaying the same `NewFile.aspx` file that you used earlier. This time, however, you are able to read the contents a bit more easily!

Figure 34-11

We won't go over the details of adding the event handlers for the Open File dialog box, because they are basically the same as with the earlier `BinaryFileReader` example. As with that example, opening a new file causes the `DisplayFile()` method to be called. The only real difference between this example

**1217**

and the previous one is the implementation of `DisplayFile` as well as that you now have the option to save a file. This is represented by another menu option, Save. The handler for this option calls another method you've added to the code, `SaveFile()`. (Note that the new file always overwrites the original file; this example does not have an option to write to a different file.)

You'll look at `SaveFile()` first, because that is the simplest function. You simply write each line of the text box, in turn, to a `StreamWriter` stream, relying on the `StreamReader.WriteLine()` method to append the trailing carriage return and line feed at the end of each line:

```
void SaveFile()
{
    StreamWriter sw = new StreamWriter(chosenFile, false, Encoding.Unicode);

    foreach (string line in textBoxContents.Lines)
        sw.WriteLine(line);
    sw.Close();
}
```

`chosenFile` is a string field of the main form, which contains the name of the file you have read in (just as for the previous example). Notice that you specify Unicode encoding when you open the stream. If you'd wanted to write files in some other format, you'd simply need to change the value of this parameter. The second parameter to this constructor would be set to `true` if you wanted to append to a file, but you don't in this case. The encoding must be set at construction time for a `StreamWriter`. It is subsequently available as a read-only property, `Encoding`.

Now you examine how files are read in. The process of reading in is complicated by the fact that you don't know until you've read in the file how many lines it is going to contain (in other words, how many `(char)13(char)10` sequences are in the file) because `char(13)char(10)` is the carriage return–line feed combination that occurs at the end of a line). You solve this problem by initially reading the file into an instance of the `StringCollection` class, which is in the `System.Collections.Specialized` namespace. This class is designed to hold a set of strings that can be dynamically expanded. It implements two methods that you will be interested in: `Add()`, which adds a string to the collection, and `CopyTo()`, which copies the string collection into a normal array (a `System.Array` instance). Each element of the `StringCollection` object will hold one line of the file.

The `DisplayFile()` method calls another method, `ReadFileIntoStringCollection()`, which actually reads in the file. After doing this, you now know how many lines there are, so you are in a position to copy the `StringCollection` into a normal, fixed-size array and feed this array into the text box. Because only the references to the strings that are copied when you actually make the copy, not the strings themselves, the process is reasonably efficient:

```
void DisplayFile()
{
    StringCollection linesCollection = ReadFileIntoStringCollection();
    string [] linesArray = new string[linesCollection.Count];
    linesCollection.CopyTo(linesArray, 0);
    this.textBoxContents.Lines = linesArray;
}
```

The second parameter of `StringCollection.CopyTo()` indicates the index within the destination array of where you want the collection to start.

## Manipulating Files and the Registry

Now you examine the `ReadFileIntoStringCollection()` method. You use a `StreamReader` to read in each line. The main complication here is the need to count the characters read in to make sure you don't exceed the capacity of the text box:

```
StringCollection ReadFileIntoStringCollection()
{
    const int MaxBytes = 65536;
    StreamReader sr = new StreamReader(chosenFile);
    StringCollection result = new StringCollection();
    int nBytesRead = 0;
    string nextLine;
    while ( (nextLine = sr.ReadLine()) != null)
    {
        nBytesRead += nextLine.Length;
        if (nBytesRead > MaxBytes)
            break;
        result.Add(nextLine);
    }
    sr.Close();
    return result;
}
```

That completes the code for this example.

If you run `ReadWriteText`, read in the `NewFile.aspx` file, and then save it, the file will be in Unicode format. You wouldn't be able to tell this from any of the usual Windows applications: Notepad, WordPad, and even the `ReadWriteText` example, will still read the file in and display it correctly under Windows NT/2000/XP/2003, although because Windows 9x doesn't support Unicode, applications like Notepad won't be able to understand the Unicode file on those platforms. (If you download the example from the Wrox Press Web site at www.wrox.com, you can try this!) However, if you try to display the file again using the earlier `BinaryFileReader` example, you can see the difference immediately, as shown in Figure 34-12. The two initial bytes that indicate the file is in Unicode format are visible, and thereafter you see that every character is represented by two bytes. This last fact is very obvious, because the high-order byte of every character in this particular file is zero, so every second byte in this file now displays x00.

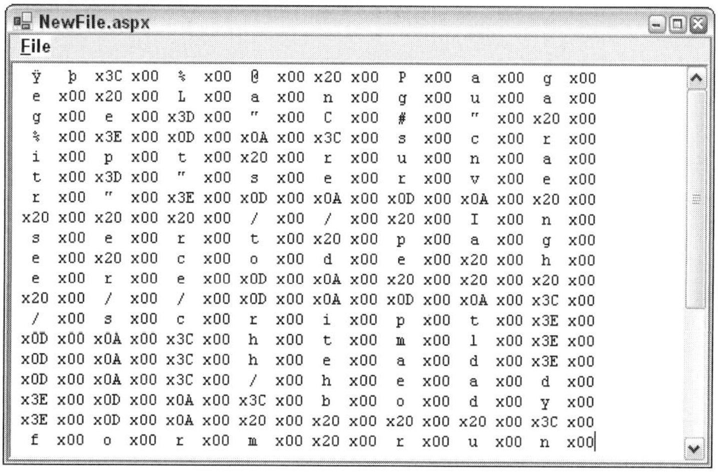

Figure 34-12

1219

# Chapter 34

# Reading Drive Information

In addition to working with files and directories, the .NET Framework 2.0 introduces the ability to read information from a specified drive. This is done using the `DriveInfo` class. The `DriveInfo` class can do a scan of a system to provide a list of available drives and then can dig in deeper, providing you with tons of details about any of the drives.

For an example of using the `DriveInfo` class, create a simple Windows Form that will list out all the available drives on a computer and then will provide details on a user-selected drive. Your Windows Form will consist of a simple `ListBox` and should look as illustrated in Figure 34-13.

**Figure 34-13**

Once you have the form all set, the code will consist of two events — one for when the form loads and another for when the end user makes drive selection in the list box. The code for this form is shown here:

```
using System;
using System.Collections.Generic;
using System.ComponentModel;
using System.Data;
using System.Drawing;
using System.Text;
using System.Windows.Forms;
using System.IO;

namespace DriveInfo
{
    partial class Form1 : Form
    {
        public Form1()
        {
            InitializeComponent();
        }

        private void Form1_Load(object sender, EventArgs e)
        {
```

# Manipulating Files and the Registry

```
        DriveInfo[] di = DriveInfo.GetDrives();

        foreach (DriveInfo itemDrive in di)
        {
            listBox1.Items.Add(itemDrive.Name);
        }
    }

    private void listBox1_SelectedIndexChanged(object sender, EventArgs e)
    {
        DriveInfo di = new DriveInfo(listBox1.SelectedItem.ToString());

        MessageBox.Show("Available Free Space: " + di.AvailableFreeSpace + "\n"
+
            "Drive Format: " + di.DriveFormat + "\n" +
            "Drive Type: " + di.DriveType + "\n" +
            "Is Ready: " + di.IsReady.ToString() + "\n" +
            "Name: " + di.Name + "\n" +
            "Root Directory: " + di.RootDirectory + "\n" +
            "ToString() Value: " + di.ToString() + "\n" +
            "Total Free Space: " + di.TotalFreeSpace + "\n" +
            "Total Size: " + di.TotalSize + "\n" +
            "Volume Label: " + di.VolumeLabel.ToString(), di.Name +
            " DRIVE INFO");
    }
}
```

The first step is to bring in the System.IO namespace with the using keyword. Within the Form1_Load event you use the DriveInfo class to get a list of all the available drives on the system. This is done using an array of DriveInfo objects and populating this array with the DriveInfo.GetDrives() method. Then using a foreach loop, you are able to iterate through each drive found and populate the list box with the results. This produces something similar to what is shown in Figure 34-14.

Figure 34-14

This form allows the end user to select one of the drives in the list. Once selected, a message box appears that contains details about the drive selected. As you can see from Figure 34-12, I have three drives on my current computer. Selecting each drive produces the following message boxes as collectively shown in Figure 34-15.

# Chapter 34

Figure 34-15

From here, you can see that these message boxes detail out three entirely different drives. The first, drive C:\, is my hard drive as the message box shows its drive type as `Fixed`. The second drive, drive D:\, is my CD/DVD drive. Here, you can even see the title of the DVD that I am viewing. The third drive, drive E:\, is my USB pen and is labeled with a drive type of `Removable`.

## File Security

When the .NET Framework 1.0/1.1 was first introduced, it didn't come with an easy way in which you could easily access and work access control lists (ACLs) for files, directories, and registry keys. To do such at that time, it usually meant some work with COM-interop, thereby also requiring a more advanced programming knowledge of working with ACLs.

This has now considerably changed with the release of the .NET Framework 2.0, because this version makes the process of working with ACLs considerably easier with a new namespace — `System.Security.AccessControl`. With this new namespace, it is now possible to manipulate security settings for files, registry keys, network shares, Active Directory objects, and more.

### Reading ACLs from a File

For an example of working with `System.Security.AccessControl`, this section takes a look at working with the ACLs for both files and directories. It starts by looking at how you would go about reviewing the ACLs for a particular file. This example is accomplished in a console application and illustrated here:

```
using System;
using System.Collections.Generic;
using System.Text;
using System.IO;
using System.Security.AccessControl;

namespace ConsoleApplication1
{
    class Program
    {
        static string myFilePath;

        static void Main(string[] args)
        {
```

# Manipulating Files and the Registry

```csharp
            Console.Write("Provide full file path: ");
            myFilePath = Console.ReadLine();

            try
            {
                using (FileStream myFile = new FileStream(myFilePath,
                    FileMode.Open, FileAccess.Read))
                {
                    FileSecurity fileSec = myFile.GetAccessControl();

                    foreach (FileSystemAccessRule fileRule in
                        fileSec.GetAccessRules(true, true,
                        typeof(System.Security.Principal.NTAccount)))
                    {
                        Console.WriteLine("{0} {1} {2} access for {3}", myFilePath,
                            fileRule.AccessControlType == AccessControlType.Allow ?
                            "provides" : "denies",
                            fileRule.FileSystemRights,
                            fileRule.IdentityReference.ToString());
                    }
                }
            }
            catch
            {
                Console.WriteLine("Incorrect file path given!");
            }

            Console.ReadLine();
        }
    }
}
```

For this example to work, the first step is to make a reference to the `System.Security.AccessControl` namespace. This will give you access to the `FileSecurity` and the `FileSystemAccessRule` classes later in the program.

After the specified file is retrieved and placed in a `FileStream` object, the ACLs of the file are grabbed using the `GetAccessControl` method now found on the `File` object. This information from the `GetAccessControl` method is then placed in a `FileSecurity` class. This class has access rights to the referenced item. Each individual access right is then in turn represented by a `FileSystemAccessRule` object. That is why a `foreach` loop is used to iterate through all the access rights found in the created `FileSecurity` object.

Running this example with a simple text file in the root directory produces something similar to the following results:

```
Provide full file path: C:\Sample.txt
C:\Sample.txt provides FullControl access for BUILTIN\Administrators
C:\Sample.txt provides FullControl access for NT AUTHORITY\SYSTEM
C:\Sample.txt provides FullControl access for PUSHKIN\Bill
C:\Sample.txt provides ReadAndExecute, Synchronize access for BUILTIN\Users
```

The next section looks at reading ACLs from a directory instead of a file.

# Chapter 34

# Reading ACLs from a Directory

Reading ACL information about a directory instead of an actual file is not much different than the preceding example. The code for this is illustrated in the following sample:

```
using System;
using System.Collections.Generic;
using System.Text;
using System.Threading;
using System.IO;
using System.Security.AccessControl;

namespace ConsoleApplication1
{
    class Program
    {
        static string mentionedDir;

        static void Main(string[] args)
        {
            Console.Write("Provide full directory path: ");
            mentionedDir = Console.ReadLine();

            try
            {
                DirectoryInfo myDir = new DirectoryInfo(mentionedDir);

                if (myDir.Exists)
                {
                    DirectorySecurity myDirSec = myDir.GetAccessControl();

                    foreach (FileSystemAccessRule fileRule in
                        myDirSec.GetAccessRules(true, true,
                        typeof(System.Security.Principal.NTAccount)))
                    {
                        Console.WriteLine("{0} {1} {2} access for {3}",
                            mentionedDir, fileRule.AccessControlType ==
                            AccessControlType.Allow ? "provides" : "denies",
                            fileRule.FileSystemRights,
                            fileRule.IdentityReference.ToString());
                    }
                }
            }
            catch
            {
                Console.WriteLine("Incorrect directory provided!");
            }

            Console.ReadLine();
        }
    }
}
```

## Manipulating Files and the Registry

The big difference with this example is that it uses the `DirectoryInfo` class, which now also includes the `GetAccessControl` method to pull information about the directory's ACLs. Running this example produces the following results.

```
Provide full directory path: C:\Test
C:\Test provides FullControl access for BUILTIN\Administrators
C:\Test provides FullControl access for NT AUTHORITY\SYSTEM
C:\Test provides FullControl access for PUSHKIN\Bill
C:\Test provides 268435456 access for CREATOR OWNER
C:\Test provides ReadAndExecute, Synchronize access for BUILTIN\Users
C:\Test provides AppendData access for BUILTIN\Users
C:\Test provides CreateFiles access for BUILTIN\Users
```

The final thing you will look at in working with ACLs is using the new `System.Security.AccessControl` namespace to add and remove items from a file's ACL.

## Adding and Removing ACLs from a File

It is also possible to manipulate the ACLs of a resource using the same objects that were used in the previous examples. The following code example changes a previous code example where a file's ACL information was read. In this example, the ACLs are read for a specified file, changed, and then read again:

```
try
{
   using (FileStream myFile = new FileStream(myFilePath,
      FileMode.Open, FileAccess.ReadWrite))
   {
      FileSecurity fileSec = myFile.GetAccessControl();

      Console.WriteLine("ACL list before modification:");

      foreach (FileSystemAccessRule fileRule in
         fileSec.GetAccessRules(true, true,
          typeof(System.Security.Principal.NTAccount)))
      {
         Console.WriteLine("{0} {1} {2} access for {3}", myFilePath,
            fileRule.AccessControlType == AccessControlType.Allow ?
            "provides" : "denies",
            fileRule.FileSystemRights,
            fileRule.IdentityReference.ToString());
      }

      Console.WriteLine();
      Console.WriteLine("ACL list after modification:");

      FileSystemAccessRule newRule = new FileSystemAccessRule(
         new System.Security.Principal.NTAccount(@"PUSHKIN\Tuija"),
         FileSystemRights.FullControl,
         AccessControlType.Allow);

      fileSec.AddAccessRule(newRule);
      File.SetAccessControl(myFilePath, fileSec);

      foreach (FileSystemAccessRule fileRule in
```

```
            fileSec.GetAccessRules(true, true,
            typeof(System.Security.Principal.NTAccount)))
    {
        Console.WriteLine("{0} {1} {2} access for {3}", myFilePath,
            fileRule.AccessControlType == AccessControlType.Allow ?
            "provides" : "denies",
            fileRule.FileSystemRights,
            fileRule.IdentityReference.ToString());
    }
  }
}
```

In this case, a new access rule is added to the file's ACL. This is done by using the `FileSystemAccessRule` object. In creating a new instance of this object, a new `NTAccount` is created and given `Full Control` to the file. Then the `AddAccessRule` method of the `FileSecurity` class is used to assign the new rule. From there, the `FileSecurity` object reference is used to set the access control to the file in question using the `SetAccessControl` method of the `File` class.

Next, the file's ACL is listed again. The following is an example of what the preceding code could produce:

```
Provide full file path: C:\Sample.txt
ACL list before modification:
C:\Sample.txt provides FullControl access for BUILTIN\Administrators
C:\Sample.txt provides FullControl access for NT AUTHORITY\SYSTEM
C:\Sample.txt provides FullControl access for PUSHKIN\Bill
C:\Sample.txt provides ReadAndExecute, Synchronize access for BUILTIN\Users

ACL list after modification:
C:\Sample.txt provides FullControl access for PUSHKIN\Tuija
C:\Sample.txt provides FullControl access for BUILTIN\Administrators
C:\Sample.txt provides FullControl access for NT AUTHORITY\SYSTEM
C:\Sample.txt provides FullControl access for PUSHKIN\Bill
C:\Sample.txt provides ReadAndExecute, Synchronize access for BUILTIN\Users
```

To remove a rule from the ACL list, there is really not much that needs to be done to the code. From the previous code example, you simply will need to change the following line:

```
fileSec.AddAccessRule(newRule);
```

to the following:

```
fileSec.RemoveAccessRule(newRule);
```

This will then remove the rule that was just added.

# Reading and Writing to the Registry

In all versions of Windows since Windows 95, the registry has been the central repository for all configuration information relating to Windows setup, user preferences, and installed software and devices. Almost all commercial software these days uses the registry to store information about itself, and COM

# Manipulating Files and the Registry

components must place information about themselves in the registry in order to be called by clients. The .NET Framework and its accompanying concept of zero-impact installation has slightly reduced the significance of the registry for applications in the sense that assemblies are entirely self-contained, so no information about particular assemblies needs to be placed in the registry, even for shared assemblies. In addition, the .NET Framework has brought the concept of isolated storage, by which applications can store information that is particular to each user in files, with the .NET Framework taking care of making sure that data is stored separately for each user registered on a machine. (Isolated storage is beyond the scope of this book, but if you are interested, you can find the relevant .NET base classes in the `System.IO.IsolatedStorage` namespace.)

The fact that applications can now be installed using the Windows Installer also frees developers from some of the direct manipulation of the registry that used to be involved in installing applications. However, despite this, the possibility exists that if you distribute any complete application, your application will use the registry to store information about its configuration. For instance, if you want your application to show up in the Add/Remove Programs dialog box in the Control Panel, this will involve appropriate registry entries. You may also need to use the registry for backward compatibility with legacy code.

As you'd expect from a library as comprehensive as the .NET library, it includes classes that give you access to the registry. Two classes are concerned with the registry, and both are in the `Microsoft.Win32` namespace. The classes are `Registry` and `RegistryKey`. Before you examine these classes, the following section briefly reviews the structure of the registry itself.

## The Registry

The registry has a hierarchical structure much like that of the file system. The usual way to view or modify the contents of the registry is with one of two utilities: regedit or regedt32. Of these, regedit comes with all versions of Windows since Windows 95 as standard. regedt32 comes with Windows NT and Windows 2000; it is less user-friendly than regedit, but allows access to security information that regedit is unable to view. Windows Server 2003 has merged regedit and regedt32 into a single new editor simply called regedit. For the discussion here, you'll use regedit from Windows XP Professional, which you can launch by typing in **regedit** at the Run dialog or command prompt.

Figure 34-16 shows what you get when you launch regedit for the first time.

Figure 34-16

1227

## Chapter 34

`regedit` has a similar tree view/list view style user interface to Windows Explorer, which matches the hierarchical structure of the registry itself. However, there are some key differences that you'll see shortly.

In a file system, the topmost-level nodes can be thought of as being the partitions on your disks, C:\, D:\, and so on. In the registry, the equivalent to a partition is the *registry hive*. It is not possible to change the existing hives — they are fixed, and there are seven of them, although only five are actually visible through regedit:

- ❑ HKEY_CLASSES_ROOT (HKCR) contains details of types of files on the system (`.txt`, `.doc`, and so on) and which applications are able to open files of each type. It also contains registration information for all COM components (this latter area is usually the largest single area of the registry, because Windows these days comes with a huge number of COM components).

- ❑ HKEY_CURRENT_USER (HKCU) contains details of user preferences for the user currently logged on to the machine locally. These settings include desktop settings, environment variables, network and printer connections, and other settings that define the user operating environment of the user.

- ❑ HKEY_LOCAL_MACHINE (HKLM) is a huge hive that contains details of all software and hardware installed on the machine. These settings are not user-specific, but are for all users that log onto the machine. This hive also includes the HKCR hive: HKCR is actually not really an independent hive in its own right but is simply a convenient mapping onto the registry key HKLM/SOFTWARE/Classes.

- ❑ HKEY_USERS (HKUSR) contains details of user preferences for all users. As you might guess, it also contains the HKCU hive, which is simply a mapping onto one of the keys in HKEY_USERS.

- ❑ HKEY_CURRENT_CONFIG (HKCF) contains details of hardware on the machine.

The remaining two keys contain information of a temporary nature, and which changes frequently:

- ❑ HKEY_DYN_DATA is a general container for any volatile data that needs to be stored somewhere in the registry.

- ❑ HKEY_PERFORMANCE_DATA contains information concerning the performance of running applications.

Within the hives is a tree structure of registry *keys*. Each key is in many ways analogous to a folder or file on the file system. However, there is one very important difference. The file system distinguishes between files (which are there to contain data), and folders (which are primarily there to contain other files or folders), but in the registry there are only keys. A key may contain both data and other keys.

If a key contains data, this will be presented as a series of values. Each value will have an associated name, data type, and data. In addition, a key can have a default value, which is unnamed.

You can see this structure by using regedit to examine registry keys. Figure 34-17 shows the contents of the key HKCU\Control Panel\Appearance, which contains the details of the chosen color scheme of the currently logged in user. regedit shows which key is being examined by displaying it with an open folder icon in the tree view.

## Manipulating Files and the Registry

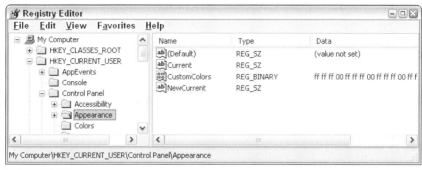

Figure 34-17

The HKCU\Control Panel\Appearance key has three named values set, although the default value does not contain any data. The column in the screenshot marked Type details the data type of each value. Registry entries can be formatted as one of three data types:

- REG_SZ (which roughly corresponds to a .NET string instance; the matching is not exact because the registry data types are not .NET data types)
- REG_DWORD (corresponds roughly to `uint`)
- REG_BINARY (array of bytes)

An application that stores data in the registry will do so by creating a number of registry keys, usually under the key HKLM\Software\<CompanyName>. Note that it is not necessary for these keys to contain any data. Sometimes the very fact of whether a key exists provides the data that an application needs.

## The .NET Registry Classes

Access to the registry is available through two classes in the `Microsoft.Win32` namespace: `Registry` and `RegistryKey`. A `RegistryKey` instance represents a registry key. This class implements methods to browse child keys, to create new keys, or to read or modify the values in the key. In other words, to do everything you would normally want to do with a registry key including setting the security levels for the key. `RegistryKey` will be the class you use for a lot your work with the registry. `Registry`, by contrast, is a class that allows for singular access to registry keys for simple operations. Another role of the `Registry` class is simply to provide you with `RegistryKey` instances that represent the top-level keys, the different hives, in order to enable you to navigate the registry. `Registry` provides these instances through static properties, and there are seven of them called, respectively, `ClassesRoot`, `CurrentConfig`, `CurrentUser`, `DynData`, `LocalMachine`, `PerformanceData`, and `Users`. It should be obvious which property corresponds to which hive.

So, for example, to obtain a `RegistryKey` instance that represents the HKLM key, you would write:

```
RegistryKey hklm = Registry.LocalMachine;
```

The process of obtaining a reference to a `RegistryKey` object is known as opening the key.

## Chapter 34

Although you might expect that the methods exposed by `RegistryKey` would be similar to those implemented by `DirectoryInfo`, given that the registry has a similar hierarchical structure to the file system, this actually isn't the case. Often, the way that you access the registry is different from the way that you would use files and folders, and `RegistryKey` implements methods that reflect this.

The most obvious difference is in how you open a registry key at a given location in the registry. The `Registry` class does not have any public constructor that you can use, nor does it have any methods that let you go directly to a key, given its name. Instead, you are expected to browse down to that key from the top of the relevant hive. If you want to instantiate a `RegistryKey` object, the only way is to start off with the appropriate static property of `Registry`, and work down from there. So, for example, if you want to read some data in the `HKLM/Software/Microsoft` key, you'd get a reference to it like this:

```
RegistryKey hklm = Registry.LocalMachine;
RegistryKey hkSoftware = hklm.OpenSubKey("Software");
RegistryKey hkMicrosoft = hkSoftware.OpenSubKey("Microsoft");
```

A registry key accessed in this way will give you read-only access. If you want to be able to write to the key (that includes writing to its values or creating or deleting direct children of it), you need to use another override to `OpenSubKey`, which takes a second parameter, of type `bool`, that indicates whether you want read-write access to the key. For example, if you want to be able to modify the `Microsoft` key (and assuming you are a systems administrator with permission to do this), you would write this:

```
RegistryKey hklm = Registry.LocalMachine;
RegistryKey hkSoftware = hklm.OpenSubKey("Software");
RegistryKey hkMicrosoft = hkSoftware.OpenSubKey("Microsoft", true);
```

Incidentally, because this key contains information used by Microsoft's applications, in most cases you probably shouldn't be modifying this particular key.

The `OpenSubKey()` method is the one you will call if you are expecting the key to be present. If the key isn't there, it will return a `null` reference. If you want to create a key, you should use the `CreateSubKey()` method (which automatically gives you read-write access to the key through the reference returned):

```
RegistryKey hklm = Registry.LocalMachine;
RegistryKey hkSoftware = hklm.OpenSubKey("Software");
RegistryKey hkMine = hkSoftware.CreateSubKey("MyOwnSoftware");
```

The way that `CreateSubKey()` works is quite interesting. It will create the key if it doesn't already exist, but if it does already exist, then it will quietly return a `RegistryKey` instance that represents the existing key. The reason for the method behaving in this manner has to do with how you will normally use the registry. The registry, on the whole, contains long-term data such as configuration information for Windows and for various applications. It's not very common, therefore, that you find yourself in a situation where you need to explicitly create a key.

What is much more common is that your application needs to make sure that some data is present in the registry — in other words create the relevant keys if they don't already exist, but do nothing if they do. `CreateSubKey()` fills that need perfectly. Unlike the situation with `FileInfo.Open()`, for example, there is no chance with `CreateSubKey()` of accidentally removing any data. If deleting registry keys is your intention, you'll need to call the `RegistryKey.DeleteSubKey()` method. This makes sense given the importance of the registry to Windows. The last thing you want is to completely break Windows accidentally by deleting a couple of important keys while you're debugging your C# registry calls!

# Manipulating Files and the Registry

Once you've located the registry key you want to read or modify, you can use the `SetValue()` or `GetValue()` methods to set or get at the data in it. Both of these methods take a string giving the name of the value as a parameter, and `SetValue()` requires an additional object reference containing details of the value. Because the parameter is defined as an object reference, it can actually be a reference to any class you want. `SetValue()` will decide from the type of class actually supplied whether to set the value as a `REG_SZ`, `REG_DWORD`, or `REG_BINARY` value. For example:

```
RegistryKey hkMine = HkSoftware.CreateSubKey("MyOwnSoftware");
hkMine.SetValue("MyStringValue", "Hello World");
hkMine.SetValue("MyIntValue", 20);
```

This code will set the key to have two values: `MyStringValue` will be of type `REG_SZ`, while `MyIntValue` will be of type `REG_DWORD`. These are the only two types you will consider here, and use in the example that presented later.

`RegistryKey.GetValue()` works in much the same way. It is defined to return an object reference, which means it is free to actually return a `string` reference if it detects the value is of type `REG_SZ`, and an `int` if that value is of type `REG_DWORD`:

```
string stringValue = (string)hkMine.GetValue("MyStringValue");
int intValue = (int)hkMine.GetValue("MyIntValue");
```

Finally, after you've finished reading or modifying the data, close the key:

```
hkMine.Close();
```

`RegistryKey` implements a large number of methods and properties. The following tables list the most useful properties.

| Property Name | Description |
| --- | --- |
| `Name` | Name of the key (read-only) |
| `SubKeyCount` | The number of children of this key |
| `ValueCount` | How many values the key contains |

The following table lists the most useful methods.

| Method Name | Purpose |
| --- | --- |
| `Close()` | Closes the key |
| `CreateSubKey()` | Creates a subkey of a given name (or opens it if it already exists) |
| `DeleteSubKey()` | Deletes a given subkey |
| `DeleteSubKeyTree()` | Recursively deletes a subkey and all its children |
| `DeleteValue()` | Removes a named value from a key |

*Table continued on following page*

| Method Name | Purpose |
|---|---|
| `GetAccessControl()` | Returns the access control list (ACL) for a specified registry key. This method is new to the .NET Framework 2.0. |
| `GetSubKeyNames()` | Returns an array of strings containing the names of the subkeys |
| `GetValue()` | Returns a named value |
| `GetValueKind()` | Returns a named value whose registry data type is to be retrieved. This method is new to the .NET Framework 2.0. |
| `GetValueNames()` | Returns an array of strings containing the names of all the values of the key |
| `OpenSubKey()` | Returns a reference to a `RegistryKey` instance that represents a given subkey |
| `SetAccessControl()` | Allows you to apply an access control list (ACL) to a specified registry key. This method is new to the .NET Framework 2.0. |
| `SetValue()` | Sets a named value |

## Example: SelfPlacingWindow

The use of the registry classes is illustrated with an application called `SelfPlacingWindow`. This example is a simple C# Windows application that has almost no features. The only thing you can do with it is click a button, which brings up a standard Windows color dialog box (represented by the `System.Windows.Forms.ColorDialog` class) to let you choose a color, which will become the background color of the form.

Despite this lack of features, the self-placing window scores over just about every other application that you have developed in this book in one important and very user-friendly way. If you drag the window around the screen, change its size, or maximize or minimize it before you exit the application, it will remember the new position, as well as the background color, so that the next time it is launched it can automatically resume the way you chose last time. It remembers this information because it writes it to the registry whenever it shuts down. In this way, it demonstrates not only the .NET registry classes themselves but also a very typical use for them, which you'll almost certainly want to replicate in any serious commercial Windows Forms application you write.

The location in which `SelfPlacingWindow` stores its information in the registry is the key HKLM\Software\WroxPress\SelfPlacingWindow. HKLM is the usual place for application configuration information, but note that it is not user-specific. If you wanted to be more sophisticated in a real application, you'd probably want to replicate the information inside the HK_Users hive as well, so that each user can have his or her own profile.

> It's also worth noting that, if you are implementing this in a real .NET application, you may want to consider using isolated storage instead of the registry to store this information. On the other hand, because isolated storage is only available in .NET, you'll need to use the registry if you need any interoperability with non-.NET apps.

# Manipulating Files and the Registry

The very first time that you run the example, it will look for this key and not find it (obviously). Therefore it is forced to use a default size, color, and position that you set in the developer environment. The example also features a list box in which it displays any information read in from the registry. On its first run, it will look similar to Figure 34-18.

Figure 34-18

If you now modify the background color and resize `SelfPlacingWindow` or move it around on the screen a bit before exiting, it will create the HKLM\Software\WroxPress\SelfPlacingWindow key and write its new configuration information into it. You can examine the information using regedit. The details are shown in Figure 34-19.

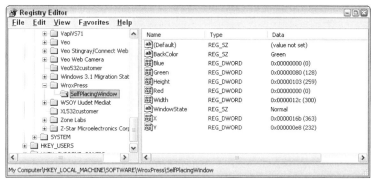

Figure 34-19

As this figure shows, `SelfPlacingWindow` has placed a number of values in the registry key.

The values Red, Green, and Blue give the color components that make up the selected background color (see Chapter 25, "Graphics with GDI+"). For now, just take it that any color display on the system can be completely described by these three components, which are each represented by a number between 0 and 255 (or 0x00 and 0xff in hexadecimal). The values given here make up a bright green color. There are also four more REG_DWORD values, which represent the position and size of the window: X and Y are the coordinates of top left of the window on the desktop — that is to say the numbers of pixels across from the top left of the screen and the numbers of pixels down. Width and Height give the size of the

1233

window. WindowsState is the only value for which you have used a string data type (REG_SZ), and it can contain one of the strings Normal, Maximized, or Minimized, depending on the final state of the window when you exited the application.

When you launch SelfPlacingWindow again, it will read this registry key and automatically position itself accordingly (see Figure 34-20).

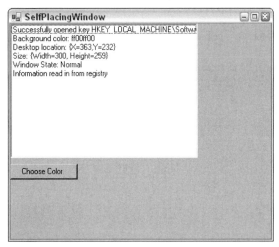

**Figure 34-20**

This time when you exit SelfPlacingWindow, it will overwrite the previous registry settings with whatever new values are relevant at the time that you exit it. To code the example, you create the usual Windows Forms project in Visual Studio .NET and add the list box and button, using the developer environment's toolbox. You will change the names of these controls, respectively, to listBoxMessages and buttonChooseColor. You also need to ensure that you use the Microsoft.Win32 namespace:

```
using System;
using System.Drawing;
using System.Collections;
using System.ComponentModel;
using System.Windows.Forms;
using System.Data;
using Microsoft.Win32;
```

You need to add one field (chooseColorDialog) to the main Form1 class, which will represent the color dialog box:

```
public class Form1 : System.Windows.Forms.Form
{
    private System.Windows.Forms.ListBox listBoxMessages;
    private System.Windows.Forms.Button buttonChooseColor;
    private ColorDialog chooseColorDialog = new ColorDialog();
```

Quite a lot of action takes place in the Form1 constructor:

# Manipulating Files and the Registry

```csharp
public Form1()
{
    InitializeComponent();
    buttonChooseColor.Click += new EventHandler(OnClickChooseColor);
    try
    {
        if (ReadSettings() == false)
            listBoxMessages.Items.Add("No information in registry");
        else
            listBoxMessages.Items.Add("Information read in from registry");
        StartPosition = FormStartPosition.Manual;
    }
    catch (Exception e)
    {
        listBoxMessages.Items.Add("A problem occurred reading in data
                                   from registry:");
        listBoxMessages.Items.Add(e.Message);
    }
}
```

In this constructor, you begin by setting up the event handler for when the user clicks the button. The handler is a method called `OnClickChooseColor`, which is covered shortly. Reading in the configuration information is done using another method that you have to write, called `ReadSettings()`. `ReadSettings()` returns `true` if it finds the information in the registry, and `false` if it doesn't (which it should be because this is the first time you have run the application). You place this part of the constructor in a `try` block, just in case any exceptions are generated while reading in the registry values (this might happen if some user has come in and played around with the registry using regedit).

The `StartPosition = FormStartPosition.Manual;` statement tells the form to take its initial starting position from the `DeskTopLocation` property instead of using the Windows default location (the default behavior). Possible values are taken from the `FormStartPosition` enumeration.

`SelfPlacingWindow` is also one of the few applications in this book in which you have a serious use for adding code to the `Dispose()` method. Remember that `Dispose()` is called whenever the application terminates normally, so this is the ideal place from which to save the configuration information to the registry. This is done using another method that you have to write, `SaveSettings()`:

```csharp
protected override void Dispose( bool disposing )
{
    if( disposing )
    {
        if (components != null)
        {
            components.Dispose();
        }
    }
    SaveSettings();
    base.Dispose( disposing );
}
```

The `SaveSettings()` and `ReadSettings()` methods are the ones that contain the registry code you are interested in, but before you examine them you have one more piece of housekeeping to do: to handle the event of the user clicking that button. This involves displaying the color dialog and setting the background color to whatever color the user chose:

```
void OnClickChooseColor(object Sender, EventArgs e)
{
    if(chooseColorDialog.ShowDialog() == DialogResult.OK)
        BackColor = chooseColorDialog.Color;
}
```

Now look at how you save the settings:

```
void SaveSettings()
{
    RegistryKey softwareKey =
            Registry.LocalMachine.OpenSubKey("Software", true);
    RegistryKey wroxKey = softwareKey.CreateSubKey("WroxPress");
    RegistryKey selfPlacingWindowKey =
            wroxKey.CreateSubKey("SelfPlacingWindow");
    selfPlacingWindowKey.SetValue("BackColor",
            (object)BackColor.ToKnownColor());
    selfPlacingWindowKey.SetValue("Red", (object)(int)BackColor.R);
    selfPlacingWindowKey.SetValue("Green", (object)(int)BackColor.G);
    selfPlacingWindowKey.SetValue("Blue", (object)(int)BackColor.B);
    selfPlacingWindowKey.SetValue("Width", (object)Width);
    selfPlacingWindowKey.SetValue("Height", (object)Height);
    selfPlacingWindowKey.SetValue("X", (object)DesktopLocation.X);
    selfPlacingWindowKey.SetValue("Y", (object)DesktopLocation.Y);
    selfPlacingWindowKey.SetValue("WindowState",
            (object)WindowState.ToString());
}
```

There's quite a lot going on here. You start off by navigating through the registry to get to the HKLM\Software\WroxPress\SelfPlacingWindow registry key using the technique demonstrated earlier, starting with the `Registry.LocalMachine` static property that represents the HKLM hive.

Then you use the `RegistryKey.OpenSubKey()` method, rather than `RegistryKey.CreateSubKey()`, to get to the HKLM/Software key. That's because you can be very confident this key already exists; if it doesn't, there's something very seriously wrong with your computer, because this key contains settings for a lot of system software! You also indicate that you need write access to this key. That's because if the `WroxPress` key doesn't already exist you will need to create it, which involves writing to the parent key.

The next key to navigate to is HKLM\Software\WroxPress — and here you are not certain whether the key already exists, so you use `CreateSubKey()` to automatically create it if it doesn't. Note that `CreateSubKey()` automatically gives you write access to the key in question. Once you have reached HKLM\Software\WroxPress\SelfPlacingWindow, it is simply a matter of calling the `RegistryKey.SetValue()` method a number of times to either create or set the appropriate values. There are, however, a couple of complications.

First, you might notice that you are using a couple of classes that you've not encountered before. The `DeskTopLocation` property of the `Form` class indicates the position of the top-left corner of the screen, and is of type `Point`. (The `Point` is discussed in Chapter 25.) What you need to know here is that it contains two `int` values, X and Y, which represent the horizontal and vertical position on the screen. You

## Manipulating Files and the Registry

also look up three member properties of the `Form.BackColor` property, which is an instance of the `Color` class: `R`, `G`, and `B`: `Color`, which represents a color, and these properties on it give the red, green, and blue components that make up the color and are all of type `byte`. You also use the `Form.WindowState` property, which contains an enumeration that gives the current state of the window: `Minimized`, `Maximized`, or `Normal`.

The other complication here is that you need to be a little careful about your casts: `SetValue()` takes two parameters: a `string` that gives the name of the key and a `System.Object` instance, which contains the value. `SetValue()` has a choice of format for storing the value — it can store it as REG_SZ, REG_BINARY, or REG_DWORD — and it is actually pretty intelligent about making a sensible choice depending on the data type that has been given. Hence for the `WindowState`, you pass it a `string` and `SetValue()` determines that this should be translated to REG_SZ. Similarly, for the various positions and dimensions you supply `int`s, which will be converted into REG_DWORD. However, the color components are more complicated as you want these to be stored as REG_DWORD too because they are numeric types. However, if `SetValue()` sees that the data is of type `byte`, it will store it as a string — as REG_SZ in the registry. To prevent this, you cast the color components to `int`s.

You've also explicitly cast all the values to the type `object`. You don't really need to do this because the cast from any other data type to `object` is implicit, but you are doing so in order to make it clear what's going on and remind yourself that `SetValue()` is defined to take just an object reference as its second parameter.

The `ReadSettings()` method is a little longer because for each value read in, you also need to interpret it, display the value in the list box, and make the appropriate adjustments to the relevant property of the main form. `ReadSettings()` looks like this:

```
bool ReadSettings()
{
    RegistryKey softwareKey =
                Registry.LocalMachine.OpenSubKey("Software");
    RegistryKey wroxKey = softwareKey.OpenSubKey("WroxPress");
    if (wroxKey == null)
       return false;
    RegistryKey selfPlacingWindowKey =
                wroxKey.OpenSubKey("SelfPlacingWindow");
    if (selfPlacingWindowKey == null)
       return false;
    else
       listBoxMessages.Items.Add("Successfully opened key " +
                selfPlacingWindowKey.ToString());
    int redComponent = (int)selfPlacingWindowKey.GetValue("Red");
    int greenComponent = (int)selfPlacingWindowKey.GetValue("Green");
    int blueComponent = (int)selfPlacingWindowKey.GetValue("Blue");
    this.BackColor = Color.FromArgb(redComponent, greenComponent,
                blueComponent);
    listBoxMessages.Items.Add("Background color: " + BackColor.Name);
    int X = (int)selfPlacingWindowKey.GetValue("X");
    int Y = (int)selfPlacingWindowKey.GetValue("Y");
    this.DesktopLocation = new Point(X, Y);
    listBoxMessages.Items.Add("Desktop location: " +
                DesktopLocation.ToString());
    this.Height = (int)selfPlacingWindowKey.GetValue("Height");
```

```
            this.Width = (int)selfPlacingWindowKey.GetValue("Width");
            listBoxMessages.Items.Add("Size: " + new
                    Size(Width,Height).ToString());
            string initialWindowState =
                    (string)selfPlacingWindowKey.GetValue("WindowState");
            listBoxMessages.Items.Add("Window State: " + initialWindowState);
            this.WindowState = (FormWindowState)FormWindowState.Parse
                    (WindowState.GetType(), initialWindowState);
            return true;
        }
```

In `ReadSettings()` you first have to navigate to the HKLM/Software/WroxPress/SelfPlacingWindow registry key. In this case, however, you are hoping to find the key there so that you can read it. If it's not there, it's probably the first time you have run the example. In this case, you just want to abort reading the keys, and you certainly don't want to create any keys. Now you use the `RegistryKey.OpenSubKey()` method all the way down. If at any stage `OpenSubkey()` returns a `null` reference then you know that the registry key isn't there and you can simply return the value `false` back to the calling code.

When it comes to actually reading the keys, you use the `RegistryKey.GetValue()` method, which is defined as returning an object reference (which means this method can actually return an instance of literally any class it chooses). Like `SetValue()`, it will return a class of object appropriate to the type of data it found in the key. Hence, you can usually assume that the REG_SZ keys will give you a string and the other keys will give you an `int`. You also cast the return reference from `SetValue()` accordingly. If there is an exception, say someone has fiddled with the registry and mangled the value types, then your cast will cause an exception to be thrown — which will be caught by the handler in the `Form1` constructor.

The rest of this code uses one more data type, the `Size` structure. This is similar to a `Point` structure, but is used to represent sizes rather than coordinates. It has two member properties, `Width` and `Height`, and you use the `Size` structure here simply as a convenient way of packaging up the size of the form for displaying in the list box.

# Summary

In this chapter, you have examined how to use the .NET base classes to access the file system and registry from your C# code. You've seen that in both cases the base classes expose simple, but powerful, object models that make it very simple to perform almost any kind of action in these areas. In the case of the file system, these are copying files; moving, creating, and deleting files and folders; and reading and writing both binary and text files; and in the case of the registry, these are creating, modifying, or reading keys.

This chapter assumed that you are running your code from an account that has sufficient access rights to do whatever the code needs to do. Obviously, the question of security is an important one, and it is discussed in Chapter 16, ".NET Security."

# 35
# Accessing the Internet

Chapters 26 through 28 discuss how you can use C# to write powerful, efficient, and dynamic Web pages using ASP.NET and XML Web services. For the most part, the clients accessing ASP.NET pages will be users running Internet Explorer or other Web browsers such as Opera or FireFox. However, you might want to add Web-browsing features to your own application, or need your applications to programmatically obtain information from a Web site. In this latter case, it is usually better for the site to implement a Web service. However, if you are accessing public Internet sites you might not have any control over how the site is implemented.

This chapter covers facilities provided through the .NET base classes for using various network protocols, particularly HTTP and TCP, to access networks and the Internet as a client. In particular, this chapter covers:

- ❑ Downloading files from the World Wide Web
- ❑ Using the new Web Browser control in a Windows Forms application
- ❑ Manipulating IP addresses and performing DNS lookups
- ❑ Socket programming with TCP, UDP, and socket classes

The two namespaces of most interest for networking are the `System.Net` and the `System.Net.Sockets` namespaces. The `System.Net` namespace is generally concerned with higher-level operations, for example, downloading and uploading files, and making Web requests using HTTP and other protocols, whereas `System.Net.Sockets` contains classes to perform lower-level operations. You will find these classes more useful when you want to work directly with sockets or protocols such as TCP/IP. The methods in these classes closely mimic the Windows socket (Winsock) API functions derived from the Berkeley sockets interface.

This chapter takes a fairly practical approach, mixing examples with a discussion of the relevant theory and networking concepts as appropriate. This chapter is not a guide to computer networking but an introduction to using the .NET Framework for network communication.

You also take a look at using the new Web Browser control in a Windows Forms environment and how it can make accomplishing some specific Internet access tasks easier for you to accomplish.

However, the chapter starts with the simplest case of sending a request to a server and storing the information sent back in the response. (As is the case with the other chapters, you can download the sample code for this chapter from the Wrox Web site at www.wrox.com.)

# The WebClient Class

If you only want to request a file from a particular URI, you will find that the easiest .NET class to use is System.Net.WebClient. This is an extremely high-level class designed to perform basic operations with only one or two commands. The .NET Framework currently supports URIs beginning with http:, https:, and file: identifiers.

> *It is worth noting that the term URL (uniform resource locator) is no longer in use in new technical specifications, and URI (uniform resource identifier) is now preferred. URI has roughly the same meaning as URL, but is a bit more general because URI does not imply you are using one of the familiar protocols, such as HTTP or FTP.*

## Downloading Files

Two methods are available for downloading a file using WebClient. The method you choose depends on how you want to process the file contents. If you simply want to save the file to disk you use the DownloadFile() method. This method takes two parameters: the URI of the file and a location (path and file name) to save the requested data:

```
WebClient Client = new WebClient();
Client.DownloadFile("http://www.reuters.com/", "ReutersHomepage.htm");
```

More commonly, your application will want to process the data retrieved from the Web site. To do this, you use the OpenRead() method. OpenRead() returns a Stream reference you can then use to retrieve the data into memory:

```
WebClient Client = new WebClient();
Stream strm = Client.OpenRead("http://www.reuters.com/");
```

## Basic Web Client Example

The first example demonstrates the WebClient.OpenRead() method. You will display the contents of the downloaded page in a ListBox control. To begin, create a new project as a standard C# Windows Forms Application and add a ListBox called listBox1 with the docking property set to DockStyle.Fill. At the beginning of the file, you will need to add the System.Net and System.IO namespaces references to your list of using directives. You then make the following changes to the constructor of the main form:

```
public Form1()
{
    InitializeComponent();
```

# Accessing the Internet

```
    System.Net.WebClient Client = new WebClient();
    Stream strm = Client.OpenRead("http://www.reuters.com");
    StreamReader sr = new StreamReader(strm);
    string line;
    while ( (line=sr.ReadLine()) != null )
    {
        listBox1.Items.Add(line);
    }

    strm.Close();
}
```

In this example, you connect a `StreamReader` class from the `System.IO` namespace to the network stream. This allows you to obtain data from the stream as text through the use of higher-level methods, such as `ReadLine()`. This is an excellent example of the point made in Chapter 34, "Manipulating Files and the Registry," about the benefits of abstracting data movement into the concept of a stream.

Figure 35-1 shows the results of running this sample code.

Figure 35-1

The `WebClient` class also has an `OpenWrite()` method. This method returns a writeable stream for you to send data to a URI. You can also specify the method used to send the data to the host; the default method is POST. The following code snippet assumes a writeable directory named `accept` on the local machine. The code will create a file in the directory with the name `newfile.txt` and the contents `Hello World`:

```
WebClient webClient = new WebClient();

Stream stream = webClient.OpenWrite("http://localhost/accept/newfile.txt", "PUT");

StreamWriter streamWriter = new StreamWriter(stream);
streamWriter.WriteLine("Hello World");
streamWriter.Close();
```

## Uploading Files

The `WebClient` class also features `UploadFile()` and `UploadData()` methods. `UploadFile()` uploads a file to a specified location given the local file name, whereas `UploadData()` uploads binary data supplied as an array of bytes to the specified URI (there is also a `DownloadData()` method for retrieving an array of bytes from a URI):

```
WebClient client = new WebClient();
client.UploadFile("http://www.ourwebsite.com/NewFile.htm",
              "C:\\WebSiteFiles\\NewFile.htm");
byte[] image;
// code to initialise image so it contains all the binary data for
// some jpg file
client.UploadData("http://www.ourwebsite.com/NewFile.jpg", image);
```

# WebRequest and WebResponse Classes

Although the `WebClient` class is very simple to use, it has very limited features. In particular, you cannot use it to supply authentication credentials — a particular problem with uploading data is that not many sites will accept uploaded files without authentication! It is possible to add header information to requests and to examine any headers in the response, but only in a very generic sense — there is no specific support for any one protocol. This is because `WebClient` is a very general-purpose class designed to work with any protocol for sending a request and receiving a response (such as HTTP or FTP). It cannot handle any features specific to any one protocol, such as cookies, which are specific to HTTP. If you want to take advantage of these features you need to use a family of classes based on two other classes in the `System.Net` namespace: `WebRequest` and `WebResponse`.

You start off by seeing how to download a Web page using these classes. This is the same example as before, but using `WebRequest` and `WebResponse`. In the process you will uncover the class hierarchy involved, and then see how to take advantage of extra HTTP features supported by this hierarchy.

The following code shows the modifications you need to make to the `BasicWebClient` sample to use the `WebRequest` and `WebResponse` classes:

```
public Form1()
{
    InitializeComponent();

    WebRequest wrq = WebRequest.Create("http://www.reuters.com");
    WebResponse wrs = wrq.GetResponse();
    Stream strm = wrs.GetResponseStream();
    StreamReader sr = new StreamReader(strm);
    string line;
    while ( (line = sr.ReadLine()) != null)
    {
        listBox1.Items.Add(line);
    }
    strm.Close();
}
```

# Accessing the Internet

In the code example, you start by instantiating an object representing a Web request. You don't do this using a constructor, but instead call the static method `WebRequest.Create()`. As you learn in more detail later in this chapter, the `WebRequest` class is part of a hierarchy of classes supporting different network protocols. In order to receive a reference to the correct object for the request type, a factory mechanism is in place. The `WebRequest.Create()` method will create the appropriate object for the given protocol.

The `WebRequest` class represents the request for information to send to a particular URI. The URI is passed as a parameter to the `Create()` method. A `WebResponse` represents the data you retrieve from the server. By calling the `WebRequest.GetResponse()` method, you actually send the request to the Web server and create a `WebResponse` object to examine the return data. As with the `WebClient` object, you can obtain a stream to represent the data, but in this case you use the `WebResponse.GetResponseStream()` method.

## Other WebRequest and WebResponse Features

This section briefly discusses a couple of the other areas supported by `WebRequest`, `WebResponse`, and other related classes.

### HTTP header information

An important part of the HTTP protocol is the ability to send extensive header information with both request and response streams. This information can include cookies and the details of the particular browser sending the request (the user agent). As you would expect, the .NET Framework provides full support for accessing the most significant data. The `WebRequest` and `WebResponse` classes provide some support for reading the header information. However, two derived classes provide additional HTTP-specific information: `HttpWebRequest` and `HttpWebResponse`. As you will see in more detail later, creating a `WebRequest` with an HTTP URI results in an `HttpWebRequest` object instance. Because `HttpWebRequest` is derived from `WebRequest`, you can use the new instance whenever a `WebRequest` is required. In addition, you can cast the instance to an `HttpWebRequest` reference and access properties specific to the HTTP protocol. Likewise, the `GetResponse()` method call will actually return an `HttpWebResponse` instance as a `WebResponse` reference when dealing with HTTP. Again, you can perform a simple cast to access the HTTP-specific features.

You can examine a couple of the header properties by adding the following code before the `GetResponse()` method call:

```
WebRequest wrq = WebRequest.Create("http://www.reuters.com");
HttpWebRequest hwrq = (HttpWebRequest)wrq;

listBox1.Items.Add("Request Timeout (ms) = " + wrq.Timeout);
listBox1.Items.Add("Request Keep Alive = " + hwrq.KeepAlive);
listBox1.Items.Add("Request AllowAutoRedirect = " + hwrq.AllowAutoRedirect);
```

The `Timeout` property is specified in milliseconds, and the default value is 100,000. You can set the `Timeout` property to control how long the `WebRequest` object will wait on the response before throwing a `WebException`. You can check the `WebException.Status` property to view the reason for an exception. This enumeration includes status codes for timeouts, connection failures, protocol errors, and more.

The `KeepAlive` property is a specific extension to the HTTP protocol, so you access this property through an `HttpWebRequest` reference. `KeepAlive` allows multiple requests to use the same connection, saving time in closing and reopening connections on subsequent requests. The default value for this property is `true`.

The `AllowAutoRedirect` property is also specific to the `HttpWebRequest` class. Use this property to control whether the Web request should automatically follow redirection responses from the Web server. Again, the default value is `true`. If you want to allow only a limited number of redirections, set the `MaximumAutomaticRedirections` property of the `HttpWebRequest` to the desired number.

Although the request and response classes expose most of the important headers as properties, you can also use the `Headers` property itself to view the entire collection of headers. Add the following code after the `GetResponse()` method call to place all of the headers in the `ListBox` control:

```
WebRequest wrq = WebRequest.Create("http://www.reuters.com");
WebResponse wrs = wrq.GetResponse();
WebHeaderCollection whc = wrs.Headers;
for(int i = 0; i < whc.Count; i++)
{
    listBox1.Items.Add("Header " + whc.GetKey(i) + " : " + whc[i]);
}
```

This example code produces the list of headers shown in Figure 35-2.

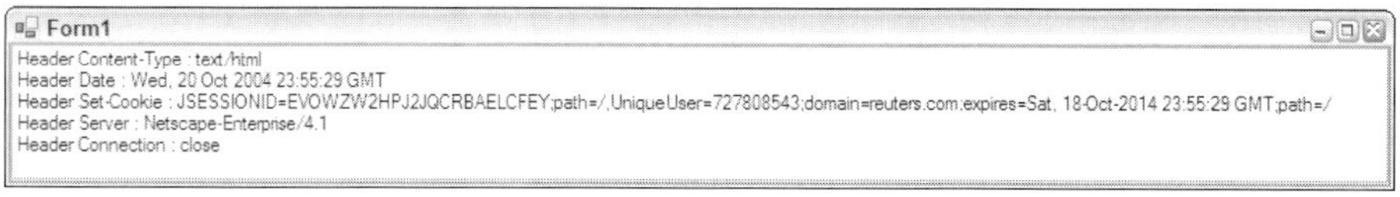

**Figure 35-2**

## Authentication

A further property in the `WebRequest` class is the `Credentials` property. If you needed authentication credentials to accompany your request, you could create an instance of the `NetworkCredential` class (also from the `System.Net` namespace) with a username and password. You could place the following code *before* the call to `GetResponse()`.

```
NetworkCredential myCred = new NetworkCredential("myusername", "mypassword");
wrq.Credentials = myCred;
```

## Asynchronous page requests

An additional feature of the `WebRequest` class is the ability to request pages asynchronously. This feature is significant because there can be quite a long delay between sending a request off to a host and receiving the response. Methods such as `WebClient.DownloadData()` and `WebRequest.GetResponse()` will not return until the response from the server is complete. You might not want your application frozen due to a long period of inactivity, and in such scenarios it is better to use the `BeginGetResponse()` and `EndGetResponse()` methods. `BeginGetResponse()` works asynchronously and returns almost immediately. Under the covers, the runtime will asynchronously manage a background thread to retrieve the response from the server. Instead of returning a `WebResponse` object, `BeginGetResponse()` returns an object implementing the `IAsyncResult` interface. With this interface you can poll or wait for the response to become available and then invoke `EndGetResponse()` to gather the results.

You can also pass a callback delegate into the `BeginGetResponse()` method. The target of a callback delegate is a method returning `void` and accepting an `IAsyncResult` reference as a parameter. When

# Accessing the Internet

the worker thread is finished gathering the response, the runtime invokes the callback delegate to inform you of the completed work. As shown in the following code, calling `EndGetResponse()` in the callback method allows you to retrieve the `WebResponse` object:

```
public Form1()
{
    InitializeComponent();

    WebRequest wrq = WebRequest.Create("http://www.reuters.com");
    wrq.BeginGetResponse(new AsyncCallback(OnResponse), wrq);
}

protected void OnResponse(IAsyncResult ar)
{
    WebRequest wrq = (WebRequest)ar.AsyncState;
    WebResponse wrs = wrq.EndGetResponse(ar);

    // read the response ...
}
```

Notice that you can retrieve the original `WebRequest` object by passing the object as the second parameter to `BeginGetResponse()`. The third parameter is an object reference known as the state parameter. During the callback method you can retrieve the same state object using the `AsyncState` property of `IAsyncResult`.

## Displaying Output as an HTML Page

The examples show how the .NET base classes make it very easy to download and process data from the Internet. However, so far you have only displayed files as plain text. Quite often you will want to view an HTML file in an Internet Explorer–style interface where the rendered HTML allows you to see what the Web document actually looks like. Unfortunately, there is not a .NET version of Microsoft's Internet Explorer, but that doesn't mean that you can't easily accomplish this task. Before the release of the .NET Framework 2.0, you could make reference to a COM object that was an encapsulation of Internet Explorer and use the .NET interop capabilities to have aspects of your application work as a browser. Now, using the .NET Framework 2.0, you can use the new built-in `WebBrowser` control available for your Windows Forms applications.

The `WebBrowser` control encapsulates the COM object even further for you making tasks that were once more complicated even easier. Besides using the `WebBrowser` control, another option is to use the programmatic ability to call up Internet Explorer instances from your code.

When not using the new `WebBrowser` control, you can programmatically start an Internet Explorer process and navigate to a Web page using the `Process` class in the `System.Diagnostics` namespace:

```
Process myProcess = new Process();
myProcess.StartInfo.FileName = "iexplore.exe";
myProcess.StartInfo.Arguments = "http://www.wrox.com";
myProcess.Start();
```

However, the preceding code launches Internet Explorer as a separate window. Your application has no connection to the new window and therefore cannot control the browser.

On the other hand, using new WebBrowser control allows you to display and control the browser as an integrated part of your application. The new WebBrowser control is quite sophisticated, featuring a large number of methods, properties, and events.

## Allowing Simple Web Browsing from Your Applications

For the sake of simplicity, start by creating a Windows Form application that simply has a TextBox control and a WebBrowser control. You will build the application so that the end user will simply enter in a URL into the text box, press Enter, and the WebBrowser control will do all the work of fetching the Web page and displaying the resulting document.

In the Visual Studio 2005 designer, your application should look as shown in Figure 35-3.

**Figure 35-3**

With this application, when the end user types in a URL and presses the Enter key, this key will register with the application and the WebBrowser control will go off to retrieve the requested page, which will then be subsequently displayed in the control itself.

The code behind this application is illustrated here:

```
using System;
using System.Collections.Generic;
using System.ComponentModel;
using System.Data;
using System.Drawing;
using System.Text;
```

# Accessing the Internet

```
using System.Windows.Forms;

namespace CSharpInternet
{
    partial class Form1 : Form
    {
        public Form1()
        {
            InitializeComponent();
        }

        private void textBox1_KeyPress(object sender, KeyPressEventArgs e)
        {
            if (e.KeyChar == (char)13)
            {
                webBrowser1.Navigate(textBox1.Text);
            }
        }
    }
}
```

From this example, you can see that each key press the end user makes in the text box is captured by the textBox1_KeyPress event and if the character inputted is a carriage return (a press of the Enter key, which is (char)13), then you take action with the WebBrowser control. Using the WebBrowser control's Navigate method, you specify the URL (as a string) through the use of the textBox1.Text property. The end result is shown in Figure 35-4.

Figure 35-4

## Launching Internet Explorer Instances

It might be that you are not interested in hosting a browser inside of your application as shown in the previous section but instead are only interested in allowing the user to find your Web site in a typical browser (for example, by clicking a link inside of your application). For an example of this task, create a Windows Form application that has a `LinkLabel` control on it. For instance, you can have a form that has a `LinkLabel` control on it that states "Visit our company website!"

Once you have this control in place, use the following code to launch your company's Web site in an independent browser as opposed to directly being in the form of your application:

```
private void linkLabel1_LinkClicked(object sender, LinkLabelLinkClickedEventArgs e)
{
   WebBrowser wb = new WebBrowser();
   wb.Navigate("http://www.wrox.com", true);
}
```

In this example, when the `LinkLabel` control is clicked by the user, a new instance of the `WebBrowser` class is created. Then, using the `WebBrowser` class's `Navigate` method, the code specifies the location of the Web page as well as a boolean value that specifies whether this end-point should be opened within the Windows Form application (a `false` value) or from within an independent browser (using a `true` value). By default, this is set to `false`. With the preceding construct, when the end user clicks the link found in the Windows application, a browser instance will be instantiated and the Wrox Web site will be immediately launched.

## Giving Your Application More IE Type Features

You will notice that when working with the previous example, in which you used the `WebBrowser` control directly in the Windows Form application, when you clicked on the links the text within the `TextBox` control was not updated to show the URL of where exactly you were in the browsing process. You can fix this by listening for events coming from the `WebBrowser` control and adding handlers to the control.

Updating the form's title with the HTML page's title is an easy thing to accomplish. You just have to create `DocumentTitleChanged` event and update the `Text` property of the form:

```
private void webBrowser1_DocumentTitleChanged(object sender, EventArgs e)
{
   this.Text = webBrowser1.DocumentTitle.ToString();
}
```

In this case, when the `WebBrowser` control notices that the page title has changed (due to changing the page viewed), the `DocumentTitleChanged` event will fire. In this case, you change the form's text box based on the complete URL of the page being viewed. To do this, you can use the `WebBrowser` control's `Navigated` event:

```
private void webBrowser1_Navigated(object sender, WebBrowserNavigatedEventArgs e)
{
   textBox1.Text = webBrowser1.Url.ToString();
}
```

# Accessing the Internet

In this case, when the requested page is finished being downloaded in the `WebBrowser` control, the `Navigated` event is fired. In your case, you simply update the `Text` value of the `textBox1` control to be the URL of the page. This means that once a page is loaded in the `WebBrowser` control's HTML container and if the URL changes in this process (for instance, if there is a redirect), then the new URL will be shown in the text box. If you employ these steps and navigate to the Wrox Web site (http://www.wrox.com), you will notice that the page's URL will immediately change to http://www.wrox.com/WileyCDA/. This process also means that if the end user clicks one of the links contained within the HTML view, the URL of the newly requested page will also be shown in the text box as well.

Now if you run the application with the preceding changes put into place, you'll find that the form title and address bar work as they do in Microsoft's Internet Explorer, as demonstrated in Figure 35-5.

Figure 35-5

The next step is to create an IE-like toolbar that will allow the end user to control the `WebBrowser` control a little more. This means that you will incorporate buttons such as Back, Forward, Stop, Refresh, and Home.

Rather than using the `ToolBar` control, you'll just add a set of `Button` controls at the top of the form where you currently have the address bar. Add five buttons to the top of the control as illustrated in Figure 35-6.

In this example, the text on the button face is changed to indicate the function of the button. Of course, you can even go as far as to use a screen capture utility to "borrow" button images from IE and use those. The buttons should be named `buttonBack`, `buttonForward`, `buttonStop`, `buttonRefresh`, and `buttonHome`. To get the resizing to work properly, make sure you set the `Anchor` property of the three buttons on the right to `Top, Right`.

## Chapter 35

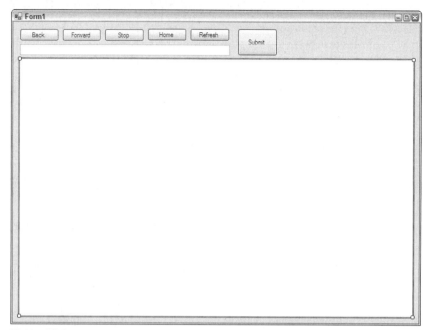

Figure 35-6

On startup, `buttonBack`, `buttonForward`, and `buttonStop` should be disabled because there is no point to the buttons if there is no initial page loaded in the `WebBrowser` control. You will later tell the application when to enable and disable the Back and Forward buttons yourself, depending on where the user is in the page stack. Also, when a page is being loaded, you will need to enable the Stop button — but also, you will need to disable the Stop button once the page has finished being loaded.

First off though, you'll add the functionality behind the buttons. The `WebBrowser` class itself has all of the methods that you need, so this is all very straightforward:

```
using System;
using System.Collections.Generic;
using System.ComponentModel;
using System.Data;
using System.Drawing;
using System.Windows.Forms;

namespace CSharpInternet
{
    partial class Form1 : Form
    {
        public Form1()
        {
            InitializeComponent();
        }

        private void webBrowser1_DocumentTitleChanged(object sender, EventArgs e)
        {
```

## Accessing the Internet

```csharp
        this.Text = webBrowser1.DocumentTitle.ToString();
    }

    private void textBox1_KeyPress(object sender, KeyPressEventArgs e)
    {
        if (e.KeyChar == (char)13)
        {
            webBrowser1.Navigate(textBox1.Text);
        }
    }

    private void webBrowser1_Navigated(object sender,
        WebBrowserNavigatedEventArgs e)
    {
        textBox1.Text = webBrowser1.Url.ToString();
    }

    private void Form1_Load(object sender, EventArgs e)
    {
        buttonBack.Enabled = false;
        buttonForward.Enabled = false;
        buttonStop.Enabled = false;
    }

    private void buttonBack_Click(object sender, EventArgs e)
    {
        webBrowser1.GoBack();
        textBox1.Text = webBrowser1.Url.ToString();
    }

    private void buttonForward_Click(object sender, EventArgs e)
    {
        webBrowser1.GoForward();
        textBox1.Text = webBrowser1.Url.ToString();
    }

    private void buttonStop_Click(object sender, EventArgs e)
    {
        webBrowser1.Stop();
    }

    private void buttonHome_Click(object sender, EventArgs e)
    {
        webBrowser1.GoHome();
        textBox1.Text = webBrowser1.Url.ToString();
    }

    private void buttonRefresh_Click(object sender, EventArgs e)
    {
        webBrowser1.Refresh();
    }

    private void buttonSubmit_Click(object sender, EventArgs e)
    {
```

```csharp
            webBrowser1.Navigate(textBox1.Text);
        }

        private void webBrowser1_CanGoBackChanged(object sender, EventArgs e)
        {
            if (webBrowser1.CanGoBack == true)
            {
                buttonBack.Enabled = true;
            }
            else
            {
                buttonBack.Enabled = false;
            }
        }

        private void webBrowser1_CanGoForwardChanged(object sender, EventArgs e)
        {
            if (webBrowser1.CanGoForward == true)
            {
                buttonForward.Enabled = true;
            }
            else
            {
                buttonForward.Enabled = false;
            }
        }

        private void webBrowser1_Navigating(object sender,
            WebBrowserNavigatingEventArgs e)
        {
            buttonStop.Enabled = true;
        }

        private void webBrowser1_DocumentCompleted(object sender,
            WebBrowserDocumentCompletedEventArgs e)
        {
            buttonStop.Enabled = false;
        }
    }
}
```

A lot of different activities are going on in this example because there are so many options for the end user when using this application. First off, for each of the button-click events, there is a specific WebBrowser class method assigned as the action to initiate. For instance, for the Back button on the form, you simply use the WebBrowser control's GoBack() method. And for the other buttons, it is the same — for the Forward button you have the GoForward() method and for the other buttons, you have methods such as Stop(), Refresh(), and GoHome(). This makes it fairly simple and straightforward to create a toolbar that will give you similar action as that of Microsoft's Internet Explorer.

When the form is first loaded, the Form1_Load event disables the appropriate buttons. From there, the end user can enter in a URL into the text box and click the Submit button to have the application retrieve the desired page.

# Accessing the Internet

To manage the enabling and disabling of the buttons, you have to key into a couple of events. As mentioned before, whenever downloading begins you need to enable the Stop button. For this, you simply added an event handler for the `Navigating` event to enable the Stop button:

```
private void webBrowser1_Navigating(object sender,
    WebBrowserNavigatingEventArgs e)
{
    buttonStop.Enabled = true;
}
```

Then the Stop button is again disabled when the document is finished being loaded:

```
private void webBrowser1_DocumentCompleted(object sender,
    WebBrowserDocumentCompletedEventArgs e)
{
    buttonStop.Enabled = false;
}
```

To enable and disable the appropriate Back and Forward buttons, it really depends on the ability to go backward or forward in the page stack. This is achieved using both the `CanGoForwardChanged()` and the `CanGoBackChanged()` events:

```
private void webBrowser1_CanGoBackChanged(object sender, EventArgs e)
{
    if (webBrowser1.CanGoBack == true)
    {
        buttonBack.Enabled = true;
    }
    else
    {
        buttonBack.Enabled = false;
    }
}

private void webBrowser1_CanGoForwardChanged(object sender, EventArgs e)
{
    if (webBrowser1.CanGoForward == true)
    {
        buttonForward.Enabled = true;
    }
    else
    {
        buttonForward.Enabled = false;
    }
}
```

Run the project now and visit a Web page and click through a few links. You should also be able to use the toolbar to enhance your browsing experience. The end product is shown in Figure 35-7.

## Chapter 35

# Showing Documents Using the WebBrowser Control

You are not just limited to Web pages for use within the `WebBrowser` control. In fact, you can allow the end user to view many different types of documents. So far, you have seen how to use the `WebBrowser` control to access documents that have been purely accessible by defining a URL. However, the `WebBrowser` control also allows you to use an absolute path and define end points to files such as Word documents, Excel documents, PDFs, and more.

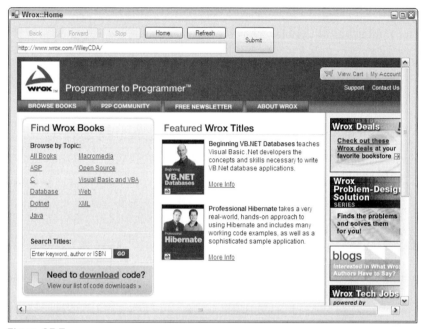

**Figure 35-7**

For instance, suppose that you are using the following code snippet:

```
webBrowser1.Navigate("C:\\Financial Report.doc");
```

This would open the Word document in your application. Not only would the document appear in the `WebBrowser` control, but the Word toolbar would also be present. This is illustrated in Figure 35-8.

In Figure 35-9 is the `WebBrowser` control showing an Adobe PDF file.

In addition to simply opening up specific documents in the control, users have the ability to drag-and-drop documents onto the `WebBrowser` control's surface and the document dropped will automatically be opened within the control. To turn off this ability (which is enabled by default), you will have to set the `WebBrowser` control's `AllowWebBrowserDrop` property to `false`.

# Accessing the Internet

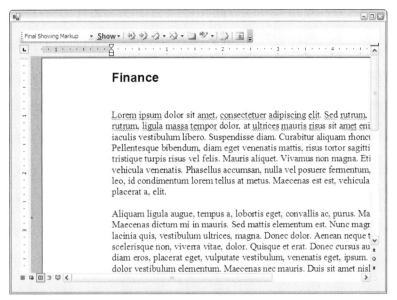

Figure 35-8

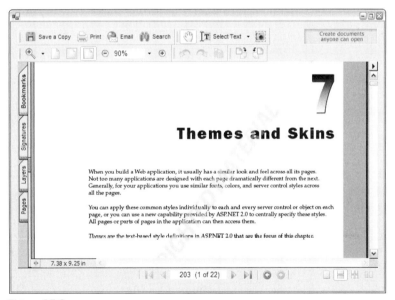

Figure 35-9

## Printing Using the WebBrowser Control

Not only can users use the `WebBrowser` control to view pages and documents; they can also use the control to send these pages and documents to the printer for printing. To print the page or document being viewed in the control, simply use the following construct:

```
webBrowser1.Print();
```

Like before, you don't have to view the page or document in order to print it. For instance, you can use the `WebBrowser` class to load an HTML document and print it without even displaying the loaded document. This would be accomplished as shown here:

```
WebBrowser wb = new WebBrowser();
wb.Navigate("http://www.wrox.com");
wb.Print();
```

## Displaying the Code of a Requested Page

In the beginning of this chapter, you used the `WebRequest` and the `Stream` classes to get at a remote page to display the code of the requested page. You used this code to accomplish this task:

```
public Form1()
{
    InitializeComponent();

    System.Net.WebClient Client = new WebClient();
    Stream strm = Client.OpenRead("http://www.reuters.com");
    StreamReader sr = new StreamReader(strm);
    string line;
    while ( (line=sr.ReadLine()) != null )
    {
        listBox1.Items.Add(line);
    }

    strm.Close();
}
```

Now, however, with the introduction of the `WebBrowser` control, it is quite easy to accomplish the same results. To accomplish this, change the browser application that you have been working on thus far in this chapter. For this change, simply add a single line to the `Document_Completed` event as illustrated here:

```
private void webBrowser1_DocumentCompleted(object sender,
    WebBrowserDocumentCompletedEventArgs e)
{
    buttonStop.Enabled = false;
    textBox2.Text = webBrowser1.DocumentText.ToString();
}
```

In the application itself, add another `TextBox` control below the `WebBrowser` control. The idea is that when the end user requests a page not only will you display the visual aspect of the page, but the code for the page as well in the `TextBox` control. The code of the page is displayed simply using the `DocumentText` property of the `WebBrowser` control, which will give you the entire page's content as a `String`. The other option is to get the contents of the page as a `Stream` using the `DocumentStream` property. The end result of the adding the second `TextBox` to display the contents of the page as a `String` is shown in Figure 35-10.

# Accessing the Internet

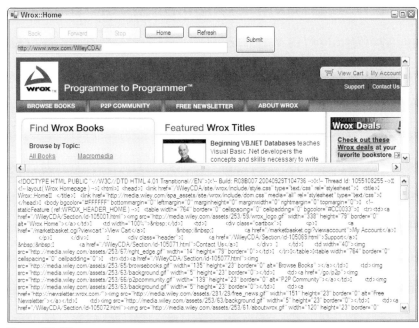

Figure 35-10

## The WebRequest and WebResponse Hierarchy

In this section you take a closer look at the underlying architecture of the `WebRequest` and `WebResponse` classes.

Figure 35-11 illustrates the inheritance hierarchy of the classes involved.

The hierarchy contains more than just the two classes you have used in your code. You should also know that the `WebRequest` and `WebResponse` classes are both abstract and cannot be instantiated. These base classes provide general functionality for dealing with Web requests and responses independent of the protocol used for a given operation. Requests are made using a particular protocol (HTTP, FTP, SMTP, and so on) and a derived class written for the given protocol will handle the request. Microsoft refers to this scheme as *pluggable protocols*. Remember in the code you examined earlier, your variables are defined as references to the base classes; however, `WebRequest.Create()` actually gives you an `HttpWebRequest` object, and the `GetResponse()` method actually returns an `HttpWebResponse` object. This factory-based mechanism hides many of the details from the client code, allowing support for a wide variety of protocols from the same code base.

The fact that you need an object specifically capable of dealing with the HTTP protocol is clear from the URI that you supply to `WebRequest.Create()`. `WebRequest.Create()` examines the protocol specifier in the URI to instantiate and return an object of the appropriate class. This keeps your code free from having to know anything about the derived classes or specific protocol used. When you need to access specific features of a protocol, you might need the properties and methods of the derived class, in which case you can cast your `WebRequest` or `WebResponse` reference to the derived class.

# Chapter 35

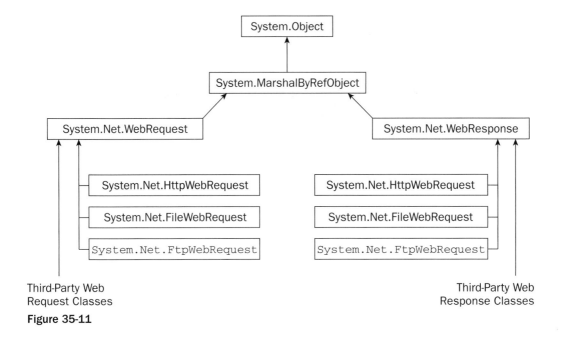

**Figure 35-11**

With this architecture you should be able to send requests using any of the common protocols. However, Microsoft currently only provides derived classes to cover the HTTP, HTTPS, FTP, and FILE protocols. The FTP option is the latest option provided by the .NET Framework 2.0. If you want to utilize other protocols, for example, SMTP, you will need to fall back on the Windows API, write your own classes, or wait for an independent software vendor to write some of the suitable .NET classes.

## Utility Classes

This section covers a couple of utility classes to make Web programming easier when dealing with URIs and IP addresses.

### URIs

`Uri` and `UriBuilder` are two classes in the `System` (not `System.Net`) namespace, and they are both intended to represent a URI. `UriBuilder` allows you to build a URI given the strings for the component parts, and the `Uri` class allows you to parse, combine, and compare URIs.

For the `Uri` class, the constructor requires a completed URI string:

```
Uri MSPage = new
            Uri("http://www.Microsoft.com/SomeFolder/SomeFile.htm?Order=true");
```

The class exposes a large number of read-only properties. A `Uri` object is not intended to be modified once it has been constructed:

# Accessing the Internet

```
    string Query = MSPage.Query;                      // Order=true;
    string AbsolutePath = MSPage.AbsolutePath;        // SomeFolder/SomeFile.htm
    string Scheme = MSPage.Scheme;                    // http
    int Port = MSPage.Port;                           // 80 (the default for http)
    string Host = MSPage.Host;                        // www.Microsoft.com
    bool IsDefaultPort = MSPage.IsDefaultPort;        // true since 80 is default
```

URIBuilder, on the other hand, implements fewer properties; just enough to allow you to build up a complete URI. These properties are read-write.

You can supply the components to build up a URI to the constructor:

```
    Uri MSPage = new
        UriBuilder("http", "www.Microsoft.com", 80, "SomeFolder/SomeFile.htm");
```

Or you can build the components by assigning values to the properties:

```
    UriBuilder MSPage = new UriBuilder();
    MSPage.Scheme ="http";
    MSPage.Host = "www.Microsoft.com";
    MSPage.Port = 80;
    MSPage.Path = "SomeFolder/SomeFile.htm";
```

Once you have completed initializing the UriBuilder, you can obtain the corresponding Uri object with the Uri property:

```
    Uri CompletedUri = MSPage.Uri;
```

## IP Addresses and DNS Names

On the Internet you identify servers as well as clients by IP address or host name (also referred to as a DNS name). Generally speaking, the host name is the human-friendly name that you type in a Web browser window, such as www.wrox.com or www.microsoft.com. An IP address, on the other hand, is the identifier computers use to identify each other. IP addresses are the identifiers used to ensure Web requests and responses reach the appropriate machines. It is even possible for a computer to have more than one IP address.

For host names to work, you must first send a network request to translate the host name into an IP address, a task carried out by one or more DNS servers.

A DNS server stores a table mapping host names to IP addresses for all the computers it knows about, as well as the IP addresses of other DNS servers to look up the host names it does not know about. Your local computer should always know about at least one DNS server. Network administrators configure this information when a computer is set up.

Before sending out a request, your computer will first ask the DNS server to tell it the IP address corresponding to the host name you have typed in. Once armed with the correct IP address, the computer can address the request and send it over the network. All of this work normally happens behind the scenes while the user is browsing the Web.

# Chapter 35

## .NET classes for IP addresses

The .NET Framework supplies a number of classes that are able to assist with the process of looking up IP addresses and finding out information about host computers.

### IPAddress

`IPAddress` represents an IP address. The address itself is available as the `GetAddressBytes` property and may be converted to a dotted decimal format with the `ToString()` method. `IPAddress` also implements a static `Parse()` method, which effectively performs the reverse conversion of `ToString()` — converting from a dotted decimal string to an `IPAddress`:

```
IPAddress ipAddress = IPAddress.Parse("234.56.78.9");
byte[] address = ipAddress.GetAddressBytes();
string ipString = ipAddress.ToString();
```

In this example, the `byte` integer `address` is assigned a binary representation of the IP address, and the string `ipString` is assigned the text `"234.56.78.9"`.

`IPAddress` also provides a number of constant static fields to return special addresses. For example, the `Loopback` address allows a machine to send messages to itself, whereas the `Broadcast` address allows multicasting to the local network:

```
// The following line will set loopback to "127.0.0.1".
// the loopback address indicates the local host.
string loopback = IPAddress.Loopback.ToString();

// The following line will set broadcast address to "255.255.255.255".
// the broadcast address is used to send a message to all machines on
// the local network.
string broadcast = IPAddress.Broadcast.ToString();
```

### IPHostEntry

The `IPHostEntry` class encapsulates information relating to a particular host computer. This class makes the host name available via the `HostName` property (which returns a string), and the `AddressList` property returns an array of `IPAddress` objects. You are going to use the `IPHostEntry` class in the in next example: `DNSLookupResolver`.

### Dns

The `Dns` class is able to communicate with your default DNS server to retrieve IP addresses. The two important (static) methods are `Resolve()`, which uses the DNS server to obtain the details of a host with a given host name, and `GetHostByAddress()`, which also returns details of the host but this time using the IP address. Both methods return an `IPHostEntry` object:

```
IPHostEntry wroxHost = Dns.Resolve("www.wrox.com");
IPHostEntry wroxHostCopy = Dns.GetHostByAddress("208.215.179.178");
```

In this code, both `IPHostEntry` objects will contain details of the Wrox.com servers.

# Accessing the Internet

The Dns class differs from the IPAddress and IPHostEntry classes because it has the ability to actually communicate with servers to obtain information. In contrast, IPAddress and IPHostEntry are more along the lines of simple data structures with convenient properties to allow access to the underlying data.

## The DnsLookup example

The DNS and IP-related classes are illustrated with an example that looks up DNS names: DnsLookup (see Figure 35-12).

Figure 35-12

This sample application simply invites the user to type in a DNS name using the main text box. When the user clicks the Resolve button, the sample uses the Dns.Resolve() method to retrieve an IPHostEntry reference and display the host name and IP addresses. Note how the host name displayed may be different from the name typed in. This can occur if one DNS name (www.microsoft.com) simply acts as a proxy for another DNS name (www.microsoft.com.nsatc.net).

The DnsLookup application is a standard C# Windows application. The controls are added as shown in Figure 35-12, giving them the names txtBoxInput, btnResolve, txtBoxHostName, and listBoxIPs, respectively. Then you simply add the following method to the Form1 class as the event handler for the buttonResolve click event:

```
void btnResolve_Click (object sender, EventArgs e)
{
    try
    {
        IPHostEntry iphost = Dns.Resolve(txtBoxInput.Text);
        foreach (IPAddress ip in iphost.AddressList)
        {
            string ipaddress = ip.AddressFamily.ToString();
            listBoxIPs.Items.Add(ipaddress);
            listBoxIPs.Items.Add("   " + ip.ToString());
```

1261

```
        }
        txtBoxHostName.Text = iphost.HostName;
    }
    catch(Exception ex)
    {
        MessageBox.Show("Unable to process the request because " +
            "the following problem occurred:\n" +
             ex.Message, "Exception occurred");
    }
}
```

Notice that in this code you are careful to trap any exceptions. An exception might occur if the user types in an invalid DNS name or if the network is down.

After retrieving the `IPHostEntry` instance, you use the `AddressList` property to obtain an array containing the IP addresses, which you then iterate through with a `foreach` loop. For each entry, you display the IP address as an integer and as a string, using the `IPAddress.AddressFamily.ToString()` method.

## Lower-Level Protocols

This section briefly discusses some of the .NET classes used to communicate at a lower level.

Network communications work on several different levels. The classes you have seen in this chapter so far work at the highest level: the level at which specific commands are processed. It is probably easiest to understand this concept if you think of file transfer using FTP. Although today's GUI applications hide many of the FTP details, it was not so long ago when you executed FTP from a command-line prompt. In this environment you explicitly typed commands to send to the server for downloading, uploading, and listing files.

FTP is not the only high-level protocol relying on textual commands. HTTP, SMTP, POP, and other protocols are based on a similar type of behavior. Again, many of the modern graphical tools hide the transmission of commands from the user, so you are generally not aware of them. For example, when you type a URL into a Web browser, and the Web request goes off to a server, the browser is actually sending a (plain text) `GET` command to the server, which fulfills a similar purpose as the FTP `get` command. It can also send a `POST` command, which indicates that the browser has attached other data to the request.

However, these protocols are not sufficient by themselves to achieve communication between computers. Even if both the client and the server understand, for example, the HTTP protocol, it will still not be possible for them to understand each other unless there is also agreement on exactly how to transmit the characters: What binary format will be used? And getting down to the lowest level, what voltages will be used to represent 0s and 1s in the binary data? Because there are so many items to configure and agree upon, developers and hardware engineers in the networking field often refer to a *protocol stack*. When you list all of the various protocols and mechanisms required for communication between two hosts, you create a protocol stack with high-level protocols on the top and low-level protocols on the bottom. This approach results in a modular and layered approach to achieving efficient communication.

Luckily, for most development work, you don't need to go far down the stack or work with voltage levels, but if you are writing code that requires efficient communication between computers, it's not

# Accessing the Internet

unusual to write code that works directly at the level of sending binary data packets between computers. This is the realm of protocols such as TCP, and Microsoft has supplied a number of classes that allow you to conveniently work with binary data at this level.

## Lower-Level Classes

The `System.Net.Sockets` namespace contains the relevant classes. These classes, for example, allow you to directly send out TCP network requests or to listen to TCP network requests on a particular port. The following table explains the main classes.

| Class | Purpose |
| --- | --- |
| Socket | Low-level class that deals with managing connections. Classes such as `WebRequest`, `TcpClient`, and `UdpClient` use this class internally. |
| NetworkStream | Derived from `Stream`. Represents a stream of data from the network. |
| TcpClient | Enables you to create and use TCP connections. |
| TcpListener | Enables you to listen for incoming TCP connection requests. |
| UdpClient | Enables you to create connections for UDP clients. (UDP is an alternative protocol to TCP, but is much less widely used, mostly on local networks.) |

### Using the TCP classes

The transmission control protocol (TCP) classes offer simple methods for connecting and sending data between two endpoints. An endpoint is the combination of an IP address and a port number. Existing protocols have well-defined port numbers, for example, HTTP uses port 80, while SMTP uses port 25. The Internet Assigned Number Authority, IANA, (http://www.iana.org/) assigns port numbers to these well-known services. Unless you are implementing a well-known service, you will want to select a port number above 1,024.

TCP traffic makes up the majority of traffic on the Internet today. TCP is often the protocol of choice because it offers guaranteed delivery, error correction, and buffering. The `TcpClient` class encapsulates a TCP connection and provides a number of properties to regulate the connection, including buffering, buffer size, and timeouts. Reading and writing is accomplished by requesting a `NetworkStream` object via the `GetStream()` method.

The `TcpListener` class listens for incoming TCP connections with the `Start()` method. When a connection request arrives, you can use the `AcceptSocket()` method to return a socket for communication with the remote machine, or use the `AcceptTcpClient()` method to use a higher-level `TcpClient` object for communication. The easiest way to demonstrate the `TcpListener` and `TcpClient` classes working together is to work through an example.

### The TcpSend and TcpReceive examples

To demonstrate how these classes work you need to build two applications. Figure 35-13 shows the first application, `TcpSend`. This application opens a TCP connection to a server and sends the C# source code for itself.

1263

Figure 35-13

Once again you create a C# Windows application. The form consists of two text boxes (txtHost and txtPort) for the host name and port, respectively, as well as a button (btnSend) to click and start a connection. First, you ensure that you include the relevant namespaces:

```
using System.Net;
using System.Net.Sockets;
using System.IO;
```

The following code shows the event handler for the button's click event:

```
private void btnSend_Click(object sender, System.EventArgs e)
{
   TcpClient tcpClient = new TcpClient(txtHost.Text, Int32.Parse(txtPort.Text));
   NetworkStream ns = tcpClient.GetStream();
   FileStream fs = File.Open("..\\..\\form1.cs", FileMode.Open);

   int data = fs.ReadByte();
   while(data != -1)
   {
      ns.WriteByte((byte)data);
      data = fs.ReadByte();
   }

   fs.Close();
   ns.Close();
   tcpClient.Close();
}
```

This example creates the TcpClient using a host name and a port number. Alternatively, if you have an instance of the IPEndPoint class, you can pass the instance to the TcpClient constructor. After retrieving an instance of the NetworkStream class, you open the source code file and begin to read bytes. Like many of the binary streams, you need to check for the end of the stream by comparing the return value of the ReadByte() method to -1. After your loop has read all of the bytes and sent them along to the network stream, you make sure to close all of the open files, connections, and streams.

On the other side of the connection, the TcpReceive application displays the received file after the transmission is finished (see Figure 35-14).

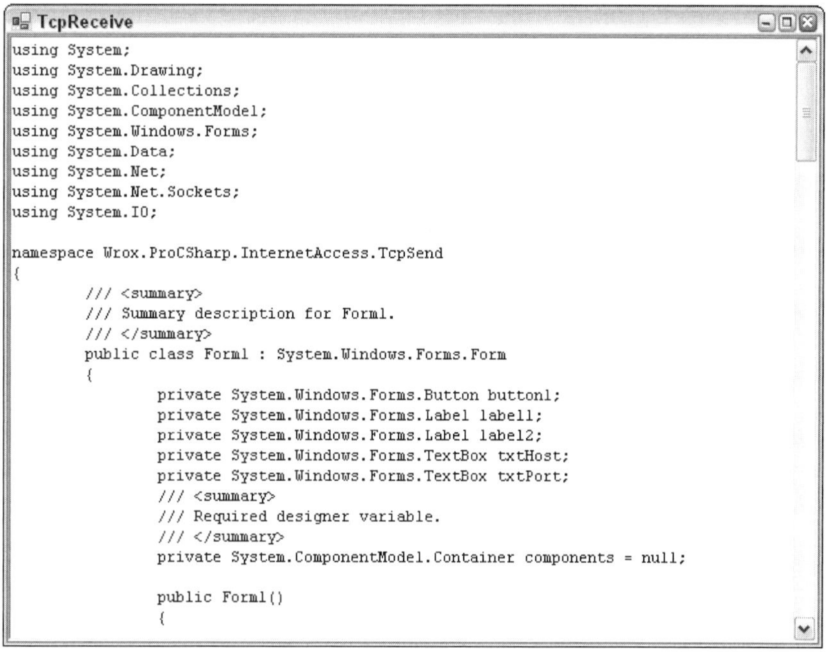

# Accessing the Internet

```
TcpReceive
using System;
using System.Drawing;
using System.Collections;
using System.ComponentModel;
using System.Windows.Forms;
using System.Data;
using System.Net;
using System.Net.Sockets;
using System.IO;

namespace Wrox.ProCSharp.InternetAccess.TcpSend
{
        /// <summary>
        /// Summary description for Form1.
        /// </summary>
        public class Form1 : System.Windows.Forms.Form
        {
                private System.Windows.Forms.Button button1;
                private System.Windows.Forms.Label label1;
                private System.Windows.Forms.Label label2;
                private System.Windows.Forms.TextBox txtHost;
                private System.Windows.Forms.TextBox txtPort;
                /// <summary>
                /// Required designer variable.
                /// </summary>
                private System.ComponentModel.Container components = null;

                public Form1()
                {
```

**Figure 35-14**

The form consists of a single TextBox control, named `txtDisplay`. The `TcpReceive` application uses a `TcpListener` to wait for the incoming connection. To avoid freezing the application interface, you use a background thread to wait for and then read from the connection. Thus, you need to include the `System.Threading` namespace as well:

```
using System.Net;
using System.Net.Sockets;
using System.IO;
using System.Threading;
```

Inside the form's constructor, you spin up a background thread:

```
public Form1()
{
   InitializeComponent();

   Thread thread = new Thread(new ThreadStart(Listen));
   thread.Start();
}
```

The remaining important code is this:

```
public void Listen()
{
   IPAddress localAddr = IPAddress.Parse("127.0.0.1");
   Int32 port = 2112;
```

```csharp
    TcpListener tcpListener = new TcpListener(localAddr, port);
    tcpListener.Start();

    TcpClient tcpClient = tcpListener.AcceptTcpClient();

    NetworkStream ns = tcpClient.GetStream();
    StreamReader sr = new StreamReader(ns);
    string result = sr.ReadToEnd();
    Invoke(new UpdateDisplayDelegate(UpdateDisplay),
            new object[] {result} );

    tcpClient.Close();
    tcpListener.Stop();
}

public void UpdateDisplay(string text)
{
    txtDisplay.Text= text;
}

protected delegate void UpdateDisplayDelegate(string text);
```

The thread begins execution in the `Listen()` method and allows you to make the blocking call to `AcceptTcpClient()` without halting the interface. Notice that the IP address (127.0.0.1) and the port number (2112) are hard-coded into the application, so you will need to enter the same port number from the client application.

You use the `TcpClient` object returned by `AcceptTcpClient()` to open a new stream for reading. Similar to the earlier example, you create a `StreamReader` to convert the incoming network data into a string. Before you close the client and stop the listener, you update the form's text box. You do not want to access the text box directly from your background thread, so you use the form's `Invoke()` method with a delegate and pass the result string as the first element in an array of `object` parameters. `Invoke()` ensures your call is correctly marshaled into the thread owning the control handles in the user interface.

## TCP versus UDP

The other protocol covered in this section is UDP (user datagram protocol). UDP is a simple protocol with few features but also little overhead. Developers often use UDP in applications where the speed and performance requirements outweigh the reliability needs, for example, video streaming. In contrast, TCP offers a number of features to confirm the delivery of data. TCP provides error correction and re-transmission in the case of lost or corrupted packets. Last, but hardly least, TCP buffers incoming and outgoing data and also guarantees a sequence of packets scrambled in transmission are reassembled before delivery to the application. Even with the extra overhead, TCP is the most widely used protocol across the Internet because of the higher reliability.

## The UDP class

As you might expect, the `UdpClient` class features a smaller and simpler interface compared to `TcpClient`. This reflects the relatively simpler nature of the protocol in comparison to TCP. Though both TCP and UDP classes use a socket underneath the covers, the `UdpClient` client does not contain

## Accessing the Internet

a method to return a network stream for reading and writing. Instead, the member function `Send()` accepts an array of bytes as a parameter, and the `Receive()` function returns an array of bytes. Also, Because UDP is a connectionless protocol, you can wait to specify the endpoint for the communication as a parameter to the `Send()` and `Receive()` methods, instead of earlier in a constructor or `Connect()` method. You can also change the endpoint on each subsequent send or receive.

The following code fragment uses the `UdpClient` class to send a message to an echo service. A server with an echo service running accepts TCP or UDP connections on port 7. The echo service simply echoes any data sent to the server back to the client. This service is useful for diagnostics and testing, although many system administrators disable echo services for security reasons:

```
using System;
using System.Text;
using System.Net;
using System.Net.Sockets;

namespace Wrox.ProCSharp.InternetAccess.UdpExample
{
    class Class1
    {
        [STAThread]
        static void Main(string[] args)
        {
            UdpClient udpClient = new UdpClient();

            string sendMsg = "Hello Echo Server";
            byte [] sendBytes = Encoding.ASCII.GetBytes(sendMsg);

            udpClient.Send(sendBytes, sendBytes.Length, "SomeEchoServer.net", 7);

            IPEndPoint endPoint = new IPEndPoint(0,0);
            byte [] rcvBytes = udpClient.Receive(ref endPoint);
            string rcvMessage = Encoding.ASCII.GetString(rcvBytes,
                                                         0,
                                                         rcvBytes.Length);

            // should print out "Hello Echo Server"
            Console.WriteLine(rcvMessage);
        }
    }
}
```

You make heavy use of the `Encoding.ASCII` class to translate strings into arrays of `byte` and vice versa. Also note that you pass an `IPEndPoint` by reference into the `Receive()` method. Because UDP is not a connection-oriented protocol, each call to `Receive()` might pick up data from a different endpoint, so `Receive()` populates this parameter with the IP address and port of the sending host.

Both `UdpClient` and `TcpClient` offer a layer of abstraction over the lowest of the low-level classes: the `Socket`.

## Chapter 35

### The Socket class

The `Socket` class offers the highest level of control in network programming. One of the easiest ways to demonstrate the class is to rewrite the `TcpReceive` application with the `Socket` class. The updated `Listen()` method is listed in this example:

```
public void Listen()
{
    Socket listener = new Socket(AddressFamily.InterNetwork,
                                 SocketType.Stream,
                                 ProtocolType.Tcp);
    listener.Bind(new IPEndPoint(IPAddress.Any, 2112));
    listener.Listen(0);

    Socket socket = listener.Accept();
    Stream netStream = new NetworkStream(socket);
    StreamReader reader = new StreamReader(netStream);

    string result = reader.ReadToEnd();

    Invoke(new UpdateDisplayDelegate(UpdateDisplay),
           new object[] {result} );
    socket.Close();
    listener.Close();
}
```

The `Socket` class requires a few more lines of code to complete the same task. For starters, the constructor arguments need to specify an IP addressing scheme for a streaming socket with the TCP protocol. These arguments are just one of the many combinations available to the `Socket` class, and the `TcpClient` class configured these settings for you. You then bind the listener socket to a port and begin to listen for incoming connections. When an incoming request arrives you can use the `Accept()` method to create a new socket for handling the connection. You ultimately attach a `StreamReader` instance to the socket to read the incoming data, in much the same fashion as before.

The `Socket` class also contains a number of methods for asynchronously accepting, connecting, sending, and receiving. You can use these methods with callback delegates in the same way you used the asynchronous page requests with the `WebRequest` class. If you really need to dig into the internals of the socket, the `GetSocketOption()` and `SetSocketOption()` methods are available. These methods allow you to see and configure options, including timeout, time-to-live, and other low-level options.

## Summary

In this chapter you reviewed the .NET Framework classes available in the `System.Net` namespace for communication across networks. You have seen some of the .NET base classes that deal with opening client connections on the network and Internet, and how to send requests to and receive responses from servers (the most obvious use of this being to receive HTML pages). By taking advantage of the new `WebBrowser` control in .NET 2.0, you can easily make use of Internet Explorer from your desktop applications.

## Accessing the Internet

As a rule of thumb, when programming with classes in the `System.Net` namespace, you should always try to use the most generic class possible. For instance, using the `TCPClient` class instead of the `Socket` class isolates your code from many of the lower-level socket details. Moving one step higher, the `WebRequest` class allows you to take advantage of the pluggable protocol architecture of the .NET Framework. Your code will be ready to take advantage of new application-level protocols as Microsoft and other third-party developers introduce new functionality.

Finally, you learned the use of the asynchronous capabilities in the networking classes, which give a Windows Forms application the professional touch of a responsive user interface.

# Windows Services

Windows Services are programs that can be started automatically at boot-time without the need of anyone logging on to the machine. After reading this chapter, you can modify the server processes from Chapter 29, ".NET Remoting," and Chapter 35, "Accessing the Internet," to be started automatically.

In the following pages, you learn:

- ❑ The architecture of Windows Services; the functionality of a service program, service control program, and service configuration program.
- ❑ How to implement a Windows Service with the classes found in the `System.ServiceProcess` namespace.
- ❑ Installation programs to configure the Windows Service in the registry.
- ❑ How to write a program to control the Windows Service using the `ServiceController` class.
- ❑ How to implement event handling.
- ❑ How to add event logging to other application types.
- ❑ How to implement performance monitoring for a Windows Service.

The first section explains the function of a Windows Service. (You can download the code for this chapter from the Wrox Web site at `www.wrox.com`.)

## What Is a Windows Service?

Windows Services are applications that can be automatically started when the operating system boots. They can run without having an interactive user logged on to the system. You can configure a Windows Service to be run from a specially configured user account; or from the system user account—a user account that has even more privileges than that of the system administrator.

# Chapter 36

> Windows Services don't run on Windows 95, 98, or ME; the NT kernel is a requirement. They do run on Windows 2000, Windows XP, and Windows Server 2003.

*Unless otherwise noted, when we refer to a service, we are referring to a Windows Service.*

Here are a few examples of services:

- Simple TCP/IP Services is a service program that hosts some small TCP/IP servers: echo, daytime, quote, and others
- World Wide Publishing Service is the service of the Internet Information Server (IIS)
- Event Log is a service to log messages to the event log system
- Microsoft Search is a service that creates indexes of data on the disk

You can use the Services administration tool, shown in Figure 36-1, to see all of the services on a system. On a Windows 2003 Server this program can be accessed be selecting Start ⇨ Programs ⇨ Administrative Tools ⇨ Services; on Windows 2000 Professional and Windows XP the program is accessible through Settings ⇨ Control Panel ⇨ Administrative Tools ⇨ Services.

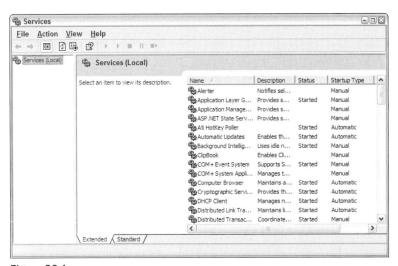

Figure 36-1

# Windows Services Architecture

Three program types are necessary to operate a Windows Service:

# Windows Services

- ❑ A service program
- ❑ A service control program
- ❑ A service configuration program

The *service program* itself provides the actual functionality you are looking for. With a *service control* program, it's possible to send control requests to a service, such as start, stop, pause, and continue. With a *service configuration* program, a service can be installed; it's copied to the file system, written into the registry, and configured as a service. Although .NET components can be installed simply with an xcopy, because they don't need to write information to the registry, installation for services requires registry configuration. A service configuration program can also be used to change the configuration of that service at a later point.

These three ingredients of a Windows Service are discussed in the following subsections.

## *Service Program*

Before looking at the .NET implementation of a service, take a look at it from an independent point of view and discover what the Windows architecture of services looks like and what the inner functionality of a service is.

The service program implements the functionality of the service. It needs three parts:

- ❑ A main function
- ❑ A service-main function
- ❑ A handler

Before discussing these parts, you must be introduced to the *Service Control Manager* (SCM). The SCM plays an important role for services, sending requests to your service to start and to stop it.

### *Service Control Manager*

The SCM is the part of the operating system that communicates with the service. Figure 36-2 illustrates how this communication works with a UML sequence diagram.

> At boot time, each process for which a service is set to start automatically is started, and so the main function of this process gets called. The service has the responsibility to register the service-main function for each of its services. The main function is the entry point of the service program, and in this function the entry points for the service-main functions must be registered with the SCM.

### *Main function, service-main, and handlers*

The main function of the service might register more than one service-main function. The service must register a service-main function for each service it provides. A service program can provide a lot of services in a single program; for example, `<windows>\system32\services.exe` is the service program that includes Alerter, Application Management, Computer Browser, and DHCP Client, among others.

1273

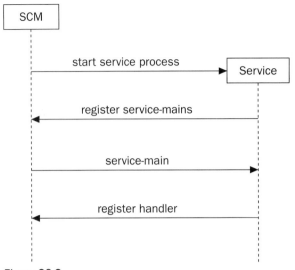

Figure 36-2

The SCM now calls the service-main function for each service that should be started. The *service-main* function contains the actual functionality of the service. One important task of the service-main function is to register a handler with the SCM.

The *handler* function is the third part of service program. The handler must respond to events from the SCM. Services can be stopped, suspended, and resumed, and the handler must react to these events.

Once a handler has been registered with the SCM, the service control program can post requests to the SCM to stop, suspend, and resume the service. The service control program is independent of the SCM and the service itself. You get many service control programs with the operating system; one is the MMC Services snap-in that you've seen earlier. You can also write your own service control program; a good example of this is the SQL Server Service Manager shown in Figure 36-3.

Figure 36-3

## Service Control Program

As the name suggests, with a service control program you can control the service. For stopping, suspending, and resuming the service, you can send control codes to the service, and the handler should react to these events. It's also possible to ask the service about the actual status and to implement a custom handler that responds to custom control codes.

## Service Configuration Program

You can't use xcopy installation with services, because services must be configured in the registry. You can set the startup type to automatic, manual, or disabled. You have to configure the user of the service program and dependencies of the service — for example, the services that must be started before this one can start. All these configurations are made within a service configuration program. The installation program can use the service configuration program to configure the service, but this program can also be used at a later time to change service configuration parameters.

# System.ServiceProcess Namespace

In the .NET Framework, you can find service classes in the System.ServiceProcess namespace that implement the three parts of a service:

- ❏ You have to inherit from the ServiceBase class to implement a service. The ServiceBase class is used to register the service and to answer start and stop requests.

- ❏ The ServiceController class is used to implement a service control program. With this class you can send requests to services.

- ❏ The ServiceProcessInstaller and ServiceInstaller classes are, as their names suggest, classes to install and configure service programs.

Now you are ready to create a new service.

# Creating a Windows Service

The service that you create will host a quote server. With every request that is made from a client, the quote server returns a random quote from a quote file. The first part of the solution uses three assemblies, one for the client and two for the server. Figure 36-4 gives an overview of the solution. The assembly QuoteServer holds the actual functionality. The service reads the quote file in a memory cache, and answers requests for quotes with the help of a socket server. The QuoteClient is a Windows Forms rich-client application. This application creates a client socket to communicate with the QuoteServer. The third assembly is the actual service. The QuoteService starts and stops the QuoteServer; the service controls the server:

Before creating the service part of your program, create a simple socket server in an extra C# class library that will be used from your service process.

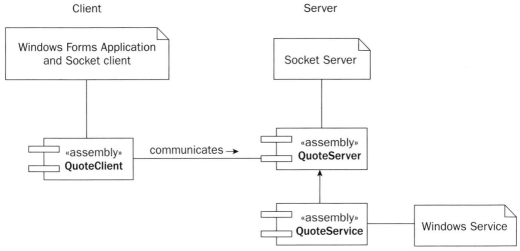

Figure 36-4

## A Class Library Using Sockets

You could build any functionality in the service, such as scanning for files to do a backup or a virus check or starting a .NET Remoting server, for example. However, all service programs share some similarities. The program must be able to start (and to return to the caller), stop, and suspend. This section looks at such an implementation using a socket server.

With Windows XP, the Simple TCP/IP Services can be installed as part of the Windows components. Part of the Simple TCP/IP Services is a "quote of the day," or qotd, TCP/IP server. This simple service listens to port 17 and answers every request with a random message from the file <windir>\system32\drivers\etc\quotes. With the sample service a similar server will be built. The sample server returns a Unicode string, in contrast to the good old qotd server that returns an ASCII string.

First, create a Class Library called QuoteServer and implement the code for the server. The following steps through the source code of your QuoteServer class in the file QuoteServer.cs:

```
using System;
using System.IO;
using System.Threading;
using System.Net;
using System.Net.Sockets;
using System.Text;
using System.Collections.Generic;

namespace Wrox.ProCSharp.WinServices
{
    public class QuoteServer
    {
        private TcpListener listener;
        private int port;
```

# Windows Services

```
private string filename;
private List<string> quotes;
private Random random;
private Thread listenerThread;
```

The constructor `QuoteServer()` is overloaded, so that a file name and a port can be passed to the call. The constructor where just the file name is passed uses the default port 7890 for the server. The default constructor defines the default file name for the quotes as quotes.txt:

```
public QuoteServer() : this ("quotes.txt")
{
}
public QuoteServer(string filename) : this(filename, 7890)
{
}
public QuoteServer(string filename, int port)
{
    this.filename = filename;
    this.port = port;
}
```

`ReadQuotes()` is a helper method that reads all the quotes from a file that was specified in the constructor. All the quotes are added to the `StringCollection` quotes. In addition, you are creating an instance of the `Random` class that will be used to return random quotes:

```
protected void ReadQuotes()
{
    quotes = new List<string>();
    Stream stream = File.OpenRead(filename);
    StreamReader streamReader = new StreamReader(stream);
    string quote;
    while ((quote = streamReader.ReadLine()) != null)
    {
        quotes.Add(quote);
    }
    streamReader.Close();
    stream.Close();
    random = new Random();
}
```

Another helper method is `GetRandomQuoteOfTheDay()`. This method returns a random quote from the `StringCollection` quotes:

```
protected string GetRandomQuoteOfTheDay()
{
    int index = random.Next(0, quotes.Count);
    return quotes[index];
}
```

In the `Start()` method, the complete file containing the quotes is read in the `StringCollection` quotes by using the helper method `ReadQuotes()`. After this, a new thread is started, which immediately calls the `Listener()` method — similar to the `TcpReceive` example in Chapter 35.

Here a thread is used because the `Start()` method cannot block and wait for a client; it must return immediately to the caller (SCM). The SCM would assume that the start failed if the method didn't return to the caller in a timely fashion (30 seconds). The listener thread is set as a background thread so that the application can exit without stopping this thread. The `Name` property of the thread is set because this helps with debugging, as the name will show up in the debugger:

```
public void Start()
{
   ReadQuotes();
   listenerThread = new Thread(
      new ThreadStart(ListenerThread));
   listenerThread.IsBackground = true;
   listenerThread.Name = "Listener";
   listenerThread.Start();
}
```

The thread function `ListenerThread()` creates a `TcpListener` instance. The `AcceptSocket()` method waits for a client to connect. As soon as a client connects, `AcceptSocket()` returns with a socket associated with the client. Next, `GetRandomQuoteOfTheDay()` is called to send the returned random quote to the client using `socket.Send()`:

```
protected void ListenerThread()
{
   try
   {
      IPAddress ipAddress = Dns.GetHostEntry("localhost").AddressList[0];
      listener = new TcpListener(ipAddress, port);
      listener.Start();
      while (true)
      {
         Socket clientSocket = listener.AcceptSocket();
         string message = GetRandomQuoteOfTheDay();
         UnicodeEncoding encoder = new UnicodeEncoding();
         byte[] buffer = encoder.GetBytes(message);
         clientSocket.Send(buffer, buffer.Length, 0);
         clientSocket.Close();
      }
   }
   catch (SocketException ex)
   {
      Console.WriteLine(ex.Message);
   }
}
```

In addition to the `Start()` method, the following methods are needed to control the service: `Stop()`, `Suspend()`, and `Resume()`:

```
public void Stop()
{
   listener.Stop();
}
```

# Windows Services

```csharp
        public void Suspend()
        {
            listener.Stop();
        }
        public void Resume()
        {
            Start();
        }
```

Another method that will be publicly available is `RefreshQuotes()`. If the file containing the quotes changes, the file is re-read with this method:

```csharp
        public void RefreshQuotes()
        {
            ReadQuotes();
        }
    }
}
```

Before building a service around the server, it is useful to build a test program that just creates an instance of the `QuoteServer` and calls `Start()`. This way, you can test the functionality without the need to handle service-specific issues. This test server must be started manually, and you can easily walk through the code with a debugger.

The test program is a C# console application, `TestQuoteServer`. You have to reference the assembly of the `QuoteServer` class. The file containing the quotes must be copied to the directory c:\ProCSharp\Services (or you have to change the argument in the constructor to specify where you have copied the file). After calling the constructor, the `Start()` method of the `QuoteServer` instance is called. `Start()` returns immediately after having created a thread, so the console application keeps running until `Return` is pressed:

```csharp
        static void Main(string[] args)
        {
            QuoteServer qs = new QuoteServer(
                @"c:\ProCSharp\WindowsServices\quotes.txt", 4567);
            qs.Start();
            Console.WriteLine("Hit return to exit");
            Console.ReadLine();
            qs.Stop();
        }
```

Note that `QuoteServer` will be running on port 4567 on localhost using this program—you will have to use these settings in the client later.

## TcpClient Example

The client is a simple Windows application where you can enter the host name and the port number of the server. This application uses the `TcpClient` class to connect to the running server, and receives the returned message, displaying it in a multiline text box. There's also a status strip at the bottom of the form (see Figure 36-5).

Figure 36-5

You have to add the following `using` directives to your code:

```
using System;
using System.Drawing;
using System.Collections;
using System.ComponentModel;
using System.Windows.Forms;
using System.Data;
using System.Net;
using System.Net.Sockets;
using System.Text;
```

The remainder of the code is automatically generated by the IDE, so we won't go into detail here. The major functionality of the client lies in the handler for the click event of the Get Quote button:

```
protected void OnGetQuote(object sender, System.EventArgs e)
{
    statusStrip.Text = "";
    string server = textHostname.Text;
    try
    {
        int port = Convert.ToInt32(textPortNumber.Text);
    }
    catch (FormatException ex)
    {
        statusStrip.Text = ex.Message;
        return;
    }
    TcpClient client = new TcpClient();
    NetworkStream stream = null;
    try
    {
        client.Connect(textHostname.Text,
                    Convert.ToInt32(textPortNumber.Text));
```

# Windows Services

```
        stream = client.GetStream();
        byte[] buffer = new Byte[1024];
        int received = stream.Read(buffer, 0, 1024);
        if (received <= 0)
        {
            statusStrip.Text = "Read failed";
            return;
        }
        textQuote.Text = Encoding.Unicode.GetString(buffer);
    }
    catch (SocketException ex)
    {
        statusStrip.Text = ex.Message;
    }
    finally
    {
        if (stream != null)
            stream.Close();
        if (client.IsConnected)
            client.Close();
    }
}
```

After starting the test server and this Windows application client, you can test the functionality. Figure 36-6 shows a successful run of this application.

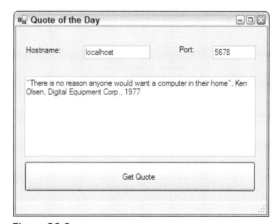

**Figure 36-6**

Next you implement the service functionality in the server. The program is already running, so what else do you need? Well, the server program should be automatically started at boot-time without anyone logged on to the system. You want to control this by using service control programs.

## *Windows Service Project*

Using the new project wizard for C# Windows Services, you can now start to create a Windows Service. For the new service use the name QuoteService (see Figure 36-7).

1281

# Chapter 36

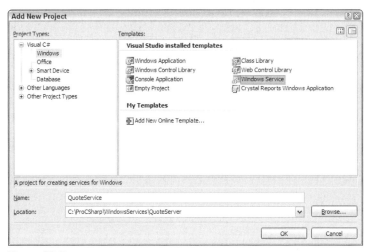

Figure 36-7

After you click the OK button to create the Windows Service application, you will see the Designer surface (just like with Windows Forms applications). However, you can't insert any Windows Forms components, because the application cannot directly display anything on the screen. The Designer surface is used later in this chapter to add other components, such as performance counters and event logging.

Selecting the properties of this service opens up the Properties editor window (see Figure 36-8).

Figure 36-8

# Windows Services

With the service properties, you can configure the following values:

- `AutoLog` specifies that events are automatically written to the event log for starting and stopping the service.
- `CanPauseAndContinue`, `CanShutdown`, and `CanStop` specify pause, continue, shutdown, and stop requests.
- `ServiceName` is the name of the service written to the registry and is used to control the service.
- `CanHandlePowerEvent` is a very useful option for services running on a laptop. If this option is enabled, the service can react to low power events, and change the behavior of the service accordingly.

> The default service name is `WinService1`, regardless of what the project is called. You can install only one WinService1 service. If you get installation errors during your testing process, you might already have installed one WinService1 service. Therefore, make sure that you change the name of the service with the Properties editor to a more suitable name at the beginning of the service development.

Changing these properties with the Properties editor sets the values of your `ServiceBase`-derived class in the `InitalizeComponent()` method. You already know this method from Windows Forms applications. With services it's used in a similar way.

A wizard generates the code, but change the file name to `QuoteService.cs`, the name of the namespace to `Wrox.ProCSharp.WinServices`, and the class name to `QuoteService`. The code of the service is discussed in detail shortly.

## The ServiceBase class

The `ServiceBase` class is the base class for all Windows services developed with the .NET Framework. The class `QuoteService` derives from `ServiceBase`; this class communicates with the SCM using an undocumented helper class, `System.ServiceProcess.NativeMethods`, which is just a wrapper class to the Win32 API calls. The class is private, so it cannot be used in your code.

The sequence diagram in Figure 36-9 shows the interaction of the SCM, the class `QuoteService`, and the classes from the `System.ServiceProcess` namespace. In the sequence diagram you can see the lifelines of objects vertically and the communication going on in the horizontal direction. The communication is time-ordered from top to bottom.

The SCM starts the process of a service that should be started. At startup, the `Main()` method is called. In the `Main()` method of the sample service the `Run()` method of the base class `ServiceBase` is called. `Run()` registers the method `ServiceMainCallback()` using `NativeMethods.StartServiceCtrlDispatcher()` in the SCM and writes an entry to the event log.

Next, the SCM calls the registered method `ServiceMainCallback()` in the service program. `ServiceMainCallback()` itself registers the handler in the SCM using `NativeMethods.RegisterServiceCtrlHandler[Ex]()` and sets the status of the service in the SCM. Then the `OnStart()` method is called. In `OnStart()` you have to implement the startup code. If `OnStart()` is successful, the string "Service started successfully" is written to the event log.

1283

# Chapter 36

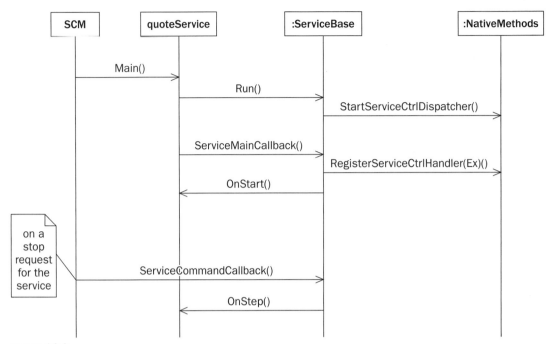

Figure 36-9

The handler is implemented in the `ServiceCommandCallback()` method. The SCM calls this method when changes are requested from the service. The `ServiceCommandCallback()` method routes the requests further to `OnPause()`, `OnContinue()`, `OnStop()`, `OnCustomCommand()`, and `OnPowerEvent()`.

## Main function

This section looks into the application wizard–generated main function of the service process. In the main function, an array of `ServiceBase` classes, `ServicesToRun`, is declared. One instance of the `QuoteService` class is created and passed as the first element to the `ServicesToRun` array. If more than one service should run inside this service process, it is necessary to add more instances of the specific service classes to the array. This array is then passed to the static `Run()` method of the `ServiceBase` class. With the `Run()` method of `ServiceBase`, you are giving the SCM references to the entry points of your services. The main thread of your service process is now blocked and waits for the service to terminate.

Here's the automatically generated code:

```
// The main entry point for the process
static void Main()
{
    ServiceBase[] ServicesToRun;

    // More than one user Service may run within the same process. To
    // add another service to this process, change the following line
    // to create a second service object. For example,
    //
```

1284

# Windows Services

```
    //    ServicesToRun = New System.ServiceProcess.ServiceBase[]
    //    {
    //       new Service1(), new MySecondUserService()
    //    };
    //
    ServicesToRun = new ServiceBase[]
    {
       new QuoteService()
    };
    ServiceBase.Run(ServicesToRun);
}
```

If there's only a single service in the process, the array can be removed; the `Run()` method accepts a single object derived from the class `ServiceBase`, so the `Main()` method can be reduced to this:

```
System.ServiceProcess.ServiceBase.Run(new QuoteService());
```

The service program Services.exe includes multiple services. If you have a similar service where more than one service is running in a single process where you must initialize some shared state for multiple services, the shared initialization must be done before the `Run()` method. With the `Run()` method the main thread is blocked until the service process is stopped, and any following instructions would not be reached before the end of the service.

The initialization shouldn't take longer than 30 seconds. If the initialization code were to take longer than this, the service control manager would assume that the service startup failed. You have to take into account the slowest machines where this service should run within the 30-second limit. If the initialization takes longer, you could start the initialization in a different thread so that the main thread calls `Run()` in time. An event object can then be used to signal that the thread has completed its work.

## Service start

At service start the `OnStart()` method is called. In this method, you can start the previously created socket server. You must reference the QuoteServer assembly for the use of the QuoteService. The thread calling `OnStart()` cannot be blocked; this method must return to the caller, which is the `ServiceMainCallback()` method of the `ServiceBase` class. The `ServiceBase` class registers the handler and informs the SCM that the service started successfully after calling `OnStart()`:

```
protected override void OnStart(string[] args)
{
    quoteServer = new QuoteServer(
        @"c:\ProCSharp\WindowsServices\quotes.txt", 5678);
    quoteServer.Start();
}
```

The `quoteServer` variable is declared as a private member in the class:

```
namespace Wrox.ProCSharp.WinServices
{
    public partial class QuoteService : ServiceBase
    {
        private QuoteServer quoteServer;
```

## Handler methods

When the service is stopped, the `OnStop()` method is called. You should stop the service functionality in this method:

```
protected override void OnStop()
{
    quoteServer.Stop();
}
```

In addition to `OnStart()` and `OnStop()`, you can override the following handlers in the service class:

- `OnPause()` is called when the service should be paused.
- `OnContinue()` is called when the service should return to normal operation after being paused. To make it possible for the overridden methods `OnPause()` and `OnContinue()` to be called, the `CanPauseAndContinue` property must be set to `true`.
- `OnShutdown()` is called when Windows is undergoing system shutdown. Normally, the behavior of this method should be similar to the `OnStop()` implementation; if more time were needed for a shutdown, you can request additional time. Similar to `OnPause()` and `OnContinue()`, a property must be set to enable this behavior: `CanShutdown` must be set to `true`.
- `OnCustomCommand()` is a handler that can serve custom commands that are sent by a service control program. The method signature of `OnCustomCommand()` has an int argument where you get the custom command number. The value can be in the range from 128 to 256; values below 128 are system-reserved values. In your service you are re-reading the quotes file with the custom command 128:

```
protected override void OnPause()
{
    quoteServer.Suspend();
}
protected override void OnContinue()
{
    quoteServer.Resume();
}
protected override void OnShutdown()
{
    OnStop();
}
public const int commandRefresh = 128;
protected override void OnCustomCommand(int command)
{
    switch (command)
    {
        case commandRefresh:
            quoteServer.RefreshQuotes();
            break;
        default:
            break;
    }
}
```

# Windows Services

## Threading and Services

With services, you have to deal with threads. As stated earlier, the SCM will assume that the service failed if the initialization takes too long. To deal with this, you have to create a thread.

The `OnStart()` method in your service class must return in time. If you call a blocking method like `AcceptSocket()` from the `TcpListener` class, you have to start a thread for doing this. With a networking server that deals with multiple clients, a thread pool is also very useful. `AcceptSocket()` should receive the call and hand the processing off to another thread from the pool. This way, no one waits for the execution of code and the system seems responsive.

## Service Installation

A service must be configured in the registry. All services can be found in HKEY_LOCAL_MACHINE\System\CurrentControlSet\Services. You can view the registry entries by using `regedit`. The type of the service, display name, path to the executable, startup configuration, and so on are all found here. Figure 36-10 shows the registry configuration of the Alerter service.

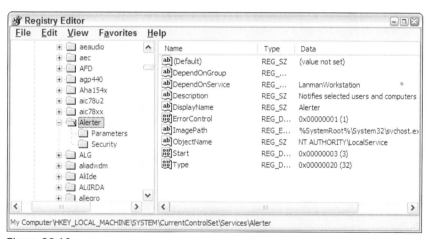

Figure 36-10

This configuration can be done by using the installer classes from the `System.ServiceProcess` namespace, as discussed in the following section.

## Installation Program

You can add an installation program to the service by switching to the design view with Visual Studio and then selecting the Add Installer option from the context menu. With this option a new `ProjectInstaller` class is created, and a `ServiceInstaller` and a `ServiceProcessInstaller` instance are created.

Figure 36-11 shows the class diagram of the installer classes for services.

With this diagram in mind, let's go through the source code in the file ProjectInstaller.cs that was created with the Add Installer option.

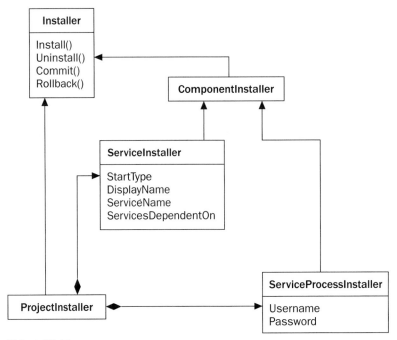

Figure 36-11

## The Installer class

The class `ProjectInstaller` is derived from `System.Configuration.Install.Installer`. This is the base class for all custom installers. With the `Installer` class, it's possible to build transaction-based installations. With a transaction-based installation, it's possible to roll back to the previous state if the installation fails, and any changes made by this installation up to that point will be undone. As you can see in Figure 36-11, the `Installer` class has `Install()`, `Commit()`, `Rollback()`, and `Uninstall()` methods, and they are called from installation programs.

The attribute `[RunInstaller(true)]` means that the class `ProjectInstaller` should be invoked when installing an assembly. Custom action installers as well as installutil.exe (which will be used later) check for this attribute.

Similar to Windows Forms applications, `InitializeComponent()` is called inside the constructor of the `ProjectInstaller` class:

```
using System;
using System.Collections;
using System.ComponentModel;
using System.Configuration.Install;

namespace Wrox.ProCSharp.WinServices
{
    [RunInstaller(true)]
    public partial class ProjectInstaller : Installer
```

# Windows Services

```
    {
        public ProjectInstaller()
        {
            InitializeComponent();
        }
    }
}
```

## The ServiceProcessInstaller and ServiceInstaller classes

Within the implementation of `InitializeComponent()`, instances of the `ServiceProcessInstaller` class and the `ServiceInstaller` class are created. Both of these classes derive from the `ComponentInstaller` class, which itself derives from `Installer`.

Classes derived from `ComponentInstaller` can be used with an installation process. Remember that a service process can include more than one service. The `ServiceProcessInstaller` class is used for the configuration of the process that defines values for all services in this process, and the `ServiceInstaller` class is for the configuration of the service, so one instance of `ServiceInstaller` is required for each service. If three services are inside the process, you have to add `ServiceInstaller` objects — three `ServiceInstaller` instances are needed in that case.

```
    partial class ProjectInstaller
    {
        /// <summary>
        ///    Required designer variable.
        /// </summary>
        private System.ComponentModel.Container components = null;

        /// <summary>
        ///    Required method for Designer support - do not modify
        ///    the contents of this method with the code editor.
        /// </summary>
        private void InitializeComponent()
        {
            this.serviceProcessInstaller1 =
                    new System.ServiceProcess.ServiceProcessInstaller();
            this.serviceInstaller1 =
                    new System.ServiceProcess.ServiceInstaller();
            //
            // serviceProcessInstaller1
            //
            this.serviceProcessInstaller1.Password = null;
            this.serviceProcessInstaller1.Username = null;
            //
            // serviceInstaller1
            //
            this.serviceInstaller1.ServiceName = "QuoteService";
            //
            // ProjectInstaller
            //
            this.Installers.AddRange(
               new System.Configuration.Install.Installer[]
                  {this.serviceProcessInstaller1,
                   this.serviceInstaller1});
```

```
            }
            private System.ServiceProcess.ServiceProcessInstaller
                        serviceProcessInstaller1;
            private System.ServiceProcess.ServiceInstaller serviceInstaller1;
    }
```

`ServiceProcessInstaller` installs an executable that implements the class `ServiceBase`. `ServiceProcessInstaller` has properties for the complete process. The following table explains the properties shared by all the services inside the process.

| Property | Description |
| --- | --- |
| Username, Password | Indicates the user account under which the service runs if the `Account` property is set to `ServiceAccount.User`. |
| Account | With this property you can specify the account type of the service. |
| HelpText | `HelpText` is a read-only property that returns the help text for setting the username and password. |

The process that is used to run the service can be specified with the `Account` property of the `ServiceProcessInstaller` class using the `ServiceAccount` enumeration. The following table explains the different values of the `Account` property.

| Value | Meaning |
| --- | --- |
| LocalSystem | Setting this value specifies that the service uses a highly privileged user account on the local system, but this account presents an anonymous user to the network. Thus it doesn't have rights on the network. |
| LocalService | This account type presents the computer's credentials to any remote server. |
| NetworkService | Similar to `LocalService`, this value specifies that the computer's credentials are passed to remote servers, but unlike `LocalService` such a service acts as a non-privileged user on the local system. As the name implies, this account should be used only for services that need resources from the network. |
| User | Setting the `Account` property to `ServiceAccount.User` means that you can define the account that should be used from the service. |

`ServiceInstaller` is the class needed for every service; it has the following properties for each service inside a process: `StartType`, `DisplayName`, `ServiceName`, and `ServicesDependedOn`, as described in the following table.

# Windows Services

| Property | Description |
|---|---|
| StartType | The StartType property indicates whether the service is manually or automatically started. Possible values are ServiceStartMode.Automatic, ServiceStartMode.Manual, and ServiceStartMode.Disabled. With ServiceStartMode.Disabled the service cannot be started. This option is useful for services that shouldn't be started on a system. You might want to set the option to Disabled if, for example, a required hardware controller is not available. |
| DisplayName | DisplayName is the friendly name of the service that is displayed to the user. This name is also used by management tools that control and monitor the service. |
| ServiceName | ServiceName is the name of the service. This value must be identical to the ServiceName property of the ServiceBase class in the service program. This name associates the configuration of the ServiceInstaller to the required service program. |
| ServicesDependentOn | Specifies an array of services that must be started before this service can be started. When the service is started, all these dependent services are started automatically, and then your service will start. |

> If you change the name of the service in the ServiceBase-derived class, also change the ServiceName property in the ServiceInstaller object!

*In the testing phases, set StartType to Manual. This way, if you can't stop the service (for example, when it has a bug), you still have the possibility to reboot the system. But if you have StartType set to Automatic, the service would be started automatically with the reboot! You can change this configuration at a later time when you're sure that it works.*

## *The ServiceInstallerDialog class*

Another installer class in the System.ServiceProcess.Design namespace is ServiceInstallerDialog. This class can be used if you want the System Administrator to enter the username and password during the installation.

If you set the Account property of the class ServiceProcessInstaller to ServiceAccount.User and the Username and Password properties to null, you will see the Set Service Login dialog box at installation time (see Figure 36-12). You can also cancel the installation at this point.

## *installutil*

After adding the installer classes to the project, you can use the installutil.exe utility to install and uninstall the service. This utility can be used to install any assembly that has an Installer class. The installutil.exe utility calls the method Install() of the class that derives from the Installer class for installation, and Uninstall() for the *deinstallation*.

# Chapter 36

Figure 36-12

The command-line inputs for the installation and deinstallation of our service are:

```
installutil quoteservice.exe
installutil /u quoteservice.exe
```

> If the installation fails, be sure to check the installation log files InstallUtil.InstallLog and <servicename>.InstallLog. Often you can find very useful information, such as "The specified service already exists."

## Client

After the service has been successfully installed, you can start the service manually from the Services MMC (see next section for further details), and then you can start the client application. Figure 36-13 shows the client accessing the service.

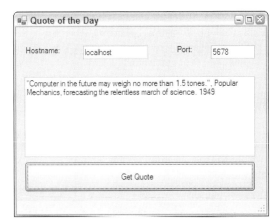

Figure 36-13

# Monitoring and Controlling the Service

To monitor and control services you can use the Services MMC snap-in that is part of the Computer Management administration tool. With every Windows system you also get a command-line utility,

1292

# Windows Services

net.exe, which allows you to control services. Another command-line utility is sc.exe. This utility has much more functionality than net.exe, which is part of the Platform SDK. In this section you create a small Windows application that makes use of the `System.ServiceProcess.ServiceController` class to monitor and control services.

## MMC Computer Management

Using the Services snap-in to the Microsoft Management Console (MMC), you can view the status of all services (see Figure 36-14). It's also possible to send control requests to services to stop, enable, or disable them, as well as to change their configuration. The Services snap-in is a service control program as well as a service configuration program.

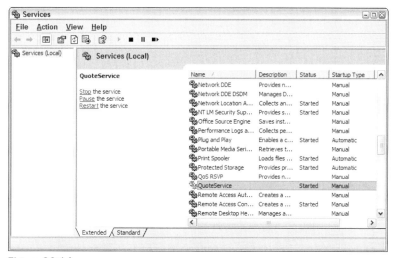

Figure 36-14

If you double-click QuoteService, you'll get the Properties dialog box shown in Figure 36-15. This dialog box enables you to view the service name, the description, the path to the executable, the startup type, and the status. The service is currently started. The account for the service process can be changed with the Log On tab in this dialog.

## net.exe

The Services snap-in is easy to use, but the system administrator cannot automate it, because it's not usable within an administrative script. To control services, you can use the command-line utility net.exe: net start shows all running services, net start servicename starts a service, net stop servicename sends a stop request to the service. It's also possible to pause and to continue a service with net pause and net continue (only if the service allows it, of course).

Figure 36-16 shows the result of net start in the console window.

1293

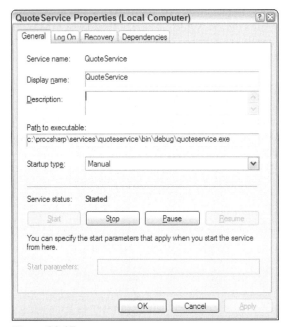

Figure 36-15

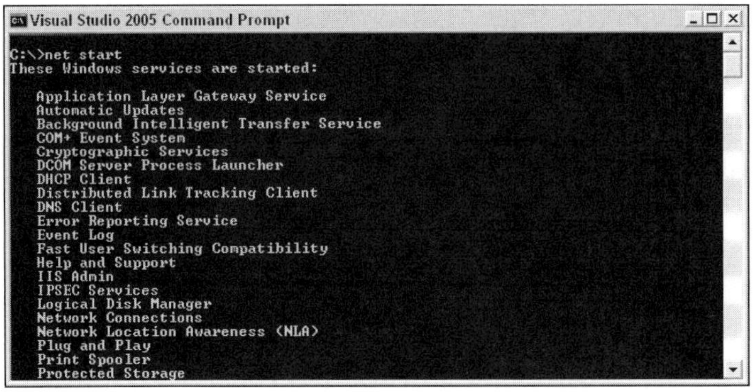

Figure 36-16

## sc.exe

There's a little-known utility delivered with Visual Studio, but starting with Windows XP is also part of the operating system: sc.exe.

sc.exe is a great tool to play with services. A lot more can be done with sc.exe compared to the net.exe utility. With sc.exe, it's possible to check the actual status of a service, or configure, remove, and add services as Figure 36-17 shows. This tool also facilitates the deinstallation of the service, if it fails to function correctly.

# Windows Services

Figure 36-17

## Visual Studio Server Explorer

It is also possible to control services using the Server Explorer within Visual Studio; Services is below Servers and the name of your computer. By selecting a service and opening the context menu a service can be started and stopped. This context menu can also be used to add a `ServiceController` class to the project. If you want to control a specific service in your application, drag and drop a service from the Server Explorer to the Designer: a `ServiceController` instance is added to the application. The properties of this object are automatically set to access the selected service, and the assembly System.ServiceProcess is referenced. You can use this instance to control a service in the same way as you can with the application that you develop in the next section.

## ServiceController Class

In this section, you create a small Windows application that uses the `ServiceController` class to monitor and control Windows Services.

Create a Windows Forms application with a user interface (see Figure 36-18). The user interface of this application has a list box to show all services, four text boxes to display the display name, status, type, and name of the service, and four buttons to send control events.

Because the class `System.ServiceProcess.ServiceController` is used, you must reference the assembly System.ServiceProcess.

# Chapter 36

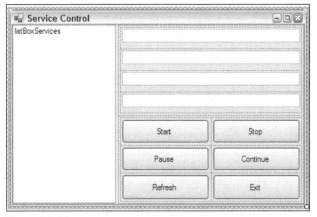

**Figure 36-18**

Create and implement the method `RefreshServiceList()` that lists all services in the list box with the following code. This method is called within the constructor of the class `ServiceControlForm`. In the implementation this method fills a `ListBox` control with the display names of all services. `GetServices()` is a static method of the `ServiceController` class, and it returns a `ServiceController` array representing all Windows Services. The `ServiceController` class also has the static method `GetDevices()` that returns a `ServiceController` array representing all device drivers.

The `ListBox` is filled by simply binding `ServiceController.GetServices()` to the `ListBox`:

```
private System.ServiceProcess.ServiceController[] services;

public ServiceControlForm()
{
    InitializeComponent();
    RefreshServiceList();
}
protected void RefreshServiceList()
{
    services = ServiceController.GetServices();
    listBoxServices.DisplayMember = "DisplayName";
    listBoxServices.DataSource = services;
}
```

Now, all Windows Services are displayed in the list box. Next, you must get the information about a service that is displayed in the text boxes.

## Monitoring the service

Using the `ServiceController` class, you can get the information about each service. The following table shows the properties of the `ServiceController` class.

1296

# Windows Services

| Property | Description |
|---|---|
| CanPauseAndContinue | If pause and continue requests can be sent to the service, true is returned. |
| CanShutdown | Returns true if the service has a handler for a system shutdown. |
| CanStop | Returns true if the service is stoppable. |
| DependentServices | Returns a collection of dependent services. If the service is stopped, all dependent services are stopped beforehand. |
| ServicesDependentOn | Returns a collection of the services that this service depends on. |
| DisplayName | Specifies the name that should be displayed for this service. |
| MachineName | Specifies the name of the machine that the service runs on. |
| ServiceName | Specifies the name of the service. |
| ServiceType | Specifies the type of the service. The service can be run inside a shared process where more than one service uses the same process (Win32ShareProcess), or run in that way that there's just one service in a process (Win32OwnProcess). If the service can interact with the desktop, the type is InteractiveProcess. |
| Status | Specifies the status of the service. The status can be running, stopped, paused, or in some intermediate mode like start pending, stop pending, and so on. The status values are defined in the enumeration ServiceControllerStatus. |

In the sample application, the properties DisplayName, ServiceName, ServiceType, and Status are used to display the service information. Also, CanPauseAndContinue and CanStop are used to enable or disable the Pause, Continue, and Stop buttons.

The status and type of the service cannot be set that easily because a string should be displayed instead of a number, which is what the ServiceController class returns. To get a string for the status and type two helper functions are implemented: SetServiceStatus() and GetServiceTypeName().

The method GetServiceTypeName() returns a string that represents the type of the service. Depending on the type that is passed with the ServiceType argument, a string is returned. The ServiceType you get from the property ServiceController.ServiceType represents a set of flags that can be combined by using the bitwise OR operator. The InteractiveProcess bit can be set together with Win32OwnProcess and Win32ShareProcess. So at first it checks if the InteractiveProcess bit is set before continuing to check for the other values. With services the string returned will be "Win32 Service Process", or "Win32 Shared Process":

```
protected string GetServiceTypeName(ServiceType type)
{
    string serviceType = "";
    if ((type & ServiceType.InteractiveProcess) != 0)
    {
        serviceType = "Interactive ";
        type -= ServiceType.InteractiveProcess;
```

```csharp
            }
            switch (type)
            {
                case ServiceType.Adapter:
                    serviceType += "Adapter";
                    break;
                case ServiceType.FileSystemDriver:
                case ServiceType.KernelDriver:
                case ServiceType.RecognizerDriver:
                    serviceType += "Driver";
                    break;
                case ServiceType.Win32OwnProcess:
                    serviceType += "Win32 Service Process";
                    break;
                case ServiceType.Win32ShareProcess:
                    serviceType += "Win32 Shared Process";
                    break;
                default:
                    serviceType += "unknown type " + type.ToString();
                    break;
            }
            return serviceType;
        }
```

The method `SetServiceStatus()` sets the current status of the service in the text box `textServiceStatus`. Also, the Start/Stop/Pause/Continue buttons will be enabled or disabled depending on the status of the service:

```csharp
        protected void SetServiceStatus(ServiceController controller)
        {
            buttonStart.Enabled = true;
            buttonStop.Enabled = true;
            buttonPause.Enabled = true;
            buttonContinue.Enabled = true;
            if (!controller.CanPauseAndContinue)
            {
                buttonPause.Enabled = false;
                buttonContinue.Enabled = false;
            }
            if (!controller.CanStop)
            {
                buttonStop.Enabled = false;
            }
            ServiceControllerStatus status = controller.Status;
            switch (status)
            {
                case ServiceControllerStatus.ContinuePending:
                    textServiceStatus.Text = "Continue Pending";
                    buttonContinue.Enabled = false;
                    break;
                case ServiceControllerStatus.Paused:
                    textServiceStatus.Text = "Paused";
```

# Windows Services

```csharp
                buttonPause.Enabled = false;
                buttonStart.Enabled = false;
                break;
            case ServiceControllerStatus.PausePending:
                textServiceStatus.Text = "Pause Pending";
                buttonPause.Enabled = false;
                buttonStart.Enabled = false;
                break;
            case ServiceControllerStatus.StartPending:
                textServiceStatus.Text = "Start Pending";
                buttonStart.Enabled = false;
                break;
            case ServiceControllerStatus.Running:
                textServiceStatus.Text = "Running";
                buttonStart.Enabled = false;
                buttonContinue.Enabled = false;
                break;
            case ServiceControllerStatus.Stopped:
                textServiceStatus.Text = "Stopped";
                buttonStop.Enabled = false;
                break;
            case ServiceControllerStatus.StopPending:
                textServiceStatus.Text = "Stop Pending";
                buttonStop.Enabled = false;
                break;
            default:
                textServiceStatus.Text = "Unknown status";
                break;
        }
    }
```

`OnSelectedIndexChanged()` is the handler for the `ListBox` event `SelectedIndexChanged`. This handler is called when the user selects a service in the `ListBox` event. In `OnSelectedIndexChanged()` the display and the service name is set directly with properties of the `ServiceController` class. The service type is set by calling the helper method `GetServiceTypeName()`:

```csharp
    protected void OnSelectedIndexChanged (object sender,
            System.EventArgs e)
    {
        ServiceController controller =
                (ServiceController)listBoxServices.SelectedItem;
        textDisplayName.Text = controller.DisplayName;
        textServiceType.Text = GetServiceTypeName(controller.ServiceType);
        textServiceName.Text = controller.ServiceName;
        SetServiceStatus(controller);
    }
```

## Controlling the service

With the `ServiceController` class, you can also send control requests to the service. The following table explains the methods that can be applied.

## Chapter 36

| Method | Description |
|---|---|
| Start() | Start() tells the SCM that the service should be started. In the example service program OnStart() is called. |
| Stop() | Stop() calls OnStop() in the example service program with the help of the SCM if the property CanStop is true in the service class. |
| Pause() | Pause() calls OnPause() if the property CanPauseAndContinue is true. |
| Continue() | Continue calls OnContinue() if the property CanPauseAndContinue is true. |
| ExecuteCommand() | With ExecuteCommand() it's possible to send a custom command to the service. |

The following code controls the services. Because the code for starting, stopping, suspending, and pausing is similar, only one handler is used for the four buttons:

```
protected void buttonCommand_Click(object sender, System.EventArgs e)
{
    Cursor.Current = Cursors.WaitCursor;
    ServiceController controller =
                    (ServiceController)listBoxServices.SelectedItem;
    if (sender == this.buttonStart)
    {
        controller.Start();
        controller.WaitForStatus(ServiceControllerStatus.Running);
    }
    else if (sender == this.buttonStop)
    {
        controller.Stop();
        controller.WaitForStatus(ServiceControllerStatus.Stopped);
    }
    else if (sender == this.buttonPause)
    {
        controller.Pause();
        controller.WaitForStatus(ServiceControllerStatus.Paused);
    }
    else if (sender == this.buttonContinue)
    {
        controller.Continue();
        controller.WaitForStatus(ServiceControllerStatus.Running);
    }
    int index =listBoxServices.SelectedIndex;
    RefreshServiceList();
    listBoxServices.SelectedIndex = index;
    Cursor.Current = Cursors.Default;
}

protected void buttonExit_Click(object sender, System.EventArgs e)
{
    Application.Exit();
}
```

# Windows Services

```
protected void buttonRefresh_Click(object sender, System.EventArgs e)
{
   RefreshServiceList();
}
```

Because the action of controlling the services can take some time, the cursor is switched to the wait cursor in the first statement. Then a `ServiceController` method is called depending on the pressed button. With the `WaitForStatus()` method, you are waiting to check that the service changes the status to the requested value, but you only wait 10 seconds maximum. After this time, the information in the `ListBox` is refreshed; and the same service as before is selected, and the new status of this service is displayed.

Figure 36-19 shows the completed, running application.

**Figure 36-19**

## Troubleshooting

Troubleshooting services is different from troubleshooting normal applications. This section covers troubleshooting topics such as:

- ❏ The problems of interactive services
- ❏ Event logging
- ❏ Performance monitoring

The best way to start building a service is to create an assembly with the functionality you want and a test client, before the service is actually created. Here you can do normal debugging and error handling. As soon as the application is running, you can build a service by using this assembly. Of course, there might still be problems with the service:

- ❏ Don't display errors in a message box from the service (except for interactive services that are running on the client system). Instead, use the event logging service to write errors to the event log. Of course, you can display a message box to inform the user about errors in the client application that uses the service.

# Chapter 36

- The service cannot be started from within a debugger, but a debugger can be attached to the running service process. Open the solution with the source code of the service and set breakpoints. From the Visual Studio Debug menu, select Processes and attach the running process of the service.

- The Performance Monitor can be used to monitor the activity of services. You can add your own performance objects to the service. This can add some useful information for debugging. For example, with the Quote service, you could set up an object to give the total number of quotes returned, the time it takes to initialize, and so on.

## Interactive Services

If an interactive service runs with a logged-on user it can be helpful to display message boxes to the user. If the service should run on a server that is locked inside a computer room, the service should never display a message box. When you open a message box to wait for some user input, the user input probably won't happen for some days because nobody is looking at the server in the computer room; but it can get even worse than that: If the service isn't configured as an interactive service, the message box opens up on a different, hidden, window station. In this case, no one can answer that message box because it is hidden and the service is blocked.

> Never open dialog boxes for services running on a server system. Nobody will answer them.

In cases where you really want to interact with the user, an interactive service can be configured. Some examples of such interactive services are the Print Spooler that displays paper-out messages to the user, and the NetMeeting Remote Desktop Sharing service.

To configure an interactive service, you must set the option "Allow service to interact with desktop" in the Services configuration tool (see Figure 36-20). This changes the type of the service by adding the `SERVICE_INTERACTIVE_PROCESS` flag to the type.

## Event Logging

Services can report errors and other information by adding events to the event log. A service class derived from `ServiceBase` automatically logs events when the `AutoLog` property is set to `true`. The `ServiceBase` class checks this property and writes a log entry at start, stop, pause, and continue requests.

In this section, you explore the following:

- Error-logging architecture
- Classes for event logging from the `System.Diagnostics` namespace
- Adding event logging to services and to other application types
- Creating an event-log listener with the `EnableRaisingEvents` property of the `EventLog` class

Figure 36-21 shows an example of a log entry from a service.

## Windows Services

**Figure 36-20**

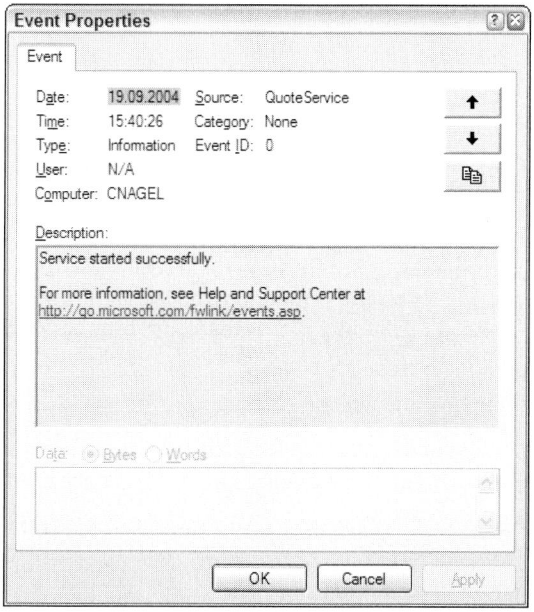

**Figure 36-21**

For custom event logging, you can use classes from the `System.Diagnostics` namespace.

# Chapter 36

## *Event Logging architecture*

By default, the event log is stored in three log files: Application, Security, and System. Looking at the registry configuration of the event log service, you'll notice three entries under HKEY_LOCAL_MACHINE\System\CurrentControlSet\Services\Eventlog with configurations pointing to the specific files. The System log file is used from the system and device drivers. Applications and services write to the Application log. The Security log is a read-only log for applications. The auditing feature of the operating system uses the Security log.

You can read these events by using the administrative tool Event Viewer. The Event Viewer can be started directly from the Server Explorer of Visual Studio by right-clicking on the Event Logs item and selecting the Launch Event Viewer entry from the context menu. The Event Viewer is shown in Figure 36-22.

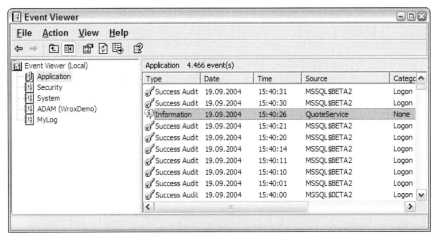

Figure 36-22

In the event log, you can see this information:

- ❑ The type can be Information, Warning, or Error. Information is an infrequent successful operation, Warning a problem that's not immediately significant, and Error a major problem. Additional types are FailureAudit and SuccessAudit, but these types are used only for the Security log.

- ❑ Date and Time show the time when the event occurred.

- ❑ The Source is the name of the software that logs the event. The source for the Application log is configured in:

    HKEY_LOCAL_MACHINE\System\CurrentControlSet\Services\ Eventlog\Application\ [ApplicationName]

- ❑ Below this key the value EventMessageFile is configured to point to a resource DLL that holds error messages.

- ❑ A Category can be defined so that event logs can be filtered when using the Event Viewer. Categories can be defined by an event source.

- ❑ The Event identifier specifies a particular event message.

# Windows Services

## Event Logging classes

The `System.Diagnostics` namespace has some classes for event logging:

- With the `EventLog` class you can read and write entries in the event log, and establish applications as event sources.
- The `EventLogEntry` class represents a single entry in the event log. With the `EventLogEntryCollection` you can iterate through `EventLogEntry` items.
- The `EventLogInstaller` class is the installer for an `EventLog` component. `EventLogInstaller` calls `EventLog.CreateEventSource()` to create an event source.
- With the help of the `EventLogTraceListener`, traces can be written to the event log. This class implements the abstract class `TraceListener`.

## Adding event logging

If the `AutoLog` property of the `ServiceBase` class is set to `true`, event logging is automatically turned on. The `ServiceBase` class logs an informational event at startup, stop, pause, and continue requests of the service. In the `ServiceInstaller` class an `EventLogInstaller` instance is created so that an event log source is configured. This event log source has the same name as the service. If you want to write events you can use the `WriteEntry()` method of the `EventLog` class. The `Source` property was already set in the `ServiceBase` class:

```
eventLog.WriteEntry("event log message");
```

This method logs an informational event. If warning or error events should be created, an overloaded method of `WriteEvent()` can be used to specify the type:

```
eventLog.WriteEntry("event log message", EventLogEntryType.Warning);
eventLog.WriteEntry("event log message", EventLogEntryType.Error);
```

## Adding event logging to other application types

With services, the `ServiceBase` class automatically adds event-logging features. If you would like to use event logging within other application types, you can easily do that by using Visual Studio.

- Use the toolbox to add an EventLog component to the Designer.
- Set the Log property of the EventLog component to Application and the Source property to a name of your choice. This name is typically the name of the application that shows up in the Event Viewer.
- Logs can now be written with the `WriteEntry()` method of the `EventLog` instance.
- An installer can be added from the Add Installer context menu item of the EventLog component. This creates the `ProjectInstaller` class that configures the event source in the registry.
- The application can now be registered with the `installutil` command. `installutil` calls the `ProjectInstaller` class and registers the event source.

If you do an xcopy-installation the last two steps are not really necessary. If the `Source` property for the `EventLog` instance is set, this source is automatically registered when an event log is written the first time, which is really easy to do. However, for a real application, you are better off adding the installer. With `installutil /u` the event log configuration is unregistered. If the application is just deleted, this registry key remains unless `EventLog.DeleteEventSource()` is called.

## Adding event logging to the QuoteServer

The library QuoteServer used from the QuoteService currently doesn't have event logging included but this can easily be changed. To use the Visual Studio Designer to drag and drop the EventLog component to the class, you have to add designer support to the class.

> *To add designer support to the class you have to derive the class from the base class* `System.ComponentModel.Component`, *and invoke the method* `InitializeComponent()` *inside the constructor of the class. The method* `InitializeComponent()` *that will be used from the Designer to set the properties of the components will be added automatically as soon as the first component is dropped onto the Designer surface, but you have to invoke this method yourself.*

After you change the code of the `QuoteServer` class in the library `QuoteServer` with a derivation from the base class `System.ComponentModel.Component`, you can switch Visual Studio to the design view:

```csharp
public class QuoteServer : System.ComponentModel.Component
{
    //...

    public QuoteServer() : this ("quotes.txt")
    {
    }

    public QuoteServer(string filename) : this(filename, 7890)
    {
    }

    public QuoteServer(string filename, int port)
    {
        this.filename = filename;
        this.port = port;

        InitializeComponent();
    }
```

After this change, you can drag and drop the EventLog component from the toolbox to the design view, where an instance of the `EventLog` class is created. Change the `Log` property of the object to `Application` and the `Source` property to `QuoteService`.

Then you can change the implementation of the method `ListenerThread()` in the class `QuoteServer`, so that an event log entry is written in case an exception is generated:

```csharp
protected void ListenerThread()
{
    try
```

# Windows Services

```
        {
            IPAddress ipAddress = Dns.Resolve("localhost").AddressList[0];
            listener = new TcpListener(ipAddress, port);
            listener.Start();
            while (true)
            {
                Socket clientSocket = listener.AcceptSocket();
                string message = GetRandomQuoteOfTheDay();
                UnicodeEncoding encoder = new UnicodeEncoding();
                byte[] buffer = encoder.GetBytes(message);
                clientSocket.Send(buffer, buffer.Length, 0);
                clientSocket.Close();
            }
        }
        catch (SocketException ex)
        {
            string message = "Quote Server failed in Listener: "
                            + ex.Message;
            eventLog.WriteEntry(message, EventLogEntryType.Error);
        }
    }
```

## Trace

It's also possible that all your trace messages are redirected to the event log. You shouldn't really do this, because on a normal running system the event log gets overblown with trace messages, and the system administrator could miss the really important logs if this happens. Turning on trace messages to the event log can be useful when testing features for problematic services. Tracing is possible with debug as well as with release code.

To send trace messages to the event log you must create an `EventLogTraceListener` object and add it to the listener's list of the `Trace` class:

```
        EventLogTraceListener listener = new EventLogTraceListener(eventLog1);
        Trace.Listeners.Add(listener);
```

Now, all trace messages are sent to the event log:

```
        Trace.WriteLine("trace message");
```

## Creating an event log listener

Next, you write an application that receives an event when a service encounters a problem. Create a simple Windows application that monitors the events of your `Quote` service. This Windows application consists of a list box and an Exit button only, as shown in Figure 36-23.

Add an `EventLog` component to the design view by dragging and dropping it from the toolbox. Set the `Log` property to `Application`, and the `Source` to the source of your service, `QuoteService`. The `EventLog` class also has a property, `EnableRaisingEvents`. The default value is `false`; setting it to `true` means that an event is generated each time this event occurs, and you can add an event handler for the `EntryWritten` event of the `EventLog` class. Add a handler with the name `OnEntryWritten()` to this event.

**Figure 36-23**

The `OnEntryWritten()` handler receives an `EntryWrittenEventArgs` object as argument, from which you can get the complete information about an event. With the `Entry` property an `EventLogEntry` object with information about the time, event source, type, category, and so on is returned:

```
protected void OnEntryWritten (object sender,
    System.Diagnostics.EntryWrittenEventArgs e)
{
    DateTime time = e.Entry.TimeGenerated;
    string message = e.Entry.Message;
    listBoxEvents.Items.Add(time + " " + message);
}
```

The running application displays all events for the QuoteService as shown in Figure 36-24.

**Figure 36-24**

# Windows Services

## Performance Monitoring

Performance monitoring can be used to get information about the normal running of the service. Performance monitoring is a great tool that helps you understand the workload of the system, and observe changes and trends.

Microsoft Windows has a lot of performance objects, such as `System`, `Memory`, `Objects`, `Process`, `Processor`, `Thread`, `Cache`, and so on. Each of these objects has many counts to monitor. For example, with the `Process` object, the user time, handle count, page faults, thread count, and so on can be monitored for all processes, or for specific process instances. Some applications, such as SQL Server, also add application-specific objects.

For the quote service sample application it might be interesting to get information about the number of client requests, the size of the data sent over the wire, and so on.

### Performance monitoring classes

The `System.Diagnostics` namespace provides these classes for performance monitoring:

- `PerformanceCounter` can be used both to monitor counts and to write counts. New performance categories can also be created with this class.
- `PerformanceCounterCategory` enables you to step through all existing categories as well as create new ones. You can programmatically get all the counters of a category.
- `PerformanceCounterInstaller` is used for the installation of performance counters. The use is similar to the `EventLogInstaller` we discussed previously.

### Performance Counter Builder

You can create a new performance counter category by selecting the performance counters in the Server Explorer and by selecting the menu entry Create New Category on the context menu. This launches the Performance Counter Builder (see Figure 36-25).

Set the name of the performance counter category to `Quote Service`. The following table shows all performance counters of the quote service.

| Name | Description | Type |
| --- | --- | --- |
| # of Bytes sent | Total # of bytes sent to the client | `NumberOfItems32` |
| # of Bytes sent/sec | # of bytes sent to the client in one second | `RateOfCountsPerSecond32` |
| # of Requests | Total # of requests | `NumberOfItems32` |
| # of Requests/sec | # of requests in one second | `RateOfCountsPerSecond32` |

The Performance Counter Builder writes the configuration to the performance database. This can also be done dynamically by using the `Create()` method of the `PerformanceCounterCategory` class in the `System.Diagnostics` namespace. An installer for other systems can easily be added later using Visual Studio.

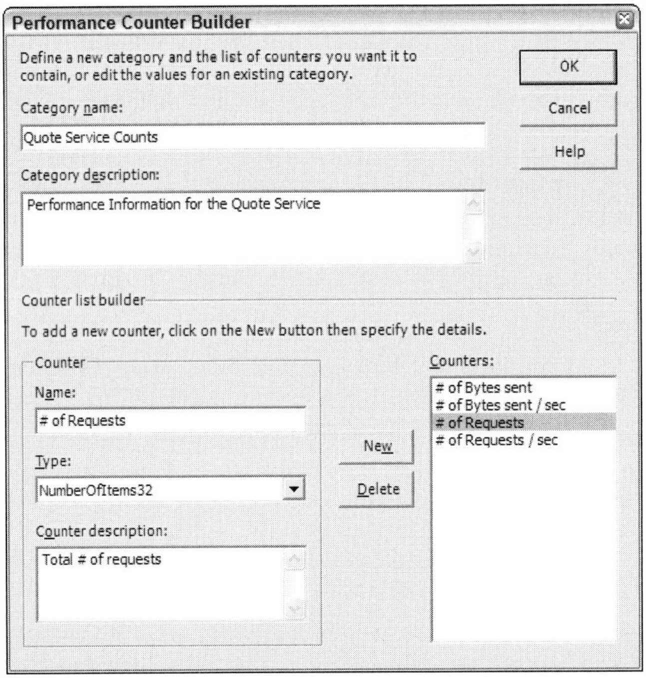

Figure 36-25

## Adding PerformanceCounter components

Now you can add PerformanceCounter components from the toolbox. Instead of using the components from the toolbox category Components, you can directly drag and drop the previously created performance counts from the Server Explorer to the design view. This way the instances are configured automatically: the `CategoryName` property is set to "Quote Service Count" for all objects, and the `CounterName` property is set to one of the values available in the selected category. Because with this application the performance counts will not be read but written, you have to set the `ReadOnly` property to `false`.

Here is a part of the code generated into `InitalizeComponent()` by adding the PerformanceCounter components to the Designer and by setting the properties as indicated previously:

```
private void InitializeComponent()
{
    //...
    // performanceCounterRequestsPerSec
    //
    this.performanceCounterRequestsPerSec.CategoryName =
        "Quote Service Counts";
    this.performanceCounterRequestsPerSec.CounterName = "# of Requests / sec";
    this.performanceCounterRequestsPerSec.MachineName = "cnagel";
    this.performanceCounterReqeustsPerSec.ReadOnly = false;
```

# Windows Services

```
            //
            // performanceCounterBytesSentTotal
            //
            this.performanceCounterBytesSentTotal.CategoryName =
               "Quote Service Counts";
            this.performanceCounterBytesSentTotal.CounterName = "# of Bytes sent";
            this.performanceCounterBytesSentTotal.MachineName = "cnagel";
            this.performanceCounterBytesSentTotal.ReadOnly = false;
            //
            // performanceCounterBytesSentPerSec
            //
            this.performanceCounterBytesSentPerSec.CategoryName =
               "Quote Service Counts";
            this.performanceCounterBytesSentPerSec.CounterName =
               "# of Bytes sent / sec";
            this.performanceCounterBytesSentPerSec.MachineName = "cnagel";
            this.performanceCounterBytesSentPerSec.ReadOnly = false;
            //
            // performanceCounterRequestsTotal
            //
            this.performanceCounterRequestsTotal.CategoryName =
               "Quote Service Counts";
            this.performanceCounterRequestsTotal.CounterName = "# of Requests";
            this.performanceCounterRequestsTotal.MachineName = "cnagel";
            this.performanceCoutnerRequestsTotal.ReadOnly = false;
            //...
         }
```

For the calculation of the performance values, you have to add the fields `requestsPerSec` and `bytesPerSec` to the class `QuoteServer`:

```
      public class QuoteServer : System.ComponentModel.Component
      {
         // Performance monitoring counts
         private int requestsPerSec;
         private int bytesPerSec;
```

The performance counts that show the total values are incremented directly in the `ListenerThread()` method (shown in the following code) of the `QuoteServer` class. You can use `PerformanceCounter.Increment()` to count the number of total requests, and `IncrementBy()` to count the number of bytes sent.

For the performance counts that show the value by seconds, just the two variables, `requestsPerSec` and `bytesPerSec`, are updated in the `ListenerThread()` method:

```
            protected void ListenerThread()
            {
               try
               {
                  listener = new TCPListener(port);
                  listener.Start();
```

```csharp
            while (true)
            {
                Socket clientSocket = listener.Accept();
                string message = GetRandomQuoteOfTheDay();
                UnicodeEncoding encoder = new UnicodeEncoding();
                byte[] buffer = encoder.GetBytes(message);
                clientSocket.Send(buffer, buffer.Length, 0);
                clientSocket.Close();

                performanceCounterRequestsTotal.Increment();
                performanceCounterBytesSentTotal.IncrementBy(buffer.Length);

                requestsPerSec++;
                bytesPerSec += buffer.Length;
            }
        }
        catch (SocketException ex)
        {
            string message = "Quote Server failed in Listener: "
                  + ex.Message;
            EventLog.WriteEntry("QuoteService", message);
        }
    }
```

To show updated values every second, add a Timer component. Set the `OnTimer()` method to the `Elapsed` event of this component. The `OnTimer()` method is called once per second if you set the Interval property to 1000. In the implementation of this method, set the performance counts by using the `RawValue` property of the `PerformanceCounter` class:

```csharp
    protected void OnTimer (object sender, System.Timers.ElapsedEventArgs e)
    {
        performanceCounterBytesSentPerSec.RawValue = bytesPerSec;
        performanceCounterRequestsPerSec.RawValue = requestsPerSec;
        bytesPerSec = 0;
        requestsPerSec = 0;
    }
```

## *perfmon.exe*

Now you can monitor the service. You can start the Performance tool by selecting Administrative Tools ⇨ Performance. By pressing the + button in the toolbar, you can add performance counts. The Quote Service shows up as a performance object. All the counters that have been configured show up in the counter list as shown in Figure 36-26.

After you've added the counters to the performance monitor, you can see the actual values of the service over time (see Figure 36-27). Using this performance tool, you can also create log files to analyze the performance at a later time.

# Windows Services

Figure 36-26

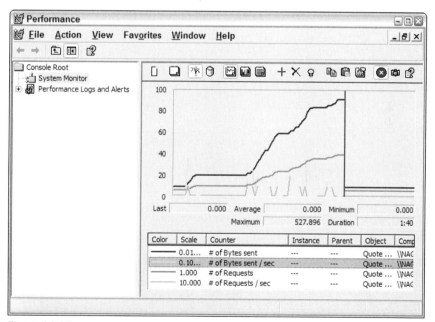

Figure 36-27

# Chapter 36

# Power Events

The Windows service can react when the power status changes. One example of a power event is when the system is hibernated — all the memory content is written to the disk, so a faster boot is possible. It's also possible to suspend the system in order to reduce the power consumption, but it can be awakened automatically on demand.

For all power events, the service can receive the control code SERVICE_CONTROL_POWEREVENT with additional parameters. The reason for the event is passed through these parameters. The reason could be low battery power, or the system is going to a suspended state, or a power status change. Depending on the circumstance the service should slow down, suspend background threads, close network connections, close files, and so on.

The classes in the `System.ServiceProcess` namespace have support for power events. In the same way as you can configure a service so that it reacts to pause and continue events with the `CanPauseAndContinue` property, you can also set a property for power management: `CanHandlePowerEvent`. Windows services that handle power events are registered in the SCM with the Win32 API method `RegisterServiceCtrlHandlerEx()`.

If you set the property `CanHandlePowerEvent` to `true`, the method `OnPowerEvent()` of the class `ServiceBase` is called. You can override this method to receive power events and to react with your service implementation accordingly. The reason for the power event is passed in an argument of type `PowerBroadcastStatus`. The possible values of this enumeration are listed in the following table.

| Value | Description |
| --- | --- |
| BatteryLow | The battery power is low. You should reduce the functionality of the service to a minimum. |
| PowerStatusChange | A switch from battery power to A/C happened, or the battery power slips below a threshold, and so on. |
| QuerySuspend | The system requests permissions to go into a suspended mode. You could deny the permissions, or prepare to go into the suspended mode by closing files, disconnecting network connections, and so on. |
| QuerySuspendFailed | Change into the suspended mode was denied for the system. You can go on with the functionality as before. |
| Suspend | Nobody denied the request to go into the suspended mode. The system will be suspended soon. |

# Summary

In this chapter, you have seen what Windows Services are and how you can create them with the .NET Framework. Applications can start automatically at boot-time with Windows Services, and you can use a privileged system account as the user of the service.

# Windows Services

The .NET Framework has great support for Windows Services. All the plumbing code that's necessary for building, controlling, and installing services is built into the .NET Framework classes in the `System.ServiceProcess` namespace. By deriving a class from `ServiceBase`, you can override methods that are invoked when the service is paused, resumed, or stopped. For installation of services, the classes `ServiceProcessInstaller` and `ServiceInstaller` deal with all registry configurations needed for services.

Support technologies such as event logging and performance monitoring can easily be used with .NET applications with classes in the `System.Diagnostics` namespace: `EventLog` and `PerformanceCounter`.

# Index

## SYMBOLS AND NUMERICS

**& (ampersand), as address operator for pointers, 207**
**\* (asterisk)**
  as indirection operator for pointers, 207
  for multi-line comments (/\* and \*/), 31, 67–68
**@ (at sign) indicating identifiers, 74**
**\ (backslash)**
  preceding escape sequences, 44, 238
  for searching for escape meta-characters, 240
**: (colon)**
  for disabling `Group` object with regular expressions (?:), 243
  as namespace alias qualifier (::), 60–61
  preceding format specifiers, 230
  in ternary operator (?:), 136–137
**, (comma) in derived class or struct declarations, 113**
**{ } (curly braces)**
  with `if` statements, 47, 48
  joining statements in blocks, 31
**" (double quotes), string literals enclosed by, 46**
**= (equals sign)**
  as assignment operator, 34, 134–135
  as comparison operator (==), 48, 134–135, 147
**- (minus sign)**
  as decrement operator (--), 135–136
  for removing method calls from multicast delegates, 183
**( ) (parentheses) for groups, 241–242**
**+ (plus sign)**
  in for loop iterator, 52
  as increment operator (++), 135–136
  regular expression groups and, 242

**# (pound symbol) for preprocessor directives, 70–73**
**? (question mark)**
  for disabling `Group` object with regular expressions (?:), 243
  in null coalescing operator (??), 139–140
  in ternary operator (?:), 136–137
**; (semicolon)**
  ending C# statements, 31
  preprocessor directives not ended by, 71
**' (single quotes), `char` literals enclosed by, 44, 46**
**/ (slash)**
  for multi-line comments (/\* and \*/), 31, 67–68
  for single-line comments (//), 31, 67
**[ ] (square brackets) for arrays, 57**
**32-bit processors, pointers and, 207–208**

## A

`Abort()` **method**
  `MessageQueueTransaction` object, 1121–1122
  `Thread` class, 354
**aborting threads, 354**
`abstract` **modifier, 117, 125**
`AcceptSocket()` **method (`QuoteServer` class), 1278**
**access control lists.** *See* **ACLs**
**access modifiers, 94, 97**
`Account` **class, 297–299**
`Accumulate()` **method**
  Account class, 298–299
  Action generic delegate, 299–300
  described, 644
  implementing for user-defined aggregates, 644–645
`AccumulateIf()` **method, 300–301**

# AccumulateSimple() method (Account class)

`AccumulateSimple()` **method (`Account` class), 298**
**acknowledgement message queues, 1120**
**ACLs (access control lists)**
  adding and removing from a file, 1225–1226
  namespace for, 1222
  reading from a directory, 1224–1225
  reading from a file, 1222–1223
`Action` **generic delegate, 299–301**
`ActionCancelEventArgs` **class**
  `BusEntity` class with, 190–191
  `Cancel` property, 188
  code listing, 189
  derivation of, 188
  `Message` property, 188
  `OnAction` method, 189–190
  using, 190–192
`ActionEventHandler` **delegate, 188**
`Activator` **class**
  `CreateInstance()` method, 1027, 1028, 1029
  `GetObject()` method, 1027, 1028, 1029, 1030
  overview, 1027
**activator for .NET Remoting client, 1012**
**Active Directory**
  accessing native ADSI objects, 735–736
  accessing properties directly by name, 731
  Active Directory Domains and Trusts MMC snap-in, 721
  Active Directory Sites and Services MMC snap-in, 721
  Active Directory Users and Computers MMC snap-in, 721–722
  ADSI (Active Directory Service Interfaces), 723–724
  ADSI Edit tool, 721, 722–723
  architecture, 714–720
  authentication, 729
  binding, 725–729
  cache, 732–733
  configuration, 716
  creating new objects, 733
  data characteristics, 719
  defined, 713
  domain, 716
  domain controllers, 716
  domain tree, 717
  DSML with, 724, 745–748
  features, 714–715
  finding message queues, 1103–1104
  forest, 717
  GC (global catalog), 717–718
  getting directory entries, 730–731
  hierarchical data organization, 714, 719
  multimaster replication, 714, 718
  object collections, 731–732
  objects, defined, 715
  read-mostly access, 719, 736
  replication latency, 718
  replication notification, 718
  replication topology, 714
  scheduled replication, 718
  schemas, 715, 719–720
  searching in, 736–745
  security, 714–715
  sites, 717
  strong typing for objects, 715, 719
  `System.DirectoryServices` namespace, 723, 725
  updating directory entries, 734
  `UserSearch` application, 740–745
  uses for, 713
**Active Directory Service Interfaces.** *See* **ADSI**
**Active Server Pages (ASP)**
  ASP.NET and, 22, 903
  defined, 21
  limitations of, 21–22
**ActiveX controls in Windows Forms**
  ActiveX Control Importer for, 1168
  ActiveX controls, defined, 1168
  creating a Windows Forms application, 1169–1171
**ActiveX Data Objects (ADO) versus ADO.NET, 580**
`Add()` **method**
  `ArrayList` class, 251, 272
  `Hashtable` class, 261
  `List<T>` generic class, 279
  `SortedList` class, 258
`AddCulturesToTree()` **method, 520–522**
`AddDocument()` **method**
  `DocumentManager` class, 284, 294
  `PriorityDocumentManager` class, 290
`AddRange()` **method (`ArrayList` class), 252**
`AddResource()` **method (`ResourceWriter` class), 527**
**address operator for pointers, 207**
`AddToMessage()` **method, 323**
`AddToOutput()` **method, 319**
**ADO (ActiveX Data Objects) versus ADO.NET, 580**
**ADO.NET.** *See also* **data binding; `DataSet` class; event-booking application; viewing .NET data**
  ADO (ActiveX Data Objects) versus, 580
  alias names to database factory objects, 585
  calling stored procedures, 594–597
  closing database connections, 583, 585–588
  commands, defined, 589
  `CommandType` enumeration, 590

# arguments

constructing commands, 590
converting relational data to XML, 694–696
converting single table data to XML, 689–694
converting XML to ADO.NET data, 696–699
copying a `DataSet`, 625–626
data access provided for C# by, 25
data reader, 597–600
database authentication, 583, 584
database-specific classes, 581–582
defining a database connection string, 584
deleting database records, 591, 595–596
ensuring resources are released, 585–588
`ExecuteNonQuery()` method, 591
`ExecuteReader()` method, 591–592
`ExecuteScalar()` method, 592–593
`ExecuteXmlReader()` method, 593–594
executing commands, 590–594
getting a single result from a SQL statement, 592–593
inserting database records, 591, 596–597
isolation level for transactions, 588–589
for key generation with SQL Server, 627–629
managing data and relationships with `DataSet` class, 600–612
managing database connection strings, 584–585
namespaces for, 580
naming conventions, 629–630
.NET versions and, 582
OLE DB provider with, 597–600
opening database connections, 583
overview, 580–582
persisting `DataSet` changes, 620–625, 691–692
populating a `DataSet`, 619–620
reading database records, 591–592, 593–594, 597–600
reading `DiffGram` XML documents, 699–701
shared classes, 581
for tiered development, 625–627
transactions, 588–589
`try...catch...finally` blocks for releasing resources, 586, 587–588
updating database records, 591, 594–595
using database connections, 582–589
`using` statement for releasing resources, 586–587, 588
Web Forms and, 926–939
XML schemas, 612–618

**ADSI (Active Directory Service Interfaces)**
accessing native objects, 735–736
ADSI Providers, 724
cache, 732–733
defined, 724
namespace for, 723

**ADSI Edit tool (Active Directory), 721, 722–723**

**aggregates**
defined, 643
user-defined, 644–645
using `AVG` aggregate, 643

**algorithms**
bubble-sorting, 180
for dictionaries, 260, 262–263
sorting, globalization and, 524–525

**aliases**
to factory objects for databases, 585
for namespaces, 60–61

**ampersand (&), as address operator for pointers, 207**

`AnalyzeType()` **method, 318–319**

**anonymous methods**
`BubbleSorter` example, 180–182
defined, 176
defining delegates with, 176
`delegateTest` example, 176–177
event handlers, 187–188
multicast delegates with, 183–185
rules for, 177
`SimpleDelegate` example, 177–180
threading and, 353

`AppDomain` **class, 414–416**

`Append()` **method (**`StringBuilder` **class), 227**

`AppendFormat()` **method (**`StringBuilder` **class), 231**

`Application` **class**
`EnableVisualStyles` method, 785–786
methods and properties, 753
`Run()` method overloads, 753

**application configuration files for assemblies, 450, 453–456**

**application domains.** *See also* **.NET Remoting**
`AppDomain` class for, 414–416
application domain-bound objects, 1031
assemblies and, 413–416
contexts, 1015
processes and, 14–16, 413
remote objects confined to, 1017
for SQL Server 2005 databases, 634
strong data typing in IL and, 14–16
usefulness of, 14
using, 414–416

`ApplyResources()` **method (**`ResourceManager` **class), 537**

**arguments.** *See* **parameters**

1489

## arithmetic operators

arithmetic operators
    overloading, 148, 151–152, 153–155
    pointers and, 210–211
    table listing, 134
array lists. *See also* `ArrayList` **class**
    adding elements, 251, 252
    arrays versus, 250
    boxing and unboxing and, 272
    converting to arrays, 253
    copying range of items to new list, 253
    dynamic growth of, 250–251
    elements as `object` references, 251
    indexers, 251
    performance compared to dictionaries, 259
    removing elements, 251–253
    setting capacity of, 250, 251
`ArrayList` **class.** *See also* **array lists**
    `Add()` method, 251, 272
    `AddRange()` method, 252
    dynamic growth of, 250–251
    `GetRange()` method, 253
    instantiating, 250
    `RemoveAt()` method, 251
    `RemoveRange()` method, 252–253
    setting capacity of, 250, 251
    `StringBuilder` class compared to, 250
arrays
    accessing elements, 58
    advantages and disadvantages of, 245
    array lists versus, 250
    `ArraySegment<T>` generic struct and, 303–304
    as collections, 247–248
    converting array lists to, 253
    `DataGridView` control for displaying data, 804–805
    finding number of elements in, 58
    `foreach` statements for iterating through items, 54
    initializing with specific dimensions, 58
    overview, 57–58
    pointers to, not allowed, 208
    as reference types, 58
    square brackets used for, 57
    stack-based, using pointers, 219–222
    `StreamReader` class with, 1215–1216
    `System.Array` as parent class for, 245
`ArraySegment<T>` **generic struct, 303–304**
`as` **operator, 138**
**ASP (Active Server Pages)**
    ASP.NET and, 22, 903
    defined, 21
    limitations of, 21–22

**ASP.NET.** *See also* `PCSDemoSite` **application; Web Forms**
    ADO.NET and data binding with, 926–939
    application configuration, 939–941
    ASP and, 22, 903
    client-side code, 905–906
    code model, 909
    `code-behind` feature, 22
    COM objects in, 1171
    control palette, 913–914
    creating applications using C#, 21–23
    creating files in Visual Studio, 906
    Crystal Reports Web server controls, 914
    custom controls, 944, 952–956
    data Web server controls, 917–918
    DHTML versus, 22
    features, 22
    file extensions for code, 909
    forms authentication, 964–969
    further information, 910
    HTML server controls, 910
    IIS and, 904
    localization using, 544–545
    login system implementation, 969–970
    login Web server controls, 970–971
    master pages, 956–960
    navigation Web server controls, 960–963
    .NET Remoting servers for, 1050–1051
    overview, 904–905
    pages as classes, 22
    PCSWebApp1 example, 906–908, 909
    performance improvements over ASP, 22
    restricting directory access, 971–973
    `runat="server"` attribute, 905, 910
    `<script>` elements, 905
    security, 963–973
    server control example, 920–925
    similar technologies, 903
    standard Web server controls, 914–917
    state management in, 905
    themes, 974–979
    user controls, 944–952
    as user interface medium, 25
    validation Web server controls, 918–920
    viewstate field, 905
    WCF and, 1146
    Web Forms, 23
    Web server controls, 23, 910–925
    Web services issues, 1126
    WebParts Web server controls, 920
    XML Web services, 23

**assemblies.** *See also* **configuring assemblies**
  adding resources to, 528–530
  as answer to DLL Hell, 412–413
  application domains and, 413–416
  attributes, 423–425
  building, 423–425
  calculating permissions required for, 481, 483–484
  code access security, 464–478
  creating using Visual Studio, 423–425
  defined, 17, 411, 412
  executable versus library code and, 17
  features, 413
  global assembly cache, 19, 413, 438–441
  ildasm symbols, 420–421
  installing, 412
  manifests, 418
  marking as CLS-compliant, 437
  metadata in, 18
  modules versus, 421–422
  namespaces and, 419
  obtaining details of types in, 319–320
  overview, 411–416
  primary interop assemblies for COM, 1166
  private, 18, 412–413, 419
  private versus shared, 412–413
  probing to find, 451
  reflection and, 19
  satellite assemblies for languages, 538
  shared, 19, 413, 419, 441–449
  structure of, 417–418
  using CLS for language independence, 427–436
  versioning, 412–413, 451–460
  viewing assemblies, 420–421
  viewing code access permissions for, 473–476
  viewing code groups for, 469–471
  Visual Basic .NET not case-sensitive, 77
**Assembly Cache Viewer, 439–440**
`Assembly` **class, 319–320, 452**
`AssemblyInfo.cs` **project, 423**
**asserting permissions, 486–487**
**assignment operator**
  assigning values to variables, 34
  comparison versus assignment, 48, 134–135
  shortcut operators, 135–136
**asterisk (*)**
  as indirection operator for pointers, 207
  for multi-line comments (/* and */), 31, 67–68
**asynchronous .NET Remoting, 1053–1054**
**at sign (@) indicating identifiers, 74**
**ATL Project Wizard (Visual Studio), 1159–1160**

**atomicity of Enterprise Services transactions, 1078**
**attributes.** *See also* **reflection**
  of assemblies, 423–425
  assembly, defined with Enterprise Services applications, 1071
  COM and, 17
  COM interop attributes, 1175–1178
  of contexts (.NET Remoting), 1015–1016
  custom, 306–313
  for custom controls (Windows Forms), 787–788
  of Enterprise Services transactions, 1079
  .NET support for, 17
  for user controls (ASP.NET), 947
  for user controls (Windows Forms), 798–799
`AttributeUsage` **attribute, 307–309**
**authentication**
  in Active Directory binding path, 729
  `AuthenticateUser()` method, 1002
  database authentication with ADO.NET, 583, 584
  `Login()` method for obtaining token, 1002–1003, 1005
  for shared assemblies, 442
  for Web Forms, 964–969
**automatic transactions, 1068, 1078**
`AVG` **aggregate, 643**

# B

**backslash (\\)**
  preceding escape sequences, 44, 238
  for searching for escape meta-characters, 240
**base classes**
  areas covered by, 20
  casts between derived classes and, 163–164
  default, 113
  defined, 19
  for generics, 277–278
  overview, 19–20
  for serialization, 1187
  for streams, 1206
`BasicWebClient` **example**
  using `WebClient` class, 1240–1241
  using `WebRequest` and `WebResponse` classes, 1242–1243
*Beginning XML* **(Wiley Publishing, Inc.), 659**
`BeginReceive()` **method (`MessageQueue` class), 1110**
`BeginTransaction()` **methods, 588**
**binary code reuse by generics, 273–274**
`BinaryFileReader` **application, 1210–1213**

`BinaryReader` class, 1207
`BinaryWriter` class, 1207
binding (Active Directory)
  authentication in binding path, 729
  defined, 725
  with `DirectoryEntry` class, 729
  distinguished name (DN) in binding path, 727–728, 729
  downlevel logon and, 729
  example path for, 725
  items specified with, 725–726
  port number in binding path, 726
  protocol in binding path, 726
  server name in binding path, 726
  user name in binding path, 728–729
  user principal name (UPN), 729
`Binding` class, 819–820
binding methods (COM), 1155
binding .NET data. See data binding
binding (WCF), 1141–1143
`BindingContext` class, 818–819
`BitBlt` (bitmap block transfer), 873–874
`Blacklist()` method (`CustomerTable` class), 837
blittable data types, 638
blocks of code
  curly braces for, 31
  `fixed` blocks, 213–214
  marking `unsafe`, 206
  showing and hiding in Visual Studio 2005, 388–390
`BookOfTheDayForm.cs`, 534–539
`books.xml` file
  code listing, 662
  MSXML example, 662–663
  retrieving attribute data, 668
  transforming XML into HTML, 684–686
  validating XSD schema with `XmlReader`, 669–670
  XSD schema generated from, 668–669
`bool` type
  casting not permitted for, 144
  as `if` statement return type, 48–49
  overview, 43
Boolean properties of `Type` class, 315
boxing and unboxing
  array lists and, 272
  avoided by `List<T>` generics class, 272–273
  casts, 164–165
  comparing value types for equality, 147
  overview, 145–146
  performance impacts, 272
`break` statement, 49, 55

breakpoints, setting in Visual Studio 2005, 404
`Brush` class, 866–867
`btnTwo_Click` method, 187
`BubbleSorter` class, 180–182
bubble-sorting algorithm, 180
building. See also compiling
  assemblies, 421–425
  debug and release builds, 399–401
  defined, 399
  dictionaries, requirements for, 260
  projects in Visual Studio 2005, 399–403
`BusEntity` class, 190–191
business object tier, 25
`Button` control (Windows Forms)
  in application example, 756
  for IE-like toolbar, 1249–1253
  images on buttons, 763
  overview, 762–763
  `PerformClick` method, 763
`ButtonBase` class (Windows Forms)
  `Button` control derived from, 762–764
  `CheckBox` control derived from, 764
  `RadioButton` control derived from, 764
`Button_Click` method, 186–187
`byte` type, 41, 42

# C

C++. See also Visual C++ 2005; Visual C++ 6; Visual C++ .NET
  advantages over C#, 6–7
  class for CLS example, 427–432
  CLR memory type safety tests and, 7
  constants in C# versus, 38
  destructors, 200
  memory management, 13
  templates compared to C# generics, 272
`CalculateDocumentSize()` method, 886–887
`CalculateLineWidths()` method, 886
calculating permissions required for an assembly, 481, 483–484
`calendar_DayRender()` event handler, 930–931
`calendar_SelectionChanged()` event handler, 930
call contexts (.NET Remoting), 1062–1064
callback functions, 171. See also delegates
camel casing, 76–77
`CapsEditor` example
  appearance, 880–881
  `CalculateDocumentSize()` method, 886–887
  `CalculateLineWidths()` method, 886

coordinate transforms, 889–890
CreateFonts() helper method, 883–884
extending for print functionality, 893–899
File menu, 880
Form1 class fields, 882
functionality, 880
initialization, 883
Invalidate() method, 884–886
LineIndexToPageCoordinates() method, 890
LineIndexToWorldCoordinates() method, 889
LoadFile() method, 884
main menu, 883–884
OnPaint() method, 887–888
PageCoordinatesToLineIndex() method, 890, 893
responding to user input, 890–893
TextLineInformation class and, 882–883
using statements, 881–882
WorldCoordinatesToLineIndex() method, 889
WorldYCoordinateToLineIndex() method, 889
**case of names**
camel casing, 76–77
IL case sensitivity, 12
Pascal casing, 76, 77
Visual Basic .NET not case-sensitive, 77
**caspol.exe (Code Access Security Policy tool)**
applying full trust, 492, 502
changing code group permissions, 494–495
creating and applying permissions sets, 495–497
creating code group using strong name, 498
creating custom code groups, 493–494
deleting code groups, 494
Execution Checking setting, 468
getting code group labels, 491
labels for code groups, 469
listing code groups and descriptions, 466–467
listing code groups compactly, 468
listing options for, 466
Policy change prompt option, 469
resetting security policy, 493
specifying trust level for code groups, 468
turning security on and off, 493
verifying the trust level, 503
viewing code access permissions for assemblies, 474–476
viewing code groups at enterprise level, 477–478
viewing code groups at user level, 476–477
viewing code groups for assemblies, 469–471, 503–504
viewing permission sets, 497

**casting.** *See also* **user-defined casts**
array list elements, 251
compilation and, 165–166
converting array element to struct member variable, 144
converting nullable types, 144
converting primitive types, 143–144
dangers of, 143
data loss from, 143–144, 166–167
limitations of, 144
between numeric and string types, 144–145
between pointer types, 208–209
pointers to integer types, 208–209
QueryInterface() method and, with COM, 1154–1155
catch **blocks**
defined, 330
error trapping process and, 330
exceptions not handled and, 338
MortimerColdCall example, 342–343
multiple blocks, 331, 332–336
omitting, 331
for releasing database resources, 586, 587–588
in SimpleExceptions class, 335–336
syntax, 331
throwing an exception and, 331
throwing exceptions from, 339
CCOMDemo **class, 1161, 1162–1163, 1167**
**CCW (COM callable wrapper), 1172**
**certificates.** *See* **digital certificates**
**channels (.NET Remoting)**
created on both server and client side, 1021
defined, 1012, 1020
delayed loading of client channels, 1046
getting configuration information for, 1022–1023
HTTP channel, 1021
interfaces for, 1022
IPC channel, 1021
listening to multiple channel by server, 1021–1022
marshal-by-value classes and, 1031
pluggability of, 1024–1025
predefined, 1041–1042
server-side creation, 1021
setting properties for, 1023–1024
ShowChannelProperties() method, 1023
TCP channel, 1021
ChannelServices **class, 1012, 1025–1026**
char **type, 42, 43–44**
CheckBox **control (Windows Forms), 764**
checked **operator, 137, 162**

# CheckedListBox control (Windows Forms)

CheckedListBox **control (Windows Forms), 765**
**chktrust.exe utility, 501**
**class hierarchies**
   for data-binding objects, 817–818
   DataGridView control, 813–816
   for exceptions, 329–330
   for streams, 1206
   for WebRequest and WebResponse classes, 1257–1258
   for Windows Forms, 757–758
**class id (CLSID) for COM objects, 1155**
class **keyword, 32**
**Class View window (Visual Studio 2005), 396–397**
**classes.** *See also* **class hierarchies; derived classes;** *specific classes and members*
   abstract, 117
   accessing fields outside the object, 37–38
   ADO.NET, 581–582
   ASP.NET pages as, 22
   constructors not required for, 95
   context attribute classes, 1015–1016
   context property classes, 1016
   data members, 85
   declaring instances, 84
   default initialization of variables in, 34
   defined, 84
   for file system operations, 1188
   for fonts and font families, 877
   formatter classes (.NET Remoting), 1025
   function members, 85–99
   generic collection classes, 276–277
   generic, custom, 293–296
   generic .NET base classes, 277–278
   marking members unsafe, 205
   members, defined, 85
   namespaces for, 21, 58–59
   .NET base classes, 19–20
   .NET Remoting and, 1031–1032
   non-compliant with CLS, 426
   not-remotable, 1032
   partial, 104–106
   Pascal casing for, 76
   for performance monitoring, 1309
   pointers to members, 212–214
   pointers to, not allowed, 208, 212
   readonly fields, 99–101
   as reference types, 40, 84
   registry classes, 1229–1232
   for regular expressions, 223
   for resources, 527–528, 533–534

   sealed, 117–118
   static, 106
   stored in the heap, 84
   structs versus, 84, 102
   System.DirectoryServices namespace, 725
   System.Xml.XPath namespace, 679
   in Visual Studio 2005 Class View window, 396–397
   in Visual Studio 2005 Object Browser window, 397–398
   for Windows Services, 1275
   XML-related, 660–661
ClearAllFields() **method**
   FileProperties application, 1194
   FilePropertiesAndMovement application, 1201
**ClickOnce deployment technology, 568–569**
   advanced options, 570–576
   application cache, 569
   Custom Actions Editor, 573–575
   dialog box types available, 572–573
   File System Editor, 570
   File Types Editor, 571
   Launch Conditions Editor, 575–576
   mage.exe command-line tool, 568
   mageUI.exe gui tool, 568
   overview, 553, 567
   properties for actions, 575
   publishing an application, 568
   Registry Editor, 570–571
   security settings, 569–570
   settings, 568–569
   User Interface Editor, 571–573
   Windows Installer compared to, 567–568
   XML-based manifest files, 567
**client applications**
   ASP.NET client-side code, 905–906
   COM client creation, 1179–1181
   COM client with a sink object, 1182–1183
   creating Web service clients, 991–992
   for DatabaseResourceReader class, 549
   event-booking client, 993–997
   fat-client, 22, 24
   hardware requirements for deployment, 553
   .NET Remoting simple client, 1019–1020
   using a COM component from a .NET client, 1159–1171
   using a .NET component from a COM client, 1171–1183
   using UDTs from client-side code, 642–643
   WCF, 1144
ClientActivated_Client.config **file (.NET Remoting), 1044**

## collections

`ClientActivated_Server.config` **file (.NET Remoting), 1043–1044**
**clipping region, 848–850**
**closing**
   database connections with ADO.NET, 583, 585–588
   forms, 782
   streams, 1209, 1215
**CLR (Common Language Runtime)**
   application domains, 634
   C++ and memory safety tests, 7
   CLR Object Remoting, 1011
   code access permissions provided by, 471–472
   compilation steps for, 4
   defined, 4
   demanding permissions and, 478
   enabling .NET code to run with SQL Server, 634
   garbage collector, 13–14
   heap maintained by, 13
   Identity Permissions, 472–473
   managed code advantages, 4–7
   passing arguments to `Main()`, 63
   stored procedures with SQL Server, 646–647
   Virtual Execution System, 465
**CLS (Common Language Specification)**
   C# class for example, 434–436
   C++/CLI class for example, 427–432
   `CLSCompliant` attribute, 437
   CTS and, 425–426
   defined, 12
   language independence using, 427–436
   language interoperability and, 425, 426
   marking assemblies as CLS-compliant, 437
   non-compliant classes and methods, 426
   overview, 12–13
   requirements, 436–438
   rules for compliance, 438
   Visual Basic class for example, 432–434
   writing non-CLS-compliant code, 12
`CLSCompliant` **attribute, 437**
**CLSID (class id) for COM objects, 1155**
**code access security.** *See also* **code groups; permissions for code access**
   caspol.exe (Code Access Security Policy tool), 466–471
   code groups, 464, 465–471
   as code-based security, 14
   distributing code using certificates, 499–504
   distributing code using strong names, 497–499
   importance of, 464
   overview, 464
   permissions, 464, 471–476
   policy levels, 476–478
   Virtual Execution System and, 465
**Code Access Security Policy tool.** *See* **caspol.exe**
**code bloat, generics and, 274**
**code groups.** *See also* **permissions for code access**
   applying full trust, 492, 502
   caspol.exe (Code Access Security Policy tool), 466–471
   changing permissions for, 494–495
   creating custom, 493–494
   deleting, 494
   evidence, 464
   getting labels for, 491
   labels for, 469
   levels, 470
   listing compactly, 468
   listing with descriptions, 466–467
   managing, 492
   membership conditions, 465–466
   overview, 464
   specifying trust level, 468
   viewing code groups at enterprise level, 477–478
   viewing code groups at user level, 476–477
   viewing for assemblies, 469–471
   Zone condition, 465, 504–506
`code-behind` **feature (ASP.NET)**
   event-booking application code-behind file, 929–930
   overview, 22
   PCSWebApp1 example code-behind file, 909
`ColdCallFileFormatException`**, 341, 346–347**
`ColdCallFileReader` **class**
   declaring variables, 343
   described, 341
   `Dispose()` method, 344, 345–346
   `NPeopleToRing` property, 345
   `Open()` method, 343–344
   `ProcessNextPerson()` method, 344–345
   using, 342
**collections**
   Active Directory object collections, 731–732
   arrays as, 247–248
   `Current` property of elements, 247
   defined, 246
   enumerators, 246–247, 248
   `foreach` loops for iterating through, 54, 246
   generic, displaying with `DataGridView` control, 811–813
   `ICollection` interface for, 247
   `IEnumerable` interface for, 246–247
   `Reset()` method for returning to start, 247
   `Vector` struct example, 248–250

**colon (:)**
   for disabling Group object with regular expressions (?:), 243
   as namespace alias qualifier (::), 60–61
   preceding format specifiers, 230
   in ternary operator (?:), 136–137
`Color` **struct, 863**
**colors in graphics applications**
   GDI+ struct for representing, 863
   graphics display modes and, 865
   named colors, 864–865
   palettes, 865–866
   RGB values, 863–864, 865
   safety palette, 866
**COM**
   ActiveX controls in Windows Forms, 1168–1171
   apartment models, 1156–1157, 1166
   attributes and, 17
   casting and `QueryInterface()` method, 1154–1155
   class id (CLSID) for objects, 1155
   connection points, 1166–1168, 1181–1182
   creating a client with a sink object, 1182–1183
   creating a COM callable wrapper (CCW), 1172
   creating a component, 1159–1163
   creating a runtime callable wrapper (RCW), 1163–1166
   creating a simple client, 1179–1181
   custom interfaces, 1153
   data types, 1155
   debugging issues, 9
   delegate for, 1181
   dispatch interfaces, 1153–1154
   dual interfaces, 1154
   Enterprise Services history and, 1066
   error handling, 1158
   event handling, 1158, 1166–1168, 1181–1182
   freeing memory, 1153
   `_ICompletedEvents` client interface, 1166–1167
   `IDispatch` interface, 1163, 1164
   `IMath` interface, 1162, 1174, 1177–1178
   instantiating components, 1165
   interfaces, .NET interfaces versus, 8, 126
   interfaces overview, 1153–1155
   interop attributes, 1175–1178
   interoperability with .NET (overview), 7
   `IUnknown` interface, 1163, 1164
   `IWelcome` interface, 1160–1161, 1162, 1174, 1177–1178
   language interoperability and, 8–9, 425
   marshaling, 1159
   memory management, 13
   metadata, 1152
   method binding, 1155
   MSXML based on, 662
   multi-threaded apartment (MTA), 1157, 1166
   namespace for objects, 1151
   .NET and, 1152–1159
   performance losses with, 8
   primary interop assemblies, 1166
   prog id for objects, 1155
   registration, 1155, 1178–1179
   releasing components, 1165
   running Windows Forms controls in Internet Explorer, 1183
   similar concepts in .NET, 1152
   single-threaded apartment (STA), 1156–1157, 1166
   threading, 1156–1157, 1166
   tlbexp utility, 1173
   tlbimp utility, 1163
   type library for, 1173–1175
   using a COM component from a .NET client, 1159–1171
   using a .NET component from a COM client, 1171–1183
   using objects in ASP.NET, 1171
**COM callable wrapper (CCW), 1172**
**COM+**
   contexts, .NET contexts compared to, 1014
   Enterprise Services history and, 1066
   interoperability with .NET (overview), 7
   simple Enterprise Services application, 1070–1073
**combined characters. See Unicode characters**
`ComboBox` **control (Windows Forms), 765, 767**
**comma (,) in derived class or struct declarations, 113**
**comments**
   multi-line, 31, 67–68
   single-line, 31, 67
   within source files, 67–68
   XML documentation, 68–70
**Common Language Runtime. See CLR**
**Common Language Specification. See CLS**
**Common Type System. See CTS**
**comparison operators**
   assignment versus comparison, 48, 134–135
   comparing reference types for equality, 147
   comparing value types for equality, 147
   overloading, 148, 155–157
   table listing, 134
**compiling. See also building**
   casts combined during, 165–166
   class library example, 64–65

## Console.WriteLine() method

constructors and, 95, 119–120
`csc.exe` command-line compiler for, 31
custom attributes and, 306–307
destructors and, 199, 200
hiding methods and errors in, 116
inlining by compiler, 94–95
JIT (Just-In-Time) compilation, 5
modules, 421
MSIL code to native code, 439
multiple `Main()` methods and, 61–62
operators and, 149–150
optimization in Visual Studio 2005, 399–400
`/out` option for output file specification, 64
performance improvement with IL, 5
pointer arithmetic and, 210
preprocessor directives for, 70–73
`PrintingCapsEdit` project, 898
`/reference` or `/r` switch for reference types, 64
rules for identifiers and, 73–75
steps in .NET, 4
`/target` or `/t` switch for file type, 63–64
`TypeView` assembly, 319
usage conventions and, 75
from Visual Studio 2005, 372, 399–403
XML comments, 68–70
`Component` **class, 755**
**Component Services explorer, 1075–1077**
**Computer Management MMC snap-in, 1101–1102**
**concatenation, operator overloads for, 224**
**conditional statements, 47.** *See also* `if` **statements;**
  `switch...case` **statements**
**configuration files (.NET Remoting)**
  client code using, 1045
  client configuration file for event handling, 1061
  client configuration for client-activated objects, 1044
  client configuration for well-known objects, 1043
  debugging, 1046–1047
  delayed loading of client channels, 1046
  example online, 1039–1040
  formatter providers, 1047–1048
  lifetime services, 1047
  main elements and attributes, 1040–1041
  .NET Framework Configuration tool for, 1048–1050
  .NET platform files versus, 1039
  overview, 1039–1041
  predefined channels, 1041–1042
  `RemotingConfiguration.Configure()` method and, 1046
  server code using, 1044–1045
  server configuration file for event handling, 1059

server configuration for client-activated objects, 1043–1044
server configuration for well-known objects, 1042–1043
`Configure()` **method (**`RemotingConfiguration` **class), 1044, 1045, 1046**
**configuring assemblies**
  application configuration files, 450, 453–456
  categories, 450
  `<codeBase>` configuration, 460–461
  configuration files used instead of registry, 449
  directories, 460–462
  machine configuration files, 450
  overview, 450–451
  `<probing>` configuration, 461–462
  publisher policy files, 450, 456–458
  remoting settings, 450
  runtime settings, 450
  runtime version, 459–460
  security settings, 450
  startup settings, 450
  versioning, 451–460
`Connect()` **method (**`RemotingServices` **class), 1028, 1029, 1030**
**connection points (COM), 1166–1168, 1181–1182**
**Connection Properties dialog box (Visual Studio), 822–824**
**consistency of Enterprise Services transactions, 1078**
**console applications**
  creating in Visual Studio 2005, 377–383
  defined, 21
  for Enterprise Services client, 1077
  first C# program, 30–33
  .NET Remoting client, 1019–1020
  .NET Remoting server, 1018–1019
  role-based security example, 508–509
  `TestQuoteServer`, 1279
  threading with `ThreadPool` class, 365–368
  uses for, 21
**console I/O**
  displaying formatted output, 65–67
  format strings, 66–67
  method for reading, 65
  methods for writing, 65
  placeholder characters for output, 67
`Console.ReadLine()` **method, 65**
`Console.Write()` **method, 65**
`Console.WriteLine()` **method**
  displaying formatted output, 65–67
  formatting expressions, 229–230, 231

1497

const keyword, 38, 85
constants
  advantages of using, 38–39
  associating with classes, 85
  in C++ versus C#, 38
  characteristics, 38
  as data members of classes, 85
  declaring, 38, 85
  defined, 38
  Pascal casing for, 76
  `readonly` fields versus, 99
constraints, database
  naming conventions, 630
  setting update and delete constraints, 611–612
constructors
  calling from other constructors, 98–99
  compiler generation of, 95, 119–120
  defined, 86
  of derived classes, 118–124
  `FileStream` class, 1208–1209
  initializers, 99
  instance and static in same class, 97
  no-parameter, adding in a hierarchy, 120–122
  not required for classes, 95
  overloading, 95
  with parameters, adding in a hierarchy, 122–124
  public or protected, 96
  `QuoteServer` class, 1277
  static, 96–98
  `StreamReader` class, 1214
  `StreamWriter` class, 1216
  for structs, 104
  syntax, 95
  `Thread` class, 352
  of Windows Form classes, 755–756
consuming Web services, 990–993
`ContextDataRow` class, 834
`ContextMenuAttribute`, 834, 835, 837
`ContextMenuStrip` class (Windows Forms), 779
contexts (.NET Remoting)
  activation, 1015
  attributes, 1015–1016
  call contexts, 1062–1064
  COM+ contexts compared to, 1014
  communication between, 1016
  context-bound objects, 1015
  Enterprise Services and, 1067–1068
  interceptors, 1015
  overview, 1014–1015
  properties, 1015, 1016

`continue` statement, 55
`Control` class
  appearance properties, 760
  as base class for controls, 759
  `Form` class inheritance from, 780
  miscellaneous functionality, 762
  overview, 759
  size and location properties, 759–760
  user interaction and, 760–761
  Windows functionality, 761–762
control palette (ASP.NET), 913–914
`ControlBindingsCollection` class, 817, 819
`ConvertAll()` method (`List<T>` generic class), 282–283
converting. See also generics
  ADO.NET relational data to XML, 694–696
  ADO.NET single table data to XML, 689–694
  array lists to arrays, 253
  enumerations from strings, 57
  explicit type conversions, 142–145
  implicit type conversions, 141–142
  need for type conversions, 141
  nullable types and, 142
  between numeric and string types, 144–145
  types with `List<T>` generic class, 282–283
  UDTs to and from strings, 640–641
  between value and reference types, 145–146
  to Visual Studio 2005 projects from previous versions, 374–376
  XML to ADO.NET data, 696–699
`CookieContainer` class, 1004–1005
`Coordinate` struct
  changing User-Defined Type template for, 637
  constructors to initialize variables, 639
  converting from a string, 641
  converting to a string, 640–641
  deploying, 642
  `get` accessor, 640
  `INullable` interface, 637
  `IsNull` property, 640
  `Null` property, 640
  `Orientation` enumeration for, 639
  serialization formats, 637–638
  `[SqlUserDefinedType]` attribute, 637, 638
  using from client-side code, 642–643
coordinates
  converting relative to client area, 861–862
  device coordinates, 863
  page coordinates, 863
  `Point` and `PointF` structs for, 851–852

`Rectangle` and `RectangleF` structs for, 853–854
`Region` struct for, 854–855
`Size` and `SizeF` structs for, 852–853
`System.Drawing` structs for, 850
transforms in `CapsEditor` example, 889–890
world coordinates, 863
`Copy()` **method (`File` class), 1197**
**Copy Web tool, deployment using, 552, 555**
**copying files, 1197–1201**
`CopyTo()` **method (`FileInfo` class), 1197**
`Course` **class, 1111–1112**
**course order application (Message Queuing)**
  assemblies, 1111
  class library, 1111–1113
  `Course` class, 1111–1112
  `CourseOrder` class, 1113
  `CourseOrderSender` application, 1114
  `Customer` class, 1112–1113
  `Invoke()` method, 1117
  `LableIdMapping` class, 1117–1118
  message receiver, 1116–1119
  message sender, 1114
  `OnOrderSelectionChanged()` method, 1118–1119
  `OnSubmitCourseOrder()` method, 1114
  `PeekMessages()` method, 1116–1117
  `ReceivedById()` method, 1119
  sending priority and recoverable messages, 1115
`CourseOrder` **class, 1113**
`Create()` **method**
  `MessageQueue` class, 1103, 1121
  `XmlReader` class, 665
`CreateFonts()` **helper method, 883–884**
`CreateGraphics()` **method (`Form` class), 845**
`CreateInstance()` **method (`Activator` class), 1027, 1028, 1029**
`CreateSubKey()` **method (`RegistryKey` class), 1230**
**cross-language support.** *See* **CLS (Common Language Specification); language interoperability with .NET**
**Crystal Reports Web server controls (ASP.NET), 914**
**.cs file extension, 30**
`csc.exe` **command-line compiler**
  compiling programs using, 31
  creating modules using, 421
**CTS (Common Type System)**
  CLS and, 425–426
  hierarchy of types, 11–12
  language interoperability and, 425
  overview, 10–12
**culturalization.** *See* **globalization; localization**
`CultureAndRegionInfoBuilder` **class, 549–550**

`CultureInfo` **class, 515, 518**
**curly braces ({ })**
  with `if` statements, 47, 48
  joining statements in blocks, 31
`Currency` **struct, 159–162**
`CurrencyManager` **class, 819, 820–822**
`Current` **property of collection elements, 247**
**Custom Actions Editor (ClickOnce), 573–575**
**custom attributes**
  `AttributeUsage` attribute and, 307–309
  compilation and, 306–307
  emitted as metadata, 306
  `FieldName` attribute example, 307–310
  finding dependencies for, 320
  required specifications, 307
  for serializing objects in XML, 702
  specifying optional parameters, 309–310
  specifying required parameters, 309
  `WhatsNewAttributes` example, 310–313
**custom controls (ASP.NET)**
  complexity of, 952
  deriving from `WebControl` class, 952
  .NET Framework and, 944
  `RainbowLabel` example, 953–956
  `<%@ Register %>` directive for, 952–953
  user controls versus, 952
  using in ASP.NET pages, 952–953
  `using` statements, 953
**custom controls (Windows Forms)**
  attributes useful to add to, 787–788
  deriving from existing controls, 787
  requirements for, 788
  starting from scratch, 787
  `TreeView`-based example, 788–794
  user controls, 794–799
**custom cultures, 549–550**
**custom generic classes**
  constraints, 294–296
  default values, 294
  defining, 293
  `DocumentManager` class example, 293–294
**custom interfaces (COM), 1153**
`Customer` **class, 1112–1113**
`CustomerTable` **class, 835–837**
`Cycle()` **method, 954**

# D

**data access with .NET.** *See* **ADO.NET; viewing .NET data; Visual Studio .NET and data access**

## data adapters

data adapters
- deleting rows with, 623
- flexibility of, 621
- inserting new rows with, 621–623
- populating a `DataSet` with stored procedure in, 619–620
- `UpdateRowSource` property and, 622–623
- updating existing rows with, 623

data binding. *See also* `DataGridView` **control; event-booking application**
- `Binding` class, 819–820
- `BindingContext` class, 818–819
- class hierarchy for objects, 817–818
- `CurrencyManager` class, 819, 820–822
- data display with templates, 935–936
- data-binding objects, 817–822
- `DataGridView` control capabilities, 801–802
- defined, 816
- Dialog Data Exchange (DDX) versus, 816–817
- `PropertyManager` class, 819, 820–822
- `ScrollingDataBinding` example, 821–822
- simple binding, 816–817
- Web Forms and, 926–939

data members of classes, 85–86. *See also* **constants; events; fields (member variables)**

data types. *See also* **reference types; UDTs (user-defined types); value types;** *specific types*
- blittable, 638
- casting, 143–145
- COM, 1155
- CTS and, 10–12, 40–41
- enumerations, 55–57
- explicit conversions, 142–145
- hierarchy of, 11–12
- implicit conversions, 141–142
- modifiers and, 124–125
- namespaces for, 21, 59
- naming generic types, 274
- nesting, 125
- nullable types, 139, 142, 144, 301–302
- pointers and, 208
- predefined, 41–46
- primitive types as .NET structs, 40–41
- strong typing in IL, 9–16
- strongly typed resources, 531–533
- type library for COM, 1173–1175
- type safety, 7, 134, 140–146
- user-defined casts, 157–169
- value types versus reference types, 9, 39–40

- variable declarations and, 34
- for Web services, 990

**data Web server controls (ASP.NET)**
- data display controls, 918
- data source controls, 917–918
- templates with, 935–939

**database access.** *See* **ADO.NET; viewing .NET data; Visual Studio .NET and data access**

**database connections**
- closing with ADO.NET, 583, 585–588
- creating with Visual Studio .NET, 822–825
- ensuring resources are released, 583–588
- managing connection strings with ADO.NET, 584–585
- opening with ADO.NET, 583

**database server.** *See* **SQL Server 2005**

`DatabaseResourceManager` **class, 548–549**

`DatabaseResourceReader` **class**
- client application for, 549
- creating, 546–547
- database columns and values for example, 545–546

`DatabaseResourceSet` **class, 547–548**

`DataColumn` **class**
- generated for XSD schema, 831–832
- naming conventions for columns, 629
- overview, 602–603

`DataGrid` **control**
- `DataGridView` control versus, 801
- getting selected row with, 839–840

`DataGridView` **control**
- for array data display, 804–805
- binding capabilities, 801–802
- class hierarchy, 813–816
- constructing columns for, 814–816
- `DataGrid` control versus, 801
- `DataGridViewColumn` objects utilized by, 814
- DataMember property, 804
- for `DataSet` display, 809–811
- DataSource property capabilities, 803
- for `DataTable` display, 805
- for `DataView` display, 806–809
- `DisplayTabularData` application, 802–803
- for generic collection display, 811–813
- `IListSource` and `IList` interfaces with, 811

`DataList` **control, 937–938**

`DataRow` **class**
- altering data, 605–606
- generated for XSD schema, 830–831
- overview, 603–604
- for pop-up menu for a database row, 832

1500

## declaring

`RowState` property, 605
versioning by, 604–605
`DataSet` class. *See also* `DataColumn` class; `DataRow` class; `DataTable` class
 converting relational data to XML, 694–696
 converting single table data to XML, 689–694
 converting XML to ADO.NET data, 696–699
 copying a `DataSet`, 625–626
 data columns, 602–603
 data constraints, 609–612
 data relationships, 608–609
 data rows, 603–606
 data tables, 601–602
 `DataGridView` control for displaying data, 805, 809–810, 814–816
 `DataViewManager` for displaying data, 810–811
 overview, 600–601
 persisting `DataSet` changes, 620–625, 691–692
 populating a `DataSet`, 619–620
 `ReadXml()` method, 620, 696–697
 `ReadXmlSchema()` method, 697
 `Recordset` object versus, 609
 schema generation, 606–608, 691
 tiered development and, 625–626
 Web services with `DataSet` objects, 997
 `WriteXml()` method, 624–625, 690–691
 writing XML output, 623–625, 690–691
**DataSource property (`DataGridView` control)**
 arrays as data source for, 804–805
 capabilities, 803
 `DataSet` class as data source for, 809–811
 `DataTable` class as data source for, 805
 `DataView` object as data source for, 806–809
 generic collections as data source for, 811–813
`DataTable` **class**
 binding column to `TextBox`, 816–817
 creating `DataView` from existing `DataTable`, 806
 data-access methods, 835–837
 `DataGridView` control for displaying data, 805
 generated for XSD schema, 829–830
 naming conventions for tables, 629
 overview, 601–602
 for pop-up menu for a database row, 832
 properties of objects, 602
 setting a foreign key, 610–611
 setting a primary key, 610
 setting update and delete constraints, 611–612
`DataView` **object, 806–809**

`DataViewManager`, **displaying** `DataSet` **data in, 810–811**
**date formatting**
 for `DateTimePicker` control, 767
 for globalization, 519–520
`DateTime` **structure, 519**
`DateTimePicker` **control (Windows Forms)**
 hosting on a `ToolStrip`, 777–779
 overview, 765
**DCOM protocol, 1126**
**DCs (device contexts) of GDI+, 843–844**
**DDX (Dialog Data Exchange), 816–817**
**deadlocks, avoiding, 361–363, 364**
**debugging**
 COM issues for, 9
 configuration files (.NET Remoting), 1046–1047
 debug builds for, 399–401
 exceptions and, 406–407
 graphics and, 855–856
 removing debugging commands (Visual Studio), 401
 setting breakpoints, 404
 symbols in Visual Studio, 400–401
 Visual Studio 2005 debugger for, 9, 373, 404–407
 Watch window for (Visual Studio), 405–406
 Windows Services, 1301–1302
`decimal` **type**
 overview, 42–43
 placeholder characters for output, 67
**declarative security**
 for code access, 488
 role-based, 509–510
**declaring.** *See also* **instantiating**
 abstract classes and functions, 117
 constants, 38, 85
 custom generic classes, 293
 delegates, 173–174
 enumerations, 55, 56
 events, 188
 methods, 86–87
 permissions (declarative security), 488
 pointers, 206–207
 properties, 93
 role-based security, 509–510
 `sealed` classes and methods, 117–118
 user-defined casts, 158–159
 variables, 33–34
 virtual methods, 114
 virtual properties, 114

# #define preprocessor directive

`#define` **preprocessor directive, 70, 71**
**defining.** *See* **declaring**
**delegates.** *See also* **events**
   with anonymous methods, 176–185
   with asynchronous .NET Remoting, 1053–1054
   `BubbleSorter` example, 180–182
   for COM, 1181
   declaring, 173–174
   `delegateTest` example, 176–177
   `EventHandler` example, 186–188
   `EventHandler<TEventArgs>` generic delegate, 302–303
   for events, 185
   generic, 299–301
   instantiating, 173–174, 176–177
   interfaces and, 181
   multicast, 183–185
   in .NET Framework, 188
   passing without parameters, 179
   proxy class for, 838
   `SimpleDelegate` example, 177–180
   syntax, 173
   for threading, 352, 353, 366
   type safety and, 172, 174
   uses for, 171–172
   using, 174–176
`delegateTest` **delegate, 176–177**
`Delete()` **method, 1197**
**deleting or removing**
   array list elements, 251–253
   code groups, 494
   database records with ADO.NET, 591, 595–596
   database rows with data adapters, 623
   debugging commands with Visual Studio, 401
   dictionary items, 261
   files, 1197–1201
   folders, 1197
   method calls from multicast delegates, 183
   setting delete constraints for databases, 611–612
**demanding permissions, 478, 479–480**
**denying permissions, 485–486**
**deployment**
   automatic, for Enterprise Services components, 1073
   ClickOnce technology for, 553, 567–576
   Copy Web tool for, 552, 555
   designing for, 551–552
   including deployment project in applications solution, 563–564
   installing client from Web server, 566–567
   manual, for Enterprise Services components, 1073–1074
   No Touch Deployment (NTD), 566–567
   options available to .NET developers, 552–553
   publishing Web sites for, 552, 555–556
   requirements, 553
   simple deployment, 554–556
   simple Web application installer, 564–565
   of triggers for SQL Server, 650
   of UDTs, 642
   of user-defined aggregates, 645
   Windows Installer for, 552, 556–567
   xcopy for, 552, 554–555
`Dequeue()` **method (`Queue` class), 256**
**derived classes**
   calling base versions of methods, 116–117
   casts between, 162–163
   casts between base and derived classes, 163–164
   commas in declarations, 113
   constructors, 118–124
   instantiating, 120
   from interfaces, 126–127
   `Object` class as parent of all classes, 106
   syntax, 113
**derived interfaces, 131–132**
**derived structs, 113**
**Design View window (Visual Studio 2005), 391–394**
**destructors.** *See* **finalizers**
**device contexts (DCs) of GDI+, 843–844**
**device coordinates, 863**
**DHTML versus ASP.NET, 22**
**Dialog Data Exchange (DDX), 816–817**
**dictionaries**
   adding objects to, 261, 262
   algorithm for, 260, 262–263
   defined, 259
   getting details from, 259–260, 261
   `Hashtable` class for, 261–262
   how they work, 262–264
   `key` class for, 262–263
   keys, 260, 262
   `MortimerPhonesEmployees` example, 264–269
   in .NET, 261–262
   overriding `Equals` method for, 264, 266
   overriding `GetHashCode()` method for, 263–264, 266–267
   performance compared to array lists, 259
   real-life dictionaries compared to, 260
   removing items from, 261

requirements for building, 260
uses for, 259, 260
`DiffGram` **documents**
  defined, 699
  reading, 700–701
  uses for, 699
  writing, 699–700
**digital certificates**
  applying FullTrust permission to assemblies, 502
  buying versus creating, 499
  checking code groups for your assembly, 503–504
  configuring the test certificate, 501
  creating a test certificate, 499
  distributing code using, 499–504
  getting a hexadecimal representation, 502
  signing assemblies with, 499–501
  verifying the trust level, 501, 503
**directories.** *See* **folders or directories**
`Directory` **class**
  `Delete()` method, 1197
  described, 1188
  `DirectoryInfo` class versus, 1189
  `Move()` method, 1197
**Directory Services Markup Language.** *See* **DSML**
`DirectoryEntries` **class, 733**
`DirectoryEntry` **class**
  binding Active Directory with, 729
  `CommitChanges()` method, 733, 734
  `RefreshCache()` method, 733
`DirectoryInfo` **class**
  `Delete()` method, 1197
  described, 1188
  `Directory` class versus, 1189
  `Exists` property, 1189–1190
  instantiating, 1189
  methods, 1191–1192
  properties, 1190, 1191
  streams versus, 1206
`DirectorySearcher` **class**
  filters, 736–737
  LDAP provider required for, 736
  `PropertiesToLoad`, 737
  read-mostly access and, 736
  `SearchRoot`, 736
  `SearchScope`, 737
  setting search limits, 737–740
`DisableMoveFeatures` **utility function, 1201**
**dispatch interfaces (COM), 1153–1154**
`DisplayAtStartup` **example, 844–847**

`DisplayFileInfo()` **method, 1194–1195, 1196**
`DisplayFolderList()` **method**
  `FileProperties` application, 1195, 1196, 1197
  `FilePropertiesAndMovement` application, 1200–1201
`DisplayImage` **project, 871–873**
**displaying images**
  example, 870–873
  issues when manipulating images, 873–874
`DisplayNames()` **method, 525**
`DisplayTabularData` **application, 802–803**
`DisplayText` **example, 874–876**
`DisplayTypeInfo()` **method, 322–323**
`Dispose()` **method**
  `ColdCallFileReader` class, 344, 345–346
  `Component` class, 755
  `Form1` class, 872
  `IDisposable` interface, 201–202
**distinguished name (DN) in Active Directory, 727–728, 729**
**distributed identity of remote objects, 1017**
**distributed programming's future.** *See* **WCF; Web services specifications**
**distributed transactions (Enterprise Services), 1068**
**distributing code**
  certificates for, 499–504
  strong names for, 497–499
**DLLs**
  assemblies as answer to DLL Hell, 412–413
  problems with (DLL Hell), 411–412
  side-by-side feature for, 412
**DN (distinguished name) in Active Directory, 727–728, 729**
`Dns` **class, 1260–1261**
**DNS servers**
  `Dns` class, 1260–1261
  `DnsLookup` application, 1261–1262
  IP addresses and, 1259
`DnsLookup` **application, 1261–1262**
`Document` **class**
  `LinkedList<T>` generic class example, 287, 289
  `Queue<T>` generic class example, 284
**document management applications**
  using custom generic class, 293–296
  using `LinkedList<T>` generic class, 287–292
  using `Queue<T>` generic class, 283–286
`DocumentManager` **class**
  custom generic class example, 293–294
  `Queue<T>` generic class example, 284–285

DocumentTitleChanged event, 1248–1249
DOM (document object model)
  using MSXML 4.0 in .NET, 661–663
  XmlDocument class as implementation of, 659, 673
DotnetComponent class, 1172–1173, 1175, 1181–1182
double quotes ("), string literals enclosed by, 46
double type, 42
do...while statements, 53–54
DownloadFile() method (WebClient class), 1240
DrawEllipse() method, overloading, 845
DrawImage() method (Graphics class), 874
DrawImageUnscaled() method (Graphics class), 873
drawing. See also graphics
  lines, 868–870
  scrollable windows, 856–862
  shapes, 844–847, 868–870
  text, 874–880
DrawRectangle() method, overloading, 845
DrawString() method (Graphics class), 874, 875–876
DriveInfo class, 1188, 1220–1222
drives, reading information from, 1220–1222
DSML (Directory Services Markup Language)
  configuration scenario for Active Directory, 745–746
  namespace for, 724, 745
  searching Active Directory objects with, 746–748
  standardized Web interfaces for, 724
  System.DirectoryServices.Protocols classes, 746
dual interfaces (COM), 1154
durability of Enterprise Services transactions, 1078

# E

early binding (COM), 1155
#elif preprocessor directive, 71–72
#else preprocessor directive, 71–72
EnableVisualStyles method (Application class), 785–786
#endif preprocessor directive, 71–72
EndOfStreamException class, 329
EndReceive() method (MessageQueue class), 1111
#endregion preprocessor directive, 72–73
Enterprise Services
  automatic transactions, 1068, 1078
  business service layer for, 1067
  client application, 1077–1078
  Component Services explorer for, 1075–1077
  contexts and, 1067–1068
  current issues, 1126
  data service layer for, 1067
  defined, 1065
  deployment, 1073–1075
  distributed transactions, 1068
  history of, 1066
  installer packages for, 1074–1075
  loosely coupled events, 1069
  Microsoft Application Center Server and, 1067
  object pooling, 1068
  overview, 1065–1069
  presentation service layer for, 1067
  queued components, 1069
  role-based security, 1068
  sample application, 1080–1090
  ServiceConfig class, 1090–1091
  ServiceDomain class, 1090, 1091
  services without components, 1069, 1090–1093
  simple COM+ application, 1070–1073
  transactions, 1068, 1078–1080
  WCF and, 1146–1147
enumerations (enums)
  benefits of using, 56
  collection enumerators, 246–247
  converting from a string, 57
  defining, 55, 56
  described, 55
  EnumFontFamilies example, 878–880
  FileStream class, 1208
  instantiated as structs, 57
  for messages in message queues, 1109–1110
  retrieving string representations, 57
  retrieving values, 57
  TimeOfDay example, 56
enumerators for collections, 248
EnumFontFamilies example, 878–880
Equals() method
  comparing reference types for equality, 146–147
  comparing value types for equality, 147, 148
  described, 107
  overriding for comparisons, 146–147, 148
  overriding for dictionaries, 264, 266, 267
  static version, 147
  virtual version, 146–147
equals sign (=)
  as assignment operator, 34, 134–135
  as comparison operator (==), 48, 134–135, 147

# event-booking application

error handling. *See also* exceptions
   `catch` blocks, defined, 330
   catching exceptions from other code, 336–337
   catching exceptions from predefined classes, 330–340
   catching user-defined exceptions, 341–343
   choosing exception type to throw, 334–335
   for code access permissions, 472
   COM, 1158
   defining your own exception classes, 346–348
   exceptions for, 16–17
   exceptions not handled and, 338
   `finally` blocks, defined, 330
   handling different exceptions in different places, 340
   modifying the type of exception, 340
   multiple catch blocks for, 331, 332–336
   nested `throw` statements for, 332
   nested `try` blocks for, 338–340
   for overflow and array out-of-bounds, 331–332
   process for, 330
   for releasing database resources, 586, 587–588
   `SimpleExceptions` class, 333–336
   syntax, 330–331
   `SystemException` properties for, 337
   throwing an exception, defined, 331
   throwing user-defined exceptions, 343–346
   for thrown `SecurityException`, 480, 482, 492
   `try` blocks, defined, 330
   for Windows Forms controls, 767–769
`#error` **preprocessor directive, 72**
`ErrorProvider` **component (Windows Forms)**
   clearing, 768
   overview, 767–768
   using one error provider per form, 768–769
**escape sequences**
   for regular expressions, 236, 238–240
   searching for escape meta-characters, 240
   table summarizing, 44, 239
`EvaluateException`, **807**
**event logging for services**
   adding for other application types, 1305–1306
   adding for service classes derived from `ServiceBase`, 1302, 1305
   adding to QuoteServer, 1306–1307
   architecture, 1304
   `AutoLog` property of `ServiceBase` class for, 1302, 1305
   classes, 1305
   creating an event log listener, 1307–1308
   custom event logging, 1303

   example log entry, 1302–1303
   trace messages and, 1307
**event sink library (.NET Remoting), 1059–1060**
`EventArgs` **class, 188–189, 832**
**event-booking application**
   `AddEvent()` method, 995
   adding events to the database, 931–933
   ADO.NET and data binding for, 926–933
   `Application_Start()` event handler, 994
   `attendeeList` control, 928
   `Attendees` table, 926–927
   binding to controls on the Web page, 999
   binding to the database, 927–928
   `calendar_DayRender()` event handler, 930–931
   `calendar_SelectionChanged()` event handler, 930
   client for Web service extension, 997–1001
   code-behind file, 929–930
   creating the Web site, 920–921, 926
   customizing the calendar control, 928–931
   data binding for client application, 1000
   data display with templates, 935–939
   database for, 926–927
   `DataList` control, 937–938
   `DataSet` objects with Web services, 997
   declaring objects needed for database access, 995–996
   deleting data sources for client application, 998
   event list display, 933–935
   `EventList` control, 936–937
   `EventList_SelectedChanged()` method, 1001
   `Events` table, 927
   `ExecuteNonQuery()` method, 932–933
   extracting event data, 930
   form for, 920–923
   `FormView` control, 936, 937–938
   `GetData()` method, 994–995
   `GetFreeDate()` method, 929–930, 933
   `GridView` control, 933–934
   `Label` control, 920
   `Lock()` and `Unlock()` methods, 996
   `MRBEventData` control, 929
   `MRBService` service, 994–995
   `Page_Load()` event handler, 924
   `queryResult` with, 996–997
   `resultLabel` control, 924
   results of a submission, 924–925
   `roomList` control, 928
   `Rooms` table, 927
   `SqlDataSource` controls, 927–928
   storing the `DataSet` for client application, 998–999

**1505**

## event-booking application (continued)

event-booking application (continued)
  submitButton_Click() event handler,
    924, 931–932, 934, 1000–1001
  using statements, 995
  ValidationSummary control, 921
  Web server controls for, 921–924
  Web service for, 993–997
  web.config file, 993
EventHandler **delegate, 186–188**
EventHandler<TEventArgs> **generic delegate,**
    **302–303**
EventList **control, 936–937**
EventLog **component, 1307–1308**
**events**
  Click event example, 186–188
  COM event handling, 1158, 1166–1168, 1181–1182
  as data members of classes, 85
  defining, 188
  delegates for, 185
  described, 85
  focus, gaining and losing for controls, 761
  generating, 188–192
  keyboard events, 760–761
  messages wrapped in, 185
  methods for handling, 186–188
  mouse events, 760
  names of event handlers, 187
  .NET Remoting and, 1056–1062
  receiver's view of, 185–188
  senders for, 185–186, 188
  threading workaround using, 350
  user control event handler, 797–798
  for user controls (ASP.NET), 948
  for Windows Form user interaction, 760–761
  Windows Services event logging, 1302–1308
**exceptions.** *See also* **error handling**
  for aborting threads, 354
  base class exception classes, 328–330
  catching from predefined classes, 330–340
  catching user-defined exceptions, 341–343
  choosing type to throw, 334–335
  class hierarchy, 329–330
  debugging and, 406–407
  handling different exceptions in different places, 340
  modifying the type of, 340
  multiple catch blocks for, 331, 332–336
  nested throw statements for, 332
  in .NET, 16–17
  not handled, outcome of, 338

  SimpleExceptions class, 333–336
  throwing, defined, 331
  throwing from catch and finally blocks, 339
  throwing user-defined exceptions, 343–346
  user-defined exception classes, 340–348
ExecuteNonQuery() **method, 591, 932–933**
ExecuteReader() **method, 591–592**
ExecuteScalar() **method, 592–593**
ExecuteXmlReader() **method, 593–594**
Exists() **method (**MessageQueue **class),**
    **1104–1105**
**explicit type conversions, 142–145, 158.** *See also*
    **user-defined casts**
**exposing Web services, 987–990**
extern **modifier, 125**
**extracting characters from strings, 224**

## F

**fat-client applications, 22, 24**
FieldName **attribute example**
  AttributeUsage attribute, 307–309
  code listing, 307
  specifying optional parameters, 309–310
  specifying required parameters, 309
**fields (member variables).** *See also* **properties**
  accessing instance fields outside the class, 38
  accessing static fields outside the object, 37–38
  casing of, 76–77
  as data members of classes, 85
  defined, 85
  marking unsafe, 206
  pointers to, 212–214
  public, in structs, 102
  readonly fields, 99–101
  scope, 35
  scope clashes for local variables and, 37–38
  usage conventions, 81
**FIFO (First In Last Out) structure**
  Queue class, 256
  Queue<T> generic class, 283
**file associations, setting with ClickOnce, 571**
File **class**
  Copy() method, 1197
  Delete() method, 1197
  described, 1188
  FileInfo class versus, 1189
  Move() method, 1197
**file management.** *See* **file system operations**

**File System Editor (ClickOnce), 570**
**file system operations.** *See also specific classes*
  buffered streams, 1207
  classes for, 1188
  file browser example, 1192–1197
  file security, 1187, 1222–1226
  `FilePropertiesAndMovement` application, 1197–1201
  moving and deleting folders, 1197
  moving, copying, and deleting files, 1197–1201
  namespace for, 1187
  reading and writing to binary files, 1208–1213
  reading and writing to text files, 1213–1219
  reading from files, 1201, 1202–1204
  streams, 1205–1207
  writing to files, 1201, 1204–1205
**File Types Editor (ClickOnce), 571**
`FileInfo` **class**
  `CopyTo()` method, 1197
  `Delete()` method, 1197
  described, 1188
  `Exists` property, 1189–1190
  `File` class versus, 1189
  instantiating, 1189
  methods, 1191–1192
  `MoveTo()` method, 1197
  properties, 1190, 1191
  streams versus, 1206
`FileProperties` **application**
  `ClearAllFields()` method, 1194
  `currentFolderPath` member field, 1194
  `DisplayFileInfo()` method, 1194–1195, 1196
  `DisplayFolderList()` method, 1195, 1196, 1197
  event handlers, 1195–1197
  events, 1194
  overview, 1192–1193
  `using` statements, 1193–1194
`FilePropertiesAndMovement` **application**
  `ClearAllFields()` method, 1201
  controls, 1198
  `DisableMoveFeatures` utility function, 1201
  `DisplayFolderList()` method, 1200–1201
  enabling and disabling controls, 1200
  event handlers, 1199–1200
  overview, 1197–1198
`FileStream` **class**
  `BinaryFileReader` application, 1210–1213
  closing streams, 1209
  constructors, 1208–1209
  described, 1207
  enumerations, 1208
  information required for instantiating, 1208
  reading data, 1209
  `StreamReader` class with, 1215
  `StreamWriter` class with, 1216
  writing data, 1209–1210
`FileSystemInfo` **class, 1188**
`Finalize()` **method**
  for compiled destructors, 199, 200
  described, 107, 108
**finalizers (destructors)**
  in C++ versus C#, 200
  defined, 86
  as `Dispose()` method backup, 202–203
  overview, 199–200
  performance and, 200
  syntax, 200
`finally` **blocks**
  defined, 330
  error trapping process and, 330
  `MortimerColdCall` example, 343
  omitting, 331
  for releasing database resources, 586, 587–588
  in `SimpleExceptions` class, 334
  syntax, 331
  throwing exceptions from, 339
`Find()` **method (**`List<T>` **generic class), 280**
`FindAll()` **method (**`List<T>` **generic class), 280**
**finding message queues, 1103–1104**
**First In Last Out (FIFO) structure**
  `Queue` class, 256
  `Queue<T>` generic class, 283
`fixed` **keyword for pointers, 213–214**
`float` **type**
  converting integers to, 159–162
  overview, 42
**floating-point types, 42.** *See also specific types*
**flow control.** *See also specific statements*
  conditional statements, 47–51
  jump statements, 54–55
  loops, 51–54
`FlowLayoutPanel` **control (Windows Forms), 774–775**
**focus, gaining and losing for controls, 761**
**folders or directories.** *See also* **file system operations**
  configuring for assemblies, 460–462
  defined, 1188
  securing with ASP.NET, 971–973

# FolderTree custom control (Windows Forms)

FolderTree **custom control (Windows Forms)**
  adding an image for Toolbox display, 794
  adding properties for handling files and folders, 791–792
  deriving from `TreeView` control, 789
  `FileNode` class for loading files, 789–790
  `FolderNode` class for loading folders, 789, 790–791
  further enhancements possible for, 794
  initializing file system loading, 792–794
  testing the control, 794
`Font` **class**
  `Height` property, 879–880
  overview, 877
`FontFamily` **class, 877, 879**
**fonts and font families**
  classes for, 877
  defined, 876
  enumerating font families, 878–880
  measuring size of text, 876
  selecting fonts, 877
  terminology, 876–877
`for` **statements**
  overview, 51–53
  scope of local variables declared in, 36–37
`ForEach()` **method (`List<T>` generic class), 281**
`foreach` **statements**
  iterating through collections with, 54, 246
  overview, 54
  for reading `Stack` values, 254
  as syntactical shortcuts, 248
`Form` **class**
  application example using, 752
  closing forms, 782
  controlling appearance of forms, 784–786
  `FormBorderStyle` property, 785
  `Icon` property, 785
  inheritance from `Control` class, 780
  initialization, 781
  instantiating, 781
  `Invalidate()` method, 884–886
  methods for keyboard events, 891
  methods for mouse events, 890
  properties relating to form startup, 782
  setting colors for forms, 785
  `Show()` method, 782
  `ShowDialog()` method, 782–784
  `ShowInTaskbar` property, 782
  system menu and, 784–785
  user interaction with, 782–784
  visibility of forms and, 781, 782

`Format()` **method (`String` class), 231**
**formatter provider (.NET Remoting), 1012, 1047–1048**
**formatters**
  Message Queuing, 1107–1108
  .NET Remoting, 1012, 1025
**formatting expressions**
  format specifiers, 230
  `FormatVector` example, 233–235
  how strings are formatted, 231–233
  interfaces for, 223
  need for, 229
`FormatVector` **struct, 233–235**
**forms. See Web Forms; Windows Forms**
`FormView` **control, 936, 937–938**
`FromFile()` **method (`Image` class), 871**
**FTP, as high-level protocol, 1262**
**function pointers, 171. See also delegates**
**functions. See also constructors; finalizers (destructors); methods; properties**
  abstract, 117
  association with class required for, 86
  calling base versions, 116–117
  defining for structs, 101–102
  function members of classes, 85–86
  methods versus, 86
  overview, 86
  standard function calls, 78–80
**future of distributed programming. See WCF; Web services specifications**

# G

**GAC. See global assembly cache**
**gacutil (Global Assembly Cache Utility), 441, 446, 449**
**garbage collection**
  closing forms and, 782
  destructors and, 199
  efficiency of, 193–194
  `fixed` keyword for pointers and, 213–214
  forcing, 199
  managed heap and, 13, 198–199
  not deterministic, 14
  overview, 198–199
  strong data typing in IL and, 13–14
  `System.GC` class for, 199
**GDI (graphical device interface), 842. See also GDI+**
**GDI+. See also graphics**
  color representation in, 863
  described, 841
  device contexts (DCs), 843–844

1508

displaying images using, 870–873
GDI versus, 842
Graphics class and, 844
huge number of features provided by, 842
namespaces for, 843
responding to user input, 890–893
Generate() **method (**ResourceWriter **class), 528**
GenericCustomer **class, 119–124**
**generics**
 ArraySegment<T> struct, 303–304
 binary code reuse by, 273–274
 C++ templates compared to, 272
 code bloat and, 274
 collection classes and their functionality, 276–277
 creating custom generic classes, 293–296
 delegates, 299–301
 displaying collections with DataGridView control, 811–813
 EventHandler<TEventArgs> delegate, 302–303
 interfaces and their functionality, 275–276
 introduction of, 269, 271
 LinkedList<T> class, 287–292
 List<T> class, 272–273, 278–283
 methods, 297–299
 namespace for, 270
 naming guidelines, 274
 .NET base classes for, 277–278
 Nullable<T> struct, 301–302
 performance advantages of, 272–273
 Queue<T> class, 283–286
 strong typing provided by, 269
 type safety of, 273
get **accessor of properties, 93, 94**
GetAssemblyFullName() **method, 452**
GetAttribute() **method (**XmlReader **class), 668**
GetChannel() **method (**ChannelServices **class), 1026**
GetCustomAttributes() **method (**Assembly **class), 320, 323**
GetDocument() **method (**DocumentManager **class), 284, 294**
GetEnumerator() **method (**IEnumerable **interface), 246–247**
GetFreeDate() **method, 929–930, 933**
GetHashCode() **method, 107, 263–264**
GetKeyList() **method (**SortedList **class), 258**
GetMembers() **method, 319**
GetMethods() **method (**Type **class), 323**
GetObject() **method (**Activator **class), 1027, 1028, 1029, 1030**

GetRandomQuoteOfTheDay() **method (**QuoteServer **class library), 1277**
GetRange() **method (**ArrayList **class), 253**
GetRowType() **method (**CustomerTable **class), 836**
GetType() **method (**Type **class), 107, 108, 314**
GetTypes() **method (**Assembly **class), 319–320, 322**
GetValue() **method (**RegistryKey **class), 1231**
GetValueList() **method (**SortedList **class), 258**
**global assembly cache**
 adding publisher policy assembly to, 457
 Assembly Cache Viewer for, 439–440
 ClickOnce limitations and, 567
 COM registration using, 1178
 defined, 19, 413, 438
 gacutil (Global Assembly Cache Utility), 441, 446, 449
 Ngen.exe native image generator, 438–439
**Global Assembly Cache Utility (gacutil), 441, 446, 449**
**globalization.** See also **localization**
 creating custom cultures, 549–550
 CultureInfo class for, 515
 CurrentCulture and CurrentUICulture properties for, 516–517, 518, 519
 date formatting, 519–520
 defined, 513
 localization versus, 513
 namespace for, 513, 514
 number formatting, 517–519
 RegionInfo class for, 515
 sorting and, 524–526
 specific, neutral, and invariant cultures and, 515–516
 Unicode issues, 514–515
 Windows Forms culture demo application, 520–524
**globally unique identifier (GUID) in Active Directory, 728**
goto **statement, 50, 55**
**graphical device interface (GDI), 842.** See also **GDI+**
**graphics.** See also CapsEditor **example; GDI+**
 clipping region and, 848–850
 colors, 863–866
 debugging and, 855–856
 device coordinates for, 863
 display modes, colors and, 865
 displaying images, 870–873
 drawing scrollable windows, 856–862
 drawing shapes and lines, 868–870
 drawing shapes, application for, 844–847
 drawing text, 874–880
 editing a text document, 880–893
 enumerating font families, 878–880
 fonts and font families, 876–880
 hidden window parts and, 846–847

## graphics (continued)

graphics (continued)
- issues when manipulating images, 873–874
- measuring coordinates and areas, 850–855
- page coordinates for, 863
- painting shapes, 847–848
- pens and brushes for, 866–868
- printing, 893–899
- simple text example, 874–876
- world coordinates for, 863

`Graphics` class
- `DrawImage()` method, 874
- `DrawImageUnscaled()` method, 873
- `DrawString()` method, 874, 875–876
- GDI+ and, 844
- `MeasureString()` method, 874, 893
- methods, 868–869

`GregorianCalendar` class, 522–523
grouping characters with regular expressions, 240–243
groups of objects. *See also* generics; *specific functionalities*
- array lists, 250–253
- collections, 246–250
- dictionaries, 259–269
- .NET functionality supporting, 245–246
- queues, 256–257
- `SortedList` collections, 257–259
- stacks, 253–256

GUID (globally unique identifier) in Active Directory, 728

## H

hash tables. *See* dictionaries
`Hashtable` class, 261–262
heap. *See* managed heap
`HelpProvider` component (Windows Forms), 769
hiding methods, 115–116
hosting with WCF, 1143–1144
HTML
- in ASP.NET code model, 909
- displaying output as HTML page, 1245–1258
- naming tags for user controls (ASP.NET), 946
- `<%@ Page %>` tag, 908
- server controls (ASP.NET), 910

HTTP performance issues, 1133

## I

IANA (Internet Assigned Number Authority), 1263
`IBankAccount` interface, 127–130
`IChannel` interface, 1022
`ICollection` interface, 247

`_ICompletedEvents` client interface (COM), 1166–1167
IDE for .NET. *See* Visual Studio 2005
identifiers, 74–75
Identity Permissions, 472–473
`IDispatch` interface (COM), 1163, 1164
`IDisposable` interface
- deriving classes from, 126–127
- destructors as backup for, 202–203
- `Dispose()` method, 201–202
- implementing, 202–204
- overview, 201–202

`IEnumerable` interface, 246–247, 1109–1110
`#if` preprocessor directive, 71–72
`if` statements
- overview, 47–49
- ternary operator, 136–137

`IFormattable` interface, 231–232
IIS (Internet Information Server), ASP.NET and, 904
IL or MSIL (Microsoft Intermediate Language)
- application domains and, 14–16, 413
- attributes, 17
- case sensitivity, 12
- CLS and language interoperability, 12–13
- compilation steps in .NET and, 4
- compiling to native code, 439
- CTS and data types, 10–12
- defined, 3
- error handling with exceptions, 16–17
- garbage collection and, 13–14
- important features, 8
- interfaces supported by, 8–9
- language interoperability with, 5–7
- as managed code, 4
- object orientation supported by, 8–9
- performance improvement with, 5
- platform independence with, 4–5
- security and strong typing, 14
- strong data typing, 9–16
- value types versus reference types, 9

ildasm utility
- checking `.mresource` attribute, 528
- symbols used in, 420–421
- viewing assemblies with, 420

`IList` interface, 811
`IListSource` interface, 811
`Image` class, 871
`ImageList` component (Windows Forms), 769
images. *See* graphics; resources
`IMath` interface (COM), 1162, 1174, 1177–1178

## internationalization

IMessageSink **interface, 1031**
**implementation inheritance**
  abstract classes and functions, 117
  calling base versions of functions, 116–117
  hiding methods, 115–116
  not supported by structs, 112
  overview, 111–112
  sealed classes and methods, 117–118
  syntax, 113
  virtual methods, 114–115
**implicit permission, 484–485**
**implicit type conversions, 141–142**
**indexers**
  for array lists, 251
  defined, 86
**indexes to XML types, 656–657**
**indirection operator for pointers, 207**
**inheritance.** *See also* **derived classes;** *specific kinds*
  abstract classes and functions, 117
  calling base versions of functions, 116–117
  constructors of derived classes, 118–124
  derived interfaces, 131–132
  hiding methods, 115–116
  implementation inheritance, 111–112, 113–124
  interface inheritance, 112, 126–132
  modifiers, 124–125
  multiple, 112
  from Object class, 106
  sealed classes and methods, 117–118
  structs and, 103, 112–113
  virtual methods, 114–115
Init() **method, 644–645**
**initialization**
  of arrays with specific dimensions, 58
  CapsEditor example, 883
  of constructors, 99
  of FolderTree custom control (Windows Forms), 792–794
  of Form class, 781
  of structs, 103
  of user controls (Windows Forms), 798
  of variables, 34–35
InitializeComponent() **method**
  Localizable property for, 536
  setting minimum document size with, 858–859
  shape-drawing application, 844–845
**inserting records with ADO.NET, 591, 596–597**
**installallutil.exe utility, 1291–1292**
InstalledFontCollection **class, 877**

**installing.** *See also* **Windows Installer projects**
  assemblies, 412
  message queues, 1122
  shared assemblies, 446, 451
  Windows Services, 1287–1292
**instantiating**
  ArrayList class, 250
  classes and structs, 84
  COM components, 1165
  delegates, 173–174, 176–177
  derived classes, 120
  DirectoryInfo class, 1189
  enumerations, 57
  FileInfo class, 1189
  Form class, 781
  reference objects, 35
  SortedList class, 258
int **type, 41, 42**
**integer types.** *See also specific types*
  casting pointers to, 208–209
  converting between string type and, 144–145
  converting to floats, 159–162
  enumerations, 55–57
  overview, 41–42
**interfaces**
  for channels (.NET Remoting), 1022
  COM, 1153–1155
  for database connections, 825
  defining and implementing, 127–130
  delegates and, 181
  derived, 131–132
  for formatters (.NET Remoting), 1025
  for formatting expressions, 223
  for generic base classes, 278
  for generics, 275–276
  IL support for, 8–9
  inheritance, 112–113
  for List<T> generic class, 278
  for message sinks, 1031
  .NET Remoting, 1052
  .NET versus COM, 8, 126
  overview, 126–127
  partial, 104
  references, 130
**Intermediate Language.** *See* **IL or MSIL (Microsoft Intermediate Language)**
internal **modifier, 124, 125**
**internationalization.** *See* **globalization**

## Internet access

**Internet access**
  displaying output as HTML page, 1245–1258
  displaying the code of a requested page, 1256–1257
  DNS servers and, 1259
  `DnsLookup` application, 1261–1262
  downloading files, 1240
  giving applications IE-type features, 1248–1253
  IP addresses and, 1259
  launching Internet Explorer instances, 1248
  lower-level classes, 1263–1268
  lower-level protocols, 1262–1263
  .NET classes for IP addresses, 1260–1261
  printing using `WebBrowser` control, 1255–1256
  showing documents using `WebBrowser` control, 1254–1255
  simple Web browsing from applications, 1246–1247
  `Socket` class, 1263, 1268
  starting an Internet Explorer process programmatically, 1245–1246
  `System.Net.Sockets` namespace classes, 1263
  TCP classes, 1263
  TCP versus UDP, 1266
  `TcpReceive` application, 1264–1266, 1268
  `TcpSend` application, 1263–1264
  `UdpClient` class, 1266–1267
  uploading files, 1242
  `Uri` class, 1258–1259
  `UriBuilder` class, 1258, 1259
  utility classes, 1258–1262
  `WebClient` class, 1240–1242
  `WebRequest` and `WebResponse` hierarchy, 1257–1258
  `WebRequest` class, 1242–1245
  `WebResponse` class, 1242–1245
**Internet Assigned Number Authority (IANA), 1263**
**Internet Explorer**
  giving applications IE-type features, 1248–1253
  launching instances, 1248
  running Windows Forms controls in, 1183
  starting a process programmatically, 1245–1246
  threading by, 349–350
**Internet Information Server (IIS), ASP.NET and, 904**
**Internet resources**
  COM interoperability sample code, 1151
  event-booking application example, 920
  Internet Assigned Number Authority (IANA), 1263
  Microsoft Application Center Server information, 1067
  Mono project, 5
  `PrintingCapsEdit` project, 895
  SharePoint Web sites information, 920

  Web services specifications, 1127
  WROX Web site, 895, 920, 1151
  `INullable` **interface, 637**
  `Invalidate()` **method (`Form` class), 884–886**
**invariant cultures, 516**
  `Invoke()` **method, 1117**
**invoking methods**
  generic methods, 297
  overview, 87–89
**IP addresses**
  `Dns` class, 1260–1261
  DNS servers and, 1259
  `DnsLookup` application, 1261–1262
  `IPAddress` class, 1260
  `IPHostEntry` class, 1260
  `IPAddress` **class, 1260**
  `IPHostEntry` **class, 1260**
  `is` **operator, 138**
**isolation levels for ADO.NET transactions, 588–589**
**isolation of Enterprise Services transactions, 1078**
  `IsStyleAvailable()` **method (`FontFamily` class), 879**
  `IsTransparentProxy()` **method (`RemotingServices` class), 1029**
  `ITransferBankAccount` **interface, 131–132**
  `IUnknown` **interface (COM), 1163, 1164**
  `IWelcome` **interface (COM), 1160–1161, 1162, 1174, 1177–1178**

## J

**J++, reading in projects to Visual Studio 2005, 387**
**JIT (Just-In-Time) compilation, 5**
  `Join()` **method (`Thread` class), 354**
**JScript .NET, interoperability with .NET, 7**
**jump statements.** *See also specific statements*
  anonymous methods and, 177
  overview, 54–55

## K

**key generation with SQL Server, 627–629**
**keyboard events**
  methods for, 891
  overview, 760–761
**keys, database**
  generation with SQL Server, 627–629
  setting a foreign key, 610–611
  setting a primary key, 610
**keys, registry, 1228–1229**

**keywords.** *See also specific keywords*
  names and, 74, 78–80
  reserved keywords, 74
  using as identifiers, 74

# L

`Label` **control**
  Web Forms, 920
  Windows Forms, 769–770
`LableIdMapping` **class, 1117–1118**
`LandLineSpyFoundException`, **341, 346**
**language interoperability with .NET.** *See also* **CLS (Common Language Specification)**
  COM and COM+, 7, 8–9, 425
  CTS and, 425
  defined, 5, 9
  scripting languages, 7
  strong data typing's importance for, 10–13
  Visual Basic 2005, 5–6
  Visual C++ 2005, 6–7
  Visual J# 2005, 7
  XML namespace and, 661
**Last In First Out (LIFO) structure of** `Stack` **class, 253–254**
`LastModifiedAttribute` **class, 311–312**
**late binding (COM), 1155**
**Launch Conditions Editor (ClickOnce), 575–576**
**lifetime management (.NET Remoting)**
  changing default lease configurations, 1038–1039
  classes for, 1037
  getting lease information, 1037–1038
  lease renewals, 1036–1037
  leasing configuration values, 1037
  overview, 1036
  services in configuration files, 1046–1047
**LIFO (Last In First Out) structure of** `Stack` **class, 253–254**
**line breaks in string literals, 46**
`#line` **preprocessor directive, 73**
`LineIndexToPageCoordinates()` **method, 890**
`LineIndexToWorldCoordinates()` **method, 889**
**lines**
  `ScrollMoreShapes` example, 869–870
  `System.Drawing.Graphics` methods for, 868–869
`LinkedList<T>` **generic class**
  advantages and disadvantages of, 287
  doubly linked list diagram, 287
  example using, 287, 289–292
`LinkLabel` **control (Windows Forms), 1248**

`ListBox` **control (Windows Forms), 765–767**
`ListControl` **class (Windows Forms)**
  `CheckedListBox` control derived from, 765
  `ComboBox` control derived from, 765, 767
  `ListBox` control derived from, 765–767
`ListenerThread()` **thread function (**`QuoteServer` **class), 1278**
`List<T>` **generic class**
  `Add()` method, 279
  boxing and unboxing avoided by, 272–273
  example using `Racer` class as elements for, 278–279
  finding elements, 280
  interfaces implemented by, 278
  with `LinkedList<T>` class, 287, 289
  performing an action with every element, 281
  sorting elements, 281–282
  type conversion using, 282–283
`ListView` **control (Windows Forms)**
  adding columns for details view, 771–772
  adding items to `ComboBox` `(cbView)`, 771
  `Alignment` property, 772
  `CheckBoxes` property, 772
  `CountryList` example, 770–771
  overview, 770
**literals, 44, 46**
`Load()` **method (**`Assembly` **class), 319**
`LoadFile()` **method**
  `CapsEditor` example, 884
  `PrintingCapsEdit` project, 895
`LoadFrom()` **method (**`Assembly` **class), 319**
**local variables**
  scope, 35–36
  scope clashes for fields and, 37–38
  scope clashes for variables with same name, 36–37
  unsafe, 206
`Localizable` **property of Windows Forms, 536, 537**
**localization.** *See also* **globalization; resources**
  automatic fallback for resources, 542
  changing the culture programmatically, 539–541
  creating custom cultures, 549–550
  `CurrentCulture` and `CurrentUICulture` properties for, 539
  custom resource messages for, 541–542
  custom resource reader, 545–549
  defined, 513
  globalization versus, 513
  namespace for, 513, 534
  outsourcing translations, 543–544
  satellite assemblies for languages, 538
  using ASP.NET, 544–545

## localization (continued)

localization (continued)
  using Visual Studio, 534–555
  winres.exe (Windows Resource Localization Editor), 543
`lock` statement
  deadlocks, avoiding, 361–363, 364
  overusing, avoiding, 361
  race conditions, avoiding, 363–364
  using, 360–361
logging Windows Services events. *See* event logging for services
login
  maintaining using SOAP headers, 1001–1007
  system implementation, 969–970
  Web server controls (ASP.NET), 970–971
`Login()` **method, 1002–1003, 1005**
`long` **type, 41, 42**
`LookUpWhatsNew` **assembly, 310, 321–324**
loops. *See also* specific statements
  `break` statement in nested loops, 55
  overview, 51
  scope of local variables declared in, 36–37

# M

machine configuration files for assemblies, 450
`machine.config` **file, 1041, 1046**
mage.exe ClickOnce tool, 568
mageUI.exe ClickOnce tool, 568
`Main()` method
  for Finnish sorting example, 525
  first thread started at, 350
  `MortimerColdCall` example, 341–343
  overview, 32–33, 61
  passing arguments to, 63
  `PriorityDocumentManager` class, 292
  `QuoteService` example, 1284–1285
  single entry point provided by, 349
  `TypeView` assembly example, 318
  using multiple `Main()` methods, 61–62
  Windows Form application, 752–753
  for Windows Services, 1273–1274
making. *See* building; compiling
managed code. *See also* IL or MSIL (Microsoft Intermediate Language)
  language interoperability with, 5–7
  performance improvement with, 5
  platform independence with, 4–5
managed heap
  garbage collector and, 13, 198–199
  reference types stored in, 9, 39, 196–198
  stack and, 196–198
  structs stored in, 9
  value types declared within reference types stored in, 9
manifests of assemblies, 418
manufactured tables and rows
  dispatching methods for, 837–838
  getting the selected row, 839–840
  required methods for, 835–837
  using an attribute, 837
maps. *See* dictionaries
marshal-by-reference classes, 1031–1032
`MarshalByRefObject` **class, 1188**
marshal-by-value classes, 1031
marshaling
  COM, 1159
  .NET Remoting, 1032–1034
`MaskedTextBox` **control (Windows Forms), 773, 774**
master pages (ASP.NET)
  `Content` controls and, 958
  `.master` file extension for, 956
  modifying `.aspx` pages to use, 957
  in `PCSDemoSite` application, 958–960
  requirements for `.aspx` pages using, 958
  selecting when adding `.aspx` pages to Web site, 957–958
  standard `.aspx` pages compared to, 956–957
  uses for, 956
`MathOperations` class
  multicast delegate with, 183–184
  simple delegate with, 177–179
`MathTest` **class, 87–89**
MDI (Multiple Document Interface), 786–787
`MeasureString()` **method (**`Graphics` **class), 874, 893**
member variables. *See* fields
`MemberwiseClone()` **method, 107, 108**
memory management. *See also* managed heap; stack
  in C++, 13
  in COM, 13, 1153
  destructors for, 199–200, 202–203
  freeing unmanaged resources, 199–204
  garbage collection, 13–14, 193–194, 198–199
  `IDisposable` interface for, 201–204
  reference types and, 196–198
  value types and, 194–195
  virtual addressing and virtual memory, 194
  Windows platform methods for, 13
memory (RAM)
  freeing in COM, 1153
  requirements for application deployment, 553

1514

MenuCommand **proxy class, 838**
**menus (Windows Forms)**
  ContextMenuStrip class for, 779
  MenuStrip control for, 779
  ToolStrip control for, 776
  ToolStripManager class for, 780
  ToolStripMenuItem class for, 779–780
MenuStrip **control (Windows Forms), 779**
Merge() **method, 644–645**
**Message Queuing**
  acknowledgement messages, 1099
  acknowledgement queues, 1120
  administration queues, 1100
  administrative tools, 1101–1102
  architecture, 1099–1101
  asynchronous operation of, 1095–1096
  asynchronous read, 1110–1111
  components available for, 1098
  connected and disconnected programming, 1096
  course order application, 1111–1119
  creating message queues programmatically, 1103
  creating message queues with Computer Management tool, 1101
  dead-letter queues, 1100, 1105
  enumerating messages, 1109–1110
  express delivery mode, 1099
  features, 1098
  finding a queue, 1103–1104
  installing message queues, 1122
  journal queues, 1100, 1105
  message formatter, 1107–1108
  message queue properties, 1101–1102
  message queues overview, 1100–1101
  messages overview, 1099–1100
  opening known queues by format name, 1105–1106
  opening known queues by path name, 1104–1105
  overview, 1095–1098
  priorities for messages, 1099
  private queues, 1100, 1105
  public queues, 1100, 1105
  receiving messages, 1109–1111
  receiving results, 1120–1121
  recoverable delivery mode, 1099–1100
  report messages, 1099
  report queues, 1100
  response messages, 1099
  response queues, 1100, 1120–1121
  sending messages, 1106–1109
  service for, 1098–1099
  system queues, 1100
  transactional messages, 1100
  transactional queues, 1121–1122
  uses for, 1096–1097
  WCF and, 1147
**message sinks (.NET Remoting)**
  defined, 1012, 1015
  overview, 1030–1031
MessageArrived **handler method (**MessageQueue **class), 1110–1111**
MessageEnumerator **class, 1110**
MessageQueue **class**
  BeginReceive() method, 1110
  Create() method, 1103, 1121
  EndReceive() method, 1111
  Exists() method, 1104–1105
  IEnumerable interface implemented by, 1109–1110
  MessageArrived handler method, 1110–1111
  Receive() method, 1109, 1110
  Send() method, 1106, 1108
**messages.** *See also* **events; Message Queuing**
  defined, 185
  .NET Remoting, 1012, 1030
  wrapped in events, 185
**metadata**
  in assemblies, 18
  COM, 1152
  custom attributes emitted as, 306
**methods.** *See also* **delegates; properties;** *specific methods*
  abstract, 117
  anonymous, delegates with, 176–185
  Application class, 753
  binding (COM), 1155
  calling base versions, 116–117
  calling in Web services with SOAP, 984–985
  for combined characters, 515
  declaring, 86–87
  defined, 86
  DirectoryInfo class, 1191–1192
  for drawing shapes and lines, 868–869
  event handlers, 186–188
  FileInfo class, 1191–1192
  format of definitions, 33
  functions versus, 86
  generic, 297–299
  of generic classes, 276–277
  of generic interfaces, 275–276
  hiding, 115–116
  initialization required for variables local to, 35
  invoking, 87–89

1515

## methods (continued)

methods (continued)
- for keyboard events, 891
- making accessible through Web services, 988
- for manufactured tables and rows, 835–838
- marking `unsafe`, 205
- for mouse events, 890
- multicast delegates and, 183–185
- non-compliant with CLS, 426
- `Object` class, 106–109
- of `object` type, 45
- overloading, 92
- overriding virtual methods, 114–115
- passing parameters to, 89–91
- `public` versus `static`, 33
- `Queue` class, 257
- for reading from console, 65
- `Registry` class, 1231–1232
- `return` statement for exiting, 55
- return type required for, 87
- `sealed`, 117–118
- `ServiceController` class, 1300
- `ServicedComponent` class, 1072
- `SortedList` class, 258–259
- `Stack` class, 255–256
- `String` class, 224–225
- `StringBuilder` class, 228–229
- `System.Type` class, 315–316
- usage conventions, 80
- virtual, 114–115
- in Visual Studio 2005 Object Browser window, 397–398
- for writing to console, 65
- `XPathNavigator` class, 679–680

**Microsoft Application Center Server, 1067**
**Microsoft Intermediate Language. See IL or MSIL**
**Microsoft Management Console. See MMC**
**Microsoft SQL Server Database Engine (MSDE), connecting to local database, 823**
`Microsoft.SqlServer.Server` **namespace, 635**
**minus sign (-)**
- as decrement operator (--), 135–136
- for removing method calls from multicast delegates, 183

**MMC (Microsoft Management Console)**
- Active Directory Domains and Trusts snap-in, 721
- Active Directory Sites and Services snap-in, 721
- Active Directory Users and Computers snap-in, 721–722
- Computer Management snap-in, 1101–1102
- Services snap-in, 1293

**mobile code, 463**

**modifiers.** *See also specific modifiers*
- interface members and, 126
- visibility modifiers, 124–125

**modules**
- assemblies versus, 421–422
- creating, 421
- defined, 421
- purpose of, 423

**Mono project, 5**

`MortimerColdCall` **example**
- catching user-defined exceptions, 341–343
- `ColdCallFileFormatException`, 341, 346–347
- `ColdCallFileFormatException` handler, 343
- `ColdCallFileReader` class, 341, 342, 343–346
- defining exception classes, 346–348
- `FileNotFound` exception, 341, 342–343
- `LandLineSpyFoundException`, 341, 346
- `Main()` method, 341–343
- overview, 340–341
- testing, 347–348
- throwing user-defined exceptions, 343–346
- `UnexpectedException`, 341, 347

`MortimerPhonesEmployees` **dictionary example, 264–269**

**mouse events**
- `CapsEditor` example, 890–893
- methods for, 890
- overview, 760

`Move()` **method (`File` and `Directory` classes), 1197**
`MoveTo()` **method (`FileInfo` and `DirectoryInfo` classes), 1197**

**moving**
- files, 1197–1201
- folders, 1197

`.mresource` **attribute, 528, 538**

**MSDE (Microsoft SQL Server Database Engine), connecting to local database, 823**

**MSIL. See IL or MSIL (Microsoft Intermediate Language)**

**MSXML parser**
- `System.Xml` namespace advantages over, 664
- using in .NET, 661–663

**MTA (multi-threaded apartment) in COM, 1157, 1166**
**multicast delegates, 183–185**
**Multiple Document Interface (MDI), 786–787**
**multiple inheritance, 112**
**multitasking. See threading**
`MyFirstCSharpClass` **class, 30–33**

## N

**names**
- Active Directory distinguish names (DNs), 727–728
- Active Directory user names, 728–729
- ADO.NET naming conventions, 629–630
- aliases, 60–61, 585
- camel casing, 76–77
- code group labels, 469
- for colors, 864–865
- distributing code using strong names, 497–499
- of event handlers, 187
- generics naming guidelines, 274
- of HTML tags for user controls (ASP.NET), 946
- IL case sensitivity, 12
- of interfaces, 128
- of namespaces, 59, 77
- .NET guidelines and philosophy, 75–76
- Pascal casing, 76, 77
- of properties, 93
- reserved keywords, 74
- rules for identifiers, 73–75
- strong, for shared assemblies, 441–443, 444–445
- styles for, 77
- variable prefixes, 75
- Visual Basic .NET not case-sensitive, 77

**`namespace` keyword, 32**

**namespaces**
- for ACLs, 1222
- for Active Directory, 723
- for ADO.NET, 580
- aliases, 60–61
- assemblies and, 419
- for classes, 32, 58–59
- for COM objects, 1151
- defined, 21
- for DSML, 724, 745
- for event senders, 188
- for file system operations, 1187
- for GDI+, 843
- for generics, 270
- for globalization, 513, 514
- for localization, 513, 534
- names for, 59, 77
- nesting, 21, 59
- for .NET Remoting, 1009
- Pascal casing for, 76
- for performance monitoring, 1309
- for power events support, 1314
- for registry operations, 1187
- for serialization base classes and interfaces, 1187
- for serializing objects in XML, 701–702
- shared assemblies and, 442
- `soap` namespace, 984–985
- for SQL Server 2005, 635
- for `Stack` class, 254
- `System.Xml.XPath`, 678–684
- `System.Xml.Xsl`, 684–689
- for threading, 351, 366
- types defined in, 21, 59
- `using` statement for, 32, 59–61
- for Windows Forms, 751
- for Windows Services, 1275
- for XML, 659, 660–661

**navigation Web server controls (ASP.NET), 960–963**

**nesting**
- `break` statement in nested loops, 55
- `for` loops, 52
- namespaces, 21, 59
- partials, 105–106
- `throw` statements in `try` blocks, 332
- `try` blocks, 338–340
- types, 125

**.NET data access.** *See* ADO.NET; viewing .NET data; Visual Studio .NET and data access

**.NET Framework.** *See also* ASP.NET; CLR (Common Language Runtime); IL or MSIL (Microsoft Intermediate Language)
- application domains, 14–16, 413–416
- assemblies, 17–19
- attributes, 17
- base classes, 19–20, 277–278
- benefits of C# and, 25
- compilation steps in, 4
- C#'s relationship to, 3, 4
- C#'s role in enterprise architecture, 24–26
- delegates defined in, 188
- error handling with exceptions, 16–17
- garbage collector, 13–14
- installation base lacking for, 24
- namespaces, 21
- open source implementation, 5
- operating systems supported, 553
- security advantages of, 14
- server platforms supported, 553
- similar concepts in COM, 1152
- usage conventions, 75–81
- using a COM component from a .NET client, 1159–1171

## .NET Framework (continued)

.NET Framework (continued)
 using a .NET component from a COM client, 1171–1183
 Windows Controls and, 24
 Windows Forms and, 24
 Windows Services and, 24
 XML standards supported, 660
.NET Framework Configuration tool, 1048–1050
.NET IDE. *See* Visual Studio 2005
.NET Remoting
 activator for client, 1012
 application types and, 1010
 asynchronous, 1053–1054
 call contexts, 1062–1064
 channels, 1012, 1020–1025, 1041–1042, 1046
 `ChannelServices` class, 1012, 1025–1026
 client-side process, 1012–1014
 CLR Object Remoting, 1011
 configuration files, 1039–1050, 1059, 1061
 contexts, 1014–1016
 defined, 1010
 delegates with, 1053–1054
 directional attributes, 1035–1036
 events and, 1056–1062
 formatter provider, 1012, 1047–1048
 formatters, 1012, 1025
 hosting servers in ASP.NET, 1050–1051
 interfaces, 1052
 key architecture elements, 1012, 1013
 lifetime management, 1036–1039, 1046–1047
 major classes for example, 1016–1017
 marshal-by-reference classes, 1031–1032
 marshal-by-value classes, 1031
 marshaling, 1032–1034
 message sinks, 1012, 1015, 1030–1031
 messages, 1012, 1030
 namespaces for, 1009
 not-remotable classes, 1032
 object activation, 1027–1030
 `OneWay` attribute, 1054
 overview, 1011–1014
 passing objects in remote methods, 1031–1036
 protocols, 1010–1011
 proxies, 1012
 remote objects, 1012, 1017–1018, 1056–1058
 `RemotingConfiguration` class, 1012, 1026
 `RemotingServices` class, 1026
 security, 1035, 1054–1055, 1126
 serialized objects and security, 1035
 server for client-activated objects, 1026–1027
 server for well-known objects, 1026
 server-side process, 1014
 simple client example, 1019–1020
 simple server example, 1018–1019
 Soapsuds utility, 1052–1053
 unbound classes, 1031
 uses for, 1011
 WCF and, 1145–1146
 XML Web services with, 1010
.NET security. *See* security
**net.exe utility, 1293–1294**
**neutral cultures, 515–516**
new **keyword**
 declaring class and struct instances, 84
 hiding methods, 116
 as modifier for function members, 125
 for object activation (.NET Remoting), 1027
 reference types and, 196
 structs versus classes and, 103
`NewRowFromBuilder()` **method (**`CustomerTable` **class), 836–837**
**Ngen.exe native image generator, 438–439**
**No Touch Deployment (NTD), 566–567**
**Northwind database example (ADO.NET).** *See* **ADO.NET**
**Northwind database example (Enterprise Services)**
 C# component library for, 1081
 client application, 1089–1090
 entity classes, 1081–1084
 `Order` class, 1081–1083
 `OrderControl` component, 1080–1081, 1084–1085
 `OrderData` component, 1081, 1085–1088
 `OrderLine` class, 1083–1084
 `OrderLineData` component, 1081, 1088–1089
 overview, 1080–1081
**NT Services.** *See* **Windows Services**
**NTD (No Touch Deployment), 566–567**
`null` **values**
 comparing reference types for equality, 147
 null coalescing operator, 139–140
 for reference types, 40
**nullable types**
 converting, 144
 implicit type conversions and, 142
 `Nullable<T>` generic struct and, 301–302
 operators and, 139
 special syntax for, 302
`Nullable<T>` **generic struct, 301–302**
**number formatting for globalization, 517–519**
`NumberFormatInfo` **class, 518**

# O

**object activation (.NET Remoting)**
  `Activator` class for, 1027
  for client-activated objects, 1028–1029
  messages, 1030
  `new` operator for, 1027
  proxy objects and, 1027, 1029
  specifying the application URL, 1027
  for well-known objects, 1027–1028
**Object Browser window (Visual Studio 2005), 397–398**
`Object` **class**
  all .NET classes derived from, 106
  as default base class, 113
  `Equals()` method, 107
  `Finalize()` method, 107, 108
  `GetHashCode()` method, 107
  `GetType()` method, 107, 108
  `MemberwiseClone()` method, 107, 108
  `ToString()` method, 106, 108–109
`object` **type, 44–45**
**object-oriented programming (OOP), 30**
**OLE DB provider with ADO.NET, 597–600**
`OnAction` **method, 189–190**
`OnContinue()` **method (**`QuoteService` **assembly), 1286**
`OnCustomCommand()` **method (**`QuoteService` **assembly), 1286**
`OnDisplayButtonClick` **event handler, 1195–1196**
`OnDoubleClick()` **event handler, 892–893**
`OnListBoxFilesSelected` **event handler, 1196**
`OnListBoxFoldersSelected` **event handler, 1196**
`OnMouseDown()` **method, 892**
`OnOrderSelectionChanged()` **method, 1118–1119**
`OnPaint()` **method**
  `CapsEditor` example, 887–888
  clipping region and, 848–850
  `DisplayImage` project, 872
  `DisplayText` example, 874–875
  `EnumFontFamilies` example, 879, 880
  painting shapes using, 847–848
  scroll bars and, 859–860, 862
  `ScrollMoreShapes` example, 870
`OnPause()` **method (**`QuoteService` **assembly), 1286**
`OnPowerEvent()` **method (**`ServiceBase` **class), 1314**
`OnSelectCulture()` **method, 522**
`OnShutdown()` **method (**`QuoteService` **assembly), 1286**
`OnStart()` **method (**`QuoteService` **assembly), 1285, 1286, 1287**
`OnSubmitCourseOrder()` **method, 1114**
`OnUpButtonClick` **event handler, 1197**
**OOP (object-oriented programming), 30**
`Open()` **method (**`ColdCallFileReader` **class), 343–344**
**opening**
  database connections with ADO.NET, 583
  message queues, 1104–1106
  projects from previous versions in Visual Studio 2005, 374–376
`OpenRead()` **method (**`WebClient` **class), 1240–1241**
`OpenSubKey()` **method (**`RegistryKey` **class), 1230**
`OpenWrite()` **method (**`WebClient` **class), 1241**
**operating systems supported by .NET, 553**
**operators.** *See also specific operators*
  `as`, 138
  assignment versus comparison, 48, 134–135
  `checked` and `unchecked`, 137
  comparison, 48, 134–135, 147
  compiler and, 149–150
  defined, 86
  `is`, 138
  null coalescing, 139–140
  nullable types and, 139
  overloading, 148–157
  pointer member access operator, 212
  for pointers, 207
  precedence, 140
  for removing method calls from multicast delegates, 183
  shortcut assignment operators, 135–136
  `sizeof`, 138
  table summarizing, 134
  ternary, 136–137
  `typeof`, 139
  unsafe, 134
`Order` **class, 1081–1083**
`OrderControl` **component, 1080–1081, 1084–1085, 1091–1092**
`OrderData` **component, 1081, 1085–1088, 1092–1093**
`OrderLine` **class, 1083–1084**
`OrderLineData` **component, 1081, 1088–1089**
`/out` **option for compiler output file specification, 64**
`out` **parameters**
  anonymous methods and, 177
  passing to methods, 91
**outsourcing translations, 543–544**

# OverflowException class

OverflowException class, 329
overloading constructors, 95
overloading methods
   DrawEllipse() method, 845
   DrawRectangle() method, 845
   overview, 92
   Run() method, 753
   Write() method, 1216–1217
overloading operators
   arithmetic operators, 148, 151–152, 153–155
   comparison operators, 148, 155–157
   compiler and, 149–150
   for concatenating strings, 224
   operators supporting overloading, 157
   public and static declaration required for, 152
   uses for, 148, 149
   Vector struct example, 150–157
override modifier, 125
overriding
   Equals method for comparisons, 146–147, 148
   Equals method for dictionaries, 264, 266, 267
   GetHashCode() method for dictionaries, 263–264, 266–267
   OnPaint() method, scrolling windows and, 859–860, 862
   Render() method for custom control, 954–955
   virtual methods and properties, 114–115

# P

page coordinates, 863
PageCoordinatesToLineIndex() method, 890, 893
Page_Load() event handler
   event-booking application, 924
   login application using SOAP headers, 1004, 1006
PaintEventArgs class, 848
painting shapes. *See also* OnPaint() method
   clipping region and, 848–850
   overview, 847–848
Panel control (Windows Forms), 774
parameters
   camel casing for, 76
   constructors with, adding in a hierarchy, 122–124
   constructors without, adding in a hierarchy, 120–122
   for custom attributes, specifying, 309–310
   out parameters, 91
   overloading methods and, 92
   passing by reference versus by value, 89
   passing to Main(), 63
   passing to methods, 89–91
   ref parameters, 90–91

ParameterTest class, 89–90
parentheses [( )] for groups, 241–242
Parse() method, 641
partial keyword, 104–106
Pascal casing, 76, 77
passing methods. *See* delegates
Path class, 1188, 1191–1192
PCSDemoSite application (ASP.NET)
   downloading, 944
   master pages in, 958–960
   navigation in, 962–963
   security, 972–973
   themes in, 975–979
   user controls in, 950–952
PCSWebApp1 example
   adding server controls, 911–913
   code-behind file, 909
   creating in Visual Studio, 906–908
PeekMessages() method, 1116–1117
Pen class, 866, 867–868
perfmon.exe utility, 1312–1313
performance
   array lists versus dictionaries, 259
   ASP.NET versus ASP, 22
   boxing and unboxing impacts on, 272
   COM issues for, 8
   demanding permissions and, 478
   destructors and, 200
   generics advantages for, 272–273
   IL and improvements in, 5
   monitoring Windows Services, 1308–1313
   optimization in Visual Studio 2005, 399–400
   pointer use for improving, 204, 219–222
   processes versus application domains and, 15
   properties and, 94–95
   reference types and, 197
   stack-based arrays for, 219–222
   structs and, 103
   value types and, 40
   Web services specifications and, 1133–1134
performance monitoring for services
   classes for, 1309
   overview, 1309
   perfmon.exe utility for, 1312–1313
   performance counters for, 1309–1312
permcacl.exe permission-calculation tool, 481, 483–484
permissions for code access
   changing for code groups, 494–495
   creating and applying permissions sets, 495–497
   creating custom, 487–488
   defined, 464

error handling blocks for, 472
Identity Permissions, 472–473
managing, 492
named sets of, 473
permission classes provided by CLR, 471–472
policy levels, 476–478
SQL Server assemblies, 634–635
viewing for assemblies, 473–476

**permissions in .NET Framework**
asserting permissions, 486–487
CLR and demands for permissions, 478
creating custom code access permissions, 487–488
demanding permissions, 478, 479–480
denying permissions, 485–486
implicit permission, 484–485
performance issues, 478
requesting permissions, 480–484
specifying declaratively, 488

`PictureBox` **control (Windows Forms), 772**
**pictures. See graphics; resources**
**platform independence, IL and, 4–5**
**pluggability (.NET Remoting)**
of channels, 1024–1025
of proxy objects, 1029

**plus sign (+)**
in for loop iterator, 52
as increment operator (++), 135–136
regular expression groups and, 242

`Point` **struct, 851–852**
**pointer member access operator, 212**
**pointers. See also delegates**
address operator, 207
arithmetic, 210–211
for backward compatibility, 204
bugs introduced due to complexity of, 205
casting between pointer types, 209
casting to integer types, 208–209
to class members, 212–214
data types and, 208
declaring, 206–207
defined, 204
`fixed` keyword for, 213–214
function pointers, 171
high level trust needed at runtime, 205
indirection operator, 207
not allowed for arrays and classes, 208
for performance improvements, 204, 219–222
pointer member access operator, 212
`PointerPlayaround` example, 214–219
reference types compared to, 40, 204

`sizeof` operator with, 211
stack allocation for, 207–208
stack pointer, 194–195
stack-based arrays using, 219–222
to structs, 211–212
32-bit processors and, 207–208
`unsafe` keyword for, 205–206
`void`, 209

`PointF` **struct, 851–852**
**policy levels for security**
overview, 476
viewing code groups at enterprise level, 477–478
viewing code groups at user level, 476–477

`Pop()` **method (**`Stack` **class), 254**
**pop-up menu for a database row**
code listing, 833–834
context menu functionality and, 832
`ContextDataRow` class for, 834
`ContextMenuAttribute` for, 834, 835
`DataRow` and `DataTable` classes for, 832
filtering methods on current object, 834
`PopupMenu` method for, 834–835
ways of providing, 832

`PopupMenu` **method, 834–835**
**pound symbol (#) for preprocessor directives, 70–73**
**power events, Windows Services and, 1314**
`#pragma` **preprocessor directive, 73**
**precedence of operators, 140**
**pre-emptive multitasking, 350**
**prefixes for variable names, 75**
**preprocessor directives**
`#define`, 70, 71
defined, 70
`#elif`, 71–72
`#else`, 71–72
`#endif`, 71–72
`#endregion`, 72–73
`#error`, 72
`#if`, 71–72
`#line`, 73
not ended by semicolon, 71
pound symbol beginning, 70
`#pragma`, 73
`#region`, 72–73
`#undef`, 71
`#warning`, 72

**printing**
displaying to screen versus, 894
graphics, 893–899
`WebBrowser` control for, 1255–1256

`PrintingCapsEdit` **project**
  compiling and testing, 898–899
  downloading, 895
  event handlers, 896–897
  `Form1` class `pagesPrinted` field, 896
  `LoadFile()` method, 895
  `using` statements, 898
**priorities for threads, 358–359**
`PriorityDocumentManager` **class**
  `AddDocument()` method, 290
  `AddDocumentToPriorityNode()` method, 290–291
  code listing, 289–290
  `GetDocument()` method, 291–292
  `LinkedList<Document>` collection in, 289
  `List<LinkedListNode<Document>>` collection in, 289
  `Main()` method, 292
**private assemblies**
  overview, 18, 412–413, 419
  versioning and, 412–413, 451
  zero impact installation, 18
**private member fields, camel casing for, 76**
`private` **modifier, 124**
`ProcessDocuments` **class**
  custom generic class example, 294–296
  `Queue<T>` generic class example, 285–286
**processes, application domains and, 14–16, 413**
`ProcessNextPerson()` **method** (`ColdCallFileReader` **class), 344–345**
**processors**
  JIT compilation for, 5
  pointers and 32-bit processors, 207–208
  pre-emptive multitasking and, 350
  requirements for application deployment, 553
*Professional ASP.NET 1.1* **(Wiley Publishing, Inc.), 910, 940**
**prog id for COM objects, 1155**
**programming guidelines for C#**
  rules for identifiers, 73–75
  usage conventions, 75–81
`ProgressBar` **control (Windows Forms), 772**
`ProjectInstaller` **class, 1288–1289**
**properties**
  access modifiers, 94
  for accessing user controls (ASP.NET), 947–948
  adding to user controls, 796–797
  `Application` class, 753
  casing of, 76–77
  of contexts (.NET Remoting), 1015, 1016
  defining, 93
  described, 86, 92
  `DirectoryInfo` class, 1190
  `FileInfo` class, 1190
  of generic classes, 276–277
  of generic interfaces, 275–276
  `get` accessor, 93
  of message queues, 1101–1102
  naming conventions, 93
  performance and, 94–95
  quote server application, 1282–1283
  read-only, 94
  `Registry` class, 1231
  `ServiceController` class, 1297
  `set` accessor, 93
  setting for channels (.NET Remoting), 1023–1024
  `System.SystemException` class, 337
  `System.Type` class, 314–315
  usage conventions, 80
  virtual, 114
  Visual Studio 2005 Properties window, 394–396
  write-only, avoiding, 81, 94
**Properties window (Visual Studio 2005), 394–396**
`PropertyManager` **class, 819, 820–822**
`PropertyValueCollection` **class, 734**
`protected internal` **modifier, 124, 125**
`protected` **modifier, 96, 124**
**protocol stack, 1262**
**proxy classes**
  for delegates, 838
  for .NET Remoting, 1012
  transparent versus real proxy, 1012
  for Web services, 990–992
**proxy objects, .NET Remoting object activation and, 1027, 1029**
`public` **keyword**
  for constructors, 96
  described, 124
  for methods, 33
**publisher policy files for assemblies, 450, 456–458**
**publishing Web sites, deployment using, 552, 555–556**
`Push()` **method (**`Stack` **class), 254**

# Q

`QueryInterface()` **method, 1154–1155**
**question mark (?)**
  for disabling `Group` object with regular expressions (`?:`), 243

in null coalescing operator (??), 139–140
in ternary operator (?:), 136–137
`Queue` **class, 256–257**
`Queue<T>` **generic class, 283–286**
`QueueUserWorkItem()` **method (**`ThreadPool` **class), 366**
`QuickArray` **example, 221–222**
**quote server application.** See also *specific classes and assemblies*
  adding event logging, 1306–1308
  handler methods, 1286
  installation program, 1287–1292
  overview, 1275–1276
  project wizard for, 1281–1283
  properties, 1282–1283
  `QuoteClient` assembly, 1275, 1276, 1279–1281
  `QuoteServer` class, 1275, 1276–1279
  `QuoteService` assembly, 1275, 1276, 1281–1287
  service start, 1285
  `ServiceBase` class, 1283–1284
  starting manually, 1292
  `TestQuoteServer` console application, 1279
`QuoteServer` **class**
  `AcceptSocket()` method, 1278
  adding event logging, 1306–1308
  constructor, 1277
  creating, 1276–1279
  `GetRandomQuoteOfTheDay()` method, 1277
  `ListenerThread()` thread function, 1278
  overview, 1275, 1276
  `ReadQuotes()` method, 1277
  `RefreshQuotes()` method, 1279
  `Resume()` method, 1278–1279
  `Start()` method, 1277–1278
  `Stop()` method, 1278
  `Suspend()` method, 1278–1279
`QuoteService` **assembly**
  handler methods, 1286
  `Main()` method, 1284–1285
  `OnContinue()` method, 1286
  `OnCustomCommand()` method, 1286
  `OnPause()` method, 1286
  `OnShutdown()` method, 1286
  `OnStart()` method, 1285, 1287
  `OnStop()` method, 1286
  project wizard for, 1281–1283
  service start, 1285
  `ServiceBase` class, 1283–1284

# R

`/r` **or** `/reference` **switch for compiler, 64**
**race conditions, avoiding, 363–364**
`Racer` **class, 278–279**
`RadioButton` **control (Windows Forms), 764**
`RainbowLabel` **custom control (ASP.NET)**
  `Color` enumeration, 953
  creating Web site for, 953
  `Default.aspx.cs` code for, 955
  enabling color cycling, 954
  modifying `Default.aspx` for, 955
  `Render()` method override, 954–955
  using, 955–956
  `using` statements, 953
**RAM.** See also **memory management**
  freeing memory in COM, 1153
  requirements for application deployment, 553
**RCW (runtime callable wrapper) in COM, 1163–1166**
**RDN (relative distinguished name) in Active Directory, 727**
`Read()` **method (**`XmlReader` **class), 665**
`ReadElementString()` **method (**`XmlReader` **class), 665–667**
**reading drive information, 1220–1222**
**reading files**
  binary files, 1208–1213
  overview, 1201
  text files, 1213–1219
  Windows Forms for, 1202–1204
`ReadLine()` **method (**`StreamReader` **class), 1215**
`readonly` **fields, 99–101**
**read-only properties, 94**
`ReadQuotes()` **method (**`QuoteServer` **class library), 1277**
`ReadStartElement()` **method (**`XmlReader` **class), 665**
`ReadToEnd()` **method (**`StreamReader` **class), 1215**
`ReadValueAs` **methods (**`XmlReader` **class), 667**
`ReadWriteText` **application, 1217–1219**
`ReadXml()` **method (**`DataSet` **class), 620, 696–697**
`ReadXmlSchema()` **method (**`DataSet` **class), 697**
`Receive()` **method (**`MessageQueue` **class), 1109, 1110**
`ReceivedById()` **method, 1119**
`Rectangle` **struct, 853–854**
`RectangleF` **struct, 853–854**
**Red-Green-Blue (RGB) values for colors, 863–864, 865**

1523

# ref parameters

ref **parameters**
  anonymous methods and, 177
  passing to methods, 90–91
**refactoring, 408–410**
**reference objects, instantiating, 35**
/reference **or** /r **switch for compiler, 64**
**reference types.** See also specific types
  arrays as, 58
  classes as, 40
  comparing for equality, 146–147
  compiler switch for, 64
  complex data types as, 40
  converting between value types and, 145–146
  defined, 9
  memory management, 196–198
  null value for, 40
  objects not created by, 39–40
  passing parameters to methods as, 90–91
  performance overhead, 197
  predefined, 41, 44–46
  stored in the heap, 9, 39, 196–198
  System.Type class for holding, 314
  value types versus, 9, 39–40
ReferenceEquals() **method, 146, 147**
**references to shared assemblies, 449**
**reflection.** See also **attributes**
  assemblies and, 19
  Assembly class, 319–320
  custom attributes, 306–313
  defined, 19, 305
  example applications described, 305–306
  System.Type class, 314–319
  uses for, 305
RefreshQuotes() **method (**QuoteServer **class),** 1279
**regasm utility, 1179**
**regedit utility, 1227–1228**
**regedit32 utility, 1227**
#region **preprocessor directive, 72–73**
Region **struct, 854–855**
RegionInfo **class, 515**
<%@ Register %> **directive (ASP.NET)**
  for custom controls, 952–953
  for user controls, 946
RegisterActivatedClientType() **method**
  (RemotingConfiguration **class), 1027, 1029**
RegisterChannel() **method (**ChannelServices **class), 1025**
RegisterWellKnownClientType() **method**
  (RemotingConfiguration **class), 1028**
RegisterWellKnownServiceType() **method**
  (RemotingConfiguration **class), 1026, 1028**
Registry **class, 1229, 1230**
**Registry Editor (ClickOnce), 570–571**
**registry operations**
  COM registration, 1155, 1178–1179
  hierarchical structure of registry, 1227–1229
  keys, 1228–1229
  namespace for, 1187
  prevalence of registry use, 1226–1227
  regedit utility, 1227–1228
  regedit32 utility, 1227
  Registry class, 1229, 1230
  registry hive, 1228
  registry overview, 1226–1229
  RegistryKey class, 1229–1232
  security and, 1187
  SelfPlacingWindow application, 1232–1238
RegistryKey **class**
  CreateSubKey() method, 1230
  described, 1229
  GetValue() method, 1231
  methods, 1231–1232
  OpenSubKey() method, 1230
  properties, 1231
  reading registry keys, 1230
  Registry class versus, 1230
  SetValue() method, 1231
  writing to registry keys, 1230
**regular expressions**
  capturing sections from URIs, 242–243
  defined, 235
  disabling Group object in returns, 243
  displaying results, 240–241
  efficiency of, 236
  escape sequences, 236, 238–240
  groups, 240–243
  .NET classes supporting, 223, 236
  prevalence of, 235
  RegularExpressionsPlayaround example, 237–241
  searching for escape meta-characters, 240
  uses for, 236
  WriteMatches() method for, 240
RegularExpressionsPlayaround **example, 237–241**
**relative distinguished name (RDN) in Active Directory, 727**
**releasing COM components, 1165**
**reliability, Web services specifications and, 1129–1131**

**remote objects**
  defined, 1012
  distributed identity, 1017
  event handling and, 1056–1058
  overview, 1017–1018
`RemoteObject` **class, 1056–1058**
`RemotingConfiguration` **class**
  `Configure()` method, 1044, 1045, 1046
  described, 1012, 1026
  predefined channels in, 1041
  `RegisterActivatedClientType()` method, 1027, 1029
  `RegisterWellKnownClientType()` method, 1028
  `RegisterWellKnownServiceType()` method, 1026, 1028
`RemotingServices` **class**
  `Connect()` method, 1028, 1030
  described, 1026
  `IsTransparentProxy()` method, 1029
  registering a well-known object to, 1026
`Remove()` **method (**`Hashtable` **class), 261**
`RemoveAt()` **method (**`ArrayList` **class), 251**
`RemoveRange()` **method (**`ArrayList` **class), 252–253**
**removing.** See **deleting or removing**
`Render()` **method, overriding, 954–955**
`Replace()` **method**
  `String` class, 226
  `StringBuilder` class, 228
**requesting permissions**
  adding permissions as assembly attributes, 482
  calculating permissions required for an assembly, 481, 483–484
  options for applications, 483
  permission sets, 484
  reasons for, 480–481
  `SecurityAction` enumeration values, 482–483
  ways of requesting, 480
`Reset()` **method, 247**
**Resgen.exe (Resource File Generator) utility, 527, 543–544**
**resource readers**
  custom, 545–549
  .NET Framework, 545
  `ResourceReader` class, 534
  `ResXResourceReader` class, 534
`ResourceDemoForm` **class, 530–533**
`ResourceManager` **class, 530–531, 533, 537**
`ResourceReader` **class, 534**

**resources.** See also **localization**
  accessing embedded resources, 530–531
  adding to assemblies, 528–530
  automatic fallback for, 542
  creating resource files, 526–528
  custom messages for, 541–542
  custom resource reader, 545–549
  outsourcing translations, 543–544
  Resource File Generator (Resgen.exe) utility, 527
  `ResourceDemoForm` class for, 531–533
  `ResourceManager` class for, 530–531, 533
  `ResourceReader` class for, 534
  `ResourceSet` class for, 533
  `ResourceWriter` class for, 527–528, 534
  .`resX` files for, 526, 527–528
  `ResXResourceReader` class for, 534
  `ResXResourceSet` class for, 534
  `ResXResourceWriter` class for, 527–528, 534
  strongly typed, 531–533
  `System.Resources` namespace classes for, 533–534
  text files for, 526
  using resource files, 528–533
  Windows Forms, disposing of, 755
`ResourceSet` **class, 533**
`ResourceWriter` **class, 527–528, 534**
**response message queues, 1100, 1120–1121**
`Resume()` **method**
  `QuoteServer` class library, 1278–1279
  `Thread` class, 354
**resuming threads, 353, 354**
.`resX` **files for resources, 526, 527–528**
`ResXResourceReader` **class, 534**
`ResXResourceSet` **class, 534**
`ResXResourceWriter` **class, 527–528, 534**
`return` **statement, 55**
**RGB (Red-Green-Blue) values for colors, 863–864, 865**
`RichTextBox` **control (Windows Forms), 773–774**
**role-based security**
  declarative, 509–510
  defined, 14, 506
  Enterprise Services and, 1068
  principal for, 507
  roles, 509
  uses for, 506–507
  `WindowsPrincipal` example, 508–509
`Run()` **method (**`Application` **class), overloading, 753**
`runat="server"` **attribute (ASP.NET), 905, 910**
**runtime callable wrapper (RCW) in COM, 1163–1166**

# safety checking

## S

**safety checking.** *See* **type safety**
**safety palette for colors, 866**
**SAX versus `XmlReader` class, 664**
`sbyte` **type, 41, 42**
**sc.exe utility, 1294–1295**
**schemas (Active Directory)**
   domain tree and, 717
   getting the naming context for, 741–742
   overview, 715, 719–720
**schemas (database)**
   building an XSD schema, 827–832
   defined, 601
   hand-coded, 606–608
   runtime generation of, 606
   XLM schemas, 612–618, 691
**SCM (Service Control Manager), 1273, 1274**
**scope of variables**
   clashes for fields and local variables, 37–38
   clashes for local variables, 36–37
   defined, 35
   fields (member variables), 35
   general rules, 35–36
   local variables, 35–36
   managed heap and, 197–198
   reference variables, 197–198
   stack and, 194–195, 197–198
   `using` statement and, 202
**scripting languages, interoperability with .NET, 7**
**scrolling windows in graphics applications**
   adding scroll bars, 858–859
   converting coordinates relative to client area, 861–862
   determining document size, 858–859
   `Form1` class for, 856–857
   `OnPaint()` method override and, 859–860, 862
   screen redraw and, 860–861
   setting minimum document size at startup, 858–859
   standard controls and, 857–858
**SDI (Single Document Interface), 781**
`sealed` **modifier, 117–118, 125**
**searching in Active Directory**
   with DSML, 746–748
   filters for, 736–737
   `PropertiesToLoad`, 737
   read-mostly access and, 736
   `SearchRoot`, 736
   `SearchScope`, 737
   setting search limits, 737–740
   `UserSearch` application, 740–745

**security.** *See also* **authentication**
   ACLs, 1222–1226
   Active Directory, 714–715
   ASP.NET, 963–973
   asserting permissions, 486–487
   ClickOnce settings, 569–570
   code access security, 464–478
   configuration file, 489–492
   declarative, 488, 509–510
   demanding permissions, 478, 479–480
   denying permissions, 485–486
   Enterprise Services, 1068
   file security, 1222–1226
   implicit permission, 484–485
   mobile code issues, 463
   .NET Framework support for, 478–488
   .NET Remoting, 1035, 1054–1055, 1126
   performance issues, 478
   policy management, 489–506
   public key cryptography, 442–443
   requesting permissions, 480–484
   role-based, 506–510, 1068
   role-based versus code-based, 14
   strong data typing in IL and, 14
   turning on and off, 493
   Web services specifications and, 1128–1129
**security policies.** *See also* **caspol.exe (Code Access Security Policy tool)**
   applying full trust, 492
   changing permissions for code groups, 494–495
   creating and applying permissions sets, 495–497
   creating custom code groups, 493–494
   deleting code groups, 494
   distributing code using certificates, 499–504
   distributing code using strong names, 497–499
   files storing, 489
   managing, 489–506
   managing code groups and permissions, 492
   managing zones, 504–506
   resetting, 493
   security configuration file, 489–492
   viewing code groups at enterprise level, 477–478
   viewing code groups at user level, 476–477
**Security Wizard (ASP.NET), 964–969**
`SecurityException`, **480, 482, 492**
**secutil.exe tool, 498–499, 502**
`SelfPlacingWindow` **application, 1232–1238**
**semicolon (;)**
   ending C# statements, 31
   preprocessor directives not ended by, 71

Send() method (MessageQueue class), 1106, 1108
serializing. *See also* serializing objects in XML
  base classes and interfaces for, 1187
  defined, 1187
  UDTs, 637–638
serializing objects in XML
  custom attributes for, 702
  namespace for, 701–702
  .NET Remoting security and, 1035
  serializing, defined, 701
  simple application for, 702–708
  without source code access, 708–711
  xsd.exe tool for, 702
server controls (ASP.NET)
  adding to PCSWebApp1 example, 911–913
  control palette, 913–914
  Crystal Reports Web server controls, 914
  data Web server controls, 917–918
  event handlers for, 911–912
  example using, 920–925
  further information, 910
  HTML server controls, defined, 910
  icon in system tray, 912
  login Web server controls, 970–971
  navigation Web server controls, 960–963
  runat="server" attribute, 910
  standard Web server controls, 914–917
  validation Web server controls, 918–920
  Web server controls, defined, 910
  WebParts Web server controls, 920
Server Explorer (Visual Studio), 1295
Server Explorer window (Visual Studio 2005), 398
server platforms supported by .NET, 553
Service Control Manager (SCM), 1273, 1274
ServiceBase class, 1283–1284, 1302, 1305, 1314
ServiceController class
  application using, 1295–1296
  controlling services using, 1299–1301
  methods, 1300
  monitoring services using, 1296–1299
  properties, 1297
ServicedComponent class, 1070
ServiceInstaller class, 1289, 1290–1291
ServiceInstallerDialog class, 1291
ServiceProcessInstaller class, 1289–1290
Services administration tool, 1272
set accessor of properties
  access modifiers, 94
  overview, 93
  for user controls (ASP.NET), 948

SetDateAndNumber() method, 535–536
setreg.exe utility, 501
setup programs. *See* Windows Installer projects
SetValue() method (RegistryKey class), 1231
shapes. *See also* graphics
  application for drawing, 844–847
  drawing, 868–870
  painting, 847–848
  ScrollMoreShapes example, 869–870
  System.Drawing.Graphics methods for, 868–869
shared assemblies
  Authenticode signatures for, 442
  creating, 444–449
  defined, 19
  delayed signing of, 448
  global assembly cache for, 19, 413, 438–441
  installing, 446, 451
  integrity using strong names, 443
  namespaces for classes and, 442
  overview, 413, 419
  public key cryptography, 442–443
  references, 449
  risks, 19
  strong names for, 441–443, 444–445
  using, 446–448
  versioning, 412, 413, 451–460
SharePoint Web sites information, 920
short type, 41, 42
Show() method (Form class), 782, 845
ShowActivatedServiceTypes() method, 1044–1045
ShowChannelProperties() method, 1023
ShowDialog() method (Form class), 782–784
ShowRegionInformation() method, 524
ShowSamples() method, 523
ShowWellKnownServiceTypes() method, 1044–1045
signcode.exe utility, 499
signtool.exe wizard, 499–501
Simple Object Access Protocol. *See* SOAP
SimpleClientApp solution
  adding the assembly, 560–561
  application properties and values, 559–560
  Configuration Properties setting, 557
  creating a desktop shortcut, 561
  creating folders for deployment, 561
  deployment project as separate solution, 558–562
  deployment project in same solution, 563–564
  project properties, 561–562
SimpleComponent class, 1072–1073

# SimpleDelegate delegate

`SimpleDelegate` **delegate, 177–180**
`SimpleExceptions` **class, 333–336**
`SimpleServer` **application (Enterprise Services)**
  assembly attributes, 1071
  creating C# library application for, 1070
  creating the component, 1072–1073
  `ServicedComponent` class, 1070, 1072
  signing the assembly, 1070
  `SimpleComponent` class, 1072–1073
**SimpleWebApp solution, 564–565**
**Single Document Interface (SDI), 781**
**single quotes ('),** char **literals enclosed by, 44, 46**
**single-threaded apartment (STA) in COM,**
    **1156–1157, 1166**
`SiteMapPath` **control, 960–962**
`Size` **struct, 852–853**
`SizeF` **struct, 852–853**
`sizeof` **operator, 138, 211**
**slash (/)**
  for multi-line comments (/* and */), 31, 67–68
  for single-line comments (//), 31, 67
`Sleep()` **method (**`Thread` **class), 355**
`sn` **(strong name tool), 442**
`soap` **namespace, 984–985**
**SOAP (Simple Object Access Protocol)**
  calling a method in a Web service, 984–985
  declaring custom header for Web service, 1002
  defined, 983
  exchanging data using SOAP headers, 1001–1007
  overview, 984–985
  performance issues, 1133
  RM sequence in messages, 1130–1131
  sending data over HTTP and, 984–985
  `SoapHeaderAttribute` attribute, 1002, 1003
  SOAP-over-UDP, 1133–1134
  Soapsuds utility, 1052–1053
  WCF message contract for, 1137, 1139
  WS-Addressing specification with, 1134
**Soapsuds utility, 1052–1053**
`Socket` **class, 1263, 1268**
`Sort()` **method**
  `Array` class, 525
  `BubbleSorter` class, 180–181
  globalization and, 525
  `List<T>` generic class, 281–282
`SortedList` **class, 257–259**
**sorting.** See also `Sort()` **method**
  bubble-sorting algorithm, 180
  `DataView` rows, 807–809
  globalization and, 524–526
  **specific cultures, 515–516**

`SplitContainer` **control (Windows Forms), 775**
**SQL Server 2005**
  key generation with, 627–629
  namespace for, 635
  as .NET runtime host, 634–635
  stored procedures, 645–647
  triggers, 648–650
  user-defined aggregates, 643–645
  user-defined functions, 647–648
  user-defined types (UDTs), 636–643
  XML data type, 650–657
`SqlContext` **class, 635**
`SqlPipe` **class, 635**
`SqlTriggerContext` **class, 635**
**square brackets ([ ]) for arrays, 57**
**STA (single-threaded apartment) in COM,**
    **1156–1157, 1166**
**stack**
  classes stored on, 9
  creating stack-based arrays, 219–222
  defined, 194
  managed heap and, 196–198
  pointer allocation on, 207–208
  scope of variables and, 194–195
  stack pointer, 194–195
  value types stored on, 9, 39, 194–195
`Stack` **class**
  `foreach` loops for reading values, 254
  LIFO (Last In First Out) structure of stacks, 253–254
  methods, 255–256
  namespace for, 254
  `Pop()` method for pulling items permanently, 254–255
  `Push()` method for adding items, 254
  `Queue` class versus, 256
  uses for, 253
`stackalloc` **command, 219–220, 221**
`StackOverflowException` **class, 329**
`Start()` **method**
  `QuoteServer` class, 1277–1278
  `Thread` class, 352
**static classes, 106**
**static constructors**
  example, 97–98
  execution of, 96–97
  instance constructor in same class, 97
`static` **keyword, 33, 125**
`Stop()` **method (**`QuoteServer` **class), 1278**
**stored procedures**
  calling in ADO.NET, 594–597
  creating for SQL Server, 645–646
  naming conventions, 630

## structs

for populating a `DataSet`, 619–620
triggers for SQL Server, 648–650
using with SQL Server, 646–647
`StreamReader` **class**
  byte code markers, 1213
  closing streams, 1215
  constructors, 1214
  described, 1207
  encoding and, 1213, 1214–1215
  `FileStream` class versus, 1213
  hooking up to a `FileStream`, 1215
  methods for reading or writing one line at a time, 1213
  options, 1214
  reading in arrays, 1215–1216
  `ReadLine()` method, 1215
  `ReadToEnd()` method, 1215
  `ReadWriteText` application, 1217–1219
**streams.** *See also specific classes*
  base class for, 1206
  `BinaryFileReader` application, 1210–1213
  `BinaryReader` class, 1207
  `BinaryWriter` class, 1207
  buffered streams, 1207
  class hierarchy, 1206
  defined, 1205
  directions of data transfer, 1205
  `FileStream` class, 1207, 1208–1210
  outside source for, 1205–1206
  overview, 1205–1207
  `ReadWriteText` application, 1217–1219
  `StreamReader` class, 1207, 1213, 1214–1216
  `StreamWriter` class, 1207, 1213–1214, 1216–1217
`StreamWriter` **class**
  byte code markers, 1213
  constructors, 1216
  described, 1207
  encoding and, 1213–1214
  `FileStream` class versus, 1213
  hooking up to a `FileStream`, 1216
  methods for reading or writing one line at a time, 1213
  `ReadWriteText` application, 1217–1219
  `Write()` method overloads, 1216–1217
  writing data into a new file, 1216
`String` **class**
  `Format()` method, 231
  inefficiency for repeated modifications, 223, 225–226
  methods, 224–225
  `Replace()` method, 226
  `StringBuilder` class versus, 223, 226
string **keyword, 45**

**string tables.** *See resources*
string **type**
  `char` type and, 44
  converting between numeric types and, 144–145
  new `string` objects created by changes, 45–46
  other reference types versus, 45–46
  overview, 45–46
  stored in the heap, 45
`StringBuilder` **class**
  `Append()` method, 227
  `AppendFormat()` method, 231
  `ArrayList` class compared to, 250
  memory allocation for, 226–227
  methods, 228–229
  `Replace()` method, 228
  `String` class versus, 223, 226
  `ToString()` method, 229
`StringInfo` **class methods, 514–515**
**strings.** *See also* **text, graphical**
  concatenating using operator overloads, 224
  extracting characters, 224
  formatting expressions, 223, 229–235
  `Type` class properties for retrieving, 314–315
**strong data typing in IL**
  application domains and, 14–16
  CLS and, 12–13
  CTS and, 10–12
  defined, 9
  garbage collection and, 13–14
  generics and, 269
  importance for interoperability, 10–13
  security and, 14
  VB6 typing versus, 9–10
**strong name tool (`sn`), 442**
**strong names**
  distributing code using, 497–499
  integrity using, 443
  for shared assemblies, 441–443, 444–445
**strongly typed objects in Active Directory, 715, 719**
**strongly typed resources, 531–533**
**strongly typed XML, 656–657**
**structs**
  accessing fields outside the object, 37–38
  `ArraySegment<T>` generic struct, 303–304
  classes versus, 84, 102
  for color representation, 863
  constructors, 104
  for coordinate representation, 850
  declaring instances, 84, 101
  default initialization of variables in, 34
  defined, 84

1529

## structs (continued)

structs (continued)
  defining functions for, 101–102
  derived-struct syntax, 113
  enumerations instantiated as, 57
  inheritance and, 103, 112–113
  initialization, 103
  `Nullable<T>` generic struct, 301–302
  partial, 104
  performance and, 103
  pointers to, 211–212
  primitive types as .NET structs, 40–41
  public fields in, 102
  stored on the stack, 84
  uses for, 101
  as value types, 84, 102–103
style of names, 77
`StyleSheetTheme` **(ASP.NET), 974–975**
`submitButton_Click()` **event handler, 924, 931–932, 934**
`SupportsWhatsNewAttribute` **class, 311–312**
`Suspend()` **method**
  `QuoteServer` class, 1278–1279
  `Thread` class, 353, 354
**suspending threads, 353–354**
`Swap<T>` **generic method, 297**
`switch...case` **statements**
  overview, 49–51
  for user control event handler, 797–798
**synchronization in threading**
  deadlocks, avoiding, 361–363, 364
  defined, 360
  importance of, 359
  overusing, avoiding, 361
  race conditions, avoiding, 363–364
**syntax of C#, 360–361**
`System` **namespace, .NET types in, 32**
`System.ApplicationException` **class, 328**
`System.Array` **class, 245**
`System.AttributeUsage` **attribute, 307–309**
`System.Data` **namespace, 580, 581**
`System.Data.Common` **namespace, 580, 581**
`System.Diagnostics` **namespace, 1309**
`System.DirectoryServices` **namespace**
  accessing native ADSI objects, 735–736
  ADSI COM object wrappers, 723
  classes, 725
`System.DirectoryServices.Protocols` **namespace**
  classes, 746
  described, 724, 745

`System.Drawing` **namespace**
  `Color` struct, 863
  described, 843
  `Graphics` methods, 868–869
  `Image` class, 871
  structs defined in, 850
`System.GC.Collect()` **method, 199**
`System.Globalization` **namespace**
  `CultureInfo` class, 515
  overview, 514, 523
  `RegionInfo` class, 515
`System.Net.Sockets` **namespace, 1263**
`System.Resources` **namespace, 533–534**
`System.Security.Permissions` **namespace, 479**
`System.ServiceProcess` **namespace, 1275**
`System.SystemException` **class, 328, 337**
`System.Type` **class**
  for holding reference types, 314
  methods, 315–316
  obtaining a `Type` reference, 314
  properties, 314–315
  `TypeView` example, 316–319
`System.Xml` **namespace.** *See also specific classes*
  advantages over MSXML, 664
  classes for handling XML, 661
  classes for reading and writing XML, 660–661
  language interoperability and, 659
  MSXML 3.0 model and, 664
  overview, 659
  `XmlDocument` class, 661, 673–678
  `XmlNode` class, 661, 672
  `XmlReader` class, 660, 664–670
  `XmlTextReader` class, 661, 664
  `XmlTextWriter` class, 661, 664
  `XmlWriter` class, 660, 664, 670–672
`System.Xml.Serialization` **namespace, 701–702**
`System.Xml.XPath` **namespace**
  described, 678
  key classes in, 679
  using classes from, 681–684
  `XPathDocument` class, 678
  `XPathNavigator` class, 678, 679–680
  `XPathNodeIterator` class, 678, 680–681
`System.Xml.Xsl` **namespace**
  invoking methods during XML transforms, 686–689
  overview, 684
  transforming XML into HTML, 684–686
  `XsltArgumentList`, 686–689

# T

`/t` or `/target` **switch for compiler file type, 63–64**
`TabControl` **control (Windows Forms), 776**
`TableLayoutPanel` **control (Windows Forms), 774, 775**
`TabPages` **control (Windows Forms), 776**
`/target` or `/t` **switch for compiler file type, 63–64**
**taskbar, showing forms in, 782**
**TCP classes, 1263**
**TCP versus UDP, 1266**
`TcpClient` **class**
  overview, 1263
  Windows Services example, 1279–1281
`TcpListener` **class, 1263**
`TcpReceive` **application, 1264–1266, 1268**
`TcpSend` **application, 1263–1264**
`Terminate()` **method, 644–645**
**ternary operator, 136–137**
`TestQuoteServer` **console application, 1279**
`TestSchema.cs` **example**
  adding elements, 829
  `DataColumn` for, 831–832
  `DataRow` for, 830–831
  `DataTable` for, 829
  `EventArgs` for, 832
  initial code, 828
**text, graphical.** See also `CapsEditor` **example**
  drawing, 874–880
  editing a text document, 880–893
  enumerating font families, 878–880
  fonts and font families, 876–880
  simple example, 874–876
`TextBox` **control (Windows Forms)**
  adding controls to user control, 795–796
  in application example, 756
  `DataBindings` property, 816–817
  overview, 773
  `WebBrowser` control with, 1246–1247
`TextBoxBase` **class (Windows Forms)**
  `MaskedTextBox` control derived from, 773, 774
  `RichTextBox` control derived from, 773–774
  `TextBox` control derived from, 773
`TextLineInformation` **class, 882–883**
**themes (ASP.NET)**
  applying to pages, 974–975
  defining, 975
  overview, 974
  in `PCSDemoSite` application, 975–979
**thick-client applications, 22, 24**

**32-bit processors, pointers and, 207–208**
`this` **keyword, 38, 96**
`Thread` **class**
  `Abort()` method, 354
  constructor, 352
  `CurrentCulture` and `CurrentUICulture` properties, 516–517, 518, 519, 539
  `Join()` method, 354
  namespace for, 366
  overview, 351
  `Resume()` method, 354
  `Sleep()` method, 355
  `Start()` method, 352
  `Suspend()` method, 353, 354
  `ThreadPool` class versus, 365
  ways of manipulating, 355
`ThreadAbortException`, **354**
**threading**
  aborting threads, 354
  anonymous methods for, 353
  COM, 1156–1157, 1166
  deadlocks, avoiding, 361–363, 364
  first thread started at `Main()` method, 350
  by Internet Explorer, 349–350
  `lock` statement, 360–361
  namespace for, 351, 366
  passing information to methods, 352
  pre-emptive multitasking for, 350
  priorities for threads, 358–359
  problems with workarounds to avoid, 350
  putting threads to sleep, 355
  race conditions, avoiding, 363–364
  resuming threads, 353, 354
  starting threads, 351–353
  suspending threads, 353–354
  synchronization of access to variables, 359–364
  thread, defined, 349
  `ThreadPlayaround` example, 355–358
  `ThreadPool` class for, 364–368
  `ThreadStart` delegate, 352, 353
  time slice of threads, 351
  waiting for a thread to terminate, 354
  Windows Services and, 1287
  worker threads, 352
`ThreadPlayaround` **example, 355–358**
`ThreadPool` **class**
  described, 364
  maximum threads per processor, 364
  namespace for, 366
  `QueueUserWorkItem()` method, 366

## ThreadPool class (continued)

ThreadPool **class (continued)**
  Thread class versus, 365
  uses for, 364
  using, 365–368
  WaitCallback delegate, 366
ThreadStart **delegate, 352, 353**
**throwing exceptions**
  from catch and finally blocks, 339
  choosing type to throw, 334–335
  defined, 331
  nested throw statements for, 332
  user-defined exceptions, 343–346
**tiered development with ADO.NET, 625–627**
**time slice of threads, 351**
**tlbexp utility, 1173**
**tlbimp utility, 1163**
ToolStrip **control (Windows Forms)**
  controls derived from, 776–777
  described, 776
  formatting text, 776
  ToolStripControlHost control, 777–779
  ToolStripDropDownItem control, 777
  using as a toolbar, 776
ToolStripContainer **control (Windows Forms), 780**
ToolStripControlHost **control (Windows Forms), 777–779**
ToolStripDropDownItem **control (Windows Forms), 777**
ToolStripManager **class (Windows Forms), 780**
ToolStripMenuItem **class (Windows Forms), 779–780**
ToString() **method**
  called by AppendFormat() method, 231
  date formatting for globalization using, 519
  described, 106
  of IFormattable interface, 232
  number formatting for globalization using, 517–518
  outputting StringBuilder class contents as a String, 229
  for UDTs, 640–641
  using, 108–109
TrackBar **control, 820–822**
**transactional message queues, 1121–1122**
**transactions**
  in ADO.NET, 588–589
  Enterprise Services, 1068, 1078–1080
  Web services specifications and, 1131–1133
TreeView **control (ASP.NET), 960, 961**
TreeView **control (Windows Forms)**
  custom control based on, 788–794

  described, 788, 789
**triggers for SQL Server**
  creating, 649–650
  defined, 648
  overview, 648–649
  using, 650
**troubleshooting Windows Services**
  debugging, 1301–1302
  event logging, 1302–1308
  interactive services, 1302
  performance monitoring, 1308–1313
try **blocks**
  defined, 330
  error trapping process and, 330
  exceptions not handled and, 338
  handling different exceptions in different places, 340
  modifying the type of exception, 340
  MortimerColdCall example, 342
  nested throw statements in, 332
  nested try blocks, 338–340
  for releasing database resources, 586, 587–588
  in SimpleExceptions class, 334
  syntax, 330
  throwing an exception and, 331
**T-SQL, 645**
Type **class**
  for holding reference types, 314
  methods, 315–316
  obtaining a Type reference, 314
  properties, 314–315
  TypeView example, 316–319
**type safety**
  boxing and unboxing, 145–146
  CLR memory safety tests, 7
  delegates and, 172, 174
  generics advantages for, 273
  strong typing in IL, 9–16
  type conversions, 140–145
  unsafe operators, 134
typeof **operator, 139**
**types. See data types**
TypeView **assembly**
  AddToOutput() method, 319
  AnalyzeType() method, 318–319
  code listing, 318–319
  compiling, 319
  GetMembers() method, 319
  Main() method, 318
  overview, 316–318
  using statements, 318

# U

**UDP protocol**
  SOAP-over-UDP, 1133–1134
  TCP versus, 1266
  `UdpClient` class, 1266–1267
**UDTs (user-defined types).** *See also* `Coordinate struct`
  converting from a string, 641
  converting to a string, 640–641
  creating, 636–641
  deploying, 642
  enumerations, 55–57
  limitations on, 636
  `object` type as parent, 44
  overview, 636
  serialization formats, 637–638
  `[SqlUserDefinedType]` attribute, 637, 638
  using from client-side code, 642–643
  Visual Studio template for, 636–637
**unboxing.** *See* **boxing and unboxing**
`unchecked` **operator, 137**
`#undef` **preprocessor directive, 71**
`UnexpectedException`**, 341, 347**
**Unicode characters**
  combining, 514
  globalization issues, 514–515
  in identifiers, 74–75
  `StringInfo` methods for combined characters, 515
**unsafe code.** *See also* **pointers; type safety**
  anonymous methods and, 177
  unsafe operators, 134
`unsafe` **keyword, 205–206**
**updating Active Directory entries, 733**
**updating data sources with Visual Studio .NET, 826**
**updating records with ADO.NET**
  calling stored procedures, 594–595
  `ExecuteNonQuery()` method for, 591
  setting update constraints, 611–612
  using data adapters, 621–623
`UploadData()` **method (**`WebClient` **class), 1242**
`UploadFile()` **method (**`WebClient` **class), 1242**
**UPN (user principal name) in Active Directory, 729**
`Uri` **class, 1258–1259**
`UriBuilder` **class, 1258, 1259**
**URIs, capturing sections with regular expressions, 242–243**
**usage conventions**
  casing of names, 76–77
  compilation and, 75
  fields, 81
  name styles, 77
  names and keywords, 78–80
  namespace names, 77
  .NET guidelines and naming philosophy, 75–76
  properties and methods, 80
  variable prefixes, 75
**user controls (ASP.NET)**
  adding methods, 949–950
  attributes for, 947
  creating Web site for, 945
  custom controls versus, 952
  defined, 944
  defining default state for, 946
  event handlers, 948, 950
  file extensions for code, 945
  graphics for card suit display, 946
  naming HTML tag for, 946
  overview, 944–945
  in `PCSDemoSite` application, 950–952
  properties for accessing, 947–948
  `<%@ Register %>` directive for, 946
  simple example, 945–950
  using in Web pages, 950
**user controls (Windows Forms)**
  adding properties, 796–797
  adding `TextBox` controls, 795–796
  attributes for, 798–799
  creating the container control, 795
  further enhancements possible for, 799
  `get` methods for properties, 797
  initialization, 798
  `set` methods for properties, 797–798
  `TextChanged` event handler, 797–798
  uses for, 794
**user interaction.** *See also* **events**
  `CapsEditor` example, 890–893
  `Control` class and, 760–761
  with `Form` class, 782–784
  interactive Windows Services, 1302
**User Interface Editor (ClickOnce), 571–573**
**user principal name (UPN) in Active Directory, 729**
**user-defined aggregates**
  creating, 644–645
  deploying, 645
  uses for, 643
  using, 645
**user-defined casts**
  between base and derived classes, 163–164
  boxing and unboxing, 164–165

**user-defined casts (continued)**
  compilation and, 165–166
  converting integers to floats, 159–162
  between derived classes, 162–163
  implementing, 159–165
  implicit versus explicit casts and, 157–158
  multiple casting, 165–169
  syntax, 158–159
**user-defined exception classes**
  catching user-defined exceptions, 341–343
  defining, 346–348
  `MortimerColdCall` example, 340–348
  throwing user-defined exceptions, 343–346
**user-defined functions with SQL Server, 647–648**
**user-defined types.** *See* **UDTs**
`UserSearch` **Active Directory application**
  described, 740
  getting the schema naming context, 741–742
  getting `user` class property names, 742–743
  searching for `user` objects, 743–745
  user interface, 740–741
`using` **statements**
  `CapsEditor` example, 881–882
  for custom controls (ASP.NET), 953
  `Dispose()` method and, 201–202
  for Enterprise Services client, 1077
  for event-booking application, 995
  `FileProperties` application, 1193–1194
  making `OleDB` classes available, 597
  for namespace aliases, 60–61
  for namespaces, 32, 59–60
  `PrintingCapsEdit` project, 898
  `QuoteClient` assembly, 1280
  for releasing database resources, 586–587, 588

# V

**validation Web server controls (ASP.NET), 918–920**
`ValidationSummary` **control, 921**
**value types.** *See also* **specific types**
  basic data types as, 40
  for Boolean values, 43
  comparing for equality, 147–148
  converting between reference types and, 145–146
  `decimal` type, 42–43
  defined, 9
  floating-point types, 42
  integer types, 41–42
  memory management, 194–195
  performance and, 40

  predefined, 41–44
  reference types versus, 9, 39–40
  for single characters, 43–44
  stored on the stack, 9, 39, 194–195
**variables.** *See also* **constants**
  anonymous methods and, 177
  assigning values, 34
  declaring, 33–34
  initialization, 34–35
  prefixes for names, 75
  scope, 35–38, 194–195
  unsafe local variables, 206
`Vector` **struct**
  adding collection support, 248–250
  adding formatting expressions, 233–235
  overloading operators, 150–157
`VectorClass` **assembly, 310, 312–313**
`VectorEnumerator` **struct, 248–250**
**versioning assemblies**
  application configuration files, 453–456
  getting the version programmatically, 452–453
  importance for shared assemblies, 412, 413, 451
  private assemblies and, 412–413, 451
  publisher policy files, 456–458
  runtime version, 459–460
  version numbers, 451–452
**viewing .NET data.** *See also* **ADO.NET;** *specific topics*
  data binding, 816–822
  `DataGridView` control for, 801–816
  Visual Studio .NET and data access, 822–840
**viewstate field (ASP.NET), 905**
**virtual addressing, 194**
**Virtual Execution System of CLR, 465**
`virtual` **keyword, 114–115, 125**
**virtual memory, 194.** *See also* **managed heap; stack**
**visibility modifiers, 124–125**
**visibility of forms, 781**
**Visual Basic 2005**
  development of, 5–6
  interoperability with .NET, 5–6
**Visual Basic 6**
  class for CLS example, 432–434
  converting to Visual Basic 2005, 6
  data typing versus IL data typing, 9–10
  reading in projects to Visual Studio 2005, 387
  unsuitability for .NET, 5–6
**Visual Basic .NET**
  extensive changes from VB6, 6
  not case-sensitive, 77

**Visual C++ 2005.** *See also* **C++**
  advantages over C#, 6–7
  CLR memory type safety tests and, 7
  interoperability with .NET, 6–7
  mixing managed and unmanaged types in, 6
**Visual C++ 6.** *See also* **C++**
  Microsoft-specific extensions, 6
  reading in projects to Visual Studio 2005, 387
**Visual C++ .NET, 6.** *See also* **C++**
**Visual J# 2005, 7**
**Visual Studio .NET and data access.** *See also* **Visual Studio 2005**
  building an XSD schema, 827–832
  creating a database connection, 822–825
  manufactured tables and rows, 835–840
  providing a pop-up menu for a row, 832–835
  selecting data from a database, 825–826
  updating the data source, 826
**Visual Studio 2005.** *See also* **Visual Studio .NET and data access**
  accessing other programs from, 373
  adding projects to solutions, 385–386
  adding TextBox controls to forms, 392–394
  for ASP.NET file creation, 906
  ATL Project Wizard, 1159–1160
  building projects, 399–403
  changes from previous versions, 373–374
  Class View window, 396–397
  compiling from, 372
  console project, 381–383
  converting VB6 to Visual Basic 2005 and, 6
  creating assemblies using, 423–425
  creating installers in, 557–567
  creating projects, 377–383
  creating UDTs, 636–641
  creating Web Forms, 906–908
  debug and release builds with, 399–401
  debugger, 9, 373, 404–407
  debugger symbols, 400–401
  Design View window, 372, 391–394
  designer-generated code separated by, 754–755
  design-time debugging, 390
  editing configurations, 402–403
  Exceptions dialog box, 407
  features, 371–373
  folding editor (default code editor), 388–390
  localization example using, 534–555
  MSDN help integrated with, 373
  Object Browser window, 397–398
  opening projects from previous versions in, 374–376
  pinning and unpinning windows, 398–399
  project, defined, 383
  project files created by, 382–383
  project types available, 379–381
  Properties window, 394–396
  RCW creation, 1164
  reading in Visual Studio 6 projects, 387
  refactoring tools, 408–410
  removing debugging commands, 401
  selecting a project type, 377–381
  selecting configuration for, 401–402
  Server Explorer window, 398
  setting breakpoints, 404
  setting the startup project, 386
  showing and hiding blocks of code, 388–390
  simple client application, deployment project as separate solution, 558–562
  simple client application, deployment project in same solution, 563–564
  solution, defined, 383
  solutions versus projects, 383–384
  supporting windows, 372
  text editor, 371
  Toolbox, 391–392
  upgrade wizard, 374–376
  User-Defined Type template, 636–637
  Visual J# 2005 and, 7
  Watch window, 405–406
  Web Forms, 23
  Windows application code, 387
  Windows Form applications and, 754–755
`void` **pointers, 209**

# W

`WaitCallback` **delegate, 366**
`#warning` **preprocessor directive, 72**
**WCF (Windows Communication Foundation)**
  architecture, 1135
  ASP.NET and, 1146
  binding, 1141–1143
  client applications, 1144
  contracts, defined, 1137
  data contract, 1137, 1138
  described, 1125
  Enterprise Services and, 1146–1147
  features, 1134–1135
  hosting, 1143–1144
  layers of applications, 1135, 1136
  message contract, 1137, 1139

1535

## WCF (Windows Communication Foundation) (continued)

**WCF (Windows Communication Foundation) (continued)**
   Message Queuing and, 1147
   .NET Remoting and, 1145–1146
   overview, 1134–1136
   preparing for, 1145–1147
   programming with, 1137–1144
   service contract, 1137–1138
   service implementation, 1139–1141
   ways of sending messages, 1135
   Web services contract, 1137

**Web Forms.** *See also* **ASP.NET**; `PCSDemoSite` **application (ASP.NET)**
   ADO.NET and data binding for, 926–939
   application configuration, 939–941
   authentication using Security Wizard, 964–969
   creating files with text editor, 905
   creating in Visual Studio 2005, 906–908
   creating with C#, 23
   defined, 23
   design considerations, 905–908
   IDEs for, 905
   `Label` control, 920
   login system implementation, 969–970
   `<%@ Page %>` tag, 908
   PCSWebApp1 example, 906–908, 909
   process after user requests, 909
   restricting directory access, 971–973
   security, 963–973
   server control example, 920–925
   state management in ASP.NET and, 905
   Web server controls for, 23

**Web server, client deployment from, 566–567**

**Web server controls (ASP.NET).** *See also* **event-booking application**
   adding to PCSWebApp1 example, 911–913
   binding to the database, 927–928
   Crystal Reports controls, 914
   data controls, 917–918
   defined, 23, 910
   login controls, 970–971
   navigation controls, 960–963
   `runat="server"` attribute, 910
   standard controls, 914–917
   validation controls, 918–920
   WebParts controls, 920

**Web Service Description Language.** *See* **WSDL**

**Web services.** *See also* **Web services specifications**
   adding a method accessible through, 988
   consuming, 990–993
   `CookieContainer` class with, 1004–1005
   creating client for, 991–992
   declaring custom SOAP header, 1002
   defined, 983
   event-booking application, 993–1001
   exchanging data using SOAP headers, 1001–1007
   exposing, 987–990
   with .NET Remoting, 1010
   proxy class for, 990–992
   SOAP for, 983, 984–985
   types available for, 990
   viewing WSDL for, 990
   WCF contract for, 1137
   WSDL for, 983, 985–987
   WSDL.exe tool, 991

**Web services specifications**
   current issues, 1126–1127
   performance and, 1133–1134
   for transactions, 1131–1133
   WS-Addressing, 1134
   WS-AtomicTransactions, 1131
   WS-BusinessActivity, 1131–1133
   WS-Coordination, 1131
   WS-Federation, 1127
   WS-ReliableMessaging, 1129–1131
   WS-SecureConversation, 1128–1129
   WS-Security, 1128

`WebBrowser` **control (Windows Forms)**
   displaying the code of a requested page, 1256–1257
   giving applications IE-type features, 1248–1253
   printing using, 1255–1256
   showing documents using, 1254–1255
   for simple Web browsing from applications, 1246–1247
   starting an Internet Explorer process programmatically, 1245–1246

`WebClient` **class**
   `BasicWebClient` example, 1240–1241
   `DownloadFile()` method, 1240
   `OpenRead()` method, 1240–1241
   `OpenWrite()` method, 1241
   overview, 1240
   `UploadData()` method, 1242
   `UploadFile()` method, 1242

`web.config` **file**
   ASP.NET application configuration, 940
   for event-booking application, 993
   `<globalization>` element, 544
   hosting .NET Remoting servers in ASP.NET and, 1050–1051

**WebParts Web server controls (ASP.NET), 920**

# Windows Forms

WebRequest **class**
  asynchronous page requests, 1244–1245
  authentication, 1244
  BasicWebClient example, 1242–1243
  class hierarchy, 1257–1258
  HTTP header information support, 1243–1244
  WebClient class versus, 1242
WebResponse **class**
  BasicWebClient example, 1242–1243
  class hierarchy, 1257–1258
  HTTP header information support, 1243–1244
  WebClient class versus, 1242
WelcomeMessage() **method, 535, 536, 541–542**
Wellknown_Client.config **file (.NET Remoting), 1043**
Wellknown_Server.config **file (.NET Remoting), 1042–1043**
WhatsNewAttributes **example**
  LookUpWhatsNew assembly, 310, 321–324
  overview, 310–311
  VectorClass assembly, 310, 312–313
  WhatsNewAttributes library assembly, 310, 311–312
WhatsNewChecker **class, 321–322**
while **statements**
  overview, 53
  scope of local variables declared in, 36
  in SimpleExceptions class, 334
**Wiley Publishing, Inc.**
  *Beginning XML*, 659
  *Professional ASP.NET 1.1*, 910, 940
**Windows Controls, 24**
**Windows Forms.** *See also* **events; graphics;** *specific classes, controls, and components*
  ActiveX controls in, 1168–1171
  appearance properties for controls, 760
  application for ActiveX controls, 1169–1170
  Button control, 762–763, 1249–1253
  CheckBox control, 764
  CheckedListBox control, 765
  class hierarchy, 757–758
  ComboBox control, 765, 767
  ContextMenuStrip class, 779
  Control class, 759–762
  controlling appearance of forms, 784–786
  creating an application, 752–757
  custom controls, 787–799
  DateTimePicker control, 765
  disposing of forms, 755
  ErrorProvider component, 767–769

  FlowLayoutPanel control, 774–775
  focus, gaining and losing for controls, 761
  FolderTree custom control, 789–794
  Form class, 752, 780–786
  Form, defined, 780
  globalization demo application, 520–524
  grouping controls on tab pages, 776
  Height property, 92–93
  HelpProvider component, 769
  ImageList component, 769
  Label control, 769–770
  LinkLabel control, 1248
  ListBox control, 765–767
  ListView control, 770–772
  Localizable property, 536, 537
  localization application, 520–524
  MaskedTextBox control, 773, 774
  MDI (Multiple Document Interface), 786–787
  MenuStrip control, 779
  namespaces for, 751
  overview, 24
  Panel control, 774
  PictureBox control, 772
  ProgressBar control, 772
  RadioButton control, 764
  reading drive information, 1220–1222
  reading from files, 1202–1204
  RichTextBox control, 773–774
  running controls in Internet Explorer, 1183
  SDI (Single Document Interface), 781
  setting colors for forms, 785
  shape-drawing application, 844–847
  showing forms in taskbar, 782
  size and location properties for controls, 759–760
  SplitContainer control, 775
  standard controls and components, 762–780
  system menu for forms, 784–785
  TabControl control, 776
  TableLayoutPanel control, 774, 775
  TabPages control, 776
  TextBox control, 773, 1246–1247
  ToolStrip control, 776–779
  ToolStripContainer control, 780
  ToolStripControlHost control, 777–779
  ToolStripDropDownItem control, 777
  ToolStripManager class, 780
  ToolStripMenuItem class, 779–780
  TreeView control, custom control based on, 788–794
  user interaction, 760–761, 782–784
  UserSearch Active Directory application, 740–745

1537

## Windows Forms (continued)

**Windows Forms (continued)**
- visibility of forms, 781, 782
- visual styles for forms, 785–786
- `WebBrowser` control, 1245–1247, 1248–1257
- Windows functionality and, 761–762
- writing to files, 1204–1205

**Windows Installer projects**
- ClickOnce compared to Windows Installer, 567–568
- creating installers, 557–567
- for Enterprise Services, 1074–1075
- installing client from Web server, 566–567
- No Touch Deployment (NTD), 566–567
- options for deployment, 552
- project types available, 556
- simple client application, deployment project as separate solution, 558–562
- simple client application, deployment project in same solution, 563–564
- simple Web application, 564–565
- Windows Installer overview, 556–557
- for Windows Services, 1287–1292

**Windows Resource Localization Editor (winres.exe), 543**

**Windows Services.** *See also* **quote server application**
- architecture, 1272–1275
- class library using sockets, 1276–1279
- creating as service, 1275–1292
- defined, 1271
- event logging, 1302–1308
- example services, 1272
- handler methods, 1274
- installing, 1287–1292
- interactive services, 1302
- monitoring and controlling services, 1292–1301
- namespace for, 1275
- net.exe utility, 1293–1294
- overview, 24
- performance monitoring, 1308–1313
- power events and, 1314
- project wizard for, 1281–1283
- `QuoteService` example, 1281–1286
- sc.exe utility, 1294–1295
- service configuration program, 1275
- Service Control Manager (SCM), 1273, 1274
- service control program, 1275
- service program, 1273–1274
- service start, 1285
- `ServiceBase` class, 1283–1284
- `ServiceController` class, 1295–1301
- service-main function, 1273–1274

- Services administration tool, 1272
- Services MMC snap-in, 1293
- `TcpClient` example, 1279–1281
- threading and, 1287
- troubleshooting, 1301–1313
- viewing all services on a system, 1272
- Visual Studio Server Explorer, 1295

`Windows.Forms` **namespace, 188**
**winres.exe (Windows Resource Localization Editor), 543**
**worker threads, 352**
**world coordinates, 863**
`WorldCoordinatesToLineIndex()` **method, 889**
`WorldYCoordinateToLineIndex()` **method, 889**
`WriteAttributeInfo()` **method, 323**
`WriteMatches()` **method, 240**
**write-only properties, avoiding, 81, 94**
`WriteXml()` **method (**`DataSet` **class), 624–625, 690–691**
**writing to files**
- binary files, 1208–1213
- overview, 1201
- text files, 1213–1219
- Windows Forms for, 1204–1205

**WROX Web site, 895, 920, 1151**
**WS-Addressing specification, 1134**
**WS-AtomicTransactions specification, 1131**
**WS-BusinessActivity specification, 1131–1133**
**WS-Coordination specification, 1131**
**WSDL (Web Service Description Language)**
- described, 983
- overview, 985–987
- type-definition section, 985–986
- viewing for Web services, 990
- as WCF contract, 1137
- as XML-compliant syntax, 985

**WSDL.exe tool, 991**
**WS-Federation specification, 1127**
**WS-ReliableMessaging specification, 1129–1131**
**WS-SecureConversation specification, 1128–1129**
**WS-Security specification, 1128**

#

**xcopy deployment, 552, 554–555**
**XML.** *See also* **XML data type (SQL Server)**
- ASP.NET server control syntax based on, 910
- comments, 68–70
- converting ADO.NET relational data to, 694–696
- converting ADO.NET single table data to, 689–694
- converting to ADO.NET data, 696–699

DiffGram documents, 699–701
further information, 659
namespace for, 659, 660–661
Office applications supporting, 651
populating a DataSet from, 620
reading streamed XML, 664–670
relational data and, 651
.resX files for resources, 526, 527–528
serializing objects in, 701–711
standards supported in .NET, 660
transforming into HTML, 684–686
using MSXML 4.0 in .NET, 661–663
using the DOM in .NET, 672–678
writing output with DataSet, 623–625, 690–691
writing streamed XML, 670–672
WSDL compliance with, 985
XmlReader with ADO.NET, 593–594
XPathNavigators, 678–689

**XML Data Modification Language (XML DML), 654–655**

**XML data type (SQL Server)**
introduction of, 650
Office applications supporting XML, 651
querying data, 653–654
relational data and, 651
strongly typed XML, 656–657
tables with XML data, 651–653
XML Data Modification Language (XML DML), 654–655
XML indexes, 655–656

**XML DML (XML Data Modification Language), 654–655**

**XML schema definition (XSD) schemas.** *See* **XSD schemas**

**XML Web services, 23**
XmlAttributeOverrides **class, 708–710**
XmlAttributes **class, 708–710**
XmlCharacterData **class, 672, 674**
XmlDataDocument **class, 692–693**
XmlDocument **class**
converting ADO.NET data to XML, 689–694
creating a document from scratch, 677–678
described, 661
DOM representation using, 673
inserting nodes, 675–678
using, 673–675
XmlElement **class, 676**
XmlLinkedNode **class**
classes extending, 673
described, 672
inheritance diagram for, 674

XmlNode **class**
classes based on, 672
described, 661, 672
inheritance diagram for, 674
XmlNodeReader **class, 664**
XmlReader **class**
classes derived from, 664
Create method for, 665
described, 660
GetAttribute() method, 668
properties for controlling processing of nodes and values, 665
Read() method, 665
ReadElementString() method, 665–667
ReadStartElement() method, 665
ReadValueAs methods, 667
retrieving attribute data, 668
SAX versus, 664
simple example, 665
validating XML to an XSD schema, 668–670
XmlReaderSettings **class, 665, 668, 670**
XmlSerializer **class, 703**
XmlTextReader **class**
described, 661, 664
EOF property, 666
XmlTextWriter **class**
described, 661, 664
using, 670–671, 677
XmlValidatingReader **class, 664**
XmlWriter **class**
classes derived from, 664
described, 660
using, 670–671
XmlWriterSettings **class, 670, 671**
XPathDocument **class, 678**
XPathException **class, 679**
XPathExpression **class, 679, 682**
XPathNavigator **class**
described, 678
move methods, 679–680
select methods, 680
using, 681–683
**XPathNavigators.** *See also specific namespaces*
defined, 678
System.Xml.XPath namespace for, 678–684
System.Xml.Xsl namespace for, 684–689
XPathNodeIterator **class**
described, 678
properties and methods, 680–681
using, 682, 683–684

**xsd command**
  converting XSD files into code, 613
  output for Products schema, 613–618
  switches, 613

**XSD (XML schema definition) schemas.** *See also* xsd command
  adding elements, 829
  building with Visual Studio .NET, 827–832
  `DataColumn` for, 831–832
  `DataRow` for, 830–831
  `DataTable` for, 829–830
  `EventArgs` for, 832
  generating from `books.xml` file, 668–669
  overview, 612–613
  Schema view versus XML view, 828
  `TestSchema.cs` example, 828–832
  validating XML to, 668–670
  `XmlReader` class for validating, 669–670

**xsd.exe tool, 702**

# Z

**zero impact installation of private assemblies, 18**